EIGHTH EDITION

MEN'S LIVES

Michael S. Kimmel

State University of New York—Stony Brook

Michael A. Messner

University of Southern California

Allyn & Bacon

Boston   New York   San Francisco
Mexico City   Montreal   Toronto   London   Madrid   Munich   Paris
Hong Kong   Singapore   Tokyo   Cape Town   Sydney

Publisher: *Karen Hanson*
Series Editorial Assistant: *Courtney Shea*
Marketing Manager: *Kelly May*
Production Editor: *Pat Torelli*
Editorial Production Service: *Publishers' Design and Production Services, Inc.*
Manufacturing Buyer: *Debbie Rossi*
Electronic Composition: *Publishers' Design and Production Services, Inc.*
Cover Administrator: *Joel Gendron*
Cover Designer: *Jennifer Hart*

Library of Congress Cataloging-in-Publication data unavailable at time of publication

10 9 8 7 6 5 4 3 2   HAM   13 12 11 10

Allyn & Bacon
is an imprint of

www.pearsonhighered.com

ISBN-10: 0-205-69294-X
ISBN-13: 978-0-205-69294-1

For Bob Blauner, friend and mentor

Why Do You Need This New Edition?

20 good reasons why you should buy this new edition of *Men's Lives* . . .

Edited by two of the field's most prominent researchers, this best-selling reader on men and masculinity contains the most current articles available. Here is a sampling of just some of the topics included in this new edition:

- Parents' responses to children's gender nonconformity

- Gendering the transition to adulthood

- Sexual fitness and the aging male body

- Gender and the meanings of adolescent romantic relationships

- Gay men of color and the racial politics of exclusion

- Athletic violence and aggression in hockey and interpersonal relationships

- Wielding masculinity inside Abu Ghraib

PEARSON

CONTENTS

Preface **ix**

Introduction **xi**

PART ONE   Perspectives on Masculinities 1

ARTICLE 1   Caveman Masculinity: Finding an Ethnicity in Evolutionary Science **Martha McCaughey 3**

ARTICLE 2   The Male Privilege Checklist **Barry Deutsch 14**

ARTICLE 3   All Men Are *Not* Created Equal: Asian Men in U.S. History **Yen Le Espiritu 17**

ARTICLE 4   "Macho": Contemporary Conceptions **Alfredo Mirandé 26**

PART TWO   Boyhood 37

ARTICLE 5   Warrior Narratives in the Kindergarten Classroom: Renegotiating the Social Contract? **Ellen Jordan and Angela Cowan 39**

ARTICLE 6   "No Way My Boys Are Going to Be Like That!": Parents' Responses to Children's Gender Nonconformity **Emily W. Kane 52**

ARTICLE 7   "Dude, You're a Fag": Adolescent Masculinity and the Fag Discourse **C. J. Pascoe 70**

ARTICLE 8   The Act Like-a-Man Box **Paul Kivel 83**

ARTICLE 9   Memories of Same-Sex Attractions **Ritch C. Savin-Williams 86**

ARTICLE 10   Making a Name for Yourself: Transgressive Acts and Gender Performance **Ann Ferguson 104**

PART THREE   Collegiate Masculinities: Privilege and Peril 117

ARTICLE 11   Guyland: Gendering the Transition to Adulthood **Michael Kimmel 119**

ARTICLE 12   The Measure of a Man: Conceptualizations of Masculinity among High-Achieving African American Male College Students **Shaun R. Harper 134**

ARTICLE 13   The Fraternal Bond as a Joking Relationship: A Case
Study of the Role of Sexist Jokes in Male Group Bonding
Peter Lyman   147

ARTICLE 14   Why College Men Drink: Alcohol, Adventure, and the Paradox of
Masculinity **Rocco L. Capraro   157**

ARTICLE 15   The Starbucks Intervention **Greg Bortnichak   171**

PART FOUR   Men and Work   175

ARTICLE 16   The Glass Escalator: Hidden Advantages for Men in the "Female"
Professions **Christine L. Williams   177**

ARTICLE 17   "Why Marcia You've Changed!": Male Clerical Temporary
Workers Doing Masculinity in a Feminized Occupation
Kevin D. Henson and Jackie Krasas Rogers   192

ARTICLE 18   Sexual Harassment and Masculinity: The Power and Meaning of
"Girl Watching" **Beth A. Quinn   208**

ARTICLE 19   Just One of the Guys?: How Transmen Make Gender Visible at Work
Kristen Schilt   221

PART FIVE   Men and Health   241

ARTICLE 20   Masculinities and Men's Health: Moving toward Post-Superman Era
Prevention **Don Sabo   243**

ARTICLE 21   Old Gay Men's Bodies and Masculinities **Kathleen F. Slevin and
Thomas J. Linneman   261**

ARTICLE 22   If Men Could Menstruate **Gloria Steinem   280**

ARTICLE 23   Fixing Broken Masculinity: Viagra as a Technology for the Production
of Gender and Sexuality **Meika Loe   282**

ARTICLE 24   It Takes Balls: Lance Armstrong and the Triumph of American
Masculinity **Monica Casper and Lisa Jean Moore   289**

PART SIX   Men in Relationships   301

ARTICLE 25   "I'm Not Friends the Way She's Friends": Ideological and
Behavioral Constructions of Masculinity in Men's Friendships
Karen Walker   303

ARTICLE 26   The Politics of Gay Men's Friendships **Peter M. Nardi   316**

ARTICLE 27   The Girl Hunt: Urban Nightlife and the Performance of Masculinity as Collective Activity **David Grazian 320**

ARTICLE 28   Gender and the Meanings of Adolescent Romantic Relationships: A Focus on Boys **Peggy C. Giordano, Monica A. Longmore, and Wendy D. Manning 338**

PART SEVEN   Male Sexualities 369

ARTICLE 29   Becoming 100 Percent Straight **Michael A. Messner 371**

ARTICLE 30   The Heterosexual Questionnaire **M. Rochlin 377**

ARTICLE 31   A Pornographic World [What Is Normal?] **Robert Jensen 378**

ARTICLE 32   They Don't Want to Cruise Your Type: Gay Men of Color and the Racial Politics of Exclusion **Chong-suk Han 384**

ARTICLE 33   Fantasy Islands: Exploring the Demand for Sex Tourism **Julia O'Connell Davidson and Jacqueline Sanchez Taylor 397**

PART EIGHT   Men in Families 411

ARTICLE 34   Strategies Men Use to Resist **Francine M. Deutch 413**

ARTICLE 35   Ethnicity, Race, and Difference: A Comparison of White, Black, and Hispanic Men's Household Labor Time **Anne Shelton and Daphne John 420**

ARTICLE 36   Fathering: Paradoxes, Contradictions, and Dilemmas **Scott Coltrane 432**

ARTICLE 37   Cruising to Familyland: Gay Hypergamy and Rainbow Kinship **Judith Stacey 450**

PART NINE   Masculinities in the Media and Popular Culture 463

ARTICLE 38   The Male Consumer as Loser: Beer and Liquor Ads in Mega Sports Media Events **Michael A. Messner and Jeffrey Montez de Oca 465**

ARTICLE 39   When in Rome: Heterosexism, Homophobia, and Sports Talk Radio **David Nylund 479**

ARTICLE 40   Retrofitting Frontier Masculinity for Alaska's War against Wolves **Sine Anahita and Tamara L. Mix 504**

ARTICLE 41   "A Walking Open Wound": Emo Rock and the "Crisis" of Masculinity in America **Sarah F. Williams   521**

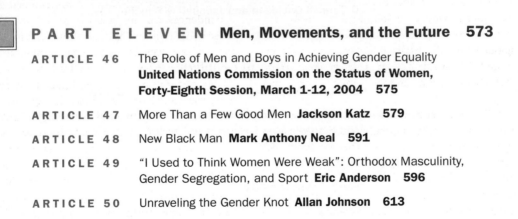

PART TEN   Violence and Masculinities   533

ARTICLE 42   Athlete Aggression on the Rink and off the Ice: Athlete Violence and Aggression in Hockey and Interpersonal Relationships **Nick T. Pappas, Patrick C. McKenry, and Beth Skilken Catlett   535**

ARTICLE 43   Culture, Gender, and Violence: "We Are Not Women" **James Gilligan   551**

ARTICLE 44   Men on Rape **Tim Beneke   559**

ARTICLE 45   Wielding Masculinity inside Abu Ghraib: Making Feminist Sense of an American Military Scandal **Cynthia Enloe   565**

PART ELEVEN   Men, Movements, and the Future   573

ARTICLE 46   The Role of Men and Boys in Achieving Gender Equality **United Nations Commission on the Status of Women, Forty-Eighth Session, March 1-12, 2004   575**

ARTICLE 47   More Than a Few Good Men **Jackson Katz   579**

ARTICLE 48   New Black Man **Mark Anthony Neal   591**

ARTICLE 49   "I Used to Think Women Were Weak": Orthodox Masculinity, Gender Segregation, and Sport **Eric Anderson   596**

ARTICLE 50   Unraveling the Gender Knot **Allan Johnson   613**

Contributors   **623**

PREFACE

Over the past twenty years, we have been teaching courses on the male experience, or "men's lives." Our courses have reflected both our own education and recent research by feminist scholars and profeminist men in U.S. society. (By profeminist men, we mean active supporters of women's efforts against male violence and claims for equal opportunity, political participation, sexual autonomy, family reform, and equal education.) Gender, scholars have demonstrated, is a central feature of social life—one of the chief organizing principles around which our lives revolve. Gender shapes our identities and the institutions in which we find ourselves. In the university, women's studies programs and courses about women in traditional disciplines have explored the meaning of gender in women's lives. But what does it mean to be a man in contemporary U.S. society?

This anthology is organized around specific themes that define masculinity and the issues men confront over the course of their lives. In addition, a social-constructionist perspective has been included that examines how men actively construct masculinity within a social and historical context. Related to this construction and integrated in our examination are the variations that exist among men in relation to class, race, and sexuality.

We begin Part One with issues and questions that unravel the "masculine mystique" and reveal various dimensions of men's position in society and their relationships with women and with other men. Parts Two through Ten examine the different issues that emerge for men at different times of their lives and the ways in which their lives change over time. We touch on central moments related to boyhood, adolescence, sports, occupations, marriage, and fatherhood, and we explore men's emotional and sexual relationships with women and with other men. We also include a section on Violence and Masculinities. We have done so because violence remains the single behavior, attitude, or trait for which there are overwhelming, significant, and seemingly intractable gender differences. It affects so many other arenas of our lives that we have decided that we need to highlight this important feature of men's lives. The final part, "Men, Movements, and the Future," explores some of the ways in which men are changing and some possible directions in which they might continue to change.

Although a major component of the traditional, normative definition of masculinity is independence, we are pleased to acknowledge those colleagues and friends whose criticism and support have been a constant help throughout our work on this project. Karen Hanson and Jeff Lasser, our editors at Allyn and Bacon, inherited this project and have embraced it as their own, facilitating our work at every turn. Chris Cardone and Bruce Nichols, our original editors, were supportive from the start and helped get the project going. Many other scholars who work on issues of masculinity, such as Bob Blauner, Robert Brannon, Harry Brod, Rocco Capraro, Raewyn Connell, James Harrison, Jeff Hearn, Joe Pleck, Tony Rotundo, Don Sabo, and Peter Stein, have contributed to a supportive intellectual community in which to work.

Colleagues at the State University of New York at Stony Brook and the University of Southern California have been supportive of this project. We are especially grateful to Diane Barthel-Bouchier, John Gagnon, Barry Glassner, Norman Goodman, Carol Jacklin, and Barrie Thorne. A fellowship from the Lilly Foundation supported Kimmel's work on pedagogical issues of teaching about men and masculinity.

This book is the product of the profeminist men's movement as well—a loose network of men who support a feminist critique of traditional masculinity and women's struggles to enlarge the scope of their personal autonomy and public power. These men are engaged in a variety of efforts to transform masculinity in ways that allow men to live fuller, richer, and healthier lives. The editors of *Changing Men* (with whom we worked as Book Review Editor and Sports Editor), the late Mike Biernbaum and Rick Cote, labored for more than a decade to provide a forum for antisexist men. We acknowledge their efforts with gratitude and respect.

Our families, friends, and colleagues have provided a rare atmosphere that combines intellectual challenge and emotional support. We thank the reviewers of this edition: Kelly Eitzen Smith, University of Arizona; Jennifer L. Emmerich, Western Michigan University; Elizabeth Erbaugh, Grinnell College; Marcia Hernandez, University of the Pacific; Michael J. Murphy, Washington University in St. Louis. We want especially to acknowledge our fathers and mothers for providing such important models—not of being women or men, but of being adults capable of career competence, emotional warmth, and nurturance (these are not masculine or feminine traits).

Finally, we thank Amy Aronson and Pierette Hondagneu-Sotelo, who have chosen to share our lives, and our sons, who didn't have much of a choice about it. Together they fill our lives with so much joy.

M.S.K.
M.A.M.

INTRODUCTION

This is a book about men. But unlike other books about men, which line countless library shelves, this is a book about men *as men*. It is a book in which men's experiences are not taken for granted as we explore the "real" and significant accomplishments of men, but a book in which those experiences are treated as significant and important in themselves.

Men as "Gendered Beings"

But what does it mean to examine men "as men"? Most courses in a college curriculum are about men, aren't they? But these courses routinely deal with men only in their public roles, so we come to know and understand men as scientists, politicians, military figures, writers, and philosophers. Rarely, if ever, are men understood through the prism of gender.

But listen to some male voices from some of these "ungendered" courses. Take, for example, composer Charles Ives, debunking "sissy" types of music; he said he used traditional tough guy themes and concerns in his drive to build new sounds and structures out of the popular musical idiom (cf. Wilkinson 1986: 103). Or architect Louis Sullivan, describing his ambition to create "masculine forms": strong, solid, commanding respect. Or novelist Ernest Hemingway, retaliating against literary enemies by portraying them as impotent or homosexual.

Consider also political figures, such as Cardinal Richelieu, the seventeenth-century French First Minister to Louis XIII, who insisted that it was "necessary to have masculine virtue and do everything by reason" (cited in Elliott 1984: 20). Closer to home, recall President Lyndon Baines Johnson's dismissal of a political adversary: "Oh him. He has to squat to piss!" Or President Johnson's boast that during the Tet offensive in the Vietnam War, he "didn't just screw Ho Chi Minh. I cut his pecker off!"

Democrats have no monopoly on unexamined gender coloring their political rhetoric. Indeed, recent political campaigns have revolved, in part, around gender issues, as each candidate attempted to demonstrate that he was not a "wimp" but was a "real man." (Of course, female politicians face the double task of convincing the electorate that they are not the "weak-willed wimps" that their gender implies in the public mind while at the same time demonstrating that they are "real women.")

These are just a few examples of what we might call gendered speech, language that uses gender terms to make its case. And these are just a few of the thousands of examples one could find in every academic discipline of how men's lives are organized around gender issues and how gender remains one of the organizing principles of social life. We come to know ourselves and our world through the prism of gender—only we act as if we didn't know it.

Fortunately, in recent years, the pioneering work of feminist scholars, both in traditional disciplines and in women's studies, and of feminist women in the political arena has made us aware of the centrality of gender in our lives. In the social sciences, gender has now taken its place alongside class and race as one of the three central mechanisms by which power and resources are distributed in our society and the three central themes out of which we fashion the meanings of our lives.

We certainly understand how this works for women. Through women's studies courses and also in courses about women in traditional disciplines, students have explored the complexity of women's lives, the hidden history of exemplary women, and the daily experiences of women in the routines of their lives. For women, we know how gender works as one of the formative elements out of which social life is organized.

The Invisibility of Gender: A Sociological Explanation

Too often, though, we treat men as if they had no gender, as if only their public personae were of interest to us as students and scholars, as if their interior experience of gender was of no significance. This became evident when one of us was in a graduate seminar on feminist theory several years ago. A discussion between a white woman and a black woman revolved around the question of whether their similarities as women were greater than their racial differences as black and white. The white woman asserted that the fact that they were both women bonded them, in spite of their racial differences. The black woman disagreed.

"When you wake up in the morning and look in the mirror, what do you see?" she asked.

"I see a woman," replied the white woman.

"That's precisely the issue," replied the black woman. "I see a black woman. For me, race is visible every day, because it is how I am not privileged in this culture. Race is invisible to you, which is why our alliance will always seem somewhat false to me."

Witnessing this exchange, Michael Kimmel was startled. When he looked in the mirror in the morning, he saw, as he put it, "a human being: universally generalizable. The generic person." What had been concealed—that he possessed both race and gender—had become strikingly visible. As a white man, he was able not to think about the ways in which gender and race had affected his experiences.

There is a sociological explanation for this blind spot in our thinking: the mechanisms that afford us privilege are very often invisible to us. What makes us marginal (unempowered, oppressed) are the mechanisms that we understand, because those are the ones that are most painful in daily life. Thus, white people rarely think of themselves as "raced" people, and rarely think of race as a central element in their experience. But people of color are marginalized by race, and so the centrality of race both is painfully obvious and needs study urgently. Similarly, middle-class people do not acknowledge the importance of social class as an organizing principle of social life, largely because for them class is an invisible force that makes everyone look pretty much the same. Working-class people, on the other hand, are often painfully aware of the centrality of class in their lives. (Interestingly, upper-class people are often more aware of class dynamics than are middle-class people. In part, this may be the result of the emphasis on status within the upper class, as lineage, breeding, and family honor take center stage. In part, it may also be the result of a peculiar marginalization of the upper class in our society, as in the overwhelming number of television shows and movies that are ostensibly about just plain [i.e., middle-class] folks.)

In this same way, men often think of themselves as genderless, as if gender did not matter in the daily experiences of our lives. Certainly, we can see the biological sex of individuals, but we rarely understand the ways in which *gender*—that complex of social meanings that is attached to biological sex—is enacted in our daily lives. For example, we treat male scientists as if their being men had nothing to do with the organization of their experiments, the logic of scientific inquiry, or the questions posed by science itself. We treat male political figures as if masculinity were not even remotely in their consciousness as they do battle in the political arena.

This book takes a position directly opposed to such genderlessness for men. We believe that men are also "gendered" and that this gendering process, the transformation of biological males into socially interacting men, is a central experience for men. That we are unaware of it only helps to perpetuate the inequalities based on gender in our society.

In this book, we will examine the various ways in which men are gendered. We have gathered together some of the most interesting, engaging, and convincing materials from the past decade that have been written about men. We believe that *Men's Lives* will allow readers to explore the meanings of masculinity in contemporary U.S. culture in a new way.

Earlier Efforts to Study Men

Certainly researchers have been examining masculinity for a long time. Historically, there have been three general models that have governed social scientific research on men and masculinity. *Biological models* have focused on the ways in which innate biological differences between males and females program different social behaviors. *Anthropological models* have examined masculinity cross-culturally, stressing the variations in the behaviors and attributes associated with being a man. And, until recently, *sociological models* have stressed how socialization of boys and girls includes accommodation to a "sex role" specific to one's biological sex. Although each of these perspectives helps us to understand the meaning of masculinity and femininity, each is also limited in its ability to explain fully how gender operates in any culture.

Relying on differences in reproductive biology, some scholars have argued that the physiological organization of males and females makes inevitable the differences we observe in psychological temperament and social behaviors. One perspective holds that differences in endocrine functioning are the cause of gender difference, that testosterone predisposes males toward aggression, competition, and violence, whereas estrogen predisposes females toward passivity, tenderness, and exaggerated emotionality. Others insist that these observed behavioral differences derive from the differences between the size or number of sperm and eggs. Since a male can produce 100 million sperm with each ejaculation, whereas a female can produce fewer than 200 eggs capable of producing healthy offspring over the course of her life, these authors suggest that men's "investment" in their offspring is signifi-

cantly less than women's investment. Other authors arrive at the same conclusion by suggesting that the different size of egg and sperm, and the fact that the egg is the source of the food supply, impels temperamental differences. Reproductive "success" to males means the insemination of as many females as possible; to females, reproductive success means carefully choosing one male to mate with and insisting that he remain present to care for and support their offspring. Still other authors argue that male and female behavior is governed by different halves of the brain; males are ruled by the left hemisphere, which controls rationality and abstract thought, whereas females are governed by the right hemisphere, which controls emotional affect and creativity. (For examples of these works, see Trivers 1972; Goldberg 1975; Wilson 1976; and Goldberg, 1986.)

Observed normative temperamental differences between women and men that are assumed to be of biological origin are easily translated into political prescriptions. In this ideological sleight of hand, what is *normative* (i.e., what is prescribed) is translated into what is *normal*, and the mechanisms of this transformation are the assumed biological imperative. George Gilder, for example, assembles the putative biological differences between women and men into a call for a return to traditional gender roles. Gilder believes that male sexuality is, by nature, wild and lusty, "insistent" and "incessant," careening out of control and threatening anarchic disorder, unless it can be controlled and constrained. This is the task of women. When women refuse to apply the brakes to male sexuality—by asserting their own or by choosing to pursue a life outside the domestic sphere—they abandon their "natural" function for illusory social gains. Sex education, abortion, and birth control are all condemned as facilitating women's escape from biological necessity. Similarly, he argues against women's employment, since the "unemployed man can contribute little to the community and will often disrupt it, but the woman may even do more good without a job than with one" (Gilder 1986: 86).

The biological argument has been challenged by many scholars on several grounds. The implied causation between two observed sets of differences (biological differences and different behaviors) is misleading, since there is no logical reason to assume that one caused the other, or that the line of causation moves only from the biological to the social. The selection of biological evidence is partial, and generalizations from "lower" animal species to human beings are always suspect. One sociologist asks, if these differences are "natural," why must their enforcement be coercive, and why must males and females be forced to assume the rules that they are naturally supposed to play (see Epstein 1986: 8)? And one primatologist argues that the evidence adduced to support the current status quo might also lead to precisely the opposite conclusions, that biological differences would impel female promiscuity and male fragility (see Hrdy 1981). Biological differences between males and females would appear to set some parameters for differences in social behavior, but would not dictate the temperaments of men and women in any one culture. These psychological and social differences would appear to be the result far more of the ways in which cultures interpret, shape, and modify these biological inheritances. We may be born males or females, but we become men and women in a cultural context.

Anthropologists have entered the debate at this point, but with different positions. For example, some anthropologists have suggested that the universality of gender differences comes from specific cultural adaptations to the environment, whereas others describe the cultural variations of gender roles, seeking to demonstrate the fluidity of gender and the primacy of cultural organization. Lionel Tiger and Robin Fox argue that the sexual division of labor is universal because of the different nature of bonding for males and females. "Nature," they argue, "intended mother and child to be together" because she is the source of emotional security and food; thus, cultures have prescribed various behaviors for women that emphasize nurturance and emo-

tional connection (Tiger and Fox 1984: 304). The bond between men is forged through the necessity of "competitive cooperation" in hunting; men must cooperate with members of their own tribe in the hunt and yet compete for scarce resources with men in other tribes. Such bonds predispose men toward the organization of the modern corporation or governmental bureaucracy.

Such anthropological arguments omit as much as they include, and many scholars have pointed out problems with the model. Why didn't intelligence become sex linked, as this model (and the biological model) would imply? Such positions also reveal a marked conservatism: The differences between women and men are the differences that nature or cultural evolution intended and are therefore not to be tampered with.

Perhaps the best-known challenge to this anthropological argument is the work of Margaret Mead. Mead insisted that the variations among cultures in their prescriptions of gender roles required the conclusion that culture was the more decisive cause of these differences. In her classic study, *Sex and Temperament in Three Primitive Societies* (1935), Mead observed such wide variability among gender role prescriptions—and such marked differences from our own—that any universality implied by biological or anthropological models had to be rejected. And although the empirical accuracy of Mead's work has been challenged in its specific arguments, the general theoretical arguments remain convincing.

Psychological theories have also contributed to the discussion of gender roles, as psychologists have specified the developmental sequences for both males and females. Earlier theorists observed psychological distancing from the mother as the precondition for independence and autonomy or suggested a sequence that placed the capacity for abstract reason as the developmental stage beyond relational reasoning. Because it is normative for males to exhibit independence and the capacity for abstract reason, it was argued that males are more successful at negotiating these psychological passages and implied that women somehow lagged behind men on the ladder of developmental success. (Such arguments may be found in the work of Freud, Erikson, and Kohlberg.)

But these models, too, have been challenged, most recently by sociologist Nancy Chodorow (1978), who argued that women's ability to connect contains a more fundamentally human trait than the male's need to distance, and by psychologist Carol Gilligan (1982), who claimed that women's predisposition toward relational reasoning may contain a more humane strategy of thought than recourse to abstract principles. Regardless of our assessment of these arguments, Chodorow and Gilligan rightly point out that the highly ideological assumptions that make masculinity the normative standard against which the psychological development of *both* males and females was measured would inevitably make femininity problematic and less fully developed. Moreover, Chodorow explicitly insists that these "essential" differences between women and men are socially constructed and therefore subject to change.

Finally, sociologists have attempted to synthesize these three perspectives into a systematic explanation of "sex roles." These are the collection of attitudes, attributes, and behaviors that is seen as appropriate for males and appropriate for females. Thus, masculinity is associated with technical mastery, aggression, competitiveness, and cognitive abstraction, whereas femininity is associated with emotional nurturance, connectedness, and passivity. Sex role theory informed a wide variety of prescriptive literature (self-help books) that instructed parents on what to do if they wanted their child to grow up as a healthy boy or girl.

The strongest challenge to all these perspectives, as we have seen, has come from feminist scholars, who have specified the ways in which the assumptions about maturity, development, and health all made masculinity the norm against which both genders were measured. In all the social sciences, these feminist scholars have stripped these early studies of their academic fa-

cades to reveal the unexamined ideological assumptions contained within them. By the early 1970s, women's studies programs began to articulate a new paradigm for the study of gender, one that assumed nothing about men or women beforehand and that made no assumptions about which gender was more highly developed.

Thinking about Men: The First Generation

In the mid-1970s, the first group of works on men and masculinity appeared that was directly influenced by these feminist critiques of the traditional explanations for gender differences. Some books underscored the costs to men of traditional gender role prescriptions, exploring how some aspects of men's lives and experiences are constrained and underdeveloped by the relentless pressure to exhibit other behaviors associated with masculinity. Books such as Marc Feigen-Fasteau's *The Male Machine* (1974) and Warren Farrell's *The Liberated Man* (1975) discussed the costs of the traditional male sex role to men's health—both physical and psychological—and to the quality of relationships with women, other men, and their children.

Several anthologies explored the meanings of masculinity in the United States by adopting a feminist-inspired prism through which to view men and masculinity. For example, Deborah David and Robert Brannon's *The Forty-Nine Percent Majority* (1976) and Joseph Pleck and Jack Sawyer's *Men and Masculinity* (1974) presented panoramic views of men's lives from within a framework that accepted the feminist critique of traditional gender arrangements. Elizabeth Pleck and Joseph Pleck's *The American Man* (1980) suggested a historical evolution of contemporary themes. These works explored both the costs and the privileges of being a man in modern U.S. society.

Perhaps the single most important book to criticize the normative organization of the male sex role was Joseph Pleck's *The Myth of Masculinity*

(1981). Pleck carefully deconstructed the constituent elements of the male sex role and reviewed the empirical literature for each component part. After demonstrating that the empirical literature did not support these normative features, Pleck argued that the male sex role model was incapable of describing men's experiences. In its place, he posited a male "sex role strain" model that specified the contemporary sex role as problematic, historically specific, and also an unattainable ideal.

Building on Pleck's work, a critique of the sex role model began to emerge. Sex roles had been cast as the static containers of behaviors and attitudes, and biological males and females were required to fit themselves into these containers, regardless of how ill-fitting these clusters of behaviors and attitudes felt. Such a model was ahistorical and suggested a false cultural universalism, and was therefore ill equipped to help us understand the ways in which sex roles change, and the ways in which individuals modify those roles through the enactments of gender expectations. Most telling, however, was the way in which the sex role model ignored the ways in which definitions of masculinity and femininity were based on, and reproduced, relationships of power. Not only do men as a group exert power over women as a group, but the definitions of masculinity and femininity reproduce those power relations. Power dynamics are an essential element in both the definition and the enactments of gender.

This first generation of research on masculinity was extremely valuable, particularly since it challenged the unexamined ideology that made masculinity the gender norm against which both men and women were measured. The old models of sex roles had reproduced the domination of men over women by insisting on the dominance of masculine traits over feminine traits. These new studies argued against both the definitions of either sex and the social institutions in which those differences were embedded. Shapers of the new model looked at "gender relations" and understood how the definition of either masculinity or femininity was relational, that is, how

the definition of one gender depended, in part, on the understanding of the definition of the other.

In the early 1980s, the research on women again surged ahead of the research on men and masculinity. This time, however, the focus was not on the ways in which sex roles reproduce the power relations in society, but rather on the ways in which femininity is experienced differently by women in various social groups. Gradually, the notion of a single femininity—which was based on the white middle-class Victorian notion of female passivity, langorous beauty, and emotional responsiveness—was replaced by an examination of the ways in which women differ in their gender role expectations by race, class, age, sexual orientation, ethnicity, region, and nationality.

The research on men and masculinity is now entering a new stage, in which the variations among men are seen as central to the understanding of men's lives. The unexamined assumption in earlier studies had been that one version of masculinity—white, middle-aged, middle-class, heterosexual—was the sex role into which all men were struggling to fit in our society. Thus, working-class men, men of color, gay men, and younger and older men were all observed as departing in significant ways from the traditional definitions of masculinity. Therefore, it was easy to see these men as enacting "problematic" or "deviant" versions of masculinity. Such theoretical assertions, however, reproduce precisely the power relationships that keep these men in subordinate positions in our society. Not only does middle-class, middle-aged, heterosexual white masculinity become the standard against which all men are measured, but this definition, itself, is used against those who do not fit as a way to keep them down. The normative definition of masculinity is not the "right" one, but it is the one that is dominant.

The challenge to the hegemonic definition of masculinity came from men whose masculinity was cast as deviant: men of color, gay men, and ethnic men. We understand now that we cannot speak of "masculinity" as a singular term, but must examine *masculinities*: the ways in which different men construct different versions of masculinity. Such a perspective can be seen in several recent works, such as Harry Brod's *The Making of Masculinities* (1987), Michael Kimmel's *Changing Men: New Directions in Research on Men and Masculinity* (1987), and Tim Carrigan, R. W. Connell, and John Lee's "Toward a New Sociology of Masculinity" (1985). R. W. Connell's *Gender and Power* (1987) and Jeff Hearn's *The Gender of Oppression* (1987) represent the most sophisticated theoretical statements of this perspective. Connell argues that the oppression of women is a chief mechanism that links the various masculinities, and that the marginalization of certain masculinities is an important component of the reproduction of male power over women. This critique of the hegemonic definition of masculinity as a perspective on men's lives is one of the organizing principles of our book, which is the first college-level text in this second generation of work on men and masculinities.

Now that we have reviewed some of the traditional explanations for gender relations and have situated this book within the research on gender in general, and men in particular, let us briefly outline exactly the theoretical perspective we have employed in the book.

The Social Construction of Masculinities

Men are not born, growing from infants through boyhood to manhood, to follow a predetermined biological imperative encoded in their physical organization. To be a man is to participate in social life as a man, as a gendered being. Men are not born; they are made. And men make themselves, actively constructing their masculinities within a social and historical context.

This book is about how men are made and how men make themselves in contemporary U.S. society. It is about what masculinity means, about how masculinity is organized, and about the social institutions that sustain and elaborate it. It is

a book in which we will trace what it means to be a man over the course of men's lives.

Men's Lives revolves around three important themes that are part of a social scientific perspective. First, we have adopted a *social constructionist* perspective. By this, we mean that the important fact of men's lives is not that they are biological males, but that they become men. Our sex may be male, but our identity as men is developed through a complex process of interaction with the culture in which we both learn the gender scripts appropriate to our culture and attempt to modify those scripts to make them more palatable. The second axis around which the book is organized follows from our social constructionist perspective. As we have argued, the experience of masculinity is not uniform and universally generalizable to all men in our society. Masculinity differs dramatically in our society, and we have organized the book to illustrate the *variations* among men in the construction of masculinity. Third, we have adopted a *life course* perspective, to chart the construction of these various masculinities in men's lives and to examine pivotal developmental moments or institutional locations during a man's life in which the meanings of masculinity are articulated. Social constructionism, variations among men, and the life course perspective define the organization of this book and the criteria we have used to select the articles included.

The Social Constructionist Model

The social constructionist perspective argues that the meaning of masculinity is neither transhistorical nor culturally universal, but rather varies from culture to culture and within any one culture over time. Thus, males become men in the United States in the early twenty-first century in a way that is very different from men in Southeast Asia, or Kenya, or Sri Lanka.

Men's lives also vary within any one culture over time. The experience of masculinity in the contemporary United States is very different from that experience 150 years ago. Who would argue that what it meant to be a "real man" in seventeenth-century France (at least among the upper classes)—high-heeled patent leather shoes, red velvet jackets covering frilly white lace shirts, lots of rouge and white powder makeup, and a taste for the elegant refinement of ornate furniture—bears much resemblance to the meaning of masculinity among a similar class of French men today?

A perspective that emphasizes the social construction of gender is, therefore, both *historical* and *comparative*. It allows us to explore the ways in which the meanings of gender vary from culture to culture, and how they change within any one culture over historical time.

Variations among Men

Masculinity also varies *within* any one society according to the various types of cultural groups that compose it. Subcultures are organized around other poles, which are the primary way in which people organize themselves and by which resources are distributed. And men's experiences differ from one another according to what social scientists have identified as the chief structural mechanisms along which power and resources are distributed. We cannot speak of masculinity in the United States as if it were a single, easily identifiable commodity. To do so is to risk positing one version of masculinity as normative and making all other masculinities problematic.

In the contemporary United States, masculinity is constructed differently by class culture, by race and ethnicity, and by age. And each of these axes of masculinity modifies the others. Black masculinity differs from white masculinity, yet each of them is also further modified by class and age. A 30-year-old middle-class black man will have some things in common with a 30-year-old middle-class white man that he might not share with a 60-year-old working-class black man, although he will share with him elements of masculinity that are different from those of the white man of his class and age. The resulting matrix of *masculinities* is complicated by crosscutting elements; without understanding this, we

risk collapsing all masculinities into one hegemonic version.

The challenge to a singular definition of masculinity as the normative definition is the second axis around which the readings in this book revolve.

The Life Course Perspective

The meaning of masculinity is not constant over the course of any man's life but will change as he grows and matures. The issues confronting a man about proving himself and feeling successful and the social institutions in which he will attempt to enact his definitions of masculinity will change throughout his life. Therefore, we have adopted a *life course perspective* to discuss the ways in which different issues will emerge for men at different times of their lives and the ways in which men's lives, themselves, change over time. The life course perspective that we have employed will examine men's lives at various pivotal moments in their development from young boys to adults. As in a slide show, these points will freeze the action for a short while, to afford us the opportunity to examine in more detail the ways in which different men in our culture experience masculinity at any one time.

The book's organization reflects these three concerns. Part One sets the context through which we shall examine men's lives. Parts Two through Ten follow those lives through their full course, examining central moments experienced by men in the United States today. Specifically, Parts Two and Three touch on boyhood and adolescence, discussing some of the institutions organized to embody and reproduce masculinities in the United States, such as fraternities, the Boy Scouts, and sports groups. Part Four, "Men and Work," explores the ways in which masculinities are constructed in relation to men's occupations. Part Five, "Men and Health," deals with heart attacks, stress, AIDS, and other health problems among men. Part Six, "Men in Relationships," describes men's emotional and sexual relationships. We deal with heterosexuality and homosexuality, mindful of the ways in which variations are based on specific lines (class, race, ethnicity). Part Seven, "Male Sexualities," studies the normative elements of heterosexuality and probes the controversial political implications of pornography as a source of both straight and gay men's sexual information. Part Eight, "Men in Families," concentrates on masculinities within the family and the role of men as husbands, fathers, and senior citizens. Part Nine, "Masculinities in the Media," explores the different ways the media present modes of masculinity. Part Ten, "Violence and Masculinities," looks at violence as the most obdurate, intractable behavioral gender difference. Part Eleven, "Men, Movements, and the Future," examines some of the ways in which men are changing and points to some directions in which men might continue to change.

Our perspective, stressing the social construction of masculinities over the life course, will, we believe, allow a more comprehensive understanding of men's lives in the United States today.

References

Brod, Harry, ed. *The Making of Masculinities*. Boston: Unwin, Hyman, 1987.

Carrigan, Tim, Bob Connell, and John Lee. "Toward a New Sociology of Masculinity" in *Theory and Society*, 1985, 5(14).

Chodorow, Nancy. *The Reproduction of Mothering*. Berkeley: University of California Press, 1978.

Connell, R. W. *Gender and Power*. Stanford, CA: Stanford University Press, 1987.

David, Deborah, and Robert Brannon, eds. *The Forty-Nine Percent Majority*. Reading, MA: Addison-Wesley, 1976.

Elliott, J. H. *Richelieu and Olivares*. New York: Cambridge University Press, 1984.

Epstein, Cynthia Fuchs. "Inevitability of Prejudice" in *Society*, Sept./Oct., 1986.

Farrell, Warren. *The Liberated Man*. New York: Random House, 1975.

Feigen-Fasteau, Marc. *The Male Machine*. New York: McGraw-Hill, 1974.

Gilligan, Carol. *In a Different Voice*. Cambridge, MA: Harvard University Press, 1982.

Gilder, George. *Men and Marriage*. Gretna, LA: Pelican Publishers, 1986.

Goldberg, Steven. *The Inevitability of Patriarchy*. New York: William Morrow & Co., 1975.

—— "Reaffirming the Obvious" in *Society*, Sept./Oct., 1986.

Hearn, Jeff. *The Gender of Oppression*. New York: St. Martin's Press, 1987.

Hrdy, Sandra Blaffer. *The Woman That Never Evolved*. Cambridge, MA: Harvard University Press, 1981.

Kimmel, Michael S., ed. *Changing Men: New Directions in Research on Men and Masculinity*. Newbury Park, CA: Sage Publications, 1987.

Mead, Margaret. *Sex and Temperament in Three Primitive Societies*. New York: McGraw-Hill, 1935.

Pleck, Elizabeth, and Joseph Pleck, eds. *The American Man*. Englewood Cliffs, NJ: Prentice-Hall, 1980.

Pleck, Joseph. *The Myth of Masculinity*. Cambridge, MA: M.I.T. Press, 1981.

—— and Jack Sawyer, eds. *Men and Masculinity*. Englewood Cliffs, NJ: Prentice-Hall, 1974.

Tiger, Lionel, and Robin Fox. *The Imperial Animal*. New York: Holt, Rinehart & Winston, 1984.

Trivers, Robert. "Parental Investment and Sexual Selection" in *Sexual Selection and the Descent of Man* (B. Campbell, ed.). Chicago: Aldine Publishers, 1972.

Wilkinson, Rupert. *American Tough: The Tough Guy Tradition and American Character*. New York: Harper & Row, 1986.

Wilson, E. O. *Sociobiology: The New Synthesis*. Cambridge, MA: Harvard University Press, 1976.

PART ONE

Perspectives on Masculinities

A quick glance at any magazine rack or television talk show is enough to make you aware that these days, men are confused. What does it mean to be a "real man"? How are men supposed to behave? What are men supposed to feel? How are men to express their feelings? Who are we supposed to be like: Eminem or Boyz II Men? Jimmy Kimmel or Carson Kressley? Derek Jeter or Kobe Bryant? Rhett Butler or Ashley Wilkes?

We are bombarded daily with images and handy rules to help us negotiate our way through a world in which all the rules seem to have suddenly vanished or changed. Some tell us to reassert traditional masculinity against all contemporary challenges. But a strength that is built only on the weakness of others hardly feels like strength at all. Others tell us that men are in power, the oppressor. But if men are in power as a group, why do individual men often feel so powerless? Can men change?

These questions will return throughout this book. These articles in Part One begin to unravel the "masculine mystique" and suggest various dimensions of men's position in society, their power, their powerlessness, and their confusion.

But we cannot speak of "masculinity" as some universal category that is experienced in the same ways by each man. "All men are alike" runs a popular saying. But are they really? Are gay men's experiences with work, relationships, love, and politics similar to those of heterosexual men? Do black and Chicano men face the same problems and conflicts in their daily lives that white men face? Do middle-class men have the same political interests as blue-collar men? The answers to these questions, as the articles in this part suggest, are not simple.

Although earlier studies of men and masculinity focused on the apparently universal norms of masculinity, recent work has attempted to demonstrate how different the worlds of various men are. Men are divided along the same lines that divide any other group: race, class, sexual orientation, ethnicity, age, and geographic region. Men's lives vary in crucial ways, and understanding these variations will take us a long way toward understanding men's experiences.

Earlier studies that suggested a single universal norm of masculinity reproduced some of the problems they were trying to solve. To be sure, *all* benefit from the inequality between women and men; for example, think of how rape jokes or male-exclusive sports culture provide contexts for the bonding of men across class, race, and ethnic lines while denying full participation to women.

But the single, seemingly universal masculinity obscured ways in which some men hold and maintain power over other men in our society, hiding the fact that men do not all share equally in the fruits of gender inequality.

Here is how sociologist Erving Goffman put it in his important book *Stigma* (New York: Doubleday, 1963, p. 128):

> In an important sense there is only one complete unblushing male in America: a young, married, white, urban, northern, heterosexual Protestant father of college education, fully employed, of good complexion, weight, and height, and a recent record in sports. Every American male tends to look out upon the world from this perspective, this constituting one sense in which one can speak of a common value system in America. Any male who fails to qualify in any one of these ways is likely to view himself—during moments at least—as unworthy, incomplete, and inferior.

As Goffman suggests, middle-class, white, heterosexual masculinity is used as the marker against which other masculinities are measured, and by which standard they may be found wanting. What is *normative* (prescribed) becomes translated into what is *normal*. In this way, heterosexual men maintain their status by the oppression of gay men; middle-aged men can maintain their dominance over older and younger men; upper-class men can exploit working-class men; and white men can enjoy privileges at the expense of men of color.

The articles in this section explore this idea of masculinities as plural. Alfredo Mirande and Yen Le Espiritu focus on the different ways in which different groups of men (Latino and Asian American) experience masculinities. They suggest that an understanding of class, ethnic, and racial minorities requires an understanding of how political, social, and economic factors shape and constrain the possibilities and personal lifestyle choices for different groups of men. Calls for "changing masculinities," these articles suggest, must involve an emphasis on *institutional* transformation.

And yet despite all these differences among men, men also share some important common characteristics. Barry Deutsch suggests that all men, regardless of race, class, ethnicity, sexuality, or age, benefit from a set of privileges that are so ordinary that they are invisible. Martha McCaughey shows how the new "science" of evolutionary psychology has rushed in to shore up a biological and evolutionary foundation for male dominance and violence.

Martha McCaughey

Caveman Masculinity:
Finding an Ethnicity in Evolutionary Science

The Caveman as Retrosexuality

Most of us can call up some image of prehistoric man and his treatment of women. He's a shaggy, well-muscled caveman, whose name is Thor, and we might picture him, club in hand, approaching a scrawny but curvaceous woman, whom he bangs over the head and drags by the hair into a cave to mate. I'm sure the majority of readers recognize this imagery. Indeed, today an image of modern men as guided by such prehistoric tendencies is even celebrated on T-shirts sold to American men on websites that allow people to post and sell their own designs. One such image for sale on the cafepress website features a version of Thor, wearing a fur pelt and holding a club, accompanied by the slogan "ME FIND WOMAN!" Another image available for T-shirts, boxer shorts, baseball caps, and coffee mugs features a man dressed in a one-shoulder fur pelt, with his club, smiling behind a cavewoman who is wearing a fur bikini outfit and cooking a skinned animal on a spit, with the saying "MEN'S PRIORITYS [sic]: 10,000 YEARS LATER AND STILL ON THE HUNT FOR FOOD AND SEX!" Another image features only the club, with the saying, "caveman: primitive pimpin'."

Everywhere we look we can find applications of an increasingly fashionable academic exercise—the invocation of evolutionary theory to explain human male behaviors, particularly de-

plorable behaviors such as sexual harassment, rape, and aggression more generally. The familiar portrayals of sex differences based in evolution popularize and legitimize an academic version of evolutionary thought known increasingly as evolutionary psychology, a field referred to as the "science of the mind."[1] The combination of scholarly and popular attention to evolution and human male sexuality has increasingly lodged American manhood in an evolutionary logic. The discourse of evolutionary science has become part of popular consciousness, a sort of cultural consensus about who men are.

The evolutionary theory is that our human male ancestors were in constant competition with one another for sexual access to fertile women, who were picky about their mate choices given the high level of parental investment required of the human female for reproduction—months of gestation, giving birth, and then years of lactation and care for a dependent child. The human male's low level of parental investment required for reproduction, we are told, resulted in the unique boorishness of the hairier sex: He is sexually promiscuous; he places an enormous emphasis on women's youth and beauty, which he ogles every chance he gets; he either cheats on his wife or wants to; and he can be sexually aggressive to the point of criminality.

We find references to man's evolutionary heritage not only on T-shirts but in new science textbooks, pop psychology books on relationships, men's magazine, and Broadway shows. There are caveman fitness plans and caveman diets. *Saturday Night Live*'s hilarious "Unfrozen Caveman Lawyer" and the affronted caveman of the

Geico car insurance ads joke about the ubiquity of caveman narratives. More disturbingly, the Darwinian discourse also crops up when men need an excuse for antisocial behavior. One man, who was caught on amateur video participating in the Central Park group sexual assaults in the summer of 2000, can be heard on video telling his sobbing victim, "Welcome back to the caveman times." How does a man come to think of himself as a caveman when he attacks a woman? What made so many American men decide that it's the DNA, rather than the devil, that makes them do it?

Using the late sociologist Pierre Bourdieu's theory of habitus, or the account of how cultural ideas are taken up in the form of bodily habits and tastes that reinforce behavioral norms and social inequality, I suggest that scientific theories find their way into both popular culture and men's corporeal habits and attitudes. Evolution has become popular culture, where popular culture is more than just media representations but refers to the institutions of everyday life: family, marriage, school, work—all sites where gender and racial knowledges are performed according to images people have available to them in actionable repertoires, scripts, and narratives. As popular culture, evolutionary narratives offer men a way to embody male sexuality.

That an evolutionary account of heterosexual male desire has captured the popular imagination is obvious from *Muscle & Fitness* magazine's article on "Man the visual animal," which explains why men leer at women. Using a theory of the evolved difference between human male and female sexual psychologies developed by leading evolutionary psychologist Donald Symons, the article offers the following explanation under the subheading "Evolution Happens":

> Not much has changed in human sexuality since the Pleistocene. In his landmark book *The Evolution of Human Sexuality* (Oxford University Press, 1979), Symons hypothesizes that the male's sexual response to visual cues has been so rewarded by evolution that it's become innate.[2]

Such stories provide a means by which heterosexual male readers can experience their sexuality as acultural, primal: "The desire to ogle is your biological destiny."[3]

Evolution may happen (or may have happened), but these stories do not just happen. Their appeal seems to lie precisely in the sense of security provided by the imagined inevitability of heterosexual manhood. In a marketplace of masculine identities, the caveman ethos is served up as Viagra for the masculine soul. Just as the 1950s women suffering what Betty Friedan famously called the "feminine mystique" were supposed to seek satisfaction in their Tupperware collections and their feminine figures, men today have been offered a way to think of their masculinity as powerful, productive, even aggressive—in a new economic and political climate where real opportunities to be rewarded for such traits have slipped away.[4]

It's hardly that most men today find themselves raising children at home while female partners bring home the bacon. But, like the fifties housewife, more men must now find satisfaction despite working below their potential (given that their job skills have lost their position to technology or other labor sources) in a postindustrial service economy that is less rewarding both materially and morally. As Susan Faludi puts it in her book *Stiffed*: "The fifties housewife, stripped of her connections to a wider world and invited to fill the void with shopping and the ornamental display of her ultrafemininity, could be said to have morphed into the nineties man, stripped of his connections to a wider world and invited to fill the void with consumption and a gym-bred display of his ultra-masculinity."[5]

On top of the economic changes affecting men, during the 1990s a growing anti-rape movement also challenged men, taking them to task for the problem of violence against women. More state and federal dollars supported efforts to stop such violence, and men increasingly feared complaints and repercussions for those complaints. The rape trials of Mike Tyson and William Kennedy Smith, Jr., the increasingly common school shootings (executed overwhelmingly by boys), the sexual harassment of women by men at the Citadel, the media attention given to the notorious Spurr Posse (a gang of guys who sought sex for "points" at almost all costs), the local sexual assault trials of countless high school and college athletic stars, the sexual harassment allegations against Supreme Court Justice nominee Clarence Thomas, and the White House sex scandals involving Bill Clinton meant more lost ground. Indeed, the 1990s saw relentless—though not necessarily ill-founded—criticism of men's sexual violence and other forms of aggression.

Right-wing leaders were as upset with men as feminists and other progressives. Those opposing abortion rights argued that sexual intercourse without procreation was undermining male responsibility, and those opposing women's equal-rights legislation argued that women's liberation would only allow men to relinquish their economic obligations to their families, sending women and children into divorce-induced poverty. Considering that critics of men came from the political right and left, and from among men as well as women, it seems fair to say that in turn-of-the century America, moral disdain for men, whatever their age, race, or economic rank, had reached an all-time high.

For some men, the response was to cultivate a rude-dude attitude—popularized by Howard Stern, *The Man Show*, and MTV's endless shows about college spring break vacations. For some others, the response was to face, with a sense of responsibility and urgency, men's animal natures and either accept or reform their caveman ways. While some men were embracing the role of consumers and becoming creatures of ornamentation—the "metrosexuals"—other men revolted against metrosexuality, embracing a can-do virility that Sara Stewart in *The New York Post* referred to as "retrosexuality," or that "cringe-inducing backlash of beers and leers."[6] Caveman masculinity, with its focus on men's irrepressible heterosexuality and natural vigor, is a scientifically authorized form of retrosexuality.

The Caveman as Popular Scientific Story

Popular culture is a political Petri dish for Darwinian ideas about sex. Average American guys don't read academic evolutionary science, but many do read about science in popular magazines and in best-selling books about the significance of the latest scientific ideas. As such, it is worth examining—even when magazine writers and television producers intentionally "dumb down" relatively sophisticated academic claims. In this section, I look at the way some popular texts make sense of evolutionary claims about men. Later I suggest that the caveman ideology, much of which centers on men's aggressive heterosexuality, gets embodied and thereby reproduced.[7]

In September of 1999, *Men's Health* magazine featured a caveman fitness program. Readers are shown an exercise routine that corresponds to the physical movements their ancestors would have engaged in: throwing a spear, hauling an animal carcass, honing a stone. A nice looking clean-shaven young man is shown exercising, his physical posture mirrored by a scruffy animal skin–clad caveman behind him in the photo. Each day of the week-long routine is labeled according to the caveman mystique: building the cave home; the hunt; the chase; the kill; the long trek home; preparing for the feast; and rest. That an exercise plan is modeled after man-as-caveman reveals the common assumption that being a caveman is good for a man, a healthy existence.

Another issue of *Men's Health* magazine explains "the sex science facts" to male readers interested in "the biology of attraction." We follow the steps of a mating dance, but don't quite understand that's what we're doing. Indeed, we must learn the evolutionary history of sex to see why men feel the way they do when they notice a beautiful woman walking down the street:

Of course, out there in the street, you have no thoughts about genetic compatibility or child-bearing. Probably the farthest thing from your mind is having a child with that beautiful woman. But that doesn't matter. What you think counts for almost nothing. In the environment that crafted your brain and body, an environment in which you might be dead within minutes of spotting this beauty, the only thing that counted was that your clever neocortex—your seat of higher reason—be turned off so that you could quickly select a suitable mate, impregnate her, and succeed in passing on your genes to the next generation.[8]

The article proceeds to identify the signals of fertility that attract men: youth, beauty, big breasts, and a small waistline. Focusing on the desire for youth in women, the article tells men that "the reason men of any age continue to like young girls is that we were designed to get them pregnant and dominate their fertile years by keeping them that way. . . . When your first wife has lost the overt signals of reproductive viability, you desire a younger woman who still has them all."[9] And, of course, male readers are reminded that "your genes don't care about your wife or girlfriend or what the neighbors will say."[10]

Amy Alkon's *Winston-Salem Journal* advice column, "The Advice Goddess," uses an evolutionary theory of men's innate loutishness to comfort poor "Feeling Cheated On," who sent a letter complaining that her boyfriend fantasizes about other women during their lovemaking. The Advice Goddess cited a study by Bruce J. Ellis and Donald Symons (whose work was also mentioned in *Muscle & Fitness*) to conclude that "male sexuality is all about variety. Men are hard-wired to want you, the entire girls' dorm next door, and the entire girls' dorm next to that."[11]

Popular magazines tell men that they have a biological propensity to favor women with the faces of 11½ year-old girls (where the eyes and chin are close together) and a waist-to-hip ratio of .7 (where the waist measures 70% that of the hips). Men are told that their sexist double standard concerning appearance is evolutionary. Some of this research is very speculative—for instance, in some studies, men are simply shown photos of women with specific waist-to-hip ratios and then asked, "Would you like to spend the rest of your life with this woman?"—as though such

staged answers reveal something about the individuals' real-life choices (or genes). But the results of this research make great copy.

Men's Health magazine in 1999 offers an article called "The Mysteries of Sex . . . Explained!" and relies on evolutionary theory, quoting several professors in the field, to explain "why most women won't sleep with you." The article elucidates:

> Stop blaming your wife. The fault lies with Mother Nature, the pit boss of procreation. Neil M. Malamuth, Ph.D., professor of psychology at UCLA, explains. "You're in Las Vegas with 10 grand. Your gambling strategy will depend on which form your money takes. With 10 chips worth $1,000 each, you'd weigh each decision cautiously. With 10,000 $1 chips, you'd throw them around." That's reproductive strategy in a nutshell.[12]

Popular magazine articles like this follow a standard formula. They quote the scientists, reporting on the evolutionary theorists' research, and offer funny anecdotes about male sexuality to illustrate the research findings. This *Men's Health* article continues to account for men's having fetishes: "Men are highly sexed creatures, less interested in relationship but highly hooked on visuals, says David Givens, Ph.D., an anthropologist. 'Because sex carries fewer consequences for men, it's easier for us to use objects as surrogate sexual partners.' Me? I've got my eye on a Zenith, model 39990."[13]

It's not just these popular and often humorous accounts of men that are based in some version of evolutionary theory. Even serious academic arguments rely on evolutionary theories of human behavior. For example, Steven Rhoads, a member of the University of Virginia faculty in public policy, has written *Taking Sex Differences Seriously* (2004), a book telling us why gender equity in the home and the workplace is a feminist pipedream. Rhoads argues that women are wrong to expect men to take better care of children, do more housework, and make a place for them as equals at work because, he states, "men and women still have different natures and, generally speaking, different preferences, talents and interests."[14] He substantiates much of his argument about the divergent psychological predispositions in men and women with countless references to studies done by evolutionary scholars.

News magazines and television programs have also spent quite a bit of time popularizing evolutionary science and its implications for understanding human sex differences. The ABC news program *Day One* reported in 1995 on evolutionary psychologist David Buss's new book, *The Evolution of Desire.*[15] Buss appeared on the show, which elaborated his theory by presenting us with super model Cindy Crawford and Barbie (the doll), presumably as representations of what men are wired to find desirable. As Buss explained in the interview, our evolutionary fore-brothers who did not prefer women with high cheekbones, big eyes, lustrous hair, and full lips did not reproduce. As Buss puts it, those men who happened to like someone who was older, sicker, or infertile "are not our ancestors. We are all the descendants of those men who preferred young healthy women and so as offspring, as descendants of those men, we carry with us their desires."[16] On that same television show, *Penthouse* magazine publisher Bob Guccioni was interviewed and explained that men are simply biologically designed to enjoy looking at sexy women: "This may be very politically incorrect but that's the way it is. . . . It's all part of our ancestral conditioning."[17] Evolutionary narratives clearly work for publishers of pornography marketed to men.

Newsweek's 1996 cover story, "The Biology of Beauty: What Science has Discovered about Sex Appeal," argues that the beautylust humans exhibit "is often better suited to the Stone Age than to the Information Age; the qualities we find alluring may be powerful emblems of health, fertility and resistance to disease. . . ."[18] Though "beauty isn't all that matters in life," the article asserts, "our weakness for 'biological quality' is the cause of endless pain and injustice."[19]

Sometimes the magazines and TV shows covering the biological basis of sexual desire give a nod to the critics. The aforementioned *Newsweek*

article, for instance, quotes feminist writer Katha Pollitt, who insists that "human beings cannot be reduced to DNA packets."[20] And then, as if to affirm Pollitt's claim, homosexuality is invoked as an example of the countless non-adaptive delights we desire: "Homosexuality is hard to explain as a biological adaptation. So is stamp collecting. . . . We pursue countless passions that have no direct bearing on survival."[21] So when there is a nod to ways humans are not hardwired, homosexual desires are framed as oddities having no basis in nature, while heterosexual attraction along the lines of stereotypical heterosexual male fantasy is framed as biological. Heterosexual desire enjoys a *biologically correct* status.

Zoologist Desmond Morris explains how evolutionary theory applies to humans in his 1999 six-part television series, *Desmond Morris' The Human Animal: A Personal View of the Human Species.*[22] The first show in the series draws from his book, *The Naked Ape,* explaining that humans are relatively hairless with little to protect themselves besides their big brains.[23] This is stated as we watch two naked people, one male and one female, walk through a public place where everyone else is dressed in modern-day clothing. Both are white, both are probably 25 to 30 years old, both look like models (the man with well-chiseled muscles, a suntan, and no chest hair; the woman thin, yet shapely with larger than average breasts, shaved legs, and a manicured pubic region). This presentation of man and woman in today's aesthetically ideal form as the image of what all of us were once like is *de rigueur* for any popular representation of evolutionary theory applied to human sexuality. No woman is flabby, flat chested, or has body hair; no man has pimples or back hair. These culturally mandated ideal body types are presented as the image of what our human ancestors naturally looked like. In this way and others, such shows posit modern aesthetic standards as states of nature.

Time magazine's 1994 cover story on "Our Cheating Hearts" reports that "the emerging field known as evolutionary psychology" gives us "fresh detail about the feelings and thoughts that draw us into marriage—or push us out."[24] After

explaining the basics about men being less discriminating about their sexual partners than
women, the article moves on to discuss why people divorce, anticipating resistance to the evolutionary explanation:

> Objections to this sort of analysis are pre-
> dictable: "But people leave marriages for emo-
> tional reasons. They don't add up their offspring
> and pull out their calculators." But emotions
> are just evolution's executioners. Beneath the
> thoughts and feelings and temperamental dif-
> ferences marriage counselors spend their time
> sensitively assessing are the stratagems of the
> genes—cold, hard equations composed of sim-
> ple variables: social status, age of spouse, num-
> ber of children, their ages, outside romantic
> opportunities, and so on. Is the wife really
> duller and more nagging than she was 20 years
> ago? Maybe, but maybe the husband's tolerance
> for nagging has dropped now that she is 45 and
> has no reproductive future.[25]

In case *Time* readers react to the new evolutionary psychology as part of a plot to destroy
the cherished nuclear family, they are told that
"progress will also depend on people using the
explosive insight of evolutionary psychology in a
morally responsible way. . . . We are potentially
moral animals—which is more than any other animal can say—but we are not naturally moral animals. The first step to being moral is to realize
how thoroughly we aren't."[26]

While many accounts of evolution's significance for male sexuality seem simply to ratio-
nalize sexist double standards and wallow in
men's loutishness, a number of pop-Darwinist
claims have the moral purpose of liberating men
from being controlled by their caveman natures.
Their message: Men can become enlightened
cavemen. These popular versions of man as caveman make an attempt to liberate men by getting
them to see themselves differently. They tell men
that they are cavemen with potential. They either make fun of men's putatively natural shortcomings or encourage them to cage the caveman
within through a kind of scientific consciousness-
raising.

Rob Becker's one-man show, *Defending the
Caveman*, played Broadway and elsewhere from
1993 to 2005. This performance piece poking fun
at sex differences is the longest running solo play
in Broadway history. It relies on a longstanding
man-the-hunter and woman-the-gatherer framework, from which modern sex differences follow.
Cavemen hunted and focused on their prey until
killing it. Cavewomen gathered things to use in
the cave home. Men are thus strong silent types
while women are into communication and togetherness. More significantly, *Defending the Caveman*'s creator and performer believes men have a
bad rap. Becker points out that women say "men
are all assholes" with a kind of feminist cultural
authority men no longer enjoy when they make
derogatory remarks about women. Rob Becker
thus echoes the common sentiment among American men today that men are in the untenable position of being both hated and ignorant. They
may want to try but they are unable to succeed.
The show validates many people's observations of
the behavior patterns and sex battles in their daily
lives, and seems to poke fun at men's shortcomings—all the while affirming a vision of men as
being as similar as peas in a primordial pea soup.

Evolution as Ideology

A critical examination of evolutionary science in
its popular cultural manifestations over the past
15 to 20 years—the way most men come to know
of the theory about their sexuality—allows us to
ask how men come to know what they know
about themselves. This type of analysis assumes
that evolution is an ideology—which is not to suggest that humans got here via God's creation or
some means other than evolution by natural selection. Positioning evolutionary arguments
about human nature as an ideology is to understand that people think and act in ways that take
evolutionary theory, however they construe it, as
a self-evident truth. Furthermore, positioning evolutionary theory applied to humans as an ideology allows us to examine the way evolutionary
ideas about male sexuality circulate in our culture. It is on this basis that I challenge the conve-

nient innocence with which men invoke science to explain their bodies and their actions.

The caveman is certainly not the only form of masculine identity in our times. But the emergence of a caveman masculinity tells us much about the authority of science, the flow of scientific ideas in our culture, and the embodiment of those ideas. In *Science, Culture and Society* Mark Erickson explains the connection between science and society in our times:

> We live with science: science surrounds us, invades our lives, and alters our perspective on the world. We see things from a scientific perspective, in that we use science to help us make sense of the world—regardless of whether or not that is an appropriate thing to do—and to legitimize the picture of the world that results from such investigations.[27]

In a culture so attached to scientific authority and explication, it is worth examining the popular appeal of evolutionary theory and its impact on masculine embodiment. The popularity of the scientific story of men's evolved desires—however watered down or distorted the science becomes as enthusiasts popularize it—can tell us something about the appeal and influence of that story.

The Caveman as Embodied Ethos

If the evolutionary stories appeal to many men, and it seems they do indeed, it's because they ring true. Many men feel like their bodies are aggressive. They feel urges, at a physical level, in line with evolutionary theoretical predictions. With a naïve understanding of experience, men can see affect as having an authenticity and empirical validity to it. In other words, the men who feel like cavemen do not see their identity as a fiction; it is their bodily reality and is backed by scientific study.

Certainly, evolutionary scholars would argue that the actual evolved psychologies make men feel like cavemen, or at least make those feelings emerge or affect behavior in particular environ-

ments. I argue that this explanation too simplistically separates men's bodies from discourse.

The work of Pierre Bourdieu provides a tool for understanding how power is organized at the level of unconscious embodiment of cultural forces. I suggest that popular manifestations of scientific evolutionary narratives about men's sexuality have a real material effect on many men. Bourdieu's theory of practice develops the concepts of *habitus* and *field* to describe a reciprocally constitutive relationship between bodily dispositions and dominant power structures. Bourdieu concerned himself primarily with the ways in which socioeconomic class is incorporated at the level of the body, including class-based ways of speaking, postures, lifestyles, attitudes, and tastes.

Significant for Bourdieu is that people acquire tastes that mark them as members of particular social groups and particular social levels.[28] Membership in a particular social class produces and reproduces a class sensibility, what Bourdieu (1990) called "practical sense."[29] Habitus is "a somatized social relationship, a social law converted into an embodied law."[30] The process of becoming competent in the everyday life of a society or group constitutes habitus. Bourdieu's notion of embodiment can be extended to suggest that habitus, as embodied field, amounts to "the pleasurable and ultimately erotic constitution of [the individual's] social imaginary."[31]

Concerning the circulation of evolutionary narratives, we can see men taking erotic pleasure in the formation of male identity and the performance of accepted norms of heterosexual masculinity using precisely these tools of popular evolutionary science. Put differently, pop-Darwinism is a discourse that finds its way into men's bones and boners. The caveman story can become a man's practical sense of who he is and what he desires. This is so because masculinity is a dimension of embodied and performative practical sensibility—because men carry themselves with a bodily comportment suggestive of their position as the dominant gender, and they invest themselves in particular lifestyle practices, consumption patterns, attire, and bodily comportment. Evolutionary narratives thus enter the so-called habitus, and an aestheticized discourse and image of the caveman circulates through popular culture becoming part of natural perception, and consequently is reproduced by those embodying it.

In his study of the overwhelmingly white and male workspace of the Options Exchange floor, sociologist Richard Widick uses Bourdieu's theory to explain the traders' physical and psychical engagement with their work. Widick holds that "the traders' inhabitation and practical mastery of the trading floor achieves the bio-physical psycho-social state of a natural identity."[32] Hence the traders describe their manner as a "trading instinct." In a similar way, American men with what we might call a caveman instinct can be said to have acquired a "pre-reflexive practical sense" of themselves as heterosexually driven.[33]

Bourdieu gives the name "symbolic violence" to that process by which we come to accept and embody power relations without ever accepting them in the conscious sense of knowing them and choosing them. We hold beliefs that don't need to be thought—the effects of which can be "durably and deeply embedded in the body in the form of dispositions."[34] From this perspective, the durable dispositions of evolutionary discourse are apparent in our rape culture, for example, when a member of the group sexual assault in New York tells the woman he's attacking, "Welcome back to the caveman times." Embodying the ideology of irrepressible heterosexual desire makes such aggression appear to be natural.

Bourdieu's theory allows us to see that both cultural and material forces reveal themselves in the lived reality of social relations.[35] We can see on men's bodies the effects of their struggle with slipping economic privilege and a sense of entitlement to superiority over women. If men live out power struggles in their everyday experiences, then caveman masculinity can be seen as an imagined compensation for men's growing sense of powerlessness.[36] To be sure, some men have more social and economic capital than others. Those with less might invest even more in their bodies and appearances.[37]

Sociologist R. W. Connell discusses the significance of naturalizing male power. He states:

> The physical sense of maleness is not a simple thing. It involves size and shape, habits of posture and movement, particular physical skills and the lack of others, the image of one's own body, the way it is presented to other people and the ways they respond to it, the way it operates at work and in sexual relations. In no sense is all this a consequence of XY chromosomes, or even of the possession on which discussions of masculinity have so lovingly dwelt, the penis. The physical sense of maleness grows through a personal history of social practice, a life-history-in-society.[38]

We see and believe that men's power over women is the order of nature because "power is translated not only into mental body-images and fantasies, but into muscle tensions, posture, the feel and texture of the body."[39] Scientific discourse constitutes the field for some men in the constructed figure of the caveman, enabling those men to internalize such an identity. The caveman thus becomes an imaginative projection that is experienced and lived as real biological truth.

In his book, *Cultural Boundaries of Science,* Thomas Gieryn comments on the cultural authority of science, suggesting that "if 'science' says so, we are more often than not inclined to believe it or act on it—and to prefer it to claims lacking this epistemic seal of approval."[40] To his observation I would add that we are also more likely to *live* it. Ideas that count as scientific, regardless of their truth value, become lived ideologies. It's how modern American men have become cavemen and how the caveman ethos enjoys reproductive success.

Cultural anthropologist Paul Rabinow gives the name "biosociality" to the formation of new group and individual identities and practices that emerge from the scientific study of human life.[41] Rabinow offers the example of neurofibromatosis groups whose members have formed to discuss their experiences, educate their children, lobby for their disease, and "understand" their fate. And in the future, he points out, ". . . [i]t is not hard to imagine groups formed around the chromosome 17, locus 16,256, site 654,376 allele variant with a guanine substitution."[42] Rabinow's concept of biosociality is instructive here; for the discourse of the caveman offers this form of biosociality. The caveman constitutes an identity based on new scientific "facts" about one's biology.

Of course, evolutionary psychologists would have us think that men's desires are, in some final instance, biological properties of an internal psyche or sexual psychology. I am suggesting, in line with Bourdieu, that men's desires are always performed in relation to the dominant discourses in circulation within their cultural lifeworlds, either for or against the representations that permeate those lifeworlds. We can see that a significant number of men are putting the pop-Darwinian rhetoric to good use in social interactions. The scientific discourse of the caveman (however unscientific we might regard it by the time it gets to everyday guys reading magazines and watching TV) is corporealized, quite literally incorporated into living identities, deeply shaping these men's experience of being a man.

The Caveman as Ethnicity

I recognize the lure of the caveman narrative. After all, it provides an explanation for patterns we do see and for how men do feel in contemporary society, tells men that they are beings who are the way they are for a specific reason, offers them an answer about what motivates them, and carries the authority of scientific investigation about their biological makeup. Evolutionary theory offers an origin story. Plus, it's fun: thinking of the reasons you might feel a certain way because such feelings might have been necessary for your ancestors to survive a hostile environment back in the Pleistocene can be a satisfying intellectual exercise.

In telling men a story about who they are, naturally, pop-Darwinism has the normalizing, disciplinary effect of forging a common, biologi-

cal identity among men. Embodying ideology allows men to feel morally exonerated while they reproduce that very ideology. The discourse of male biological unity suppresses many significant differences among men, and of course many ways in which men would otherwise identify with women's tastes and behaviors. The evolutionary explanation of men's sexual behavior is an all encompassing narrative enabling men to frame their own thoughts and experiences through it. As such it's a *grand narrative,* a totalizing theory explaining men's experiences as though all men act and feel the same ways, and as though the ideas of Western science provide a universal truth about those actions and feelings.

I'm skeptical of this kind of totalizing narrative about male sexuality because evolution applied to human beings does not offer that sort of truth. The application of evolutionary theory to human behavior is not as straightforwardly scientific as it might seem, even for those of us who believe in the theory of evolution by natural selection. It is a partial, political discourse that authorizes certain prevalent masculine behaviors and a problematic acceptance of those behaviors. I think there are better—less totalizing, and differently consequential—discourses out there that describe and explain those same behaviors. I'm also skeptical of men's use of the evolutionary narrative because, at its best, it can only create "soft patriarchs"—kinder, gentler cavemen who resist the putative urges of which evolutionary science makes them aware.[43]

Caveman masculinity has become an "ethnic option," a way of identifying and living one's manhood. Mary C. Waters explains that ethnic identity is "far from the automatic labeling of a primordial characteristic" but instead is a complex, socially created identity.[44] As an ethnicity, caveman masculinity is seen as not only impossible but also undesirable to change.[45] The caveman as an ethnicity reveals an embrace of biology as a reaction to social constructionist understandings of masculinity, feminist demands on men, and the changing roles of men at work and in families.

To repeat: My quarrel is not limited to evolutionary theorists alone. Darwinian ideas are often spread by enthusiasts—secondary school teachers, science editors of various newspapers and magazines, and educational television show producers—who take up evolutionary theorists' ideas and convey them to mass audiences. Evolutionary thinking has become popular in part because it speaks to a publicly recognized predicament of men. Changing economic patterns have propelled men's flight from marriage and breadwinning, in conjunction with women's increased (albeit significantly less prosperous) independence. If a man today wants multiple partners with as little commitment as possible, evolutionary rhetoric answers why this is so.

Evolutionary science doesn't tell a flattering story about men. But more significantly, many people don't understand that it's *a story*. Evolution has become not only a grand narrative but also a lived ideology. Maleness and femaleness, like heterosexuality and homosexuality, are not simply identities but *systems of knowledge*.[46] And those systems of knowledge inform thinking and acting. Bourdieu's concept of habitus explains the ways in which culture and knowledge, including evolutionary knowledge, implant themselves at the level of the body, becoming a set of attitudes, tastes, perceptions, actions, and reactions. The status of science as objective, neutral knowledge helps make evolution a lived ideology because it feels truthful, natural, real.

Taking the historical and cultural changes affecting men seriously and embracing the diversity among men demand new understandings of masculinity, identity, and science. In gaining such a sociological perspective, men might resist making gender a new ethnicity and instead take a great leap forward to become new kinds of men.

Notes

1. For defenses of the study of the popularization of scientific discourse, and exemplary studies of the popularization of Darwinian discourse in different eras, see Alfred Kelly, *The Descent of Darwin: The Popularization of Darwinism in Germany, 1860–1914* (Chapel Hill: University of North Carolina Press, 1981) and Alvar Ellegård, *Darwin and the General Reader: The Reception of Darwin's Theory of Evolution in the British Press, 1859–1872* (Chicago: University of Chicago Press, 1990).

2. Mary Ellen Strote, "Man the Visual Animal," *Muscle & Fitness* (February 1994): 166.

3. Ibid., 166.

4. Betty Friedan, *The Feminine Mystique* (New York: Dell Publishing Company, 1963).

5. Susan Faludi, *Stiffed: The Betrayal of the American Man* (New York: HarperCollins, 1999), 40.

6. Sara Stewart, "Beasty Boys—'Retrosexuals' Call for Return of Manly Men; Retrosexuals Rising," *The New York Post*, July 18, 2006).

7. My argument here parallels a study of the pervasive iconography of the gene in popular culture. In *The DNA Mystique: The Gene As a Cultural Icon*, Dorothy Nelkin and M. Susan Lindee (New York: W. H. Freeman and Company, 1995, 11) explain that popular culture provides "narratives of meaning." Those narratives filter complex ideas, provide guidance, and influence how people see themselves and evaluate other people, ideas, and policies. In this way, Nelkin and Lindee argue, DNA works as an ideology to justify boundaries of identity and legal rights, as well as to explain criminality, addiction, and personality. Of course addict genes and criminal genes are misnomers—the definitions of what counts as an addict and what counts as a crime have shifted throughout history. Understanding DNA stories as ideological clarifies why, for example, people made sense of Elvis's talents and shortcomings by referring to his genetic stock (Ibid., 79-80). To call narratives of DNA ideological, then, is *not* to resist the scientific argument that deoxyribonucleic acid is a double-helix structure carrying information forming living cells and tissues, but to look at the way people make sense of DNA and use DNA to make sense of people and events in their daily lives.

8. Laurence Gonzales, "The Biology of Attraction," *Men's Health* 20.7 (2005): 186–93.

9. Ibid., 192.

10. Ibid., 193.

11. Amy Alkon, "Many Men Fantasize During Sex, But It Isn't a Talking Point," *Winston-Salem Journal*, 29 September 2005, p. 34.

12. Greg Gutfeld, "The Mysteries of Sex . . . Explained!," *Men's Health* April: 1999, 76.

13. Ibid., 76.

14. Steven E. Rhoads, *Taking Sex Differences Seriously* (San Francisco: Encounter Books, 2004), 4.

15. David M. Buss, *The Evolution of Desire: Strategies of Human Mating* (New York: BasicBooks, 1994).

16. *Day One* reported in 1995. ABC News.

17. Ibid.

18. Geoffrey Cowley, "The Biology of Beauty," *Newsweek* 127 (1996): 62.

19. Ibid., 64.

20. Ibid., 66.

21. Ibid.

22. *Desmond Morris' The Human Animal: A Personal View of the Human Species* ["Beyond Survival"]. Clive Bromhall, dir. (Discovery Communication/TLC Video, 1999).

23. Desmond Morris, *The Naked Ape* (New York: Dell Publishing, 1967).

24. Robert Wright, *The Moral Animal: Evolutionary Psychology and Everyday Life* (New York: Pantheon Books, 1994), 15.

25. Ibid., 50.

26. Ibid., 52.

27. Mark Erickson, *Science, Culture and Society* (Cambridge: Polity Press, 2005), 224.

28. Pierre Bourdieu, *Distinction: A Social Critique of the Judgment of Taste* (Cambridge: Harvard University Press, 1984).

29. Pierre Bourdieu, *The Logic of Practice* (Stanford: Stanford University Press, 1990).

30. Pierre Bourdieu, *Masculine Domination* (Stanford: Sanford University Press, 2001).

31. Richard Widick, "Flesh and the Free Market: (On Taking Bourdieu to the Options Exchange)," *Theory and Society* 32 (2003): 679–723, 716.

32. Widick, 701.

33. Ibid.

34. Bourdieu, *Masculine*, 39.

35. Lois McNay, "Agency and Experience: Gender As a Lived Relation," in *Feminism After Bourdieu*, ed. Lisa Adkins and Bev Skeggs (Oxford: Blackwell, 2004), 177.

36. See McNay 175–90 for a discussion of emotional compensation and lived experience.

37. See Beverley Skeggs, *Formations of Class and Gender: Becoming Respectable* (London: Sage, 1997) for a study pointing this out about working class women.

38. R. W. Connell, *Gender and Power: Society, the Person and Sexual Politics* (Cambridge: Polity Press, 1987), 84.

39. Ibid., 85.

40. Thomas F. Gieryn, *Cultural Boundaries of Science: Credibility on the Line* (Chicago: University of Chicago Press, 1999), 1.

41. Paul Rabinow, *Making PCR, A Story of Biotechnology* (Chicago: University of Chicago Press, 1996), 101–102.

42. Ibid., 102.

43. I am appropriating W. Bradford Wilcox's term, from his book *Soft Patriarchs, New Men: How Christianity Shapes Fathers and Husbands* (Chicago: University of Chicago Press, 2004). Wilcox argues that the Christian men's movement known as the Promise Keepers encourages men to spend more time with their wives and children without ever challenging the fundamental patriarchal family structure that places men at the top.

44. Mary C. Waters, *Ethnic Options: Choosing Identities in America,* Berkeley: University of California Press, 1990), 16.

45. See Michael S. Kimmel, *Manhood in America: A Cultural History* (New York: Free Press, 1996), 127–137.

46. Steven Seidman, *Difference Troubles: Queering Social Theory and Sexual Politics* (Cambridge, UK: Cambridge University Press, 1997), 93.

Barry Deutsch

The Male Privilege Checklist*

In 1990, Wellesley College professor Peggy McIntosh wrote an essay called "White Privilege: Unpacking the Invisible Knapsack." McIntosh observes that whites in the U.S. are "taught to see racism only in individual acts of meanness, not in invisible systems conferring dominance on my group." To illustrate these invisible systems, McIntosh wrote a list of 26 invisible privileges whites benefit from.

As McIntosh points out, men also tend to be unaware of their own privileges as men. In the spirit of McIntosh's essay, I thought I'd compile a list similar to McIntosh's, focusing on the invisible privileges benefiting men.

Due to my own limitations, this list is unavoidably U.S. centric. I hope that writers from other cultures will create new lists, or modify this one, to reflect their own experiences.

Since I first compiled it, the list has been posted many times on internet discussion groups. Very helpfully, many people have suggested additions to the checklist. More commonly, of course, critics (usually, but not exclusively, male) have pointed out men have disadvantages too—being drafted into the army, being expected to suppress emotions, and so on. These are indeed bad things—but I never claimed that life for men is all ice cream sundaes.

Obviously, there are individual exceptions to most problems discussed on the list. The existence of individual exceptions does not mean that *general problems* are not a concern.

Pointing out that men are privileged in no way denies that bad things happen to men. Being privileged does not mean men are given every-thing in life for free; being privileged does not mean that men do not work hard, do not suffer. In many cases—from a boy being bullied in school, to a soldier dying in war—the sexist society that maintains male privilege also does great harm to boys and men.

In the end, however, it is men and not women who make the most money; men and not women who dominate the government and the corporate boards; men and not women who dominate virtually all of the most powerful positions of society. And it is women and not men who suffer the most from intimate violence and rape; who are the most likely to be poor; who are, on the whole, given the short end of patriarchy's stick.

Several critics have also argued that the list somehow victimizes women. I disagree; pointing out problems is not the same as perpetuating them. It is not a "victimizing" position to acknowledge that injustice exists; on the contrary, without that acknowledgment it isn't possible to fight injustice.

An internet acquaintance of mine once wrote, "The first big privilege which whites, males, people in upper economic classes, the able bodied, the straight (I think one or two of those will cover most of us) can work to alleviate is the privilege to be oblivious to privilege." This checklist is, I hope, a step towards helping men to give up the "first big privilege."

The Male Privilege Checklist

1. My odds of being hired for a job, when competing against female applicants, are probably skewed in my favor. The more prestigious the job, the larger the odds are skewed.

*An Unabashed Imitation of an article by Peggy McIntosh
From the author's website: www.amptoons.com/blog/the-male-priviledge-checklist/. Reprinted by permission.

2. I can be confident that my co-workers won't think I got my job because of my sex—even though that might be true.

3. If I am never promoted, it's not because of my sex.

4. If I fail in my job or career, I can feel sure this won't be seen as a black mark against my entire sex's capabilities.

5. I am far less likely to face sexual harassment at work than my female co-workers are.

6. If I do the same task as a woman, and if the measurement is at all subjective, chances are people will think I did a better job.

7. If I'm a teen or adult, and if I can stay out of prison, my odds of being raped are relatively low.

8. On average, I am taught to fear walking alone after dark in average public spaces much less than my female counterparts are.

9. If I choose not to have children, my masculinity will not be called into question.

10. If I have children but do not provide primary care for them, my masculinity will not be called into question.

11. If I have children and provide primary care for them, I'll be praised for extraordinary parenting if I'm even marginally competent.

12. If I have children and a career, no one will think I'm selfish for not staying at home.

13. If I seek political office, my relationship with my children, or who I hire to take care of them, will probably not be scrutinized by the press.

14. My elected representatives are mostly people of my own sex. The more prestigious and powerful the elected position, the more this is true.

15. When I ask to see "the person in charge," odds are I will face a person of my own sex. The higher-up in the organization the person is, the surer I can be.

16. As a child, chances are I was encouraged to be more active and outgoing than my sisters.

17. As a child, I could choose from an almost infinite variety of children's media featuring positive, active, non-stereotyped heroes of my own sex. I never had to look for it; male protagonists were (and are) the default.

18. As a child, chances are I got more teacher attention than girls who raised their hands just as often.

19. If my day, week or year is going badly, I need not ask of each negative episode or situation whether or not it has sexist overtones.

20. I can turn on the television or glance at the front page of the newspaper and see people of my own sex widely represented, every day, without exception.

21. If I'm careless with my financial affairs, it won't be attributed to my sex.

22. If I'm careless with my driving, it won't be attributed to my sex.

23. I can speak in public to a large group without putting my sex on trial.

24. Even if I sleep with a lot of women, there is no chance that I will be seriously labeled a "slut," nor is there any male counterpart to "slut-bashing."

25. I do not have to worry about the message my wardrobe sends about my sexual availability or my gender conformity.

26. My clothing is typically less expensive and better-constructed than women's clothing for the same social status. While I have fewer options, my clothes will probably fit better than a woman's without tailoring.

27. The grooming regimen expected of me is relatively cheap and consumes little time.

28. If I buy a new car, chances are I'll be offered a better price than a woman buying the same car.

29. If I'm not conventionally attractive, the disadvantages are relatively small and easy to ignore.

30. I can be loud with no fear of being called a shrew. I can be aggressive with no fear of being called a bitch.

31. I can ask for legal protection from violence that happens mostly to men without being seen as a selfish special interest, since that kind of violence is called "crime" and is a

general social concern. (Violence that happens mostly to women is usually called "domestic violence" or "acquaintance rape," and is seen as a special interest issue.)

32. I can be confident that the ordinary language of day-to-day existence will always include my sex. "All men are created equal," mailman, chairman, freshman, he.

33. My ability to make important decisions and my capability in general will never be questioned depending on what time of the month it is.

34. I will never be expected to change my name upon marriage or questioned if I don't change my name.

35. The decision to hire me will never be based on assumptions about whether or not I might choose to have a family sometime soon.

36. Every major religion in the world is led primarily by people of my own sex. Even God, in most major religions, is pictured as male.

37. Most major religions argue that I should be the head of my household, while my wife and children should be subservient to me.

38. If I have a wife or live-in girlfriend, chances are we'll divide up household chores so that she does most of the labor, and in particular the most repetitive and unrewarding tasks.

39. If I have children with a wife or girlfriend, chances are she'll do most of the childrearing, and in particular the most dirty, repetitive and unrewarding parts of childrearing.

40. If I have children with a wife or girlfriend, and it turns out that one of us needs to make career sacrifices to raise the kids, chances are we'll both assume the career sacrificed should be hers.

41. Magazines, billboards, television, movies, pornography, and virtually all of media is filled with images of scantily-clad women intended to appeal to me sexually. Such images of men exist, but are rarer.

42. In general, I am under much less pressure to be thin than my female counterparts are. If I am fat, I probably suffer fewer social and economic consequences for being fat than fat women do.

43. If I am heterosexual, it's incredibly unlikely that I'll ever be beaten up by a spouse or lover.

44. Complete strangers generally do not walk up to me on the street and tell me to "smile."

45. On average, I am not interrupted by women as often as women are interrupted by men.

46. I have the privilege of being unaware of my male privilege.

Yen Le Espiritu

All Men Are *Not* Created Equal: Asian Men in U.S. History

Today, virtually every major metropolitan market across the United States has at least one Asian American female newscaster. In contrast, there is a nearly total absence of Asian American men in anchor positions (Hamamoto, 1994, p. 245; Fong-Torres, 1995). This gender imbalance in television news broadcasting exemplifies the racialization of Asian American manhood: Historically, they have been depicted as either asexual or hypersexual; today, they are constructed to be less successful, assimilated, attractive, and desirable than their female counterparts (Espiritu, 1996, pp. 95–98). The exclusion of Asian men from Eurocentric notions of the masculine reminds us that not all men benefit—or benefit equally—from a patriarchal system designed to maintain the unequal relationship that exists between men and women. The feminist mandate for gender solidarity tends to ignore power differentials among men, among women, and between white women and men of color. This exclusive focus on gender bars traditional feminists from recognizing the oppression of men of color: the fact that there are men, and not only women, who have been "feminized" and the fact that some white middle-class women hold cultural power and class power over certain men of color (Cheung, 1990, pp. 245–246; Wiegman, 1991, p. 311). Presenting race and gender as relationally constructed, King-Kok Cheung (1990) exhorted white scholars to acknowledge that, like female voices, "the voices of many men of color have been historically silenced or dismissed" (p. 246). Along the same line, black feminists have referred to "racial patriarchy"—a concept that calls attention to the white/patriarch master in U.S. history and his dominance over the black male as well as the black female (Gaines, 1990, p. 202).

Throughout their history in the United States, Asian American men, as immigrants and citizens of color, have faced a variety of economic, political, and ideological racism that have assaulted their manhood. During the pre–World War II period, racialized and gendered immigration policies and labor conditions emasculated Asian men, forcing them into womanless communities and into "feminized" jobs that had gone unfilled due to the absence of women. During World War II, the internment of Japanese Americans stripped *Issei* (first generation) men of their role as the family breadwinner, transferred some of their power and status to the U.S.-born children, and decreased male dominance over women. In the contemporary period, the patriarchal authority of Asian immigrant men, particularly those of the working class, has also been challenged due to the social and economic losses that they suffered in their transition to life in the United States. As detailed below, these three historically specific cases establish that the material existences of Asian American men have historically contradicted the Eurocentric, middle-class constructions of manhood.

Asian Men in Domestic Service

Feminist scholars have argued accurately that domestic service involves a three-way relationship between privileged white men, privileged white women, and poor women of color (Romero, 1992). But women have not been the only domestic workers. During the pre–World War II period, racialized and gendered immigration policies and labor conditions forced Asian men into "feminized" jobs such as domestic service, laundry work, and food preparation.[1] Due to their noncitizen status, the closed labor market, and the shortage of women, Asian immigrant men, first Chinese and later Japanese, substituted to some extent for female labor in the American West. David Katzman (1978) noted the peculiarities of the domestic labor situation in the West in this period: "In 1880, California and Washington were the only states in which a majority of domestic servants were men" (p. 55).

At the turn of the twentieth century, lacking other job alternatives, many Chinese men entered into domestic service in private homes, hotels, and rooming houses (Daniels, 1988, p. 74). Whites rarely objected to Chinese in domestic service. In fact, through the 1900s, the Chinese houseboy was the symbol of upper-class status in San Francisco (Glenn, 1986, p. 106). As late as 1920, close to 50 percent of the Chinese in the United States were still occupied as domestic servants (Light, 1972, p. 7). Large numbers of Chinese also became laundrymen, not because laundering was a traditional male occupation in China, but because there were very few women of any ethnic origin—and thus few washerwomen—in gold-rush California (Chan, 1991, pp. 33–34). Chinese laundrymen thus provided commercial services that replaced women's unpaid labor in the home. White consumers were prepared to patronize a Chinese laundryman because as such he "occupied a status which was in accordance with the social definition of the place in the economic hierarchy suitable for a member of an 'inferior race' " (cited in Siu, 1987, p. 21). In her autobiographical fiction *China Men*, Maxine Hong Kingston presents her father and his partners as engaged in their laundry business for long periods each day—a business considered so low and debased that, in their songs, they associate it with the washing of menstrual blood (Goellnicht, 1992, p. 198). The existence of the Chinese house-

boy and launderer—and their forced "bachelor" status—further bolstered the stereotype of the feminized and asexual or homosexual Asian man. Their feminization, in turn, confirmed their assignment to the state's labor force which performed "women's work."

Japanese men followed Chinese men into domestic service. By the end of the first decade of the twentieth century, the U.S. Immigration Commission estimated that 12,000 to 15,000 Japanese in the western United States earned a living in domestic service (Chan, 1991, pp. 39–40). Many Japanese men considered housework beneath them because in Japan only lower-class women worked as domestic servants (Ichioka, 1988, p. 24). Studies of Issei occupational histories indicate that a domestic job was the first occupation for many of the new arrivals; but unlike Chinese domestic workers, most Issei eventually moved on to agricultural or city trades (Glenn, 1986, p. 108). Filipino and Korean boys and men likewise relied on domestic service for their livelihood (Chan, 1991, p. 40). In his autobiography *East Goes West*, Korean immigrant writer Younghill Kang (1937) related that he worked as a domestic servant for a white family who treated him "like a cat or a dog" (p. 66).

Filipinos, as stewards in the U.S. Navy, also performed domestic duties for white U.S. naval officers. During the ninety-four years of U.S. military presence in the Philippines, U.S. bases served as recruiting stations for the U.S. armed forces, particularly the navy. Soon after the United States acquired the Philippines from Spain in 1898, its navy began actively recruiting Filipinos—but only as stewards and mess attendants. Barred from admissions to other ratings, Filipino enlistees performed the work of domestics, preparing and serving the officers' meals, and caring for the officers' galley, wardroom, and living spaces. Ashore, their duties ranged from ordinary housework to food services at the U.S. Naval Academy hall. Unofficially, Filipino stewards also have been ordered to perform menial chores such as walking the officers' dogs and acting as personal servants for the officers' wives (Espiritu, 1995, p. 16).

As domestic servants, Asian men became subordinates of not only privileged white men but also privileged white women. The following testimony from a Japanese house servant captures this unequal relationship:

> Immediately the ma'am demanded me to scrub the floor. I took one hour to finish. Then I had to wash windows. That was very difficult job for me. Three windows for another hour! ... The ma'am taught me how to cook.... I was sitting on the kitchen chair and thinking what a change of life it was. The ma'am came into the kitchen and was so furious! It was such a hard work for me to wash up all dishes, pans, glasses, etc., after dinner. When I went into the dining room to put all silvers on sideboard, I saw the reflection of myself on the looking glass. In a white coat and apron! I could not control my feelings. The tears so freely flowed out from my eyes, and I buried my face with my both arms (quoted in Ichioka, 1988, pp. 25–26).

The experiences of Asian male domestic service workers demonstrate that not all men benefit equally from patriarchy. Depending on their race and class, men experience gender differently. While male domination of women may tie all men together, men share unequally in the fruits of this domination. For Asian American male domestic workers, economic and social discriminations locked them into an unequal relationship with not only privileged white men but also privileged white women (Kim, 1990, p. 74).

The racist and classist devaluation of Asian men had gender implications. The available evidence indicates that immigrant men reasserted their lost patriarchal power in racist America by denigrating a weaker group: Asian women. In *China Men*, Kingston's immigrant father, having been forced into "feminine" subject positions, lapses into silence, breaking the silence only to utter curses against women (Goellnicht, 1992, pp. 200–201). Kingston (1980) traces her father's abuse of Chinese women back to his feeling of emasculation in America: "We knew that it was to feed us you had to endure demons and physical labor" (p. 13). On the other hand, some men

brought home the domestic skills they learned on the jobs. Anamaria Labao Cabato relates that her Filipino-born father, who spent twenty-eight years in the navy as a steward, is "one of the best cooks around" (Espiritu, 1995, p. 143). Leo Sicat, a retired U.S. Navy man, similarly reports that "we learned how to cook in the Navy, and we brought it home. The Filipino women are very fortunate because the husband does the cooking. In our household, I do the cooking, and my wife does the washing" (Espiritu, 1995, p. 108). Along the same line, in some instances, the domestic skills which men were forced to learn in their wives' absence were put to use when husbands and wives reunited in the United States. The history of Asian male domestic workers suggests that the denigration of women is only one response to the stripping of male privilege. The other is to institute a revised domestic division of labor and gender relations in the families.

Changing Gender Relations: The Wartime Internment of Japanese Americans

Immediately after the bombing of Pearl Harbor, the incarceration of Japanese Americans began. On the night of 7 December 1941, working on the principle of guilt by association, the Federal Bureau of Investigation (FBI) began taking into custody persons of Japanese ancestry who had connections to the Japanese government. On 19 February 1942, President Franklin Delano Roosevelt signed Executive Order 9066, arbitrarily suspending civil rights of U.S. citizens by authorizing the "evacuation" of 120,000 persons of Japanese ancestry into concentration camps, of whom approximately 50 percent were women and 60 percent were U.S.-born citizens (Matsumoto, 1989, p. 116).

The camp environment—with its lack of privacy, regimented routines, and new power hierarchy—inflicted serious and lasting wounds on Japanese American family life. In the crammed twenty-by-twenty-five-foot "apartment" units, tensions were high as men, women, and children struggled to recreate family life under very trying conditions. The internment also transformed the balance of power in families: husbands lost some of their power over wives, as did parents over children. Until the internment, the Issei man had been the undisputed authority over his wife and children: he was both the breadwinner and the decision maker for the entire family. Now "he had no rights, no home, no control over his own life" (Houston and Houston, 1973, p. 62). Most important, the internment reverted the economic roles—and thus the status and authority—of family members. With their means of livelihood cut off indefinitely, Issei men lost their role as breadwinners. Despondent over the loss of almost everything they had worked so hard to acquire, many Issei men felt useless and frustrated, particularly as their wives and children became less dependent on them. Daisuke Kitagawa (1967) reports that in the Tule Lake relocation center, "the [Issei] men looked as if they had suddenly aged ten years. They lost the capacity to plan for their own futures, let alone those of their sons and daughters" (p. 91).

Issei men responded to this emasculation in various ways. By the end of three years' internment, formerly enterprising, energetic Issei men had become immobilized with feelings of despair, hopelessness, and insecurity. Charles Kikuchi remembers his father—who "used to be a perfect terror and dictator"—spending all day lying on his cot: "He probably realizes that he no longer controls the family group and rarely exerts himself so that there is little family conflict as far as he is concerned" (Modell, 1973, p. 62). But others, like Jeanne Wakatsuki Houston's father, reasserted their patriarchal power by abusing their wives and children. Stripped of his roles as the protector and provider for his family, Houston's father "kept pursuing oblivion through drink, he kept abusing Mama, and there seemed to be no way out of it for anyone. You couldn't even run" (Houston and Houston, 1973, p. 61). The experiences of the Issei men underscore the intersections of racism and sexism—the fact that men of color live in a society that creates sex-based norms and expectations (i.e., man as breadwinner)

which racism operates simultaneously to deny (Crenshaw, 1989, p. 155).

Camp life also widened the distance and deepened the conflict between the Issei and their U.S.-born children. At the root of these tensions were growing cultural rifts between the generations as well as a decline in the power and authority of the Issei fathers. The cultural rifts reflected not only a general process of acculturation, but were accelerated by the degradation of everything Japanese and the simultaneous promotion of Americanization in the camps (Chan, 1991, p. 128; see also Okihiro, 1991, pp. 229–232). The younger *Nisei* also spent much more time away from their parents' supervision. As a consequence, Issei parents gradually lost their ability to discipline their children, whom they seldom saw during the day. Much to the chagrin of the conservative parents, young men and women began to spend more time with each other unchaperoned—at the sports events, the dances, and other school functions. Freed from some of the parental constraints, the Nisei women socialized more with their peers and also expected to choose their own husbands and to marry for "love"—a departure from the old customs of arranged marriage (Matsumoto, 1989, p. 117). Once this occurred, the prominent role that the father plays in marriage arrangements—and by extension in their children's lives—declined (Okihiro, 1991, p. 231).

Privileging U.S. citizenship and U.S. education, War Relocation Authority (WRA) policies regarding camp life further reverted the power hierarchy between the Japan-born Issei and their U.S.-born children. In the camps, only Nisei were eligible to vote and to hold office in the Community Council; Issei were excluded because of their alien status. Daisuke Kitagawa (1967) records the impact of this policy on parental authority: "In the eyes of young children, their parents were definitely inferior to their grown-up brothers and sisters, who as U.S. citizens could elect and be elected members of the Community Council. For all these reasons many youngsters lost confidence in, and respect for, their parents" (p. 88). Similarly, the WRA salary scales were based on English-speaking ability and on citizenship status. As a result, the Nisei youths and young adults could earn relatively higher wages than their fathers. This shift in earning abilities eroded the economic basis for parental authority (Matsumoto, 1989, p. 116).

At war's end in August 1945, Japanese Americans had lost much of the economic ground that they had gained in more than a generation. The majority of Issei women and men no longer had their farms, businesses, and financial savings; those who still owned property found their homes dilapidated and vandalized and their personal belongings stolen or destroyed (Broom and Riemer, 1949). The internment also ended Japanese American concentration in agriculture and small businesses. In their absence, other groups had taken over these ethnic niches. This loss further eroded the economic basis of parental authority since Issei men no longer had businesses to hand down to their Nisei sons (Broom and Riemer, 1949, p. 31). Historian Roger Daniels (1988) declared that by the end of World War II, "the generational struggle was over: the day of the Issei had passed" (286). Issei men, now in their sixties, no longer had the vigor to start over from scratch. Forced to find employment quickly after the war, many Issei couples who had owned small businesses before the war returned to the forms of manual labor in which they began a gen eration ago. Most men found work as janitors, gardeners, kitchen helpers, and handymen; their wives toiled as domestic servants, garment workers, and cannery workers (Yanagisako, 1987, p. 92).

Contemporary Asian America: The Disadvantaged

Relative to earlier historical periods, the economic pattern of contemporary Asian America is considerably more varied, a result of both the postwar restructured economy and the 1965 Immigration Act.[2] The dual goals of the 1965 Immigration Act—to facilitate family reunification and to admit educated workers needed by the U.S. econ-

omy—have produced two distinct chains of emigration from Asia: one comprising the relatives of working-class Asians who had immigrated to the United States prior to 1965; the other of highly trained immigrants who entered during the late 1960s and early 1970s (Liu, Ong, and Rosenstein, 1991). Given their dissimilar backgrounds, Asian Americans "can be found throughout the income spectrum of this nation" (Ong, 1994, p. 4). In other words, today's Asian American men both join whites in the well-paid, educated, white collar sector of the workforce *and* join Latino immigrants in lower-paying secondary sector jobs (Ong and Hee, 1994). This economic diversity contradicts the model minority stereotype—the common belief that most Asian American men are college educated and in high-paying professional or technical jobs.

The contemporary Asian American community includes a sizable population with limited education, skills, and English-speaking ability. In 1990, 18 percent of Asian men and 26 percent of Asian women in the United States, age 25 and over, had less than a high school degree. Also, of the 4.1 million Asians 5 years and over, 56 percent did not speak English "very well" and 35 percent were linguistically isolated (U.S. Bureau of the Census, 1993, Table 2). The median income for those with limited English was $20,000 for males and $15,600 for females; for those with less than a high school degree, the figures were $18,000 and $15,000, respectively. Asian American men and women with both limited English-speaking ability and low levels of education fared the worst. For a large portion of this disadvantaged population, even working full-time, full-year brought in less than $10,000 in earnings (Ong and Hee, 1994, p. 45).

The disadvantaged population is largely a product of immigration: Nine tenths are immigrants (Ong and Hee, 1994). The majority enter as relatives of the pre-1956 working-class Asian immigrants. Because immigrants tend to have socioeconomic backgrounds similar to those of their sponsors, most family reunification immigrants represent a continuation of the unskilled and semiskilled Asian labor that emigrated before

1956 (Liu, Ong, and Rosenstein, 1991). South-east Asian refugees, particularly the second-wave refugees who arrived after 1978, represent another largely disadvantaged group. This is partly so because refugees are less likely to have acquired readily transferable skills and are more likely to have made investments (in training and education) specific to the country of origin (Chiswick, 1979; Montero, 1980). For example, there are significant numbers of Southeast Asian military men with skills for which there is no longer a market in the United States. In 1990, the overall economic status of the Southeast Asian population was characterized by unstable, minimum-wage employment, welfare dependency, and participation in the informal economy (Gold and Kibria, 1993). These economic facts underscore the danger of lumping all Asian Americans together because many Asian men do not share in the relatively favorable socioeconomic outcomes attributed to the "average" Asian American.

Lacking the skills and education to catapult them into the primary sector of the economy, disadvantaged Asian American men and women work in the secondary labor market—the labor-intensive, low-capital service, and small manufacturing sectors. In this labor market, disadvantaged men generally have fewer employment options than women. This is due in part to the decline of male-occupied manufacturing jobs and the concurrent growth of female-intensive industries in the United States, particularly in service, microelectronics, and apparel manufacturing. The garment industry, microelectronics, and canning industries are top employers of immigrant women (Mazumdar, 1989, p. 19; Takaki, 1989, p. 427; Villones, 1989, p. 176; Hossfeld, 1994, pp. 71–72). In a study of Silicon Valley (California's famed high-tech industrial region), Karen Hossfeld (1994) reported that the employers interviewed preferred to hire immigrant women over immigrant men for entry-level, operative jobs (p. 74). The employers' "gender logic" was informed by the patriarchal and racist beliefs that women can afford to work for less, do not mind dead-end jobs, and are more suited physiologically to certain kinds of detailed

and routine work. As Linda Lim (1983) observes, it is the "*comparative disadvantage* of women in the wage-labor market that gives them a comparative advantage vis-à-vis men in the occupations and industries where they are concentrated—so-called female ghettoes of employment" (p. 78). A white male production manager and hiring supervisor in a California Silicon Valley assembly shop discusses his formula for hiring:

> Just three things I look for in hiring [entry-level, high-tech manufacturing operatives]: small, foreign, and female. You find those three things and you're pretty much automatically guaranteed the right kind of work force. These little foreign gals are grateful to be hired—very, very grateful—no matter what (Hossfeld, 1994, p. 65).

Refugee women have also been found to be more in demand than men in secretarial, clerical, and interpreter jobs in social service work. In a study of Cambodian refugees in Stockton, California, Shiori Ui (1991) found that social service agency executives preferred to hire Cambodian women over men when both had the same qualifications. One executive explained his preference, "It seems that some ethnic populations relate better to women than men.... Another thing is that the pay is so bad" (cited in Ui, 1991, p. 169). As a result, in the Cambodian communities in Stockton, it is often women—and not men—who have greater economic opportunities and who are the primary breadwinners in their families (Ui, 1991, p. 171).

Due to the significant decline in the economic contributions of Asian immigrant men, women's earnings comprise an equal or greater share of the family income. Because the wage each earns is low, only by pooling incomes can a husband and wife earn enough to support a family (Glenn, 1983, p. 42). These shifts in resources have challenged the patriarchal authority of Asian men. Men's loss of status and power—not only in the public but also in the domestic arena—places severe pressure on their sense of well-being. Responding to this pressure, some men accepted the new division of labor in the family (Ui, 1991, pp. 170–173); but many others resorted to spousal abuse and divorce (Luu, 1989, p. 68). A Korean immigrant man describes his frustrations over changing gender roles and expectations:

> In Korea [my wife] used to have breakfast ready for me.... She didn't do it any more because she said she was too busy getting ready to go to work. If I complained she talked back at me, telling me to fix my own breakfast.... I was very frustrated about her, started fighting and hit her (Yim, 1978, quoted in Mazumdar, 1989, p. 18).

Loss of status and power has similarly led to depression and anxieties in Hmong males. In particular, the women's ability—and the men's inability—to earn money for households "has undermined severely male omnipotence" (Irby and Pon, 1988, p. 112). Male unhappiness and helplessness can be detected in the following joke told at a family picnic, "When we get on the plane to go back to Laos, the first thing we will do is beat up the women!" The joke—which generated laughter by both men and women—drew upon a combination of "the men's unemployability, the sudden economic value placed on women's work, and men's fear of losing power in their families" (Donnelly, 1994, pp. 74–75). As such, it highlights the interconnections of race, class, and gender—the fact that in a racist and classist society, working-class men of color have limited access to economic opportunities and thus limited claim to patriarchal authority.

Conclusion

A central task in feminist scholarship is to expose and dismantle the stereotypes that traditionally have provided ideological justifications for women's subordination. But to conceptualize oppression only in terms of male dominance and female subordination is to obscure the centrality of classism, racism, and other forms of inequality in U.S. society (Stacey and Thorne, 1985, p. 311). The multiplicities of Asian men's lives indicate

that ideologies of manhood and womanhood have as much to do with class and race as they have to do with sex. The intersections of race, gender, and class mean that there are also hierarchies among women and among men and that some women hold power over certain groups of men. The task for feminist scholars, then, is to develop paradigms that articulate the complicity among these categories of oppression, that strengthen the alliance between gender and ethnic studies, and that reach out not only to women, but also to men, of color.

Notes

1. One of the most noticeable characteristics of pre–World War II Asian America was a pronounced shortage of women. During this period, U.S. immigration policies barred the entry of most Asian women. America's capitalist economy also wanted Asian male workers but not their families. In most instances, families were seen as a threat to the efficiency and exploitability of the workforce and were actively prohibited.

2. The 1965 Immigration Act ended Asian exclusion and equalized immigration rights for all nationalities. No longer constrained by exclusion laws, Asian immigrants began arriving in much larger numbers than ever before. In the 1980s, Asia was the largest source of U.S. legal immigrants, accounting for 40 percent to 47 percent of the total influx (Min, 1995, p. 12).

References

Broom, Leonard and Ruth Riemer. 1949. *Removal and Return: The Socio-Economic Effects of the War on Japanese Americans.* Berkeley: University of California Press.

Chan, Sucheng. 1991. *Asian Americans: An Interpretive History.* Boston: Twayne.

Cheung, King-Kok. 1990. "The Woman Warrior Versus the Chinaman Pacific: Must a Chinese American Critic Choose Between Feminism and Heroism?" In *Conflicts in Feminism*, edited by Marianne Hirsch and Evelyn Fox Keller (pp. 234–251). New York and London: Routledge.

Chiswick, Barry. 1979. "The Economic Progress of Immigrants: Some Apparently Universal

Patterns." In *Contemporary Economic Problems* edited by W. Fellner (pp. 357–399). Washington, DC: American Enterprise Institute.

Crenshaw, Kimberlee. 1989. "Demarginalizing the Intersection of Race and Sex: A Black Feminist Critique of Antidiscrimination Doctrine, Feminist Theory and Antiracist Politics." In *University of Chicago Legal Forum: Feminism in the Law: Theory, Practice, and Criticism* (pp. 139–167). Chicago: University of Chicago Press.

Daniels, Roger. 1988. *Asian America: Chinese and Japanese in the United States Since 1850*. Seattle: University of Washington Press.

Donnelly, Nancy D. 1994. *Changing Lives of Refugee Hmong Women*. Seattle: University of Washington Press.

Espiritu, Yen Le. 1995. *Filipino American Lives*. Philadelphia: Temple University Press.

Espiritu, Yen Le. 1996. *Asian American Women and Men: Labor, Laws, and Love*. Thousand Oaks, CA: Sage.

Fong-Torres, Ben. 1995. "Why Are There No Male Asian Anchor*men* on TV?" In *Men's Lives*, 3rd ed., edited by Michael S. Kimmel and Michael A. Messner (pp. 208–211). Boston: Allyn and Bacon.

Gaines, Jane. 1990. "White Privilege and Looking Relations: Race and Gender in Feminist Film Theory." In *Issues in Feminist Film Criticism*, edited by Patricia Erens (pp. 197–214). Bloomington: Indiana University Press.

Glenn, Evelyn Nakano. 1983. "Split Household, Small Producer and Dual Wage Earner: An Analysis of Chinese-American Family Strategies." *Journal of Marriage and the Family*, February: 35–46.

Glenn, Evelyn Nakano. 1986. *Issei, Nisei, War Bride: Three Generations of Japanese American Women at Domestic Service*. Philadelphia: Temple University Press.

Goellnicht, Donald C. 1992. "Tang Ao in America: Male Subject Positions in *China Men*." In *Reading the Literatures of Asian America*, edited by Shirley Geok-lin-Lim and Amy Ling (pp. 191–212). Philadelphia: Temple University Press.

Gold, Steve and Nazli Kibria. 1993. "Vietnamese Refugees and Blocked Mobility." *Asian and Pacific Migration Review* 2:27–56.

Hamamoto, Darrell. 1994. *Monitored Peril: Asian Americans and the Politics of Representation*. Minneapolis: University of Minnesota Press.

Hossfeld, Karen J. 1994. "Hiring Immigrant Women: Silicon Valley's 'Simple Formula.' " In *Women of Color in U.S. Society*, edited by Maxine Baca Zinn and Bonnie Thornton Dill (pp. 65–93). Philadelphia: Temple University Press.

Houston, Jeanne Wakatsuki and James D. Houston. 1973. *Farewell to Manzanar*. San Francisco: Houghton Mifflin.

Ichioka, Yuji. 1988. *The Issei: The World of the First Generation Japanese Immigrants, 1885–1924*. New York: The Free Press.

Irby, Charles and Ernest M. Pon. 1988. "Confronting New Mountains: Mental Health Problems Among Male Hmong and Mien Refugees. *Amerasia Journal* 14: 109–118.

Kang, Younghill. 1937. *East Goes West*. New York: C. Scribner's Sons.

Katzman, David. 1978. "Domestic Service: Women's Work." In *Women Working: Theories and Facts in Perspective*, edited by Ann Stromberg and Shirley Harkess (pp. 377–391). Palo Alto: Mayfield.

Kim, Elaine. 1990. " 'Such Opposite Creatures': Men and Women in Asian American Literature." *Michigan Quarterly Review*, 68–93.

Kingston, Maxine Hong. 1980. *China Men*. New York: Knopf.

Kitagawa, Daisuke. 1967. *Issei and Nisei: The Internment Years*. New York: Seabury Press.

Kitano, Harry H. L. 1991. "The Effects of the Evacuation on the Japanese Americans." In *Japanese Americans: From Relocation to Redress*, edited by Roger Daniels, Sandra C. Taylor, and Harry Kitano (pp. 151–162). Seattle: University of Washington Press.

Light, Ivan. 1972. *Ethnic Enterprise in America: Business and Welfare Among Chinese, Japanese, and Blacks*. Berkeley and Los Angeles: University of California Press.

Lim, Linda Y. C. 1983. "Capitalism, Imperialism, and Patriarchy: The Dilemma of Third-World Women Workers in Multinational Factories." In *Women, Men, and the International Division of Labor*, edited by June Nash and Maria Patricia Fernandez-Kelly (pp. 70–91). Albany: State University of New York.

Liu, John, Paul Ong, and Carolyn Rosenstein. 1991. "Dual Chain Migration: Post-1965 Filipino Immigration to the United States." *International Migration Review* 25 (3): 487–513.

Luu, Van. 1989. "The Hardships of Escape for Vietnamese Women." In *Making Waves: An Anthology of Writings by and About Asian American Women*, edited by Asian Women United of California (pp. 60–72). Boston: Beacon Press.

Matsumoto, Valerie. 1989. "Nisei Women and Resettlement During World War II." In *Making Waves: An Anthology of Writings by and about Asian American Women*, edited by Asian Women United of California (pp. 115–126). Boston: Beacon Press.

Mazumdar, Sucheta. 1989. "General Introduction: A Woman-Centered Perspective on Asian American History." In *Making Waves: An Anthology by and about Asian American Women*, edited by Asian Women United of California (pp. 1–22). Boston: Beacon Press.

Min, Pyong Gap. 1995. "Korean Americans." In *Asian Americans: Contemporary Trends and Issues*, edited by Pyong Gap Min (pp. 199–231). Thousand Oaks, CA: Sage.

Modell, John, ed. 1973. *The Kikuchi Diary: Chronicle from an American Concentration Camp*. Urbana: University of Illinois Press.

Montero, Darrell. 1980. *Vietnamese Americans: Patterns of Settlement and Socioeconomic Adaptation in the United States*. Boulder, CO: Westview.

Okihiro, Gary Y. 1991. *Cane Fires: The Anti-Japanese Movement in Hawaii, 1865–1945*. Philadelphia: Temple University Press.

Ong, Paul. 1994. "Asian Pacific Americans and Public Policy." In *The State of Asian Pacific America: Economic Diversity, Issues, & Policies*, edited by Paul Ong (pp. 1–9). Los Angeles: LEAP Asian Pacific American Public Policy Institute and UCLA Asian American Studies Center.

Ong, Paul and Suzanne Hee. 1994. "Economic Diversity." In *The State of Asian Pacific America: Economic Diversity, Issues, & Policies*, edited by Paul Ong (pp. 31–56). Los Angeles: LEAP Asian Pacific American Public Policy Institute and UCLA Asian American Studies Center.

Romero, Mary. 1992. *Maid in the U.S.A.* New York: Routledge.

Siu, Paul. 1987. *The Chinese Laundryman: A Study in Social Isolation*. New York: New York University Press.

Stacey, Judith and Barrie Thorne. 1985. "The Missing Feminist Revolution in Sociology." *Social Problems* 32: 301–316.

Takaki, Ronald. 1989. *Strangers from a Different Shore: A History of Asian Americans*. Boston: Little, Brown.

Ui, Shiori. 1991. " 'Unlikely Heroes': The Evolution of Female Leadership in a Cambodian Ethnic Enclave." In *Ethnography Unbound: Power and Resistance in the Modern Metropolis*, edited by Michael Burawoy et al. (pp. 161–177). Berkeley: University of California Press.

U.S. Bureau of the Census. 1993. *We the American Asians*. Washington, DC: U.S. Government Printing Office.

Villones, Rebecca. 1989. "Women in the Silicon Valley." In *Making Waves: An Anthology of Writings by and About Asian American Women*, edited by Asian Women United of California (pp. 172–176). Boston: Beacon Press.

Wiegman, Robyn. 1991. "Black Bodies/American Commodities: Gender, Race, and the Bourgeois Ideal in Contemporary Film." In *Unspeakable Images: Ethnicity and the American Cinema*, edited by Lester Friedman (pp. 308–328). Urbana and Chicago: University of Illinois Press.

Yanagisako, Sylvia Junko. 1987. "Mixed Metaphors: Native and Anthropological Models of Gender and Kinship Domains." In *Gender and Kinship: Essays Toward a Unified Analysis*, edited by Jane Fishburne Collier and Sylvia Junko Yanagisako (pp. 86–118). Palo Alto, CA: Stanford University Press.

Alfredo Mirandé

"Macho": Contemporary Conceptions

Mi Noche Triste

My own *noche triste* occurred when my father returned from location on the film *Capitán de Castilla* (Captain from Castille). I remember that he had been gone for a long time, that he came back from Morelia with a lot of presents, and that at first, I was very happy to see him. Then there was a big fight; my parents argued all night, and they separated shortly thereafter. One night when my mother was very sad and depressed, she went to *el árbol de la noche triste*. As she cried by the tree she thought about how she and Hernán Cortés both had been in the same situation: depressed, weeping, and alone.

After my parents separated, my brothers and I went with my father and moved to Tacubaya to live with his mother, Anita, and her mother (my great-grandmother), Carmela (Mamá Mela). Grandmother Anita, or *Abillá*, as we called her, was a petite, energetic little woman, but Mamá Mela was tall, dark, and stately. In Tacubaya we were also surrounded by family, but now it was my father's family, Mirandé-Salazar. His family was smaller because he was an only child and because his father's two siblings, Concha (Consuelo) and Lupe (Guadalupe), never married or had children. My grandfather, Alfredo, died when I was about two years old, but I remember him.

In Tacubaya we first lived in a big, long house with a large green entrance, *El Nueve* (nine), on a

street called Vicente Eguía, before moving to an apartment house, *El Trece* (thirteen), down the street. At *El Trece* we lived in the first apartment, and my great-aunts, Concha and Lupe, lived in *El Seis* (six). Concha had been an elementary school teacher and Lupe was an artist. They were retired but very active; both did a lot of embroidering and Lupe was always painting. I was very fond of *las tías*. To me *las tías* always seemed old and very religious, but I was very close to my aunts and loved them deeply. They wore black shawls and went to church early each morning. When I wasn't playing in the courtyard, I was often visiting with my aunts. They taught me catechism, and Tía Lupe was my *madrina*, or godmother, for my first communion.

I would spend hours with *las tías*, fascinated by their conversation. It seemed that every minute was filled with stories about the Mexican Revolution and about my grandfather, Alfredo. I especially liked it when they spoke about him, as I had been named Alfredo and identified with him. They said he was a great man and that they would be very proud and happy if I grew up to be like him someday. No, it was actually that I had no choice—I was destined to be like him. Because I had the good fortune of being named after Alfredo, I had to carry on his name, and, like him, I too would be a great man someday. I should add that my aunts stressed *man* when they talked about him. In other words, I had a distinct impression that my grandfather and I were linked not only because we were both named Mirandé and Alfredo, but also because we were both men. I did not realize it at the time, but my teachers (who were mostly women)—*las tías*, my *Abillá*,

Mamá Mela, and my mother—were socializing me into my "sex role." But I don't remember anyone describing Grandfather Alfredo as "macho." Perhaps my *tías* took his being "macho" for granted, since he was obviously male.

I do not know very much about Alfredo's family, except that his father, Juan, or *Jean*, came to Mexico from France and married a *mexicana*, María. I also learned from my mother that Alfredo was of humble origins and was, in a very real sense, a self-made man who studied and pursued a career as a civil engineer. He was committed to bringing about social justice and distributing the land held by the *hacendados* (landowners) among the Mexican *peones*. As a civilian he served under Emiliano Zapata, making cannons and munitions. According to historian John Womack . . . , Alfredo Mirandé was one of Zapata's key assistants and worked as a spy in Puebla for some time under the code name "Delta." While he was in hiding, my *Abillú* would take in other people's clothes to mend and to launder to earn money so that the family could survive. My grandfather grew to be disillusioned, however, as the Revolution did not fulfill its promise of bringing about necessary economic and social reforms.

My *tías* had a photograph of Alfredo standing proudly in front of a new, experimental cannon that he had built. They related that a foolish and headstrong general, anxious to try out the new cannon, pressured Alfredo to fire it before it was ready. My grandfather reluctantly complied and received severe burns all over his body, almost dying as a result of the explosion. It took him months to recover from the accident.

As I think back, most of the stories they told me had a moral and were designed, indirectly at least, to impart certain values. What I learned from my *tías* and, indirectly, from my grandfather was that although one should stand up for principles, one should attempt to avoid war and personal conflicts, if at all possible. One should also strive to be on a higher moral plane than one's adversaries. Alfredo was intelligent, strong, and principled. But what impressed me most is that he

was said to be incredibly just and judicious. Everyone who knew him said he treated people of varying educational and economic levels fairly, equally, and with dignity and respect.

I realize that Alfredo lived in a society and a historical period in which women were relegated to an inferior status. Yet I also know that he and my grandmother shared a special intimacy and mutual respect such as I have never personally encountered. By all accounts they loved and respected each other and shared an incredible life together. I have read letters that my grandfather wrote to my grandmother when they were apart, and they indicate that he held her in very high regard and treated her as an equal partner.

"Macho": An Overview

Mexican folklorist Vicente T. Mendoza suggested that the word "macho" was not widely used in Mexican songs, *corridos* (folk ballads), or popular culture until the 1940s. . . . Use of the word was said to have gained in popularity after Avila Camacho became president. The word lent itself to use in *corridos* because "macho" rhymed with "Camacho."

While "macho" has traditionally been associated with Mexican or Latino culture, the word has recently been incorporated into American popular culture, so much so that it is now widely used to describe everything from rock stars and male sex symbols in television and film to burritos. When applied to entertainers, athletes, or other "superstars," the implied meaning is clearly a positive one that connotes strength, virility, masculinity, and sex appeal. But when applied to Mexicans or Latinos, "macho" remains imbued with such negative attributes as male dominance, patriarchy, authoritarianism, and spousal abuse. Although both meanings connote strength and power, the Anglo macho is clearly a much more positive and appealing symbol of manhood and masculinity. In short, under current usage the Mexican macho oppresses and coerces women, whereas his Anglo counterpart appears to attract and seduce them.

This [reading] focuses on variations in perceptions and conceptions of the word "macho" held by Mexican and Latino men. Despite all that has been written and said about the cult of masculinity and the fact that male dominance has been assumed to be a key feature of Mexican and Latino culture, very little research exists to support this assumption. Until recently such generalizations were based on stereotypes, impressionistic evidence, or the observations of ethnographers such as Oscar Lewis . . . , Arthur Rubel . . . , and William Madsen. . . . These Anglo ethnographers were criticized by noted Chicano folklorist Américo Paredes . . . for the persistent ignorance and insensitivity to Chicano language and culture that is reflected in their work. Paredes contended, for example, that although most anthropologists present themselves as politically liberal and fluent in Spanish, many are only minimally fluent and fail to grasp the nuance and complexity of Chicano language. There is, it seems, good reason to be leery of their findings and generalizations regarding not only gender roles but also all aspects of the Mexican/Latino experience.

Utilizing data obtained through qualitative open-ended questions, I look in this chapter at how Latino men themselves perceive the word "macho" and how they describe men who are considered "*muy machos*." Although all of the respondents were living in the United States at the time of the interviews, many were foreign-born and retained close ties with Mexican/Latino culture. Since they had been subjected to both Latino and American influences, I wondered whether they would continue to adhere to traditional Mexican definitions of "macho" or whether they had been influenced by contemporary American conceptions of the word.

Specifically, an attempt was made in the interviews to examine two polar views. The prevailing view in the social science literature of the Mexican macho is a negative one. This view holds that the origins of the excessive masculine displays and the cult of masculinity in México and other Latino countries can be traced to the Spanish Conquest, as the powerless colonized man at-

tempted to compensate for deep-seated feelings of inadequacy and inferiority by assuming a hypermasculine, aggressive, and domineering stance. There is a second and lesser-known view that is found in Mexican popular culture, particularly in film and music, one that reflects a more positive, perhaps idyllic, conception of Mexican culture and national character. Rather than focusing on violence and male dominance, this second view associates macho qualities with the evolution of a distinct code of ethics.

Un hombre que es macho is not hypermasculine or aggressive, and he does not disrespect or denigrate women. Machos, according to the positive view, adhere to a code of ethics that stresses humility, honor, respect of oneself and others, and courage. What may be most significant in this second view is that being "macho" is not manifested by such outward qualities as physical strength and virility but by such inner qualities as personal integrity, commitment, loyalty, and, most importantly, strength of character. Stated simply, a man who acted like my Tío Roberto would be macho in the first sense of the word but certainly not in the second. It is not clear how this code of ethics developed, but it may be linked to nationalist sentiments and Mexican resistance to colonization and foreign invasion. Historical figures such as Cuauhtémoc, *El Pipíla, Los Niños Héroes*, Villa, and Zapata would be macho according to this view. In music and film positive macho figures such as Pedro Infante, Jorge Negrete, and even Cantinflas are patriots, but mostly they are *muy hombres*, men who stand up against class and racial oppression and the exploitation of the poor by the rich.

Despite the apparent differences between the two views, both see the macho cult as integral to Mexican and Latino cultures. Although I did not formulate explicit hypotheses, I entered the field expecting that respondents would generally identify with the word "macho" and define it as a positive trait or quality in themselves and other persons. An additional informal hypothesis proposed was that men who had greater ties to Latino culture and the Spanish language would be more likely to identify and to have positive associations with the word. I expected, in other words, that respondents would be more likely to adhere to the positive view of macho.

Findings: Conceptions of Macho

Respondents were first asked the following question: "What does the word 'macho' mean to you?" The interviewers were instructed to ask this and all other questions in a neutral tone, as we wanted the respondents to feel that we really were interested in what they thought. We stressed in the interviews that there were no "right" or "wrong" answers to any of the questions. This first question was then followed by a series of follow-up questions that included: "Can you give me an example (or examples) of someone you think is really macho?"; "What kinds of things do people who are really macho do?"; and "Can a woman be macha?"

Each person was assigned an identification number, and the responses to the above questions were typed on a large index card. Three bilingual judges, two men and one woman, were asked to look at the answers on the cards and to classify each respondent according to whether they believed the respondent was generally "positive," "negative," or "neutral" toward the word "macho." Those respondents classified as "positive" saw the term as a desirable cultural or personal trait or value, identified with it, and believed that it is generally good to be, or at least to aspire to be, macho. But those respondents classified as "negative" by the judges saw it as an undesirable or devalued cultural or personal trait, did not identify with being macho, and believed that it is generally bad or undesirable to be macho. In the third category, respondents were classified as "neutral" if they were deemed to be indifferent or ambivalent or to recognize both positive and negative components of the word "macho." For these respondents, macho was "just a word," or it denoted a particular male feature without imputing anything positive or negative about the feature itself.

Overall there was substantial agreement among the judges. In 86 percent of 105 cases the judges were in complete agreement in their classifications, and in another 12 percent two out of three agreed. In other words, in only two instances was there complete disagreement among the judges in which one judge ranked the respondents positive, another negative, and still another neutral.

One of the most striking findings is the extent to which the respondents were polarized in their views of macho. Most had very strong feelings; very few were neutral or indifferent toward the word. In fact, only 11 percent of the 105 respondents were classified as neutral by our judges. No less surprising is the fact that, contrary to my expectations, very few respondents viewed the word in a positive light. Only 31 percent of the men were positive in their views of macho, compared to 57 percent who were classified as negative. This means, in effect, that more than two-thirds of the respondents believed that the word "macho" had either negative or neutral connotations.

My expectation that those individuals with greater ties to Latino culture would be more likely to identify and to have positive associations with "macho" was also not supported by the data. Of the thirty-nine respondents who opted to be interviewed in Spanish, only 15 percent were seen as having a positive association with macho, whereas 74 percent were negative and 10 percent were neutral toward the term. In contrast, of the sixty-six interviewed in English, 41 percent were classified as positive, 47 percent as negative, and 12 percent as neutral toward the term.

Although negative views of the word "macho" were more prevalent than I had expected, the responses closely parallel the polar views of the word "macho" discussed earlier. Responses classified as "negative" by our judges are consistent with the "compensatory" or "deficit" model, which sees the emphasis on excessive masculinity among Mexicans and Latinos as an attempt to conceal pervasive feelings of inferiority among native men that resulted from the Conquest and the ensuing cultural, moral, and spiritual rape of the indigenous population. Those classified as "positive," similarly, are roughly consistent with an "ethical" model, which sees macho behavior as a positive, nationalist response to colonization, foreign intervention, and class exploitation.

Negative Conceptions of "Macho"

A number of consistent themes are found among the men who were classified as viewing the word "macho" in a negative light. Though I divide them into separate themes to facilitate the presentation of the findings, there is obviously considerable overlap between them.

Negative Theme 1: Synthetic/Exaggerated Masculinity   A theme that was very prevalent in the responses is that machos are men who are insecure in themselves and need to prove their manhood. It was termed a "synthetic self-image," "exaggerated masculinity," "one who acts tough and is insecure in himself," and an "exaggerated form of manliness or super manliness." One respondent described a macho as

> one who acts "bad." One who acts tough and who is insecure of himself. I would say *batos* [dudes] who come out of the *pinta* [prison] seem to have a tendency to be insecure with themselves, and tend to put up a front. [They] talk loud, intimidate others, and disrespect the meaning of a man.

Another person described it as

> being a synthetic self-image that's devoid of content. . . . It's a sort of facade that people use to hide the lack of strong, positive personality traits. To me, it often implies a negative set of behaviors. . . . I have a number of cousins who fit that. I have an uncle who fits it. He refuses to have himself fixed even though he was constantly producing children out of wedlock.

Negative Theme 2: Male Dominance Authoritarianism   A second, related theme is that of male dominance, chauvinism, and the double standard for men and women. Within the family, the macho figure is viewed as authoritarian, es-

pecially relative to the wife. According to one respondent, "They insist on being the dominant one in the household. What they say is the rule. They treat women as inferior. They have a dual set of rules for women and men." Another respondent added:

> It's someone that completely dominates. There are no two ways about it; it's either his way or no way. My dad used to be a macho. He used to come into the house drunk, getting my mother out of bed, making her make food, making her cry.

A Spanish-speaker characterized the macho as follows:

> *Una persona negativa completamente. Es una persona que es irresponsable en una palabra. Que anda en las cantinas. Es no es hombre. Si, conozco muchos de mi tierra; una docena. Toman, pelean. Llegan a la case gritando y golpeando a la señora, gritando, cantando. Eso lo vi yo cuando era chavalillo y se me grabó. Yo nunca vi a mi papá que golpeara a mi mamá* (A completely negative person. In a word, it's a person who is irresponsible. Who is out in the taverns. That's not a man. Yes, I know many from my homeland; a dozen. They drink, fight. They come home yelling and hitting the wife, yelling, singing. I saw this as a child and it made a lasting impression on me. I never saw my father hit my mother).

Negative Theme 3: Violence/Aggressiveness   A third, related theme is macho behavior manifested in expressions of violence, aggressiveness, and irresponsibility, both inside and outside the family. It is "someone that does not back down, especially if they fear they would lose face over the most trivial matters." Another person saw macho as the exaggeration of perceived masculine traits and gave the example of a fictional figure like Rambo and a real figure like former president Ronald Reagan. This person added that it was "anyone who has ever been in a war," and "it's usually associated with dogmatism, with violence, with not showing feelings." A Spanish-speaking man summarized it succinctly as "*el* *hombre que sale de su trabajo los vierns, va a la cantina, gasta el cheque, y llega a su casa gritando, pegándole a su esposa diciendo que él es el macho"* (the man who gets out of work on Friday, goes to a bar, spends his check, and comes home yelling and hitting his wife and telling her that he is the macho [i.e., man]). Still another felt that men who were macho did such things as "drinking to excess," and that associated with the word "macho" was "the notion of physical prowess or intimidation of others. A willingness to put themselves and others at risk, particularly physically. For those that are married, the notion of having women on the side."

One of our Spanish-speaking respondents mentioned an acquaintance who lost his family because he would not stop drinking. *"Él decía, 'La mujer se hizo para andar en la casa y yo pa' andar en las cantinas'"* (He used to say, "Woman was made to stay at home and I was made to stay in taverns"). This respondent also noted that men who are real machos tend not to support their families or tend to beat them, to get "dandied up," and to go out drinking. Another said that they "drink tequila" and "have women on their side kissing them."

Negative Theme 4: Self-Centeredness/*Egoismo*

Closely related is the final theme, which views someone who is macho as being self-centered, selfish, and stubborn, a theme that is especially prevalent among respondents with close ties to México. Several men saw machismo as *un tipo de egoísmo* (a type of selfishness) and felt that it referred to a person who always wanted things done his way—*a la mía*. It is someone who wants to impose his will on others or wants to be right, whether he is right or not. It is viewed, for example, as

> *un tipo de egoísmo que nomás "lo mío" es bueno y nomás mis ideas son buenas. Como se dice, "Nomás mis chicharrones truenan."* . . . *Se apegan a lo que ellos creen. Todo lo que ellos dicen está correcto. Tratan que toda la gente entre a su manera de pensar y actuar, incluyendo hijos y familia* (A type of selfishness where only "mine" is good and only

my ideas are worthwhile. As the saying goes, "Whatever I say goes." . . . They cling to their own beliefs. Everything they say is right. They try to get everyone, including children and family, to think and act the way they do).

Some respondents who elaborated on the "self-centeredness" or *egoísta* theme noted that some men will hit their wives "just to prove that they are machos," while others try to show that they "wear the pants" by not letting their wives go out. One person noted that some men believe that wives and daughters should not be permitted to cut their hair because long hair is considered "a sign of femininity," and another made reference to a young man who actually cut off a finger in order to prove his love to his sweetheart.

Because the word "macho" literally means a "he-mule" or a "he-goat," respondents often likened macho men to a dumb animal such as a mule, goat, or bull: "Somebody who's like a bull, or bullish"; "The man who is strong as though he were an animal"; "It's an ignorant person, like an animal, a donkey or mule"; and "It's a word that is outside of that which is human." One person described a macho as

> the husband of the mule that pulls the plow. A macho is a person who is dumb and uneducated. *Hay tienes a* [There you have] Macho Camacho [the boxer]. He's a wealthy man, but that doesn't make a smart man. I think he's dumb! . . . They're aggressive, and they're harmful, and insensitive.

Another respondent said, "Ignorant, is what it means to me, a fool. They're fools, man. They act bully type." Another similarity linked it to being "ignorant, dumb, stupid," noting that they "try to take advantage of their physical superiority over women and try to use that as a way of showing that they are right."

Given that these respondents viewed "macho" in a negative light, it is not surprising to find that most did not consider themselves macho. Only eight of the sixty men in this category reluctantly acknowledged that they were "somewhat" macho. One said, "Yes, sometimes when I drink, I get loud and stupid," and another, "Yes, to an extent because I have to be headstrong, and bullish as a teacher."

Positive Conceptions of Macho: Courage, Honor, and Integrity

As previously noted, only about 30 percent of the respondents were classified as seeing macho as a desirable cultural or personal trait or value, and those who did so were much more apt to conduct the interview in English. Some 82 percent of the men who had positive conceptions were interviewed in English.

As was true of men who were classified as negative toward the word "macho," several themes were discernible among those classified as positive. And as with the negative themes, they are separate but overlapping. A few respondents indicated that it meant "masculine" or "manly" (*varonil*), a type of masculinity (*una forma de masculinidad*), or male. The overriding theme, however, linked machismo to internal qualities like courage, valor, honor, sincerity, respect, pride, humility, and responsibility. Some went so far as to identify a distinct code of ethics or a set of principles that they saw as being characteristic of machismo.

Positive Theme 1: Assertiveness/Standing Up for Rights   A more specific subtheme is the association of machismo with being assertive, courageous, standing up for one's rights, or going "against the grain" relative to other persons. The following response is representative of this view:

> To me it means someone that's assertive, someone who stands up for his or her rights when challenged. . . . Ted Kennedy because of all the hell he's had to go through. I think I like [Senator] Feinstein. She takes the issues by the horns. . . . They paved their own destiny. They protect themselves and those that are close to them and attempt to control their environment versus the contrast.

It is interesting to note that this view of being macho can be androgynous. Several respondents mentioned women who exemplified "macho qualities" or indicated that these qualities may be found among either gender. Another man gave John Kennedy and Eleanor Roosevelt as examples and noted that people who are macho

> know how to make decisions because they are confident of themselves. They know their place in the world. They accept themselves for what they are and they are confident in that. They don't worry about what others think. . . . They know what to do, the things that are essential to them and others around them.

A Spanish-speaking respondent added:

> *En respecto a nuestra cultra es un hombre que defiende sus valores, en total lo físico, lo emocional, lo psicológico. En cada mexicano hay cierto punto de macho. No es arrogante, no es egoísta excepto cuando tiene que defender sus valores. No es presumido* (Relative to our culture, it's a man that stands up for what he believes, physically, emotionally, and psychologically. Within every Mexican there is a certain sense of being macho. He is not arrogant, not egotistic, except when he has to defend his values. He is not conceited).

Positive Theme 2: Responsibility/Selflessness
A second positive macho theme is responsibility, selflessness, and meeting obligations. In direct opposition to the negative macho who is irresponsible and selfish, the positive macho is seen as having a strong sense of responsibility and as being very concerned with the welfare and well-being of other persons. This second positive macho theme was described in a number of ways: "to meet your obligations"; "someone who shoulders responsibility"; "being responsible for your family"; "a person who fulfills the responsibility of his role. . . irrespective of the consequences"; "they make firm decisions . . . that take into consideration the well-being of others." According to one respondent:

> A macho personality for me would be a person that is understanding, that is caring, that is trustworthy. He is all of those things and prac-

tices them as well as teaches them, not only with family but overall. It encompasses his whole life.

It would be a leader with compassion. The image we have of Pancho Villa. For the Americans it would be someone like Kennedy, as a strong person, but not because he was a womanizer.

Positive Theme 3: General Code of Ethics

The third theme we identified embodies many of the same traits mentioned in the first and second themes, but it differs in that respondents appear to link machismo not just to such individual qualities as selflessness but to a general code of ethics or a set of principles. One respondent who was married to an Israeli woman offered a former defense minister of Israel as exemplifying macho qualities. He noted that

It's a man responsible for actions, a man of his word. . . . I think a macho does not have to be a statesman, just a man that's known to stand by his friends and follow through. A man of action relative to goals that benefit others, not himself.

Another said that it means living up to one's principles to the point of almost being willing to die for them. One of the most extensive explications of this code of ethics was offered by the following respondent:

To me it really refers to a code of ethics that I use to relate values in my life and to evaluate myself in terms of my family, my job, my community. My belief is that if I live up to my code of ethics, I will gain respect from my family, my job, and my community. Macho has nothing to do with how much salsa you can eat, how much beer you can drink, or how many women you fuck!

They have self-pride, they hold themselves as meaningful people. You can be macho as a farmworker or judge. It's a real mixture of pride and humility. Individualism is a part of it—self-awareness, self-consciousness, responsibility.

Positive Theme 4: Sincerity/Respect

The final positive theme overlaps somewhat with the others and is often subsumed under the code of ethics or principles. A number of respondents associated the word "macho" with such qualities as respect for oneself and others, acting with sincerity and respect, and being a man of your word. One of our interviewees said,

Macho significa una persona que cumple con su palabra y que es un hombre total. . . . Actúan con sinceridad y con respeto (Macho means a person who backs up what he says and who is a complete man. . . . They act with sincerity and respect).

Another mentioned self-control and having a sense of oneself and the situation.

Usually they are reserved. They have kind of an inner confidence, kind of like you know you're the fastest gun in town so you don't have to prove yourself. There's nothing to prove. A sense of self.

Still another emphasized that physical prowess by itself would not be sufficient to identify one as macho. Instead, "It would be activities that meet the challenge, require honor, and meet obligations." Finally, a respondent observed:

Macho to me means that you understand your place in the world. That's not to say that you are the "he-man" as the popular conception says. It means you have respect for yourself, that you respect others.

Not surprisingly, all of the respondents who viewed machismo in a positive light either already considered themselves to have macho qualities or saw it as an ideal they hoped to attain.

Neutral Conceptions of Macho

Twelve respondents could not be clearly classified as positive or negative in their views of "macho." This so-called neutral category is somewhat of a residual one, however, because it includes not only men who were, in fact, neutral but also those who gave mixed signals and about whom the judges could not agree. One said that "macho" was just a word that didn't mean anything; another said that it applied to someone strong like a boxer or a wrestler, but he did not know anyone who was macho, and it was not clear whether he considered it to be a positive or negative trait. Others were either ambivalent or pointed to both positive and negative components of being macho. A street-wise young man in his mid-twenties, for example, indicated that

> The word macho to me means someone who won't take nothing from no one. Respects others, and expects a lot of respect from others. The person is willing to take any risk. . . . They always think they can do anything and everything. They don't take no shit from no one. They have a one-track mind. Never want to accept the fact that women can perform as well as men.

Significantly, the judges were divided in classifying this respondent; one classified him as negative, another as positive, and the third as neutral. The fact is that rather than being neutral, this young man identifies both positive ("respects others and self") and negative ("never want to accept the fact that women can perform as well as men") qualities with being macho.

Another person observed that there were at least two meanings of the word—one, a brave person who is willing to defend his ideals and himself, and the other, a man who exaggerates his masculinity—but noted that "macho" was not a term that he used. Another respondent provided a complex answer that distinguished the denotative (i.e., macho) and connotative (i.e., machismo) meanings of the term. He used the word in both ways, differentiating between being macho or male, which is denotative, and machismo, which connotes male chauvinism. He considered himself to be macho but certainly not *machista*.

> *Ser macho es ser valiente o no tener miedo. La connotación que tiene mal sentido es poner los intereses del hombre adelante de los de la mujer o del resto de*

la familia. Representa egoísmo. . . . Macho significa varón, hombre, pero el machismo es una manera de pensar, y es negativo (To be macho is to be brave or to not be afraid. The connotation that is negative is to put the interests of the man ahead of those of the woman or the rest of the family. It represents selfishness. . . . Macho means male, man, but machismo is a way of thinking, and it is negative).

Another person similarly distinguished between being macho and being *machista*.

> *Pues, en el sentido personal, significa el sexo masculino y lo difiere del sexo femenino. La palabra machismo existe solamente de bajo nivel cultural y significa un hombre valiente, borracho y pendenciero* (Well, in a personal sense, it means the masculine gender and it distinguishes it from the feminine. The word machismo exists only at a low cultural level and it means a brave man, a drunkard, and a hell-raiser).

Six of the twelve respondents who were classified as neutral considered themselves to be at least somewhat macho.

Regional and Socioeconomic Differences in Conceptions of Macho

Conceptions of the word "macho" do not vary significantly by region, but there are significant differences according to socioeconomic status. Men with more education, with a higher income, and in professional occupations were more likely to have a positive conception of the word. This is not to suggest that they are necessarily more *machista*, or chauvinistic, but that they simply see the word in a more positive light. Almost half (42 percent) of the respondents who were professionals associated the word "macho" with being principled or standing up for one's rights, whereas only 23 percent of nonprofessionals had a positive conception of the word.

Place of birth and language were also significantly associated with attitudes toward machismo, but, ironically, those respondents who were born in the United States and those who were interviewed in English were generally more positive toward the word "macho." Forty-two percent of those born in the United States have positive responses, compared with only 10 percent of those who were foreign-born.

An English-speaking respondent said that "macho equals to me chivalry associated with the Knights of the Round Table, where a man gives his word, defends his beliefs, etc." Another noted that machos were people who "stand up for what they believe, try things other people are afraid to do, and defend the rights of others." But one Mexican man saw it as the opposite—"*Mexicanos que aceptan que la mujer 'lleve los pantalones,' irresponsables, les dan mas atención a sus aspectos sociales que a sus responsabilidades*" (Mexicans who accept that the women "wear the pants," they are irresponsible, these men pay more attention to their social lives than to their responsibilities).

Regional and Socioeconomic Differences in "How Machos Act"

After defining the word "macho," respondents were asked to give an example of how people who are macho act or behave. The answers ranged from drinking to excess, acting "bad" or "tough," being insecure in themselves, to having a "synthetic self-image," a code of ethics, and being sincere and responsible. Because responses typically were either negative or positive rather than neutral or indifferent, they were grouped into two broad categories.

Regional differences were not statistically significant, although southern Californians were more likely than Texans or northern Californians to see macho behavior as aggressive or negative and to associate it with acting tough, drinking, or being selfish.

The general pattern that was observed with regard to occupation, education, and income was that professionals, those with more education, and those with higher incomes were less likely to associate the word "macho" with negative behaviors such as drinking and trying to prove one's masculinity.

Place of birth and the language in which the interview was conducted were also related to the type of behavior that was associated with the word "macho." Men born in the United States and those who opted to conduct the interview in English were significantly more likely to associate such positive behaviors as being responsible, honorable, or respectful of others with people they considered to be macho.

Conclusion

These data provide empirical support for two very different and conflicting models of masculinity. The compensatory model sees the cult of virility and the Mexican male's obsession with power and domination as futile attempts to mask feelings of inferiority, powerlessness, and failure, whereas the second perspective associates being macho with a code of ethics that organizes and gives meaning to behavior. The first model stresses external attributes such as strength, sexual prowess, and power; the second stresses internal qualities like honor, responsibility, respect, and courage.

Although the findings are not conclusive, they have important implications. First, and most importantly, the so-called Mexican/Latino masculine cult appears to be a more complex and diverse phenomenon than is commonly assumed. But the assumption that being macho is an important Mexican cultural value is seriously called into question by the findings. Most respondents did not define macho as a positive cultural or personal trait or see themselves as being macho. Only about one-third of the men in the sample viewed the word "macho" positively. If there is a cultural value placed on being macho, one would expect that those respondents with closer ties to Latino culture and the Spanish language would be more apt to identify and to have positive associations with macho, but the opposite tendency was found to be true. Respondents who preferred to be interviewed in English were much more likely to see macho positively and to identify with it, whereas the vast majority of those who elected to be interviewed in Spanish viewed it negatively.

A major flaw of previous conceptualizations has been their tendency to treat machismo as a unitary phenomenon. The findings presented here suggest that although Latino men tend to hold polar conceptions of macho, these conceptions may not be unrelated. In describing the term, one respondent observed that there was almost a continuum between a person who is responsible and one who is chauvinistic. If one looks more closely at the two models, moreover, it is clear that virtually every trait associated with a negative macho trait has its counterpart in a positive one. Some of the principal characteristics of the negative macho and the positive counterparts are highlighted in Table 4.1.

The close parallel between negative and positive macho traits is reminiscent of Vicente T. Mendoza's distinction between genuine and false macho. According to Mendoza, the behavior of a genuine machismo is characterized by true brav-

■ **TABLE 4.1**
Negative and Positive Macho Traits

Negative	Positive
Bravado	Brave
Cowardly	Courageous
Violent	Self-defensive
Irresponsible	Responsible
Disrespectful	Respectful
Selfish	Altruistic
Pretentious	Humble
Loud	Soft-spoken
Boastful	Self-effacing
Abusive	Protective
Headstrong/bullish	Intransigent
Conformist	Individualistic
Chauvinistic	Androgynous
Dishonorable	Honorable
External qualities	Internal qualities

ery or valor, courage, generosity, stoicism, heroism, and ferocity; the negative macho simply uses the appearance of semblance of these traits to mask cowardliness and fear. . . .

From this perspective much of what social scientists have termed "macho" behavior is not macho at all, but its antithesis. Rather than attempting to isolate a modal Mexican personality type of determining whether macho is a positive or a negative cultural trait, social scientists would be well served to see Mexican and Latino culture as revolving around certain focal concerns or key issues such as honor, pride, dignity, courage, responsibility, integrity, and strength of character. Individuals, in turn, are evaluated positively or negatively according to how well they are perceived to respond to these focal concerns. But because being macho is ultimately an internal quality, those who seek to demonstrate outwardly that they are macho are caught in a double bind. A person who goes around holding his genitals, boasting about his manliness, or trying to prove how macho he is would not be considered macho by this definition. In the final analysis it is up to others to determine the extent to which a person lives up to these expectations and ideals.

It is also important to note that to a great extent, the positive internal qualities associated with the positive macho are not the exclusive domain of men but extend to either gender. One can use the same criteria in evaluating the behavior of women and employ parallel terminology such as *la hembra* (the female) and *hembrismo* (femaleness). *Una mujer que es una hembra* (a woman who is a real "female") is neither passive and submissive nor physically strong and assertive, for these are external qualities. Rather, *una hembra* is a person of strong character who has principles and is willing to defend them in the face of adversity. Thus, whereas the popular conception of the word "macho" refers to external male characteristics such as exaggerated masculinity or the cult of virility, the positive conception isolated here sees being macho as an internal, androgynous quality.

PART TWO

Boyhood

"**O**ne is not born, but rather becomes, a woman," wrote the French feminist thinker Simone de Beauvoir in her ground-breaking book *The Second Sex* (New York: Vintage, 1958). The same is true for men. And the social processes by which boys become men are complex and important. How does early childhood socialization differ for boys and girls? What specific traits are emphasized for boys that mark their socialization as different? What types of institutional arrangements reinforce those traits? How do the various institutions in which boys find themselves—school, family, and circles of friends—influence their development? What of the special institutions that promote "boys' life" or an adolescent male subculture?

During childhood and adolescence, masculinity becomes a central theme in a boy's life. *New York Times* editor A. M. Rosenthal put the dilemma this way: "So there I was, 13 years old, the smallest boy in my freshman class at DeWitt Clinton High School, smoking a White Owl cigar. I was not only little, but I did not have longies—long trousers—and was still in knickerbockers. Obvi-ously, I had to do something to project my fierce sense of manhood" (*New York Times*, 26 April 1987). That the assertion of manhood is part of a boy's natural development is suggested by Roger Brown, in his textbook *Social Psychology* (New York: Free Press, 1965, p. 161):

> In the United States, a real boy climbs trees, disdains girls, dirties his knees, plays with sol-diers, and takes blue for his favorite color. When they go to school, real boys prefer man-ual training, gym, and arithmetic. In college the boys smoke pipes, drink beer, and major in en-gineering or physics. The real boy matures into a "man's man" who plays poker, goes hunting, drinks brandy, and dies in the war.

The articles in this section address the ques-tion of how boys develop, focusing on the institu-tions that shape boys' lives. Ellen Jordan and Angela Cowan describe the gender socialization of schooling, both inside and outside the classroom. Ritch Savin-Williams and Ann Ferguson examine these issues from the perspectives of different groups of boys—both those who feel different and those who are made to feel different.

As anyone walking down any hallway in middle school or high school in the United States would probably tell you, the most common put down is "that's so gay." Homophobia is one of the found-ing principles of masculinity, as the articles by C. J. Pascoe and Emily Kane, and the exercise de-veloped by Paul Kivel, detail. Asked recently about

Photo by Mike Messner.

why he is constantly rapping about "faggots," one of our favorite contemporary gender theorists, Eminem, said:

> The lowest degrading thing you can say to a man when you're battling him is to call him a faggot and try to take away his manhood. Call him a sissy, call him a punk. Faggot to me doesn't necessarily mean gay people. Faggot to me just means taking away your manhood.

The association between sexual orientation and gender begins early in boys' lives, and continues as they grow to be men.

Ellen Jordan
Angela Cowan

Warrior Narratives in the Kindergarten Classroom: Renegotiating the Social Contract?

Since the beginning of second wave feminism, the separation between the public (masculine) world of politics and the economy and the private (feminine) world of the family and personal life has been seen as highly significant in establishing gender difference and inequality (Eisenstein 1984). Twenty years of feminist research and speculation have refined our understanding of this divide and how it has been developed and reproduced. One particularly striking and influential account is that given by Carole Pateman in her book *The Sexual Contract* (1988).

Pateman's broad argument is that in the modern world, the world since the Enlightenment, a "civil society" has been established. In this civil society, patriarchy has been replaced by a fratriarchy, which is equally male and oppressive of women. Men now rule not as fathers but as brothers, able to compete with one another, but presenting a united front against those outside the group. It is the brothers who control the public world of the state, politics, and the economy. Women have been given token access to this world because the discourses of liberty and universalism made this difficult to refuse, but to take part they must conform to the rules established to suit the brothers.

This public world in which the brothers operate together is conceptualized as separate from the personal and emotional. One is a realm where

there is little physicality—everything is done rationally, bureaucratically, according to contracts that the brothers accept as legitimate. Violence in this realm is severely controlled by agents of the state, except that the brothers are sometimes called upon for the supreme sacrifice of dying to preserve freedom. The social contract redefines the brawling and feuding long seen as essential characteristics of masculinity as deviant, even criminal, while the rest of physicality—sexuality, reproduction of the body, daily and intergenerationally—is left in the private sphere. Pateman quotes Robert Unger, "The dichotomy of the public and private life is still another corollary of the separation of understanding and desire. . . . When reasoning, [men] belong to a public world. . . . When desiring, however, men are private beings" (Pateman 1989, 48).

This is now widely accepted as the way men understand and experience their world. On the other hand, almost no attempt has been made to look at how it is that they take these views on board, or why the public/private divide is so much more deeply entrenched in their lived experience than in women's. This article looks at one strand in the complex web of experiences through which this is achieved. A major site where this occurs is the school, one of the institutions particularly characteristic of the civil society that emerged with the Enlightenment (Foucault 1980, 55–57). The school does not deliberately condition boys and not girls into this dichotomy, but it is, we believe, a site where what Giddens (1984, 10–13) has called a cycle of

From *Gender & Society* 9(6): 727–743. Copyright © 1995 by Sage Publications. Reprinted by permission of Sage Publications, Inc.

practice introduces little boys to the public/private division.

The article is based on weekly observations in a kindergarten classroom. We examine what happens in the early days of school when the children encounter the expectations of the school with their already established conceptions of gender. The early months of school are a period when a great deal of negotiating between the children's personal agendas and the teacher's expectations has to take place, where a great deal of what Genovese (1972) has described as accommodation and resistance must be involved.

In this article, we focus on a particular contest, which, although never specifically stated, is central to the children's accommodation to school: little boys' determination to explore certain narratives of masculinity with which they are already familiar—guns, fighting, fast cars—and the teacher's attempts to outlaw their importation into the classroom setting. We argue that what occurs is a contest between two definitions of masculinity: what we have chosen to call "warrior narratives" and the discourses of civil society—rationality, responsibility, and decorum—that are the basis of school discipline.

By "warrior narratives," we mean narratives that assume that violence is legitimate and justified when it occurs within a struggle between good and evil. There is a tradition of such narratives, stretching from Hercules and Beowulf to Superman and Dirty Harry, where the male is depicted as the warrior, the knight-errant, the superhero, the good guy (usually called a "goody" by Australian children), often supported by brothers in arms, and always opposed to some evil figure, such as a monster, a giant, a villain, a criminal, or, very simply, in Australian parlance, a "baddy." There is also a connection, it is now often suggested, between these narratives and the activity that has come to epitomize the physical expression of masculinity in the modern era: sport (Duthie 1980, 91–94; Crosset 1990; Messner 1992, 15). It is as sport that the physicality and desire usually lived out in the private sphere are permitted a ritualized public presence. Even though

the violence once characteristic of the warrior has, in civil society and as part of the social contract, become the prerogative of the state, it can still be re-enacted symbolically in countless sporting encounters. The mantle of the warrior is inherited by the sportsman.

The school discipline that seeks to outlaw these narratives is, we would suggest, very much a product of modernity. Bowles and Gintis have argued that "the structure of social relations in education not only inures the student to the discipline of the work place, but develops the types of personal demeanor, modes of self-presentation, self-image, and social-class identifications which are the crucial ingredients of job adequacy" (1976, 131). The school is seeking to introduce the children to the behavior appropriate to the civil society of the modern world.

An accommodation does eventually take place, this article argues, through a recognition of the split between the public and the private. Most boys learn to accept that the way to power and respectability is through acceptance of the conventions of civil society. They also learn that warrior narratives are not a part of this world; they can only be experienced symbolically as fantasy or sport. The outcome, we will suggest, is that little boys learn that these narratives must be left behind in the private world of desire when they participate in the public world of reason.

The Study

The school where this study was conducted serves an old-established suburb in a country town in New South Wales, Australia. The children are predominantly Australian born and English speaking, but come from socioeconomic backgrounds ranging from professional to welfare recipient. We carried out this research in a classroom run by a teacher who is widely acknowledged as one of the finest and most successful kindergarten teachers in our region. She is an admired practitioner of free play, process writing, and creativity. There was no gender definition of games in her classroom. Groups composed of both girls and boys had turns at playing in the Doll Corner, in the Construction Area, and on the Car Mat.

The research method used was nonparticipant observation, the classic mode for the sociological study of children in schools (Burgess 1984; Thorne 1986; Goodenough 1987). The group of children described came to school for the first time in February 1993. The observation sessions began within a fortnight of the children entering school and were conducted during "free activity" time, a period lasting for about an hour. At first we observed twice a week, but then settled to a weekly visit, although there were some weeks when it was inconvenient for the teacher to accommodate an observer.

The observation was noninteractive. The observer stationed herself as unobtrusively as possible, usually seated on a kindergarten-sized chair, near one of the play stations. She made pencil notes of events, with particular attention to accurately recording the words spoken by the children, and wrote up detailed narratives from the notes, supplemented by memory, on reaching home. She discouraged attention from the children by rising and leaving the area if she was drawn by them into any interaction.

This project thus employed a methodology that was ethnographic and open-ended. It was nevertheless guided by certain theories, drawn from the work on gender of Jean Anyon, Barrie Thorne, and R. W. Connell, of the nature of social interaction and its part in creating personal identity and in reproducing the structures of a society.

Anyon has adapted the conceptions of accommodation and resistance developed by Genovese (1972) to understanding how women live with gender. Genovese argued that slaves in the American South accommodated to their contradictory situation by using certain of its aspects, for example, exposure to the Christian religion, to validate a sense of self-worth and dignity. Christian beliefs then allowed them to take a critical view of slavery, which in turn legitimated certain forms of resistance (Anyon 1983, 21). Anyon lists

a variety of ways in which women accommodate to and resist prescriptions of appropriate feminine behavior, arguing for a significant level of choice and agency (Anyon 1983, 23–26).

Thorne argues that the processes of social life, the form and nature of the interactions, as well as the choices of the actors, should be the object of analysis. She writes, "In this book I begin not with individuals, although they certainly appear in the account, but with *group life*—with social relations, the organization and meanings of social situations, the collective practices through which children and adults create and recreate gender in their daily interactions" (1993, 4).

These daily interactions, Connell (1987, 139–141) has suggested, mesh to form what Giddens (1984, 10–13) has called "cyclical practices." Daily interactions are neither random nor specific to particular locations. They are repeated and recreated in similar settings throughout a society. Similar needs recur, similar discourses are available, and so similar solutions to problems are adopted; thus, actions performed and discourses adopted to achieve particular ends in particular situations have the unintended consequence of producing uniformities of gendered behavior in individuals.

In looking at the patterns of accommodation and resistance that emerge when the warrior narratives that little boys have adapted from television encounter the discipline of the classroom, we believe we have uncovered one of the cyclical practices of modernity that reveal the social contract to these boys.

Warrior Narratives in the Doll Corner

In the first weeks of the children's school experience, the Doll Corner was the area where the most elaborate acting out of warrior narratives was observed. The Doll Corner in this classroom was a small room with a door with a glass panel opening off the main area. Its furnishings—stove, sink, dolls' cots, and so on—were an attempt at a literal re-creation of a domestic setting, revealing the school's definition of children's play as a preparation for adult life. It was an area where the acting out of "pretend" games was acceptable.

Much of the boys' play in the area was domestic:

Jimmy and Tyler were jointly ironing a tablecloth. "Look at the sheet is burnt, I've burnt it," declared Tyler, waving the toy iron above his head. "I'm telling Mrs. Sandison," said Jimmy worriedly. "No, I tricked you. It's not really burnt. See," explained Tyler, showing Jimmy the black pattern on the cloth. (February 23, 1993)

"Where is the baby, the baby boy?" Justin asked, as he helped Harvey and Malcolm settle some restless teddy babies. "Give them some potion." Justin pretended to force feed a teddy, asking "Do you want to drink this potion?" (March 4, 1993)

On the other hand, there were attempts from the beginning by some of the boys and one of the girls to use this area for nondomestic games and, in the case of the boys, for games based on warrior narratives, involving fighting, destruction, goodies, and baddies.

The play started off quietly, Winston cuddled a teddy bear, then settled it in a bed. Just as Winston tucked in his bear, Mac snatched the teddy out of bed and swung it around his head in circles. "Don't hurt him, give him back," pleaded Winston, trying vainly to retrieve the teddy. The two boys were circling the small table in the center of the room. As he ran, Mac started to karate chop the teddy on the arm, and then threw it on the floor and jumped on it. He then snatched up a plastic knife, "This is a sword. Ted is dead. They all are." He sliced the knife across the teddy's tummy, repeating the action on the bodies of two stuffed dogs. Winston grabbed the two dogs, and with a dog in each hand, staged a dog fight. "They are alive again." (February 10, 1993)

Three boys were busily stuffing teddies into the cupboard through the sink opening. "They're in jail. They can't escape," said Malcolm. "Let's pour water over them." "Don't do that. It'll hurt them," shouted Winston, rushing into the Doll

Corner. "Go away, Winston. You're not in our group," said Malcolm. (February 12, 1993)

The boys even imported goodies and baddies into a classic ghost scenario initiated by one of the girls:

"I'm the father," Tyler declared. "I'm the mother," said Alanna. "Let's pretend it's a stormy night and I'm afraid. Let's pretend a ghost has come to steal the dog." Tyler nodded and placed the sheet over his head. Tyler moaned, "ooooOOOOOOOAHHHH!!!" and moved his outstretched arms toward Alanna. Jamie joined the game and grabbed a sheet from the doll's cradle, "I'm the goody ghost." "So am I," said Tyler. They giggled and wrestled each other to the floor. "No! you're the baddy ghost," said Jamie. Meanwhile, Alanna was making ghostly noises and moving around the boys. "Did you like the game? Let's play it again," she suggested. (February 23, 1993)

In the first two incidents, there was some conflict between the narratives being invoked by Winston and those used by the other boys. For Winston, the stuffed toys were the weak whom he must protect knight-errant style. For the other boys, they could be set up as the baddies whom it was legitimate for the hero to attack. Both were versions of a warrior narrative.

The gender difference in the use of these narratives has been noted by a number of observers (Paley 1984; Clark 1989, 250–252; Thorne 1993, 98–99). Whereas even the most timid, least physically aggressive boys—Winston in this study is typical—are drawn to identifying with the heroes of these narratives, girls show almost no interest in them at this early age. The strong-willed and assertive girls in our study, as in others (Clark 1990, 83–84; Walkerdine 1990, 10–12), sought power by commandeering the role of mother, teacher, or shopkeeper, while even the highly imaginative Alanna, although she enlivened the more mundane fantasies of the other children with ghosts, old widow women, and magical mirrors, seems not to have been attracted by warrior heroes.[1]

Warrior narratives, it would seem, have a powerful attraction for little boys, which they lack for little girls. Why and how this occurs remains unexplored in early childhood research, perhaps because data for such an explanation are not available to those doing research in institutional settings. Those undertaking ethnographic research in preschools find the warrior narratives already in possession in these sites (Paley 1984, 70–73, 116; Davies 1989, 91–92). In this research, gender difference in the appeal of warrior narratives has to be taken as a given—the data gathered are not suitable for constructing theories of origins; thus, the task of determining an explanation would seem to lie within the province of those investigating and theorizing gender differentiation during infancy, and perhaps, specifically, of those working in the tradition of feminist psychoanalysis pioneered by Dinnerstein (1977) and Chodorow (1978). Nevertheless, even though the cause may remain obscure, there can be little argument that in the English-speaking world for at least the last hundred years—think of Tom Sawyer playing Robin Hood and the pirates and Indians in J. M. Barrie's *Peter Pan*—boys have built these narratives into their conceptions of the masculine.

Accommodation through *Bricolage*

The school classroom, even one as committed to freedom and self-actualization as this, makes little provision for the enactment of these narratives. The classroom equipment invites children to play house, farm, and shop, to construct cities and roads, and to journey through them with toy cars, but there is no overt invitation to explore warrior narratives.

In the first few weeks of school, the little boys un-self-consciously set about redressing this omission. The method they used was what is known as *bricolage*—the transformation of objects from one use to another for symbolic purposes (Hebdige 1979, 103). The first site was the Doll Corner. Our records for the early weeks contain a number of examples of boys rejecting the usages ascribed to the various Doll Corner objects by the teacher and by the makers of equipment and assigning a

different meaning to them. This became evident very early with their use of the toy baby carriages (called "prams" in Australia). For the girls, the baby carriages were just that, but for many of the boys they very quickly became surrogate cars:

> Mac threw a doll into the largest pram in the Doll Corner. He walked the pram out past a group of his friends who were playing "crashes" on the Car Mat. Three of the five boys turned and watched him wheeling the pram toward the classroom door. Mac performed a sharp three-point turn; raced his pram past the Car Mat group, striking one boy on the head with the pram wheel. (February 10, 1993)

> "Brrrrmmmmmm, brrrrrmmmmm," Tyler's revving engine noises grew louder as he rocked the pram back and forth with sharp jerking movements. The engine noise grew quieter as he left the Doll Corner and wheeled the pram around the classroom. He started to run with the pram when the teacher could not observe him. (March 23, 1993)

The boys transformed other objects into masculine appurtenances: knives and tongs became weapons, the dolls' beds became boats, and so on.

> Mac tried to engage Winston in a sword fight using Doll Corner plastic knives. Winston backed away, but Mac persisted. Winston took a knife but continued to back away from Mac. He then put down the knife, and ran away half-screaming (semi-seriously, unsure of the situation) for his teacher. (February 10, 1993)

In the literature on youth subcultures, bricolage is seen as a characteristic of modes of resistance. Hebdige writes:

> It is through the distinctive rituals of consumption, through style, that the subculture at once reveals its "secret" identity and communicates its forbidden meanings. It is predominantly the way commodities are *used* in subculture which mark the subculture off from more orthodox cultural formations. . . . The concept of *bricolage* can be used to explain how subcultural styles are constructed. (1979, 103)

In these early weeks, however, the boys did not appear to be aware that they were doing anything more than establishing an accommodation between their needs and the classroom environment.

This mode of accommodation was rejected by the teacher, however, who practiced a gentle, but steady, discouragement of such bricolage. Even though the objects in this space are not really irons, beds, and cooking pots, she made strong efforts to assert their cultural meaning, instructing the children in the "proper" use of the equipment and attempting to control their behavior by questions like "Would you do that with a tea towel in your house?" "Cats never climb up on the benches in *my* house." It was thus impressed upon the children that warrior narratives were inappropriate in this space.

The children, our observations suggest, accepted her guidance, and we found no importation of warrior narratives into the Doll Corner after the first few weeks. There were a number of elaborate and exciting narratives devised, but they were all to some degree related to the domestic environment. For example, on April 20, Justin and Nigel used one of the baby carriages as a four-wheel drive, packed it with equipment and went off for a camping trip, setting out a picnic with Doll Corner tablecloths, knives, forks, and plates when they arrived. On May 18, Matthew, Malcolm, Nigel, and Jonathan were dogs being fed in the Doll Corner. They then complained of the flies, and Jonathan picked up the toy telephone and said, "Flycatcher! Flycatcher! Come and catch some flies. They are everywhere." On June 1, the following was recorded:

> "We don't want our nappies [diapers] changed," Aaron informed Celia, the mum in the game. "I'm poohing all over your clothes mum," Mac declared, as he grunted and positioned himself over the dress-up box. Celia cast a despairing glance in Mac's direction, and went on dressing a doll. "I am too; poohing all over your clothes mum," said Aaron. "Now mum will have to clean it all up and change my nappy," he informed Mac, giggling. He turned to the dad

> [Nigel], and said in a baby voice, "Goo-goo; give him [Mac] the feather duster." "No! give him the feather duster; he did the longest one all over the clothes," Mac said to Nigel. (June 1, 1993)

Although exciting and imaginative games continued, the bricolage virtually disappeared from the Doll Corner. The intention of the designer of the Doll Corner equipment was increasingly respected. Food for the camping trip was bought from the shop the teacher had set up and consumed using the Doll Corner equipment. The space invaded by flies was a domestic space, and appropriate means, calling in expert help by telephone, were used to deal with the problem. Chairs and tables were chairs and tables, clothes were clothes and could be fouled by appropriate inhabitants of a domestic space, babies. Only the baby carriages continued to have an ambiguous status, to maintain the ability to be transformed into vehicles of other kinds.

The warrior narratives—sword play, baddies in jail, pirates, and so on—did not vanish from the boys' imaginative world, but, as the later observations show, the site gradually moved from the Doll Corner to the Construction Area and the Car Mat. By the third week in March (that is, after about six weeks at school), the observer noticed the boys consistently using the construction toys to develop these narratives. The bricolage was now restricted to the more amorphously defined construction materials.

> Tyler was busy constructing an object out of five pieces of plastic straw (clever sticks). "This is a water pistol. Everyone's gonna get wet," he cried as he moved into the Doll Corner pretending to wet people. The game shifted to guns and bullets between Tyler and two other boys. "I've got a bigger gun," Roger said, showing off his square block object. "Mine's more longer. Ehehehehehehehe, got you," Winston yelled to Roger, brandishing a plastic straw gun. "I'll kill your gun," Mac said, pushing Winston's gun away. "No Mac. You broke it. No," cried Winston. (March 23, 1993)

Two of the boys picked up swords made out of blue- and red-colored plastic squares they had displayed on the cupboard. "This is my sword," Jamie explained to Tyler. "My jumper [sweater] holds it in. Whichever color is at the bottom, well that's the color it shoots out. Whoever is bad, we shoot with power out of it." "Come on Tyler," he went on. "Get your sword. Let's go get some baddies." (March 30, 1993)

The toy cars on the Car Mat were also pressed into the service of warrior narratives:

Justin, Brendan, and Jonathan were busy on the Car Mat. The game involved police cars that were chasing baddies who had drunk "too much beers." Justin explained to Jonathan why his car had the word "DOG" written on the front. "These are different police cars, for catching robbers taking money." (March 4, 1993)

Three boys, Harvey, Maurice, and Marshall, were on the Car Mat. "Here comes the baddies," Harvey shouted, spinning a toy car around the mat. "Crasssshhhhh everywhere." He crashed his car into the other boys' cars and they responded with laughter. "I killed a baddie everyone," said Maurice, crashing his cars into another group of cars. (May 24, 1993)

A new accommodation was being proposed by the boys, a new adaptation of classroom materials to the needs of their warrior narratives.

Classroom Rules and Resistance

Once again the teacher would not accept the accommodation proposed. Warrior narratives provoked what she considered inappropriate public behavior in the miniature civil society of her classroom. Her aim was to create a "free" environment where children could work independently, learn at their own pace, and explore their own interests, but creating such an environment involved its own form of social contract, its own version of the state's appropriation of violence. From the very first day, she began to establish a series of classroom rules that imposed constraints on violent or disruptive activity.

The belief underlying her practice was that firmly established classroom rules make genuine free play possible, rather than restricting the range of play opportunities. Her emphasis on "proper" use of equipment was intended to stop it being damaged and consequently withdrawn from use. She had rules of "no running" and "no shouting" that allowed children to work and play safely on the floor of the classroom, even though other children were using equipment or toys that demanded movement, and ensured that the noise level was low enough for children to talk at length to one another as part of their games.

One of the outcomes of these rules was the virtual outlawing of a whole series of games that groups of children usually want to initiate when they are playing together, games of speed and body contact, of gross motor self-expression and skill. This prohibition affected both girls and boys and was justified by setting up a version of public and private spaces: The classroom was not the proper place for such activities, they "belong" in the playground.[2] The combined experience of many teachers has shown that it is almost impossible for children to play games involving car crashes and guns without violating these rules; therefore, in this classroom, as in many others (Paley 1984, 71, 116), these games were in effect banned.

These rules were then policed by the children themselves, as the following interchange shows:

"Eeccccchceeeceheeeeh!" Tyler leapt about the room. A couple of girls were saying, "Stop it Tyler" but he persisted. Jane warned, "You're not allowed to have guns." Tyler responded saying, "It's not a gun. It's a water pistol, and that's not a gun." "Not allowed to have water pistol guns," Tony reiterated to Tyler. "Yes, it's a water pistol," shouted Tyler. Jane informed the teacher, who responded stating, "NO GUNS, even if they are water pistols." Tyler made a spear out of Clever Sticks, straight after the banning of gun play. (March 23, 1993)

The boys, however, were not prepared to abandon their warrior narratives. Unlike gross motor activities such as wrestling and football, they were not prepared to see them relegated to the playground, but the limitations on their expression and the teacher disapproval they evoked led the boys to explore them surreptitiously; they found ways of introducing them that did not violate rules about running and shouting.

As time passed, the games became less visible. The warrior narratives were not so much acted out as talked through, using the toy cars and the construction materials as a prompt and a basis:

> Tyler was showing his plastic straw construction to Luke. "This is a Samurai Man and this is his hat. A Samurai Man fights in Japan and they fight with the Ninja. The bad guys who use cannons and guns. My Samurai is captain of the Samurai and he is going to kill the sergeant of the bad guys. He is going to sneak up on him with a knife and kill him." (June 1, 1993)

> Malcolm and Aaron had built boats with Lego blocks and were explaining the various components to Roger. "This ship can go faster," Malcolm explained. "He [a plastic man] is the boss of the ship. Mine is a goody boat. They are not baddies." "Mine's a steam shovel boat. It has wheels," said Aaron. "There it goes in the river and it has to go to a big shed where all the steam shovels are stopping." (June 11, 1993)

It also became apparent that there was something covert about this play. The cars were crashed quietly. The guns were being transformed into water pistols. Swords were concealed under jumpers and only used when the teacher's back was turned. When the constructed objects were displayed to the class, their potential as players in a fighting game was concealed under a more mundane description. For example:

> Prior to the free play, the children were taking turns to explain the Clever Stick and Lego Block constructions they had made the previous afternoon. I listened to Tyler describe his Lego robot to the class: "This is a transformer robot. It can do things and turn into everything." During free play, Tyler played with the same robot explaining its capacities to Winston: "This is a terminator ship. It can kill. It can turn into a robot and the top pops off." (March 23, 1993)

Children even protested to one another that they were not making weapons, "This isn't a gun, it's a lookout." "This isn't a place for bullets, it's for petrol."

The warrior narratives, it would seem, went underground and became part of a "deviant" masculine subculture with the characteristic "secret" identity and hidden meanings (Hebdige 1979, 103). The boys were no longer seeking accommodation but practicing hidden resistance. The classroom, they were learning, was not a place where it was acceptable to explore their gender identity through fantasy.

This, however, was a message that only the boys were receiving. The girls' gender-specific fantasies (Paley 1984, 106–108; Davies 1989, 118–122) of nurturing and self-display—mothers, nurses, brides, princesses—were accommodated easily within the classroom. They could be played out without contravening the rules of the miniature civil society. Although certain delightful activities—eating, running, hugging, and kissing (Best 1983, 110)—might be excluded from this public sphere, they were not ones by means of which their femininity, and thus their subjectivity, their conception of the self, was defined.

Masculinity, the School Regime, and the Social Contract

We suggest that this conflict between warrior narratives and school rules is likely to form part of the experience of most boys growing up in the industrialized world. The commitment to such narratives was not only nearly 100 percent among the boys we observed, but similar commitment is, as was argued above, common in other sites. On the other hand, the pressure to preserve a decorous classroom is strong in all teachers (with the possible exception of those teaching in "alternative" schools) and has been since the beginnings of compulsory education. Indeed, it is only in classrooms where there is the balance of freedom and constraint we observed that such narratives are likely to surface at all. In more formal situations, they would be defined as deviant and forced underground from the boys' first entry into school.

If this is a widely recurring pattern, the question then arises: Is it of little significance or is it what Giddens (1984, 10–3) would call one of the "cyclical practices" that reproduce the structures of our society? The answer really depends on how little boys "read" the outlawing of their warrior narratives. If they see it as simply one of the broad constraints of school against which they are continually negotiating, then perhaps it has no significance. If, on the other hand, it has in their minds a crucial connection to the definition of gender, to the creation of their own masculine identity, to where they position particular sites and practices on a masculine to feminine continuum, then the ostracism of warrior narratives may mean that they define the school environment as feminine.

There is considerable evidence that some primary school children do in fact make this categorization (Best 1983, 14–15; Brophy 1985, 118; Clark 1990, 36), and we suggest here that the outlawry of the masculine narrative contributes to this. Research by Willis (1977) and Walker (1988) in high schools has revealed a culture of resistance based on definitions of masculinity as *antagonistic* to the demands of the school, which are construed as feminine by the resisters. It might therefore seem plausible to see the underground perpetuation of the warrior narrative as an early expression of this resistance and one that gives some legitimacy to the resisters' claims that the school is feminine.

Is the school regime that outlaws the warrior narratives really feminine? We would argue, rather, that the regime being imposed is based on a male ideal, an outcome of the Enlightenment and compulsory schooling. Michel Foucault has pointed out that the development of this particular regime in schools coincided with the emergence of the prison, the hospital, the army barracks, and the factory (Foucault 1980, 55–57).

Although teachers in the first years of school are predominantly female, the regime they impose is perpetuated by male teachers (Brophy 1985, 121), and this preference is endorsed by powerful and influential males in the society at large. The kind of demeanor and self-management that teachers are trying to inculcate in the early school years is the behavior expected in male-dominated public arenas like boardrooms, courtrooms, and union mass meetings.[3]

Connell (1989, 291) and Willis (1977, 76, 84) provide evidence that by adolescence, boys from all classes, particularly if they are ambitious, come to regard acquiescence in the school's demands as compatible with constructing a masculine identity. Connell writes:

> Some working class boys embrace a project of mobility in which they construct a masculinity organized around themes of rationality and responsibility. This is closely connected with the "certification" function of the upper levels of the education system and to a key form of masculinity among professionals. (1989, 291)

Rationality and responsibility are, as Weber argued long ago, the primary characteristics of the modern society theorized by the Enlightenment thinkers as based on a social contract. This prized rationality has been converted in practice into a bureaucratized legal system where "responsible" acceptance by the population of the rules of civil society obviates the need for individuals to use physical violence in gaining their ends or protecting their rights, and where, if such violence is necessary, it is exercised by the state (Weber 1978, 341–354). In civil society, the warrior is obsolete, his activities redefined bureaucratically and performed by the police and the military.

The teacher in whose classroom our observation was conducted demonstrated a strong commitment to rationality and responsibility. For example, she devoted a great deal of time to showing that there was a cause and effect link between the behavior forbidden by her classroom rules and classroom accidents. Each time an accident occurred, she asked the children to determine the cause of the accident, its result, and how it could have been prevented. The implication throughout was that children must take responsibility for the outcomes of their actions.

Mac accidentally struck a boy, who was lying on the floor, in the head with a pram wheel. He was screaming around with a pram, the victim was playing on the Car Mat and lying down to obtain a bird's eye view of a car crash. Mac rushed past the group and struck Justin on the side of the head. Tears and confusion ensued. The teacher's reaction was to see to Justin, then stop all play and gain children's attention, speaking first to Mac and Justin plus Justin's group:

T. How did Justin get hurt?

M. [No answer]

T. Mac, what happened?

M. I was wheeling the pram and Justin was in the way.

T. Were you running?

M. I was wheeling the pram.

The teacher now addresses the whole class:

T. Stop working everyone, eyes to me and listen. Someone has just been hurt because someone didn't remember the classroom rules. What are they, Harvey?

(Harvey was listening intently and she wanted someone who could answer the question at this point.)

H. No running in the classroom.

T. Why?

Other children offer an answer.

Chn. Because someone will get hurt.

T. Yes, and that is what happened. Mac was going too quickly with the pram and Justin was injured. Now how can we stop this happening next time?

Chn. No running in the classroom, only walk. (February 10, 1993)

Malcolm, walking, bumped Winston on the head with a construction toy. The teacher intervened:

T. [To Malcolm and Winston] What happened?

W. Malcolm hit me on the head.

M. But it was an accident. I didn't mean it. I didn't really hurt him.

T. How did it happen?

M. It was an accident.

W. He [Malcolm] hit me.

T. Malcolm, I know you didn't mean to hurt Winston, so how did it happen?

M. I didn't mean it.

T. I know you didn't mean it, Malcolm, but why did Winston get hurt?

Chn. Malcolm was running.

M. No I wasn't.

T. See where everyone was sitting? There is hardly enough room for children to walk. Children working on the floor must remember to leave a walking path so that other children can move safely around the room. Otherwise someone will be hurt, and that's what has happened today. (February 23, 1993)

This public-sphere masculinity of rationality and responsibility, of civil society, of the social contract is not the masculinity that the boys are bringing into the classroom through their warrior narratives. They are using a different, much older version—not the male as responsible citizen, the producer and consumer who keeps the capitalist system going, the breadwinner, and caring father of a family. Their earliest vision of masculinity is the male as warrior, the bonded male who goes out with his mates and meets the dangers of the world, the male who attacks and defeats other males characterized as baddies, the male who turns the natural products of the earth into weapons to carry out these purposes.

We would argue, nevertheless, that those boys who aspire to become one of the brothers who wield power in the public world of civil society ultimately realize that conformity to rationality and responsibility, to the demands of the school, is the price they must pay. They realize that although the girls can expect one day to become the brides and mothers of their pretend games, the boys will never, except perhaps in time of war, be allowed to act out the part of warrior hero in reality.

On the other hand, the school softens the transition for them by endorsing and encouraging the classic modern transformation and domestication of the warrior narrative, sport (Connell 1987, 177; Messner 1992, 10–12). In the school where this observation was conducted, large playground areas are set aside for lunchtime cricket, soccer, and basketball; by the age of seven, most boys are joining in these games. The message is conveyed to them that if they behave like citizens in the classroom, they can become warriors on the sports oval.

Gradually, we would suggest, little boys get the message that resistance is not the only way to live out warrior masculinity. If they accept a public/private division of life, it can be accommodated within the private sphere; thus, it becomes possible for those boys who aspire to respectability, figuring in civil society as one of the brothers, to accept that the school regime and its expectations are masculine and to reject the attempts of the "resisters" to define it (and them) as feminine. They adopt the masculinity of rationality and responsibility as that appropriate to the public sphere, while the earlier, deeply appealing masculinity of the warrior narratives can still be experienced through symbolic reenactment on the sports field.

Conclusion

We are not, of course, suggesting that this is the only way in which the public/private division becomes part of the lived awareness of little boys. We do, however, believe that we have teased out one strand of the manner in which they encounter it. We have suggested that the classroom is a major site where little boys are introduced to the masculinity of rationality and responsibility charac-

teristic of the brothers in civil society; we have been looking at a "cycle of practice" where, in classroom after classroom, generation after generation, the mode of masculinity typified in the warrior narratives is first driven underground and then transferred to the sports field. We are, we would suggest, seeing renegotiated for each generation and in each boy's own life the conception of the "social contract" that is characteristic of the era of modernity, of the Enlightenment, of democracy, and of capitalism. We are watching reenacted the transformation of violence and power as exercised by body over body, to control through surveillance and rules (Foucault 1977, 9; 1984, 66–67), the move from domination by individual superiors to acquiescence in a public sphere of decorum and rationality (Pateman 1988).

Yet, this is a social *contract*, and there is another side to the bargain. Although they learn that they must give up their warrior narratives of masculinity in the public sphere, where rationality and responsibility hold sway, they also learn that in return they may preserve them in the private realm of desire as fantasy, as bricolage, as a symbolic survival that is appropriate to the spaces of leisure and self-indulgence, the playground, the backyard, the television set, the sports field. Although this is too large an issue to be explored in detail here, there may even be a reenactment in the school setting of what Pateman (1988, 99–115) has defined as the sexual contract, the male right to dominate women in return for accepting the constraints of civil society. Is this, perhaps, established for both boys and girls by means of the endemic misogyny—invasion of girls' space (Thorne 1986, 172; 1993, 63–88), overt expressions of aversion and disgust (Goodenough 1987, 422; D'Arcy 1990, 81), disparaging sexual innuendo (Best 1983, 129; Goodenough 1987, 433; Clark 1990, 38–46)—noted by so many observers in the classrooms and playgrounds of modernity? Are girls being contained by the boys' actions within a more restricted, ultimately a private, sphere because, in the boys' eyes, they have not earned access to the public sphere by sharing their ordeal of repression, resistance, and ultimate symbolic accommodation of their gender-defining fantasies?

Author's Note: The research on which this article is based was funded by the Research Management Committee of the University of Newcastle. The observation was conducted at East Maitland Public School, and the authors would like to thank the principal, teachers, and children involved for making our observer so welcome.

Notes

1. Some ethnographic studies describe a "tomboy" who wants to join in the boys' games (Best 1983, 95–97; Davies 1989, 93, 123; Thorne 1993, 127–129), although in our experience, such girls are rare, rarer even than the boys who play by choice with girls. The girls' rejection of the warrior narratives does not appear to be simply the result of the fact that the characters are usually men. Bronwyn Davies, when she read the role-reversal story *Rita the Rescuer* to preschoolers, found that many boys identified strongly with Rita ("they flex their muscles to show how strong they are and fall to wrestling each other on the floor to display their strength"), whereas for most girls, Rita remained "other" (Davies 1989, 57–58).

2. This would seem to reverse the usual parallel of outdoor/indoor with public/private. This further suggests that the everyday equation of "public" with "visible" may not be appropriate for the specialized use of the term in sociological discussions of the public/private division. Behavior in the street may be more visible than what goes on in a courtroom, but it is nevertheless acceptable for the street behavior to be, to a greater degree, personal, private, and driven by "desire."

3. There are some groups of men who continue to reject these modes of modernity throughout their lives. Andrew Metcalfe, in his study of an Australian mining community, has identified two broad categories of miner, the "respectable," and the "larrikin" (an Australian slang expression carrying implications of nonconformism, irreverence, and impudence). The first are committed to the procedural decorums of union meetings, sporting and hobby clubs, welfare groups, and so on; the others relate more strongly to the less disciplined masculinity of the pub, the brawl, and the racetrack (Metcalfe 1988, 73–125). This distinction is very similar to that noted by Paul Willis in England between the "ear'oles" and the "lads" in a working-class secondary school (Willis 1977). It needs to be noted that this is not a *class* difference and that demographically the groups are identical. What distinguishes them is, as Metcalfe points out, their relative commitment to the respectable modes of accommodation and resistance characteristic of civil society of larrikin modes with a much longer history, perhaps even their acceptance or rejection of the social contract.

References

Anyon, Jean. 1983. Intersections of gender and class: Accommodation and resistance by working-class and affluent females to contradictory sex-role ideologies. In *Gender, class and education*, edited by Stephen Walker and Len Barton. Barcombe, Sussex: Falmer.

Best, Raphaela. 1983. *We've all got scars: What girls and boys learn in elementary school*. Bloomington: Indiana University Press.

Bowles, Samuel, and Herbert Gintis. 1976. *Schooling in capitalist America: Educational reform and the contradictions of economic life*. London: Routledge and Kegan Paul.

Brophy, Jere E. 1985. Interactions of male and female students with male and female teachers. In *Gender influences in classroom interaction*, edited by L. C. Wilkinson and C. B. Marrett. New York: Academic Press.

Burgess, R. G., ed. 1984. *The research process in educational settings: Ten case studies*. Lewes: Falmer.

Chodorow, Nancy. 1978. *The reproduction of mothering: Psychoanalysis and the sociology of gender*. Berkeley: University of California Press.

Clark, Margaret. 1989. Anastasia is a normal developer because she is unique. *Oxford Review of Education* 15:243–255.

———. 1990. *The great divide: Gender in the primary school*. Melbourne: Curriculum Corporation.

Connell, R. W. 1987. *Gender and power: Society, the person and sexual politics*. Sydney: Allen and Unwin.

———. 1989. Cool guys, swots and wimps: The interplay of masculinity and education. *Oxford Review of Education* 15:291–303.

Crosset, Todd. 1990. Masculinity, sexuality, and the development of early modern sport. In *Sport, men and the gender order*, edited by Michael E. Messner and Donald F. Sabo. Champaign, IL: Human Kinetics Books.

D'Arcy, Sue. 1990. Towards a non-sexist primary classroom. In *Dolls and dungarees: Gender issues in the primary school curriculum*, edited by Eva Tutchell. Milton Keynes: Open University Press.

Davies, Bronwyn. 1989. *Frogs and snails and feminist tales: Preschool children and gender*. Sydney: Allen and Unwin.

Dinnerstein, Myra. 1977. *The mermaid and the minotaur: Sexual arrangements and human malaise*. New York: Harper and Row.

Duthie, J. H. 1980. Athletics: The ritual of a technological society? In *Play and culture*, edited by Helen B. Schwartzman. West Point, NY: Leisure.

Eisenstein, Hester. 1984. *Contemporary feminist thought*. London: Unwin Paperbacks.

Foucault, Michel. 1977. *Discipline and punish: The birth of the prison*. Translated by Alan Sheridan. New York: Pantheon.

———. 1980. Body/power. In *power/knowledge: Selected interviews and other writings 1972–1977*, edited by Colin Gordon. Brighton: Harvester.

———. 1984. Truth and power. In *The Foucault reader*, edited by P. Rabinow. New York: Pantheon.

Genovese, Eugene F. 1972. *Roll, Jordan, roll: The world the slaves made*. New York: Pantheon.

Giddens, Anthony. 1984. *The constitution of society: Outline of the theory of structuration*. Berkeley: University of California Press.

Goodenough, Ruth Gallagher. 1987. Small group culture and the emergence of sexist behaviour: A comparative study of four children's groups. In *Interpretive ethnography of education*, edited by G. Spindler and L. Spindler. Hillsdale, NJ: Lawrence Erlbaum.

Hebdige, Dick. 1979. *Subculture: The meaning of style*. London: Methuen.

Messner, Michael E. 1992. *Power at play: Sports and the problem of masculinity*. Boston: Beacon.

Metcalfe, Andrew. 1988. *For freedom and dignity: Historical agency and class structure in the coalfields of NSW*. Sydney: Allen and Unwin.

Paley, Vivian Gussin. 1984. *Boys and girls: Superheroes in the doll corner*. Chicago: University of Chicago Press.

Pateman, Carole. 1988. *The sexual contract*. Oxford: Polity.

———. 1989. The fraternal social contract. In *The disorder of women*. Cambridge: Polity.

Thorne, Barrie. 1986. Girls and boys together . . . but mostly apart: Gender arrangements in elementary schools. In *Relationships and development*, edited by W. W. Hartup and Z. Rubin. Hillsdale, NJ: Lawrence Erlbaum.

———. 1993. *Gender play: Girls and boys in school*. New Brunswick, NJ: Rutgers University Press.

Walker, J. C. 1988. *Louts and legends: Male youth culture in an inner-city school*. Sydney: Allen and Unwin.

Walkerdine, Valerie. 1990. *Schoolgirl fictions*. London: Verso.

Weber, Max. 1978. *Selections in translation*. Edited by W. G. Runciman and translated by Eric Matthews. Cambridge: Cambridge University Press.

Willis, Paul. 1977. *Learning to labour: How working class kids get working class jobs*. Farnborough: Saxon House.

Emily W. Kane

"No Way My Boys Are Going to Be Like That!": Parents' Responses to Children's Gender Nonconformity

Parents begin gendering their children from their very first awareness of those children, whether in pregnancy or while awaiting adoption. Children themselves become active participants in this gendering process by the time they are conscious of the social relevance of gender, typically before the age of two. I address one aspect of this process of parents doing gender, both for and with their children, by exploring how parents respond to gender nonconformity among preschool-aged children. As West and Zimmerman (1987, 136) note, "to 'do' gender is not always to live up to normative conceptions of femininity or masculinity; it is to engage in behavior *at the risk of gender assessment.*" I argue that many parents make efforts to stray from and thus expand normative conceptions of gender. But for their sons in particular, they balance this effort with conscious attention to producing a masculinity approximating hegemonic ideals. This balancing act is evident across many parents I interviewed regardless of gender, race/ethnicity, social class, sexual orientation, and partnership status. But I also argue that within that broader pattern are notable variations. Heterosexual fathers play a particularly central role in accomplishing their sons' masculinity and, in the process, reinforce their own as well. Their expressed motivations for that accomplishment

work often involve personal endorsement of hegemonic masculinity. Heterosexual mothers and gay parents, on the other hand, are more likely to report motivations that invoke accountability to others for crafting their sons' masculinity in accordance with hegemonic ideals.

Three bodies of literature provide foundations for this argument. Along with the body of work documenting parental behaviors in relation to gendering children, I draw on interactionist approaches that view gender as a situated accomplishment and scholarship outlining the contours of normative conceptions of masculinity. These latter two literatures offer a framework for understanding the significance of the patterns evident in my analysis of interview data.

Parents and the Social Construction of Gender

Scholars of gender and childhood are increasingly interested in the role of peers in the process of gendering children, viewing children themselves as active agents rather than passive recipients of adult influence. However, they also continue to recognize parents as important in the gendering of children (Coltrane and Adams 1997; Maccoby 1998). Lytton and Romney's (1991) meta-analysis of the substantial quantitative and experimental literature on gender and parents' behavior toward their sons and daughters documents that parents do not always enforce gendered expectations for their children, nor do they consistently treat sons

From *Gender & Society* 20(2):149–176. Copyright © 2006 Sociologists for Women in Society. Reprinted by permission of Sage Publications, Inc.

and daughters differently. Some researchers have highlighted subgroups of parents who actively seek to disrupt traditional gendered expectations for their children (Quoss, Ellis, and Stromberg 1987; Risman 1998; Risman and Myers 1997; Stacey and Biblarz 2001). But as a whole, the literature documents definite parental tendencies toward gendered treatment of children. These tendencies are evident beginning at birth and in the early childhood years. For example, the literature indicates differential treatment of sons and daughters in terms of parental selection of toys (Etaugh and Liss 1992; Pomerleau et al. 1990), clothing (Cahill 1989), and décor for children's rooms (Pomerleau et al. 1990), as well as parental emphasis on emotions versus autonomy in family stories (Fiese and Skillman 2000; Reese, Haden, and Fivush 1996). Across this literature, gender typing by parents is well documented, as are two patterns within that gender typing. First, fathers appear to engage in more differential treatment of sons and daughters and more enforcement of gender boundaries than do mothers; second, for both mothers and fathers, such boundary maintenance appears to be more evident in the treatment of sons than daughters (Antill 1987, Coltrane and Adams 1997; Maccoby 1998).

The large literature on gender typing by parents is predominantly quantitative and often based on experiments, closed-ended surveys, and/or counting the frequency of various parental behaviors. This literature is valuable in documenting the role that parents play in gendering their children. However, it does less to explore the nuances of how parents make meaning around gender, to document in detail what kinds of attributes and behaviors are accepted and sanctioned by parents of young children, to reveal what motivates parents as they participate in the social construction of their children's gender, or to illuminate how aware parents are of their role in these processes. Parents are clearly gendering their children, but what are the subtleties of the gendered outcomes they seek to construct, why do they seek to construct those, and how aware are they of that construction process?

Doing Gender: Accomplishment and Accountability

The interactionist approach to gender as accomplishment (West and Fenstermaker 1993, 1995; West and Zimmerman 1987) provides a powerful framework for understanding what I heard about gender nonconformity in my interviews with parents of young children. This approach allows us to view parents not simply as agents of gender socialization but rather as actors involved in a more complex process of accomplishing gender with and for their children. Along with the notion of gender as accomplished, equally central is the concept of accountability. Accountability is relevant not only when people are doing gender in accordance with the expectations of others but also when they resist or stray from such expectations. This claim, present in West and Zimmerman's (1987) earlier formulation, is one to which Fenstermaker and West (2002) return in defending the approach against criticism that it does not allow for resistance and social change. They note that their focus on the process by which gender is accomplished places activity, agency, and the possibility of resistance in the foreground. But the accomplishment of such change takes place within the context of, and is constrained by, accountability to gendered assessment. Fenstermaker and West (2002, 212) have recently argued that accountability is "the most neglected aspect of our formulation. . . . Few of those who have used our approach have recognized the essential contribution that accountability makes to it."

While accomplishment and accountability are key concepts framing my analysis of parents' responses to their children's gender nonconformity, it is also crucial to note the importance of normative conceptions. Fenstermaker and West (2002) have extended their approach to address not only gender but other categories of difference. "In the accomplishment of difference [including gender], accountability is the driving motivator; the specifics of the normative order provide the content, with social interaction the medium" (Fenstermaker and West 2002, 213-14). They refer to the "content" provided by the normative order as *normative conceptions* and view these as historically and locally variable. Normative conceptions of appropriate masculine conduct are particularly relevant to my analysis, and to explore that domain, I turn briefly to scholarship on the history of masculinity as a social construct.

Normative Conceptions of Masculinity: Hegemonic Masculinity

Connell (1995, 77) has argued persuasively that "at any given time, one form of masculinity rather than others is culturally exalted." This hegemonic masculinity is cross-culturally and historically variable and offers a clear example of a locally specific normative conception of gender. It stands as a normative conception to which men are accountable, a form of masculinity in relation to which subordinated masculinities, as well as femininities, are defined. Connell (1987, 187) argues that there is no need for a concept of hegemonic femininity, because the fundamental purpose of hegemonic masculinity is to legitimate male domination. The subordination of nonhegemonic masculinities is crucial as well, as it allows hegemonic masculinity to legitimate not only male privilege but also race, class, and sexual orientation–based privileges as well.

Several elements of Connell's theory are especially relevant to my analysis of how parents think about their preschool sons' gender nonconformity. He argues that among the features of hegemonic masculinity in this particular time and place are aggression, limited emotionality, and heterosexuality. In addition, he and other scholars interested in the social construction of masculinity emphasize its relational meaning: " 'masculinity' does not exist except in contrast with 'femininity' " (Connell 1995, 68). As Kimmel notes, the "notion of anti-femininity lies at the heart of contemporary and historical constructions of manhood, so that masculinity is defined more by what one is not rather than who one is" (1994, 119). Passivity and excessive emotionality, as well as more material adornments of

femininity, are precisely what must be avoided in this hegemonic version of masculinity. Both Connell and Kimmel view homophobia as central to this rejection of femininity. Connell (1987, 186) states this bluntly when he notes that "the most important feature of contemporary hegemonic masculinity is that it is heterosexual. . . . Contempt for homosexuality and homosexual men. . . . is part of the ideological package of hegemonic masculinity."

Data and Method

Participants and Interviewing

The analyses presented here are based on data from 42 interviews with a diverse sample of parents, each of whom has at least one preschool-aged child (three to five years old). Interviews focused on parents' perceptions of their children's gendered attributes and behaviors. The preschool age range is emphasized because this is the period when most children begin to develop a clear understanding of the gender expectations around them, as evidenced in the development of gender identity and the tendency to engage in more gender-typed patterns of behavior (Maccoby 1998; Weinraub et al. 1984).

Interviews were conducted primarily in southern and central Maine (with a small number conducted elsewhere in New England), over a period ranging from the summer of 1999 to the fall of 2002. Participants were recruited through postings in local child care centers, parents' resource organizations, community colleges, local businesses, and public housing projects and through personal networks (though none of the participants were people I knew prior to the interviews). Recruiting materials included general reference to "parents' experiences raising sons and daughters" and did not emphasize gender conformity or nonconformity. Thus, recruitment was focused not on trying to find parents struggling with significant gender-related issues but rather on finding a cross-section of parents. None of those eventually participating reported seeking any professional intervention related to their children's gender identity or gendered behaviors.

The process of participation began with a brief written questionnaire, which was followed by a semistructured interview. Particular emphasis was on a focal child between the ages of three and five, although questions were asked about any other children the respondents lived with as well. The major focus of the interview questions was on the current activities, toys, clothes, behaviors, and gender awareness of the focal child and the parents' perceptions of the origins of these outcomes, as well as their feelings about their children's behaviors and characteristics in relation to gendered expectations. Interviews ended with some general questions about the desirability and feasibility of gender neutrality in childhood. The interviews were taped and transcribed, although some minor smoothing of quotes used in the analyses presented below was conducted to increase clarity. The length of interviews was generally from one to two hours. Most interviews were conducted in the interviewees' homes, but 7 of the 42 interviewees preferred their place of employment or some other neutral site such as a restaurant or my office. Even for those interviews conducted in the home, it is important to note that sometimes a child or children were present and other times not. Therefore, I had no consistent opportunity to observe parents' behavior with their children. The project focuses on parents' perceptions and self-reports, and I am not able to compare those to evidence on actual parental behavior. Interviews were conducted either by myself or by a research assistant. Participants were paid a modest honorarium ($25 to $35, depending on the year of the interview) for their time and participation, funded by a series of small internal research grants, and were ensured complete confidentiality.

The 42 interviewees include 24 mothers and 18 fathers. Four of the fathers are married to women interviewed for the study as mothers. Although geographically specific primarily to northern New England, interviewees come from a relatively diverse range of family types (single-parent and two-parent families, with some of the latter being blended families), class locations (ranging from those self-identifying as poor/low income to upper middle class), racial/ethnic groups (including white, Asian American, and African American interviewees), and sexual orientations (including heterosexual and gay parents).[1] These parents' children include biological children, adopted children, step-children, and foster children. Interviewees' educational backgrounds range from having completed less than a high school education to holding a doctorate, with the average years of formal schooling falling between high school graduate and college graduate. Ages range from 23 to 49 years, with the average age at 35 years. All of the men interviewed work outside the home for pay; among those in heterosexual partnerships, their female partners were roughly equally split among full-time homemakers, those employed part-time in the paid labor force, and those employed full-time. Among the mothers interviewed, about one in three are full-time homemakers, with the remainder employed part-time or full-time in the paid labor force. Interviewees average 2.5 children (with the mode being 2) and are split among those having only daughters (11), only sons (12), or at least one of each (23). The focal children on whom interviews focused include 22 sons and 20 daughters.

Coding and Analysis

I began with a general interest in how parents responded to gender nonconformity, but otherwise my reading and rereading of the transcripts was inductive, coding for issues addressed by all interviewees in response to the structure of the questions as well as for other themes that arose. For the particular focus of this analysis, parental responses to perceived gender nonconformity, I began by identifying all instances in which a parent commented on items, activities, attributes, or behaviors—whether actual or hypothetical—of one of their children as more typical of a child of the other sex. Given that many of the interview questions specifically addressed whether the parent considers their child(ren)'s toys, clothes, activities, and attributes stereotypically gender linked, much of the interview focused on the parents' perception of gender typicality and atypicality. As a result, for the coding relevant to this analysis, I did not identify particular activities or attributes as stereotypically male or female. Instead, I was able to focus only on instances in which the parent himself or herself explicitly noted something as more typical of the other sex, allowing me to document what parents themselves view as atypical. Most of these mentions involved actual instances of perceived nonconformity, but some involved hypothetical outcomes.

Among these mentions of gender atypicality or nonconformity, I then narrowed my focus to just those quotes addressing a parental response. Such responses fell into two broad groups: feelings and actions related to gender nonconformity. Parental feelings were defined as any reported emotional response and were further divided into positive/neutral (e.g., "I love it," "I think it's great," "it's fine with me") versus negative (e.g., "I worry about. . . . ," "it bothers me when. . . ."). Actions were defined as reports of actually doing something about gender nonconformity, acting in some way to either encourage or discourage it. These too were coded as positive/neutral versus negative. Examples of positive and neutral actions include actively encouraging use of an atypical toy or just allowing something atypical because the child really wanted it. Negative actions included a range of reported efforts to discourage or even forbid gender-atypical choices. Once I had coded all of the transcripts for these categories, I coded each interviewee for whether his or her responses to perceived gender nonconformity were all positive/neutral, all negative, or a combination of both. This coding was done separately for sons and daughters because the patterns of positive/neutral and negative responses varied markedly by the child's gender. On the basis of that coding, I decided to focus this article primarily on parents' responses regarding their sons.

Combinations of positive/neutral and negative responses toward children's gender nonconformity varied by gender of child and gender of parent. But they did not vary consistently by parents' racial/ethnic background or class location, perhaps indicating that geographic similarity outweighs such variation in my particular sample. Scholars of gender have clearly documented the inseparability of race, class, gender, and sexual orientation, and I endeavor to consider each within the context of my interview data. But it is also important to note that the size of my interview sample limits my ability to fully consider those intersections. While some variations by race and class are evident within the broader interview project from which this particular analysis is drawn, such variations are generally absent in terms of parental responses to gender nonconformity. Therefore, although I indicate the race, class, and sexual orientation of each parent quoted, I analyze variations only by sexual orientation, and only when those are evident.

Responses to Gender Nonconformity

Mothers and fathers, across a variety of social locations, often celebrated what they perceived as gender nonconformity on the part of their young daughters. They reported enjoying dressing their daughters in sports-themed clothing, as well as buying them toy cars, trucks, trains, and building toys. Some described their efforts to encourage, and pleased reactions to, what they considered traditionally male activities such as t-ball, football, fishing, and learning to use tools. Several noted that they make an effort to encourage their young daughters to aspire to traditionally male occupations and commented favorably on their daughters as "tomboyish," "rough and tumble," and "competitive athletically." These positive responses were combined with very little in the way of any negative response. The coding of each interviewee for the combination of positive/neutral and negative responses summarizes this pattern clearly: Among parents commenting about daughter(s), the typical combination was to express only positive responses. For example, a white, middle-class, heterosexual mother noted approvingly that her five-year-old daughter "does a lot of things that a boy would do, and we encourage that," while a white, upper-middle-class, lesbian mother reported that she and her partner intentionally "do [a lot] of stuff that's not stereotypically female" with their daughter. Similarly, a white, upper-middle-class, heterosexual father indicated with relief that his daughter is turning out to be somewhat "boyish": "I never wanted a girl who was a little princess, who was so fragile. . . . I want her to take on more masculine characteristics." An African American, working-class, heterosexual father also noted this kind of preference: "I don't want her just to color and play with dolls, I want her to be athletic."

A few parents combined these positive responses with vague and general negative responses. But these were rare and expressed with little sense of concern, as in the case of an African American, low-income, heterosexual mother who offered positive responses but also noted limits regarding her daughter: "I wouldn't want her to be too boyish, because she's a girl." In addition, no parents expressed only negative responses. These various patterns suggest that parents made little effort to accomplish their daughters' gender in accordance with any particular conception of femininity, nor did they express any notable sense of accountability to such a conception. Instead, parental responses may suggest a different kind of gendered phenomenon closely linked to the pattern evident in responses toward sons: a devaluing of traditionally feminine pursuits and qualities. Although many parents of daughters reported positive responses to what they consider typical interests and behaviors for a girl, most also celebrated the addition of atypical pursuits to their daughters' lives, and very few noted any negative response to such additions.

It is clear in the literature that there are substantial gendered constraints placed on young girls, and any devaluation of the feminine is potentially such a constraint. But the particular constraint of negative responses by parents to perceived gender nonconformity was not evident in my interview results. It is possible that negative response from parents to perceived departures from traditional femininity would be more notable as girls reach adolescence. Pipher (1998, 286) argues that parents of young girls resist gender stereotypes for their daughters but that "the time to really worry is early adolescence. That's when the gender roles get set in cement, and that's when girls need tremendous support in resisting cultural definitions of femininity." Thorne (1994, 170) invokes a similar possibility, claiming that girls are given more gender leeway than boys in earlier childhood, "but the lee-way begins to tighten as girls approach adolescence and move into the heterosexualized gender system of teens and adults." The question of whether negative parental responses might be less gender differentiated in adolescence cannot be addressed with my interview data and remains instead an intriguing question for future research.

In stark contrast to the lack of negative response for daughters, 23 of 31 parents of sons expressed at least some negative responses, and 6 of these offered only negative responses regarding what they perceived as gender nonconformity. Of 31 parents, 25 did indicate positive responses as well, but unlike references to their daughters, they tended to balance those positive feelings and actions about sons with negative ones as well.[2] The most common combination was to indicate both positive and negative responses.

Domestic Skills, Nurturance, and Empathy

Parents accepted, and often even celebrated, their sons' acquisition of domestic abilities and an orientation toward nurturance and empathy. Of the 25 parents of sons who offered positive/neutral responses, 21 did so in reference to domestic skills, nurturance, and/or empathy. For example, they reported allowing or encouraging traditionally girl toys such as dolls, doll houses, kitchen centers, and tea sets, with that response often revolving around a desire to encourage domestic competence, nurturance, emotional openness, empathy, and nonviolence as attributes they considered nontraditional but positive for boys. These parents were reporting actions and sentiments oriented toward accomplishing gender in what they considered a less conventional manner. One white, low-income, heterosexual mother taught her son to cook, asserting that "I want my son to know how to do more than boil water, I want him to know how to take care of himself." Another mother, this one a white, working-class, heterosexual parent, noted that she makes a point of talking to her sons about emotions: "I try to instill a sense of empathy in my sons and try to get them to see how other people would feel." And a white, middle-class, heterosexual father emphasized domestic competence when he noted that it does not bother him for his son to play with dolls at his cousin's house: "How then are they going to learn to take care of their children if they don't?" This positive response to domestic activities is consistent with recent literature on parental coding of toys as masculine, feminine, or neutral, which indicates that parents are increasingly coding kitchens and in some cases dolls as neutral rather than exclusively feminine (Wood, Desmarais, and Gugula 2002).

In my study, mothers and fathers expressed these kinds of efforts to accomplish gender differently for their sons with similar frequency, but mothers tended to express them with greater certainty, while fathers were less enthusiastic and more likely to include caveats. For example, this mother described her purchase of a variety of domestic toys for her three-year-old son without ambivalence: "One of the first big toys [I got him] was the kitchen center. . . . We cook, he has an apron he wears. . . . He's got his dirt devil vacuum and he's got his baby [doll]. And he's got all the stuff to feed her and a highchair" (white, low-income, heterosexual mother).

Some mothers reported allowing domestic toys but with less enthusiasm, such as a white, low-income, heterosexual mother who said, regarding her three-year-old son, "He had been curious about dolls and I just said, you know, usually girls play with dolls, but it's okay for you to do it too." But this kind of caution or lack of enthusiasm, even in a response coded as positive

or neutral due to its allowance of gender-atypical behavior, was more evident among fathers, as the following quote illustrates: "Occasionally, if he's not doing something, I'll encourage him to maybe play with his tea cups, you know, occasionally. But I like playing with his blocks better anyway" (white, middle-class, heterosexual father).

Thus, evident among both mothers and fathers, but with greater conviction for mothers, was widespread support among parents for working to "undo" gender at the level of some of their sons' skills and values. However, this acceptance was tempered for many parents by negative responses to any interest in what I will refer to as iconic feminine items, attributes, or activities, as well as parental concern about homosexuality.

Icons of Femininity

A range of activities and attributes considered atypical for boys were met with negative responses, and for a few parents (3 of 31 parents of sons) this even included the kind of domestic toys and nurturance noted above. But more common were negative responses to items, activities, or attributes that could be considered icons of femininity. This was strikingly consistent with Kimmel's (1994, 119) previously noted claim that the "notion of anti-femininity lies at the heart of contemporary and historical constructions of manhood," and it bears highlighting that this was evident among parents of very young children. Parents of sons reported negative responses to their sons' wearing pink or frilly clothing; wearing skirts, dresses, or tights; and playing dress up in any kind of feminine attire. Nail polish elicited concern from a number of parents too, as they reported young sons wanting to have their fingernails or toenails polished. Dance, especially ballet, and Barbie dolls were also among the traditionally female activities often noted negatively by parents of sons. Of the 31 parents of sons, 23 mentioned negative reactions to at least one of these icons.

In relation to objects such as clothing and toys, the following responses are typical of the many concerns raised and the many indications of actions parents had taken to accomplish gender with and for their sons:

> He's asked about wearing girl clothes before, and I said no. . . . He likes pink, and I try not to encourage him to like pink just because, you know, he's not a girl. . . . There's not many toys I wouldn't get him, except Barbie, I would try not to encourage that. (white, low-income, heterosexual mother)

> If we go into a clothing store. . . . I try to shy my son away from the Power Puff Girls shirt or anything like that. . . . I would steer him away from a pink shirt as opposed to having him wear a blue shirt. (Asian American, middle-class, heterosexual father)

These quotes are typical of many instances in which parents not only specify the items that strike them as problematic but clearly indicate the actions they take in accomplishing gender. In the first quote, the mother indicates her actions in encouraging and discouraging various outcomes, while in the second, the father reports "shying away" and "steering" his young son.

Playing with nail polish and makeup, although tolerated by some parents, more often evoked negative responses like this one, from a white, upper-middle-class, gay father, speaking about his four-year-old son's use of nail polish: "He put nail polish on himself one time, and I said 'No, you can't do that, little girls put nail polish on, little boys don't.'"

Barbie dolls are an especially interesting example in that many parents reported positive responses to baby dolls, viewing these as encouraging nurturance and helping to prepare sons for fatherhood. Barbie, on the other hand, an icon of femininity, struck many parents of sons as more problematic. Barbie was often mentioned when parents were asked whether their child had ever requested an item or activity more commonly associated with the other gender. Four parents—three mothers and one father—indicated that they had purchased a Barbie at their son's request, but more often parents of sons noted that they would avoid letting their son have or play with Barbie dolls.

Sometimes this negative response was categorical, as in the quote above in which a mother of a three-year-old son noted that "there's not many toys I wouldn't get him, except Barbie." A father offers a similar negative reaction to Barbie in relation to his two young sons: "If they asked for a Barbie doll, I would probably say no, you don't want [that], girls play with [that], boys play with trucks" (white, middle-class, heterosexual father).

In other cases, parents reported that they would compromise in ways that strike me as designed to minimize Barbie's iconic status. These instances are particularly pointed examples of carefully crafted parental accomplishment of gender: "I would ask him 'What do you want for your birthday?'. . . . and he always kept saying Barbie. . . . So we compromised, we got him a NASCAR Barbie" (white, middle-class, heterosexual mother).

Another father reported that his five-year-old son likes to play Barbies with his four-year-old sister and expressed relief that his son's interest is more in Ken than Barbie: "He's not interested in Barbie, he's interested in Ken. . . . He plays with Ken and does boy things with him, he has always made clear that he likes Ken. . . . If he was always playing with dolls and stuff like this then I would start to worry and try to do something to turn it around. But he plays with Ken and it doesn't go much further than that, so I'm fine" (white, upper-middle-class, heterosexual father).

Notable throughout these comments is the sense that parents are carefully balancing an openness to some crossing of gender boundaries but only within limits, as the father in the final quote indicated when he said that he would "do something to turn it around" if his son's interest were in Barbie rather than Ken. A similar balancing act in the accomplishment of masculinity is evident for a white, middle-class, heterosexual father who noted that if his son "really wanted to dance, I'd let him. . . . , but at the same time, I'd be doing other things to compensate for the fact that I signed him up for dance."

Along with material markers of femininity, many parents expressed concern about excessive emotionality (especially frequent crying) and passivity in their sons. For example, a white, upper-middle-class, heterosexual father, concerned about public crying, said about his five-year-old son, "I don't want him to be a sissy. . . . I want to see him strong, proud, not crying like a sissy." Another father expressed his frustration with his four-year-old son's crying over what the father views as minor injuries and indicated action to discourage those tears: "Sometimes I get so annoyed, you know, he comes [crying], and I say, 'you're not hurt, you don't even know what hurt is yet,' and I'm like 'geez, sometimes you are such a little wean,' you know?" (white, middle-class, heterosexual father).

Passivity was also raised as a concern, primarily by fathers. For example, one white, middle-class, heterosexual father of a five-year-old noted that he has told his son to "stop crying like a girl," and also reported encouraging that son to fight for what he wants: "You just go in the corner and cry like a baby. I don't want that. If you decide you want [some] thing, you are going to fight for it, not crying and acting like a baby and hoping that they're going to feel guilty and give it to you."

A mother who commented negatively about passivity even more directly connected her concern to how her son might be treated: "I do have concerns. . . . He's passive, not aggressive. . . . He's not the rough and tumble kid, and I do worry about him being an easy target" (white, working-class, heterosexual mother).

Taken together, these various examples indicate clearly the work many parents are doing to accomplish gender with and for their sons in a manner that distances those sons from any association with femininity. This work was not evident among all parents of sons. But for most parents, across racial, class, and sexual orientation categories, it was indeed evident.

Homosexuality

Along with these icons of feminine gender performance, and arguably directly linked to them, is the other clear theme evident among some parents' negative responses to perceived gender non-conformity on the part of their sons: fear that a son either would be or would be perceived as gay. Spontaneous connections of gender nonconformity and sexual orientation were not evident in parents' comments about daughters, nor among gay and lesbian parents, but arose for 7 of the 27 heterosexual parents who were discussing sons. The following two examples are typical of responses that invoked the possibility of a son's being gay, with explicit links to performance of femininity and to the parents' own role in accomplishing heterosexuality:

> If he was acting feminine, I would ask and get concerned on whether or not, you know, I would try to get involved and make sure he's not gay. (white, low-income, heterosexual mother)

> There are things that are meant for girls, but why would it be bad for him to have one of them? I don't know, maybe I have some deep, deep, deep buried fear that he would turn out, well, that his sexual orientation may get screwed up. (white, middle-class, heterosexual father)

The first comment explicitly indicates that feminine behavior, even in a three-year-old boy, might be an indicator of an eventual nonheterosexual orientation. The second comment raises another possibility: that playing with toys "that are meant for girls" might not indicate but rather shape the son's eventual sexual orientation. In both cases, though, the parent is reporting on actions, either actual or hypothetical, taken to discourage homosexuality and accomplish heterosexuality. Another quote from a father raises a similar concern and further exemplifies parental responsibility for the accomplishment of masculinity as linked to heterosexuality. This father had noted throughout the interview that his five-year-old son tends to show some attributes he considers feminine. At one point, he mentioned that he sometimes wondered if his son might be gay, and he explained his reaction to that possibility in the following terms: "If [he] were to be gay, it would not make me happy at all. I would probably see that as a failure as a dad. . . . , as a failure because I'm raising him to be a boy, a man" (white, upper-middle-class, heterosexual father). This comment suggests that the parent does not view masculinity as something that naturally unfolds but rather as something he feels responsible for crafting, and he explicitly links heterosexual orientation to the successful accomplishment of masculinity.

The fact that the connection between gender performance and sexual orientation was not raised for daughters, and that fear of homosexuality was not spontaneously mentioned by parents of daughters whether in connection to gender performance or not, suggests how closely gender conformity and heterosexuality are linked within hegemonic constructions of masculinity. Such connections might arise more by adolescence in relation to daughters, as I noted previously regarding other aspects of parental responses to gender nonconformity. But for sons, even among parents of very young children, heteronormativity appears to play a role in shaping parental responses to gender nonconformity, a connection that literature on older children and adults indicates is made more for males than females (Antill 1987; Hill 1999; Kite and Deaux 1987; Sandnabba and Ahlberg 1999). Martin's (2005) recent analysis also documents the importance of heteronormativity in the advice offered to parents by experts. She concludes that expert authors of child-rearing books and Web sites are increasingly supportive of gender-neutral child rearing. But especially for sons, that expert support is limited by implicit and even explicit invocations of homosexuality as a risk to be managed. As McCreary (1994, 526) argues on the basis of experimental work on responses to older children and adults, "the asymmetry in people's responses to male and female gender role deviations is motivated, in part, by the implicit assumption that male transgressions are symptomatic of a homosexual orientation." This implicit assumption appears to motivate at least some parental gender performance management among heterosexual parents, even for children as young as preschool age. Given the connections between male heterosexuality and the rejection of femininity noted previously as evident in theories of hegemonic masculinity, the tendency for parents to associate gender performance and sexual orientation for sons more than daughters may also reflect a more general devaluation of femininity.

Mothers versus Fathers in the Accomplishment of Masculinity

In documenting parental work to accomplish masculinity with and for young sons, I have focused on the encouragement of domestic skills, nurturance, and empathy; discouragement of icons of femininity; and heterosexual parents' concerns about homosexuality. Within all three of these arenas, variation by parental gender was evident. Although both mothers and fathers were equally likely to express a combination of positive and negative responses to their sons' perceived gender nonconformity, with domestic skills and empathy accepted and icons of femininity rejected, the acceptance was more pointed for mothers, and the rejection was more pointed for fathers. More fathers (11 of 14) than mothers (12 of 17) of sons indicated negative reactions to at least one of the icons discussed. Fathers also indicated more categorically negative responses: 7 of the 14 fathers but only 2 of the 17 mothers reported simply saying "no" to requests for things such as Barbie dolls, tea sets, nail polish, or ballet lessons, whether actual requests or hypothetical ones. Although fewer parents referred to excessive emotionality and passivity as concerns, the 6 parents of sons who did so included 4 fathers and 2 mothers, and here too, the quotes indicate a more categorical rejection by fathers.

Another indication of more careful policing of icons of femininity by fathers is evident in comments that placed age limitations on the acceptability of such icons. Four fathers (but no mothers) commented with acceptance on activities or interests that they consider atypical for boys but went on to note that these would bother them if they continued well past the preschool age range. The following quote from a father is typical of these responses. After noting that his four-year-old son sometimes asks for toys he thinks of as "girl toys," he went on to say, "I don't think it will ruin his life at this age but. . . . if he was 12 and asking for it, you know, My Little Pony or Barbies, then I think I'd really worry" (white, middle-class, heterosexual father). While comments like this one were not coded as negative responses, since they involved acceptance, I mention them here as they are consistent with the tendency for fathers to express particular concern about their sons' involvement with icons of femininity.

Three of 15 heterosexual mothers and 4 of 12 heterosexual fathers of sons responded negatively to the possibility of their son's being, or being perceived as, gay. These numbers are too small to make conclusive claims comparing mothers and fathers. But this pattern is suggestive of another arena in which fathers—especially heterosexual fathers—may stand out, especially taken together with another pattern. Implicit in the quotes offered above related to homosexuality is a suggestion that heterosexual fathers may feel particularly responsible for crafting their sons' heterosexual orientation. In addition, in comparison to mothers, their comments are less likely to refer to fears for how their son might be treated by others if he were gay and more likely to refer to the personal disappointment they anticipate in this hypothetical scenario. I return to consideration of these patterns in my discussion of accountability below.

Parental Motivations for the Accomplishment of Masculinity

The analysis I have offered thus far documents that parents are aware of their role in accomplishing gender with and for their sons. Although some parents did speak of their sons as entirely "boyish" and "born that way," many reported efforts to craft a hegemonic masculinity. Most parents expressed a very conscious awareness of normative conceptions of masculinity (whether

explicitly or implicitly). Many, especially heterosexual mothers and gay parents, expressed a sense that they felt accountable to others in terms of whether their sons live up to those conceptions. In numerous ways, these parents indicated their awareness that their sons' behavior was at risk of gender assessment, an awareness rarely noted with regard to daughters. Parents varied in terms of their expressed motivations for crafting their sons' masculinity, ranging from a sense of measuring their sons against their own preferences for normative masculinity (more common among heterosexual fathers) to concerns about accountability to gender assessment by peers, other adults, and society in general (more common among heterosexual mothers and gay parents, whether mothers or fathers).

Heterosexual Fathers

Some parents expressed negative feelings about a son's perceived gender nonconformity that were personal, invoking a sense of accountability not so much to other people as to their own moral or normative framework. Among fathers, twice as many expressed personal accountability than accountability toward others (six versus three). Some references that were personal did arise among mothers, such as this response from a white, working-class, heterosexual mother talking about how she would feel if one of her sons asked for a toy more typically associated with girls: "I'd rather have my girls playing with bows and arrows and cowboys and Indians than the boys to play with dolls and dresses and stuff, you know? . . . . I don't think it's normal that boys play with dolls and Barbies and dress them, it's not in their gender."

But, as noted, such references to a personal normative framework dominated the negative responses offered by fathers. Among fathers, this was the case for the two major themes documented previously as eliciting negative response: icons of feminine gender performance and homosexuality. For example, one white, middle-class, heterosexual father referred to this general issue in two separate portions of the interview.

These comments were in relation to his four-year-old son's interest in what he considered "girly" toys.

FATHER: I don't want him to be a little "quiffy" thing, you know. . . . It's probably my own insecurities more than anything. I guess it won't ruin his life. . . . It's probably my own selfish feeling of like "no way, no way my kids, my boys, are going to be like that."

INTERVIEWER: Is it a reflection on you as a parent, do you think?

FATHER: As a male parent, yeah, I honestly do.

This comment suggests the interviewee's belief that fathers are responsible for crafting appropriately masculine sons. A similar sense of responsibility is evident in relation to homosexuality in a quote presented earlier, from the father who indicated that he would see himself as a failure if his son were gay because "he is raising him to be a boy, a man." Sometimes this invocation of a father's own sense of normative gender for his son was offered more casually, as in the case of an Asian American, middle-class, heterosexual father who said regarding his four-year-old son, "I wouldn't encourage him to take ballet or something like that, 'cause I guess in my own mind that's for a girl."

Although not all heterosexual fathers made these kinds of comments, they were more likely than heterosexual mothers or gay and lesbian parents to situate themselves as the reference point in their concerns about gender nonconformity among their sons. Their motivation for accomplishing hegemonic masculinity with and for their sons is more often expressed as personal, a pattern consistent with the role both Connell and Kimmel argue heterosexual men play in maintaining hegemonic masculinity. In some cases, these heterosexual fathers even explicitly judge their success as a father based on the degree to which they are raising adequately masculine sons. This suggests that passing along that normative conception to their sons may be part of how they accomplish their own masculinity. Not just their sons but their own execution of fatherhood in raising those sons are at risk of gender assessment if they do not approximate the ideal of hegemonic masculinity.

Heterosexual Mothers, Lesbian Mothers, and Gay Fathers

Heterosexual mothers, lesbian mothers, and gay fathers were involved in the same balancing act in accomplishing gender with and for their sons, but their expressed motivations tended to invoke accountability to others. Rather than expressing a sense of commitment directly to the ideal of hegemonic masculinity, they were more likely to express fear for how their sons would be assessed by others if they did not approximate that ideal. The focus was more often on the child and the others to whom they assumed their son's gender performance would be accountable rather than on the parent. Some heterosexual fathers did express concern about accountability to others, but as noted previously, such concerns were outnumbered two to one by their references to their own normative framework. But for heterosexual mothers and gay and lesbian parents, explanations for concern more often invoked accountability in terms of how others might react to breaches both of the icons of femininity and of heteronormativity. It is also worth noting that very few of the parents reported experiencing any specific problems for their young sons. Instead, they seemed to view this preschool age as an important, foundational moment in accomplishing their sons' gender, often projecting into the future as they expressed concern about the risk of gender assessment.

Among both heterosexual and lesbian mothers, a substantial number (11 of 17 mothers of sons) expressed fear that their sons might be treated negatively by adults and/or their peers if they did not approximate hegemonic masculinity. One mother indicated that she would encourage her three-year-old son to wear styles and colors of clothing typically associated with boys, explaining her reasoning in terms of her fear for how her son would feel if others treated him negatively: "This stupid world cares about what we look like, unfortunately. . . . You know, it shouldn't, probably shouldn't matter. It's a piece of cloth, but that's the way the world is and I wouldn't want him to feel out of place" (white, low-income, heterosexual mother).

About half of such comments by mothers referred in this way to society in general, or the adult world, while the other half referred to peers. Six mothers of sons referred to peers, whether through explicit mention of other children or more implicitly through the use of language suggestive of children's peer groups, while only two fathers did so. The following quote is typical of the various responses invoking the risk of gender assessment within a son's peer group: "I would worry if he had too many feminine characteristics, that would worry me. I just want him to be a boy and play with the boys, not to like girl things. If he did that, the boys would think he's weird, and then he'd be lonely" (African American, low-income, heterosexual mother).

Another mother offered a particularly dramatic example of her sense of accountability to others, in this case with concern expressed both for her son and herself, when describing an incident that occurred about a year before the interview. Her son was two years old at the time and sustained an injury while playing dress up with his older sister. He was dressed in a pink princess costume, and once they arrived at the hospital, the mother began to feel concerned about gender assessment:

> People can be so uptight about things, I was worried they were going to think I was some kind of nut and next thing you know, send a social worker in. . . . You never know what people will think, and in a hospital, someone has the power to go make a phone call to a social worker or someone, someone who doesn't realize he's two years old and it doesn't matter. . . . It was totally obvious that it was a little boy dressing up in silly clothing but there are people out there who would think that's really

wrong, and I was afraid. (white, upper-middle-class, heterosexual mother)

A sense of accountability regarding the reactions of others was expressed in relation to sexual orientation as well. When heterosexual mothers raised the issue, they were more likely to invoke fear regarding the reactions of others. In fact, all three mothers who were coded as offering a negative response to the possibility of a son's being gay or being perceived as gay included at least some reference to concern about the reactions that her child might have to face from others, while all four fathers who were coded in this category included at least some reference to their own personal negative reactions, as documented in the previous section.[3] Typical of mothers' concerns is the following quote, which refers to a son's being perceived as gay if he does not conform to masculine expectations (but others also referred to fears for a son who actually does grow up to identify as gay): "If he's a nurse or something he must be gay, you know, [people] label you instantly that there must be something wrong with you if you're doing this 'cause men should be like construction workers and women should be nurses and things like that. Yeah, it's very difficult in society. . . . I don't want people to think something of me that I'm not. I don't want them to think that on my children either, I don't want my children to be hurt by that in the future, you know?" (white, low-income, heterosexual mother). This comment, and others like it, demonstrates that parents—especially mothers—feel accountable to others in fulfilling heteronormative expectations for their sons and expect that gender nonconformity and sexual orientation will be linked in the assessments those others make of their sons.

Also notable among the comments expressing accountability to others were reports by gay and lesbian parents who felt under particular scrutiny in relation to their sons' (but not their daughters') gender performance. Although my sample is diverse in terms of parents' sexual orientation, all five of the gay and lesbian parents interviewed are white, partnered, and identify as middle or upper middle class. In most ways, their responses to gender nonconformity paralleled those of heterosexual parents. But there are two particular ways in which heterosexual parents differed from gay and lesbian parents. As noted previously, only heterosexual parents raised fears or concerns about their sons' eventual sexual orientation. In addition, four of the five gay and lesbian parents I interviewed had at least one son, and all four of those reported at least some concern that they were held accountable for their sons' gender conformity. One white, upper-middle-class, lesbian mother of two sons noted that she feels "under more of a microscope" and that her sons "don't have as much fluidity" because she has "loaded the dice. . . . in terms of prejudice they will face because of who their parents are." Similar sentiments are evident in the following quote from another interviewee: "I feel held up to the world to make sure that his masculinity is in check or something. . . . It's a big rap against lesbian parents, how can you raise sons without a masculine role model in the house, and that's something I always feel up against" (white, upper-middle-class, lesbian mother).

Although stated in less detail, a similar concern is invoked in the following quote from a gay father of a three-year-old son: "I mean I think we have to be a little bit conscious of going too far, you know, as gay men the last thing we want to do is put him in anything that's remotely girly" (white, middle-class, gay father).

Some past research has emphasized the lack of any variation in gender typing by sexual orientation of parents (Golombock and Tasker 1994; Gottman 1990; Patterson 1992). Stacey and Bibliarz (2001) have more recently offered a compelling case that gay and lesbian parents tend to allow their children more freedom in terms of gendered expectations. But the concern these parents express indicates yet another social price they pay in a homophobic society, and it is one that seems to arise for sons more so than for daughters.

I cannot offer any conclusive claims about how gay and lesbian parents feel about gender conformity based on only four interviews. However, the fact that all of the gay and lesbian parents with sons spontaneously mentioned this sense of additional accountability regarding their sons' masculinity offers strong suggestive evidence that gay and lesbian parents feel under particular scrutiny.

Another intriguing pattern in terms of accountability was evident among heterosexual mothers, and this pattern further indicates the unique role that heterosexual fathers play in accomplishing gender for their sons. No specific questions were asked about each interviewee's partner or ex-partner, but 12 of the 15 heterosexual mothers of sons spontaneously mentioned either actual or potential negative reactions to a boy's gender nonconformity on the part of their son's father (while only 2 mentioned any such paternal reactions to a daughter's nonconformity, and of those, one was a positive response by the father). The negative responses these mothers reported are similar to those previously described in quotes from heterosexual fathers themselves. Sometimes these responses were hypothetical, as in the following example: "I love dance, and I would give him the opportunity and let him decide. But I think my husband has a stereotype that boy dancers are more feminine. He definitely, you know, has said that. I don't think he would want his son in ballet" (white, upper-middle-class, heterosexual mother). Other references to fathers' negative responses were reports of actual situations: "My son, when he gets upset, he will cry at any child, boy or girl, and my husband has made the comment about that being, you know, a girl thing, crying like a girl" (white, low-income, heterosexual mother).

One comment offered by a nonpartnered mother resonates with this theme and is interesting in terms of what it suggests about partnership status for heterosexual women. She encourages her sons to play with a wide range of toys, both stereotypically male and stereotypically female ones. But she noted that many other people do not do this and that it would be difficult to encourage most people to relax gender constraints on their sons for the following reason: "I tend to think that you have the most difficulty when you have fathers around, they're the ones. . . . I have the final say here, but when you've got a husband to deal with it's harder" (white, low-income, heterosexual mother).

This notion is speculative, as it did not arise consistently among nonpartnered mothers. But taken together with the frequent mentions of male partners' reactions among heterosexually partnered mothers, it bolsters the contention that accountability to fathers is felt strongly by heterosexual mothers as they assess their sons' gender performance. This may influence their approach to accomplishing gender. For example, one white, middle-class, heterosexual mother recounted defending her clothing purchases to her husband after having a stranger assume her then-infant son was a girl: "I had a few people think the baby was a girl, which is kind of irritating, because I would think 'Oh my God, am I buying clothes that are too feminine looking?' The first time it happened I went right to [my husband] and said 'I bought this in the boys' department at Carter's, I'm telling you, I really did.' "

Another heterosexual mother, this one a white, working-class parent, reported not just defending her actions to her husband but changing a purchase decision based on what her husband might think. When her five-year-old son asked for a Barbie suitcase at the store, she told him, "No, you can't have that, your father wouldn't like it." This mother may be steering her son in a direction that avoids the need for his father to become aware of, or react to, gender-atypical preferences in his son. Direct actions to accomplish masculinity by fathers are certainly evident in my analyses, but accountability to fathers indicates an indirect path through which heterosexual men may further influence the accomplishment of their sons' gender.

Conclusion

The interviews analyzed here, with New England parents of preschool-aged children from a diverse array of backgrounds, indicate a considerable endorsement by parents of what they perceive as gender nonconformity among both their sons and their daughters. This pattern at first appears encouraging in terms of the prospects for a world less constrained by gendered expectations for children. Many parents respond positively to the idea of their children's experiencing a greater range of opportunities, emotions, and interests than those narrowly defined by gendered stereotypes, with mothers especially likely to do so. However, for sons, this positive response is primarily limited to a few attributes and abilities, namely, domestic skills, nurturance, and empathy. And it is constrained by a clear recognition of normative conceptions of masculinity (Connell 1987, 1995). Most parents made efforts to accomplish, and either endorsed or felt accountable to, an ideal of masculinity that was defined by limited emotionality, activity rather than passivity, and rejection of material markers of femininity. Work to accomplish this type of masculinity was reported especially often by heterosexual fathers; accountability to approximate hegemonic masculinity was reported especially often by heterosexual mothers, lesbian mothers, and gay fathers. Some heterosexual parents also invoked sexual orientation as part of this conception of masculinity, commenting with concern on the possibility that their son might be gay or might be perceived as such. No similar pattern of well-defined normative expectations or accountability animated responses regarding daughters, although positive responses to pursuits parents viewed as more typically masculine may well reflect the same underlying devaluation of femininity evident in negative responses to gender nonconformity among sons.

In the broader study from which this particular analysis was drawn, many parents invoked biology in explaining their children's gendered tendencies. Clearly, the role of biological explanations in parents' thinking about gender merits additional investigation. But one of the things that was most striking to me in the analyses presented here is how frequently parents indicated that they took action to craft an appropriate gender performance with and for their preschool-aged sons, viewing masculinity as something they needed to work on to accomplish. These tendencies are in contrast to what Messner (2000) summarizes eloquently in his essay on a gender-segregated preschool sports program. He observes a highly gender-differentiated performance offered by the boys' and girls' teams during the opening ceremony of the new soccer season, with one of the girls' teams dubbing themselves the Barbie Girls, while one of the boys' teams called themselves the Sea Monsters. He notes that parents tended to view the starkly different approaches taken by the boys and girls as evidence of natural gender differences. "The parents do not seem to read the children's performances of gender as social constructions of gender. Instead, they interpret them as the inevitable unfolding of natural, internal differences between the sexes" (Messner 2000, 770).

I agree with Messner (2000) that this tendency is evident among parents, and I heard it articulated in some parts of the broader project from which the present analysis is drawn. I began this project expecting that parents accept with little question ideologies that naturalize gender difference. Instead, the results I have presented here demonstrate that parents are often consciously aware of gender as something that they must shape and construct, at least for their sons. This argument extends the literature on the routine accomplishment of gender in childhood by introducing evidence of conscious effort and awareness by parents as part of that accomplishment. This awareness also has implications for efforts to reduce gendered constraints on children.

Recognition that parents are sometimes consciously crafting their children's gender suggests the possibility that they could be encouraged to shift that conscious effort in less gendered directions.

In addition to documenting this parental awareness, I am also able to extend the literature by documenting the content toward which parents' accomplishment work is oriented. The version of hegemonic masculinity I have argued underlies parents' responses is one that includes both change and stability. Parental openness to domestic skills, nurturance, and empathy as desirable qualities in their sons likely represents social change, and the kind of agency in the accomplishment of gender to which Fenstermaker and West (2002) refer. As Connell (1995) notes, hegemonic masculinity is historically variable in its specific content, and the evidence presented in this article suggests that some broadening of that content is occurring. But the clear limits evident within that broadening suggest the stability and power of hegemonic conceptions of masculinity. The parental boundary maintenance work evident for sons represents a crucial obstacle limiting boys' options, separating boys from girls, devaluing activities marked as feminine for both boys and girls, and thus bolstering gender inequality and heteronormativity.

Finally, along with documenting conscious awareness by parents and the content toward which their accomplishment work is oriented, my analysis also contributes to the literature by illuminating the process motivating parental gender accomplishment. The heterosexual world in general, and heterosexual fathers in particular, play a central role in that process. This is evident in the direct endorsement of hegemonic masculinity many heterosexual fathers expressed and in the accountability to others (presumably heterosexual others) many heterosexual mothers, lesbian mothers, and gay fathers expressed. Scholarly investigations of the routine production of gender in childhood, therefore, need to pay careful attention to the role of heterosexual fathers as enforcers of gender boundaries and to the role of accountability in the process of accomplishing gender. At the same time, practical efforts to loosen gendered constraints on young children by expanding their parents' normative conceptions of gender need to be aimed at parents in general and especially need to reach heterosexual fathers in particular. The concern and even fear many parents—especially heterosexual mothers, lesbian mothers, and gay fathers—expressed about how their young sons might be treated if they fail to live up to hegemonic conceptions of masculinity represent a motivation for the traditional accomplishment of gender. But those reactions could also serve as a motivation to broaden normative conceptions of masculinity and challenge the devaluation of femininity, an effort that will require participation by heterosexual fathers to succeed.

Notes

1. Details regarding key social locations are as follows: 7 of the interviewees are people of color, and a total of 12 come from families who are of color or are multiracial (including white parents who have adopted children of color); 4 interviewees are poor/low income, 13 working class, 17 middle class, and 8 upper middle class; 5 interviewees are gay, including 2 gay fathers and 3 lesbian mothers.

2. One explanation for the paucity of negative responses could be that a broader range of actions, objects, and attributes are considered appropriate for girls than for boys. But this seems unlikely given that a similar number of parents offered positive or neutral comments about sons and daughters, indicating that they were equally likely to identify a range of actions, attributes, and objects as atypical for each gender.

3. This pattern is also consistent with the results of the literature on heterosexual men's and women's attitudes toward homosexuality, which documents that heterosexual men tend to hold more negative attitudes (Kane and Schippers 1996) and that homophobic attitudes are especially notable toward gay men as compared with lesbians (Herek 2002).

References

Antill, John K. 1987. Parents' beliefs and values about sex roles, sex differences, and sexuality. *Review of Personality and Social Psychology* 7:294–328.

Cahill, Spencer. 1989. Fashioning males and females. *Symbolic Interaction* 12:281–98.

Coltrane, Scott, and Michele Adams. 1997. Children and gender. In *Contemporary parenting*, edited by Terry Arendell. Thousand Oaks, CA: Sage.

Connell, R. W. 1987. *Gender and power*. Stanford, CA: Stanford University Press.

———. 1995. *Masculinities*. Berkeley: University of California Press.

Etaugh, Claire, and Marsha B. Liss. 1992. Home, school, and playroom: Training grounds for adult gender roles. *Sex Roles* 26:129–47.

Fenstermaker, Sarah, and Candace West, eds. 2002. *Doing gender, doing difference*. New York: Routledge.

Fiese, Barbara H., and Gemma Skillman. 2000. Gender differences in family stories. *Sex Roles* 43:267–83.

Golombock, Susan, and Fiona Tasker. 1994. Children in lesbian and gay families: Theories and evidence. *Annual Review of Sex Research* 5:73–100.

Gottman, Julie Schwartz. 1990. Children of gay and lesbian parents. *Marriage and Family Review* 14:177–96.

Herek, Gregory. 2002. Gender gaps in public opinion about lesbians and gay men. *Public Opinion Quarterly* 66:40–66.

Hill, Shirley A. 1999. *African American children*. Thousand Oaks, CA: Sage.

Kane, Emily W., and Mimi Schippers. 1996. Men's and women's beliefs about gender and sexuality. *Gender & Society* 10:650–65.

Kimmel, Michael S. 1994. Masculinity as homophobia. In *Theorizing masculinities*, edited by Harry Brod. Thousand Oaks, CA: Sage.

Kite, Mary E., and Kay Deaux. 1987. Gender belief systems: Homosexuality and the implicit inversion theory. *Psychology of Women Quarterly* 11:83–96.

Lytton, Hugh, and David M. Romney. 1991. Parents' differential socialization of boys and girls. *Psychological Bulletin* 109:267–96.

Maccoby, Eleanor E. 1998. *The two sexes: Growing up apart, coming together*. Cambridge, MA: Harvard University Press.

Martin, Karin A. 2005. William wants a doll, can he have one? Feminists, child care advisors, and gender-neutral child rearing. *Gender & Society* 20:1–24.

McCreary, Donald R. 1994. The male role and avoiding femininity. *Sex Roles* 31:517–31.

Messner, Michael. 2000. Barbie girls versus sea monsters: Children constructing gender. *Gender & Society* 14:765–84.

Patterson, Charlotte J. 1992. Children of lesbian and gay parents. *Child Development* 63:1025–42.

Pipher, Mary. 1998. *Reviving Ophelia*. New York: Ballantine Books.

Pomerleau, Andree, Daniel Bolduc, Gerard Malcuit, and Louise Cossette. 1990. Pink or blue: Environmental gender stereotypes in the first two years of life. *Sex Roles* 22:359–68.

Quoss, Bernita, Godfrey J. Ellis, and Frances Stromberg. 1987. Sex-role preferences of young children reared by feminist parents and parents from the general population. *Free Inquiry in Creative Sociology* 15:139–44.

Reese, Elaine, Catherine Haden, and Robyn Fivush. 1996. Gender differences in autobiographical reminiscing. *Research on Language and Social Interaction* 29:27–56

Risman, Barbara. 1998. *Gender vertigo*. New Haven, CT: Yale University Press

Risman, Barbara J., and Kristen Myers. 1997. As the twig is bent: Children reared in feminist households. *Qualitative Sociology* 20:229–52.

Sandnabba, N. Kenneth, and Christian Ahlberg. 1999. Parents' attitudes and expectations about children's cross-gender behavior. *Sex Roles* 40:249–63.

Stacey, Judith, and Timothy J. Bibliarz. 2001. (How) does the sexual orientation of parents matter? *American Sociological Review* 66:159–83.

Thorne, Barrie. 1994. *Gender play*. New Brunswick, NJ: Rutgers University Press.

Weinraub, Marsha, Lynda P. Clemens, Alan Sockloff, Teresa Ethridge, Edward Gracely, and Barbara Myers. 1984. The development of sex role stereotypes in the third year. *Child Development* 55:1493–1503.

West, Candace, and Sarah Fenstermaker. 1993. Power, inequality and the accomplishment of gender. In *Theory on gender/feminism on theory*, edited by Paula England. New York: Aldine de Gruyter.

———. 1995. Doing difference. *Gender & Society* 9:8–37.

West, Candace, and Don Zimmerman. 1987. Doing gender. *Gender & Society* 1:124–51.

Wood, Eileen, Serge Desmarais, and Sara Gugula. 2002. The impact of parenting experience on gender stereotyped toy play of children. *Sex Roles* 47:39–49.

C. J. Pascoe

"Dude, You're a Fag": Adolescent Masculinity and the Fag Discourse

"There's a faggot over there! There's a faggot over there! Come look!" yelled Brian, a senior at River High School, to a group of 10-year-old boys. Following Brian, the 10-year-olds dashed down a hallway. At the end of the hallway Brian's friend, Dan, pursed his lips and began sashaying towards the 10-year-olds. He minced towards them, swinging his hips exaggeratedly and wildly waving his arms. To the boys Brian yelled, "Look at the faggot! Watch out! He'll get you!" In response the 10-year-olds raced back down the hallway screaming in terror. (From author's fieldnotes)

The relationship between adolescent masculinity and sexuality is embedded in the specter of the faggot. Faggots represent a penetrated masculinity in which "to be penetrated is to abdicate power" (Bersani, 1987: 212). Penetrated men symbolize a masculinity devoid of power, which, in its contradiction, threatens both psychic and social chaos. It is precisely this specter of penetrated masculinity that functions as a regulatory mechanism of gender for contemporary American adolescent boys.

Feminist scholars of masculinity have documented the centrality of homophobic insults to masculinity (Lehne, 1998; Kimmel, 2001) especially in school settings (Wood, 1984; Smith, 1998; Burn, 2000; Plummer, 2001; Kimmel, 2003). They argue that homophobic teasing often characterizes masculinity in adolescence and early adulthood, and that anti-gay slurs tend to primarily be directed at other gay boys.

This article both expands on and challenges these accounts of relationships between homo-

From *Sexualities*. Copyright © 2005 Sage Publications (London, Thousand Oaks, CA, and New Delhi). Vol. 8(3):329–346.

phobia and masculinity. Homophobia is indeed a central mechanism in the making of contemporary American adolescent masculinity. This article both critiques and builds on this finding by (1) pointing to the limits of an argument that focuses centrally on homophobia, (2) demonstrating that the fag is not only an identity linked to homosexual boys[1] but an identity that can temporarily adhere to heterosexual boys as well and (3) highlighting the racialized nature of the fag as a disciplinary mechanism.

"Homophobia" is too facile a term with which to describe the deployment of "fag" as an epithet. By calling the use of the word "fag" homophobia—and letting the argument stop with that point—previous research obscures the gendered nature of sexualized insults (Plummer, 2001). Invoking homophobia to describe the ways in which boys aggressively tease each other overlooks the powerful relationship between masculinity and this sort of insult. Instead, it seems incidental in this conventional line of argument that girls do not harass each other and are not harassed in this same manner.[2] This framing naturalizes the relationship between masculinity and homophobia, thus obscuring the centrality of such harassment in the formation of a gendered identity for boys in a way that it is not for girls.

"Fag" is not necessarily a static identity attached to a particular (homosexual) boy. Fag talk and fag imitations serve as a discourse with which boys discipline themselves and each other through joking relationships.[3] Any boy can temporarily become a fag in a given social space or interaction. This does not mean that those boys who identify as or are perceived to be homosexual are not subject to intense harassment. But becoming a fag has as much to do with failing at the masculine tasks of competence, heterosexual prowess and strength or in any way revealing weakness or femininity, as it does with a sexual identity. This fluidity of the fag identity is what makes the specter of the fag such a powerful disciplinary mechanism. It is fluid enough that boys police most of their behaviors out of fear of having the fag identity permanently adhere and definitive enough so that boys recognize a fag behavior and strive to avoid it.

The fag discourse is racialized. It is invoked differently by and in relation to white boys' bodies than it is by and in relation to African-American boys' bodies. While certain behaviors put all boys at risk for becoming temporarily a fag, some behaviors can be enacted by African-American boys without putting them at risk of receiving the label. The racialized meanings of the fag discourse suggest that something more than simple homophobia is involved in these sorts of interactions. An analysis of boys' deployments of the specter of the fag should also extend to the ways in which gendered power works through racialized selves. It is not that this gendered homophobia does not exist in African-American communities. Indeed, making fun of "Negro faggotry seems to be a rite of passage among contemporary black male rappers and filmmakers" (Riggs, 1991: 253). However, the fact that "white women and men, gay and straight, have more or less colonized cultural debates about sexual representation" (Julien and Mercer, 1991: 167) obscures varied systems of sexualized meanings among different racialized ethnic groups (Almaguer, 1991; King, 2004).

Theoretical Framing

The sociology of masculinity entails a "critical study of men, their behaviors, practices, values and perspectives" (Whitehead and Barrett, 2001: 14). Recent studies of men emphasize the multiplicity of masculinity (Connell, 1995) detailing the ways in which different configurations of gender practice are promoted, challenged or reinforced in given social situations. This research on how men do masculinities has explored gendered practices in a wide range of social institutions, such as families (Coltrane, 2001), schools (Skelton, 1996; Parker, 1996; Mac an Ghaill, 1996; Francis and Skelton, 2001), workplaces (Cooper, 2000), media (Craig, 1992), and sports (Messner, 1989; Edly and Wetherel, 1997; Curry, 2004). Many of these studies have developed specific typologies of masculinities: gay, Black, Chicano, working class, middle class, Asian, gay Black, gay Chicano, white working class, militarized, transnational business, New Man, negotiated, versatile, healthy, toxic, counter, and cool masculinities, to name a few (Messner, 2004). In this sort of model the fag could be (and often has been) framed as a type of subordinated masculinity attached to homosexual adolescent boys' bodies.

Heeding Timothy Carrigan's admonition that an "analysis of masculinity needs to be related as well to other currents in feminism" (Carrigan et al., 1987: 64), in this article I integrate queer theory's insights about the relationships between gender, sexuality, identities and power with the attention to men found in the literature on masculinities. Like the sociology of gender, queer theory destabilizes the assumed naturalness of the social order (Lemert, 1996). Queer theory is a "conceptualization which sees sexual power as embedded in different levels of social life" and interrogates areas of the social world not usually seen as sexuality (Stein and Plummer, 1994). In this sense queer theory calls for sexuality to be looked at not only as a discrete arena of sexual practices and identities, but also as a constitutive element of social life (Warner, 1993; Epstein, 1996).

While the masculinities' literature rightly highlights very real inequalities between gay and straight men (see for instance Connell, 1995), this emphasis on sexuality as inhered in static identities attached to male bodies, rather than major organizing principles of social life (Sedgwick, 1990), limits scholars' ability to analyze the myriad ways in which sexuality, in part, constitutes gender. This article does not seek to establish that there are homosexual boys and heterosexual boys and the homosexual ones are marginalized. Rather this article explores what happens to theories of gender if we look at a *discourse* of sexualized identities in addition to focusing on seemingly static identity categories inhabited by men. This is not to say that gender is reduced only to sexuality, indeed feminist scholars have demonstrated that gender is embedded in and constitutive of a multitude of social structures—the economy, places of work, families and schools. In the tradition of post-structural feminist theorists of race and gender who look at "border cases" that explode taken-for-granted binaries of race and gender (Smith, 1994), queer theory is another tool which enables an integrated analysis of sexuality, gender and race.

As scholars of gender have demonstrated, gender is accomplished through day-to-day interactions (Fine, 1987; Hochschild, 1989; West and Zimmerman, 1991; Thorne, 1993). In this sense gender is the "activity of managing situated conduct in light of normative conceptions of attitudes and activities appropriate for one's sex category" (West and Zimmerman, 1991: 127). Similarly, queer theorist Judith Butler argues that gender is accomplished interactionally through "a set of repeated acts within a highly rigid regulatory frame that congeal over time to produce the appearance of substance, of a natural sort of being" (Butler, 1999: 43). Specifically she argues that gendered beings are created through processes of citation and repudiation of a "constitutive outside" (But-

ler, 1993: 3) in which is contained all that is cast out of a socially recognizable gender category. The "constitutive outside" is inhabited by abject identities, unrecognizably and unacceptably gendered selves. The interactional accomplishment of gender in a Butlerian model consists, in part, of the continual iteration and repudiation of this abject identity. Gender, in this sense, is "constituted through the force of exclusion and abjection, on which produces a constitutive outside to the subject, an abjected outside, which is, after all, 'inside' the subject as its own founding repudiation" (Butler, 1993: 3) This repudiation creates and reaffirms a "threatening specter" (Butler, 1993: 3) of failed, unrecognizable gender, the existence of which must be continually repudiated through interactional processes.

I argue that the "fag" position is an "abject" position and, as such, is a "threatening specter" constituting contemporary American adolescent masculinity. The fag discourse is the interactional process through which boys name and repudiate this abjected identity. Rather than analyzing the fag as an identity for homosexual boys, I examine uses of the discourse that imply that any boy can become a fag, regardless of his actual desire or self-perceived sexual orientation. The threat of the abject position infuses the faggot with regulatory power. This article provides empirical data to illustrate Butler's approach to gender and indicates that it might be a useful addition to the sociological literature on masculinities through highlighting one of the ways in which a masculine gender identity is accomplished through interaction.

Method

Research Site

I conducted fieldwork at a suburban high school in north-central California which I call River High.[4] River High is a working class, suburban 50-year-old high school located in a town called Riverton. With the exception of the median household income and racial diversity (both of which are elevated due to Riverton's location in

California), the town mirrors national averages in the percentages of white collar workers, rates of college attendance and marriages, and age composition (according to the 2000 census). It is a politically moderate to conservative, religious community. Most of the students' parents commute to surrounding cities for work.

On average Riverton is a middle-class community. However, students at River are likely to refer to the town as two communities: "Old Riverton" and "New Riverton." A busy highway and railroad tracks bisect the town into these two sections. River High is literally on the "wrong side of the tracks," in Old Riverton. Exiting the freeway, heading north to Old Riverton, one sees a mix of 1950s-era ranch-style homes, some with neatly trimmed lawns and tidy gardens, others with yards strewn with various car parts, lawn chairs and appliances. Old Riverton is visually bounded by smoke-puffing factories. On the other side of the freeway New Riverton is characterized by wide sidewalk-lined streets and new walled-in home developments. Instead of smokestacks, a forested mountain, home to a state park, rises majestically in the background. The teens from these homes attend Hillside High, River's rival.

River High is attended by 2000 students. River High's racial/ethnic breakdown roughly represents California at large: 50 percent white, 9 percent African-American, 28 percent Latino and 6 percent Asian (as compared to California's 46, 6, 32, and 11 percent respectively, according to census data and school records). The students at River High are primarily working class.

Research

I gathered data using the qualitative method of ethnographic research. I spent a year and a half conducting observations, formally interviewing 49 students at River High (36 boys and 13 girls), one male student from Hillside High, and conducting countless informal interviews with students, faculty and administrators. I concentrated on one school because I explore the richness rather than the breadth of data (for other examples of this method see Willis, 1981; MacLeod, 1987; Eder et al., 1995; Ferguson, 2000).

I recruited students for interviews by conducting presentations in a range of classes and hanging around at lunch, before school, after school and at various events talking to different groups of students about my research, which I presented as "writing a book about guys." The interviews usually took place at school, unless the student had a car, in which case he or she met me at one of the local fast food restaurants where I treated them to a meal. Interviews lasted anywhere from half an hour to two hours.

The initial interviews I conducted helped me to map a gendered and sexualized geography of the school, from which I chose my observation sites. I observed a "neutral" site—a senior government classroom, where sexualized meanings were subdued. I observed three sites that students marked as "fag" sites—two drama classes and the Gay/Straight Alliance. I also observed two normatively "masculine" sites—auto-shop and weightlifting.[5] I took daily field notes focusing on how students, faculty and administrators negotiated, regulated and resisted particular meanings of gender and sexuality. I attended major school rituals such as Winter Ball, school rallies, plays, dances and lunches. I would also occasionally "ride along" with Mr. Johnson (Mr J.), the school's security guard, on his battery-powered golf cart to watch which, how and when students were disciplined. Observational data provided me with more insight to the interactional processes of masculinity than simple interviews yielded. If I had relied only on interview data I would have missed the interactional processes of masculinity which are central to the fag discourse.

Given the importance of appearance in high school, I gave some thought as to how I would present myself, deciding to both blend in and set myself apart from the students. In order to blend in I wore my standard graduate student gear—comfortable, baggy cargo pants, a black t-shirt or sweater and tennis shoes. To set myself apart I carried a messenger bag instead of a back-pack, didn't wear makeup, and spoke slightly differently than the students by using some slang, but re-fraining from uttering the ubiquitous "hecka" and "hella."

The boys were fascinated by the fact that a 30-something white "girl" (their words) was interested in studying them. While at first many would make sexualized comments asking me about my dating life or saying that they were going to "hit on" me, it seemed eventually they began to forget about me as a potential sexual/romantic partner. Part of this, I think, was related to my knowledge about "guy" things. For instance, I lift weights on a regular basis and as a result the weightlifting coach introduced me as a "weight-lifter from U.C. Berkeley" telling the students they should ask me for weight-lifting advice. Additionally, my taste in movies and television shows often coincided with theirs. I am an avid fan of the movies *Jackass* and *Fight Club*, both of which contain high levels of violence and "bathroom" humor. Finally, I garnered a lot of points among boys because I live off a dangerous street in a nearby city famous for drug deals, gang fights and frequent gun shots.

What Is a Fag?

"Since you were little boys you've been told, 'hey, don't be a little faggot,'" explained Darnell, an African-American football player, as we sat on a bench next to the athletic field. Indeed, both the boys and girls I interviewed told me that "fag" was the worst epithet one guy could direct at another. Jeff, a slight white sophomore, explained to me that boys call each other fag because "gay people aren't really liked over here and stuff." Jeremy, a Latino junior, told me that this insult literally reduced a boy to nothing, "To call someone gay or fag is like the lowest thing you can call someone. Because that's like saying that you're nothing."

Most guys explained their or others' dislike of fags by claiming that homophobia is just part of what it means to be a guy. For instance Keith, a white soccer-playing senior, explained, "I think guys are just homophobic." However, it is not just homophobia, it is a *gendered* homophobia. Sev-

eral students told me that these homophobic insults only applied to boys and not girls. For example, while Jake, a handsome white senior, told me that he didn't like gay people, he quickly added, "Lesbians, okay that's *good*." Similarly Cathy, a popular white cheerleader, told me "Being a lesbian is accepted because guys think 'oh that's cool.' " Darnell, after telling me that boys were told not to be faggots, said of lesbians, "They're [guys are] fine with girls. I think it's the guy part that they're like ewwww!" In this sense it is not strictly homophobia, but a gendered homophobia that constitutes adolescent masculinity in the culture of this school. However, it is clear, according to these comments, that lesbians are "good" because of their place in heterosexual male fantasy not necessarily because of some enlightened approach to same-sex relationships. It does however, indicate that using only the term homophobia to describe boys' repeated use of the word "fag" might be a bit simplistic and misleading.

Additionally, girls at River High rarely deployed the word "fag" and were never called "fags." I recorded girls uttering "fag" only three times during my research. In one instance, Angela, a Latina cheerleader, teased Jeremy, a well-liked white senior involved in student government, for not ditching school with her, "You wouldn't 'cause you're a faggot." However, girls did not use this word as part of their regular lexicon. The sort of gendered homophobia that constitutes adolescent masculinity does not constitute adolescent femininity. Girls were not called dykes or lesbians in any sort of regular or systematic way. Students did tell me that "slut" was the worst thing a girl could be called. However, my field notes indicate that the word "slut" (or its synonym "ho") appears one time for every eight times the word "fag" appears. Even when it does occur, "slut" is rarely deployed as a direct insult against another girl.

Highlighting the difference between the deployment of "gay" and "fag" as insults brings the gendered nature of this homophobia into focus. For boys and girls at River High "gay" is a fairly common synonym for "stupid." While this word shares the sexual origins of "fag," it does not *consistently* have the skew of gender-loaded meaning. Girls and boys often used "gay" as an adjective referring to inanimate objects and male or female people, whereas they used "fag" as a noun that denotes only un-masculine males. Students used "gay" to describe anything from someone's clothes to a new school rule that the students did not like, as in the following encounter:

> In auto-shop Arnie pulled out a large older version black laptop computer and placed it on his desk. Behind him Nick said "That's a gay laptop! It's five inches thick!"

A laptop can be gay, a movie can be gay or a group of people can be gay. Boys used "gay" and "fag" interchangeably when they refer to other boys, but "fag" does not have the non-gendered attributes that "gay" sometimes invokes.

While its meanings are not the same as "gay," "fag" does have multiple meanings which do not necessarily replace its connotations as a homophobic slur, but rather exist alongside. Some boys took pains to say that "fag" is not about sexuality. Darnell told me "It doesn't even have anything to do with being gay." J.L., a white sophomore at Hillside High (River High's crosstown rival) asserted "Fag, seriously, it has nothing to do with sexual preference at all. You could just be calling somebody an idiot you know?" I asked Ben, a quiet, white sophomore who wore heavy metal t-shirts to auto-shop each day, "What kind of things do guys get called a fag for?" Ben answered "Anything. . . . literally, anything. Like you were trying to turn a wrench the wrong way, 'dude, you're a fag.' Even if a piece of meat drops out of your sandwich, 'you fag!' " Each time Ben said "you fag" his voice deepened as if he were imitating a more masculine boy. While Ben might rightly *feel* like a guy could be called a fag for "anything . . . literally, anything," there are actually specific behaviors which, when enacted by most boys, can render him more vulnerable to a fag epithet. In this instance Ben's comment high-

lights the use of "fag" as a generic insult for incompetence, which in the world of River High, is central to a masculine identity. A boy could get called a fag for exhibiting any sort of behavior defined as non-masculine (although not necessarily behaviors aligned with femininity) in the world of River High: being stupid, incompetent, dancing, caring too much about clothing, being too emotional or expressing interest (sexual or platonic) in other guys. However, given the extent of its deployment and the laundry list of behaviors that could get a boy in trouble it is no wonder that Ben felt like a boy could be called "fag" for "anything."

One-third (13) of the boys I interviewed told me that, while they may liberally insult each other with the term, they would not actually direct it at a homosexual peer. Jabes, a Filipino senior, told me

> I actually say it [fag] quite a lot, except for when I'm in the company of an actual homosexual person. Then I try not to say it at all. But when I'm just hanging out with my friends I'll be like, "shut up, I don't want you hear you any more, you stupid fag."

Similarly J.L. compared homosexuality to a disability, saying there is "no way" he'd call an actually gay guy a fag because

> There's people who are the retarded people who nobody wants to associate with. I'll be so nice to those guys and I hate it when people make fun of them. It's like, "bro do you realize that they can't help that." And then there's gay people. They were born that way.

According to this group of boys, gay is a legitimate, if marginalized, social identity. If a man is gay, there may be a chance he could be considered masculine by other men (Connell, 1995). David, a handsome white senior dressed smartly in khaki pants and a white button-down shirt said, "Being gay is just a lifestyle. It's someone you choose to sleep with. You can still throw around a football and be gay." In other words there is a possibility, however slight, that a boy can be gay and masculine. To be a fag is, by definition, the opposite of masculine, whether or not the word is deployed with sexualized or non-sexualized meanings. In explaining this to me, Jamaal, an African-American junior, cited the explanation of popular rap artist, Eminem,

> Although I don't like Eminem, he had a good definition of it. It's like taking away your title. In an interview they were like, "you're always capping on gays, but then you sing with Elton John." He was like "I don't mean gay as in gay."

This is what Riki Wilchins calls the "Eminem Exception. Eminem explains that he doesn't call people 'faggot' because of their sexual orientation but because they're weak and unmanly" (Wilchins, 2003). This is precisely the way in which this group of boys at River High uses the term "faggot." While it is not necessarily acceptable to gay, at least a man who is gay can do other things that render him acceptably masculine. A fag, by the very definition of the word, indicated by students' usages at River High, cannot be masculine. This distinction between "fag" as an unmasculine and problematic identity and "gay" as a possibly masculine, although marginalized, sexual identity is not limited to a teenage lexicon, but is reflected in both psychological discourses (Sedgwick, 1995) and gay and lesbian activism.

Becoming a Fag

"The ubiquity of the word faggot speaks to the reach of its discrediting capacity" (Corbett, 2001: 4). It is almost as if boys cannot help but shout it out on a regular basis—in the hallway, in class, across campus as a greeting, or as a joke. In my fieldwork I was amazed by the way in which the word seemed to pop uncontrollably out of boys' mouths in all kinds of situations. To quote just one of many instances from my fieldnotes:

> Two boys walked out of the P.E. locker room and one yelled "fucking faggot!" at no one in particular.

This spontaneous yelling out of a variation of "fag" seemingly apropos of nothing happened repeatedly among boys throughout the school.

The fag discourse is central to boys' joking relationships. Joking cements relationships between boys (Kehily and Nayak, 1997; Lyman, 1998) and helps to manage anxiety and discomfort (Freud, 1905). Boys invoked the specter of the fag in two ways: through humorous imitation and through lobbing the epithet at one another. Boys at River High imitated the fag by acting out an exaggerated "femininity," and/or by pretending to sexually desire other boys. As indicated by the introductory vignette in which a predatory "fag" threatens the little boys, boys at River High link these performative scenarios with a fag identity. They lobbed the fag epithet at each other in a verbal game of hot potato, each careful to deflect the insult quickly by hurling it toward someone else. These games and imitations make up a fag discourse which highlights the fag not as a static but rather as a fluid identity which boys constantly struggle to avoid.

In imitative performances the fag discourse functions as a constant reiteration of the fag's existence, affirming that the fag is out there; at any moment a boy can become a fag. At the same time these performances demonstrate that the boy who is invoking the fag is *not* a fag. By invoking it so often, boys remind themselves and each other that at any point they can become fags if they are not sufficiently masculine.

> Mr McNally, disturbed by the noise outside of the classroom, turned to the open door saying "We'll shut this unless anyone really wants to watch sweaty boys playing basketball." Emir, a tall skinny boy, lisped "I wanna watch the boys play!" The rest of the class cracked up at his imitation.

Through imitating a fag, boys assure others that they are not a fag by immediately becoming masculine again after the performance. They mock their own performed femininity and/or same-sex desire, assuring themselves and others that such an identity is one deserving of derisive laughter.

The fag identity in this instance is fluid, detached from Emir's body. He can move in and out of this "abject domain" while simultaneously affirming his position as a subject.

Boys also consistently tried to put another in the fag position by lobbing the fag epithet at one another.

> Going through the junk-filled car in the auto-shop parking lot, Jay poked his head out and asked "Where are Craig and Brian?" Neil, responded with "I think they're over there," pointing, then thrusting his hips and pulling his arms back and forth to indicate that Craig and Brian might be having sex. The boys in auto-shop laughed.

This sort of joke temporarily labels both Craig and Brian as faggots. Because the fag discourse is so familiar, the other boys immediately understand that Neil is indicating that Craig and Brian are having sex. However these are not necessarily identities that stick. Nobody actually thinks Craig and Brian are homosexuals. Rather the fag identity is a fluid one, certainly an identity that no boy wants, but one that a boy can escape, usually by engaging in some sort of discursive contest to turn another boy into a fag. However, fag becomes a hot potato that no boy wants to be left holding. In the following example, which occurred soon after the "sex" joke, Brian lobs the fag epithet at someone else, deflecting it from himself:

> Brian initiated a round of a favorite game in auto-shop, the "cock game." Brian quietly, looking at Josh, said, "Josh loves the cock," then slightly louder, "Josh loves the cock." He continued saying this until he was yelling "JOSH LOVES THE COCK!" The rest of the boys laughed hysterically as Josh slinked away saying "I have a bigger dick than all you mother fuckers!"

These two instances show how the fag can be mapped, momentarily, on to one boy's body and how he, in turn, can attach it to another boy, thus deflecting it from himself. In the first instance Neil makes fun of Craig and Brian for simply hanging out together. In the second instance Brian goes from being a fag to making Josh into a fag, through the "cock game." The "fag" is transferable. Boys move in and out of it by discursively creating another as a fag through joking interactions. They, somewhat ironically, can move in and out of the fag position by transforming themselves, temporarily, into a fag, but this has the effect of reaffirming their masculinity when they return to a heterosexual position after imitating the fag.

These examples demonstrate boys invoking the trope of the fag in a discursive struggle in which the boys indicate that they know what a fag is—and that they are not fags. This joking cements bonds between boys as they assure themselves and each other of their masculinity through repeated repudiations of a non-masculine position of the abject.

Racing the Fag

The fag trope is not deployed consistently or identically across social groups at River High. Differences between white boys' and African-American boys' meaning making around clothes and dancing reveal ways in which the fag as the abject position is racialized.

Clean, oversized, carefully put together clothing is central to a hip-hop identity for African-American boys who identify with hip-hop culture.[6] Richard Majors calls this presentation of self a "cool pose" consisting of "unique, expressive and conspicuous styles of demeanor, speech, gesture, clothing, hairstyle, walk, stance and handshake" developed by African-American men as a symbolic response to institutionalized racism (Majors, 2001: 211). Pants are usually several sizes too big, hanging low on a boy's waist, usually revealing a pair of boxers beneath. Shirts and sweaters are similarly oversized, often hanging down to a boy's knees. Tags are frequently left on baseball hats worn slightly askew and perched high on the head. Meticulously clean, unlaced athletic shoes with rolled up socks under the tongue complete a typical hip-hop outfit.

This amount of attention and care given to clothing for white boys not identified with hip-hop culture (that is, most of the white boys at River High) would certainly cast them into an abject, fag position. White boys are not supposed to appear to care about their clothes or appearance, because only fags care about how they look. Ben illustrates this:

> Ben walked in to the auto-shop classroom from the parking lot where he had been working on a particularly oily engine. Grease stains covered his jeans. He looked down at them, made a face and walked toward me with limp wrists, laughing and lisping in a in a high pitch sing-song voice "I got my good panths all dirty!"

Ben draws on indicators of a fag identity, such as limp wrists, as do the boys in the introductory vignette to illustrate that a masculine person certainly would not care about having dirty clothes. In this sense, masculinity, for white boys, becomes the carefully crafted appearance of not caring about appearance, especially in terms of cleanliness.

However, African-American boys involved in hip-hop culture talk frequently about whether or not their clothes, specifically their shoes, are dirty:

> In drama class both Darnell and Marc compared their white Adidas basketball shoes. Darnell mocked Marc because black scuff marks covered his shoes, asking incredulously "Yours are a week old and they're dirty—I've had mine for a month and they're not dirty!" Both laughed.

Monte, River High's star football player, echoed this concern about dirty shoes when looking at the fancy red shoes he had lent to his cousin the week before, and told me he was frustrated because after his cousin used them, the "shoes are hella scuffed up." Clothing, for these boys, does not indicate a fag position, but rather defines membership in a certain cultural and racial group (Perry, 2002).

Dancing is another arena that carries distinctly fag associated meanings for white boys and masculine meanings for African-American boys who participate in hip-hop culture. White boys often associate dancing with "fags." J.L. told me that guys think "'nSync's gay" because they can dance. 'nSync is an all white male singing group known for their dance moves. At dances white boys frequently held their female dates tightly, locking their hips together. The boys never danced with one another, unless engaged in a round of "hot potato." White boys often jokingly danced together in order to embarrass each other by making someone else into a fag:

> Lindy danced behind her date, Chris. Chris's friend, Matt, walked up and nudged Lindy aside, imitating her dance moves behind Chris. As Matt rubbed his hands up and down Chris's back, Chris turned around and jumped back startled to see Matt there instead of Lindy. Matt cracked up as Chris turned red.

However dancing does not carry this sort of sexualized gender meaning for all boys at River High. For African-American boys dancing demonstrates membership in a cultural community (Best, 2000). African-American boys frequently danced together in single sex groups, teaching each other the latest dance moves, showing off a particularly difficult move or making each other laugh with humorous dance moves. Students recognized K.J. as the most talented dancer at the school. K.J. is a sophomore of African-American and Filipino descent who participated in the hip-hop culture of River High. He continually wore the latest hip-hop fashions. K.J. was extremely popular. Girls hollered his name as they walked down the hall and thrust urgently written love notes folded in complicated designs into his hands as he sauntered to class. For the past two years K.J. won first place in the talent show for dancing. When he danced at assemblies the room reverberated with screamed chants of "Go K.J.! Go K.J.! Go K.J.!" Because dancing for African-American boys places them within a tradition of masculinity, they are not at risk of becoming a fag for this particular gendered practice. Nobody called K.J. a fag. In fact in several of my interviews boys of multiple racial/ethnic backgrounds spoke admiringly of K.J.'s dancing abilities.

Implications

These findings confirm previous studies of masculinity and sexuality that position homophobia as central to contemporary definitions of adolescent masculinity. These data extend previous research by unpacking multilayered meanings that boys deploy through their uses of homophobic language and joking rituals. By attending to these meanings I reframe the discussion as one of a fag discourse, rather than simply labeling this sort of behavior as homophobia. The fag is an "abject" position, a position outside of masculinity that actually constitutes masculinity. Thus, masculinity, in part, becomes the daily interactional work of repudiating the "threatening specter" of the fag.

The fag extends beyond a static sexual identity attached to a gay boy. Few boys are permanently identified as fags; most move in and out of fag positions. Looking at "fag" as a discourse rather than a static identity reveals that the term can be invested with different meanings in different social spaces. "Fag" may be used as a weapon with which to temporarily assert one's masculinity by denying it to others. Thus "fag" becomes a symbol around which contests of masculinity take place.

The fag epithet, when hurled at other boys, may or may not have explicit sexual meanings, but it always has gendered meanings. When a boy calls another boy a fag, it means he is not a man, not necessarily that he is a homosexual. The boys in this study know that they are not supposed to call homosexual boys "fags" because that is mean. This, then, has been the limited success of the mainstream gay rights movement. The message absorbed by some of these teenage boys is that "gay men can be masculine, just like you." Instead of challenging gender inequality, this particular discourse of gay rights has reinscribed it. Thus we need to begin to think about how gay

men may be in a unique position to challenge gendered as well as sexual norms.

This study indicates that researchers who look at the intersection of sexuality and masculinity need to attend to the ways in which racialized identities may affect how "fag" is deployed and what it means in various social situations. While researchers have addressed the ways in which masculine identities are racialized (Connell, 1995; Ross, 1998; Bucholtz, 1999; Davis, 1999; Price, 1999; Ferguson, 2000; Majors, 2001) they have not paid equal attention to the ways in which "fag" might be a racialized epithet. It is important to look at when, where and with what meaning "the fag" is deployed in order to get at how masculinity is defined, contested, and invested in among adolescent boys.

Research shows that sexualized teasing often leads to deadly results, as evidenced by the spate of school shootings in the 1990s (Kimmel, 2003). Clearly the fag discourse affects not just homosexual teens, but all boys, gay and straight. Further research could investigate these processes in a variety of contexts: varied geographic locations, sexualized groups, classed groups, religious groups and age groups.

Acknowledgments

The author would like to thank Natalie Boero, Leslie Bell, Meg Jay and Barrie Thorne for their comments on this article. This work was supported by the Center for the Study of Sexual Culture at University of California, Berkeley.

Notes

1. While the term "homosexual" is laden with medicalized and normalizing meanings, I use it instead of "gay" because "gay" in the world of River High has multiple meanings apart from sexual practices or identities.

2. Girls do insult one another based on sexualized meanings. But in my own research I found that girls and boys did not harass girls in this manner with the same frequency that boys harassed each other through engaging in joking about the fag.

3. I use discourse in the Foucauldian sense, to describe truth producing practices, not just text or speech (Foucault, 1978).

4. The names of places and respondents have been changed.

5. Auto-shop was a class in which students learned how to build and repair cars. Many of the students in this course were looking into careers as mechanics.

6. While there are several white and Latino boys at River High who identify with hip-hop culture, hip-hop is identified by the majority of students as an African-American cultural style.

References

Almaguer, Tomas (1991) "Chicano Men: A Cartography of Homosexual Identity and Behavior," *Differences* 3: 75–100.

Bersani, Leo (1987) "Is the Rectum a Grave?" *October* 43: 197–222.

Best, Amy (2000) *Prom Night: Youth, Schools and Popular Culture.* New York: Routledge.

Bucholtz, Mary (1999) "'You Da Man': Narrating the Racial Other in the Production of White Masculinity," *Journal of Sociolinguistics* 3/4: 443–60.

Burn, Shawn M. (2000) "Heterosexuals' Use of 'Fag' and 'Queer' to Deride One Another: A Contributor to Heterosexism and Stigma," *Journal of Homosexuality* 40: 1–11.

Butler, Judith (1993) *Bodies That Matter.* Routledge: New York.

Butler, Judith (1999) *Gender Trouble.* New York: Routledge.

Carrigan, Tim, Connell, Bob and Lee, John (1987) "Toward a New Sociology of Masculinity," in Harry Brod (ed.) *The Making of Masculinities: The New Men's Studies,* pp. 188–202. Boston, MA: Allen & Unwin.

Coltrane, Scott (2001) "Selling the Indispensable Father," paper presented at *Pushing the Boundaries Conference: New Conceptualizations of Childhood and Motherhood,* Philadelphia.

Connell, R.W. (1995) *Masculinities.* Berkeley: University of California Press.

Cooper, Marianne (2000) "Being the 'Go-to Guy': Fatherhood, Masculinity and the Organization of Work in Silicon Valley," *Qualitative Sociology* 23: 379–405.

Corbett, Ken (2001) "Faggot = Loser," *Studies in Gender and Sexuality* 2: 3–28.

Craig, Steve (1992) *Men, Masculinity and the Media.* Newbury Park: Sage.

Curry, Timothy J. (2004) "Fraternal Bonding in the Locker Room: A Profeminist Analysis of Talk about Competition and Women," in Michael Messner and Michael Kimmel (eds.) *Men's Lives.* Boston, MA: Pearson.

Davis, James E. (1999) "Forbidden Fruit, Black Males' Constructions of Transgressive Sexualities in Middle School," in William J. Letts IV and James T. Sears (eds.) *Queering Elementary Education: Advancing the Dialogue about Sexualities and Schooling,* pp. 49 ff. Lanham, MD: Rowan & Littlefield.

Eder, Donna, Evans, Catherine and Parker, Stephen (1995) *School Talk: Gender and Adolescent Culture* New Brunswick, NJ: Rutgers University Press.

Edly, Nigel and Wetherell, Margaret (1997) "Jockeying for Position: The Construction of Masculine Identities," *Discourse and Society* 8: 203–17.

Epstein, Steven (1996) "A Queer Encounter," in Steven Seidman (ed.) *Queer Theory / Sociology,* pp. 188–202. Cambridge, MA: Blackwell.

Ferguson, Ann (2000) *Bad Boys: Public Schools in the Making of Black Masculinity.* Ann Arbor: University of Michigan Press.

Fine, Gary (1987) *With the Boys: Little League Baseball and Preadolescent Culture.* Chicago, IL: University of Chicago Press.

Foucault, Michel (1978) *The History of Sexuality, Volume I.* New York: Vintage Books.

Francis, Becky and Skelton, Christine (2001) "Men Teachers and the Construction of Heterosexual Masculinity in the Classroom," *Sex Education* 1: 9–21.

Freud, Sigmund (1905) *The Basic Writings of Sigmund Freud,* (translated and edited by A.A. Brill). New York: The Modern Library.

Hochschild, Arlie (1989) *The Second Shift.* New York: Avon.

Julien, Isaac and Mercer, Kobena (1991) "True Confessions: A Discourse on Images of Black Male Sexuality," in Essex Hemphill (ed.) *Brother to Brother: New Writings by Black Gay Men,* pp. 167–73. Boston, MA: Alyson Publications.

Kehily, Mary Jane and Nayak, Anoop (1997) "Lads and Laughter: Humour and the Production of

Heterosexual Masculinities," *Gender and Education* 9: 69–87.

Kimmel, Michael (2001) "Masculinity as Homophobia: Fear, Shame, and Silence in the Construction of Gender Identity," in Stephen Whitehead and Frank Barrett (eds.) *The Masculinities Reader,* pp. 166–187. Cambridge: Polity.

Kimmel, Michael (2003) "Adolescent Masculinity, Homophobia, and Violence: Random School Shootings, 1982–2001," *American Behavioral Scientist* 46: 1439–58.

King, D. L. (2004) *Double Lives on the Down Low.* New York: Broadway Books.

Lehne, Gregory (1998) "Homophobia among Men: Supporting and Defining the Male Role," in Michael Kimmel and Michael Messner (eds.) *Men's Lives,* pp. 237–49. Boston, MA: Allyn and Bacon.

Lemert, Charles (1996) "Series Editor's Preface," in Steven Seidman (ed.) *Queer Theory / Sociology.* Cambridge, MA: Blackwell.

Lyman, Peter (1998) "The Fraternal Bond as a Joking Relationship: A Case Study of the Role of Sexist Jokes in Male Group Bonding," in Michael Kimmel and Michael Messner (eds.) *Men's Lives,* pp. 171–93. Boston, MA: Allyn and Bacon.

Mac an Ghaill, Martain (1996) "What about the Boys—School, Class and Crisis Masculinity," *Sociological Review* 44: 381–97.

MacLeod, Jay (1987) *Ain't No Makin It: Aspirations and Attainment in a Low Income Neighborhood.* Boulder, CO: Westview Press.

Majors, Richard (2001) "Cool Pose: Black Masculinity and Sports," in Stephen Whitehead and Frank Barrett (eds.) *The Masculinities Reader,* pp. 208–17. Cambridge: Polity.

Messner, Michael (1989) "Sports and the Politics of Inequality," in Michael Kimmel and Michael Messner (eds.) *Men's Lives.* Boston, MA: Allyn and Bacon.

Messner, Michael (2004) "On Patriarchs and Losers: Rethinking Men's Interests," paper presented at Berkeley *Journal of Sociology* Conference, Berkeley.

Parker, Andrew (1996) "The Construction of Masculinity within Boys' Physical Education," *Gender and Education* 8: 141–57.

Perry, Pamela (2002) *Shades of White: White Kids and Racial Identities in High School.* Durham, NC: Duke University Press.

Plummer, David C. (2001) "The Quest for Modern Manhood: Masculine Stereotypes, Peer Culture and the Social Significance of Homophobia," *Journal of Adolescence* 24: 15–23.

Price, Jeremy (1999) "Schooling and Racialized Masculinities: The Diploma, Teachers and Peers in the Lives of Young, African-American Men," *Youth and Society* 31: 224–63.

Riggs, Marlon (1991) "Black Macho Revisited: Reflections of a SNAP! Queen," in Essex Hemphill (ed.) *Brother to Brother: New Writings by Black Gay Men,* pp. 153–260. Boston, MA: Alyson Publications.

Ross, Marlon B. (1998) "In Search of Black Men's Masculinities," *Feminist Studies* 24: 599–626.

Sedgwick, Eve K. (1990) *Epistemology of the Closet.* Berkeley: University of California Press.

Sedgwick, Eve K. (1995) " 'Gosh, Boy George, You Must be Awfully Secure in Your Masculinity!' " in Maurice Berger, Brian Wallis and Simon Watson (eds.) *Constructing Masculinity,* pp. 11–20. New York: Routledge.

Skelton, Christine (1996) "Learning to be Tough: The Fostering of Maleness in One Primary School," *Gender and Education* 8: 185–97.

Smith, George W. (1998) "The Ideology of 'Fag': The School Experience of Gay Students," *The Sociological Quarterly* 39: 309–35.

Smith, Valerie (1994) "Split Affinities: The Case of Interracial Rape," in Anne Herrmann and Abigail Stewart (eds.) *Theorizing Feminism,* pp. 155–70. Boulder, CO: Westview Press.

Stein, Arlene and Plummer, Ken (1994) " 'I Can't Even Think Straight': 'Queer' Theory and the Missing Sexual Revolution in Sociology," *Sociological Theory* 12: 178 ff.

Thorne, Barrie (1993) *Gender Play: Boys and Girls in School.* New Brunswick, NJ: Rutgers University Press.

Warner, Michael (1993) "Introduction," in Michael Warner (ed.) *Fear of a Queer Planet: Queer Politics and Social Theory,* pp. vii–xxxi. Minneapolis: University of Minnesota Press.

West, Candace and Zimmerman, Don (1991) "Doing Gender," in Judith Lorber (ed.) *The Social Construction of Gender,* pp. 102–21. Newbury Park: Sage.

Whitehead, Stephen and Barrett, Frank (2001) "The Sociology of Masculinity," in Stephen

Whitehead and Frank Barrett (eds.) *The Masculinities Reader,* pp. 472–6. Cambridge: Polity.

Wilchins, Riki (2003) "Do You Believe in Fairies?" *The Advocate,* 4 February.

Willis, Paul (1981) *Learning to Labor: How Working Class Kids Get Working Class Jobs.* New York: Columbia University Press.

Wood, Julian (1984) "Groping Toward Sexism: Boy's Sex Talk," in Angela McRobbie and Mica Nava (eds.) *Gender and Generation.* London: Macmillan Publishers.

Paul Kivel

The Act-Like-a-Man Box

How are boys trained in the United States? What is the predominant image of masculinity that boys must deal with while growing up?

From a very early age, boys are told to "Act Like a Man." Even though they have all the normal human feelings of love, excitement, sadness, confusion, anger, curiosity, pain, frustration, humiliation, shame, grief, resentment, loneliness, low self-worth, and self-doubt, they are taught to hide the feelings and appear to be tough and in control. They are told to be aggressive, not to back down, not to make mistakes, and to take charge, have lots of sex, make lots of money, and be responsible. Most of all, they are told not to cry.

My colleagues and I have come to call this rigid set of expectations the "Act-Like a Man" box because it feels like a box, a 24-hour-a-day, seven-day-a-week box that society tells boys they must fit themselves into. One reason we know it's a box is because every time a boy tries to step out he's pushed back in with names like wimp, sissy, mama's boy, girl, fag, nerd, punk, mark, bitch, and others even more graphic. Behind those names is the threat of violence.

These words are little slaps, everyday reminders designed to keep us in the box. They are also fighting words. If someone calls a boy a "wimp" or a "fag," he is supposed to fight to prove that he is not. Almost every adult man will admit that as a kid, he had to fight at least once to prove he was in the box.

The columns on either side of the box show the expectations our society holds for men. The abuse, pressure, and training boys receive to meet these expectations and stay in the box produce a lot of feelings, some of which are listed in the middle of the box above. Yet they have to cover over those feelings and try to act like a man because one of the strictures of being a man is not to show your feelings.

Notice that many of the words we get called refer to being gay or feminine. This feeds into two things we're taught to fear: (1) that we are not manly enough and (2) that we might be gay. Homophobia, the fear of gays or of being taken for gay, is an incredibly strong fear we learn as boys and carry with us throughout our lives. Much too often we try to relieve our fears of being gay or effeminate by attacking others.

There is other training that keeps us in the box. Besides getting into fights, we are ostracized and teased, and girls don't seem to like us when we step out of the box. Many adults keep pushing us to be tough, and that process begins early. They seem convinced that if they "coddle" us, we will be weak and vulnerable. Somehow, with drawal of affection is supposed to toughen us and prepare us for the "real" world. Withdrawal of affection is emotional abuse. And that's bad enough. But it often does not stop there. One out of every six of us is sexually abused as a child. Often, the verbal, physical, and sexual abuse continues throughout our childhood.

There are many cultural variations of this theme, but its prevalence in Western cultures is striking. All boys have different strategies for trying to survive in the box. Some might even sneak

"Act-Like-a-Man" Box

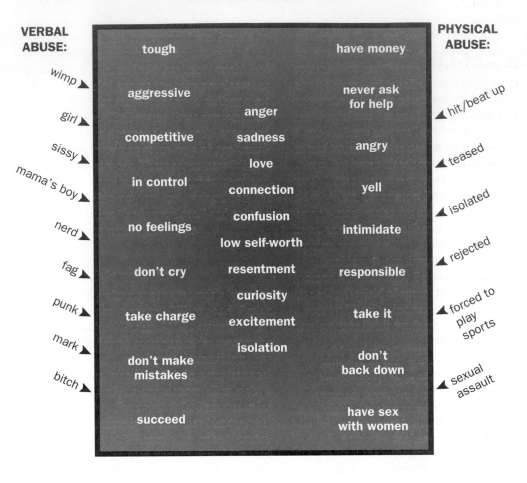

VERBAL ABUSE:

wimp
girl
sissy
mama's boy
nerd
fag
punk
mark
bitch

PHYSICAL ABUSE:

hit/beat up
teased
isolated
rejected
forced to play sports
sexual assault

tough
aggressive
anger
competitive
sadness
love
in control
connection
confusion
no feelings
low self-worth
don't cry
resentment
curiosity
take charge
excitement
isolation
don't make mistakes
succeed

have money
never ask for help
angry
yell
intimidate
responsible
take it
don't back down
have sex with women

out of it at times, but the scars from living within the walls of the box are long-lasting and painful.

If we pay attention we can easily see the box's effects on boys. Just watch a group of them together. They are constantly challenging each other, putting each other down, hitting each other, testing to see who is in the box. They are never at ease, always on guard. At an early age they start to hide their feelings, toughen up, and will make a huge emotional effort not to cry. They stop wearing colorful clothing or participating in activities that they think might make them vulnerable to being labeled gay. They walk more stiffly, talk more guardedly, move more aggressively. Behind this bravura they are often confused, scared, angry, and wanting closeness with others. But being in the box precludes closeness and makes intimacy unlikely.

The key to staying in the box is control. Boys are taught to control their bodies, control their feelings, control their relationships—to protect themselves from being vulnerable. Although the box is a metaphor for the pressures all boys must respond to, the possibility that a boy will have control over the conditions of his life varies depending on his race, class, and culture.

Being in control is not the same as being violent. In Western societies hitting people is frowned upon except in particular sports or military settings. It is deemed much more refined to retain control by using verbal, emotional, or psychological means rather than physical force. Financial manipulation, coercion and intimidation, and sexual pressure are also condoned as long as no one is physically injured.

Clearly, the more money, education, and connections a man has, the easier it is for him to buy or manipulate what he wants. Wealthy and upper- or middle-class white men are generally promoted and celebrated for being in control and getting what they want. Poor or working-class men and men of color are usually punished for these same behaviors, especially, but not only, if they use physical force.

Why are boys trained to be in control? Most boys will end up with one of three roles in society—to be workers, consumers, or enforcers. A small percentage of boys are trained to give orders—to be bosses, managers, or officers. The box trains boys for the roles they will play, whether they will make decisions governing the lives of others or carry out the decisions made by those at the top. The box prepares boys to be police officers, security cops, deans, administrators, soldiers, heads of families, probation officers, prison guards—the roles that men, primarily white men, are being trained to fill. Men of color, along with women and young people, are the people more often being controlled.

Many men are under the illusion that being in the box is like being in an exclusive club. No girls allowed. All men are equal. For working- and middle-class white men and for those men of color who aspire to be accepted by them, the box creates a false feeling of solidarity with men in power and misleads many of them into thinking they have more in common with the corporate executives, political and religious leaders, generals, and bosses than they have with women.

Nobody is born in the Act-Like-a-Man box. It takes years and years of enforcement, name-calling, fights, threats, abuse, and fear to turn us into men who live in this box. By adolescence we believe that there are only two choices—we can be a man or a boy, a winner or a loser, a bully or a wimp, a champ or a chump.

Nobody wants to live in a box. It feels closed in; much of us is left out. It was a revelation to realize how I had been forced into the box. It was a relief to understand how it had been accomplished and to know it didn't have to be that way. Today, it inspires me to see adult men choose to live outside the box. It is a choice each of us can, and must make—to step outside the box and back into our families and communities.

Ritch C. Savin-Williams

Memories of Same-Sex Attractions

Recalling their childhood, gay/bisexual youths often report the pervasiveness of distinct, early memories of same-sex attractions. They remember particular feelings or incidents from as young as four or five years of age that, in retrospect, reflect the first manifestations of sexual orientation. These memories often comprise some of the youths' earliest recollections of their lives, present in some rudimentary form for many years before the ability to label sexual feelings and attractions emerges, usually after pubertal onset.[1]

Indeed, over 80 percent of the interviewed youths reported same-sex attractions prior to the physical manifestations of puberty. By the completion of puberty, all youths recalled attractions that they later labeled as "homosexual." Nearly half noted that their feelings for other males were some of their very first memories, present prior to beginning elementary school. Revelation for one youth came through his kindergarten naps: "Dreams of naked men and curious about them. Really wanting to look at them." Another youth was acting on his sexually charged feelings at age four: "I particularly remember an incident with a cousin in the bathroom and we both having hardons and feeling a tingling sensation when we rubbed against each other. I wanted to repeat it, and did!"

The origins of these feelings and their meanings are difficult to discern because prepubertal children are seldom asked if they have sexual attractions for other boys or girls. Thus, clinicians, educators, researchers, and other interested pro-

fessionals must rely on retrospective data from adolescents and young adults. Although these later recollections may be distorted by an awareness of current sexual identity, they provide an invaluable source of information.

Gay/bisexual youths often recall a vague but distinct sense of *being different* from other boys. Indeed, characterizing most developmental models of sexual identity is an introductory stage in which an individual has an unequivocal cognitive and/or emotional realization that he or she is "different" from others. An individual may feel alienated from others with very little awareness that homosexuality is the relevant issue.[2] For example, sociologist and sex educator Richard Troiden proposes a coming-out model that begins with an initial sense that one is marginalized in conjunction with perceptions of being different from peers.[3] This undeniable feeling may be the first internal, emotional revelation of sexual orientation, although it is not likely to be perceived initially as sexual but rather as a strongly experienced sense of not fitting in or of not having the same interests as other boys/girls.

The existence of these early feelings implies that youths have both an awareness of a normative standard of how boys are supposed to act, feel, and behave and a belief that they violate this ideal. Troiden describes this conflation of feeling different and gender inappropriate:

> It is not surprising that "prehomosexuals" used gender metaphors, rather than sexual metaphors, to interpret and explain childhood feelings of difference. . . . Children do not appear to define their sexual experimentation in heterosexual or homosexual terms. The socially created categories of homosexual, heterosex-

ual, and bisexual hold little or no significance for them. (p. 52)

Retrospectively, the gay/bisexual youths interviewed for this book reported three somewhat overlapping sources as a basis for their initial awareness of differentness:

- a pervasive and emotional captivation with other boys that felt passionate, exotic, consuming, and mysterious;
- a strongly felt desire to engage in play activities and to possess traits usually characteristic of girls;
- disinterest or, in more extreme cases, a revulsion in typical boys' activities, especially team sports and rough-and-tumble physical play.[4]

These three sources are not mutually exclusive—many youths recalled instances of all three during their childhood. For example, one youth who felt apart and isolated during his childhood was obsessed with wanting to be around adult men, frequently developed crushes on male teachers, and spent considerable time with neighborhood girls, particularly enjoying their games of hopscotch and jump rope. He was called "sissy" and "girly" by other boys, and he detested team sports and all things athletic, especially locker rooms.

The prevalence of these three is difficult to determine because few researchers have systematically asked boys the relevant questions that probe these issues. It also bears noting that not all gay or bisexual individuals recall this sense of being different during childhood and adolescence and that these feelings and attractions are not solely the domain of sexual-minority youths. Heterosexual boys may also feel different, have same-sex attractions or desires, enjoy feminine activities, and avoid aggressive pursuits.

Youths interviewed for this book easily and at times graphically remembered these same-sex attractions that emanated from their earliest childhood memories. Despite the dramatic significance that these early homoerotic attractions would have, at the time they felt natural, om-

nipresent. Many recalled these attractions to other males by identifying concrete, distinct memories prior to first grade. Without great fanfare, with no clashing of cymbals, and with no abiding shock, later homoerotic attractions were felt to be contiguous with these early feelings.

Captivation with Masculinity

Of the three sources for feeling different, the vast majority of the gay/bisexual youths interviewed for this book attributed to themselves an early sense that in some fundamental way they differed from other boys. This difference was an obsession of always wanting to be near other males. Most boys did not at the time believe that these attractions were sexually motivated; they were just overwhelmed with an all-consuming desire to be with other males. Some became flushed or excited when they made contact, especially physical, with other boys or men; some arranged their lives so as to increase time spent with males, while others avoided males because they were frightened by the male aura. Above all else, their obsession with males was mysterious and pervasive. It was also present from an early age, from first memories.

One youth's childhood was one massive memory of men. He decided that the death of his father ten years earlier was the reason that he would always need guys in his life.

I can remember wanting the men who visited us to hug me when I was real little, maybe three or four. I've always wanted to touch and be touched by guys, and I was a lot. Guys loved to manhandle me. They would throw me up in the air and I'd touch the ceiling and I'd scream and would love it and would do anything to make it happen more and more. It never was enough and I'd tire them out or I'd go to someone else who would toss me. Sometimes I would be teased for the "little points" [erections] in my pants, but no one, including myself, made much of it.

I think I spent my childhood fantasizing about men, not sexually of course, but just being close to them and having them hold me or hug me.

I'd feel safe and warm. My dad gave me this and my older brother Mitchell gave me this but all of this was never enough. With the other men I'd feel flushed, almost hot. Maybe those were hot flashes like what women get! Those were good days.

Although he may have been an extreme case, other youths also recalled distinct attractions to men that a decade or more later were still vivid, emotional, and construed as significant. This obsession with males remained at the time nameless for the following three youths:

I was seven at the time and Will, who was working for us doing yard work, was twenty-one and a college student/athlete. One night when my parents went to a hotel for their anniversary dinner and whatever, they asked Will to stay the night to watch over me. He was in a sleeping bag on the floor and I knew he was nude and he was next to my bed and I kept wondering what was in the sleeping bag. I just knew that I wanted to get in with him but I didn't know why or that I could because I didn't want to bother him. I didn't sleep the whole night.

Maybe it was third grade and there was an ad in the paper about an all-male cast for a movie. This confused me but fascinated—intrigued—me so I asked the librarian and she looked all flustered, even mortified, and mumbled that I ought to ask my parents.

It was very clear to me around six years of age. There was a TV beer commercial which featured several soccer players without shirts on. I mentioned to my brother how much I liked this TV show because the guys didn't have shirts on. I remember this but I'm sure I had thoughts before this.

Those who monopolized their attention were occasionally same-age boys, but were more often older teenagers and adults—male teachers, coaches, cousins, or friends of the family. Public male figures were also sources of fantasies—Superman, Scott Baio, Duran Duran, John Ritter, Bobby Ewing, and Hulk Hogan. Others turned pages in magazines and catalogs to find male models in various stages of undress; especially popular were underwear advertisements. The captivation with men had a familiar tone—a drive for male contact or the male image from an early age with little understanding of what it meant—and a common emotional quality—excitement, euphoria, mystery.

These same-sex attractions were not limited to gay boys. Bisexual youths recalled similar early homoerotic captivation with men.

Technically it could be either male or female, no matter. I just was into naked bodies. I had access and took, without him knowing it, dad's *Penthouse* magazines. Such a big fuss, but actually in them and whatever else I could find, turned on by both the girls and the men. The men I recall most vividly. It was the hairless, feminine guys with big penises and made-up faces. I loved make-up on my guys, the eyelashes and the eyes, blue shadow, but mostly it was the look. Tight jeans, lean bodies.

Homoerotic desires were often interpreted as natural and hence characteristic of all boys. Many youths articulated that their desire for the "male touch" was deeply embodied in their natural self. By this they implied that their attractions to boys were not a matter of choice or free will but were of early and perhaps, they speculated, genetic origins. For example, one youth never felt that he had a choice regarding his intense attractions to adult males:

My infatuation with my day camp counselor I didn't choose. Why him and not his girlfriend? I never chose my love objects but I was always attracted to guys. In all of my early dreams and fantasies I always centered on guys whether they were sexual or not. What I wanted to do was to get close to them and I knew that innately, perhaps even by the age of six or seven. I felt it was okay because God said it was okay.

Similarly, many other youths noted that their homoerotic desires were never a matter of choice but "just were." Most believed that they were gay or bisexual in large part because of genetic factors or the "way the cards were dealt—luck of the draw, like something in the neuro-structure or hormonal."

> I'd dream of my uncle and wake up all euphoric and sweaty and eroticized. Another dream that I had at six was of my [boy] classmates playing around in their underwear with these big cocks sticking out. It just happened. How could I choose these things to dream about, to check out the cocks in my mom's *Playgirl*, and to cut out pictures of guys from movie magazines? I was very intrigued by all of this and knew somehow it related to me.

> Maybe my child sex play taught me how to be gay but then maybe it only reinforced what already was. I know that I've been gay for a long time, probably I was born with it. I assumed when I was young that all people had a pee pee. It doesn't have to be genetic but then it could happen during the first year of life. I think I was born being gay, leaning toward homosexuality, and development just sort of pushed it further.

> My brother is gay, my uncle is gay, my father acts like he is gay sometimes, and my mother is hanging out with feminist support groups and really butch-looking women. Did I really have a choice?!

> I can't stand the smell of women. Who really cares? I could have gone straight but it would have been torture. I am what I am, from birth.

Some youths simply assumed, based on the egocentric principle that their thoughts and feelings were shared by others, that all boys must feel as they do but were simply not talking about their desires. With age, however, they came to realize that perhaps they were more "into it."

> I guess I was pretty touchable—and I still am based on what guys I know or am with tell me. I didn't understand why because I thought all kids liked it. Others have told me that they liked it too but somehow I think I liked it more. I craved and adored it and my day would not be a good one unless I had this contact. Only later did I find out why I liked being touched by guys.

Another youth decided that he would simply "outgrow" his obsession with males. He was not, however, going to let this future keep him from enjoying this wonderful pleasure at the moment.

> As a child I knew I was attracted to males. I was caught by my mother looking at nude photographs of men in her magazines and I heard my father say to her that, "He'll grow out of it," and so I thought and hoped I would. But until then I just settled back and enjoyed my keen curiosity to see male bodies.

> You see, it did not feel threatening because (a) it felt great, and (b) father said I would grow out of it, and he was always right. So why not enjoy it until it went away?

Other youths, however, recognized that these undeniably homoerotic attractions were not typical of other boys. They knew they were extreme cases but they "could not help it."

> Even at eight I could tell that my interest in guys was way beyond normal. Like this time that we were out with my friend Chad's big brother catching fireflies and he took off his shirt and I forgot about the fireflies and just stared at his chest. Chad got really irritated and called out, "Hey homo give me the jar!" I'm sure I blushed.

> When we played truth-or-dare I always wanted to be dared to kiss one of the guys. No one ever dared me to do that, probably because they knew that I'd like it. And I would have! I knew it was strange of me and that they didn't want to kiss boys. They all knew that too but I really didn't care.

Eventually, most youths understood that these undeniable attractions were the wrong ones to have. Despite the belief that they had no choice in matters of their attractions, most inevitably came to appreciate that they should hide their attractions. Snide remarks made by peers, prohibitions taught by parents, and the silence imposed by religion and by teachers all contributed to this realization. Thus, although early obsessions with males were experienced as instinctive, most of the gay/bisexual youths acknowledged from an early age that their impulses were somehow "wrong" but not necessarily "bad."

Despite the presence of an older gay brother, one youth was vulnerable to society's negative messages about homosexuality. His concern centered on being "strike two" for his mother.

> Well, I knew enough to hide Sean's *Jock* after I looked at it. It was not guilt—it was too much fun!—but fear that I felt. I was afraid if mother found out that she would feel bad that she had two failures and that Sean would kill me for getting into his stockpile.

Very few youths made the connection during their childhood that these attractions that felt so natural and significant placed them in the stigmatized category of "homosexual." Although most had a passing acquaintance with the concept and had seen "homosexuals" displayed in the media, relatively few would have situated themselves in this category at this point in their lives. One youth believed that "it" was something to be outgrown: "I thought maybe that it was just a stage that I was going through. But if it wasn't a stage then it was probably no problem for me to worry about now." Other youths, however, were worried.

> Something was different about me. I knew that. I was afraid of what it meant, and I prayed to God that whatever it was that He would take it away. It was a burden but I liked it, and so I felt guilty about liking it.

It was not until many years later, with the onset of sexual maturations that these attractions would be fully linked with sexuality and perhaps a sexual identity. Homosensuality for these youths was not foreign but natural, a lifelong intrigue with men's bodies. However, as the societal wrongness of their intuitive obsession with masculinity became increasingly apparent, many youths hoped that their attractions were a phase to be outgrown or that their feelings would make sense in some distant future.

The feared repercussions from family members and peers if they were known to have gay traits served as a powerful reason for the boys to feel that their same-sex desires and acts were improper and should not be shared with others. Acting on them was thought to be wrong because if caught, punishment would likely ensue. Balancing desire and fear became a significant dilemma. Eventually, many of the youths recognized that others rarely shared or understood their same-sex desires. This pact of secrecy with themselves was a major theme for many of the youths. It did not, however, always inhibit their sexual behavior; a significant number of the boys acted on their sexual desires during childhood. . . .

Acting Like a Girl

A second source of feeling different, not explicitly linked with same-sex attractions, involved cultural definitions of gender—how a boy should *not* act, think, and feel. Characteristics deemed not appropriate for boys included observable behaviors such as play with girl-typed toys, especially dolls; involvement in female activities and games; cross-dressing; sex-role motor behavior including limp wrists, high-pitched voices, and dramatic gestures; and stated interests such as wishing to be a girl, imagining self as dancer or model, and preferring female friends and being around older women. These boys did not wonder, "Why am I gay?" but "Why do I act like a girl?"[5] For example, one youth recalled his childhood in the following way:

> I knew that a boy wasn't supposed to kiss other boys, although I did. I knew it was wrong, so this must be some indication that I knew. I also knew that I wasn't supposed to cross my legs at the knees, but I wouldn't like quickly uncross my legs whenever that was the case. So this is certainly at a young age that I noticed this. I think I knew that it was sort of a female thing, sort of an odd thing, and I knew that boys weren't supposed to do that.

Many boys who fit the category of gender bending were at once erotically drawn to boys and men (the first source) but were repelled by their behavior, their standard of dress and cleanliness, and their barbarian nature. They felt ambivalent regarding their attractions to males; intrigued by male bodies and the masculinity mystique, these youths saw men as enigmatic and unapproachable.

Psychotherapist Richard Isay characterizes this sense of gender atypicality in some pregay boys: "They saw themselves as more sensitive than other boys; they cried more easily, had their feelings more readily hurt, had more aesthetic interests, enjoyed nature, art, and music, and were drawn to other 'sensitive' boys, girls, and adults" (p. 23).[6] Indeed, research amply demonstrates that gender nonconformity is one of the best childhood predictors of adult homosexuality in men.[7] Findings from prospective studies are fairly straightforward: The proportion of *extremely* feminine boys who eventually profess a same-sex sexual orientation approaches 100 percent. However, the fraction of these gender-nonconforming boys in the total population remains considerably below that of gay men. Thus, while the vast majority of extremely feminine boys eventually adopt a gay or bisexual identity in adulthood, so do an unknown number of boys who are not particularly feminine.

Feeling more similar to girls than to boys, one youth described his experience "as if I was from a different planet than other boys." He was not alone; a substantial proportion of the gay/bisexual youths recalled that this "girl-like syndrome" was the basis of how they differed from their male peers. Of all boys interviewed, over one-third described their self-image as being more similar to that of girls than boys, and nearly all of these boys reported that this sense of themselves permeated areas of their lives.

One consequence of having more culturally defined feminine than masculine interests was that many boys with gender-atypical characteristics felt most comfortable in the company of girls and women or preferred spending time alone. Two youths described their gender nonconformity during their childhood years.

> I had mostly friends who were girls and I can remember playing jump rope, dolls, and hopscotch with them, and I can remember being very interested in hairstyling and practicing on dolls. I got into sewing and knitting. I played make-believe, read spy and adventure stories, house with my sisters. I had a purse and dolls that they gave me. We did everything together. I was never close with my brother and we never did anything together. I was always accepted by girls and few other boys were.

> Thinking back I did play with girls in the neighborhood a lot. I loved actually to kiss girls and I was always wanting to kiss girls and I thought this might be a little strange or weird because I liked girls so much at such a young age. I just felt very comfortable with them. I felt more self-conscious around boys because I always wondered what they were thinking about.

The extent to which such behavior could produce a gender-bender who is accepted by girls as one of them is illustrated by a third youth:

> I was even invited to slumber parties and I always went. They were so much fun! Just the five of us in our gowns, with lace and bows that my mom had made for my sister and I "borrowed," laughing, sneaking cigarettes, and gossiping about other girls.

Thus, almost without exception boys who displayed early gender-atypical behavior strongly preferred hanging out with girls rather than with boys. Girls were far less likely to reject the "feminine" boys, a reaction that has been confirmed by research studies.[8] If such youths had male friends it was usually one best friend, perhaps a neighbor who also disliked masculine activities.

> I have always been gay although I did not know what that meant at the time. But I knew that I always felt queer, out of place in my hometown. . . . Mostly I spent my time alone in the

house or with girls at school. We ate lunch together and talked in between classes. I always felt that girls received the short end of the stick. I really did not have many friends because I lived in a rural area. I felt rejected and I feared being rejected.

I have usually had one best male friend, who might change every other year or so but who always was like me in hating sports. Like Tim who was one of my best friends because he lived across the street and was handy, someone so I would not be alone. We spent time together but I am not sure what else we ever did. Otherwise I hung with girls.

Not uncommonly, boys who displayed interest in gender-atypical pursuits fervently expressed strong preferences for solo activities such as reading and make-believe games, or for artistic endeavors.

But my major activity during childhood was drawing and I was sort of known as "The Artist," even as early as third and fourth grades. Today I can see some very gay themes in my drawings! Whenever anyone in the class wanted anything drawn then they asked me. No matter how much they had ridiculed me I agreed to do it.

A second youth made up plays for the neighborhood, role-played TV characters, and cartooned.

I took part in dance, ballet, singing, and had good manners. I liked Broadway musicals, Barbra, Bette, Joan, Liz, Judy, and Greta. . . . I did drama, lots and lots of drama! Anything pretend. I did lots of skits for the Mickey Mouse Club, play writing, and office decorating.

Unclear from these accounts is whether the decision to spend time alone was one freely chosen by the gay/bisexual youths or was a consequence of exclusion dictated by others. That is, were they loners by choice or by circumstance? Although most evidence supports the banishment hypothesis, time alone may have been desired and pursued for creative reasons; time alone may have enhanced their creative efforts. One youth found

that he spent a lot of time "doing nothing, just being alone, playing the violin, planting flowers, and arranging flowers." Another youth loved "building and creating things like castles and bridges and rivers in the backyard. Maybe it was because I was an only child but I was into any kind of art and I also composed on the piano." When asked about his childhood activities, a third youth was merely succinct: "Shopped. Homework. Masturbated. Read."

Most difficult for many gender-atypical gay/bisexual boys was the almost universal harassment they received from their peers. As a consequence of associating with girls and not boys, spending considerable time alone, and appreciating female activities, they faced almost daily harassment from peers, usually boys but sometimes girls, teachers, parents, and siblings. Perhaps most insufferable to their male peers was the gay/bisexual boys' feminine gross and fine motor behavior. Their hand gestures, standing and sitting posture, leg and hip movement, voice pitch and cadence, and head tilt conveyed to others that these boys were girllike and hence weak and deplorable. The reactions they received from peers went beyond mere teasing, which most youths receive during childhood and adolescence as a mechanism for social bonding, to outright verbal abuse that was harassing and sometimes extremely destructive to a sense of self. The abuse was occasionally physically expressed and always had emotional and self-image consequences.

Below is a list of names that boys with gender-atypical characteristics reported that they were called by age mates. Not all youths recalled or wanted to remember the exact names.

• sissy	• clumsy	• bitchy	• fag
• queer	• little girl	• super fem	• queer bait
• gayson	• faggot	• fruit	• gay
• fruitcake	• wimpy	• gaylord	• Janus
• schoolboy	• pansy	• girl	• fag boy
• fairy	• softy	• cocksucker	• lisp
• girly	• homo	• Avon Lady	• Safety
• wimp	• gay guy	• mommy's	Girl
• Tinkerbell	• flamer	boy	

One youth reported that in grammar school he was voted "The Person Most Likely to Own a Gay Bar."

The specific provocation that elicited these names during school, on the bus, and in the neighborhood varied, but several patterns are discernible. The abuse usually occurred because a boy was perceived as a misfit, as acting too much "like a girl." Three youths provided testimonies from their lives:

> Because I was somewhat effeminate in my behavior and because I wore "girly" shoes. Some said that I was a little girl because I couldn't play baseball. I played the clarinet in school and this was defined as a female instrument so I got some teasing for that. I thought I could control my behavior but it got so bad that my family decided to pull me out of the public school to go to a private Catholic school where the teasing receded.

> Because I was weak and a cry baby. I was not in the "in" crowd. Also because of the way I dressed and that I got good grades. I was very thin and got every disease that came around. I had all sorts of allergies and was always using all sorts of drugs. I was told I looked like a girl. I played with Barbies and taught her how to sit up and later how to fly. I just wasn't masculine enough I guess.

> People thought that perhaps I might be gay because they thought I was just way too nice and also because I was flamboyant. They really didn't think I was like homosexually gay. It was just a term they used for me because it seemed to fit my personality. People said I'm gay because of my mannerisms, also because I slur my s's and I'm so flamboyant. I think it's the way that I walked, the way I talked, the way I carried myself. I had a soft voice. Lots of boys blew me kisses. My voice is just not masculine. Also I tended to be very giggly and flighty and flaky and silly at times.

One youth believed that "most kids were just looking for a laugh" and that he was the easiest target, because of his femininity, they could find. He was their "amusement for the day."

In no story were girls the only ones who verbally abused a youth for being gender nonconforming. On many occasions, however, boys acted alone. Perhaps the most usual pattern was for boys, or a subset of boys, to be the persistent ridiculers with a few girls chiming in when present.

> Some of the jocks really bothered me but mostly it was these three guys every day making my life miserable. Always done by males who really had this pecking order. Real bullies!

> This was mostly males—this one guy seemed to have it out for me. But some of the girls who hung out with him also did it. The girls thought I was bitchy and called me "fag" and "homo."

Although reactions to being victimized by peer ridicule were diverse, the most common responses, illustrated by three youths, were to ignore, withdraw, or cry.

> I took it without saying anything back. I'd pretend that I didn't hear them or hide my feelings. I hated it but didn't say anything back. Guess I was benign to it. Just sat there and took it. I did that for protection. I was so much of a misfit that bullies did it to me. I offended them in some way. Just a horrible, wrenching experience.

> I became more withdrawn and thus more of an outcast. I'd cower and keep my distance, keeping it inside myself. I did nothing or remained silent or said "leave me alone." Once I fought back and lost, which made me withdraw even more.

> I was very, very sensitive and would cry very easily. I had very little emotional control at the time. Cry, yell at them, cry some more. I would tell my mother and cry and she'd try to comfort me or she'd just dismiss it all. I would tell the guys that I had told my mother and they would make more fun of me.

Not all boys reacted so passively to the verbal assault. Several developed innovative, self-enhancing ways to cope with peer harassment. For example, one youth noted an unusual situation:

All my boyfriends, the jock types, always protected me and punished those who teased me. I would just turn away as if I never gave notice because I knew that I would be protected by all the guys, the jocks, that I was having sex with. I never did try to get back at them [the harassers]. Once they realized this then they kept quiet.

Another used his intelligence and experience as strategies for coping with peer harassment.

I think it was because I was so flamboyant and I was not so sports-oriented. If they said it to my face then I would say "get out of my face!" Or I would point out their stupidity. I considered them to be rather stupid, so immature. I'd been around the world and I knew I could say things that would damage them because I was smarter than them and because I had so many female friends. I tried to ignore it because I knew that I was better than them. I sort of got respect for not fighting back or sometimes I would say, "I like girls! What's *your* problem?"

It is difficult to ascertain the true impact on a youth of this constant bombardment of negative peer review. Few of the boys thought it was anything but negative. Most felt that the most significant effect of the verbal harassment was what it did to their personality: They became increasingly withdrawn from social interactions, despondent, and self-absorbed. The aftermath for the four youths below was a decrease in their self-image and self-worth.

I felt very conscious about my voice and somewhat shameful that I wasn't masculine enough. I actually just sort of retreated more and became more introverted. I felt rejected and it hurt my self-esteem. I took the ridicule to heart and I blamed myself.

Because I knew that indeed I had the attractions to guys I knew that they were right and that I was a disgusting human being. I just spent a lot more time alone to avoid the pain. I just sort of blocked it all internally because it hurt so much. I just sort of erased all my memories

of my childhood so I can't give you much detail.

A real nightmare! I really felt like I had no friends. It really did lower my self-esteem and it made me focus on sort of my outer appearance and ignore the inner. It devastated me because I felt everything they said was true. I was quiet and kept it inside.

Heightened my sense of being different. Caused me to withdraw and not feel good about myself. Cut off from people and became shy. Became introverted, guilty. I hated that time. Childhood was supposed to be happy times but it was not. Later, I dropped out of school, thought about suicide, and ran away from home.

Although none of the boys felt that the labeling made him gay, many believed that the name-calling contributed to their negative image of homosexuality. Hence, the ridicule became a central factor in who they are. The abuse also kept them in the closet for a considerably longer period of time. These effects are apparent in the two narratives below:

It just sort of reinforced that men are scum. I viewed being a fag as so negative that it hurt my self-image for them to call me that. I didn't like myself, so being gay is bad and what they're saying I knew it to be true because I am bad and being gay is bad and I'm gay. It's made me think of males only as sex objects because I wanted to be hated by men because I didn't like myself. I started back in elementary school to believe it was true.

I had such a hostile view towards homosexuality, so it was hard to come out as a result of this stigma because I had really low self-esteem. It affected me by not having a positive attitude about homosexuality in general. I needed at least a positive or even neutral point of view and that would have made my gay life so much easier. I continue to suppress things.

It was the rare youth for whom anything positive emerged from the verbal ridicule. One youth noted that "teasing sort of helped me to deal with my gay identity at a very early age because everyone was calling my attention to it." He was proud to be effeminate; he reported that the teasing made him stronger and was thus beneficial.

> I wore stylish clothes and was my own individual self. My teachers appreciated this but not the slobs. Because of this a lot of them said that I was gay and so I thought I must be, although I did not know what this meant except that it meant I would not be shoveling cow shit!

Unfortunately, few youths could recall such positive aspects to their gender atypicality. More often, the consequences of being true to their nature were that other boys viewed them as undesirable playmates and as "weird." Labeled sissy or effeminate, they were rejected by boys, and, equally important, they had little desire to fraternize with their male peers. Because other boys did not constitute an enjoyable or safe context for play or socializing, the youths often turned to girls for activities and consolation. They preferred to dance rather than shovel shit, to sing rather than yell "hike," and to draw rather than bash heads. Thus, childhood was usually experienced as a traumatizing time by youths who did not conform to cultural sex roles. The fortunate ones sought and found girls for solace and support. Girls became their saviors, offering sources of emotional sustenance as the male world of childhood became increasingly distasteful. It was to these girls that many gay/bisexual males subsequently disclosed their sexual affiliations during middle or late adolescence. . .

Not Acting Like a Boy

A third source of feeling different among the interviewed youths originated from a disinterest or abhorrence of typical masculine activities, which may or may not have occurred in the presence of a captivation with masculinity (first source) or of high levels of femininity (second source). Thus, a lack of masculinity did not necessarily imply that such youths were fond of female activities or were drawn to or hung out with girls. Many reported never playing house, dressing up as a girl,

or having a passing acquaintance with Barbie. In the absence of typical expressions of femininity, boys without masculine interests were usually loners or spent time with one or several best male friends.

Compared with what is known about gender-atypical boys, considerably less is known concerning those who during childhood do not fit cultural images of how a boy should act, think, and feel. Characteristics labeled as unmasculine or as failure to conform to gender expectations include observable behaviors such as avoidance of rough-and-tumble play, typical boys' games, and athletic activities; no imagining of oneself as a sports figure; and no desire to grow up to be like one's father. These boys did not wonder, "Why am I gay?" but "Why don't I act like a boy?"[9]

Childhood activities that constitute "unmasculine" all share the characteristic of being gender neutral by North American standards, suitable for both boys and girls. Within this gender non-partisanship, active and passive patterns were evident in the interviews. Some boys were as active as masculine-inclined peers but in nonmasculine, nonathletic—at least in a team sports sense—activities.

> My friend and me made roads and gardens. I liked to sort of build cities and bridges outside and in the garden. Played in the woods, hiked in the woods, camped out, and hide and seek. Ted and I were almost inseparable for a couple of years. I also biked, swam a lot, jumped on the trampoline. Biking was my way of dealing with stress. I was into matchbox cars.

> I enjoyed playing office, playing grow-up, walking around the city basically looking at other people. Mind games and chess with my brothers. Creative imaginative play. Discovering and enjoying spending a lot of time on bike trips, going to new places. Getting out of the house and being outside, just wandering off by myself.

More common were boys who spent considerable time alone pursuing passive activities. This passivity should not be equated, however, with having a bad time or having a bad childhood.

Many recalled an enjoyable if unconventional life during childhood.

> At school I hung out with myself but on weekends it was primarily guys in the neighborhood and we would like watch TV and videos. They were like my best friends and we were not really into moving sports. We were more into passive activities like music and cards. I've always been in the band. Hanging out at the mall. A couple of us guys would do this.

> Very quiet pursuits, stamps, cooking, which my mother liked. Guess I played verbal games, board games with the family, Risk and Candyland, and crossword puzzles. Did a lot with my family, like family vacations, visiting historical things. I read, played with Lincoln Logs, fantasizing, spending time by myself, drawing, and swinging. I loved the freedom of the swing and I'd do it for hours. Oh yes, I loved croquet!

> I read a lot—like the encyclopedia, the phone book, science fiction, science, mystery, and gothic novels. I had a comic book collection and Star Wars cards. I spent most of my other time drawing maps. I was really into getting any information anywhere I could, even from the atlas or an almanac. I can remember actually setting out to read the dictionary, although I don't think I got very far. Almost every book in the public library later on.

Most explicitly, unmasculine youths felt particularly ill at ease with archetypal male sports, especially loathing team sports such as baseball, basketball, and football. If they became involved in competitive, aggressive sports it was in response to family or peer pressure. Perhaps forced by a father or coach to participate in sports as a right fielder, a defensive back, or a bench warmer, they deeply resented such coercion and their inevitable failure. Severely repulsed by many typical masculine pursuits, this source of trauma was to be avoided at all costs, even at the price of disappointing parents. Unmasculine youths often shared with the following very gender-atypical youth his rejection of masculine activities and hence of masculinity.

> I did not play basketball or wrestle and I was not a farmer nor a slob nor did I shovel cow shit like my classmates. Girl, they would come in smelling like they looked and you can be sure it was not a number Chanel ever heard of! There was no way that I was going to let this be a part of what I wanted for my life.

> Well they [parents] wanted me to try at least one sport but I was always sort of the last chosen. I knew I was effeminate and clumsy and my father ridiculed me for it. So I avoided sports and I did this by going home for lunch and visiting my female friends rather than playing sports with the other guys during recess.

For one youth, the appeal or even logic of sports baffled and befuddled him.

> I really did not care about most sports and I still do not. I liked more intellectual than physical things. I enjoyed more talking philosophy, writing poetry, and drawing than spending time throwing stupid balls away, then running after the stupid balls, trying to find the stupid balls, and then throwing the stupid balls back to the same person so that he could throw it away again and have somebody run after it, find it, and throw it back to him again. Sounds real intelligent does it not?! Doing these stupid ball tricks made Bill [twin brother] real popular and me really unpopular. Where is the fairness in that?

> I only played sports during recess when I had to. I hated little boy games such as basketball, kickball, football, baseball, or anything that had a ball or a peck order. It was very aggressive and used all of the wrong parts of my anatomy and my personality.

The most aversive aspect of sports was its aggressive, dominant, physical nature. One youth remarked that in sports someone always has to lose—"and it was usually me!" This reflected not only his own personal experience of losing but also an antipathy to his life philosophy of peace, harmony, cooperation. Another youth astutely recognized another reason not to become involved in sports—his true nature might emerge and become figuratively and physically visible.

I was not on any team sport because I was so self-conscious about being around other males. I was afraid of how I might be looked upon by them and what I might do or say or look at if I was around them a lot. What would I do in the locker room? What would happen to "George," who has a mind of his own? Maybe my feelings might come out and then where would I be?

Other youths reported that they wanted to participate in sports but could not because of physical problems. One noted, "I could never much be a sports person because I had a coordination problem because of my vision that caused me to be physically awkward." Another compensated by reading about sports: "Well, I read the sports pages and sports books! I hated gym because I was overweight. I could not do sports because I felt so evil watching men strip naked in the locker room and I couldn't take it." A third youth was on the swim team before getting pneumonia, forcing him to quit. His restitution was to remain active: "I hung out at the beach (yes, looking at the guys!), played Atari, skateboarded, and played Pogo."

Those who became involved in sports almost preferred individual to team sports. These "jocks" included the two youths below.

Some track, cross-country, swimming. I never liked the team sports. I had to do soccer in fourth grade because my best friends were into it but I disliked it immensely. Guess I was mid-level in ability and lower than that in interest but it gave me something to do and kept me around guys. I lived in a very sex-segregated rural area. I gave all of these up in junior high, except swimming in the Scout pool.

I was really into sports. Let's see. Gymnastics in fourth to sixth grades; bowling in third; darts in third; ping pong whenever; dodge the ball in second to fourth; volleyball in sixth.

Perhaps because of their paltry athleticism and low levels of masculine interests, these boys were not immune to peer ridicule and teasing. They were not, however, ridiculed nearly to the degree that gender-nonconforming boys were. They were often teased for non-gender-related characteristics or for individualized perceived deficits in physical features ("fatty"), in normative masculine behavior ("wimp"), or in desirable kinds of intelligence ("nerd"). Some were also called names more typical of effeminate youths ("fag") without, they almost universally acknowledged, the connotation of sexuality. One youth defended himself by asserting, "Being called a fag really was not a sexual thing. It was more that it reflected on my low self-esteem and that I was so wimpy."

The most common name callers were same-age, same-sex peers, although occasionally girls also participated. One youth had an unusual experience. Called "nerd" by three girls who were making his life miserable, "several boys seemed to go out of their way to protect me and shield me from this kind of teasing. Of course I was giving them answers on their exams!" Otherwise he simply withdrew. Because ridicule was seemingly random and seldom daily, it was sometimes difficult for unmasculine youths to understand what provoked the name calling.

One youth reported that he enjoyed his life as a loner and that others seemed more upset than he was that he was spending so much time alone. With his involvement in computers, the complaints lessened, perhaps, he guessed, because others envied his knowledge and saw it as a means to earn a good living. He was subject, however, to the taunts of male peers. Occasionally he was ridiculed by several boys on the school bus and during recess for reasons that were beyond his control.

At first I didn't understand why they were on my case, but since I didn't fit in in a lot of ways, they had their way. It was just the usual thing. Probably because I wasn't good at sports but I can't remember what I was called. In gym classes primarily by macho males. Nothing I didn't want to remember. I really can't remember too much of it or certainly not the names. It just seemed like I was teased about as much as anyone else was. Not every day, maybe once a month, and I just sort of reacted passively. Never really a major thing or very threatening, just sort of stupid kids' stuff. Just sort of let it go away.

I didn't fit in because I was against the intellectualism of the smart kids and I wasn't a jock. Hence I was not respected. I have no real memories of the exact names but I think they weren't happy ones because I was thin and, oh yes, my ears stuck out so I was called "monkey face."

The name-calling message might be that the boy was too feminine or not masculine enough, but more commonly it was because he was simply different or had undesirable characteristics. Very few felt that being gay was a cause of the verbal abuse. The following youths recounted the reasons they believed they suffered at the hands of their peers.

I was awkward and wore glasses. I had a speech impediment and a birthmark. I was ostracized, sort of left out because I wasn't conforming and I was very shy. I was sort of known as an only child and thus a spoiled brat with very little social skills. I was never teased about being gay.

For being fat and overweight. Maybe I was teased more than average. It did hurt. I reacted by just crying because I really couldn't ignore it. It was a weight issue and not a sexual identity issue.

Because I was quiet, shy, and geekish. For being physically awkward, being different, bookish. As a kid I was teased for having cow eyes because my eyes were large. For not going to church. Very low-class assholes, mostly males. Then I went to a school for gifted children and it stopped.

I was ridiculed about being a softy and brain box because I was so intellectual or consumed in the books. They said I got good grades because I was kissing teachers' asses. I think I was just different from all of them and the teachers liked me because I liked learning. Perhaps it happened because I went to an all-male Catholic school.

I was shy and I got called Spock a lot because of my eyes which were real dark. They thought I was wearing eye shadow.

The most common response of the youths was to remain silent. One youth felt scared and frightened but "later it just got to be an annoyance. My response was to remain rather stoic." Another hated gym because he was not "graceful" and because of a particular nemesis.

A classic case of one guy on my case which I usually ignored. But one day he threw me to the gym floor but a guy came to my rescue. He was bigger than me so my reaction was basically to brave it, to try to show that it did not affect me by just walking away. I would usually not talk back and I would not cry.

A second common response was to simply avoid situations where one might be ridiculed. This was not always an easy task.

Being not good at sports, I tried to avoid all sporting situations if at all possible. I just felt like I was left out of everything. I sort of internalized it but I can't really remember how I reacted. I dreaded going to the gym. I was afraid and felt that I was bullied. I was not verbally equipped to deal with this kind of teasing. I really didn't fight back until high school.

A third response, somewhat less prevalent, was to feel extremely hurt and cry, either publicly or in private. One youth grew to hate and fear school. "It was very painful and I was upset by it and I cried. In fact, so much so I didn't want to go to school." Another cried in private.

I was teased for being very heavy and for being slow. I reacted by being very hurt; I couldn't accept it. I cried a lot, not in front of them but in the bathroom or my room. My out was always, "Well, I'm smart."

Finally, several youths reported that they surprised their tormentors by behaving in a very masculine way, fighting back against the name-calling.

I rode the bus. I felt singled out and ridiculed. Initially what I did was simply relax and ignore it but then at one point I actually fought back, physically and verbally attacking sort of the main person who was ridiculing me the most. If I did fight back, which was the case occasionally, I would usually win. Because it was a small school, the word got out and after that I had no problems. I gained in popularity and the teasing tapered off to almost nothing.

There were rumors about me being gay. I got teasing when my friend told others that we had slept together. I confronted these people but it didn't help. I ended up going back at others or attacking them. I confronted them, "Why are you so interested in my sexuality?" After awhile they left me alone. I denied being gay but I knew I was. I wasn't ashamed but I wanted the ridiculing to stop. I was very wicked to others.

The immediate effects of the ridicule are difficult to determine. However, based on their reports, consequences appear far less severe than they were for youths who enacted femininity, perhaps because the ridicule was not as frequent and did not focus on a central aspect of their sexuality. For example, one youth noted that the name-calling had no repercussion on his sexuality because he did not interpret the ridicule as emanating from his unconventional sexuality. He did not feel that the abuse made him gay or caused him to delay self-identifying as gay. He felt, however, that the ridicule contributed to this tendency to withdraw from social settings, causing him to be more introverted and self-effacing.

It had no real implications for my sexual identification. Everybody in my school was teased; everyone was called faggot, so I really didn't feel like I was singled out. But it made me trust people less. Hurt my self-esteem. I still need to be liked by others and if not, it upsets me. Maybe why I spent so much time alone. People hurt you. On the good side, I developed good sarcastic skills and a dry wit.

Including those who had many feminine characteristics during childhood, as many as three-quarters of the gay/bisexual youths interviewed had few interests or characteristics usually attributed to men in North American culture. Being *neither* particularly masculine *nor* feminine resulted in youths occupying the middle rung of the peer-group status hierarchy. When not alone, they were usually with a best buddy or a small group of male friends with whom they spend considerable time. Although they were seldom as frequently ridiculed by peers as were youths who were gender atypical in their lifestyle, such youths still faced verbal abuse, usually from same-age boys. The personal characteristics that became targets of abuse were notably analogous to those that heterosexual boys also receive teasing about if they are "unconventional": physical features, personality characteristics, and intelligence. Similar to other gay/bisexual youths, however, most recalled early, intense, natural attractions to other boys and men.

Acting Like a Boy

Not all of the gay/bisexual boys felt different from peers, acted in gender-atypical ways, expressed effeminate gestures and postures, or disliked team sports during their childhood. One in ten was masculine in appearance, behavior, and interests—nearly indistinguishable from their childhood masculine heterosexual peers. Although these relatively rare boys recalled, in retrospect, that they might have had "nonsexual" attractions to males during early childhood, they had few memories of *sexual* attractions to girls, boys, or anything else. Now, however, they believe that their same-sex attractions have always been a natural part of who they are.

Many of these youths reminisced that as children they chased girls, but this was more of a game that they joined with other boys than a statement about their sexuality or their true sexual interests. As adolescents they were simply disinterested in sexual relations with girls, in being emotionally intimate with girls, or in developing romantic relationships with girls. Most never fantasized about girls. The gay youths with masculine characteristics often had difficulty articulating precisely what it was about sexuality that excited them. Many failed to recall any prepubertal sexual or erotic attractions; thus, in some respects, they appeared to be asexual, especially during the years preceding adolescence. One youth reported "a vague sense that although I did not desire intimate relations with girls, I was not sure what I wanted." Unsure of how they "became gay," the youths characterized their life before puberty as "sexless" and as deeply invested in masculine activities, especially sports.

One youth, who would later run track and play high-school baseball and football, remembered his childhood as his "glory years." Girls were not an integral part of his life.

> As a child I used to run a lot, just everywhere I could, and play tag, swimming, kickball, and softball. Loved making forts. Building blocks, Legos, war games. Just like my best buddy, which changed from time to time, well at least every year I would develop a best buddy, and it was always the best looking guy in my class who was my best friend—always an athlete. I hung around totally guys.

> Maybe I just did not have time but I was not into sex. I would have to say that I was sexless because I cannot remember any sexual thoughts. I was not interested in girls even though I had several girlfriends. In general I felt left out of what my teammates said they were going through.

When asked during the interview to elaborate *any* aspect of his childhood sexuality, he drew a blank. He had many stories of athletic exploits but no sexual ones. Years after pubertal onset he discovered his sexuality and expressed wonderment regarding the location of his sexual desires during childhood.

Similar to this youth, others appeared in most respects to be the traditional, heterosexual boy next door. This was especially evident in their play activities and partners. They enjoyed their popularity with other boys, and they often developed a best friendship with another boy, usually a teammate on a sports team. One swimmer noted that the time he spent "with Jared and the other guys on the swim team was the happiest time of my life."

The sports acumen of these youths was equal or superior to many of their heterosexual peers. However, a distinct bias existed in terms of liking and participating in individual rather than team sports. While many played competitive team sports, their participation appeared more obligatory as an important aspect of male culture than a real choice. Their true love was more apparent in individual sports, especially swimming, track, tennis, and wrestling. Similar to other gay/bisexual youths, many disliked the aggressive, competitive nature of team sports.

> For Dad I did baseball—and it wasn't that I was bad, because I made the team and started—but I just couldn't get into it. Like I refused to slide because I was afraid I'd hurt the other guy, and I was just not going to go crashing into fences to catch a ball! I didn't like being challenged at sports because I was afraid I wasn't good enough so I went into individual sports like tennis, track, and swimming. Dad and I reached a compromise with my track, especially when I won the state 1000M.

> As a child I really liked horseplay, tag, and wrestling. I have to admit that I hated the Little League but as a kid I played Little League for five years, usually at second base. Later tennis, two years of which were on varsity and I lettered. Also track and lifted weights. I was accepted by everyone, but the baseball guys who were so cutthroat; every game was the end of the universe for them!

As a result of their peer status, few of these boys were teased by others. When they were, it was usually within the context of normative male bonding—teasing in good humor. Although relatively few heard references to being gay, they nonetheless dreaded such accusations. One youth feared that his friends would notice his head turning when a good-looking guy passed by.

In contrast to the gay/bisexual youths previously discussed, masculine youths by disposition looked and acted like other boys their age, participated in typical masculine pursuits, and "fooled" peers into believing that they were heterosexual. They claimed no memories of homoerotic or even sexual attractions during childhood, perhaps, one might speculate, because the realization that the true objects of their sexual desires were boys would have caused them considerable grief and confusion. They were often perceived to be social butterflies and they actively engaged in male–male competitive sports, although their preference was individual sports. Their male friendships were critical to maintain; they wanted and needed to be members of the "male crowd." From all appearances they succeeded in creating a facade of heterosexuality, in being accepted as "one of the guys."

Reflections on the Childhood of Gay/Bisexual Youths

From an early age, the vast majority of the gay/bisexual youths believed that they were different from other boys their age and that regardless of the source of this feeling, it was a natural, instinctual, and omnipresent aspect of themselves. The pattern that most characterized the youths' awareness, interpretation, and affective responses to childhood attractions consisted of an overwhelming desire to be in the company of men. They wanted to touch, smell, see, and hear masculinity. This awareness originated from earliest childhood memories; in this sense, they "always felt gay."

Most ultimately recognized, however, that these feelings were not typical of other boys and that it would be wrong or unwise to express them because of family and peer prohibitions. Others simply assumed that all boys felt as they did and could not understand why their friends were not as preoccupied as they were with homoerotic desires. Although these attractions may have felt natural, the youths were told by parents, friends, religious leaders, teachers, and dogma that such desires were evil and sinful. Many knew that their homosensuality was ill-advised, but they did not thus conclude that it made them sick or immoral.

Beyond this common pattern, two other sources of "feeling different" characterized the vast majority of the gay/bisexual youths. Many were dominated by an overwhelming sense that their difference was attributed to their feminine appearance, behavior, and interests. In many respects these characteristics typify the stereotype that many, gay and nongay alike, have of gay males. Youths so feminized felt natural and true to self, despite the fact that their gender noncomformity was frequently and severely punished with ostracism. Most of these youths detested cultural definitions of masculinity and felt at odds with other boys because they did not share their peers' interest in team sports, competition, and aggressive pursuits. Being an outcast in the world of male peers was usually felt to be unfair and unnecessary, but also inevitable. To avoid becoming expatriated, these boys developed friendships with girls, perhaps because of common interests such as attractions to boys and appreciation of the arts, creativity, clothing, and manners. They felt more comfortable and had greater comradery with girls than with boys. Few wanted to change either their genitalia or their behavior; they did not view themselves as women in disguise—they were simply repulsed by the "grossness" of masculinity and attracted to the sensitivities of femininity.

Other youths failed to duplicate standard masculine characteristics without necessarily assuming feminine traits. In this they may well have resembled heterosexual peers who were also neither particularly masculine nor feminine in behavior. They differed, however, in the direction of their sexual attractions. Being disinterested in team sports and other typical aggressive and competitive pursuits caused them to feel unmasculine, but they did not thus necessarily construe themselves as feminine. Relatively few spent time with girls or participated in girl games. Rather, their activities can be characterized as "appropriate" for either girls or boys.

Many of these youths felt that they simply faded into the background when with peers. Most were loners for a considerable period during their childhood; when they socialized with peers they were usually with one or two male friends. Although they were spared the vicious, pervasive verbal abuse that their effeminate counterparts received during childhood, they were not immune from harassment. Boys still ridiculed them for their physical features, lack of ability in athletic pursuits, and unconventional behavior or intelligence.

In contrast to these gay/bisexual youths was a much smaller group of youths who were nearly indistinguishable from masculine heterosexual boys their age. Constituting at least one of every ten youths interviewed, their participation in typical masculine pursuits, especially individual and team sports, blended them into the fabric of male culture. Many were socially active and one might speculate that their male friendships were an enjoyable sublimation of homoerotic attractions that they only later, often during adolescence or young adulthood, recognized. Their failure to recognize any sexual feelings during childhood could be attributed to the direction their sexual attractions might take if they were allowed into consciousness. In this respect, their psychic investment was to conceal this secret from themselves and others.

Unknown is the etiology of these patterns and their long-term effects on other aspects of development, including participation in sexual activities, self-recognition of a sexual identity, disclosure of that identity to others, romantic relationships with other males, and developing a positive sense of self.

Although several of the interviewed youths experienced same-sex attractions as arising abruptly and unexpectedly, for the vast majority these feelings emerged as gradual, inevitable, and not particularly surprising. In this sense, these findings are at odds with the theme of this book—diversity in developmental patterns. Few if any youths believed that they could control the direction of their sexual feelings and no youth believed

that he ultimately chose his sexual orientation or sexual attractions. The incorporation of the various masculine and feminine behavioral patterns was felt by youths to be less a matter of choice than an experienced naturalness that was derived from their biological heritage and, less commonly, from early socialization processes beyond their control. On his emerging sexuality, one youth reflected, "It was like being visited by an old friend." This awareness may have emerged early or late, surfaced gradually or arrived instantaneously, felt normal or wrong, motivated sexual activity or abstinence—but it was one aspect of the self that was present without invitation. Future development [...] was simply an unfolding of that which was already present, with puberty playing a crucial turning point for many youths in clarifying for them that their homosensuality had a sexual component. From this awareness often loomed first sexual encounters, which occurred during the earliest years of childhood or waited until young adulthood. They too were interpreted by the youths in diverse ways, thus having a differential impact on the eventual incorporation of a gay or bisexual identity.

Notes

1. See early account in A. P. Bell, M. S. Weinberg, and S. K. Hammersmith (1981), *Sexual Preference: Its Development in Men and Women* (Bloomington, IN: Indiana University Press). For data on gay youths see G. Herdt and A. Boxer (1993), *Children of Horizons: How Gay and Lesbian Teens Are Leading a New Way Out of the Closet* (Boston: Beacon) and R. C. Savin-Williams (1990), *Gay and Lesbian Youth: Expressions of Identity* (New York: Hemisphere).

2. J. Sophie presents a synthesis of coming-out models in her 1985–1986 article, "A Critical Examination of Stage Theories of Lesbian Identity Development," *Journal of Homosexuality, 12,* 39–51.

3. Revised in his 1989 article, R. R. Troiden, "The Formation of Homosexual Identities," *Journal of Homosexuality, 17,* 43–73. Additional empirical evidence is available in references in note 1 and B. S. Newman and P. G. Muzzonigro (1993), "The Effects of Tradi-

tional Family Values on the Coming Out Process of Gay Male Adolescents," *Adolescence, 28,* 213–226, and S. K. Tellijohann and J. P. Price (1993), "A Qualitative Examination of Adolescent Homosexuals' Life Experiences: Ramifications for Secondary School Personnel," *Journal of Homosexuality, 26,* 41–56.

4. For a comprehensive review of this literature, see J. M. Bailey and K. J. Zucker (1995), "Childhood Sex-Typed Behavior and Sexual Orientation: A Conceptual Analysis and Quantitative Review," *Developmental Psychology, 31,* 43–55.

5. For a review of studies using these measures, see note 4 and J. M. Bailey (1996), "Gender Identity," in R. C. Savin-Williams and K. M. Cohen (Eds.), *The Lives of Lesbians, Gays, and Bisexuals: Children to Adults,* pp. 71–93 (Fort Worth, TX: Harcourt Brace); R. Green (1987), *The "Sissy Boy Syndrome" and the Development of Homosexuality* (New Haven: Yale University Press); G. Phillips and R. Over (1992), "Adult Sexual Orientation in Relation to Memories of Childhood Gender Conforming and Gender Nonconforming Behaviors," *Archives of Sexual Behavior, 21,* 543–558; and B. Zuger (1984), "Early Effeminate Behavior in Boys: Outcome and Significance for Homosexuality," *Journal of Nervous and Mental Disease, 172,* 90–97.

6. From R. A. Isay (1989), *Being Homosexual: Gay Men and Their Development* (New York: Farrar Straus Grove).

7. See sources in notes 1 and 4.

8. Experimental evidence is supplied in K. J. Zucker, D. N. Wilson-Smith, J. A. Kurita, and A. Stern (1995), "Children's Appraisals for Sex-Typed Behavior in their Peers," *Sex Roles, 33,* 703–725.

9. See references in notes 4 and 5.

Ann Ferguson

Making a Name for Yourself: Transgressive Acts and Gender Performance

Though girls as well as boys infringe the rules, the overwhelming majority of violations in every single category, from misbehavior to obscenity, are by males. In a disturbing tautology, transgressive behavior is that which constitutes masculinity. Consequently, African American males in the very act of identification, of signifying masculinity, are likely to be breaking rules.

I use the concept of sex/gender not to denote the existence of a stable, unitary category that reflects the presence of fundamental, natural biological difference, but as a socially constructed category whose form and meaning [vary] culturally and historically. We come to know ourselves and to recognize others as of a different sex through an overdetermined complex process inherent in every sphere of social life at the ideological and discursive level, through social structures and institutional arrangements, as well as through the micropolitics of social interactions.[1] We take sex difference for granted, as a natural form of difference as we look for it, recognize it, celebrate it; this very repetition of the "fact" of difference produces and confirms its existence. Indeed, assuming sex/gender difference and identifying as one or the other gender is a precursor of being culturally recognizable as "human."

While all these modes of constituting gender as difference were palpable in the kids' world, in the following analysis of sex/gender as a heightened and highly charged resource for self-fashioning and making a name for oneself, the phenomenological approach developed by ethnomethodologists and by poststructuralist feminist Judith Butler is the most productive one to build on. Here gender is conceptualized as something we do in a performance that is both individually and socially meaningful. We signal our gender identification through an ongoing performance of normative acts that are ritually specific, drawing on well-worked-over, sociohistorical scripts and easily recognizable scenarios.[2]

Butler's emphasis on the coerced and coercive nature of these performances is especially useful. Her work points out that the enactment of sex difference is neither voluntary nor arbitrary in form but is a compulsory requirement of social life. Gender acts follow sociohistorical scripts that are policed through the exercise of repression and taboo. The consequences of an inadequate or bad performance are significant, ranging from ostracism and stigmatization to imprisonment and death. What I want to emphasize in the discussion that follows are the rewards that attach to this playing out of roles; for males, the enactment of masculinity is also a thoroughly embodied display of physical and social power.

Identification as masculine through gender acts, within this framework, is not simply a matter of imitation or modeling, but is better understood as a highly strategic attachment to a social category that has political effects. This attachment involves narratives of the self and of Other, constructed within and through fantasy and imagination, as well as through repetitious, referential acts. The performance signals the individual as socially

From *Bad Boys: Public Schools in the Making of Black Masculinity*, by Ann Ferguson. Ann Arbor: University of Michigan Press, 2000. © University of Michigan. Reprinted with permission.

connected, embedded in a collective membership that always references relations of power.

African American boys at Rosa Parks School use three key constitutive strategies of masculinity in the embrace of the masculine "we" as a mode of self-expression. These strategies speak to and about power. The first is that of heterosexual power, always marked as male. Alain's graffiti become the centerpiece of this discussion. The second involves classroom performances that engage and disrupt the normal direction of the flow of power. The third strategy involves practices of "fighting." All three invoke a "process of iterability, a regularized and constrained repetition of norms," in doing gender, constitute masculinity as a natural, essential, corporeal style; and involve imaginary, fantasmatic identifications.[3]

These three strategies often lead to trouble, but by engaging them a boy can also make a name for himself as a real boy, the Good Bad Boy of a national fantasy. All three illustrate and underline the way that normative male practices take on a different, more sinister inflection when carried out by African American boys. Race makes a significant difference both in the form of the performance as well as its meaning for the audience of adult authority figures and children for whom it is played.

Heterosexual Power: Alain's Graffiti

One group of transgressions specifically involves behavior that expresses sexual curiosity and attraction. These offenses are designated as "personal violations" and given more serious punishment. Inscribed in these interactions are social meanings about relations of power between the sexes as well as assumptions about male and female difference at the level of the physical and biological as well as the representational. It is assumed that females are sexually passive, unlikely to be initiators of sexual passes, while males are naturally active sexual actors with strong sexual drives. Another assumption is that the feminine is a contaminated, stigmatizing category in the sex/gender hierarchy.

Typically, personal violations involved physical touching of a heterosexual nature where males were the "perpetrators" and females the "victims." A few examples from the school files remind us of some of the "normal" displays of sexual interest at this age.

- Boy was cited with "chasing a girl down the hall" [punishment: two days in the Jailhouse].
- Boy pulled a female classmate's pants down during recess [punishment: one and a half days in the Jailhouse].
- Boy got in trouble for, "touching girl on private parts. She did not like" [punishment: a day in the Jailhouse].
- Boy was cited for "forcing girl's hand between his legs" [punishment: two and a half days in the Jailhouse].

In one highly revealing case, a male was cast as the "victim" when he was verbally assaulted by another boy who called him a girl. The teacher described the "insult" and her response to it on the referral form in these words:

> During the lesson, Jonas called Ahmed a girl and said he wasn't staying after school for detention because "S" [another boy] had done the same thing. Since that didn't make it ok for anyone to speak this way, I am requesting an hour of detention for Jonas. I have no knowledge of "S" saying so in my presence.

This form of insult is not unusual. When boys want to show supreme contempt for another boy they call him a girl or liken his behavior to female behavior. What is more troubling is that adults capitulate in this stigmatization. The female teacher takes for granted that a comment in which a boy is called a girl is a symbolic attack, sufficiently derogatory to merit punishment. All the participants in the classroom exchange witness the uncritical acknowledgment of adult authority to a gender order of female debasement.

Of course, this is not news to them. Boys and girls understand the meaning of being male and being female in the field of power; the binary opposition of male/female is always one that expresses a norm, maleness, and its constitutive outside, femaleness. In a conversation with a group of boys, one of them asserted and then was supported by others that "a boy can be a girl, but a girl can never be a boy." Boys can be teased, controlled, punished by being accused of being "a girl." A boy faces the degradation of "being sissified," being unmanned, transferred to the degraded category of female. Girls can be teased about being a tomboy. But this is not the same. To take on qualities of being male is the access to and performance of power. So females must now fashion themselves in terms of male qualities to partake of that power. Enactments of masculinity signal value, superiority, power.

Let us return to Alain, the 11-year-old boy who while cooling off and writing lines as a punishment in the antechamber of the Punishing Room, writes on the table in front of him: "Write 20 times. I will stop fucking 10 cent teachers and this five cent class. Fuck you. Ho! Ho! Yes Baby." Alain's message can be read in a number of ways. The most obvious way is the one of the school. A child has broken several rules in one fell swoop and must be punished: he has written on school property (punishable); he has used an obscenity (punishable); he has committed an especially defiant and disrespectful act because he is already in the Punishing Room and therefore knows his message is likely to be read (punishable). Alain is sent home both as a signal to him and to the other witnesses as well as to the students and adults who will hear it through the school grapevine that he cannot get away with such flagrant misbehavior.

An alternative reading looks at the content of the message itself and the form that Alain's anger takes at being sent to the Punishing Room. Alain's anger is being vented against his teacher and the school itself, expressing his rejection, his disidentification with school that he devalues as monetarily virtually worthless. His message expresses his anger through an assertion of sexual power—to fuck or not to fuck—one sure way that a male can conjure up the fantasmatic as well as the physical specter of domination over a female of any age. His assertion of this power mocks the authority of the teacher to give him orders to write lines. His use of "baby" reverses the relations of power, teacher to pupil, adult to child; Alain allies himself through and with power as the school/teacher becomes "female," positioned as a sex object, as powerless, passive, infantilized. He positions himself as powerful through identification with and as the embodiment of male power as he disidentifies with school. At this moment, Alain is not just a child, a young boy, but taking the position of "male" as a strategic resource for enacting power, for being powerful. At the same time, this positioning draws the admiring, titillated attention of his peers.

These moments of sex trouble exemplify some of the aspects of the performance of sex/gender difference that is naturalized through what is deemed punishable as well as punishment practices. Judging from the discipline records, girls do not commit sexual violations. It is as if by their very nature they are incapable. To be female is to be powerless, victimizable, chased down the hallway, an object to be acted upon with force, whose hand can be seized and placed between male legs. To be female is also to be sexually passive, coy, the "chaste" rather than the chaser, in relation to male sexual aggressiveness. In reality, I observed girls who chased boys and who interacted with them physically. Girls, in fact, did "pants" boys, but these acts went unreported by the boys. For them to report and therefore risk appearing to be victimized by a girl publicly would be a humiliating outcome that would only undermine their masculinity. In the production of natural difference, boys' performances work as they confirm that they are active pursuers, highly sexualized actors who must be punished to learn to keep their burgeoning sexuality under control. There is a reward for the behavior even if it may be punished as a violation. In the case of African American boys, sex trouble is treated as egregious conduct.

African American males have historically been constructed as hypersexualized within the national imagination. Compounding this is the process of the adultification of their behavior. Intimations of sexuality on their part, especially when directed toward girls who are bused in—white girls from middle-class families—are dealt with as grave transgressions with serious consequences.

Power Reversals: Class Acts

Performance is a routine part of classroom work. Students are called upon to perform in classes by teachers to show off their prowess or demonstrate their ineptitude or lack of preparation. They are required to read passages aloud, for example, before a highly critical audience of their peers. This display is teacher initiated and reflects the official curricula; they are command performances with well-scripted roles, predictable in the outcome of who has and gets respect, who is in control, who succeeds, who fails.

Another kind of performance is the spontaneous outbreaks initiated by the pupils generally defined under the category of "disruption" by the school. These encompass a variety of actions that punctuate and disrupt the order of the day. During the school year about two-thirds of these violations were initiated by boys and a third by girls. Here are some examples from the discipline files of girls being "disruptive":

- Disruptive in class—laughing, provoking others to join her. Purposely writing wrong answers, being very sassy, demanding everyone's attention.
- Constantly talking; interrupting; crumpling paper after paper; loud.

Some examples of boys' disruption:

- Constant noise, indian whoops, face hiccups, rapping.
- Chanting during quiet time—didn't clean up during art [punishment: detention].
- Joking, shouting out, uncooperative, disruptive during lesson.

From the perspective of kids, what the school characterizes as "disruption" on the referral slips is often a form of performance of the self: comedy, drama, melodrama become moments for self-expression and display. Disruption adds some lively spice to the school day; it injects laughter, drama, excitement, a delicious unpredictability to the classroom routine through spontaneous, improvisational outbursts that add flavor to the bland events.

In spite of its improvisational appearance, most performance is highly ritualized with its own script, timing, and roles. Teachers as well as students engage in the ritual and play their parts. Some kids are regular star performers. Other kids are audience. However, when a substitute is in charge of the class and the risk of being marked as a troublemaker is minimal, even the most timid kids "act up." These rituals circulate important extracurricular knowledge about relations of power.

These dramatic moments are sites for the presentation of a potent masculine presence in the classroom. The Good Bad Boy of our expectations engages power, takes risks, makes the class laugh, and the teacher smile. Performances mark boundaries of "essential difference"—risk taking, brinkmanship. The open and public defiance of the teacher in order to get a laugh, make things happen, take center stage, be admired, is a resource for doing masculinity.

These acts are especially meaningful for those children who have already been marginalized as outside of the community of "good," hard-working students. For the boys already labeled as troublemakers, taking control of the spotlight and turning it on oneself so that one can shine, highlights, for a change, one's strengths and talents. Already caught in the limelight, these kids put on a stirring performance.

Reggie, one of the Troublemakers, prides himself on being witty and sharp, a talented performer. He aspires to two careers: one is becoming a Supreme Court justice, the other an actor. He had recently played the role of Caliban in the school production of *The Tempest* that he described excitedly to me:

> I always try to get the main characters in the story 'cause I might turn out to be an actor

because I'm really good at acting and I've already did some acting. Shakespeare! See I got a good part. I was Caliban. I had to wear the black suit. Black pants and top. Caliban was a beast! In the little picture that we saw, he looks like the . . . the . . . [searching for image] the beast of Notre Dame. The one that rings the bells like *fing! fing! fing!*

Here is one official school activity where Reggie gets to show off something that he is "good at." He is also proud to point out that this is not just a role in any play, but one in a play by Shakespeare. Here his own reward, which is not just doing something that he is good at, but doing it publicly so that he can receive the attention and respect of adults and peers, coincides with the school's educational agenda of creating an interest in Shakespeare among children.

Reggie also plays for an audience in the classroom, where he gets in trouble for disruption. He describes one of the moments for me embellished with a comic imitation of the teacher's female voice and his own swaggering demeanor as he tells the story:

The teacher says [he mimics a high-pitched fussy voice], "You not the teacher of this class." And then I say [adopts a sprightly cheeky tone], "Oh, yes I am." Then she say, "No, you're not, and if you got a problem, you can just leave." I say, "Okay" and leave.

This performance, like others I witnessed, are strategies for positioning oneself in the center of the room in a face-off with the teacher, the most powerful person up to that moment. Fundamental to the performance is engagement with power; authority is teased, challenged, even occasionally toppled from its secure heights for brief moments. Children-generated theatrics allow the teasing challenge of adult power that can expose its chinks and weaknesses. The staged moments heighten tension, test limits, vent emotions, perform acts of courage. For Reggie to have capitulated to the teacher's ultimatum would have been to lose what he perceives as the edge in the strug-

gle. In addition, he has won his escape from the classroom.

Horace describes his challenge to the teacher's authority in a summer school math class:

Just before the end of the period he wrote some of our names on the board and said, "Whoever taught these students when they were young must have been dumb." So I said, "Oh, I didn't remember that was you teaching me in the first grade." Everyone in the room cracked up. I was laughing so hard, I was on the floor. He sent me to the office.

Horace is engaging the teacher in a verbal exchange with a comeback to an insult rather than just passively taking it. In this riposte, Horace not only makes his peers laugh at the teacher, but he also defuses the insult through a quick reversal. The audience in the room, raised on TV sitcom repartee and canned laughter, is hard to impress, so the wisecrack, the rejoinder, must be swift and sharp. Not everyone can get a laugh at the teachers' expense, and to be topped by the teacher would be humiliating, success brings acknowledgment, confirmation, applause from one's peers. For Horace, this is a success story, a moment of gratification in a day that brings few his way.

The tone of the engagement with power and the identity of the actor is highly consequential in terms of whether a performance is overlooked by the teacher or becomes the object of punishment. In a study of a Texas high school, Foley documents similar speech performances.[4] He describes how both teacher and students collaborate to devise classroom rituals and "games" to help pass the time given the context of routinized, alienating classroom work. He observes that upper-middle-class male Anglo students derail boring lessons by manipulating teachers through subtle "making out" games without getting in trouble. In contrast, low-income male Hispanic students, who were more likely to challenge teachers openly in these games, were punished. Foley concluded that one of the important lessons learned by all participants in these ritual games was that the subtle manipulation of authority was a much more effective way of getting your way than openly confronting power.

Style becomes a decisive factor in who gets in trouble. I am reminded of comments made by one of the student specialists at Rosa Parks who explained the high rate of black kids getting in trouble by remarking on their different style of rule breaking: "The white kids are sneaky, black kids are more open."

So why are the black kids "more open" in their confrontations with power? Why not be really "smart" and adopt a style of masculinity that allows them to engage in these rituals that spice the school day and help pass time, but carry less risk of trouble because it is within certain mutually understood limits?

These rituals are not merely a way to pass time, but are also a site for constituting a gendered racial subjectivity. For African American boys, the performance of masculinity invokes cultural conventions of speech performance that draw on a black repertoire. Verbal performance is an important medium for black males to establish a reputation, make a name for yourself, and achieve status.[5] Smitherman points out that black talk in general is

> a functional dynamic that is simultaneously a mechanism for learning about life and the world and a vehicle for achieving group recognition. Even in what appears to be only casual conversation, whoever speaks is highly conscious of the fact that his personality is on exhibit and his status at stake.[6]

Oral performance has a special significance in black culture for the expression of masculinity. Harper points out that verbal performance functions as an identifying marker for masculinity only when it is delivered in the vernacular and that "a too-evident facility in white idiom can quickly identify one as a white-identified uncle Tom who must also be therefore weak, effeminate, and probably a fag."[7] Though the speech performances that I witnessed were not always

delivered in the strict vernacular, the nonverbal, bodily component accompanying it was always delivered in a manner that was the flashy, boldly flamboyant popular style essential to a good performance. The body language and spoken idiom openly engage power in a provocative competitive way. To be indirect, "sly," would not be performing masculinity.

This nonstandard mode of self-representation epitomizes the very form the school seeks to exclude and eradicate. It is a masculine enactment of defiance played in a black key that is bound for punishment. Moreover, the process of adultification translates the encounter from a simple verbal clash with an impertinent child into one interpreted as an intimidating threat.

Though few white girls in the school were referred to the office for disruptive behavior, a significant number of African American girls staged performances, talked back to teachers, challenged authority, and were punished. But there was a difference with the cultural framing of their enactments and those of the boys. The bottom line of Horace's story was that "everyone in the room cracked up." He engaged authority through a self-produced public spectacle with an eye for an audience that is at home with the cultural icon of the Good Bad Boy as well as the "real black man." Boys expect to get attention. Girls vie for attention too, but it is perceived as illegitimate behavior. As the teacher described it in the referral form, the girl is "demanding attention." The prevailing cultural framework denies her the rights for dramatic public display.

Male and female classroom performance is different in another respect. Girls are not rewarded with the same kind of applause or recognition by peers or by teachers. Their performance is sidelined; it is not given center stage. Teachers are more likely to "turn a blind eye" to such a display rather than call attention to it, for girls are seen as individuals who operate in cliques at most and are unlikely to foment insurrection in the room. Neither the moral nor the pragmatic principle prods teachers to take action. The behavior is not taken seriously; it is rated as "sassy" rather than symptomatic of a more dangerous disorder. In some classrooms, in fact, risk taking and "feistiness" on the part of girls is subtly encouraged given the prevailing belief that what they need is to become more visible, more assertive in the classroom. The notion is that signs of self-assertion on their part should be encouraged rather than squelched.

Disruptive acts have a complex, multifaceted set of meanings for the male Troublemakers themselves. Performance as an expression of black masculinity is a production of a powerful subjectivity to be reckoned with, to be applauded; respect and ovation are in a context where none is forthcoming. The boys' anger and frustration as well as fear motivate the challenge to authority. Troublemakers act and speak out as stigmatized outsiders.

Ritual Performances of Masculinity: Fighting

Each year a substantial number of kids at Rosa Parks get into trouble for fighting. It is the most frequent offense for which they are referred to the Punishing Room. Significantly, the vast majority of the offenders are African American males.[8]

The school has an official position on fighting; it is the wrong way to handle any situation, at any time, no matter what. Schools have good reasons for banning fights: kids can get hurt and when fights happen they sully the atmosphere of order, making the school seem like a place of danger, of violence.

The prescribed routine for schoolchildren to handle situations that might turn into a fight is to tell an adult who is then supposed to take care of the problem. This routine ignores the unofficial masculine code that if someone hits you, you should solve the problem yourself rather than showing weakness and calling an adult to intervene. However, it is expected that girls with a problem will seek out an adult for assistance. Girls are assumed to be physically weaker, less aggressive, more vulnerable, more needy of self-

protection; they must attach themselves to adult (or male) power to survive. This normative gender distinction, in how to handle both problems of a sexual nature and physical aggression, operates as a "proof" of a physical and dispositional gender nature rather than behavior produced through discourses and practices that constitute sex difference.

Referrals of males to the Punishing Room, therefore, are cases where the unofficial masculine code for problem resolution has prevailed. Telling an adult is anathema to these youth. According to their own codes, the act of "telling" is dangerous for a number of reasons. The most practical of these sets it as a statement to the "whole world" that you are unable to deal with a situation on your own—to take care of yourself—an admission that can have disastrous ramifications when adult authority is absent. This is evident from the stance of a Troublemaker who questions the practical application of the official code by invoking knowledge of the proper male response when one is "attacked" that is shared with the male student specialist charged with enforcing the regulation: "I said, 'Mr. B, if somebody came up and hit you, what would you do?' 'Well,' he says, 'We're not talking about me right now, see.' That's the kind of attitude they have. It's all like on you."

Another reason mentioned by boys for not relying on a teacher to take care of a fight situation is that adults are not seen as having any real power to effectively change the relations among kids:

> If someone keep messing with you, like if someone just keep on and you tell them to leave you alone, then you tell the teacher. The teacher can't do anything about it because, see, she can't hit you or nothing. Only thing she can do is tell them to stop. But then he keep on doing it. You have no choice but to hit 'em. You already told him once to stop.

This belief extends to a distrust of authority figures by these young offenders. The assumption that all the children see authority figures such as teachers, police, and psychologists as acting on their behalf and trust they will act fairly may be true of middle- and upper-class children brought up to expect protection from authority figures in society. This is not the case with many of the children at the school. Their mistrust of authority is rooted in the historical and locally grounded knowledge of power relations that come from living in a largely black and impoverished neighborhood.

Fighting becomes, therefore, a powerful spectacle through which to explore trouble as a site for the construction of manhood. The practice takes place along a continuum that ranges from play—spontaneous outbreaks of pummeling and wrestling in fun, ritualistic play that shows off "cool" moves seen on video games, on TV, or in movies—to serious, angry socking, punching, fistfighting. A description of some of these activities and an analysis of what they mean provides the opportunity for us to delve under the surface of the ritualized, discrete acts that make up a socially recognizable fight even into the psychic, emotional, sensuous aspects of gender performativity. The circular, interactive flow between fantasmatic images, internal psychological processes, and physical acts suggest the dynamics of attachment of masculine identification.

Fighting is one of the social practices that add tension, drama, and spice to the routine of the school day. Pushing, grabbing, shoving, kicking, karate chopping, wrestling, fistfighting engage the body and the mind. Fighting is about play and games, about anger and pain, about hurt feelings, about "messing around." To the spectator, a fight can look like serious combat, yet when the combatants are separated by an adult, they claim, "We were only playing." In fact, a single fight event can move along the continuum from play to serious blows in a matter of seconds. As one of the boys explained, "You get hurt and you lose your temper."

Fighting is typically treated as synonymous with "aggression" or "violence," terms that already encode the moral, definitional frame that obscures the contradictory ways that the practice,

in all its manifestations, is used in our society. We, as good citizens, can distance ourselves from aggressive and violent behavior. "Violence" as discourse constructs "fighting" as pathological, symptomatic of asocial, dangerous tendencies, even though the practice of "fighting" and the discourses that constitute this practice as "normal," are in fact taken for granted as ritualized resources for "doing" masculinity in the contemporary United States.

The word *fighting* encompasses the "normal" as well as the pathological. It allows the range of meanings that the children, specifically the boys whom I interviewed and observed, as well as some of the girls, bring to the practice. One experience that it is open to is the sensuous, highly charged embodied experience before, during, and after fighting; the elating experience of "losing oneself" that I heard described in fight stories.

War Stories

I began thinking about fights soon after I started interviews with the Troublemakers and heard "fight stories." Unlike the impoverished and reluctantly told accounts of the school day, these stories were vivid, elaborate descriptions of bodies, mental states, and turbulent emotional feelings. They were stirring, memorable moments in the tedious school routine.

Horace described a fight with an older boy who had kept picking on him. He told me about the incident as he was explaining how he had broken a finger one day when we were trading "broken bones" stories.

> When I broke this finger right here it really hurted. I hit somebody in the face. It was Charles. I hit him in the face. You know the cafeteria and how you walk down to go to the cafeteria. Right there. That's where it happened. Charles picked me up and put me on the wall, slapped me on the wall, and dropped me. It hurt. It hurt bad. I got mad because he used to be messing with me for a long time so I just swung as hard as I could, closed my eyes, and just *pow,* hit him in the face. But I did like

a roundhouse swing instead of doing it straight and it got the index finger of my right hand. So it was right there, started right here, and all around this part [he is showing me the back of his hand] it hurt. It was swollen. Oooh! It was like this! But Charles, he got hurt too. The next day I came to school I had a cast on my finger and he had a bandage on his ear. It was kinda funny, we just looked at each other and smiled.

The thing that most surprised and intrigued me about Horace's story was that he specifically recalled seeing Charles the next day and that they had looked at each other and smiled. Was this a glance of recognition, of humor, of recollection of something pleasing, of all those things? The memory of the exchanged smile derailed my initial assumption that fighting was purely instrumental. This original formulation said that boys fight because they have to fight in order to protect themselves from getting beaten up on the playground. Fighting from this instrumental perspective is a purely survival practice. Boys do fight to stave off the need to fight in the future, to stop the harassment from other boys on the playground and in the streets. However, this explains only a small group of boys who live in certain environments; it relegates fighting to the realm of the poor, the deviant, the delinquent, the pathological. This position fails to address these physical clashes as the central normative practice in the preparation of bodies, of mental stances, of self-reference for manhood and as the most effective form of conflict resolution in the realm of popular culture and international relations.

I listened closely to the stories to try to make sense of behavior that was so outside of my own experience, yet so familiar a part of the landscape of physical fear and vulnerability that I as a female walked around with every day. I asked school adults about their own memories of school and fighting. I was not surprised to find that few women seemed to recall physical fights at school, though they had many stories of boys who teased them or girlfriends whom they were always "fighting" with. This resonated with my own experience. I was struck, however, by the fact that all of

the men whom I talked to had had to position themselves in some way with regard to fighting. I was also struck that several of these men framed the memory of fighting in their past as a significant learning experience.

Male adults in school recall fighting themselves, but in the context both of school rules and of hindsight argue that they now know better. One of the student specialists admitted that he used to fight a lot. I found it significant that he saw "fighting" as the way he "learned":

> I used to fight a lot. [Pause.] I used to fight a lot and I used to be real stubborn and silent. I wouldn't say anything to anybody. It would cause me a lot of problems, but that's just the way I learned.

The after-school martial arts instructor also admitted to fighting a lot when he was younger:

> There were so many that I had as a kid that it's hard to remember all of them and how they worked out. But yes, I did have a lot of arguments and fights. A lot of times I would lose my temper, which is what kids normally do, they lose their temper, and before they have a chance to work things out they begin punching and kicking each other. Right? Well I did a lot of those things so I know from experience those are not the best thing to do.

As I explored the meaning of fighting I began to wonder how I, as female, had come to be shaped so fighting was not a part of my own corporeal or mental repertoire. A conversation with my brother reminded me of a long forgotten self that could fight, physically, ruthlessly, inflict hurt, cause tears. "We were always fighting," he recalled. "You used to beat me up." Memories of these encounters came back. I am standing with a tuft of my brother's hair in my hand, furious tears in my eyes. Full of hate for him. Kicking, scratching, socking, feeling no pain. Where had this physical power gone? I became "ladylike," repressing my anger, limiting my physical contact to shows of affection, fearful. I wondered about the meaning of being female in a society in which to be female is to be always conscious of men's physical power and to consciously chart one's everyday routines to avoid becoming a victim of this power, but to never learn the bodily and mental pleasure of fighting back.

Bodily Preparations: Pain and Pleasure

Fighting is first and foremost a bodily practice. I think about fighting and physical closeness as I stand observing the playground at recess noticing a group of three boys, bodies entangled, arms and legs flailing. In another area, two boys are standing locked closely in a wrestling embrace. Children seem to gravitate toward physical contact with each other. For boys, a close, enraptured body contact is only legitimate when they are positioned as in a fight. It is shocking that this bodily closeness between boys would be frowned on, discouraged if it were read as affection. Even boys who never get in trouble for "fighting" can be seen engaging each other through the posturing and miming, the grappling of playfight encounters.

This play can lead to "real" fights. The thin line between play and anger is crossed as bodies become vulnerable, hurt, and tempers are lost. One of the white boys in the school who was in trouble for fighting describes the progression this way:

> Well we were messing with each other and when it went too far, he started hitting me and then I hit him back and then it just got into a fight. It was sorta like a game between me, him and Thomas. How I would get on Thomas's back an—he's a big guy—and Stephen would try to hit me and I would wanta hit him back. So when Thomas left it sorta continued and I forgot which one of us wanted to stop—but one of us wanted to stop and the other one wouldn't.

Fighting is about testing and proving your bodily power over another person, both to yourself and to others through the ability to "hurt" someone as well as to experience "hurt."

> HORACE: You know Claude. He's a bad boy in the school. When I was in the fifth grade, he was in the fifth grade. I intercepted his pass and he threw the ball at my head and then I said, "You're mad," and I twisted the ball on the floor. I said, "Watch this," and y'know spiraled it on the floor, and he kicked it and it hit my leg, and I said, "Claude, if you hit me one more time with the ball or anything I'm going to hurt you." He said. "What if you do?" I said, "Okay, you expect me not to do anything, right?" He said, "Nope." Then I just *pow, pow, pow,* and I got him on the floor and then I got him on his back. I wanted to hurt him badly but I couldn't.

> ANN: Why couldn't you?

> HORACE: I didn't want to get in trouble. And if I did really hurt him it wouldn't prove anything anyway. But it did. It proved that I could hurt him and he didn't mess with me anymore.

Pain is an integral part of fighting. Sometimes it is the reason for lashing out in anger. This description by Wendell also captures the loss of self-control experienced at the moment of the fight:

> Sometimes it starts by capping or by somebody slams you down or somebody throws a bullet at you. You know what a bullet is, don't you? [He chuckles delightedly because I think of a bullet from a gun.] The bullet I am talking about is a football! You throw it with all your might and it hits somebody. It just very fast and they call it bullets. You off-guard and they throw it at your head, and bullets they throw with all their might so it hurts. Then that sorta gets you all pissed off. Then what happens is, you kinda like, "Why you threw it?" " 'Cause I wanted to. Like, so?" "So you not going to do that to me." Then: "So you going to do something about it?" Real smart. "Yeah!" And then you tap the person on the shoulder and your mind goes black and then *shweeeee* [a noise and hand signal that demonstrates the evaporation of thought] you go at it. And you don't stop until the teacher comes and stops it.

Fighting is a mechanism for preparing masculinized bodies through the playful exercise of bodily moves and postures and the routinized rehearsal of sequences and chains of stances of readiness, attack, and defense. Here it is crucial to emphasize that while many boys in the school never ever engage in an actual physical fight with another boy or girl during school hours, the majority engage in some form of body enactments of fantasized "fight" scenarios. They have observed boys and men on TV, in the movies, in video games, on the street, in the playground adopting these stances.

These drills simultaneously prepare and cultivate the mental states in which corporeal styles are grounded. So for instance, boys are initiated into the protocol of enduring physical pain and mental anguish—"like a man"—through early and small infusions of the toxic substance itself in play fights. The practice of fighting is the site for a hot-wiring together of physical pain and pleasure, as components of masculinity as play and bodily hurt inevitably coincide.

Consequently, it also engages powerful emotions. Lindsey described the feelings he experienced prior to getting into a fight:

> Sometimes it's play. And sometimes it's real. But that's only sometimes, because they can just suddenly make you angry and then, it's like they take control of your mind. Like they manipulate your mind if you angry. Little by little you just lose it and you get in a temper.

One of the white boys in the school who had gotten in trouble for fighting described his thoughts and feelings preceding a fight and the moment of "just going black" in a loss of self:

> My mind would probably be going through how I would do this. If I would stop it now or if I would follow through with it. But once the fight actually happens I sort of go black and just fight 'em.

Fighting is a practice, like sports, that is so symbolically "masculine" that expressions of emotion or behavior that might call one's man-

hood into question are allowed without danger of jeopardizing one's manliness. Even crying is a permissible expression of "masculinity" under these circumstances. One of the boys who told me he never cried, corrected himself:

> But if I be mad, I cry. Like if I get into a fight or something like that, I cry because I lose my temper and get so mad. But sometimes, I play football and if I cry that mean I'm ready to tumble—throw the ball to me because I'm going.

Fighting in school is a space in which boys can feel free to do emotional work.[9] In a social practice that is so incontrovertibly coded as masculine, behaviors marked as feminine, such as crying, can be called upon as powerful wellsprings for action.

One of the questions that I asked all the boys about fighting came out of my own ignorance. My query was posed in terms of identity work around the winning and losing of fights. Did you ever win a fight? Did you ever lose a fight? How did you feel when you lost? How did you feel when you won? I found the answers slippery, unexpected, contradictory. I had anticipated that winning would be described in proud and boastful ways, as success stories. But there seemed to be a surprising reluctance to embellish victory. I learned that I was missing the point by posing the question the way I had in terms of winning and losing. Trey enlightened me when he explained that what was at stake was not winning or losing per se but in learning about the self:

> I won a lot of fights. You know you won when they start crying and stuff or when they stop and leave. I lost fights. Then you feel a little okay. At least you lost. I mean like you ain't goin' win every fight. At least you fought back instead of just standing there and letting them hit you.

Another boy expressed the function that fighting played in establishing yourself as being a particular kind of respectable person:

> It's probably like dumb, but if somebody wants to fight me, I mean, I don't care even if I know I can't beat 'em. I won't stop if they don't stop.

I mean I'm not scared to fight anybody. I'm not a coward. I don't let anybody punk me around. If you let people punk you around, other peoples want to punk you around.

Proving yourself to others is like a game, a kind of competition:

Me and Leslie used to fight because we used to be the biggest boys, but now we don't care anymore. We used to get friends and try and fight each other. I fought him at Baldwin school all the time. We stopped about the fifth grade [the previous year]. Just got tired, I guess.

Standing and proving yourself today can be insurance against future harassment in the yard as you make a name for yourself through readiness to fight: "Like if somebody put their hands on you, then you have to, you have to hit them back. Because otherwise you going be beat up on for the rest of your life."

Eddie, who has avoided fights because he does not want to get in trouble, is now seen as a target for anyone to beat up, according to one of his friends, who characterized Eddie's predicament this way: "He can't fight. *He can't fight.* Every girl, every boy in the whole school fixing to beat him up. Badly. They could beat him up badly."

Eddie explains his own perspective on how he has come to actually lose a reputation.

Yeah, I won a fight in preschool. Like somebody this tall [his gesture indicates a very tall someone] I had to go like this [reaches up to demonstrate] so I could hit him. He was older than me. He was the preschool bully. Till I mess him up.

But Eddie's parents came down hard on him for getting in trouble for fighting in elementary school:

Yeah, I lost fights. See when I got to Rosa Parks my parents told me not to fight unless I had to—so I lost my face. 'Cause I was so used to telling them to stop, don't fight, don't fight.

In constructing the self through fight stories, it is not admirable to represent oneself as the aggressor or initiator in a fight. All the boys whom I talked to about fighting presented themselves as responding to a physical attack that had to be answered in a decisive way. No one presented himself as a "bully," though I knew that Horace had that reputation. Yet he told me that "only fights I been in is if they hit me first."

There are, however, times when it is legitimate to be the initiator. When verbal provocation is sufficient. This is when "family" has been insulted. Talking about "your momma" is tantamount to throwing down the gauntlet:

Mostly I get in fights if somebody talk about my grandfather because he's dead. And I loved my grandfather more than I love anybody and then he died. [Tears are in Jabari's eyes as we talk.] That's why I try to tell people before they get ready to say anything, I'm like, "Don't say anything about my grandfather, 'cause if you say something about him, I'm goin' hit you."

The boys talked about how they learned to fight. How one learns to fight and what one learns about the meaning of fighting—why fight, to fight or not to fight—involved both racial identity and class positioning. Ricky and Duane, two of the Schoolboys, have been enrolled by their parents in martial arts classes. Fighting remains a necessary accoutrement of masculinity that is "schooled," not a "natural" acquisition of doing. As such, it becomes a marker of higher class position. Fighting takes place in an institutionalized arena rather than spontaneously in just any setting. The mind seems to control the body here, rather than vice versa.

Horace, on the other hand, like the majority of boys with whom I talked, explained that he had learned to fight through observation and practice:

I watched people. Like when I was younger, like I used to look up to people. I still do. I look up to people and they knew how to fight so I just watched them. I just like saw people fight on TV, you know. Boxing and stuff.

Another boy told me that he thought kids learned to fight "probably from theirselves. Like their mom probably say, if somebody hit you, hit them back." This advice about proper behavior is grounded in the socialization practices that are brought into school as ways of responding to confrontations.

Gender Practice and Identification

Fighting acts reproduce notions of essentially different gendered natures and the forms in which this "difference" is grounded. Though class makes some difference in when, how, and under what conditions it takes place, fighting is the hegemonic representation of masculinity. Inscribed in the male body—whether individual males fight or not, abjure fighting or not—is the potential for this unleashing of physical power. By the same token, fighting for girls is considered an aberration, something to be explained.

Girls do get in fights at school. Boys asserted that girls can fight, even that "sometimes they get in fights easier. Because they got more attitude." Indeed, girls do make a name for themselves this way. One of the girls at Rosa Parks was in trouble several times during the school year for fighting. Most of her scrapes were with the boys who liked to tease her because she was very tall for her age. This, however, was not assumed to be reflective of her "femaleness" but of her individuality. Mr. Sobers, for example, when I asked him about her, made a point of this singularity rather than explaining her in terms of race, class, or gender: "Oh, Stephanie is just Stephanie."

Notes

1. Here are a very few examples of the enormous body of work concerned with the production of gender differences in the last two decades. At the ideological and discursive level see Mullings, "Images, Ideology"; Teresa de Lauretis, *Technologies of Gender: Essays on Theory, Film, and Fiction* (Bloomington: Indiana University Press, 1987); and Michele Barrett, *Women's Oppression Today: Problems in Marxist Feminist Analysis* (London: New Left Books, 1980). For processes of social structure and institutional arrange-

ments see R. W. Connell et al., *Making the Difference: Schools, Families, and Social Division* (London: George Allen and Unwin, 1982); Mariarosa Dalla Costa, "Women and the Subversion of the Community," in *The Power of Women and the Subversion of Community,* ed. Mariarosa Dalla Costa and Selma James (Bristol, England: Falling Wall Press, 1973); Catharine A. MacKinnon, *Feminism Unmodified: Discourses on Life and Law* (Cambridge: Harvard University Press, 1987). For micropolitics see Arlie Russell Hochschild, *The Second Shift: Working Parents and the Revolution at Home* (New York: Viking, 1989); Donna Eder, Catherine Colleen Evans, and Stephen Parker, *School Talk: Gender and Adolescent Culture* (New Brunswick, N.J.: Rutgers University Press, 1995); and Candace West and Don H. Zimmerman, "Doing Gender," *Gender & Society* 1, no. 2 (1987).

2. Judith Butler, "Performative Acts and Gender Constitution: An Essay in Phenomenology and Feminist Theory," *Theatre Journal* 40, no. 4 (1988).

3. Judith Butler, *Bodies That Matter: On the Discursive Limits of "Sex"* (New York: Routledge, 1993), 95.

4. Douglas E. Foley, *Learning Capitalist Culture: Deep in the Heart of Tejas* (Philadelphia: University of Pennsylvania, 1990).

5. Geneva Smitherman, *Talkin and Testifyin: Language of Black America* (Detroit: Wayne State University Press, 1977); Lawrence Levine, *Black Culture and Black Consciousness: Afro-American Folk Thought from Slavery to Freedom* (New York: Oxford University Press, 1977); Philip Brian Harper, *Are We Not Men? Masculine Anxiety and the Problem of African-American Identity* (New York: Oxford University Press, 1996); Keith Gilyard, *Voices of the Self: A Study of Language Competence* (Detroit: Wayne State University Press, 1991).

6. Smitherman, *Talkin and Testifyin,* 80.

7. Harper, *Are We Not Men?* 11.

8. One-quarter of the 1,252 referrals to the Punishing Room were for fighting; four-fifths of the incidents involved boys, nine out of ten of whom were African Americans. All except three of the girls who were in fights were black.

9. Arlie Russell Hochschild, *The Managed Heart: Commercialization of Human Feeling* (Berkeley and Los Angeles: University of California Press, 1983). Hochschild explores the feeling rules that guide and govern our own emotional displays as well as how we interpret the emotional expression of others.

PART THREE

Collegiate Masculinities: Privilege and Peril

The old social science orthodoxy about sex role socialization, from the 1950s until today, held that three institutions—family, church, and school—formed the primary sites of socialization, and the impact of education, family values, and religious training was decisive in shaping people's lives. This view tended to emphasize the centrality of adults in boys' lives. Because adults themselves were constructing the models of socialization, this conclusion seems understandable. But as social scientists began to ask boys and girls about the forces that influenced them, they heard about the increasing importance of peer groups and the media—two arenas where adults had far less reach. In recent years, researchers have begun to explore how homosocial peer groups affect men's lives.

The articles in Part Three focus on masculinities in college, a place Michael Kimmel calls "Guyland," where the all-male peer group is especially salient. How does collegiate life organize and reproduce the definitions of masculinity that we learn as young boys? How do specific all-male subcultures develop within these institutions, and what roles do they play?

Peter Lyman looks at fraternities and the special male-bonding that takes place there, while Shaun R. Harper discusses the particular challenges that African American men face in college life. Rocco Capraro provides a fascinating gender analysis of male drinking culture in college. And Greg Bortnichak describes how, while working as a barista in a local Starbucks, he decided to do something about what he saw.

Photo courtesy of Barbara Kruger.

Michael Kimmel

Guyland: Gendering the Transition to Adulthood

The period between childhood and adulthood has been expanding for centuries. "Our society has passed from a period which was ignorant of adolescence to a period in which adolescence is the favorite age," wrote the French historian Philippe Aires (1962: 30). "We now want to come to it early and linger in it as long as possible."

Recently a body of research has emerged that expands this stage of development beyond the boundaries of what had been considered adolescence. Drawing on current empirical research on postadolescent development, a new group of social and behavioral scientists have identified what they call the "transition to adulthood." Although this new body of research has mapped the broadest parameters of this stage of development, the initial analytic forays have been astonishingly lacking in any analysis of gender. This lacuna is more striking because it is during the transition to adulthood that gender plays perhaps its most central role. To understand this new stage and to better map its gendered topography, it makes some sense to begin by remembering how deeply gendered was the initial study of adolescence.

The Invention of Adolescence

In 1904, G. Stanley Hall published his massive two-volume tome, *Adolescence: Its Psychology and*

Its Relations to Physiology, Anthropology, Sociology, Sex, Crime, Religion, and Education. Almost immediately, the word *adolescence* entered the common vocabulary to describe a stage of development poised anxiously between childhood puerility and adult virility. Hall saw adolescence, roughly coincident with the biological changes of puberty (ages 12–15), as a time of transition—a time when boys and girls develop their adult identity, test themselves, and find out who they really are.

No one could accuse Hall of failing to pay attention to gender. He was preoccupied with it. While he was generally eager to shield adolescents from entering the adult world prematurely, his chief interest was in boys' development. Concerned that boys were becoming feminized, in part by overprotective mothers and largely because of the increasingly coeducational environment of school and church, Hall wanted to rescue boys—from both the feminizing tendencies of girls and the enervating world of work, hoping that adolescent boys could be immersed in supportive, controlled, adult-monitored homosocial environments. Hall opposed coeducation, which he believed turned boys gay as it "diluted the mystic attraction of the opposite sex," and proposed a host of masculinity-building activities like sports, vigorous exertion in the outdoors, and even fighting and bullying others. He championed the Boy Scouts (founded in 1910) and the YMCA (founded in 1844 and revamped in the early 1900s) as vehicles to stem the tide of enervation.[1]

Hall generalized to all adolescents from only a tiny fraction of America's youth. When his book was published, only 6% of American teenagers actually graduated from high school.

By contrast, 18% of youth between 10 and 14 worked in factories or stores, and millions more were working on family farms. But Hall was on to something important. In the first decades of the twentieth century, the structural foundations of a prolonged adolescence were established, as an industrializing nation sought to stabilize its progress. Apprenticeships declined and child labor laws pushed young people out of the labor force. Compulsory education laws gave them someplace else to go if they couldn't work.

High school became the single defining experience for children of the middle and professional classes. While as late as 1920, only 16% of 17-year-old males had graduated from high school, by 1936 the majority of American teenagers attended high school. A new high school opened every day for the first 30 years of the century.[2]

With the increased universality of high school, a new word, "teenager," entered the American vocabulary in 1941, on the eve of our entrance into World War II. Critics worried that this "sudden and dramatic prolongation of adolescence" meant that over half of those who had "passed the terminal age of adolescence" were not acting as adults—physically, socially, economically, as E. C. Cline, the high school principal in Richmond, Indiana, worried.[3]

And Americans have been worrying about teenagers ever since. Some worried about teen sexuality, especially after the publication of the two volumes of Kinsey's studies of American sexual behavior. Some worried about "juvenile delinquency," another new term from the era— lonely disaffected boys who sought the approval of their fellows by participating in increasingly dangerous stunts and petty crime. "Let's Face It" read the cover of *Newsweek* in 1956, "Our Teenagers Are Out of Control." Many youths, the magazine reported, "got their fun" by "torturing helpless old men and horsewhipping girls they waylaid in public parks."

By the 1950s, many cultural critics followed Hall's lead and blamed mothers—works by Philip Wylie and Edward Strecker identified "momism" as the cultural illness that resulted in emasculated

boys and henpecked husbands. Others blamed the absent or emasculated fathers, the men in the grey flannel suits, like Jim Backus in *Rebel without a Cause*; its author, Robert Lindner, argued that "almost every symptom that delineates the psychopath clinically is to be found increasingly in the contemporary adolescent."[4]

Two Breakthroughs in Psychology and Sociology

Into this cultural controversy stepped psychologist Erik H. Erikson and sociologist James Coleman. Taken together, their writings helped to normalize adolescence, to neutralize and naturalize it. In his path-breaking book, *Childhood and Society* (1950) and later in *Identity: Youth and Crisis* (1968), Erikson identified the seven life-stages of individual psychological development that became a mantra in Developmental Psychology classes for decades. By labeling adolescence as a "moratorium"—a sort of prolonged time-out between childhood and adulthood—Erikson tamed and sanitized Hall's fears that adolescence was a maelstrom, a chaos of uncontrolled passions.

To Erikson, the moratorium of adolescence was a time for regrouping, reassessing, and regenerating oneself before undertaking the final quest for adult identity, "a vital regenerator in the process of social evolution," as he put it. Rather than rushing headlong into work and family lives, as children did in earlier societies, adolescents slow down the process to accomplish certain identity tasks. The venerable institutions that structured a young person's socialization—family, church, school—began to recede in their importance as the adolescent began to strike out on his or her own, plagued by doubts, taking tentative steps towards autonomy, and faced with a set of adult responsibilities looming ominously ahead.[5]

In his treatise, *The Adolescent Society* (1961), sociologist James Coleman had a somewhat less sanguine view of the displacement of education, religion, and family as the primary institutions of socialization. He noticed in high schools that teachers and administrators had lost most of their credibility as agents of socialization—they were more like agents of repression, as far as the kids were concerned. Parental scrutiny waned, and the influence of religion dissipated. As a result, he argued, adolescents developed a distinct peer culture, toward which they oriented their activities and from which they derived their sense of identity. Anti-intellectualism abounded, sports reigned supreme, and everyone wanted to be popular! Hardly tremulous individualists, Coleman saw adolescents as frighteningly dependent on peer culture, and boys, especially, desperate to prove their masculinity in the eyes of other boys.[6]

By the 1960s and 1970s, observers had a more optimistic view of late adolescence. While many shared Coleman's sense that peer groups had replaced parents as the primary source of socialization, they saw this simply as the attenuation of socialization, not its resolution. Indeed, Yale psychoanalyst Kenneth Keniston warned in 1971 that if the "conformity to peer group norms merely replaces conformity to parental norms . . . adolescent development is foreclosed before real self-regulation and independence are achieved." Reliance on peers was just another late hurdle on the way to autonomy and adulthood.[7]

As we will see, contemporary psychologists have tended to follow Erickson and Keniston. And, as we will see, Coleman was far more prescient.

Postwar Adolescence as Anomaly

One problem with Erikson and others' theories of adolescence was that although they insisted that they described eternal—or at least reliably consistent historical—trajectories, they were written during a period that is now understood to have been anomalous. The immediate postwar era was, in many ways, an era utterly unlike our own. It's the stuff of nostalgic longings, and the screen against which we often project our anxieties about the contemporary era.[8]

For adolescents, the period was no less anomalous. It was the only time when all the developmental markers were in perfect alignment

with all the social and institutional frameworks in which development takes place. Those developmental psychological indicators—increased autonomy, the capacity for intimacy, a commitment to a career and the development of a life plan—all coincided with the social and cultural markers that have typically denoted adulthood.

How different that world seems now—and how different were the motivations of men and women who were in the 18–26 age group. For one thing, Americans had just emerged from a calamitous war, in which millions of young men had been killed or wounded. The generation of men that came of age in 1950 had just experienced the horrors of the beaches in Normandy or the South Pacific, the randomness of death and destruction as the guys next to them were gunned down. They couldn't wait to get married, settle down into stable adulthood, to forget the terrors of war, to silence their nightmares. They rushed into careers, married their high schools sweethearts, moved to the suburbs, and started their families. The housing boom spurred by rapid suburbanization was accompanied by an education boom and a baby boom. No wonder the "Greatest Generation" almost instantly morphed into the bland conformity of the "man in the gray flannel suit."

Adolescence Starts Earlier and Ends Later

Adolescence today stretches out in both directions; it starts earlier and ends later. Children are becoming adolescents earlier and earlier, both biologically and socially. Typically we mark adolescence by the onset of puberty—which today occurs 4–5 years earlier than it did in the mid-nineteenth century. Improvements in nutrition, sanitation, and health care have lowered the average age of puberty about one year for every 25 years of development. Each generation enters puberty about a year earlier than its predecessor. In the years just before the Civil War, the average age for the onset of puberty was 16 for girls and 18 for boys; today it is about 12 for girls and 14 for boys.

Since the average age of marriage in the mid-nineteenth century was about the same—16 for girls and 18 for boys—there was really no "stage of development" during which time a youth was both single and sexually active. It wouldn't be far-fetched to say that before the twentieth century, there were no "teenagers" in America.

But just as adolescence reaches us earlier and earlier, it also seems to stretch longer and longer. Biologically, just as puberty is beginning at earlier ages, full physiological maturation doesn't take place until well into our 20s. At 18, neuropsychological development is far from complete; the brain continues to grow and develop into the early 20s. In a bit of stretch, one biologist suggests that this immature brain lacks the "wiring" for placing long-term benefits over shorter-term gains, which explains how we are "hard-wired" for high-risk behaviors like drug taking, smoking, and drinking.[9]

Young people today seem almost determined not to grow up too fast, to give the lie to George Bernard Shaw's famous dictum that "youth is wasted on the young." They may move directly from the "crisis" of adolescence to their "quarter-life crisis" and right into a "mid-life crisis" without ever having settled into a stage of life that wasn't a crisis!

Over the past two years, I interviewed about 400 college students at more than 40 colleges and universities across the United States. While in no way a nationally representative sample, my interviews provide compelling empirical evidence of the transition to adulthood as a new and previously unnoticed stage of development poised between adolescence and adulthood, and the ways that it is deeply and determinatively gendered.

"I feel like my whole life has been one long exercise in delayed gratification," says Matt, a graduate student in psychology at University of Wisconsin:

> I mean, in high school, I had to get good grades, study hard, and do a bunch of extracurricular things so I could get into a good college. OK, I did that. Went to Brown. Then, in college, I had to work really hard and get good grades so I could get into a good graduate school. OK, I did that. I'm here at Wisconsin. Now, though, I have to work really hard, publish my research, so I can get a good tenure track job somewhere. And then, I'll have to work really hard for six years just to get tenure. I mean, by the time I can exhale and have a little fun, I'll be in my mid-30s—and that's too old to have fun anymore!

When do young people become adults? How do they know? What are the markers of adulthood now? Is it when you can legally drink? Get married? Drive a car? Rent a car? Vote? Serve in the military? Have an abortion without parental consent? Consider how disparate these ages are. More than 50,000 Americans get married each year before their 18th birthday—that is, they are legally allowed to have sex before they can legally watch it on a video. We can buy cars before we are legally allowed to drive them and long before we can rent them.

Markers of Adulthood

Demographers today typically cite five life-stage events to mark the transition to adulthood: leaving home, completing one's education, starting work, getting married, and becoming a parent. Just about all adolescents live at home, go to high school, experience puberty, and are unmarried. "Adults," by contrast, have completed their educations, live away from home, are married, and have children and stable careers. (Of course, not all adults would actually check off all those markers, but they represent a pattern, a collection of indicators.) In 1950, when Erikson and Coleman wrote, all those markers clicked at almost exactly the same time.

Let's look at what happened to each of those markers of the transition from adolescence to adulthood. Let's begin with the narrative of one baby boomer:

> My parents married in 1948, after my father returned from the wartime Navy, and both he and my mother began their careers. At first, like so many of their generation, they lived in the bottom floor of my grandparents' home, saving

their money to flee the city and buy a house in the New York suburbs—part of the great wave of suburban migration of the early to mid-1950s. My mother, and her five closest lifelong friends, all had their first children within two years of their weddings, and their second child three years later—all within five years of graduating from college. And all of their friends did the same.

That baby boomer is me. And that pattern is a distant memory today. Baby boomers began to expand the timeframe of these markers of adulthood, attenuating education, prolonging singlehood as a permanent life stage, and drifting toward settled careers. The U.S. census shows a steady and dramatic decline in the percentage of young adults, under 30, who have finished school, left home, gotten married, had a child, and entered the labor force sufficiently to develop financial independence of their parents. In 2000, 46% of women and 31% of men had reached those markers by age 30. In 1960, just forty years earlier, 77% of women and 65% of men had reached them.[10]

Marriage and Family Life

In 1950, the average age of marriage was 20.3 for women and 22.8 for men. Close to half of all women were married by age 20. Even by 1975, the median age for marriage was 21.1 for women and 23.5 for men. The age of marriage has climbed steadily and today, the median age of marriage is 27.1 for men and 25.3 for women.[11]

And young people are having their first child four years later than they did in 1970. In 1970, the average age at which people had their first child was 21.4 years. By 2000, it was 24.9. (Massachusetts had the highest mean age for first birth; Mississippi had the lowest.)[12]

Today's young people live much less stable and settled family lives than their own parents did. They're far more likely to have been raised in a single-parent home. Their reticence is the result of high expectations for their own relationships and fears that their love lives will resemble those of their parents. Afraid to commit and desperate to do so, they make great cross-sex friends and casually hook up sexually. Their parents understand neither phenomenon.

"Serial Jobogamy"

They feel similarly about their careers. They know that their career is supposed to be more than a job, that it is supposed to be financially rewarding, be emotionally rich and satisfying, and offer them a sense of accomplishment and inner satisfaction. Work, for them, is an "identity quest." "Emerging adults want more out of work than a decent wage and a steady paycheck. They want their work to be an expression of themselves, to fit well their interests and abilities, to be something they find satisfying and enjoyable," writes Arnett.[13] And they expect that; they feel *entitled* to it. And why shouldn't they? They put up with four years of college, and maybe even some years of professional or graduate school, just to enhance their career prospects. Many have utterly unrealistic expectations about the range of jobs they might find satisfying. They all seem to want to write for television, become famous actors, or immediately become dot.com entrepreneurs. One employment recruiter calls them "the Entitlement Generation" since they have such "shockingly high expectations for salary, job flexibility, and duties but little willingness to take on grunt work or remain loyal to a company."[14]

But in a way, their bloated expectations may be a response to the very different economic climate in which they're coming of age. For one thing, the secure economic foundation on which previous generations have come of age has eroded. Globalization, the decline in manufacturing jobs, the decline in union protections for workers, and the increase in the supply of service sector jobs has changed all that. They know that corporations are no longer loyal to their employees—just consider all those companies that picked up and moved out of towns they had helped to build, watching indifferently as entire communities unraveled. So why should they be loyal to the company?

They're lucky to find a job at all. In 2000, 72.2% of Americans aged 20–24 were employed; four years later it was barely two-thirds (67.9%). "Younger workers have just been crushed," commented Andrew Sum, the director of the Center for Labor Market Studies at Northeastern University.[15] Unlike virtually every single previous generation of Americans, the income trajectory for the current generation of young people is downwards. Between 1949 and 1973, during that postwar economic boom, men's earnings doubled and the income gap narrowed. But since the early 1970s, annual earnings for men, aged 25–34 with full-time jobs has steadily declined, dropping 17% from 1971 to 2002. Of male workers with only a high school diploma, the average wage decline from 1975 to 2002 was 11%. Only half of all Americans in their mid-20s earn enough to support a family. Two-thirds of this current generation "are not living up to their parents' standard of living," commented Professor Sum.[16]

And the gap between college-educated and non-college-educated has increased as well. In the late 1970s, male college graduates earned about 33% more than high school graduates; by the end of the 1980s, that gap had increased to 53%.[17] Nor do they have much protection. Once they're 18 or 19, young people are rarely covered as dependents on their parents' health and medical care plans. And many work at low-wage, temporary, low-benefit jobs, or remain dependent on their parents. As a result, in 1999, over half (53%) of all young adults (aged 18–21) had no health insurance at all—all the more striking when compared with those 35–44 (16.5% had no health care) and 45–54 (13.4% uninsured), according to the General Accounting Office. Another 12.9% are covered by Medicare or other public insurance. Fewer than 10% (8.8%) were covered by their employer.

This generation of young people is downwardly mobile. Gen Xers and Gen Yers will earn less than their parents did—at every single age marker. Of all age groups, the 18–25 year olds are the lowest ranked in earned income of all age groups. Their household income is the second

lowest (right above 65 and older). "On most socioeconomic measures, the young were the worst off age group in 1997—and the gap has widened since," notes Tom Smith, the director of the General Social Survey.[18]

The only economic sector in which jobs are being created is entry-level service and sales. In *Generation X*, author Douglas Coupland calls it "McJob"—"low paying, low-prestige, low-dignity, no future job in the service sector. Frequently considered a satisfying career choice by people who have never held one."[19] Young people, along with immigrants, minorities, and the elderly, are the bulk of workers in the new service economy. Half of all workers in restaurants, grocery stores, and department stores are under 24. As one journalist recently put it, "hundred of thousands of young people are spending hours making decaf lattes, folding jeans, grilling burgers or unpacking boxes of books and records for minimum wage." And their poverty rates are twice the national average.[20]

As a result, young people rarely commit to a career right out of college. They don't have their eyes on the prize; it's really more like their "eyes on the fries," as a recent documentary film put it. The increased instability of their employment prospects coupled with their sense that jobs must be emotionally and financially fulfilling leads to a volatile career trajectory. Many experience the "two-month itch" and switch jobs as casually as they change romantic partners. They take "stop-gap jobs," engaging in what I like to call "serial jobogamy." Listen to Jon, a 1992 Rutgers grad, who told a journalist about his career cluelessness:

> I had absolutely no idea what I wanted to do right out of college. I was clueless and fell blindly into a couple of dead-end jobs, which were just there for me to make money and figure out what I wanted to do. When I had no idea what I wanted to do, I couldn't even picture myself doing anything because I was so clueless about what was out there. I had so little direction. I was hanging on to these completely dead-end jobs thinking that maybe something would turn up. I was unhappy about

the situation, and the only thing that made it better was that all of my friends out of college were in the same boat. We would all come home and complain about our jobs together. We were all still drunks back then.[21]

And remember, this is the kid who is moving back home after graduation!

Education for What?

In 1900, only a small fraction of male teens attended secondary schools. About half were involved in agricultural labor and the rest were employed in resource, manufacturing, or the service sector, making nearly a living wage. Many lived with their families, and when they did, they made considerable financial contributions to family income. In fact, for many working-class families, the family's most prosperous years were the years their children were living at home with them.[22]

A century later, in most western nations, the vast majority of teens attended secondary school. In 2000, over 88% of all people aged 25–29 had completed high schools and nearly 30% (29.1%) had a BA—up from 17% only thirty years ago. This is the most highly educated group of young people in history.[23]

But they're taking their time getting that education. Four years after high school, 15% of the high school graduating class of 1972 had obtained their degree. Ten years later, the percentage had been cut by more than half—less than 7% had obtained a degree. Today, it's closer to 4%.

And also the least financially independent generation. Two-thirds of all college graduates owe more than $10,000 when they graduate; the average debt is nearly $20,000 and 5% owe more than $100,000. Recent college graduates owe 85% more in student loans alone than graduates a decade ago according to the Center for Economic and Policy research. Credit card debt for the age group 18–24 more than doubled between 1992 and 2001.[25]

The twentieth century has seen these kids move from being productive citizens to dependents on their families, the educational system, and the state. Less than one-third of this age group are employed enough to make them potentially financially independent. Those who live with their parents make virtually no contribution to family income. More than one-third of youth aged 18–34 receive cash from their parents, and nearly half (47%) receive time-help from their parents in any given year—averaging about $3,410 in cash and about 367 hours of help from their parents. At home, adolescents in many families are not treated as equal adults but as "indulged guests," writes psychologist Jeffrey Arnett. And away, young people who "swim" are able to do so "because families provide significant material and emotional support."[25]

No wonder two-thirds of all young people 18 to 24 live with their parents or other relatives and one-fifth of all 25-year-old Americans still live at home. And no wonder that 40% of all college graduates return to live with their parents for at least some period of time in that age span. Only 25% of men aged 25 live independently; 38% of women do. Eighteen million Americans between 20 and 34 live with their parents. Forget the empty nest syndrome—for one in five American families, it's still a "full nest."

And we're not the only country where this is happening. In Britain, for example, they're talking about nesters, boomerang children, co-resident adults, or "kippers"—Kids In Pockets, Eroding Retirement Savings, which pretty much sums up what their parents think of the 50% of college graduates who have returned home. In Japan, 70% of women between age 30 and 35 live with their parents, and in Australia, only 14% of people in their early 20s are independent.[26]

The Upward Age Spiral

These five classic demographic markers—education, marriage, parenthood, career and residential independence—have not simply shifted over the past generation. They've exploded, scattered across a time span that now stretches to more than a decade for a large swath of American youth. And they feed back on each other, reinforcing their separation and pushing the boundaries even further. "Because people are delaying marriage, they're living with their parents longer," writes Farnsworth Riche, in an article in *American Demographics*. "They are delaying marriage longer because they are going to school. They're going to school because most well-paying jobs now require a college degree." The National Marriage Project found that 86% of 20–29 year olds agree that "it is extremely important to be economically set before you get married."

Surely, then, it makes little sense to speak of this entire period, from early teens to late 20s, as a single identifiable period called "adolescence." The developmental tasks of a 13 year old are just too different from those of a 23 year old—even if they both are single, unemployed, and live with their parents. We need to identify this new stage of development, between adolescence and adulthood, that both captures the developmental characteristics of this life stage and locates it within important social and cultural shifts in American life, including the historical decrease in the number of males under 25 who are married or fathers; the increased number of young males who are extending their educations beyond college, to professional or graduate school; and, the increased percentage of young males under 25 who are living with their parents.

We need to see the stage from 18–26 as a distinct stage of development, a unique period. We need to map its contours, explore its boundaries, and understand its meaning. "In another 10 or 20 years, we're not going to be talking about this as a delay," says Tom Smith, director of the General Social Survey. "We're going to be talking about this as a normal trajectory."[27]

Thirty Is the New Twenty

Recently, some social scientists have begun to pay attention to this period between the end of adolescence and the beginning of adulthood. In September, 2004, a front page story in *USA Today* noticed that something was happening; a few months later, *Time* made it their cover story, calling them "twixters"—neither kids nor adults, but betwixt and between.[28]

The *Time* story, and the subsequent letters the magazine published offer a glimpse of our national confusion about this age. The twixters wrote eloquently about their situation. One moved back home after college because she couldn't find a job that paid enough to live on her own—only to find that "the majority of my high school class had done the same thing." But, she insisted, "we are not lazy. We want to work and make our way in the world." Another pointed out that her generation is "overwhelmed by indecision. We have the necessary tools, but now have too many options and not enough options at the same time. We are stuck." Another painted a nearly inspirational picture. Given that half their "parents are divorced, have financial problems or are stuck in jobs they loathe," she wrote, the twixters might instead be seen as "a generation that refuses to fall into the same archaic conventions that have led to so many dysfunctional families."

Adult letter writers were uniformly unsympathetic. They blamed the kids themselves, as if somehow the disastrous economy, sky-high housing costs, and high aspirations with no ways to fulfill them were somehow the fault of job seekers, not job suppliers—namely the adults themselves. "If only their parents had cut the golden apron strings and left them to their own devices, they would have learned to be more independent," wrote one. "There's not a single thing wrong with the young adults who live off their parents that a stint in the U.S. Marine Corps couldn't fix," wrote another. "Why do we need to come up with a new label for kids who stay home with their parents while figuring out what to do?" asked another, before reminding us that "we've had a name for that for years: moocher."[29]

Ironically, *all* of the twixter letters were from women, and *all* of the adult respondents were male. (*Time* did not seem to notice this interesting gender difference.) But it's an important element in our conversation: it is fathers—far more than mothers—who deeply resent the return of their college graduate children. The empty nest is experienced differently by fathers and mothers. Mothers may, for a time, mourn the absence of their children, as if their world has suddenly lost its center of gravity and spins aimlessly off its axis. Fathers, by contrast, often celebrate their new freedom from child-care responsibilities—they buy new golf clubs, load up on Viagra, and talk about this being, finally, their "turn." Similarly, mothers may be ambivalent about the "full nest" syndrome, but their husbands seem to be universally unhappy about it.

Developmental psychologists and sociologists have also tried to map this newly emerging stage of life. Sociologist James Cote calls the period "youthhood," while Terri Apter, a British social psychologist calls them "thresholders," who suffer from the neglect and scorn from parents who mistake their need for support and guidance as irresponsibility and immaturity. Recently, the John D. and Catherine T. MacArthur Foundation convened an academic panel on the "Transition to Adulthood."

Perhaps the most ambitious effort to map this postadolescent terra incognita has been Jeffrey Arnett's studies of what he calls "emerging adulthood." Following Erickson, Arnett sees this developmental stage as a gradual unfolding of a life plan, a "time for serious self-reflection, for thinking about what kind of life you want to live and what your Plan should be for your life" (p. 181). It's a period of increased independence—including independence from the preordained roles that they inherited from their elders. So, "they are not constrained by gender roles that prescribe strict rules for how they may meet and get to know each other" (p. 94). They are moving deliberately if unevenly toward intimate relationships, a steady and stable career path, and family lives, and along the way they are developing closer friendships with their parents, since the old issues of adolescent rebellion have been resolved by time and experience.

Yet Arnett's view of this stage of life is so sanguine, so sanitized, it's hardly recognizable. It's hard to square becoming better friends with your parents and an increasing sense of auton-

omy (and a decreasing reliance on peer groups for validation) with the fraternity initiations, binge drinking, athletic hazing, and date rape and other forms of sexual predation that often fill the exposes of campus life.

It's also hard to square this gradual easing into adulthood with the observations of other cultural critics. For example, Christopher Lasch observed more than twenty years ago that college students have a "certain protective shallowness, a fear of binding commitments, a willingness to pull up roots whenever the need arises, a dislike of depending on anyone, an incapacity for loyalty or gratitude."[30]

So, what do psychologists and sociologists know about this stage of development? For one thing, it's a stage of life characterized by indeterminacy. Many young adults feel they are just treading water, waiting to find the right job, the right person, the right situation, to reveal itself. "I'm just sitting around waiting for my life to begin, while it's all just slippin' away," sings Bruce Springsteen on "Better Days."

All the established markers of adulthood feel more ephemeral, more transient, and less reliable—both as events and as markers of adulthood. They're children of divorce, of family instability or dysfunction. They're unsure what to think about their parents. Some, mostly young women, describe their parents (mothers) as their best friend, others see their parents as exactly who they don't want to end up like.

"I'm in no rush to get married, and even less in a rush to have a kid," says Jeff, a 22-year-old senior at Indiana University interviewed 2/23/05. "I watched my own parents divorce, and it became pretty clear that they got married and started having kids—namely me—before they were ready. I'm not going to make that mistake."

It's a time of perhaps the greatest mismatch between their ambitions and their accomplishments. They graduate from college filled with ideas about changing the world, making their contribution, finding their place, and they enter a job market at the bottom, where work is utterly unfulfilling, boring, and badly paid. "It concerns me that of the many gifted people I went to school with, so few of them are actually doing what they really want to do," said one.[31] They are among the most entitled and underappreciated people in America. This was a generation that was told from the get-go that each of them was special, in which their self-esteem was so inflated they became light-headed, in which they were rewarded for every normal developmental milestone as if they were Mozart.

They're extremely other-directed, taking their cues from outside. They perform to please grown-ups—parents, teachers—but exhibit little capacity for self-reflection or internal motivation. They have high self-esteem, but little self-awareness. Many suspect that their self-esteem, so disconnected from actual achievement, is a bit of a fraud. Many lack a moral compass to help negotiate their way in the world.

It's unstable and uncertain. They drink more than they think they should, take more drugs, and probably get involved in more hook ups and bad relationships than they think they should. And they also get more down on themselves, because at this stage they also think they should know better. Their suicide rate is the highest for any age group except men over 70.[32]

As a result, they're more disconnected. They are less likely to read a newspaper, attend church, belong to a religion or a union, vote for president, or identify with a political party than any other age group, according to the General Social Survey. They're more cynical or negative about other people and less trusting. They are less likely to believe that people are basically trustworthy, helpful, fair, or that human beings are naturally good.[33]

Nor do they have any particular confidence in social, economic, or political institutions. They don't trust corporations, the way their parents did, because they've seen how such loyalty is rewarded with layoffs, downsizing, outsourcing, and moving overseas. They've watched as corporate executives lined their pockets with the pension funds of their own employees. They believe the only way to get rich in this culture is not by working hard, saving, and sacrificing, but by winning the

lottery. And they don't trust the government, which they believe is filled with people who are venal and self-aggrandizing, out of touch with the needs of their constituents.

On the other hand, there is plenty of good news. For one thing, they're developing friendships, especially across sex, the likes of which their parents do not understand. Young people constantly told me of trying to explain their cross-sex friendships to their parents. "My father just doesn't get it," said Kim, a 21-year-old senior at Oakland University in suburban Detroit. "I keep saying that they're my 'guy friends' and he's like, 'Wait. He's a boy and he's your friend, but he's not your boyfriend?' And I'm like 'Dad, chill. He's a boy. He's my friend. He is not my boyfriend.' And so he asks 'Does Jeff [her boyfriend] know?' "

Young adults go out in groups, hang out together, maybe even hook up. But they are friends first. And this bodes well in two ways. First, friendships are based on mutuality and equality, which assumes, at least in part, a more equal relationship between women and men than is offered either by the sexual predatory conquest model and its corollary, the passionate-swept-off-the-feet model, or even the chivalric code of gentlemen and ladies. And second, gender equality in marriage—marriages based on models of friendship and partnership—are far sturdier and more successful than those based on those other sexual passion-attractiveness models, according to psychologist John Gottman.

For some, friends are the new family. Think, actually, of the hit television sit-com *Friends*. Six friends share their mutual befuddlement about being grown-ups, relationships, careers, and life in general until they suddenly realize that everything they ever wanted in a life partner is right there next to them. And they then spend the next two seasons sorting out which one goes with whom. Or consider the HBO show, *Sex and the City*, the story of a quartet of single, sexually active women on the loose in New York City, each one hoping and struggling through relationships with the opposite sex, all the while aware that their real "family" was each other.

For others, our families become friends. Arnett suggests that some young adults become closer to their parents, and develop cross-generational friendships that surprise both parent and child. Over half of all Americans aged 18–29 talk to their parents every day, according to a January, 2005, article in *TIME*. But it is also true that the half who do speak to their parents every day are daughters—and the parents they are speaking to are their mothers.

There is more potentially good news. Students of domestic violence have recently noted a significant downward trend—lower and lower rates of domestic violence seem to be popping up in the United States, Canada, and Britain. For a long time, social scientists worried that a host of factors—increasing attention to the problem, better reporting of the crimes, better police and hospital evaluations, more stringent arrest mandates —would actually drive the rates higher, creating the irony that the more we talked about it, the more it seemed to increase. But the decrease in domestic violence seems to come less from the increased constraints placed on men, or even the increased deterrence of stronger laws, better enforced with mandatory sentencing. It seems to stem, instead, from the increased age of women entering into marriage (younger women are battered more often than older women) and the host of dramatic changes in women's lives (work outside the home leads to increased economic resources to leave a dangerous situation; women feel entitled not to be battered; playing sports and working outside the home correlate with higher self-esteem, which leads them to put up with less, etc.). It may be that the older women are when they marry, the lower their chances of being battered when they do.

Situational Maturity

If the demographic markers of adulthood have scattered across a decade or more, young people today are turning to more attitudinal indicators of when they become adults. In a 1994 study, Jeffrey Arnett asked students at a large Midwestern university "Do you think you have reached adult-

hood?" Twenty-seven per cent said "yes," 10% said "no" and 63% said "in some respects yes, in some respects no." Interestingly, the students no longer used traditional markers to categorize themselves. Completing education, entering the labor force, marriage, and parenthood all got low ratings, from 14% for parenthood to 27% for entering the labor force. Marriage and completing education were only identified by 15%, having a child by 14% as indicators of adulthood.

On the other hand, psychological criteria received much higher endorsements. "Accept responsibility for the consequences of your actions" led the list at 93%. Being able to "decide on personal beliefs and values independently of parents or other influences" was noted by 81%, the same percentage that identified becoming "less self-oriented, develop greater consideration for others."[34]

They become adults when they *feel* like adults. They experience a "situational maturity." Sometimes they want to be treated like adults, sometimes they want to be treated like children. "You don't get lectures about what life is like after college," comments Brandon to journalist Alexandra Robbins. "You don't have a textbook that tells you what you need to do to find success." "People have to invent their own road map," commented another.[35]

And they don't experience a calamitous break with their childhoods, since there is no one time when all five transitional indicators are achieved. By spreading them out, adulthood becomes a gradual process, a series of smaller decisions. One looks back suddenly and realizes one is actually an adult. The General Social Survey found that most people believe the transition to adulthood should be completed by age 26, a number that seems to rise every year.

The Missing Conversation: Gender

Perhaps one reason Arnett and his colleagues are so sanguine about emerging adulthood is because there is nary a word about gender in their work. The word *masculinity*—or, for that matter *femininity* —does not appear in his book's index; there's scant mention of gender gaps in attitudes. And that's about it.[36]

How can one possibly discuss the age group 16–26 and not talk about gender? In fact, this is perhaps the most gendered stage of a person's development—for one simple reason: It is a time that is utterly unmapped. The older institutions of socialization exert far less influence, although same-sex peers and media often pick up some of the slack. It is a time when there are no road maps, no blueprints, no primers that tell the young person what to do, how to understand this period. That's why none of the terms given to this stage of development—"emergent adulthood," "transition to adulthood," "twixters," "thresholders," and the like—have any resonance whatever to the young men and women I speak to on college campuses and in workplaces around the country.

Almost all of them call themselves—and call each other—"guys." It's both a generic catch-all term that goes beyond this age group and a specific term demarcating it from "kids" and "grown-ups." While it's gender-specific, women use it too. Watch a group of college women sitting around wondering what to do that evening: "What do you guys want to do?" "I don't know, what do you guys want to do?" One hardly needs a man around to whom the term would refer. (This "generic" term is also gender-specific, and we'll look at the ways that the term itself implies the gender inequality that characterizes this stage of life. Girls live in Guyland—*not* the other way around.)

In fact, this is a period of what sociologists James Cote and Anton Allahar call "gender intensification"—the assertion of "exaggerated notions associated with the different roles that still hold many men and women in separate spheres of endeavor."[37] It's when the struggle to prove manhood becomes even more intense—in part because it is only peers who are watching—and judging.

That the territory remains so unmapped actually exacerbates the emphasis on gender. Part of the definition of masculinity is, after all, to act

as if one knows exactly where one is going. If men have a difficult time asking for directions when they get lost driving their cars, imagine what they'll do when they feel lost and adrift on the highway of life! One acts as if one knows where one is going, even if it isn't true. And it's this posture, and the underlying sense that one is a fraud, that leaves young men most vulnerable to manipulation by the media and by their peers. If I just follow along and don't ask any questions, everyone will assume I have it all together—and I won't be exposed.

Guyland thus becomes the terrain in which young men so relentlessly seem to act out, seem to take the greatest risks, and do the stupidest things. It's also the time when they need the involvement of their parents—especially their fathers. Fathers often fade out of the picture, thinking their job of child-rearing and role-modeling is over once their offspring graduate from high school. For many guys, their fathers are a "shadowy presence."[38] Their kids have survived, so now, fathers seem to say, it's time for "us."

It's not entirely true that fathers are just self-ish; they're also encouraged to think selfishly for the first time in a long time, by an advertising industry that has recently discovered empty nesters as an emerging market—they've finally shed all the financial responsibilities of child-rearing and college, giving them some disposable income for the first time in decades. And they're ready to find something other than their children to fulfill them.

All the advice books about boys' development offer little guidance here. Although they may be useful when they discuss boys' development up until they turn 16 or so, they all end just at the cusp of "guyland." It's pretty difficult to talk to a 17- or 22-year-old guy about what the books say about being a man when the books top out at 16!

And so, directionless and clueless, we come to rely increasingly on our peers. And our peers often have some interesting plans for what we have to endure to prove to them that we are real men. The "penalty for not living up to the norms of being tough, being 'cool' is severe," writes Marie Richmond-Abbott.[39] Is it "rejection or simply being ignored."

Beyond Guyland

Guyland is both a social space and a stage of life. It's unlikely to disappear. If anything, the stage of life is likely to become more firmly entrenched. There are positive reasons for delaying marriage, exploring different career paths, playing the field, traveling, hanging out, exploring one's self and who one wants to be, and become, in this lifetime. But it must be time well spent.

Most guys drift out of Guyland by their late 20s, as they commit to careers or girlfriends, and begin to enter the world of responsible adulthood. But still, they do so with few rules and fewer signposts to help them on their journeys.

Our task, as a society, is to disengage the stage of life with that social space—to enable young men to live through this stage more consciously, more honorably, and with greater resilience—to inject into that anomic and anarchic space called Guyland a code of ethics, of emotional responsiveness, and of wholesome occasional irresponsibility.

Some of Guyland's most celebrated inhabitants seem to be getting that message—and passing it on. In response to the death of Scott Krueger (a pledge at MIT) during a drinking and hazing ritual, the national office of Phi Gamma Delta has produced a well-conceived video about high-risk drinking that is required for all their chapters. The local chapter of another fraternity accepts openly gay men and then works to make other brothers' homophobia the problem to be addressed. Sigma Phi Epsilon has embraced a new "balanced man program," which the fraternity developed in the 1990s to combat a culture of "boozing, drugging and hazing." They've simply and unilaterally done away with the pledge system; new members have virtually all the rights and privileges of brothers. The brothers are *presumed* to be men when they begin; they don't have to prove their manhood to their peers. Scott

Thompson, the fraternity's national spokesman, told a journalist:

> New members don't pledge for a certain period of time, get hazed, get initiated, and then show up for parties until they graduate. In the Balanced Man Program, men join, and they are developed from the time they join until the time they graduate. Part of that development focuses on building a sound mind and sound body, a simple philosophy that we took from the ancient Greeks.[40]

Here, in the words of a former frat guy, lies the hope of guys everywhere: that the culture of entitlement can become a culture of integrity—in which guys know that each person's integrity is equal to his own. That guys can be valued for their integrity and encouraged to be good, whole human beings. That the culture of silence can become a culture of honor, in which each guy feels honor bound to speak up, to act ethically, and to defend his core beliefs with respect for the simple dignity of his friends. That the culture of protection can become a culture of love, in which each guy feels surrounded by support and care, knows that he is not alone, and that having left Guyland far behind, he has nothing left to prove.

Notes

1. G. Stanley Hall, *Adolescence: Its Psychology and Its Relations to Physiology, Anthropology, Sociology, Sex, Crime, Religion, and Education* (New York: Appleton, 1904). In an earlier essay, he explained that "the boy's bullying is the soul-germ of the man's independence." He defended one boy who was "overbearing and cruel" to his sister, whom he had "perfectly terrorized."

2. See Steven Mintz, "Adolescence's Neglected Anniversary" op-ed at Ascribe Newswire, January 10, 2005; archived at www.contemporaryfamilies.org/media/news%2099.htm

3. E. C. Cline, "Social Implications of Modern Adolescent Problems" in *The School Review*, September 1941, pp. 511–514.

4. Edward Strecker, *Their Mothers' Sons: The Psychiatrist Examines an American Problem* (Philadelphia:

Lippincott, 1946) and Philip Wylie, *Generation of Vipers* (New York: Rinehart, 1942).

5. Erik Erikson, *Childhood and Society* (New York: W. W. Norton, 1950) and *Identity: Youth and Crisis* (New York: W. W. Norton, 1968).

6. James Coleman, *The Adolescent Society* (New York: The Free Press, 1961). See also James Coleman, *Adolescents and Schools* (New York: Basic Books, 1965).

7. Kenneth Keniston, *Young Radicals: Notes on a Committed Youth*. (New York: Harcourt, 1968).

8. See Stephanie Coontz, *The Way We Never Were* (New York: Basic, 1992).

9. See Caroline Stanley, "Why Teens Do Dumb Things" in www.healthykids.com, accessed October 23, 2004, describing the research of Dr. James Bjork.

10. Sharon Jayson, "It's Time to Grow Up—Later" in *U.S.A. Today*, September 30, 2004, p. 1D.

11. U.S. Bureau of the Census, Table MS-2: "Estimated Median Age at First Marriage by Sex, 1890 to Present" released September 15, 2004. In the first part of the century, the median age of first marriage fluctuated as the economy expanded and contracted; now, however, the median age creeps up steadily, seemingly disconnected from and uninfluenced by external factors.

12. T. J. Mathews, and Brady Hamilton, "Mean Age of Mother, 1970–2000" *National Vital Statistics Reports*, 51 (1), December, 2002.

13. Jeffrey Jensen Arnett, *Emerging Adulthood: The Winding Road from the Late Teens through the Twenties* (New York: Oxford University Press, 2004), p. 162.

14. Martha Irvine, "Young Workers Want It All, Now" in *Seattle-Post-Intelligencer*, June 27, 2005; available at: http://seattlepi.nwsource.com/business/230177_entitlement27.html (accessed 6/28/05).

15. Bob Herbert, "The Young and the Jobless" in *The New York Times*, May 12, 2005.

16. Cited in Herbert, "The Young and the Jobless," *ibid.*

17. Mary Corcoran and Jordan Matsudaira, "Is it Getting Harder to Get Ahead? Economic Attainment in Early Adulthood for Two Cohorts" in *On the Frontier of Adulthood: Theory, Research and Public Policy*, Richard Settersten, Jr., Frank F. Furstenberg, Jr., and Ruben G. Rumbaut, eds. (Chicago: University of Chicago Press, 2005), p. 357.

18. Tom Smith, "Generation Gaps in Attitudes and Values from the 1970s to the 1990s" in *On the Frontier of Adulthood: Theory, Research and Public Policy*, Richard Settersten, Jr., Frank F. Furstenberg, Jr., and Ruben G. Rumbaut, eds. (Chicago: University of Chicago Press, 2005), p. 182.

19. Douglas Coupland, *Generation X: Tales for an Accelerated Culture*. (New York: St. Martin's Press, 1991).

20. Elana Berkowitz, "Eyes on the Fries: Young People are Coming of Age in the Era of the McJob," published by CampusProgress.org on March 31, 2005.

21. Cited in Alexandra Robbins and Abby Wilner, *Quarterlife Crisis* (New York: Jeremy Tarcher, 2001), p. 113.

22. William Reese, *The Origins of the American High School* (New Haven: Yale University Press, 1995).

23. Elizabeth Fussell and Frank F. Furstenberg, Jr., "The Transition to Adulthood during the Twentieth Century: Race, Nativity, and Gender" in *On the Frontier of Adulthood*, p. 38.

24. Lou Dobbs, "The Generation Gap" in *U.S. News and World Report*, May 23, 2005, p. 58.

25. Schoeni and Ross, 402; Settersten, 2005, p. 535; Jeffrey Jensen Arnett, "Are College Students Adults? Their Conceptions of the Transition to Adulthood" in *Journal of Adult Development* 1, 1994, p. 162.

26. Edi Smockum, "Done with College? Come back to the Fold" in *The Financial Times*, September 10, 2005, p. 23.

27. As cited in Tom Smith, "Generation Gaps in Attitudes and Values from the 1970s to the 1990s" in *On the Frontier of Adulthood: Theory, Research, and Public Policy*, edited by Richard Settersten, Frank Furstenberg and Richard Rumbault (Chicago: University of Chicago Press, 2005), p. 182.

28. Sharon Jayson, "It's Time to Grow Up — Later" in *USA Today*, September 30, 2004, p. 1D; Lev Grossman, "Grow Up? Not So Fast" in *Time*, January 24, 2005, p. 42–54.

29. Letters, *Time*, February 14, 2005, p. 6.

30. *Haven in a Heartless World*, 1979, no page given

31. In Jeffrey Arnett, *Emerging Adulthood*, p. 41.

32. James E. Cote and Anton L. Allahar, *Generation on Hold: Coming of Age in the Late Twentieth Century* (New York: New York University Press, 1996), p. 59.

33. Tom Smith, "Generation Gaps in Attitudes and Values from the 1970s to the 1990s" in *On the Frontier of Adulthood: Theory, Research, and Public Policy*, edited

by Richard Settersten, Frank Furstenberg and Richard Rumbault (Chicago: University of Chicago Press, 2005), p. 182.

34. Jeffrey Jensen Arnett, "Are College Students Adults?"; see also Arnett, *Emerging Adulthood* p. 210.

35. Alexandra Robbins and Amy Willner, *Quarterlife Crisis*, p. 121, 6.

36. Neither of the two major works cited here—Arnett's *Emerging Adulthood* and the MacArthur-sponsored *On the Frontier of Adulthood*—has a single reference to "masculinity," "manhood," or even "men" in the index.

37. James Cote and Anton Allahar, *Generation on Hold*, p. 84.

38. Larson and Richard, 1994, p. 164.

39. Marie Richmond-Abbott, *Masculine and Feminine: Gender Roles over the Life Cycle* (2nd ed). McGraw-Hill, 1992, p. 121.

40. Benoit Denizet-Lewis, "Ban of Brothers" in *The New York Times Magazine*, January 9, 2005, p. 74.

Shaun R. Harper

The Measure of a Man: Conceptualizations of Masculinity among High-Achieving African American Male College Students

Previous inquiry confirms that a healthy, conflict-free masculine identity leads to a strong self-concept and positive outcomes in a wide array of areas, including academics (Gilbert and Gilbert 1998; Price 2000). Despite this, little attention has been given to exploring identity development and conceptualizations of masculinity among male students on college and university campuses. Research regarding within-group variations among 18–24 year-old African American male collegians is virtually nonexistent, and the intersection between race and gender among this population remains particularly understudied. The proverbial saying, "Boys will be boys," has not been adequately disaggregated by race and ethnicity within various age groups in much of the mainstream literature on masculinity. Theoretical perspectives on masculine identity development in schools have been largely based on data collected from White male students, thus offering limited applicability to men of color. Consequently, structured efforts to assist African American male students in developing strong masculine identities that lead to academic, social, and long-term post-undergraduate success have not been implemented at most postsecondary educational institutions. Given that two-thirds of all African American men who start college never graduate (Mortenson 2001), it is essential to explore the nexus between identity development, definitions of self, and outcomes, including academic achievement and retention.

African American college students have received considerable attention in the social-science literature over the past 30 years (Sedlacek 1987). However, few studies focus exclusively on African American men, and even fewer examine the needs and experiences of high-achieving African American male undergraduates (Bonner 2001; Fries-Britt 1997, 1998). As a result, current scholarship contains limited insight into the gender politics and peer interactions of African American male college students. To help address the paucity of research on this population, this article explores definitions of masculinity among African American male college students, and perceptions of those definitions by high-achievers within this group.

Literature Review

Previous research on masculinity and its role in identity development has almost exclusively been based on data collected from young boys, adolescents, and male adults who were not enrolled in college during the time at which the studies were conducted. Therefore, the majority of the literature reviewed in this section is not specific to traditional-aged college students.

Social Context and Masculine Identity Formation

Many foundational studies on masculinity suggest that identity development among boys is primarily characterized by autonomy, achievement concerns, competence, mastery, supremacy, and

Reprinted by permission of the author.

competitiveness (Gilligan 1993). This body of literature provides many of the generally accepted theories regarding masculine identity development, and consistently confirms that same-sex peers are largely influential in the development of masculine identities among young boys, which help shape long-lasting definitions of what it means to be a man (Blos 1962, 1979; Chodorow 1978; LaVoire 1976; Stoller 1964; Wainrib 1992). Connell (1993) suggests that men of all ages and ethnicities are often forced to negotiate their masculinities with other males—meaning that their manhood must be approved and validated by their peers. Morrison and Eardley's (1985) assertions fully capture and describe what most of the published literature reports about the impact of peers on identity development in young boys:

> Boys grow up to be wary of each other. We are taught to compete with one another at school, and to struggle to prove ourselves outside it, on the street, the playground and the sports field. Later we fight for status over sexual prowess, or money, or physical strength or technical know-how . . . the pressure is on to act tough. We fear humiliation or exclusion, or ultimately the violence of other boys if we fail to conform (19).

These claims are supported by Gilligan (1993) and Head (1999), who also suggest that men are more competitive, less apt to collaborate with one another, and far more rule- and authority-bound than women. Accordingly, male peer group interactions typically result in some sort of contest to see who can outpace, outrun, and overpower the others.

For boys at almost all levels of schooling, peer promotion of sports and athleticism play an influential role in the shaping of their masculine identities (Morrison & Eardley 1985). Quite often, interests beyond football and active outdoor play for young boys are seen as abnormal and unacceptable by peers (Harris 1995). Alternative expressions of manliness, such as doing well in school or participating in non-sports related school activities, must be approved by other male peer group members. Gilbert and Gilbert (1998:

63) contend that rule-based sports both afford boys the opportunity to rehearse their masculinities and also factor into what it means to be deemed "cool" by peers: "Unfortunately, this image of the cool sociable sportsman is constantly set against the picture of the boy whose interests might be to read a book, a practice most often associated with girls." They posit that sports are chief among the masculine endeavors that conflict with a commitment to school achievement.

Through the adolescence and young adulthood periods, being good at sports becomes more important than simple participation. Usually, the "coolest guys" on campus are those who are standouts on the athletic field or court (Askew & Ross 1988; Gilbert & Gilbert 1998). By contrast, rarely, if ever, is the class president or smartest student in the class considered the most "manly" by his peers—unless of course he also participates in sports. Furthermore, those who can overpower opponents in athletic competition are also usually more sought after for romantic relationships by young women than male students who demonstrate leadership in other areas on campus and make good grades. Kunjufu (1988) asserts that African American boys must make a choice between school achievement and peer acceptance. The title of his book, *To Be Popular or Smart: The Black Peer Group,* captures the essence of this struggle. To this end, young men generally prefer to identify themselves as standout athletes instead of academic achievers or campus leaders.

This fascination with sports, accumulating points, beating out opponents, and demonstrating masculinity and superiority through competitive exercises has an enduring effect on the male identity, which extends into the college years. For example, the accumulation of points to surpass others in childhood games usually turns into a motivation to accumulate wealth, power, and monetary status during adulthood (Wainrib 1992). Likewise, most boys who strive for autonomy and superiority during the childhood years develop identities characterized by a desire to compete with and outperform others through the mastery of non-collaborative tasks. The peer influences discussed herein are largely shaped by perceivably rigid societal standards regarding male-appropriate behaviors (Askew & Ross 1988; Gilbert & Gilbert 1998; Harris 1995; Head 1999; Martino & Meyenn 2001).

Westwood (1990: 58) argues that society has provided "the insistence of 'the male role' against which all men must be measured." Society has historically suggested that boys should play sports, suppress outward displays of emotion, and compete rigorously against each other. Parents have also been influenced by these societal indices of masculinity, as many communicate messages of power, toughness, and competitiveness to their young sons. No father wants his son to grow up being a "pussy," "sissy," "punk," or "softy"—terms commonly associated with boys and men who fail to live up to the traditional standards of masculinity in America. Masculine identity is largely impacted by societal messages that say men should be the breadwinners for and protectors of their families; should be legends in college and professional sports; and should be leaders and executives in the organizations by which they are employed.

Expressions of Masculinity among African American Males

Harris (1995) argues that the traditional pathway to masculine identity development is limited in its applicability to African American men, and offers the following:

> Pressures to meet European American standards of manhood as provider, protector, and disciplinarian are representative of such a dilemma for African American men . . . Inequities in earning potential and employment and limited access to educational opportunities prevent the expression of these behaviors . . . To compensate for feelings of powerlessness, guilt, and shame that result from the inability to enact traditional masculine roles, some African American male youth have redefined masculinity to emphasize sexual promiscuity, toughness, thrill seeking, and the use of violence in interpersonal interactions (279–280).

Harris suggests that traditionally White masculine ideals are often unattainable for African American men due to the material constraints of race, and that expectations for African American men to assume these seemingly unachievable masculine roles exacerbate identity conflicts. In turn, these perceptions and experiences force them to find alternative ways to prove their manliness. Instead of the mainstream definitions of masculinity—accumulation of wealth, status, and power—Oliver (1988, 1989) asserts that masculinity for African American men is often characterized by two primary orientations: "tough guy" and "player of women."

Tough guys are those who are good at fighting, are not afraid to defend themselves, and incite fear in others. Although most boys attempt to exude toughness and are generally "naughty by nature," displays of hyperactivity and roughness among African American males of all ages are perceived as dangerous and disproportionately lead to a harsher set of penalties in schools and society (Ferguson 2000). In a national study of more than 25 million public school students, Gregory (1997) found that African American males were more likely to be punished at school, suspended, or expelled than any other racial/ethnic group. In fact, they were 16 times more likely than their White female counterparts to experience disciplinary actions or school expulsion. Davis and Jordan (1994) found a nexus between school discipline, suspensions, grade retention, and academic failure. Despite these negative outcomes, African American males often set the standards for popularity, hip-hop culture, and athleticism at school (Davis 2003). Those who are perceived as tough, rough, and athletically talented enjoy peer admiration and respect, but usually garner negative reactions from teachers and school administrators.

The "player of women" concept is usually more prevalent in the teenage and young adulthood years, and is often linked to the "tough guy" orientation. Having multiple girlfriends and sexual partners typifies the "player." Those who are unsuccessful at these aims are generally made fun of, have their heterosexuality questioned, or are considered less masculine than their peers. Again, this characteristic also applies to men of different races and ethnicities, but it is extremely common among African Americans. Media and commercial images overwhelmingly depict, popularize, and celebrate certain types of African American men—namely pimps, rappers, and athletes, who are surrounded by attractive women (usually more than one at a time) and appear to be financially prosperous. In turn, young African American boys are socialized to believe that these behaviors are in fact indicative of Black masculinity and success. Those who are glorified usually share a certain communication and self-presentation style and approach to interacting with women. Majors and Billson (1992) introduced the term "cool pose," which is displayed by many African American men of all ages. Trendy and baggy clothing (usually urban wear), an overall relaxed look and informal presence, and a "pimp-style" strut are characteristic of this pose.

The African American male middle school students in Davis' (2001) study had developed a strict masculine code of conduct in their school that was characterized by various elements of the aforementioned "player of women" and "cool pose" concepts. He offers the following analysis:

> Boys who do not adhere to the prescribed rigid masculine orthodoxy are victimized . . . Black boys who dare to verbalize alternative views on masculinity and any aspect of the code in effect violate the masculine code. These actions conflict with the notions of what is appropriately male, and thus he is usually expelled from the confines and benefits of boy networks at the school (177–178).

These findings are consistent with Connell's (1993: 193) assertion that masculinity "must be seen as an active process of construction, occurring in a field of power relations that is often tense and contradictory, and often involving negotiation of alternative ways of being masculine." Connell calls for more inquiry that examines the masculine identities of African American men

who assume roles other than the cool posing tough guys, players of women, and athletes.

As previously mentioned, insight into within-group masculine negotiations among African American men in college is scarce, as most research has been conducted either with young African American boys or with White male students. How do those who choose to excel in postsecondary education resolve the conflicts noted above? How do African American men on college and university campuses define masculinity? Do high-achieving African American male undergraduates ignore societal and peer messages regarding what is masculine, or are their identities in conflict? The paucity of research regarding masculine variability among this population makes the investigation of these questions especially interesting and important. The present study seeks to fill this void. Exploring and understanding the ways in which masculine identities are conceptualized and negotiated among African American male undergraduates could offer practical implications that lead to more positive academic and psychosocial outcomes.

Methodology

This article is based on a larger qualitative data set regarding the experiences of high-achieving African American undergraduate men. The phenomenological study sought to understand what it is like to be a high-achieving African American male college student at a large, predominantly White university, and included questions regarding the ways in which the participants deemed themselves different from other African American male undergraduates on their campuses. The phenomenology tradition in qualitative research focuses on understanding and describing the "lived experiences" of the participants involved in the study (Moustakas 1994). This type of qualitative study usually provides full, detailed descriptions of the phenomenon under study (Denzin & Lincoln 2000; Miles & Huberman 1994). The aim of the present study was to capture, in the students' words, what they had experienced and observed within their same-race male peer groups at their respective institutions.

Sites

This study was conducted at six large, public research universities in the Midwest—Indiana University, Michigan State University, Purdue University, The Ohio State University, the University of Illinois, and the University of Michigan. These six institutions are similar in terms of size, age, reputation, and selectivity; they are also in close geographic proximity to each other and are affiliated with the same athletic conference. On average, 6.3 percent of the students at the institutions were African American during the time at which the data were collected, with African American undergraduate enrollments ranging from 3.1 percent to 8.8 percent. Approximately 34 percent of the African American students at these universities were male.

Sample

Key administrators on the six campuses (i.e., deans, vice presidents, and directors of campus programs) were asked to identify African American male students who had made the most of their college experience. This was defined as earning cumulative grade point averages above 3.0; establishing lengthy records of leadership and involvement in multiple campus organizations; earning the admiration of their peers (as determined by peer elections to campus leadership positions); developing quality relationships with faculty and high-ranking campus administrators; participating in enriching educational experiences (e.g., study abroad programs, internships, and summer research programs); and earning numerous collegiate awards and honors. Using these criteria, 32 high-achieving African American undergraduate men were identified and selected for participation in this study.

The sample included four sophomores, 12 juniors, and 16 seniors, representing a wide variety of academic majors. The mean GPA for the sample was 3.32. All of the participants were between the ages of 18–22 years old and single with no

dependents. Twelve participants grew up in single-parent homes and the remaining 20 were from homes with two parents. Collectively, they had been awarded more than $489,000 in merit-based scholarship awards. The participants expressed high educational and career aspirations, with 72 percent indicating the intent to someday earn a doctoral degree (including the J.D.). The remaining 28 percent planned to pursue master's degrees, usually in business. None of the high-achievers were student athletes. All but two identified themselves as heterosexual—one was openly gay and the other was privately bisexual.

Data Collection Procedures

Each of the 32 African American men was asked to participate in a 2–3 hour face-to-face interview, and at least two follow-up interviews via telephone. I visited each campus at least once to conduct the first-round individual interviews; four campuses were visited twice. A semi-structured interview technique was used in the face-to-face interview sessions, which enabled me to gather information without making the dialogue exchange inflexible and restrictive (Holstein & Gubrium 1995). Although specific questions and interview protocol were used in this study, the discussions often became conversational, thus allowing the participants to reflect upon the experiences, perceptions, and observations they deemed most important. Transcripts from all sessions were sent to each participant for confirmation within eight weeks following his interviews.

Data Analysis

Several techniques prescribed by Moustakas (1994) were used to analyze the data collected from interviews with the 32 participants. I first bracketed out my thoughts and assumptions as I read each line of the participants' transcripts. The margins of the transcripts were marked with reflective comments regarding my own presumptions and experiences. After bracketing, the transcripts were sorted and key phases were linearly arranged under tentative headings in NVivo®. This process resulted in the identification of 36 invariant constituents, which were sub-themes that did not vary more than 84.7 percent of the time (Moustakas, 1994). The invariant constituents were helpful for understanding the participants' experiences, and were later clustered into thematic categories. I identified seven thematic categories that captured the essence of the participants' shared experiences.

Findings

Participants on the six campuses consistently noted that their African American male peers used a limited number of variables to describe masculinity—dating and pursuing romantic (oftentimes sexual) relationships with women; any type of athletic activity (organized sports, individual exercise and bodybuilding, etc.); competition, namely through sports and video games; and the accumulation and showing off of material possessions. Some participants added fraternity membership to the list based on the observation that fraternity members seemed to attract and date more women. The participants were convinced that activities in which they were engaged—such as, holding multiple leadership positions; achieving top academic honors in the classroom; and maintaining a high-profile status on campus—would not have made it into the African American undergraduate male portfolio of masculinity. One University of Illinois student commented:

> Playing basketball in the rec. center, lifting weights, shooting hoops, partying, and showing off . . . they think those are masculine activities. I can be blunt, right? How many girls they can screw and who they've slept with. Those are the activities that most brothas' on this campus would use to define masculinity. You'll find them talking about these things in a boastful way all the time. I don't believe that holding a leadership position in student government has quite found its way onto the list of masculinity.

Participants from the other five campuses consistently reported similar ways of thinking among their fellow African American male peers.

Lenny, a senior at Purdue, was dumbfounded when asked if other African American male students would perceive leadership and out-of-class involvement as masculine. Instead of speculating, he posed the following question in return: "He's slept with 30 girls or he's the Vice President in an organization on campus . . . which would you think the majority of 18–21 year-old Black males would consider more masculine?" The participants believed their peers were seeking validation from other African American males, and had something to prove by attempting to date and have sex with as many women as possible. Reportedly, competition to see who could sleep with the most female students on campus was commonplace—extra points were awarded for interracial sexual encounters. Males who successfully conquered the most women were considered "the big men on campus."

Because of their active pursuit of dating opportunities and attention from the opposite sex, many of their male peers spent a significant amount of time in the gym working out and enhancing their physiques. Michael, a student at Michigan State, believed women somehow occupied most African American male students' time on campus. "Women probably take a good 80 percent of that time because when they aren't actually spending time with women, they're working out to look good for the ladies." One Indiana University student noted that one of his closest male friends spent more time lifting weights and playing basketball in the campus fitness center than the combined hours he spent attending class and doing homework. "Sure, his body is on point, but his grades and resume are not," the participant added.

Second to women, competition influenced many of their peers' perceptions of masculinity. Specifically, defeating opponents at video games and on the basketball court were two key ways in which "real men" could flaunt their manhood. Marshawn, another Indiana University student, observed that competition among African American males, while quite prevalent on campus, was not "cutthroat." That is, his peers derived tremendous satisfaction from outpacing each other in intramural and recreational sports and outscoring each other on video games. Thus, they did not seek to bring about harm, injury, or widespread insult to other African American males. Instead, Marshawn noticed that competition on his campus had more to do with building masculine reputations and earning respect. An Ohio State student remembered an excerpt from a speech given by a visiting lecturer who was directly addressing the African American males in the audience:

> He was like, when you're on the basketball court and you're about to take someone to the hole, you're talking trash and grabbing your [genitals] like, 'bring it on'! Now, why is it when brothas' are in the classroom, they act like 'little punks?' You can be hard out there, but then you get in here and you're a 'little punk'!

The participants also thought other African American male students on their campuses defined masculinity and achievement through the accumulation and exhibition of material possessions. Anyone who appeared to have a pocket full of money earned the respect of other African American males on campus. Nice cars with flashy rims were at the top of the list. One student shared the following story:

> I've sat down with different brothas' and asked them why they were here. This one African American guy told me something that really shocked me. He said he was here in college so he could get a good enough job to buy a Ford Excursion [sports utility vehicle]. This really shocked me. His idea of achievement was to have this truck with some rims on it. That was his sole reason for attending college.

In addition to cars, the participants' African American male peers also relied on expensive clothing and shoes to show they were excelling and doing well, the participants claimed. Those who sported the "flyest gear" were often dubbed coolest among the African American students on campus. The participants considered their peers to be quite materialistic and disproportionately focused on showing off to impress women and other male students.

By contrast, the participants in this study offered different definitions of masculinity. Though they too enjoyed playing recreational sports and pursuing romantic relationships (time permitting), the high-achievers did not consider those activities paradigmatic examples of masculinity. Instead, their shared definition overwhelmingly included "taking care of business." For example, many participants talked about the importance of working hard to secure their futures, and handling the business that would protect them from dropping out or failing out of school. Failing to do well and having to return home to their mothers did not strike them as being very masculine, especially for men who called themselves adults.

They also strongly believed that leadership and community advancement had been historically associated with men. Bryant, a senior at the University of Michigan commented: "Real men assume responsibility and take the lead on making improvements; they don't leave problems for others to solve. College is the place where you learn to be a leader." The participants also acknowledged that most of the historical icons and celebrated figures in the African American community were male leaders. "Look at Dr. Martin Luther King, Malcolm X, Jesse Jackson, Louis Farrakhan . . . they're masculine; they weren't athletes, but they were out in the streets fighting for the rights of Black folks. To me, that's masculine."

Reportedly, the participants' African American male peers (though uninvolved themselves) supported, appreciated, and applauded the participants' display of leadership on the six campuses. In fact, both their African American male and female peers elected them to serve in a variety of important leadership capacities in minority and mainstream student organizations. Keely, a junior at the University of Illinois, commented, "They don't really know what the organization does, but because they feel this camaraderie with another African American student who's running for a particular leadership position, they're going to vote for that student because he or she is Black." The participants felt a special sense of support from other African American males on campus and believed their peers would not have elected them to major leadership positions if they deemed such activities inappropriately "unmasculine." "When I ran for student body president, brothas' turned out in record numbers to cast their ballots in my favor; they wouldn't have done that if they didn't at least respect me as an African American male peer who could be their leader," a Purdue student added.

The participants believed their previous track records for contributing to the advancement of the minority and African American student communities on campus helped them win favor with their fellow African American male peers. Though they were involved in an array of clubs and student organizations on their campuses, the high-achievers primarily held leadership positions in African American and minority student organizations. Their involvement enabled them to programmatically address issues and communicate the concerns of the African American community to university administrators. The participants often likened their roles to leading a family. In essence, their fellow African American peers comprised a "family" that these student leaders were providing for and protecting from social isolation, racism, and discrimination on their predominantly White campuses.

Regarding masculinity, the participants strongly believed that being a man had a lot to do with preparing to take care of a family. They often asked what good would a man who wasted his time in college and consequently ended up in dead-end jobs for the rest of his life be to his family and community. Or how useful was a man who did not stand up for his family and attempt to make their lives better. Robert's remarks provided an excellent synopsis of the high-achievers' shared opinion:

First of all, a real man honors God. Secondly, a real man takes care of his family and the people he is directly or indirectly responsible for . . . to me, anything outside of that is not very masculine. If you're not a person who's honoring God, you're not a man. If you're not doing things right now to take care of the family you're going to have in the future because you're so bent on self-gratification, you're not a man. Real men know that most decisions they make today will affect the family they're going to have in the future.

The participants believed they would be better off in the long-term by striving to become like older African American male leaders from their communities, instead of validating their manhood through their fellow African American college peers who would presumably achieve limited success later in life.

Although their definitions of masculinity were relatively unconventional and the activities in which they were most engaged were not part of the traditional African American male portfolio of manliness, the participants indicated that their masculinities were never questioned or challenged by their African American male peers or anyone else. This even held true for the gay and bisexual men in the sample. They had never been the victims of ridicule because they chose to spend their out-of-class time differently. The high-achievers received an incredible amount of support and praise from other African American male students on their campuses, including the uninvolved. "Though the things that I'm involved in wouldn't be in their criteria for being a man, they wouldn't look at me and say, 'Cullen isn't masculine.'"

The high-achievers had a different perspective on the perceived nexus between masculinity, materialism, and achievement. For instance, one participant from the University of Michigan noted:

Being "the man" isn't about the money, the clothes, and the cars that you have right now. You're "the man" when you're at a company and you're in a position to hire other African

Americans; when you're in a position to give dollars back to the Black community; when you have time to go be a mentor to young African American boys in your city, that's masculine . . . to me, being an executive someday who's able to reach back and help other African Americans is the measure of a man.

Discussion

The 32 high-achieving African American men's conceptualizations of masculinity, in comparison to their fellow African American male peers, offer several intriguing contrasts to previous inquiries on this topic. The participants were comfortable with themselves and had apparently developed conflict-free masculine identities, despite their unconventional views and the ways in which their out-of-class time was spent. Morrison and Eardley (1985) contend that boys who fail to live up to traditional standards of masculinity usually experience ridicule and sometimes become victims of violent acts committed by their male peers. The experiences of these 32 high-achievers contradicted that claim. Instead they felt extremely supported by other African American male students on their campuses, and were not ridiculed or deemed heterosexually-suspect because of the decisions they made regarding the allocation of their out-of-class time. This held true for the openly gay student in the sample. He believed his African American male peers fully supported and treated him with an enormous amount of respect. The sexual orientation of the one bisexual participant remained private and undisclosed among his African American male peers, and he too experienced no ridicule from other men on his campus. Reportedly, this was largely due in part to their previous track records of service, leadership, and contributions to the African American communities at their universities.

These reports of peer approval coincide with Connell's (1993) claim that masculinities must be negotiated within male peer groups. It appears that committing one's time to the advancement of the African American community and assuming responsibility for bringing about changes that would improve the quality of life for minority students were the primary ways by which the high-achievers were able to negotiate with their uninvolved male peers who would ultimately benefit from the improved campus conditions.

Unlike Kunjufu's (1988) characterization, the participants did not have to choose between being popular or smart—they were accepted as both. That they were elected to multiple campus leadership positions suggests the participants were popular and highly-regarded by their peers. Gilligan (1993) and Head (1999) found that most men were competitive and generally disinterested in collaboration. In the present study, competitiveness manifested itself vis-à-vis the participants' reports of vying for multiple leadership positions on campus. However, collaboration is a necessary attribute of a successful undergraduate student leader. In fact, this was one of the key skills the participants deemed important for future success.

The high-achievers devoted a sizeable portion of their out-of-class time to purposeful activities—participating in clubs and organizations, leading various student groups on campus, studying and preparing for class, interacting with university administrators, and so on. In contrast, most of their African American male peers spent their time in residence hall rooms doing nothing, pursuing romantic (oftentimes sexual) relationships with women, exercising in the campus recreation facility, and playing video games and intramural sports. This finding is consistent with previous reports of traditionally African American masculine activities (Askew & Ross 1988; Head 1999; Martino & Meyenn 2001).

It does appear, however, that the high-achievers held certain beliefs and aspired to roles that are consistent with traditional, mainstream White definitions of masculinity (i.e. provider, family man, and executive). At the same time, their motives were strikingly different. They were involved in leadership roles for selfless reasons and believed their work as student leaders was central to the advancement of the African American community on their campuses. Even in discussing their aspirations of becoming top executives and leaders in their future professions, the participants consistently emphasized the importance of being in a position to help, hire, and provide opportunities to other African Americans. There was no mention of solely personal gain or competing for the sake of simply being on top. This social commitment is inconsistent with the self-serving, ultra-competitive depiction of White men who subscribe to traditional definitions of masculinity. Moreover, the high-achievers' views of masculinity were clearly alternative and inconsistent with those of fellow African American male peers.

Oliver (1988, 1989) found that many African American men take on the "tough guy" or "players of women" identities to compensate for their inability to meet traditional White standards of masculinity. While there was no mention of "tough guys" or violent peers, many African American men on the six campuses reportedly devoted tremendous time and energy to romantic and sexual conquests with female students (oftentimes multiple women simultaneously). Although 30 participants identified themselves as heterosexual and admittedly engaged in romantic and sexual endeavors with women, they did not deem the high priority and disproportionate emphasis that their peers placed on opposite sex relationships healthy or productive. Moreover, instead of relying on indicators such as money, cars, and the exhibition of material possessions to define masculinity, the participants' conceptualizations included campus involvement, community improvement, and the indemnity of long-term career success beyond the undergraduate years.

Implications and Recommendations

According to data from Mortenson (2001), 67.6 percent of all African American men who started college in 1996 withdrew before completing their bachelor's degrees in 2000, compared to 56 percent of African American women and 58.1 percent of White male undergraduates. Mortenson's findings also indicate that African American men had the lowest retention rates among both sexes and all racial/ethnic groups in higher education in 2000. While the causes of student attrition are extensive and complex (Tinto 1993), identity conflict—confusion about who one is, challenges with fitting into a community within the college environment, and unresolved psychosocial insecurities—is largely responsible for a significant number of student departures from the college campus (Evans, Forney, & Guido-DiBrito 1998). In fact, Gilbert and Gilbert (1998) and Price (2000) suggest that a healthy, conflict-free masculine identity positively affects a variety of student outcomes, including academic achievement. If colleges and universities are to improve retention and graduation rates for African American male undergraduates, faculty and administrators must implement effective programs that will assist these students in resolving identity conflicts and developing masculinities with which they are comfortable.

Highly-involved African American male student leaders, such as the participants in the present study, should be used as a resource in efforts to broaden or redefine within-group conceptualizations of masculinities. Programs and structured dialogues in which students candidly share their perspectives on manhood may broaden the scope of masculine attitudes and behaviors that are deemed acceptable by and garner respect from peers.

Organizations specifically designed for African American male students are also important, as they typically attract many men who would otherwise remain completely uninvolved. Programs that focus on masculine identity issues and diversified conceptualizations of what it means to be a man would naturally complement the mission of this type of student organization. These initiatives must be student-led with some faculty and administrative guidance, as undergraduates are more likely to listen to peers who challenge them to see issues in a different light. Given that fraternity membership was occasionally deemed highly masculine among men on the six campuses, it would be advantageous for advisors and administrators to encourage the African American fraternities to sponsor semi-structured programs that focus on explorations of masculinity.

It is also important to connect African American male undergraduates to African American mentors who can expose them to alternative definitions of what it means to be a man. These mentors could include male faculty, staff, administrators, and graduate students, as well as alumni who serve in important positions in their professions and are actively involved in their communities. These mentors could share their personal success stories, encourage mentees to spend their out-of-class time more meaningfully, deconstruct longstanding myths about masculinity and help undergraduates understand how the choices they make today will affect future success and employability. These mentoring relationships are especially critical for African American male students who come from single-parent homes or communities where they were not exposed to African American male professionals and leaders.

Campus counseling centers should also consider approaches that focus on masculinity for African American men. Private, individualized sessions and small group therapy may help these students unpack their identity issues and come to terms with their alternative conceptualizations of masculinity. Given the sexual promiscuity that the study participants described among their peers, campus health centers should expand their safe-sex campaigns to include information about masculinity. Programs and materials that emphasize to male students (African American and otherwise) that being a man is not all about sex would likely inspire some students to rethink their priorities. A "men's only" session at new student orientation would be an appropriate venue for spreading this message. African American male student leaders could also participate in these orientation sessions and suggest to newcomers that they balance their romantic and sexual pursuits with out-of-class activities that will yield meaningful post-college outcomes. Gender-specific orientation sessions would also give advanced male student leaders the opportunity to share with new students their definitions of what it means to be a man and provide recommendations for how to survive in college despite peer pressure to live up to traditional standards of masculinity. These sessions would also confirm that it is possible to maintain intact masculine reputations without participating in sports, showing off material possessions, and constantly pursuing women.

Similar to women's centers that exist on hundreds of college and university campuses across the country, administrators should also consider devoting financial and staff resources to the establishment of men's centers. These centers could provide activities, resources, and support for male students. In addition to regularly sponsoring structured dialogues regarding identity and definitions of masculinity, the centers could also offer information and programs on rape prevention, aggression, health and wellness, sexuality, and male/female relationships, and facilitate opportunities for the cultivation of friendships and male bonding. If resources are not available to start this type of center, perhaps multicultural affairs offices could expand their scope to include programming on gender, particularly men's issues. These and other initiatives designed to address identity issues and definitions of masculinity among undergraduate men in general and African American male students specifically, would help students feel better about their definitions of self. The resolution of identity issues is necessary for retention and success in college, and is especially critical for African American male undergraduates.

Limitations

The most glaring limitation of this study is the reliance on self-reported data of peer perceptions. Interviews were only conducted with the 32 high-achieving African American undergraduate men, not their peers. Although the participants believed their African American male peers held certain views regarding masculinity or disproportionately devoted their out-of-class time to traditionally masculine activities, their peers may have reported something different. Also, the participants believed their peers perceived them to be masculine and never questioned their heterosexuality; no data were collected to confirm these speculations.

References

Askew, S., and Ross, C. 1988. *Boys don't cry: Boys and sexism in education.* Philadelphia, PA: Open University Press.

Blos, P. 1962. *On adolescence.* New York: Free Press.

———.1979. *The adolescence passage.* New York: International Universities Press.

Bonner II, F.A. 2001. *Gifted African American male college students: A phenomenological study.* Storrs, CT: The National Research Center on the Gifted and Talented.

Chodorow, N. 1978. *The reproduction of mothering.* Berkeley, CA: University of California Press.

Connell, R.W. 1993. "Disruptions: Improper masculinities." In *Beyond silenced voices.* Edited by L. Weis and M. Fine, 191–208. Albany, NY: State University of New York Press.

Davis, J.E. 2001. "Black boys at school: Negotiating masculinities and race." In *Educating our Black children: New directions and radical approaches.* Edited by R. Majors, 169–182. New York: RoutledgeFalmer.

———.2003. Early schooling and academic achievement of African American males. *Urban Education, 38*(5): 515–533.

Davis, J.E., and Jordan, W.J. 1994. The effects of school context, structure, and experience on African American males in middle and high school. *Journal of Negro Education, 63:* 570–587.

Denzin, N., and Lincoln, Y. 2000. Introduction: The discipline and practice of qualitative research. In *Handbook of qualitative research 2nd ed.,* Edited by N. Denzin & Y. Lincoln, 1–28. Thousand Oaks, CA: Sage.

Evans, N.J., Forney, D.S., and Guido-DiBrito, F. 1998. *Student development in college: Theory, research, and practice.* San Francisco: Jossey-Bass.

Fries-Britt, S. 1997. Identifying and supporting gifted African American men. In *Helping African American men succeed in college. New Directions for Student Services, No. 80.* Edited by M.J. Cuyjet, 65–78. San Francisco: Jossey-Bass.

———.1998. Moving beyond Black achiever isolation: Experiences of gifted Black collegians. *Journal of Higher Education, 69*(5): 556–576.

Ferguson, A.A. 2000. *Bad boys: Public schools in the making of black male masculinity.* Ann Arbor: The University of Michigan Press.

Gilbert, R., and Gilbert, P. 1998. *Masculinity goes to school.* New York: Routledge.

Gilligan, C. 1993. *In a different voice: Psychological theory and women's development.* Cambridge, MA: Harvard University Press.

Gregory, J.F. 1997. Three strikes and they're out: African American boys and American schools' responses to misbehavior. *International Journal of Adolescence and Youth, 7*(1), 25–34.

Harris, S.M. 1995. Psychosocial development and Black male masculinity: Implications for counseling economically disadvantaged African American male adolescents. *Journal of Counseling and Development, 73,* 279–287.

Head, J. 1999. *Understanding the boys: Issues of behaviour and achievement.* London: Falmer Press.

Holstein, J.A., and Gubrium, J.F. 1995. *The active interview. Qualitative research method series, No. 37.* Thousand Oaks, CA: Sage.

Kunjufu, J. 1988. *To be popular or smart: The Black peer group.* Chicago: African American Images.

LaVoire, J. 1986. Ego identity formation in middle adolescence. *Journal of Youth and Adolescence, 5:* 371–385.

Majors, R., and Billson, J.M. 1992. *Cool pose: The dilemmas of Black manhood in America.* New York: Lexington Press.

Martino, W., and Meyenn, B., eds. 2001. *What about the boys? Issues of masculinity in schools.* Philadelphia, PA: Open University Press.

Miles, M.B., and Huberman, A.M. 1994. *Qualitative data analysis: An expanded sourcebook, 2nd ed.* Thousand Oaks, CA: Sage.

Morrison, P., and Eardley, T. 1985. *About men.* Philadelphia, PA: Open University Press.

Mortenson Research Seminar on Public Policy Analysis of Opportunity for Postsecondary Education. 2001, July. College participation by gender age 18 to 24, 1967 to 2000. *Postsecondary Education Opportunity, 109:* 1–16.

Moustakas, C. 1994. *Phenomenological research methods.* Thousand Oaks, CA: Sage.

Oliver, W. 1988. Black males and social problems: Prevention through Afrocentric socialization. *Journal of Black Studies, 24:* 379–390.

———.1989. Sexual conquest and patterns of Black-on-Black violence: A structural-cultural perspective. *Violence and Victims, 4:* 257–273.

Price, J.N. 2000. *Against the odds: The meaning of school and relationships in the lives of six young African-American men.* Stamford, CT: Ablex.

Sedlacek, W.E. 1987. Black students on White campuses: 20 years of research. *Journal of College Student Personnel,* 28: 484–495.

Stoller, R.J. 1964. A contribution to the study of gender identity. *International Journal of Psychoanalysis,* 45: 220–226.

Tinto, V. 1993. *Leaving college: Rethinking the causes and cures of student attrition,* 2nd ed. Chicago: University of Chicago Press.

Wainrib, B.R. 1992. *Gender issues across the lifecycle.* New York, Springer.

Westwood, S. 1990. Racism, Black masculinity and the politics of space. In *Men, masculinities and social theory.* Edited by J. Hearn and D. Morgan, 55–71. Cambridge, MA: Unwin Hyman.

Peter Lyman

The Fraternal Bond as a Joking Relationship: A Case Study of the Role of Sexist Jokes in Male Group Bonding

One evening during dinner, 45 fraternity men suddenly broke into the dining room of a nearby campus sorority, surrounded the 30 women residents, and forced them to watch while one pledge gave a speech on Freud's theory of penis envy as another demonstrated various techniques of masturbation with a rubber penis. The women sat silently, staring downward at their plates, and listened for about 10 minutes, until a woman law student who was the graduate resident in charge of the house walked in, surveyed the scene and demanded, "Please leave immediately!" As she later described that moment, "There was a mocking roar from the men, 'It's tradition.' I said, 'That's no reason to do something like this, please leave!' And they left. I was surprised. Then the women in the house started to get angry. And the guy who made the penis-envy speech came back and said to us, 'That was funny to me. If that's not funny to you I don't know what kind of sense of humor you have, but I'm sorry.'"

That night the women sat around the stairwell of their house discussing the event, some angry and others simply wanting to forget the whole thing. They finally decided to ask the university to require that the men return to discuss the event. When university officials threatened to take action, the men agreed to the meeting. I had served as a faculty resident in student housing for

two years and had given several talks in the dorm about humor and gender, and was asked by both the men and the women involved to attend the discussion as a facilitator, and was given permission to take notes and interview the participants later, provided I concealed their identities.

The penis-envy ritual had been considered a successful joke in previous years by both "the guys and the girls," but this year it failed, causing great tension between two groups that historically had enjoyed a friendly joking relationship. In the women's view, the joke had not failed because of its subject; they considered sexual jokes to be a normal part of the erotic joking relationship between men and women. They thought it had failed because of its emotional structure, the mixture of sexuality with aggression and the atmosphere of physical intimidation in the room that signified that the women were the object of a joking relationship between the men. A few women argued that the failed joke exposed the latent domination in men's relation to women, but this view was labeled "feminist" because it endangered the possibility of reconstituting the erotic joking relationship with the men. Although many of the men individually regretted the damage to their relationship with women friends in the group, they argued that the special male bond created by sexist humor is a unique form of intimacy that justified the inconvenience caused the women. In reinterpreting these stories as social constructions of gender, I will focus upon the way the joke form and joking relationships reveal the emotional currents underlying gender in this situation.

From *Changing Men*, Michael Kimmel (ed.). Newbury Park, CA: Sage Publications, 1987. Reprinted by permission.

The Sociology of Jokes

Although we conventionally think of jokes as a meaningless part of the dramaturgy of everyday life, this convention is part of the way that the social function of jokes is concealed and is necessary if jokes are to "work." It is when jokes fail that the social conflicts that the joke was to reconstruct or "negotiate" are uncovered, and the tensions and emotions that underlie the conventional order of everyday social relations are revealed.

Joking is a special kind of social relationship that suspends the rules of everyday life in order to preserve them. Jokes indirectly express the emotions and tensions that may disrupt everyday life by "negotiating" them (Emerson 1969, 1970), reconstituting group solidarity by shared aggression and cathartic laughter. The ordinary consequences of forbidden words are suspended by meta-linguistic gestures (tones of voice, facial expressions, catch phrases) that send the message "this is a joke," and emotions that would ordinarily endanger a social relationship can be spoken safely within the micro-world created by the "the joke form" (Bateson 1972).

Yet jokes are not just stories, they are a theater of domination in everyday life, and the success or failure of a joke marks the boundary within which power and aggression may be used in a relationship. Nearly all jokes have an aggressive content, indeed shared aggression toward an outsider is one of the primary ways by which a group may overcome internal tension and assert its solidarity (Freud 1960, p. 102). Jokes both require and renew social bonds; thus Radcliffe-Brown pointed out that "joking relationships" between mothers-in-law and their sons-in-law provide a release for tension for people structurally bound to each other but at the same time feeling structural conflict with each other (Radcliffe-Brown 1959). Joking relationships in medicine, for example, are a medium for the indirect expression of latent emotions or taboo topics that if directly expressed would challenge the physician's authority or disrupt the need to treat life and death situations as ordinary work (see Coser 1959; Emerson 1969, 1970).

In each of the studies cited above, the primary focus of the analysis was upon the social function of the joke, not gender, yet in each case the joke either functioned through a joking relationship between men and women, such as in Freud's or Radcliffe-Brown's analysis of mother-in-law jokes, or through the joking relationship among men. For example, Coser describes the role of nurses as a safe target of jokes: as a surrogate for the male doctor in patient jokes challenging medical authority; or as a surrogate for the patient in the jokes with which doctors expressed anxiety. Sexist jokes, therefore, should be analyzed not only in general terms of the function of jokes as a means of defending social order, but in specific terms as the mechanism by which the order of gender domination is sustained in everyday life. From this perspective, jokes reveal the way social organizations are gendered, namely, built around the emotional rules of male bonding. In this case study, gender is not only the primary content of men's jokes, but the emotional structures of the male bond is built upon a joking relationship that "negotiates" the tension men feel about their relationship with each other, and with women.

Male bonding in everyday life frequently takes the form of a group joking relationship by which men create a serial kind of intimacy to "negotiate" the latent tension and aggression they feel toward each other. The humor of male bonding relationships generally is sexual and aggressive, and frequently consists of sexist or racist jokes. As Freud (1960, p. 99) observed, the jokes that individual men direct toward women are generally erotic, tend to clever forms (like the double entendre), and have a seductive purpose. The jokes that men tell about women in the presence of other men are sexual and aggressive rather than erotic and use hostile rather than clever verbal forms; and, this paper will argue, have the creation of male group bonding as their purpose. While Freud analyzed jokes in order to reveal the unconscious, in this article, relationships will be analyzed to uncover the emotional dynamics of male friendships.

The failed penis-envy joke reveals two kinds of joking relationships between college men and women. First, the attempted joke was part of an ongoing joking relationship between "the guys and the girls," as they called each other. The guys used the joking relationship to negotiate the tension they felt between sexual interest in the girls and fear of commitment to them. The guys contrasted their sense of independence and play in male friendships to the sense of dependence they felt in their relationships with women, and used hostile joking to negotiate their fear of the "loss of control" implied by intimacy. Second, the failure of the joke uncovered the use of sexist jokes in creating bonds between men; through their own joking relationships (which they called friendship), the guys negotiated the tension between their need for intimacy with other men and their fear of losing their autonomy as men to the authority of the work world.

The Girls' Story

The women frequently had been the target of fraternity initiation rites in the past, and generally enjoyed this joking relationship with the men, if with a certain ambivalence. "There was a naked Christmas Carol event, they were singing 'We wish you a Merry Christmas,' and 'Bring on the hasty pudding' was the big line they liked to yell out. And we had five or six pledges who had to strip in front of the house and do naked jumping jacks on the lawn, after all the women in the house were lined up on the steps to watch." The women did not think these events were hostile because they had been invited to watch, and the men stood with them watching, suggesting that the pledges, not the women, were the targets of the joke. This made the joke sexual, not sexist, and part of the normal erotic joking relationship between the guys and girls. Still, these jokes were ritual events, not real social relationships; one woman said, "We were just supposed to watch, and the guys were watching us watch. The men

set up the stage and the women are brought along to observe. They were the controlling force, then they jump into the car and take off."

At the meeting with the men, two of the women spoke for the group while 11 others sat silently in the center, surrounded by about 30 men. Each tried to explain to the men why the joke had not been funny. The first began, "I'm a feminist, but I'm not going to blame anyone for anything. I just want to talk about my feelings." When she said, "these guys pile in, I mean these huge guys," the men exploded in loud cathartic laughter, and the women joined in, releasing some of the tension of the meeting. She continued, "Your humor was pretty funny as long as it was sexual, but when it went beyond sexual to sexist, then it became painful. You were saying 'I'm better than you.' When you started using sex as a way of proving your superiority it hurt me and made me angry."

The second woman speaker criticized the imposition of the joke form itself, saying that the men's raid had the tone of a symbolic rape. "I admit we knew you were coming over, and we were whispering about it. But it went too far, and I felt afraid to say anything. Why do men always think about women in terms of violating them, in sexual imagery? You have to understand that the combination of a sexual topic with the physical threat of all of you standing around terrified me. I couldn't move. You have to realize that when men combine sexuality and force it's terrifying to women." This woman alluded to having been sexually assaulted in the past, but spoke in a nonthreatening tone that made the men listen silently.

The women spoke about feeling angry about the invasion of their space, about the coercion of being forced to listen to the speeches, and about being used as the object of a joke. But they reported their anger as a psychological fact, a statement about a past feeling, not an accusation. Many began by saying, "I'm not a feminist, but . . . ," to reassure the men that although they felt angry, they were not challenging traditional gender relations. The women were caught in a double-bind; if they spoke angrily to the men they would violate the taboo against the expression of anger by women (Miller 1976, p. 102). If they said nothing, they would internalize their anger, and traditional feminine culture would encourage them to feel guilty about feeling angry at all (Bernardez 1978; Lerner 1980). In part they resolved the issue by accepting the men's construction of the event as a joke, although a failed joke; accepting the joke form absolved the men of responsibility, and transformed a debate about gender into a debate about good and bad jokes.

To be accepted as a joke, a cue must be sent to establish a "frame" [for] the latent hostility of the joke content in a safe context; the men sent such a cue when they stood next to the women during the naked jumping jacks. If the cue "this is a joke" is ambiguous, or is not accepted, the aggressive content of the joke is revealed and generally is responded to with anger or aggression, endangering the relationship. In part the women were pointing out to the men that the cue "this is a joke" had not been given in this case, and the aggressive content of the joke hurt them. If the cue is given properly and accepted, the everyday rules of social order are suspended and the rule "this is fun" is imposed on the expression of hostility.

Verbal aggression mediated by the joke form generally will be [accepted] without later consequences in the everyday world, and will be judged in terms of the formal intention of jokes, shared play marked by laughter in the interest of social order. By complaining to the university, the women had suspended the rules of joke culture, and attempted to renegotiate them by bringing in an observer; even this turned out to be too aggressive, and the women retreated to traditional gender relationships. The men had formally accepted this shift of rules in order to avoid punishment from the university, however their defense of the joke form was tacitly a defense of traditional gender rules that would define male sexist jokes toward women as erotic, not hostile.

In accepting the construction of the event as "just a joke" the women absolved the men of responsibility for their actions by calling them "little boys." One woman said, "It's not wrong, they're just boys playing a prank. They're little boys, they don't know what they're doing. It was unpleasant, but we shouldn't make a big deal out of it." In appealing to the rules of the joke form the men were willing to sacrifice their relationship to the women to protect the rules. In calling the men "little boys" the women were bending the rules trying to preserve the relationship through a patient nurturing role (see Gilligan 1982, p. 44).

In calling the guys "little boys," the girls had also created a kind of linguistic symmetry between "the boys and the girls." With the exception of the law student, who called the girls "women," the students called the men "guys" and the women "girls." Earlier in the year the law student had started a discussion about this naming practice. The term "women" had sexual connotations that made "the girls" feel vulnerable, and "gals," the parallel to "guys," connoted "older women" to them. While the term "girls" refers to children, it was adopted because it avoided sexual connotations. Thus the women had no term like "the guys," which is a bonding term that refers to a group of friends as equals; the women often used the term "the guys" to refer to themselves in a group. As the men's speeches were to make clear, the term "guys" refers to a bond that is exclusively male, which is founded upon the emotional structure of the joke form, and which justifies it.

The Guys' Story

Aside from the roar of laughter when a woman referred to their intimidating size, the men interrupted the women only once. When a woman began to say that the men obviously intended to intimidate them, the men loudly protested that the women couldn't possibly judge their intentions, that they intended the whole event only as a joke, and the intention of a joke is, by definition, just fun.

At this point the two black men in the fraternity intervened to explain the rules of male joke culture to the women. The black men said that in a sense they understood what the women meant, it is painful being the object of aggressive jokes. In fact, they said, the collective talk of the fraternity at meals and group events was made up of nothing but jokes, including many racist jokes. One said, "I know what you mean. I've had to listen to things in the house that I'd have hit someone for saying if I'd heard them outside." There was again cathartic laughter among the guys, for the male group bond consisted almost entirely of aggressive words that were barely contained by the responsibility absolving rule of the joke form. A woman responded, "Maybe people should be hit for saying those things, maybe that's the right thing to do." But the black speaker was trying to explain the rules of male joke culture to the women, "if you'd just ignored us, it wouldn't have been any fun." To ignore a joke, even though it makes you feel hurt or angry, is to show strength or coolness, the two primary masculine ideals of the group.

Another man tried to explain the failure of the joke in terms of the difference between the degree of "crudeness" appropriate among the guys and between "guys and girls." He said, "As I was listening at the edge of the room, near the door, and when I looked at the guys I was laughing but when I looked at the girls I was embarrassed. I could see both sides at the same time. It was too crude for your sense of propriety. We have a sense of crudeness you don't have. That's a cultural aspect of the difference between girls and guys."

The other men laughed as he mentioned "how crude we are at the house," and one of the black men added, "you wouldn't believe how crude it gets." Many of the men said privately that while they individually found the jokes about women vulgar, the jokes were justified because they were necessary for the formation of the fraternal bond. These men thought the mistake had been to reveal their crudeness to the women, this was "in bad taste."

In its content, the fraternal bond was almost entirely a joking relationship. In part, the joking was a kind of "signifying" or "dozens," a ritual exchange of insults that functioned to create group solidarity. "If there's one theme that goes on, it's the emphasis on being able to take a lot of ridicule, of shit, and not getting upset about it. Most of the interaction we have is verbally abusing each other, making disgusting references to your mother's sexuality, or the women you were seen with, or your sex organ, the size of your sex organ. And you aren't cool unless you can take it without trying to get back." Being cool is an important male value in other settings as well, such as sports or work; the joke form is a kind of male pedagogy in that, in one guy's words, it teaches "how to keep in control of your emotions."

But the guys themselves would not have described their group as a joking relationship or even as a male bond; they called it friendship. One man said he had found perhaps a dozen guys in the house who were special friends, "guys I could cry in front of." Yet in interviews, no one could recall any of the guys actually crying in front of each other. One said, "I think the guys are very close, they would do nearly anything for each other, drive each other places, give each other money. I think when they have problems about school, their car, or something like that, they can talk to each other. I'm not sure they can talk to each other about problems with women though." The image of crying in front of the other guys was a moving symbol of intimacy to the guys, but in fact crying would be an admission of vulnerability, which would violate the ideals of "strength" and "being cool."

Although the fraternal bond was idealized as a unique kind of intimacy upon which genuine friendship was built, the content of the joking relationship was focused upon women, including much "signifying" talk about mothers. The women interpreted the sexist jokes as a sign of vulnerability. "The thing that struck me the most about our meeting together," one said, "was when the men said they were afraid of trusting women, afraid of being seen as jerks." According to her, this had been the women's main reaction to the meeting by the other women, "How do you tell men that they don't have to be afraid, and what do you do with women who abuse that kind of trust?" One of the men on the boundary of the group remarked that the most hostile misogynist jokes came from the men with the fewest intimate relationships with women. "I think down deep all these guys would love to have satisfying relationships with women. I think they're scared of failing, of having to break away from the group they've become comfortable with. I think being in a fraternity, having close friendships with men is a replacement for having close relationships with women. It'd be painful for them because they'd probably fail."

Joking mobilized the commitment of the men to the group by policing the individual men's commitments to women and minimized the possibility of dyadic withdrawal from the group (see Slater 1963). "One of the guys just acquired a girlfriend a few weeks ago. He's someone I don't think has had a woman to be friends with, maybe ever, at least in a long time. Everybody has been ribbing him intensely the last few weeks. It's good natured in tone. Sitting at dinner they've invented a little song they sing to him. People yell questions about his girlfriend, the size of her vagina, does she have big breasts."

Since both the jokes and the descriptions of the parties have strong homoerotic overtones, including the exchange of women as sexual partners, jokes were also targeted at homosexuality, to draw an emotional line between the homosocial male bond and homosexual relationships. Being called "queer," however, did not require a sexual relationship with another man, but only visible signs of vulnerability or nurturing behavior.

Male Bonding as a Joking Relationship

Fraternal bonding is an intimate kind of male group friendship that suspends the ordinary rules and responsibilities of everyday life through joking relationships. To the guys, dyadic friendship with a woman implied "loss of control," namely, responsibility for work and family. In dealing with women, the group separated intimacy from sex, defining the male bond as intimate but not sexual (homosocial), and relationships with women as sexual but not intimate (heterosexual). The intimacy of group friendship was built upon shared spontaneous action, "having fun," rather than the self-disclosure that marks women's friendships (see Rubin 1983, p. 13). One of the men had been inexpressive as he listened to the discussion, but spoke about fun in a voice filled with emotion, "The penis-envy speech was a hilarious idea, great college fun. That's what I joined the fraternity for, a good time. College is a stage in my life to do crazy and humorous things. In 10 years when I'm in the business world I won't be able to carry on like this [again cathartic laughter from the men]. The initiation was intended to be humorous. We didn't think through how sensitive you women were going to be."

This speech gives the fraternal bond a specific place in the life cycle. The joking relationship is a ritual bond that creates a male group bond in the transition between boyhood and manhood, after the separation from the family, where the authority of mothers limits fun, but before becoming subject to the authority of work. One man later commented on the transitional nature of the male bond, "I think a lot of us are really scared of losing total control over our own lives. Having to sacrifice our individuality. I think we're scared of work in the same way we're scared of women." In this sense individuality is associated with what the guys called "strength," both the emotional strength suggested by being cool, and the physical strength suggested by facing the risks of sports and the paramilitary games they liked to play.

The emotional structure of the joking relationship is built upon the guys' latent anger about the discipline that middle-class male roles imposed upon them, both marriage rules and work rules. The general relationship between organization of men's work and men's domination of women was noted by Max Weber (1958, pp. 345–346), who described "the vocational specialist" as a man mastered by the rules of organization that create an impersonal kind of dependence, and who therefore seeks to create a feeling of independence through the sexual conquest of women. In each of the epochs of Western history, Weber argues, the subordination of men at work has given rise to a male concept of freedom based upon the violation of women. Although Weber tied dependence upon rules to men's need for sexual conquest through seduction, this may also be a clue to the meaning of sexist jokes and joking relationships among men at work. Sexist jokes may not be simply a matter of recreation or a means of negotiating role stress, they may be a reflection of the emotional foundations of organizational life for men. In everyday work life, sexist jokes may function as a ritual suspension of the rules of responsibility for men, a withdrawal into a microworld in which their anger about dependence upon work and women may be safely expressed.

In analyzing the contradictions and vulnerabilities the guys felt about relationships with women and the responsibilities of work, I will focus upon three dimensions of the joking relationship: (1) the emotional content of the jokes; (2) the erotics of rule breaking created by the rules of the joke form; and (3) the image of strength and "being cool" they pitted against the dependence represented by both women and work.

The Emotional Dynamic of Sexist Jokes

When confronted by the women, the men defended the joke by asserting the formal rule that the purpose of jokes is play, then by justifying the jokes as necessary in order to create a special male bond. The defense that jokes are play defines aggressive behavior as play. This defense was far more persuasive to the men than to the women, since many forms of male bonding play are rule-governed aggression, as in sports and games. The second defense, asserting the relation between sexist jokes and male bonds, points out the social function of sexist jokes among the guys, to control the threat that individual men might form intimate emotional bonds with women and withdraw from the group. Each defense poses a

puzzle about the emotional dynamics of male group friendship, for in each case male group friendship seems more like a defense against vulnerability than a positive ideal.

In each defense, intimacy is split from sexuality in order to eroticize the male bond, thereby creating an instrumental sexuality directed at women. The separation of intimacy from sexuality transforms women into "sexual objects," which both justifies aggression at women by suspending their relationships to the men and devalues sexuality itself, creating a disgust at women as the sexual "object" unworthy of intimate attention. What is the origin of this conjunction between the devaluation of sexuality and the appropriation of intimacy for the male bond?

Chodorow (1978, p. 182) argues that the sense of masculine identity is constructed by an early repression of the son's erotic bond with his mother; with this repression the son's capacity for intimacy and commitment is devalued as feminine behavior. Henceforth men feel ambivalent about intimate relationships with women, seeking to replicate the fusion of intimacy and sexuality that they had experienced in their primal relationships to their mothers, but at the same time fearing engulfment by women in heterosexual relationships, like the engulfment of their infant selves by their mothers (Chodorow 1976). Certainly the content of the group's joke suggests this repression of the attachment to the mother, as well as hostility to her authority in the family. One man reported, "There're an awful lot of jokes about people's mothers. If any topic of conversation dominates the conversation it's 'heard your mother was with Ray [one of the guys] last night.' The guys will say incredibly vulgar things about their mothers, or they'll talk about the anatomy of a guy's girlfriends, or women they'd like to sleep with." While the guys' signifying mother jokes suggest the repression Chodorow describes, the men realized that their view of women made it unlikely that marriage would be a positive experience. One said, "I think a lot of us expect to marry someone pretty enough that other men will think we got a good catch, someone who is at least marginally interesting to chat with, but not someone we'd view as a friend. But at the same time, a woman who will make sufficient demands that we won't be able to have any friends. So we'll be stuck for the rest of our lives without friends."

While the emotional dynamic of men's "heterosexual knots" may well begin in this primordial separation of infant sons from mothers, its structure is replicated in the guys' ambivalence about their fathers, and their anger about the dependence upon rules in the work world. Yet the guys themselves described the fraternal bond as a way of creating "strength" and overcoming dependence, which suggests a positive ideal of male identity. In order to explore the guys' sense of the value of the male bond, their conception of strength and its consequences for the way they related to each other and to women has to be taken seriously.

Strength

Ultimately the guys justified the penis-envy joke because it created a special kind of male intimacy, but while the male group is able to appropriate its members' needs for intimacy and commitment, it is not clear that it is able to satisfy those needs, because strength has been defined as the opposite of intimacy. "Strength" is a value that represents solidarity rather than intimacy, the solidarity of a shared risk in rule-governed aggressive competition; its value is suggested by the cathartic laughter when the first woman speaker said, "These guys poured in, these huge guys."

The eros detached from sexuality is attached to rules, not to male friends; the male bond consists of an erotic toward rules, and yet the penis-envy joke expresses most of all the guys' ambivalence about rules. Like "the lads," the male gangs who roam the English countryside, "getting in trouble" by enforcing social mores in unsocial ways (Peters 1972), "the guys" break the rules in rule-governed ways. The joke form itself suggests this ambivalence about rules and acts as a kind of pedagogy about the relationship

between rules and aggression in male work culture. The joke form expresses emotions and tensions that might endanger the order of the organization, but that must be spoken lest they damage social order. Jokes can create group solidarity only if they allow dangerous things to be said; allow a physical catharsis of tension through laughter; or create the solidarity of an "in group" through shared aggression against an "out group." In each case there is an erotic in joke forms: an erotic of shared aggression, of shared sexual feeling, or an erotic of rule breaking itself.

It has been suggested that male groups experience a high level of excitement and sexual arousal in public acts of rule breaking (Thorne & Luria 1986). The penis-envy speech is precisely such an act, a breaking of conventional moral rules in the interest of group arousal. In each of the versions of the joking relationship in this group there is such an erotic quality: in the sexual content of the jokes, in the need for women to witness dirty talk or naked pledges, in the eros of aggression of the raid and jokes themselves. The penis-envy speech, a required event for all members of the group, is such a collective violation of the rules, and so is the content of their talk, a collective dirty talking that violates moral rules. The cathartic laughter that greeted the words, "You wouldn't believe what we say at the house," testifies to the emotional charge invested in dirty talk.

Because the intimacy of the guys' bond is built around an erotic of rule breaking, it has the serial structure of shared risk rather than the social structure of shared intimacy. In writing about the shared experience of suffering and danger of men at war, J. Glenn Gray (1959, pp. 89–90) distinguishes two kinds of male bonding, comradeship and friendship. Comradeship is based upon an erotic of shared danger, but is based upon the loss of an individual sense of self to a group identity, while friendship is based upon an individual's intellectual and emotional affinity to another individual. In the eros of friendship one's sense of self is heightened; in the eros of comradeship a sense of self is replaced by a sense of group membership. In this sense the guys were seeking comradeship, not friendship, hence the group constructed its bond through an erotic of shared activities with an element of risk, shared danger, or rule breaking: in sports, in paramilitary games, in wild parties, in joking relations. The guys called the performance of these activities "strength," being willing to take risks as a group and remaining cool.

Thus the behavior that the women defined as aggressive was seen by the men as a contest of strength governed by the rules of the joke form, to which the proper response would have been to remain "cool." To the guys, the masculine virtue of "strength" has a positive side, to discover oneself and to discover a sense of the other person through a contest of strength that is governed by rules. To the guys, "strength" is not the same as power or aggression because it is governed by rules, not anger; it is anger that is "uncool."

"Being Cool"

It is striking that the breaking of rules was not spontaneous, but controlled by the rules of the joke form: that aggressive talk replaces action; that talk is framed by a social form that requires the consent of others; that talk should not be taken seriously. This was the lesson that the black men tried to teach the women in the group session: In the male world, aggression is not defined as violent if it is rule governed rather than anger governed. The fraternal bond was built upon this emotional structure, for the life of the group centered upon the mobilization of aggressive energies in rule-governed activities (in sports, games, jokes, parties). In each arena aggression was highly valued (strength) only when it was rule governed (cool). Getting angry was called "losing control" and the guys thought they were most likely to lose control when they experienced themselves as personally dependent, as in relationships with women and at work.

Rule-governed aggression is a conduct that is very useful to organizations, in that it mobilizes aggressive energies but binds them to order by rules (see Benjamin 1980, p. 154). The male sense of order is procedural rather than substantive because the male bond is formal (rule governed), rather than personal (based upon intimacy and commitment). Male groups in this sense are shame cultures, not guilt cultures, because the male bond is a group identity that subordinates the individual to the rules, and because social control is imposed through collective judgments about self-control, such as "strength" and "cool." The sense of order within such male groups is based upon the belief that all members are equally dependent upon the rules and that no personal dependence is created within the group. This is not true of the family or of relations with women, both of which are intimate, and, from the guys' point of view, are "out of control" because they are governed by emotion.

The guys face contradictory demands from work culture about the use of aggressive behavior. Aggressive conduct is highly valued in a competitive society when it serves the interests of the organization, but men also face a strong taboo against the expression of anger at work when it is not rule governed. "Competition" imposes certain rules upon aggressive group processes: Aggression must be calculated, not angry; it must be consistent with the power hierarchy of the organization, serving authority and not challenging it; if expressed, it must be indirect, as in jokes; it must serve the needs of group solidarity, not of individual autonomy. Masculine culture separates anger from aggression when it combines the value "strength" with the value "being cool." While masculine cultures often define the expression of anger as "violent" or "loss of control," anger, properly defined, is speech, not action; angry speech is the way we can defend our sense of integrity and assert our sense of justice. Thus it is anger that challenges the authority of the rules, not aggressive behavior in itself, because anger defends the self, not the organization.

The guys' joking relationship taught them a pedagogy for the controlled use of aggression in the work world, to be able to compete aggressively without feeling angry. The guys recognized the relationship between their male bond and the work world by claiming that "high officials of the university know about the way we act and they understand what we are doing." While this might be taken as evidence that the guys were internalizing their fathers' norms and thus inheriting the mantle of patriarchy, the guys described their fathers as slaves to work and women, not as patriarchs. The guys also asserted themselves against the authority of their fathers by acting out against the authority of rules in the performance of "strength."

The guys clearly benefited from the male authority that gave them the power to impose the penis-envy joke upon the women with essentially no consequences. Men are allowed to direct anger and aggression toward women because social norms governing the expression of anger or humor generally replicate the power order of the group. It is striking, however, that the guys would not accept the notion that men have more power than women do; to them it is not men who rule, but rules that govern men. These men had so internalized the governing of male emotions by rules that their anger itself could emerge only indirectly through rule-governed forms, such as jokes and joking relationships. In these forms their anger could serve only order, not their sense of self or justice.

References

Bateson, G. (1972). A theory of play and fantasy. In *Steps toward an ecology of mind* (pp. 177–193). New York: Ballantine.

Benjamin, J. (1978). Authority and the family revisited, or, A world without fathers. *New German Critique, 4*(3), 13, 35–57.

Benjamin, J. (1980). The bonds of love: Rational violence and erotic domination. *Feminist Studies, 6*(1), 144–174.

Berndardez, T. (1978). Women and anger. *Journal of the American Medical Women's Association, 33*(5), 215–219.

Bly, R. (1982). What men really want: An interview with Keith Thompson. *New Age,* pp. 30–37, 50–51.

Chodorow, N. (1976). Oedipal asymmetries, heterosexual knots. *Social Problems, 23,* 454–468.

Chodorow, N. (1978). *The reproduction of mothering.* Berkeley: University of California Press.

Coser, R. (1959). Some social functions of laughter: A study of humor in a hospital setting. *Human Relations, 12,* 171–182.

Emerson, J. (1969). Negotiating the serious import of humor. *Sociometry, 32,* 169–181.

Emerson, J. (1970). Behavior in private places. In H. P. Dreitzel (Ed.), *Recent sociology: Vol. 2. Patterns in communicative behavior.* New York: Macmillan.

Freud, S. (1960). *Jokes and their relation to the unconscious.* New York: Norton.

Gilligan, C. (1982). *In a different voice.* Cambridge, MA: Harvard University Press.

Gray, G. J. (1959). *The warriors: Reflections on men in battle.* New York: Harper & Row.

Lerner, H. E. (1980). Internal prohibitions against female anger. *American Journal of Psychoanalysis, 40,* 137–148.

Miller, J. B. (1976). *Toward a new psychology of women.* Boston: Beacon.

Peters, E. L. (1972). Aspects of the control of moral ambiguities. In M. Gluckman (Ed.), *The allocation of responsibility* (pp. 109–162). Manchester: Manchester University Press.

Radcliffe-Brown, A. (1959). *Structure and function in primitive society.* Glencoe, IL: Free Press.

Rubin, L. (1983). *Intimate strangers.* New York: Harper & Row.

Slater, P. (1963). On social regression. *American Sociological Review, 28,* 339–364.

Thorne, B., & Luria, Z. (1986). Sexuality and gender in children's daily worlds. *Social Problems, 33*(3), 176–190.

Weber, M. (1958). Religions of the world and their directions. In H. Gerth & C. W. Mills (Eds.), *From Max Weber.* New York: Oxford University Press.

Rocco L. Capraro

Why College Men Drink: Alcohol, Adventure, and the Paradox of Masculinity

And you drink this burning liquor like your life
Your life which you drink like an eau-de-vie.

Apollinaire[1]

Though terror speaks to life and death and distress makes of the world a vale of tears,
yet shame strikes deepest into the heart of man.

Tomkins[2]

Given the magnitude of the negative consequences of some college men's drinking—for themselves and for those around them—on campuses across the nation,[3] college health professionals and alcohol prevention educators might well wonder: "Why *do* college men drink?" Because most college men drink in unproblematic ways and only to be sociable,[4] those men who drink in a way that is likely to be harmful to themselves or others are actually the central focus of this article—that is, those men "for whom drinking has become a central activity in their way of life."[5(p100)]

Writing from a men's health studies perspective, I articulate what is necessarily only a tentative answer to the question of men's problem drinking by offering a model for conceptualizing the complex connections between college men and alcohol. Men's health studies, a subfield of men's studies, describes and analyzes men's experience

of health, injury, morbidity, and mortality in the context of masculinity.[6,7] I also suggest an answer to the companion question that immediately presents itself to us: "What can we do about it?"

Part one of this article discusses the connections between alcohol, men, and masculinity generally; part two, the cultural and developmental aspects of men in a college setting; and part three, conceptual and programmatic responses to the men's problem drinking.

In general, I conclude that when college men drink, they are simply *being* men in college: that is the best context for understanding why they drink. I further conclude, in what is perhaps my central insight in this article, that college men's drinking appears to be profoundly paradoxical in a way that seems to replicate a larger paradox of masculinity itself: that men's alcohol use is related to both men's power and men's powerlessness. Stated most succinctly, my interpretation of a variety of evidence suggests that many college men may be drinking not only to enact male privilege but also to help them negotiate the emotional hazards of being a man in the contemporary American college.

From *Journal of American College Health* 48: 307–315. Copyright © 2000. Reprinted with permission of the Helen Dwight Reid Foundation. Published by Heldref Publication, Washington, DC.

Alcohol and Masculinity

Drinking as a Male Domain

If we want to understand why college men drink, then we might embed drinking and college in masculinity and ask in what ways each might be seen as a specific male experience.[6] When we look for connections between drinking, men, and masculinity, we observe that the most prominent feature on the social landscape of drinking is that drinking is a "male domain."[3(p6)] By *male domain,* I suggest that drinking is male dominated, male identified, and male centered.[8]

Men outnumber women in virtually every category of drinking behavior used in research for comparison—prevalence, consumption, frequency of drinking and intoxication, incidence of heavy and problem drinking, alcohol abuse and dependence, and alcoholism.[4,9–12] Although most college men and women say they drink to be sociable, men are more likely than women to say they drink for escapism or to get drunk.[4(p125)]

These findings hold true for the categories of age, ethnicity, geographic region, religion, education, income, and marital status.[9] Although there has been some speculation that changing gender roles may be narrowing the gap between women and men vis-á-vis alcohol, discussed by scholars as the *convergence hypothesis,* research tends to reject that proposition.[3]

In a classic and often-cited article, Lemle and Miskind[9] asked, "Why should it be that males drink and abuse alcohol in such magnitude and in such marked contrast to females?" Citing empirical research that placed men mostly in the company of other men in the life course of their drinking, they suggested that drinking was a symbol of masculinity and speculated that men may drink to be manly.[9(p215)] They found little or no empirical evidence to support many of the theoretical possibilities they discussed, particularly for any theories concerned with men's abusive drinking, yet they remained intrigued with the idea that men were affirming their manliness by drinking.

More recently, McCreary et al.[10] ask what *specific* aspects of the male gender role correlate with alcohol involvement. In addition to the personality traits of instrumentality and expressiveness, they explore the traits of traditional male-role attitudes and masculine gender-role stress. For their research, traditional male-role attitudes represent a "series of beliefs and assumptions that men should be in high-status positions in society, act in physically and emotionally toughened ways, and avoid anything stereotypically feminine." *Masculine gender-role stress* is a term used to "describe the stress resulting from a man's belief that he is unable to meet society's demands of what is expected from men or the male role or from having to respond to a situation in a feminine-typed manner."[10(pp111–112)]

McCreary et al.[10] identify traditional male-role attitudes as the *one* aspect of the male gender role they studied that predicts alcohol *use* among men. Alcohol use itself correlates with alcohol problems. However, masculine gender-role stress, while statistically unrelated to alcohol *use,* does predict alcohol *problems* for men (p. 121). In short, this study suggests that, from the point of view of masculinity or culture of manhood as a factor among many others, men *qua* men might arrive at alcohol problems by two routes: one route starts at traditional male-role attitudes, passes through alcohol use, and ends in alcohol problems; another route starts at masculine gender-role stress and ends directly in alcohol problems.

Variations on a Theme: Conflict and Strain, Shame and Fear, Depression, and the Paradox of Masculinity

The Paradox of Masculinity   Traditional male-role attitudes and masculine gender-role stress are actually not very far apart; in some aspects, they are correlated.[10,13] Their correlation reveals the contradictory nature of masculinity.[14] Reflecting upon the contradictory nature of the male role, researchers in the field of men's studies have articulated the paradox of masculinity, or the paradox of men's power, as follows: *men are powerful and powerless.*[15–18]

What is the resolution of the apparent contradiction that constitutes the paradox? How can men be both powerful and powerless? Men's studies observe two aspects of men's lives. First, in objective social analysis, *men as a group have power over women as a group:* but, in their subjective experience of the world, *men as individuals do not feel powerful.* In fact, they feel powerless. As at first articulated, and then later resolved by men's studies, the concept of a paradox of men's power offers an important insight into men's lives, one that seems to capture and to explain many of the contradictory claims made by and about men.

Ironically, it is men themselves who make the "rules of manhood" by which men as individuals are "disempowered."[17(p138)] Kaufman[16] aptly concludes that men's power is actually the cause of men's pain: "men's social power is the source of individual power and privilege . . . it is also the source of the individual experience of pain and alienation."[16(pp142-143)]

The paradoxical nature of masculinity is further illuminated in other men's studies research on at least three critical psychosocial aspects of masculinity: gender-role conflict and strain, shame and fear, and depression. Interestingly, those same aspects of masculinity are themselves important possible connections between men and alcohol. Consequently, the concept of the paradox of men's power draws us to an important conceptual understanding of some men's connections to alcohol.

Conflict and Strain O'Neil[19] provides a useful series of interlocking definitions that locate gender-role conflict and strain in relation to the gender role itself. Gender roles are "behaviors, expectations, and values defined by society as masculine or feminine," or "as appropriate behavior for men and women." Gender-role conflict is "a psychological state in which gender roles have negative consequences on the individual or others" through the restriction, devaluation, or violation of oneself or others. Gender-role strain is "physical or psychological tension experienced as an outcome of gender-role

conflict." At the bottom of gender-role strain is a "discrepancy between the real self and the gender role" (pp. 24, 25). Strain can follow from both conformity and nonconformity to the male role.

In his writings on strain, Pleck[14,20] provides additional insight into the relation between the masculine gender role and conflict or strain. Pleck maintains that the masculine gender role itself is "dysfunctional,"[14(p147)] fraught with contradictions and negative consequences. Even when men live up to the role, they suffer well-documented adverse consequences. But, very often, men do not live up to the role. In fact, conflict and strain are inherent in the role, and they are actually the best rubrics under which to understand most men's identity and experience.

In Pleck's[14] role-strain paradigm, social approval and situational adaptation replace innate psychological need as the social and psychological mechanisms by which men achieve manhood. Violating gender roles (norms and stereotypes) results in social condemnation, a negative consequence experienced as sex-role strain and anxiety, a negative psychological consequence (pp. 145, 146). At least one study has connected role conflict and alcohol use. Blazina and Watkins[21] found that masculine gender-role conflict, in particular the factor cluster of "success, power, and competition," were significantly related to college men's reported use of alcohol.

Shame and Fear Krugman,[22] reflecting on Pleck's foundational work on gender-role strain, characterizes male-role strain, with its grounding in feelings of inadequacy and inferiority, as a shame-based experience. "Role strain generates shame affect as males fail to live up to the cultural and peer group standards they have internalized."[22(p95)] The essence of shame for Krugman is "painful self-awareness" or "a judgment against the self" (p. 99). He advises that shame is active in both male gender-role strain and normal male socialization.

Recent research suggests that normative male socialization employs shame to shape boys' and men's behaviors and attitudes.[22,23] In common and nonpathological forms, shame becomes integrated into the self and transformed into a cue that tells us when to modify our behaviors and feelings in response to shame's messages about their appropriateness. But although shame may be the powerful leverage to enforce boys' and men's conformity to the male role, men are less likely than women to transform shame because they find shame to be *repugnant* to their masculinity. Consequently, for Krugman,[22] boys and men internalize male gender roles to avoid shame; but they also learn that dependency needs, for example, are shameful, especially under the gaze of their peer group.

Shame is related to fear.[2] Shame can magnify fear by linking similar episodes of fear into what Tomkins refers to as a family of episodes, creating a behavioral template in which fear can be anticipated and become more pervasive. In adversarial cultures, and I would include our own society generally in that category, fear and shame are conjoined, resulting in the mutually reinforcing "fear of shame" and "shame of fear."[2(p538)]

Kimmel[17] places fear and shame at the very center of the social construction of men's identity. For him, men "fear that other men will unmask us, emasculate us, reveal to us and the world that we do not measure up, that we are not real men. Fear makes us ashamed" (p. 131). To avoid shame, Kimmel writes, men distance themselves from the feminine and all associations with it, including mothers, the world of feelings, nurturing, intimacy, and vulnerability.

Without the transformation of shame, men learn to manage shame in other ways. Alcohol is one of the significant ways men manage shame: drinking is a "maladaptive male solution to the pressure of undischarged shame."[22(p120)] Speaking metaphorically, Krugman observes that alcohol "dissolves acute shame" (p. 94). Referring to Lansky's study of shame in families, Krugman reports that alcohol, as a disinhibitor, is used by some men "to handle vulnerable and exposed states that generate shameful feelings." Krugman, citing M. Horowitz, advises that alcohol "softens ego criticism" and "facilitates interpersonal con-

nections and self-disclosures" (p. 120). Drinking may also reduce fear.[2] It seems to me that shame may also be the mechanism that leads men directly to alcohol, which is used to instill conformity to the dictates of traditional masculinity that encourage men to drink.

Depression   In addition to anxiety and shame, male gender-role strain and conflict make themselves known in the lives of men in depression. Depression is significantly related to all four aspects of gender-role conflict: (a) success, power, and competition; (b) restrictive emotionality; (c) restrictive affectionate behavior between men; and (d) conflicts between work and family relations.[13,24] Traditional masculinity insidiously puts men at risk for depression and also masks the depression, should it actually develop.[25,26]

Whereas Kaufman[16] uses a discourse of power to explain men's unacknowledged emotions, Lynch and Kilmartin[25] offer an alternative approach to the pitfalls of masculinity drawn from the point of view of social relations. Men's socialization encourages them to disconnect, or dissociate, from their feelings. An emotionally restrictive masculinity permits men to show their feelings only "in disguised form," and so they become "mostly unrecognized, unexpressed, and misunderstood by self and others" (p. 45). Men, instead, express their feelings in indirect ways, often through behavior that is destructive to themselves or others. Dissociation from feelings and destructive behavior are the two major characteristics of what Lynch and Kilmartin refer to as "masculine depression."[25(pp9,10)]

Heavy drinking, or binge drinking, is one of the ways some depressed men may act out, or manifest, their depression.[4] Lynch and Kilmartin[25] cite research indicating that depression is a strong risk factor for substance abuse problems. Krugman[22] notes a study showing strong correlations between alcohol abuse and major depression, especially among men. Although they do not cite empirical evidence for it, Blazina and Watkins[21] speculate that traditional men may "self-medicate their pain and depression with alcohol" (p. 461). Although research findings suggest only a possible correlation between alcohol use or abuse and depression, perhaps alcohol use or abuse may actually precede depression. Alcohol and depression are certainly connected in the lives of some men.

Alcohol and the Paradox of Men's Power

Men in our society are supposed to be powerful.[27] According to the empirical findings of McClelland et al.,[28] when men are not powerful, they may often compensate for their lack of power or seek an "alternative to obtaining social power" with alcohol. Stated most dramatically by McClelland, drinking is "part of a cluster of actions which is a principal manifestation of the need for power" (p. 119). For this research, feeling powerful means "feeling that one is vigorous and can [have] an impact on others" (p. 84). But men's power motivation can be personalized (i.e., for "the greater glory or influence of the individual") or socialized for "the good of others" (p. 137).

According to McClelland,[28] a few drinks will stimulate socialized power thoughts for most men, and that is one of the reasons they like to drink. Higher levels of drinking tend to decrease inhibitions and stimulate personalized power thoughts. Heavy drinking in men is uniquely associated with personalized power, McClelland says. Heavy drinking makes men feel strong and assertive and, I would argue, the way they are supposed to feel.

Drinking may be related to men's power in a more profound and paradoxical way. In the aggregate, the connection between some men and heavy or problem drinking appears to be of two sorts: (a) that which follows from simple, apparently uncomplicated, conformity to traditional masculinity—drinking simply because men are supposed to drink; and (b) that which is informed by complex, perceived inadequacy as men, either from men's own point of view, or from that of society. If they do not feel inadequate, then at least they experience a kind of doubt, or a sense of falling short of the cultural ideal of manhood—drinking because of gender-role conflicts.

This distinction may be, after all, only a conceptual, or theoretical, distinction; in practice, the two sorts of connection co-occur. I wonder if traditional masculinity does not contain within it, socially constructed over time in the course of men's history, the use of alcohol to accommodate gender-role conflict. Given the way traditional masculinity has been constructed, is not gender-role conflict of the sort described by Pleck[14] and O'Neil[19] and documented in the lives of the men studied by Tomkins,[2] Krugman,[21] Lynch and Kilmartin,[25] Real,[26] and Kimmel[17] inherent in most men's lives? Have not men as historical agents, therefore, made provision for taking care of their own? If so, traditional masculine drinking would encompass conflicted drinking; certainly, in the culture of manhood, it does.

If heavy and problem drinking is associated with conformity, overconformity, or conflicted or strained resistance to the imperatives of traditional masculinity, why should this be the case? It would appear that drinking is a kind of fatally flawed defense mechanism, or compensatory behavior. It protects men's objective power as a group, even as it reveals men's subjective powerlessness as individuals and results in a diminution of men's power, particularly through the loss of control of emotions, health, and a variety of other negative consequences.

If this is the case, then drinking would have much in common with other documented psychological defense mechanisms that correlate with male gender-role conflict. And gender-role conflict, following from either conformity or nonconformity, might itself be seen as a defense mechanism that "protects a man's sense of wellbeing."[29(p253)] Like men's silence,[30] men's drinking turns out to be in the interest of men's power, even as it disempowers individual men. And alcohol, in my view, is the paradoxical drug that is a part of the larger whole, a trope, of a paradoxical masculinity.

As I ponder this material, then, it seems to me that a significant part of men's drinking, like male gender-role stress and strain, men's shame, and masculine depression themselves, is a reflection of both men's power and men's powerlessness about men's privilege and men's pain. Heavy and problem drinking join other aspects of masculinity as they, too, come to be seen as manifestations of the paradox of masculinity. Drinking thus falls into a line of masculine icons, including body building, sexual assault, and pornography, that reveal the paradoxical nature of masculinity itself.[31–34] As I review those icons, it strikes me that at those times men *appear* most powerful socially, they *feel* most powerless personally.

College and Masculinity

College Drinking

What happens when we look at *college* men? College students, mostly men, are among the heavy drinkers in Rorabaugh's[35] history of drinking in early American society. Contemporary college men drink more than they did in high school and more heavily than their noncollege counterparts, and the gap is widening.[3,36–38] Men have been the primary public purveyors of alcohol to the college campus. All of the differences in drinking behavior for men and women generally hold true for college men and women.[3,4]

Given today's college students' preference for alcohol, one could not really imagine most colleges void of alcohol.[39] However, given the great variety of colleges and universities, the diversity of today's student populations, and the sweeping nature of the concerns I express in this article, most of what follows must necessarily speak primarily to an ideal type, represented for me by the relatively small, residential liberal arts college, occupied by a mostly traditionally aged student population.[40] In the following pages, I shall discuss critical aspects of college that seem to define college men's experience and help explain much of the presence of alcohol on college campuses: adventure, adult development, and permissiveness.

College as Adventure

Green[41] conceptualizes adventure as a domain of transgression. For Green, adventure takes shape around the themes of "eros" and "potestas"—love and power. Following Bataille, Green asks us to think about civil society "as based on the purposes and values of work, which means the denial of all activities hostile to work, such as both the ecstasies of eroticism and those of violence." Adventure lies in the conceptual space where heroes, "men acting with power," break free of ordinary restraints and "sample the repressed pleasures of sex and violence."[42(p17)]

Although Green[41] makes no reference to drinking in his essays on adventure, we can easily recognize that the terrain of adventure is the same terrain as that of alcohol: "a boy's first drink, first prolonged drinking experience, and first intoxication tend to occur with other boys away from home."[9(p214)] Sports and the military are contexts for both adventure and drinking. Drinking games "are an important factor in the socialization of new students into heavy use," particularly for men.[42(p105)] Drinking, in general, can be an adventure, insofar as it takes men through a "breach" of the social contract and into the realms of violence, sex, and other adventure motifs.

In what way might college be conceptualized as an adventure? College is not literally, or predominantly, a scene of eros and potestas. It is, however, a time and place of an imaginative assertion of manhood outside of civil society, away from home and family, where a kind of heroism is possible. By analogy, we can observe that student life in 19th-century American colleges developed outside of the civil society represented by the faculty and administration in what I would regard as the realm of adventure. Horowitz[43] argues that what we think of as student life was actually "born in revolt" (p. 23) against the faculty and administration. It is a "world made by the undergraduates," she says (p. 3).

Levine and Cureton[39] find that colleges today are occupied by a transitional generation that reflects the changing demographics of contemporary American society. Horowitz's history, however, employs a simple tripartite typology of college students that is still largely applicable as a model for understanding students on many campuses in more recent times. That typology deeply resonates with my own many years of experience in student affairs: (a) college men—affluent men in revolt against the faculty and administration who created campus life as "the culture of the college man" (p. 32); (b) outsiders—hardworking men who identify with the faculty (p. 14); and (c) rebels—creative, modernist, and expressive men who conform neither to campus life nor to the faculty (p. 15). Horowitz[43] observes that these three student types were distinctly *male* when they first made their appearance, but their female counterparts eventually found their place alongside the men.

Nuwer[44] argues that there are historical links between traditional male undergraduate life and danger, a key adventure motif. Social interactions initiating students into various campus communities have continuously subjected college men to high risk. Acceptance by their peers is granted in exchange for successfully undertaking the risk involved. A variety of college rituals and traditions often mix danger and alcohol.[44] Alcohol, itself, is associated with risk in men's lives.[9] Seen this way, college and campus life become an adventure-scape, where young men (college men) imagine their manhood in a developmental moment that is socially dominated by alcohol.

Green[41] identifies a number of arenas or institutions of adventure: manhood before marriage, hunting, battle, travel, sports, and politics, to name a few. Although there may be feminine variants, Green links adventure to masculinity because society gives men the freedom to "apply forces to the world to assert power and identity." Adventure is an act of assertion by which men "imagine themselves" in "a breach of the social contract" (p. 19).

College as a Male Developmental Moment

Beyond seeing the sociology of college and student life organized as adventure, we must also consider the role of individual developmental psychology in the college environment. Paradoxically, just at the moment the great adventure begins, college men feel the most vulnerable.

Rotundo[45] observes that in the 19th century, "male youth culture" made its appearance in men's development as the vehicle for the transition from boyhood to manhood. Boys' principal developmental task was disengagement from home, which created conflict between the imperatives of worldly ambition young men's psychological needs for attachment. Young men of Rotundo's period gathered in business districts and colleges. Wherever they gathered, a "special culture" developed to support them in a time of need (pp. 56–62).

Lyman[46] carries us forward from Rotundo's[45] historical analysis to the present. In his essay on male bonding in fraternities, he locates college as a developmental time and place between the authority of home and family (in the high school years), and that of work and family (after graduation). He identifies college men's anger, their "latent anger about the discipline that middle-class male roles impose upon them, both marriage rules and work rules" (p. 157). Their great fear is loss of control and powerlessness. Lyman concludes that joking relationships (banter, sexual humor, etc.) among men allow a needed connection without being self-disclosive or emotionally intimate, that is, with little vulnerability. Recent research on first-year college men has characterized their transition to college as often involving separation anxiety and loss, followed by grieving. Among the significant responses that may manifest some college men's grief, we find self-destructive behaviors, including alcohol use.[47]

Shame theory advises that to avoid shame, boys need to distance themselves from their mothers because of the "considerable discomfort with dependency needs at the level of the peer group."[22(p107)] College men in groups, such as Lyman's fraternity men, perceive homosexuality and intimate emotional relationships with women to be a threat to their homosocial world. Thus, men are encouraged to treat women as sexual objects, which confirms their heterosexuality, but prevents true intimacy with women.

Alcohol plays a role in men's emotional management under these conditions. Drinking remains a "socially acceptable way for men to satisfy their dependency needs while they maintain a social image of independence,"[48(p187)] even as it masks those needs. For example, recent research on drinking games suggests they are actually an environmental context for drinking where a variety of students' social and psychological needs come into play.[49] When men (and women) give reasons for playing drinking games, they are likely to be "tapping into more general motives for drinking" (p. 286). Alcohol may be an effective way to cope in the short term, but it is ultimately "self-destructive."[48(p191)]

For Nuwer,[44] as was true for Horowitz,[43] fraternities are the quintessential emblems of traditional college life. They provide a "feeling of belonging" for students who "crave relationships and acceptance" in their college years (p. 38). They are also the riskiest environments for heavy and problem drinking.[4] Nationally, just over 80 percent of fraternity residents binge drink, whereas just over 40 percent of all college students binge.[50] Drinking in fraternities is perhaps best understood as an extreme on a continuum of college men's drinking, dramatizing what may be going on to a lesser extent in traditional student life among a range of men. From the point of view of men's needs assessments, we have much to learn from the psychology of brotherhood.

Permissiveness—Real and Imagined

Alcohol is "one of the oldest traditions in the American college," and alcohol-related problems have also been a benchmark of campus life. Until very recently, though, college administrations have been permissive about alcohol, voicing "official condemnation tempered by tacit toleration."[51(pp81–83)] Myers[52] provides a model for "institutional (organizational) denial" of the presence (or extent) of alcohol abuse that could easily apply to college campuses nationally (p. 43). In 1995, Wechsler[11] was explicit about the widespread denial about alcohol on college campuses.

With the increase in the drinking age from 18 to 21 years and increased awareness of the dangers of alcohol abuse, colleges now "typically

have policies which promote responsible drinking" and attempt the "management of student drinking and its consequences."[51(pp84–88)] My own informal observations are that liability case law, awareness of the negative impact of alcohol on the achievement of educational mission, and enrollment management concerns for retention have also encouraged colleges to be more vigilant about the role of alcohol in campus cultures.

But among students, permissiveness persists, both in drinking behavior and in attitudes toward drinking. Permissiveness itself is, in part, the result of students' own misperceptions of campus norms for alcohol behavior and attitudes.[53,54] With reference to the consumption of alcohol and the acceptability of intoxication, students generally perceive themselves to be in a permissive environment. In reality, the environment is not as permissive as they think. Misperceiving the norm leads students who are inclined to drink to consume more alcohol than they otherwise would drink were they to perceive the norm correctly.[55] This social norms research indicates that correcting the misperception through public information campaigns can reduce both problem drinking and binge drinking on college campuses.[56,57]

How well do social norms approaches work with college men who are heavy drinkers? How are masculinity, permissive attitudes about drinking, and misperceptions of the norm related? How accurately do college men perceive their campus norms? For social norms theory and research, the heaviest drinking results from the interaction of the most permissive personal attitudes toward alcohol and the greatest misperception of the norm as more permissive than it actually is. Men as a group are the heaviest drinkers on campus. We might conclude that the heaviest drinking men have the most permissive attitudes about drinking and that they misperceive the norm at the greatest rates. But, theoretically, they should also be most susceptible to the benefits of social norms approaches.

However, in one study, the heaviest drinking college men proved to be the least susceptible to social norms interventions. From 1995 to 1998

Western Washington University implemented a campus-wide social norms approach. Although most students on the campus changed their patterns of drinking in positive ways, the "students reporting they had seven or more drinks on peak occasions [the most consumed at one time in the past month] remained virtually unchanged [at about 35 percent]." The most recalcitrant students at Western Washington were underage men: "nearly two thirds of the underage men still reported having seven or more drinks on a peak occasion. Only one third of the underage women reporting the same"[56(p3)] level of consumption.

In view of the significance of personal attitudes toward alcohol,[55] permissive personal attitudes about alcohol in the group of recalcitrant underage men might have been so robust that they simply overwhelmed any other perceptions of the environment. Prentice and Miller[58] found that men and women in their study did respond differently to corrections of misperceptions. Perhaps, in the case of at least some college men, personal attitudes about drinking and misperception of the campus norm are so inextricably linked that research and prevention work that addresses the one (personal attitudes) must necessarily be done in conjunction with the same kind of work on the other (misperception of the norm).

Perkins once characterized "the perceived male stereotype of heavy use as a misperception to which males do not need to conform."[3(p6)] Some college men's misperceptions of their campus alcohol norms may be "contained" in their personal attitudes about drinking. Baer found that differences in the perception of campus drinking norms among students in different housing situations on one campus "already existed prior to college enrollment"[42(p98)] [emphasis mine]. Certainly, if "the impact of public behavior and conversation" on campus can generate misperceptions of the norm,[54(p17)] a lifetime of powerful messages about the connection between alcohol and manhood would produce great distortions of its own.

Social norms theory, research, and strategies would be enhanced by a closer look at gender in the creation of drinking attitudes and behaviors, in possible differences in the misperception of norms, and in the social mechanisms that lie behind the actual norms. Social norms research surveys should include measures of traditional masculine role strain and should look for correlations between attitudes and perceptions of the norm and actual drinking behavior.

In addition, surveys should replace the generic "college student" with "male student" or "female student" when asking college students about how much students are drinking and asking about their attitudes toward drinking. So, for example, we should ask, "How many drinks does a *male* [or *female*] student typically have at a party on this campus?" instead of "do *students* typically have" or "Is it acceptable for men [or women] to drink with occasional intoxication as long as it does not interfere with other responsibilities?"[54(p15)]

The results would have implications for norms-based prevention programs. It would make sense if, in fact, masculinity were found to predispose men to misperceive the norm because assumptions and attitudes about drinking and how drinking relates to manhood are built into masculinity. It would also make sense that the actual and perceived social norms be gender specific.

What Is to Be Done?
Concrete Responses

Men, alcohol, and college are connected by the paradoxical nature of men's power. What can we do about college men's frequent, heavy, and problem drinking? Following from the model that has been developed in this essay, nothing short of radical reconstruction of masculinity and a reimagining of the college experience are likely to bring about significant change in college men's drinking. The same paradox that characterizes college men's drinking also provides a pedagogy for change. This is because, while the paradox acknowledges men's pain and powerlessness, it also discourages men from seeing themselves simply as victims, and it insists that men take responsibility for their actions.

Colleges, in collaboration with high schools and community agencies, should integrate gender awareness into alcohol education, prevention, and risk-reduction programs. For men, I recommend a comprehensive educational program that addresses four central themes in men's lives: friendship, health, life/work/family, and sexual ethics (see also, Good and Mintz[24(p20)]).

As in the case of effective rape prevention education workshops for men, the pedagogy should be workshops that are all male, small group, interactive, and peer facilitated. Such programs have been shown to change some men's attitudes and values that are associated with the perpetration of rape.[59] It may be that the rape prevention workshops are changing attitudes because they correct men's misperceived norm of other men's attitudes about women, or vice versa.[60]

Attitudes and values associated with problem drinking could be similarly changed. Developing what Lynch and Kilmartin[25] refer to as "healthy masculinity" that connects men in healthy relationships with other men, family, and intimate partners would be a succinct statement of the goal of such programming (pp. 46, 47).

The transition to college is a critical juncture in the consumption of alcohol.[4] Programming should therefore begin early in the first year and continue well beyond orientation week. Broad-based, fully integrated, social norms educational programs, interventions, and public information initiatives should be implemented.[55] I would add that such programs should be gender-informed along the lines I have suggested in this article. College men should understand how the paradoxical masculinity I have discussed may orient them to alcohol use and abuse.

College students should be strongly encouraged to get involved in clubs and organizations on campus, to run for office, and to be involved in sports as ways of meeting power orientation needs in socially responsible ways.[23] Those activities themselves must have alcohol education components; otherwise, involvement could have the ironic consequence of promoting heavier drinking.[3] Associations between men and beer in campus media should be discouraged.[61,62] Given their powerful influence over men's drinking in the first year,[43] the hazards of drinking games should be especially discussed in educational programming.

In general, college as adventure is a theme that should be discouraged. A "boys will be boys" permissiveness should be rejected. Recognizing and affirming that alcohol does harm, colleges must assert themselves as "moral communities" and move from permissive to restrictive stances on alcohol by first articulating what the harm is, then establishing policies to prevent college community members from harming themselves or others.[51(pp135,150–159)] Wechsler and associates[63] recommend a comprehensive approach to alcohol use on college campuses, including scrutiny of alcohol marketing, more alcohol-free events and activities, and more restrictive policies that control the flow of alcohol on campus. Their recommendation would benefit from more deeply gendered approaches to the problem because the problem, itself, is deeply gendered.

In addition to promoting social norms approaches, preventive education, and risk-reduction education, college administrators should require that frequent violators of alcohol policy seek treatment or seek their education elsewhere. Although critics of treatment may say it addresses the symptoms and not the real problem, which is the campus culture itself, colleges must offer treatment as part of a comprehensive program for renewed campus life. Treatment should seamlessly integrate men's health studies approaches.[66,67] Unfortunately, some college men will be untouched and untouchable by education or treatment, and they must lose the privilege of attending their chosen college and be asked to leave.

Conceptual Responses

Speaking most globally about solving the problem of college men's drinking and solving the problem of the connections between alcohol and masculinity, I would paraphrase what I have previously written about the problem of rape: Our understanding of the specific act of drinking should be embedded in our understanding of masculinity. Drinking is not an isolated behavior; it is a behavior linked to larger systems of attitudes, values, and modalities of conduct in men's lives that constitute masculinity and men's social position relative to women. In this model, alcohol prevention work with men begins with them *as* men, and with men's questioning of prevailing assumptions about masculinity and what it means to be a man. I am extremely skeptical of any alcohol prevention work that proposes solutions to the problem of drinking that leave masculinity, as we know it, largely intact.[68(p22)]

The educational challenge, which is really the psychological and political resistance to this solution, lies in the fact that alcohol benefits men as a group, even as it injures men as individuals. Men are likely to resist this global approach because we fear losing the benefits of masculinity conferred upon the group. The path to a reconstructed masculinity or alternatives to the dominant masculinity that includes more variety of men's identities and experiences may look something like Helms's[69] stage-development model for a positive racial-cultural identity for minority groups. It will not be easy getting there.

In the meantime, in our work with college men who drink, we must look to the bottom of their glasses and find the *men* inside. For when college men drink, they are simply being men at college, or what they perceive men at college to be. By this I mean that the most useful way to interpret their behavior is not so much in its *content*, but in its *context*—first, the imperatives of manhood, then the psychosocial particulars of college life, both of which put men at risk for drinking. Basically, at the bottom of heavy and problematic drinking among college men are the paradoxical nature of masculinity and the corresponding paradoxical nature of alcohol in men's lives. Once we know college men *as* men, we will know more about why they drink and what we can do about it.

Acknowledgment

This article is dedicated to Alan D. Berkowitz, longtime friend and colleague. I would also like to thank others for their extremely helpful and supportive readings of its various drafts: John Lynch, H. Wesley Perkins, Jan E. Regan, David A. Diana, and David DeVries.

References

1. Apollinaire G. Zone. In: *Selected Writings of Guillaume Apollinaire* (trans. Roger Shattuck). New York: New Directions, 1971.

2. Tomkins S. *Affect, Imagery, Consciousness.* Vol 3, 1962–1992. New York: Springer, 1991.

3. Perkins H. W. Gender patterns in consequences of collegiate alcohol abuse: A 10-year study of trends in an undergraduate population. *J Stud Alcohol.* 1992, September: 458–462.

4. Berkowitz A. D., Perkins H. W. Recent research on gender differences in collegiate alcohol use. *J Am Coll Health.* 1987, 36:123–129.

5. Fingarette H. *Heavy Drinking: The Myth of Alcoholism as a Disease.* Berkeley, CA: University of California Press, 1989.

6. Brod H. The case for men's studies. In: Brod H., ed. *The Making of Masculinities: The New Men's Studies.* Boston: Allen Unwin, 1987.

7. Sabo D., Gordon D. F. Rethinking men's health and illness. In: Sabo D., Gordon D. F. eds. *Men's Health and Illness: Gender, Power, and the Body.* Thousand Oaks, CA: Sage, 1995.

8. Johnson A. G. *The Gender Knot: Unraveling Our Patriarchal Legacy.* Philadelphia: Temple University Press, 1997.

9. Lemle R., Mishkind M. E. Alcohol and masculinity. *Journal of Substance Abuse Treatment.* 1989, 6:213–222.

10. McCreary D. R., Newcomb M. D., Sadave S. The male role, alcohol use, and alcohol problems. *Journal of Counseling Psychology.* 1999, 46(1): 109–124.

11. Wechsler H., Deutsch C., Dowdell G. Too many colleges are still in denial about alcohol abuse. (1995) http://www.hsph.harvard.edu/cas/test/articles/chronicle2.shtm/.

12. Courtenay W. H. Behavioral factors associated with disease, injury, and death among men: Evidence and implications for prevention. *The Journal of Men's Studies.* In press.

13. Sharpe M. J. Heppner P. P. Gender role, gender-role conflict, and psychological well-being in men. *Journal of Counseling Psychology.* 1991, 39(3): 323–330.

14. Pleck J. H. *The Myth of Masculinity.* Cambridge, MA: The MIT Press, 1981.

15. Pleck J. Men's power with women, other men, and society: A men's movement analysis. In: Kimmel M. S., Messner M. A. eds. *Men's Lives.* New York: Macmillan, 1989.

16. Kaufman M. Men, feminism, and men's contradictory experiences of power. In: Brod H., Kaufman M., eds. *Theorizing Masculinities.* Newbury Park, CA: Sage, 1994.

17. Kimmel M. S. Masculinity as homophobia: Fear, shame, and silence in the construction of gender identity. In: Brod H., Kaufman M., eds. *Theorizing Masculinities.* Newbury Park, CA: Sage, 1994.

18. Capraro R. L. Review of *Theorizing Masculinities.* Brod H., Kaufman M., eds. Sage; 1994. *Journal of Men's Studies.* 1995, 4(2):169–172.

19. O'Neil J. Assessing men's gender role conflict. In: Moore D., Leafgren F., eds. *Problem Solving Strategies and Interventions for Men in Conflict.* Alexandria, VA: American Association for Counseling and Development, 1990.

20. Pleck J. The gender role strain paradigm: An update. In: Levant R. L., Pollack W. S., eds. *A New Psychology of Men.* New York: Basic, 1995.

21. Blazina C., Watkins C. E. Masculine gender role conflict: Effects on college men's psychological well-being, chemical substance usage, and attitudes toward help-seeking. *Journal of Counseling Psychology.* 1995, 43(4):461–465.

22. Krugman S. Male development and the transformation of shame. In: Levant R. F., Pollack W. S., eds. *A New Psychology of Men.* New York: Basic, 1995.

23. Pollack W. *Real Boys.* New York: Henry Holt, 1999.

24. Good G. E., Mintz L. Gender role conflict and depression in college men: Evidence for compounded risk. *Journal of Counseling and Development.* 1990, 69 (September/October):17–21.

25. Lynch J., Kilmartin C. *The Pain Behind the Mask: Overcoming Masculine Depression.* New York: Haworth, 1999.

26. Real T. *I Don't Want to Talk About It.* New York: Simon & Schuster, 1997.

27. David D. S., Brannon R., eds. *The Forty-Nine Percent Majority: The Male Sex Role.* New York: Random House, 1976.

28. McClelland D. C., David W. N., Kalin R., Wanner E. *The Drinking Man.* New York: The Free Press, 1972.

29. Mahalik J. R., Cournoyer R. J., DeFran W., Cherry M., Napolitano J. M. Men's gender role conflict in relation to their use of psychological defenses. *Journal of Counseling Psychology.* 1998, 45(3):247–255.

30. Sattel J. W. Men, inexpressiveness, and power. In: Thorne K. H. *Language, Gender and Society.* Newbury House, 1983.

31. Fussell W. S. *Muscle: Confessions of an Unlikely Body-builder.* New York: Avon Books, 1991.

32. Berkowitz A. D., Burkhart B. R., Bourg S. E. *Research on College Research and Prevention Education in Higher Education.* San Francisco: Jossey-Bass, 1994.

33. Brod H. Pornography and the alienation of male sexuality. In: Hearn J., Morgan D., eds. *Men, Masculinities and Social Theory.* London: Unwin Hyman, 1990.

34. Kimmel M. S. *Men Confront Pornography.* New York: Crown, 1990.

35. Rorabaugh W. J. *The Alcoholic Republic: An American Tradition.* New York: Oxford University Press, 1981.

36. Maddox G. L., ed. *The Domesticated Drug: Drinking Among Collegians.* New Haven: College and University Press, 1970.

37. Bacon S. D., Strauss R. *Drinking in College.* New Haven: Yale University Press, 1953.

38. Johnston L., Bachman J. G., O'Malley P. M. *Monitoring the Future.* Health and Human Services Dept., US Public Health Service, National Institutes of Health, National Institute of Drug Abuse, 1996.

39. Levine A., Cureton J. S. *When Hope and Fear Collide: A Portrait of Today's College Student.* San Francisco: Jossey-Bass, 1998.

40. *Daedalus.* Distinctively American: The residential liberal arts colleges. Winter 1999.

41. Green M. *The Adventurous Male: Chapters in the History of the White Male Mind.* University Park, PA: The Pennsylvania State University Press, 1993.

42. Adams C. E., Nagoshi C. T. Changes over one semester in drinking game playing and alcohol use and problems in a college sample. *Subst Abuse.* 1999, 20(2):97–106.

43. Horowitz H. L. *Campus Life: Undergraduate Cultures from the End of the Eighteenth Century to the Present.* Chicago: University of Chicago Press, 1987.

44. Nuwer H. *Wrongs of Passage: Fraternities, Sororities, Hazing, and Binge Drinking.* Bloomington, IN: Indiana University Press, 1999.

45. Rotundo E. A. *American Manhood: Transformations in Masculinity from the Revolution to the Modern Era.* New York: HarperCollins, 1993.

46. Lyman P. The fraternal bond as a joking relationship. In: Kimmel M. S., ed. *Changing Men: New Directions in Research on Men and Masculinity.* Newbury Park, CA: Sage, 1987.

47. Gold J., Neururer J., Miller M. Disenfranchised grief among first-semester male university students: Implications for systemic and individual interventions. *Journal of the First Year Experience.* 2000, 12(1): 7–27.

48. Burda P. C., Tushup R. J., Hackman P. S. Masculinity and social support in alcoholic men. *Journal of Men's Studies.* 1992, 1(2):187–193.

49. Johnson T. J., Hamilton S., Sheets V. L. College students' self-reported reasons for playing drinking games. *Addict Behav.* 1999, 24(2):279–286.

50. Wechsler H., Dowdall G. W., Maener G., Gledhill-Hoyt J., Lee H. Changes in binge drinking and related problems among American college students between 1993 and 1997. *J Am Coll Health.* 1998, 47:57–68.

51. Hoekema D. A. *Campus Rules and Moral Community: In Place of In Loco Parentis.* Lanham, MD: Rowman & Littlefield, 1994.

52. Myers P. L. Sources and configurations of institutional denial. *Employee Assistance Quarterly.* 1990, 5(3):43–53.

53. Berkowitz, A. D. From reactive to proactive prevention: Promoting an ecology of health on campus. In: Rivers P. C., Shore E. R., eds. *Substance Abuse on Campus: A Handbook for College and University Personnel.* Westport, CT: Greenwood Press, 1997.

54. Perkins H. W. Confronting misperceptions of peer drug use norms among college students: An alternative approach for alcohol and other drug education programs. In: *The Higher Education Leaders/Peer Network Peer Prevention Resource Manual.* US Dept. of Education, FIPSE Drug Prevention Program, 1991.

55. Perkins H. W., Wechsler H. Variation in perceived college drinking norms and its impact on alcohol abuse: A nationwide study. *Journal of Drug Issues.* 1996, 26(4):961–974.

56. Fabiano P. M., McKinney G. R., Hyun Y.-R., Mertz H. K., Rhoads K. Lifestyles, 1998: Patterns of alcohol and drug consumption and consequences among Western Washington University students—An extended executive study. *Focus: A Research Summary.* 1999, 4(3):1–8.

57. Haines M. *A Social Norms Approach to Preventing Binge Drinking at Colleges and Universities.* Newton, MA: The Higher Education Center for Alcohol and Other Drug Prevention, 1998.

58. Prentice D. A., Miller D. T. Pluralistic ignorance and alcohol use on campus: Some consequences of misperceiving the social norms. *J Pers Soc Psychol.* 1993, 65:243–256.

59. Berkowitz A. D. A model acquaintance rape prevention program for men. In: Berkowitz A. D., ed. *Men and Rape: Theory, Research, and Prevention Education in Higher Education.* San Francisco: Jossey-Bass, 1994.

60. Berkowitz A. D. Applications of social norms theory to other health and social justice issues. Paper presented at: Annual Social Norms Conference. July 28–30, 1999, Big Sky, Mont.

61. Postman N., Nystrom C., Strate L., Weingartner C. *Myths, Men, and Beer: An Analysis of Beer Commercials on Broadcast Television, 1987.* Washington, DC: AAA Foundation for Traffic Safety, undated.

62. Courtenay W. H. Engendering health: A social constructionist examination of men's health beliefs and behaviors. *Psychology of Men and Masculinity.* In press.

63. Wechsler H., Kelley K., Weitzman E. R., San Giovanni J. P., Seebring M. What colleges are doing about student binge drinking: A survey of college administrators. (March 2000) http://www.hsph.Harvard.edu/cas/test/alcohol/surveyrpt.shtm/.

64. Scher M., Steven M., Good G., Eichenfield G. A. *Handbook of Counseling and Psychotherapy with Men.* Newbury Park, CA: Sage, 1987.

65. Moore D., Leafgren F., eds. *Problem Solving Strategies and Intervention for Men in Conflict.* Alexandria, VA: American Association for Counseling and Development, 1990.

66. Levant R. F., Pollack, W. S., eds. *A New Psychology of Men.* New York: Basic, 1995.

67. Mahalik M. R. Incorporating a gender role strain perspective in assessing and treating men's cognitive distortions. *Professional Psychology: Research and Practice.* 1999, 30(4):333–340.

68. Capraro R. L. Disconnected lives: Men, masculinity, and rape prevention. In: Berkowitz A. D., ed. *Men and Rape: Theory, Research, and Prevention Programs in Higher Education.* San Francisco: Jossey-Bass, 1994.

69. Helms J. An Update of Helms' *White and People of Color Racial Identity Models.* In: Ponterretto J., et al., eds. *Handbook of Multicultural Counseling.* Newbury Park, CA: Sage, 1995.

Greg Bortnichak

The Starbucks Intervention

I'm the kind of twenty-something guy you would expect to work in a coffee shop. I play guitar and cello in an experimental punk band and have some cool downloads on MySpace. I'm tall and lean, with an explosive mess of dark hair that makes me look like the love child of Edward Scissorhands and Blacula. Most people correctly guess that I'm artistic and a bit to the political left. What they may not realize is that I am a self-defined male feminist. Being a feminist is mighty powerful stuff because staying true to ideals about equality and justice involves consciously altering the way I behave. The bottom line is that I try to reject personal acts of subjugation, and I do my best to combat the systems that enable others to be oppressive. As the saying goes, the personal is political.

My brand of feminism is all about not imposing patriarchal power on the women in my life, and hoping to set an example for the boys and men I meet. From the time I was seven and too short to play ball with big kids, to the time I was 13 and too sensitive to party with the cool kids, to now when I struggle with masculinist ideology, I have always felt that the dominant culture only truly benefits a select few. So I do my best to reject it. I do it for me. I do it for my partner, and for every man who feels alienated by the expectations that culture places on guys who do not quite fit the "man's man" mold. I do it for

anyone who feels constrained by the music videos on MTV because they see both women and men reduced to sexual commodities. But the question remains, how do I do my feminism? And, more important, how am I a male feminist?

It's tricky. And the truth is that a lot of the time I feel friction between being a man and being a feminist. Problems come up when I want more than anything to take feminist action—to act in defense of someone who is being victimized by patriarchal power—but my aid is unwelcome or inappropriate or potentially does more political harm than good.

Allow me to illustrate: I work at Starbucks. I spend roughly 20 hours each week serving coffee to strangers, sometimes as many as several hundred each day. And you better believe I see it all. Customers reveal all kinds of personal details. So do my coworkers. I put up with a lot from them: sexist and racist jokes, routine descriptions of masculinist sexploitation, flat-out ridicule for my feminist views. And at the end of the day when my feet feel like they're ready to fall off and my entire body reeks of espresso grinds, I think back and try to make sense of it.

One day a customer comes in and begins telling us about this scheme he has to buy a wife. What he really wants to do is hire a housekeeper, but he thinks it's funnier if he tells us that he's "wife shopping" today. He complains about doing housework, saying he'd pay a cute, young girl 20 bucks an hour to do his chores for him rather than do them himself, or worse, get remarried to have yet another woman sit at home all day, take his money, and bitch at him when gets home from work. He keeps saying there is nothing worse than married life, to which the guys I'm working with chuckle in agreement. The only girl working at the time, Joy, is offended. She tells the customer that marriage won't be bad at all for her husband—she will do all the housework and more (wink, wink). For free. Joy wants to be a housewife, and she gives me a hard time for being feminist. The customer tells Joy that she's sweet but that she won't be sweet forever. He's expecting his purchased "wife" to be totally obedient and pleasant every hour of every day. Then, as an afterthought, he mentions that he has no problem getting his "non-domestic" (wink, wink) needs met elsewhere for not much more than it's going to cost him to buy this wife of his.

Later, my girlfriend, Ana, decides to come by and do some homework, keeping me company as I work. She is sitting alone in a far corner, completely engrossed in her studies. A man with slicked-back silver hair, white guy, probably in his fifties, and appearing to be quite wealthy (gold jewelry, designer golf shirt, the works) steps into line and begins staring at Ana. He makes no effort to hide this, and gets out of line to walk around behind her and get a better look. Then he gets back into line and cranes his neck to see down her shirt and up her dress. I see all of this, and I'm simultaneously disgusted and pissed off. He's such trash. I would love to call him out, or lay him out right then and there, but I risk losing my job if I'm rude to the customers. So I bite my tongue. It gets to be his turn in line and he still won't stop staring at her, not even to place his order. He's holding up the line, people behind him are starting to get flustered, and I lose it.

"What's so interesting over there, sir? You seem to be looking very intently at something," I ask as innocently as I possibly can. "That girl in the corner," he says like he's ready to eat her. He doesn't take his eyes off Ana once. "Oh yeah, what do you think?" I'm trying now to sound as sleazy as I possibly can in an attempt to lead him to believe that I'm going along with the shameless objectification of Ana. "I think she's a real pretty girl in that little dress of hers." He licks his ugly thin lips and makes a face that screams "pervert."

I've caught him red-handed at his patriarchal bullshit, and at this point, I'm done: "Well, I think she's a friend of mine, and I think she'd feel violated if she knew you were staring at her like that." I say it low and threateningly beneath my breath so as not to cause a scene. "I think she should get used to it," he replies. There is no hint of apology in his tone. It's like I'm wrong for telling him not to lech at a girl who could be his fucking granddaughter! I glare at him like I want to burn a hole in his face with my eyes and growl, "I think you need to learn a little respect." He leaves. I'm shaking.

I go to Ana and ask her if she saw what just transpired. She says no, that she was completely unaware. When I tell her what happened she is visibly upset. She thanks me for sticking up for her and waits for me to finish my shift without returning to her homework. The woman in line behind the silver-haired man approaches me before leaving and wishes me goodnight, smiling at me in a way that I could only interpret as solidarity.

That night I had nightmares about the silver-haired man. He was so ruthless in how he visually dismembered Ana that he put me in touch with a very distinct fear. No one had ever made me so mad, or provoked such a reaction from me. But was it even my place to step in on Ana's behalf? Was I being overprotective?

Despite Ana's appreciation for my fast action, I still could not get this encounter out of my mind. The silver-haired man obviously saw nothing wrong with what he did. I even had a coworker poke fun at me for bothering that "poor old man." The woman in line behind the silver-haired man was my best assurance—as iffy as it was—that speaking up was the right thing to do. Yet I could not help but feel unsettled about how I chose to respond. After all, I don't doubt that if Ana looked up at the right time, she would have reacted more strongly and defended herself far better than I. And if Ana had been the one to terminate the encounter, perhaps she would have a stronger feeling of closure or justice. I had to wonder what it meant that I defended Ana instead of simply bringing her attention to what was happening. Did my chivalrous feminism reflect some duty I feel to protect her? And if so, does that mean that on some level I think she is incapable of protecting herself? Even worse, what if my actions actually revealed a sense of possession or ownership over Ana? And what about that burst of anger I felt? How stereotypically masculine to feel angry in light of something another man did to my girlfriend.

This encounter with the silver-haired man raises so many difficult questions for me about whether profeminist men ought to step in to help women or instead focus our efforts on enabling women to protect themselves. On the night of the scuffle in Starbucks, Ana happened to be wearing a gorgeous dress that was short, with a very low neckline. She has gotten upset in the past over men leering at her when she wears this dress. Sometimes I think about gently suggesting to Ana that she shelve the dress, but I don't think it's my place to say so. I do not want Ana to continue feeling violated by these tactless creeps but, at the same time, I do not want her to compromise her own sense of beauty, self-expression, and sexuality. I also don't want to be perceived as controlling or paternalistic. It is not Ana's fault that some men feel it's their right to stare crudely at young women. But still, it upsets Ana, and it happens less when she does not wear this particular dress. It is clear who is at fault. It's the voyeurs like that silver-haired man at Starbucks. But if men like that deny responsibility, and if women have the right to wear whatever they damn well please, and

if I happen to see what's going on, then shouldn't I step in and speak my mind?

I've run into a dilemma: It's true that men can deflect unwanted attention, but in doing so we risk offending or patronizing women who are capable of protecting themselves, or insulting women who like this sort of thing. I know that some women rely on the male gaze to feel attractive and some may dress in ways to get attention on purpose. Women have the right to express themselves through their clothes and demeanor in any way they see fit. But I risk sounding sexist if I advise a woman not to go to certain parts of the city looking a certain way, and I risk feeling guilty knowing someone could get hurt if I don't speak up.

The problem lies in knowing when it's okay to intervene; in knowing when to act on my personal feminist beliefs, and knowing when to hold back. Mastering this discretion is something I grapple with each day. Sometimes I get to thinking that I'm setting myself up for an unconquerable task by trying to live the life of an active male feminist. Sometimes it feels so daunting that I consider giving up. But then I remember what got me here in the first place, and it gives me hope. Feminism is something I embrace because it helps me think more clearly about who I am and how I behave as a man in this society. When I keep this in mind, I understand that I'm not about to defeat the patriarchy overnight, but that I can feel a little better knowing I'm not letting it defeat me little by little, each and every day.

PART FOUR

Men and Work

In what ways is work tied to male identity? Do men gain a sense of fulfillment from their work, or do they view it as necessary drudgery? How might the organization of workplaces play on, reinforce, or sometimes threaten the types of masculinity that males have already learned as youngsters? How does the experience of work (or of not having work) differ for men of different social classes, ethnicities, and sexual preference groups? And how do recent structural changes in society affect the masculinity–work relationship? The articles in this section address these issues and more.

The rise of urban industrial capitalism saw the creation of separate "public" and "domestic" spheres of social life. As women were increasingly relegated to working in the home, men were increasingly absent from the home, and the male "breadwinner role" was born. The sexual division of labor, this gendered split between home and workplace, has led to a variety of problems and conflicts for women and for men. Women's continued movement into the paid labor force, higher levels of unemployment, and the rise of a more service-oriented economy have led to dramatic shifts in the quality and the quantity of men's experiences in their work.

Articles by Christine Williams and Kevin Henson and Jackie Krasas Rogers explore how men who do women's work also "do" gender by ensuring that their masculinity is also validated. Kristin Schilt finds that gendered world of work is never more apparent when people change their gender.

The work world has also become an arena of the battle between the sexes, as the continuing debates over sexual harassment make clear. The article by Beth Quinn examines sexual harassment in that most commonplace behavior—girl watching.

Christine L. Williams

The Glass Escalator: Hidden Advantages for Men in the "Female" Professions

The sex segregation of the U.S. labor force is one of the most perplexing and tenacious problems in our society. Even though the proportion of men and women in the labor force is approaching parity (particularly for younger cohorts of workers) (U.S. Department of Labor 1991:18), men and women are still generally confined to predominantly single-sex occupations. Forty percent of men or women would have to change major occupational categories to achieve equal representation of men and women in all jobs (Reskin and Roos 1990:6), but even this figure underestimates the true degree of sex segregation. It is extremely rare to find specific jobs where equal numbers of men and women are engaged in the same activities in the same industries (Bielby and Baron 1984).

Most studies of sex segregation in the work force have focused on women's experiences in male-dominated occupations. Both researchers and advocates for social change have focused on the barriers faced by women who try to integrate predominantly male fields. Few have looked at the "flip-side" of occupational sex segregation: the exclusion of men from predominantly female occupations (exceptions include Schreiber 1979; Zimmer 1988; Williams 1989). But the fact is that men are less likely to enter female sex-typed occupations than women are to enter male-dominated jobs (Jacobs 1989). Reskin and Roos, for exam-

ple, were able to identify 33 occupations in which female representation increased by more than nine percentage points between 1970 and 1980, but only three occupations in which the proportion of men increased as radically (1990:20–21).

In this paper, I examine men's underrepresentation in four predominantly female occupations—nursing, librarianship, elementary school teaching, and social work. Throughout the twentieth century, these occupations have been identified with "women's work"—even though prior to the Civil War, men were more likely to be employed in these areas. These four occupations, often called the female "semi-professions" (Hodson and Sullivan 1990), today range from 5.5 percent male (in nursing) to 32 percent male (in social work). (See Table 16.1.) These percentages have not changed substantially in decades. In fact, as Table 16.1 indicates, two of these professions—librarianship and social work—have experienced declines in the proportions of men since 1975. Nursing is the only one of the four experiencing noticeable changes in sex composition, with the proportion of men increasing 80 percent between 1975 and 1990. Even so, men continue to be a tiny minority of all nurses.

Although there are many possible reasons for the continuing preponderance of women in these fields, the focus of this paper is discrimination. Researchers examining the integration of women into "male fields" have identified discrimination as a major barrier to women (Reskin and Hartmann 1986; Reskin 1988; Jacobs 1989). This discrimination has taken the form of laws or

■ **TABLE 16.1**
Percent Male in Selected Occupations,
Selected Years

Profession	1990	1980	1975
Nurses	5.5	3.5	3.0
Elementary teachers	14.8	16.3	14.6
Librarians	16.7	14.8	18.9
Social workers	31.8	35.0	39.2

Source: U.S. Department of Labor. Bureau of Labor
Statistics. *Employment and Earnings* 38:1 (January 1991),
Table 22 (Employed civilians by detailed occupation), 185;
28:1 (January 1981), Table 23 (Employed persons by
detailed occupation), 180; 22:7 (January 1976), Table 2
(Employed persons by detailed occupation), 11.

institutionalized rules prohibiting the hiring or
promotion of women into certain job specialties.
Discrimination can also be "informal," as when
women encounter sexual harassment, sabotage,
or other forms of hostility from their male coworkers resulting in a poisoned work environment (Reskin and Hartmann 1986). Women in
nontraditional occupations also report feeling
stigmatized by clients when their work puts them
in contact with the public. In particular, women
in engineering and blue-collar occupations
encounter gender-based stereotypes about their
competence which undermine their work performance (Martin 1980; Epstein 1988). Each of
these forms of discrimination—legal, informal,
and cultural—contributes to women's underrepresentation in predominantly male occupations.

The assumption in much of this literature is
that any member of a token group in a work setting will probably experience similar discriminatory treatment. Kanter (1977), who is best known
for articulating this perspective in her theory of
tokenism, argues that when any group represents
less than 15 percent of an organization, its members will be subject to predictable forms of discrimination. Likewise, Jacobs argues that "in
some ways, men in female-dominated occupations experience the same difficulties that women
in male-dominated occupations face" (1989:167),
and Reskin contends that any dominant group in

an occupation will use their power to maintain a
privileged position (1988:62).

However, the few studies that have considered men's experience in gender-atypical
occupations suggest that men may not face discrimination or prejudice when they integrate predominantly female occupations. Zimmer (1988)
and Martin (1988) both contend that the effects of
sexism can outweigh the effects of tokenism
when men enter nontraditional occupations. This
study is the first to systematically explore this
question using data from four occupations. I
examine the barriers to men's entry into these professions; the support men receive from their
supervisors, colleagues, and clients; and the reactions they encounter from the public (those outside their professions).

Methods

I conducted in-depth interviews with 76 men and
23 women in four occupations from 1985–1991.
Interviews were conducted in four metropolitan
areas: San Francisco/Oakland, California; Austin,
Texas; Boston, Massachusetts; and Phoenix, Arizona. These four areas were selected because they
show considerable variation in the proportions of
men in the four professions. For example, Austin
has one of the highest percentages of men in
nursing (7.7 percent), whereas Phoenix's percentage is one of the lowest (2.7 percent) (U.S.
Bureau of the Census 1980). The sample was generated using "snowballing" techniques. Women
were included in the sample to gauge their feelings and responses to men who enter "their"
professions.

Like the people employed in these professions generally, those in my sample were predominantly white (90 percent).[1] Their ages
ranged from 20 to 66 and the average age was 38.
The interview questionnaire consisted of several
open-ended questions on four broad topics: motivation to enter the profession; experiences in
training; career progression; and general views
about men's status and prospects within these
occupations. I conducted all the interviews,

which generally lasted between one and two hours. Interviews took place in restaurants, my home or office, or the respondent's home or office. Interviews were tape-recorded and transcribed for the analysis.

Data analysis followed the coding techniques described by Strauss (1987). Each transcript was read several times and analyzed into emergent conceptual categories. Likewise, Strauss's principle of theoretical sampling was used. Individual respondents were purposively selected to capture the array of men's experiences in these occupations. Thus, I interviewed practitioners in every specialty, oversampling those employed in the *most* gender atypical areas (e.g., male kindergarten teachers). I also selected respondents from throughout their occupational hierarchies—from students to administrators to retirees. Although the data do not permit within-group comparisons, I am reasonably certain that the sample does capture a wide range of experiences common to men in these female-dominated professions. However, like all findings based on qualitative data, it is uncertain whether the findings generalize to the larger population of men in nontraditional occupations.

In this paper, I review individuals' responses to questions about discrimination in hiring practices, on-the-job rapport with supervisors and co-workers, and prejudice from clients and others outside their profession.

Discrimination in Hiring

Contrary to the experience of many women in the male-dominated professions, many of the men and women I spoke to indicated that there is a *preference* for hiring men in these four occupations. A Texas librarian at a junior high school said that his school district "would hire a male over a female."

I: Why do you think that is?

R: Because there are so few, and the . . . ones that they do have, the library directors

seem to really . . . think they're doing great jobs. I don't know, maybe they just feel they're being progressive or something, [but] I have had a real sense that they really appreciate having a male, particularly at the junior high. . . . As I said, when seven of us lost our jobs from the high schools and were redistributed, there were only four positions at the junior high, and I got one of them. Three of the librarians, some who had been here longer than I had with the school district, were put down in elementary school as librarians. And I definitely think that being male made a difference in my being moved to the junior high rather than an elementary school.

Many of the men perceived their token status as males in predominantly female occupations as an *advantage* in hiring and promotions. I asked an Arizona teacher whether his specialty (elementary special education) was an unusual area for men compared to other areas within education. He said,

> Much more so. I am extremely marketable in special education. That's not why I got into the field. But I am extremely marketable because I am a man.

In several cases, the more female-dominated the specialty, the greater the apparent preference for men. For example, when asked if he encountered any problem getting a job in pediatrics, a Massachusetts nurse said,

> No, no, none. . . . I've heard this from managers and supervisory-type people with men in pediatrics: "It's nice to have a man because it's such a female-dominated profession."

However, there were some exceptions to this preference for men in the most female-dominated specialties. In some cases, formal policies actually barred men from certain jobs. This was the case in some rural Texas school districts, which refused to hire men in the youngest grades (K–3). Some nurses also reported being excluded from positions in obstetrics and gynecology wards, a policy encountered more frequently in private Catholic hospitals.

But often the pressures keeping men out of certain specialties were more subtle than this. Some men described being "tracked" into practice areas within their professions which were considered more legitimate for men. For example, one Texas man described how he was pushed into administration and planning in social work, even though "I'm not interested in writing policy; I'm much more interested in research and clinical stuff." A nurse who is interested in pursuing graduate study in family and child health in Boston said he was dissuaded from entering the program specialty in favor of a concentration in "adult nursing." A kindergarten teacher described the difficulty of finding a job in his specialty after graduation: "I was recruited immediately to start getting into a track to become an administrator. And it was men who recruited me. It was men that ran the system at that time, especially in Los Angeles."

This tracking may bar men from the most female-identified specialties within these professions. But men are effectively being "kicked upstairs" in the process. Those specialties considered more legitimate practice areas for men also tend to be the most prestigious, better paying ones. A distinguished kindergarten teacher, who had been voted city-wide "Teacher of the Year," told me that even though people were pleased to see him in the classroom, "there's been some encouragement to think about administration, and there's been some encouragement to think about teaching at the university level or something like that, or supervisory-type position." That is, despite his aptitude and interest in staying in the classroom, he felt pushed in the direction of administration.

The effect of this "tracking" is the opposite of that experienced by women in male-dominated occupations. Researchers have reported that many women encounter a "glass ceiling" in their efforts to scale organizational and professional hierarchies. That is, they are constrained by invisible barriers to promotion in their careers, caused mainly by sexist attitudes of men in the highest positions (Freeman 1990).[2] In contrast to the "glass ceiling," many of the men I interviewed seem to encounter a "glass escalator." Often, despite their intentions, they face invisible pressures to move up in their professions. As if on a moving escalator, they must work to stay in place.

A public librarian specializing in children's collections (a heavily female-dominated concentration) described an encounter with this "escalator" in his very first job out of library school. In his first six-months' evaluation, his supervisors commended him for his good work in storytelling and related activities, but they criticized him for "not shooting high enough."

> Seriously. That's literally what they were telling me. They assumed that because I was a male—and they told me this—and that I was being hired right out of graduate school, that somehow I wasn't doing the kind of management-oriented work that they thought I should be doing. And as a result, really they had a lot of bad marks, as it were, against me on my evaluation. And I said I couldn't believe this!

Throughout his ten-year career, he has had to struggle to remain in children's collections.

The glass escalator does not operate at all levels. In particular, men in academia reported some gender-based discrimination in the highest positions due to their universities' commitment to affirmative action. Two nursing professors reported that they felt their own chances of promotion to deanships were nil because their universities viewed the position of nursing dean as a guaranteed female appointment in an otherwise heavily male-dominated administration. One California social work professor reported his university canceled its search for a dean because no minority male or female candidates had been placed on their short list. It was rumored that other schools on campus were permitted to go forward with their searches—even though they also failed to put forward names of minority candidates—because the higher administration perceived it to be "easier" to fulfill affirmative action goals in the social work school. The interviews provide greater evidence of the "glass escalator" at work in the lower levels of these professions.

Of course, men's motivations also play a role in their advancement to higher professional positions. I do not mean to suggest that the men I talked to all resented the informal tracking they experienced. For many men, leaving the most female-identified areas of their professions helped them resolve internal conflicts involving their masculinity. One man left his job as a school social worker to work in a methadone drug treatment program not because he was encouraged to leave by his colleagues, but because "I think there was some macho shit there, to tell you the truth, because I remember feeling a little uncomfortable there . . . ; it didn't feel right to me." Another social worker, employed in the mental health services department of a large urban area in California, reflected on his move into administration:

> The more I think about it, through our discussion, I'm sure that's a large part of why I wound up in administration. It's okay for a man to do the administration. In fact, I don't know if I fully answered a question that you asked a little while ago about how did being male contribute to my advancing in the field. I was saying it wasn't because I got any special favoritism as a man, but . . . I think . . . because I'm a man, I felt a need to get into this kind of position. I may have worked harder toward it, may have competed harder for it, than most women would do, even women who think about doing administrative work.

Elsewhere I have speculated on the origins of men's tendency to define masculinity through single-sex work environments (Williams 1989). Clearly, personal ambition does play a role in accounting for men's movement into more "male-defined" arenas within these professions. But these occupations also structure opportunities for males independent of their individual desires or motives.

The interviews suggest that men's underrepresentation in these professions cannot be attributed to discrimination in hiring or promotions. Many of the men indicated that they received preferential treatment because they were men. Although men mentioned gender discrimination in the hiring process, for the most part they were channelled into the more "masculine" specialties within these professions, which ironically meant being "tracked" into better paying and more prestigious specialties.

Supervisors and Colleagues: The Working Environment

Researchers claim that subtle forms of workplace discrimination push women out of male-dominated occupations (Reskin and Hartmann 1986; Jacobs 1989). In particular, women report feeling excluded from informal leadership and decision-making networks, and they sense hostility from their male co-workers, which makes them feel uncomfortable and unwanted (Carothers and Crull 1984). Respondents in this study were asked about their relationships with supervisors and female colleagues to ascertain whether men also experienced "poisoned" work environments when entering gender atypical occupations.

A major difference in the experience of men and women in nontraditional occupations is that men in these situations are far more likely to be supervised by a member of their own sex. In each of the four professions I studied, men are overrepresented in administrative and managerial capacities, or, as in the case of nursing, their positions in the organizational hierarchy are governed by men (Grimm and Sterm 1974; Phenix 1987; Schmuck 1987; York, Henley, and Gamble 1987; Williams 1989). Thus, unlike women who enter "male fields," the men in these professions often work under the direct supervision of other men.

Many of the men interviewed reported that they had good rapport with their male supervisors. Even in professional school, some men reported extremely close relationships with their male professors. For example, a Texas librarian described an unusually intimate association with two male professors in graduate school:

> I can remember a lot of times in the classroom there would be discussions about a particular topic or issue, and the conversation would spill over into their office hours, after the class was over. And even though there were . . . a couple of the other women that had been in on the discussion, they weren't there. And I don't know if that was preferential or not . . . it certainly carried over into personal life as well. Not just at the school and that sort of thing. I mean, we would get together for dinner . . .

These professors explicitly encouraged him because he was male:

> **I:** Did they ever offer you explicit words of encouragement about being in the profession by virtue of the fact that you were male? . . .
>
> **R:** Definitely. On several occasions. Yeah. Both of these guys, for sure, including the Dean who was male also. And it's an interesting point that you bring up because it was, oftentimes, kind of in a sign, you know. It wasn't in the classroom, and it wasn't in front of the group, or if we were in the student lounge or something like that. It was . . . if it was just myself or maybe another one of the guys, you know, and just talking in the office. It's like . . . you know, kind of an opening-up and saying, "You know, you are really lucky that you're in the profession because you'll really go to the top real quick, and you'll be able to make real definite improvements and changes. And you'll have a real influence," and all this sort of thing. I mean, really, I can remember several times.

Other men reported similar closeness with their professors. A Texas psychotherapist recalled his relationships with his male professors in social work school:

> I made it a point to make a golfing buddy with one of the guys that was in administration. He

and I played golf a lot. He was the guy who kind of ran the research training, the research part of the master's program. Then there was a sociologist who ran the other part of the research program. He and I developed a good friendship.

This close mentoring by male professors contrasts with the reported experience of women in nontraditional occupations. Others have noted a lack of solidarity among women in nontraditional occupations. Writing about military academies, for example, Yoder describes the failure of token women to mentor succeeding generations of female cadets. She argues that women attempt to play down their gender difference from men because it is the source of scorn and derision.

> Because women felt unaccepted by their male colleagues, one of the last things they wanted to do was to emphasize their gender. Some women thought that, if they kept company with other women, this would highlight their gender and would further isolate them from male cadets. These women desperately wanted to be accepted as cadets, not as *women* cadets. Therefore, they did everything from not wearing skirts as an option with their uniforms to avoiding being a part of a group of women. (Yoder 1989:532)

Men in nontraditional occupations face a different scenario—their gender is construed as a *positive* difference. Therefore, they have an incentive to bond together and emphasize their distinctiveness from the female majority.

Close, personal ties with male supervisors were also described by men once they were established in their professional careers. It was not uncommon in education, for example, for the male principal to informally socialize with the male staff, as a Texas special education teacher describes:

> Occasionally I've had a principal who would regard me as "the other man on the campus" and "it's us against them," you know? I mean, nothing really that extreme, except that some male

principals feel like there's nobody there to talk to except the other man. So I've been in that position.

These personal ties can have important consequences for men's careers. For example, one California nurse, whose performance was judged marginal by his nursing supervisors, was transferred to the emergency room staff (a prestigious promotion) due to his personal friendship with the physician in charge. A Massachusetts teacher acknowledged that his principal's personal interest in him landed him his current job.

> **I:** You had mentioned that your principal had sort of spotted you at your previous job and had wanted to bring you here [to this school]. Do you think that has anything to do with the fact that you're a man, aside from your skills as a teacher?
>
> **R:** Yes, I would say in that particular case, that was part of it. . . . We have certain things in common, certain interests that really lined up.
>
> **I:** Vis-à-vis teaching?
>
> **R:** Well, more extraneous things—running specifically, and music. And we just seemed to get along real well right off the bat. It is just kind of a guy thing; we just liked each other . . .

Interviewees did not report many instances of male supervisors discriminating against them, or refusing to accept them because they were male. Indeed, these men were much more likely to report that their male bosses discriminated against the *females* in their professions. When asked if he thought physicians treated male and female nurses differently, a Texas nurse said:

> I think yeah, some of them do. I think the women seem like they have a lot more trouble with the physicians treating them in a derogatory manner. Or, if not derogatory, then in a very paternalistic way than the men [are treated]. Usually if a physician is mad at a male nurse, he just kind of yells at him. Kind of like

an employee. And if they're mad at a female nurse, rather than treat them on an equal basis, in terms of just letting their anger out at them as an employee, they're more paternalistic or there's some sexual harassment component to it.

A Texas teacher perceived a similar situation where he worked:

> I've never felt unjustly treated by a principal because I'm a male. The principals that I've seen that I felt are doing things that are kind of arbitrary or not well thought out are doing it to everybody. In fact, they're probably doing it to the females worse than they are to me.

Openly gay men may encounter less favorable treatment at the hands of their supervisors. For example, a nurse in Texas stated that one of the physicians he worked with preferred to staff the operating room with male nurses exclusively—as long as they weren't gay. Stigma associated with homosexuality leads some men to enhance, or even exaggerate their "masculine" qualities, and may be another factor pushing men into more "acceptable" specialties for men.

Not all men who work in these occupations are supervised by men. Many of the men interviewed who had female bosses also reported high levels of acceptance—although levels of intimacy with women seemed lower than with other men. In some cases, however, men reported feeling shut-out from decision making when the higher administration was constituted entirely by women. I asked an Arizona librarian whether men in the library profession were discriminated against in hiring because of their sex:

> Professionally speaking, people go to considerable lengths to keep that kind of thing out of their [hiring] deliberations. Personally, is another matter. It's pretty common around here to talk about the "old girl network." This is one of the few libraries that I've had any intimate knowledge of which is actually controlled by women. . . . Most of the department heads and upper level administrators are women. And

there's an "old girl network" that works just like the "old boy network," except that the important conferences take place in the women's room rather than on the golf course. But the political mechanism is the same, the exclusion of the other sex from decision making is the same. The reasons are the same. It's somewhat discouraging . . .

Although I did not interview many supervisors, I did include 23 women in my sample to ascertain their perspectives about the presence of men in their professions. All of the women I interviewed claimed to be supportive of their male colleagues, but some conveyed ambivalence. For example, a social work professor said she would like to see more men enter the social work profession, particularly in the clinical specialty (where they are underrepresented). Indeed, she favored affirmative action hiring guidelines for men in the profession. Yet, she resented the fact that her department hired "another white male" during a recent search. I questioned her about this ambivalence:

I: I find it very interesting that, on the one hand, you sort of perceive this preference and perhaps even sexism with regard to how men are evaluated and how they achieve higher positions within the profession, yet, on the other hand, you would be encouraging of more men to enter the field. Is that contradictory to you, or . . . ?

R: Yeah, it's contradictory.

It appears that women are generally eager to see men enter "their" occupations. Indeed, several men noted that their female colleagues had facilitated their careers in various ways (including mentorship in college). However, at the same time, women often resent the apparent ease with which men advance within these professions, sensing that men at the higher levels receive preferential treatment which closes off advancement opportunities for women.

But this ambivalence does not seem to translate into the "poisoned" work environment described by many women who work in male-dominated occupations. Among the male interviewees, there were no accounts of sexual harassment. However, women do treat their male colleagues differently on occasion. It is not uncommon in nursing, for example, for men to be called upon to help catheterize male patients, or to lift especially heavy patients. Some librarians also said that women asked them to lift and move heavy boxes of books because they were men. Teachers sometimes confront differential treatment as well, as described by this Texas teacher:

As a man, you're teaching with all women, and that can be hard sometimes. Just because of the stereotypes, you know. I'm real into computers . . . and all the time people are calling me to fix their computer. Or if somebody gets a flat tire, they come and get me. I mean, there are just a lot of stereotypes. Not that I mind doing any of those things, but it's . . . you know, it just kind of bugs me that it is a stereotype, "A man should do that." Or if their kids have a lot of discipline problems, that kiddo's in your room. Or if there are kids that don't have a father in their home, that kid's in your room. Hell, nowadays that'd be half the school in my room (laughs). But you know, all the time I hear from the principal or from other teachers, "Well, this child really needs a man . . . a male role model" (laughs). So there are a lot of stereotypes that . . . men kind of get stuck with.

This special treatment bothered some respondents. Getting assigned all the "discipline problems" can make for difficult working conditions, for example. But many men claimed this differential treatment did not cause distress. In fact, several said they liked being appreciated for the special traits and abilities (such as strength) they could contribute to their professions.

Furthermore, women's special treatment sometimes enhanced—rather than poisoned—the men's work environments. One Texas librarian said he felt "more comfortable working with women than men" because "I think it has something to do with control. Maybe it's that women will let me take control more than men will."

Several men reported that their female colleagues often cast them into leadership roles. Although not all savored this distinction, it did enhance their authority and control in the workplace. In subtle (and not-too-subtle) ways, then, differential treatment contributes to the "glass escalator" men experience in nontraditional professions.

Even outside work, most of the men interviewed said they felt fully accepted by their female colleagues. They were usually included in informal socializing occasions with the women—even though this frequently meant attending baby showers or Tupperware parties. Many said that they declined offers to attend these events because they were not interested in "women's things," although several others claimed to attend everything. The minority men I interviewed seemed to feel the least comfortable in these informal contexts. One social worker in Arizona was asked about socializing with his female colleagues:

> **I:** So in general, for example, if all the employees were going to get together to have a party, or celebrate a bridal shower or whatever, would you be invited along with the rest of the group?
>
> **R:** They would invite me, I would say, somewhat reluctantly. Being a black male, working with all white females, it did cause some outside problems. So I didn't go to a lot of functions with them . . .
>
> **I:** You felt that there was some tension there on the level of your acceptance . . . ?
>
> **R:** Yeah. It was OK working, but on the outside, personally, there was some tension there. It never came out, that they said, "Because of who you are we can't invite you" (laughs), and I wouldn't have done anything anyway. I would have probably respected them more for saying what was on their minds. But I never felt completely in with the group.

Some single men also said they felt uncomfortable socializing with married female colleagues because it gave the "wrong impression." But in general, the men said that they felt very comfortable around their colleagues and described their workplaces as very congenial for men. It appears unlikely, therefore, that men's underrepresentation in these professions is due to hostility towards men on the part of supervisors or women workers.

Discrimination from "Outsiders"

The most compelling evidence of discrimination against men in these professions is related to their dealings with the public. Men often encounter negative stereotypes when they come into contact with clients or "outsiders"—people they meet outside of work. For instance, it is popularly assumed that male nurses are gay. Librarians encounter images of themselves as "wimpy" and asexual. Male social workers describe being typecast as "feminine" and "passive." Elementary school teachers are often confronted by suspicions that they are pedophiles. One kindergarten teacher described an experience that occurred early in his career which was related to him years afterwards by his principal:

> He indicated to me that parents had come to him and indicated to him that they had a problem with the fact that I was a male. . . . I recall almost exactly what he said. There were three specific concerns that the parents had: One parent said, "How can he love my child; he's a man." The second thing that I recall, he said the parent said, "He has a beard." And the third thing was, "Aren't you concerned about homosexuality?"

Such suspicions often cause men in all four professions to alter their work behavior to guard against sexual abuse charges, particularly in those specialties requiring intimate contact with women and children.

Men are very distressed by these negative stereotypes, which tend to undermine their self-esteem and to cause them to second-guess their motivations for entering these fields. A California teacher said,

> If I tell men that I don't know, that I'm meeting for the first time, that that's what I do, . . .

sometimes there's a look on their faces that, you know, "Oh, couldn't get a real job?"

When asked if his wife, who is also an elementary school teacher, encounters the same kind of prejudice, he said,

> No, it's accepted because she's a woman. . . . I think people would see that as a . . . step up, you know. "Oh, you're not a housewife, you've got a career. That's great . . . that you're out there working. And you have a daughter, but you're still out there working. You decided not to stay home, and you went out there and got a job." Whereas for me, it's more like I'm supposed to be out working anyway, even though I'd rather be home with [my daughter].

Unlike women who enter traditionally male professions, men's movement into these jobs is perceived by the "outside world" as a step down in status. This particular form of discrimination may be most significant in explaining why men are underrepresented in these professions. Men who otherwise might show interest in and aptitudes for such careers are probably discouraged from pursuing them because of the negative popular stereotypes associated with the men who work in them. This is a crucial difference from the experience of women in nontraditional professions: "My daughter, the physician," resonates far more favorably in most people's ears than "My son, the nurse."

Many of the men in my sample identified the stigma of working in a female-identified occupation as the major barrier to more men entering their professions. However, for the most part, they claimed that these negative stereotypes were not a factor in their own decisions to join these occupations. Most respondents didn't consider entering these fields until well into adulthood, after working in some related occupation. Several social workers and librarians even claimed they were not aware that men were a minority in their chosen professions. Either they had no well-defined image or stereotype, or their contacts and mentors were predominantly men. For example,

prior to entering library school, many librarians held part-time jobs in university libraries, where there are proportionally more men than in the profession generally. Nurses and elementary school teachers were more aware that mostly women worked in these jobs, and this was often a matter of some concern to them. However, their choices were ultimately legitimized by mentors, or by encouraging friends or family members who implicitly reassured them that entering these occupations would not typecast them as feminine. In some cases, men were told by recruiters there were special advancement opportunities for men in these fields, and they entered them expecting rapid promotion to administrative positions.

> **I:** Did it ever concern you when you were making the decision to enter nursing school, the fact that it is a female-dominated profession?
>
> **R:** Not really. I never saw myself working on the floor. I saw myself pretty much going into administration, just getting the background and then getting a job someplace as a supervisor and then working, getting up into administration.

Because of the unique circumstances of their recruitment, many of the respondents did not view their occupational choices as inconsistent with a male gender role, and they generally avoided the negative stereotypes directed against men in these fields.

Indeed, many of the men I interviewed claimed that they did not encounter negative professional stereotypes until they had worked in these fields for several years. Popular prejudices can be damaging to self-esteem and probably push some men out of these professions altogether. Yet, ironically, they sometimes contribute to the "glass escalator" effect I have been describing. Men seem to encounter the most vituperative criticism from the public when they are in the most female-identified specialties. Public concerns sometimes result in their being shunted into more "legitimate" positions for men. A librarian formerly in charge of a branch library's children's collection, who now works in the reference department of the city's main library, describes his experience:

> **R:** Some of the people [who frequented the branch library] complained that they didn't want to have a man doing the storytelling scenario. And I got transferred here to the central library in an equivalent job . . . I thought that I did a good job. And I had been told by my supervisor that I was doing a good job.
>
> **I:** Have you ever considered filing some sort of lawsuit to get that other job back?
>
> **R:** Well, actually, the job I've gotten now . . . well, it's a reference librarian; it's what I wanted in the first place. I've got a whole lot more authority here. I'm also in charge of the circulation desk. And I've recently been promoted because of my new stature, so . . . no, I'm not considering trying to get that other job back.

The negative stereotypes about men who do "women's work" can push men out of specific jobs. However, to the extent that they channel men into more "legitimate" practice areas, their effects can actually be positive. Instead of being a source of discrimination, these prejudices can add to the "glass escalator effect" by pressuring men to move *out* of the most female-identified areas, and *up* to those regarded as more legitimate and prestigious for men.

Conclusion: Discrimination Against Men

Both men and women who work in nontraditional occupations encounter discrimination, but the forms and consequences of this discrimination are very different. The interviews suggest that unlike "nontraditional" women workers, most of the discrimination and prejudice facing men in the "female professions" emanates from outside those professions. The men and women interviewed for the most part believed that men are given fair—if not preferential—treatment in hiring and promotion decisions, are accepted by supervisors and colleagues, and are well-integrated into the workplace subculture. Indeed, subtle mechanisms seem to enhance men's position in these professions—a phenomenon I refer to as the "glass escalator effect."

The data lend strong support for Zimmer's (1988) critique of "gender neutral theory" (such as Kanter's [1977] theory of tokenism) in the study of occupational segregation. Zimmer argues that women's occupational inequality is more a consequence of sexist beliefs and practices embedded in the labor force than the effect of numerical underrepresentation per se. This study suggests that token status itself does not diminish men's occupational success. Men take their gender privilege with them when they enter predominantly female occupations: this translates into an advantage in spite of their numerical rarity.

This study indicates that the experience of tokenism is very different for men and women. Future research should examine how the experience of tokenism varies for members of different races and classes as well. For example, it is likely that informal workplace mechanisms similar to the ones identified here promote the careers of token whites in predominantly black occupations. The crucial factor is the social status of the token's group—not their numerical rarity—that determines whether the token encounters a "glass ceiling" or a "glass escalator."

However, this study also found that many men encounter negative stereotypes from persons not directly involved in their professions. Men who enter these professions are often considered "failures" or sexual deviants. These stereotypes may be a major impediment to men who otherwise might consider careers in these occupations. Indeed, they are likely to be important factors whenever a member of a relatively high status group crosses over into a lower status occupation. However, to the extent that these stereotypes contribute to the "glass escalator effect" by channeling men into more "legitimate" (and higher paying) occupations, they are not discriminatory.

Women entering traditionally "male" professions also face negative stereotypes suggesting they are not "real women" (Epstein 1981; Lorber 1984; Spencer and Podmore 1987). However, these stereotypes do not seem to deter women to the same degree that they deter men from pursuing nontraditional professions. There is ample historical evidence that women flock to male-identified occupations once opportunities are available (Cohn 1985; Epstein 1988). Not so with men. Examples of occupations changing from predominantly female to predominantly male are very rare in our history. The few existing cases—such as medicine—suggest that redefinition of the occupations as appropriately "masculine" is necessary before men will consider joining them (Ehrenreich and English 1978).

Because different mechanisms maintain segregation in male- and female-dominated occupations, different approaches are needed to promote their integration. Policies intended to alter the sex composition of male-dominated occupations—such as affirmative action—make little sense when applied to the "female professions." For men, the major barriers to integration have little to do with their treatment once they decide to enter these fields. Rather, we need to address the social and cultural sanctions applied to men who do "women's work" which keep men from even considering these occupations.

One area where these cultural barriers are clearly evident is in the media's representation of men's occupations. Women working in traditionally male professions have achieved an unprecedented acceptance on popular television shows. Women are portrayed as doctors ("St. Elsewhere"), lawyers ("The Cosby Show," "L.A. Law"), architects ("Family Ties"), and police officers ("Cagney and Lacey"). But where are the male nurses, teachers, and secretaries? Television rarely portrays men in nontraditional work roles, and when it does, that anomaly is made the central focus—and joke—of the program. A comedy series (1991–1992) about a male elementary school teacher ("Drexell's Class") stars a lead character who *hates children!* Yet even this negative portrayal is exceptional. When a prime-time hospital drama series ("St. Elsewhere") depicted a male orderly striving for upward mobility, the show's writers made him a "physician's assistant," not a nurse or nurse practitioner—the much more likely "real life" possibilities.

Presenting positive images of men in nontraditional careers can produce limited effects. A few social workers, for example, were first inspired to pursue their careers by George C. Scott, who played a social worker in the television drama series, "Eastside/Westside." But as a policy strategy to break down occupational segregation, changing media images of men is no panacea. The stereotypes that differentiate masculinity and femininity, and degrade that which is defined as feminine, are deeply entrenched in culture, social structure, and personality (Williams 1989). Nothing short of a revolution in cultural definitions of masculinity will effect the broad scale social transformation needed to achieve the complete occupational integration of men and women.

Of course, there are additional factors besides societal prejudice contributing to men's underrepresentation in female-dominated professions. Most notably, those men I interviewed mentioned as a deterrent the fact that these professions are all underpaid relative to comparable "male" occupations, and several suggested that instituting a "comparable worth" policy might attract more men. However, I am not convinced that improved salaries will substantially alter the sex composition of these professions unless the cultural stigma faced by men in these occupations diminishes. Occupational sex segregation is remarkably resilient, even in the face of devastating economic hardship. During the Great Depression of the 1930s, for example, "women's jobs" failed to attract sizable numbers of men (Blum 1991:154). In her study of American Telephone and Telegraph (AT&T) workers, Epstein (1989) found that some men would rather suffer unemployment than accept relatively high paying "women's jobs" because of the damage to their identities this would cause. She quotes one unemployed man who refused to apply for a female-identified telephone operator job:

> I think if they offered me $1000 a week tax free, I wouldn't take that job. When I . . . see those guys sitting in there [in the telephone operating room], I wonder what's wrong with them. Are they pansies or what? (Epstein 1989: 577)

This is not to say that raising salaries would not affect the sex composition of these jobs. Rather, I am suggesting that wages are not the only—or perhaps even the major—impediment to men's entry into these jobs. Further research is needed to explore the ideological significance of the "woman's wage" for maintaining occupational stratification.[3]

At any rate, integrating men and women in the labor force requires more than dismantling barriers to women in male-dominated fields. Sex segregation is a two-way street. We must also confront and dismantle the barriers men face in predominantly female occupations. Men's experiences in these nontraditional occupations reveal just how culturally embedded the barriers are, and how far we have to travel before men and women attain true occupational and economic equality.

Author's Note: This research was funded in part by a faculty grant from the University of Texas at Austin. I also acknowledge the support of the sociology departments of the University of California, Berkeley; Harvard University; and Arizona State University. I would like to thank Judy Auerbach, Martin Dutton, Robert Nye, Teresa Sullivan, Debra Umberson, Mary Waters, and the reviewers at *Social Problems* for their comments on earlier versions of this paper.

Notes

1. According to the U.S. Census, black men and women comprise 7 percent of all nurses and librarians, 11 percent of all elementary school teachers, and 19 percent of all social workers (calculated from U.S. Census 1980: Table 278, 1–197). The proportion of blacks in social work may be exaggerated by these statistics. The occupational definition of "social worker" used by the Census Bureau includes welfare workers and pardon and parole officers, who are not considered "professional" social workers by the National Association of Social Workers. A study of degreed professionals found that 89 percent of practitioners were white (Hardcastle 1987).

2. In April 1991, the Labor Department created a "Glass Ceiling Commission" to "conduct a thorough study of the underrepresentation of women and minorities in executive, management, and senior decision-making positions in business" (U.S. House of Representatives 1991:20).

3. Alice Kessler-Harris argues that the lower pay of traditionally female occupations is symbolic of a patriarchal order that assumes female dependence on a male breadwinner. She writes that pay equity is fundamentally threatening to the "male worker's sense of self, pride, and masculinity" because it upsets his individual standing in the hierarchical ordering of the sexes (1990:125). Thus, men's reluctance to enter these occupations may have less to do with the actual dollar amount recorded in their paychecks, and more to do with the damage that earning "a woman's wage" would wreak on their self-esteem in a society that privileges men. This conclusion is supported by the interview data.

References

Bielby, William T., and James N. Baron
1984. "A woman's place is with other women: Sex segregation within organizations." In *Sex Segregation in the Workplace: Trends, Explanations, Remedies*, ed. Barbara Reskin, 27–55. Washington, D.C.: National Academy Press.

Blum, Linda M.
1991. *Between Feminism and Labor: The Significance of the Comparable Worth Movement*. Berkeley and Los Angeles: University of California Press.

Carothers, Suzanne C., and Peggy Crull
1984. "Contrasting sexual harassment in female-dominated and male-dominated occupations." In *My Troubles Are Going to have Trouble with Me: Everyday Trials and Triumphs of Women Workers*, ed. Karen B. Sacks and Dorothy Remy, 220–227. New Brunswick, N.J.: Rutgers University Press.

Cohn, Samuel

1985. *The Process of Occupational Sex-Typing*. Philadelphia: Temple University Press.

Ehrenreich, Barbara, and Deirdre English

1978. *For Her Own Good: 100 Years of Expert Advice to Women*. Garden City, N.Y.: Anchor Press.

Epstein, Cynthia Fuchs

1981. *Women in Law*. New York: Basic Books.

1988. *Deceptive Distinctions: Sex, Gender and the Social Order*. New Haven: Yale University Press.

1989. "Workplace boundaries: Conceptions and creations." *Social Research* 56: 571–590.

Freeman, Sue J. M.

1990. *Managing Lives: Corporate Women and Social Change*. Amherst, Mass.: University of Massachusetts Press.

Grimm, James W., and Robert N. Stern

1974. "Sex roles and internal labor market structures: The female semi-professions." *Social Problems* 21: 690–705.

Hardcastle, D. A.

1987. "The social work labor force." Austin, Tex.: School of Social Work, University of Texas.

Hodson, Randy, and Teresa Sullivan

1990. *The Social Organization of Work*. Belmont, Calif.: Wadsworth Publishing Co.

Jacobs, Jerry

1989. *Revolving Doors: Sex Segregation and Women's Careers*. Stanford, Calif.: Stanford University Press.

Kanter, Rosabeth Moss

1977. *Men and Women of the Corporation*. New York: Basic Books.

Kessler-Harris, Alice

1990. *A Woman's Wage: Historical Meanings and Social Consequences*. Lexington, Ky.: Kentucky University Press.

Lorber, Judith

1984. *Women Physicians: Careers, Status, and Power*. New York: Tavistock.

Martin, Susan E.

1980. *Breaking and Entering: Police Women on Patrol*. Berkeley, Calif.: University of California Press.

1988. "Think like a man, work like a dog, and act like a lady: Occupational dilemmas of policewomen." In *The Worth of Women's Work: A Qualitative Synthesis*, ed. Anne Statham, Eleanor M. Miller, and Hans O. Mauksch, 205–223. Albany, N.Y.: State University of New York Press.

Phenix, Katharine

1987. "The status of women librarians." *Frontiers* 9: 36–40.

Reskin, Barbara

1988. "Bringing the men back in: Sex differentiation and the devaluation of women's work." *Gender & Society* 2: 58–81.

Reskin, Barbara, and Heidi Hartmann

1986. *Women's Work, Men's Work: Sex Segregation on the Job*. Washington, D.C.: National Academy Press.

Reskin, Barbara, and Patricia Roos

1990. *Job Queues, Gender Queues: Explaining Women's Inroads into Male Occupations*. Philadelphia: Temple University Press.

Schmuck, Patricia A.

1987. "Women school employees in the United States." In *Women Educators: Employees of Schools in Western Countries*, ed. Patricia A. Schmuck, 75–97. Albany, N.Y.: State University of New York Press.

Schreiber, Carol

1979. *Men and Women in Transitional Occupations*. Cambridge, Mass.: MIT Press.

Spencer, Anne, and David Podmore

1987. *In a Man's World: Essays on Women in Male-Dominated Professions*. London: Tavistock.

Strauss, Anselm L.

1987. *Qualitative Analysis for Social Scientists*. Cambridge, England: Cambridge University Press.

U.S. Bureau of the Census

1980. *Detailed Population Characteristics*, Vol. 1, Ch. D. Washington, D.C.: Government Printing Office.

U.S. Congress. House

1991. *Civil Rights and Women's Equity in Employment Act of 1991*. Report. (Report 102-40, Part I.) Washington, D.C.: Government Printing Office.

U.S. Department of Labor. Bureau of Labor Statistics

1991. *Employment and Earnings*. January. Washington, D.C.: Government Printing Office.

Williams, Christine L.

1989. *Gender Differences at Work: Women and Men in Nontraditional Occupations*. Berkeley, Calif.: University of California Press.

Yoder, Janice D.

1989. "Women at West Point: Lessons for token women in male-dominated occupations." In

Women: A Feminist Perspective, ed. Jo Freeman, 523–537. Mountain View, Calif.: Mayfield Publishing Company.

York, Reginald O., H. Carl Henley, and Dorothy N. Gamble

1987. "Sexual discrimination in social work: Is it salary or advancement?" *Social Work* 32: 336–340.

Zimmer, Lynn

1988. "Tokenism and women in the workplace." *Social Problems* 35: 64–77.

Kevin D. Henson
Jackie Krasas Rogers

"Why Marcia You've Changed!": Male Clerical Temporary Workers Doing Masculinity in a Feminized Occupation

To say that organizations are gendered has many meanings, from gender segregation at work to the part organizations play in the cultural reproduction of gender inequality (Acker 1990; Britton 2000). We know that "advantage and disadvantage, exploitation and control, action and emotion, meaning and identity are patterned through and in terms of a distinction between male and female, masculine and feminine" (Acker 1990, 146). Interaction and identity are but two means through which gender is constituted and reproduced in the workplace. Men and women "do gender" (West and Fenstermaker 1995; West and Zimmerman 1987) at work in organizations that are themselves gendered, and organizational imperatives shape interaction that "naturalizes" and essentializes cultural constructions of masculinity and femininity for men and women. This study provides a look at men doing gender in the highly feminized context of temporary clerical employment.

Doing gender "appropriately" in the workplace has consequences, including material ones, for both women and men. A significant portion of the existing sociological literature explores how women are required to do gender at work, including emotional labor, which often reinforces vulnerability and inequality (Hochschild 1983; Leidner 1993; Pierce 1995; Williams 1989, 1995; Rogers and Henson 1997). Yet, men are also

From *Gender & Society* 15(2): 218–238. Copyright ©
2001 Sociologists for Women in Society.

required to do gender on the job, and although less well documented, men do perform emotional labor, albeit subject to a different set of constraints, expectations, and outcomes than women's emotional labor (Pierce 1995; Cheng 1996). Indeed, emotional work is implicated in the microprocesses of doing gender that reinforce, uphold, and even naturalize male dominance and hegemonic masculinity (Collinson and Hearn 1996).[1]

In contrast with Kanter's (1977) position that any token, male or female, is subject to a distinct set of negative experiences, a recent avenue of inquiry has demonstrated how some men "benefit" from their token status in "women's work"— riding the "glass escalator" to more prestigious, better-paid positions within women's professions (Pierce 1995; Williams 1995; Maume 1999). Although men who cross over into women's work are often seen as less manly, this disadvantage has paled in comparison to the material benefits available to (white) male tokens, who self-segregate (or are pushed) into higher pay and higher status specialties or administrative positions in female-dominated professions (see Williams 1989, 1995).

What happens, however, when men find themselves in a female-dominated occupation with limited opportunities to ride the glass escalator? Temporary clerical work is such an occupation. As externalized employment that institutionalizes limited access to internal labor markets, there is no glass escalator to ride in temporary clerical work. Temporary clerical work does not provide the opportunities for men (or women) to elevate their status through additional credentialing, specialization, or promotions. Indeed, upward mobility into permanent employment—hailed as a major benefit by the temporary industry—is extremely elusive (Smith 1998; Rogers 2000).[2] Therefore, male tokens in female-dominated temporary clerical work present an interesting case concerning the gendered nature of work. How does men's gender privilege operate in the absence of opportunities for upward mobility? Does men's presence in a dead-end, female-dominated occupation disrupt the gender order and challenge hegemonic masculinity?

In this article, we argue that although men's presence in temporary clerical work has the potential to challenge the "naturalness" of the gendered organization of work, in everyday practice it is assumed to say more about the essential nature of the individual men. Male clerical temporaries, as with other men who cross over into women's work, fall increasingly short of the ideals of hegemonic masculinity on at least two fronts. First, they face gender assessment through their lack of a "real" job (i.e., a full-time career in "men's work"). Second, their location in a feminized occupation that requires the performance of emphasized femininity, including deference and caretaking behaviors, calls into question their presumed heterosexuality. The resulting gender strategies (Hochschild 1989) these men adopt reveal how male clerical temporary workers "do masculinity" to reassert the feminine identification of the job while rejecting its application to them. In particular, we argue that men in clerical temporary work do masculinity through renaming and reframing the work, distancing themselves from the work with a cover story, and resisting the demands to perform deference. Paradoxically, rather than disrupting the gender order, the gender strategies adopted help reproduce and naturalize the gendered organization of work and reinvigorate hegemonic masculinity and its domination over women and subaltern men.

The Gendered Character of Temporary Clerical Employment

While temporary employment has increased dramatically in the past 15 years in response to employers' demands (Golden and Appelbaum 1992), researchers have only recently begun to systematically document the effects of this trend for workers and workplace relations. The rapid expansion of temporary employment is profoundly changing the experience, meaning, and conditions of work for temporaries who, like other contingent workers, fall through the cracks of existing workplace protections and provision of benefits (Parker 1994; Henson 1996; Rogers and Henson 1997; Rogers 2000).

The clerical sector of temporary employment, like the permanent clerical sector, is predominantly composed of women (Bureau of Labor Statistics 1995). Historically, this association of temporary work with women's work was reflected in the common inclusion of the infantilizing term *girl* in the names of the earliest temporary agencies (e.g., Kelly Girl). While temporary agencies have formally modernized their names (i.e., Kelly Girl became Kelly Services), the continued popular usage of the outdated names accurately reflects the gendered composition of the temporary clerical workforce. Indeed, a survey by the National Association of Temporary Services (1992) estimated that 80 percent of member agency temporaries were women. A recent government survey concluded that "workers employed by temporary help agencies in February 1997 were more likely than other workers to be young, female, Black or Hispanic" (Cohany 1998, 13).

Contemporary clerical temporary employment, like permanent clerical work, is so completely identified as women's work that until recently, it was considered inappropriate employment for a man, even by the temporary industry. Until the 1960s, in fact, it was common policy within the industry not to accept male applicants for clerical temporary work (Moore 1963, 35).

Men, it was asserted, should be seeking a permanent, full-time career-type job—a "real job"—that would allow them to work hard, be financially successful, and take on the idealized (male) breadwinner role (Connell 1987, 1995; Cheng 1996).

Recently, however, men have come to constitute a greater proportion of temporary agency workers, although they are still more likely to be working as industrial than clerical temporaries (see Parker 1994). In fact, the continued numerical predominance of women in both the permanent and temporary clerical workforce often leads to the assumption that clerical temporary workers are women. Indeed, the job of clerical temporary worker is gendered—more specifically feminized—as women's work. Consequently, temporary work, clerical work, and especially temporary clerical work are perceived as women's work.

Given temporaries' low status and vulnerability to work deprivation, the expectations of temporary agencies and clients become de facto job requirements that shape temporary workers' interactions in such a way that one's gender and sexuality are prominently featured as aspects of the work (see Rogers and Henson 1997). For example, the demands of temporary agencies and client companies for particular (gendered or sexy) physical presentations, and the embedded expectations for deference and caretaking behaviors, highlight the gendered (feminized) and sexualized nature of temporary clerical work (Henson 1996; Rogers and Henson 1997). Indeed, the common association of temporary work with promiscuity, or "occupational sleeping around," highlights the ways in which clerical work and temporary work intersect to create a highly feminized job (see Rogers 2000 for a discussion of the gendering of temporary versus clerical work). In other words, temporary clerical work is a gendered (as well as raced, classed, aged, and heterosexualized) occupation that requires workers to do gender (and race, class, and so forth) in certain forms, recreating them and making them appear natural (see West and Zimmerman 1987; Acker 1990, West

and Fenstermaker 1995). The type of gender one must "do" in clerical temporary work is primarily white, middle-class, heterosexual femininity. Consequently, while certain exceptions are made, it is nearly impossible to do this brand of femininity appropriately if you are a man or a woman of color. After describing our research methodology, we examine the gendered (feminized) context of clerical temporary employment, the institutionalized challenges to masculinity such employment poses for token men, and the gender strategies token men adopt to buttress their sense of masculinity. Finally, we discuss how these gender strategies reproduce rather than challenge the gender order.

Method

This research is based on in-depth interviews and extensive participant observation from two broader studies on temporary clerical work we conducted in Chicago in 1990–1991 (Henson 1996) and Los Angeles in 1993–1994 (Rogers 2000). During the participant observation component of our studies, each of us worked as a clerical temporary worker for more than one year on a variety of assignments in many different types of organizations. We entered our temporary employment with many common characteristics such as relatively high educational attainment, whiteness, and youthfulness (Kevin was 26; Jackie was 28), yet our different respective genders affected our temporary work experiences in many dissimilar and revealing ways.

In addition to our participant–observation work, each of us conducted open-ended, semi-structured interviews with temporaries and agency personnel, yielding 68 interviews in all (35 in Chicago and 33 in Los Angeles). Our interview participants included 10 temporary agency personnel and one client company representative, but the majority (57) were temporary clerical workers. We located participants of this highly fluid and difficult-to-access workforce through a variety of methods—personal contacts made on assignment, responses to fliers placed at temporary agency offices, and personal referrals. We pursued a grounded theory approach in our research, including an emphasis on theoretical sampling (Glaser and Strauss 1965, 1967). Consequently, we sought out participants who maximized the range of temporary work experiences we studied rather than pursuing a strictly representative sample of the temporary workforce. In the end, our sample of temporary clerical workers included a relatively diverse group of participants, including 20 men and 37 women ranging in age from 20 to 60 (see Table 17.1).[3] Indeed, our sample approximates the age and race distribution of the general temporary workforce. However, our sample differs in at least one important way from the general clerical temporary workforce. We deliberately oversampled for men in this female-dominated occupation. Collectively, our interview participants had worked through more than 40 temporary agencies with individual tenure in temporary employment ranging from a few months to more than 10 years.

We followed flexible open-ended interview schedules, addressing themes that we had identified as salient during our participant-observation work and pursued new themes as they emerged. We both interviewed women and men in our respective locales, and although evidence of participants' negotiation of the "gendered context of the [interview] interaction" emerged (e.g., men talked directly about feeling "less manly" to Jackie but talked more abstractly about feeling

■ **TABLE 17.1**
Race/Ethnicity and Gender of
Temporary Clerical Workers

Race/Ethnicity	Men	Women
White	13	28
African American	3	7
Asian	1	2
Latino/Latina	1	0
Other	2	0
Total	20	37

like "failures" to Kevin), there was a remarkable overlap and consistency in the substance of participants' responses (see Williams and Heikes 1993). We tape-recorded, transcribed, and analyzed all of the interviews. Although at first we pursued an open coding process focusing on general concepts such as stigmatization and coping strategies, eventually our analysis revealed consistent gendered patterns in our data. All names indicated in the body of the article are pseudonyms.

What's He Doing Here?

Male temporary clerical workers initially disrupt the gendered landscape of an organization since both the permanent and temporary clerical workforces are female dominated. This is reflected in the consistency with which token male clerical temporaries were met with surprise on the job. Indeed, the reaction to token men highlights the almost complete feminization of the work and the associated expectation that temporary workers will be women. The male temporaries we interviewed, for example, universally commented on their experiences as token men in women's work:

> There are areas where I felt that I did not fit in properly because I was a man on a temp assignment. (Michael Glenn, 26-year-old Asian American man)

> People are looking at me like, "What are you doing here?" Like they're thinking, "Gee, what's the deal? Shouldn't you be, I don't know, doing something else?" I mean it's like it's sort of fine if you're just out of school. They kind of expect well, you're doing this until you get a regular job. (Harold Koenig, 29-year-old white man)

Similarly, Henson was conscious on more than one of his assignments of steady streams of chuckling female workers conspicuously moving past his workstation, (apparently) to see the male receptionist. While there might be socially acceptable reasons for a young man's location in temporary work (e.g., "just out of school" or "until you get a regular job"), for men, it is generally employment requiring an explanation.[4]

In fact, the disruption of the taken-for-granted naturalness of workplace gender segregation by the presence of male temporaries was often a source of humor for permanent workers. For example, Henson repeatedly encountered variants of a joke that played on themes of gender and mistaken identity. Permanent workers, especially men, upon seeing him for the first time at a (female) permanent worker's desk, would declare with mock seriousness, "Why (Marcia, Faye, Lucy) you've changed!" The humor of this joke, apparently, derived from the mismatch between the expected gender of the worker and Henson's gender. Another widespread joke, playing on similar themes, was to knowingly misattribute ownership of a permanent female employee's personal (and feminine) belongings to a male temporary through a mock compliment such as, "Nice pumps." Jackie, however, experienced neither the need to explain her employment nor the jokes.

The feminized nature of the work was further highlighted when others failed to recognize a male temporary as the secretary, mistaking him for someone with higher organizational status. Jon Carter, for example, described the confusion callers experienced when they heard his masculine voice at the receptionist's desk: "I get a lot of people, you know, that are confused as to who I am because it's a male voice" (23-year-old gay white man). Henson also experienced being mistaken for a permanent (higher status) new hire. One coworker, realizing his error after warmly welcoming Kevin and introducing himself, quickly pulled back his extended hand and retreated in embarrassment.

Finally, the feminized nature of temporary work was revealed by the extent to which "male" continues to be the verbally marked category. Note, for example, Linda Schmidt's verbal marking of both "male secretaries" and "male temps":

Roger Piderat. He was a male secretary. He was very good. And then we had a male temp come in. And he was English. He was a nice guy. And he did reception for a while. And he worked at Anne's desk for a while. But he was a very pleasant person too. So we've had male secretaries before. (Linda Schmidt, 38-year-old white woman)

As with women in nontraditional occupations (e.g., female doctors or female lawyers), men in nontraditional (secretarial and clerical) work are the marked category.

The expectation, indeed assumption, that (requested) temporary workers will be women sometimes is expressed as an overt preference for women—or aversion to men—in these positions. Although temporary agencies are legally required to operate under equal opportunity employer legislation (i.e., to hire workers without regard to race, sex, or age), temporaries are nevertheless often placed for non-skill-specific characteristics including their race, gender, age, and physical attractiveness (Henson 1996; Rogers and Henson 1997; Rogers 2000). Cindy Beitz, a temporary counselor, described how client companies sometimes explicitly, and quite illegally, requested female temporaries:

> You can call them and say, "We have a young gentleman who will be coming in there tomorrow for you." And sometimes they will say . . . they'll come out and say, "Well, I don't want him. I told you I wanted a woman." (Cindy Beitz, 33-year-old white woman)

Without prompting, approximately half of the agency representatives mentioned similar illegal requests. Similarly, temporary workers like Irene Pedersen, who were privy to client company–agency interactions, reported overhearing illegal requests:

> I worked on a temp assignment somewhere in the Personnel Department at this company, and the client wanted a temp receptionist. And he would come in and beat on the personnel man-

ager, he didn't want a man. He didn't want anybody who was Black, he didn't want anybody who was this. (Irene Pedersen, 25-year-old white woman)

Temporary workers were often aware, or at least suspected, that personal characteristics such as gender determined their access to jobs. Arnold Finch, for example, hypothesized that he had lost a job because of his gender:

> I was working a temp job and I left there. I did really good work. They wouldn't call me back. The only reason why, I was a male. They only wanted females to work that job. . . . It's just that I guess companies that . . . when somebody comes in the door, they want a pretty, happy, smiling female face behind the counter. (Arnold Finch, 23-year-old white man)

In addition, Henson lost at least one clerical assignment admittedly on the basis of his gender: "The client isn't sure if they want a male temporary or not. Whoever placed the order is going to check and see if it's okay" (Henson's field notes, 1990). Although Kevin had cross trained in preparation at the agency's office on a specific word processing program (without pay), the assignment was withdrawn. Neither Rogers nor any of the women we interviewed experienced a negative gender screening similar to Henson's—they were the right gender.[5]

Not only is clerical temporary work feminized, it is also heterosexualized, especially for women. Clients, for example, often included demands for particular feminized (even sexy) physical presentations when placing an order for temporary help:

> When we get a position like that in where they say, "She should wear this outfit" or "She should look like this." Whatever. We'll still recommend . . . we can still call men in too, but . . . (Cindy Beitz, 33-year-old white woman)

They'll ask for blond and blue eyes and stuff like that. Always for the front office. We tell them that we'll send the best qualified. If we send a qualified person and they send 'em back because they're not blond, we obviously wouldn't be able to fill that order. They'll go to another agency that will. (Regina Mason, 44-year-old Latina agency manager)

Indeed, female temporary secretaries, like women serving higher status men in other traditional women's work (MacKinnon 1979; Hall 1993), were often expected to make an offering of their gender, including their sexual attractiveness, as part of the job. Since the agencies' interests are in pleasing clients, even some of the more egregious requests for female temporary workers as sex objects (e.g., for a young, blond woman with great legs) are often honored (Henson 1996; Rogers and Henson 1997; Rogers 2000). Because temporary agencies depend on client companies for revenue, they are under considerable pressure to comply with these client requests. Agencies that assiduously follow the law risk losing their clients.

However, it would be inaccurate to describe the preference for women in temporary secretarial work as simply the desire to employ women as sexual objects. The employers' preference for women is partially explained by employers' essentialized understandings of gender as it relates to workers' capabilities. In other words, client companies and agencies often use a "gender logic" when matching workers with assignments (Hossfeld 1990). Women, in this logic, are often assumed to be innately superior at work calling for certain emotional and relational skills (Hochschild 1983; Leidner 1993; Pierce 1995). In fact, temporary secretaries, as part of the job, are expected to perform emotional labor—to be deferential and nurturing toward managers, coworkers, clients, and agency personnel (Henson 1996; Rogers and Henson 1997). As Pierce (1995, 89) has argued about another feminized occupation (paralegals), "The feminization of this occupation . . . is created not only by employer preference for women, but by the fact that the occupation itself—formally or not—calls for women to cater to men's emotional needs."

Challenges to Masculinity

Men who cross over to work in highly feminized occupations face institutionalized challenges to their sense of masculinity, that is, the extent to which they measure up to the dictates of hegemonic masculinity (Pringle 1993; Pierce 1995; Williams 1989, 1995). Male clerical temporary workers, for example, face gender assessment—highlighting their failure to live up to the ideals of hegemonic masculinity—on at least two fronts. First, they are working temporary rather than permanent, higher paying, full-time jobs ("He should have a real job"), which limits their ability to assume the male breadwinner role. Second, they are doing clerical work (i.e., women's work), including demands for deference and caretaking, which challenges their presumed heterosexuality ("He could be gay"). Yet, unlike the situation of male nurses or elementary schoolteachers (Williams 1989, 1995), clerical temporary work is not a semiprofession with institutionalized room for upward mobility via the glass escalator.

He Should Have a Real Job

Male temporary clerical workers' individual failings, when faced with gender assessment, included questions about their drive, motivation, and competence for male career success (i.e., "Why doesn't he have a real job?"). Indeed, permanent work providing a sufficient financial base to assume the male breadwinner role is a core component of hegemonic masculine identity (Connell 1987, 1995; Kimmel 1994; Cheng 1996). Consequently, men who have jobs that do not allow them to assume the breadwinner role—such as those in part-time or temporary work—are perceived as "less manly" (Epstein et al. 1999; Rogers 2000).

Indeed, the assumption that men, but not women, should hold or desire permanent employment was widely shared by temporary workers, temporary agency staff, and client company supervisors. For example, Dorothy Brooke, a temporary worker, expressed the idea that temporary work was acceptable for women but that men should be striving to get real jobs. In other words, temporary jobs are unsatisfactory jobs that no real man (i.e., white, heterosexual, and middle-class) would or should accept:

> I was surprised by how many older men were working as temporaries. I guess I expected to just see women. But I asked one of these guys if he was looking for full-time work. And he said he was just hoping that one of his temp jobs was going to turn into a full-time job. I thought you've got to have more spunk than that to get a job. (Henson's field notes, 1991)

Likewise, Regina Mason, a temporary agency manager, struggling to explain the anomalous presence of men in temporary work, tapped into gendered industry rhetoric portraying the work as good for women—a "flexible, secondary wage earning job"—but inadequate for men, except on a truly temporary basis (Henson 1996):

> I think that's the trend that men have never thought of working temporary. I mean that's a new thing to men to go work temp. It's the old attitude that men are breadwinners you know so they gotta have stability, permanency, a real job. But we still have a few men working. I think a lot of housewives don't want anything permanent. So they prefer to come in and just do temping so that they can take off when they want to. (Regina Mason, 44-year-old Latina agency manager)

Ironically, while men in temporary employment are curiosities to be pitied, the low-pay, impermanence, and dead-end nature of these jobs is seen as natural or unproblematic for women. Consequently, an agency manager can bemoan the difficulties she has telling men, but not women, "they'd only be getting maybe $8 an hour and not necessarily steady work" (Rogers's field notes, 1994).

The irregularity, uncertainty, and poor remuneration of clerical temporary work challenged male temporaries' abilities to live up to the breadwinner, and self-sufficiency, ideals contained in hegemonic masculinity. Without prompting, most men in the study detailed the challenges temping presented to their sense of masculinity. Kirk Stevens, for example, felt guilty and ashamed about his inability to take on the idealized (male) breadwinner role. An inadequate supply of assignments left Kirk financially dependent on his girlfriend:

> So far, this summer, Natalie, my girlfriend, has been supporting us both. I really can't stand it. She leaves at eight thirty and gets home at five thirty or six and she's totally exhausted. She can't stay up past eleven at night. And I feel really guilty 'cause she wouldn't have to be working quite so crazy if I were getting any money in at all. But it's difficult for both of us. (Kirk Stevens, 27-year-old white man)

While financial dependence is seen as an unproblematic aspect of low-wage temporary employment for women (i.e., the income is assumed to be secondary), this same dependence among men often challenges male temporary workers' sense of masculinity. In other words, not only is the male temporary worker unable to provide for others but he also finds himself in the painful position of dependence.

The lack of respect accorded to men who fail to live up to the career orientation ideals embodied in hegemonic masculinity was not lost on male temporary workers. Albert Baxter, for example, described his belief that male temporary workers received less respect than female temporaries:

> I think men get a little less respect if they're temping. There's that expectation that they should be like career oriented and like moving up in the world and being a businessman and moving himself forward in business. Where women can do that but it's not an expectation. And so I think that, I think that's where that Kelly Girl image, that temporaries are women is. I have noticed that there is a certain amount, looking down upon. I think that's true of temps in general. They're somewhat looked down upon. I think the men maybe more. (Albert Baxter, 31-year-old white man)

Accordingly, male temporary workers sometimes experienced feelings of inferiority and inadequacy when recognized (and judged) as temporary secretaries by others. Denny Lincoln, for example, articulated feelings of inferiority when others assessed him on the basis of his low-wage, low-status temporary employment:

> Why are all these people taking $6.50 and $7.00 an hour jobs? Why? Why can't they go out and get a real job? And I think that's what goes through people's minds. Like you have a college degree! What the hell's going on here? There must be something wrong with this guy. He can't hold a job, he's working for 7 bucks an hour stuffing envelopes. (Denny Lincoln, 39-year-old white man)

Similarly, Bob Johnson described the embarrassment he felt when recognized on a temporary assignment by old college classmates:

> Where I work there's a lot of people who I graduated [from college] with on staff. And when they see me, you know, they go, "What are you doing? Why are you working as a secretary?" And you have to explain yourself. Well, I'm trying to find the ideal job. Maybe it's all in my mind because I feel sort of inferior to that because they're kind of established. I feel really inadequate. (Bob Johnson, 23-year-old gay white man)

Bob's reaction reveals his embarrassment about both the impermanence of his employment ("they're kind of established") and its feminization ("Why are you working as a secretary?").

He Could Be Gay

Male temporary workers' failing, when faced with gender assessment, does not stop with questioning their drive, motivation, and competence for male career success. Their location in a female-dominated occupation that requires and produces emphasized femininity, including deferential and nurturing behaviors, also calls into question their presumed heterosexuality, a core component of hegemonic masculinity. When men do deference and caretaking, they are popularly defined as feminine—like women—and therefore gay. As Donaldson (1993, 648) has noted, any type of powerlessness quickly becomes conflated with the popular stereotype of homosexuality. Male clerical temporaries, as with male secretaries (Pringle 1993), nurses (Williams 1989), elementary schoolteachers (Williams 1995), and paralegals (Pierce 1995), are regularly stereotyped as gay. Patsy Goodrich, for example, accepted the construction of male temporary clerical workers, but not male temporary industrial workers, as gay:

> But, yeah, I think most of the people [in temporary work] that I know have either been gay men or women. Or lesbian women. I don't really know. I can't think of a straight man that I know that's done it. Except for my brother. But he did the kind where it's like the industrial side. (Patsy Goodrich, 27-year-old white lesbian woman)

Similarly, in searching for an explanation for the presence of some men in temporary clerical work, Connie Young described the male temporary workers in her office as unmasculine or effeminate in appearance:

> We've had male temporaries come in to answer the phones and do whatever typing jobs. And, for some reason, all the male temps we've gotten didn't have any masculine features. They're very longhaired, ponytailed, very artsy look. And the men in business suits would look at them and kind of not take them seriously actually. You know like, "Oh, he has an earring." (Connie Young, 25-year-old Asian American woman)

In addition, male temporary workers are feminized as they enter and interact in an organizational environment that requires the performance of emphasized femininity, including deference. Male temporaries' discomfort with the demands for deference, although more limited than the deferential demands made of female temporaries, revealed both the gendered nature of the work and its implicit threat to their sense of masculinity:

> It's a manly thing to be in charge. And men should want to be, supposedly in charge and delegating things. If you're a man and you're being delegated to, it somehow makes you less manly. You know what I'm saying? Whereas it seems to be okay for the person delegating to women. And the women, maybe they're just projecting that to get by. It seems that they're more okay with that than men are. I guess I'm saying that it makes me feel less of the manly kind of qualities, like I'm in charge, you know. And men should be like takin' meetings and barking orders instead of just being subservient. (Harold Koenig, 29-year-old heterosexual white man)

Several male temporary workers remarked that they were surprised by the deferential demands of temporary work—as men with male privilege, they had rarely experienced the requirement to enact deference.

Similarly, Kirk Stevens was outraged when he was asked to perform the subservient work of cleaning bathrooms:

> I got a phone call saying there was this company that needed me to go out and change the light bulbs And I met the guy and he gives me, you know, the obligatory tour. . . . And then he gives me a bucket and a mop, some rubber gloves, and he says, "Now what I'd really like you to do, just to start off, is clean, if you could, the bathrooms need cleaning. Could you clean this bathroom?" And it didn't even . . . I just . . . I just can't believe that I didn't just say. "Go to hell. I'm not going to clean your goddamn bathrooms." (Kirk Stevens, 27-year-old heterosexual white man)

While someone has to clean bathrooms (often work relegated to poor women of color), Kirk Stevens believed he was not the type of person (e.g., white, educated, and male) who should be asked to do so. The negative reactions to deferential demands were strongest (but not exclusive) among white, heterosexual, college-educated men who would fall closest to the cultural ideal of hegemonic masculinity (see Connell 1987, 1995).

Male temporary workers, heterosexual and gay, were aware of the construction of the male temporary as gay. A noted exception, Michael Glenn, positively rather than negatively framed and accepted an essentialized construction of temporary workers as gay:

> But temps usually are women or homosexual men. Um, it's not to say that some heterosexual men don't make good temps, but I think it's harder to find. And then you get into the whole psychology of heterosexual men I suppose. *Men are from Mars* and all of that. But heterosexual men are not as great at being people-people. . . . you have to be flexible. And there's more of a rigidity to a heterosexual male. And then again in the gradations, I would say there's more rigidity for a homosexual male than for a woman. And I'm not even gonna try to place homosexual women. (Michael Glenn, 26-year-old Asian American gay man)

Note how Michael's assertion that gay men excel over heterosexual men at the emotional and relational demands of the job (being flexible and being "people-people") leads him to the conclusion that gay men are more suited to temporary clerical work. Ironically, while gay men come closer than straight men to naturally making good temps in his account, they still do not measure up to (real, i.e., heterosexual) women, leaving the natural gender order intact.

Gender Strategies/Hegemonic Bargains

The male temporaries we interviewed, faced with gender assessment, adopted three primary gender strategies—renaming and reframing the work, distancing themselves from the work with a cover story, as well as the more risky strategy of resisting demands for deference—to do masculinity in a feminized occupation. Ironically, rather than disrupting the gender order, each of these strate-

gies "enables men to maintain a sense of themselves as different from and better than women—thus contributing to the gender system that divides men from women in a way that privileges men" (Williams 1995, 123). Indeed, each of these gender strategies represents what Chen (1999, 600), modifying Kandiyoti's (1988) "patriarchal bargain" concept, has described as a "hegemonic bargain"—a situation in which a man's "gender strategy involves trading on (or benefiting from) the advantages conferred by his race, gender, sexuality, class, accent, and/or generational status to achieve "unblushing" manhood."

Doing Masculinity—Renaming and Reframing

One of the primary gender strategies male temporaries use to maintain their sense of masculinity is to distance themselves from the feminized aspects of the occupation by renaming or reframing the work. Male temporary secretaries, similar to men in other feminized occupations (Pierce 1995; Pringle 1993; Williams 1989, 1995), described their work in terms perceived to be more masculine, or at the very least, gender-neutral (e.g., word processor, administrative assistant, proofreader, bookkeeper). Steve Woodhead, a 35-year-old white gay man, for example, characterized his temporary work assignment as *bookkeeping*. Steven did not mention the temporary nature of his job, framing it more as an independent contracting arrangement. Indeed, male temporaries displayed an almost pathological avoidance of the term *secretarial*. In contrast, most of the female temporaries we interviewed described their work without hesitation as secretarial.

Occasionally, agency personnel and clients also participated in this project of renaming the work in more masculine terms. For example, on one of Henson's temporary assignments, the supervisor wondered aloud how to refer to the position in a more masculine or gender-neutral way: "Word processor? What should we call you? We're not going to call you secretary" (Henson's field notes, 1990). Whether this renaming was simply a courtesy to individual male temporary workers or a way of reconciling clients' discomfort in seeing men crossing over into women's work is unclear.[6]

In addition, some male temporary workers attempted to reframe the work as masculine by focusing on the technical competencies required on their temporary assignments. Indeed, to be technically competent is to be masculine (Cockburn 1985; Messerschmidt 1996; Wright 1996). Bob Johnson, for example, described his work in terms of the computer environment of software he was required to use on his (secretarial) work assignments:

> That was mostly work with IBM. You know, cause IBM is incredibly popular. So I used my WordPerfect a lot. And then when they didn't have any WordPerfect, they sent me out on proofreading assignments. To proofread these books that no one would ever, ever read. Basically, it's been a lot of word processing. (Bob Johnson, 23-year-old gay white man)

This focus on the technological aspects (computer) of the work, however, is not just a refusal to name the work. As Cynthia Cockburn (1985, 12) has noted, "Femininity is incompatible with technological competence; to feel technically competent is to feel manly." Therefore, focusing on the technological aspects of the work is part of a gender strategy that bolsters one's sense of power at the same time it reinforces segregation between men's and women's work.

Another reframing technique male temporaries use to maintain their masculinitiy is to borrow the prestige of the employing organization (Pierce 1995; Williams 1995) when describing their work to outsiders, especially other men. A male paralegal in Pierce's (1995) study of gender in law firms described how he used the name of the law firm rather than his job title to impress outsiders. Similarly, Bob Johnson described the unit he was assigned to at a consulting firm in elaborate detail rather than his specific work tasks when asked about his temporary job:

I work for six managers . . . in the change management services division. Companies hire them to do consulting work and they sort of do a lot of work with organizations that are going through organizational change. Implementing new systems. Both in the workforce and in terms of like information technology. Sort of reeducating them and reorganizing them around different responsibilities and different organizational hierarchies. And the other division I work for is integration services. And they're really technical experts. In terms of different [computer] hardware and software configuration systems. (Bob Johnson, 23-year-old gay white man)

Only in follow-up questions did he detail his more mundane day-to-day secretarial tasks: "I do support work. It's a lot of typing up correspondence between clients and interoffice correspondence. A lot of filing. A lot of typing. Answering phones a lot. Most of the time."

Doing Masculinity—Telling the Cover Story

Male temporaries, almost universally, invoked the "cover story" as a gender strategy to buttress their challenged sense of masculinity. The cover story, told to both self and others, invokes an alternative identity and defines one as truly temporary or occupationally transient (Henson 1996). Male clerical temporaries, through telling the cover story both on and off the job, provide an explanation for their apparent lack of drive or competence in obtaining a real (male) job. Steve Woodhead, for example, described how he strategically used his cover story on new assignments: "Oh, I always told them I was an actor. Immediately. Immediately. And they were, like, 'Great! This is wonderful.' So maybe that's what cut the ice, you know. They knew I wasn't just waiting to get a *real job*. 'Why doesn't this guy have a *real job* yet?'" (35-year-old gay white man). Likewise, Harold Koenig said, "I always wanna tell people that I'm just doing this because I'm a writer and I'm really here because of that. But they really don't want to know that. It's like to save your ego" (29-year-old white man). The cover story, then, explains why a man in clerical temporary employment does not have a real job and asserts a more valuable (masculine) social identity.

While permanent workers might also define themselves as occupationally transient (Williams 1989; Garson 1994; Pierce 1995), the organization of temporary work provided workers with the ready-made temporary label. For example, Pierce (1995, 170) noted that male paralegals frequently asserted their occupational transience despite their permanent, full-time status ("I'm planning to go to law school after working as a legal assistant for a few years"). The organization of their work as permanent, however, required that these workers simultaneously demonstrate commitment and noncommitment to their work.

The organization of temporary work, however, presupposes that male temporary workers are uncommitted and facilitates the assumption that there is an underlying reason to be revealed. Note, for example, Henson's failed use of his cover story, in response to direct questioning, in this field note excerpt:

> Someone asked me if I just temped all the time or what I did. And I said, "Well no. I'm a graduate student in Sociology at Northwestern." She asked what I was studying and I said, "Clerical temporary work." Which she thought was really funny. I saw her in the elevator today and she asked, "How's your little study going?" Like, "Sure. That's just your little story." And it is. Because I'm [also] doing it for money. So it is just my little story. But I felt really belittled because she just wasn't taking me seriously. (Henson's field notes, 1991)

Coworkers commonly elicited cover stories from men, but seldom from women. While some women did offer cover stories, their use appeared to be motivated by class rather than gender anxieties (i.e., "What am I doing here with a college degree?").[7] In fact, since women's presence in clerical temporary employment is naturalized, coworkers rarely pressed them for explanations

of any sort. On the few occasions when this happened, the question was precipitated by the temporary worker's efforts or exceptional work performance. During her fieldwork, for example, Rogers's presence in temporary clerical work was questioned only once when she was found to possess unusually detailed knowledge about insurance benefits.

Doing Masculinity—Refusing to Do Deference

Finally, men in clerical temporary work often adopted the risky gender strategy of resisting demands for deference in an effort to do masculinity. Deference, however, is part of being a "good" temporary worker for both male and female temporaries (Rogers 1995; Henson 1996; Rogers and Henson 1997). Temporaries must enact subservience and deference, for example, to continue getting assignments. While other researchers (Hochschild 1983; Pierce 1995; Williams 1995) have argued that men in women's work are not required to do deference (or at least in the same way), we believe that there are occupations in which men are required to do deference, including clerical temporary work. While the demands for deference may be different for women and men (and different within genders along dimensions of race, age, and sexual orientation), men were still expected to provide deferential services as clerical temporary workers.

While none of the men reported ever being asked to get coffee, a request many women reported with great irritation, they were still expected to provide deferential services—smiling, waiting, taking orders, and tolerating the bad moods of their supervisors. In other words, women were asked to provide more of the nurturing and caretaking components of deference than men, especially when working for older and more established men. Helen, for example, reported receiving (and resisting) a particularly egregious request for caretaking behavior on one of her assignments:

They had this glass candy jar this big. And like, "You're supposed to keep that filled with chocolate." Like, "Where do I get the chocolate from?" "Well, you know, just pick something up. Something cheap." Yeah. Like I'm supposed to go and buy a bag of Hershey's Kisses so that the executives can add to their waistlines. I'm like no. And it's been empty ever since I've been there. [Laughs]. (Helen Weinberg, 24-year-old white woman)

Helen, unlike many of the women we interviewed, resisted the most demeaning caretaking requests through a passive "forgetfulness" strategy. Although both female and male temporaries are generally passive in their resistance (Rogers 2000), the significance of deference in temporary employment for masculinity is heightened when we realize that most opportunities for resistance are passive ones.

The refusal to do deference, as doing masculinity, may be so important that male temporary workers risk losing the job rather than feel demeaned. Contrast Helen's forgetfulness strategy above with Bob's overt refusal to do deferential tasks, notably for a female superior:

At my long-term assignment, this one permanent secretary was out sick. I had my own desk and I had things that had to be done. And this woman comes up to me and she hands me a stack of photocopying to do. And I said, "Excuse me." And she said, "Well this is for you to do." And I said, "Well, thank you, but I have my own work to do. This work has to be done by 5." And she goes, "Well, you are just a temp and blah, blah, blah, blah, blah." I said, "Wait a minute. I am a temporary worker, but I do have a desk and assigned work that has to be done." And she threw this little fit. And throughout the day she was really terse and really just a real bitch to me. . . . She was just awful. You know that whole mentality of "just a temp, just a temp." (Bob Johnson, 23-year-old gay white man)

Similarly, Pierce (1995, 92) reports a story of a male paralegal who did not successfully do def-

erence and appropriately "manage his own anger" with an ill-behaved male attorney. He confronted the attorney on his abusive behavior, was removed from the case, and eventually pushed to a peripheral position within the firm.

Similarly, Henson discovered the risks in resisting demands for deference when he failed to adopt a submissive demeanor and was removed from an assignment. Near the end of his first week on a (scheduled) long-term assignment at a small medical college, Henson arrived to find a typed message from Shirley, his work-site supervisor, on his chair. The note clearly asserted the hierarchy of power and demanded deference and submission—especially since Shirley worked only a few feet from Henson's desk and could have easily communicated her request verbally:

"Kevin. RE: Lunch today (12/5). My plans are to be out of the office from about 11:45 AM to 1:00 PM. (If you get hungry early, I suggest you have a snack before I leave at 11:45 AM). Thanks. Shirl."

This annoys me: patronizing and hostile—at least that's the way I take it. So, I very casually and fully aware of the politics, walk to Shirley's door with the note in hand and say, "Oh, about lunch. . . . That's great! That works out fine with my plans too. No problem." I'm upbeat and polite, but I'm framing it as giving permission or at least as an interaction between equals. (Henson's field notes, 1990)

At the end of the day, Henson said good night to Shirley and left with every intention of returning in the morning. That evening, however, he received a call from his agency counselor: "Hi Kevin. This is Wendy. I don't know how to tell you this, but the college called us today and they said they just didn't think things were working out. They don't want you to come back tomorrow." While Henson had completed the formal work adequately, he had consciously resisted adopting the appropriate submissive demeanor. By refusing to perform deference and doing masculinity instead, he had lost the assignment.

Demands for deference seemed to be the breaking point for the male temporaries in this study. They were no longer able to reframe their way out of their feminized position. Male privilege no longer protected these men from the requirements of the job, including the performance of feminine styles of emotional labor and deference. While men do perform emotional labor and even deference on the job (Hochschild 1983; Pierce 1995), they typically do so in ways that are compatible with hegemonic notions of masculinity. In contrast, male temporaries were required to enact feminine modes of deference. Thus, men's refusals to do deference in temporary clerical work come to serve as proof that men are not suited for temporary clerical work.

Conclusion

Male clerical temporaries, as with other men who cross over into women's work, fail to conform to the dictates of hegemonic masculinity on at least two fronts. First, they are working temporary rather than permanent, higher paying, full-time jobs (i.e., a real job), which limits their ability to assume the male breadwinner role. Second, they are doing clerical work (i.e., women's work), including demands for deference and caretaking, which challenges their presumed heterosexuality.

At first glance, men's presence in a female-dominated job such as temporary clerical work might appear to disrupt the gendered landscape of the workplace. Unlike men in women's semiprofessions, however, these men cannot exercise their male privilege by riding the glass escalator to higher paying, more prestigious work. Work that is female dominated and very low status does not provide the credential system and internal labor market necessary for the operation of the glass escalator. Here, occupational specificity makes all the difference in understanding men's interactions in female-dominated work. The experience of male temporary clerical workers neither conforms wholly to Kanter's (1977) theory of tokenism nor to Williams's (1992) glass escalator theory. Rather, these men experience a gendered set of token-related problems that center on maintaining the ideals of hegemonic masculinity.

With little organizational opportunity for upward mobility, men do gender in such a way that they reassert the feminine identification of the job while rejecting its application to them. Through renaming and reframing their individual duties, men distance themselves from the most feminized aspects of the job. Through telling their cover story, men construct their presence in temporary work as truly transient while naturalizing women's numerical dominance in the job. While men's refusal to do female-typed deference places them at risk of job loss individually, the meanings attributed to those actions once again reproduce the gender order as men are confirmed as unsuited for temporary clerical work. Through their gender strategies, male temporary clerical workers strike a hegemonic bargain, retracing the lines of occupational segregation and reinvigorating hegemonic masculinity and its domination over women and subaltern men.

Author's Note: An earlier version of this article was presented at the 1999 meeting of the American Sociological Association in Chicago, Illinois. We would like to thank Marjorie L. DeVault, Ronnie J. Steinberg, Judith Wittner, Anne Figert, Christine Bose, and the reviewers of *Gender & Society* for their comments on earlier drafts of this article.

Notes

1. Connell (1987, 1995) argues that hegemonic masculinity is not a static and homogeneous trait or role but is the ascendant (dominant) definition of masculinity at any one time to which other men are measured and, almost invariably, found wanting. Although the specific dictates of hegemonic masculinity vary over time, it is "chiefly, though not exclusively, associated with men located in the uppermost reaches of a society's ascriptive hierarchies" (Chen 1999, 587). The power of hegemonic masculinity lies not so much in the extent to which men actually conform to its (impossible) expectations but rather in the practice of masculinity and the patriarchal dividend they collect (Connell 1987, 1995).

2. Nevertheless, men may have different rates of exit from temporary work into permanent employment gained from sources other than temporary agencies.

3. Although we did not systematically collect data on the sexual orientation of respondents, two women and 10 men in our sample self-identified as lesbian and gay. While we make no claims regarding generalizability on this front, we have marked sexual orientation of the interviewee where it is directly relevant as indicated by the respondents.

4. We would specify white men here, if our sample permitted, since race is theoretically an important part of the construction of the socially acceptable male temporary clerical worker.

5. Women did report negative screenings on the basis of race, age, and perceived attractiveness.

6. We documented no systematic pay differences for jobs that were renamed in more masculine terms. In fact, pay increases were seldom reported and difficult to negotiate (Rogers 2000).

7. Class anxiety is apparent in the men's comments as well. While class is an important component of hegemonic masculinity, it is difficult to unravel gender and class at this intersection.

References

Acker, Joan. 1990. Hierarchies, jobs, bodies: A theory of gendered organizations. *Gender & Society* 4:139–158.

Britton, Dana M. 2000. The epistemology of the gendered organization. *Gender & Society* 14: 418–434.

Bureau of Labor Statistics. 1995. *Handbook of labor statistics.* Washington, DC: Government Printing Office.

Chen, Anthony S. 1999. Lives at the center of the periphery, lives at the periphery of the center: Chinese American masculinities and bargaining with hegemony. *Gender & Society* 13:584–607.

Cheng, Cliff. 1996. *Masculinities in organizations.* Thousand Oaks, CA: Sage.

Cockburn, Cynthia. 1985. *Machinery of dominance: Women, men, and technical know-how.* Boston: Northeastern University Press.

Cohany, Sharon R. 1998. Workers in alternative employment arrangements: A second look. *Monthly Labor Review* 121:3–21.

Collinson, David L., and Jeff Hearn. 1996. *Men as managers, managers as men: Critical perspectives on men, masculinities and managements.* Thousand Oaks, CA: Sage.

Connell, R. W. 1987. *Gender and power.* Palo Alto, CA: Stanford University Press.

———. 1995. *Masculinities.* Berkeley: University of California Press.

Donaldson, Mike. 1993. What is hegemonic masculinity? *Theory and Society* 22:643–657.

Epstein, C. F., C. Seron, B. Oglensky, and R. Saute. 1999. *The part-time paradox: Time norms, professional life, family and gender.* New York: Routledge.

Garson, Barbara. 1994. *All the livelong day: The meaning and demeaning of routine work.* Rev. 2d ed. New York: Penguin.

Glaser, Barney G., and Anselm L. Strauss. 1965. *Awareness of dying.* Chicago: Aldine.

———. 1967. *The discovery of grounded theory: Strategies for qualitative research.* Chicago: Aldine.

Golden, Lonnie, and Eileen Appelbaum. 1992. What was driving the 1982–88 boom in temporary employment: Preferences of workers or decisions and power of employers? *Journal of Economics and Society* 51:473–494.

Hall, Elaine, J. 1993. Smiling, deferring, and flirting: Doing gender by giving "good service." *Work & Occupations* 20:452–471.

Henson, Kevin, D. 1996. *Just a temp.* Philadelphia: Temple University Press.

Hochschild, Arlie R. 1983. *The managed heart: Commercialization of human feeling.* Berkeley: University of California Press.

———. 1989. *The second shift.* New York: Avon.

Hossfeld, Karen. 1990. Their logic against them: Contradictions in sex, race, and class in Silicon Valley. In *Women workers and global restructuring,* edited by K. Ward, Ithaca, NY: ILR Press.

Kandiyoti, Deniz. 1988. Bargaining with patriarchy. *Gender & Society* 2:274–290.

Kanter, Rosabeth M. 1977. *Men and women of the corporation.* New York: Basic Books.

Kimmel, Michael S. 1994. Masculinity as homophobia: Fear, shame, and silence in the construction of gender identity. In *Theorizing masculinities,* edited by Harry Brod and Michael Kaufman. Thousand Oaks, CA: Sage.

Leidner, Robin. 1993. *Fast food, fast talk: Service work and the routinization of everyday life.* Berkeley: University of California Press.

MacKinnon, Catharine A. 1979. *Sexual harassment of working women: A case of sex discrimination.* New Haven and London: Yale University Press.

Maume, David J. Jr. 1999. Glass ceilings and glass escalators: Occupational segregation and race and sex differences in managerial promotions. *Work & Occupations* 26:483–509.

Messerschmidt, James W. 1996. Managing to kill: Masculinities and the space shuttle Challenger explosion. In *Masculinities in organizations,* edited by C. Cheng. Thousand Oaks, CA: Sage.

Moore, Mack. A. 1963. The role of temporary help-services in the clerical labor market. Ph.D. diss., University of Wisconsin–Madison.

National Association of Temporary Services. 1992. *Report on the temporary help services industry.* Alexandria, VA: DRI/McGraw-Hill.

Parker, Robert E. 1994. *Flesh peddlers and warm bodies: The temporary help industry and its workers.* New Brunswick, NJ: Rutgers University Press.

Pierce, Jennifer. 1995. *Gender trials: Emotional lives in contemporary law firms.* Berkeley: University of California Press.

Pringle, Rosemary. 1993. Male secretaries. In *Doing "women's work": Men in nontraditional occupations,* edited by C. L. Williams. Newbury Park, CA: Sage.

Rogers, Jackie K. 1995. Just a temp: Experience and structure of alienation in temporary clerical employment. *Work and Occupations* 22:137–166.

———. 2000. *Temps: The many faces of the changing workplace.* Ithaca, NY: Cornell University Press.

Rogers, Jackie K., and Kevin D. Henson. 1997. "Hey, why don't you wear a shorter skirt?" Structural vulnerability and the organization of sexual harassment in temporary clerical employment. *Gender & Society* 11:215–237.

Smith, Vicki. 1998. The fractured world of the temporary worker: Power, participation, and fragmentation in the contemporary workplace. *Social Problems* 45:411–430.

West, Candace, and Sarah Fenstermaker. 1995. Doing difference. *Gender & Society* 1:8–37.

West, Candace, and Don H. Zimmerman. 1987. Doing gender. *Gender & Society* 1:125–151.

Williams, Christine L. 1989. *Gender differences at work: Women and men in nontraditional occupations.* Berkeley: University of California Press.

———. 1992. The glass escalator: Hidden advantages for men in the "female" professions. *Social Problems* 39:253–267.

———. 1995. *Still a man's world: Men who do women's work.* Berkeley: University of California Press.

Williams, Christine L., and Joel E. Heikes. 1993. The importance of researcher's gender in the in-depth interview: Evidence from two case studies of male nurses. *Gender & Society* 7:280–291.

Wright, Rosemary. 1996. The occupational masculinity of computing. In *Masculinities in organizations,* edited by C. Cheng. Thousand Oaks, CA: Sage.

Beth A. Quinn

Sexual Harassment and Masculinity: The Power and Meaning of "Girl Watching"

Confronted with complaints about sexual harassment or accounts in the media, some men claim that women are too sensitive or that they too often misinterpret men's intentions (Buckwald 1993; Bernstein 1994). In contrast, some women note with frustration that men just "don't get it" and lament the seeming inadequacy of sexual harassment policies (Conley 1991; Guccione 1992). Indeed, this ambiguity in defining acts of sexual harassment might be, as Cleveland and Kerst (1993) suggested, the most robust finding in sexual harassment research.

Using in-depth interviews with 43 employed men and women, this article examines a particular social practice—"girl watching"—as a means to understanding one way that these gender differences are produced. This analysis does not address the size or prevalence of these differences, nor does it present a direct comparison of men and women; this information is essential but well covered in the literature.[1] Instead, I follow Cleveland and Kerst's (1993) and Wood's (1998) suggestion that the question may best be unraveled by exploring how the "subject(ivities) of perpetrators, victims, and resistors of sexual harassment" are "discursively produced, reproduced, and altered" (Wood 1998, 28).

This article focuses on the subjectivities of the perpetrators of a disputable form of sexual harassment, "girl watching." The term refers to the act of men's sexually evaluating women, often in the company of other men. It may take the form of a verbal or gestural message of "check it

From *Gender & Society* 16(3): 386–402. Copyright © 2002 Sociologists for Women in Society.

out," boasts of sexual prowess, or explicit comments about a woman's body or imagined sexual acts. The target may be an individual woman or group of women or simply a photograph or other representation. The woman may be a stranger, coworker, supervisor, employee, or client. For the present analysis, girl watching within the workplace is [the focus].

The analysis is grounded in the work of masculinity scholars such as Connell (1987, 1995) in that it attempts to explain the subject positions of the interviewed men—not the abstract and genderless subjects of patriarchy but the gendered and privileged subjects embedded in this system. Since I am attempting to delineate the gendered worldviews of the interviewed men, I employ the term "girl watching," a phrase that reflects their language ("they watch girls").

I have chosen to center the analysis on girl watching within the workplace for two reasons. First, it appears to be fairly prevalent. For example, a survey of federal civil employees (U.S. Merit Systems Protection Board 1988) found that in the previous 24 months, 28 percent of the women surveyed had experienced "unwanted sexual looks or gestures," and 35 percent had experienced "unwanted sexual teasing, jokes, remarks, or questions." Second, girl watching is still often normalized and trivialized as only play, or "boys will be boys." A man watching girls—even in his workplace—is frequently accepted as a natural and commonplace activity, especially if he is in the presence of other men.[2] Indeed, it may be required (Hearn 1985). Thus, girl watching sits on the blurry edge between fun and harm, joking and harassment. An understanding of the process of identifying behavior as sexual harassment, or of rejecting this label, may be built on this ambiguity.

Girl watching has various forms and functions, depending on the context and the men involved. For example, it may be used by men as a directed act of power against a particular woman or women. In this, girl watching—at least in the workplace—is most clearly identified as harassing by both men and women. I am most interested, however, in the form where it is characterized as only play. This type is more obliquely motivated and, as I will argue, functions as a game men play to build shared masculine identities and social relations.

Multiple and contradictory subject positions are also evidenced in girl watching, most notably that between the gazing man and the woman he watches. Drawing on Michael Schwalbe's (1992) analysis of empathy and the formation of masculine identities, I argue that girl watching is premised on the obfuscation of this multiplicity through the objectification of the woman watched and a suppression of empathy for her. In conclusion, the ways these elements operate to produce gender differences in interpreting sexual harassment and the implications for developing effective policies are discussed.

Previous Research

The question of how behavior is or is not labeled as sexual harassment has been studied primarily through experimental vignettes and surveys.[3] In both methods, participants evaluate either hypothetical scenarios or lists of behaviors, considering whether, for example, the behavior constitutes sexual harassment, which party is most at fault, and what consequences the act might engender. Researchers manipulate factors such as the level of "welcomeness" the target exhibits, and the relationship of the actors (supervisor–employee, coworker–coworker).

Both methods consistently show that women are willing to define more acts as sexual harassment (Gutek, Morasch, and Cohen 1983; Padgitt and Padgitt 1986; Powell 1986; York 1989; but see Stockdale and Vaux 1993) and are more likely to see situations as coercive (Garcia, Milano, and Quijano 1989). When asked who is more to blame in a particular scenario, men are more likely to blame, and less likely to empathize with, the victim (Jensen and Gutek 1982; Kenig and Ryan 1986). In terms of actual behaviors like girl watching, the U.S. Merit Systems Protection Board (1988) survey found that 81 percent of the women surveyed considered "uninvited sexually suggestive looks or gestures" from a supervisor to be sexual harassment. While the majority of men (68 percent) also defined it as such, significantly more men were willing to dismiss such behavior. Similarly, while 40 percent of the men would not consider the same behavior from a coworker to be harassing, more than three-quarters of the women would.

The most common explanation offered for these differences is gender role socialization. This conclusion is supported by the consistent finding that the more men and women adhere to traditional gender roles, the more likely they are to deny the harm in sexual harassment and to consider the behavior acceptable or at least normal (Pryor 1987; Malovich and Stake 1990; Popovich et al. 1992; Gutek and Koss 1993; Murrell and Dietz-Uhler 1993; Tagri and Hayes 1997). Men who hold predatory ideas about sexuality, who are more likely to believe rape myths, and who are more likely to self-report that they would rape under certain circumstances are less likely to see behaviors as harassing (Pryor 1987; Reilly et al. 1992; Murrell and Dietz-Uhler 1993).

These findings do not, however, adequately address the between-group differences. The more one is socialized into traditional notions of sex roles, the more likely it is for both men and women to view the behaviors as acceptable or at least unchangeable. The processes by which gender roles operate to produce these differences remain underexamined.

Some theorists argue that men are more likely to discount the harassing aspects of their behavior because of a culturally conditional tendency to misperceive women's intentions. For example, Stockdale (1993, 96) argued that "patriarchal norms create a sexually aggressive belief system in some people more than others, and this belief system can lead to the propensity to misperceive." Gender differences in interpreting sexual harassment, then, may be the outcome of the acceptance of normative ideas about women's inscrutability and indirectness and men's role as sexual aggressors. Men see harmless flirtation or sexual interest rather than harassment because they misperceive women's intent and responses.

Stockdale's (1993) theory is promising but limited. First, while it may apply to actions such as repeatedly asking for dates and quid pro quo harassment,[4] it does not effectively explain motivations for more indirect actions, such as displaying pornography and girl watching. Second, it does not explain why some men are more likely to operate from these discourses of sexual aggression contributing to a propensity to misperceive.

Theoretical explanations that take into account the complexity and diversity of sexual harassing behaviors and their potentially multifaceted social etiologies are needed. An account of the processes by which these behaviors are produced and the active construction of their social meanings is necessary to unravel both between- and within-gender variations in behavior and interpretation. A fruitful framework from which to begin is an examination of masculine identities and the role of sexually harassing behaviors as a means to their production.

Method

I conducted 43 semistructured interviews with currently employed men and women between June 1994 and March 1995. Demographic characteristics of the participants are reported in Table 18.1. The interviews ranged in length from one to three hours. With one exception, interviews were audiotaped and transcribed in full.

Participants were contacted in two primary ways. Twenty-five participants were recruited from "Acme Electronics," a Southern California electronic design and manufacturing company. An additional 18 individuals were recruited from an evening class at a community college and a university summer school class, both in Southern California. These participants referred three more individuals. In addition to the interviews, I conducted participant observation for approximately one month while on site at Acme. This involved observations of the public and common spaces of the company.

At Acme, a human resources administrator drew four independent samples (salaried and hourly women and men) from the company's approximately 300 employees. Letters of invitation were sent to 40 individuals, and from this group, 13 women and 12 men agreed to be interviewed.[5]

The strength of organizationally grounded sampling is that it allows us to provide context for individual accounts. However, in smaller organizations and where participants occupy unique positions, this method can compromise participant anonymity when published versions of the research are accessed by participants. Since this is the case with Acme, and since organizational context is not particularly salient for this analysis, the identity of the participant's organization is sometimes intentionally obscured.

The strength of the second method of recruitment is that it provides access to individuals employed in diverse organizations (from self-employment to multinational corporations) and in a range of occupations (e.g., nanny, house painter, accounting manager). Not surprisingly, drawing from college courses resulted in a group with similar educational backgrounds; all participants from this sample had some college, with 22 percent holding college degrees. Student samples and snowball sampling are not particularly robust in terms of generalizability. They are, nonetheless, regularly employed in qualitative studies (Connell 1995; Chen 1999) when the goal is theory development—as is the case here—rather than theory testing.

The interviews began with general questions about friendships and work relationships and progressed to specific questions about gender rela-

■ **TABLE 18.1**
Participant Demographic Measures

Variable	Men		Women		Total	
	n	%	n	%	n	%
Student participants and referrals	6	33	12	67	18	42
Racial/ethnic minority	2	33	2	17	4	22
Mean age	27.2		35		32.5	
Married	3	50	3	25	6	33
Nontraditional job	1	17	4	33	5	28
Supervisor	0	0	6	50	6	33
Some college	6	100	12	100	18	100
Acme participants	12	48	13	52	25	58
Racial/ethnic minority	2	17	3	23	5	20
Mean age	42.3		34.6		38.6	
Married	9	75	7	54	16	64
Nontraditional job	0	0	4	31	4	16
Supervisor	3	25	2	15	5	20
Some college	9	75	9	69	18	72
All participants	18	42	25	58	43	100
Racial/ethnic minority	4	22	5	20	9	21
Mean age	37.8		34.9		36.2	
Married	12	67	10	40	22	51
Nontraditional job	1	6	8	32	9	21
Supervisor	3	17	8	32	11	26
Some college	15	82	21	84	36	84

tions, sexual harassment, and the policies that seek to address it.[6] Since the main aim of the project was to explore how workplace events are framed as sexual harassment (and as legally bounded or not), the term "sexual harassment" was not introduced by the interviewer until late in the interview.

While the question of the relationship between masculinity and sexual harassment was central, I did not come to the research looking expressly for girl watching. Rather, it surfaced as a theme across several men's interviews in the context of a gender reversal question:

> It's the end of an average day. You get ready for bed and fall to sleep. In what seems only a moment, the alarm goes off. As you awake, you find your body to be oddly out of sorts. . . . To your surprise, you find that you have been transformed into the "opposite sex." Even stranger,

no one in your life seems to remember that you were ever any different.

Participants were asked to consider what it would be like to conduct their everyday work life in this transformed state. I was particularly interested in their estimation of the impact it would have on their interactions with coworkers and supervisors. Imagining themselves as the opposite sex, participants were forced to make explicit the operation of gender in their workplace, something they did not do in their initial discussions of a typical workday.

Interestingly, no man discussed girl watching in initial accounts of his workplace. I suspect that they did not consider it to be relevant to a discussion of their average *work* day, even though it became apparent that it was an integral daily activity for some groups of men. It emerged only when men were forced to consider themselves as explicitly gendered workers through the hypothetical question, something they were able initially to elide.[7]

Taking guidance from Glaser and Strauss's (1967) grounded theory and the methodological insights of Dorothy Smith (1990), transcripts were analyzed iteratively and inductively, with the goal of identifying the ideological tropes the speaker used to understand his or her identities, behaviors, and relationships. Theoretical concepts drawn from previous work on the etiology of sexual harassment (Bowman 1993; Cleveland and Kerst 1993), the construction of masculine identities (Connell 1995, 1987), and sociolegal theories of disputing and legal consciousness (Bumiller 1988; Conley and O'Barr 1998) guided the analysis.

Several related themes emerged and are discussed in the subsequent analysis. First, girl watching appears to function as a form of gendered play among men. This play is productive of masculine identities and premised on a studied lack of empathy with the feminine other. Second, men understand the targeted woman to be an object rather than a player in the game, and she is most often not the intended audience. This obfuscation of a woman's subjectivity, and men's refusal to consider the effects of their behavior, means men are likely to be confused when a woman complains. Thus, the production of masculinity though girl watching, and its compulsory disempathy, may be one factor in gender differences in the labeling of harassment.

Findings: Girl Watching as "Hommo-Sexuality"

[They] had a button on the computer that you pushed if there was a girl who came to the front counter. . . . It was a code and it said "BAFC"—Babe at Front Counter. . . . If the guy in the back looked up and saw a cute girl come in the station, he would hit this button for the other dispatcher to [come] see the cute girl.

—Paula, police officer

In its most serious form, girl watching operates as a targeted tactic of power. The men seem to want everyone—the targeted woman as well as coworkers, clients, and superiors—to know they are looking. The gaze demonstrates their right, as men, to sexually evaluate women. Through the gaze, the targeted woman is reduced to a sexual object, contradicting her other identities, such as that of competent worker or leader. This employment of the discourse of asymmetrical heterosexuality (i.e., the double standard) may trump a woman's formal organizational power, claims to professionalism, and organizational discourses of rationality (Collinson and Collinson 1989; Yount 1991; Gardner 1995).[8] As research on rape has demonstrated (Estrich 1987), calling attention to a woman's gendered sexuality can function to exclude recognition of her competence, rationality, trustworthiness, and even humanity. In contrast, the overt recognition of a man's (hetero)sexuality is normally compatible with other aspects of his identity; indeed, it is often required (Hearn 1985; Connell 1995). Thus, the power of sexuality is asymmetrical, in part, because being seen as sexual has different consequences for women and men.

But when they ogle, gawk, whistle and point, are men always so directly motivated to disempower their women colleagues? Is the target of the gaze also the intended audience? Consider, for example, this account told by Ed, a white, 29-year-old instrument technician.

When a group of guys goes to a bar or a nightclub and they try to be manly. . . . A few of us always found [it] funny [when] a woman would walk by and a guy would be like, "I can have her." [pause] "Yeah, OK, we want to see it!" [laugh]

In his account—a fairly common one in men's discussions—the passing woman is simply a visual cue for their play. It seems clear that it is a game played by men for men; the woman's participation and awareness of her role seem fairly unimportant.

As Thorne (1993) reminded us, we should not be too quick to dismiss games as "only play." In her study of gender relations in elementary schools, Thorne found play to be a powerful form of gendered social action. One of its "clusters of meaning" most relevant here is that of "dramatic performance." In this, play functions as both a source of fun and a mechanism by which gendered identities, group boundaries, and power relations are (re)produced.

The metaphor of play was strong in Karl's comments. Karl, a white man in his early thirties who worked in a technical support role in the Acme engineering department, hoped to earn a degree in engineering. His frustration with his slow progress—which he attributed to the burdens of marriage and fatherhood—was evident throughout the interview. Karl saw himself as an undeserved outsider in his department and he seemed to delight in telling on the engineers.

Girl watching came up as Karl considered the gender reversal question. Like many of the men I interviewed, his first reaction was to muse about premenstrual syndrome and clothes. When I inquired about the potential social effects of the transformation (by asking him, Would it "be easier dealing with the engineers or would it be harder?") he haltingly introduced the engineers' "game."

Karl: Some of the engineers here are very [pause] they're not very, how shall we say? [pause] What's the way I want to put this? They're not very, uh [pause] what's the word? Um. It escapes me.

Researcher: Give me a hint?

Karl: They watch women but they're not very careful about getting caught.

Researcher: Oh! Like they ogle?

Karl: Ogle or gaze or [pause] stare even, or [pause] generate a commotion of an unusual nature.

His initial discomfort in discussing the issue (with me, I presume) is evident in his excruciatingly formal and hesitant language. The aspect of play, however, came through clearly when I pushed him to describe what generating a commotion looked like: " 'Oh! There goes so-and-so. Come and take a look! She's wearing this great outfit today!' Just like a schoolboy. They'll rush out of their offices and [cranes his neck] and check things out." That this is as a form of play was evident in Karl's boisterous tone and in his reference to schoolboys. This is not a case of an aggressive sexual appraising of a woman coworker but a commotion created for the benefit of other men.

At Acme, several spatial factors facilitated this form of girl watching. First, the engineering department is designed as an open-plan office with partitions at shoulder height, offering a maze-like geography that encourages group play. As Karl explained, the partitions offer both the opportunity for sight and cover from being seen. Although its significance escaped me at the time, I was directly introduced to the spatial aspects of the engineers' game of girl watching during my first day on site at Acme. That day, John, the current human resources director, gave me a tour of the facilities, walking me through the departments and offering informal introductions. As we entered the design engineering section, a rhythm of heads emerged from its landscape of partitions, and movement started in our direction. I was definitely aware of being on display as several men gave me obvious once-overs.

Second, Acme's building features a grand stairway that connects the second floor—where the engineering department is located—with the lobby. The stairway is enclosed by glass walls, offering a bird's eye view to the main lobby and the movements of visitors and the receptionists (all women). Robert, a senior design engineer, specifically noted the importance of the glass walls in his discussion of the engineers' girl watching.

There's glass walls around the upstairs right here by the lobby. So when there's an attractive young female . . . someone will see the girl in the area and they will go back and inform all the men in the area. "Go check it out." [laugh] So we'll walk over to the glass window, you know, and we'll see who's down there.

One day near the end of my stay at Acme, I was reminded of his story as I ventured into the first-floor reception area. Looking up, I saw Robert and another man standing at the top of the stairs watching and commenting on the women gathered around the receptionist's desk. When he saw me, Robert gave me a sheepish grin and disappeared from sight.

Producing Masculinity

I suggest that girl watching in this form functions simultaneously as a form of play and as a potentially powerful site of gendered social action. Its social significance lies in its power to form identities and relationships based on these common practices for, as Cockburn (1983, 123) has noted, "patriarchy is as much about relations between man and man as it is about relations between men and women." Girl watching works similarly to the sexual joking that Johnson (1988) suggested is a common way for heterosexual men to establish intimacy among themselves.

In particular, girl watching works as a dramatic performance played to other men, a means by which a certain type of masculinity is produced and heterosexual desire displayed. It is a means by which men assert a masculine identity to other men, in an ironic "hommo-sexual" practice of heterosexuality (Butler 1990).[9] As Connell (1995) and others (West and Zimmerman 1987; Butler 1990) have aptly noted, masculinity is not a static identity but rather one that must constantly be reclaimed. The content of any performance—and there are multiple forms—is influenced by a hegemonic notion of masculinity. When asked what "being a man" entailed, many of the men and women I interviewed triangulated toward notions of strength (if not in muscle, then in character and job performance),

dominance, and a marked sexuality, overflowing and uncontrollable to some degree and natural to the male "species." Heterosexuality is required, for just as the label "girl" questions a man's claim to masculine power, so does the label "fag" (Hopkins 1992; Pronger 1992). I asked Karl, for example, if he would consider his sons "good men" if they were gay. His response was laced with ambivalence; he noted only that the question was "a tough one."

The practice of girl watching is just that—a practice—one rehearsed and performed in everyday settings. This aspect of rehearsal was evident in my interview with Mike, a self-employed house painter who used to work construction. In locating himself as a born-again Christian, Mike recounted the girl watching of his fellow construction workers with contempt. Mike was particularly disturbed by a man who brought his young son to the job site one day. The boy was explicitly taught to catcall, a practice that included identifying the proper targets: women and effeminate men.

Girl watching, however, can be somewhat tenuous as a masculine practice. In their acknowledgment (to other men) of their supposed desire lies the possibility that in being too interested in women the players will be seen as mere schoolboys giggling in the playground. Taken too far, the practice undermines rather than supports a masculine performance. In Karl's discussion of girl watching, for example, he continually came back to the problem of men not being careful about getting caught. He referred to a particular group of men who, though "their wives are [pause] very attractive—very much so," still "gawk like schoolboys." Likewise, Stephan explained that men who are obvious, who "undress [women] with their eyes" probably do so "because they don't get enough women in their lives. Supposedly." A man must be interested in women, but not too interested; they must show their (hetero) sexual interest, but not overly so, for this would be to admit that women have power over them.

The Role of Objectification and (Dis)Empathy

As a performance of heterosexuality among men, the targeted woman is primarily an object onto which men's homosocial sexuality is projected. The presence of a woman in any form—embodied, pictorial, or as an image conjured from words—is required, but her subjectivity and active participation is not. To be sure, given the ways the discourse of asymmetrical sexuality works, men's actions may result in similarly negative effects on the targeted woman as that of a more direct form of sexualization. The crucial difference is that the men's understanding of their actions differs. This difference is one key to understanding the ambiguity around interpreting harassing behavior.

When asked about the engineers' practice of neck craning, Robert grinned, saying nothing at first. After some initial discussion, I started to ask him if he thought women were aware of their game ("Do you think that the women who are walking by . . . ?"). He interrupted, misreading my question. What resulted was a telling description of the core of the game:

> It depends. No. I don't know if they enjoy it. When I do it, if I do it, I'm not saying that I do. [big laugh] . . . If they do enjoy it, they don't say it. If they don't enjoy it—wait a minute, that didn't come out right. I don't know if they enjoy it or not [pause]; that's not the purpose of us popping our heads out.

Robert did not want to admit that women might not enjoy it ("that didn't come out right") but acknowledged that their feelings were irrelevant. Only subjects, not objects, take pleasure or are annoyed. If a women did complain, Robert thought "the guys wouldn't know what to say." In her analysis of street harassment, Gardner (1995, 187) found a similar absence, in that "men's interpretations seldom mentioned a woman's reaction, either guessed at or observed."

The centrality of objectification was also apparent in comments made by José, a Hispanic man in his late 40s who worked in manufactur-

ing. For José, the issue came up when he considered the topic of compliments. He initially claimed that women enjoy compliments more than men do. In reconsidering, he remembered girl watching and the importance of intent.

> There is [pause] a point where [pause] a woman can be admired by [pause] a pair of eyes, but we're talking about "that look." Where, you know, you're admiring her because she's dressed nice, she's got a nice figure, she's got nice legs. But then you also have the other side. You have an animal who just seems to undress you with his eyes and he's just [pause], there's those kind of people out there too.

What is most interesting about this statement is that in making the distinction between merely admiring and an animal look that ravages, José switched subject position. He spoke in the second person when describing both forms of looking, but his consistency in grammar belies a switch in subjectivity: you (as a man) admire, and you (as a woman) are undressed with his eyes. When considering an appropriate, complimentary gaze, José described it from a man's point of view; the subject who experiences the inappropriate, violating look, however, is a woman. Thus, as in Robert's account, José acknowledged that there are potentially different meanings in the act for men and women. In particular, to be admired in a certain way is potentially demeaning for a woman through its objectification.

The switch in subject position was also evident in Karl's remarks. Karl mentioned girl watching while imagining himself as a woman in the gender reversal question. As he took the subject position of the woman watched rather than the man watching, his understanding of the act as a harmless game was destabilized. Rather than taking pleasure in being the object of such attention, Karl would take pains to avoid it.

> So with these guys [if I were a woman], I would probably have to be very concerned about my attire in the lab. Because in a lot of cases, I'm working at a bench and I'm hunched over, in which case your shirt, for example, would open

at the neckline, and I would just have to be concerned about that.

Thus, because the engineers girl watch, Karl feels that he would have to regulate his appearance if he were a woman, keeping the men from using him in their game of girl watching. When he considered the act from the point of view of a man, girl watching was simply a harmless antic and an act of appreciation. When he was forced to consider the subject position of a woman, however, girl watching was something to be avoided or at least carefully managed.

When asked to envision himself as a woman in his workplace, like many of the individuals I interviewed, Karl believed that he did not "know how to be a woman." Nonetheless, he produced an account that mirrored the stories of some of the women I interviewed. He knew the experience of girl watching could be quite different—in fact, threatening and potentially disempowering—for the woman who is its object. As such, the game was something to be avoided. In imagining themselves as women, the men remembered the practice of girl watching. None, however, were able to comfortably describe the game of girl watching from the perspective of a woman and maintain its (masculine) meaning as play.

In attempting to take up the subject position of a woman, these men are necessarily drawing on knowledge they already hold. If men simply "don't get it"—truly failing to see the harm in girl watching or other more serious acts of sexual harassment—then they should not be able to see this harm when envisioning themselves as women. What the interviews reveal is that many men—most of whom failed to see the harm of many acts that would constitute the hostile work environment form of sexual harassment—did in fact understand the harm of these acts when forced to consider the position of the targeted woman.

I suggest that the gender reversal scenario produced, in some men at least, a moment of empathy. Empathy, Schwalbe (1992) argued, requires two things. First, one must have some knowledge of the other's situation and feelings.

Second, one must be motivated to take the position of the other. What the present research suggests is that gender differences in interpreting sexual harassment stem not so much from men's not getting it (a failure of the first element) but from a studied, often compulsory, lack of motivation to identify with women's experiences.

In his analysis of masculinity and empathy, Schwalbe (1992) argued that the requirements of masculinity necessitate a "narrowing of the moral self." Men learn that to effectively perform masculinity and to protect a masculine identity, they must, in many instances, ignore a woman's pain and obscure her viewpoint. Men fail to exhibit empathy with women because masculinity precludes them from taking the position of the feminine other, and men's moral stance vis-à-vis women is attenuated by this lack of empathy.

As a case study, Schwalbe (1992) considered the Thomas–Hill hearings, concluding that the examining senators maintained a masculinist stance that precluded them from giving serious consideration to Professor Hill's claims. A consequence of this masculine moral narrowing is that "charges of sexual harassment . . . are often seen as exaggerated or as fabricated out of misunderstanding or spite" (Schwalbe 1992, 46). Thus, gender differences in interpreting sexually harassing behaviors may stem more from acts of ignoring than states of ignorance.

The Problem with Getting Caught

But are women really the untroubled objects that girl watching—viewed through the eyes of men—suggests? Obviously not; the game may be premised on a denial of a woman's subjectivity, but an actual erasure is beyond men's power! It is in this multiplicity of subjectivities, as Butler (1990, ix) noted, where "trouble" lurks, provoked by "the unanticipated agency of a female 'object' who inexplicably returns the glance, reverses the gaze, and contests the place and authority of the masculine position." To face a returned gaze is to get caught, an act that has the power to undermine the logic of girl watching as simply a game among men. Karl, for example, noted that when caught, men are often flustered, a reaction suggesting that the boundaries of usual play have been disturbed.[10]

When a woman looks back, when she asks, "What are you looking at?" she speaks as a subject, and her status as mere object is disturbed. When the game is played as a form of hommosexuality, the confronted man may be baffled by her response. When she catches them looking, when she complains, the targeted woman speaks as a subject. The men, however, understand her primarily as an object, and objects do not object.

The radical potential of sexual harassment law is that it centers women's subjectivity, an aspect prompting Catharine MacKinnon's (1979) unusual hope for the law's potential as a remedy. For men engaged in girl watching, however, this subjectivity may be inconceivable. From their viewpoint, acts such as girl watching are simply games played with objects: women's bodies. Similar to Schwalbe's (1992) insight into the senators' reaction to Professor Hill, the harm of sexual harassment may seem more the result of a woman's complaint (and law's "illegitimate" encroachment into the everyday work world) than men's acts of objectification. For example, in reflecting on the impact of sexual harassment policies in the workplace, José lamented that "back in the '70s, [it was] all peace and love then. Now as things turn around, men can't get away with as much as what they used to." Just whose peace and love are we talking about?

Reactions to Anti–Sexual Harassment Training Programs

The role that objectification and disempathy play in men's girl watching has important implications for sexual harassment training. Consider the following account of a sexual harassment training session given in Cindy's workplace. Cindy, an Italian American woman in her early 20s, worked as a recruiter for a small telemarketing company in Southern California.

> [The trainer] just really laid down the ground rules, um, she had some scenarios. Saying,

> "OK, would you consider this sexual harassment?" "Would you . . ." this, this, this? "What level?" Da-da-da. So, um, they just gave us some real numbers as to lawsuits and cases. Just that "you guys better be careful" type of a thing.

From Cindy's description, this training is fairly typical in that it focuses on teaching participants definitions of sexual harassment and the legal ramifications of accusations. The trainer used the common strategy of presenting videos of potentially harassing situations and asking the participants how they would judge them. Cindy's description of the men's responses to these videos reveals the limitation of this approach.

> We were watching [the TV] and it was [like] a studio audience. And [men] were getting up in the studio audience making comments like "Oh well, look at her! I wouldn't want to do that to her either!" "Well, you're darn straight, look at her!"

Interestingly, the men successfully used the training session videos as an opportunity for girl watching through their public sexual evaluations of the women depicted. In this, the intent of the training session was doubly subverted. The men interpreted scenarios that Cindy found plainly harassing into mere instances of girl watching and sexual (dis)interest. The antiharassment video was ironically transformed into a forum for girl watching, effecting male bonding and the assertion of masculine identities to the exclusion of women coworkers. Also, by judging the complaining women to be inferior as women, the men sent the message that women who complain are those who fail at femininity.

Cindy conceded that relations between men and women in her workplace were considerably strained after the training ("That day, you definitely saw the men bond, you definitely saw the women bond, and there was a definite separation"). The effect of the training session, rather than curtailing the rampant sexual harassment in Cindy's workplace, operated as a site of masculine performance, evoking manly camaraderie and reestablishing gender boundaries.

To be effective, sexual harassment training programs must be grounded in a complex understanding of the ways acts such as girl watching operate in the workplace and the seeming necessity of a culled empathy to some forms of masculinity. Sexually harassing behaviors are produced from more than a lack of knowledge, simple sexist attitudes, or misplaced sexual desire. Some forms of sexually harassing behaviors—such as girl watching—are mechanisms through which gendered boundaries are patrolled and evoked and by which deeply held identities are established. This complexity requires complex interventions and leads to difficult questions about the possible efficacy of any workplace training program mandated in part by legal requirements.

Conclusions

In this analysis, I have sought to unravel the social logic of girl watching and its relationship to the question of gender differences in the interpretation of sexual harassment. In the form analyzed here, girl watching functions simultaneously as only play and as a potent site where power is played. Through the objectification on which it is premised and in the nonempathetic masculinity it supports, this form of girl watching simultaneously produces both the harassment and the barriers to men's acknowledgment of its potential harm.

The implications these findings have for anti–sexual harassment training are profound. If we understand harassment to be the result of a simple lack of knowledge (of ignorance), then straightforward informational sexual harassment training may be effective. The present analysis suggests, however, that the etiology of some harassment lies elsewhere. While they might have quarreled with it, most of the men I interviewed had fairly good abstract understandings of the behaviors their companies' sexual harassment policies prohibited. At the same time, in relating stories of social relations in their workplaces, most failed to identify specific behaviors as sexual harassment when they matched the abstract def-

inition. As I have argued, the source of this contradiction lies not so much in ignorance but in acts of ignoring. Traditional sexual harassment training programs address the former rather than the latter. As such, their effectiveness against sexually harassing behaviors born out of social practices of masculinity like girl watching is questionable.

Ultimately, the project of challenging sexual harassment will be frustrated and our understanding distorted unless we interrogate hegemonic, patriarchal forms of masculinity and the practices by which they are (re)produced. We must continue to research the processes by which sexual harassment is produced and the gendered identities and subjectivities on which it poaches (Wood 1998). My study provides a first step toward a more process-oriented understanding of sexual harassment, the ways the social meanings of harassment are constructed, and ultimately, the potential success of antiharassment training programs.

Author's Note: I would like to thank the members of my faculty writing group—Lisa Aldred, Susan Kollin, and Colleen Mack-Canty—who prove again and again that cross-disciplinary feminist dialogue is not only possible but a powerful reality, even in the wilds of Montana. In addition, thanks to Lisa Jones for her thoughtful reading at a crucial time and to the anonymous reviewers who offered both productive critiques and encouragement.

Notes

1. See Welsh (1999) for a review of this literature.

2. For example, Maria, an administrative assistant I interviewed, simultaneously echoed and critiqued this understanding when she complained about her boss's girl watching in her presence: "If he wants to do that in front of other men . . . you know, that's what men do."

3. Recently, more researchers have turned to qualitative studies as a means to understand the process of labeling behavior as harassment. Of note are Collinson and Collinson (1996), Giuffre and Williams (1994), Quinn (2000), and Rogers and Henson (1997).

4. Quid pro quo ("this for that") sexual harassment occurs when a person with organizational power at-

tempts to coerce an individual into sexual behavior by threatening adverse job actions.

5. This sample was not fully representative of the company's employees; male managers (mostly white) and minority manufacturing employees were underrepresented. Thus, the data presented here best represent the attitudes and workplace tactics of white men working in white-collar, technical positions and white and minority men in blue-collar jobs.

6. Acme employees were interviewed at work in an office off the main lobby. Students and referred participants were interviewed at sites convenient to them (e.g., an office, the library).

7. Not all the interviewed men discussed girl watching. When asked directly, they tended to grin knowingly, refusing to elaborate. This silence in the face of direct questioning—by a female researcher—is also perhaps an instance of getting caught.

8. I prefer the term "asymmetrical heterosexuality" over "double standard" because it directly references the dominance of heterosexuality and more accurately reflects the interconnected but different forms of acceptable sexuality for men and women. As Estrich (1987) argued, it is not simply that we hold men and women to different standards of sexuality but that these standards are (re)productive of women's disempowerment.

9. "Hommo" is a play on the French word for man, *homme*.

10. Men are not always concerned with getting caught, as the behavior of catcalling construction workers amply illustrates; that a woman hears is part of the thrill (Gardner 1995). The difference between the workplace and the street is the level of anonymity the men have vis-à-vis the woman and the complexity of social rules and the diversity of power sources an individual has at his or her disposal.

References

Bernstein, R. 1994. Guilty if charged. *New York Review of Books,* 13 January.

Bowman, C. G. 1993. Street harassment and the informal ghettoization of women. *Harvard Law Review* 106:517–580.

Buckwald, A. 1993. Compliment a woman, go to court. *Los Angeles Times,* 28 October.

Bumiller, K. 1988. *The civil rights society: The social construction of victims.* Baltimore: Johns Hopkins University Press.

Butler, J. 1990. *Gender trouble: Feminism and the subversion of identity.* New York: Routledge.

Chen, A. S. 1999. Lives at the center of the periphery, lives at the periphery of the center: Chinese American masculinities and bargaining with hegemony. *Gender & Society* 13:584–607.

Cleveland, J. N., and M. E. Kerst. 1993. Sexual harassment and perceptions of power: An underarticulated relationship. *Journal of Vocational Behavior* 42 (1): 49–67.

Cockburn, C. 1983. *Brothers: Male dominance and technological change.* London: Pluto Press.

Collinson, D. L., and M. Collinson. 1989. Sexuality in the workplace: The domination of men's sexuality. In *The sexuality of organizations,* edited by J. Hearn and D. L. Sheppard. Newbury Park, CA: Sage.

———. 1996. "It's only Dick": The sexual harassment of women managers in insurance sales. *Work, Employment & Society* 10 (1): 29–56.

Conley, F. K. 1991. Why I'm leaving Stanford: I wanted my dignity back. *Los Angeles Times,* 9 June.

Conley, J., and W. O'Barr. 1998. *Just words.* Chicago: University of Chicago Press.

Connell, R. W. 1987. *Gender and power.* Palo Alto, CA: Stanford University Press.

———. 1995. *Masculinities.* Berkeley: University of California Press.

Estrich, S. 1987. *Real rape.* Cambridge, MA: Harvard University Press.

Garcia, L., L. Milano, and A. Quijano. 1989. Perceptions of coercive sexual behavior by males and females. *Sex Roles* 21 (9/10): 569–577.

Gardner, C. B. 1995. *Passing by: Gender and public harassment.* Berkeley: University of California Press.

Giuffre, P., and C. Williams. 1994. Boundary lines: Labeling sexual harassment in restaurants. *Gender & Society* 8:378–401.

Glaser, B., and A. L. Strauss. 1967. *The discovery of grounded theory: Strategies for qualitative research.* Chicago: Aldine.

Guccione, J. 1992. Women judges still fighting harassment. *Daily Journal,* 13 October, 1.

Gutek, B. A., and M. P. Koss. 1993. Changed women and changed organizations: Consequences of and coping with sexual harassment. *Journal of Vocational Behavior* 42 (1): 28–48.

Gutek, B. A., B. Morasch, and A. G. Cohen. 1983. Interpreting social–sexual behavior in a work setting. *Journal of Vocational Behavior* 22 (1): 30–48.

Hearn, J. 1985. Men's sexuality at work. In *The sexuality of men,* edited by A. Metcalf and M. Humphries. London: Pluto Press.

Hopkins, P. 1992. Gender treachery: Homophobia, masculinity, and threatened identities. In *Rethinking masculinity: Philosophical explorations in light of feminism,* edited by L. May and R. Strikwerda. Lanham, MD: Littlefield, Adams.

Jensen, I. W., and B. A. Gutek. 1982. Attributions and assignment of responsibility in sexual harassment. *Journal of Social Issues* 38 (4): 121–136.

Johnson, M. 1988. *Strong mothers, weak wives.* Berkeley: University of California Press.

Kenig, S., and J. Ryan. 1986. Sex differences in levels of tolerance and attribution of blame for sexual harassment on a university campus. *Sex Roles* 15 (9/10): 535–549.

MacKinnon, C. A. 1979. *The sexual harassment of working women.* New Haven: Yale University Press.

Malovich, N. J., and J. E. Stake. 1990. Sexual harassment on campus: Individual differences in attitudes and beliefs. *Psychology of Women Quarterly* 14 (1): 63–81.

Murrell, A. J., and B. L. Dietz-Uhler. 1993. Gender identity and adversarial sexual beliefs as predictors of attitudes toward sexual harassment. *Psychology of Women Quarterly* 17 (2): 169–175.

Padgitt, S. C., and J. S. Padgitt. 1986. Cognitive structure of sexual harassment: Implications for university policy. *Journal of College Students Personnel* 27:34–39.

Popovich, P. M., D. N. Gehlauf, J. A. Jolton, J. M. Somers, and R. M. Godinho. 1992. Perceptions of sexual harassment as a function of sex of rater and incident form and consequent. *Sex Roles* 27 (11/12): 609–625.

Powell, G. N. 1986. Effects of sex-role identity and sex on definitions of sexual harassment. *Sex Roles* 14:9–19.

Pronger, B. 1992. Gay jocks: A phenomenology of gay men in athletics. In *Rethinking masculinity: Philosophical explorations in light of feminism,* edited by L. May and R. Strikwerda. Lanham, MD: Littlefield Adams.

Pryor, J. B. 1987. Sexual harassment proclivities in men. *Sex Roles* 17 (5/6): 269–290.

Quinn, B. A. 2000. The paradox of complaining: Law, humor, and harassment in the everyday work world. *Law and Social Inquiry* 25 (4): 1151–1183.

Reilly, M. E., B. Lott, D. Caldwell, and L. DeLuca. 1992. Tolerance for sexual harassment related to self-reported sexual victimization. *Gender & Society* 6:122–138.

Rogers, J. K., and K. D. Henson, 1997. "Hey, why don't you wear a shorter skirt?" Structural vulnerability and the organization of sexual harassment in temporary clerical employment. *Gender & Society* 11:215–238.

Schwalbe, M. 1992. Male supremacy and the narrowing of the moral self. *Berkeley Journal of Sociology* 37:29–54.

Smith, D. 1990. *The conceptual practices of power: A feminist sociology of knowledge.* Boston: Northeastern University Press.

Stockdale, M. S. 1993. The role of sexual misperceptions of women's friendliness in an emerging theory of sexual harassment. *Journal of Vocational Behavior* 42 (1): 84–101.

Stockdale, M. S., and A. Vaux. 1993. What sexual harassment experiences lead respondents to acknowledge being sexually harassed? A secondary analysis of a university survey. *Journal of Vocational Behavior* 43 (2): 221–234.

Tagri, S., and S. M. Hayes. 1997. Theories of sexual harassment. In *Sexual harassment: Theory, research and treatment,* edited by W. O'Donohue. New York: Allyn and Bacon.

Thorne, B. 1993. *Gender play: Girls and boys in school.* Buckingham, UK: Open University Press.

U.S. Merit Systems Protection Board, 1988. *Sexual harassment in the federal government: An update.* Washington, DC: Government Printing Office.

Welsh, S. 1999. Gender and sexual harassment. *Annual Review of Sociology* 1999:169–190.

West, C., and D. H. Zimmerman, 1987. Doing gender. *Gender & Society* 1:125–151.

Wood, J. T. 1998. Saying makes it so: The discursive construction of sexual harassment. In *Conceptualizing sexual harassment as discursive practice,* edited by S. G. Bingham. Westport, CT: Praeger.

York, K. M. 1989. Defining sexual harassment in workplaces: A policy-capturing approach. *Academy of Management Journal* 32:830–850.

Yount, K. R. 1991. Ladies, flirts, tomboys: Strategies for managing sexual harassment in an underground coal mine. *Journal of Contemporary Ethnography* 19:396–422.

Kristen Schilt

Just One of the Guys?: How Transmen Make Gender Visible at Work

Theories of gendered organizations argue that cultural beliefs about gender difference embedded in workplace structures and interactions create and reproduce workplace disparities that disadvantage women and advantage men (Acker 1990; Martin 2003; Williams 1995). As Martin (2003) argues, however, the practices that reproduce gender difference and gender inequality at work are hard to observe. As these gendered practices are citations of established gender norms, men and women in the workplace repeatedly and unreflectively engage in "doing gender" and therefore "doing inequality" (Martin 2003; West and Zimmerman 1987). This repetition of well-worn gender ideologies naturalizes workplace gender inequality, making gendered disparities in achievements appear to be offshoots of "natural" differences between men and women, rather than the products of dynamic gendering and gendered practices (Martin 2003). As the active reproduction of gendered workplace disparities is rendered invisible, gender inequality at work becomes difficult to document empirically and therefore remains resistant to change (Acker 1990; Martin 2003; Williams 1995).

The workplace experiences of female-to-male transsexuals (FTMs), or transmen, offer an opportunity to examine these disparities between men and women at work from a new perspective. Many FTMs enter the workforce as women and, after transition, begin working as men.[1] As men, they have the same skills, education, and abilities

they had as women; however, how this "human capital" is perceived often varies drastically once they become men at work. This shift in gender attribution gives them the potential to develop an "outsider-within" perspective (Collins 1986) on men's advantages in the workplace. FTMs can find themselves benefiting from the "patriarchal dividend" (Connell 1995, 79)—the advantages men in general gain from the subordination of women—after they transition. However, not being "born into it" gives them the potential to be cognizant of being awarded respect, authority, and prestige they did not have working as women. In addition, the experiences of transmen who fall outside of the hegemonic construction of masculinity, such as FTMs of color, short FTMs, and young FTMs, illuminate how the interplay of gender, race, age, and bodily characteristics can constrain access to gendered workplace advantages for some men (Connell 1995).

In this article, I document the workplace experiences of two groups of FTMs, those who openly transition and remain in the same jobs (open FTMs) and those who find new jobs posttransition as "just men" (stealth FTMs).[2] I argue that the positive and negative changes they experience when they become men can illuminate how gender discrimination and gender advantage are created and maintained through workplace interactions. These experiences also illustrate that masculinity is not a fixed character type that automatically commands privilege but rather that the relationships between competing hegemonic and marginalized masculinities give men differing abilities to access gendered workplace advantages (Connell 1995).

From *Gender & Society* 26(4): 465–490. Copyright © 2006 Sociologists for Women in Society. Reprinted by permission.

Theories of Workplace Gender Discrimination

Sociological research on the workplace reveals a complex relationship between the gender of an employee and that employee's opportunities for advancement in both authority and pay. While white-collar men and women with equal qualifications can begin their careers in similar positions in the workplace, men tend to advance faster, creating a gendered promotion gap (Padavic and Reskin 2002; Valian 1999). When women are able to advance, they often find themselves barred from attaining access to the highest echelons of the company by the invisible barrier of the "glass ceiling" (Valian 1999). Even in the so-called women's professions, such as nursing and teaching, men outpace women in advancement to positions of authority (Williams 1995). Similar patterns exist among blue-collar professions, as women often are denied sufficient training for advancement in manual trades, passed over for promotion, or subjected to extreme forms of sexual, racial, and gender harassment that result in women's attrition (Byrd 1999; Miller 1997; Yoder and Aniakudo 1997). These studies are part of the large body of scholarly research on gender and work finding that white- and blue-collar workplaces are characterized by gender segregation, with women concentrated in lower-paying jobs with little room for advancement.

Among the theories proposed to account for these workplace disparities between men and women are human capital theory and gender role socialization. Human capital theory posits that labor markets are neutral environments that reward workers for their skills, experience, and productivity. As women workers are more likely to take time off from work for child rearing and family obligations, they end up with less education and work experience than men. Following this logic, gender segregation in the workplace stems from these discrepancies in skills and experience between men and women, not from gender discrimination. However, while these differences can explain some of the disparities in salaries and rank between women and men, they fail to explain why women and men with comparable prestigious degrees and work experience still end up in different places, with women trailing behind men in advancement (Valian 1999; Williams 1995).

A second theory, gender socialization theory, looks at the process by which individuals come to learn, through the family, peers, schools, and the media, what behavior is appropriate and inappropriate for their gender. From this standpoint, women seek out jobs that reinforce "feminine" traits such as caring and nurturing. This would explain the predominance of women in helping professions such as nursing and teaching. As women are socialized to put family obligations first, women workers would also be expected to be concentrated in part-time jobs that allow more flexibility for family schedules but bring in less money. Men, on the other hand, would be expected to seek higher-paying jobs with more authority to reinforce their sense of masculinity. While gender socialization theory may explain some aspects of gender segregation at work, however, it leaves out important structural aspects of the workplace that support segregation, such as the lack of workplace child care services, as well as employers' own gendered stereotypes about which workers are best suited for which types of jobs (Padavic and Reskin 2002; Valian 1999; Williams 1995).

A third theory, gendered organization theory, argues that what is missing from both human capital theory and gender socialization theory is the way in which men's advantages in the workplace are maintained and reproduced in gender expectations that are embedded in organizations and in interactions between employers, employees, and coworkers (Acker 1990; Martin 2003; Williams 1995). However, it is difficult to study this process of reproduction empirically for several reasons. First, while men and women with similar education and workplace backgrounds can be compared to demonstrate the disparities in where they end up in their careers, it could be argued that differences in achievement between them can be attributed to personal characteristics of the workers rather than to systematic gender discrimination. Second, gendered expectations about which types of jobs women and men are suited for are strengthened by existing occupational segregation; the fact that there are more women nurses and more men doctors comes to be seen as proof that women are better suited for helping professions and men for rational professions. The normalization of these disparities as natural differences obscures the actual operation of men's advantages and therefore makes it hard to document them empirically. Finally, men's advantages in the workplace are not a function of simply one process but rather a complex interplay between many factors, such as gender differences in workplace performance evaluation, gendered beliefs about men's and women's skills and abilities, and differences between family and child care obligations of men and women workers.

The cultural reproduction of these interactional practices that create and maintain gendered workplace disparities often can be rendered more visible, and therefore more able to be challenged, when examined through the perspective of marginalized others (Collins 1986; Martin 1994, 2003; Yoder and Aniakudo 1997). As Yoder and Aniakudo note, "marginalized others offer a unique perspective on the events occurring within a setting because they perceive activities from the vantages of both nearness (being within) and detachment (being outsiders)" (1997, 325–26). This importance of drawing on the experiences of marginalized others derives from Patricia Hill Collins's theoretical development of the "outsider-within" (1986, 1990). Looking historically at the experience of Black women, Collins (1986) argues that they often have become insiders to white society by virtue of being forced, first by slavery and later by racially bounded labor markets, into domestic work for white families. The insider status that results from being immersed in the daily lives of white families carries the ability to demystify power relations by making evident how white society relies on racism and sexism, rather than superior ability or intellect, to gain advantage; however, Black women are not able to become total insiders due to being visibly marked as different. Being a marginalized insider creates a unique perspective, what Collins calls "the outsider-within," that allows them to see "the con-

tradictions between the dominant group's actions and ideologies" (Collins 1990, 12), thus giving a new angle on how the processes of oppression operate. Applying this perspective to the workplace, scholars have documented the production and reproduction of gendered and racialized workplace disparities through the "outsider-within" perspective of Black women police officers (Martin 1994) and Black women firefighters (Yoder and Aniakudo 1997).

In this article, I posit that FTMs' change in gender attribution, from women to men, can provide them with an outsider-within perspective on gendered workplace disparities. Unlike the Black women discussed by Collins, FTMs usually are not visibly marked by their outsider status, as continued use of testosterone typically allows for the development of a masculine social identity indistinguishable from "bio men."[3] However, while both stealth and open FTMs can become social insiders at work, their experience working as women prior to transition means they maintain an internalized sense of being outsiders to the gender schemas that advantage men. This internalized insider/outsider position allows some transmen to see clearly the advantages associated with being men at work while still maintaining a critical view to how this advantage operates and is reproduced and how it disadvantages women. I demonstrate that many of the respondents find themselves receiving more authority, respect, and reward when they gain social identities as men, even though their human capital does not change. This shift in treatment suggests that gender inequality in the workplace is not continually reproduced only because women make different education and workplace choices than men but rather because coworkers and employers often rely on gender stereotypes to evaluate men's and women's achievements and skills.

Method

I conducted in-depth interviews with 29 FTMs in the Southern California area from 2003 to 2005. My criteria for selection were that respondents were assigned female at birth and were currently living and working as men or open transmen. These selection criteria did exclude female-bodied individuals who identified as men but had had not publicly come out as men at work and FTMs who had not held any jobs as men since their transition, as they would not be able to comment about changes in their social interactions that were specific to the workplace. My sample is made up of 18 open FTMs and 11 stealth FTMs.

At the onset of my research, I was unaware of how I would be received as a non-transgender person doing research on transgender workplace experiences, as well as a woman interviewing men. I went into the study being extremely open about my research agenda and my political affiliations with feminist and transgender politics. I carried my openness about my intentions into my interviews, making clear at the beginning that I was happy to answer questions about my research intentions, the ultimate goal of my research, and personal questions about myself. Through this openness, and the acknowledgment that I was there to learn rather than to be an academic "expert," I feel that I gained a rapport with my respondents that bridged the "outsider/insider" divide (Merton 1972).

Generating a random sample of FTMs is not possible as there is not an even dispersal of FTMs throughout Southern California, nor are there transgender-specific neighborhoods from which to sample. I recruited interviewees from transgender activist groups, transgender listservers, and FTM support groups. In addition, I participated for two years in Southern California transgender community events, such as conferences and support group meetings. Attending these community events gave me an opportunity not only to demonstrate long-term political commitment to the transgender community but also to recruit respondents who might not be affiliated with FTM activist groups. All the interviews were conducted in the respondents' offices, in their homes, or at a local café or restaurant. The interviews ranged from one and a half to four hours. All interviews were audio recorded, transcribed, and coded.

Drawing on sociological research that reports long-standing gender differences between men and women in the workplace (Reskin and Hartmann 1986; Reskin and Roos 1990; Valian 1999; Williams 1995), I constructed my interview schedule to focus on possible differences between working as women and working as men. I first gathered a general employment history and then explored the decision to openly transition or to go stealth. At the end of the interviews, I posed the question, "Do you see any differences between working as a woman and working as a man?" All but a few of the respondents immediately answered yes and began to provide examples of both positive and negative differences. About half of the respondents also, at this time, introduced the idea of male privilege, addressing whether they felt they received a gender advantage from transitioning. If the concept of gender advantage was not brought up by respondents, I later introduced the concept of male privilege and then posed the question, saying, "Do you feel that you have received any male privilege at work?" The resulting answers from these two questions are the framework for this article.

In reporting the demographics of my respondents, I have opted to use pseudonyms and general categories of industry to avoid identifying my respondents. Respondents ranged in age from 20 to 48. Rather than attempting to identify when they began their gender transition, a start date often hard to pinpoint as many FTMs feel they have been personally transitioning since childhood or adolescence, I recorded how many years they had been working as men (meaning they were either hired as men or had openly transitioned from female to male and remained in the same job). The average time of working as a man was seven years. Regarding race and ethnicity, the sample was predominantly white (17), with 3 Asians, 1 African American, 3 Latinos, 3 mixed-race individuals, 1 Armenian American, and 1 Italian American. Responses about sexual identity fell into four main categories, heterosexual (9), bisexual (8), queer (6), and gay (3). The remaining 3 respondents identified their sexual identity as celibate/asexual, "dating women," and pansexual. Finally, in terms of region, the sample included a mixture of FTMs living in urban and suburban areas. (See Table 19.1 for sample characteristics.)

The experience of my respondents represents a part of the Southern California FTM community from 2003 to 2005. As Rubin (2003) has demonstrated, however, FTM communities vary greatly from city to city, meaning these findings may not be representative of the experiences of transmen in Austin, San Francisco, or Atlanta. In addition, California passed statewide gender identity protection for employees in 2003, meaning that the men in my study live in an environment in which they cannot legally be fired for being transgender (although most of my respondents said they would not wish to be a test case for this new law). This legal protection means that California transmen might have very different workplace experiences than men in states without gender identity protection. Finally, anecdotal evidence suggests that there are a large number of transgender individuals who transition and then sever all ties with the transgender community, something known as being "deep stealth." This lack of connection to the transgender community means they are excluded from research on transmen but that their experiences with the workplace may be very different than those of men who are still connected, even slightly, to the FTM community.

Transmen as Outsiders Within at Work

In undergoing a physical gender transition, transmen move from being socially gendered as women to being socially gendered as men (Dozier 2005). This shift in gender attribution gives them the potential to develop an "outsider-within" perspective (Collins 1986) on the sources of men's advantages in the workplace. In other words, while they may find themselves, as men, benefiting from the "patriarchal dividend" (Connell 1995, 79), not being "born into it" can make vis-

ible how gendered workplace disparities are created and maintained through interactions. Many of the respondents note that they can see clearly, once they become "just one of the guys," that men succeed in the workplace at higher rates than women because of gender stereotypes that privilege masculinity, not because they have greater skill or ability. For transmen who do see how these cultural beliefs about gender create gendered workplace disparities, there is an accompanying sense that these experiences are visible to them only because of the unique perspective they gain from undergoing a change in gender attribution. Exemplifying this, Preston reports about his views on gender differences at work posttransition: "I swear they let the guys get away with so much stuff! Lazy ass bastards get away with so much stuff and the women who are working hard, they just get ignored. . . . I am really aware of it. And that is one of the reasons that I feel like I have become much more of a feminist since transition. I am just so aware of the difference that my experience has shown me." Carl makes a similar point, discussing his awareness of blatant gender discrimination at a hardware/home construction store where he worked immediately after his transition: "Girls couldn't get their forklift license or it would take them forever. They wouldn't make as much money. It was so pathetic. I would have never seen it if I was a regular guy. I would have just not seen it. . . . I can see things differently because of my perspective. So in some ways I am a lot like a guy because I transitioned younger but still, you can't take away how I was raised for 18 years." These comments illustrate how the outsider-within perspective of many FTMs can translate into a critical perspective on men's advantages at work. The idea that a "regular guy," here meaning a bio man, would not be able to see how women were passed over in favor of men makes clear that for some FTMs, there is an ability to see how gender stereotypes can advantage men at work.

However, just as being a Black woman does not guarantee the development of a Black feminist perspective (Collins 1986), having this critical

■ TABLE 19.1
Sample Characteristics

Pseudonym	Age	Race/Ethnicity	Sexual Identity	Approximate Number of Years Working as Male	Industry	Status at Work
Aaron	28	Black/White	Queer	5	Semi-Professional	Open
Brian	42	White	Bisexual	14	Semi-Professional	Stealth
Carl	34	White	Heterosexual	16	Higher Professional	Stealth
Christopher	25	Asian	Pansexual	3	Semi-Professional	Open
Colin	31	White	Queer	1	Lower Professional	Open
Crispin	42	White	Heterosexual	2	Blue-Collar	Stealth
David	30	White	Bisexual	2	Higher Professional	Open
Douglas	38	White	Gay	5	Semi-Professional	Open
Elliott	20	White	Bisexual	1	Retail/Customer Service	Open
Henry	32	White	Gay	5	Lower Professional	Open
Jack	30	Latino	Queer	1	Semi-Professional	Open
Jake	45	White	Queer	9	Higher Professional	Open
Jason	48	White/Italian	Celibate	20	Retail/Customer Service	Stealth
Keith	42	Black	Heterosexual	1	Blue-Collar	Open
Kelly	24	White	Bisexual	2	Semi-Professional	Open
Ken	26	Asian/White	Queer	6 months	Semi-Professional	Open
Paul	44	White	Heterosexual	2	Semi-Professional	Open
Peter	24	White/Armenian	Heterosexual	4	Lower Professional	Stealth
Preston	39	White	Bisexual	2	Blue-Collar	Open
Riley	37	White	Dates women	1	Lower Professional	Open
Robert	23	Asian	Heterosexual	2	Retail/Customer Service	Stealth
Roger	45	White	Bisexual	22	Lower Professional	Stealth
Sam	33	Latino	Heterosexual	15	Blue-Collar	Stealth
Simon	42	White	Bisexual	2	Semi-Professional	Open
Stephen	35	White	Heterosexual	1	Retail/Customer Service	Stealth
Thomas	42	Latino	Queer	13	Higher Professional	Open
Trevor	35	White	Gay/Queer	6	Semi-Professional	Open
Wayne	44	White/Latino	Bisexual	22	Higher Professional	Stealth
Winston	40	White	Heterosexual	14	Higher Professional	Stealth

perspective on gender discrimination in the workplace is not inherent to the FTM experience. Respondents who had held no jobs prior to transition, who were highly gender ambiguous prior to transition, or who worked in short-term, high-turnover retail jobs, such as food service, found it harder to identify gender differences at work. FTMs who transitioned in their late teens often felt that they did not have enough experience working as women to comment on any possible differences between men and women at work. For example, Sam and Robert felt they could not comment on gender differences in the workplace because they had begun living as men at the age of 15 and, therefore, never had been employed as women. In addition, FTMs who reported being very "in-between" in their gender appearance, such as Wayne and Peter, found it hard to comment on gender differences at work, as even when they were hired as women, they were not always sure how customers and coworkers perceived them. They felt unable to speak about the experience of working as a woman because they were perceived either as androgynous or as men.

The kinds of occupations FTMs held prior to transition also play a role in whether they develop this outsider-within perspective at work. Transmen working in blue-collar jobs—jobs that are predominantly staffed by men—felt their experiences working in these jobs as females varied greatly from their experiences working as men. This held true even for those transmen who worked as females in blue-collar jobs in their early teens, showing that age of transition does not always determine the ability to see gender discrimination at work. FTMs working in the "women's professions" also saw a great shift in their treatment once they began working as men. FTMs who transitioned in their late teens and worked in marginal "teenage" jobs, such as fast food, however, often reported little sense of change posttransition, as they felt that most employees were doing the same jobs regardless of gender. As a gendered division of labor often does exist in fast food jobs (Leidner 1993), it may be that these respondents worked in atypical settings,

or that they were assigned "men's jobs" because of their masculine appearance.

Transmen in higher professional jobs, too, reported less change in their experiences post-transition, as many of them felt that their workplaces guarded against gender-biased treatment as part of an ethic of professionalism. The experience of these professional respondents obviously runs counter to the large body of scholarly research that documents gender inequality in fields such as academia (Valian 1999), law firms (Pierce 1995), and corporations (Martin 1992). Not having an outsider-within perspective, then, may be unique to these particular transmen, not the result of working in a professional occupation.

Thus, transitioning from female to male can provide individuals with an outsider-within perspective on gender discrimination in the workplace. However, this perspective can be limited by the age of transition, appearance, and type of occupation. In addition, as I will discuss at the end of this article, even when the advantages of the patriarchal dividend are seen clearly, many transmen do not benefit from them. In the next section, I will explore in what ways FTMs who expressed having this outsider-within perspective saw their skills and abilities perceived more positively as men. Then, I will explore why not all of my respondents received a gender advantage from transitioning.

Transition and Workplace Gender Advantages[4]

A large body of evidence shows that the performance of workers is evaluated differently depending on gender. Men, particularly white men, are viewed as more competent than women workers (Olian, Schwab, and Haberfeld 1988; Valian 1999). When men succeed, their success is seen as stemming from their abilities while women's success often is attributed to luck (Valian 1999). Men are rewarded more than women for offering ideas and opinions and for taking on leadership roles in group settings (Butler and Geis 1990; Valian

1999). Based on these findings, it would be expected that stealth transmen would see a positive difference in their workplace experience once they have made the transition from female to male, as they enter new jobs as just one of the guys. Open FTMs, on the other hand, might find themselves denied access to these privileges, as they remain in the same jobs in which they were hired as women. Challenging these expectations, two-thirds of my respondents, both open and stealth, report receiving some type of posttransition advantage at work. These advantages fell into four main categories: gaining competency and authority, gaining respect and recognition for hard work, gaining "body privilege," and gaining economic opportunities and status.

Authority and Competency

Illustrating the authority gap that exists between men and women workers (Elliott and Smith 2004; Padavic and Reskin 2002), several of my interviewees reported receiving more respect for their thoughts and opinions posttransition. For example, Henry, who is stealth in a professional workplace, says of his experiences, "I'm right a lot more now. . . . Even with folks I am out to [as a trans-sexual], there is a sense that I know what I am talking about." Roger, who openly transitioned in a retail environment in the 1980s, discussed customers' assumptions that as a man, he knew more than his boss, who was a woman: "People would come in and they would go straight to me. They would pass her and go straight to me because obviously, as a male, I knew [sarcasm]. And so we would play mind games with them. . . . They would come up and ask me a question, and then I would go over to her and ask her the same question, she would tell me the answer, and I would go back to the customer and tell the customer the answer." Revealing how entrenched these stereotypes about masculinity and authority are, Roger added that none of the customers ever recognized the sarcasm behind his actions. Demonstrating how white men's opinions are seen to carry more

authority, Trevor discusses how, posttransition, his ideas are now taken more seriously in group situations—often to the detriment of his women coworkers: "In a professional workshop or a conference kind of setting, a woman would make a comment or an observation and be overlooked and be dissed essentially. I would raise my hand and make the same point in a way that I am trying to reinforce her and it would be like [directed at me], 'That's an excellent point!' I saw this shit in undergrad. So it is not like this was a surprise to me. But it was disconcerting to have happen to me." These last two quotes exemplify the outsider-within experience: Both men are aware of having more authority simply because of being men, an authority that happens at the expense of women coworkers.

Looking at the issue of authority in the women's professions, Paul, who openly transitioned in the field of secondary education, reports a sense of having increased authority as one of the few men in his work environment:

I did notice [at] some of the meetings I'm required to attend, like school district or parent involvement [meetings], you have lots of women there. And now I feel like there are [many times], mysteriously enough, when I'm picked [to speak]. . . . I think, well, why me, when nobody else has to go to the microphone and talk about their stuff? That I did notice and that [had] never happened before. I mean there was this meeting . . . a little while ago about domestic violence where I appeared to be the only male person between these 30, 40 women and, of course, then everybody wants to hear from me.

Rather than being alienated by his gender tokenism, as women often are in predominantly male workplaces (Byrd 1999), he is asked to express his opinions and is valued for being the "male" voice at the meetings, a common situation for men in "women's professions" (Williams 1995). The lack of interest paid to him as a woman in the same job demonstrates how women in predominantly female workspaces can encourage their coworkers who are men to take more authority and space in these careers, a situation that can lead to the promotion of men in women's professions (Williams 1995).

Transmen also report a positive change in the evaluation of their abilities and competencies after transition. Thomas, an attorney, relates an episode in which an attorney who worked for an associated law firm commended his boss for firing Susan, here a pseudonym for his female name, because she was incompetent—adding that the "new guy" [i.e., Thomas] was "just delightful." The attorney did not realize that Susan and "the new guy" were the same person with the same abilities, education, and experience. This anecdote is a glaring example of how men are evaluated as more competent than women even when they do the same job in careers that are stereotyped requiring "masculine" skills such as rationality (Pierce 1995; Valian 1999). Stephen, who is stealth in a predominantly male customer-service job, reports, "For some reason just because [the men I work with] assume I have a dick, [they assume] I am going to get the job done right, where, you know, they have to second guess that when you're a woman. They look at [women] like well, you can't handle this because you know, you don't have the same mentality that we [men] do, so there's this sense of panic . . . and if you are a guy, it's just like, oh, you can handle it." Keith, who openly transitioned in a male-dominated blue-collar job, reports no longer having to "cuddle after sex," meaning that he has been able to drop the emotional labor of niceness women often have to employ to when giving orders at work. Showing how perceptions of behavior can change with transition, Trevor reports, "I think my ideas are taken more seriously [as a man]. I had good leadership skills leaving college and um . . . I think that those work well for me now. . . . Because I'm male, they work better for me. I was 'assertive' before. Now I'm 'take charge.' " Again, while his behavior has not changed, his shift in gender attribution translates into a different kind of evaluation. As a man, being assertive is consistent with gendered expectations for men, meaning his same leadership

skills have more worth in the workplace because of his transition. His experience underscores how women who take on leadership roles are evaluated negatively, particularly if their leadership style is perceived as assertive, while men are rewarded for being aggressive leaders (Butler and Geis 1990; Valian 1999).[5]

This change in authority is noticeable only because FTMs often have experienced the reverse: being thought, on the basis of gender alone, to be less competent workers who receive less authority from employers and coworkers. This sense of a shift in authority and perceived competence was particularly marked for FTMs who had worked in blue-collar occupations as women. These transmen report that the stereotype of women's incompetence often translated into difficulty in finding and maintaining employment. For example, Crispin, who had worked as a female construction worker, reports being written up by supervisors for every small infraction, a practice Yoder and Aniakudo (1997, 330) refer to as "pencil whipping." Crispin recounts, "One time I had a field supervisor confront me about simple things, like not dotting i's and using the wrong color ink. . . . Anything he could do, he was just constantly on me. . . . I ended up just leaving." Paul, who was a female truck driver, recounts, "Like they would tell [me], 'Well we never had a female driver. I don't know if this works out.' Blatantly telling you this. And then [I had] to go, 'Well let's see. Let's give it a chance, give it a try. I'll do this three days for free and you see and if it's not working out, well then that's fine and if it works out, maybe you want to reconsider [not hiring me].' " To prove her competency, she ended up working for free, hoping that she would eventually be hired.

Stephen, who was a female forklift operator, described the resistance women operators faced from men when it came to safety precautions for loading pallets:

[The men] would spot each other, which meant that they would have two guys that would close down the aisle . . . so that no one could go on that aisle while you know you were up there [with your forklift and load] . . . and they wouldn't spot you if you were a female. If you were a guy . . . they got the red vests and the safety cones out and it's like you know—the only thing they didn't have were those little flashlights for the jets. It would be like God or somebody responding. I would actually have to go around and gather all the dykes from receiving to come out and help and spot me. And I can't tell you how many times I nearly ran over a kid. It was maddening and it was always because [of] gender.

Thus, respondents described situations of being ignored, passed over, purposefully put in harm's way, and assumed to be incompetent when they were working as women. However, these same individuals, as men, find themselves with more authority and with their ideas, abilities, and attributes evaluated more positively in the workforce.

Respect and Recognition

Related to authority and competency is the issue of how much reward workers get for their workplace contributions. According to the transmen I interviewed, an increase in recognition for hard work was one of the positive changes associated with working as a man. Looking at these stories of gaining reward and respect, Preston, who transitioned openly and remained at his blue-collar job, reports that as a female crew supervisor, she was frequently short staffed and unable to access necessary resources yet expected to still carry out the job competently. However, after his transition, he suddenly found himself receiving all the support and materials he required:

> I was not asked to do anything different [after transition]. But the work I did do was made easier for me. [Before transition] there [were] periods of time when I would be told, "Well, I don't have anyone to send over there with you." We were one or two people short of a crew or the trucks weren't available. Or they would send me people who weren't trained. And it got to the point where it was like, why do I have to fight about this? If you don't want your freight,

you don't get your freight. And, I swear it was like from one day to the next of me transitioning [to male], I need this, this is what I want and [snaps his fingers]. I have not had to fight about anything.

He adds about his experience, "The last three [performance] reviews that I have had have been the absolute highest that I have ever had. New management team. Me not doing anything different than I ever had. I even went part-time." This comment shows that even though he openly transitioned and remained in the same job, he ultimately finds himself rewarded for doing less work and having to fight less for getting what he needs to effectively do his job. In addition, as a man, he received more positive reviews for his work, demonstrating how men and women can be evaluated differently when doing the same work.

As with authority and competence, this sense of gaining recognition for hard work was particularly noticeable for transmen who had worked as women in blue-collar occupations in which they were the gender minority. This finding is not unexpected, as women are also more likely to be judged negatively when they are in the minority in the workplace, as their statistical minority status seems to suggest that women are unsuited for the job (Valian 1999). For example, Preston, who had spent time in the ROTC as a female cadet, reported feeling that no matter how hard she worked, her achievements were passed over by her men superiors: "On everything that I did, I was the highest. I was the highest-ranking female during the time I was there. . . . I was the most decorated person in ROTC. I had more ribbons, I had more medals, in ROTC and in school. I didn't get anything for that. There was an award every year called Superior Cadet, and guys got it during the time I was there who didn't do nearly what I did. It was those kinds of things [that got to me]." She entered a blue-collar occupation after ROTC and also felt that her workplace contributions, like designing training programs for the staff, were invisible and went unrewarded.

Talking about gender discrimination he faced as a female construction worker, Crispin reports,

I worked really hard. . . . I had to find myself not sitting ever and taking breaks or lunches because I felt like I had to work more to show my worth. And though I did do that and I produced typically more than three males put together—and that is really a statistic—what it would come down to a lot of times was, "You're single. You don't have a family." That is what they told me. "I've got guys here who have families.". . . And even though my production quality [was high], and the customer was extremely happy with my work . . . I was passed over lots of times. They said it was because I was single and I didn't have a family and they felt bad because they didn't want Joe Blow to lose his job because he had three kids at home. And because I was intelligent and my qualities were very vast, they said, "You can just go get a job anywhere." Which wasn't always the case. A lot of people were—it was still a boy's world and some people were just like, uh-uh, there aren't going to be any women on my job site. And it would be months . . . before I would find gainful employment again.

While she reports eventually winning over many men who did not want women on the worksite, being female excluded her from workplace social interactions, such as camping trips, designed to strengthen male bonding.

These quotes illustrate the hardships that women working in blue-collar jobs often face at work: being passed over for hiring and promotions in favor of less productive male coworkers, having their hard work go unrecognized, and not being completely accepted.[6] Having this experience of being women in an occupation or industry composed mostly of men can create, then, a heightened appreciation of gaining reward and recognition for job performance as men.

Another form of reward that some transmen report receiving posttransition is a type of bodily respect in the form of being freed from unwanted sexual advances or inquiries about sexuality. As Brian recounts about his experience of working as a waitress, that customer service involved "having my boobs grabbed, being called 'honey' and 'babe.' " He noted that as a man, he no longer has to worry about these types of experiences. Jason reported being constantly harassed by men bosses for sexual favors in the past. He added, "When I transitioned . . . it was like a relief! [laughs] . . . I swear to God! I am not saying I was beautiful or sexy but I was always attracting something." He felt that becoming a man meant more personal space and less sexual harassment. Finally, Stephen and Henry reported being "obvious dykes," here meaning visibly masculine women, and added that in blue-collar jobs, they encountered sexualized comments, as well as invasive personal questions about sexuality, from men uncomfortable with their gender presentation, experiences they no longer face posttransition. Transitioning for stealth FTMs can bring with it physical autonomy and respect, as men workers, in general, encounter less touching, groping, and sexualized comments at work than women. Open FTMs, however, are not as able to access this type of privilege, as coworkers often ask invasive questions about their genitals and sexual practices.

Economic Gains

As the last two sections have shown, FTMs can find themselves gaining in authority, respect, and reward in the workplace posttransition. Several FTMs who are stealth also reported a sense that transition had brought with it economic opportunities that would not have been available to them as women, particularly as masculine women.

Carl, who owns his own company, asserts that he could not have followed the same career trajectory if he had not transitioned:

I have this company that I built, and I have people following me; they trust me, they believe in me, they respect me. There is no way I could have done that as a woman. And I will tell you that as just a fact. That when it comes to business and work, higher levels of management, it is different being a man. I have been on both sides [as a man and a woman], younger obviously, but I will tell you, man, I could have never done what I did [as a female]. You can take the same personality and it wouldn't have happened. I would have never made it.

While he acknowledges that women can be and are business entrepreneurs, he has a sense that his business partners would not have taken his business venture idea seriously if he were a woman or that he might not have had access to the type of social networks that made his business venture possible. Henry feels that he would not have reached the same level in his professional job if he were a woman because he had a nonnormative gender appearance:

> If I was a gender normative woman, probably. But no, as an obvious dyke, I don't think so . . . which is weird to say but I think it's true. It is interesting because I am really aware of having this job that I would not have had if I hadn't transitioned. And [gender expression] was always an issue for me. I wanted to go to law school but I couldn't do it. I couldn't wear the skirts and things females have to wear to practice law. I wouldn't dress in that drag. And so it was very clear that there was a limit to where I was going to go professionally because I was not willing to dress that part. Now I can dress the part and it's not an issue. It's not putting on drag; it's not an issue. I don't love putting on a tie, but I can do it. So this world is open to me that would not have been before just because of clothes. But very little has changed in some ways. I look very different but I still have all the same skills and all the same general thought processes. That is intense for me to consider.

As this response shows, Henry is aware that as an "obvious dyke," meaning here a masculine-appearing woman, he would have the same skills and education level he currently has, but those skills would be devalued due to his nonnormative appearance. Thus, he avoided professional careers that would require a traditionally feminine appearance. As a man, however, he is able to wear clothes similar to those he wore as an "obvious dyke," but they are now considered gender appropriate. Thus, through transitioning, he gains the right to wear men's clothes, which helps him in accessing a professional job.

Wayne also recounts negative workplace experiences in the years prior to his transition due to being extremely ambiguous or "gender blending" (Devor 1987) in his appearance. Working at a restaurant in his early teens, he had the following experience:

> The woman who hired me said, "I will hire you only on the condition that you don't ever come in the front because you make the people uncomfortable." 'Cause we had to wear like these uniforms or something and when I would put the uniform on, she would say, "That makes you look like a guy." But she knew I was not a guy because of my name that she had on the application. She said, "You make the customers uncomfortable." And a couple of times it got really busy, and I would have to come in the front or whatever, and I remember one time she found out about it and she said, "I don't care how busy it gets, you don't get to come up front." She said I'd make people lose their appetite.

Once he began hormones and gained a social identity as a man, he found that his work and school experiences became much more positive. He went on to earn a doctoral degree and become a successful professional, an economic opportunity he did not think would be available had he remained highly gender ambiguous.

In my sample, the transmen who openly transitioned faced a different situation in terms of economic gains. While there is an "urban legend" that FTMs immediately are awarded some kind of "male privilege" post-transition (Dozier 2005), I did not find that in my interviews. Reflecting this common belief, however, Trevor and Jake both recount that women colleagues told them, when learning of their transition plans, that they would probably be promoted because they were becoming white men. While both men discounted these comments, both were promoted relatively soon after their transitions. Rather than seeing this as evidence of male privilege, both respondents felt that their promotions were related to their job performance, which, to make clear, is not a point I am questioning. Yet these promotions show that while these two men are not benefiting undeservedly from transition, they also are not disadvantaged.[7] Thus, among the men I interviewed, it is common for both stealth and open FTMs to find their abilities and skills more valued posttransition, showing that human capital can be valued differently depending on the gender of the employee.

Is It Privilege or Something Else?

While these reported increases in competency and authority make visible the "gender schemas" (Valian 1999) that often underlie the evaluation of workers, it is possible that the increases in authority might have a spurious connection to gender transitions. Some transmen enter a different work field after transition, so the observed change might be in the type of occupation they enter rather than a gender-based change. In addition, many transmen seek graduate or postgraduate degrees posttransition, and higher education degrees afford more authority in the workplace. As Table 19.2 shows, of the transmen I interviewed, many had higher degrees working as men than they did when they worked as women. For some, this is due to transitioning while in college and thus attaining their bachelor's degrees as men. For others, gender transitions seem to be accompanied by a desire to return to school for a higher degree, as evidenced by the increase in master's degrees in the table.

A change in educational attainment does contribute to getting better jobs with increased authority, as men benefit more from increased human capital in the form of educational attainment (Valian 1999). But again, this is an additive effect, as higher education results in greater advantages for men than for women. In addition, gender advantage alone also is apparent in these experiences of increased authority, as transmen report seeing an increase in others' perceptions of their competency outside of the workplace where their education level is unknown. For example, Henry, who found he was "right a lot more" at work, also notes that in daily, nonworkplace interactions, he is assumed, as a man, to know what he is talking about and does not have to provide evidence to support his opinions. Demonstrating a similar experience, Crispin, who had many years of experience working in construction as a woman, relates the following story:

> I used to jump into [situations as a woman]. Like at Home Depot, I would hear . . . [men] be so confused, and I would just step over there and say, "Sir, I work in construction and if you don't mind me helping you." And they would be like, "Yeah, yeah, yeah" [i.e., dismissive]. But now I go [as a man] and I've got men and women asking me things and saying, "Thank you so much," like now I have a brain in my head! And I like that a lot because it was just kind of like, "Yeah, whatever." It's really nice.

His experience at Home Depot shows that as a man, he is rewarded for displaying the same knowledge about construction—knowledge gendered as masculine—that he was sanctioned for offering when he was perceived as a woman. As a further example of this increased authority

■ **TABLE 19.2**
Highest Level of Education Attained

Highest Degree Level	Stealth FTMs		Open FTMs	
	As Female	As Male	As Female	As Male
High school/GED	7	2	3	2
Associate's degree	2	3	3	3
Bachelor's degree	2	4	7	4
Master's degree	0	1	2	4
Ph.D.	0	1	1	2
J.D.	0	0	1	2
Other	0	0	1	1
Total	11	11	18	18

Note: FTMs = female-to-male transsexuals.

outside of the workplace, several FTMs report a difference in their treatment at the auto shop, as they are not assumed to be easy targets for unnecessary services (though this comes with an added expectation that they will know a great deal about cars). While some transmen report that their "feminine knowledge," such as how to size baby clothes in stores, is discounted when they gain social identities as men, this new recognition of "masculine knowledge" seems to command more social authority than prior feminine knowledge in many cases. These stories show that some transmen gain authority both in and out of the workplace. These findings lend credence to the argument that men can gain a gender advantage, in the form of authority, reward, and respect.

Barriers to Workplace Gender Advantages

Having examined the accounts of transmen who feel that they received increased authority, reward, and recognition from becoming men at work, I will now discuss some of the limitations to accessing workplace gender advantages. About one-third of my sample felt that they did not receive any gender advantage from transition. FTMs who had only recently begun transition or who had transitioned without using hormones ("no ho") all reported seeing little change in their workplace treatment. This group of respondents felt that they were still seen as women by most of their coworkers, evidenced by continual slippage into feminine pronouns, and thus were not treated in accordance with other men in the workplace. Other transmen in this group felt they lacked authority because they were young or looked extremely young after transition. This youthful appearance often is an effect of the beginning stages of transition. FTMs usually begin to pass as men before they start taking testosterone. Successful passing is done via appearance cues, such as hairstyles, clothes, and mannerisms. However, without facial hair or visible stubble, FTMs often are taken to be young boys, a mistake that intensifies with the onset of

hormone therapy and the development of peach fuzz that marks the beginning of facial hair growth. Reflecting on how this youthful appearance, which can last several years depending on the effects of hormone therapy, affected his work experience immediately after transition, Thomas reports, "I went from looking 30 to looking 13. People thought I was a new lawyer so I would get treated like I didn't know what was going on." Other FTMs recount being asked if they were interns, or if they were visiting a parent at their workplace, all comments that underscore a lack of authority. This lack of authority associated with looking youthful, however, is a time-bounded effect, as most FTMs on hormones eventually "age into" their male appearance, suggesting that many of these transmen may have the ability to access some gender advantages at some point in their careers.

Body structure was another characteristic some FTMs felt limited their access to increased authority and prestige at work. While testosterone creates an appearance indistinguishable from bio men for many transmen, it does not increase height. Being more than 6 feet tall is part of the cultural construction for successful, hegemonic masculinity. However, several men I interviewed were between 5'1" and 5'5", something they felt put them at a disadvantage in relation to other men in their workplaces. Winston, who managed a professional work staff who knew him only as a man, felt that his authority was harder to establish at work because he was short. Being smaller than all of his male employees meant that he was always being looked down on, even when giving orders. Kelly, who worked in special education, felt his height affected the jobs he was assigned: "Some of the boys, especially if they are really aggressive, they do much better with males that are bigger than they are. So I work with the little kids because I am short. I don't get as good of results if I work with [older kids]; a lot of times they are taller than I am." Being a short man, he felt it was harder to establish authority with older boys. These experiences demonstrate the importance of bringing the body back into discussions of masculinity and gender advantage, as being short can constrain men's benefits from the "patriarchal dividend" (Connell 1995).

In addition to height, race/ethnicity can negatively affect FTMs' workplace experience post-transition. My data suggest that the experiences of FTMs of color is markedly different than that of their white counterparts, as they are becoming not just men but Black men, Latino men, or Asian men, categories that carry their own stereotypes. Christopher felt that he was denied any gender advantage at work not only because he was shorter than all of his men colleagues but also because he was viewed as passive, a stereotype of Asian men (Espiritu 1997). "To the wide world of America, I look like a passive Asian guy. That is what they think when they see me. Oh Asian? Oh passive. . . . People have this impression that Asian guys aren't macho and therefore they aren't really male. Or they are not as male as [a white guy]." Keith articulated how his social interactions changed with his change in gender attribution in this way: "I went from being an obnoxious Black woman to a scary Black man." He felt that he has to be careful expressing anger and frustration at work (and outside of work) because now that he is a Black man, his anger is viewed as more threatening by whites. Reflecting stereotypes that conflate African Americans with criminals, he also notes that in his law enforcement classes, he was continually asked to play the suspect in training exercises. Aaron, one of the only racial minorities at his workplace, also felt that looking like a Black man negatively affected his workplace interactions. He told stories about supervisors repeatedly telling him he was threatening. When he expressed frustration during a staff meeting about a new policy, he was written up for rolling his eyes in an "aggressive" manner. The choice of words such as "threatening" and "aggressive," words often used to describe Black men (Ferguson 2000), suggests that racial identity and stereotypes about Black men were playing a role in his workplace treatment. Examining how race/ethnicity and appearance intersect with gender, then, illustrates that masculinity is not a fixed construct that automatically generated privilege (Connell 1995), but that white, tall men often see greater returns from the patriarchal dividend than short men, young men and men of color.

Conclusion

Sociological studies have documented that the workplace is not a gender-neutral site that equitably rewards workers based on their individual merits (Acker 1990; Martin 2003; Valian 1999, Williams 1995); rather "it is a central site for the creation and reproduction of gender differences and gender inequality" (Williams 1995, 15). Men receive greater workplace advantages than women because of cultural beliefs that associate masculinity with authority, prestige, and instrumentality (Martin 2003; Padavic and Reskin 2002; Rhode 1997; Williams 1995)—characteristics often used to describe ideal "leaders" and "managers" (Valian 1999). Stereotypes about femininity as expressive and emotional, on the other hand, disadvantage women, as they are assumed to be less capable and less likely to succeed than men with equal (or often lesser) qualifications (Valian 1999). These cultural beliefs about gender difference are embedded in workplace structures and interactions, as workers and employers bring gender stereotypes with them to the workplace and, in turn, use these stereotypes to make decisions about hiring, promotions, and rewards (Acker 1990; Martin 2003; Williams 1995). This cultural reproduction of gendered workplace disparities is difficult to disrupt, however, as it operates on the level of ideology and thus is rendered invisible (Martin 2003; Valian 1999; Williams 1995).

In this article, I have suggested that the "outsider-within" (Collins 1986) perspective of many FTMs can offer a more complex understanding of these invisible interactional processes that help maintain gendered workplace disparities. Transmen are in the unique position of having been socially gendered as both women and men (Dozier

2005). Their workplace experiences, then, can make the underpinnings of gender discrimination visible, as well as illuminate the sources of men's workplace advantages. When FTMs undergo a change in gender attribution, their workplace treatment often varies greatly—even when they continue to interact with coworkers who knew them previously as women. Some posttransition FTMs, both stealth and open, find that their coworkers, employers, and customers attribute more authority, respect, and prestige to them. Their experiences make glaringly visible the process through which gender inequality is actively created in informal workplace interactions. These informal workplace interactions, in turn, produce and reproduce structural disadvantages for women, such as the glass ceiling (Valian 1999), and structural advantages for men, such as the glass escalator (Williams 1995).

However, as I have suggested, not all of my respondents gain authority and prestige with transition. FTMs who are white and tall received far more benefits posttransition than short FTMs or FTMs of color. This demonstrates that while hegemonic masculinity is defined against femininity, it is also measured against subordinated forms of masculinity (Connell 1995; Messner 1997). These findings demonstrate the need for using an intersectional approach that takes into consideration the ways in which there are cross-cutting relations of power (Calasanti and Slevin 2001; Collins 1990; Crenshaw 1989), as advantage in the workplace is not equally accessible for all men. Further research on FTMs of color can help develop a clearer understanding of the role race plays in the distribution of gendered workplace rewards and advantages.[8]

The experiences of this small group of transmen offer a challenge to rationalizations of workplace inequality. The study provides counterevidence for human capital theories: FTMs who find themselves receiving the benefits associated with being men at work have the same skills and abilities they had as women workers. These skills and abilities, however, are suddenly viewed more positively due to this change in gender attribution. FTMs who may have been labeled "bossy" as women become "go-getting" men who seem more qualified for managerial positions. While FTMs may not benefit at equal levels to bio men, many of them do find themselves receiving an advantage to women in the workplace they did not have prior to transition. This study also challenges gender socialization theories that account for inequality in the workplace. Although all of my respondents were subjected to gender socialization as girls, this background did not impede their success as men. Instead, by undergoing a change in gender attribution, transmen can find that the same behavior, attitudes, or abilities they had as females bring them more reward as men. This shift in treatment suggests that gender inequality in the workplace is not continually reproduced only because women make different education and workplace choices than men but rather because coworkers and employers often rely on gender stereotypes to evaluate men and women's achievements and skills.

It could be argued that because FTMs must overcome so many barriers and obstacles to finally gain a male social identity, they might be likely to overreport positive experiences as a way to shore up their right to be a man. However, I have reasons to doubt that my respondents exaggerated the benefits of being men. Transmen who did find themselves receiving a workplace advantage posttransition were aware that this new conceptualization of their skills and abilities was an arbitrary result of a shift in their gender attribution. This knowledge often undermined their sense of themselves as good workers, making them continually second-guess the motivations behind any rewards they receive. In addition, many transmen I interviewed expressed anger and resentment that their increases in authority, respect, and recognition came at the expense of women colleagues. It is important to keep in mind, then, that while many FTMs can identify privileges associated with being men, they often retain a critical eye to how changes in their treatment as men can disadvantage women.

This critical eye, or "outsider-within" (Collins 1986) perspective, has implications for social change in the workplace. For gender equity at work to be achieved, men must take an active role in challenging the subordination of women (Acker 1990; Martin 2003; Rhode 1997; Valian 1999; Williams 1995). However, bio men often cannot see how women are disadvantaged due to their structural privilege (Rhode 1997; Valian 1999). Even when they are aware that men as a group benefit from assumptions about masculinity, men typically still "credit their successes to their competence" (Valian 1999, 284) rather than to gender stereotypes. For many transmen, seeing how they stand to benefit at work to the detriment of women workers creates a sense of increased responsibility to challenge the gender discrimination they can see so clearly. This challenge can take many different forms. For some, it is speaking out when men make derogatory comments about women. For others, it means speaking out about gender discrimination at work or challenging supervisors to promote women who are equally qualified as men. These challenges demonstrate that some transmen are able, at times, to translate their position as social insiders into an educational role, thus working to give women more reward and recognition at these specific work sites. The success of these strategies illustrates that men have the power to challenge workplace gender discrimination and suggests that bio men can learn gender equity strategies from the outsider-within at work.

Notes

1. Throughout this article, I endeavor to use the terms "women" and "men" rather than "male" and "female" to avoid reifying biological categories. It is important to note, though, that while my respondents were all born with female bodies, many of them never identified as women but rather thought of themselves as always men, or as "not women." During their time as female workers, however, they did have social identities as women, as coworkers and employers often were unaware of their personal gender identities. It is this social identity that I am referencing when I refer to them as "working as women," as I am discussing their social interactions in the workplace. In referring to their specific work experiences, however, I use "female" to demonstrate their understanding of their work history. I also do continue to use "female to male" when describing the physical transition process, as this is the most common term employed in the transgender community.

2. I use "stealth," a transgender community term, if the respondent's previous life as female was not known at work. It is important to note that this term is not analogous with "being in the closet," because stealth female-to-male transsexuals (FTMs) do not have "secret" lives as women outside of working as men. It is used to describe two different workplace choices, not offer a value judgment about these choices.

3. "Bio" man is a term used by my respondents to mean individuals who are biologically male and live socially as men throughout their lives. It is juxtaposed with "transman" or "FTM."

4. A note on pronoun usage: This article draws from my respondents' experiences working as both women and men. While they now live as men, I use feminine pronouns to refer to their female work histories.

5. This change in how behavior is evaluated can also be negative. Some transmen felt that assertive communication styles they actively fostered to empower themselves as lesbians and feminists had to be unlearned after transition. Because they were suddenly given more space to speak as men, they felt they had to censor themselves or they would be seen as "bossy white men" who talked over women and people of color. These findings are similar to those reported by Dozier (2005).

6. It is important to note that not all FTMs who worked blue-collar jobs as women had this type of experience. One respondent felt that he was able to fit in, as a butch, as "just one of the guys." However, he also did not feel he had an outsider-within perspective because of this experience.

7. Open transitions are not without problems, however. Crispin, a construction worker, found his contract mysteriously not renewed after his announcement. However, he acknowledged that he had many problems with his employers prior to his announcement and had also recently filed a discrimination suit. Aaron, who announced his transition at a

small, medical site, left after a few months as he felt that his employer was trying to force him out. He found another job in which he was out as a transman. Crispin unsuccessfully attempted to find work in construction as an out transman. He was later hired, stealth, at a construction job.

8. Sexual identity also is an important aspect of an intersectional analysis. In my study, however, queer and gay transmen worked either in lesbian, gay, bisexual, transgender work sites, or were not out at work. Therefore, it was not possible to examine how being gay or queer affected their workplace experiences.

References

Acker, Joan. 1990. Hierarchies, jobs, bodies: A theory of gendered organizations. *Gender & Society* 4: 139–58.

Butler, D., and F. L. Geis. 1990. Nonverbal affect responses to male and female leaders: Implications for leadership evaluation. *Journal of Personality and Social Psychology* 58:48–59.

Byrd, Barbara. 1999. Women in carpentry apprenticeship: A case study. *Labor Studies Journal* 24 (3): 3–22.

Calasanti, Toni M., and Kathleen F. Slevin. 2001. *Gender, social inequalities, and aging*. Walnut Creek, CA: Alta Mira Press.

Collins, Patricia Hill. 1986. Learning from the outsider within: The sociological significance of Black feminist thought. *Social Problems* 33 (6): S14–S31.

————. 1990. *Black feminist thought*. New York: Routledge.

Connell, Robert. 1995. *Masculinities*. Berkeley: University of California Press.

Crenshaw, Kimberle. 1989. Demarginalizing the intersection of race and sex: A Black feminist critique of antidiscrimination doctrine, feminist theory, and antiracist politics. *University of Chicago Legal Forum* 1989: 139–67.

Devor, Holly. 1987. Gender blending females: Women and sometimes men. *American Behavioral Scientist* 31 (1): 12–40.

Dozier, Raine. 2005. Beards, breasts, and bodies: Doing sex in a gendered world. *Gender & Society* 19: 297–316.

Elliott, James R., and Ryan A. Smith. 2004. Race, gender, and workplace power. *American Sociological Review* 69: 365–86.

Espiritu, Yen. 1997. *Asian American women and men*. Thousand Oaks, CA: Sage.

Ferguson, Ann Arnett. 2000. *Bad boys: Public schools in the making of Black masculinity*. Ann Arbor: University of Michigan Press.

Leidner, Robin. 1993. *Fast food, fast talk: Service work and the routinization of everyday life*. Berkeley: University of California Press.

Martin, Patricia Yancy. 1992. Gender, interaction, and inequality in organizations. In *Gender, interaction, and inequality*, edited by Cecelia L. Ridgeway. New York: Springer-Verlag.

————. 2003. "Said and done" versus "saying and doing": Gendering practices, practicing gender at work. *Gender & Society* 17: 342–66.

Martin, Susan. 1994. "Outsiders-within" the station house: The impact of race and gender on Black women police officers. *Social Problems* 41: 383–400.

Merton, Robert. 1972. Insiders and outsiders: A chapter in the sociology of knowledge. *American Journal of Sociology* 78 (1): 9–47

Messner, Michael. 1997. *The politics of masculinities: Men in movements*. Thousand Oaks, CA: Sage.

Miller, Laura. 1997. Not just weapons of the weak: Gender harassment as a form of protest for army men. *Social Psychology Quarterly* 60 (1): 32–51.

Olian, J. D., D. P. Schwab, and Y. Haberfeld. 1988. The impact of applicant gender compared to qualifications on hiring recommendations: A meta-analysis of experimental studies. *Organizational Behavior and Human Decision Processes* 41: 180–95.

Padavic, Irene, and Barbara Reskin. 2002. *Women and men at work*. 2d ed. Thousand Oaks, CA: Pine Forge Press.

Pierce, Jennifer. 1995. *Gender trials: Emotional lives in contemporary law firms*. Berkeley: University of California Press.

Reskin, Barbara, and Heidi Hartmann. 1986. *Women's work, men's work: Sex segregation on the job*. Washington, DC: National Academic Press.

Reskin, Barbara, and Patricia Roos. 1990. *Job queues, gender queues*. Philadelphia: Temple University Press.

Rhode, Deborah L. 1997. *Speaking of sex: The denial of*

gender inequality. Cambridge, MA: Harvard University Press.

Rubin, Henry. 2003. *Self-made men: Identity and embodiment among transsexual men*. Nashville, TN: Vanderbilt University Press.

Valian, Virginia. 1999. *Why so slow? The advancement of women*. Cambridge, MA: MIT Press.

West, Candace, and Don Zimmerman. 1987. Doing gender. *Gender & Society* 1: 13–37.

Williams, Christine. 1995. *Still a man's world: Men who do "women's" work*. Berkeley: University of California Press.

Yoder, Janice, and Patricia Aniakudo. 1997. Outsider within the firehouse: Subordination and difference in the social interactions of African American women firefighters. *Gender & Society* 11: 324–41.

PART FIVE

Men and Health

Why did the gap between male and female life expectancy increase from two years in 1900 to nearly eight years today? Why do men suffer heart attacks and ulcers at such a consistently higher rate than women do? Why are auto insurance rates so much higher for young males than for females of the same age? Are mentally and emotionally "healthy" males those who conform more closely to the dominant cultural prescriptions for masculinity, or those who resist those dominant ideals?

The articles in this section examine the "embodiment" of masculinity, the ways in which men's mental health and physical health expresses and reproduces the definitions of masculinity we have ingested in our society. Don Sabo offers a compassionate account of how men will invariably confront traditional stereotypes as they look for more nurturing roles. Gloria Steinem pokes holes in the traditional definitions of masculinity, especially the putative biological basis for gender expression.

Kathleen Slevin and Thomas Linneman examine the specifically gendered experiences of gay men as they age. Monica Casper and Lisa Jean Moore look at the ways that gender identity and health are all wrapped together in our images of sports heroes. And the article by Meika Loe explores the increased pressure on men to stay healthy, vital and sexually potent as they age—and how modern medicine has jumped in to cure problems that are of recent invention.

Don Sabo

Masculinities and Men's Health: Moving toward Post-Superman Era Prevention[1]

My grandfather used to smile and say, "Find out where you're going to die and stay the hell away from there." Grandpa had never studied epidemiology (i.e., the study of variations in health and illness in society) but he understood that certain behaviors, attitudes, and cultural practices can put individuals at risk for accidents, illness, or death. This chapter presents an overview of men's health that proceeds from the basic assumption that aspects of traditional masculinity can be dangerous for men's health (Sabo & Gordon, 1995; Harrison, Chin, & Ficarrotto, 1992). First, I identify some gender differences in relation to morbidity (i.e., sickness) and mortality (i.e., death). Next, I examine how the risk for illness varies from one male group to another. I then discuss an array of men's health issues and a preventive strategy for enhancing men's health.

Gender Differences in Health and Illness

When British sociologist, Ashley Montagu, put forth the thesis in 1953 that women were biologically superior to men, he shook up the prevailing chauvinistic beliefs that men were stronger, smarter, and better than women. His argument was partly based on epidemiological data that show males are more vulnerable to mortality than females from before birth and throughout the life span.

Mortality and Life Expectancy

From the time of conception, men are more likely to succumb to prenatal and neonatal death than females. Men's chances of dying during the prenatal stage of development and also the neonatal (newborn) stage are greater than those of females. A number of neonatal disorders are common to males but not females, such as bacterial infections, respiratory illness, digestive diseases, and some circulatory disorders of the aorta and pulmonary artery. Table 20.1 illustrates the disparities between male and female infant mortality rates (i.e., death during the first year of life) across a 50-year span of the 20th century (Centers for Disease Control and Prevention [CDC], 1992). Men's greater mortality rates persist through the "age 85" subgroup and, as Table 20.2 shows, male death rates are higher than female rates for

■ TABLE 20.1
Gender and Infant Mortality Rates for the United States, 1940–1989

Year	Both Sexes	Males	Females
1940	47.0	52.5	41.3
1950	29.2	32.8	25.5
1960	26.0	29.3	22.6
1970	20.0	22.4	17.5
1980	12.6	13.9	11.2
1989	9.8	10.8	8.8

Source: Adapted from Centers for Disease Control and Prevention, *Monthly Vital Statistics Report*, *40*(8, Suppl. 2), p. 41.

Note: Rates are for infant (under 1 year) deaths per 1,000 live births for all races.

■ **TABLE 20.2**

Ratio of Male to Female Age-Adjusted Death Rates, for the 15 Leading Causes of Death for the Total U.S. Population in 2002

Rank	Cause of Death	Number of Total Deaths	Percentage	Male to Female Ratio
1	Diseases of heart	710,760	29.6	1.4
2	Malignant neoplasms	553,091	23.0	1.5
3	Cerebrovascular diseases	167,661	7.0	1.0
4	Chronic lower respiratory diseases	122,009	5.1	1.4
5	Accidents (unintentional injuries)	97,900	4.1	2.2
6	Diabetes	69,301	2.9	1.2
7	Influenza and pneumonia	65,313	2.7	1.3
8	Alzheimer's disease	49,558	2.1	0.8
9	Nephritis, nephritic syndrome, nephrosis	37,251	1.5	1.4
10	Septicemia	31,224	1.3	1.2
11	Intentional harm (suicide)	29,350	1.2	4.5
12	Chronic liver disease and cirrhosis	26,552	1.1	2.2
13	Essential hypertension and hypertensive renal disease	18,073	0.8	1.0
14	Assault (homicide)	16,765	0.7	3.3
15	Pneumonitis due to solids and liquids	16,636	0.7	1.8

Source: Adapted from National Center for Health Statistics, *National Vital Statistics Report, 50*(15), September 16, 2002, Table C.

12 of the 15 leading causes of death in the United States (National Center for Health Statistics, 2002). Females have greater life expectancy than males in the United States, Canada, and post-industrial societies (Payne, 2006).

These facts suggest a female biological advantage, but a closer analysis of changing trends in the gap between women's and men's life expectancy indicates that social and cultural factors related to lifestyle, gender identity, and behavior are operating as well. Life expectancy among American females in 2004 was about 80.4 but 75.2 for males (National Center for Health Statistics, 2006). While life expectancy for U.S. citizens is now the highest in history, it has shifted a lot during the 20th century. Women's relative advantage in life expectancy over men was rather small at the beginning of the 20th century (Waldron, 1995). During the mid-20th century, female mortality declined more rapidly than male mortality, thereby increasing the gender gap in life expectancy. Whereas women benefited from the decreased maternal mortality, the mid-century trend toward elevating men's life expectancy was slowed by increasing mortality from coronary heart disease and lung cancer that were, in turn, mainly due to higher rates of cigarette smoking among males.

The recent trends show that differences between U.S. women's and men's mortality have decreased. Female life expectancy was 7.9 years greater than males in 1979, 6.9 years in 1989 (National Center for Health Statistics, 1992), and 5.2 years in 2004. Some changes in behavior between the sexes, such as increased smoking among women, have narrowed the gap between men's formerly higher mortality rates from lung cancer, chronic obstructive pulmonary disease, and ischemic heart disease (Waldron, 1995). Figures 20.1 and 20.2 illustrate shifting patterns of life expectancy by race and gender across the past four decades (Kung, Hoyert, Xu, & Murphy, 2008). In summary, both biological and sociocultural processes help to shape patterns of men's and women's mortality.

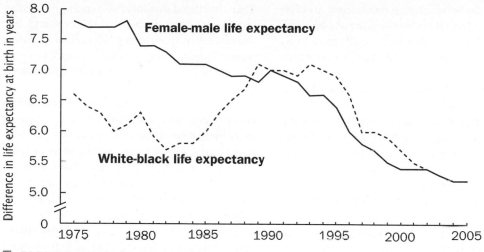

■ **FIGURE 20.1**

Difference in Life Expectancy between Males and Females, and between Black and White: United States, 1975–2005

Morbidity

While females generally outlive males, females report higher morbidity (or sickness) rates even after controlling for maternity. U. S. national health surveys show that females experience acute illnesses, such as respiratory conditions, infective and parasitic conditions, and digestive system disorders, at higher rates than males do, with the exception of injuries (Cypress, 1981; Dawson & Adams, 1987). Men's higher injury rates are partly owed to gender differences in socialization and lifestyle; for example, learning

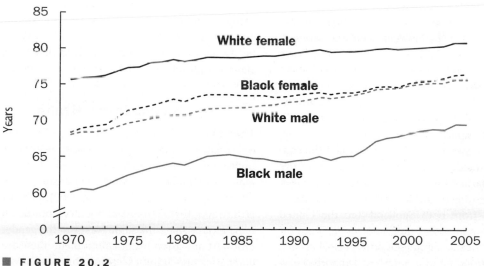

■ **FIGURE 20.2**

Life Expectancy by Race and Sex: United States, 1970–2005

to prove manhood through recklessness, involvement in contact sports, working in risky blue-collar occupations. Women are generally more likely than males to experience chronic conditions such as anemia, chronic enteritis and colitis, migraine headaches, arthritis, diabetes, and thyroid disease. However, males are more prone to develop chronic illnesses such as coronary heart disease, emphysema, and gout. While chronic conditions do not ordinarily cause death, they often limit activity or cause disability. Finally, a lot of pharmaceutical advertising aims to convince people that they are sick or need to see a doctor when, in fact, they are not clinically ill (Brownlee, 2007). Much of this type of "direct to consumer" advertising has been geared to women, but greater marketing efforts are now geared to men. Men's rate of "morbidity" may be increasing as a result.

Biology + Society + Culture = Complexity

In addition to gender, a highly complex set of global, social, cultural, psychological, racial, and ethnic factors influence variations in men's and women's health (Payne, 2006). Understanding the disparate mortality and morbidity rates between men and women is further complicated by the emphasis on gender differences itself, which, ironically, has been part of traditional patriarchal beliefs *and* much Second Wave feminist thought (Sabo, 2005). Whereas patriarchal culture exaggerated differences between men and women, and masculinity and femininity, Second Wave feminists theorized a "presumed oppositionality" between men and women, and masculinity and femininity (Digby, 1998). Epidemiologically, however, the emphasis on *differences* can sometimes hide *similarities*. For example, MacIntyre, Hunt, and Sweeting (1996) questioned the conventional wisdom that in industrialized countries men die earlier than women, and that women get sick more often than men. They studied health data sets from both Scotland and the United Kingdom and found that, after controlling for age, statistically significant differences between many of men's and women's self-reported psychological and physical symptoms disappeared.

They concluded that *both* differences and similarities in men's and women's health exist and, furthermore, that changes in gender relations during recent decades "may produce changes in men's and women's experiences of health and illness" (p. 623).

In summary, although some gender differences in mortality and morbidity are associated with biological or genetic processes, or with reproductive biology (e.g., testicular or prostate cancer), it is increasingly evident that the largest variations in men's and women's health are related to shifting social, economic, cultural, and behavioral factors (Courtenay, McCreary, & Merighi, 2002; Kandrack, Grant, & Segall, 1991). For this reason, Schofield et al. (2000) critiqued the prevailing "men's health discourse," which too often equates "men's health" to the delivery of biomedical services to men, or to private sector marketing services or products designed to enhance "men's health." They reject lumping "all men" into statistical comparisons between men's and women's health outcomes because, mainly, it is disadvantaged men (e.g., poor men, men of color, uninsured men, gay men) who disproportionately contribute to men's collective higher mortality and morbidity rates in comparison to women. As Keeling (2000) writes, "So it is that there is no single, unitary men's health—instead, sexual orientation, race, socioeconomic status, and culture all intervene to affect the overall health status of each man and of men of various classes or groups" (p. 101).

Masculinities and Men's Health

There is no such thing as masculinity; there are only masculinities (Sabo & Gordon, 1995). A limitation of early gender theory was its treatment of "all men" as a single, large category in relation to "all women" (Connell, 2000). The fact is, however, that all men are not alike, nor do all male groups share the same stakes in the gender order. At any given historical moment, there are competing masculinities—some dominant, some marginalized, and some stigmatized—each with their respective structural, psychosocial, and cultural moorings. There are substantial differences between the health options of homeless men, working-class men, underclass men, gay men, men with AIDS, prison inmates, men of color, and their comparatively advantaged middle- and upper-class, Caucasian, professional male counterparts. Similarly, there exists a wide range of individual differences between the ways that men and women act out "femininity" and "masculinity" in their everyday lives. A health profile of several male groups is discussed below.

Adolescent Males

Pleck, Sonenstein, and Ku (1992) applied critical feminist perspectives to their research on problem behaviors and health among adolescent males. A national sample of adolescent males, never-married males aged 15–19 were interviewed in 1980 and 1988. They tested whether the extent that young men identified with traditionally masculine attitudes increased their risk for an array of problem behaviors. The findings showed a significant, independent association with seven of ten problem behaviors. Specifically, traditionally masculine attitudes were associated with being suspended from school, drinking and use of street drugs, frequency of being picked up by the police, being sexually active, the number of heterosexual partners in the last year, and tricking or forcing someone to have sex. These kinds of behaviors, which are in part expressions of the pursuit of traditional masculinity, elevate boys' risk for sexually transmitted diseases, HIV transmission, and early death by accident or homicide. At the same time, however, these same behaviors can also encourage victimization of women through men's violence, sexual assault, unwanted teenage pregnancy, and sexually transmitted diseases.

Today not as many young men may buy into traditional "macho" identities. But traditional masculinities remain plentiful in media, school subcultures, locker rooms, advertising, gangs, the military, and other institutions. We can only speculate about the links between traditional masculinities and the health risk behaviors of 10–24

year-old males in the United States, for whom four main causes are responsible for 72% of their deaths: homicide, motor-vehicle accidents, suicide, and unintentional injuries (Eaton et al., 2006).

Finally, adolescence is a phase of accelerated physiological development and, contrary to many people's beliefs, more boys than girls are classified as "obese." Obesity puts adults at risk for a variety of diseases such as coronary heart disease, diabetes mellitus, joint disease, and certain cancers. Obese adolescents often become obese adults, thus elevating long-term risk for illness. Obesity among *both* boys and girls has been increasing; for example, the percentage of overweight children aged 12–19 moved from 5% in 1970 to 14% in 1999 (National Health and Nutrition Examination Survey [NHANES], 2003). Between 1988 and 1994, about 11.3% of all boys in this age group were overweight compared with 9.7% of all girls. Adolescents from racial/ethnic minorities were especially likely to be overweight. Among non-Hispanic blacks, 10.7% of boys and 16.3% of girls were overweight, and among Mexican Americans, the corresponding proportions were 14.1% for boys and 13.5% for girls (NHANES, 2003). In 2007, 16.3% of high school males were obese compared with 9.6% of females (Eaton et al., 2006).

Men of Color

Patterns of health and illness among men of color can be partly understood against the historical and social context of economic inequality. Generally, because African Americans, Hispanics, and Native Americans are disproportionately poor, they are more apt to work in low-paying and dangerous occupations, live in polluted environments, be exposed to toxic substances, experience the threat and reality of crime, and worry about meeting basic needs. Cultural barriers can also complicate their access to available health care. Poverty is correlated with lower educational attainment which, in turn, works against adoption of preventive health behaviors.

Compared with Caucasians, African Americans experience twice as much infant mortality, are twice as likely to die from diabetes-related complications, have 80% more strokes, have 20–40% higher rates of cancer, and have 5–7 years less life expectancy (Burrus, Liburd, & Burroughs, 1998; Chin, Zhang, & Merrell, 1998; Straub, 1994; Wingo et al., 1996). The age-adjusted death rate is greater for men in all racial/ethnic groups: 1.7 times greater among African Americans, 1.8 times greater among Asians, and 1.5 times greater among Latinos/Hispanics (Collins, Hall, & Neuhaus, 1999; Courtenay, McCreary & Merighi, 2002).

The neglect of the public health in the United States is particularly pronounced in relation to African Americans (Polych & Sabo, 2001). Even though African American men have higher rates of alcoholism, infectious diseases, and drug-related conditions, for example, they are less apt to receive health care and, when they do, they are more apt to receive inferior care (Bullard, 1992). The statistics below document the woeful state of African-American men's health.

- The leading cause of death among 18–34 year-old African American males is homicide (National Vital Statistics Reports, 2006).
- While 21% of nonelderly Asian men and 16% of non-Hispanic Caucasian men had no health insurance in 2005, 25% of African American men had no coverage (CDC, April 2, 2006).
- When it comes to HIV/AIDS, heart disease, prostate cancer, colon cancer, and lung cancer, African American males have higher death rates than men from other racial groups (Kaiser Family Foundation, 2007).

The health profile of many other men of color is also poor. Compared to the "all race" population, for example, Native American youth exhibit more serious problems in the areas of depression, suicide, anxiety, alcohol and substance use, and general health status (Blum et al., 1992). The health problems facing American and Canadian natives are correlates of poverty and social marginalization such as school drop-out, sense of hopelessness, experience of prejudice, poor nutrition, and lack of regular health care. Hispanic males also show more signs of ill health than their Caucasian counterparts. One explanation is that the growing numbers of both documented and undocumented Hispanic males in the U.S. work force in recent decades, particularly in blue-collar jobs (e.g., construction, agriculture, warehousing), contributed to high rates of work-related injuries and deaths between 1992–2006 (Mortality and Morbidity Weekly Report [MMWR], 2008). Those who care about men's health, therefore, need to be attuned to the interplay between gender, race/ethnicity, cultural differences, and economic conditions when working with diverse populations.

Gay and Bisexual Men

Gay and bisexual men are estimated to be anywhere from 5 to 10 percent of the male population. In the past, gay men have been viewed as evil, sinful, sick, emotionally immature, and socially undesirable. Many health professionals and the wider public have harbored mixed feelings and homophobic attitudes toward gay and bisexual men. Gay men's identity, their lifestyles, and the social responses to homosexuality can impact the health of gay and bisexual men. Stigmatization and marginalization, for example, may lead to emotional confusion and suicide among gay male adolescents. For gay and bisexual men who are "in the closet," anxiety and stress can tax emotional and physical health. When seeking medical services, gay and bisexual men must often cope with the homophobia of health care workers or deal with the threat of losing health care insurance if their sexual orientation is made known.

Whether they are straight or gay, men tend to have more sexual contacts than women do, which heightens men's risk for STD's. Men's sexual attitudes and behaviors are closely tied to the way masculinity has been socially constructed. For example, "real" men are taught to suppress their emotions, which can lead to a separation of sex from feeling. Traditionally, men are also encouraged to be daring, which can lead to risky sexual decisions. In addition, contrary to common myths about gay male effeminacy, masculinity also plays a powerful role in shaping gay and bisexual men's identity and behavior. To the extent that traditional masculinity informs sexual activity of men, masculinity can be a barrier to safer sexual behavior among men.

Although rates of sexually transmitted disease declined in the 1980s among American men who had sex with men (MSM), data gathered in some cities indicate a resurgent trend toward increased prevalence rates since 1993 (Fox et al., 2001). These latter data may mean that more MSM are engaging in sexual behaviors that elevate risk for contagion, such as unprotected anal and oral sex. Other researchers suggest that some risky sexual behaviors among MSM are related to polysubstance abuse. One American Medical Association council report (1996) estimated the prevalence of substance abuse among gay men and lesbians at 28–35%, compared with a 10–21% rate for heterosexuals. Some studies of gay communities have found higher rates of substance use (e.g., heavy drinking, amphetamines, heroin, and Ecstasy) than among heterosexual males (Crosby, Stall, Paul, & Barrett, 1998; Klitzman, Pope, & Hudson, 2000).

In the United States and Canada, MSM remain a large risk group for HIV transmission (especially among Caucasian men). For gay and bisexual men who are infected by the HIV virus, the personal burden of living with an AIDS diagnosis is made heavier by the stigma associated with homosexuality. The cultural meanings associated with AIDS can also filter into gender and sexual identities. Tewksbury's (1995) interviews with 45 HIV+ gay men showed how masculinity, sexuality, stigmatization, and interpersonal commitment mesh in the decision making around risky sexual behavior. Most of the men practiced celibacy in order to prevent others from contracting the disease, others practiced safe sex, and a few went on having unprotected sex.

Prison Inmates

In 2006 there were 2,258,983 prisoners in federal or state prisons or in local jails (U.S. Department of Justice, 2006). The United States has the highest rate of incarceration of any nation in the world, and racial and ethnic minorities are overrepresented among those behind bars. In many states, black and Hispanic males comprise the majority of prisoners (Mauer, 1999). Among African American males born between 1965 and 1969, for example, 20% spent time in prison in their teens or twenties (Treadwell & Nottingham, 2005).

The prison system acts as a pocket of risk, within which men already at greater risk of a preexisting Acquired Immune Deficiency Syndrome (AIDS) infection, are, because of prison conditions, yet again exposed to heightened risk of contracting Human Immunodeficiency Virus (HIV) or other infections such as tuberculosis (TB) or hepatitis (Polych & Sabo, 2001). The corrections system is part of an institutional chain that facilitates transmission of HIV and other infections in certain North American populations, particularly among poor, inner-city, men of color. Prisoners are burdened not only by social disadvantage but also by high rates of physical illness, mental disorder, and substance use that jeopardize their health.

HIV/AIDS prevalence is markedly higher among state and federal inmates than in the general U.S. population (Maruschak, 2003; McQuillan, Kottiri, & Kruszon-Moran, 2007). Many men already have AIDS at the time of admission (Mumola, 2007). Inside prisons, the HIV virus is primarily transmitted between adults by unprotected penetrative sex, or needle sharing without bleaching, with an infected partner. Sexual contacts between prisoners occur mainly through consensual unions and secondarily through sexual assault and rape (Kupers, 2001). The amount of IV drug use behind prison walls is unknown, although it is known to be prevalent, and that the scarcity of needles often leads to needle and sharps sharing.

The failure to provide comprehensive health education and treatment interventions in prisons is not only putting more inmates at risk for HIV infections, but also the public at large. Prisons are not hermetically sealed enclaves set apart from the community, but an integral part of society. Prisoners regularly move in and out of the prison system, and this means that they often return to their communities after having served their sentences. Indeed, several hundred thousand prisoners are released each year, while hundreds of thousands return to the prison system. The extent to which the drug-related social practices and sexual activities of released and/or paroled inmates who are HIV positive is putting others at risk upon return to their communities is unresearched and unknown (Polych & Sabo, 2001).

Many prison sentences became longer during the past few decades. One consequence is that more prisoners are now age 50 or older. The "graying" of the prison population is placing more demands on the system to attend to both the physical and mental health needs of men behind bars (Day, 2003). Heart disease, cancer, and liver diseases are likely to top the list of ailments for this aging population (Mumola, 2007). Many older men will also be among the more than half of U.S. prison and jail prisoners who are dealing with a mental illness (James & Glaze, 2006).

Male Athletes

Injury is everywhere in sport. It is evident in the lives and bodies of athletes who regularly experience bruises, torn ligaments, broken bones, aches, lacerations, muscle tears, and so forth. There were an estimated 1,442,533 injuries to U.S. high school athletes in nine popular sports during the 2005–06 school year (*MMWR*, Sept. 29, 2006a). Football players and wrestlers had the highest injury rates. Critics of violent contact sports claim that athletes are paying too high a physical price for their participation. George D. Lundberg (1994), former editor of the *Journal of the American Medical Association*, called for a ban on boxing in the Olympics and in the United States military.

His editorial entreaty, while based on clinical evidence for neurological harm from boxing, was also couched in a wider critique of the exploitative economics of the sport.

Injuries are basically unavoidable in sports but, in traditional men's sports, there has been a tendency to glorify pain and injury, to inflict injury on others, and to sacrifice one's body in order to "win at all costs." Some men's sport subcultures such as football, hockey, and rodeo raise risk-taking to the level of male heroism (Frey, Preston & Bernhard, 2004). The "no pain, no gain" philosophy, which is rooted in traditional cultural equations between masculinity and sports, can jeopardize the health of athletes who conform to its ethos (Sabo, 2004). It is often difficult for injured athletes to figure out when to push themselves to compete or to back off and heal. For example, Tiger Woods played in pain and won the 2008 U. S. Open only weeks after knee surgery. Right after the event, he admitted that doctors had told him it might not be a good idea to play. When asked why he played in spite of the pain and risks for complication, he explained, "You just keep playing. Like one of my buddies, we always used to joke 'How many reps you got?' And we used to say 'Four? No, it's forever'." (Golf Channel & Yahoo.com videoclip, June 17, 2008). Hopefully, his decision will not contribute to serious future medical complications. But for some young athletes the mind-over-matter and macho-over-medicine credo of "hang tough" leads to permanent damage and a sad end to their dreams.

The connections between sport, masculinity, and health risks are also evident in Klein's (1993) study of how bodybuilders use anabolic steroids, overtrain, and engage in extreme dietary practices. He spent years as an ethnographic researcher in the muscled world of the bodybuilding subculture, where masculinity is equated to maximum muscularity and men's striving for bigness and physical strength hide emotional insecurity and low self-esteem. Klein lays bare a tragic irony in American culture; that is, that the powerful male athlete, a symbol of strength and health, has often sacrificed his health in pursuit of ideal masculinity (Messner & Sabo, 1994).

An early nationwide survey of American male high school seniors found that 6.6% used or had used anabolic steroids. About two-thirds of the steroid users were athletes (Buckley et al., 1988). Since that time extensive use of anabolic steroids has been uncovered in professional baseball and football, Olympic weight lifting, and international cycling. Anabolic steroid use is now also happening among boys (and girls) involved with youth and recreational sports (Bahrke et al., 2000). Anabolic steroid use has been linked to physical health risks such as liver disease, kidney problems, atrophy of the testicles, elevated risk for injury, and premature skeletal maturation. The use of anabolic steroid by young males makes it more likely that they engage in other health risk behaviors such as fighting, driving without a seatbelt, drug and alcohol use, and suicide (Miller et al., 2002).

Finally, high school athletic participation is associated with a variety of health benefits for boys. Male high school athletes are less likely than nonathletes to use marijuana, cocaine, crack cocaine, and inhalants (Miller et al., 2001). Fewer athletes than nonathletes start smoking cigarettes (Melnick et al., 2001). High school athletes also have higher odds of using seatbelts than their nonathletic counterparts (Melnick et al., 2005). A key question for men's health is whether youthful involvement with sport gets translated into greater physical activity in older men's lives. Physical activity helps adult males (and females) reduce their overall risk for heart disease and certain cancers. Regretfully, however, little is known about the extent that youthful involvement with sports contributes to a physically active lifestyle among adults.

Infertile Men

Millions of American couples experience difficulty conceiving a pregnancy. Although factors related to infertility can be found in both sexes, the bulk of extant research focuses on the psychosocial aspects of women's experiences with involuntary childlessness and in vitro fertilization (Daniluk, 1997; Nachtigall, Becker, & Wozny, 1992). In one of the few studies of men's experiences, Webb and Daniluk (1999) interviewed men who had never biologically fathered a child and were the sole cause of the infertility in their marriages. They found that men experienced a "tremendous blow to their masculine identities" (p. 21), profound grief and loss, loss of control, personal inadequacy, isolation, a sense of foreboding, and a desire to overcome and survive. They recommend that both "infertile men and women receive compassionate support when faced with negotiating this challenging life transition" (p. 23).

Men's Health Issues

Advocates for men's health have identified a variety of issues that impact directly on men's lives. Some of these issues may concern you or men you care about.

Testicular Cancer

Though relatively rare in the general population (1% of all cancers in men), it is the most common cancer among 15–34 year-old males (American Cancer Society, 2005). The incidence of testicular cancer is increasing, doubling during the past 40 years, and accounting for about 8,000 new cases and 390 deaths per year (Ibid.). If detected early, the cure rate is high, while delayed diagnosis can be life-threatening. Regular testicular self-examination (TSE), therefore, is a potentially effective preventive means for insuring early detection and successful treatment. Regretfully, however, most physicians do not teach TSE techniques.

Although testicular cancer rates are increasing in many countries, mortality rates have declined in the European Union, Eastern Europe, Japan, the United States, and Canada (Levi, LaVecchia, Boyle, Lucchini, & Negri, 2001). Declining mortality is likely due to advances in medical diagnosis and treatment, early detection, TSE, and greater educational awareness among males. Finally, survivors of testicular cancer generally go on to have physically and emotionally healthy lives (Rudberg, Nilsson, & Wikblad, 2000).

Denial may influence men's perceptions of testicular cancer and TSE (Blesch, 1986). Studies show that most males are not aware of testicular cancer and, even among those who are aware, many are reluctant to examine their testicles as a preventive measure. Even when symptoms are recognized, men sometimes postpone seeking treatment. Moreover, men who are taught TSE are often initially receptive, but the practice of TSE decreases over time. Men's resistance to TSE has been linked to awkwardness about touching themselves, associating touching genitals with homosexuality or masturbation, or the idea that TSE is not a manly behavior. And finally, men's individual reluctance to discuss testicular cancer partly derives from the widespread cultural silences that envelope it. The penis is a cultural symbol of male power, authority, and sexual domination. Its symbolic efficacy in traditional, male-dominated gender relations, therefore, would be eroded or neutralized by the realities of testicular cancer.

Diseases of the Prostate

Middle-aged and elderly men are likely to develop medical problems with the prostate gland. The older men get, the more likely it is that they will develop prostate cancer. Some men may experience benign prostatic hyperplasia, an enlargement of the prostate gland that is associated with symptoms such as dribbling after urination, frequent urination, or incontinence. Others may develop infections (prostatitis) or malignant prostatic hyperplasia (prostate cancer). Prostate cancer is diagnosed more frequently in Canada and the United States than any other cancer (McDavid, Lee, Fulton, Tonita, & Thompson, 2004). One in six men develop this cancer during their lifetime, with African American males showing a higher prevalence rate than their Caucasian counterparts (American Cancer Society, 2007; Jones et al., 2007). While the incidence of prostate cancer has been increasing in recent

decades, earlier diagnosis and treatment have reduced mortality.

Treatments for prostate problems depend on the specific diagnosis and may range from medication to radiation and surgery. As is the case with testicular cancer, survival from prostate cancer is enhanced by early detection. Raising men's awareness about the health risks associated with the prostate gland, therefore, may prevent unnecessary morbidity and mortality. Finally, more invasive surgical treatments for prostate cancer can produce incontinence and impotence, so men should diligently explore their medical options. Men are also beginning to talk about their physical, emotional, and sexual experiences following treatment for prostate cancer (Gray, 2005).

Alcohol Use

While social and medical problems stemming from alcohol abuse involve both sexes, males comprise the largest segment of alcohol abusers. Some researchers have begun exploring the connections between traditional masculinity and alcohol abuse. Mass media often sensationalize links between booze and male bravado. For decades male stereotypes have been used in beer commercials to promote beer drinking as a reward for a job well done or to glorify daring, male friendship, or romantic success with women (Postman, Nystrom, Strate, & Weingartner, 1987). The combination of beer and liquor ads with sports imagery is a common advertising ploy to entice males to consume alcohol products (Messner & Montez de Oca, 2005).

Alcohol use is now highly prevalent among U.S. teenagers. More than half (55%) of youth in 2007 reported they had gotten drunk "at least once" in their lives by 12th grade, compared to about 1 in 5 (18%) of 8th graders (Johnston, O'Malley, Bachman, & Schulenberg, 2008). While boys typically have showed higher rates of heavy drinking in the past, 8th and 10th grade girls now match boys' rates (Ibid).

Findings from a 1999 Harvard School of Public Health nationwide survey of U.S. college students found that 44% engaged in "binge drinking," defined as drinking five drinks in rapid succession for males and four drinks for females (Wechsler, 2005). Males were more apt to report binge drinking during the past two weeks than females; 51% and 40% respectively. Males who were frequent binge-drinkers were more likely than non-binge-drinking males to report driving after drinking, missing class, engaging in unplanned sexual behavior, falling behind in school work, being hurt or injured and having trouble with campus police.

Between 1999 and 2005, about twice as many men as women died from alcohol-induced causes (National Vital Statistics Reports, 2006). Alcohol-related automobile accidents are the top cause of death among 16–24 year-olds. The number of automobile fatalities among male adolescents that result from a mixture of alcohol abuse and masculine daring is unknown. Alcohol use is frequently involved with the four leading causes of death among youth and young adults—motor vehicle accidents, unintentional injuries, homicide, and suicide (Eaton et al., 2006). However, readers can assess the links between alcohol use and men's greater risks for accidents in this context. Even though heart disease is the leading health risk for U.S. men *across all* age groups, from childhood through age 44 it is unintentional injuries that are the greatest threats to men's lives (Mayo Clinic, 2008).

Men and HIV/AIDS

Human immunodeficiency virus (HIV) infection became a major cause of death among U.S. males in the 1980s. By 1990, among men aged 25–44, HIV infection was the second leading cause of death, compared to the sixth leading cause of death among same-age women (MMWR, 1993a). It is now estimated that about one million persons in the United States live with HIV. Among reported cases of acquired immunodeficiency syndrome (AIDS) for adolescent and adult men at the end of 2006, 59% were men who had sex with other men, 20% percent were injecting drug users, 11% percent were exposed through heterosexual sexual contact, 8% percent were

men who had sex with men and injected drugs (Noble, 2008). Among U.S. adolescent and adult women living with AIDS in 2006, 65% were exposed through heterosexual contact, 33% were injecting drug users, and 3% had other or unknown risks (MMWR, 2006b).

Because most AIDS cases have been among men who have sex with other men, perceptions of the epidemic and its victims have been tinctured by sexual attitudes. In North American cultures, the stigma associated with AIDS is fused with stigma complicated by homophobia. Thoughts and feelings about men with AIDS are also influenced by attitudes toward race, ethnicity, drug abuse, and social marginality. CDC data show, for example, that African Americans, who are about 14% of the total U.S. population, comprised 49% of both new HIV cases and new AIDS diagnoses in 2006 (Noble, 2008). African Americans (not Hispanic) were 38.2% of all the estimated adult and adolescent males living with AIDS between 1981 and 2006 (MMWR, 2006b). (The corresponding estimate for African American (not Hispanic) females is 62%.) Courtenay (2008) reports that one in four males who die from HIV infection is African American, and among college age African American men, the HIV infection rate is three times greater than the rate of their Caucasian American counterparts. The high rate of AIDS among racial and ethnic minorities can kindle racial prejudices in some minds, and AIDS is sometimes seen as a "minority disease." While African American or Hispanic males may be at greater risk of contracting HIV/AIDS, just as yellow fingers do not cause lung disease, it is not their race or ethnicity that confers risk, but the behaviors they engage in and the social circumstances of their lives (Polych & Sabo, 2001).

Perceptions of HIV/AIDS can also be influenced by attitudes toward poverty and poor people (Zieler & Krieger, 1997). HIV infection is linked to economic problems that include community disintegration, unemployment, homelessness, eroding urban tax bases, mental illness, substance use, and criminalization (Wallace,

1991). For example, males comprise the majority of homeless persons and runaway children. Poverty and adult homelessness and running away from home among children overlap with drug addiction and sexual victimization which, in turn, are linked to HIV infection.

Suicide

Centers for Disease Control data show that males are more likely than females to commit suicide (Suicide.org, 2008). In 2001 an estimated 1.3% of all deaths were due to suicide, with one 15–24 year-old dying by suicide every 97 minutes. Suicide is the eleventh leading cause of death among Americans, and the second leading cause of death for college students. For each one female to die by suicide, there are four males who do so. Among racial and ethnic groups, it is Caucasian males have are most likely to commit suicide, especially if they are elderly, accounting for 73% of all suicide deaths during 2001. During 2004 elderly males (65+) in the United States committed suicide more than seven times more often than elderly females (respectively, 29 suicides per 100,000 versus 3.8 per 100,000) (Suicide.org, 2008). Compared to females, males typically deploy more violent means of attempting suicide (e.g., guns or hanging versus pills) and are more likely to complete the act. Men's selection of more violent methods to kill themselves is consistent with traditionally masculine behavior

Canetto (1995) interviewed male survivors of suicide attempts in order to better understand sex differences in suicidal behavior. While she recognizes that men's psychosocial reactions and adjustments to nonfatal suicide vary by race/ethnicity, socioeconomic status, and age, she also finds that gender identity is an important factor in men's experiences. Suicide data show that men attempt suicide less often than women but are more likely to die than women. Canetto indicates that men's comparative "success" rate points toward a tragic irony in that, consistent with gender stereotypes, men's failure even at suicide undercuts the cultural mandate that men are supposed to succeed at everything. A lack of embroilment in traditionally masculine expectations, she

suggests, may actually increase the likelihood of surviving a suicide attempt for some men.

Erectile Dysfunction

Erectile Dysfunction is basically a partial or complete inability to get and maintain an erection. Men often joke about their penises or tease one another about penis size and erectile potency (i.e., "not getting it up"). In contrast, they rarely discuss their concerns about erectile dysfunction (ED) in a serious way. Men's silences about ED are regrettable in that many men, both young and old, experience recurrent or periodic difficulties getting or maintaining an erection. ED usually has physical causes, happens mostly to older men, and is frequently treatable. Estimates of the number of American men with erectile disorders range from 10 million to 30 million (Minnesota Men's Health Center, 2008). Some main risk factors for ED are diabetes, smoking, and aging.

During the 1960s and 1970s, erectile disorders were largely thought to stem from psychological problems such as depression, financial worries, or work-related stress. Masculine stereotypes about male sexual prowess, phallic power, or being in charge of lovemaking were also said to put too much pressure on some males to perform. Today, however, physiological explanations of ED and medical treatments have been increasingly emphasized.

Finally, the marketing and availability of drugs like Viagra to treat ED have inadvertently spawned a wave of recreational drug use (Brownlee, 2007). Younger men may mix Viagra with other club drugs at rave parties or for all-night sex. Some evidence shows that Viagra use is greater among MSMs and heterosexuals who use other kinds of drugs during sex which, in turn, can lead to other forms of sexual risk taking (Fisher et al., 2006).

Men's Violence

Men's violence is a major public health problem. The traditional masculine ideal calls on males to be aggressive and tough. Anger is a by-product of aggression and toughness and, ultimately, part of the inner terrain of traditional masculinity.

Images of angry young men are compelling vehicles used by some males to separate themselves from women and to measure their status in respect to other males. Men's anger and violence derive, in part, from sex inequality. Men use the threat and/or application of violence to maintain their political and economic advantage over women and lower-status men. Male socialization reflects and reinforces these larger patterns of domination.

The homicide rate is highest among U.S. 15–19 year-old males (13/100,000 standard population) followed by 25–34 year-olds (11/8100,000) (Kung, Hoyert, Xu, & Murphy, 2008). In 2005 males were almost four times more likely than females to die from homicide (9.8/100,000 and 2.5/100,000, respectively). The convergence of race, ethnicity, and economic inequalities also shapes risk for death from homicide, with death rates among African American males at 39.7/100,000, Caucasian males at 5.4/100,000, and Hispanic males at 13.6/100,000. Finally, 65.3% of men's homicide victims in 2005 were *other men* (U.S. Department of Justice, 2008).

Women are especially victimized by men's anger and violence in the form of rape, date rape, wife beating, assault, sexual harassment on the job, and verbal harassment (Katz, 2006). That the reality and potential of men's violence impacts women's mental and physical health is safely assumed. However, men's violence also exacts a toll on men themselves in the forms of fighting, gang clashes, hazing, gay-bashing, intentional infliction of injury, homicide, suicide, and organized warfare.[?]

War, a form of institutionalized violence, has always been a predominantly male activity (Malszecki & Carver, 2001) that exacted high rates of morbidity and mortality among its participants. Warriors were taught to conform to a type of traditional masculinity that embodies violence-proneness, toughness, and obedience to male authority. The negative health consequences of war for both sexes are painfully evident. Many boys and men, who are disproportionately enlisted to fight in wars, are killed or physically and psychologically maimed, whereas elite male groups may profit or solidify political power through warfare. Men's violence on the patriarchal battlefields also often spills over into civilian populations, where women and children are victimized (Brownmiller, 1975; Chang, 1997). As Sen (1997) observed, "Historically, wars between nations, classes, castes, races, have been fought on the battlefield on the bodies of men, and off the battlefield on the bodies of women" (p. 12). Recent expressions of the militarization of men's violence, partly inspired and fueled by traditional masculinities, can be found in the Taliban of Afghanistan, the Darfur region of Sudan, terrorist movements, and the war in Iraq.

Male Victims of Sexual Assault

Sexual violence typically involves a male perpetrator and female victim. Whereas researchers and public health advocates began to recognize the sexual victimization of women in Western countries during the late 1960s, it was not until the latter 1990s that the sexual abuse of males began to receive systematic scrutiny from human service professionals and gender researchers (O'Leary, 2001). Recognition of the issue in Canada was spurred by media coverage of the sexual abuse of youth hockey players by their coaches (Robinson, 1998). Prison reformers have recently decried man on man rape in North American prisons (see www.stopprisonerrape. org). The alleged cover-ups by Catholic bishops in the United States, in relation to some priests' pedophilic exploitation of boys, and the activism and litigation of victims have expanded public awareness of the problem. Despite growing public recognition, research in this area is rare, and little is know about the prevalence of sexual abuse of boys and its psychosocial effects (Dhaliwal, Gauzas, Antonowicz, & Ross, 1996). Some studies show that males who suffer sexual victimization as children experience lasting self-blame, feelings of powerlessness and stigmatization, suspicion of others, and confusion about sexual identity, and some eventually repeat the cycle by victimizing others as adolescents and adults (Messerschmidt, 2000; O'Leary, 2001).

Summary

Traditional images of muscled, invulnerable, daring, unemotional, and risk-taking masculinity are still a big part of the culture. Each summer Hollywood pumps old patriarchal blood into the newest cinemagraphic renderings of superheroes like the Hulk, Iron Man, Spiderman, the X-Men, and Fantastic Four. It is ironic, however, that two of the best known actors who portrayed Superman met with real-life disaster. George Reeves, who starred in the original black-and-white television show, committed suicide, and Christopher Reeves, who portrayed the "man of steel" in recent film versions, was paralyzed by an accident during a high-risk equestrian event. Perhaps one lesson to be learned here is that, behind the cultural facade of mythic masculinity, men are vulnerable. Indeed, as we have seen in this chapter, some of the cultural messages sewn into the cloak of masculinity can put men at risk for illness and early death. A sensible preventive health strategy for men today is to critically evaluate the Superman legacy, that is, to challenge the negative aspects of traditional masculinity that endanger their health, while hanging on to the positive aspects of masculinity and men's lifestyles that heighten men's physical vitality. Hey guys, enjoy the movies, play with the myths, but don't buy into messages about masculinity that put your well-being at risk.

The promotion of men's health requires a sharper recognition that the sources of men's risks for many diseases do not strictly reside in men's psyches, gender identities, or the activities that they enact in daily life. Men's activities, routines, and relations with others are fixed in the historical and structural relations that constitute the larger gender order. As we have seen, not all men or male groups share the same access to social resources, educational attainment, and opportunity that, in turn, can influence their health options. Yes, men need to pursue personal change in order to enhance their health, but without changing the political, economic, and ideological structures of the gender order, the subjective gains and insights forged within individuals can easily erode and fade away. If men are going to pursue self-healing, therefore, they need to create an overall preventive strategy that at once seeks to change potentially harmful aspects of traditional masculinity as well as meeting the health needs of lower-status men.

Notes

1. This overview of men's health issues and concerns was updated during summer of 2008. Special thanks to Jill Church at D'Youville College for her library research expertise.

2. For a list of ten ways to stop men's violence go to http://www.jacksonkatz.com/topten.html

References

American Cancer Society. (2007). *Cancer facts and figures 2007*. Altanta, GA: Author.

American Cancer Society. (2005). *Cancer facts and figures 2005*. American Cancer Society, Inc. Available at www.cancer.org/downloads/STT/CAFF2005f4PWsecured.pdf

American Medical Association. (1996). Health care needs of gay men and lesbians in the United States. *Journal of the American Medical Association, 275,* 1354–1359.

Bahrke, M. S., Yesalis, C. E., Kopstein, A. N., & Stephens, J. A. (2000). Risk factors associated with anabolic-androgenic steroid use among adolescents. *Sports Medicine, 29*(6):397–405.

Blesch, K. (1986). Health beliefs about testicular cancer and self-examination among professional men. *Oncology Nursing Forum, 13*(1):29–33.

Blum, R., Harman, B., Harris, L., Bergeissen, L., & Restrick, M. (1992). American Indian–Alaska native youth health. *Journal of American Medical Association, 267* (12):1637–44.

Brownlee, S. (2007). *Overtreated: Why too much medicine is making us sicker and poorer*. New York: Bloomsbury.

Brownmiller, S. (1975). *Against our will: Men, women, and rape*. New York: Simon and Schuster.

Buckley, W. E., Yesalis, C. E., Friedl, K. E., Anderson, W. A., Streit, A. L., & Wright, J. E. (1988). Estimated prevalence of anabolic steroid use among male high school seniors. *Journal of the American Medical Association, 260* (23): 3441–46.

Bullard, R. D. (1992). Urban infrastructure: Social, environmental, and health risks to African-Americans. In Tidwell, B. J. (Ed.) *The state of Black America*. New York: National Urban League, pp. 183–196.

Burrus, B. B., Liburd, L. C., & Burroughs, A. (1998). Maximizing participation by Black Americans in population-based diabetes research: The Project Direct pilot experience. *Journal of Community Health, 23,* 15–37.

Canetto, S. S. (1995). Men who survive a suicidal act: Successful coping or failed masculinity? In D. Sabo & D. Gordon (Eds.) (1995). *Men's Health and Illness*. Newbury Park, CA: Sage.

Centers for Disease Control and Prevention (2006). *HIV/AIDS Surveillance Report 2006, (Vol. 18)*

Centers for Disease Control and Prevention (1992). *Monthly Vital Statistics Report, 40*(8, Suppl. 2), p. 41.

Chang, I. (1997). *The rape of Nanking: The forgotten holocaust of World War II*. New York: Penguin Books.

Chin, M. H., Zhang, J. X., & Merrell, K. (1998). Diabetes in the African-American Medicare population *Diabetes Care, 21,* 1090–1095.

Collins, K. S., Hall, A., & Neuhaus, C. (1999). *US minority health: A chartbook*. New York: The Commonwealth Fund.

Connell, R. W. (2000). *The men and the boys*. Berkeley, CA: University of California Press

Courtenay, W. H. (2008). Men's Health Consulting website. See www.menshealth.org

Courtenay, W. H., McCreary, D. R., & Merighi, J. R. (2002). Gender and ethnic differences in health beliefs and behaviors. *Journal of Health Psychology, 7*(3), 219–231.

Crosby, G. M., Stall, R. D., Paul, J. P., & Barrett, D. C. (1998). Alcohol and drug use patterns have declined between generations of younger gay-bisexual men in San Francisco. *Drug and Alcohol Dependence, 52,* 177–182.

Cypress, B. (1981). *Patients' reasons for visiting physicians: National ambulatory medical care survey, U.S. 1977–78*. DHHS Publication No. (PHS) 82-1717, Series 13, No. 56. Hyattsville, MD: National Center for Health Statistics, December, 1981a.

Daniluk, J. C. (1997). Gender and infertility. In S. R. Leiblum (ed.), *Infertility: Psychological issues and counseling strategies* (pp. 103–125). New York: Wiley.

Dawson, D. A., & Adams, P. F. (1987). *Current estimates from the national health interview survey: U.S., 1986*. Vital Health Statistics Series, Series 10, No. 164. DHHS Publication No. (PHS) 87-1592, Public Health Service, Washington, D.C., U.S. Government Printing Office.

Day, R. H. (2003). *Aging prisoners: Crisis in American corrections*. New York: Praeger.

Dhaliwal, G. K., Gauzas, L., Antonowicz, D. H., & Ross, R. R. (1996). Adult male survivors of childhood sexual abuse: Prevalence, sexual abuse characteristics, and long-term effects *Clinical Psychology Review, 16*(7), 616–639.

Digby, T. (Ed.) (1998). *Men doing feminism*. New York: Routledge.

Eaton, D. K., Kann, L., Kinchen, S., et al. (2006). Youth risk behavior survey surveillance—United States, 2005. *Journal of School Health, 76,* 353–372.

Fisher, G. F., Malow, R., Rosenberg, R., Reynolds, G. L., Farrell, N., & Jaffe, A. (2006). Recreational Viagra use and sexual risk among drug abusing men. *American Journal of Infectious Diseases, 2*(2): 107–114.

Fox, K. K., del Rio, C., Holmes, K. K., Hook, E .W. III, Judson, F. N., Knapp, J. S., Procop, G. W., Wang, S. A., Whittington, W. L., & Levine, W. C. (2001). Gonorrhea in the HIV era: A reversal in trends among men who have sex with men, *American Journal of Public Health, 91,* 959–964.

Frey, J. H., Preston, F. W., & Bernhard, B. J. (2004). Risk and injury: A comparison of football and rodeo subcultures. In Young, K. (Ed.) *Sporting bodies, damaged selves: Sociological studies of sports-related injury*, pp. 211–222. Boston: Elsevier.

Gibbs, J. T. (Ed.) (1988). *Young, black, and male in America: An endangered species*. Dover, MA: Auburn House.

Gray, R. E. (2005). *Prostate tales: Men's experiences with prostate cancer*. Harriman, TN: Men's Studies Press.

Harrison, J., Chin, J., & Ficarrotto, T. (1992). Warning: Masculinity may be dangerous to your health. In M. S. Kimmel & M. A. Messner (Eds.) *Men's Lives*, pp. 271–285. New York: Macmillan.

James, D. J., & Glaze, L. E. (2006). Mental health problems of prison and inmates. *Bureau of Jus-*

tice Statistics Special Report. September, NCJ 213600.

Johnston, L. D., O'Malley, P. M., Bachman, J. G., & Schulenberg, J. E. (2008). *Monitoring the future national results on adolescent drug use: Overview of key findings, 2007* (NIH Publication No. 08-6418). Bethesda, MD: National Institute on Drug Abuse.

Jones, R. A., Underwood, S. A., & Rivers, B. M. (2007). Reducing prostate cancer morbidity and mortality in African American men: Issues and challenges. *Clinical Journal of Oncology Nursing, 11*(6):865–872.

Kaiser Family Foundation. (2007). Race, ethnicity & health care fact sheet. Publication #7630 available on the Kaiser Family Foundation's website at www.kff.org.

Kandrack, M., Grant, K. R., & Segall, A. (1991). Gender differences in health-related behavior: Some unanswered questions. *Social Science & Medicine, 32*(5), 579–590.

Katz, J. (2006). *The macho paradox: Why some men hurt women and how all men can help.* Naperville, IL: Sourcebooks.

Keeling, R. R. (2000). College health: Biomedical and beyond. *Journal of American College Health, 49,* 101–104.

Klein, A. (1993). *Little Big Men: Bodybuilding Subculture and Gender Construction.* Albany, NY: SUNY Press.

Klitzman, R., Pope, H., & Hudson, J. (2000). Ecstasy abuse and high risk sexual behaviors among 169 gay and bisexual men. *American Journal of Psychiatry, 157,* 1162–1164.

Kupers, T. A. (2001). Rape and the prison code. In Sabo, D., Kupers, T. A., & London, W. (Eds.), *Prison Masculinities,* pp. 111–17. Philadelphia: Temple University Press.

Kung, H. C., Hoyert, D. L., Xu, J. & Murphy, S. L. (2008). Deaths: Final data for 2005. *National Vital Statistics Reports, 56*(10), April 24.

Levi, F., LaVecchia, C., Boyle, P., Lucchini, F., & Negri, E. (2001). Western and Eastern European trends in testicular cancer mortality. *Lancet, 357,* 1853–1854.

Lundberg, G. D. (1994) Let's stop boxing in the Olympics and the United States military. *Journal of the American Medical Association, 271* (22), p. 1790.

MacIntyre, S., Hunt, K., & Sweeting, H. (1996). Gender differences in health: Are things really as simple as they seem? *Social Science of Medicine, 42*(2), 617–624.

Malszecki, G., & Carver, T. (2001). Men, masculinities, war, and sport. In N. Mandell (Ed.), *Feminist issues: Race, class, and sexuality* (pp. 166–192). Toronto: Pearson Education Canada.

Manton, K. G., Blazer, D. G., & Woodbury, M. A. (1987). Suicide in middle age and later life: Sex and race specific life table and cohort analyses. *Journal of Gerontology, 42,* 219–227.

Maruschak L. M. (2003). *HIV in prisons.* Bureau of Justice Statistics bulletin. Washington, DC: US Department of Justice, Office of Justice Programs; September 2005. Publication no. NCJ 210344.

Mauer, M. (1999). *Race to incarcerate.* New York: The New Press.

Mayo Clinic. (2008). *Men's top 10 health threats: Mostly preventable.* Retrieved online at http://www.mayoclinic.com/health/mens-health/MC00013

McDavid, K., Lee, J., Fulton, J. P., Tonita, J., & Thompson, T. D. (2004). *Prostate cancer incidence and mortality rates and trends in the United States and Canada.* U.S. Department of Health and Human Services; Public Health Report 2004: 119: 174–186.

McQuillan, G. M., Kottiri, B. J., & Kruszon-Moran, D. (2007). The prevalence of HIV in the United States household population: The national health and nutrition examination surveys, 1988 to 2002. Presented at the 12th Conference on Retroviruses and Opportunistic Infections, Boston, MA; Abstract no. 166.

Melnick, M., Miller, K., Sabo, D., Barnes, G., & Farrell, M. P. (2005). "Athletic Participation and Seat Belt Use Among U.S. Teenagers: A National Study." Paper presented at the Annual Conference of the North American Society for the Study of Sport, Winston-Salem, NC.

Melnick, M., Miller, K., Sabo, D., Farrell, M.P., & Barnes, G. (2001). Tobacco use among high school athletes and nonathletes: Results of the 1997 Youth Risk Behavior Survey. *Adolescence, 36*(144):727–747.

Messerschmidt, J. W. (2000). *Nine lives: Adolescent masculinities, the body, and violence.* Boulder, CO: Westview.

Messner, M. A., & Montez de Oca, J. (2005) The male consumer as loser: Beer and liquor ads in mega sports media events. *Signs: Journal of Women in Culture and Society 30*, 1879–1909.

Messner, M. A., and Sabo, D. (1994). *Sex, violence, and power in sports: Rethinking masculinity*. Freedom, CA: Crossing Press.

Miller, K., Barnes, G., Sabo, D. F., Melnick, M. J., & Farrell, M. P. (2002). Anabolic-androgenic steroid use and other adolescent problem behaviors: Rethinking the male athlete assumption. *Sociological Perspectives, 44*(4):467–489.

Miller, K., Sabo, D., Melnick, M., Farrell, M. P., & Barnes, G. (2001). *The Women's Sports Foundation Report: Health risks and the teen athlete*. East Meadow, New York: The Women's Sports Foundation. See www.womenssportsfoundation.org

Minnesota Men's Health Center (2008). *Facts about Erectile Dysfunction*. Retrieved online at http://www.mmhc-online.com/articles/impotency.html

Montagu, A. (1953). *The natural superiority of women*. New York: MacMillan.

Morbidity and Mortality Weekly Report (2008). *Work-related injury deaths among Hispanics—United States, 1992–2006*, 57(22), June 6, pp. 597–600.

——— (2006a). *Sports related injuries among high school athletes— United States, 2005–06 school year*, 55(38), September 29, retrieved online.

——— (2006b). *Twenty-five years of HIV/AIDS United States, 1981–2006*, 55(21): 585–589.

——— (1993a). *Update: Mortality attributable to HIV infection/AIDS among persons aged 25–44 years— United States, 1990–91*, 42(25), July 2, pp. 481–486.

——— (1993b). *Summary of notifiable diseases United States, 1992*, 41 (55), September 24.

Mumola, C. J. (2007). Medical causes of death in state prisons, 2001–2004. *Bureau of Justice Statistics Data Brief*. January, NCJ 215340.

Nachtigall, R. D., Becker, G., & Wozny, M. (1992). The effects of gender-specific diagnosis on men's and women's response to infertility. *Fertility and Sterility, 57*, 113–121.

National Center for Health Statistics (2006). *Deaths: Preliminary data for 2004*. Health e-stat. Retrieved online at www.cdc.gov/nchs/pressroom/06facts/preliminarydeaths04.htm

National Center for Health Statistics (2002). *National Vital Statistics Report, 50*(15), September 16, 2002, Table C.

National Center for Health Statistics (1992). Advance report of final mortality statistics, 1989. *Monthly Vital Statistics Report, 40* (8): supplement 2 (DHHS Publication No. (PHS) 92–1120).

National Health and Nutrition Examination Survey (NHANES). (2003). *Overweight among U.S. children and adolescents*. Hyattsville, MD: Department of Health and Human Services, Centers for Disease Control and Prevention. Retrieved from www.cdc.gov/nchs/nhanes.htm

National Vital Statistics Reports (2006). *Leading causes of death by age group, black males—United States, 2004*. Retrieved online at http://www.cdc.gov/nchs/datawh/statab/unpubd/mortabs.htm

Noble, R. (2008). *AVERT (Averting HIV and AIDS), United States Statistics Summary*. Retrieved online at http://www.avert.org/statsum.htm

O'Leary, P. (2001). Working with males who have experienced childhood sexual abuse. In B. Pease & P. Camilleri (Eds.), *Working with men in the human services* (pp. 80–92). New South Wales, Australia: Allen & Unwin.

Payne, S. (2006). *The health of men and women*. Malden, MA: Polity Press.

Pleck, J., Sonenstein, F. L., & Ku, L. C. (1992). In Ketterlinus, R. & Lamb, M. E. (Eds.). *Adolescent problem behaviors*. Hillsdale, NJ: Lawrence Erlbaum Associates.

Polych, C., & Sabo, D. (2001). Sentence—Death by lethal infection: IV-drug use and infectious disease transmission in North American prisons. In Sabo, D., Kupers, T. A., & London, W. *Prison masculinities*. Philadelphia: Temple University Press, pp. 173–83.

Postman, N, Nystrom, C., Strate, L. & Weingartner, C. (1987). *Myths, men and beer: An analysis of beer commercials on broadcast television, 1987*. Falls Church, VA: Foundation for Traffic Safety.

Robinson, L. (1998). *Crossing the line: Violence and sexual assault in Canada's national sport*. Toronto: McClelland and Stewart.

Rudberg, L., Nilsson, S., & Wikblad, K. (2000). Health-related quality of life in survivors of testicular cancer 3 to 13 years after treatment. *Journal of Psychosocial Oncology, 18*, 19–31.

Sabo, D. (2005). The Study of Masculinities and Men's Health: An Overview (2005). In M. Kimmel, J. Hearn, & R. W. Connell (Eds.). *Handbook of men's studies.* Newbury Park, CA: Sage Publications. Pp. 326–352.

Sabo, D. (2004). The politics of sports injury: Hierarchy, power, and the pain principle. In Young, K. (Ed.). *Sporting bodies, damaged selves: Sociological studies of sports-related injury.* Boston: Elsevier, pp. 59–79.

Sabo, D., & Gordon, D. (1995). *Men's health & illness: Gender, power & the body.* Newbury Park: Sage.

Schofield, T., Connell, R. W., Walker, L., Wood, J. F., & Butland, D. L. (2000). Understanding men's health and illness: A gender relations approach to policy, research and practice. *Journal of American College Health, 48*(6), 247–256.

Sen, G. (1997, June). *Globalization in the 21st century: Challenges for civil society.* The UVA Development Lecture, delivered at the University of Amsterdam.

Stillion, J. (1995). Premature death among males: Rethinking links between masculinity and health. In D. Sabo & D. Gordon (Eds.), *Men's health and illness.* Newbury Park, CA: Sage.

Straub, N. R. (1994, Winter). African Americans: Their health and the health care system. *The Pharos,* pp. 18–20.

Suicide.org (2008). U. S. Suicide Rates, 1950–2003. See http://www.suicide.org/suicide-statistics.html

Tewksbury, (1995). Sexual adaptation among gay men with HIV. In D. Sabo & D. Gordon, *Men's health & illness: Gender, power & the body.* Newbury Park: Sage, pp. 222–245.

Torres, R. A., Mani, S., Altholz, J., & Brickner, P. W. (1990). HIV infection among homeless men in a New York City shelter. *Archives of Internal Medicine, 150*: 2030–2036.

Treadwell, H. M., & Nottingham, J. H. (2005). Editor's choice: Standing in the gap. *American Journal of Public Health, 95*(10): 1676.

U. S. Department of Justice (2008). Bureau of Justice Statistics, Homicide trends in the U. S.: Trends by gender. Retrieved online http://www.ojp.usdoj.gove/bjs/homicide/gender.htm

U. S. Department of Justice (2006). Bureau of Justice Statistics, Prison statistics, December 31, 2006. Retrieved online http://www.ojp.usdoj.gov/bjs/prisons.htm

Waldron, I. (1995). Contributions of changing gender differences in behavior and social roles to changing gender differences in mortality. In D. Sabo & D. Gordon (Eds.), *Men's health and illness,* Newbury Park, CA: Sage.

Wallace, R. (1991). Traveling waves of HIV infection on a low dimensional 'socio-geographic' network. *Social Science Medicine, 32*(7), 847–852.

Watson, J. (2000). *Male bodies: Health, culture and identity.* Philadelphia: Open University Press.

Webb, R. E., & Daniluk, J. C. (1999). The end of the line: Infertile men's experiences of being unable to produce a child. *Men and Masculinities, 2*(1), 6–25.

Weinreb, L. F., & Bassuk, E. L. (1990). Substance abuse: A growing problem among homeless families. *Family and Community Health, 13*(1), 55–64.

Wechsler, H. (2005). *Harvard School of Public Health College Alcohol Study, 1999* [Computer file]. ICPSR03818-v2. Boston, MA: Harvard School of Public Health [producer], 2005. Ann Arbor, MI: Inter-university Consortium for Political and Social Research [distributor], 2005-11-22.

Wingo, P. A., Bolden, S., Tong, T., Parker, S. L., Martin, L. M., & Heath, C. W. (1996). Cancer statistics for African Americans, 1996. *CA: A Cancer Journal for Clinicians, 46,* 113–125.

Zierler, S., & Krieger, N. (1997). Reframing women's risk: Social inequalities and HIV infection. *Annual Review of Public Health, 18*(1), 401–436.

Kathleen F. Slevin
Thomas J. Linneman

Old Gay Men's Bodies and Masculinities

Introduction

There is a relative lack of literature regarding old[1] gay men. One reason is that this important population is not easily accessible to researchers. Another factor is the invisibility of these men—not only in society in general but also within gay communities themselves. Consequently, this paper addresses a much-needed topic for discussion—not only in the social science literature but also in the masculinities literature.

Within the growing literature on masculinities, several claims deserve note. First, given the focus of this paper, it is important to register that notions of masculinity are embodied: the body plays a critical role in how men understand and practice what it means to be a man (Connell 2002). Second, multiple forms of masculinity exist: there are many ways to be a man, based on the various intersections of race/ethnicity, age, class, and sexuality. Given this plurality of masculinities, it is also the case that some forms of manhood are more honored than others. Hence, hegemonic masculinity which, while not assumed to be statistically representative among populations of men, presents exalted ideals or exemplars of masculinity, of the ideal man (e.g., the professional sports star in contemporary U.S.). Yet, as Connell and Messerschmidt remind us in their recent historical review of the concept of hegemonic masculinity, scholars need to "eliminate any usage of hegemonic masculinity as a fixed, transhistorical model" (Connell and Messerschmidt 2005, 838). Accordingly, understanding

masculinities requires that we acknowledge the complex ways that notions of manhood are dynamic. As well as being shaped by social locations, they are also influenced by local, regional, and global practices (Connell and Messerschmidt 2005). Thus, in any particular historical moment, men and boys construct, produce, negotiate, and re-negotiate what it means to be a man. Age relations are centrally important for at least two reasons: first, because hegemonic masculinity honors what is youthful and, second, notions of manhood are not only influenced by age but also are likely to change over an individual's life course. In addition, gender plays a powerful role in how men construct their notions of manhood; masculinity is invariably defined relationally, against the feminine (Hennen 2005). Also worthy of note is the recent documentation of subordinate or subaltern masculinities that are considered to be inferior variants of the masculine ideal: non-white masculinities, working-class masculinities, older masculinities, and gay masculinities (Chen 1999, Connell 1995, Nardi 2000). Often, researchers analyze each of these masculinities separately, examining how old men are demasculinized (Meadows and Davidson 2006), or how gay men are feminized (Linneman 2008). Increasingly, however, scholars are focusing on the intersections of these subaltern forms (Barrett 2000, Han 2000).

It is to this latter development that this paper contributes by studying the masculinities of old, white, privileged gay men. The use of an intersectionality perspective allows us to explore the complexities of how the intersections of various locations such as race, class, gender, sexuality and age shape the ways the men interviewed for this

Paper presented at the annual meetings of the American Sociological Association, New York, August 2008. Reprinted by permission of Kathleen Slevin and Tom Linneman.

study experience what it means to be old men who are both advantaged and disadvantaged by these interlocking systems of power and oppression. Our attention to age relations and sexuality adds a new perspective to the traditional dominant statuses of race, class, and gender that typically represent intersectional analyses (Collins, 2000; Crenshaw, 1991). Indeed, age inequalities are widely ignored, even in feminist literatures (Calasanti and Slevin 2006).

Through narrative analysis, this paper explores how ten old gay men talk about their masculinities, and specifically the masculinities of their aging bodies. This qualitative approach, often missing in extant literature, allows these old gay men to tell us how they understand themselves as men. It also allows us to make explicit the connections between men's bodies and masculinity (Connell 1995).Thus, we draw attention to old men and their aging bodies—topics largely ignored by scholars (Katz 2005; Calasanti and King 2005; Faircloth 2003; Calasanti and Slevin 2001). Through a focus on this largely ignored group, we explore how the intersections of race, class, gender, and sexual orientation intersect with age to influence notions of masculinity and aging. We also uncover how old gay men talk about their self-identities as men who are both old and gay, as men with at least two negatively "marked identities" (Brekhus 2003:11). Thus, through them we gain insights into how their notions of embodied masculinity are constructed within a cultural context that stigmatizes both being old and being gay while glorifying youthful and heterosexual notions of masculinity. Narrative analysis provides us a window through which we can glimpse "the contradictory and shifting nature of hegemonic discourse" (Chase 2005). Such analysis allows us to see how these men both create meaning and make sense of what it means to grow old and to be old gay men. It provides us a mechanism to explore the contradictions and messiness of lived experiences, uncovering how "hegemonic masculinity may not be the lived form of masculinity at all" despite the fact that it is a powerful, even dominant script,

against which men judge themselves and others (Thompson and Whearty 2004: 6). As well, these men's narratives allow us to illustrate the complicated nature of how old gay men who are privileged by class and race experience their aging bodies; through their voices we understand better how they work to create and sustain biographical continuity as they sort through and integrate the forces that shape and re-shape their lives. Finally, their stories reveal common threads among the men but they also highlight their diverse and unique experiences.

Old Masculinities

In our culture growing old and being old is nowadays constructed as a problem—albeit one that we are told is increasingly solvable (Cruikshank 2003). Nowadays consumer society targets the body as central to age-resisting practices and strategies; fighting aging, resisting growing old or looking old is big business (Slevin 2006; Calasanti and Slevin, 2001; Gilleard and Higgs 2000). As well, the body is central to ageist notions and practices (Slevin 2006); and, as Laws (1995) reminds us, ageism is an embodied form of oppression. Yet, despite all attempts to fight aging, bodies are more than social constructions, they are subject to biological and physiological constraints and they decline (Turner 1996). The male body at the height of its productive capacities is held up as an ideal form of masculinity. This production occurs at a number of sites: economic, athletic, and sexual, to name a few. As men enter old age, their productivity within these sites decreases markedly. As Calasanti and Slevin point out: "old age does in fact confer a loss of power, even for those advantaged by other social locations" (Calasanti and Slevin 2001, 191). A common cultural belief holds that men gain power and become men when they achieve the status of economic producers (Emslie et al. 2004). But, as men enter old age and face a new set of socially constructed gender norms, they find themselves increasingly moving from sites of economic production such as the workplace to the feminized sphere of the home (Meadows and

Davidson 2006). Their contributions to the economy occur primarily through consumption and not through production (Calasanti and King 2005).

The sporting arena is another institution typically associated with masculinity (Messner 1992). The finely tuned male body is idealized both on the playing field and in advertisements. Though the aging male body indeed may successfully maintain some presence within certain sporting activities, men must take greater care as their bodies begin their inevitable physical decline (Calasanti 2004). As with economic production, their participation on the sporting field moves to the sidelines and towards consumption. Furthermore, approaches to inevitable physical decline are complicated by gender because seeking health care (a common need in old age) is inconsistent with hegemonic masculinity (McVittie and Willock 2006).

Just as male bodily performance decreases on the playing field, many men experience a similar decline in the bedroom. Sexual performance among old men certainly has entered the public consciousness through the development of Viagra and similar drugs that aim to re-sex the aging male body (Marshall 2006; Loe 2003). A multibillion dollar industry has grown around the new expectation that aging men are expected now to "keep it up" as long as possible, and to age more "successfully" than previous generations of old men (Calasanti and King 2005). Recent survey data does show that the old have sex more frequently than previously believed (Lindau et al. 2007). However, loss of ability to perform sexually, and loss of interest in sex, remain key indicators of old age (Marshall and Katz 2002). As a consequence of these losses and declines the ability of old men to correspond to the widespread ideals of ideal manhood are both compromised and jeopardized.

At every turn, then, the aging male body faces the likelihood of demasculinization. Yet, as Spector-Mercel argues, scholars of masculinity, while focusing on the varied influences of, for example, race, class, culture and sexual orienta-

tion, have largely disregarded the critical role played by age and life course (Spector-Mersel 2006). She reminds us that the scripts for masculinity in old age are ambiguous and ill-formed; old men not only constitute an ambiguous social category, but also they "live in a hybrid-state" (Spector-Mercel 2006, 68). Thompson further concludes: "To many people, aging is a negation of masculinity, and thus older men become effeminate over time" (Thompson 1994, 13). But, given the dearth of empirical literature on the lived bodily experiences of old people in general what all of this means for their *subjective* experiences of aging and aging bodies is quite unexplored (Slevin 2006). Indeed, we must be wary of assuming that dominant social values, such as those that characterize the aging body as negative, are synonymous with what old men and women actually experience (Oberg 2003).

Gay Masculinities

The hegemonic form of masculinity is youthful *and* heterosexual. Consequently, homosexuality is routinely associated with gender inversion (Rosenfeld 2003). When a man reveals his homosexuality, regardless of his gender performance, many question his masculinity because of his sexual desires (Kimmel 1996). Accordingly, much of the demasculinization associated with gay men takes the form of feminization. There is a long history of gay men's feminization. Indeed, the arbiters of this feminizing are often gay men themselves. In the introduction to his important volume on gay masculinities, Nardi titles his introduction "Anything for a Sis, Mary," quoting from the classic gay play "The Boys in the Band." Feminizing camp has a long tradition in gay male culture (Dyer 2002). Even today, the feminization of gay men remains prevalent. For example, the popular pro-gay show "Will & Grace" consistently engaged in feminizing its gay characters hundreds of times, often in moments of conflict where the goal was castigation of the gay men (Linneman 2008). It is important to maintain the distinction between feminization and demasculinization, for even if a gay man is not feminized, he still is often not considered able to live up to the true standards of masculinity. Indeed, openly gay men are virtually shut out of bastions of hegemonic masculinity, such as corporate boardrooms, professional sports teams, and the military. There are communities of gay men, such as the radical faeries and the bears, who actively disrupt the connections between homosexuality and femininity (Hennen 2008), but given that these groups are doubly marginalized (by hetero-sexuals and by gay cultures), the effect of such efforts is minor.

As attention to gay masculinities has grown, researchers have begun to study various forms of gay masculinities. Nardi's volume contains pieces on the masculinities of working-class gay men (Barrett 2000), Latino gay men (Cantu 2000), and Asian American gay men (Han 2000). However, the masculinities of old gay men make no appear-ance. In fact, as Jones and Pugh point out, the oldest respondent in any of the studies in Nardi's volume was 56 (Jones and Pugh 2005).

The Masculinities of Old Gay Men

Reinforcing the need for studies such as our own, we note the limited research available on the mas-culinities of old gay men. Brekhus's seminal work on gay suburban men, while not focusing on old men, does suggest that the intersection of these identities creates complicated identity work that requires various strategies and struggles to accom-plish some sense of authenticity (Brekhus 2003). Yet, while acknowledging the role of stigma in old gay men's lives, it is equally important to note that cultural domination is never complete; those who are stigmatized—either by age or sexual ori-entation—may elect in various ways to resist ageist or homophobic messages and to create alternative notions of manhood. Managing mul-tiple identities (positive and negative) requires much work and in exposing this on-going iden-tity work, we begin to uncover how the old gay men in this study work hard to counteract and resist stigmatized identities. The fact that they are privileged by race and class provides them resources that most likely would be unavailable

to men of color or those who are in lower social classes.

Another common theme in the literature on older gay men is that of "accelerated aging" (Wahler and Gabbay 1997). Indeed, some schol-ars argue that gay men become arbiters of their own oppression (Chen 1999). Gay male culture, in many of its commodified forms, holds up as its masculine ideal the young, muscular man, even more so than in heterosexual male culture. Because of this, gay men are considered old much sooner than in non-gay culture:

> Because of the gay community's emphasis on youth, homosexual men are considered mid-dle-aged and elderly by other homosexual men at an earlier age than heterosexual men in the general community. Since these age-status norms occur earlier in the gay sub-culture, the homosexual man thinks of himself as middle-aged and old before his heterosexual counter-part does. (Bennett and Thompson 1991, 66)

A cursory look at gay culture corroborates this: glossy gay newsmagazines consistently fea-ture young men on their covers, and gay pornog-raphy treats older men as a marginalized fetish. However, empirical data regarding how real gay men experience this phenomenon are scarce and contradictory (Jones and Pugh 2005).

Also inconsistent are findings regarding the effects of involvement in gay communities. Quam and Whitford (1992) found that many of the older gay men they studied were both involved in gay communities and experienced high levels of life satisfaction. In contrast, one of the more provocative findings of Hostetler's empirical research is that a high level of involvement in a gay community was associated with increased concern over aging (Hostetler 2004). However, the nature of the relationship is uncertain, and the causal argument may go both ways. It could be that old gay men, through their involvement in the gay community, may experience ageism as they interact with younger members of the com-munity (Heaphy 2007). Alternatively, concern over aging could prompt some gay men to seek involvement in their community. Further complicating the matter, it is necessary to keep in mind the multiplicity of gay communities and the wide variation among such communities with regard to the extent to which they stigmatize old age.

A prominent argument that highlights some positive consequences of being gay reminds us that at various points in their lives gay men learn to cope with stigma because they are denied the privileges that accompany normative notions of masculinity. Yet, of course, some gay men also benefit to a degree from the privileges of being white men who are relatively affluent. Indeed, gay men often can pass for heterosexual and thus insure that they are still beneficiaries of the privileges associated with being heteronormative men. That said, if they live their lives out of the closet, a loss of privilege is a distinct possibility. Thus, having learned to live with one marked identity (being gay), they are potentially positioned to adapt better to a second stigmatized or marked identity (being old). If this is the case, and their narratives lend some credence to this proposition, they might be less likely to miss these privileges when they are denied them in old age. Thus, by the time they reach their 60s and 70s, gay men have had decades of experience dealing with demasculinization and stigma, and therefore have a battery of coping skills at the ready:

> The gay man who has successfully navigated the coming-out process arrives at the knowledge that how he constructs his reality need most importantly be acceptable to himself, according to the dictates of his own needs. Gay men frequently report a greater sense of freedom from cultural norms. This may mean a highly adaptive flexibility in terms of which roles and role expectations are "acceptable." This translates into more flexibility in meeting the challenges of aging, and leads to individuals who may be better equipped to construct an interpersonal reality that meets their needs not just as gay people but as old people. (Wahler and Gabbay 1997, 14)

In contrast, aging heterosexual men experience demasculinization for perhaps the first time in their lives (Meadows and Davidson 2006). Thus, old gay men may indeed be ahead of their heterosexual peers in some ways as they face the daily challenges of inhabiting older bodies. In sum, exploring how being gay shapes men's embodied experiences of masculinity, and trying to understand how these notions are shaped by other intersecting social relations such as race, class, and age, is likely to reveal a complicated picture that differs for each man and reveals multiple, varying factors that shape their notions of what it means to be a man, to be gay, to be old, and to be an old gay man.

Methods

Based on intensive interviews with ten gay men aged 60 to 85, this study explores the narrative accounts of how they conceive of embodied masculinity in old age. The study is part of a larger study in which the lead author, between 2002 and 2004, conducted intensive interviews with 26 men (16 heterosexual; 10 homosexual) and 31 women (22 heterosexual; 9 lesbian) in their 60s, 70s and 80s about how they experienced their bodies in old age. The researcher used a snowball sampling method to obtain interviewees from different backgrounds. Such a sampling method is very appropriate for locating this invisible population (Carpenter 2002). The intensive, exploratory interviews addressed a variety of topics related to aging and the body. Questions were broad and there were lots of invited opportunities to "think out loud" about the topics that were the focus of the interviews. This sort of narrative inquiry made sense for a number of reasons. First, because so little is known empirically about the topics under investigation, such inquiry is most likely to capture "retrospective meaning making—the shaping or ordering of past experience" (Chase 2005). Second, it allows the researcher to explore very broadly the lived experiences of individuals who are willing to talk about their own biographical particulars, and it allows for "the uniqueness of each human action and event rather than their common properties"

(Chase 2005). As well, narrative inquiry provides us the opportunity to seek similarities and differences across narratives on topics that are difficult to explore. It is especially suited not only to the subject matter but also to recruitment of members of "hard to find" populations, especially those who are reluctant to reveal their sexual identities and, are often *only* accessible through person-to-person recruitment. Thus, the word-of-mouth support for this research (which was critical, given the snowball nature of the sample) was enhanced by the fact that future participants learned from those already interviewed that they would have an opportunity to "tell their story" to a sympathetic listener. Finally, narrative inquiry is particularly well suited for exploring and deepening our understanding of various oppressions but especially ageism, which (unlike racism, sexism, and homophobia) is "more often invoked than analyzed" (Cruikshank 2003, 135).

Topics addressed concerns about aging in general and specifically about looking and feeling old, preventing the aging process, body image issues, sexuality/ageism/attractiveness issues, masculinity/femininity issues, and the media and aging. In the case of these old gay men, they were asked at various times throughout the interviews to reflect upon how being gay shaped their responses to various issues. All interviews took place in the homes of the respondents and lasted between one and a half to two and a half hours. The interviews were taped and later transcribed. Interviews and transcripts were read and re-read to identify themes within the interviews.

All of the old gay interviewees lived in a mid-Atlantic state and the majority, seven, lived in mid-sized cities. The remaining three lived in small towns. All were born between 1922 and 1947 and all came of age when to be homosexual was to experience stigma and fear of reprisal on multiple fronts. Consequently, they were part of a cohort that grew up in especially stigmatized conditions. Two were previously married to heterosexual women and one had children during this marriage; both divorced and came out in their forties. The eight remaining men were "lifetime" gay

men. Two were living with partners at the time of the interviews. All of the interviewees were white and very well educated: all had bachelor's degrees and the majority, seven, also had earned graduate degrees. While one man had spent his working life as a religious pastor, the majority, six, were employed in various fields of education: two were teachers, four held administrative positions. The remaining three interviewees were executives in various organizations. Eight of the men were formally retired from the workforce, one was employed full-time, and one was working part-time. All of the men were financially secure and their lifetimes in professional jobs provide them with financial and health benefits that ensured secure retirements.

Findings

The narratives of these ten gay men provided numerous insights about how they experience and make sense of their bodies as they age and as they relate to their masculinities, to their identities, and to the gay communities in which they interact. Below, we recount several themes that emerged from the interviews. All of these themes point to the complexities inherent in the relationships among masculinities and the intersections of race, class, gender, age, and sexualities.

Aging and Acceptance of Self/Body

While one interviewee, Bart (67)[2], claims that over the decades of his life there has been consistency in his sense of himself as masculine, the rest of the respondents talked about how they had changed over the years. Most talked about how they have, over time, become more accepting of who they are, both as men and as gay men. Taken-for-granted and totally unnoted in conversations, however, are the race and class privileges that provide them useful resources—social, educational, and financial—to address many of the disadvantages stemming from their sexual orientation and from growing old. For instance, these men have the time and financial resources to avail of therapy, and they are, by and large, surrounded by friends and others who value a therapeutic culture of self-reflection as well as individual therapy. Consequently, it is not surprising that most of the interviewees are very explicit about how they have worked hard to recognize, accept, and be comfortable with themselves as they are, not as others might have them be. In general, the interviewees appear to have reflected long and hard on who they are. In old age they have arrived, for the most part, at a notable level of comfort with themselves. Analysis of conversations about masculinity and changes over time, as well as about general life changes, reveals an interesting and complicated picture. In part, their conversations suggest that aging itself has contributed to a growing comfort level. Glen (85) captures this notion when he comments that "Most mature men have become more thoughtful." Raymond (67) reinforces this notion when he comments: "I'm so much wiser now . . . I like being where I am." Yet, the comments of Glen and Raymond, positive as they are, also illuminate an embedded ageism that manifests itself in notions of "sageism"—the idea that old people are wiser than young people simply because they are older.

Given their race and class privileges—and the fact that they are very well educated—it is hardly surprising that most of these men consciously explored these issues through therapy and through a growing political awareness or engagement in gay issues, and are cognizant of the fact that mainstream society has become significantly less anti-gay throughout their lives (Loftus 2001). In these ways class and race privilege intertwine with sexual orientation in shaping how these old men approach their identities and, for the most part, ensures that they are both thoughtful and articulate about who they are and about the identity shifts that have accompanied various life transitions and societal changes. Still, an intersectionality lens also requires that we account for disadvantages and that we recognize how structural inequalities create multiple (dis)advantages. Consequently, while our interviewees grew up as white, upper-middle-class men who were advantaged by those societal positions, it is also the case

that they are disadvantaged by their sexual orientation. They grew up and lived many decades of their lives in a cultural milieu where being gay was both denigrated and dangerous. Their comments convey some of what they faced as they tried to make sense of their multiple identities and their narratives remind us of the complicated nature of identity construction. Aging, and especially retirement from a labor force where most had to hide their sexual identities, provides for different perspectives and allows us to glimpse how identities shift over the life course. For instance, Glen (85) captures some of this identity struggle with these words, "Getting older has made me more real . . . I am freer now to say 'Hey, I am not a gay, just a gay. That does not fit me. I'm a man before I'm a gay man . . .'" Glen's words provide us a window into the tenuous and elastic interplay between identities; they hint at a blurring of boundaries, a blending of identities. His words remind us of the need to recognize how identities are nuanced and ambivalent. Indeed, they serve as a caution not to jump easily into classifying certain identities as fixed master statuses. Finally, his comments shed light on the tensions between his masculine and gay identities and they allow us to appreciate that old age has allowed him to find some authenticity in an accommodation of *both* identities.

Raymond (67) also alludes to a journey toward greater self-acceptance. His story underscores how identity work is an on-going and fluid process that reflects a larger cultural narrative that includes a growing emphasis on self-reflection, as well as shifting messages about masculinity and homosexuality. Thus, he spoke of how, in his early 40s, he shifted from Western to Eastern philosophies of life and how the shift had helped him become more self-accepting. He goes on to explain how his sense of masculinity changed as he grew older. For Raymond, the journey described is of a gay man keenly aware of his body's role in shaping masculine identity. His story is also one that highlights his aim to approximate the ideal images of masculinity that he grew up with. Here is how he talks about his 40s and how at that time he came closer to approximating ideal standards of masculine strength: "I filled out and so I was no longer emaciated looking. I began to look like all those men I guess I had seen [in] those movies and so, because I did, I no longer felt so bad about myself. I felt like a male." Raymond talks at considerable length about how, over the years, he grew to be much more accepting of himself. He is emphatic that he needs to see himself as masculine. Indeed, being masculine is critical to his overall well-being. Thus, it is hardly surprising that he claims to have "worked very hard over the years to make myself feel masculine." His journey ultimately has led to a more positive self-image of himself as a man: "My sense of masculinity now is very strong." Interestingly, coming to accept that he is gay was, in his own mind, critical to reaching a more positive image of himself as a man: "When I realized I was gay, I began to feel much better about myself as a male."

While on its face it may appear paradoxical that Raymond achieves a greater sense of himself as masculine once he accepts that he is gay, it is critical to consider Raymond's analysis of the shifts in his masculine identity over his life. Raymond's narrative reveals the struggles he has undergone over decades and it allows us to hear how he works to repair his identity. His is a story that also highlights the need to understand both how notions of masculinity shift with age as well as how gay men develop coping skills that help them manage the stigma of their sexual identity. Thus, with age and time he has negotiated the tensions between his notions of masculinity as heteronormative and his own sexual identity. Like Glen, getting older has also allowed him to develop notions of manhood that incorporate his masculine and gay identities. Indeed, he hints at this when he says "I felt so un-male for so many years growing up because my maleness was measured by all those things I could not achieve." Nowadays, Raymond has adopted a biological minimum for being a man: "If you have a penis and testicles, you're male." Such a biologically reductionist argument flattens the hierarchies of

masculinities: Raymond is gay and old, but his male body speaks for itself. While this equation may seem at first overly simplistic, taking into account Raymond's long-standing work on his masculinity gives this statement a power that it otherwise might not have.

Constructing/Managing Identities

For several of the men interviewed, the secret to greater self-acceptance appears to lie in their abilities to negotiate what it means to be a man. Social class privileges provide them not only the material means to explore their identities (through therapy, supportive others, leisure time to think about these sorts of issues, etc.) but also provide them a language to communicate their identity work to others. Through their voices we glimpse the dynamics of how they construct notions of self; we learn how they reject exaggerated masculinity in favor of a more authentic masculinity or what Connell and Messerschmidt (2005, 848) refer to as "nonhegemonic patterns of masculinity." For instance, four of the interviewees are very explicit about the fact that they recognize that they combine both masculine and feminine traits. For example, Eric (60), talks about the need to recognize and accept the "ying-yang or balance" between masculinity and femininity in himself. Peter (62), who at various points in the interview refers to himself as "queenish," uses similar language to Eric and argues that masculine and feminine traits co-exist for him: "I know I have female points of view . . . I've always been a combination of the two. It won't shift. Well, it never has." Unlike Peter, Eric's acceptance of his masculine and feminine sides has come in mid-life. A level of comfort has developed over time, he claims. He goes on to register that he has "always been aware that I was not masculine—now [I am] more comfortable with it." Richard (69), who is very religious, talks about how he works with his spiritual director in order to "accept the feminine side of myself." Asked how he feels about his masculinity, he responds: "[I am] probably not the most masculine out there. [I] accept my femininity. [I am] OK with the blending—whatever that looks like I have no idea yet." Still, Richard's next observation illuminates how notions of masculinity are defined relationally: "When I am creative, I'm feminine. [I am] masculine when I do butch things at the gym." Richard ends his comments on the topic by suggesting that the very terms *masculine* and *feminine* become less important as one grows old. In keeping with his deep religiosity, he concludes that growing old makes one "more prepared for the next life, where being masculine and feminine don't matter." Gary (64) has a slightly different angle on this issue and his comments reinforce ageist notions of old men and women as sexless. He ascribes to the view that "men and women, as they get older, become . . . less feminine [and] . . . less masculine. They just become old people." Thus, Gary would have us believe that growing old makes gender matter less.

But even those who resisted rigid notions of what it means to be a man spoke of managing their public persona in order to avoid being perceived as what Freitas and others (1997: 329) refer to as "visual caricatures." Conversations about public presentations of self sensitize us to "the complicated work of appearance management and identity border construction" (Freitas et al., 1997: 325). Yet, we caution that this drive to distance themselves from "a perceived stereotypical aesthetic" (Freitas et al., 1997:329) does not represent a desire to distance themselves from gay culture. Similarly, this disassociation from stereotypical effeminacy does not signal that these men embraced heterosexuality. When asked whether they presented themselves differently when spending time with gay men and lesbians versus heterosexuals, many told stories that illustrate that they manage their presentations of self very carefully. By contrast, all spoke in one way or another of being "more free," "more comfortable," "more open" around other gay people: free to dress as they wished, free to physically express themselves as they desired. Bart (67) captures a common sentiment when he claims that he has a "great sense of relaxation with other gays." Some

talked of monitoring their physical presentations of self in public spaces, of being careful with their "non-verbal cues." For instance, Eric (60), who has a deep, male voice and who strikes the interviewer as "typically male" in his embodiment, illuminates how critical the body is to "reading" sexual orientation, specifically homosexuality. He spoke of being very aware that others look at body movement to assess masculinity and, by extension, to ascribe sexual orientation. Thus, he pays particular attention to not being seen to "flit around the grocery store." Similarly, he avoids public gestures that are seen as stereotypically feminine such as resting his hands on his hips. Yet, as Hennen (2005) reminds us, such attention to not being seen as effeminate signals more than concerns about the complex negotiations of gendered and sexed spaces; it also signals a rejection and devaluation of the feminine and demonstrates a gendered hierarchy that remains central to the logic of hegemonic masculinity.

Achieving Masculinity

Gary (64) in some ways mirrors Raymond's lifetime battle to achieve a greater sense of himself as masculine. Both have struggled with heteronormative ideals and both have tried in some fundamental ways to aspire to those ideals while also accepting that being gay may compromise these ideals, if only in the eyes of others. Thus, Gary, like Raymond, talks at some length about the "long fight" to live up to dominant notions of manhood and to achieve some sense of normative masculinity. Both highlight how, in negotiating notions of effeminacy, they reject what is feminine and they shape their own masculine ideals by calling on the standards of hegemonic masculinity. For instance, Gary emphatically claims that he is "very much into masculinity and not being limp-wristed." Another interesting angle on issues of masculinity and sexual orientation is revealed in a story told by James (64). His partner of 22 years recently died and James, at one point in the discussion about masculinity, comments that the absence of his partner in his life has led to his feeling more masculine. Upon further discussion, James explains that his partner was more masculine than he was because: "He could fix more things." Consequently, James's partner's death has caused him to be "more self-sufficient, to mow the lawn, to fix things." As this explanation suggests, James's notions of manhood are intimately tied to normative notions of the man as doer and fixer and his comments imply that his personal loss now allows him to embrace an identity that is more masculine.

The oldest interviewee, Glen (85), calls on classic notions of masculinity when he talks about what sorts of things make him feel masculine. He has already established that his best friend is a heterosexual man who loves to work on cars and his answer implies that heterosexual men define conventional masculinity. Indeed, he talks about how just being around heterosexual men shores up his own sense of masculinity—the very act of associating with a heterosexual man reinforces a sense of manhood that might otherwise be lacking. Thus, feeling masculine for Glen is about "football, phoning my best friend . . . [and] I feel most masculine when I watch him repair cars, when I have my car oiled and greased and I realize I'm with these [heterosexual] guys." As Glen's comments suggest, the essence of masculinity is embodied in his friend and his masculine activities; his friend is a sort of talisman for masculine ideals. As Connell and Messerschmidt remind us: "hegemony works in part through the production of exemplars of masculinity, symbols that have authority despite the fact that most men and boys do not fully live up to them" (2005, 846).

Disapproval/Distancing

Despite the fact that several of the men interviewed expressed a range of openness and acceptance for themselves when it came to androgynous or feminine traits and characteristics, it is especially interesting to explore what some of the interviewees have to say about masculinity and its perceived presence or absence in other men. This sort of analysis allows us to highlight the complicated ways that ambivalence manifests itself in the lives of most of these old gay men. In many ways, the uncovered ambivalence allows us to glimpse how these men use strategies of separation in order to establish who they are not. As Freitas and others (1997:324) remind us, such attention also "fosters an awareness of actions and transaction that enables individuals to vie for preferred identities in the face of stigmatizing or discrediting social labels." Additionally, our analysis illuminates the insidiousness of hegemonic masculinity; it underscores how old gay men may contribute to their own oppression through their rejection of men who do not adhere to hegemonic ways of being male. Finally, we are reminded again of the importance of gender relations and how masculinity is defined relationally, against what is feminine.

Despite, or perhaps because of his own acknowledged struggles with masculinity, Gary (64) is among the most vocal in his disapproval of men who do not measure up to heteronormative ideals of masculinity. He is clear that he likes masculine-looking men: those, as he says, who demonstrate a "lack of physical feminine characteristics." Gary also highlights another component of ideal masculinity when he identifies sexual activity and sexual attractiveness as important. Indeed, when asked what makes a man masculine, he responds by exclaiming that for him the epitome of masculinity is a "hot guy." He further elaborates in a way that highlights how notions of embodied masculinity shift when we consider sexual orientation. Thus, when asked to elaborate on his notion that "a guy who is hot is masculine," Gary obliges with this analysis wherein he objectifies and sexualizes the male body in ways similar to how heterosexual men often objectify female bodies: "It has to do with the way he moves, to a certain extent with the way he dresses." Gary seems to be criticizing here what Hennen describes as "kinesthetic effeminacy, wherein a man is judged by prevailing standards as either moving or using his voice 'like a woman'" (Hennen 2008). To be considered "hot" by Gary one must sufficiently discipline the body to comport to hegemonic standards of masculinity.

On the other hand, not all of the men interviewed were disapproving of gay men who did not uphold ideal notions of masculinity or who sometimes exhibited what some would describe as feminine characteristics. The story here is complicated, however. On one hand, the narratives underscore that these old men are not monolithic and also that we must consider context as important. Thus, some of the men interviewed spoke of responding one way in a particular context and another way when circumstances were different. For instance, Bart (67) responded to the question about whether masculinity was important to him with a loud "Oh, Yes," and even went on to exclaim that "[I] like my men to look like men." This claim describes Bart's personal desires about ideal partners and, as such, differs from his willingness to be accepting of more feminine men in contexts beyond those of personal desire. Consequently, he reinforces this distinction when he later talks openly and warmly about the gay world he inhabits where gay drag queens and "gay peacocks" are acceptable and welcome. Jake (78) also is very open about his own presentation of self, especially around other gays. He exclaims at one point: "I'm an effeminate person and more so with gays." At other times as we talk, he refers comfortably to h   as "an old queen." On the other hand, s   a different approach and the   the tensions and   their own notions   tor (71) exemplifies   that masculinity is not   et he is also clear that he   in men. Indeed, not only do   such characteristics with drag quee   ords suggest a negative association wit   s feminine. Thus, he claims that he has "never been comfortable with 'nelly queens.' [I] don't enjoy drag." At another point in the interview, Victor is more explicit in his negative connection of effeminacy in gay men with lower-class women. He talks about not liking gay men who are "slutty [and who wear] ridiculously tight pants." Conversations such as those with Victor, increase our awareness of how distancing strate-

gies work. Accordingly, we see how some gay men protect their own identities by choosing to disidentify with gay men who represent "visual caricatures" (Freitas et al.1997). Nonetheless, as we have argued already, Victor and others who use distancing tactics are not engaged in wholesale rejection of homosexuals or homosexuality. Rather, such responses illustrate the complicated work of stigma management. Such work brings to mind Goffman's seminal work on stigma and his insight about ambivalence toward similar others: "he can neither embrace his group nor let it go" (Goffman 1963:109).

Ageism in Gay Communities

A predominant theme that interviewees cited repeatedly was the youth obsession of gay culture and of its consequences for themselves and others. Glen (85), for instance, talked at length when we first met about these issues and, as a political activist for gay issues, it is clear that he thinks a lot about these concerns. He is extremely well-networked and well-known in the gay communities of his city and well beyond. Asked to respond to what he sees as the level of ageism among gays, Glen puts into words a sentiment that the others share: "gays are much more ageist than straights." Eric (60) sees this ageism as having to do with how gay culture "really accentuates youth and body and physical conditions." Guy goes on to talk about gay social life and the dominance of "the bar scene" in urban areas, and he makes the point that "in many a bar, a man over 40 would not be looked at because he is too old." At least in part because they face ageism in this social setting, he argues that, in his experience many gay men become increasingly socially isolated. Here is how he responds to a question about what happens to gay men in their 60s, 70s, and 80s: "Well, such men stop going to bars, [they] become isolated, [they] become introverted, [they] become loners, [they] become peculiar people. From being in their 30s where they had a number of friends, as each decade comes they have fewer friends and go out less." Nevertheless, unmentioned in this narrative is the role that cohort plays in how these particular old gay men experience growing old. As well, what Glen is not explicit about at this point in the interview—although he later raises this issue—is the importance of having a partner and how this can mitigate the loneliness of being old and gay. Others raise this issue and underscore the varying strategies adopted by these old gay men to ensure a viable social or sexual life in the face of the ageism they see in the gay communities around them. For instance, Victor (71) talks about his current situation with his life partner of 22 years (who is 24 years younger than he is): "Well, if I had to go out and compete for sexual partners like I did years ago, that would be a definite concern. But I've got what I want and he accepts me as I am."

As well as having partners, some of the men interviewed are also involved with a group called "Prime Timers" which several describe as a social group for "older gay men and their [younger] admirers." The extent to which this organization is joined by men who are white, middle class and beyond is not known to us but comments made by the interviewees suggest that the chapters attended by these men predominantly meet these class and race profiles. On the international group's website, Prime Timers are described as "Older gay or bisexual men (and younger men who admire mature men)" (www.primetimer-sww.org/about.htm). Glen, who is heavily involved with this national organization (which has numerous local chapters), tells us that these younger admirers are not ageist because they like men older than themselves. Yet, and several interviewees make this point, Prime Timers is an organization that in many ways highlights the ageism of gay culture by reinforcing hegemonic ideals of what constitutes an attractive man. Consequently, even if inadvertently, this organization reproduces the notion that youth and youthful attractiveness and sexual vitality are the coins of the realm. Here is what Victor (71) tells us in these regards:

> I think, like most aging or older gay men, I find younger men attractive. I think that's why a lot of Prime Timers don't get together with each other. The majority of them would say that they would love to have a partner and most of them don't . . . they want somebody younger and that's the way it is . . . I can walk into a room of 100 Prime Timers and I might be very fond of most of them but I don't want to go to bed with any of them . . . I think they are all very aware of that.

Gary (64) also tells a story that not only reinforces the ageism suggested above but also hints at his attempts to cover up his real age, to use the strategy of passing as younger than his chronological age. When asked if he is comfortable telling his age, he responds: "It depends on the people . . . if I am trying to chat up some man I have to figure out: 'Now, if I tell you the truth' is he going to find out that I'm too old." Thus, Gary illustrates his own internalization of ageist notions and his narrative also portrays the stigma older gay men experience when they seek to find partners—especially younger men—for sexual pleasure. Victor and Gary's comments also underscore the importance of sex in the gay world, even among old men. These comments allow us to glimpse how they construct gayness. Indeed, Eric (60) is explicit in this regard: "Gays [are] defined in terms of sex. It's what defines us."

Richard (69), who has taken a vow of celibacy, is not as accepting as Victor and others of the ageist self-denigration within Prime Timers. He has recently decided not to attend their functions because "when an admirer [a young man] walks in [to the room] and everybody flocks around him, I can't stand this." Eric (60) also resists what he sees as the youth obsession of exclusively gay groups and allows: "I don't socialize just with gays." He has recently experienced a break up with his younger partner and learned from close friends that the partner saw Eric's being older as a negative. Yet, illustrating how pervasive is the social value placed on youthful attractiveness and how insidious ageism is, Eric admits that he does not date men over 50. He tells of how he has had several arguments with close lesbian friends who accuse him of being ageist in his choice of partners. He acknowledges his own ageism but still observes that he was recently "flattered to hell and back when a 27-year-old model wanted to see me."

Negotiating Old Bodies: Resisting Old Age

What can we learn from these gay men's masculinity and about how their various social locations shape how they inhabit and negotiate old bodies? How do they make sense of what it means to be physically old, and to look old, in a world that denigrates old age? How does being white and relatively affluent influence their experiences with old bodies? How do they negotiate and respond to masculinity scripts that glorify young bodies, especially in gay culture? The picture is far from being a straightforward one. The narratives of these men uncover the complications and ambivalences of managing stigmatized identities. What we learn is that in coping with the stigmas of being old gay men there is no one script that all follow. In some ways, as gay men who spend time in gay communities, they have had the experience of being defined as old for many more years than would be the case if they were heterosexual; they have learned to deal with this marked identity in a variety of ways.

High levels of education and other life privileges that accompany being white and economically secure provide these men with the wherewithal to resist aging and to be more positive about some aspects of being old. Coping with the stigmas of being gay has also taught them some valuable life lessons about oppression, how to manage it and, ideally, how to resist it. Nevertheless, there are commonalities among these men that illustrate the oppressive nature of age relations. Their accounts reveal strategies they employ to manage the ageism that shapes their responses to their own bodies and the bodies of others.

At age 64 Gary is a large, bearded man who lives alone but also within what he calls a "gay world, not community." Gary talks frequently throughout our interview about sex and his

desire to have frequent sex. He is keenly aware that his age is a distinct disadvantage in the gay world he moves in, especially when seeking sex partners. For instance, when asked whether he is comfortable telling his age, he is the only man interviewed who suggests that he sometimes hides his age or, at the very least, avoids talking about it. Gary's motivation to avoid telling his age is intimately connected to his desire to find a sex partner and the fact that he feels it necessary to hide his real age underscores the ageism that exists within the gay world. Gary's strategy of passing or covering also illustrates how he works to minimize the impact of his stigmatized status as an old man.

As Gary's narrative demonstrates, ageism gets reinforced and reproduced through ideas that to be old is bad and to be seen as more youthful than one's chronological age is good. Covering or passively "passing" as younger than one's real age is a strategy sometimes used by our interviewees and they provide us evidence that they use this strategy specifically to accommodate the ageism they encounter in their daily lives. Thus, while in one voice they tell us that they are comfortable with where they are in their lives, that being old brings a measure of contentment, they also echo this sentiment of Peter (62): "I do not feel old, so when I hear the word 'old' I can't relate to it." Put another way, Bart (67) says: "I don't like the term 'old.' . . . I hate [the term] 'senior citizens'." Gary (64) illustrates another form of denial: "I do not admit that my body has slowed down." Victor (71) also refuses to see himself as "old" and all of the negative things that that implies. Indeed, he exhibits a level of denial and ambivalence that is typical of almost all of the men interviewed. Unwilling to use the word "old" in reference to himself, he claims: "I do not see myself as an older person. I do not feel like an older person. I don't feel much different than I can remember feeling 40 to 50 years ago. I am thrilled with that. I'm so glad that is the case." At least for Victor, but we suspect for others too, acceptance of being gay comes more easily than acceptance of being old.

Illuminating the complex ways that gay culture reinforces youthful and hegemonic masculinity and how old gay men, even if unwittingly, adhere to such notions, several talk about how gay men age better than heterosexual men because they pay more attention to keeping youthful bodies through exercise and disciplining their bodies. Responses vary as to why this might be the case. For instance, Eric (60) makes a general claim that "appearance is more of a concern with gay men." Gary (64) who is, by his own assessment, 75 pounds overweight, supports this same notion by laughingly explaining that "straight men age quicker than gay men do. I think gay men take better care of themselves." This notion of paying attention to one's appearance, doing the work necessary to "look good" (meaning youthful) is also captured in this comment of Bart's (67): "Many, many heterosexual friends, some younger than I, look twice as old as I am because they have given up." Raymond is quite explicit about the ageism that underscores this obligatory dictate of keeping up appearances: "old gay men feel compelled to do everything they can to hide the ravages of their body. They dye their hair, they have facelifts, they wear clothing that they think makes them look younger . . . they do a lot of exercise." However, Raymond and others do not reflect upon how their social class (and race) privileges provide them with the means to consume more youthful lifestyles, to exercise, and to look younger for more years than their less affluent peers.

Peter (62) also claims that gay men age better than heterosexual men: "if you were to compare heterosexual men my age to homosexual men my age, the homosexual men are much more interested in what they look like. They have not gone to pot, to seed. They are snappy dressers . . . they are conscious of their physical appearance." Peter's comparison of older gay and heterosexual men's appearances highlights his ageist and class-specific notions of how gay men are more concerned than heterosexual men with embracing youthful bodies and youthful fashion as ways to avoid being seen as old. Yet, underscoring the often contradictory and ambivalent nature of such responses, Peter also claims that gay men do not chase youthful bodies as they age. Indeed, he decries such stereotypes—at least in his own circle of friends: "The gay men I know are not like that. They do not work out and wear youthful clothes. They are not in the 'silly old fool syndrome.' The gay people I know are content with their ages."

In keeping with the story above, others also told stories that left no doubt that they were ambivalent about growing old and especially about looking old. Their stories provide us a picture of the ambivalences and contradictions that are ongoing in the management of stigmatized identities. For instance, Raymond (67), who is generally very positive about being old, tells us of another strategy for coping with old age, one that highlights how old age is "contagious" and thus, must be avoided. Consequently, Raymond tells how he avoids others who are old: "All of the friends I have from the time that I was 40 are much younger than I am." Perhaps by associating with younger people, one can stave off the inevitable, because Raymond is also quite sure that getting older makes a man less masculine: "I think most men think that. Because most men tie masculinity to their physical prowess. And once they sit in a wheelchair and can't feed themselves anymore, I think they feel very . . . emasculated." Raymond's sentiment about embodied old age and the resulting diminution of masculinity is shared by James (64) who also sees masculinity and independence as inevitably compromised by old age. In response to the question about whether of not being old makes men less masculine, he claims: "Yea, I think it does in that they become dependent. When you lose that element of dignity, I think of the product called 'Depends'."

For affluent consumers, especially those who are white, cosmetic surgery offers a way to regain or sustain a more youthful appearance, to cover signs of aging and to pass as younger than one's chronological age. Such surgery illuminates the strategies of ongoing appearance management that can be called upon in the face of "stigmatizing or discrediting social labels" (Freitas et al., 1997:324). This analysis allows us to glimpse how some of these men actively work to acquire a preferred embodied identity of being not old—or at least not looking as old as they are. Seeking to maintain a youthful appearance through cosmetic surgery was something that four of these interviewees were willing to consider. For instance, James (64) claimed that "If I had lots of money, I guess I would. I'd have a body makeover." Eric (60) was similarly inclined and he admitted that he had been "seriously considering it for a year or two." He told how he had gone so far as to get the name of a local cosmetic surgeon; he was interested in both a facelift and liposuction around the abdominal area. Victor talked about how he had considered cosmetic eye surgery to reduce the bags under his eyes ten or fifteen years ago but had never gotten around to doing it. Cost was a disincentive but also "discomfort," plus the fact that "I don't trust it. I don't know that it's safe." Gary (64) had this to say about cosmetic surgery: "you've got to deal with what you've got . . . next time I go to Brazil, I'm going to have some face work done." "I have no interest in plastic surgery and tightening up and getting rid of wrinkles, " he claimed. Instead, Gary wanted to remove some other signs of aging: "The liver spots I'll get removed and some of the moles." Using makeup provides a cheaper and less intrusive way to hide certain signs of aging, such as the liver or age spots referred to by Gary. Bart (67), for instance, talked openly about how "a good five years ago I tried to cover up some aging marks" by using makeup. He was especially proud of the fact that he was so adept at using it that "you'd never know I had it on." Yet, underscoring how complex and sometimes paradoxical are approaches to aging, Bart told of how he had stopped using makeup to hide his aging because "I am pretty much trying to be honest with myself and to others." By revealing his true physiological self, and accepting the embodied stigma(ta) of old age, Bart also moves himself away from engaging in feminine behavior (wearing makeup). Sto-

ries such as Bart's shed some light on the shifting and fluid nature of how some old gay men negotiate multiple stigmatized identities.

Even among this small number of old gay men, the reactions to the aging process are impressively wide-ranging: it is clear that there is no one way for gay men to grow old. In fact, given their widely varying life histories, the multiple forms of masculinity at play, and the variety of involvement in gay communities, it is quite possible that old gay men's experiences with aging may be even more diverse than those of their heterosexual peers.

Conclusions

This study gives voice to the experiences of a group of men who rarely have been heard. We trust that their voices will help illuminate the experiences of other old gay men like them, and provoke further discussion on the ways such men grapple with their sexuality, with aging, with masculinities, and with how their bodies are critical to their sense-making of all of these. Through the use of an intersectionality perspective that highlights not only race, class, and gender but also age and sexuality, we uncover how privileges and disadvantages are negotiated; we begin to understand how gender, race, and class privileges help mitigate forms of oppression stemming from sexuality and old age.

As well, the narrative analysis used in this paper allows us to explore in some depth how a small, privileged group of old, white, relatively affluent gay men experience key corporeal aspects of growing old in a culture that glorifies hegemonic masculinity and its key components of youthfulness and heterosexuality. Again, we come to understand how they have forms of capital (through class, race, and gender privileges) that allow them to resist aging and, sometimes, to pass as younger than their chronological ages. Our focus on this marginalized population brings attention that is much needed in studies of masculinities. We learn firsthand how many struggle to live up to hegemonic ideals of what it means to be a man and to look like one. In addition, we also come to appreciate the diversity of their approaches to manhood as they strive to accomplish some sense of authenticity.

Additionally, we appreciate the complicated and contradictory nature of their approaches to being men who are old and gay. Narrative analysis proves particularly salient as a method that exposes the ways that the body is central to notions of masculinity; the voices of the interviewees allow us to glimpse the contradictions and messiness of how they grapple with embodied masculinity throughout the life course. As well, the narratives attest to a long-standing assumption about gay culture: ageism is prominent, and much of this ageism is related to the body. Indeed, their words lend credence to Laws's (1995) claim that ageism is an embodied form of oppression. This should come as no surprise, given that gay male culture puts a very specific body on a pedestal, and this body is in no way old. Regardless of their many successes in other areas of their lives, many of these men have experienced the stigmatization of their aging bodies.

We gain, too, a greater understanding of how age relations render the body a site of struggle and ambivalence. These struggles and ambivalences demonstrate themselves in myriad ways. For instance, we hear over and over again how, despite a declared comfort with themselves, that comfort has more to do with being gay than with being old; most subscribe to negative notions of being old and looking old. That they frequently enact these negative notions when they interact with other old gay men reinforces Chen's (1999) claim that gay men become arbiters of their own oppression. As relatively affluent retirees, most feel fairly keenly the continuous obligation to consume products and lifestyles (exercising, dieting, youthful clothes, etc.) that reinforce ageist notions of old bodies as undesirable bodies. Even though the men sometimes positively framed contrasts to heterosexual men, who they see as having "given up" on stopping their bodily declines, there is a subtext to the narratives, one that sees old age as something to avoid or resist. Indeed, they confirm

what Cruikshank (2003) reminds us of: old age is increasingly pathologized in our culture.

We suggest that the interviewees, as white professional men, have much in common with similarly situated heterosexual men, especially when they discuss their aging bodies (Slevin, forthcoming). As we argued in the introduction, in addition to the socially constructed nature of aging in all its permutations, a fact glares: the physical body ages and at some point begins to break down. An aching joint and a non-responsive penis know no sexual orientation. Nowadays, consumer society encourages all men to chase youthful ideals—whether they are 30 or 80. Class and race privileges allow some men to postpone the inevitabilities of aging bodies and to adhere to hegemonic masculine ideals for longer than less affluent men. Yet, there are some differences in the way gay men react to the bodily changes that accompany aging. For example, few heterosexual men would dare to use makeup, as Bart (67) admitted to doing. Though these men face little discrimination due to their sexual orientation, they do face significant discrimination as old men in gay communities. And in the bitterest of ironies, some of this discrimination is carried out by other old gay men as they continually attempt to construct positive identities through strategies that distance themselves from other old men.

We see fruitful possibilities for researchers interested in the lives of old gay men. The first and most promising avenue for research leads directly to the group Prime Timers. As noted, some of the interview respondents in this study had heated views of this organization, and questioned the role that it plays within the older gay male community. While some see the group as an oasis from invisibility, there are signs that Prime Timers chapters (or at least some of the men involved in them) perpetuate and reinforce the very ageism that they seek to address. A large-scale, multi-site study of Prime Timers and its membership could make great strides in advancing our understanding of the complexities we identified above. Studying the membership experiences of men at a variety of stages of old age could help us to understand the various points at which these men develop problematic relationships with the organization. Do younger Prime Timers have more positive experiences than those who are at a more advanced stage of old age? What steps does the organization, or specific chapters within the organization, take to address these issues among its constituencies?

Those who "admire" old gay men (as some of the interviewees put it, and as the organization explicitly states) are also worthy of study. For example, we recounted a story from Ed (60), who had a 27-year-old admirer, and a male model at that. Who is this young man, and how does he conceive of his admiration for older men? If the goal is to decrease the ageism that old gay men face in gay communities, in-depth analyses of such young men certainly would be a place to start. In addition to delineating what they find attractive about older men, another topic of interest would be the stigma such men might themselves face from others in the gay community. The common, immediate assumption that such a man simply must be a gold-digger is yet another window into the ageism of the gay community.

In addition to Prime Timers, one might explore other options for old gay men to be involved in gay communities. Of course old gay men may (and do) become involved in all aspects of gay communities, but their presence in two subcultures is particularly striking: the bears and the sadomasochism communities. The bear community rejects the strict body norms (washboard abs, hairless torsos) that the broader gay community tends to value. Therefore, it should be no surprise that some old gay men find the bears a welcome respite, as their aging bodies will be treated with a greater level of admiration than elsewhere in the gay community. Some old gay men find a place in the SM community, serving in the role of a "daddy" to submissive (and usually younger) participants. This community actually may allow old gay men to turn their aging into a distinct advantage. A comparative study of these three communities (Prime Timers, bears, and SM), and why various men seek out each of these

communities would offer some understanding of the way old gay men see themselves and their places within gay culture. Hennen's groundbreaking study of communities of faeries, bears, and leathermen (2008) is replete with insights about gay masculinities, but he does not deal with age in any in-depth fashion. Thus, these groups are worthy of much more attention.

A final possibility for continuing this line of research involves an expansion of the study to middle-aged gay men. Are these men indeed considered old within their gay communities, and do they in some ways buy into this perception? The rising generation of middle-aged gay men offers unique research opportunities, as these men are among the first to come of age in a culture with markedly less stigma attached to gay identities, as well as less imminent concern over AIDS. Their aging may look quite different from the aging of their gay brothers a generation before them. We should not pass up the opportunity to study this process as it occurs.

Notes

1. Because "old" carries a unique stigma in our culture we want to reclaim its positive connotations, to naturalize and neutralize it. Thus, we use it throughout this article (rather than "older") in an activist manner. See Calasanti and Slevin 2001 (pp. 9–10) for a more detailed discussion.

2. Throughout the paper, we use pseudonyms to protect the identities of the respondents.

References

Barrett, D. 2000. Masculinity among working-class gay males. In *Gay masculinities*, edited by P. Nardi, 176–205. Thousand Oaks, CA: Sage.

Bennett, K.C., and N. L. Thompson. 1991. Accelerated aging and male homosexuality: Australian evidence in a continuing debate. *Journal of Homosexuality* 20: 65–75.

Brekhus, W. 2003. *Peacocks, chameleons, centaurs: Gay suburbia and the grammar of social identity*. Chicago: University of Chicago Press.

Calasanti, T. M. 2004. Feminist gerontology and old men. *Journal of Gerontology* 59B: 305–314.

Calasanti, T. M. and N. King. 2005. Firming the floppy penis: Age, class, and gender relations in the lives of old men. *Men and Masculinities* 8: 3–23.

Calasanti, T. M., and K. F. Slevin. 2006. Introduction: Age matters. In *Age matters: Realigning feminist thinking,* edited by T. M. Calasanti and K. F. Slevin, 1–17. New York, Routledge.

Calasanti, T. M., and K. F. Slevin. 2001. *Gender, social inequalities, and aging.* Walnut Creek, CA: AltaMira Press.

Cantu, L. 2000. Entre hombres/between men: Latino masculinities and homosexualities. In *Gay masculinities,* edited by P. Nardi, 224–246. Thousand Oaks, CA: Sage.

Carpenter, L. M. 2002. Gender and the social construction of virginity loss in the contemporary United States. *Gender & Society* 16: 345–365.

Chase, S. E. 2005. Narrative inquiry: Multiple lenses, approaches, voices. In *Qualitative research,* 3rd ed., edited by N. K. Denzin and Y. Lincoln, 651–679. Thousand Oaks, CA: Sage.

Chen, A. S. 1999. Lives at the center of the periphery, lives at the periphery of the center: Chinese American masculinity and bargaining with hegemony. *Gender & Society* 13: 584–607.

Collins, P. H. 2000. *Black feminist thought: Knowledge, consciousness, and the politics of empowerment.* New York: Routledge.

Connell, R. W. 1995. *Masculinities.* Berkeley: University of California Press.

Connell, R. W. and J. W. Messerschmidt. 2005. Hegemonic masculinity: Rethinking the concept. *Gender & Society* 19: 829–859.

Crenshaw, K. 1991. Mapping the margins: Intersectionality, identity politics, and violence against women of color. *Stanford Law Review* 46: 1241–99.

Cruikshank, M. 2003. *Learning to be old: Gender, culture, and aging.* Lanham, MD: Rowman and Littlefield.

Dyer, R. 2002. *The culture of queers.* New York: Routledge.

Emslie, C., K. Hunt, and R. O'Brien. 2004. Masculinities in older men: A qualitative study in the west of Scotland. *The Journal of Men's Studies* 12: 207–226.

Faircloth, C. A., ed. 2003. *Aging bodies: Images and everyday experience.* Walnut Creek, CA: AltaMira Press.

Freitas, A., S. Kaiser, D. J. Chandler, D. C. Hall, J. Kim, and T. Hammidi. 1997. Appearance management as border construction: Least favorite clothing, group distancing, and identity not! *Sociological Inquiry* 67: 323–335.

Gilleard, C., and P. Higgs. 2000. *Cultures of ageing: Self, citizen and the body.* Harlow, England: Prentice Hall.

Goffman, E. 1963. *Stigma: Notes on the management of spoiled identity.* Englewood Cliffs, NJ: Prentice-Hall.

Han, S. 2000. Asian American gay men's (dis)claim on masculinity. In *Gay masculinities,* edited by P. Nardi, 206–223. Thousand Oaks, CA: Sage.

Heaphy, B. 2007. Sexualities, gender and ageing. *Current Sociology* 55: 193–210.

Hennen, P. 2008. *Faeries, bears, and leathermen: Men in community queering the masculine.* Chicago: University of Chicago Press.

Hennen, P. 2005. Bear bodies, bear masculinity: Recuperation, resistance, or retreat? *Gender & Society* 19: 25–43.

Hostetler, A. J. 2004. Old, gay, and alone? The ecology of well-being among middle-aged and older single gay men, in *Gay and lesbian aging: Research and future directions.* Edited by G. Herdt and B. De Vries. New York: Springer.

Jones, J. and S. Pugh. 2005. Ageing gay men. *Men and Masculinities* 7: 248–260.

Katz, S. 2005. *Cultural aging: Life course, lifestyle, and senior worlds.* Ontario, Canada: Broadview Press.

Kimmel, M. 1996. *Manhood in America: A cultural history.* New York: The Free Press.

Laws, G. 1995. Understanding ageism: Lessons from feminism and postmodernism. *The Gerontologist* 35(1): 112–18.

Lindau, S. T., L. P. Schumm, E. O. Laumann, W. Levinson, C. A. O'Muircheartaigh, and L. J. Waite. 2007. A study of sexuality and health among older adults in the United States. *New England Journal of Medicine* 375: 762–774.

Linneman, T. 2008. How do you solve a problem like Will Truman? The feminization of gay men on Will & Grace. *Men and Masculinities* 10: 583–603

Loe, M. 2003. *The rise of Viagra: How the little blue pill changed sex in America*. New York: New York University Press.

Loftus, J. 2001. America's liberalization in attitudes toward homosexuality, 1973 to 1998. *American Sociological Review* 66:762–782.

Marshall, B. L. 2006. The new virility: Viagra, male aging and sexual function. *Sexualities* 9: 345–362.

Marshall, B. L., and S. Katz. 2002. Forever functional: Sexual fitness and the ageing male body. *Body & Society* 8: 43–70.

McVittie, C., and J. Willock 2006. 'You can't fight windmills': How older men do health, ill health, and masculinities. *Qualitative Health Research* 16: 788–801.

Meadows, R. and K. Davidson 2006. Maintaining manliness in later life: Hegemonic masculinities and emphasized femininities. In *Age matters: Realigning feminist thinking*, edited by T. M. Calasanti and K. F. Slevin, 295–312. New York: Routledge.

Messner, M. A. 1992. *Power at play: Sports and the problem of masculinity*. Boston: Beacon Press.

Nardi, P. 2000. 'Anything for a sis, Mary': An introduction to gay masculinities. In *Gay masculinities*, edited by P. Nardi, 1–11. Thousand Oaks, CA: Sage.

Oberg, P. 2003. Images vs. experiences of the aging body. In *Aging bodies: Images and everyday experience*. Edited by C. A. Faircloth, 103–39. Walnut Creek, CA: AltaMira Press.

Prime Timers World Wide. 2008. *Prime Timers World Wide*. http://www.primetimersww.org/about.htm (accessed January 13, 2008).

Quam, J. K., and Whitford, G. S. 1992. Adaptation and age-related expectations of older gay and lesbian adults. *The Gerontologist* 32: 367–374.

Rosenfeld, D. 2003. The homosexual body in lesbian and gay elders' narratives. In *Aging bodies: Images and everyday experience*, edited by C. A. Faircloth, 171–203. Walnut Creek, CA: AltaMira Press.

Slevin, K. F. in-progress. Disciplining bodies: The aging experiences of old heterosexual and gay men. *Generations*.

Slevin, K. F. 2006. The embodied experiences of old lesbians. In *Age matters: Realigning feminist thinking*, edited by T. M. Calasanti and K. F. Slevin, 247–268. New York, Routledge.

Spector-Mersel, G. 2006. Never-aging stories: Western hegemonic masculinity scripts. *Journal of Gender Studies* 15: 67–82.

Thompson, E. H., Jr., and Whearty, P. M. 2004. Older men's social participation: The importance of masculinity ideology. *The Journal of Men's Studies* 13: 5–24.

Thompson, E. H. 1994. Older men as invisible men in contemporary society. In *Older men's lives*, edited by E. H. Thompson, 1–21. London: Sage.

Turner, B. S. 1996. *The body and society*. 2nd ed. London: Sage.

Wahler, J., and S. G. Gabbay. 1997. Gay male aging: A review of the literature. *Journal of Gay & Lesbian Social Services* 6: 1–20.

Gloria Steinem

If Men Could Menstruate

A white minority of the world has spent centuries conning us into thinking that a white skin makes people superior—even though the only thing it really does is make them more subject to ultraviolet rays and to wrinkles. Male human beings have built whole cultures around the idea that penis-envy is "natural" to women—though having such an unprotected organ might be said to make men vulnerable, and the power to give birth makes womb-envy at least as logical.

In short, the characteristics of the powerful, whatever they may be, are thought to be better than the characteristics of the powerless—and logic has nothing to do with it.

What would happen, for instance, if suddenly, magically, men could menstruate and women could not?

The answer is clear—menstruation would become an enviable, boastworthy, masculine event:

Men would brag about how long and how much.

Boys would mark the onset of menses, that longed-for proof of manhood, with religious rituals and stag parties.

Congress would fund a National Institute of Dysmenorrhea to help stamp out monthly discomforts.

Sanitary supplies would be federally funded and free. (Of course, some men would still pay for the prestige of commercial brands such as John Wayne Tampons, Muhammad Ali's Rope-a-dope Pads, Joe Namath Jock Shields—"For Those Light Bachelor Days," and Robert "Baretta" Blake Maxi-Pads.)

Military men, right-wing politicians, and religious fundamentalists would cite menstruation ("*men*-struation") as proof that only men could serve in the Army ("you have to give blood to take blood"), occupy political office ("can women be aggressive without that steadfast cycle governed by the planet Mars?"), be priests and ministers ("how could a woman give her blood for our sins?"), or rabbis ("without the monthly loss of impurities, women remain unclean").

Male radicals, left-wing politicians, and mystics, however, would insist that women are equal, just different; and that any woman could enter their ranks if only she were willing to self-inflict a major wound every month ("you *must* give blood for the revolution"), recognize the preeminence of menstrual issues, or subordinate her selfness to all men in their Cycle of Enlightenment.

Street guys would brag ("I'm a three-pad man") or answer praise from a buddy ("Man, you lookin' *good!*") by giving fives and saying, "Yeah, man, I'm on the rag!"

TV shows would treat the subject at length. ("Happy Days": Richie and Potsie try to convince Fonzie that he is still "The Fonz," though he has missed two periods in a row.) So would newspapers. (SHARK SCARE THREATENS MENSTRUATING MEN. JUDGE CITES MONTHLY STRESS IN PARDONING RAPIST.) And movies. (Newman and Redford in "Blood Brothers"!)

Men would convince women that intercourse was *more* pleasurable at "that time of the month." Lesbians would be said to fear blood and therefore life itself—though probably only because they needed a good menstruating man.

Of course, male intellectuals would offer the most moral and logical arguments. How could a woman master any discipline that demanded a sense of time, space, mathematics, or measurement, for instance, without that in-built gift for measuring the cycles of the moon and planets—and thus for measuring anything at all? In the rarefied fields of philosophy and religion, could women compensate for missing the rhythm of the universe? Or for their lack of symbolic death-and-resurrection every month?

Liberal males in every field would try to be kind: the fact that "these people" have no gift for measuring life or connecting to the universe, the liberals would explain, should be punishment enough.

And how would women be trained to react? One can imagine traditional women agreeing to all these arguments with a staunch and smiling masochism. ("The ERA would force housewives to wound themselves every month": Phyllis Schlafly. "Your husband's blood is as sacred as that of Jesus—and so sexy, too!": Marabel Morgan.) Reformers and Queen Bees would try to imitate men, and *pretend* to have a monthly cycle. All feminists would explain endlessly that men, too, needed to be liberated from the false idea of Martian aggressiveness, just as women needed to escape the bonds of menses-envy. Radical feminists would add that the oppression of the nonmenstrual was the pattern for all other oppressions. ("Vampires were our first freedom fighters!") Cultural feminists would develop a bloodless imagery in art and literature. Socialist feminists would insist that only under capitalism would men be able to monopolize menstrual blood. . . .

In fact, if men could menstruate, the power justifications could probably go on forever.

If we let them.

Meika Loe

Fixing Broken Masculinity: Viagra as a Technology for the Production of Gender and Sexuality

This essay centers on the turn of the century heterosexual male body as a new site for medicalization, technological enhancement, and cultural and personal crisis. Using ethnographic data, I explore the ways in which masculinity and heterosexuality are constructed and problematized in light of the Viagra phenomenon. I expose the ways in which consumers and practitioners actively make sense of Viagra in terms of "trouble" and "repair." And I argue that Viagra is both a cultural and material tool used in the production and achievement of gender and sexuality. For the first time in American history, biotechnology is being used to "fix" or enhance heterosexual male confidence and power and thus avert masculinity "in crisis."

In this article I draw from fifty-one interviews (twenty-five male consumers and twenty-six medical professionals) conducted between 1999–2001. All names have been changed to insure confidentiality. The male consumers I spoke with are a self-selected group who responded to my requests for interviews through internet postings, newspaper advertisements, practitioner referrals, senior citizens organizations, personal contacts, and prostate cancer support group meetings. They represent a diverse sample in terms of ethnicity, sexual orientation, and age (seventeen to eighty-six years old. The majority are middle class. Semi-structured con-

From *Sexuality & Culture* 5(3) Summer 2001. Reprinted with kind permission from Springer Science and Business Media.

versational consumer interviews were primarily conducted over the phone or the internet (for anonymity and confidentiality reasons) with the in-person interview as the exception. In addition, I interviewed twenty-six medical professionals from Boston, Massachusetts, and Beverly Hills, California, two medically sophisticated urban areas with extremely different medical scenes. The majority of these interviews were in-person, semi-structured conversations, with phone conversations as the exception. All interviews were transcribed, and then coded and analyzed using qualitative data analysis software.

Turn of the Century Troubled Masculinity

Problematic Package

In the age of Viagra, most practitioners and consumers agree that loss of erectile function appears to be synonymous with loss of manhood. Early on, some urologists learned that they couldn't treat the penis in isolation from the man. To treat the penis on its own, one prominent psychiatrist commented, was not to see masculinity as a whole package.

> Certainly [the discovery of a chemical injection that could produce an erection] started a new era in understanding sexual response. This really excited urologists who thought they could isolate the erection from the man. Now they have learned they can't detach the man from his penis. [Baker, psychiatrist]

It quickly became clear to many practitioners that masculinity was intimately tied to erectile functioning. A growing field of scholarship on male sexual bodies suggests that sexuality is a proving ground for masculinity (Bordo 1999; Connell 1995; Fasteau 1975; Kimmel 1996; Potts 2000). Thus, for males, gender and sexuality may be difficult to separate out. Masculinity requires sexuality and vice versa.

This conversation between a doctor, his patient, and myself exposes the close relationship between masculinity and erectile function.

Doctor: You see, sexual dysfunction in males is peculiar. I'm sure if someone is a paraplegic and can't walk, he would feel psychologically deprived. But beyond the great obvious lack—people who don't see or hear as well, they don't feel like they have lost their manhood, you see. I must tell you, and I'm not a psychiatrist, but I think it is far more prevalent in males than it would be in females. The fact that if women don't have sexual gratification, or don't have it [sex?], it isn't that they don't miss it, but they don't have the psychological burden that males seem to have. Maybe it's a throwback to the time when the caveman went and dragged a woman out on his shoulder. [Bending, internist]

Me: So sexuality is integral to male identity?

Patient: Absolutely! [My wife and I] talked about it for a long time—well a couple of weeks before the [prostate] operation itself. We talked about its possible we may not be able to have sex because the apparatuses they had out didn't necessarily work. So you could go for the rest of your life without having sex. And [the doctor] is so right. You feel part of your manhood is gone. [Gray, consumer]

Above, a practitioner and his patient agree that the "trouble" associated with erectile dysfunction is a psychological burden and loss of manhood. Most of my interview subjects were in

agreement on this point; that if the penis is in trouble, so is the man.

> You probably wouldn't understand it—it's a big part of manhood. Ever since you're a little boy growing up that's a part of your masculinity. And whether its right or wrong, and however you deal with it—that's, well, I'm dealing with it and I seem to be okay. If a man gets an erection, or the boys in the shower compare each other, that's your masculinity. A lot of men don't like to admit it. [Phil, consumer]

In this way sexuality, or "erectile health," is compulsory for men; integral to achieving manhood. "Every man must pump up for phallocracy" (Potts 2000, 98).

While many men may not discuss their masculinity problems openly with a doctor, the doctor-patient dialogue above and Viagra's recent blockbuster success are representative of a new global concern for the "broken," or impotent male. If gender is "accomplished" in daily life (West and Fenstermaker 1995), then the accomplishment of masculinity is situated, to some extent, in erectile achievement. Fixing the male machine and ensuring erectile functioning, for the patients quoted above and countless others, is to ensure masculinity. Viagra is a technology, or a tool, used to fix the broken machine.

The Poorly Functioning Male Machine

Donna Haraway argues that the postmodern subject is a cyborg, a hybrid creature composed of both organism and machine who populates a world ambiguously natural and crafted (1991, 149). Medical language about the body reflects the overlap between humans and machines as consumers and practitioners describe bodies using mechanical terminology such as "functioning" and "maintenance." The metaphor of the body as a smoothly functioning machine is central to Viagra constructions. In her research into 20th century understandings of health and the body, Emily Martin (1994) found that the human body is commonly compared to a disciplined machine. Like a machine, the body is made up of parts that can break down. Illness, then, refers to a broken body part. To fix this part ensures the functioning of the machine. Drawing on interviews with consumers and practitioners, I argue in this section that the popularity of Viagra has exposed and created a masculinity crisis of sorts. In this section, consumers and practitioners employ industrial and technological metaphors to make sense of body and gender trouble, or masculinity in crisis.

In this section, customers and practitioners make sense of "trouble" by attempting to locate problems in the male body or machine. Such industrial metaphors are regularly used by Dr. Irwin Goldstein, a media-friendly urologist and Pfizer consultant, known for describing erectile functioning as "all hydraulics" and suggesting that dysfunction requires "rebuilding the male machine." Following this metaphor, common treatment protocols for "erectile dysfunction" center on treating the penis (broken part) separately from the body (machine). Physicians are encouraged (by Pfizer representatives) to center their doctor/patient dialogue around the patient's erectile "performance"—asking the patient to rate their erections in terms of penetrability, hardness, maintenance, and satisfaction levels. This construction of the penis as dysfunctional and fixable is exemplified in the following quotes.

> What I do is say [to patients complaining of erectile dysfunction], "Tell me about the erections. When you were 20 years old let's say they were a 10, rock hard. Where would they be now on a scale from 1–10?" So I give them some objectible evidence that they can give me. They'll say, oh, now it's a 2. A lot of guys say its now a 7 or 8. I say "Can you still perform with a 7 or 8?" They say, "Yeah, but its not as good as it was." [Curt, urologist]

The medical professionals I spoke with were clear that if a patient experiences "deficiency" or complete lack of erectile function, Viagra might be of help. But "dysfunction" may not be as black and white. As Pfizer Inc. and its promotional information suggests, "erectile dysfunction" lies on a continuum from complete inability to achieve erection, to consistent ability to achieve an erection. Many patients who are currently looking for treatment for erectile dysfunction inhabit the gray area (in terms of performance rankings from 1 to 10), and appear to be concerned with restoring their "machine" to a "normal," or near-perfect level of functioning. Optimal performance, or the ability to penetrate one's partner and sustain an erection, is desired, as reflected in the above quotes.

Trouble with Normal

While rigidity is the goal, part of optimal penile performance is to appear malleable. In a twentieth century postmodern world, flexibility is a trait cherished and cultivated in all fields, including health (Martin 1994). Thus, the healthiest bodies are disciplined machines which also exhibit current cultural ideals such as reliability, fitness, and elasticity (Martin 1994). Viagra is constructed as a tool used to achieve the ideal flexible body—a body that is always "on call."

In some cases, Viagra is used by consumers who feel that normal penile functioning is not good enough. While these consumers claim they do not "need" Viagra, they are more satisfied with their performance when they do use it. In the quotes below, Bill and Stan imply that the pre-Viagra penis is slow, unpredictable, and uncertain, and thus, problematic.

> I noticed that if I get titillated, [after using Viagra] then the penis springs to attention. Not atypically. But more facile. It's easier. It's more convincing. It's not like maybe I'll get hard and maybe I won't. It's like "Okay, here I am!" [Stanford, consumer]

For these consumers, the Viagra-body may be preferable to the natural body, because it is consistent and predictable. The "on-call" Viagra penis will consistently respond when it is needed, whereas the "natural" body is constructed as too unpredictable.

> Erections are a lot more temperamental than people are willing to admit. But we have this

image of masculinity and expectations of male sexuality as being virile and always ready to go and being the conqueror. And I think that this pill allows people to finally live out that myth (laughs). [Stu, consumer]

As Stu points out, Viagra exposes the flawed "natural" body and enables a man to achieve mythic masculinity. In this way, the Viagra story is one that slips between artificial and natural, and even beyond to super-natural levels. For many, the promise of Viagra is the fact that it can deliver "optimal" results, pushing the consumer beyond his own conceptions of "normal" functioning. In this way, practitioners and customers construct Viagra as a miracle cure because it not only "fixes" the problem, but makes things "better." Below, Viagra is constructed as an enhancement drug.

> With Viagra we say it's for a medical condition, not for just anyone. However I know a fellow who was fine who took a Viagra to get himself extra-normal. [Bastine, psychiatrist]

Practitioners and consumers collaborate in constructing Viagra as a magic bullet that can "extend" the realm of "normal," and push people to the next level: extra-normality, or superhumanness. By pushing the boundaries of erectile function, performance, and sexuality, Viagra sets new standards and constructs countless male bodies in need of repair. Consumers and practitioners use technological metaphors to construct the ways in which Viagra can be used to repair the broken male machine.

Repairing the Broken Male

There is no doubt that at the turn of the century, males may be feeling emasculated, powerless, and lifeless for any number of reasons. For those who are feeling this way, Viagra comes to the rescue, with the potential to avert or repair personal and/or cultural troubles. Acknowledging that culture, the media, or relationships can be a source of trouble is not part of the medical model and appears too complicated to fix. However, when

the problem is located solely in the body (as in medical discourse), individualized, and treated as a physiological dysfunction, it can be easier to repair. Even clinical psychologists, who acknowledge that the trouble can be psychological, social, or relational, may join medical practitioners in seeing Viagra as a tool for regaining body function and repairing confidence, and masculinity.

In the face of troubled masculinity, Viagra is commonly constructed by consumers and practitioners as a pill for masculinity-repair or instruction, to be used either in extreme erectile dysfunction cases where manhood appears to be "lost," to more common "mild E.D." situations where manhood needs a "jump-start" or an extra boost. In this way, Viagra itself is a technology for the production of gender and sexuality. Viagra can be understood as a tool for the repair and/or production of hegemonic masculinity and sexuality. Some consumers take Viagra hoping not only to restore or supplement "natural" physiological function, but also "normal" masculinity and heterosexuality. Others choose not to use Viagra, claiming that Viagra is more "trouble" than solution by producing an artificial and "uncontrollable" body. This idea of trouble will be developed further in a later section.

Techno-Fix and the Viagra "Tool"

With the embrace of Viagra as a biotechnological "wonder," Viagra is invested with myriad technological metaphors. As we have seen, Viagra can be understood as a tool for fixing the broken male machine. The term "jump-start" is used by many practitioners and consumers to understand Viagra's effect on the body, and to symbolize an energetic positive step forward, with biotechnology backing-up and assuring performance. Viagra can jump-start the body and the mind to produce a self-assured masculinity.

> Even the ones with psychological problems, they still try the Viagra to help convince them that everything works okay. I'll give it to them. You need this to *jump-start* your system. See how it works. If it gives you the confidence that

you can get an erection, it can work. Then you can taper off of it. [Curt, urologist]

Viagra is employed by practitioners as a tool, similar to jumper cables, to "jump-start" the male machine—to get the patient performing again. In the first quote above, the urologist renders the whole body affected by erectile dysfunction as lifeless, like a dead battery. The urologist and consumers quoted after him use the same metaphor (although they don't know one another) and advocate a rapid return to normal erections, normal performance, and thus, normal masculinity. Below, a consumer uses the same terminology as practitioners to reveal how Viagra works in the body.

> Viagra is a miracle product for men with performance problems. And partners love it too. I've found that it really *jump-starts* things, physiologically. I've talked to many people who say this. But where I'm at right now, with my diet and tantra work, Viagra just doesn't suit me anymore. But I think for some people it might be great to take once in a while to jump-start things. [Bradley, consumer]

Technology-based metaphors pervade practitioner and consumer explanations of Viagra's relationship to the male body. Many medical professionals choose to use machine or automobile-related metaphors to construct the type of treatment now available with Viagra. Here, Viagra does optional repair work (on the male machine) and erections are seen as enhancements or "attachments" to the basic body.

> Viagra has a snap-on component to it. People want it now. It is a metaphor for our culture. [Redding, psychotherapist]

Consumers use similar industrial metaphors to describe how penises are repaired, transformed, and enhanced after using Viagra.

> [My friend] Jack, on the other hand, claimed victory that night and said the little blue confidence pill helped him achieve "pink steel," which impressed his occasional girlfriend, at least that night. [Lue, consumer]

Viagra's promise is one of corporeal techno-logical enhancement—in the form of a snap-on, an accessory, and a ready-made erection. By making such comparisons (car, steel, weapon), consumers attribute masculine characteristics such as power, resilience, hardness, and strength to the Viagra penis, essentially constructing Viagra as a tool for producing masculinity, and enforcing social meanings. In this way, myth and tool mutually constitute each other (Haraway 1991, 164).

Repair = Trouble

Not all consumers buy into the techno-fix model. Some consumers commented that although Viagra may promise bodily repair it can actually cause more trouble than its worth. In this section, Viagra constructs problems, not solutions. Below, Viagra is constructed as techno-trouble, constructing the male body as increasingly out of control.

> I don't ever want to try [Viagra] again. The thing about it is, the side-effects could be very dangerous for someone a little older than I am. Because you do end up with palpitation. Your body is just not your body. So if [your functioning is] not normal, I think its better to just let it go at that. Or make pills that are much much weaker. But I wouldn't recommend it for anybody. [Joel, consumer]

As we saw earlier, some men see Viagra as a tool to create the ideal flexible body. For other consumers, Viagra may produce a body that is overly rigid and inflexible. At this point, the Viagra-effect becomes "unnatural" and uncontrollable, and consequently undesirable.

> Well, I also didn't like it because it was unnatural. Like you were hard and you stayed hard. And I also didn't like the fact that it guaranteed things would be sexual until you weren't hard. [Dusty, consumer]

Rather than lose control of their bodies or experience trouble through repair, these consumers construct alternatives to the pharmaceutical fix model, accepting their bodies as they are or just "leaving it alone." Despite overwhelming evidence that Viagra is associated with the production of normal and/or mythic masculinity, these men work hard at reconstructing masculinity as separate from "erectile health." They insist that masculinity can be achieved without the help of Viagra, or consideration of erectile potential.

> I've talked to a lot of different men about this. Some cannot live without sex. They feel their sex makes them the man that they are. And I'm not sure how important that is to me. I'm a man anyways. It's about self-esteem. What do you think about yourself to begin with? [Ollie, consumer]

For many, Viagra fits perfectly in a society that is known for pushing the limits of normal. Consumers may be critical of American culture and Viagra's role in perpetuating the endless pursuit of the quick-fix. Consumers warn of a hedonistic, money-driven, artificial world, where there is a pill for everything. Viagra exists in this world as a crutch or band-aid solution to larger social problems.

> I think there is a gross overuse of drugs for "happiness and well-being." Feeling depressed, get a script for a mood enhancer . . . feeling tired, get a pill for energy . . . want to have better sex, get some blue magic. What about the age-proven solution of removing or reducing the problems or stress factors affecting your life and then seeing if pharmacological agents are still needed? [Miles, consumer]

Here, consumers construct society as pharmacologically-infused, producing individuals who are dependent upon pills for health and happiness. Consumers are critical of capitalist and biotechnological attempts at constructing needs, desires, and easy markets for products.

> I just see that society is just driving us crazy, making us jump through hoops and do things we really don't need to do. So—a drug for everything. Even if you don't want to do it, you are driven if you pay attention to what's going on. I'm not that kind of person. I just don't believe in it. [Ollie, consumer]

In many ways, consumers are critical of Viagra's potential to enforce social and gendered meanings and realities. Savvy consumers refuse to "buy into" mythic masculinity, and see through problematic discourses of medical progress and widespread public health crises. In this way consumers resist and reframe masculinity, biotechnology, and medicalization in ways that make sense to them. Rather than construct their bodies and masculinities as troubled, with Viagra as a techno-fix or magical solution, these consumers construct Viagra as problematic, contributing to larger social troubles.

Masculinity, Technology, and Resistance

As my interview data reveals, Viagra can and is being used by consumers and practitioners to enforce and perpetuate such ideal and corporeal masculinities. In this way consumers collaborate with medical professionals and pharmaceutical companies in an attempt to understand and fix "broken" bodies. Perhaps of more interest, my data also reveals consumers and practitioners struggling with the necessity of the Viagra-enhanced body, and what that represents. As they negotiate their relationship to this product, mainstream ideas about sexuality, masculinity, and health are both reinforced and redefined in important ways. For example, some insist that "doing" masculinity does not require sexual performance. Others are critical of a society that increasingly promotes and depends upon biotechnology for achieving health and happiness. This paper reveals men constructing their own ideas about manhood, medicalization, and biotechnology, and creating "various and competing masculinities" in Viagra's midst (Messner 1997).

References

Basalmo, Anne. (1996). *Technologies of the Gendered Body: Reading Cyborg Women*. Duke University Press.

Bordo, Susan. (1999). *The Male Body: A New Look At Men in Public and Private*. New York: Farrar, Straus, and Giroux.

Bullough, Vern. (1987). Technology for the prevention of "les maladies produites par la masturbation." *Technology and Culture, 28*(4): 828–32.

Connell, R. W. (1995). *Masculinities*. Berkeley: University of California Press.

Conrad, Peter & Joseph Schneider. (1980). *Deviance and Medicalization: From Badness to Sickness*. London: Mosby.

Davis, Angela. (1981). *Women, Race & Class*. New York: Vintage.

DeLauretis, Teresa. (1987). *Technologies of Gender*. Indiana: Indiana University Press.

D'Emilio, John & Estelle Freedman. [1988] 1997. *Intimate Matters: A History of Sexuality in America*. Chicago: University of Chicago Press.

Ehrenreich, Barbara & Dierdre English. (1973). *Complaints and Disorders. The Sexual Politics of Sickness*. New York: The Feminist Press.

———. (1979). *For Her Own Good: 150 Years of the Expert's Advice to Women*. New York: Anchor.

Faludi, Susan. (1999). *Stiffed: The Betrayal of the American Man*. New York: Morrow and Co.

Fasteau, Marc Feigen. (1975). *The Male Machine*. New York: Dell.

Foucault, Michel. (1973). *The Birth of the Clinic, an Archaeology of Medical Perception*. New York: Vintage.

———. (1977). *Discipline and Punish: The Birth of the Prison*. New York: Pantheon Books.

———. (1978). *The History of Sexuality, an Introduction*. New York: Random House.

Franklin, Sarah & Helena Ragone. (1998). Introduction. In *Reproducing Reproduction: Kinship, Power, and Technological Innovation*. Eds. Sarah Franklin and Helena Ragone. Philadelphia: University of Pennsylvania Press.

Groneman, Carol. (1994). Nymphomania: The historical construction of female sexuality. *Signs: Journal of Women in Culture and Society, 19*:2.

Hausman, Bernice. (1995). *Changing Sex: Transsexuailsm, Technology, and the Idea of Gender*. London: Duke University Press.

Haraway, Donna Jeanne. (1991). *Simians, Cyborgs, and Women: The Reinvention of Nature*. New York: Routledge.

———. (1999). The virtual speculum in the new world order. In *Revisioning Women, Health, and Healing: Feminist, Cultural, and Technoscience Perspectives*, Eds. Adele E. Clarke and Virginia L. Olesen. New York: Routledge.

Irvine, Janice. (1990). *Disorders of Desire: Sex and Gender in Modern American Sexology*. Temple University Press.

Jacobson, Nora. (2000). *Cleavage: Technology, Controversy and the Ironies of the Man-Made Breast*. New Jersey: Rutgers University Press.

Kimmel, Michael. (1996). *Manhood in America: A Cultural History*. New York: Free Press.

———. & Michael Messner. [1989] 1995. *Men's Lives*. Boston: Allyn and Bacon.

Maines, Rachel. (1999). *The Technology of Orgasm: "Hysteria," the Vibrator, and Women's Sexual Satisfaction*. Johns Hopkins.

Messner, Michael. (1997). *The Politics of Masculinities: Men in Movements*. Thousand Oaks: Sage Publications.

Martin, Emily. (1994). *Flexible Bodies*. Boston: Beacon Press.

Mumford, Kevin. (1992). Lost manhood found: Male sexual impotence and Victorian culture in the United States. *Journal of the History of Sexuality, 3*(1).

Potts, Annie. (2000). The essence of the hard on. *Men and Masculinities, 3*(1): 85–103.

Raymond, Janice. (1994). *The Transsexual Empire: The Making of the She-Male*. New York: Athene.

Reissman, Catherine Kohler. (1983). Women and medicalization: A new perspective. *Social Policy, 14*(1).

Sawicki, Jana. (1991). *Disciplinary Foucault: Feminism, Power, and the Body*. New York: Routledge.

Terry, Jennifer. (1995). The seductive power of science in the making of deviant subjectivity. In *Posthuman Bodies*, eds. Judith Halberstam and Ira Livingston, Bloomington: Indiana University Press.

Tiefer, Leonore. (1998). Doing the Viagra tango. *Radical Philosophy, 92*.

———. (1994). The medicalization of impotence: Normalizing phallocentrism. *Gender & Society, 8*(3).

Watkins, Elizabeth. (1998). *On the Pill: A Social History of Oral Contraceptions, 1950–1970*. Baltimore: Johns Hopkins University Press.

West, Candace & Sarah Fenstermaker. (1995). Doing difference. *Gender & Society, 9*(1): 8–38.

Monica Casper

Lisa Jean Moore

It Takes Balls: Lance Armstrong and the Triumph of American Masculinity

"What's the deal with that name, anyway? Lance Armstrong. Is that a comic-book hero or a bendable action figure? Once somebody gives you a name like that, how hard can life be? Lance Armstrong. Wasn't he the star of those 1950s boys' sports books? Lance Armstrong, All-American Hero!" Rick Reilly, Sports Illustrated, *2002*

What Lies Between

Human bodies are fragmented, divided into specific parts for unique purposes. In allopathic medicine, for example, we rarely have our entire bodies x-rayed or examined; rather, body parts are isolated as part of the doctrine of specific etiology, considered apart from the organism as a whole. We suffer headaches, stomachaches, and backaches, the pain displaying corporeal regionalism. When we exercise at the gym, we work particular muscles, one day our biceps and the next our quads. We know how, thanks to fitness magazines, exercise shows, and the ever-present instructors and trainers. In pornography, we see only body parts shown in exquisite detail, the full body often not making the frame. The camera lens zooms in on penises, vaginas, and breasts, writhing, heaving, spread open for visual consumption. Our body parts, the pieces that comprise the human machine, each have a history. Some, such as breasts and faces, are highly visible, while others are hidden, tucked away in our cellular folds and blood-rich cavities. All body parts are laden with significance. The story of our own breasts, for example, could be framed as a narrative about girlhood, puberty, sexual florescence,

pleasure and anxiety, body image, infant feeding, aging, and health.

In this chapter, we are especially interested in meanings of male anatomy. The human scrotum, for example, is not an everyday topic of conversation. Outside of sex, pornography, and the omnipresent television image of professional athletes adjusting their cups on the playing field, testicles—the spherical glands dangling inside the scrotum—are invisible. Sometimes packaged creatively to enhance size and appearance . . . men's balls are nonetheless routinely hidden inside clothing and absent as body parts from public discourse. Pornography, when it does focus on male genitalia, tends to emphasize the phallus in all its rigid glory and not the "family jewels" gilding the sword. Diseases of men's bodies (e.g., prostate and testicular cancers) are not nearly as well known or oft discussed as those affecting women's bodies. Indeed, testicles are more popular as a metaphor denoting masculinity: having balls means being a man. Correspondingly, having no balls, like Jessica Lynch, means that one is feminized, a so-called "pussy".

Lance Armstrong, the subject of our inquiry here, has legendary balls. This is entirely appropriate given that his name conjures up images of spears, javelins, and, dare we say it, another thrusting object: the phallus. Few professional athletes have achieved the mega-superstardom and instant name recognition of the seven-time

Tour de France champion. While his achievements on a racing bike are unparalleled and the stuff of sporting legend, his identity as a testicular cancer survivor has further propelled Armstrong into the public eye. Indeed, he remarks often in media interviews that he would prefer to be known first as a survivor and second as a Tour champion. Certainly many athletes have donated their names to various causes, but no athlete has achieved the kind of commingled integration of sport, charity, and celebrity embodied—literally—by Armstrong. And few athletes have been more entrepreneurial: Lance Armstrong™ is an icon relentlessly self-fashioned—physically, mentally, and culturally.

Commenting in 2003 on an Annie Leibovitz photograph of the famous cyclist . . . , journalist Rachel Koper writes, "When I look at Lance Armstrong's thighs I get weak in the knees. The sinuous calf, the knee straining like a neck . . . then those thighs. Naked, with tan lines, head down in the rain on the bike . . . Since the picture was actually shot indoors and not at an actual race, the lighting is fairly even and bright, and Lance becomes a breathing emblem of toughness—an avatar of endurance. It's easy to ignore the tan lines from those goofy spandex tights and the fake rain because those thighs don't lie." The Austin, Texas, reporter is not the only person obsessed with Armstrong's ripped thighs. *Sports Illustrated's* Rick Reilly describes a black-tie event in Las Vegas at which golfer Tiger Woods, himself no slouch in the fame and fortune department, asked Armstrong if he could feel his legs. "And Tiger took his hands and put them on Armstrong's concrete thighs. 'Man!' he said, squeezing. 'I mean, man!' "

As alluring as Armstrong's thighs may be—and we admit to a certain regret that we have never fondled them in the name of science—we are equally interested in what lies *between* the man's awesome quads. The story of Lance Armstrong, über-cyclist, cannot be told outside of the story of Lance Armstrong, testicular cancer survivor. And in media accounts, autobiographies, biographies, and Lance Armstrong Foundation materials, this is exactly how the legend is nar-

rated. Both these battles—to overcome advanced cancer and to become a champion athlete—have intertwined to make Armstrong into a mythic (and lucrative) figure.[1] In some ways, it's a familiar trope: an ordinary young man in his prime is struck down by cancer, undergoes aggressive treatment, recovers miraculously, and is a changed man, better than he ever was as a person and an athlete. As the cyclist himself writes, "The truth is that cancer was the best thing that ever happened to me."

But Lance Armstrong's illness narrative, just like Jessica Lynch's rescue tale, is no simple fable: it is complicated and fueled by his celebrity, which begins and ends with that legendary, much-photographed physique. Whether vulnerable in disease or triumphant in victory, his body and its extraordinary visibility in popular culture have contributed to the making of the man and the myth. Journalist Martin Dugard describes "chasing Lance": following Armstrong and the other cyclists around France, with the man in yellow typically pedaling furiously at the front of the *peloton*. It seems to us that everyone has been chasing Lance Armstrong: rival athletes, photographers, attractive women and men, curious and awestruck children, sponsors, journalists, cancer survivors, scientists, and a couple of sociologists. What can one famous body and its highly visible machinations tell us about masculinity, illness, sport, philanthropy, and the redemption of American national identity in wartime?

Testicular Cancer and the Politics of Men's Health

Testicular cancer is the most common type of cancer in young American men ages 15 to 34. It is highly treatable, compared to many other cancers, if diagnosed early. The disease is characterized by development of a malignancy (or malignancies) in the testicles, which are located inside the scrota underneath the penis. The testes produce sex hormones and sperm cells for reproduction. Causes of testicular cancer are unknown, although there is some evidence that it may be linked to environmental toxins (Daniels 2006).

For example, the U.S. Centers for Disease Control and Prevention (CDC) suggests a connection between pregnant women's use of diethylstilbesterol (DES) and development of testicular cancer in male offspring.[2] The age-adjusted incidence rate in the U.S. from 2000–2004 was 5.3 per 100,000, and the median age at death for testicular cancer was 40 years of age. Unlike many other diseases where incidence and mortality are higher in African Americans (as with infant mortality rates), for testicular cancer the incidence among white men is significantly higher, at 6.3 per 100,000 for whites as compared to 1.4 per 100,000 for African Americans.[3]

Men's health issues, especially those concerning the genitals, historically have been invisible, and only recently has a men's health movement emerged to rival the women's health movement (Clatterbaugh 2000; White 2002). As sociologists Dana Rosenfeld and Christopher Faircloth suggest, studying medicalization, men's bodies, and men's health can enhance our understanding of masculinity and gender relations. For example, in *Sperm Counts*, Lisa chronicled practices involving sperm in medicine and culture, including interpretations of semen and male genitalia, noting a clear connection between sperm and constructions of masculinity. All too often, serious discussions of male anatomy (despite visualization in pornography, for example) are shrouded in secrecy, denial, and shame. Men do not often talk about their health, seek care on their own, or undertake preventive practices such as testicular self-exam (TSE). For example, our classroom suggestions to male students that they should be practicing such exams have been routinely met with discomfort and embarrassment. This general neglect of men's health "generates considerable pain and suffering, along with sizeable and avoidable health care costs" (Meyer 2003).

The consequences of testicular cancer may be significant, even when the disease is not fatal. In a qualitative study of men's most humiliating experiences, the rankings were, from the most to the least: not maintaining an erection during sex, *losing a testicle to cancer*, being teased about penis size, having a rectal exam, being diagnosed as

sterile, being left by an intimate partner, and being seen naked by male friends (emphasis added).

Canadian psychologist Maria Gurevich and her colleagues assert "testicular cancers occur at a point in a man's life when the impact on sexuality, identity and fertility may be significant." Drawing on earlier studies suggesting important links between "testicular integrity" and "the coherence of male (sexual) identity," the authors interviewed forty men diagnosed with testicular cancer. They found that the loss of a testicle was interpreted as a challenge to masculinity; the anatomical structure served as an important marker of identity. In their words, "the routes to readings of masculinity inevitably pass through anatomy . . . [and] anatomically intact bodies are designated as anatomically and socio-culturally 'correct' bodies" (Gurevich et al. 2003:1604).

In a comparative analysis of breast, testicular, and prostate cancer, medical sociologist Juanne Clarke (2003:549) found in media portrayals "the threat of the disease seems to be less a threat to life itself than a threat to the proper, i.e., gendered enactment of life." Coverage of testicular cancer, in particular, emphasized early detection and aggressive treatment while also couching genital terminology in colloquialisms such as "nuts," "balls," and "family jewels." Testicles were frequently associated with manhood and masculinity, and the disease and its treatment often discussed in militarized metaphors (Clarke 2003). Reference is made in this article to Armstrong's autobiography, in which he describes "the war on cancer" and the disease as "just like a big race". Moreover, in Clarke's study, testicular cancer was found to be associated with sexuality, fertility, and relationships with women. This type of media coverage causes Clarke to ask, "Why are breast, testicular, and prostate cancers portrayed as threats to masculinity, femininity and sexuality rather than as mechanical and organic failures that could have life-threatening consequences?"

Journalist Arthur Allen (1999) reports "advances in chemotherapy and other treatment nearly assure survival for most of the patients diagnosed with testicular cancer nowadays, a fact obscured by Armstrong—and most of the press—when they proclaimed his accomplishment as downright miraculous." According to oncologist Bruce Roth, however, "it is absolutely not a miracle" (quoted in Allen 1999). Testicular cancer is quite survivable, even when it is advanced. But "this is not to say that [it] is a walk in the park," writes Allen (1999). Orchiectomy, or amputation of the testicle(s), is one common treatment for testicular cancer, and potentially the one with the most lasting emotional consequences. Chemotherapy and radiation are also key weapons and may reconfigure the body while destroying malignancies. The overall message of testicular cancer is that it is often silent, rarely deadly, but can have enormous implications for a man's sense of masculinity.

"Two Lance Armstrongs": The Making of a Champion and a Cause

In 1996, when Armstrong was 25 years old, his strong, young body betrayed him by developing cancer. He did not pay attention when his right testicle swelled and became painful. In fact, he assumed it was a bike-related injury and, like many men, ignored it. In his autobiography, *It's Not About the Bike*, he writes, "Of *course* I should have known that something was wrong with me. But athletes, especially cyclists, are in the business of denial. You deny all the aches and pains because you have to in order to finish the race" (Armstrong and Jenkins 2000:5). He continued to compete, winning the Flèche-Wallonne (the first American to do so) and the Tour Du Pont. He was frequently exhausted, but told himself to "suck it up." That year, he dropped out of the Tour de France after just five days, too tired and sore to be a viable contender. In September, he experienced a "brain-crushing" headache, and one day soon after he began to cough up blood. He thought perhaps his sinuses were acting up. It was not until his right testicle had expanded to the size of an orange that he sought medical care (testicles are typically about the size of a plum). The diagnosis: stage 3 testicular cancer, which had already metastasized to his lungs, abdomen, and brain.

Armstrong describes his illness as "humbling and starkly revealing", forcing him to consider aspects of his life with "an unforgiving eye" (2000:4). Indeed, the narrative of *It's Not About the Bike* follows Armstrong's cancer experience from shocking diagnosis to incredible recovery, with a brief sojourn through his personal history including his strong bond with his mother, Linda, who raised him on her own. The subtext of the book, co-written with prolific sports journalist Sally Jenkins, is about how a champion is forged from adversity, both on and off the bike. In Armstrong's case, that adversity comes in the form of a personal and public war against testicular cancer.

The story is suffused with elements of masculinity, from Armstrong's characteristically male denial of his illness, to his relationship with his now ex-wife ("Don't be a skirt", he tells her when she drives too cautiously), to his abundant and renowned cycling achievements. The take-home message is that "there are two Lance Armstrongs, pre-cancer and post"; both are men, but only one can become a superhero. Ironically, Armstrong had to lose a testicle to gain the kind of symbolic balls that turned an ordinary, if highly successful, athlete into a mega-star. Dugard (2005:81) puts it this way: "The cancer had reshaped Armstrong's body, stripping away all that upper body musculature. In its place was the stick-thin torso the world has come to know so well. His heart, by contrast, was bigger—not physically, but metaphysically. Lance Armstrong had faced death and miraculously returned to life. He knew what it was to race against time."

In Armstrong's own story, cancer is deeply transformative: "I left my house on October 2, 1996, as one person and came home another. I was a world-class athlete with a mansion on a riverbank, keys to a Porsche, and a self-made fortune in the bank. I was one of the top riders in the world and my career was moving along a perfect arc of success. I returned a different person, literally. In a way, the old me did die, and I was given a second life" (Armstrong and Jenkins 2000:4). One of the most striking aspects of Armstrong's account is the fear and self-doubt that consumed him after he received his cancer diagnosis. Before cancer, he believed himself to be "an indestructible 25-year-old, bulletproof" (Armstrong and Jenkins 2000:14). He worried not only that cancer might take his career and his life, but also that it would change his very definition of *self*. He writes, "There were gallons of sweat all over every trophy and dollar I had ever earned, and now what would I do? Who would I be if I wasn't Lance Armstrong, world-class cyclist?" Immediately post-diagnosis, he was reduced to a frighteningly monolithic identity: "sick person" (Armstrong and Jenkins 2000:14).

Armstrong sought and received aggressive treatment for his advanced cancer, from October through December 1996 at Indiana University Medical Center. He underwent two surgeries, one to remove his affected testicle and the other to remove cancerous tissue from his brain. In his autobiography, Armstrong writes: "I spent the first weekend on the couch recovering from the surgery. The anesthesia made me woozy, and the incision was excruciating. I rested and watched football while my mother cooked for me, and we both read up on cancer, exhaustively" (2000:84). He experienced two rounds of chemotherapy, and later was hailed by pharmaceutical manufacturers as a poster child for their products.[4] These chemical cocktails also came to have a starring role in the doping scandals and allegations by the French media of Armstrong's use of performance enhancing supplements. "I had no life other than chemo," Armstrong recalls (2000:132). "My old forms of keeping dates and time fell by the wayside, substituted by treatment regimens."

An important part of Armstrong's cancer narrative is confronting his low sperm count and future reproductive capacity. He eventually banked his sperm, and post-treatment, he fathered three children with whom he is frequently photographed. Only after he retired from competitive cycling did he divorce their mother and begin a succession of relationships with celebrity women. A significant portion of *It's Not About the Bike* and its sequel, *Every Second Counts*, is devoted to Armstrong's quest for his lost masculinity. This process began with his successful efforts, with

then-wife Kik, to produce children through *in vitro fertilization* but it certainly did not end there. Armstrong's life, as detailed in these books, is devoted to hard bodily work, pain and suffering through sport, the annihilation of his opponents in the Tour, and a series of risky practices including diving headfirst off a 50-foot bluff into Dead Man's Hole near his home in Texas, just to remind himself that he's still alive. His is an epic quest, framed in the language of conquest. Or, as journalist Daniel Coyle (2006) terms it, *Lance Armstrong's War: One Man's Battle Against Fate, Fame, Love, Death, Scandal, and a Few Other Rivals on the Road to the Tour de France.*

Lance Armstrong was not the first celebrity to struggle against testicular cancer and probably he will not be the last. In 1970, the Chicago Bears' Brian Piccolo died at age 26 from the disease, inspiring a book and made-for-TV movie, *Brian's Song*. As sportscaster Bob Costas has pointed out, viewing *Brian's Song* is practically a male rite of passage with requisite emotional catharsis: "There's no question that Brian Piccolo's story was amplified by the movie. And now generations later, you don't know how many guys who ordinarily would be loath to admit that they shed a tear, will tell you at the drop of a hat, I still cry every time I see *Brian's Song*."[5] Emotional displays aside, the movie does not mention testicular cancer or make any overt reference to the type of cancer that Piccolo died from.

In 2000, comedian Tom Green turned his testicular cancer into television entertainment, offering real-time coverage of his surgery and filming several public service announcements. And Olympic figure skater Scott Hamilton underwent treatment in 2003 for advanced testicular cancer, accompanied by significant media exposure. Yet "it wasn't until Lance Armstrong . . . won the Tour de France [in 1999] that the disease again received mass attention" (Vastag 1999). This time around, it was an unprecedented amount, fueled by our collective fascination with sport and disease, and by increasing public attention to men's health (White 2002). Health educator Samantha King (2006:xvii) argues that Armstrong's "very public battle with testicular cancer has helped strengthen the profile of men's cancers in general." Or, as Allen (1999) puts it, "Skater Scott Hamilton, subway shooter Bernard Goetz, Alexander Solzhenitsyn and the panda Hsing-Hsing all survived testicular cancer, but none stepped forward as role models. Armstrong has gripped the role with gusto."

Like the family and friends of football player Piccolo, who established the Brian Piccolo Foundation for testicular cancer research, Armstrong set up his own organization, the Lance Armstrong Foundation (LAF). He did so during his treatment for the disease and before he knew if he would recover. Consider the self-promotional language used on the LAF website: "this marked the beginning of Lance's life as an advocate for people living with cancer and a world representative for the cancer community."[6] The LAF supports research on testicular cancer, particularly the after-effects of treatment, and it has helped to solidify Armstrong's role as an authority in the war on cancer. In 2005, it awarded 27 grants to 21 institutions across the U.S., totaling more than $5 million. It also provides resources for support and care of cancer sufferers; for example, the afflicted (and their families) can download or order materials to help them guide and organize their treatment. In 2005, more than 28,000 survivorship notebooks were distributed.[7]

Clearly, Armstrong's "balls" have been incredibly productive. He is not just a survivor and a winner, but is a champion *for* people with cancer. He transformed his illness experience—and his considerable earnings—into an effective, financially sound advocacy organization. How effective can be measured, in part, by the unexpected success of the yellow silicon LiveStrong bracelets worn by cancer survivors, athletes, youth, gymrats, cycling fans, soccer moms, presidential candidates, and health care professionals around the country. The bracelets hit the market in 2004 at various outlets (Niketown, Foot Locker, etc.), selling for $1 each. With corporate sponsorship from Nike, 100% of the proceeds of the first five million bracelets went directly to the LAF. The bracelets sold out before that summer's Tour de France had ended—illustrating an emergent and profitable alliance between

corporations and philanthropies.[8] Why so successful? *New York Times* consumer journalist Rob Walker suggests "there's nothing even vaguely controversial or political or even provocative about a visible declaration of concern about cancer. Perhaps more crucial, the item is associated not just with a cause, but also with a heroic athlete at the peak of his popularity."

Celebrity cases draw attention to disease, and they may help to spawn social movements and change. But as physician and author Barron Lerner (2006) points out, the ways in which illnesses affect celebrities may be quite different than for ordinary people. For example, while Armstrong may fit the demographic for testicular cancer incidence, he is quite unusual in other respects. For one, he survived a rare form of advanced cancer that might have killed a "lesser" human, somebody not wealthy, privileged, and extremely fit. Anthropologist and bioethicist Barbara Koenig (2001) argues, "Armstrong's dramatic recovery is atypical . . . Over 1,500 Americans die each day from cancer. No commercials trumpet their needs or remind us that once 'saved' from cancer we will necessarily die of something else . . . It's the miracles that sell, repeating the heroic narratives of success we are so fond of."

In Armstrong's epic recovery, our insatiable desire for evidence of medicine's achievements collides seamlessly with our need for everyday miracles and invincible heroes. But what makes Armstrong so special, aside from his considerable fame and fortune? How is it possible that he actually *survived* advanced cancer? Is he, indeed, superhuman? How was he able to redeem his masculinity despite amputation of one of his testicles? In addressing these questions, we turn next to bodily obsessions, or the ongoing cultural examination of what makes Lance tick.

"The Lance Armstrong Effect": Scrutinizing the Unbeatable Body

In *It's Not About the Bike*, peppered among descriptions of grueling cancer treatment and the challenges of recovery, Armstrong details the surprisingly positive changes wrought upon his body by the disease. He writes, "There was one unforeseen benefit of cancer: it had completely reshaped my body. I now had a much sparer build. In old pictures, I looked like a football player with my thick neck and big upper body . . . Now I was almost gaunt, and the result was a lightness I'd never felt on the bike before. I was leaner in body and more balanced in spirit" (2000:224). Ironically, testicular cancer and its physical aftermath transformed Armstrong from a decent athlete into a superstar, in part by chemically resculpting his body, paring it down to perfectly meet the demands of competitive cycling. Media coverage routinely notes the cancer as a signal moment in which Armstrong shifted from merely racing to becoming a champion, marking corporeal changes as part of the legend. Dugard (2005: 207) declares, "Before the cancer, Lance had been just another bike racer."

Reilly (2002) asserts, "Among professional athletes Armstrong is mythic." Opinion seems mixed as to whether Armstrong's success is due to one of three factors: enhancement, genetics, or sheer will. Science writer Gina Kolata (2005) argues in the *New York Times*, "The urban legends about Lance Armstrong have been circulating for years: He's superhuman, a genetic freak, the one person on the planet so perfectly made to ride the Tour de France that competitors don't have a chance." Others have described the cyclist as Herculean, evoking mythical strength. Yet we are not invested here in resolving these disagreements; we do not particularly care what makes the Lance machine run like the Energizer Bunny® or whether he in fact used performance enhancing drugs. Rather, we want to focus on what public discussions about Armstrong's famous physique can tell us about sport, embodiment, and masculinity. We have detected a certain obsession with the cyclist's body on the part of sports writers, scientists, cyclists, and the media. They all want to know one thing: how a man who survived stage 3 cancer became one of the greatest athletes of all time.

Few athletes are as frequently measured and evaluated as Armstrong. Indeed, the detailed analysis of Armstrong's body represents a whole new order of fragmentation. Journalist Michael Specter (2002) writes, "Every ounce of fat, bone, and muscle on Armstrong's body is regularly inventoried, analyzed, and accounted for. I asked him if he felt it was necessary to endure the daily prodding and poking required to provide all this information, and to adhere so rigidly to his training schedules. 'Depends on whether you want to win,' he replied. 'I do.'" This scrutiny is most evident in the doping controversy surrounding Armstrong. Coyle (2005: 184) observes, "As the world's premier cyclist, he was treated with unparalleled levels of suspicion. Armstrong was tested thirty, forty times a year, both in competition and out . . . In 2001–02 the Postal team had been the subject of a twenty-one-month French judicial inquiry that was eventually dropped for lack of evidence."

Tested randomly in the U.S., France, and elsewhere over a period of many years, the cyclist has always turned up clean. Moreover, he has repeatedly and publicly denied drug use. In a clever television ad for Nike produced in 2000, he stated "Everybody wants to know what I'm on. What am I on? I'm on my bike, busting my ass six hours a day. What are you on?" (Specter 2002). In *Every Second Counts*, Armstrong avowed, "I wanted all the tests, because I knew they would come back pure. They were my only means of vindication" (2003:80). But the accusations continue to fly, especially from the French who he perpetually beat (seven times) on their own turf (Dugard 2005; CBS News 2006). Surely, no "ordinary" human being could accomplish what Armstrong did without enhancement, according to this camp.

Other commentators, outraged by allegations of doping, believe that Armstrong is a singularly phenomenal natural athlete endowed with superior qualities. In *How Lance Does It*, for example, his longtime friend Brad Kearns blends self-help and hagiography to position Armstrong as "genetically superior." Specter (2002) describes Armstrong's body as "specially constructed for cycling," noting that, "his thigh bones are unusually long . . . which permits him to apply just the right amount of torque to the pedals." He also points out that "Armstrong's heart is almost a third larger than that of an average man." (And here we assume he means physically, not metaphysically.) Coyle remarked about Armstrong in one interview, "He's the proof that Darwinism works." Here, evolutionary theory is marshaled in the service of celebrity.

A group of scientists were so impressed by the cyclist's stunning ability to recover from metastatic testicular cancer that they coined the term "the Lance Armstrong Effect" to describe such "astounding therapeutic success" (Coffey et al. 2006). The subtext of the article, which examines cellular and molecular factors related to Armstrong's survival, is: If Lance can do it, so perhaps can other patients diagnosed with testicular cancer (assuming they have some of the same physical attributes as Armstrong). This is a theme repeated often in LAF materials designed to inspire other cancer survivors. But as Armstrong himself notes, "Basically, I can endure more physical stress than most people can, and I don't get as tired while I'm doing it. So I figure maybe that helped me live. I was lucky—I was born with an above-average capacity for breathing" (Armstrong and Jenkins 2000: 4).

A third category of Lance-chasers eschews genetic explanations while also dismissing allegations of doping. This camp believes there is an obvious explanation for Armstrong's success: he works harder and "trains more than his competitors" (Specter 2002). Reilly says, "It's not Armstrong's body that wins Tours. It's his will." Armstrong has described his bike as his office: "It's my job . . . I love it, and I wouldn't ride if I didn't. But it's incredibly hard work, full of sacrifices. And you have to be able to go out there every single day" (quoted in Specter 2002). The cyclist is known for his fixation on every detail about diet (including how much each morsel weighs), watts burned while riding, his weight, speed, aerodynamics, his heart rate at rest and in motion, lactic acid levels, aerobic and anaerobic abilities, and other performance-related minutiae. His workouts are legendary and have been featured in books for the masses (e.g., *The Lance Armstrong Performance Program*). On Armstrong's

success, kinesiologist Ed Coyle reports: "As it turns out, it wasn't drugs or any other artificial enhancement—it was just a simple matter of determination, natural-born physical gifts and a training ethic that 99 percent of us don't come anywhere close to having."

All of these perspectives on "how Lance does it" share two important features: they agree that the champ was (and perhaps still is) relentlessly unbeatable, and they focus on the cyclist's legendary body. We are not suggesting here that Armstrong is the only American athlete ever to be so dissected by press and pundits. Others, such as Michael Jordan and Barry Bonds, have had their share of the media spotlight, including emphasis on extraordinary physical capabilities. However, Armstrong's body represents a unique conglomeration of factors. His experiences with testicular cancer and his identity as a survivor are layered inextricably with his unprecedented success as a seven-time Tour de France champion and his celebrity. His body, and his testicles specifically, represent male vulnerability at the same time that they embody the superhuman. He is one of us, but crucially not. Not only is his body perceived to be superior to the bodies of most athletes (much less vis-à-vis ordinary people), but so too is his drive to win and succeed. Regardless of which perspective one adopts regarding what makes Lance tick, all are focused on the same goal: explaining his post-cancer success and articulating a unified theory about his extraordinary physical capabilities.

Consider Discovery Education's lesson plans for grades 9–12, "The Science of Lance Armstrong." (The cyclist was initially sponsored by the U.S. Postal Service, and later by the Discovery Channel.) Objectives of the lesson plans include: learning that science is essential in athletic training; researching examples of sports science; explaining how new technologies have changed sports; and discovering careers in sports science. Modules of the plan focus on physiology, equipment, psychology, and training/strategy. Armstrong's body is the material used to illustrate each module. For example, under physiology the plan reads: "Heart can pump more blood per minute and beat more times than the average heart"; "He was 20 pounds lighter after cancer but with the same strength"; and "Has very high lung efficiency and aerobic capacity."[9] So while the lesson plan is geared toward explaining various aspects of training and strategy, contained within it are assumptions about Armstrong's corporeal uniqueness and superiority. He becomes that anomaly which sports science must *explain*. High school students can learn about drafting, drag, and lactic acid, but they will also learn that Lance Armstrong is special. There is nobody quite like him.

Armstrong's body, then, is both literally and figuratively taken apart and displayed by educators, medical professionals, the media, the LAF, high school students, and his supporters and rivals. The physical vulnerability showcased by his testicular cancer is reframed, over and over again, as an *opportunity*. In the end, Armstrong still has only one ball (his friend, the comedian Robin Williams, jokingly calls him the Uni-Baller),[10] but he has *balls*, and thus his masculinity is redeemed. The reality of Armstrong's body as "deformed" (i.e., missing a testicle) is erased; the most gendered physical consequence of testicular cancer—amputation of the balls—is hidden from view. We suspect that a woman athlete who undergoes mastectomy would not be able to overcome public scrutiny and be seen as whole, nor would she forever be identified positively (much less humorously) as the one-breasted champion. Yet we see Lance Armstrong's body as whole, and then some. He is not reduced to a missing testicle, but becomes even *more than* the sum of his parts—magnificent thighs, giant heart, outsized lungs, and imposing will.

These dynamics are not only gendered, but they are also thoroughly racialized. Consider the figure of Barry Bonds, the bad boy of baseball. Unlike Armstrong, who has deflected allegations of steroid use like so much Teflon while lesser men (and women) have fallen, Bonds has been unable to dodge accusations of chemical enhancement. And where Armstrong embodies the straight, white, male American hero that everyone (except the French) admires, Bonds is

unavoidably Black. He is routinely portrayed in the media as a liar and a criminal, and much is made of his arrogance and lack of polish. As author and critic John Ridley points out, Bonds is just not that "likeable"; little wonder that a biography of the famous hitter is called *Love Me, Hate Me: Barry Bonds and the Making of an Antihero*. Bloggers have picked up on the distinctions between the cyclist and the baseball giant, noting that Armstrong is often portrayed as the "anti-Barry Bonds." Not only is Bonds already culturally suspect by virtue of his race, he did not overcome a near-fatal disease nor has he been seen bicycling among the wildflowers with Dubya. His philanthropy, the Bonds Family Foundation, helps underprivileged youth (read Black) in the San Francisco Bay Area, not cancer survivors. And the lived realities of poor kids' lives cannot compare to the glamour of celebrity diseases and charities.

Lance Armstrong is, to borrow Rick Reilly's words, a bendable action figure. He is a superman for our times. And if "it's not about the bike", then it really must be about the balls, or rather the structural arrangements of gender that are routinely advantageous to men, particularly white men, and disadvantageous to women and men of color. As Christi Anderson of Eurosport tells Dugard (2005:173) in *Chasing Lance*: "It's all about having a big set . . . The upper ten percent of the riders all have a big set of balls. Lance only has one, but it's a very big one." And in our enduring national quest for heroes, bigger really is better.

Holding Out for a (National) Hero

In 2006, the U.S. Navy announced that its elite SEAL (sea, air, and land) unit would begin recruiting from within the ranks of accomplished athletes including snow boarders, surfers, ice climbers, and water polo players (Hsu 2007). Due to conflicts in Afghanistan and Iraq, in which the SEALs are heavily involved, there is an ongoing need for new recruits who can successfully complete the rigorous training. The SEALs are known as one of the toughest and fittest military units in the country; "the Navy Special Warfare Command figures that ultra-athletes have the physical and mental toughness to get through SEAL training's legendary Hell Week and thrive in the secretive, intensely demanding world of special ops" (Liewer 2006). Because less than 25 percent of each class of trainees graduates, the Navy has become more creative in how it seeks and retains recruits. This means targeting men who "are already living an athletic lifestyle" (Liewer 2006), men just like Lance Armstrong who would make the perfect Navy SEAL (he was once a competitive swimmer)—except that he is now several years past the cutoff age (28 years old) for new recruits.

Armstrong's physique and its visibility evoke a dream of the perfect soldier: a lean, mean fighting machine, capable of withstanding extraordinary challenges. Armstrong is a kind of weaponized cyborg, ready to be deployed down (or up) a mountain—his memoirs are full of military metaphors involving conquests and battles. His body has been (re)crafted from a potent mix of chemicals, exercise, training, strategy, supplements, measurements of all kinds, food, and a perfect melding of his muscular frame to the technology of a super light bicycle. No surprise that "he was the first cyclist in the Tour to use aerodynamically tapered handlebars for the final time trial" (Specter 2002). Indeed, according to Specter, one of the things the French do not like much about Armstrong is that he embodies a "technological renaissance" that troubles many traditionalists who believe the Tour should be won by sweat alone. Armstrong the cyborg is more like the soldier of the future, genetically and technically enhanced, than he is like the Tour de France riders of old (see Thompson 2006).

A bionic man for the 21st century, Armstrong first won the Tour in 1999, *after* recovering from testicular cancer; his seventh and final victory came in 2005. In March 2003, President Bush launched an invasion of Iraq, and just a few short weeks later, Pfc. Jessica Lynch was "rescued" by U.S. troops. Later that month, in April 2003, Secretary of State Colin Powell warned France that there would be consequences of its refusal to support military action against Iraq. According to BBC News, "the idea would be to send a signal to the French that relations are in the freezer. President Chirac should not expect an invitation to the White House" (BBC News 2003). French goods and services—including wine, cheese, and hotels—faced a backlash from American consumers who supported the invasion (Bhatnagar 2003). Foods such as French fries were temporarily renamed Freedom Fries, a move that the U.S. Congress supported. In such tense times, it was terribly satisfying for many Americans when Armstrong beat France on its own geopolitical terrain.

As sportswriter Andrew Hood (2003) reported, "What could be more galling to the Gauls on July 27 than to see Lance Armstrong—whose record, cocksure manner and red-white-and-blue, government-sponsored U.S. Postal Service team screams American domination—atop the podium on the Champs-Elysées for a historic fifth straight time? After all, Armstrong has not just dominated their Tour the last four years, he has changed its character by introducing private jets, bodyguards, and retractable barriers to a sport whose charm was once rooted in the accessibility of its champions." It mattered little that Armstrong publicly stated his opposition to the invasion of Iraq, especially after he was photographed bicycling with his friend George W. Bush on his Texas ranch.

Like Jessica Lynch, who left the war with significant injuries requiring technical intervention, Armstrong, too, has become a pop culture cybernetic organism. Feminist historian of science Donna Haraway's cyborg was meant to be gender-free, a kind of explosion of binary categories such as male and female and an opportunity for hopefulness about the dismantling of gender through technological integration and innovation. Yet we want to argue here that cyborgs are profoundly gendered; they may deepen gender differences and cleavages rather than erase them. Jessica Lynch and Lance Armstrong both are cyborgs, to be sure, but they are very different kinds of cyborgs: One a girl soldier, configured as a fragile, injured princess to be rescued, the embodiment of "messy hardware", and the other a superhero for our times, a soldier of the future (and of fortune), remade stronger than ever before.

In closing, we want to talk about what happens when visually privileged superheroes become human again. In 2006, Armstrong took on a different challenge: he ran the New York City Marathon, a grueling 26.2-mile race through Manhattan. By his own admission, he had not really prepared, other than engaging in his usual post-retirement workouts, and he stumbled across the finish line exhausted, sweaty, and obviously in pain. He finished the race in the middle of the pack, with a time of two hours, 59 minutes and 36 seconds—"good stockbroker or schoolteacher time", as he put it. Signaled out among 37,000 runners by his celebrity, a "Lance Cam" captured his efforts for a live webcast. One marathoner said, "I don't know how Lance's race went, but I almost hope it was pretty tough on him, because that gives us more credibility". There was grumbling among serious racers about the marathon being "hijacked" by celebrities; one remarked, "There were two American Olympic medalists in this race and you hardly knew it. If Madonna wants to run next year, what are you going to do?" Armstrong himself remarked upon finishing, "The two-hour guys in front. I don't know how they do it".

But even with his now "imperfect" body clad in baggy shorts and his less-than-championship finish, Armstrong is redeemed as a genuine hero. Perhaps not as strong as he was in his Tour days, to at least one commentator, he is still a winner: "So when he crossed the finish line yesterday on a perfect Technicolor fall day . . . it was not only a victory for a first-time marathon runner, but for thousands of cancer patients like me and survivors everywhere . . . I applaud him every day for what he has done for the thousands of cancer patients and survivors worldwide who look to him for daily inspiration. The fact is, people with cancer run a marathon every day, whether it's going to work or walking a block to the subway or doing laps around the hospital ward after a grueling surgery. So if he inspires us to get out and walk or move or live, he deserves a lot of credit" (Terrazzano 2006).

In victory or defeat, with just one actual testicle but a collectively recognized set of symbolic cojones, Lance Armstrong is a mythical hero for our time, in ways that Jessica Lynch, with her delicate femininity and failure as a soldier, could never be. Okay, so the über-jock did not win the New York City Marathon, nor is he likely to be recruited by the SEALs for Operation Iraqi Freedom. But his elevation to national superstardom, both in the cycling world and in the war on cancer, is predicated on his technically enhanced, exuberantly displayed, visually choreographed masculinity. He is a "man's man," a frequent subject in magazines catering to men's interests and the very picture of the valiant warrior from children's fairy tales. After beating cancer, Armstrong wrote, "I want to die at a hundred years old with an American flag on my back and the star of Texas on my helmet, after screaming down an Alpine descent on a bicycle at 75 miles per hour" (Armstrong and Jenkins 2000:1). This sure sounds to us like the embodiment of glorious, red blooded, American masculinity, reproduced and celebrated in the name of national allegiance.

Notes

1. Forbes estimates Armstrong's annual earnings between June 2004 and June 2005 as $28 million; see www.forbes.com.

2. See www.cdc.gov.

3. See www.cancer.gov.

4. The first was a combination of Bleomycin, Etoposide, and Platinol, and the second a combination of Ifosfamide, Etoposide, and Platinol.

5. ESPN Classic's SportsCentury series.

6. See www.livestrong.org.

7. For financial data on the Foundation, see Annual Report 2005, available at www.livestrong.org.

8. The bracelets were so popular that they spawned numerous copycats in a rainbow of colors demonstrating myriad diseases and causes and have also become fashion accessories.

9. See www.DiscoveryEducation.com

10. See Reilly.

References

Abt, Samuel. 2005. "News Analysis: Who Do You Believe, Lance or France?" *International Herald Tribune*, September 5.

Allen, Arthur. 1999. "Triumph of the Cure." *Salon*, July 29, www.salon.com.

Armstrong, Lance and Sally Jenkins. 2000. *It's Not About the Bike: My Journey Back to Life*. New York: G.P. Putnam's Sons.

Armstrong, Lance and Sally Jenkins. 2003. *Every Second Counts*. New York: Broadway Books.

Bhatnagar, Parija. 2003. "French Goods Face U.S. Backlash." CNNMoney.com, March 17.

Clarke, Juanne Nancarrow. 2004. "A Comparison of Breast, Testicular and Prostate Cancer in Mass Print Media (1996–2001)." *Social Science and Medicine* 59:541–551.

Clatterbaugh, Kenneth. 2000. *Contemporary Perspectives on Masculinity: Men, Women, and Politics in Modern Society*. Boulder, CO: Westview Press.

Coffey, Donald S., Robert H. Getzenberg, and Theodore L. De Weese. 2006. "Hyperthermic Biology and Cancer Therapies: A Hypothesis for the 'Lance Armstrong Effect'." *Journal of the American Medical Association* 296(4):445–448.

Coyle, Daniel. 2006. *Lance Armstrong's War: One Man's Battle Against Fate, Fame, Love, Death, Scandal, and a Few Other Rivals on the Road to the Tour de France*. New York: Harper.

Daniels, Cynthia R. 2006. *Exposing Men: The Science and Politics of Male Reproduction*. New York: Oxford University Press.

Dugard, Martin. 2005. *Chasing Lance: The 2005 Tour de France and Lance Armstrong's Ride of a Lifetime*. New York: Little, Brown and Company.

Gurevich, Maria, Scott Bishop, Jo Bower, Monika Malka, and Joyce Nyhof-Young. 2004. "(Dis)Embodying Gender and Sexuality in Testicular Cancer." *Social Science and Medicine* 58:1597–1607.

Hood, Andrew. 2003. "Lance de France." *Time*, June 29.

Hsu, Andrea. 2007. "Navy SEALs Seek to Build Up Their Ranks." National Public Radio, October 16.

Kearns, Brad. 2007. *How Lance Does It: Put the Success Formula of a Champion into Everything You Do*. New York: McGraw Hill.

King, Samantha. 2006. *Pink Ribbons, Inc.: Breast Cancer and the Politics of Philanthropy*. Minneapolis: University of Minnesota Press.

Koenig, Barbara. 2001. "When the Miracles Run Out in America, Care for Dying Patients Fails to Measure Up." *San Jose Mercury News*, August 7.

Kolata, Gina. 2005. "Super, Sure, But Not More Than Human." *New York Times*, July 24.

Koper, Rachel. 2003. "Piece of Work: Lance Armstrong by Annie Leibovitz." *Austin Chronicle*, November 7.

Lerner, Barron. 2006. "Famous Patients and the Lessons They Teach." *New York Times*, November 14.

Liewer, Steve. 2006. "SEALs Looking for Ultra-Athletes." *San Diego Union-Tribune*, July 29.

Meyer, Jack A. 2003. "Improving Men's Health: Developing a Long-Term Strategy." *American Journal of Public Health* 93(5):709–711.

Moore, Lisa Jean. 2007. *Sperm Counts: Overcome by Man's Most Precious Fluid*. New York: New York University Press.

Reaves, Jessica. 2001. "Tour de France: Vive Le Lance!" *Time*, July 27.

Reilly, Rick. 2002. "Sportsman of the Year: Lance Armstrong." *Sports Illustrated*, December 16, 97(24):52–59.

Ridley, John. 2007. "The Unforgivable Blackness of Barry Bonds." National Public Radio, July 23.

Rosenfeld, Dana and Christopher A. Faircloth, eds. 2006. *Medicalized Masculinities*. Philadelphia, PA: Temple University Press.

Specter, Michael. 2002. "The Long Ride." *The New Yorker*, July 15.

Terrazzano, Lauren. 2006. "Armstrong an Inspiration to All with Cancer." *Newsday*, November 6, D9.

Thompson, Christopher S. 2006. *The Tour de France: A Cultural History*. Berkeley: University of California Press.

Vastag, Brian. 1999. "High-Profile Cancer Cases Prompt Awareness Efforts." *Journal of the National Cancer Institute* 91(21):1802.

White, Rob. 2002. "Social and Political Aspects of Men's Health." *Health* 6(3):267–285.

PART SIX

Men in Relationships

Why do many men have problems establishing and maintaining intimate relationships with women? What different forms do male–female relational problems take within different socioeconomic groups? How do men's problems with intimacy and emotional expressivity relate to power inequities between the sexes? Are rape and domestic violence best conceptualized as isolated deviant acts by "sick" individuals, or are they the illogical consequences of male socialization? This complex web of male–female relationships, intimacy, and power is the topic of this section.

And what is the nature of men's relationships with other men? Do men have close friendships with men, or do they simply "bond" around shared activities and interests? How do competition, ho-

mophobia, and violence enter into men's relationships with each other? For example, a student recently commented that when he goes to the movies with another male friend, they always leave a seat between them, where they put their coats, because they don't want anyone to think they are there "together."

But what are the costs of this emotional and physical distance? And what are the costs of maintaining emotionally impoverished relationships with other men? How is this emotional distance connected to men's intimate relationships with women? Is it related to Billy Crystal's line in *When Harry Met Sally* that women and men can never be friends because "the sex thing always gets in the way"?

Karen Walker and Peter Nardi explore the gender of friendships, whether comparing women and men or gay men and heterosexual men. David Grazian exposes the elaborate pregame rituals that precede the "spontaneous" hooking up and bar-dating scenes where men search for romantic and sexual partners. Finally, Peggy Giordano and her colleagues describe how adolescent boys are far more romantic than we often give them credit for being, although this romanticism often leads to a certain "learned helplessness" when it comes to actually working on a relationship.

"We've been wandering in the desert for forty years. But he's a man—would he ever ask directions?"

Karen Walker

"I'm Not Friends the Way She's Friends": Ideological and Behavioral Constructions of Masculinity in Men's Friendships

Contemporary ideologies about men's friendships suggest that men's capacity for intimacy is sharply restricted. In this view, men have trouble expressing their feelings with friends. Whether due to the development of the masculine psyche or cultural prescriptions, men are viewed as highly competitive with friends. Because of their competition, they are unlikely to talk about intimate matters such as feelings and relationships. The literature on gender differences in friendship suggests that the ideologies reflect actual behavior. Researchers have found that men limit verbal self-disclosure with friends, especially when compared to women (Caldwell & Peplau 1982; Rubin 1985; Sherrod 1987; Aukett, Ritchie, & Mill 1988; Swain 1989; Reid & Fine 1992). Men share activities with friends (Rubin 1985; Swain 1987). On the other hand, there are also suggestions that the degree of self-disclosure among men may be underestimated (Hacker 1981; Wright 1982; Rawlins 1992), particularly among men from particular groups (Franklin 1992). My research on friendship shows that men and women share the stereotypes about gender differences in friendship, but in specific friendships, men discuss their relationships and report relying on men friends for emotional support and intimacy (Walker 1994). In addition, many activities of friendship—seeing friends for dinner, sharing ritual events, and visiting—are things both men and women do.

Barry Wellman (1992) argues that there has been a widespread "domestication" of male friendship, with men seeing friends in their home in much the same way women do.

In much of the literature on gender differences in friendship, ideology has been mistaken for behavior. In part, researchers seem to have made this mistake because they have asked general, instead of specific, questions about friendship.[1] As a result, they have elicited good representations of what respondents *believe* their behavior is— beliefs that are shaped by the respondents' own ideologies. What they have sometimes failed to elicit is information about specific friendships in which variations from the ideologies may be substantial. Because researchers report what respondents tell them, it is easy to understand why researchers make this mistake. What becomes more difficult to understand is how the confusion between the ideology of friendship and friendship behavior comes to be constructed in everyday life. Why do men maintain their belief that men are less open than women in the face of considerable evidence that they do discuss their feelings with their friends? This is even more crucial because the stereotype of intimate friendship that men believe characterizes women's friendship is currently highly valued. Feminist scholars and writers have successfully revalued women's intimate relationships to the detriment of earlier ideals that privileged male bonding. While not all respondents in this study positively evaluated the stereotype of women's openness with friends, many did, as evidenced by one professional man who said:

From *Masculinities* 2(2): 38–55. Copyright © 1994 by Men's Studies Association. Reprinted with permission.

I mean, we [men] talk about sports and politics sometimes, any kind of safe [topic], if you will. Not that any [every] kind of interaction needs to be intimate or this and that, but it's much different when you talk to women. Women catch on. I remember once seeing Robert Bly, and he said something that is really so in my experience, that women get to the heart of things and that they get there so quickly that it makes you, uh, it can put men into a rage because women are able to articulate these kinds of things that men can't.

Given the belief that being intimate and "getting to the heart of things" is good, and given the evidence that men are more intimate in practice than the ideology suggests, *why don't men challenge the ideology?*

There seem to be several answers to this question. First, when men do not conform to the masculine ideals about how they should act with their friends, they are occasionally censured. In the practice of masculine friendship, the positive evaluation of feminine intimacy disappears. Because of their friends' reactions, men come to see their behavior as anomalous and bad, and they do not reevaluate the extent to which the ideology of masculine friendship accurately reflects behavior.

Second, social class influences men's capacities for conforming to gender ideologies. Professional men are somewhat more likely than working-class men to conform to gendered norms with respect to intimate behavior (Franklin 1992; Walker 1994). Also, professional men's social class makes them—with other middle-class men—the primary groups on which cultural stereotypes are based. Literature written specifically about men's friendships often relies on research of middle-class men, particularly college-aged men (Caldwell and Peplau 1982; Rubin 1985; Swain 1989; Rawlins 1992; Reid and Fine 1992). Very recently, some researchers have noted that men who are other than middle-class or white may have different types of friendships from the ideology (Franklin 1992; Hansen 1992), but the knowledge of the existence of other forms of mas-culine friendship among working-class African American and white men has not influenced the ideology of friendship.

Third, there *are* gender differences in behavior, and these differences reinforce stereotypes about gendered forms of friendship, even if the differences differ substantively from the substance of the ideology. For instance, male respondents in this study used the telephone somewhat differently from the ways women used it. Through their use of the telephone men constructed their masculinity, and in so doing they reinforced their notions that men are not open. As I will show, men claimed they called their friends for explicitly instrumental reasons—to make plans, get specific information, and so on—but not to find out how friends were, which they connected to women's telephone use. These practices generally supported the idea that women were better at maintaining friendships and talking to friends about feelings even though men's telephone conversations often included talk about personal matters. But a desire to talk to friends about personal matters was rarely the motive for phone calls.

In this article I examine the ways gender ideology about friendships is maintained through four behaviors and men's interpretations of those behaviors: telephone use, jokes, the use of public space, and how men talk about women. It is only when we understand how men behaviorally construct gender within friendship that we can begin to understand how men use these behavioral constructions to support ideological constructions of masculine friendship practices.

Method of Study

This paper relies on research from a study of men's and women's same-gender and cross-gender friendships. I interviewed 9 working-class and 10 professional men (as well 18 working- class and 15 middle-class women). Within each class I individually interviewed some men who were friends with other respondents in the study. Interviewing friends allowed me to gather information on group interaction that would have been unavailable had I interviewed isolated individuals. In addition, I was able to explore issues that were most salient to groups of friends. Finally, by interviewing friends I could examine the extent to which friends agree on what their interactions were like. This was particularly important when there was a discrepancy between behavior and ideology: Some men did not report on behavior that contradicted the masculine ideology of friendship either because they were unwilling to disclose that their behavior did not match the cultural ideal or because such behavior was somewhat meaningless to them, and they forgot it.

Respondents ranged in age from 27 to 48. Class location was determined by both lifestyle and individuals' work. Thus, working-class respondents tended to have high school educations or less, although one self-employed carpenter had a four-year degree in accounting. Working-class men were in construction and some service occupations. Most working-class men lived in densely populated urban neighborhoods in row houses or twins in Philadelphia. Professional respondents had graduate degrees, and they worked as academics, administrators, lawyers, and therapists. Professionals lived in the suburbs of Philadelphia or in urban apartments.

Interviews were semistructured, and respondents answered both global questions about their friendship patterns as well as questions about activities and topics of conversations in which they engaged with each friend they named. The use of in-depth interviews that included both global and specific questions allowed me to gather data indicating the frequent discrepancies between cultural ideologies of masculine friendships and actual behaviors. In addition, in-depth interviews allowed me to compare working-class and professional respondents' experiences.

Recently, Christine Williams and Joel Heikes (1993) have observed that male nurses shaped responses to interview questions in ways that took into account the gender of the interviewer. In this study, my status as a woman interviewer appeared to have both positive and negative implications for data collection. On the one hand, being a woman made it more likely that men admitted

behavior that contradicted gender ideology. Sociologists studying gender and friendship have consistently argued that men do not engage in self-disclosure with other men (Caldwell & Peplau 1982; Reid & Fine 1992). Other research shows that men are likely to be more self-disclosing with women than with men (Rubin 1985; O'Meara 1989). While my research shows that men engaged in self-disclosure more frequently with friends than the literature suggests, they did so with men they considered close friends. Frequently close friends were people they knew for a long time or people with whom they spent much time. Wright (1982) notes that long-time men friends engage in self-disclosure. I suspected that certain kinds of disclosures that men made during the interviews might have been more difficult to make to an unknown man instead of to me, an unknown woman.

On the other hand, respondents suggested that they more heavily edited their responses to questions about how they discussed women with their men friends than they did other questions. They frequently sprinkled their responses with comments recognizing my gender, "You don't have a gun in there, do you? (laugh)" or "I don't mean to be sexist here." I suspected that responses were much more benign than they would have been if I were a man. Thus, when I discuss men's talk about women below I believe that my data underestimate the extent to which men's talk about women constructs gender tensions.

Behavioral Construction of Masculinity

In recent years sociologists of gender have come to emphasize the active construction of gender. Gender is seen as an ongoing activity fundamental to all aspects of social life rather than a static category in which we place men or women (Connell 1987; West & Zimmerman 1987; Leidner 1991). One advantage of a social constructionist perspective is that it allows researchers to explore both the ideological as well as the behavioral construction of gender. Gender is constructed *ideologically* when men and women believe that certain qualities, such as intimacy, characterize one gender rather than another. The way men and women interpret life and its meaning for them is deeply influenced by their ideological beliefs. Gender is constructed *behaviorally* in the activities men and women do and the way they do them.

Sometimes ideology and behavior match—such as when men talk about gender differences in telephone use and report behavior that differs from women's behavior. Sometimes ideology and behavior do not match. When there is a mismatch, the interesting problem of how ideology is sustained when behavior contradicts it emerges. I argue that, in the specific case of friendship, specific behaviors supported men's gendered ideologies. Men discounted or ignored altogether evidence that discredited a distinctly masculine model of friendship. This occurred because gender is a category culturally defined by multiple qualities. When men included themselves in the masculine gender category based on some behavior, they tended unreflectively to accept as given the cultural boundaries of the entire category *even if other of their behaviors contradicted those boundaries*.

Among respondents there were several ways masculinity was constructed in the activities of friendship. First, where men met, particularly working-class men, became a mark of masculinity. Second, the way men used the telephone distinguished masculine from feminine behavior. Third, men used jokes in particular ways to establish masculinity and also to manage tensions between actual behavior and gender ideologies. Finally, men friends talked about women in ways that emphasized the differences and tensions between men and women.

There are class differences in the behaviors that form particular patterns of masculinity. Differential financial constraints, the social expectations of particular kinds of work, and lifestyle differences played roles in shaping particular forms of masculinity. The use of jokes was somewhat more elaborated among working-class men than among professional men, but reports of

jokes and joking behavior emerged in both groups. Professional men talked about wives and the strains of work and family differently from working-class men; as I will discuss, this resulted from different work experiences.

Besides class differences, which I will address throughout the article, there were individual differences. All men did not engage in all the behaviors that I argue contribute to the construction of masculinity. One professional man said that while he talked "about what specific women are like," he did not talk about women in general and men who talked about what women are generally like "would not be my friends." Other men did not report the use of jokes and joking behavior in their friendships. Sociology frequently avoids discussion about individuals who do not participate in the behaviors that the sociologist argues shows the existence of meaningful social patterns. Unfortunately, doing so often reifies behavioral differences. This is a particular problem in the discussion of gender because there is currently (and happily for the existence of a lively, informed debate) a very close link between the results of social research on gender and broad social and political debates about men's and women's differences.

I wish, therefore, to give the reader a general indication of the individual variability in the gendered behaviors in which men engaged. In all the behaviors discussed below at least half, and frequently more, of the men participated in the behaviors whereas few women did. There were, however, individual exceptions to these behaviors, and those exceptions point to a flexibility in gendered behavior that, while not as expansive as many would wish, is broader than we frequently recognize. Current social theory about gender emphasizes the agentic nature of the construction of gender. It is a practice in which men and women have a considerable range of actions from which to choose. At given historical points, certain actions may be dictated more than others, and therefore individual men and women may frequently act in ways that conform to current ideology. But even when cultural ideology demands close adherence to particular practices, the practical nature of gender means that some individuals will not conform. Further, the multiplicity of practices that create gender enables individuals to maintain their positions within gender categories without much difficulty.

Men's Use of Public Space

The use of public space for informal and apparently unplanned socializing is much more common among men than among women, and it marks the gender boundaries between men and women. The frequent use of public space by working-class men for informal socializing emerges in ethnographies of men's groups (Liebow 1967; Kornblum 1974; Anderson 1976; Whyte 1981). Working-class men in this study met in public spaces such as local bars and playgrounds. There they talked about work and family, and they made informal connections with other men. Sometimes they picked up side work, sometimes they hung out. At the time of our interview, one working-class man said that he spent some of his time at a local bar selling advertisements in a book to raise money for a large retirement dinner for a long-time coach of a community football team. He also spent time there drinking and talking to friends.

Working-class men also met in semipublic spaces such as gyms or clubs. While membership in these spaces was frequently restricted, the spaces themselves functioned in similar ways to public spaces. Men met regularly and informally in public and semipublic spaces one or more times a week. Unlike women who made definite plans to meet friends occasionally in bars, the men assumed because of past practice that on particular nights of the week they would meet friends.

Wellman (1992) suggests that the use of public space for male socializing is diminishing, and men's friendships are becoming domesticated as their friendships move into the home and hence more like women's. This phenomenon of domestication was evident among professional respondents, most of whom reported socializing infrequently in public spaces. But it was not evident among the working-class respondents in this study. All but one of the working-class respondents had been brought up in the same communities in which they lived when I interviewed them. Among these men there were long-time, continuous patterns of public socializing. While Wellman's point is important, the domestication of male friendship seems to be influenced by circumstances in men's lives and is probably occurring unevenly. Further, barring significant structural changes in working-class men's formal and informal work lives, the domestication of male friendships is unlikely to be complete.

Men's Telephone Use

Discussions of men's telephone use as a construction of gender make the most sense when contrasted with women's telephone use. Many men noted that their wives used the telephone very differently from them. A few, primarily working-class men, stated that they disliked talking on the telephone, and they used it only for instrumental reasons (e.g., to make appointments or get specific information). Other men, both professional and working class, said their wives called friends just to see how they were doing and then talked for a long time, whereas men did not do so. Thus men ideologically constructed gender through their understandings of telephone practices. In addition, both men and women constructed gender behaviorally through using the telephone in different ways.

Telephone use differed slightly by class and work experiences, but even accounting for the effects of class and work, there were substantial gender differences. Men frequently reported that the purpose of their most recent telephone calls with friends was instrumental: lawyers discussed cases, men discussed upcoming social plans, and some working-class men made plans to do side work together. Because of this instrumental motive for telephone calls to friends, many professional men reported that their frequent telephone contact was from their offices during working hours. Men rarely reported that they called friends just to say "hi" and find out how they were. One professional man, Mike,[2] reported differences between his wife and himself in being friends:

> I'm not friends the way she's friends. *How are you friends differently?* I don't work on them. I don't pick the phone up and call people and say, "How are you?"

While Mike reported that, in fact, he did call one friend to find out how he was doing at least once a year, most telephone contact was initiated when friends made plans to visit from out of town or he had business matters to discuss with friends. One result of this behavior was tremendous attrition in his friendship network over time. Mike was a gregarious man who reported many past and current friends, but he tended to lose touch with past friends once business reasons for keeping in touch with them diminished, even those who continued to live in Philadelphia. He only reported talking to two friends six or more times a year on the telephone. One of those friends was a man with whom he had professional ties, and they called one another when they did business. The other friend, Gene, was one of the few men who called friends for social conversations. The fairly frequent calls between Gene and Mike may have been initiated by Gene.

Gil, a working-class man, usually spoke to friends on the phone to arrange meetings. Although he kept in touch with two friends largely through telephone use (he worked two jobs during the week and one of his friends worked on weekends—theirs was a telephone friendship), he said:

> I don't talk to them a long time because I'm not a phone person. I'd rather see them in person because I don't like holding the phone and talking because you really can't think of things to say too often on the phone, but when you're in person you can think of more things, cause I like prefer sitting and talking to a person face-to-face . . . I'll talk to people 10, 15 minutes sometimes, but I prefer not to if I can. But some

you just can't get off the phone, no matter what you do. And you're like, "Uh, great, well, I'll talk to you a little bit later." And they go into another story. You know [my friend] Cindy will do that, Cindy is great for that. Now Joanne [my wife] can talk on the phone for two to three hours . . . And then the person she's with is not too far away so she could just walk over and talk, you know.

Peter, a young working-class man, reported that he "avoided the phone as much as possible." He did not call friends to chat, and he only used the telephone for social chats with one friend, a woman:

> I'm not a phone person, but yeah, I do [talk to a specific friend] because she talks on the phone, she likes the phone so . . . She'll talk and I'll yes and no (laughs).

Peter did not do side jobs with other men, thus his reasons for using the telephone were sharply limited. Peter and Gil both reported that their telephone preferences were different from those of women they knew. Their general comment "I'm not a phone person" was a representation of their identity, and it was substantiated by their behavior that differs from women's behavior. Typically, working-class men spoke on the telephone once or twice a week to those with whom they did side jobs. One man who ran a bookmaking business with a friend reported that they spoke several times a day about business. Men spoke much less frequently than that to friends for other reasons.

Although most men reported calling friends for instrumental reasons, many men reported that their telephone conversations were not limited to the reason for the call. During telephone calls men discussed their families or their work after they finished with their business. During telephone calls made to discuss social plans several men discussed infertility problems with their wives. Another complained to a friend about his marital problems during a phone call initiated to plan side work. One man called a friend to make plans for a birthday dinner for the caller's wife.

During the conversation he told his friend how many feelings the interview I had with him had stirred up (the friend had referred me to him). These conversations, then, had several functions for men's friendships. The telephone was primarily considered a tool for business or to make social plans, but it was also used as means of communicating important personal information. Most men, however, deemphasized the telephone's function in the communication of personal information.

About one fourth of the men reported that they did call friends simply to find out how they were. Most of the time these men reported calling out-of-town friends with whom they lacked other regular means of contact, and most of the time their calls were infrequent— one to three times a year. In one exception, a professional man regularly called friends to see how they were (and sometimes became irritated and upset when the friends did not reciprocate by initiating some percentage of the telephone calls). He talked with one local friend once a week for no other reason than to keep in touch, but this pattern was unique. The friend he called had limited mobility, and the men rarely saw one another. The telephone was a primary vehicle for their friendship. In this instance, the two men's calls differed little from some women's calls.

There was tremendous variation in telephone use among men, but the variation does not erase the differences across genders. While only one quarter of the men in this study reported that they ever called friends to visit over the telephone and three quarters called for instrumental reasons, over four-fifths of the women reported that they called friends to visit. Also, men's reported frequency of telephoning friends was consistently lower than women's. Whereas two-thirds of all women reported that they spoke with at least one friend three or more times a week, less than one quarter of the men did so.

The finding that men use the telephone less than women and that women use it for social visiting has been noted by others (Rakow 1991; Fischer 1992). Fischer (1992) argues:

research shows that, discounting their fewer opportunities for social contact, women are more socially adept and intimate than men, for whatever reasons—psychological constitution, social structure, childhood experiences or cultural norms. The telephone therefore fits the typical female style of personal interaction more closely than it does the typical male style (p. 235).

Fischer's comments may hold a clue about how ideologies of gender are maintained despite the evidence of intimate behaviors among men. Men and women both see the telephone as something women use more than men, and they see it as a way women are intimate. Men's telephone practices provided evidence to respondents that men are incapable of intimacy whereas women are very intimate with friends. Although women used the telephone more often for intimate conversation than men, men used opportunities at work and in public hangouts to talk intimately (one respondent reported that when they got together in the bar "we're worse than a bunch of girls when it comes to that [talking about their spouses]!"). Although telephone patterns are a poor measure of intimacy in friendship, men used them as such. Several men commented on hearing their wives call friends and talk about personal information. Doing so substantiated their impressions of women's friendships. Also, because the men focused on the reasons for their calls rather than on the contents of telephone calls, telephone use acted to provide confirmation that stereotypes about friendship are true.

Men's Jokes

Men's use of jokes is another way in which men construct their masculinity. In his ethnography, *America's Working Man*, David Halle (1984) points to several functions jokes serve among men: they reaffirm values of friendship and generosity, they ritually affirm heterosexuality among men whose social circumstances create a level of physical and emotional intimacy culturally regarded as unmasculine, and they mediate disputes. These functions were evident in the way working-class men talked about jokes and humor in their friendships. They were less evident among the professional men, for reasons suggested by Halle.

Men friends, particularly working-class men, used harsh teasing as a form of social control to reinforce certain behaviors. One working-class man said that he and his friends were the worst "ball breakers" in the world. If a man did not show up at the bar or at some social event then my respondent said they heard about it from all their friends. Among these men the friendship group was highly valued, but also, like many contemporary friendships, somewhat fragile. Work and family responsibilities that kept men away from the friendship group might put a friend at risk of being teased.

Other men said that the failure to reciprocate favors, such as help with household projects, might be a basis for teasing friends. This was a particularly important way of defusing tension as well as reaffirming values of friendship for working-class men. They frequently depended on friends to help them attain higher standards of living: friends provided craft services whose prices are high in the formal market and thus many working-class people's material lives were somewhat improved through the help of friends. Failure to reciprocate had implications not only for friendship but also for family income. Jokes about a friend's failure to reciprocate became a public statement about his failure to conform to recognized norms, and they were a way for someone to handle his anger at his friend.

Another way jokes constructed masculinity was to highlight an activity that was outside the purview of men's activities that they nonetheless did. For instance, Greg and Chris were friends from law school who saw each other seven or eight times a year. One of those times was a yearly shopping trip to buy Christmas presents. Men generally claimed they did not shop—those who did usually said they went to hardware stores when they were doing a project with a friend. The shopping trip Greg and Chris went on was a traditional joke between them both. It began in law school when Greg asked Chris to go with him to

buy a negligee for Greg's girlfriend. When they got to the store Chris ran away and Greg was left feeling terribly embarrassed. Ever since, they went shopping once a year, but both men downplayed the shopping aspect of the trips and highlighted the socializing. They said they did not accomplish very much on their trips. They also said they used the time to buy gag gifts for people instead of serious gifts. Turning the shopping spree into a joke subverted the meaning of shopping as something women do, and the trip became a ritual reaffirmation of masculinity.

Jokes were sometimes used as pseudoinstrumental reasons to call friends on the phone when men lacked instrumental reasons; they thus maintained the masculinity of men's telephone practices. Men called each other and told one another jokes and then moved into more personal topics. Gene, for instance, befriended Al's lover, Ken, before Al died of AIDS. During Al's illness Gene was an important source of support for both men, and he continued to keep in touch with Ken after Al's death. They talked regularly on the telephone, but most of the conversations initiated by Ken began with jokes. After Ken and Gene had exchanged jokes the two men moved on to other topics, including their feelings for Al.

Finally, men used jokes to exaggerate gender differences and denigrate women. Gene considered himself sympathetic to women's issues. He said that he and his friends

> will tell in a joking way, tell jokes that are hostile towards feminism or hostile towards women. It's like there's two levels of it. One is, we think the joke is funny in and of itself or we think the joke is funny because it's so outrageously different from what's politically correct. You know, so we kind of laugh about it, and then we'll laugh that we even had the gall to tell it.

Not all men mentioned the importance of humor to friendship, the existence of jokes among friends, or the tendency to tease friends, but about half the respondents indicated that jokes and teasing were part of their friendship. Also, jokes and joking behavior were not limited solely to men.

A few women also told jokes and engaged in joking behavior with their friends, but men emphasized the behavior as part of their friendships, whereas women did not. Also, women reported using jokes in a much more restricted way than men. For men, jokes are an elaborated code with multiple meanings and functions.

Men Talk About Women

Finally, men constructed masculinity through their behavior with men friends through their talk about what women are like. While not every man reported that he engaged in discussions about women with his friends, most men did. Comments about women emphasized men's and women's differences. Men, for instance, discussed how their wives had higher housekeeping standards than they, their wives' greater control over child rearing, and their greater propensity to spend money impulsively; they also discussed women's needs for relationships. These comments helped men interpret their relationships with their wives and served to reassure men that their experiences were not unusual.

> We would talk about like how long it would take them to get dressed . . . my wife took exceptionally long to get dressed, four or five hours in the bathroom. Um, but I mean, I don't think I talk a whole lot about women, when I did I guess I generalized and that kind of stuff, like how a wife expects a husband to kind of do everything for her. (Working-class man)

> What we talked about was the differences, differences we have with our wives in terms of raising kids . . . And how sometimes we feel, rightly or wrongly, we both agreed that we didn't have quite as much control over the situation or say in the situation as we might have liked . . . That's something that a lot of my friends who have younger kids, I've had that discussion with. I've talked to them about it in terms of something that I think mothers, in particular, have a different input into their child's lives than do fathers. (Professional man)

Through these sorts of discussions with men friends—some brief and jocular, some more sus-

tained and serious—men defined who women are, and who they were, in contrast, as men. These discussions with friends frequently reinforced stereotypes about women and men.

Women were spendthrifts:

> One individual may call me up and say, "Geez, my wife just went out and bought these rugs. I need that like a hole in the head. You know, this is great, I have these oriental rugs now, you know, I'm only going to spill coffee on it." (Professional man)

Women attempted to control men's free time:

> [We might talk about] how much we're getting yelled at or in trouble or whatever, you know what I mean, for not doin' stuff around the house, or workin' over somebody else's house too much or staying out at the bars too late. (Working-class man)

Women were manipulative:

> Sometimes they seem, they don't know what they want, or what they want is something different than what they tell you they want. You know, tough to figure out, [we say] that they can be manipulative . . . Conniving. (Professional man)

Men evaluated women's behaviors and desires through such talk. They reported that such talk was a way of getting feedback on their marital experiences. Talking with friends frequently relieved the tensions men felt in their cross-gender relationships, and it did so without requiring men to change their behaviors vis-à-vis women. Men rarely reported that they accommodated themselves to their wives because their friends suggested that they should: in an unusual case, one working-class man said his friend told him that women needed to be told, "I love you," all the time, and he thought his friend had been helpful in mitigating some strains in his marriage through their talk.

More frequently, men's jokes and comments about women—about their demands for more housekeeping help, their ways with money, and their desires to have men home more often—

served to delegitimize women's demands. Men talked about women as unreasonable; as one man above said, "everybody needs time away." This tendency to delegitimize wives' demands was more apparent among working-class men than among the professional men. Professionals reported that their jobs, not unreasonable wives, prevented them from greater involvement in child care, and they sometimes talked with friends about this as an inevitable part of professional life. The effect, however, was similar because talk among both professional and working-class men friends supported the status quo. Instead of becoming a problem to be solved, professional men and their friends determined that professional life unfortunately, but inevitably, caused men to limit their family involvement. (One man who consistently seemed to play with the boundaries of masculinity had tried to solve the problem through scheduling his work flexibly along the lines that a friend had suggested. He reported that he still did not have enough time for his family.)

These four behaviors: using public spaces for friendship socializing, men's telephone practices, joking, and talking about women in particular ways are some ways that men construct masculinity in their friendships. There are many others. Discussions of sports, for instance, are one obvious other way men construct their masculinity, and such discussions were common among respondents. Like women's telephone use and ease with intimacy, men's talk about sports has become part of our cultural ideology about gendered friendships. Not all respondents, however, participated in such talk, and of those who did, some did not enjoy such talk but engaged in it because it was expected.

Cultural Ideology of Men and Friendship

When I began this article I asked not only how men construct masculinity through their behaviors but also why there was a discrepancy between the cultural ideology of men's friendship's, which maintains that men do not share intimate thoughts and feelings with one another, and reports of specific behaviors that show that they do. It is in part by recognizing that the construction of gender is an ongoing activity that incorporates many disparate behaviors that this question becomes answerable. While one behavior in an interaction may violate the norms of gender ideology, other behaviors are simultaneously conforming to other ideologies of masculinity. When men reflect back on their behavior they emphasize those aspects of their behavior that give truth to their self-images as men. The other behavior may be reported, but, in this study, it did not discredit men's gender ideologies.

Second, as I noted earlier, masculinity is frequently reified, and behavior that does not conform does not affect the overall picture of masculinity. Men belong in the gender category to which they were assigned at birth, and their past in that category reassures them that they belong there. Occasionally respondents recognized that men do things that contradict gender ideology. One man told me about a friend of his who "does thoughtful things for other men." When I asked what he did, and he said:

> Uh, remembers their birthdays. Will buy them gifts. Uh, and does it in a way that's real, I think, really, uh, I don't know, it's not uh, it's not uh, feminine in the sense of, feminine, maybe in the pejorative sense . . . I mean, I remember that John, uh, John's nurturing I saw, not that I was a recipient of it so much although I was in his company a lot and got to see him. Uh, I thought, boy, this guy's a, this guy's a real man, this guy. This guy's all right, you know.

Though my respondent identified his friend's behavior as different, almost feminine, he made sure to tell me that the man is a "real man." This seemed problematic for him, his language became particularly awkward, full of partial sentences. But in the end, the fact that his friend was a man and that my respondent liked and respected him enabled him to conclude, "this guy's a real man."

At other times, recognition that behavior contradicts gender ideology elicits censure instead of acceptance. When men censure one another for such behavior, they reinforce the idea that such behavior is anomalous and should not be expressed. For instance, Gene, who consciously worked at intimacy with his friends, told me about sitting and drinking with a friend of his one night when Gene was depressed. His friend asked him how things were going and Gene told him he was depressed because he was feeling financial pressures. Gene felt "house poor" and upset with himself for buying a house that would cause him to feel such pressures when he had determined that he would not do such a thing. His friend's response was, "Oh, that's the last time I ask you how you're feeling." On an earlier occasion Gene called his gay friend in California on the telephone crying because he had just broken off with a woman he had been dating. His friend comforted him at the time, but later he said, "I didn't know you had it in you [to express yourself like that]." Gene believed that men had greater difficulties with self-disclosure than women, and these events acted as support for his beliefs instead of counterexamples. In both cases friends had let him know his self-disclosing behavior was either intolerable or unusual. His gay friend seemed to admire Gene's ability to call him up in tears by giving him a back-handed compliment, but this was a man who had rejected many norms of heterosexuality, and who saw Gene as participating in hegemonic masculinity (Connell 1987) and teased him for it. Gene's interpretation of these events coincided with his friends: he was behaving in ways men normally did not.

In another case, Anna, a woman respondent, told me about her husband Tom's experience with his best friend. Anna had been diagnosed with a serious chronic illness that had profound consequences for her lifestyle, and Tom was depressed about it. One night he went out with two friends, Jim, Tom's best friend, and another man who was unhappy about his recent divorce. According to Anna, Jim commented that he wished he did not know either Tom or the other man at the time because they were both so depressed. From this, Anna said she and Tom concluded that men did

not express their feelings and were not as intimate with one another as women were.

These sorts of events reinforce men's notions that men are emotionally distant. Self-disclosure and attempts to express one's feelings are seen as anomalous, even if desirable—desirable because the contemporary evaluation on friendship as defined primarily by feminists is that women have better friendships than men. Women, by the way, also reported occasions when their friends were unsympathetic to their expressions of distress. The conclusions women and men drew about their unsympathetic friendship differed, however. Women concluded that particular friends lacked sympathy. Unlike men, they did not think their expressive behavior was inappropriate or unusual.

Conclusion

I have conceptualized gender as an ongoing social creation rather than a role individuals learn or a personality type they develop that causes differences in behavior. Individuals construct gender on an ideological and a behavioral level. On a behavioral level, many social acts contribute to the overall construction of masculinity. Men do not talk on the phone unless they have something specific they wish to find out or arrange. Men friends joke around together. Men hang out in bars. Men also talk about women and their wives in ways that distinguish women from men and define gender tensions and men's solutions to them. Some of these behaviors have become part of the cultural ideology of men's friendships. Respondents, for instance, talked generally about differences between men's and women's telephone use. Some also said that women stayed home with their friends whereas men went out. But the relationship between behavior and ideology is not so direct and simple that behaviors in which most men participate become part of the cultural ideology. To the extent that talking about women, for instance, is perceived as sharing personal information, then talking about women is something men do not recognize as characteristic of their friendships.

Because so many actions construct masculinity and gender is a practice over which individuals have some control, the failure to conform to the cultural ideology of masculine friendship does not necessarily threaten either the cultural ideology or the individual's position in the masculine gender category. This becomes particularly important in understanding why the many men who share personal information with friends continue to believe that men are inexpressive and find intimacy difficult. I have found that the exchange of intimate information is something most respondents, men and women, engaged in, but most people also did it with selected friends. Furthermore, talking about personal matters or sharing feelings frequently constituted a small portion of all friendship interactions. Thus, for men whose identities included a notion that they, as men, were not open with friends, the times when they were open were insignificant. There were many other activities of friendship that men preferred to emphasize.

It is useful to expand the debate over gender differences in friendship to include behaviors other than intimacy that has dominated the recent literature on gender and friendship (Miller 1983; Rubin 1985; Sherrod 1987; Swain 1987; Allan 1989; Rawlins 1992). The narrowness of the debate has limited our understandings of why men's friendships have been meaningful and important to them. Working-class men's reliance on friends for services and material support becomes invisible. The importance of joking behavior as a communicative style and its functions in maintaining stable relationships for both working-class and professional men disappear. Finally, the narrow debate over intimacy obscures some implications of how men talk to one another about women for gender relations and inequality.

A version of this article was presented at the 1993 annual meetings of the American Sociological Association in Miami. The author gratefully acknowledges the comments of Robin Leidner and Vicki Smith.

Notes

1. Some researchers have made this mistake as part of a more general positive evaluation of women. Some of this literature is explicitly feminist and draws on literature which emphasizes and dichotomizes gender differences.

2. All names of the respondents have been changed.

References

Allan, G. (1989). *Friendship: Developing a sociological perspective*. Boulder, CO: Westview.

Anderson, E. (1976). *A place on the corner*. Chicago: University of Chicago Press.

Aukett, R., Ritchie, J., & Mill, K. (1988). Gender differences in friendship patterns. *Sex Roles, 19*, 57–66.

Caldwell, M. A., & Peplau, L. A. (1982). Sex differences in same-sex friendships. *Sex Roles, 8*, 721–732.

Connell, R. W. (1987). *Gender and power*. Palo Alto, CA: Stanford University Press.

Fischer, C. (1992). *America calling: A social history of the telephone to 1940*. Berkeley: University of California Press.

Franklin, C. W. II (1992). Friendship among Black men. In P. Nardi (Ed.), *Men's friendships* (pp. 201–214). Newbury Park, CA: Sage.

Hacker, H. M. (1981). Blabbermouths and clams: Sex differences in self-disclosure in same-sex and cross-sex friendship dyads. *Psychology of Women Quarterly, 5*, 385–401.

Halle, D. (1984). *America's working man: Work, home, and politics among blue-collar property owners*. Chicago: University of Chicago Press.

Hansen, K. V. (1992). Our eyes behold each other: masculinity and intimate friendship in antebellum New England. In P. Nardi (Ed.), *Men's friendships* (pp. 35–58). Newbury Park, CA: Sage.

Kornblum, W. (1974). *Blue collar community*. Chicago: University of Chicago Press.

Leidner, R. (1991). Serving hamburgers and selling insurance: Gender, work, and identity in interactive service jobs. *Gender & Society, 5*, 154–177.

Liebow, E. (1967). *Tally's corner: A study of Negro street-corner men*. Boston: Little, Brown.

Miller, M. (1983). *Men and friendship*. Boston: Houghton Mifflin.

O'Meara, J. D. (1989). Cross-sex friendship: Four basic challenges of an ignored relationship. *Sex Roles, 21,* 525–543.

Rakow, L. F. (1991). *Gender on the line: Women, the telephone, and community life.* Urbana, IL: University of Illinois Press.

Rawlins, W. (1992). *Friendship matters: Communication, dialectics, and the life course.* New York: Aldine de Gruyter.

Reid, H. M., & Fine, G. A. (1992). Self-disclosure in men's friendships. In P. Nardi (Ed.), *Men's friendships* (pp. 132–152). Newbury Park, CA: Sage.

Rubin, L. (1985). *Just friends: The role of friendship in our lives.* New York: Harper & Row.

Sherrod, D. (1987). The bonds of men: Problems and possibilities in close male relationships. In H. Brod (Ed.), *The making of masculinities* (pp. 213–239). Boston: Allen and Unwin.

Swain, S. (1989). Covert intimacy: Closeness in men's friendships. In B. Risman & P. Schwartz (Eds.), *Gender and intimate relationships* (pp. 71–86). Belmont, CA: Wadsworth.

Walker, K. (1994). Men, women and friendship: what they say; what they do. *Gender & Society, 8,* 246–265.

Wellman, B. (1992). Men in networks: Private communities, domestic friendships. In P. Nardi (Ed.), *Men's friendships* (pp. 74–114). Newbury Park, CA: Sage.

West, C., & Zimmerman, D. (1987). Doing gender. *Gender & Society, 1,* 125–151.

Whyte, W. F. (1981). *Street corner society: The social structure of an Italian slum* (3rd ed.). Chicago: The University of Chicago Press.

Williams, C. L., & Heikes, E. J. (1993). The importance of researcher's gender in the in-depth interview: Evidence from two case studies of male nurses. *Gender & Society, 7,* 280–291.

Wright, P. (1982). Men's friendships, women's friendships and the alleged inferiority of the latter. *Sex Roles, 8,* 1–20.

Peter M. Nardi

The Politics of Gay Men's Friendships

Towards the end of Wendy Wasserstein's Pulitzer Prize–winning play, *The Heidi Chronicles*, a gay character, Peter Patrone, explains to Heidi why he has been so upset over all the funerals he has attended recently: "A person has so many close friends. And in our lives, our friends are our families" (Wasserstein 1990: 238). In his collection of stories, *Buddies*, Ethan Mordden (1986: 175) observes: "What unites us, all of us, surely, is brotherhood, a sense that our friendships are historic, designed to hold Stonewall together. . . . It is friendship that sustained us, supported our survival." These statements succinctly summarize an important dimension about gay men's friendships: Not only are friends a form of family for gay men and lesbians, but gay friendships are also a powerful political force.

Mordden's notion of "friends is survival" has a political dimension that becomes all the more salient in contemporary society where the political, legal, religious, economic, and health concerns of gay people are routinely threatened by the social order. In part, gay friendship can be seen as a political statement, since at the core of the concept of friendship is the idea of "being oneself" in a cultural context that may not approve of that self. For many people, the need to belong with others in dissent and out of the mainstream is central to the maintenance of self and identity (Rubin 1985). The friendships formed by a shared marginal identity, thus, take on powerful political dimensions as they organize around a stigmatized status to confront the dominant culture in solidarity. Jerome (1984: 698) believes that

friendships have such economic and political implications, since friendship is best defined as "the cement which binds together people with interests to conserve."

Suttles (1970: 116) argues that:

> The very basic assumption friends must make about one another is that each is going beyond a mere presentation of self in compliance with "social dictates." Inevitably, this makes friendship a somewhat deviant relationship because the surest test of personal disclosure is a violation of the rules of public propriety.

Friendship, according to Suttles (1970), has its own internal order, albeit maintained by the cultural images and situational elements that structure the definitions of friendship. In friendship, people can depart from the routine and display a portion of the self not affected by social control. That is, friendships allow people to go beyond the basic structures of their cultural institutions into an involuntary and uncontrollable exposure of self—to deviate from public propriety (Suttles 1970).

Little (1989) similarly argues that friendship is an escape from the rules and pieties of social life. It's about identity: who one is rather than one's roles and statuses. And the idealism of friendship "lies in its detachment from these [roles and statuses], its creative and spiritual transcendence, its fundamental skepticism as a platform from which to survey the givens of society and culture" (Little 1989: 145). For gay men, these descriptions illustrate the political meaning friendship can have in their lives and their society.

The political dimension of friendship is summed up best by Little (1989: 154–155):

> [T]he larger formations of social life—kinship, the law, the economy—must be different where there is, in addition to solidarity and dutiful role-performance, a willingness and capacity for friendship's surprising one-to-one relations, and this difference may be enough to transform social and political life. . . . Perhaps, finally, it is true that progress in democracy depends on a new generation that will increasingly locate itself in identity-shaping, social, yet personally liberating, friendships.

The traditional, nuclear family has been the dominant model for political relations and has structured much of the legal and social norms of our culture. People have often been judged by their family ties and history. But as the family becomes transformed into other arrangements, so do the political and social institutions of society. For example, the emerging concept of "domestic partnerships" has affected a variety of organizations, including insurance companies, city governments, private industry, and religious institutions (Task Force on Family Diversity final report 1988).

For many gay people, the "friends as family" model is a political statement, going beyond the practicality of developing a surrogate family in times of needed social support. It is also a way of refocusing the economic and political agenda to include nontraditional family structures composed of both romantic and nonromantic nonkin relationships.

In part, this has happened by framing the discussions in terms of gender roles. The women's movement and the emerging men's movement have highlighted the negative political implications of defining gender roles according to traditional cultural norms or limiting them to biological realities. The gay movement, in turn, has often been one source for redefining traditional gender roles and sexuality. So, for example, when gay men exhibit more disclosing and emotional interactions with other men, it demonstrates the limitations of male gender roles

typically enacted among many heterosexual male friends. By calling attention to the impact of homophobia on heterosexual men's lives, gay men's friendships illustrate the potentiality for expressive intimacy among all men.

Thus, the assumptions that biology and/or socialization have inevitably constrained men from having the kinds of relationships and intimacies women often typically have can be called into question. This questioning of the dominant construction of gender roles is in itself a sociopolitical act with major implications on the legal, religious, and economic order.

White (1983:16) also sees how gay people's lives can lead to new modes of behavior in the society at large:

> In the case of gays, our childlessness, our minimal responsibilities, the fact that our unions are not consecrated, even our very retreat into gay ghettos for protection and freedom: all of these objective conditions have fostered a style in which we may be exploring, even in spite of our conscious intentions, things as they will someday be for the heterosexual majority. In that world (as in the gay world already), love will be built on esteem rather than passion or convention, sex will be more playful or fantastic or artistic than marital—and friendship will be elevated into the supreme consolation for this continuing tragedy, human existence.

If, as White and others have argued, gay culture in the post-Stonewall, sexual liberation years of the 1970s was characterized by a continuous fluidity between what constituted a friend, a sexual partner, and a lover, then we need to acknowledge the AIDS decade of the 1980s as a source for restructuring of gay culture and the reorganization of sexuality and friendship. If indeed gay people (and men in particular) have focused attention on developing monogamous sexual partnerships, what then becomes the role of sexuality in the initiation and development of casual or close friendships? Clearly, gay culture is not a static phenomenon, unaffected by the larger social order. Certainly, as the moral order in the AIDS years encourages the re-establishment of more traditional relationships, the implications for the ways sexuality and friendships are organized similarly change.

Friends become more important as primary sources of social and emotional support when illness strikes; friendship becomes institutionally organized as "brunch buddies" dating services or "AIDS buddies" assistance groups; and self-help groups emerge centering on how to make and keep new friends without having "compulsive sex." While AIDS may have transformed some of the meanings and role of friendships in gay men's lives from the politicalization of sexuality and friendship during the post-Stonewall 1970s, the newer meanings of gay friendships, in turn, may be having some effect on the culture's definitions of friendships.

Interestingly, the mythical images of friendships were historically more male-dominated: bravery, loyalty, duty, and heroism (see Sapadin 1988). This explained why women were typically assumed incapable of having true friendships. But today, the images of true friendship are often expressed in terms of women's traits: intimacy, trust, caring, and nurturing, thereby excluding the more traditional men from true friendship. However, gay men appear to be at the forefront of establishing the possibility of men overcoming their male socialization stereotypes and restructuring their friendships in terms of the more contemporary (i.e., "female") attributes of emotional intimacy.

To do this at a wider cultural level involves major sociopolitical shifts in how men's roles are structured and organized. Friendships between men in terms of intimacy and emotional support inevitably introduce questions about homosexuality. As Rubin (1985: 103) found in her interviews with men: "The association of friendship with homosexuality is so common among men." For women, there is a much longer history of close connections with other women, so that the separation of the emotional from the erotic is more easily made.

Lehne (1989) has argued that homophobia has limited the discussion of loving male rela-

tionships and has led to the denial by men of the real importance of their friendships with other men. In addition, "the open expression of emotion and affection by men is limited by homophobia. . . . The expression of more tender emotions among men is thought to be characteristic only of homosexuals" (Lehne 1989: 426). So men are raised in a culture with a mixed message: strive for healthy, emotionally intimate friendships, but if you appear too intimate with another man you might be negatively labelled homosexual.

This certainly wasn't always the case. As a good illustration of the social construction of masculinity, friendship, and sexuality, one need only look to the changing definitions and concepts surrounding same-sex friendship during the nineteenth century (see Smith-Rosenberg 1975; Rotundo 1989). Romantic friendships could be erotic but not sexual, since sex was linked to reproduction. Because reproduction was not possible between two women or two men, the close relationship was not interpreted as being a sexual one:

> Until the 1880s, most romantic friendships were thought to be devoid of sexual content. Thus a woman or man could write of affectionate desire for a loved one of the same gender without causing an eyebrow to be raised (D'Emilio and Freedman 1988: 121).

However, as same-sex relationships became medicalized and stigmatized in the late nineteenth century, "the labels 'congenital inversion' and 'perversion' were applied not only to male sexual acts, but to sexual or romantic unions between women, as well as those between men" (D'Emilio and Freedman, 1988: 122). Thus, the twentieth century is an anomaly in its promotion of female equality, the encouragement of male–female friendships, and its suspicion of intense emotional friendships between men (Richards 1987). Yet, in ancient Greece and the medieval days of chivalry, comradeship, virtue, patriotism, and heroism were all associated with close male friendship. Manly love, as it was often called, was a central part of the definition of manliness (Richards 1987).

It is through the contemporary gay, women's, and men's movements that these twentieth century constructions of gender are being questioned. And at the core is the association of close male friendships with negative images of homosexuality. Thus, how gay men structure their emotional lives and friendships can affect the social and emotional lives of all men and women. This is the political power and potential of gay friendships.

References

D'Emilio, John, and Freedman, Estelle. (1988). *Intimate Matters: A History of Sexuality in America.* New York: Harper & Row.

Jerome, Dorothy. (1984). Good company: The sociological implications of friendship. *Sociological Review*, 32(4), 696–718.

Lehne, Gregory K. (1989 [1980]). Homophobia among men: Supporting and defining the male role. In M. Kimmel and M. Messner (Eds.), *Men's Lives* (pp. 416–429). New York: Macmillan.

Little, Graham. (1989). Freud, friendship, and politics. In R. Porter and S. Tomaselli (Eds.), *The Dialectics of Friendship* (pp. 143–158). London: Routledge.

Mordden, Ethan. (1986). *Buddies.* New York: St. Martin's Press.

Richards, Jeffrey. (1987). "Passing the love of women": Manly love and Victorian society. In J. A. Mangan and J. Walvin (Eds.), *Manliness and Morality: Middle-Class Masculinity in Britain and America (1800–1940)* (pp. 92–122). Manchester, England: Manchester University Press.

Rotundo, Anthony. (1989). Romantic friendships: Male intimacy and middle-class youth in the northern United States, 1800–1900. *Journal of Social History*, 23(1), 1–25.

Rubin, Lillian. (1985). *Just Friends: The Role of Friendship in Our Lives.* New York: Harper & Row.

Sapadin, Linda. (1988). Friendship and gender: Perspectives of professional men and women. *Journal of Social and Personal Relationships*, 5(4), 387–403.

Smith-Rosenberg, Carroll. (1975). The female world of love and ritual: Relations between women in nineteenth-century America. *Signs*, 1(1): 1–29.

Suttles, Gerald. (1970). Friendship as a social institution. In G. McCall, M. McCall, N. Denzin, G. Suttles, and S. Kurth, *Social Relationships* (pp. 95–135). Chicago: Aldine.

Task Force on Family Diversity. (1988). *Strengthening Families: A Model for Community Action.* City of Los Angeles.

Wasserstein, Wendy. (1990). *The Heidi Chronicles.* San Diego: Harcourt, Brace, Jovanovich.

White, Edmund. (1983). Paradise found: Gay men have discovered that there is friendship after sex. *Mother Jones*, June, 10–16.

David Grazian

The Girl Hunt: Urban Nightlife and the Performance of Masculinity as Collective Activity

From Chicago's jazz cabarets to New York's gay discos to Las Vegas's strip clubs, sexualized environments have historically defined downtown zones of urban nightlife (Bernstein 2001; Chatterton and Hollands 2003; Chauncey 1994; Kenney 1993; Owen 2003). Hot nightclubs and cool lounges enforce sexualized norms of dress and body adornment and invite flirtation, innuendo, and physical contact among patrons engaged in rituals of courtship. Nightspots also rely on the attractiveness of service staff and the promise of eroticized interaction to recruit customers (Allison 1994; Lloyd 2005; Spradley and Mann 1975), while sexual relations among staff are frequently the norm (Giuffre and Williams 1994). Moreover, young urbanites identify downtown clusters of nightclubs as *direct sexual marketplaces*, or markets for singles seeking casual encounters with potential sex partners (Laumann et al. 2004).

For these reasons, scenes of urban nightlife serve as particularly fitting sites for observing how men and women enact gender as a routine accomplishment in everyday life (West and Zimmerman 1987). In this article I examine girl hunting—a practice whereby adolescent heterosexual men aggressively seek out female sexual partners in nightclubs, bars, and other public arenas of commercialized entertainment. Recent sociolog-

ical studies of sexual behavior analyze courtship patterns in relatively normative terms, concentrating on the logistics of sex partnering and mate selection in cities (Laumann et al. 2004). In contrast, in this article I wish to emphasize the more performative nature of contemporary flirtation rituals by examining how male-initiated games of heterosexual pursuit function as strategies of impression management in which young men sexually objectify women to heighten their own performance of masculinity. While we typically see public sexual behavior as an interaction between *individuals*, I illustrate how these rituals operate as collective and homosocial *group* activities conducted in the company of men.

The Performance of Masculinity as Collective Activity

According to the symbolic interactionist perspective, masculinity represents a range of dramaturgical performances individuals exhibit through face-to-face interaction (Goffman 1959, 1977; West and Zimmerman 1987). Like femininity, masculinity is not innate but an accomplishment of human behavior that appears natural because gendered individuals adhere to an institutionalized set of myths they learn through everyday interactions and encounters, and thus accept as social reality (Goffman 1977; West and Zimmerman 1987). Throughout their formative years and beyond, young men are encouraged by their parents, teachers, coaches, and peers to adopt a socially constructed vision of manhood, a set of

From *Symbolic Interaction*, Vol. 30, Issue 2, pp. 221–243. Copyright © 2007 by the Society for the Study of Symbolic Interaction. All rights reserved. Reprinted by permission of the University of California Press through the Copyright Clearance Center and the author.

cultural beliefs that prescribe what men ought to be like: physically strong, powerful, independent, self-confident, efficacious, dominant, active, persistent, responsible, dependable, aggressive, courageous, and sexually potent (Donaldson 1993; Messner 2002; Mishkind et al. 1986). In the fantasies of many boys and men alike, a relentless competitive spirit, distant emotional detachment, and an insatiable heterosexual desire, all commonly (but not exclusively) displayed by the sexual objectification of women (Bird 1996), characterize idealized masculinity.

Essentialist visions of masculinity obscure how both women and men resist, challenge, and renegotiate the meanings surrounding masculinity and femininity in their everyday lives (Chapkis 1986; Connell 1987, 1992, 1993, 1995; Connell and Messerschmidt 2005; Donaldson 1993; Hollander 2002). The inevitable disconnect between dominant expectations of normative masculinity, on the one hand, and actualized efforts at what West and Zimmerman (1987) refer to as "doing gender" as a dramaturgical performance, on the other, presents a challenging problem for men, particularly because "the number of men rigorously practicing the hegemonic pattern in its entirety may be quite small" (Connell 1995:79). It is an especially acute dilemma for young men of college age (18–25) who, as "emerging adults" (Arnett 1994, 2000), display many of the physical traits of early adulthood along with the emotional immaturity, diminutive body image, and sexual insecurities of late adolescence (Mishkind et al. 1986).

The competitive ritual of *girl hunting* epitomizes this dilemma, as heterosexual adolescent males aggressively seek out female sexual partners in dance clubs, cocktail lounges, and other public arenas of commercialized entertainment in the city at night. While courtship rituals are by no means confined to nightlife settings—as evidenced by the relatively large numbers of romantic couples who meet through work and school (Michael et al. 1995:72)—in American culture, bars and nightclubs are widely considered more normative environments for actively pursuing

anonymous sexual partners in a strategic manner (Laumann et al. 2004). In contrast to occupational and educational domains in which masculine power can be signaled by professional success and intellectual superiority, sexual prowess is a primary signifier of masculinity in the context of urban nightlife.[1] Indeed, the importance placed on competitive "scoring" (Messner 2002) among men in the highly gendered universe of cocktail lounges and singles bars should not be underestimated.

However, a wealth of data suggests that, contrary to representations of urban nightlife in popular culture, such as Candace Bushnell's novel *Sex and the City* ([1996] 2001) and its HBO television spin-off, rumors of the proverbial one-night stand have been greatly exaggerated (Williams 2005). According to the National Health and Social Life Survey, relatively few men (16.7 percent) and even fewer women (5.5 percent) report engaging in sexual activity with a member of the opposite sex within two days of meeting them (Laumann et al. 1994:239).[2] About 90 percent of women aged eighteen to forty-four report that they find having sex with a stranger unappealing (Laumann et al. 1994:163–65). Findings from the Chicago Health and Social Life Survey demonstrate that, across a variety of city neighborhood types, typically less than one-fifth of heterosexual adults aged eighteen to fifty-nine report having met their most recent sexual partner in a bar, nightclub, or dance club (Mahay and Laumann 2004:74).[3]

Moreover, the efficacy of girl hunting is constrained by women's ability to resist unwanted sexual advances in public, as well as to initiate their own searches for desirable sex partners. Whereas the ideological basis of girl hunting stresses vulnerability, weakness, and submissiveness as conventional markers of femininity, young women commonly challenge these stereotypes by articulating their own physical strength, emotional self-reliance, and quick wit during face-to-face encounters with men (Duncier and Molotch 1999; Hollander 2002; Paules 1991; Snow et al. 1991).

For all these reasons, girl hunting would not seem to serve as an especially efficacious strategy for locating sexual partners, particularly when compared with other methods (such as meeting through mutual friends, colleagues, classmates, or other trusted third parties; common participation in an educational or recreational activity; or shared membership in a civic or religious organization). In fact, the statistical rareness of the one-night stand may help explain why successful lotharios are granted such glorified status and prestige among their peers in the first place (Connell and Messerschmidt 2005: 851). But if this is the case, then why do adolescent men persist in hassling women in public through aggressive sexual advances and pickup attempts (Duneier and Molotch 1999; Snow et al. 1991; Whyte 1988), particularly when their chances of meeting sex partners in this manner are so slim?

I argue that framing the question in this manner misrepresents the actual sociological behavior represented by the girl hunt, particularly since adolescent males do not necessarily engage in girl hunting to generate sexual relationships, even on a drunken short-term basis. Instead, three counterintuitive attributes characterize the girl hunt. First, the girl hunt is as much *ritualistic and performative* as it is utilitarian—it is a social drama through which young men perform their interpretations of manhood. Second, as demonstrated by prior studies (Martin and Hummer 1989; Polk 1994; Sanday 1990; Thorne and Luria 1986), girl hunting is not always a purely heterosexual pursuit but can also take the form of an inherently *homosocial* activity. Here, one's male peers are the intended audience for competitive games of sexual reputation and peer status, public displays of situational dominance and rule transgression, and in-group rituals of solidarity and loyalty. Finally, the emotional effort and logistical deftness required by rituals of sexual pursuit (and by extension the public performance of masculinity itself) encourage some young men to seek out safety in numbers by participating in the girl hunt as a kind of *collective* activity, in which they enjoy

the social and psychological resources generated by group cohesion and dramaturgical teamwork (Goffman 1959). Although tales of sexual adventure traditionally feature a single male hero, such as Casanova, the performance of heterosexual conquest more often resembles the exploits of the dashing Christian de Neuvillette and his better-spoken coconspirator Cyrano de Bergerac (Rostand 1897). By aligning themselves with similarly oriented accomplices, many young men convince themselves of the importance and efficacy of the girl hunt (despite its poor track record), summon the courage to pursue their female targets (however clumsily), and assist one another in "mobilizing masculinity" (Martin 2001) through a collective performance of gender and heterosexuality.

In this article, I focus on the ritual of girl hunting to analyze how heterosexual young men perform masculinity as a collective activity in the context of urban nightlife. Drawing on their self-reported narrative accounts, I document how these young men employ a set of collective "hunting" strategies designed to (1) reinforce what I call "the myth of the pickup" and other dominant expectations of masculine behavior; (2) boost confidence in one's performance of masculinity and heterosexual power; and (3) assist in the performance of masculinity in the presence of women. I am not suggesting that the presentation of a masculine self and its attendant peer status serves as the *only* desired or stated purpose or outcome of the girl hunt, as this activity is also clearly motivated by physical and romantic pleasure seeking (Collins 2004). It is also not my intention to suggest that all young men follow the protocols of girl hunting as collective activity in their sexual pursuits. Rather, in this article I wish to illustrate how groups of young heterosexual men employ the power of collective rituals of homosociality to perform heterosexual competence and masculine identity in the public context of urban nightlife, and to show how these rituals reproduce structures of inequality *within* as well as *across* the socially constructed gender divide between women and men.

Methods and Data

I draw on firsthand narrative accounts provided by 243 heterosexual male college students attending the University of Pennsylvania, an Ivy League research university situated in Philadelphia. These data represent part of a larger study involving approximately 600 college students (both men and women). The study was conducted at Penn among all students enrolled in one of two semester terms of a sociology course on media and popular culture taught by me during the 2003–4 academic year.[4] Respondents were directed to explore Philadelphia's downtown nightlife by attending at least one nightlife entertainment venue (i.e., restaurant, café, dance club, sports bar, cocktail lounge) located in Philadelphia's Center City district for the duration of a few evening hours' time. They were encouraged to select familiar sites where they would feel both comfortable and safe and were permitted to choose whether to conduct their outing alone or with one or more friends, relatives, intimates, or acquaintances of either gender.

Upon the conclusion of their evening, students were instructed to document their experiences in detailed narrative accounts. Although some of the materials I assigned during the course address the elaborated performance of masculinity in public (i.e., Bissinger 1990; Geertz 1973; Grazian 2003; Grindstaff 2002), students were not necessarily expected to address these themes or issues in their accounts. After submitting their typed narrative accounts electronically to a team of research assistants (who in turn read them to ensure that each adhered to proper standards of protocol), the respondents' names were removed from their submissions to protect their anonymity. These accounts were then forwarded to me; I assigned them individual case numbers and systematically coded and analyzed them separately on the basis of gender.[5] An initial read-through of accounts submitted by my male respondents revealed recurring commonalities, including a pronounced goal of seeking out young women as potential sexual and romantic partners, and an ambitiously strategic orientation toward this end. Subsequent coding of these accounts highlighted the importance of collective behavior (including the ritualistic consumption of alcohol), a codependent reliance on one's peer group, and the deployment of team-oriented strategies deemed necessary for approaching women in public.[6]

The original sample of 243 heterosexual male students consists of 21.4 percent (n = 52) freshman, 36.6 percent (n = 89) sophomores, 21.8 percent (n = 53) juniors, and 20.2 percent (n = 49) seniors. Participants ranged from 18 to 24 years of age, with a mean age of 19.9 years. Reflecting the privileged social status of Ivy League university students, the racial and ethnic makeup of the sample is as follows: 78.2 percent (n = 190) white, 11.5 percent (n = 28) Asian, 4.5 percent (n = 11) non-Hispanic black, 2.9 percent (n = 7) Hispanic, and 2.9 percent (n = 7) mixed race/other.[7] Recent available statistics (*U.S. News and World Report* 2005) estimate the proportion of minority students at the University of Pennsylvania at 17 percent Asian, 6 percent black, and 5 percent Hispanic. In terms of residence prior to college, nearly three-quarters (70 percent) of the sample lived in suburban areas, while about one-quarter hailed from urban environments (26.3 percent) and the rest from rural areas (3.7 percent). Likewise, nearly three-quarters of the sample (70.4 percent) resided in the northeastern United States, with the rest closely divided among the Midwest (5.3 percent), South (9.1 percent), West (10.7 percent), and eight countries outside the United States (3.7 percent).[8]

Studying College Men

Because young people are likely to self-consciously experiment with styles of public behavior (Arnett 1994, 2000), observing undergraduates can help researchers understand how young heterosexual men socially construct masculinity through gendered interaction rituals in the context of everyday life. But just as there is not one single mode of masculinity but many *masculinities* available to young men, respondents exhibited a variety of socially recognizable masculine roles in their accounts, including the doting boyfriend, dutiful son, responsible escort, and perfect gentleman. In the interests of exploring the girl hunt as *one among many types* of social orientation toward the city at night, the findings discussed here represent only the accounts of those heterosexual young men whose accounts revealed commonalities relevant to the girl hunt, as outlined above.

These accounts represent about one-fifth of those submitted by my 243 heterosexual male respondents. While this subgroup comprises a substantial portion of the sample, the findings it suggests by no means represents the behaviors of *all* my students, and this should not be surprising. As Connell (1995), Messner (2002), and others argue, the dominance of hegemonic masculinity is often sustained by the aggressive actions of a minority within a context of normative complicity by a more or less "silent majority" of men who nevertheless benefit from the subordination and sexual objectification of women. Insofar as the ritual of the girl hunt symbolizes a celebrated form of hegemonic masculinity, it is therefore imperative that we examine how it is practiced in the context of everyday life, even if its proponents and their activities represent only one of many possibilities within the constellation of masculine performances and sexual identities available to men. As Connell and Messerschmidt (2005:850) observe, hegemonic masculinities are "to a significant degree constituted in men's interaction with women." Accordingly, examining how girl hunting is accomplished can help clarify how group interactions link gender ideologies to everyday social behavior.

To ensure informants' anonymity and confidentiality, I have assigned pseudonyms to all persons. However, I have identified all respondents by their reported age, school year, and racial and ethnic background.

The Girl Hunt and the Myth of the Pickup

As I argue above, it is statistically uncommon for men to successfully attract and "pick up" female sexual partners in bars and nightclubs. However, as suggested by a wide selection of mass media—from erotic films to hardcore pornography—heterosexual young men nevertheless sustain fantasies of successfully negotiating chance sexual encounters with anonymous strangers in urban public spaces (Bech 1998), especially dance clubs, music venues, singles bars, cocktail lounges, and other nightlife settings. According to Aaron, a twenty-one-year-old mixed-race junior:

> I am currently in a very awkward, sticky, complicated and bizarre relationship with a young lady here at Penn, where things are pretty open right now, hopefully to be sorted out during the summer when we both have more time. So my mentality right now is to go to the club with my best bud and seek out the ladies for a night of great music, adventure and female company off of the grounds of campus.

Young men reproduce these normative expectations of masculine sexual prowess—what I call *the myth of the pickup*—collectively through homosocial group interaction. According to Brian, a nineteen-year-old Cuban sophomore:

> Whether I would get any girl's phone number or not, the main purpose for going out was to try to get with hot girls. That was our goal every night we went out to frat parties on campus, and we all knew it, even though we seldom mention that aspect of going out. *It was implicitly known that tonight, and every night out, was a girl hunt.* Tonight, we were taking that goal to Philadelphia's nightlife. In the meanwhile, we would have fun drinking, dancing, and joking around. (emphasis added)

For Brian and his friends, the "girl hunt" articulates a shared orientation toward public interaction in which the group collectively negotiates the city at night. The heterosexual desire among men for a plurality of women (hot *girls*, as it were) operates at the individual and group level. As in game hunting, young men frequently evaluate their erotic prestige in terms of their raw number of sexual conquests, like so many notches on a belt. Whereas traditional norms of feminine desire privilege the search for a singular and specified romantic interest (Prince Charming, Mr. Right, or his less attractive cousin, Mr. Right Now), heterosexual male fantasies idealize the pleasures of an endless abundance and variety of anonymous yet willing female sex partners (Kimmel and Plante 2005).

Despite convincing evidence to the contrary (Laumann et al. 2004), these sexual fantasies seem deceptively realizable in the context of urban nightlife. To many urban denizens, the city and its never-ending flow of anonymous visitors suggests a sexualized marketplace governed by transactional relations and expectations of personal noncommitment (Bech 1998), particularly in downtown entertainment zones where nightclubs, bars, and cocktail lounges are concentrated. The density of urban nightlife districts and their tightly packed venues only intensifies the pervasive yet improbable male fantasy of successfully attracting an imaginary surplus of amorous single women.

Adolescent men strengthen their belief in this fantasy of the sexual availability of women in the city— the myth of the pickup—through collective reinforcement in their conversations in the hours leading up to the girl hunt. While hyping their sexual prowess to the group, male peers collectively legitimize the myth of the pickup and increase its power as a model for normative masculine behavior. According to Dipak, an eighteen year old Indian freshman:

> I finished up laboratory work at 5:00 pm and walked to my dormitory, eagerly waiting to "hit up a club" that night. . . . I went to eat with my three closest friends at [a campus dining hall]. We acted like high school freshmen about to go to our first mixer. We kept hyping up the night and saying we were going to meet and dance with many girls. Two of my friends even bet with each other over who can procure the most phone numbers from girls that night. Essentially, the main topic of discussion during dinner was the night yet to come.

Competitive sex talk is common in male homosocial environments (Bird 1996) and often acts as a catalyst for sexual pursuit among groups of adolescent and young adult males. For example, in

his ethnographic work on Philadelphia's black inner-city neighborhoods, Anderson (1999) documents how sex codes among youth evolve in a context of peer pressure in which young black males "run their game" by women as a means of pursuing in-group status. Moreover, this type of one-upmanship heightens existing heterosexual fantasies and the myth of the pickup while creating a largely unrealistic set of sexual and gender expectations for young men seeking in-group status among their peers. In doing so, competitive sexual boasting may have the effect of momentarily energizing group participants. However, in the long run it is eventually likely to deflate the confidence of those who inevitably continue to fall short of such exaggerated expectations and who consequently experience the shame of a spoiled masculine identity (Goffman 1963).

Preparing for the Girl Hunt through Collective Ritual

Armed with their inflated expectations of the nightlife of the city and its opportunities for sexual conquest, young men at Penn prepare for the girl hunt by crafting a specifically gendered and class-conscious nocturnal self (Grazian 2003)— a presentation of masculinity that relies on prevailing fashion cues and upper-class taste emulation. According to Edward, a twenty-year-old white sophomore, these decisions are made strategically:

> I hadn't hooked up with a girl in a couple weeks and I needed to break my slump (the next girl you hook up with is commonly referred to as a "slump-bust" in my social circle). So I was willing to dress in whatever manner would facilitate in hooking up.

Among young college men, especially those living in communal residential settings (i.e., campus dormitories and fraternities), these preparations for public interaction serve as *collective rituals of confidence building*—shared activities that generate group solidarity and cohesion while elevating the personal resolve and self-assuredness of individual participants mobilizing for the girl hunt. Frank, a nineteen-year-old white sophomore, describes the first of these rituals:

> As I began observing both myself and my friends tonight, I noticed that there is a distinct pre-going-out ritual that takes place. I began the night by blasting my collection of rap music as loud as possible, as I tried to overcome the similar sounds resonating from my roommate's room. Martin seemed to play his music in order to build his confidence. It appears that the entire ritual is simply there to build up one's confidence, to make one more adept at picking up the opposite sex.

Frank explains this preparatory ritual in terms of its collective nature, as friends recount tall tales that celebrate character traits commonly associated with traditional conceptions of masculinity, such as boldness and aggression. Against a soundtrack of rap music—a genre known for its misogynistic lyrics and male-specific themes, including heterosexual boasting, emotional detachment, and masculine superiority (McLeod 1999)—these shared ritual moments of homosociality are a means of generating group resolve and bolstering the self-confidence of each participant. Again, according to Frank:

> Everyone erupted into stories explaining their "high-roller status." Martin recounted how he spent nine hundred dollars in Miami one weekend, while Lance brought up his cousins who spent twenty-five hundred dollars with ease one night at a Las Vegas bachelor party. Again, all of these stories acted as a confidence booster for the night ahead.

Perhaps unsurprisingly, this constant competitive jockeying and one-upmanship so common in male-dominated settings (Martin 2001) often extends to the sexual objectification of women. While getting dressed among friends in preparation for a trip to a local strip club, Gregory, a twenty-year-old white sophomore, reports on the banter: "We should all dress rich and stuff, so we can get us some hookers!" Like aggressive locker-room boasting, young male peers bond over competitive sex talk by laughing about real

and make-believe sexual exploits and misadventures (Bird 1996). This joking strengthens male group intimacy and collective heterosexual identity and normalizes gender differences by reinforcing dominant myths about the social roles of men and women (Lyman 1987).

After engaging in private talk among roommates and close friends, young men (as well as women) commonly participate in a more public collective ritual known among American college students as "pregaming." As Harry, an eighteen-year-old white freshman, explains,

> Pregaming consists of drinking with your "boys" so that you don't have to purchase as many drinks while you are out to feel the desired buzz. On top of being cost efficient, the actual event of pregaming can get any group ready and excited to go out.

The ritualistic use of alcohol is normative on college campuses, particularly for men (Martin and Hummer 1989), and students largely describe pregaming as an economical and efficient way to get drunk before going out into the city. This is especially the case for underage students who may be denied access to downtown nightspots. However, it also seems clear that pregaming is a bonding ritual that fosters social cohesion and builds confidence among young men in anticipation of the challenges that accompany the girl hunt. According to Joey, an eighteen-year-old white freshman:

> My thoughts turn to this girl, Jessica. . . . I was thinking about whether or not we might hook up tonight. . . . As I turn to face the door to 301, I feel the handle, and it is shaking from the music and dancing going on in the room. I open the door and see all my best friends just dancing together. . . . I quickly rush into the center of the circle and start doing my "J-walk," which I have perfected over the years. My friends love it and begin to chant, "Go Joey— it's your birthday." I'm feeling connected with my friends and just know that we're about to have a great night. . . . Girls keep coming in and out of the door, but no one really pays close attention to them. Just as the "pregame" was

getting to its ultimate height, each boy had his arms around each other jumping in unison, to a great hip-hop song by Biggie Smalls. One of the girls went over to the stereo and turned the power off. We yelled at her to turn it back on, but the mood was already lost and we decided it was time to head out.

In this example, Joey's confidence is boosted by the camaraderie he experiences in a male-bonding ritual in which women—supposedly the agreed-upon raison d'être for the evening—are ignored or, when they make their presence known, scolded. As these young men dance arm-in-arm with one another, they generate the collective effervescence and sense of social connectedness necessary to plunge into the nightlife of the city. As such, pregaming fulfills the same function as the last-minute huddle (with all hands in the middle) does for an athletic team (Messner 2002).[9] It is perhaps ironic that Joey's ritual of "having fun with my boys" prepares him for the girl hunt (or more specifically in his case, an opportunity to "hook up" with Jessica) even as it requires those boys to exclude their female classmates. At the same time, this men-only dance serves the same function as the girl hunt: it allows its participants to expressively perform hegemonic masculinity through an aggressive display of collective identification. In this sense the pregame resembles other campus rituals of male socialization and boundary maintenance, particularly those associated with fraternity life and violence against women (Boswell and Spade 1996; Martin and Hummer 1989; Sanday 1990).

During similar collective rituals leading up to the girl hunt, young men boost each other's confidence in their abilities of sexual persuasion by watching films about male heterosexual exploits in urban nightlife, such as Doug Liman's *Swingers* (1996), which chronicles the storied escapades of two best friends, Mike and Trent. According to Kevin, an eighteen-year-old white freshman:

> I knew that [my friend] Darryl needed to calm down if he wanted any chance of a second date.

At about 8:15 pm, I sat him down and showed him (in my opinion, the movie that every man should see at least once—I've seen it six times)—*Swingers*. . . . Darryl immediately related to Mike's character, the self-conscious but funny gentleman who is still on the rebound from a long-term relationship. At the same time, he took Trent's words for scripture (as I planned): "There's nothing wrong with showing the beautiful babies that you're money and that you want to party." His mind was clearly eased at the thought of his being considered "money." Instead of being too concerned with not screwing up and seeming "weird or desperate," Darryl now felt like he was in control. The three of us each went to our own rooms to get ready.

This collective attention to popular cultural texts helps peer groups generate common cultural references, private jokes, and speech norms as well as build ingroup cohesion (Eliasoph and Lichterman 2003; Fine 1977; Swidler 2001).[10] In this case, globally distributed mass-media texts (i.e., films, music recordings and videos, television programs, computer games, comic books) supply audiences with a familiar set of shared discursive strategies and symbolic resources that influence daily social behavior pertaining to gender and sexual expression at a more localized level (Connell and Messerschmidt 2005; Swidler 2001). Similar to the immersion in rap music, the incorporation of collective film viewing into the pregame ritual promotes male group solidarity. But in addition to generating a sense of collective energy, it provides a set of cultural frames useful for making sense of the girl hunt, just as Sanday (1990:129) documents how fraternity brothers habitually watch pornographic films together in their preparations for late-night parties. Of course, *Swingers* represents much tamer fare: yet like pornography, the film encourages the development of a hypermasculine identity while supplying young men with scripts for upcoming social interactions with women, reducing women to infantile objects of sexual desire ("beautiful babies"), generating collective excitement for the girl hunt, and giving young men the self-confidence necessary for competing in such a contest.[11]

Girl Hunting and the Collective Performance of Masculinity

Finally, once the locus of action moves to a more public venue such as a bar or nightclub, the much-anticipated "girl hunt" itself proceeds as a strategic display of masculinity best performed with a suitable game partner. According to Christopher, a twenty-two-year-old white senior, he and his cousin Darren "go out together a lot. We enjoy each other's company and we seem to work well together when trying to meet women." Reporting on his evening at a local dance club, Lawrence, a twenty-one-year-old white junior, illustrates how the girl hunt itself operates as collective activity:

> We walk around the bar area as we finish [our drinks]. After we are done, we walk down to the regular part of the club. We make the rounds around the dance floor checking out the girls. . . . We walk up to the glassed dance room and go in, but leave shortly because it is really hot and there weren't many prospects.

Lawrence and his friends display their elaborated performance of masculinity by making their rounds together as a pack in search of a suitable feminine target. Perhaps it is not surprising that the collective nature of their pursuit should also continue *after* such a prize has been located:

> This is where the night gets really interesting. We walk back down to the main dance floor and stand on the outside looking at what's going on and I see a really good-looking girl behind us standing on the other side of the wall with three friends. After pointing her out to my friends, I decide that I'm going to make the big move and talk to her. So I turn around and ask her to dance. She accepts and walks over. My friends are loving this, so they go off to the side and watch. . . .
>
> After dancing for a little while she brings me over to her friends and introduces me. They tell

me that they are all freshman at [a local college], and we go through the whole small talk thing again. I bring her over to my two boys who are still getting a kick out of the whole situation. . . . My boys tell me about some of the girls they have seen and talked to, and they inform me that they recognized some girls from Penn walking around the club.

Why do Lawrence and his dance partner both introduce each other to their friends? Lawrence seems to gain almost as much pleasure from his *friends'* excitement as from his own exploits, just as they are "loving" the vicarious thrill of watching their comrade succeed in commanding the young woman's attention, as if their own masculinity is validated by his success.

In this instance, arousal is not merely individual but represents a collectively shared experience as well (Thorne and Luria 1986:181). For these young men the performance of masculinity does not necessarily require successfully meeting a potential sex partner as long as one enthusiastically participates in the ritual *motions* of the girl hunt in the company of men. When Lawrence brings over his new female friend, he does so to celebrate his victory with his buddies, and in return, they appear gratified by their *own* small victory by association. (And while Lawrence celebrates with them, perhaps he alleviates some of the pressure of actually conversing with her.)

Along these lines, the collective quality of the girl hunt makes each male participant accountable to the group as well as to himself. In this manner, young single men will goad each other on to persist in the hunt, deriding those who turn away potential pickups. Michael, a nineteen-year-old white junior, reports on his evening out at McFadden's, an Irish-themed sports bar and nightclub:

> My friend Buddy beckoned to me from the dance floor. Not knowing what he wanted, I snaked my way through the crowd to join him. As I approached him, a girl several years my senior smiled at me. She looked like she wanted to start a conversation, but waited for me to initiate. Not particularly interested in her and with

my friend waiting, I awkwardly moved past with what I am sure was a weird smile on my face. *Buddy had seen this entire exchange and said he was disappointed in me for not trying to hit on her.* (emphasis added)

Through their homosocial encounters, young men make one another accountable for their interactions with women, and their vigilance increases the chances that over time these men will eventually comply with the set of practices that sustain the ideals of hegemonic masculinity, *even in instances when such men disagree with those expectations* (Connell 1995; Demetriou 2001).

As Christopher remarked above on his relationship with his cousin, the collective aspects of the girl hunt also highlight the efficacy of conspiring with peers to meet women: "We go out together a lot. We enjoy each other's company and we seem to work well together when trying to meet women." In the language of the confidence game, men eagerly serve as each other's shills (Goffman 1959; Grazian 2004; Maurer 1940) and sometimes get roped into the role unwittingly with varying degress of success. Michael continues in his report by describing Buddy's exploits:

> Buddy, a twenty-five-year-old University of Pennsylvania alumnus, is the kind of guy who is not afraid to flirt with as many girls as possible. Tonight he was putting his charm to good use, dancing with any girl who would give him the time of day. I realized he had called me over for the purpose of finding a girl for me. Turning to the girl nearest him on dance floor he said to her, "This is my friend Michael. He's a little shy." Waiting for him to introduce me to her, I realized after a moment that he didn't know these girls either. His introduction was actually one of the cheesiest pickup lines I had ever heard used that wasn't the punch line to a joke. I introduced myself to the girl whose name I found out was Rebecca, a twenty-four-year-old professional from South Philly. I talked to her for a few minutes and admitted my true age to her; surprisingly, she didn't blow me off too quickly, but her interest was definitely in Buddy rather than me at that point. Deciding to

leave the two of them to get better acquainted, I excused myself to the bar to get a second beer.

In this instance, Michael politely disengages from the interaction without challenging the ideological basis of the girl hunt itself. Rather, his passive performance amounts to what Connell (1995) refers to as "complicit masculinity," insofar as Michael is able to support his friend's interaction and thus benefit from the "patriarchal dividend" (acceptance within a male homosocial group and the status associated with such membership) gained from the promotion of the ideals of hegemonic masculinity as represented by the girl hunt (also see Demetriou 2001).

Among young people, the role of the passive accomplice is commonly referred to in contemporary parlance as a *wingman*. Popularized by the 1986 film *Top Gun*, the term literally refers to the backup fighter pilots who protect the head of a military flying formation by positioning themselves outside and behind (or on the wing of) the lead aircraft to engage enemy fire when necessary. In recent years, the term has been appropriated to refer to an accomplice who assists a designated leading man in meeting eligible single women, often at costs to his own ability to do the same. In male-oriented popular culture, the wingman has become institutionalized in men's magazines ("*Maxim's* Wingman Training Manual" 2003), literature documenting young men's real-and-imagined sex lives (i.e., Max 2006; Strauss 2005), and how-to manuals with such dubiously promising titles as *The Guide to Picking Up Girls*. This last text provides a vulgar description of the colloquialism:

> Everyone knows what a wingman must do. Your wingman must take the extra girl for you if there are two girls and you want to talk to one of them. The wingman must lay rap on your girl's friend as long as you rap with your girl. It does not matter that the girl's friend may be very ugly. The wingman must do his job at any cost. He must be able to pull his own weight and back you up. Otherwise, your girl may get pulled away by her friend whom your wingman has failed to entertain. (Fischbarg 2002:36)

In public rituals of courtship, the wingman serves multiple purposes: he provides validation of a leading man's trustworthiness, eases the interaction between a single male friend and a larger group of women, serves as a source of distraction for the friend or friends of a more desirable target of affection, can be called on to confirm the wild (and frequently misleading) claims of his partner, and, perhaps most important, helps motivate his friends by building up their confidence. Indeed, men describe the role of the wingman in terms of loyalty, personal responsibility, and dependability, traits commonly associated with masculinity (Martin and Hummer 1989; Mishkind et al. 1986). According to Nicholas, an eighteen-year-old white freshman:

> As we were beginning to mobilize ourselves and move towards the dance floor, James noticed Rachel, a girl he knew from Penn who he often told me about as a potential girlfriend. Considering James was seemingly into this girl, Dan and I decided to be good wingmen and entertain Rachel's friend, Sarah.

Hegemonic masculinity is not only expressed by competitiveness but camaraderie as well, and many young men will take their role as a wingman quite seriously and at a personal cost to their relationships with female friends. According to Peter, a twenty-year-old white sophomore:

> "It sounds like a fun evening," I said to Kyle, "but I promised Elizabeth I would go to her date party." I don't like to break commitments. On the other hand, I didn't want to leave Kyle to fend for himself at this club. . . . Kyle is the type of person who likes to pick girls up at clubs. If I were to come see him, I would want to meet other people as well. Having Elizabeth around would not only prevent me from meeting (or even just talking to) other girls, but it would also force Kyle into a situation of having no "wing man."

In the end, Peter takes Elizabeth to a nightclub where, although he *himself* will not be able to meet available women, he will at least be able to assist Kyle in meeting them:

> Behind Kyle, a very attractive girl smiles at me. Yes! Oh, wait. Damnit, Elizabeth's here. . . . "Hey, Kyle," I whisper to him. "That girl behind you just smiled at you. Go talk to her." Perhaps Kyle will have some luck with her. He turns around, takes her by the hand, and begins dancing with her. She looks over at me and smiles again, and I smile back. I don't think Elizabeth noticed. I would have rather been in Kyle's position, but I was happy for him, and I was dancing with Elizabeth, so I was satisfied for the moment.

By the end of the night, as he and Kyle chat in a taxi on the way back to campus, Peter learns that he was instrumental in securing his friend's success in an additional way:

> "So what ever happened with you and that girl?" I ask. "I hooked up with her. Apparently she's a senior." I ask if she knew he was a freshman. "Oh, yeah. She asked how old you were, though. I said you were a junior. I had to make one of us look older."

Peter's willingness to serve as a wingman demonstrates his complicity in sustaining the ideals of hegemonic masculinity, which therefore allows him to benefit from the resulting "patriarchal dividends"—acceptance as a member of his male homosocial friendship network and its attendant prestige—even when he himself does not personally seek out the sexual rewards of the girl hunt.

In addition, the peer group provides a readily available audience that can provide emotional comfort to all group members, as well as bear witness to any individual successes that might occur. As demonstrated by the preceding examples, young men deeply value the erotic prestige they receive from their conspiratorial peers upon succeeding in the girl hunt. According to Zach, a twenty-year-old white sophomore:

> About ten minutes later, probably around 2:15 am, we split up into cabs again, with the guys in one and the girls in another. . . . This time in the cab, all the guys want to talk about is me hooking up on the dance floor. It turns out that they saw the whole thing. I am not embarrassed; in fact I am proud of myself.

As an audience, the group can collectively validate the experience of any of its members and can also internalize an individual's success as a shared victory. Since, in a certain sense, a successful sexual interaction must be recognized by one's peers to gain status as an in-group "social fact," the group can transform a private moment into a celebrated public event—thereby making it "count" for the male participant and his cohorts.[12]

Of course, as argued above and elsewhere (Laumann et al. 1994) and demonstrated by the sample analyzed here, turning a heterosexual public encounter with a stranger into an immediately consummated sexual episode is a statistical rarity, especially when compared with the overwhelming degree of time, money, effort, and emotion that young men invest in such an enterprise. But if we focus on the *primary* goal of the girl hunt—the performance of normative masculinity—then it becomes clear that the collectivity of the endeavor allows peer group members to successfully enact traditional gender roles even when they ultimately fail at the sexual pursuit itself. Again, the performance of masculinity does not necessarily require *success* at picking up women, just so long as one participates in the endeavor enthusiastically in the company of men.

For instance, Sam, a twenty-two-year-old black senior, observes how one such peer group takes pleasure in one of their member's public rejection at the hands of an unimpressed woman:

> By this time it was around 1:30 am, and the party was almost over. . . . I saw a lot of the guys had their cell phones out while they were talking to the women. I figured the guys were trying to get phone numbers from the girls. So as I walked past one of the guys, I heard him ask a girl for her number. But she just laughed and walked away. That was real funny especially since his friends saw what happened and proceeded to laugh as well.

As young men discover, contrary to popular myths about femininity, it is increasingly uncommon for women to act passively during sexually charged confrontations, even those that may be physically precarious. In such situations, women often resist and challenge the advances of strange men in public through polite refusal or the expression of humor, moral outrage, outright rejection, or physical retaliation (Berk 1977; Hollander 2002; Snow et al. 1991).

Nevertheless, one participant's botched attempt at an ill-conceived pickup can solidify the male group's bonds as much as a successful one. According to Brian, the aforementioned nineteen-year-old Cuban sophomore:

> We had been in the club for a little more than half an hour, when the four of us were standing at the perimeter of the main crowd in the dancing room. It was then when Marvin finished his second Corona and by his body gestures, he let it be known that he was drunk enough and was pumped up to start dancing. He started dancing behind a girl who was dancing in a circle with a few other girls. Then the girl turned around and said "Excuse me!" Henry and I saw what happened. We laughed so hard and made so much fun of him for the rest of the night. I do not think any of us has ever been turned away so directly and harshly as that time.

In this instance, Marvin's abruptly concluded encounter with an unwilling female participant turns into a humorous episode for the rest of his peer group, leaving his performance of masculinity bruised yet intact. Indeed, in his gracelessness Marvin displays an enthusiastic male heterosexuality as emphasized by his drunken attempts to court an unsuspecting target before a complicit audience of his male peers. And as witnesses to his awkward sexual advance, Brian and Henry take pleasure in the incident, as it not only raises *their* relative standing within the group in comparison with Marvin but can also serve as a narrative focus for future "signifying" episodes (or ceremonial exchanges of insults) and other rituals of solidarity characteristic of joking relationships among male adolescents (Lyman 1987:155). Meanwhile, these young men can bask in their collective failure to attract a woman without ever actually challenging the basis of the girl hunt itself: the performance of adolescent masculinity.

In the end, young men may enjoy this performance of masculinity—the hunt itself—even more than the potential romantic or sexual rewards they hope to gain by its successful execution. In his reflections on a missed opportunity to procure the phone number of a law student, Christopher, the aforementioned twenty-two-year-old senior, admits as much: "There's something about the chase that I really like. Maybe I subconsciously neglected to get her number. I am tempted to think that I like the idea of being on the look out for her better than the idea of calling her to go out for coffee." While Christopher's excuse may certainly function as a compensatory face-saving strategy employed in the aftermath of another lonely night (Berk 1977), it might also indicate a possible acceptance of the limits of the girl hunt despite its potential opportunities for male bonding and the public display of adolescent masculinity.

Discussion

A consistent thread in symbolic interactionism concerns how structures of inequality are constituted and reproduced through recurrent patterns of ordinary social interaction. According to Collins (1981:987–88), the very foundations of the macrosocial world and its institutions can be reduced to the agglomeration of everyday face-to-face encounters conducted among humans over time. As he argues, "Strictly speaking, there is no such thing as a 'state,' an 'economy,' a 'culture,' a 'social class.' There are only collections of individual people acting in particular kinds of microsituations." Schwalbe et al. (2000) emphasize how the repetition of "generic processes" such as oppressive othering, identity work, boundary maintenance, and emotion management all contribute to the reproduction of inequality through their frequent deployment in varied social contexts.

Taken in this way, the "girl hunt" is shorthand for a composite of multiple types of collectively initiated interaction rituals capable of reproducing social inequality on the basis of gender. Group-based efforts at "mobilizing masculinity" (Martin 2001) during the pregame, and "girl watching" (Quinn 2002) in the context of nightclub interaction, operate as processes that fabricate gender difference and male superiority while transforming women into targets of the collective male gaze and objects of sexual desire. By engaging in the "mutually supportive facework" provided by wingmen, would-be suitors reproduce myths of male dominance by cooperatively creating nocturnal selves that "foster impressions of competence and trustworthiness" through strategies of impression management, deception, and guile (Schwalbe et al. 2000:424). Of course, these generic processes occur not merely in a vacuum but within a social setting in which the regularity of sexist banter and asymmetric courtship rituals encourage the replication of such behaviors, along with the continually renewed ideologies of feminine subordination they promote.

But at the same time, it is equally noteworthy that the girl hunt promotes social inequality and subordinate behavior *among men*. Among participants in the girl hunt, the most dominant men enjoy a disproportionate degree of social prestige relative to their competitors, as is the case in other sexual contests (Wright 1995). Competitive sex talk among adolescent peers in the hours leading up to the girl hunt create an unrealistic set of sexual expectations for impressionable young men, particularly those who already suffer from anxiety over their body image and sexual development (Mishkind et al. 1986). Meanwhile, the repetition of collective rituals of masculine identification successfully conditions young men to suppress empathy for females targeted by the girl hunt, just as the training regimes of military and police units serve to diminish feelings of inhibition and fear among cadets (Schwalbe et al. 2000:437). As illustrated in the last section, male peers often rely on the cultural scripts associated with girl hunting to hassle one another to perform masculinity by behaving in ways that seem to counter their actual sexual desires. In the end, the interaction rituals associated with the girl hunt reproduce structures of inequality *within* as well as *across* the socially constructed gender divide between women and men.

Conclusion

In this article, I used the ritual of girl hunting to analyze how young men employ the power of collective rituals of homosociality to perform heterosexual competence and masculine identity in public. Drawing on self-reported narrative accounts, I documented collective strategies young men employ when girl hunting, suggesting that these strategies reinforce dominant myths about masculine behavior, boost confidence in one's performance of masculinity and heterosexual power, and assist in the performance of masculinity in the presence of women. While the presentation of a heteronormative masculine self and its attendant peer status does not necessarily serve as the only desired or stated purpose of the girl hunt, my goal in this article was to isolate and therefore emphasize the *ritualistic, performative,* and *homosocial* features of girl hunting as a *collective* strategy of impression management and mobilizing masculinity.

In emphasizing the collective aspects of girl hunting and the performance of masculinity in urban nightlife, this study follows a consistent thread within sociology that recognizes how rituals of dating and mating occur within specific interpersonal networks in which shared and collective meanings of sexuality are institutionally inscribed in social space (Anderson 1999; Laumann et al. 2004; Liebow 1967; Swidler 2001; Waller 1937). More specifically, this exploration of how men collectively perform gender and heterosexuality builds on more recent symbolic interactionist approaches to homosocial group dynamics, including the maintenance of hegemonic masculinity through homosocial behavior (Bird 1996), the mobilization of masculinities in public (Martin 2001), and the practice of "girl watching" as a collective form of sexual harassment (Quinn 2002). Likewise, this analysis of girl hunting illustrates the efficacy of homosocial rituals of solidarity not only as tools for mobilizing

masculinities among men in the moment but as engines of confidence building for subsequent public encounters.

While girl hunting employs collective group dynamics found in a variety of settings, the social context in which college students participate clearly shapes the collective character of their everyday behaviors, including the performance of adolescent masculinity and the pursuit of casual sex. While by no means "total institutions" (Becker 2003; Goffman 1961), modern American colleges and universities encourage collective behavior through the segregation of persons on the basis of age (as well as other social attributes such as race and class), officially recognized student groups (including fraternities, sororities, and athletic teams), shared residential housing, and the spatial concentration of campus life. As young adults undergoing the slow transition from adolescence to adulthood, college men may be more likely than their elder counterparts to desire the protection of their peers during risky encounters with strangers in public. Meanwhile, as men grow older and gain additional markers of status (i.e., occupational prestige), they may no longer require the pregaming rituals of confidence building once considered necessary preparation for the girl hunt. At the very least, they may replace collegiate forms of "pregaming" with more adult-oriented rituals, such as happy hour cocktails shared with colleagues after work.

The nightlife setting itself also appears to invite a more collective orientation to masculine performance and sexual pursuit than other contexts. Unlike professional settings where formal guidelines and official workplace norms (at least theoretically) censure sexually suggestive talk and behavior (Dellinger and Williams 2002; Quinn 2002), nightlife settings encourage aggressive sexual interaction among participants. As a result, such an environment may prove too intimidating for individuals unprotected by a surrounding peer group. Moreover, nightclubs and singles bars feature open floor plans where populous clusters of anonymous strangers can congregate and mingle, whereas coffeehouses, bookstores, sidewalks, and other public areas conducive to public interaction are less accommodating of large groups of people. In such settings, perhaps we would expect to see men participating in the girl hunt in smaller formations of two and three (the exception being the male "girl-watchers" who line downtown sidewalks during the lunch hour; see Whyte 1988). Future research on girl hunting in alternative public contexts (and among a wider variety of populations) will undoubtedly yield interesting findings about the collective nature of masculine performance and heterosexual pursuit.

Acknowledgments: This research was supported by grants from the University of Pennsylvania Research Foundation, Alice Paul Center for Research on Women and Gender, and the Penn Institute for Urban Research. I gratefully acknowledge Rachelle Brunn, Jan Jaeger, Colette Joyce, Taryn Kudler, Abigail Platten, Georges Reiners, Lindsay Rutherford, Elizabeth Vaquera, and Yuping Zhang for their invaluable research assistance. I also wish to thank Elizabeth Armstrong, Kathleen Bogle, Wayne Brekhus, Meredith Broussard, Keith Brown, Randall Collins, Maria Kefalas, Jennifer Lena, Peggy Reeves Sanday, and the editors and reviewers at *Symbolic Interaction* for their comments on an earlier draft of this article.

Notes

1. Other such signifiers include physical dominance and assertiveness relative to other men, skill at competitive bar games, and a high tolerance for alcohol.

2. The gender discrepancy here may reflect reporting biases, with men overreporting and women underreporting their sexual behavior (Laumann et al. 1994:239n12). For a critique of the National Health and Social Life Survey and the reliability of sex research more generally, see Lewontin 1995.

3. According to the Chicago Health and Social Life Survey, the exception to this statistic is the Mexican community area called "Westside," in which 23 percent of women (but only 19 percent of men) reported having met their most recent partner at a bar, dance club, or nightclub (Mahay and Laumann 2004:81).

4. For inclusion in the sample generated for this article, male students either voluntarily self-identified as heterosexual or else were coded as such from their written narrative accounts (i.e., referenced a female

sex partner or generalized heterosexual desire). While it is certainly possible that those coded as heterosexual may *also* engage in homosexual or bisexual practices, this did not preclude them from inclusion in the sample, given the nature of the research question. (In my original pool of 267 eligible male subjects, 4 self-identified as gay and 34 opted not to disclose their sexual orientation; of the latter, 14 were eventually coded as heterosexual, while 20 remained nondescript enough to be removed from the sample.) The lack of data on the experiences of homosexual students is a clear limitation of this study; on the varied performances of gay men in the context of urban nightlife, see Brekhus 2003, Chauncey 1994, and Rupp and Taylor 2003.

5. All names were removed to ensure the anonymity and confidentiality of the participants. However, students were asked to supply basic demographic information (including gender, age, year of school, residence, racial and ethnic origin, and sexual orientation [optional]) to be used as a reference during coding and analysis, which was conducted with the help of NVivo, a qualitative data software package.

6. Of course, since these reports account for only one evening's worth of behavior and experience, I cannot validate whether they accurately characterize the lifestyles of my individual respondents, although peer-led focus groups later conducted among a smaller sample of thirty male respondents uncovered similar findings.

7. Nearly 40 percent of the Asian students in the sample are of Indian descent. While my data analysis did uncover very small differences in consumption patterns among my sample on the basis of race and ethnicity, I could not detect notable differences relevant to the arguments presented in this article. Nevertheless, for the edification of the reader I identify the ethnoracial background of all participants cited in the rest of the article.

8. Students residing in Philadelphia prior to attending the University of Pennsylvania comprise 8.2 percent of the entire sample, while 22.2 percent hail from within the Commonwealth of Pennsylvania. Of those students from outside the Northeast, a disproportionate number resided in the populous states of California and Florida prior to college. The numbers are rounded off.

9. In this context, the male ritual of jumping in unison to loud music bears a close resemblance to the "circle dance" initiated by fraternity brothers imme-

diately prior to an alleged incident of gang rape, as described in Sanday 1990.

10. Perhaps for this reason, Kevin's narrative account consistently draws on the slang employed by the film's lead characters: "Darryl, our newly decreed 'money' friend, shifts around, playing it cool, scanning the room for his tie." "Darryl was definitely in 'money' mode, because she sat close to him (after only a little to drink—so she must have seen something in him)."

11. In the last several years, my classroom surveys of undergraduate students and their favorite motion pictures reveal that male respondents consistently cite films that draw on similar themes to those in *Swingers*, including the party-hearty campus hijinks of college life (*National Lampoon's Animal House, Old School*); male vanity and the meaning of manhood (*American Psycho, Fight Club*); the camaraderie of violent men in secret societies and criminal gangs (*The Godfather, Goodfellas, Scarface, The Usual Suspects*); and the relentless pursuit of women (*There's Something About Mary*).

12. There are additional benefits to working as a collective as well. If the success of any single member can confer status on all other members, then traveling in a large group increases the odds that at least *someone* in the group will have a successful romantic encounter, provided the group does not *impede* the success of any single member by introducing competition to the setting or prove distracting to the proceedings.

References

Allison, Anne. 1994. *Nightwork: Sexuality, Pleasure, and Corporate Masculinity in a Tokyo Hostess Club.* Chicago: University of Chicago Press.

Anderson, Elijah. 1999. *Code of the Street: Decency, Violence, and the Moral Life of the Inner City.* New York: Norton.

Arnett, Jeffrey Jensen. 1994. "Are College Students Adults? Their Conceptions of the Transition to Adulthood." *Journal of Adult Development* 1(4): 213–24.

———. 2000. "Emerging Adulthood: A Theory of Development from the Late Teens through the Twenties." *American Psychologist* 55(5):469–80.

Bech, Henning. 1998. "Citysex: Representing Lust in Public." *Theory, Culture & Society* 15(3–4):215–41.

Berk, Bernard. 1977. "Face-Saving at the Singles Dance." *Social Problems* 24(5):530–44.

Becker, Howard S. 2003. "The Politics of Presentation: Goffman and Total Institutions." *Symbolic Interaction* 26(4):659–69.

Bernstein, Elizabeth. 2001. "The Meaning of the Purchase: Desire, Demand, and the Commerce of Sex." *Ethnography* 2(3):389–420.

Bird, Sharon R. 1996. "Welcome to the Men's Club: Homosociality and the Maintenance of Hegemonic Masculinity." *Gender & Society* 10(2): 120–32.

Bissinger, H. G. 1990. *Friday Night Lights: A Town, a Team, and a Dream.* Reading, MA: Addison-Wesley.

Boswell, A. Ayres and Joan Z. Spade. 1996. "Fraternities and Collegiate Rape Culture: Why Are Some Fraternities More Dangerous Places for Women?" *Gender & Society* 10(2):133–47.

Brekhus, Wayne H. 2003. *Peacocks, Chameleons, Centaurs: Gay Suburbia and the Grammar of Social Identity.* Chicago: University of Chicago Press.

Bushnell, Candace. [1996] 2001. *Sex and the City.* New York: Warner.

Chapkis, Wendy. 1986. *Beauty Secrets: Women and the Politics of Appearance.* Boston: South End.

Chatterton, Paul and Robert Hollands. 2003. *Urban Nightscapes: Youth Cultures, Pleasure Spaces, and Corporate Power.* London: Routledge.

Chauncey, George. 1994. *Gay New York: Gender, Urban Culture, and the Making of the Gay Male World, 1980–1940.* New York: Basic Books.

Collins, Randall. 1981. "On the Microfoundations of Macrosociology." *American Journal of Sociology* 86(5):984–1014.

———. 2004. *Interaction Ritual Chains.* Princeton, NJ: Princeton University Press.

Connell, R. W. 1987. *Gender and Power: Society, the Person, and Sexual Politics.* Stanford, CA: Stanford University Press.

———. 1992. "A Very Straight Gay: Masculinity, Homosexual Experience, and the Dynamics of Gender." *American Sociological Review* 57(6):735–51.

———. 1993. "The Big Picture: Masculinities in Recent World History." *Theory and Society* 22(5):597–623.

———. 1995. *Masculinities.* Berkeley: University of California Press.

Connell, R. W. and James W. Messerschmidt. 2005. "Hegemonic Masculinity: Rethinking the Concept." *Gender & Society* 19(6):829–59.

Dellinger, Kirsten and Christine L. Williams. 2002. "The Locker Room and the Dorm Room: Workplace Norms and the Boundaries of Sexual Harassment in Magazine Editing." *Social Problems* 49(2):242–57.

Demetriou, Demetrakis Z. 2001. "Connell's Concept of Hegemonic Masculinity: A Critique." *Theory and Society* 30(3):337–61.

Donaldson, Mike. 1993. "What Is Hegemonic Masculinity?" *Theory and Society* 22(5):643–57.

Duneier, Mitchell and Harvey Molotch. 1999. "Talking City Trouble: Interactional Vandalism, Social Inequality, and the 'Urban Interaction Problem.'" *American Journal of Sociology* 104(5): 1263–95.

Eliasoph, Nina and Paul Lichterman. 2003. "Culture in Interaction." *American Journal of Sociology* 108(4):735–94.

Fine, Gary Alan. 1977. "Popular Culture and Social Interaction: Production, Consumption, and Usage." *Journal of Popular Culture* 11(2):453–56.

Fischbarg, Gabe. 2002. *The Guide to Picking Up Girls*. New York: Plume.

Geertz, Clifford. 1973. "Deep Play: Notes on a Balinese Cockfight." In *The Interpretation of Cultures*. New York: Basic.

Giuffre, Patti A. and Christine L. Williams. 1994. "Boundary Lines: Labeling Sexual Harassment in Restaurants." *Gender & Society* 8(3):378–401.

Goffman, Erving. 1959. *The Presentation of Self in Everyday Life*. Garden City, NY: Anchor Books.

———. 1961. *Asylums: Essays on the Social Situation of Mental Patients and Other Inmates*. New York: Anchor.

———. 1963. *Stigma: Notes on the Management of Spoiled Identity*. New York: Simon & Schuster.

———. 1977. "The Arrangement between the Sexes." *Theory and Society* 4(3):301–31.

Grazian, David. 2003. *Blue Chicago: The Search for Authenticity in Urban Blues Clubs*. Chicago: University of Chicago Press.

———. 2004. "The Production of Popular Music as a Confidence Game: The Case of the Chicago Blues." *Qualitative Sociology* 27(2):137–58.

Grindstaff, Laura. 2002. *The Money Shot: Trash, Class, and the Making of TV Talk Shows*. Chicago: University of Chicago Press.

Hollander, Jocelyn A. 2002. "Resisting Vulnerability: The Social Reconstruction of Gender in Interaction." *Social Problems* 49(4): 474–96.

Kenney, William Howland. 1993. *Chicago Jazz: A Cultural History, 1904–1930*. New York: Oxford University Press.

Kimmel, Michael S. and Rebecca F. Plante. 2005. "The Gender of Desire: The Sexual Fantasies of Women and Men." In *The Gender of Desire: Essays on Male Sexuality*, edited by M. S. Kimmel. Albany: State University of New York Press.

Laumann, Edward O., John H. Gagnon, Robert T. Michael, and Stuart Michaels. 1994. *The Social Organization of Sexuality: Sexual Practices in the United States*. Chicago: University of Chicago Press.

Laumann, Edward O., Stephen Ellingson, Jenna Mahay, Anthony Paik, and Yoosik Youm, eds. 2004. *The Sexual Organization of the City*. Chicago: University of Chicago Press.

Lewontin, Richard C. 1995. "Sex, Lies, and Social Science." *New York Review of Books*, April 20.

Liebow, Elliot. 1967. *Tally's Corner: A Study of Negro Streetcorner Men*. Boston: Little, Brown.

Lloyd, Richard. 2005. *Neo-Bohemia: Culture and Capital in Postindustrial Chicago*. New York: Routledge.

Lyman, Peter. 1987. "The Fraternal Bond as a Joking Relationship: A Case Study of the Role of Sexist Jokes in Male Group Bonding." In *Changing Men: New Directions in Research on Men and Masculinity*, edited by M. S. Kimmel. Newbury Park, CA: Sage.

Mahay, Jenna and Edward O. Laumann. 2004. "Neighborhoods as Sex Markets." In *The Sexual Organization of the City*, edited by E. O. Laumann, S. Ellingson, J. Mahay, A. Paik, and Y. Youm. Chicago: University of Chicago Press.

Martin, Patricia Yancey. 2001. "'Mobilizing Masculinities': Women's Experiences of Men at Work." *Organization* 8(4):587–618.

Martin, Patricia Yancey and Robert A. Hummer. 1989. "Fraternities and Rape on Campus." *Gender & Society* 3(4):457–73.

Maurer, David W. 1940. *The Big Con: The Story of the Confidence Man*. New York: Bobbs-Merrill.

Max, Tucker. 2006. *I Hope They Serve Beer in Hell*. New York: Citadel. "*Maxim*'s Wingman Training Manual." 2003. *Maxim*, May.

McLeod, Kembrew. 1999. "Authenticity within Hip-Hop and Other Cultures Threatened with Assimilation." *Journal of Communication* 49(4): 134–50.

Messner, Michael A. 2002. *Taking the Field: Women, Men, and Sports*. Minneapolis: University of Minnesota Press.

Michael, Robert T., John H. Gagnon, Edward O. Laumann, and Gina Kolata. 1995. *Sex in America: A Definitive Survey*. New York: Warner Books.

Mishkind, Marc, Judith Rodin, Lisa R. Silberstein, and Ruth H. Striegel-Moore. 1986. "The Embodiment of Masculinity." *American Behavioral Scientist* 29(5):545–62.

Owen, Frank. 2003. *Clubland: The Fabulous Rise and Murderous Fall of Club Culture*. New York: Broadway.

Paules, Greta Foff. 1991. *Dishing It Out: Power and Resistance among Waitresses in a New Jersey Restaurant*. Philadelphia: Temple University Press.

Polk, Kenneth. 1994. "Masculinity, Honor, and Confrontational Homicide." In *Just Boys Doing Business? Men, Masculinities, and Crime*, edited by T. Newburn and E. A. Stanko. London: Routledge.

Quinn, Beth A. 2002. "Sexual Harassment and Masculinity: The Power and Meaning of 'Girl Watching.'" *Gender & Society* 16(3):386–402.

Rostand, Edmond. 1897. *Cyrano de Bergerac*.

Rupp, Leila and Verta Taylor. 2003. *Drag Queens at the 801 Cabaret*. Chicago: University of Chicago Press.

Sanday, Peggy Reeves. 1990. *Fraternity Gang Rape: Sex, Brotherhood, and Privilege on Campus*. New York: New York University Press.

Schwalbe, Michael, Sandra Goodwin, Daphne Holden, Douglas Schrock, Shealy Thompson, and Michele Wolkomir. 2000. "Generic Processes in the Reproduction of Inequality: An Interactionist Analysis." *Social Forces* 79 (2): 419–52.

Snow, David A., Cherylon Robinson, and Patricia L. McCall. 1991. "'Cooling Out' Men in Singles Bars and Nightclubs: Observations on the Interpersonal Survival Strategies of Women in Public Places." *Journal of Contemporary Ethnography* 19(4):423–49.

Spradley, James P. and Brenda J. Mann. 1975. *The Cocktail Waitress: Woman's Work in a Man's World*. New York: Wiley.

Strauss, Neil. 2005. *The Game: Penetrating the Secret Society of Pickup Artists*. New York: Regan Books.

Swidler, Ann. 2001. *Talk of Love: How Culture Matters*. Chicago: University of Chicago Press.

Thorne, Barrie and Zella Luria. 1986. "Sexuality and Gender in Children's Daily Worlds." *Social Problems* 33(3):176–90.

U.S. News and World Report. 2005.

Waller, Willard. 1937. "The Rating and Dating Complex." *American Sociological Review* 2(5):727–34.

West, Candace and Don H. Zimmerman. 1987. "Doing Gender." *Gender & Society* 1(2):125–51.

Whyte, William H. 1988. *City: Rediscovering the Center*. New York: Doubleday.

Williams, Alex. 2005. "Casual Relationships, Yes. Casual Sex, Not Really." *New York Times*, April 3,pp. 1, 12.

Wright, Robert. 1995. *The Moral Animal: Evolutionary Psychology and Everyday Life*. New York: Vintage.

Peggy C. Giordano
Monica A. Longmore
Wendy D. Manning

Gender and the Meanings of Adolescent Romantic Relationships: A Focus on Boys

Increased interest in heterosexual relationships has long been considered a hallmark of adolescence (Waller 1937; Sullivan 1953). Yet sociological attention to adolescent love and romance is dwarfed by the level of cultural interest, ranging from television and film portrayals to parental concerns about teenage sexuality and pregnancy. Recently, media accounts have declared the end of dating and romance among teens in favor of casual hook-ups that lack feelings of intimacy or commitment (see, e.g., Denizet-Lewis 2004). A large-scale investigation based on a national probability sample of adolescents contradicts this depiction, however: by age 18 over 80 percent of adolescents have some dating experience, and a majority of these liaisons are defined by adolescent respondents as "special romantic relationships" (Carver, Joyner, and Udry 2003). Even relatively young adolescents indicate some romantic relationship experience, and those who do not nevertheless express a strong interest in dating (Giordano, Longmore, and Manning 2001). In spite of the ubiquitous nature of dating relationships during the period, we know little about how adolescents themselves experience the transition from a social life based on same-gender friendships to one that includes romantic involvement (Brown, Feiring, and Furman 1999).

From *American Sociological Review*, Volume 71, Number 2, April 2006, pp. 260–287.

We know much more about the character, meaning, and impact of adolescent peer relations. This research not only underscores that peers and friends are critically important to children and adolescents (see, e.g., Call and Mortimer 2001; Crosnoe 2000; Youniss and Smollar 1985), but it also provides a basis for expecting gender differences in the ways in which adolescents navigate and experience romantic relationships. Maccoby (1990) emphasizes that girls more often forge intimate dyadic friendships and rely on supportive styles of communication, while boys tend to play in larger groups, use a "restrictive" interaction style, and develop a greater emphasis on issues of dominance. In light of these differences, she poses a key developmental question: "What happens, then, when individuals from these two distinctive 'cultures' attempt to interact with one another? People of both sexes are faced with a relatively unfamiliar situation to which they must adapt" (Maccoby 1990:517).

Maccoby argues that the transition to dating is easier for boys, who tend to transport their dominant interaction style into the new relationship. This is consistent with other research on peer socialization that also adapts a spillover argument. While girls are socialized to center attention on personal relationships (Gilligan 1982) and romance, boys' interactions within male peer groups often lead them to define the heterosexual world as another arena in which they can compete and score (Eder, Evans, and Parker 1995).

Studies from this peer-based research tradition thus provide a theoretical basis for expecting that as adolescents begin to date, boys will do so with greater confidence and less emotional engagement (i.e., the notion that boys want sex, girls want romance), ultimately emerging as the more powerful actors within these relationships.

Research on peer relationships has been critical to an understanding of the adolescent period, and is important in that it foreshadows some of the origins of problematic features of male-female relationships, including intimate violence and gender mistrust. Yet perspectives about dating are too heavily grounded in studies of peer interactions and concerns, rather than in research on romantic encounters themselves. In addition, prior research has focused almost exclusively on issues of sexuality, while the relational and emotional dimensions of early heterosexual experiences have often been ignored. The symbolic interactionist perspective that we develop highlights unique features of adolescent romantic relationships that provide a rich climate for additional socialization. Our view is that meanings may emerge from interaction and communication within the romantic context that significantly alter or supplant those developed through peer interactions. This perspective fosters a different view of the ways in which gender influences the crossing-over process, and suggests fundamental limitations of the focus on spillover effects. Further, depictions of girls' experiences, especially concerning issues of sexuality, have become increasingly nuanced, but in prior work boys have often been cast as especially flat or one-dimensional characters (Forster [1927] 1974). Thus, it is important to explore both girls' and boys' perspectives on romance, but our central objective here is to address consequential gaps in knowledge about boys' relationship experiences.[1] The theoretical perspective and findings presented nevertheless have implications for understanding the character and range of girls' experiences, and provide a basic foundation for additional research focused specifically on girls' perspectives.

Background

Prior Research on Adolescent Girls

Most studies of adolescent life emphasize girls' strong relational orientation (e.g., Gilligan 1982; Martin 1996), as well as fundamental gender inequalities that tend to be reproduced as girls learn to center much time and energy on their romantic attachments (Holland and Eisenhart 1990; Pipher 1994). In a study based on social life within a Midwestern middle school, Eder et al. (1995) conclude that emphases within girls' peer groups (e.g., the notion that one must always be in love, the focus on personal appearance, and concerns over reputation) foster these inequalities and serve to distance young women from their sexual feelings (see also Simon, Eder, and Evans 1992). Within their own peer networks, boys emphasize competition on many levels, and ridicule those who express caring and other positive emotions for girls. Consistent with Maccoby's (1990) spillover hypothesis, then, Eder et al. (1995) argue that these peer emphases influence the character of cross-gender relations: "[M]ost male adolescents and many adults continue to associate excitement with a sense of domination and competition . . . [while] most girls fail to develop a sense of the depth of their inner resources and power and thus remain dominated and controlled" (Eder et al. 1995:148).

Studies that explore girls' early sexual experiences draw similar conclusions about asymmetries of power within romantic relationships. Holland, Ramazanoglu, and Thomson (1996) initially theorize that there is a sense in which female and male adolescents can be considered "in the same boat" due to their relative inexperience. They subsequently discard this notion, however, based on their analysis of girls' and boys' narrative accounts of their first sexual experiences. The authors argue that girls quickly learn that sex is in large part directed to "supporting and satisfying masculine values and needs" (Holland et al. 1996:159). Thompson's (1995) study of girls' sexual narratives develops a more nuanced portrait, by highlighting significant variations in girls' sexual experiences. Focusing on the highly melodramatic character of many girls' narratives, however, Thompson (1995) concludes that within the contemporary context, the gender gap in orientations toward relationships and sexuality may even have widened. She suggests, for example, that it is no longer as necessary as in earlier eras for boys to engage in preliminary steps of relationship-building to achieve their goal of sexual access, a dynamic that could accentuate rather than diminish traditional differences in perspectives. Interestingly, Risman and Schwartz (2002) have recently developed an alternative hypothesis. Examining aggregate trends that show declining rates of sexual intercourse during the adolescent period, the authors link such changes to "the increasing power of girls in their sexual encounters" (Risman and Schwartz 2002:21), particularly to negotiate the timing and the context within which sexual behavior occurs. Thus, while interpretations of the nature and effects of these dynamic processes differ, prior research points to power as a key relationship dynamic that warrants more direct, systematic scrutiny.

In summary, the emphases of prior studies have been appropriate, as the dynamics highlighted connect in intimate ways to processes that have been limiting or injurious to young women. Areas of concern range from leveled career aspirations (Holland and Eisenhart 1990) to sexual coercion and partner violence (Eder et al. 1995). Nevertheless, this research is itself limited by the focus on the relatively public face of cross-gender relations, such as joking and teasing that occurs within school lunch-rooms or during after-school activities. Here the emphasis remains upon the dynamics of the same-gender peer group, providing only glimpses into the more private world of the romantic dyad. Many studies in this tradition also rely on small non-diverse samples, or concentrate on very young adolescents. The heavy focus on issues of sexuality also provides a restricted view of the broader relationship context within which sexual behaviors unfold; that is, of the more basic emotional and other rela-

tional dynamics that characterize these relationships. More fundamentally, this portrait of spillover effects does not sufficiently highlight the communicative strengths and relationship competencies that girls bring to these relationships, nor does this literature confront inherent limits to the idea of carry-over effects. These criticisms apply equally to prior research on boys, where similar themes emerge, even though the research base is even more sketchy and incomplete.

Studies of Boys Romantic and Sexual Lives

Boys have certainly not been ignored in prior research on adolescence. Yet within the many studies that concentrate on boys, romantic relationships have not been a frequent subject. Classic investigations of boys' lives often concentrate on group processes within boys' friendship and peer circles, either as ends in themselves (e.g., Fine 1987), or as peers influence specific outcomes such as delinquency (e.g., Cohen 1955; Sullivan 1989; Thrasher 1927) or the reproduction of the class system (e.g., MacLeod 1987; Willis 1977). These studies do, however, sometimes offer characterizations of boys' romantic attachments. For example, MacLeod (1987) in a classic study of boys' delinquency involvement suggests that "women were reduced to the level of commodities and the discussions sometimes consisted of consumers exchanging information" (MacLeod 1987:280). The relative lack of research on boys' romantic experiences, then, likely stems from scholars' interests in other areas, as well as from their views that male-female relationships are of a limited, or at least a delimited (primarily sexual), interest to adolescent boys themselves. This is consistent with the research reviewed on girls' lives, and again highlights the reach of male peer culture. A consequence, however, is that boys' views about romance are gleaned primarily from analyses of girls' narratives and/or studies based on boys' discourse within the relatively public arena of the male peer group.

A few studies have examined boys' perspectives on romance directly, again often in connection with discussions of sexuality. Wight (1994), for example, observed significant differences in boys' talk about their girlfriends and sex among their peers compared with interviews conducted in more private settings. In the latter context, the working-class Scottish youth whom he studied were much more likely to express insecurities and vulnerabilities regarding the adequacy of their own sexual performances. Nevertheless, Wight (1994:721) also concludes that only a minority of the boys were engaged emotionally in the relationship aspects of these heterosexual liaisons. He suggests that generally the boys preferred male company and "particularly dislike girls' displays of feminine emotion which make them feel extremely awkward." Despite his more layered view of boys' perspectives, then, Wight's (1994) depiction of boys' attitudes toward romance does not differ greatly from a number of other accounts: "the main excitement of girlfriends is the challenge of chatting them up and getting off with them; once this has been achieved, going out with the girl becomes tedious . . . only a few came close to expressing trust in, or loyalty to, girls in the way they sometimes did for boys" (p. 714). In contrast, Moffatt (1989), relying on older students' written accounts of their sexual lives, found that a significant number (about one third) of the young men's narratives stressed the importance of romance and love in connection with their sexual experiences. It is unclear whether these differences in findings stem from significant age differences across samples, or variations in the methods employed. Thus, it is important to examine specific aspects of the existing portrait of adolescent males' romantic relationship experiences using a larger, more heterogeneous sample of adolescents.

The present study, then, focuses on basic but foundational research questions. Do adolescent boys, as Maccoby (1990) hypothesized, more often than girls express confidence as they cross over to the heterosexual realm? Are adolescent girls more likely to be engaged emotionally, relative to their male counterparts? And, perhaps most central to existing portraits, do boys typically evidence greater power and influence within their early heterosexual liaisons? These questions are interrelated and central to the development of an age-graded, life-course perspective on how gender influences relationship processes.

A Neo-Meadian Perspective on Adolescent Romantic Relationships

In our view, prior work in this area offers an incomplete portrait of the ways in which gender influences the crossing-over process. Further, existing treatments undertheorize the extent to which the romantic relationship itself becomes a potentially important arena of socialization and site for the emergence of meanings. These relationships may occasion new perspectives that coexist with, contradict, and even negate previous peer-based messages. Mead's (1934) symbolic interaction theory and recent extensions in the sociology of emotions tradition (e.g., Collins 2004; Engdahl 2004) provide a useful framework for exploring this general idea.[a]

Two central tenets of symbolic interaction theories are that meanings emerge from the process of social interaction and that the self is continuously shaped by dynamic social processes (Mead 1934). These basic insights foster a highly unfinished, continually emerging view of development, and a caution to the notion that meanings derived from peer interactions are likely to be transported wholesale into the romantic context. As Sandstrom, Martin, and Fine (2002:10) point out, Mead (1934) and later Blumer (1969) emphasized that "social definitions guide action," but also recognized that this involves much more than a "reflex-like application of these definitions."

> We have to determine which objects or actions we need to give meaning and which we can neglect. Moreover, we must figure out which of the many meanings that can be attributed to a thing are the appropriate ones in this context. . . . [W]hen we find ourselves in some situations, particularly new and ambiguous ones,

we discover that no established meanings apply. As a result, we must be flexible enough to learn or devise new meanings. We have this flexibility because we handle the things we encounter through a dynamic and creative process of interpretation. This process allows us to generate new or different meanings and to adjust our actions accordingly.

Scholars such as Corsaro (1985) highlight these dynamics as a way to understand the character of the parents-to-peers transition that reliably occurs during childhood and adolescence (see also Corsaro and Eder 1990). Researchers point out that parental socialization efforts are never fully successful, in that young people inevitably produce novel cultural practices through interaction with their peers. These meanings fit the peer context well, as they are a product of this context. Social forces are thus deeply implicated in the production of meanings; and, as these meanings are shared, they become a further source of social solidarity and self-definition (Fine 1987). This meaning-construction process is never fully stabilized, however, because new "hooks for change" continually present themselves within the environment (Giordano, Cernkovich, and Rudolph 2002). Individuals also possess the unique capacity to develop new plans, including the capacity to carve out new social networks. Yet as Emirbayer and Goodwin (1994) note, these new affiliations will nevertheless in turn have a shaping influence.

These basic insights are integral to many discussions of child and adolescent peer networks, but researchers have not systematically applied the symbolic interactionist or interpretive framework to an understanding of the peers-to-romance transition. It is intuitive to do so for several reasons: First, adolescent romantic relationships definitely qualify as a new situation, one in which interaction and communication hold a central place. Second, the relatively private world of romantic interactions makes it likely that meanings will emerge on site, rather than simply being imported from earlier peer experiences or from the broader culture (see also Simon and

Gagnon 1986). The fundamentally reciprocal qualities of dyadic communication enhance these possibilities. Mead ([1909] 1964:101) theorized that the "probable beginning of human communication was in cooperation, not in imitation, where conduct *differed* [emphasis added] and yet where the act of the one answered to and called out the act of the other." Third, scholars point out that contemporary romantic relationships in Western nations lack the heavily scripted qualities that characterized earlier eras or courtship practices within more traditional cultural contexts (Giddens 1992). This too leads us to favor a symbolic interactionist perspective on the meaning construction process. In the following discussion, we explore three basic relationship domains—communication, emotion, and influence—that allow us to develop further this symbolic interactionist perspective on adolescent romantic relationships.

Communication.   We agree with Maccoby's (1990) key assertion that "both sexes face a relatively unfamiliar situation to which they must adapt" (p. 517), but we offer a different perspective on the ways in which gender-related experiences may influence the crossing-over process. Recall Maccoby's suggestion that the transition is easier for boys, who are seen as frequently transporting their dominant interaction style into the new relationship. A competing hypothesis is that because girls have more experience with intimate dyadic communications by virtue of their own earlier friendship experiences, boys must make what amounts to a bigger developmental leap as they begin to develop this more intimate way of relating to another.

Mead (1913:378) pointed out that when engaged in familiar, habitual actions, "the self is not self-conscious." In contrast, on those occasions when the individual's previous repertoire proves inadequate to the task at hand (what Mead termed the "problematic situation"), cognitive processes, including feelings of self-consciousness, are fully engaged. While both girls and boys are likely to experience their initial forays into heterosexual territory as instances of Mead's "problematic situation," this may be even more descriptive of boys' experience, by virtue of the especially strong contrast for boys with the form and content of their earlier peer interactions. Thus, our expectation is that boys, at least initially, will experience a greater level of *communication awkwardness* in connection with their romantic liaisons. Following Mead, this also implies that cues within the new situation will be especially important. Mead noted that while the past (here, youths' understandings derived from peer interactions) is never completely discarded, the current perspective will nevertheless be transformed in light of present circumstances and future plans (Mead 1934; see also Joas 1997: 167–98).

Movement into romantic relationships involves more than developing a level of comfort while communicating with the opposite gender. It also requires a full complement of relationship skills, most of them communication based as well. Adolescents must become familiar with the process of making initial overtures, learn how to communicate their needs to partners, manage conflict, and successfully terminate unwanted relationships. Here, too, young women may be more competent and confident in what we will call relationship navigational skills, as they have experienced generally related social dynamics in prior relationships (e.g., friendship troubles and their repair). In addition, norms about dating behavior have become more ambiguous within the contemporary context, but boys are still often expected to make the initial advances. This provides a further reason for them to be more anxious and less certain about how to proceed.

Adolescents' perceived *confidence navigating relationships* requires systematic investigation, however, as prior research has shown that boys frequently score higher on scales measuring general self-esteem and self-efficacy (Gecas and Longmore 2003). Thus focusing only on the self-esteem literature, and the notion that males occupy a position of greater societal privilege, we might expect boys simply to forge ahead with

confidence into this new terrain, with little uncertainly about a lack of expertise or preparation. This is also consistent with the idea that girls may lack confidence in their abilities to make their own needs known in relationships, particularly given socialization practices that heighten girls' sensitivities to and concern for the needs of others (Gilligan 1982).

Emotion. Researchers have recently accorded greater significance to the role of emotions in human behavior (e.g., Katz 1999; Massey 2002; Turner 2000). Theorists in the sociology of emotions tradition in particular stress the strongly social basis of emotional processes (e.g., Collins 2004; Thoits 1989). Departing from highly individualistic conceptions of emotions, many sociological treatments focus on the ways in which cultural expectations influence emotion-management as well as emotional expression (e.g., Hochschild 1983). This sociological viewpoint resonates with the peer-based literature reviewed earlier, as it stresses that boys are socialized to avoid or deny softer emotions, and are teased and ridiculed by peers if they reveal signs of weakness or emotionality. In turn, this literature suggests that boys learn to devalue relationships that might engender positive emotions, and to objectify and denigrate the young women who are their partners in romantic interactions. Overall, much previous research provides support for the idea of an emotional closing-off process, as boys are observed making crude comments in the school lunchroom (Eder et al. 1995), describing their romantic relationships as tedious (Wight 1994), or constructing relationships as a game perpetrated on young women for the purpose of sexual conquest (Anderson 1989).

The symbolic interactionist approach, in contrast, suggests that the new dyadic context opens up additional opportunities for role-taking, defined as "putting oneself in another's position and taking that person's perspective" (Shott 1979:1323). Such reciprocal interactions may promote new definitions of the situation, as well as the experience of new emotions. Scholars have recently noted that emotions have clarifying and motivational significance (Frijda 2002), in effect providing valence or energy to new lines of action (Collins 2004). Our central argument, then, is that adolescent romantic relationships become a potentially important arena of socialization and reference, one that fosters new definitions and interrelated emotions. Suggesting that girls typically experience heightened emotionality in connection with their romantic endeavors is hardly a novel assertion. In contrast, however, to the emphases within much of the existing adolescence literature, we argue that boys often develop positive emotional feelings toward partners and accord significance and positive meanings to their romantic relationships. The notion that new attitudes and feelings can emerge from these recurrent sequences of interaction is generally consistent with Thorne's (1993:133) key observation that "incidents of crossing (gender boundaries) may chip away at traditional ideologies and hold out new possibilities."

This educational process and boys' emerging interest, we believe, frequently extends beyond the sexual to include the relationship itself. To the degree that boys engage in a distinctive form of intimate self-disclosure lacking within their peer discourse, and receive both positive identity and social support from a caring female partner, boys in some respects may be seen as more dependent on these relationships than girls, who have a range of other opportunities for intimate talk and social support. Feelings of heightened emotionality or *love* for the partner can be assessed directly, as adolescents are well placed to comment on their own subjective emotional experiences. Here the private interview provides a useful supplement to observational studies of boys' interactions in public settings, as recent work on gender and emotions underscores that the public face of emotions appears more highly gendered than the personal experience of these same emotions (Fischer 2000). It is also important to obtain systematic assessments across a large, heterogeneous sample of adolescents, as most of the research reviewed earlier indicates

that some boys develop caring attitudes toward a partner and positive feelings about their romantic relationships. These researchers frequently assert, however, that this adaptation is characteristic of a small subgroup of male adolescents who represent a departure from the more common and traditionally gendered pattern (Anderson 1989; Eder et al. 1995; Wight 1994).

Influence. Social interactions are not only implicated in the production of specific emotional feelings, but as some theorists argue, these emotional processes are capable of transforming the self in more fundamental ways (MacKinnon 1994; Engdahl 2004). The social influence literature emphasizes that the more highly valued the relationship, the more individuals are willing to accede to influence attempts in order to maintain or enhance their standing with valued others (Blau 1964). Viewed from a neo-Meadian perspective, however, positive interactions with significant others influence self-feelings (emotions) and attitudes that become catalysts in the truest sense. This neo-Meadian viewpoint encompasses but also extends the notion that change is accomplished primarily as a strategic move to preserve the relationship.

If, on the other hand, positive meanings are largely constructed outside the romantic relationship (e.g., as a source of competition and basis for camaraderie with one's male peers), we may expect the romantic partner's influence to be (and to be viewed as) rather minimal (see Collins 2004:238). This is likely to be the case whether the focus is on change in relationship attitudes/behaviors, influence on other aspects of the adolescent's life, or effects on the young person's emerging identity. Thus the character of communication and levels of emotional engagement in these relationships during adolescence are critical dynamics likely to be implicated in the nature and extent of partner influence. Our expectation, following the arguments developed in the previous sections, is that adolescent girls, owing to their greater familiarity with issues of intimacy and skill in communication, will likely make influence attempts, and boys (highly interested/engaged in this new relationship form) will often be receptive to them. Consequently, we do not expect to find significant gender differences in reports of partner influence, as contrasted with the hypothesis of a highly gendered (i.e., boys have more influence) pattern.

Consistent with prior sociological treatments, it is also useful to distinguish *influence* processes, which may be quite subtle, from *power*, often defined as the ability to overcome some resistance or to exercise one's will over others (Weber 1947). Youniss and Smollar (1985) note that much of the time within same-gender friendship relations, reality is "cooperatively co-constructed." This description reflects that the initial similarity of friends favors the development of a relatively egalitarian style of mutual influence. As a close relationship, romantic relations should also entail many instances of cooperative co-construction—but these relationships to a greater extent than friendships also bridge considerable difference. Thus it is not only likely that differences in perspective and conflict will occur, but also that partners will attempt to control or change the other in some way.

It is conventional to argue that structurally based gender inequalities tend to be reproduced at the couple level. On average the male partner acquires more power and control in the relationship (Komter 1989). While these ideas originally were applied to adult marital relations, as suggested earlier, the notion of gendered inequalities of power is also a recurrent theme within the adolescence literature. These power and influence processes require more systematic study, however, because during adolescence, social forces that are generally understood as fostering gender inequalities are still somewhat at a distance (e.g., childbearing, gendered access to the labor force and to other bases of power); thus the reproduction process itself may be markedly less than complete. The symbolic interactionist framework also suggests a more situated, constantly negotiated view of power dynamics, in contrast to a straightforward male privilege argument (see, e.g., Sprey

1999). The assumption of boys' greater power and control also connects to the largely untested assumptions that: (a) boys, on average, effect a dominant interaction style in these fledgling relationships (our communication hypothesis), and (b) girls are systematically disadvantaged by their greater commitment and emotional investment in their romantic endeavors (our emotion hypothesis). Asymmetries of various kinds (demographic, relational, status) are common within adolescent romantic relationships (see Carver and Udry 1997; Giordano, Longmore, and Manning 2001). Our view, however, is that these imbalances in the contours of the relationship need not—during this phase of life—necessarily and systematically privilege male adolescents. In the current analysis, then, our goal with respect to influence and power is to assess and compare adolescent male and female reports about their romantic partner's *influence attempts, actual influence* (as perceived by the respondent), and perceptions of the *power balance* within the relationship (defined as getting one's way, given some level of disagreement).

Data and Methods

Data

The Toledo Adolescent Relationships Study (TARS) sample was drawn from the year 2000 enrollment records of all youths registered for the 7th, 9th, and 11th grades in Lucas County, Ohio, a largely urban metropolitan environment that includes Toledo (n = 1,316).[3] The sample universe encompassed records elicited from 62 schools across seven school districts. The stratified, random sample was devised by the National Opinion Research Center, and includes over-samples of African American and Hispanic adolescents. School attendance was not a requirement for inclusion in the sample, and most interviews were conducted in the respondent's home using preloaded laptops to administer the interview.

From the total sample of 1,316, we focus the present analysis on 957 respondents who reported either currently dating or having recently dated (the previous year).[4] As shown in Table 28.1, 49

■ TABLE 28.1

Means/Percentages and Standard Deviations for the Total Sample and Separately for Boys and Girls

	Total		Boys		Girls	
	Mean/%	SD	Mean/%	SD	Mean/%	SD
Dependent Variables (range)						
Communication processes						
Awkwardness (4–20)	9.87*	3.3	10.10	3.2	9.64	3.4
Confidence (3–15)	10.40*	2.8	9.92	2.8	11.03	2.7
Heightened emotionality						
Love (4–20)	14.13	3.6	13.91	3.5	14.34	3.6
Influence and power						
Influence attempts (2–10)	3.80*	1.7	4.09	1.7	3.51	1.7
Actual influence (3–15)	6.41*	2.5	6.94	2.5	5.89	2.4
Perceived power balance (4–12)	8.23*	1.8	7.63	1.8	8.80	1.7
Independent Variables						
Gender						
Boys	.49	—	—	—	—	—
Girls	.51	—	—	—	—	—
Race						
White	.69	—	.64	—	.66	—
African American	.24	—	.24	—	.23	—
Hispanic	.07	—	.12	—	.11	—
Age (12–19)	15.49	1.7	15.44	1.7	15.54	1.7
Family structure						
Married biological	.46	—	.46	—	.43	—
Single	.26	—	.25	—	.28	—
Step	.16*	—	.19	—	.14	—
Other	.12*	—	.09	—	.15	—
Mother's monitoring (6–24)	20.55*	2.8	20.17	3.0	20.92	2.4
Peer orientation (1–4)	3.16*	.9	3.25	.9	3.08	.9
Mother's education						
< 12 years	.11	—	.13	—	.12	—
(12 years)	.32	—	.31	—	.31	—
> 12 years	.57	—	.56	—	.57	—
Self-esteem (10–30)	23.80	3.6	23.92	3.4	23.60	3.8
Currently dating						
Yes	.60*	—	.52	—	.67	—
No	.40	—	.48	—	.33	—
Duration of relationship (1–8 months)	4.79*	2.1	4.62*	2.1	4.95	2.1
Sex with romantic partner						
Yes	.28	—	.30	—	.27	—
No	.72	—	.70	—	.73	—
N	957	—	469	—	488	—

Note: Mean/% = mean or percent; N = number; SD = standard deviation.

*$p < .05$ difference between boys and girls (two-tailed tests).

percent of the dating sample is male, and the average age is approximately fifteen years. The race/ethnic distribution is: 69 percent white, 24 percent African American, and 7 percent Hispanic. In-depth interviews were also conducted with a subset (n = 100) of the respondents who had participated in the structured interview. These youths were selected based on their race/gender characteristics, and having indicated some dating experience during the structured interview. This subsample is on average older than the sample as a whole, and includes 51 girls and 49 boys. Of these 40 were white, 33 African American, 26 Hispanic, and one was "other" (Filipino).[5]

Measures

Definition of a romantic relationship.
We developed a simple definition that precedes the romantic relationships section of the interview schedule: "Now we are interested in your own experiences with dating and the opposite sex. When we ask about 'dating' we mean when you like a guy, and he likes you back. This does not have to mean going on a formal date."[6] The interview schedule elicits information about a number of different types of relationships, but the items and scales that we later describe and the accompanying analyses focus on the adolescent's relationship with a current or most recent partner.

Relationship Qualities/Dynamics

Communication awkwardness.
To measure feelings of communication awkwardness or apprehension we rely on four items: "Sometimes I don't know quite what to say with X," "I would be uncomfortable having intimate conversations with X," "Sometimes I find it hard to talk about my feelings with X," and "Sometimes I feel I need to watch what I say to X" (Powers and Hutchinson 1979) (alpha = .71).

Confidence in navigating romantic relationships.
This scale was designed for the TARS study, and it includes three items that tap dating-specific dilemmas and respondents' perceptions of confidence that they would be able to communicate their wishes: "How confident are you that you could . . . refuse a date?" "tell your girlfriend/boyfriend how to treat you?" and "break up with someone you no longer like?" (alpha = .72).

Heightened emotionality.
To measure the adolescent's level of emotional engagement we use items drawn from Hatfield and Sprecher's (1986) passionate *love* scale, including "I would rather be with X than anyone else," "I am very attracted to X," "the sight of X turns me on," and "X always seems to be on my mind" (alpha = .85).

Influence.
We distinguish between the partner's influence attempts and perceptions of "actual" partner influence. *Influence attempts* are indexed by these items: "X sometimes wants to control what I do" and "X always tries to change me" (alpha = .77). "*Actual" influence* reflects the level of agreement that respondents have been influenced by or actually changed things about themselves due to their relationship with the partner. Items include "X often influences what I do," "I sometimes do things because X is doing them," and "I sometimes do things because I don't want to lose X's respect" (alpha = .71). We note that the influence scales do not require respondents to select who has the most influence in their relationship, but instead to provide an assessment of their perception that partners have made influence attempts and that they have actually made changes or adjustments that they trace to the partner's influence. We then compare girls' and boys' average scores on these indices to gauge perceptions of partner influence.

Power.
The measure of power includes a more direct comparative element, as questions focus on the likelihood of getting one's way given some disagreement. This index is modeled on Blood and Wolfe's (1960) *decision power index* revised for use with this younger sample. The scale includes

an overall assessment ("If the two of you disagree, who usually gets their way?") and also includes items that reference specific situations: "what you want to do together," "how much time you spend together," and "how far to go sexually." Responses include "X more than me," "X and me about the same," and "me more than X." Higher scores reflect the adolescent's perception of a relatively more favorable power balance, relative to the partner (alpha = .77).

Control variables. Although our primary objective is to examine similarities and differences in the experience of romantic relationships as influenced by the respondent's gender, we also include control variables in our models. This allows us to account for possible differences between the gender subgroups on other basic characteristics and features of adolescents' lives, and to assess whether these variables operate as mediators of any observed gender differences. In addition to the influence of other sociodemographic characteristics, gender differences in reports about relationships might be influenced by girls' generally higher levels of parental monitoring (Longmore, Manning, and Giordano 2001), or males' greater levels of involvement with peers (as suggested in the foregoing literature review). It is particularly important to control for self-esteem, as responses to items about relationship confidence or perceived power may be influenced by the adolescent's generally efficacious or confident self-views. This would be consistent with Maccoby's (1990) argument that boys move ahead with confidence into the heterosexual context. Thus we not only assess whether, on average, boys tend to report greater relationship confidence, but also whether high self-esteem accounts for any observed gender difference. During adolescence, romantic relationships themselves vary significantly—both in terms of duration and level of seriousness (Carver, Joyner, and Udry 2003). Thus, our models also include controls for *duration* and whether or not the relationship has become sexually intimate. Teens with romantic relationship

experience who were not dating at the time of the interview reported about a "most recent" partner; thus we also add a control for whether the referent is a current or most recent relationship.

In addition to *gender* (female = 1), controls are added for *race/ethnicity* (African American, Hispanic, and white were created), and *age*. We also include dummy variables reflecting variations in *mother's education* as a proxy for socioeconomic status (less than 12, greater than 12, where 12th grade completion is the reference category), a strategy that allows for the observation of nonlinear effects. This measure is derived from a questionnaire completed by parents, rather than from youth reports. *Family structure* is represented in the models as a set of dummy variables (single parent, stepparent, other, with married biological as the reference category). *Parental monitoring* is measured by a six-item scale completed by the parent, which includes items such as "When my child is away from home, s/he is supposed to let me know where s/he is," "I call to check if my child is where s/he said," "My child has to be home at a specific time on the weekends" (alpha = .73). A measure of *peer orientation* is included, which asks respondents, "During the past week, how many times did you just hang out with your friends?" *Self-esteem* is measured with a six-item version of Rosenberg's (1979) self-esteem scale (alpha = .71). Relationship controls include a measure of *duration* of the focal relationship in months, whether *sexual intercourse* has occurred within the relationship (1 = yes), and whether the relationship is *current* (1 = yes) or most recent.

Analytic Strategy

We estimate zero-order models with gender and then add the remaining covariates to the model. This includes the social and demographic factors (e.g., race/ethnicity, age, mother's education), other network and individual characteristics (parental monitoring, peer orientation, self-esteem), and features of the relationship described (duration, whether the relationship includes sex, whether the referent is a current relationship).

Given the nature of our dependent variables, we use ordinary least squares (OLS) to estimate our models. Although we do not develop specific hypotheses in this regard, due to the general importance of the adolescent's other social addresses, and the utility of the concept of intersectionalities as developed in prior theorizing about gender, we also test for differential effects of gender based on race/ethnicity, mother's education, and age by sequentially estimating each model introducing a series of interaction terms (gender by race, gender by mother's education, and gender by age). This allows us to document whether observed patterns of gender similarity and difference generalize across various race/ethnic, SES, and age categories. We also examine interactions between gender and other features of the focal relationship, including duration and whether intercourse has occurred, in order to determine whether the findings with regard to gender reflect a consistent pattern across relationships that vary in longevity and level of sexual intimacy. We use a Chow test to evaluate whether the influence of the total set of covariates on relationship qualities is sufficiently different for boys and girls to warrant analysis of separate models.

Qualitative Data

The in-depth relationship history narratives that we elicited from a subset of the respondents are useful as they serve to validate the quantitative findings, give depth to our conceptual arguments, and provide a starting point for reconciling our results with themes about gender and relationships that have predominated in prior research. Qualitative methods preserve respondents' own language and narrative emphasis, and thus provide an additional vantage point from which to explore the meaning and importance of these relationships from each respondent's point of view (Morse 1994).

The in-depth interviews were generally scheduled separately from the structured interview, and were conducted by a full-time interviewer with extensive experience eliciting in-depth, unstructured narratives. Areas covered in general parallel the structured protocol, but allow a more detailed consideration of respondents' complete romantic and sexual histories. The interview began by exploring the dating scene at the respondent's high school, and subsequently moved to a more personal discussion of the respondent's own dating career. The prompt stated, "Maybe it would be a good idea if you could just kind of walk me through some of your dating experiences—when did you first start liking someone?" Probes were designed to elicit detail about the overall character and any changes in a focal relationship, and about the nature of different relationships across the adolescent's romantic and sexual career. The resulting relationship narratives were tape-recorded and subsequently transcribed verbatim. We relied on Atlas.ti software to assist with the coding and analysis of the qualitative data. This program was useful in the organization of text segments into conceptual categories and refinement of the categories, while retaining the ability to move quickly to the location of the text within the more complete narrative. We also relied on shorter two-to-three-page summaries for some aspects of our analysis.

Because the current study is based on a combined analytic approach, we do not attempt an overview of the qualitative data, as the systematically collected structured data and related quantitative analyses adequately depict aggregate trends. Here we generally limit our discussion of the qualitative material to narrative segments that (a) illustrate the direction of specific quantitative findings, but that further illuminate them, particularly with reference to the conceptual areas outlined above, and (b) serve to reconcile our results with the perspectives and emphases of prior research. Consistent with our focus in this article, we draw on boys' narratives, recognizing that a comprehensive account of adolescents' heterosexual experiences requires a corollary analysis of girls' perspectives. Other analyses using the

TARS data focus specifically on issues of sexuality, both within romantic relationships (Giordano, Manning, and Longmore 2005a) and outside the traditional dating context (Manning, Longmore, and Giordano 2005).

Results

Table 28.1 presents descriptive statistics for all variables included in the analyses. In addition to the focal relationship variables to be discussed presently, results indicate that, consistent with prior research, female respondents score higher on parental monitoring, relative to their male counterparts. Young women also report relationships of significantly longer duration, and they are more likely to reference a current (rather than "most recent") partner. Male respondents score higher on the measure of time spent with peers, but self-esteem scores did not differ significantly by gender. Table 28.2 presents results of analyses of boys' and girls' reports of communication awkwardness, confidence navigating relationships, and feelings of love. Table 28.3 shows results of similar analyses focusing on partner influence attempts and "actual" influence, as well as the perceived power balance within the current/most recent relationship. Results of analyses focused on gender interactions are reported in the text.

Communication

Awkwardness.   The first column in Table 28.2 indicates that, consistent with our hypothesis, boys report significantly higher levels of communication awkwardness in connection to their relationship with a current/most recent partner. Within the context of the more complete relationship-history narratives elicited from a subset of the respondents (recall that these youths are, on average, slightly older), these communication difficulties are especially likely to surface in boys' references to the early days of their dating careers or in discussions of how a given relationship had changed over time. Jake, for example, mentioned such communication difficulties in connection to his very first romantic relationship:

Then I like talked to her on the phone, I don't know it was kind of awkward, like long silences when you're talking and stuff like that, and I don't know, then she like broke up with me a week later . . . [during their conversations] I couldn't like think of anything more to say you know . . . I really didn't know [her]; I really wasn't friends before I asked her out, so it was kind of like talking to somebody I really didn't know. . . . [Jake, 17]

Table 28.2 presents multivariate results, in which other covariates have been taken into account. Gender differences remain significant in a model that controls for race/ethnicity, age, mother's education, family structure, parental monitoring, peer orientation, self-esteem, and whether the relationship had become sexually intimate (results not shown). The gender gap is explained by the other relationship controls (specifically duration and current dating status), as shown in model 2. This indicates that girls' tendency to be involved in relationships of longer duration and their greater likelihood of referencing a current partner influence the observed gender difference in level of communication awkwardness. The addition of the relationship controls also reduces the effect of age—in the reduced model without relationship controls, age is, as expected, inversely related to perceived awkwardness, but the relationship controls reduce this to non-significance. This suggests intuitive connections between age, relationship seriousness, and perceived awkwardness in communication. Having had sex with the romantic partner is also inversely related to perceived communication awkwardness, but this does not influence the findings with regard to gender and age (not shown). Turning to gender interactions, additional analyses indicate a significant gender by race interaction—white and Hispanic male respondents score significantly higher on communication awkwardness than their female counterparts, but African American male and female respondents do not show this pattern.[7] Interactions of age, mother's education and the various relationship controls (duration, having sex, current dating status) with

■ **TABLE 28.2**

Communication and Emotion within Adolescent Romantic Relationships

Gender	Communication Awkwardness		Confidence Navigating Relationships		"Love"	
	1	2	1	2	1	2
(Male)						
Female	−.462*	−.195	1.118***	1.208***	.435	−.020
Race						
(White)	—	—	—	—	—	—
African American	—	.300	—	.167	—	−.553*
Hispanic	—	−.098	—	−.053	—	.104
Age	—	−.094	—	.159**	—	.165*
Family structure						
(Married biological)	—	—	—	—	—	—
Single	—	.002	—	.129	—	−.465
Step	—	−.061	—	.030	—	−.743*
Other	—	.410	—	−.253	—	−.788*
Parental monitoring	—	−.042	—	.033	—	.042
Peer orientation	—	−.160	—	−.022	—	.017
Mother's education						
< 12 years	—	.060	—	.258	—	−.055
(12 years)	—	—	—	—	—	—
> 12 years	—	−.230	—	.095	—	−.023
Self-esteem	—	−.116	—	.180***	—	.032
Duration of relationship	—	−.249***	—	.026	—	.486***
Sex with romantic partner						
(No)	—	—	—	—	—	—
Yes	—	.635**	—	.442*	—	.185
Currently dating						
(No)	—	—	—	—	—	—
Yes	—	1.583***	—	−.311	—	1.786***
F	4.68	11.74	40.89	8.95	3.58	16.42
R^2	.049	.158	.041	.125	.004	.208

Note: Reference category in parentheses. N = 957.

*$p < .05$; **$p < .01$; ***$p < .001$ (two-tailed tests).

gender are not significant, however, indicating that, for example, duration has a similar effect on boys' and girls' reports about communication awkwardness.

The findings reported provide general support for the hypothesis outlined, but the relationship between gender and communication awkwardness is relatively modest and not significant in the full model. Aside from the gender dif-

ferences in duration that we noted, several other factors may have influenced these results, and suggest the need to qualify the hypothesis. First, perceived communication awkwardness is a general feature of early romantic relationships, and undoubtedly characterizes girls' as well as boys' feelings about the crossing-over process. In addition, results point to some variations in the gender pattern by race/ethnicity. Finally, youths completing this section of the interview focused on a specific, and most often, ongoing relationship. While adolescent romantic relationships do contain elements of uncertainty and awkwardness, the narratives also show that the perceived ability to "really communicate" with a particular other often develops as an important basis for both boys' and girls' feelings of positive regard. Although we explore these ideas further in the sections on emotion and influence, quotes such as the following illustrate this countervailing tendency:

> A lot of the other girls I met in high school, I felt like I had to hold back from them, you know you just couldn't talk about everything with them. With Tiffany you could. Like she wants to know what is on your mind. And if there is something bothering me, you don't have to dress it up or you know, you can just be straight with her all the time. [Tim, 17]

Confidence navigating relationships. Table 28.2 also presents the results of analyses examining effects of gender on perceptions of confidence in navigating romantic relationships. This index provides a more general assessment of confidence in navigating various stages of romantic relationships, and is thus not only focused on the current/most recent partner. When we consider this more general scale, male adolescents, consistent with our hypothesis, report significantly lower levels of relationship confidence. Recall that the scale refers to confidence through such items as "to refuse a date," "tell your partner how to treat you," and "break up with someone you no longer like." Gender differences are significant for responses to each of these items examined separately, as well as for the total scale, and gender remains significant in the model that incorporates the control and other relationship variables, as well as self-esteem. As these confidence items were also completed by non-dating youths, we also assessed the perceptions of confidence of youth who had not yet entered the dating world. The gender difference is significant whether we

focus on non-daters, daters as shown in Table 28.2, or consider the total sample of over 1,300 male and female respondents. These findings thus reflect a gendered portrait, but one that contrasts with Maccoby's (1990) hypothesis about boys' relatively more confident transition into the heterosexual arena.

With regard to other covariates, race/ethnicity and socioeconomic status are not significant predictors in this model, but age is positively related to perceived confidence. Self-esteem is also positively related to these assessments of relationship confidence, and focusing on the other relationship controls, having had sex with the romantic partner is related to greater overall feelings of confidence. None of the gender interactions assessed is significant. This indicates a consistent pattern of gender differences across the various race/ethnic groups, and the lack of a significant interaction of gender and mother's education suggests that this gendered confidence gap is found across various levels of socioeconomic status. Further, while age is positively related to perceived confidence, the age by gender interaction is not statistically significant—the observed gender disparity is evident in reports of older as well as younger respondents. Similarly, while teens who had sex with their boy/girlfriend report greater feelings of confidence navigating their relationships, a gender and sexual intercourse interaction term is not significant, reflecting a consistent pattern of gender differences in "confidence navigating relationships," whether or not the respondents reported that the relationship had become sexually intimate. Duration by gender and self-esteem by gender interactions are also not significant.

As suggested previously, the relationship-history narratives give respondents the opportunity to elaborate on ways in which they have experienced different stages of a number of different relationships (e.g., as they discuss the initial phase of starting a relationship or how they experience a particular breakup). These more wide-ranging discussions align well with the gender differences described earlier. Boys frequently reflect on their lack of confidence when talking about the beginning stages of a relationship, or a desired relationship that never materialized:

> I don't know why I'm so scared to let girls know I like them . . . like I said I was always nervous at asking them out but that one experience where I crashed and burned that just killed my confidence completely and I have been scared ever since to ask girls out and stuff . . . [Michael, 17]

This excerpt is useful as it clearly depicts feelings of concern and even inadequacy, feelings that Michael connects to one unfortunate early experience. Michael makes reference earlier within his narrative to what appears to be a generally positive self-image (*I know that I'm like a good-looking guy and everything, but I just get so nervous*), even as he offers a candid description of these relationship insecurities. While Michael's discussion includes the notion that such feelings may abate with time and additional experience (e.g., *I don't know how I'm going to be later but hopefully I'll just loosen up*), this awareness does not serve to lessen current feelings of discomfort. Undoubtedly, some of these feelings connect to boys' more often being cast in the role of initiators, but the feelings that some boys describe nevertheless provide a sharp contrast to depictions of boys' confident, privileged positions within these dating situations. Young men who do not appear to possess characteristics viewed as desirable within the context of what Waller (1937) termed "the rating and dating complex" were even more likely to include references to a lack of confidence. James, a slightly built sixteen year old, originally from Latin America, stressed that "girls still think of me as a little shy guy and short . . . with an accent . . . young . . . well it's hard for me because I'm not too experienced." These quantitative and qualitative data thus add to Wight's (1994) observation that adolescent boys frequently experience feelings of anxiety about the adequacy of their sexual performances, as here we document considerable insecurity extending to the broader relationship realm.

The quantitative findings and open-ended narratives also suggest that these feelings of insecurity are not limited to the early stages of the relationship-navigation process. For example, within the context of the structured interview, boys express less confidence about "telling your partner how to treat you," an interview question that was specifically developed with girls in mind. Further, the narratives provide evidence that corresponds with the item that asks about confidence to "break up with someone you no longer like." For example, Bobby indicated that he had experienced considerable trepidation about how to go about breaking up with his girlfriend Sara:

> It really took me like a while I guess to [break up] because I didn't want to like hurt her so I kinda like waited too long to do it, which was stupid by me. I just kept on like, I couldn't do it. I felt really bad. . . . I just put myself in her shoes and I felt like awful like you know. . . . Just like she saw a girl with my sweatshirt on and she just felt like what the heck's going on and everything just probably went down for her. . . . I couldn't do it, I just kept waiting too long to do it. . . . I didn't want to like hurt her really bad which I knew it would that's why I just kept on waiting so. [Bobby, 16]

Bobby felt sufficiently uncomfortable about the prospect of breaking up that he continued to let things slide rather than speaking directly with Sara about his desire to end the relationship (for example, he repeats some version of "I just couldn't do it" eight times within the longer narrative). From an outsider's perspective, Bobby had rather callously started up a relationship with a new partner, without properly ending things with his current girlfriend. Bobby's own narrative, however, reveals feelings of insecurity and discomfort, concern for Sara's reaction, and intimate connections between these two sets of feelings. This suggests at least the rudiments of a role-taking experience, and the possibility that Bobby has learned important lessons that could be carried forward into the next relationship. When asked about what he had taken from this relationship, Bobby replied, "If I'm feeling a certain way I should just tell them and not just sit there and wait and wait and not tell her." This is consistent with our argument that for adolescent males schooled in the peer dynamics described at the outset, the romantic context itself represents an especially important arena of socialization. Bobby's own narrative does not suggest a complete aversion to such lessons, but at least a general receptivity to learning from them.

Emotion

An examination of reports of feelings of love across the total sample does not reveal a significant gender difference in these feelings of heightened emotionality in connection with the current or most recent relationship. Recall that the scale contains items such as "I would rather be with X than anyone else," "X always seems to be on my mind," and "the sight of X turns me on." The multivariate model shown in Table 28.2 mirrors the bivariate findings: boys and girls report similar levels of feelings of love in connection with the focal relationship. Race/ethnicity (African American or Hispanic, relative to white youth) is not related to reports of heightened emotionality at the bivariate level, but being African American emerges as a significant predictor in the multivariate analysis.[8] The multivariate results also reveal a developmental trend—age is positively related to reports of feelings of love for the partner. Youths living with both parents relative to those residing in single or stepparent families also scored higher on the love scale, but mother's education is not related to reports of love. Longer-duration relationships are also characterized by higher scores on this scale, and, perhaps not surprisingly, when the current partner is the referent, scores are also significantly higher. Sexual intercourse within the relationship is not, however, related to variations in adolescents' reports of feelings of love. Race/ethnicity and gender interactions are not significant, indicating that the pattern of responses by gender is similar across race/ethnic groups. Analyses indicate no significant gender interaction by mother's education. Duration has a similar effect for boys and girls,

and the gender by intercourse interaction is not statistically significant. This indicates that having sex does not exert a differential impact on reports of feelings of love provided by male and female respondents.

It could be argued that the items within the love scale capture feelings of sexual attraction as much or more than a strong emotional connection to the partner, or positive feelings about the relationship. The narratives are thus an important adjunct to the quantitative findings, as they allow us further to explore questions of meaning from respondents' own subjectively experienced and uniquely articulated points of view. Many quotes from the narratives are congruent with the quantitative results, and inconsistent with Wight's (1994) conclusion that boys have little interest in the relationship aspects of these liaisons. One index that adolescent relationships can be said to "matter" to many adolescent boys is the sheer length of the relationship-history narratives that they often produced.[9] Here we refer to total length, as well as to lengthy sections discussing particular girlfriends. Will's 74-page narrative contains a very long section about his history with his current girlfriend Jenny, including a detailed story of how they met and a discussion of the various phases within their relationship's development. Will commented directly on the relationship's importance:

I: How important is your relationship to Jenny in your life?

R: About as important as you get. You know, well, you think of it as this way, you give up your whole life, you know, know, to save Jenny's life, right? That's how I feel. I'd give up my whole life, to save any of my friends' life too. But it's a different way. Like, if I could save Jon's life, and give up my own, I would, because that is something you should, have in a friend, but I wouldn't want to live without Jenny, does that make some sense? [Will, 17]

It is important to note that such expressions of positive regard and heightened emotionality are not contained only within the narratives of white middle-class youth, since prior research on African American youth in particular often includes the notion that romance is constructed largely as a kind of disingenuous game or con (e.g., Anderson 1989). Ron and Steve, two African American respondents who participated in the in-depth interview, express intense emotional feelings about their girlfriends:

> Yeah, I ain't never, I ain't never like, felt that way about somebody. . . . I tell her that [he loves her] everyday too! Everyday, I see her. [Ron, 17]

I: So, you remember all the dates and stuff?

R: Yeah, I'm like a little girl in a relationship. . . . [at first] just seemed like every time I was around her I couldn't talk, I was getting butterflies in my stomach, I just was like, discombobulated or something. [Steve, 17]

When asked to be more specific about features of the relationship that make it special or important, many adolescent boys reference themes that have long been emphasized in the literature on intimacy and social support (e.g., Duck 1997; Prager 2000), including opportunities for self-disclosure (see e.g., Tim's quote on page 274), and the importance of having a partner who is always there for them:

> Because she was always there for me. Like with everything. Like when my parents separated, she was there for me to comfort me then. And she helped me pull up my grades up to good grades and she was just always there for me. She always comforted me when I needed a hug. [Nick, 17]

We do not believe that such statements were produced primarily to please the interviewer, since the detailed answers frequently reference concrete instances where emotional support was provided. The narrative histories also frequently include descriptions of the endings of relationships. Breakups often involve disillusionment and other negative feelings, but such discussions also telegraph feelings of loss, providing a further indi-

cation of boys' own constructions of the meanings of these relationships:

I: I mean a year and three months is a long. . .

R: I'm not doing that good but my friends and my mother, they're helping me.

I: In what ways aren't you doing so well?

R: Ah emotionally. I, I can't sleep. I really can't eat that much.

I: I'm sorry.

R: That's okay.

I: How long and this just happened?

R: About a week.

I: Oh wow. So this is very fresh . . .

I: Do you believe them [friends and mom] that you'll get over it?

R: Yes. Some, someday I'll get over this but hopefully soon. [Eric, 17]

R: She just broke it down to me like, "Yeah, we're at different schools, we're young, we need to see other people."

I: So, why were you upset that you broke up?

R: I don't know. 'Cause I loved her so much. [Derrick, 17]

> She kept insisting I wasn't going to work out and I kept insisting I wanted to try it and one night, and like I said I couldn't sleep, and I wrote her a letter, front and back, crying the whole time and then I handed the letter to her the next morning. . . . It was really emotional, like how she hurt me and how it wasn't right. [Cody, 17]

These narratives often specifically mention the emotional realm (e.g., "It was really emotional"; "I'm not doing that good"; "my feelings was hurt"), or referenced behavioral indicators of psychological distress (e.g., "can't sleep," "really can't eat"). It is, however, also important to highlight that while Derrick's narrative communicated that the breakup did have a significant effect on him, he did not possess the social knowledge that other boys may also experience similar emotions (as he attempted to explain his bad mood to his mother, "I'm on my weekly [sic] cycle.").

Influence

Table 28.3 presents results of analyses examining reports of influence attempts, actual influence, and the perceived power balance within the current or most recent romantic relationship, as constructed by these adolescent respondents. Although most of the arguments developed in the existing literature focus specifically on issues of power, it is useful to consider the power results alongside the broader and perhaps ultimately more useful dynamic of interpersonal influence. Power assumes competing interests and only one victor, while influence focuses on whether the individual has taken the partner into account and actually made some adjustments. This need not involve a strong contrary view that needs to be overcome by the assertion of a power privilege. In line with this, recall that the questions about influence do not require the respondent to make a choice about who has the most influence in the relationship, but only to indicate whether and to what degree respondents believe that they have been influenced by their partner. The power items, in contrast, require a specific comparison of the respondent's own, relative to the partner's ability to get his or her way in a disagreement.

Attempted and actual influence. Results regarding influence attempts indicate a consistent pattern of gender differences: in both the zero-order and multivariate models, male respondents score higher on partner influence attempts. In the multivariate model, lower self-esteem youth report higher levels of partner influence attempts, and all of the relationship controls are significant: youths involved in more serious relationships (as measured by duration and sexual intimacy) report higher levels of partner influence attempts. Youths also describe former partners as making more attempts to influence, relative to reports about current partners. These relationship covariates have similar effects for boys and girls (results not shown).

More surprising than this pattern, however, is the finding that boys also report higher levels of "actual" influence from the romantic partner. The second set of models in Table 28.3 show a significant gender gap in reports of "actual" partner influence. In addition to a significant effect of gender, Hispanic youth scored lower on partner influence relative to their white counterparts. Lower self-esteem is associated with greater partner influence, and youths involved in longer-duration relationships also scored higher on "actual" influence. Sexual intercourse was not related to perceptions of partner influence. The interactions of gender with other sociodemographic variables as well as other relationship measures were not significant in this model. Thus, these results indicate that the gender gap is consistent across youths who vary in developmental stage, race/ethnicity, mother's education, and seriousness of the relationship.

The scales measuring partner influence (attempts and actual) are rather general (e.g., "X influences what I do"), and thus do not provide a full picture of (a) specific mechanisms of influence, (b) the areas or domains in which boys believe they have been influenced, or (c) the nature of their reactions to various influence attempts. Although a comprehensive examination of these issues is beyond the scope of this analysis, the narrative data do provide a more in-depth portrait of these processes.[10] The specific domains referenced within the narrative accounts are of particular interest, because they indicate influence on many potentially important relationship dynamics and behavioral outcomes—ranging from boys' behavior within the romantic context to academic performance and delinquency involvement. Given boys' initial lack of familiarity and confidence with intimate ways of relating, it is perhaps not surprising to find that some boys indicate that girlfriends had influenced their ability to relate in a more intimate fashion:

> Yeah, well it was a while . . . like about three months. Her mom was having problems . . . and so like she just kept talking to me a lot you know what I'm saying, and I listened and I tried to help and I had problems and you know we just, that was somebody we could open up to each other, so it was like I could talk to her and she could talk to me. [Todd, 17]

Todd described a gradual process that began with Caroline's willingness to open up to him

■ TABLE 28.3

Influence and Power within Adolescent Romantic Relationships

Gender	Influence Attempts		'Actual' Influence		Perceived Power Balance	
	1	2	1	2	1	2
(Male)						
Female	−.583***	−.547***	−1.045***	−1.107***	1.173***	1.215***
Race						
(White)	—	—	—	—	—	—
African American	—	.043	—	−.273	—	.375*
Hispanic	—	−.083	—	−.620*	—	.287
Age	—	−.047	—	−.039	—	−.021
Family structure						
(Married biological)						
Single	—	.067	—	−.206	—	.126
Step	—	−.149	—	−.293	—	.078
Other	—	.260	—	−.060	—	−.005
Parental monitoring	—	−.015	—	−.023	—	.019
Peer orientation	—	.038	—	−.010	—	.066
Mother's education						
< 12 years	—	.283	—	.349	—	.433ᴬ
(12 years)	—	—	—	—	—	—
> 12 years	—	−.093	—	.023	—	.043
Self esteem	—	−.086***	—	−.112***	—	.024
Duration of relationship	—	.077**	—	.137**	—	−.052
Sex with romantic partner						
(No)	—	—	—	—	—	—
Yes	—	.592***	—	−.092	—	.037
Currently dating						
(No)	—	—	—	—	—	—
Yes	—	−.460***	—	−.084	—	−.023
F	28.0	8.06	44.6	6.38	111.4	9.49
R^2	.029	.114	.045	.092	.105	.132

Note: Reference category in parentheses. N = 957.

*$p < .05$; **$p < .01$; ***$p < .001$ (two-tailed tests).

about some of her own family problems. Eventually Todd found that he could not only be helpful to her, but that he also increasingly began to talk with Caroline about some of his own problems. Although he does not state this directly, Caroline may have influenced not only his willingness to

engage in intimate self-disclosure, but the way in which he chose to handle problems that the two had discussed in this more intimate fashion.

In addition to modifications in their relationship-based selves, a number of the narratives reference specific changes that the youths indicate they had made in other important areas of their lives, shifts in perspective and behavior that respondents specifically connect to the influence of their romantic partners. Consider the following narrative excerpts:

> [Julie] makes me want to do better in school and stuff. I want to do well because of her because she is really smart and she's got a real good grade point average. Mine isn't as high as hers so I try to be up there and I don't want to look stupid. I don't think she would want me to be dumb. [Rob, 18]

> For like um the past two years, you know that I've been with her it has been, you know, about school. We both are carrying 3.8 averages and stuff. You know we're both kind of you know, kind of pushing each other along like, "you should really go do this." So academically, we help each other like a lot. [Dan, 17]

> I don't know it's weird but certain things make me want to go out and do better. I don't know why . . . You know Melanie, Melanie makes me want to do a hell of a lot better you know . . . [Chad, 18][11]

As the first quote makes clear, Julie is not simply one more friend who has been added to Rob's total mix of definitions favorable to academic achievement, and this hints at potentially distinctive influence mechanisms across types of reference others (notably peers versus romantic partners). Reciprocal role-taking experiences that elicit positive emotions provide an enriched social terrain for further development, as cognitive, emotional, and behavioral changes reciprocally influence self-views, including views of self in relation to these valued others. Here the positive emotions elicited within the romantic context can be seen as providing energy and valence to compatible or even new lines of action (e.g., Collins 2004). The last quote from Chad nicely evokes this notion of an energizing component.

Theorists have often noted that similar others (e.g., close same-gender friends) are very important as a source of reference. This is a sound assertion, based on basic principles of identifica-tion. Nevertheless, relationships based in elements of difference are also potentially important, as contrasts offer more in the way of a developmental challenge (see, e.g., Cooley [1902] 1970:380), and at times a blueprint for how to make specific changes and adjustments (Giordano 1995; Giordano et al. 2002). For example, Todd learns about self-disclosure through his partner's own tendency to self-disclose, as well as her encouragement of his own efforts to do so. Yet describing romantic relationships only in terms of contrasts provides an incomplete portrait of these relationships. If difference were the only dynamic involved, individuals might not be inclined to enter into the type of sustained interaction that results in a social influence process. In short, some level of identification or social coordination necessarily precedes role-taking and in effect makes it possible (see, e.g., Engdahl 2004; Miller 1973).[12] This neo-Meadian view, along with other sociology of emotions theorizing, tends to position emotions at the center of change processes, as individuals draw inspiration from their points of connection and a new direction via the element of contrast.[13]

Perceived power balance.   The findings and discussion focus on influence processes that may be subtle and incremental. In the examples relating to school performance, Rob wants Julie to think well of him, and Dan and his romantic partner are even more in tune, both having a strong commitment to keeping up their high grade point averages. Yet not all influence attempts lead individuals in a direction they wish to go. As stated at the outset, many of the significant differences that male and female adolescents bring to romantic relationships are not entirely overcome by a developing mutuality of perspectives that we described in the previous section. When interests clearly diverge, considerations of power become especially important.

Table 28.3 presents results of analyses focused on the perceived power balance in the current or most recent relationship (who has the most say in a disagreement—overall and in relation to specific domains). In the zero-order model, the gender coefficient is statistically significant; boys' scores are lower, indicating on average a relatively less favorable (to self) view of the power balance within their relationship. It is important to point out that the modal response to each question is egalitarian (having equal say); thus these findings reflect a significant gender difference where respondents have diverged from this more common response across the four items that make up this scale. We note also, however, that gender differences are significant for each of the items making up the scale (regarding overall say in relation to decisions about what the couple does and how much time they spend together, as well as about how far to go sexually) and for the total scale score.

Turning to the multivariate results, additional statistical analyses reveal that the best fitting model is a separate model for boys and girls (results not shown).[14] Most of the covariates are similar in their effects on reports of power (youths whose mothers have less than a high school degree saw themselves as having a relatively more favorable power position, and African American youth are also likely to describe a relatively more favorable level of power in their relationships). Some gendered effects of covariates, however, are masked when a combined model is estimated. We find that relationship duration does not influence girls' reports, but longer duration of the relationship is related to *less* perceived power in the case of male respondents. In contrast, while sexual intercourse experience was again not related to girls' reports about power, boys who reported that the relationship had become sexually intimate reported a *more* favorable (to self) power balance, compared with the reports of male adolescents whose relationships had not become sexually intimate. It is important to highlight that within models focused only on the subsample of sexually active male and female youths, the overall gender difference remains significant, with boys reporting a less favorable power balance relative to similarly situated girls. Nevertheless, these intriguing interaction results warrant addi-

tional scrutiny and exploration, as we did not have a theoretical basis for expecting these patterns. In addition, it is of interest that the two findings operate in an apparently distinct fashion—the association between duration and lower perceived power on the part of boys is somewhat unexpected from a traditional inequality point of view, while the findings regarding intercourse are more consistent with the idea that sexual involvement is a more pivotal event or marker for male adolescents (Holland et al. 1996).

The quantitative findings provide indications that, in contrast to the direction of much theorizing within the adolescence literature, when male and female respondents departed from an egalitarian description of the power dynamics within their relationships, males were more likely to describe a tilt favoring the partner's greater decision-making power. A number of narratives also highlight distinct interests on the part of partners, and a perceived power balance that corresponds with the statistical results:

> I guess she was more mature than I was and I guess I wasn't on her level you know because she wanted to do it [have sex] more than I did . . . she said that I wasn't mature enough and you know all that stuff . . . I was too young, I was scared, I didn't know what I was doing I wasn't ready for it. I think I felt like I was too young . . . she was my girlfriend and that's what she wanted. [David, 18]

> She's like okay we're going out now, and I tried making plans with my friends, but Amy's like "No we're going out here and we're doing this." I just wasn't going to live with that anymore . . . there was something about her she always wanted to change me. She wanted me to do this and wear this and do that. I was like okay. Whatever. I'd do it but I don't see it [as] right. [Josh, 17]

David's longer narrative confirms that this adolescent did have sex with his girlfriend, even though he felt that he was not "ready for it." Josh also admitted that he often went along with his former girlfriend's preferences, even though his narrative clearly telegraphed that he experienced this power balance in a negative way ("I don't see it as right," "I just wasn't going to live with that anymore"). The latter quote, then, provides support for the direction of the quantitative results, while reflecting the continuing impact of traditional gender scripts.

Variations

Further support for characterizations emphasized in the peer-based literature can be found when we confront the variability in boys' orientations and relationship styles evident within the narrative histories. This heterogeneity is necessarily somewhat obscured by our focus here on aggregate trends. A symbolic interactionist framework can accommodate explorations of subtypes and variations, as theorists have emphasized that while interactions influence identities, as identities begin to solidify, they become a kind of cognitive filter for decision-making (Matsueda and Heimer 1997). Over time, these differentiated identities increasingly structure social interaction in line with these self-conceptions. For example, Donny, a 17 year old, had apparently developed a strong identity as a player within his high school. Donny's first sexual experience occurred at an early age, and this respondent estimated about 35 sexual partners. Donny was also unable to recall the names of all of the young women with whom he had become sexually intimate ("I don't know I would have to go through some letters"). While he considered some of these young women girlfriends, he nevertheless often cheated on them, and indicated that he had control within his relationships. Consistent with this portrait, Donny admitted physically abusing at least one young woman he had dated and reacted aversively to the idea of expressing his feelings ("I really don't like talking about my feelings . . . I don't know I just don't like talking about it").

Donny's narrative thus departs significantly from the aggregate portrait that emerges from the quantitative analysis; yet these types of cases and corresponding identities are important, as they are vivid representations of traditional masculinity that virtually demand attention. Thorne (1993) noted the heavy societal and even research focus on what she termed the "Big Man" social type. It has been important to highlight that the aggregate findings and many narratives do not accord with Donny's perspective; indeed a number of boys specifically position away from this social type in discussions of their own self-views. Yet the number of references to players and other traditional gender attitudes itself affirms the continuing impact of such gender scripts:

> I rather focus on one girl than a whole bunch because I don't think that I'm like some player or something and I really don't like those people that go out and have a bunch of girlfriends and stuff and they think that they're some big pimp or whatever. [Michael, 16]

Additional research on masculine styles such as the player are needed, because (a) a host of negative social dynamics are directly and indirectly associated with this orientation, and (b) adolescents apparently believe that this is a more prevalent and highly valued social role than appears to be the case. Such shared misunderstandings are consequential, and are undoubtedly heavily influenced by the character of peer interactions that have been so effectively captured in prior research. For example, Eric explained why he does not engage in intimate self-disclosure with his male friends: "most of them don't, they don't probably think the way I think or have the feelings that I, feelings that I have for girls." We also saw evidence of this in earlier quotes (e.g., Steve's admission that he is "like the little girl in the relationship," or Derrick's reference to negative emotions after his girlfriend broke up with him, "I'm on my weekly cycle."). Undoubtedly differences between discussions within peer settings and the more private experience of these relationships serves to perpetuate boys' beliefs about the uniqueness of their feelings and emotional reactions.

Conclusions

In this article, we developed a symbolic interactionist perspective on adolescent romantic relationships that draws on Mead's basic insights, as well as recent treatments of the role of emotions in social interaction and self-development processes. Relying on structured interview data collected from a large stratified random sample of adolescents, we found support for hypotheses that differ significantly from traditional accounts of the role of gender as an influence on the relationship dynamics within these romantic liaisons. Results suggest a portrait of adolescent boys as relatively less confident and yet more emotionally engaged in romantic relationships than previous characterizations would lead us to expect. The findings regarding power and influence are also unexpected from a straightforward gender inequality point of view. Although we did not specifically predict systematic gender differences in reports of power and partner influence, these results do follow logically from our conceptual discussion and fit well with the findings concerning communication and emotion.

As boys make the transition from peers to romance, they lack experience with intimate ways of relating (as evidenced by lower perceived confidence in navigating relationships and at the bivariate level, among white and Hispanic respondents, by greater perceived communication awkwardness), even as they are beginning to develop a high interest and at times strong emotional attachment to certain romantic partners (as evidenced by the absence of strong gender differences on reports of feelings of love for the current/most recent partner). In line with our symbolic interactionist framework, we argued that these relationships set up conditions favorable to new definitions, to the emergence of new emotions, and, at least within these relationship contexts, to glimpses of a different and more connected view of self. The argument that boys move in a straight line toward autonomy, or the declaration that "heterosexuality is masculinity" (Holland et al. 1996) are global assertions that do not take into account the adjustments that boys as well as girls continually make as they begin to forge this new type of intimate social relationship.

Although additional research is needed on these and other relationship processes, we do not believe that the results derive from unique peculiarities of our measurement approach. First, the

findings across various indices are themselves quite consistent. For example, differences on the power and influence scales are all significant and vary in the same direction. In addition, findings fit well with observations based on a range of methods employed during preliminary phases of the TARS study (see, e.g., Giordano et al. 2001), and are further validated by the content of indepth relationship-history narratives that we also collected and drew upon in the present analysis. We also estimated a series of interactions that in most instances support the idea that documented similarities (feelings of love) and differences (boys' lower confidence levels, perceptions of greater partner power and influence) generalize across respondents who vary significantly in race/ethnic backgrounds, socioeconomic status levels, and age. We also estimated models that contained gender by sexual intercourse and duration interactions, and the lack of significance of these interactions in most models suggests that the observed gender patterns are not strongly influenced by length of the relationship or whether it had become sexually intimate. Exceptions were associations between sexual intercourse experience and duration of the relationship and boys' reports of power, findings that warrant additional research scrutiny. Finally, controls for variations in family and peer dynamics, other basic features of the relationship, and self-esteem, although sometimes significant, did not strongly influence or attenuate these results.

The symbolic interactionist theoretical perspective described at the outset provides a generally useful framework for interpreting our results. As we have suggested throughout this analysis, it is important to avoid an adult vantage point when focusing on early heterosexual relationships. It is quite possible that as boys gain in social maturity and confidence, and links to traditional sources of inequality become more salient, dynamic features within these romantic relationships will more often and more directly correspond to traditional gender scripts. In line with this idea, prior research has shown that certain transition events such as the move from cohabitation to marriage more often depend on male rather than female preferences (see, e.g., Brown 2000). Another possibility is that the nature of reports of relationship qualities and dynamics we documented in this study reflect cohort changes associated with broader societal level transformations. This interpretation would be consistent with Risman and Schwartz's (2002) recent discussion of apparent temporal shifts in adolescent sexual behavior patterns.

More research is also needed on the heterogeneity within this and other sample groups, as briefly described earlier. Our observations of variation are similar to those described by Moffatt (1989), who found that some university men emphasized love and romance in their personal narratives, while those whom he labeled the "Neanderthals" and "Neoconservatives" held more traditionally gendered views that appeared to influence their relationship styles and sexual behaviors significantly. Since few studies had directly assessed relationship processes during adolescence (and the results provide a strong contrast with key assertions about them contained within the existing literature), our findings should provide a useful background for exploring such variations in more detail in subsequent analyses.

It would also be useful to examine factors linked to within-individual shifts and variations in the ascendance or movement away from more traditionally gendered patterns and relationship styles (Thorne 1993). This suggests a more situated (again resonant with the symbolic interactionist framework) rather than a fixed or overarching gender inequalities approach to relationship processes. Aside from connections to major life-course transitions, for example, researchers could explore how certain relationship experiences connect to such shifts in perspective. Even within a focal relationship or time period, situations that link to boys' enactment of traditional/nontraditional repertoires need to be further highlighted. As an example, some of the same boys who expressed caring sentiments about their girlfriends undoubtedly make denigrating comments about girls when in the company of their circle of friends. Some boys also

described tensions between their wish to spend time with friends and also to be responsive to their girlfriends. The fear of being seen as controlled by their girlfriends and subsequently ridiculed by friends reflects well that boys care very much what their friends think of them (a primary emphasis of prior research), but also what their girlfriends think of them (a conclusion of the present study). In line with this notion, we found that male respondents scored higher on a scale measuring perceived influence from friends as well as on the index of influence from romantic partners (results available on request). The idea of crosscurrents of social influence should in the long run prove more useful than the theme of autonomy so often highlighted as the central dynamic associated with boys' development.

The current analysis focused primarily on boys' perspectives on romance, as this was a particularly noticeable gap in the existing adolescence literature. Nevertheless, a comprehensive understanding of these social relationships obviously awaits more systematic investigations of girls' experiences. Where research has delved into the role of romantic involvement on girls' development, the focus of sociological investigations has, as suggested in the literature review, remained almost exclusively on sexuality or alternatively, negative outcomes—for example, establishing links to depression (Joyner and Udry 2000) and to relationship violence (Hagan and Foster 2001; Halpern et al. 2001), or pointing out how dating derails young women's academic pursuits (Holland and Eisenhart 1990). The conceptual framework and data presented here provide a starting point for a more multifaceted approach to girls' relationship experiences. Future research linking dating and particular outcomes needs not only to assess whether adolescents have entered the dating world, but also to capture variations in partners' attitude and behavioral profiles, as well as the qualitative features of these romantic relationships. It is important to note that girls' narratives provide support for the direction of the results reported here, while also highlighting significant variations. Some young women described what they viewed as egalitarian relationships or a favorable power balance (e.g., "he wears what I want him to wear"), but others stressed that boyfriends had engaged in a range of controlling, intrusive behaviors. The aggregate findings are an important backdrop for further exploring the impact of these variations, as the subset of girls who describe themselves as having low power may experience this power balance in an especially detrimental way (for reasons highlighted in prior work, and because such girls may compare their own situations to those of other teens whose relationships are characterized by less traditionally gendered dynamics). A full exploration from girls' points of view also requires moving beyond the immediate confines of the dating context to consider some of the indirect ways in which involvement in the heterosexual world influences girls' well-being, including concerns about weight and appearance (Pipher 1994), and connections to relationships with parents (e.g., Joyner and Udry [2000] found that some of the gender difference in the dating-depression link was associated with increases in girls' conflicts with their parents).

Finally, the symbolic interactionist perspective highlights the importance of adolescents' own constructions of the nature and meanings of their relationships. This framework recognizes that many important relationship features are inherently subjective (e.g., adolescents are better positioned than others to comment upon their own confidence levels or feelings of love). It is, however, important to supplement the perceptual accounts described here with findings based on other methodological strategies. For example, teens may report a relatively egalitarian power balance, or even greater power on the part of the female partner, but laboratory-based studies or other methods may well uncover more traditionally gendered communication and relationship dynamics that are not well appreciated by adolescents themselves. Yet we hope that researchers will continue to explore the subjectively experienced aspects of adolescent romantic relationships, as these provide an important supplement to peer-focused ethnographies and the behavioral emphasis of large-scale surveys such as the National Longitudinal Study of Adolescent Health (Add Health).

Notes

1. This analysis is also limited to a consideration of heterosexual relationships, as we are particularly interested in the process of "crossing over" from a social life based primarily on same-gender friendships to involvement with heterosexual partners. In addition, the number of respondents who self-identify as homosexual or bisexual at wave one is too small to support a separate analysis. Nevertheless, our conceptual framework and associated measurement emphasis could potentially be useful in connection with future investigations that explore the broader relationship contexts within which gay, lesbian, and bisexual youths' romantic and sexual experiences unfold.

2. The focus on emotions as an important dynamic within social interactions represents a shift from Mead's original cognitive emphasis, but it can be considered neo-Meadian since his more general ideas (e.g., the concept of role-taking and focus on self-processes) are applicable to understanding the emotional as well as cognitive realms of experience (see Engdahl 2004; MacKinnon 1994).

3. All of the schools eventually complied with our requests for these data, as this information is legally available under Ohio's Freedom of Information Act.

4. Furman and Hand (2004) found similarities in dating involvement in TARS and in their own study. Both studies document higher rates of dating involvement by age than are evident within the National Longitudinal Study of Adolescent Health (Add Health). We note that our reports of (for example) sexual intercourse by age parallel those in Add Health, but a higher percentage of respondents at each age report current romantic involvement: 32 percent of 7th, 41 percent of 9th graders, and 59 percent of 11th grade TARS respondents, compared with 17 percent, 32 percent, and 44 percent of Add Health respondents.

5. This respondent was excluded from the quantitative analysis, but included in our study of the relationship history narratives.

6. This introduction and definition were selected after extensive pre-testing and reflects contemporary trends

in dating that are less focused than in earlier eras on formal activities. In addition, the latter type of definition is strongly class-linked, and would tend to exclude lower socioeconomic-status (SES) youth. Our definition also differs from that used in Add Health, where respondents are asked whether they currently have a "special romantic relationship." We wished to avoid selecting on a relationship that the respondent specifically defines as special, since understanding the patterning of relationship qualities is a primary objective of the study.

7. Further examination of the means for all groups indicates that African American male respondents perceive significantly less communication awkwardness than African American girls. In general, this fits with Staples's (1981) hypothesis about the greater social and communication ease of African American youths, but we document a significant gender difference in this regard. These distinct patterns highlight the importance of examining the nature of relationship dynamics among diverse groups of teens, since the bulk of prior research on adolescent relationships focuses on samples of white adolescents or largely white samples of college students (see also Carver et al. 2003).

8. We note that no racial/ethnic differences are observed in multivariate models that include demographic, family, and peer controls. African American youth report relationships of longer duration, and relationships are more likely to include sexual intercourse; when these variables are introduced, the African American coefficient becomes significant. These findings suggest that African American youth may accord differential meanings and emotional significance to different types of relationships. The role of race/ethnicity warrants more systematic investigation than we give it in the current analysis (see Giordano, Manning, and Longmore 2005b for an analysis of race/ethnicity effects on romantic relationships using Add Health data).

9. Martin (1996) makes a similar point in her discussion of the length of girls' romance narratives, but she concludes from her own study that boys "rarely express the feelings of romantic love that girls do" (Martin 1996:68). Our results are not in accord with this conclusion.

10. For a more detailed discussion of specific mechanisms of influence and reactions to influence attempts, see Trella (2005).

11. These narratives provide a strong contrast with Frost's (2001) description of boys' singular concern with what peers think of them, citing Kimmel (1994:128–29): "this kind of policing of identity construction, reflects a profound need to be accepted and approved by men: 'There is no strong concern for women's approval as they are in too low a place on the social ladder.' "

12. Our own interpretation of this dynamic differs slightly from Engdahl (2004) and Miller's (1973) emphases, as we posit a level of recognition of these points of connection on the part of the actors involved.

13. Research is needed on specific domains (e.g., achievement, delinquency, sexuality), where complex portraits of partner influence and gender effects will undoubtedly emerge. TARS data document effects of romantic partners' grades on respondents' grades, net of peer and parent influences, but we find a stronger effect for boys (Phelps et al. 2006). Using Add Health data, we found an effect of partners' minor deviance on respondents' deviance for male and female respondents, but a stronger effect for girls. Effects of the romantic partner's involvement in serious delinquency were comparable for boys and girls (Haynie et al. 2005).

14. Based on statistical tests, we do not find support for separate gender models for any of the other relationship qualities (communication awkwardness, confidence navigating relationships, love, and influence attempts or 'actual' influence).

References

Anderson, Elijah. 1989. "Sex Codes and Family Life among Poor Inner-City Youths." *Annals of the American Academy of Political Social Science* 501:59–79.

Blau, Peter M. 1964. *Exchange and Power in Social Life*. New York: Wiley.

Blood, Robert O. and Donald M. Wolfe. 1960. *Husbands and Wives: The Dynamics of Married Living*. Glencoe, IL: Free Press.

Blumer, Herbert. 1969. *Symbolic Interactionism: Perspective and Method*. Berkeley, CA: University of California Press.

Brown, B. Bradford, Candice Feiring, and Wyndol Furman. 1999. "Missing the Love Boat: Why

Researchers Have Shied away from Adolescent Romance." Pp. 1–18 in *The Development of Romantic Relationships in Adolescence*, edited by W. Furman, B. B. Brown, and C. Feiring. New York: Cambridge University Press.

Brown, Susan L. 2000. "Union Transitions among Cohabitors: The Significance of Relationship Assessments and Expectations." *Journal of Marriage and the Family* 62:833–46.

Call, Kathleen T. and Jeylan T. Mortimer. 2001. *Arenas of Comfort in Adolescence: A Study of Adjustment in Context*. Mahwah, NJ: Lawrence Erlbaum Associates.

Carver, Karen P., Kara Joyner, and J. Richard Udry. 2003. "National Estimates of Adolescent Romantic Relationships." Pp. 23–56 in *Adolescent Romantic Relations and Sexual Behavior*, edited by Paul Florsheim. Mahwah, NJ: Lawrence Erlbaum Associates.

Carver, Karen P. and J. Richard Udry. 1997. *Reciprocity in the Identification of Adolescent Romantic Partners*. Presented at the annual meeting of the Population Association of America, March 28, Washington, DC.

Cohen, Albert K. 1955. *Delinquent Boys: The Culture of the Gang*. New York: Free Press.

Collins, Randall. 2004. *Interaction Ritual Chains*. Princeton, NJ: Princeton University Press.

Cooley, Charles H. [1902] 1970. *Human Nature and the Social Order*. New York: Scribner.

Corsaro, William A. 1985. *Friendship and Peer Culture in the Early Years*. Norwood, NJ: Ablex.

Corsaro, William A. and Donna Eder. 1990. "Children's Peer Cultures." *Annual Review of Sociology* 16:197–220.

Crosnoe, Robert. 2000. "Friendships in Childhood and Adolescence: The Life Course and New Directions." *Social Psychology Quarterly* 63: 377–91.

Denizet-Lewis, Benoit. 2004. "Whatever Happened to Teen Romance? (And What Is a Friend with Benefits Anyway?): Friends, Friends with Benefits and the Benefits of the Local Mall." *New York Times*, May 30, p. 30.

Duck, Steve, ed. 1997. *Handbook of Personal Relationships: Theory, Research, and Interventions*. New York: Wiley.

Eder, Donna, Catherine Evans, and Stephen Parker. 1995. *School Talk: Gender and Adolescent Culture*. New Brunswick, NJ: Rutgers University Press.

Emirbayer, Mustafa and Jeff Goodwin. 1994. "Network Analysis, Culture, and the Problem of Agency." *American Journal of Sociology* 99:1411–54.

Engdahl, Emma. 2004. "A Theory of the Emotional Self: From the Standpoint of a Neo-Meadian." Ph.D. dissertation, Department of Sociology, Örebro University, Örebro, Sweden.

Fine, Gary A. 1987. *With the Boys: Little League Baseball and Preadolescent Culture*. Chicago, IL: University of Chicago Press.

Fischer, Agneta H. 2000. *Gender and Emotion: Social Psychological Perspectives*. Cambridge, England: Cambridge University Press.

Forster, Edward M. [1927] 1974. *Aspects of the Novel, and Related Writings*. New York: Holmes and Meier.

Frijda, Nico H. 2002. "Emotions as Motivational States." Pp. 11–32 in *European Review of Philosophy: Emotion and Action*, vol. 5, edited by E. Pacherie. Stanford, CA: CSLI Publications.

Frost, Liz. 2001. *Young Women and the Body: A Feminist Sociology*. New York: Palgrave Macmillan.

Furman, Wyndol and Laura S. Hand. 2004. "The Slippery Nature of Romantic Relationships: Issues in Definition and Differentiation." Presented at the Pennsylvania State Family Symposium, October, Philadelphia, PA.

Gecas, Viktor and Monica A. Longmore. 2003. "Self-Esteem." Pp. 1419–24 in *International Encyclopedia of Marriage and Family Relationships*, 2d ed., edited by James J. Ponzetti, Jr. New York: Macmillan Reference.

Giddens, Anthony. 1992. *The Transformation of Intimacy: Sexuality, Love, and Eroticism in Modern Societies*. Stanford, CA: Stanford University Press.

Gilligan, Carol. 1982. *In a Different Voice: Psychological Theory and Women's Development*. Cambridge, MA: Harvard University Press.

Giordano, Peggy C. 1995. "The Wider Circle of Friends in Adolescence." *American Journal of Sociology* 101:661–97.

Giordano, Peggy C., Stephen A. Cernkovich, and Jennifer L. Rudolph. 2002. "Gender, Crime, and Desistance: Toward a Theory of Cognitive Transformation." *American Journal of Sociology* 107:990–1064.

Giordano, Peggy C., Monica A. Longmore, and Wendy D. Manning. 2001. "A Conceptual Portrait of Adolescent Romantic Relationships." Pp. 111–39 in *Sociological Studies of Children and*

Youth, edited by D. A. Kinney. London, England: Elsevier Science.

Giordano, Peggy C., Wendy D. Manning, and Monica A. Longmore. 2005a. "The Qualities of Adolescent Relationships and Sexual Behavior." Presented at the annual meeting of the Population Association of America, April 1, Philadelphia, PA.

———. 2005b. "The Romantic Relationships of African American and White Adolescents." *The Sociological Quarterly* 46:545–68.

Hagan, John and Holly Foster. 2001. "Youth Violence and the End of Adolescence." *American Sociological Review* 66:874–99.

Halpern, Carolyn T., Selene G. Oslak, Mary L. Young, Sandra L. Martin, and Lawrence L. Kupper. 2001. "Partner Violence among Adolescents in Opposite-Sex Romantic Relationships: Findings from the National Longitudinal Study of Adolescent Health." *American Journal of Public Health* 91:1679–85.

Hatfield, Elaine and Susan Sprecher. 1986. "Measuring Passionate Love in Intimate Relations." *Journal of Adolescence* 9:383–410.

Haynie, Dana L., Peggy C. Giordano, Wendy D. Manning, and Monica A. Longmore. 2005. "Adolescent Romantic Relationships and Delinquency Involvement." *Criminology* 43:177–210.

Hochschild, Arlie R. 1983. *The Managed Heart: Commercialization of Human Feeling*. Berkley, CA: University of California Press.

Holland, Dorothy C. and Margaret A. Eisenhart. 1990. *Educated in Romance: Women, Achievement, and College Culture*. Chicago, IL: University of Chicago Press.

Holland, Janet, Caroline Ramazanoglu, and Rachel Thomson. 1996. "In the Same Boat? The Gendered (In)experience of First Heterosex." Pp. 143–60 in *Theorizing Heterosexuality: Telling it Straight*, edited by D. Richardson. Philadelphia, PA: Open University Press.

Joas, Hans. 1997. *G. H. Mead: A Contemporary Re-examination of His Thought*. Cambridge, MA: MIT Press.

Joyner, Kara and J. Richard Udry. 2000. "You Don't Bring Me Anything but Down: Adolescent Romance and Depression." *Journal of Health and Social Behavior* 41: 369–91.

Katz, Jack. 1999. *How Emotions Work*. Chicago, IL: University of Chicago Press.

Kimmel, Michael S. 1994. "Masculinity as Homophobia: Fear, Shame, and Silence in the Construction of Gender Identity." Pp. 119–41 in *Theorizing Masculinities*, edited by H. Brod and M. Kaufman. London, England: Sage.

Komter, Aafke. 1989. "Hidden Power in a Marriage." *Gender and Society* 3:187–216.

Longmore, Monica A., Wendy D. Manning, and Peggy C. Giordano. 2001. "Preadolescent Parenting Strategies and Teens' Dating and Sexual Initiation." *Journal of Marriage and the Family* 63:322–35.

Maccoby, Eleanor. 1990. "Gender and Relationships: A Developmental Account." *American Psychologist* 45:513–20.

MacKinnon, Neil J. 1994. *Symbolic Interactionism as Affect Control*. Albany, NY: State University of New York Press.

MacLeod, Jay. 1987. *Ain't No Makin' It: Leveled Aspirations in a Low-Income Neighborhood*. Boulder, CO: Westview Press.

Manning, Wendy D., Monica A. Longmore, and Peggy C. Giordano. 2005. "Adolescents' Involvement in Non-Romantic Sexual Activity." *Social Science Research* 34:384–407.

Martin, Karin A. 1996. *Puberty, Sexuality, and the Self: Boys and Girls at Adolescence*. New York: Routledge.

Massey, David S. 2002. "A Brief History of Human Society: The Origin and Role of Emotion in Social Life." *American Sociological Review* 67:1–29.

Matsueda, Ross L. and Karen Heimer. 1997. "A Symbolic Interactionist Theory of Role-Transitions, Role-Commitments, and Delinquency." Pp. 163–213 in *Developmental Theories of Crime and Delinquency*, edited by T. P. Thornberry. New Brunswick, NJ: Transaction.

Mead, George H. [1909] 1964. "Social Psychology as Counterpart to Physiological Psychology." Pp. 94–104 in *Selected Writings: George Herbert Mead*, edited by A. J. Reck. Chicago, IL: University of Chicago Press.

———. 1913. "The Social Self." *Journal of Philosophy, Psychology, and Scientific Methods* 10:374–80.

———. 1934. *Mind, Self, and Society from the Standpoint of a Social Behaviorist*. Chicago, IL: University of Chicago Press.

Miller, David L. 1973. *George Herbert Mead: Self, Language, and the World*. Austin, TX: University of Texas Press.

Moffatt, Michael. 1989. *Coming of Age in New Jersey: College and American Culture*. New Brunswick, NJ: Rutgers University Press.

Morse, Janice M. 1994. "Designing Funded Qualitative Research." Pp. 220–35 in *Handbook of Qualitative Research*, edited by N. Denzin and Y. Lincoln. Thousand Oaks, CA: Sage.

Phelps, Kenyatta D., Peggy C. Giordano, Wendy D. Manning, and Monica A. Longmore. 2006. "The Influence of Dating Partners on Adolescents' Academic Achievement." To be presented at the annual meeting of the North Central Sociological Association, March 23–25, Indianapolis, IN.

Pipher, Mary. 1994. *Reviving Ophelia: Saving the Lives of Adolescent Girls*. New York: Ballentine.

Powers, William G. and Kevin Hutchinson. 1979. "The Measurement of Communication Apprehension in the Marriage Relationship." *Journal of Marriage and the Family* 41:89–95.

Prager, Karen J. 2000. "Intimacy in Personal Relations." Pp. 229–42 in *Close Relationships: A Sourcebook*, edited by C. Hendrick and S. S. Hendrick. Thousand Oaks, CA: Sage.

Risman, Barbara and Pepper Schwartz. 2002. "After the Sexual Revolution: Gender Politics in Teen Dating." *Contexts* 1.16–24.

Rosenberg, Morris. 1979. *Conceiving the Self*. New York: Basic Books.

Sandstrom, Kent L., Daniel D. Martin, and Gary A. Fine. 2002. *Symbols, Selves, and Social Reality: A Symbolic Interactionist Approach to Social Psychology and Sociology*. Los Angeles, CA: Roxbury.

Shott, Susan. 1979. "Emotion and Social Life: A Symbolic Interactionist Analysis." *American Journal of Sociology* 84:1317–34.

Simon, Robin W., Donna Eder, and Cathy Evans. 1992. "The Development of Feeling Norms Underlying Romantic Love among Adolescent Females." *Social Psychology Quarterly* 55:29–46.

Simon, William and John H. Gagnon. 1986. "Sexual Scripts: Permanence and Change." *Archives of Sexual Behavior* 15:97–120.

Sprey, Jetse. 1999. "Family Dynamics: An Essay on Conflict and Power." Pp. 667–85 in *Handbook of Marriage and the Family*, 2d ed., edited by M. R. Sussman, S. K. Steinmetz, and G. W. Peterson. New York: Plenum.

Staples, Robert. 1981. *The World of Black Singles: Changing Patterns of Male-Female Relationships*. Westport, CT: Greenwood.

Sullivan, Harry S. 1953. *The Interpersonal Theory of Psychiatry*. New York: Norton.

Sullivan, Mercer L. 1989. *"Getting Paid": Youth Crime and Work in the Inner City*. Ithaca, NY: Cornell University Press.

Thompson, Sharon. 1995. *Going All The Way: Teenage Girls' Tales of Sex, Romance, and Pregnancy*. New York: Hill and Wang.

Thoits, Peggy A. 1989. "The Sociology of Emotions." *Annual Review of Sociology* 15:317–42.

Thorne, Barrie. 1993. *Gender Play: Girls and Boys in School*. New Brunswick, NJ: Rutgers University Press.

Thrasher, Frederic M. 1927. *The Gang: A Study of 1,313 Gangs*. Chicago, IL: University of Chicago Press.

Trella, Deanna L. 2005. "Control and Power Dynamics in Adolescent Romantic Relationships." Masters thesis, Department of Sociology, Bowling Green State University, Bowling Green, OH.

Turner, Jonathan H. 2000. *On the Origin of Human Emotion: A Sociological Inquiry into the Evolution of Human Affect*. Stanford, CA: Stanford University Press.

Waller, Walter. 1937. "The Rating and Dating Complex." *American Sociological Review* 2:727–34.

Weber, Max. 1947. *The Theory of Social and Economic Organization*. Translated by A. M. Henderson and T. Parsons. Edited by T. Parsons. Glencoe, IL: Free Press.

Wight, Daniel. 1994. "Boys' Thoughts and Talk about Sex in a Working Class Locality of Glasgow." *Sociological Review* 42:703–38.

Willis, Paul E. 1977. *Learning to Labor*. Aldershot, England: Gower.

Youniss, James and Jacqueline Smollar. 1985. *Adolescent Relations with Mothers, Fathers and Friends*. Chicago, IL: University of Chicago Press.

PART SEVEN

Male Sexualities

How do many men learn to desire women? What are men thinking about when they are sexual with women? Are gay men more sexually promiscuous than straight men? Are gay men more obsessed with demonstrating their masculinity than straight men, or are they likely to be more "effeminate"? Recent research indicates that there are no simple answers to these questions. It is increasingly clear, however, that men's sexuality, whether homosexual, bisexual, or heterosexual, is perceived as an experience of their gender.

Since there is no anticipatory socialization for homosexuality and bisexuality, future straight and gay men receive the same socialization as boys. As a result, sexuality as a gender enactment is often a similar internal experience for all men. Early socialization teaches us—through masturbation, locker-room conversations, sex-ed classes and conversations with parents, and the tidbits that boys will pick up from various media—that sex is private, pleasurable, guilt provoking, exciting, and phallocentric, and that orgasm is the goal toward which sexual experience is oriented.

The articles in this section explore how male sexualities express the issues of masculinity. Michael Messner describes how he "became" 100 percent straight, and M. Rochlin's questionnaire humorously challenges us to question the normative elements of heterosexuality. Robert Jensen reopens the debate about whether men's consumption of pornography fuels misogyny and inspires rape and violence. Chong-suk Han suggests that racial and ethnic stereotypes remain fully operative in the world of gay male sexuality. Finally, Julia O'Connell Davidson and Jacqueline Sanchez Taylor examine the recent phenomenon of sex tourism and raise important questions about masculinity on the one hand and global sex trafficking, globalization, and consumer culture on the other.

THINK AGAIN (David John Attyah and S. A. Bachman) 1998–1999

Michael A. Messner

Becoming 100 Percent Straight

In 1995, as part of my job as the President of the North American Society for the Sociology of Sport, I needed to prepare an hour-long presidential address for the annual meeting of some 200 people. This presented a challenge to me: how might I say something to my colleagues that was interesting, at least somewhat original, and, above all, not boring. Students may think that their professors are especially dull in the classroom but, believe me, we are usually much worse at professional meetings. For some reason, many of us who are able to speak to our classroom students in a relaxed manner, using relatively jargon free language, seem to become robots, dryly reading our papers—packed with impressively unclear jargon—to our yawning colleagues.

Since I desperately wanted to avoid putting 200 sport studies scholars to sleep, I decided to deliver a talk which I entitled "Studying up on sex." The title, which certainly did get my colleagues' attention, was intended as a play on words, a double entendre. "Studying up" has one generally recognizable colloquial meaning, but in sociology it has another. It refers to studying "up" in the power structure. Sociologists have perhaps most often studied "down"—studying the poor, the blue- or pink-collar workers, the "nuts, sluts and perverts," the incarcerated. The idea of "studying up" rarely occurs to sociologists unless and until we live in a time when those who are

"down" have organized movements that challenge the institutional privileges of elites. For example, in the wake of labor movements, some sociologists like C. Wright Mills studied up on corporate elites. Recently, in the wake of racial and ethnic civil rights movements, some scholars like Ruth Frankenberg have begun to study the social meanings of "whiteness." Much of my research, inspired by feminism, has involved a studying up on the social construction of masculinity in sport. Studying up, in these cases, has raised some fascinating new and important questions about the workings of power in society.

However, I realized that when it comes to understanding the social and interpersonal dynamics of sexual orientation in sport we have barely begun to scratch the surface of a very complex issue. Although sport studies have benefited from the work of scholars such as Helen Lenskyj (1986, 1997), Brian Pronger (1990), and others who have delineated the experiences of lesbians and gay men in sports, there has been very little extension of their insights into a consideration of the social construction of heterosexuality in sport. In sport, just as in the larger society, we seem obsessed with asking "how do people become gay?" Imbedded in this question is the assumption that people who identify as heterosexual, or "straight," require no explanation, since they are simply acting out the "natural" or "normal" sexual orientation. We seem to be saying that the "sexual deviants" require explanation, while the experience of heterosexuals, because we are considered normal, seems to require no critical examination or discussion. But I knew that a closer look at the development of sexual orientation or sexual identity reveals an extremely complex process. I decided to challenge myself and my colleagues by arguing that although we have begun to "study up" on corporate elites in sport, on whiteness, on masculinity, it is now time to extend that by studying up on heterosexuality.

But in the absence of systematic research on this topic, where could I start? How could I explore, raise questions about, and begin to illuminate the social construction of heterosexuality for my colleagues? Fortunately, for the previous two years I had been working with a group of five men (three of whom identified as heterosexual, two as gay) mutually to explore our own biographies in terms of the earlier bodily experiences that helped to shape our gender and sexual identities. We modeled our project after that of a German group of feminist women, led by Frigga Haug, who created a research method which they call "memory work." In short, the women would mutually choose a body part, such as "hair," and each would then write a short story based on a particularly salient childhood memory that related to their hair (for example, being forced by parents to cut one's hair, deciding to straighten one's curly hair in order to look more like other girls, etc.). Then the group would read all of the stories and discuss them one by one in the hope of gaining a more general understanding of, and raising new questions about, the social construction of "femininity." What resulted from this project was a fascinating book called *Female Sexualization* (Haug 1987), which my men's group used as the inspiration for our project.

As a research method, memory work is anything but conventional. Many sociologists would argue that this is not really a "research method" at all. The information that emerges from the project cannot be used very confidently as a generalizable "truth," and in this sort of project the researcher is simultaneously part of what is being studied. How, my more scientifically oriented colleagues might ask, is the researcher to maintain his or her objectivity? My answer is that in this kind of project objectivity is not the point. In fact,

the strength of this sort of research is the depth of understanding that might be gained through a systematic group analysis of one's experience, one's subjective orientation to social processes. A clear understanding of the subjective aspect of social life—one's bodily feelings, emotions, and reactions to others—is an invaluable window that allows us to see and ask new sociological questions about group interaction and social structure. In short, group memory work can provide an important, productive, and fascinating insight on social reality, though not a complete (or completely reliable) picture.

As I pondered the lack of existing research on the social construction of heterosexuality in sport, I decided to draw on one of my own stories from my memory work in the men's group. Some of my most salient memories of embodiment are sports memories. I grew up as the son of a high school coach, and I eventually played point guard on my dad's team. In what follows, I juxtapose my story with that of a gay former Olympic athlete, Tom Waddell, whom I had interviewed several years earlier for a book on the lives of male athletes (Messner and Sabo 1994).

Many years ago I read some psychological studies that argued that even for self-identified heterosexuals it is a natural part of their development to have gone through "bisexual" or even "homosexual" stages of life. When I read this, it seemed theoretically reasonable, but did not ring true in my experience. I have always been, I told myself, 100 percent heterosexual! The group process of analyzing my own autobiographical stories challenged the concept I had developed of myself, and also shed light on the way in which the institutional context of sport provided a context for the development of my definition of myself as "100 percent straight." Here is one of the stories:

> When I was in the 9th grade, I played on a "D" basketball team, set up especially for the smallest of high school boys. Indeed, though I was pudgy with baby fat, I was a short 5'2", still pre-pubescent with no facial hair and a high

voice that I artificially tried to lower. The first day of practice, I was immediately attracted to a boy I'll call Timmy, because he looked like the boy who played in the *Lassie* TV show. Timmy was short, with a high voice, like me. And like me, he had no facial hair yet. Unlike me, he was very skinny. I liked Timmy right away, and soon we were together a lot. I noticed things about him that I didn't notice about other boys: he said some words a certain way, and it gave me pleasure to try to talk like him. I remember liking the way the light hit his boyish, nearly hairless body. I thought about him when we weren't together. He was in the school band, and at the football games, I'd squint to see where he was in the mass of uniforms. In short, though I wasn't conscious of it at the time, I was infatuated with Timmy—I had a crush on him. Later that basketball season, I decided—for no reason that I could really articulate then—that I hated Timmy. I aggressively rejected him, began to make fun of him around other boys. He was, we all agreed, a geek. He was a faggot.

Three years later, Timmy and I were both on the varsity basketball team, but had hardly spoken a word to each other since we were freshman. Both of us now had lower voices, had grown to around six feet tall, and we both shaved, at least a bit. But Timmy was a skinny, somewhat stigmatized reserve on the team, while I was the team captain and starting point guard. But I wasn't so happy or secure about this. I'd always dreamed of dominating games, of being the hero. Halfway through my senior season, however, it became clear that I was not a star, and I figured I knew why. I was not aggressive enough.

I had always liked the beauty of the fast break, the perfectly executed pick and roll play between two players, and especially the long twenty-foot shot that touched nothing but the bottom of the net. But I hated and feared the sometimes brutal contact under the basket. In fact, I stayed away from the rough fights for rebounds and was mostly a perimeter player, relying on my long shots or my passes to more aggressive teammates under the basket. But now it became apparent to me that time was running out in my quest for greatness: I needed to change my game, and fast. I decided one day before practice that I was gonna get aggressive. While practicing one of our standard plays, I passed the ball to a teammate, and then ran to the spot at which I was to set a pick on a defender. I knew that one could sometimes get away with setting a face-up screen on a player, and then as he makes contact with you, roll your back to him and plant your elbow hard in his stomach. The beauty of this move is that your own body "roll" makes the elbow look like an accident. So I decided to try this move. I approached the defensive player, Timmy, rolled, and planted my elbow deeply into his solar plexus. Air exploded audibly from Timmy's mouth, and he crumbled to the floor momentarily.

Play went on as though nothing has happened, but I felt bad about it. Rather than making me feel better, it made me feel guilty and weak. I had to admit to myself why I'd chosen Timmy as the target against whom to test out my new aggression. He was the skinniest and weakest player on the team.

At the time, I hardly thought about these incidents, other than to try to brush them off as incidents that made me feel extremely uncomfortable. Years later, I can now interrogate this as a sexual story, and as a gender story unfolding within the context of the heterosexualized and masculinized institution of sport. Examining my story in light of research conducted by Alfred Kinsey a half-century ago, I can recognize in myself what Kinsey saw as a very common fluidity and changeability of sexual desire over the life course. Put simply, Kinsey found that large numbers of adult, "heterosexual" men had previously, as adolescents and young adults, experienced sexual desire for males. A surprisingly large number of these men had experienced sexual contact to the point of orgasm with other males during adolescence or early adulthood. Similarly, my story invited me to consider what is commonly called the "Freudian theory of bisexuality." Sigmund Freud shocked the post-Victorian world by suggesting that all people go through a stage, early in life, when they are attracted to people of the same sex.[1] Adult experiences, Freud argued, eventually led most people to shift their sexual desire to what he called an appropriate "love object"—a person of the opposite sex. I also considered my experience in light of what lesbian feminist author Adrienne Rich called the institution of compulsory heterosexuality. Perhaps the extremely high levels of homophobia that are often endemic in boys' and men's organized sports led me to deny and repress my own homoerotic desire through a direct and overt rejection of Timmy, through homophobic banter with male peers, and the resultant stigmatization of the feminized Timmy. Eventually I considered my experience in the light of what radical theorist Herbert Marcuse called the sublimation of homoerotic desire into an aggressive, violent act as serving to construct a clear line of demarcation between self and other. Sublimation, according to Marcuse, involved the driving underground, into the unconscious, of sexual desires that might appear dangerous due to their socially stigmatized status. But sublimation involves more than simple repression into the unconscious. It involves a transformation of sexual desire into something else—often into aggressive and violent acting out toward others. These acts clarify the boundaries between oneself and others and therefore lessen any anxieties that might be attached to the repressed homoerotic desire.

Importantly, in our analysis of my story, the memory group went beyond simply discussing the events in psychological terms. The story did perhaps suggest some deep psychological processes at work, but it also revealed the importance of social context—in this case, the context of the athletic team. In short, my rejection of Timmy and the joining with teammates to stigmatize him in ninth grade stands as an example of what sociologist R. W. Connell calls a moment of engagement with hegemonic masculinity, where I actively took up the male group's task of constructing heterosexual/masculine identities in the context of sport. The elbow in Timmy's gut three years later can be seen as a punctuation mark that

occurred precisely because of my fears that I might be failing in this goal.

It is helpful, I think, to compare my story with gay and lesbian "coming out" stories in sport. Though we have a few lesbian and bisexual coming out stories among women athletes, there are very few from gay males. Tom Waddell, who as a closeted gay man finished sixth in the decathlon in the 1968 Olympics, later came out and started the Gay Games, an athletic and cultural festival that draws tens of thousands of people every four years. When I interviewed Tom Waddell over a decade ago about his sexual identity and athletic career, he made it quite clear that for many years sports was his closet:

> When I was a kid, I was tall for my age, and was very thin and very strong. And I was usually faster than most other people. But I discovered rather early that I liked gymnastics and I liked dance. I was very interested in being a ballet dancer . . . [but] something became obvious to me right away—that male ballet dancers were effeminate, that they were what most people would call faggots. And I thought I just couldn't handle that . . . I was totally closeted and very concerned about being male. This was the fifties, a terrible time to live, and everything was stacked against me. Anyway, I realized that I had to do something to protect my image of myself as a male—because at that time homosexuals were thought of primarily as men who wanted to be women. And so I threw myself into athletics—I played football, gymnastics, track and field . . . I was a jock—that's how I was viewed, and I was comfortable with that.

Tom Waddell was fully conscious of entering sports and constructing a masculine/heterosexual athletic identity precisely because he feared being revealed as gay. It was clear to him, in the context of the 1950s, that being known as gay would undercut his claims to the status of manhood. Thus, though he described the athletic closet as "hot and stifling," he remained there until several years after his athletic retirement. He even knowingly played along with locker room discussions about sex and women as part of his "cover."

> I wanted to be viewed as male, otherwise I would be a dancer today. I wanted the male, macho image of an athlete. So I was protected by a very hard shell. I was clearly aware of what I was doing . . . I often felt compelled to go along with a lot of locker room garbage because I wanted that image—and I know a lot of others who did too.

Like my story, Waddell's points to the importance of the athletic institution as a context in which peers mutually construct and reconstruct narrow definitions of masculinity. Heterosexuality is considered to be a rock-solid foundation of this concept of masculinity. But unlike my story, Waddell's may invoke a dramaturgical analysis.[2] He seemed to be consciously "acting" to control and regulate others' perceptions of him by constructing a public "front stage" persona that differed radically from what he believed to be his "true" inner self. My story, in contrast, suggests a deeper, less consciously strategic repression of my homoerotic attraction. Most likely, I was aware on some level of the dangers of such feelings, and was escaping the risks, disgrace, and rejection that would likely result from being different. For Waddell, the decision to construct his identity largely within sport was to step into a fiercely heterosexual/masculine closet that would hide what he saw as his "true" identity. In contrast, I was not so much stepping into a "closet" that would hide my identity; rather, I was stepping out into an entire world of heterosexual privilege. My story also suggests how a threat to the promised privileges of hegemonic masculinity—my failure as an athlete—might trigger a momentary sexual panic that can lay bare the constructedness, indeed, the instability of the heterosexual/masculine identity.

In either case, Waddell's or mine, we can see how, as young male athletes, heterosexual masculinity was not something we "were," but something we were doing. It is significant, I think, that although each of us was "doing heterosexuality,"

neither of us was actually "having sex" with women (though one of us desperately wanted to). This underscores a point made by some recent theorists that heterosexuality should not be thought of simply as sexual acts between women and men. Rather, heterosexuality is a constructed identity, a performance, and an institution that is not necessarily linked to sexual acts. Though for one of us it was more conscious than for the other, we were both "doing heterosexuality" as an ongoing practice through which we sought to do two things:

- avoid stigma, embarrassment, ostracism, or perhaps worse if we were even suspected of being gay;
- link ourselves into systems of power, status, and privilege that appear to be the birthright of "real men" (i.e., males who are able to compete successfully with other males in sport, work, and sexual relations with women).

In other words, each of us actively scripted our own sexual and gender performances, but these scripts were constructed within the constraints of a socially organized (institutionalized) system of power and pleasure.

Questions for Future Research

As I prepared to tell this sexual story publicly to my colleagues at the sport studies conference, I felt extremely nervous. Part of the nervousness was due to the fact that I knew some of them would object to my claim that telling personal stories can be a source of sociological insights. But a larger part of the reason for my nervousness was due to the fact that I was revealing something very personal about my sexuality in such a public way. Most of us are not accustomed to doing this, especially in the context of a professional conference. But I had learned long ago, especially from feminist women scholars, and from gay and lesbian scholars, that biography is linked to history. Part of "normal" academic discourse has been to hide "the personal" (including the fact that the researchers are themselves people with values, feelings, and yes, biases) behind a carefully constructed facade of "objectivity." Rather than trying to hide or be ashamed of one's subjective experience of the world, I was challenging myself to draw on my experience of the world as a resource. Not that I should trust my experience as the final word on "reality." White, heterosexual males like me have made the mistake for centuries of calling their own experience "objectivity," and then punishing anyone who does not share their worldview by casting them as "deviant." Instead, I hope to use my experience as an example of how those of us who are in dominant sexual/racial/gender/class categories can get a new perspective on the "constructedness" of our identities by juxtaposing our subjective experiences against the recently emerging worldviews of gay men and lesbians, women, and people of color.

Finally, I want to stress that in juxtaposition neither my own nor Tom Waddell's story sheds much light on the question of why some individuals "become gay" while others "become" heterosexual or bisexual. Instead, I should like to suggest that this is a dead-end question, and that there are far more important and interesting questions to be asked:

- How has heterosexuality, as an institution and as an enforced group practice, constrained and limited all of us—gay, straight, and bi?
- How has the institution of sport been an especially salient institution for the social construction of heterosexual masculinity?
- Why is it that when men play sports they are almost always automatically granted masculine status, and thus assumed to be heterosexual, while when women play sports, questions

are raised about their "femininity" and sexual orientation?

These kinds of questions aim us toward an analysis of the working of power within institutions—including the ways that these workings of power shape and constrain our identities and relationships—and point us toward imagining alternative social arrangements that are less constraining for everyone.

Notes

1. The fluidity and changeability of sexual desire over the life course is now more obvious in evidence from prison and military populations, and single-sex boarding schools. The theory of bisexuality is evident, for example, in childhood crushes on same-sex primary schoolteachers.

2. Dramaturgical analysis, associated with Erving Goffman, uses the theater and performance to develop an analogy with everyday life.

References

Haug, Frigga (1987) *Female Sexualization: A Collective Work of Memory*, London: Verso.

Lenskyj, Helen (1986) *Out of Bounds: Women, Sport and Sexuality*, Toronto: Women's Press.

———. (1997) "No fear? Lesbians in sport and physical education," *Women in Sport and Physical Activity Journal* 6(2): 7–22.

Messner, Michael A. (1992) *Power at Play: Sports and the Problem of Masculinity*, Boston: Beacon Press.

———. (1994) "Gay athletes and the Gay Games: An interview with Tom Waddell," in M. A. Messner and D. F. Sabo (eds), *Sex, Violence and Power in Sports: Rethinking Masculinity*, Freedom, CA: The Crossing Press, pp. 113–119.

Pronger, Brian (1990) *The Arena of Masculinity: Sports, Homosexuality, and the Meaning of Sex*, New York: St. Martin's Press.

M. Rochlin

The Heterosexual Questionnaire

1. What do you think caused your heterosexuality?

2. When and how did you decide you were a heterosexual?

3. Is it possible that your heterosexuality is just a phase you may grow out of?

4. Is it possible that your heterosexuality stems from a neurotic fear of others of the same sex?

5. If you have never slept with a person of the same sex, is it possible that all you need is a good gay lover?

6. Do your parents know that you are straight? Do your friends and/or roommate(s) know? How did they react?

7. Why do you insist on flaunting your heterosexuality? Can't you just be who you are and keep it quiet?

8. Why do heterosexuals place so much emphasis on sex?

9. Why do heterosexuals feel compelled to seduce others into their lifestyle?

10. A disproportionate majority of child molesters are heterosexual. Do you consider it safe to expose children to heterosexual teachers?

11. Just what do men and women *do* in bed together? How can they truly know how to please each other, being so anatomically different?

12. With all the societal support marriage receives, the divorce rate is spiraling. Why are there so few stable relationships among heterosexuals?

13. Statistics show that lesbians have the lowest incidence of sexually transmitted diseases. Is it really safe for a woman to maintain a heterosexual lifestyle and run the risk of disease and pregnancy?

14. How can you become a whole person if you limit yourself to compulsive, exclusive heterosexuality?

15. Considering the menace of overpopulation, how could the human race survive if everyone were heterosexual?

16. Could you trust a heterosexual therapist to be objective? Don't you feel s/he might be inclined to influence you in the direction of her/his own leanings?

17. There seem to be very few happy heterosexuals. Techniques have been developed that might enable you to change if you really want to. Have you considered trying aversion therapy?

18. Would you want your child to be heterosexual, knowing the problems that s/he would face?

Robert Jensen

A Pornographic World [What Is Normal?]

My Story

I am a normal guy in a world in which no guy is really normal. I was raised in a conventional household (two parents, three siblings, one dog) in a part of the United States not known for radical thinking or countercultural lifestyles (Fargo, North Dakota). There I was exposed to the standard US ideology of male dominance, white supremacy, the inherent superiority of capitalism, and America's role as the moral exemplar of the world. I was raised to be a nice white guy who took his place in the world, worked hard, and didn't complain too much.

At the same time, there are aspects of my biography that are not so normal, such as experiences of abuse early in my life. But it turns out, when you start talking to guys, such things happened to lots of us. My sexual profile also might, at first glance, seem outside the norm; I have had sexual relationships with men and women, though most of my life has been lived as a heterosexual. But it turns out that such sexual ambiguity isn't so unusual for lots of men either.

As a child growing up, until my late teens, I typically was the shortest boy in my class and painfully thin. As a small, "faggy" kid, I knew I was an easy target. So, I spent a lot of energy trying not to appear to be homosexual. And it turns out that a lot of the men of my generation whom I have talked to over the years—no matter how

macho they appeared on the surface—worried at some point about being tagged as gay when they were young.

Even with my lack of physical ability, I managed to be minimally competent in sports and played on baseball and basketball teams through junior high. Emotionally, I was what's typically called a "sensitive child," but I managed to fake my way through the routine interactions with other boys without getting beaten up. Other boys were not so lucky. I remember one in particular in junior high who endured endless cruelty for being a gangly, socially awkward kid. When other boys teased and attacked him, I stepped aside. I didn't actively participate in that abuse, but I never defended the boy; my fear of being similarly targeted kept me silent. As I write this, 35 years later, I can recall how deeply I empathized with his suffering, and how terrified I was of those boys turning on me.

I have never felt like a "real man," but it turns out that almost no man I know feels much confidence in that realm; even those who fit the specifications more closely rarely feel like they are fulfilling their masculine obligations. So, I wasn't normal, and at the same time I was well within the norm. Most important, I was raised to be normal. I was socialized to be a man, even if I lacked some of the physical or emotional attributes to fill the role very well. And part of that socialization involved the use of pornography.

Pornography Use

I was born in 1958, in the post-*Playboy* world. My first recollection of viewing sexual material is from early grade school, when one of the boys in my school got his hands on a biker magazine that had pictures of women with exposed breasts. I have no recollection of the specific images but do retain a clear memory of gathering in the backyard of a neighborhood boy's house to look at the magazine, which we had hidden under a leaf pile. It was at about the same time I began "playing doctor," exploring bodies with other boys and girls in the neighborhood. So, as I was consciously becoming aware of sexuality, my first recognizable cultural lesson on the subject came in a male-bonding ritual around men's use of an objectified woman, who existed only to provide sexual excitement for us.

[A footnote: This memory is so powerful that every time I see a poster called "Celebrate the Whole Boy" I am reminded of it. The picture on the poster is of five grade-school boys after football practice in the park as they listen to one of the boys playing the violin. In the picture it is fall, with leaves on the ground. Three of the boys are kneeling around the violin case, with the other two standing. The obvious irony is that a poster with a healthy message—that the culture's narrow conception of masculinity limits boys' development and that we should think of all the ways to nurture them—reminds me of the patriarchal training it is critiquing.]

That grade-school experience is the first recollection I have of what Sheila Jeffreys calls "the idea of prostitution," the notion that men can buy women's sexuality in various forms. Rather than seeing men's control and use of women for sex as natural and stemming from a biological imperative, Jeffreys argues that such behavior is socially constructed. "The idea of prostitution has to exist in a man's head first if he is to consider using a woman that way," she writes. "A necessary component of this idea is that it will be sexually exciting to so use a woman."[1]

So, let's mark my introduction into the idea of prostitution at age seven, gathered around the leaf pile, one of a group of boys experiencing our emerging sexuality in an act of male dominance, the ideological assertion of dominance made into a material reality in a picture. That magazine would decay by winter but, in those few months of fall, it taught us something about what it meant to be a man.

The story goes downhill from there.

In the 1960s and 70s, as I went through public school, the main medium for pornography was the magazine, and in my circle of friends there was a reasonably steady supply of them, tucked away under beds, shoved in the back of closets, and carefully hidden under piles of leaves. Some were pilfered from relatives—we all knew where dads and big brothers hid their stash. Others were retrieved from dumpsters; we knew when stores that sold pornography threw away out-of-date stock. Sometimes we looked at them in groups, sometimes alone.

At the end of junior high school and my first year of high school, I was hanging out with a group of guys who had learned the art of sneaking into movie theaters without paying. One of our targets was the Broadway Theater in Fargo, my hometown's only "dirty movie theater," where I saw parts of several hardcore pornographic films as a teenager. At the time I had no sexual experience beyond a few sessions of sexual experimentation with other kids (boys and girls) in grade school, and I really didn't understand much of what was happening on the screen, though I was transfixed by the intensity of my sexual reaction. At a conventional movie theater we sneaked in to see *Last Tango in Paris*, to which I had the same reaction and of which I understood even less.

[Another footnote: In one of those episodes at the Broadway, three of us approached the rear door in the alley with the intention of sneaking in. At the last minute, one of the other boys backed out, claiming to be nervous. But he encouraged us to go ahead, which we did. Once in the theater, we were extremely nervous, desperately afraid of being caught. A few minutes into the film, my companion thought he heard an usher coming toward us and decided to bolt for the exit, with me a few steps behind. He hit the exit door at full speed and met some resistance, but pushed it open and tumbled into the alley, falling over garbage cans. The friend who had stayed behind had dragged the cans in front of the door, assuming that when we tried to exit, we would find it blocked and get scared. Although we were angry at him in the moment, it never occurred to me that such a prank was quite a strange thing to do to a friend. Such cruelty was simply part of growing up male.]

In college, after becoming legally able to enter adult bookstores and theaters, I made occasional visits. Because there was only one such bookstore in Fargo and we risked being seen by friends or relatives while entering or leaving (not to mention while inside), most of those forays took place during trips to Minneapolis, again sometimes with friends and sometimes alone. While in college I also saw a few X-rated movies with friends (both all-male and mixed-gender groups), who treated the outings as campy fun, and I went to a couple of those movies on my own.

[One last footnote: One of my friends from college with whom I made a couple of those trips was a man with whom I had a sexual experience after we had graduated. He was among the most militantly heterosexual men I have ever known and, to the best of my knowledge, did not have a secret gay life. That experience is a reminder that the way most men present themselves to the world in sexual terms does not reflect the complexity of our lives, and we rarely have places to talk openly about that experience. It's one of the most obvious ways in which heterosexism/homophobia limits all men.]

In my 20s, as a working professional, I had a complex relationship to pornography. I typically did not purchase pornography to use at home, although through the years I occasionally bought magazines such as *Playboy* and *Penthouse*. I never showed pornography to women with whom I was involved, with the exception of one trip to an adult theater with a woman in college. I have never made homemade pornography or recorded sexual activity.

Throughout my 20s I would sometimes visit the stores or theaters, though I was increasingly uncomfortable using the material, I had no political critique at that point, nor did I have moral qualms about it; I was then, and remain today, a secular person and had no theological conflicts about the subject. My hesitations were emotional—it just felt wrong. I fell into what I later learned was a common pattern: I would feel intense sexual excitement, masturbate, and immediately feel a sense of shame. That experience would typically lead to a decision to stop using pornography, which would last for some weeks or months. But eventually I would find myself back in a bookstore or theater.

Pornographic Fallout

That pattern continued until I was about 30 years old, when I started graduate school and began studying the feminist critique of pornography. Since then, I have used pornography only in the course of four research projects on the content of video and internet pornography.

When people ask me the last time I used pornography—not as a researcher but as a consumer—my answer is "yesterday." By that, I don't mean that I watched a pornographic film yesterday, but that for those of us with a history of "normal" pornography use as children and young adults, quitting pornography doesn't necessarily mean we are pornography-free. My sexual imagination was in part shaped by the use of pornography. I still have in my head vivid recollections of specific scenes in pornographic films I saw 25 years ago. To the degree possible, I try to eliminate those images when I am engaging in sexual activity today (whether alone or with my partner), and I think I'm pretty successful at it. The longer I'm away from pornography, the easier it gets. But the key term is "to the degree possible."

Even with the advances in neuroscience, we really don't know all that much about human memory, consciousness, and behavior. What is pretty clear is that what goes on in our heads and bodies is far more complex than we can ever fully understand. It would not be surprising if the images and ideas that we encounter during the act of achieving orgasm—especially early in our development—would have a powerful influence on us, one that might last in various ways throughout our lives.

What goes on in my body sexually is the result of not just what I think and feel in the moment, but a lifetime of training and experience. I wish I could neatly segregate and eliminate not only the effects of my past pornography use but the effects of all the ugly sexist training I have received in my life about sexuality. I wish I could wall myself off from the sexist messages and images that are all around me today. I wish I could find a way to create a space untouched by those forces in which I could live.

But if I am to be honest, I have to admit something that is painful to face: I still struggle against those forces. I have to work to bracket out of my mind—to the degree possible—those images. I have to work to remember that I can deepen my own experience of intimacy and sexuality only when I let go of those years of training in how to dominate.

It's hard to be honest about these things, because so much of what lives within us is rooted in that domination/subordination dynamic. But it's a good rule of thumb that the things that are difficult are the most important to confront. That's easy to say but hard to practice.

The Culture's Story

When I was born in 1958, the cultural conversation on pornography took place largely within a framework of moral assertions. The obscenity law that regulated sexual material was typically defended as necessary because such uses of sex were immoral, while defenders of pornography argued that individuals should be free to use such material because there was no harm to others and the state should not make moral decisions for

people. The anti-pornography view was articulated mostly by conservative and religious people; liberals and secular people dominated the defense of pornography.

Beginning in the late 1970s, feminist anti-violence activists began to focus on the connections between men's violence against women and mass media, especially pornography. The framework for that critique was political; feminists were not arguing that any particular expression of sexuality was immoral. Instead, they focused on the political—on differences in power and men's subordination of women, and the concrete harms that followed.

By the mid-1990s, the feminist critique of pornography mostly had been pushed out of the public discussion and a new economic framework emerged. Journalists began writing routinely about pornography as an ordinary business that raised no particular moral or political concerns. These stories sometimes mentioned opposition to the industry, but simply as one aspect of doing business that pornographers had to cope with. Neither the conservative/religious objections to pornography[2] nor the feminist critique[3] has disappeared, but the shift in the framework—the predominant way in which the culture engages pornography—is revealing. Opposition to pornography in the United States, rooted either in conservative religious faith or feminist politics, must articulate that position in a society that largely takes pornography as an uncontroversial part of contemporary culture. This is the normalization or mainstreaming of pornography.

I had been observing that normalization trend for two decades when I went for the first time, in January 2005, to the Adult Entertainment Expo sponsored by *Adult Video News,* the preeminent trade magazine of the pornography industry. Although I had been studying the industry for years, I had always avoided going to the AVN convention, which is held in Las Vegas. When I went in 2005 as part of the crew for a documentary on the industry, I finally understood why I had always instinctively stayed away.

Las Vegas

My job at the AEE was to move around on the convention floor with the film's director, Miguel Picker, and talk to the pornography producers, performers, and fans about why they make, distribute, and consume sexually explicit media. As we roamed the huge Sands Expo and Convention Center, which accommodated about 300 booths and thousands of people a day, rock music pulsated from multiple directions. There were photos of naked women everywhere, video screens running porn loops scattered throughout the hall, display tables of dildos and sex dolls. And around every corner were performers in various states of undress, signing posters and posing for pictures. Flashes popped constantly as fans photographed their favorite stars.

At the end of the first day of shooting, Miguel and I were tired. We had spent the day surrounded by images of women being presented and penetrated for the sexual pleasure of men. I had listened to young men tell me that pornography had taught them a lot about what women really want sexually. I had listened to a pornography producer tell me that he thinks anal sex is popular in pornography because men like to think about fucking their wives and girlfriends in the ass to pay them back for being bitchy. And I interviewed the producer who takes great pride that his Gag Factor series was the first to feature exclusively aggressive "throat fucking."

We walked silently from the convention center to the hotel, until I finally said, "I need a drink."

I don't want to feign naïveté. I wasn't particularly shocked by anything I saw that day. There was no one thing I learned on the convention floor that surprised me, nothing anyone said that was really that new to me. I had been working on the issue for more than 15 years at that point; it would have been hard for me to find anything at AEE shocking.

We stopped at the nearest hotel bar (which didn't take long, given how many bars there are in a Las Vegas hotel). I sat down with a glass of wine, and Miguel and I started to talk, searching for some way to articulate what we had just experienced, what we felt. I struggled to hold back tears, and then finally stopped struggling.

I hadn't had some sort of epiphany about the meaning of pornography. It's just that in that moment, the reality of the industry—of the products the industry creates and the way in which they are used—all came crashing down on me. My defenses were inadequate to combat a simple fact: The pornographers had won. The feminist arguments about justice and the harms of pornography had lost. The pornographers not only are thriving, but are more mainstream and normalized than ever. They can fill up a Las Vegas convention center, with the dominant culture paying no more notice than it would to the annual boat show.

My tears at that moment were for myself, because I realized in a more visceral way than ever that the pornographers had won and are helping to construct a world that is not only dangerous for women and children, but also one in which I have fewer and fewer places to turn as a man. Fewer places to walk and talk and breathe that haven't been colonized and pornographized. As I sat there, all I could say to Miguel was, "I don't want to live in this world."

I think Miguel didn't quite know what to make of my reaction. He was nice to me, but he must have thought I was going a bit over the top. I don't blame him; I was a bit over the top. After all, we were there to make a documentary film about the industry, not live out a melodrama about my angst in a Las Vegas hotel bar. The next day Miguel and I hit the convention floor again. At the end of that day, as we walked away, I made the same request. We sat at the same bar. I had another glass of wine and cried again. I think Miguel was glad it was the last day. So was I.

Two days after we left Las Vegas, Miguel called me from New York. This time he was the one crying. He told me that he had just come to his editing studio and had put on some music that he finds particularly beautiful, and then the floodgates opened. "I understand what you meant in the bar," he said, speaking through his own tears.

I tell this story not to highlight the sensitivity of two new-age men. Miguel actually is a sensitive person, though not very new age. I'm not new age, and I don't feel particularly sensitive these days. I often feel harsh and angry. Instead, I tell the story to remind myself that I am alive, that I haven't given up, that I still feel.

I tell the story to remind myself that I'm not alone in that struggle. In a world that trains men to struggle with each other for dominance and keep their emotional distance from each other, Miguel and I could connect. He's a musician and artist from Chile; I'm a journalist and professor from North Dakota. On the surface, we don't have much in common, except our humanity.

I have to remind myself of those things because in the short term, things are grim. The feminist critique that could help this culture transcend its current crisis—on every level, from the intimate to the global—has been attacked and marginalized, and the feminists with the courage to take the critique to the public have been demonized and insulted. That's the short term. In the long term, I believe human society will move out of patriarchy and into some other organizing principle that will emerge through struggle. The problem is, as the economist John Maynard Keynes put it, in the long run we're all dead.

Hope in the long run is rational only when we are willing to face difficult analyses and action in the short term.

Notes

1. Sheila Jeffreys, *The Idea of Prostitution* (North Melbourne, Australia: Spinifex, 1997), 3.

2. See Morality in Media, http://www.morality inmedia.org/.

3. See National Feminist Antipornography Movement, http://feministantipornographymovement.org/.

Chong-suk Han

They Don't Want to Cruise Your Type: Gay Men of Color and the Racial Politics of Exclusion

Introduction

Thirty minutes after the posted starting time, men, and a handful of women, continue to wander into the second floor auditorium of a long neglected performance hall in the center of the city's gayborhood. Like many things gay, the scheduled forum on race, sponsored by one of the largest gay-identified organization in the city, begins on gay time. As the audible levels of conversations begin to wane, organizers urge the audience of some 200 men, and a handful of women, to take their seats so we can all begin. Within minutes, a representative of the host agency lays out the ground rules of discussion—most noticeably that we will not, given the limited time, try to define racism while quickly offering that, 'everyone is capable of racism', a definition that many men of color in the audience would, if given the chance, vehemently dispute. Perhaps it wouldn't have been such an issue if members of the community who were invited to help plan the forum hadn't spent weeks arguing for the need to discuss racism in the gay community, rather than focus solely on race. Or perhaps it wouldn't have been such a slight if they were asked to provide an alternative definition of racism, particularly who is able, within the larger social structure, to practise it rather than being

left with only one definition of it. In fact, the title 'Race Forum' was specifically chosen, against the suggestions offered by members of the community, so that the focus could be on 'race' rather than the trickier topic of 'racism'.

'It's like they didn't hear a thing', a member of the 'community' told me immediately after the announcement. 'Why did we go to the meetings? It's like we weren't even there. We might as well be invisible.' Though flabbergasted, he also told me that, 'It's no surprise'. It seems that for this member of the community, speaking up and being ignored has come to be a common occurrence. After all, being a gay man of color is to experience the unnerving feeling of being invited to a potluck while being told not to bring anything since nobody would be interested in what you bring, and then not being offered any food since you didn't bring anything anyway.

Looking around the audience, two things become immediately clear. First, the auditorium is noticeably empty given the tendency of other forums hosted by this agency to fill to capacity and then some. More importantly, the faces are overwhelmingly darker than those at other forums sponsored by this organization. One could conclude, if one were so inclined, that this forum on race was not as popular with many of the gay men who normally attend while bringing out other men who wouldn't normally attend events that would have a broader gay appeal. However, the composition of the audience reflects a larger picture of the broader gay community where issues of race and racism are often ignored.

From *Social Identities* 13(1) (January 2007), pp. 51–67. Reprinted by permission of the publisher (Taylor & Francis Ltd., http://www.tandf.co.uk/journals).

Looking around any gayborhood, something becomes blatantly clear. Within the queer spaces that have sprung up in once neglected and forgotten neighborhoods, inside the slick new storefronts and trendy restaurants, and on magazine covers—as well as between the covers for that matter— that are no longer covered in plain brown paper and kept behind the counter, gay America has given a whole new meaning to the term 'whitewash'.

We, as a collective, have rehabilitated homes in neglected neighborhoods. We've planted flowers, we've painted the walls, fixed old roofs, and generally have increased the 'value' of areas that were once in urban decline. Whitewash.

We've revived old storefronts, bringing a multitude of retail shops (and the accompanying tax base) to streets once reserved for activities outside the law—not that everything we do within our own houses, or behind the storefronts for that matter, are well within the comfortable boundaries of a legally sanctioned activity. Whitewash.

We've fought hard to counter the stereotypes so famous in mainstream culture of the nellie queens or the lecherous sex stalker and replace them with images that reflect the 'true' gay experience. Rather than accept the images thrown upon us by the mainstream press, we've given gay American a face we can all be proud of. Whitewash.

Whiteness in the gay community is everywhere, from what we see, what we experience, and more importantly, what we desire. The power of whiteness, of course, derives from appearing to be nothing in particular (Lipsitz, 1998). That is, whiteness is powerful precisely because it is everywhere but nowhere in particular. When we see whiteness, we process it as if it doesn't exist or that its existence is simply natural. We don't see it precisely because we see it constantly. It blends into the background and then becomes erased from scrutiny. And this whiteness is imposed from both outside and inside of the gay community. According to Allan Bérubé, the gay community is overwhelmingly portrayed in the heterosexual mind as being 'white and well-to-do'

(2001, p. 234). Media images now popular in television and film such as *Will and Grace, My Best Friend's Wedding, In and Out, Queer as Folks, Queer Eye for the Straight Guy*, etc. promote a monolithic image of the gay community as being overwhelmingly upper-middle class—if not simply rich—and white. For example, in the movie, *Boat Trip*, about the comic misadventures of two straight men booked on a gay cruise by a gay travel agent hell-bent on preserving the honor of his lover, all the gay men, with one exception, are white. The juxtaposition of Cuba Gooding Jr. as the protagonist who stumbles his way through a boat filled with hundreds of gay men, also works to mark racial boundaries. Gay men are white and the straight man is not. Clearly, in this movie, 'men of color' and 'gay' are mutually exclusive categories. While mass media will often use stereotypes to sell minority characters to majority audiences, the gay media are no less to blame for the promotion of the 'gay equals white' misconception. Even the most perfunctory glance through gay publications exposes the paucity of non-white gay images. It's almost as if no gay men of color exist outside of fantasy cruises to Jamaica, Puerto Rico, or the 'Orient'. And even then, they exist only to fulfill the sexual fantasies of gay white men. 'Exotic' vacations to far away places are marketed to rich white men and poor colored bodies are only another consumable product easily purchased with western dollars. As such, gay men of color, whether found within western borders or conveniently waiting for white arrival in the far off corners of the globe, are nothing more than commodities for consumption.

It's not just the media, both straight and gay, that robs gay men of color of equal representation, the gay 'community' is no less to blame. Gay organizations themselves promote and reinforce the whiteness of gay life. The gay movement that once embodied the ideals of liberation, freedom, and social justice quickly turned to the causes of promoting gay pride through visibility and lobbying efforts that forced established institutions—particularly media institutions—to re-examine mainstream heterosexist bias against gay men and women. Doing so, however, led to the unfortunate consequence of ignoring non-gay issues such as 'homelessness, unemployment, welfare, universal health care, union organizing, affirmative action, and abortion rights' (Bérubé, 2001, p. 235). Promoting gay issues meant promoting acceptance rather than liberation. To do so, gay activists adapted various whitening practices to sell gay America to the heartland of America by:

> *mirroring* the whiteness of men who run powerful institutions as a strategy for winning credibility, acceptance, and integration; *excluding* people of color from gay institutions; *selling* gay as white to raise money, make a profit, and gain economic power; and daily wearing the *pale protective coloring* that camouflages the unquestioned assumptions and unearned privileges of gay whiteness. (Bérubé, 2001, p. 246)

Unfortunately, this mirroring of the mainstream community to promote gay causes has meant ignoring the 'non-gay issues' that impact the lives of gay men and women of color as members of racial minority groups such as affirmative action, unemployment, educational access, etc. It has even ignored immigration debates, as is evident in a recent Advocate.com editorial which suggested that focusing on immigrant rights would take away from gay rights. What such arguments ignore is that many in the gay community are members of immigrant groups. As such, to be gay in America today is to be white. More specifically, it means to be white and well-to-do. This is obvious in the ways that gay organizations and businesses mark and market themselves to the larger community, both gay and straight. Gay publications tout the affluence of the gay community when fighting for advertising dollars. Non-profit organizations (NPO) and gay-identified businesses that serve a multi-racial clientele are marked as being raced and, in turn, mark themselves as such. For example, organizations such as Brother to Brother, Gay Asian Pacific Support Network, Hombres Latinos, etc. mark the racial borders of patronage. Gay businesses, too, mark these borders. Bars populated by non-white

clients exist merely to support white male fantasies about gay men of color are marked with appropriately fetishized names such as the Voodoo Lounge in Seattle, Papicock in New York, and Red Dragon in Los Angeles. The Blatino Bronx Factory not only marks the club as raced but also quite blatantly specifies which races they are marking. Yet gay-identified organizations with mostly, and sometimes exclusively, white clientele—both businesses and NPOs—are never marked in this way. In fact, they vehemently oppose such characterizations, arguing instead that they serve all gay people. It is never the 'Gay White Support/Social Organization', but rather, 'Gay Support/Social Organization'. In doing so, the implication is that they speak for all gay people, a claim they make while ignoring certain voices. Their concerns, those of largely gay white men, become the *de facto* concerns for gay men of color. As such, whiteness takes center stage and it becomes synonymous with gay where gay comes to mean white and white comes to mean gay.

Despite all of this, it would be a mistake to assume that whiteness is not actively maintained. Rather, the illusion of normalcy requires active maintenance of racial borders. 'White' doesn't become normal because it is so, it becomes normal because we make it so. More often than not, whiteness is maintained through active exclusion of those who are non-white. In this paper, I examine the forms of racism that are found in gay communities and show how race is implicated in the construction of gay identities. Particularly, I focus on subtle forms and blatant forms of racism that negate the existence of gay men of color and how racism affects the way we see gay men. In this way, I hope to add another dimension to Bérubé's theory about how 'gay' remains white. In addition, I examine the homophobia found in racial and ethnic communities to examine the further marginalization of gay men of color.

Of course, in discussing gay men of color, it is important to point out that this group includes people with vastly different backgrounds along every imaginable social delineation. Care should be taken when referencing the experiences of this group. At the same time, this essay is not about gay men of color as it is about racism in the larger gay community, as well as homophobia found elsewhere, and how that racism and homophobia, both subtle and overt, manifests itself. I'm not so much interested here in the values, beliefs, and cultures of gay men of color as I am with the discriminatory practices of gay white men and the institutions that they control. I'm certain that the racist discourse that justifies such behavior is uniquely modified to fit different racial/ethnic groups that are targeted. My interest is to point out that despite different constructions of race and ethnicity, the end results of exclusion and objectification are similar for racialized groups. As such, this paper should not be read as an exploration into the lives of gay men of color but to the practices of gay white men that work to marginalize the previous group.

Invisible . . . You Make Me Feel Invisible: Subtle Forms of Racism

Not surprisingly, allusions to invisibility are common in the writings and media productions created by gay men of color. For example, in *Tongues untied*, black film maker Marlon Riggs had this to say about San Francisco:

> I pretended not to notice the absence of black images in this new gay life, in bookstores, poster shops, film festivals, even my own fantasies. Something in Oz was amiss, but I tried not to notice. I was intent on my search for my reflection, love, affirmation, in eyes of blue, gray, green. Searching, I discovered something I didn't expect, something decades of determined assimilation cannot blind me to. In this great, gay Mecca, I was an invisible man. I had no shadow, no substance, no place, no history, no reflection. (Riggs, 1989)

Likewise, Joseph Beam (1986) in his work, *In the Life* wrote:

> Visibility is survival . . . It is possible to read thoroughly two or three consecutive issues of

the Advocate, the national biweekly gay newsmagazine, and never encounter, in the words or images, Black gay men . . . We ain't family. Very clearly, gay male means: White, middleclass, youthful, nautilized, and probably butch, there is no room for Black gay men within the confines of this gay pentagon. (quoted in Manalansan, 1996, p. 402)

Standing at the door of various gay bars, I've been asked, on several occasions, by doormen if I was aware that it was a gay bar. In one particular instance, one doorman added after I answered in the affirmative, 'You must really want a drink'. In these instances, unlike other instances of blatant racism that I discuss below, it just didn't occur to the doormen that being gay *and* Asian was within the realm of the possible. Following their logic, if gay men are white, non-white men must not be gay. As such, the non-white man entering this 'gay' establishment must obviously be in great need of libation rather than sexual encounter. In addition to lived experiences, this sense of invisibility is found in writings by gay Asian men as well. Song Cho writes:

> The pain of being a gay Asian, however, is not just the pain of direct discrimination but the pain of being negated again and again by a culture that doesn't acknowledge my presence . . . Not only did I have to deal with the question of sexual invisibility as a gay man, there was also the issue of racial invisibility. (Cho, 1998, p. 2)

Another writer describes his experiences at gay bathhouses in this way:

> When I go to the baths, I usually go home empty handed without even one guy having hit or making a pass at me . . . When I first started going to the baths, I could not understand why no one was interested in me. I would hang out for hours and hours and no one would give me a second look. What was more disheartening was the fact that I saw some weird combinations at the baths. Drop dead gorgeous white men would not even give me a second look, yet be with someone who (in my mind) was below average in the looks department . . . When I

came out, it never occurred to me that I would become invisible and undesirable and truly worthless in the eyes of so many gay men . . . Gay Asians are invisible to the gay white community. (Anonymous, n.d.)

At the same time that they are invisible, gay Asian men are also seen as being exotic, submissive fantasies for white men. However, being seen as exotic and submissive is yet another form of subtle racism where gay Asian men are not seen as individuals but as a consumable product for white male fantasy (Ayres, 1999).

Gay Native American men also felt this 'disconnection' from the gay community, even when they are active in gay politics. Jaline Quinto quotes one gay Native American activist as stating:

> I was doing a lot of things in the community, but feeling still that disconnection from the larger mainstream gay community because I was Native . . . There was this ideal of what constituted beauty, part of it had to do with if you don't have blonde hair and blue eyes, you don't meet the standard. (Quinto, 2003, p. 14)

Gay Latino men don't fare much better in the larger gay community. As Munoz (1999) points out, the mainstream gay community either ignores or exoticizes Latino bodies. That is to say, Latino men, like other men of color, also fall into two categories within the gay community. Either they are invisible or exist only as props for white male consumption. Miguel Flores is quoted by Joel P. Engardio as stating:

> I hate being a fetish. They don't see you as a person. Just an object, Latin meat . . . When I found out about this city, it seemed like a dream. But when I got here [San Francisco], I realized even in the gay capital of the U.S., I'm still Mexican . . . I didn't come all this way to go through the same shit. (Engardio, 1999, p. 7)

Perhaps no example of racial fetishization of gay men of color is more blatant than the use of the 'Indian' character in the 1970s disco group, Vil-

lage People. Singing songs embedded with gay metaphors, the Village People rose to cult status among both gay and straight listeners and were, perhaps, the most popular music group during the gay-active 1970s. A brain child of music producer, Jacques Morali, each 'character' in the band represented a gay fetish. While the 'Indian' was a character onto his own, representing the idea that a man of color can be a fetish just by being a man of color, the other characters were given an occupational or behavioral role often fetishized within the gay community such as cowboy, biker, construction worker, soldier, and cop. The implication, of course, is that while men of color are fetishized for what they are, white men are fetishized for what they do. Thus, white men can choose when they want to be objectified, but men are color are simply objects.

As discussed above, existing only as props for white male consumption represents another subtle form of racism. As Tony Ayres notes:

> First, there is overt belligerence: the drunk queens who shout in my face, 'Go back to your own country'; the tag line at the end of gay personal classifieds—'No Fates, Femmes, or Asians'; the guys who hissed at me in the back room, 'I'm not into Asians'. Still, these incidents are rare and easily dealt with . . . The second response is the exact opposite of this racist antagonism. It is an attraction to me because of my Asianness, my otherness . . . This has nothing to do with my individual qualities as a person . . . It is the fact that I conveniently fit into someone else's fantasy . . . They expect me to be so flattered by the attention of a white man that I will automatically bend over and grab my ankles. (1999, p. 89)

Whereas Asian men become the object of white male fantasy due to their perceived feminine qualities, Black men suffer the opposite stereotype. Rather than subservient geishas who will submissively tend to all of the white male fantasies of domination, black men are the overly sexual predators racially capable of fulfilling white male sexual lust. If Asian men are the vassals for white men's domination fantasies, black men are the tools required for white male submissive fantasies. As Frantz Fanon explains, the black 'man' no longer exists in the white sexual imagination. Instead, 'one is no longer aware of the negro, but only of a penis. The Negro is eclipsed. He is turned into a penis. He is a penis' (1970, p. 120). Rather than existing as individuals, black men exist as sexual tools, ready to fulfill, or violate, white male sexual fetishes. This fetishization of the black man's penis is perhaps most evident in nude photographs of black men, taken by white men, and meant for white (straight, gay, male and female) consumption. Perhaps nowhere is this more evident than in the photography of Robert Mapplethorpe, particularly the collection of photographs published in *Black Book*. As Mercer (1991) points out, images, such as those presented by Mapplethorpe, help to objectify and fetishize black men as being nothing more than giant penises. Ironically, whereas the objectification of Asian men is largely based on the desire to dominate, the objectification of black men is based on the fear of domination (Fung, 1991; Marriott, 2000).

They Don't Want to Cruise Your Type: Blatant Forms of Racism

Sometimes racism in the gay community takes on more explicit forms. Like racism everywhere, these forms tend to operate with the goal of excluding, in this case, men of color from gay institutions. Perhaps the most notorious has been the events surrounding Badlands, a popular bar in the Castro district in San Francisco. In the summer of 2004, Badlands became the site of weekly picketing after a group of racially diverse Bay Area residents filed a complaint with the San Francisco Human Rights Commission, the San Francisco Entertainment Commission, the California Department of Fair Employment and Housing, and the state Alcoholic Beverage Control Department claiming racial discrimination at the bar. Among the complaints were that not only was the owner practising job discrimination at the bar but also that non-white customers were being either turned away at the door

or were being expunged from the bar. According to complainants, people of color were routinely denied employment and promotional opportunities and entrance into the establishment. Most obvious incidents were the fact that black men were required to provide two forms of I.D. at the door while white men were required to only show one. Michael Kinsley, a former bouncer at the club stated:

> One of my tasks while working at the Badlands was to stand guard and judge whether or not to allow entrance into the bar. Introductory bouncer etiquette, courtesy of Les (the owner), was a short course in discriminating between 'Badlands' and 'non-Badlands' customers . . . During this introduction there were continual references to the characteristics of the undesirable customers—if they looked like 'street people' or if they were not 'dressed' like 'Badlands customers.' As a new initiate into the field of adult door monitor there were, in the first few weeks, instances where Les would politely walk a person to the door and escort them from the premises. These instances were all accompanied by an admonishing, 'This person was not a Badlands customer', or 'He had a backpack. We don't let in people with backpacks. They are often street people or have no money'. All of these individuals had one common feature and it was painfully obvious to me— everyone escorted out was black. (And Castro for All, 2004)

Max Killen, another former Badlands doorman was also quoted as stating:

> He (Les Natali, the owner) sat me down and he told me, 'There are certain types of people that we don't want in here. And those people can go across the street'. He didn't say the Pendulum (another Castro street bar with a large black clientele), but . . . it was really obvious that he was talking about the bar. He wasn't talking about hanging out in the parking lot or at the other places there. It was the Pendulum. (And Castro for All, 2004)

It is interesting to note that the racist policies are cloaked in discourses of class. By doing so, it allows gay businesses to escape the stigma of racism while ultimately maintaining racial borders. Ironically, the mirroring of the gay community with the white mainstream, as discussed earlier, contributes to such actions. Such mirroring actions allow gay business owners to mask issues of race and class under the justification of running a 'successful' business.

An isolated incident might have been easily forgotten, but the events at Badlands struck a cord with the city's non-white gay and lesbian residents. For them, it was just another incident in a long history of racial discrimination in the city's gayborhood. As Don Romesburg (2004) notes,

> The most recent troubles surrounding the Badlands [were] just the latest incarnation of a long-standing struggle in the Castro's LGBT community regarding racial discrimination and exclusion.

In fact, the policy of requiring multiple forms of I.D. from non-white patrons had a long history in the Castro, starting with the Mine Shaft, a Castro bar that required three forms of I.D. for men of color during the mid-1970s. Rodrigo Reyes, in an interview with Richard Marquez in 1991, recalls this about the early 1980s:

> There were also some racist discriminatory practices on the part of the bars in that sometimes they would ask for an inordinate amount of IDs from people of color . . . They would ask for two, three picture IDs. So it wasn't a very happy time for Latino gays . . . We were still a marginal group. The dominant group was still white gay men. (quoted in Ramirez, 2003, p. 232)

Also during the early 1980s, an informal study conducted by the Association of Lesbian and Gay Asians (ALGA) found that multiple carding was a fairly widespread practice among gay bars throughout San Francisco, not just in the Castro district. Recalling the ensuing boycott following the release of the study, Dinoa Duazo notes:

> The most insidious aspect of the whole situation was how proprietors felt completely justified to practice such casual discrimination. Unfortunately, just because a community has faced oppression, there's no guarantee that its members won't practice it themselves. (1999, p. 5)

In fact, during an on-air debate on KPFA, a local radio station, one bar owner told Randy Kikukawa, one of the organizers of the boycott, that 'Your people don't drink. We have to make money', and 'It's a cruise bar, we would lose money because they don't want to cruise your type' (Duazo, 1999, p. 5). Also, the practice of multiple carding was not unique to San Francisco. In Washington DC, two bars, Lost & Found and Grand Central, were targeted by community activists for blatantly requiring two forms of I.D. from non-white patrons while allowing white patrons easy access. In 1984, the 'Boston Bar Study' conducted by Men of All Colors Together Boston (MACTB) cited numerous examples of widespread discrimination at gay bars in Boston against black men. Similar types of discrimination have also been cited in Los Angeles and New York (Wat, 2002). Even more troubling is that this type of behavior seems to be international as well—anywhere that gay white men come into contact with gay men of color (Ridge, Hee & Minichiello, 1999). One can only imagine how many others never make it into the new stories. Rather than isolated events attributable to racist owners of single bars, the attempt to patrol the borders of whiteness in gay-owned business establishments seems to be a systematic practice to ensure only certain types of people are allowed into 'gay' bars.

I Just Want an 'All American' Boy

The primacy of white images in the gay community often leads to detrimental results for gay men of color, particularly manifested as internalized racism. In 'No blacks allowed', Keith Boykin argues that 'in a culture that devalues black males and elevates white males', black men deal with issues of self-hatred that white men do not. 'After all', he notes, 'white men have no reason to hate themselves in a society that reinforces their privilege'. Boykin argues that this racial self-hatred makes gay black men see other gay black men as unsuitable sexual partners. Obviously, such racial self-hatred rarely manifests itself as such. Instead, gay black men who don't want to date other black men simply rely on stereotypes to justify their behavior rather than confront their own self-hatred. For example, Boykin notes that most of these men justify excluding other black men as potential partners by relying on old stereotypes of the uneducated, less intelligent black male. Ironically, the same black men who rely on these stereotypes to exclude members of their own race rarely enforce them on gay white men, as evidenced by Boykin's example of the gay black man who has no problem with dating blue-collar white men but excludes black men on the assumption that they are, 'uneducated and less successful than he is'. What's worse is that not only do gay black men fail to see each other as sexual partners, white men also ignore them. In such an environment, black men compete with each other for the allusive white male partner (Boykin, 2002, p. 1).

This desire for white male companionship is not limited just to black men, and neither is racial self-hatred. Rather, it seems to be pandemic among many gay men of color. For example, Tony Ayres explains that:

> The sexually marginalized Asian man who has grown up in the West or is western in his thinking is often invisible in his own fantasies. [Their] sexual daydreams are populated by handsome Caucasian men with lean, hard Caucasian bodies. (1999, p. 91)

Likewise, Kent Chuang writes about how he tried desperately to avoid anything related to his Chinese heritage and his attempts to transform his 'shamefully slim Oriental frame . . . into a more desirable western body' (1999, p. 33) Asian men, too, rely on stereotypes to justify their exclusive attraction to white men. For example, a gay Asian man is cited as stating:

> For me, I prefer dating white men because I want something different from myself. I think that dating another Asian would be like dating

my sister. I mean, we would have so much in common, what would there be for us to learn about? Where would the excitement come from? (Han, 2005)

Here, gay Asian men rely on the old stereotype of an 'Asian mass' to justify their own prejudices towards other Asian men. All Asians are presented as homogenous masses with each person being interchangeable with another. Ironically, white men who exclusively date white men rarely rely on such tactics. There is no need to argue, from a white male position, that dating other white men would be like 'dating their brothers'. Also, the man's characterization of other Asian men as 'sister', also points to the stereotypical ways that Asian men are seen in the larger gay community. Stereotyped as overly feminine, gay Asian men become unappealing to gay men who desire men who are masculine or 'straight acting'.

Partner preference among Latino men also seems to follow the hierarchy of the 'white is best' mentality. Ramirez notes that the competition for a white 'trophy' boyfriend among gay Latino men has often hindered community formation. Rather than seeing each other as allies, gay Latino men may see each other as competitors for the attention of the few white men who prefer Latino men to other white men. For example, one Latino man was quoted as saying:

> One of the things that I saw that really bothered me and I told them, I said, 'What the problem here is everybody is after the white trophy That's the problem here. And unless two people are comadres [godmothers], you don't want to have nothing to do with each other. But that's the problem. After the white trophy, nobody has time. And it's like, you tear each other down . . . viciousness, because you're after the white trophy. And to have a white lover is ooohhh! Don't you see?' (2003, p. 229)

After complaining to other Latino men about the pedestalization of white men among gay Latino men, this particular gay Latino man was labeled a 'radical lesbian'. The implication here is that any Latino man who chooses to be with another Latino man, rather than a white man that has come to dominate gay male sexual fantasies, must be a 'lesbian', a woman who prefers other women. The limited definition of desirable masculinity within the gay community leads to white males as being 'men' while men of color are placed lower on the hierarchy much in the same way that the mainstream creates a hierarchy of men and women. As such, men of color are seen lower on the gendered hierarchy within the gay community where white masculinity is valued over all other forms of masculinity. Should they prefer other men of color, they are easily conflated with 'lesbians', two people lower on the gender hierarchy who prefer the sexual companionship of each other over that of the gender dominant group.

While information about racial preference for Native American men is scarce, Brown (1997) reported that only one of their five gay Native American male informants reported ever having a sexual relationship with another Native American male.

Rather than less, race seems to matter more to gay men than to straight men when it comes to mate selection. Examining personal ads, Phua and Kaufman (2003) found that gay men were significantly more likely to prefer one race and suggest that they may be more likely to exclude certain races as well. According to their data, gay men of color were much more likely to explicitly exclude members of their own race and much more likely to request another race (overwhelmingly white) than even gay white men.

There's No Name for This

It would be too easy to throw racism at the doorstep of gay white men and blame them for all of the problems encountered by gay men of color. But racial and ethnic communities must also take some of the blame for whatever psychological assaults gay men of color have endured. If we are invisible in the dominant gay community, perhaps we are doubly so in our racial/ethnic communities.

In the film, *There is no name for this,* produced by Ming-Yuen S. Ma and Cianna Pamintuan Stewart, Chwee Lye Chng, a gay Asian man explains:

> There are words in Malay, in Chinese, or what have you that describes, you know, that is used in the culture. But it's more akin to the word, a transvestite. We just don't know, there is no vocabulary for that and I think that's why it was so difficult to, to perhaps, come out because if I thought I'm gay, I almost have to accept the very distorted definition in the culture of, I'm going to be a cross dresser, I'm going to stand in the street corner and service me. (Ma & Stewart, 1996)

As can be noted from the above quote, the prominence of negative gay stereotypes in Asian cultures makes it difficult for them to discuss their sexual orientation with their families. In addition, the absence of vocabulary also makes it difficult to discuss sexual matters. Anna Jiang in describing the difficulty of discussing her sister's sexuality with her parents stated:

> I have some relatives who only speak Chinese. When I tried to explain Cecilia's character to them, I don't know how to do it. I don't know how to explain the term 'gay' and 'lesbian' to them. (Ma & Stewart, 1996)

Likewise, Doug Au explained:

> It's not just coming out, it's not just saying that I'm queer or that I'm gay but really being able to sit down with someone and explain to them in a way they could understand. (Ma & Stewart, 1996)

Gay and lesbian Asians are not alone in feeling invisible within their ethnic communities. One gay Latino man was quoted by Edgar Colon as stating:

> My family acts as if my sexual orientation does not exist. Moreover, I have no ongoing contact with my family. In this way, we can make sure that I remain invisible. (2001, p. 86)

In Latino cultures, much as in some Asian cultures, 'there is no positive or self-validating word for one who identifies himself as homosexual' (Manalansan, 1996, p. 399) Rather, to self-identify as 'gay' means taking on the maligned and feminine label of *maricon*, implying that one takes the passive role in sexual intercourse. Embedded within the *machisimo* framework of Latin male sexuality, the passive partner during gay intercourse is doubly stigmatized as not only being one who engages in sexual acts with other men but also as taking the feminine, passive role during execution.

Likewise, many Native American gay men have also been forced to leave reservations and families after disclosing that they are gay. As Karina Walters notes:

> In some cases, [first nations gay, lesbian, bisexual, transgendered, two-spirits] leave reservations at very young ages and with little education, eventually trading sex to survive in cities. Prejudice in [first nations] communities manifests itself in the denial of the existence of [first nations gay, lesbian, bisexual, transgendered, two-spirits], avoidance in discussing the subject, and cultural beliefs that nonheterosexual behavior is sinful, immoral, and against traditions. (Walters *et al.*, 2002, p. 317)

In black communities, much has been debated recently regarding the 'down low' phenomenon when men, who may be either bisexual or closeted homosexuals, have openly heterosexual lives but engage in covert sexual acts with other men (King, 2004). While it should be noted that black men are not the only men to engage in homosexual activity while leading heterosexual lives, the common belief is that they are more likely than white men to engage in such behavior. True, there are ample examples of homophobia in the black community. At the same time, there is evidence to indicate that it is a mistake to attribute homophobia as simply a black phenomenon, or a phenomenon specific to any racial/ethnic community. Rather, as Manalansan (1996) explains, homophobia in the black community

may have much to do with class, self-identification of gay men and women, and other situational factors associated with being a minority group in a racialized society than with blacks being inherently more homophobic than whites.

Borrow the Words but Ignore the Meaning

The irony, of course, is that even as the 'gay' community uses the language of the civil rights movement to further the cause of equality for gays and lesbians, many within the community continue to ignore the lessons that should be apparent within the language that they have adopted. For example, the National Gay and Lesbian Task Force describes itself in this way:

> Founded in 1973, the National Gay and Lesbian Task Force Foundation (the Task Force) was the first national lesbian, gay, bisexual and transgender (LGBT) civil rights and advocacy organization and remains the movement's leading voice for freedom, justice and equality. We work to build the grassroots political strength of our community by training state and local activists and leaders, working to strengthen the infrastructure of state and local allies, and organizing broad-based campaigns to build public support for complete equality for LGBT people.

The use of the terms civil rights, movement, justice, equality, grassroots, activist, etc., clearly harkens back to the language of the civil rights movement. The language of the civil rights movement has resonated with numerous 'gay' organizations and as such, they have presented the movement as being one of equality and justice rather than sexual preference. While the Task Force has done an admirable job in promoting issues of race within the gay community, and several men and women of color hold leadership positions on their board of directors, the majority of other gay organizations have not followed suit, particularly at the local level.

Predictably, the use of civil rights language has been met with contesting viewpoints about its validity when applied to gay rights. On the one hand, it has been met positively with Julian Bond, board chairman of the NAACP stating:

> Are gay rights civil rights? Of course they are. 'Civil rights' are positive legal prerogatives—the right to equal treatment before the law. These are rights shared by all—there is no one in the United States who does not—or should not—share in these rights . . . We ought to be flattered that our movement has provided so much inspiration for others, that it has been so widely imitated, and that our tactics, methods, heroines and heroes, even our songs, have been appropriated by or served as models for others . . . Many gays and lesbians worked side by side with me in the '60s Civil Rights Movement. Am I to tell them 'thanks' for risking life and limb helping me win my rights—but they are excluded because of a condition of their birth? They cannot share now in the victories they helped to win? (Bond, 2004, p. 142)

Others have been less generous with their support, such as the Reverend Fred L. Shuttlesworth, the interim president of the Southern Christian Leadership Conference:

> I was among the original five who started the Southern Christian Leadership Conference (SCLC), and our primary focus back then was to put an end to racial segregation under the Jim Crow system. As SCLC's first secretary, I never took down anything in our minutes that addressed the issue of gay rights. The issue of gay rights was not our focus, and should not be confused with the Civil Rights Movement. (Shuttlesworth, 2004, p. 142)

The problem here is that whether one supports the analogy with the civil rights movement or not, both perspectives seem to negate the possibility that people can be both gay and a racial minority, a point made clear by Mary F. Morten, the former liaison to the gay community under Chicago mayor Richard Daley, when she states:

A major problem is that gay and lesbian life is associated with privilege because it is depicted far too often from a white perspective. We have few positive images of African American gays and lesbians, and we rarely see African American gays and lesbians on TV. So for many people being gay is associated with being white . . . We have always had visibly gay and lesbian folks in our community, whether we talked about it or not . . . We need to be much more open about the reality that you live next door to some gays and lesbians, that we're in your family, that we're literally everywhere in our community. (Morten, 2004, p. 144)

Clearly, for Morten, acknowledging that racial communities include gay members and, by extension, acknowledging that gay communities include members of racial minority groups, is a top priority.

Discussion

Given the prevalence of negative racial attitudes in the larger gay community and the homophobia in racial communities, gay men of color have had to build identities along the margins of both race and sexuality. More often than not, this has been a difficult road. Looking for a space to call his own, Eric Reyes asks, while referring to Michiyo Cornell's early writing that America is a 'great lie':

> I ask which America should I call a lie. Is it the Eurocentric and heterosexual male-dominated America, the white gay male-centered Queer America, the marginalized People of Color (POC) America, or our often-romanticized Asian America? As a Queer API, I ask where is this truth situated that betrays our belief that we have a space here in this place called America? Locating this space from which we draw our strength and our meaning is the part of coming out that never ends. (Reyes, 1996, p. 85)

The difficulty for gay men of color in coming out as gay has to do with both the homophobia found in racial communities and the racism found in gay communities. True, men of color are dependent on ethnic communities. Michiyo Cornell explains, 'because of Asian American dependence on our families and Asian American communities for support, it is very difficult for us to be out of the closet' (1996, p. 83). At the same time, this 'dependence' may have more to do with lacking alternatives rather than self-inflicted internal homophobia. As Richard Fung points out:

> As is the case for many other people of color and especially immigrants, our families and our ethnic communities are a rare source of affirmation in a racist society. In coming out, we risk (or feel that we risk) losing this support. (Fung, 1991, p. 149)

Other gay men of color have also pointed out the need to maintain ties to their racial and ethnic communities in order to maintain a sense of self-esteem. In fact, the two-spirit movement among gay Native Americans has played a powerful part in bolstering self-esteem among gay Native American men and women. Rather than attempting to 'fit' into white definitions of 'gay' or 'lesbians', Native Americans have reclaimed a long cultural practice of valuing a third gender that is not rigidly linked to the European definitions of 'man' and 'woman' (Brown, 1997; Quinto, 2003; Walters, 1999) In fact, Walters demonstrates that enculturation into Native communities is critical for mental health among gay Native Americans (Walters, 1999).

In this paper, I examined both the racism found in the gay community and the homophobia found in racial and ethnic communities and argue that both racism and homophobia affect men of color negatively in ways that may be multiplicative rather than additive. That is, gay men of color don't simply experience racism because they are racial minorities and homophobia because they are sexual minorities. Instead, they experience a unique type of racism and homophobia because they are gay and of color. Certainly, gay Asian men experience these forces differently from gay black men. In addition, the mirroring of the mainstream by the gay community can also be seen to occur in communities of color, where they favor heterosexuality above homosexuality in an attempt to mirror the dominant society. Within this framework, gay men and women of color are relegated to the bottom of the hierarchy in both communities. While I have limited my discussion to gay men, it is likely that examining the lives of bisexual men of color, bisexual women of color, and lesbian women of color, would lead to a fuller understanding of multiple sites of oppression. Future research and theoretical work will need to tease out the specific experiences of multiply marginalized groups in order to truly understand how race, sexuality, class, etc. may be intersected in the lives of subaltern groups rather than focus on single categories of oppression and expect these to be additive rather than multiplicative. Only then can we truly understand the methods of domination and oppression that mark groups and the implications that such categorization may have.

References

And Castro for All. (2004). Is badlands bad? Retrieved 10 August 2005 from www.isbadlandsbad. com

Anonymous. (n.d.). *Racism or preference (at the baths?)*. Retrieved 10 February 2005 from *Bathhouse Diaries*, www.bathhouseblues.com/racism.html.

Ayres, T. (1999). China doll: The experience of being a gay Chinese Australian. In P. A. Jackson & G. Sullivan (Eds.), *Multicultural queer: Australian narratives*. New York: The Haworth Press.

Beam, J. (1986). Introduction. In J. Beam (Ed.), *In the life: A Black gay anthology*. Boston: Alyson.

Bérubé, A. (2001). How gay stays white and what kind of white it stays. In B. Brander Rasmussen, E. Klinenberg, I. J. Nexica & M. Wray (Eds.), *The making and unmaking of whiteness*. Durham, NC: Duke University Press.

Bond, J. (2004). Is gay rights a civil rights issue? Yes. *Ebony, 59*(9), 142–46.

Boykin, K. (2002). No blacks allowed. Retrieved 25 September 2005 from *Temenos*, www.temenos. net/articles/12-23-04.shtml

Brown, L. (1997). Women and men, not-men and not-women, lesbians and gays: American Indian gender style alternatives. *Journal of Gay and Lesbian Social Services, 6*(2), 5–20.

Cho, S. (1998). *Rice: Explorations into gay Asian culture and politics*. Toronto: Queer Press.

Chuang, K. (1999). Using chopsticks to eat steak. *Journal of Homosexuality, 36*(3/4), 29–41.

Colon, E. (2001). An ethnographic study of six Latino gay and bisexual men. *Journal of gay and lesbian social services, 12*(3/4), 77–92.

Cornell, M. (1996). Living in Asian America: An Asian American lesbian's address before the Washington Monument (1979). In R. Leong (Ed.), *Asian American sexualities: Dimensions of the gay and lesbian experience*. New York: Routledge.

Diaz, R. M. (1998). *Latino gay men and HIV: Culture, sexuality and risk behavior*. New York: Routledge.

Duazo, D. (1999). Looking back in homage. *Lavender Godzilla*, April, 1–5.

Engardio, J. P. (1999). You can't be gay, you're Latino: A gay Latino identity struggles to emerge, somewhere between the macho Mission and Caucasian Castro. *SF Weekly, 7.*

Fanon, F. (1970). *Black skin, white masks*. London: Paladin.

Fung, R. (1991). Looking for my penis: The eroticized Asian in gay video porn. In Bad Object-Choice (Ed.), *How do I look: Queer film and video*. Seattle: Bay Books.

Han, C.-S. (2005). Gay Asian men and negotiating race and sexual behavior. Unpublished manuscript.

King, J. L. (2004). *On the down low: A journey into the lives of 'straight' black men who sleep with men*. New York: Broadway Books.

Lipsitz, G. (1998). *Possessive investment in whiteness*. Philadelphia: Temple University Press.

Ma, M.-Y. S., & Stewart, C. P. (1997). *There is no name for this*. API Wellness Center.

Manalansan, M. R. (1996). Double minorities: Latino, black and Asian men who have sex with men. In R. Savin Williams & K. Cohen (Eds.), *The lives of lesbians, gays, and bisexuals: Developmental, clinical and cultural issues*. Forth Worth: Harcourt, Brace and Co.

Marriott, D. (2000). *On black men*. New York: Columbia University Press.

Mercer, K. (1991). Skin head sex thing: Racial difference and the homoerotic imaginary. In Bad Object-Choice (Ed.), *How do I look: Queer film and video*. Seattle: Bay Books.

Morten, M. (2004). Is gay rights a civil rights issue? Maybe. *Ebony, 59*(9), 142–46.

Munoz, J. E. (1999). *Disidentifications: Queers of color and the performance of politics*. Minneapolis: University of Minnesota Press.

National Gay and Lesbian Task Force Foundation. Retrieved from www.thetaskforce.org/aboutus/whatwedo.cfm

Phua, V., & Kaufman, G. (2003). The crossroads of race and sexuality: Date selection among men in internet 'personal' ads. *Journal of Family Issues, 24*(8), 981–94.

Quinto, J. (2003). Northwest two-spirit society. *Colors northwest, 3*(3), 12–15.

Ramirez, H. N. R. (2003). 'That's my place!': Negotiating racial, sexual, and gender politics in San Francisco's Gay Latino Alliance, 1975–1983. *Journal of the History of Sexuality, 12*(2), 224–58.

Reyes, E. (1996). Strategies for queer Asian and Pacific Islander spaces. In R. Leong (Ed.), *Asian American sexualities: Dimensions of the gay and lesbian experience*. New York: Routledge.

Ridge, D., Hee, A., & Minichiello, V. (1999). 'Asian' men on the scene: Challenges to 'gay communities'. *Journal of Homosexuality. 36*(3/4), 43–68.

Riggs, M. (1989). *Tongues untied*. MTR Production.

Romesburg, D. (2004). Racism and reaction in the Castro: A brief, incomplete history. Retrieved 20 October 2005 from www.isbadlandsbad.com/archives/000039.html

Shuttlesworth, F. (2004). Is gay rights a civil rights issue? No. *Ebony, 59*(9), 142–46.

Walters, K. (1999). Negotiating conflicts in allegiances among lesbians and gays of color: Reconciling divided selves and communities. In G. P. Mallon (Ed.), *Foundations of social work practice*. New York: Harrington Park Press.

Walters, K., Longress, J., Han, C.-S., & Icard, L. (2002). Cultural competence with gay and lesbian persons of color. In D. Lum (Ed.), *Culturally competent practice: A framework for understanding diverse groups and justice issues*. Pacific Grove, CA: Thomson Brooks/Cole.

Wat, E. C. (2002). *The making of a gay Asian community: An oral history of pre-AIDS Los Angeles*. Lanham, MD: Rowman and Littlefield.

Julia O'Connell Davidson
Jacqueline Sanchez Taylor

Fantasy Islands: Exploring the Demand for Sex Tourism

In a useful review of prostitution cross-culturally and historically, Laurie Shrage observes that "one thing that stands out but stands unexplained is that a large percentage of sex customers seek (or sought) sex workers whose racial, national, or class identities are (or were) different from their own" (Shrage 1994: 142). She goes on to suggest that the demand for African, Asian, and Latin American prostitutes by white Western men may "be explained in part by culturally produced racial fantasies regarding the sexuality of these women" and that these fantasies may be related to "socially formed perceptions regarding the sexual and moral purity of white women" (ibid: 48–50). Kempadoo also draws attention to the "over-representation of women of different nationalities and ethnicities, and the hierarchies of race and color within the [international sex] trade" and observes, "That sex industries today depend upon the eroticization of the ethnic and cultural Others suggest we are witnessing a contemporary form of exoticism which sustains postcolonial and post-cold war relations of power and dominance" (Kempadoo 1995: 75–76).

This chapter represents an attempt to build on such insights. Drawing on our research with both male and female Western heterosexual sex tourists in the Caribbean,[1] it argues that their sexual taste for "Others" reflects not so much a wish to engage in any specific sexual practice as a desire for an extraordinarily high degree of control over the management of self and others as sexual, racialized, and engendered beings. This desire, and the Western sex tourist's power to satiate it, can only be explained through reference to power relations and popular discourses that are simultaneously gendered, racialized, and economic.

White Western Men's Sex Tourism

Empirical research on sex tourism to Southeast Asia has fairly consistently produced a portrait of Western male heterosexual sex tourists as men whose desire for the Other is the flip side of dissatisfaction with white Western women, including white Western prostitute women. Lee, for example, explores the demand for sex tourism as a quest for racially fantasized male power, arguing that this is at least in part a backlash against the women's movement in the West: "With an increasingly active global feminist movement, male-controlled sexuality (or female passivity) appears to be an increasingly scarce resource. The travel advertisements are quite explicit about what is for sale: docility and submission" (Lee 1991: 90; see also Jeffreys 1997). Western sex tourists' fantasies of "docile" and "willing" Asian women are accompanied, as Kruhse-Mount Burton (1995: 196) notes, by "a desexualization of white women . . . who are deemed to be spoiled, grasping and, above all, unwilling or inferior sexual partners." These characteristics are also attributed to white prostitute women. The sex tourists interviewed by Seabrook (1997: 3) compared Thai prostitutes "very favorably with the more mechanistic and functional behavior of most

Western sex workers." Kruhse-Mount Burton states that where many impose their own boundaries on the degree of physical intimacy implied by the prostitution contract (for example refusing to kiss clients on the mouth or to engage in unprotected penetrative and/or oral sex) and are also in a position to turn down clients' requests to spend the night or a few days with them is likewise experienced as a threat to, or denial of, traditional male identity.

Though we recognize that sex tourism provides Western men with opportunities "to reaffirm, if only temporarily, the idealized version of masculine identity and mode of being," and that in this sense sex tourism provides men with opportunities to manage and control both themselves and others as engendered beings, we want to argue that there is more to the demand for sex tourism than this (ibid: 202). In the remainder of this chapter we therefore interrogate sex tourists' attitudes toward prostitute use, sexuality, gender, and "race" more closely, and further complicate matters by considering white Western women's and black Western men and women's sex tourism to the Caribbean.

Western Sexuality and Prostitute Use

Hartsock observes that there is "a surprising degree of consensus that hostility and domination, as opposed to intimacy and physical pleasure" are central to the social and historical construction of sexuality in the West (Hartsock 1985: 157). Writers in the psychoanalytic tradition suggest that the kind of hostility that is threaded through Western sexual expression reflects an infantile rage and wish for revenge against the separateness of those upon whom we depend. It is, as Stoller puts it, "a state in which one wishes to harm an object," and the harm wished upon objects of sexual desire expresses a craving to strip them of their autonomy, control, and separateness—that is, to dehumanize them, since a dehumanized sexual object does not have the power to reject, humiliate, or control (Stoller 1986: 4).

The "love object" can be divested of autonomy and objectified in any number of ways, but clearly the prostitute woman, who is in most cultures imagined and socially constructed as an "unnatural" sexual and social Other (a status which is often enshrined in law), provides a conveniently ready dehumanized sexual object for the client. The commercial nature of the prostitute–client exchange further promises to strip all mutuality and dependency from sexual relations. Because all obligations are discharged through the simple act of payment, there can be no real intimacy and so no terrifying specter of rejection or engulfment by another human being. In theory, then, prostitute use offers a very neat vehicle for the expression of sexual hostility and the attainment of control over self and others as sexual beings. Yet for many prostitute users, there is a fly in the ointment:

> Prostitute women may be socially constructed as Others and *fantasized* as nothing more than objectified sexuality, but in reality, of course, they are human beings. It is only if the prostitute is imagined as stripped of everything bar her sexuality that she can be *completely* controlled by the client's money/powers. But if she were dehumanized to this extent, she would cease to exist as a person. . . . Most clients appear to pursue a contradiction, namely to control as an object that which cannot be objectified. (O'Connell Davidson 1998: 161)

This contradiction is at the root of the complaints clients sometimes voice about Western prostitutes (Graaf et al. 1992: Plumridge and Chetwynd 1997). It is not always enough to buy access to touch and sexually use objectified body parts. Many clients want the prostitute to be a "lover" who makes no claims, a "whore" who has sex for pleasure not money, in short, a person (subject) who can be treated as an object. This reflects, perhaps, deeper inconsistencies in the discourses which surround prostitution and sexuality. The prostitute woman is viewed as acting in a way wholly inconsistent with her gender identity. Her perceived sexual agency degenders her (a woman who takes an impersonal, active, and instrumental approach to sex is not a "real" woman) and dishonors her (she trades in something which is constitutive of her personhood and cannot honorably be sold). The prostitute-using man, by contrast, behaves "in a fashion consistent with the attributes associated with his gender (he is active and sexually predatory, impersonal, and instrumental), and his sexual transgression is thus a minor infraction, since it does not compromise his gender identity" (O'Connell Davidson 1998: 127). A paradox thus emerges:

> The more that men's prostitute use is justified and socially sanctioned through reference to the fiction of biologically determined gender roles and sexuality, the greater the contradiction implicit in prostitution. In order to satisfy their "natural" urges, men must make use of "unnatural" women. (ibid: 128)

All of this helps to explain the fact that, even though their sexual interests may be powerfully shaped by a cultural emphasis on hostility and domination, prostitute use holds absolutely no appeal for many Western men.[2] Fantasies of unbridled sexual access to willingly objectified women are not necessarily fantasies of access to prostitute women. Meanwhile, those who do use prostitutes in the West imagine and manage their own prostitute use in a variety of different ways (see O'Connell Davidson 1998). At one extreme are men who are actually quite satisfied with brief and anonymous sexual use of women and teenagers who they imagine as utterly debased and objectified "dirty whores." (For them, the idea of using a prostitute is erotic in and of itself.) At the other extreme are those who regularly visit the same prostitute woman and construct a fiction of romance or friendship around their use of her, a fiction which helps them to imagine themselves as seen, chosen, and desired, even as they pay for sex as a commodity. Between these two poles are men who indulge in a range of (often very inventive) practices and fantasies designed to create the illusion of balance between sexual hostility and sexual mutuality that they personally find sexually exciting. How does this relate to the demand for sex tourism?

Let us begin by noting that not all Western male sex tourists subjectively perceive their own sexual practices abroad as a form of prostitute use. This reflects the fact that even within any one country affected by sex tourism, prostitution is not a homogeneous phenomenon in terms of its social organization. In some countries sex tourism has involved the maintenance and development of existing large-scale, highly commoditized sex industries serving foreign military personnel (Truong 1990; Sturdevant and Stoltzfus 1992; Hall 1994). But it has also emerged in locations where no such sex industry existed, for instance, in Gambia, Cuba, and Brazil (Morris-Jarra 1996; Perio and Thierry 1996; Sanchez Taylor 1997). Moreover, even in countries like Thailand and the Philippines, where tourist-related prostitution has been grafted onto an existing, formally organized brothel sector serving military demand, tourist development has *also* been associated with the emergence of an informal prostitution sector (in which prostitutes solicit in hotels, discos, bars, beaches, parks, or streets, often entering into fairly protracted and diffuse transactions with clients).

This in itself gives prostitution in sex tourist resorts a rather different character to that of prostitution in red-light districts in affluent, Western countries. The sense of difference is enhanced by the fact that, in many places, informally arranged prostitution spills over into apparently noncommercial encounters within which tourists who do not self-identify as prostitute users can draw local/migrant persons who do not self-identify as prostitutes into profoundly unequal and exploitative sexual relationships. It also means that sex tourism presents a diverse array of opportunities for sexual gratification, not all of which involve straightforward cash for sex exchanges in brothels or go-go clubs or on the streets, and so provides the sex tourist with a veritable "pic 'n' mix" of ways in which to manage himself as a sexual and engendered being. He can indulge in overt forms of sexual hostility (such as selecting a numbered brothel prostitute from those on display in a bar or brothel for "short time" or buying a cheap, speedy sexual service from one of many street prostitutes), or he can indulge in fantasies of mutuality, picking up a woman/teenager in an ordinary tourist disco, wining and dining and generally simulating romance with her for a day or two and completely denying the commercial basis of the sexual interaction. Or, and many sex tourists do exactly this, he can combine both approaches.

Now it could be argued that, given the fact that Western men are socialized into a view of male sexuality as a powerful, biologically based need for sexual "outlets," the existence of multiple, cheap, and varied sexual opportunities is, in itself, enough to attract large numbers of men to a given holiday resort. However, it is important to recognize the numerous other forms of highly sexualized tourism that could satisfy a wish to indulge in various sexual fantasies and also a desire for control over the self as a sexual and engendered being. Sex tourists could, for example, choose to take part in organized holidays designed to facilitate sexual and romantic encounters between tourists (such as Club 18–30 and other singles holidays), or they could choose to take all-inclusive holidays to resorts such as Hedonism or destinations renowned for promiscuous tourist–tourist sex, such as Ibiza or Cap d'Azur. These latter offer just as many opportunities for anonymous and impersonal sex in a party atmosphere as well as for intense but ultimately brief and noncommitted sexual romances. What they do not offer is the control that comes from paying for sex or the opportunity to indulge in racialized sexual fantasies, which helps to explain why sex tourists reject them in favor of sexual experience in what they term "Third World" countries. This brings us to questions about the relationship between the construction of "Otherness" and sex tourism.

"Otherness" and Western Men's Sex Tourism

For obvious reasons, sex tourists spend their time in resorts and *barrios* where tourist-related prostitution is widespread. Thus they constantly encounter what appear to them as hedonistic scenes— local "girls" and young men dancing "sensuously," draping themselves over and being fondled by Western tourists, drinking and joking with each other, and so on. Instead of seeing the relationship between these scenes and their own presence in the resort, sex tourists tend to interpret all this as empirical vindication of Western assumptions of "non-Western peoples living in idyllic pleasure, splendid innocence or Paradise-like conditions—as purely sensual, natural, simple and uncorrupted beings" (Kempadoo 1995: 76). Western sex tourists (and this is true of black as well as white informants) say that sex is more "natural" in Third World countries, that prostitution is not really prostitution but a "way of life," that "They" are "at it" all of the time.

This explains how men who are not and would not dream of becoming prostitute users back home can happily practice sex tourism (the "girls" are not really like prostitutes and so they themselves are not really like clients, the prostitution contract is not like the Western prostitution contract and so does not really count as prostitution). It also explains the paranoid obsession with being cheated exhibited by some sex tourists, who comment on their belief that women in certain sex tourist resorts or particular brothels or bars are "getting too commercial" and advise each other how to avoid being "duped" and "exploited" by a "real professional," where to find "brand new girls," and so on (see O'Connell Davidson 1995; Bishop and Robinson 1998).

It also points to the complex interrelations between discourses of gender, "race," and sexuality. To begin with, the supposed naturalness of prostitution in the Third World actually reassures the Western male sex tourist of his racial or cultural superiority. Thus we find that sex tourists continue a traditional Western discourse of travel which rests on the imagined opposition between the "civilized" West and the "barbarous" Other (Grewal 1996: 136; Kempadoo 1996: 76; see also Brace and O'Connell Davidson 1996). In "civilized" countries only "bad" women become prostitutes (they refuse the constraints civilization places upon "good" women in favor of earning "easy money"), but in the Third World (a corrupt and lawless place where people exist in a state of nature), "nice girls" may be driven to prostitution in order to survive ("they have to do it because they've all got kids" or "they're doing it for their families"). In the West, "nice girls" are protected and supported by their menfolk, but in the Third World, "uncivilized" Other men allow (or even demand that) their womenfolk enter prostitution. In interviews, Western male sex tourists contrast their own generosity, humanity, and chivalry against the "failings" of local men, who are imagined as feckless, faithless, wife-beaters, and pimps. Even as prostitute users, Other men are fantasized as inferior moral beings who cheat and mistreat the "girls."

In this we see that sex tourism is not only about sustaining a male identity. For white men it is also about sustaining a *white* identity. Thus, sex tourism can also be understood as a collective behavior oriented toward the restoration of a generalized belief about what it is to be white: to be truly white is to be served, revered, and envied by Others. For the black American male sex tourists we have interviewed, sex tourism appears to affirm a sense of Western-ness and so of inclusion in a privileged world. Take, for example, the following three statements from a 45-year-old black American sex tourist. He is a New York bus driver and ex-vice cop, a paid-up member of an American-owned sex tourist club, Travel & the Single Male, and he has used prostitutes in Thailand, Brazil, Costa Rica, and the Dominican Republic:

> There's two sides to the countries that I go to. There's the tourist side and then there's the real people, and I make a habit of going to the real people, I see how the real people live, and when I see something like that . . . I tend to look at the little bit I've got at home and I appreciate it. . . .
>
> I've always been proud to be an American. . . . I always tip in US dollars when I arrive. I always keep dollars and pesos, because people tend to think differently about pesos and dollars. . . .

They always say at hotels they don't want you to bring the girls in; believe me, that's crap, because you know what I do? Reach in my pocket and I go anywhere I want.

Meanwhile, sexualized racisms help the sex tourist to attain a sense of control over himself and Others as engendered and racialized sexual beings. Here it is important to recognize the subtle (or not so subtle) variations of racism employed by white Western men. The sex tourists we have interviewed in the Caribbean are not a homogeneous group in terms of their "race" politics, and this reflects differences of national identity, age, socioeconomic background, and racialized identity. One clearly identifiable subgroup is comprised of white North American men aged forty and above, who, though perhaps not actually affiliated with the Klan, espouse a white supremacist worldview and consider black people their biological, social, and cultural inferiors. They use the word "nigger" and consider any challenge to their "right" to use this term as "political correctness." As one sex tourist complained, in the States. "You can't use the N word, nigger. Always when I was raised up, the only thing was the F word, you can't use the F word. Now you can't say cunt, you can't say nigger."

For men like this, black women are imagined as the embodiment of all that is low and debased, they are "inherently degraded, and thus the appropriate partners for degrading sex" (Shrage 1994: 158). As unambiguous whores by virtue of their racialized identity, they may be briefly and anonymously used, but they are not sought out for longer term or quasi-romantic commercial sexual relationships. Thus, the sex tourist quoted above told us that when he and his cronies (all regular sex tourists to the Dominican Republic) see another American sex tourist "hanging round" with a local girl or woman who has the phenotypical characteristics they associate with African-ness, they call out to him, "How many bananas did it take to get her down out of the tree?" and generally deride him for transgressing a racialized sexual boundary which should not, in their view, be openly crossed.

The Dominican females that men like this want sexual access to are light skinned and straight haired (this is also true in Cuba and in the Latin American countries where we have undertaken fieldwork). They are not classified as "niggers" by these white racists, but instead as "LBFMs" or "Little Brown Fucking Machines," a catch-all category encompassing any female Other not deemed to be either white or "African." The militaristic and imperialist associations of this term (coined by American GIs stationed in Southeast Asia) simultaneously make it all the more offensive and hostile and all the more appealing to this type of sex tourist, many of whom have served in the armed forces (a disturbing number of whom have also been or currently are police officers in the United States) and the rest of whom are "wanna-be vets"—men who never made it to Vietnam to live out their racialized–sexualized fantasies of masculine glory.

Shrage and Kruhse-Mount Burton's comments on the relationship between fantasies of hypersexual Others and myths about white women's sexual purity are also relevant to understanding this kind of sex tourist's worldview. An extract from an article posted on an Internet site written by and for sex tourists entitled "Why No White Women?" is revealing:

Q: Is it because white women demand more (in terms of performance) from their men during Sex? and white men cannot deliver?

A: In my case, it's just that my dick is not long enough to reach up on the pedestal they like to stand on.

If whiteness is imagined as dominance, and woman is imagined as subordination, then "white woman" becomes something of a contradiction. As Young notes, "For white men, white women are both self and other: they have a floating status. They can reinforce a sense of self through common racial identity or threaten and disturb that sense through their sexual Otherness" (Young 1996: 52). White supremacists have to place white women on a pedestal (iconize them

as racially, morally, and sexually pure), since whiteness and civilization are synonymous and "civilization" is constructed as the rejection of base animalism. But keeping them on their pedestal requires men to constantly deny what they imagine to be their own needs and nature and thus white women become the object of profound resentment.

Not all Western male sex tourists to the Caribbean buy into this kind of overt, denigrating racism. In fact, many of them are far more strongly influenced by what might be termed "exoticizing" racisms. Younger white Europeans and North Americans, for example, have been exposed to such racisms through the Western film, music, and fashion industries, which retain the old-school racist emphasis on blackness as physicality but repackage and commoditize this "animalism" so that black men and women become the ultimate icons of sporting prowess, "untamed" rebelliousness, "raw" musical talent, sexual power, and so on (see hooks 1992, 1994; Young 1996). As a consequence, many young (and some not so young) white Westerners view blackness as a marker of something both "cool" and "hot."

In their own countries, however, their encounters with real live black people are not only few and far between, but also generally something of a disappointment to them. As one British sex tourist to Cuba told us, black people in Britain are "very standoffish. . . . They stick to their own, and it's a shame, because it makes divisions." What a delight it is for men like this to holiday in the Caribbean, then, where poverty combined with the exigencies of tourist development ensure that they are constantly faced by smiling, welcoming black folk. The small black boy who wants to shine their shoes; the old black woman who cleans their hotel room; the cool, young, dreadlocked black man on the beach who is working as a promoter for some restaurant or bar; the fit, young black woman soliciting in the tourist disco—all want to "befriend" the white tourist. Finally, interviews with black American male sex tourists suggest that they too sexualize and exoticize the women they sexually exploit in the Third World ("Latin women are hot," "Latin girls love sex").

Both the sexualized racism that underpins the category LBFM and the exoticizing sexualized racism espoused by other sex tourists help to construct the Other prostitute as the embodiment of a contradiction, that is, as a "whore" who does it for pleasure as much as for money, an object with a subjectivity completely attuned to their own, in short, the embodiment of a masturbatory fantasy. Time and again Western sex tourists have assured us that the local girls really are "hot for it," that Third World prostitutes enjoy their work and that their highest ambition is to be the object of a Western man's desire. Their belief that Third World prostitutes are genuinely economically desperate rather than making a free choice to prostitute for "easy money" is clearly inconsistent with their belief that Third World prostitutes are actually acting on the basis of mutual sexual desire, but it is a contradiction that appears to resolve (at least temporarily) an anxiety they have about the relationship between sex, gender, sexuality, and "race."

The vast majority of the sex tourists we have interviewed believe that gender attributes, including sexual behavior, are determined by biological sex. They say that it is natural for women to be passive and sexually receptive as well as to be homemakers, child rearers, dependent upon and subservient toward men, which is why white Western women (prostitute and nonprostitute alike) often appear to them as unsexed. Thus the sex tourist quoted at the beginning of this chapter could only explain women's presence on traditional male terrain by imagining them as sexually "unnatural" ("Most of these girls are dykes anyways"). White women's relative economic, social, and political power as well as their very whiteness makes it hard for Western male sex tourists to eroticize them as nothing more than sexual beings. Racism/ethnocentrism can collapse such tensions. If black or Latin women are naturally physical, wild, hot, and sexually powerful, there need be no anxiety about enjoying them as pure

sex. Equally, racism settles the anxieties some men have about the almost "manly" sexual power and agency attributed to white prostitutes. A Little Brown Fucking Machine is not unsexed by prostituting, she is "just doing what comes naturally." Since the Other woman is a "natural" prostitute, her prostitution does not make her any the less a "natural woman." All these points are also relevant to understanding the phenomenon of female sex tourism.

"Otherness" and Female Sex Tourism

Western women's sexual behavior abroad (both historically and contemporaneously) is often viewed in a rather different light compared to that of their male counterparts, and it is without doubt true that Western women who travel to Third World destinations in search of sex differ from many of the Western male sex tourists discussed above in terms of their attitudes toward prostitution and sexuality. Few of them are prostitute users back home, and few of them would choose to visit brothels while abroad or to pay street prostitutes for a quick "hand job" or any other sexual service (although it should be noted that some women do behave in these ways). But one of the authors' (Sanchez Taylor) ongoing interview and survey research with female sex tourists in Jamaica and the Dominican Republic suggests that there are also similarities between the sexual behavior of Western women and men in sex tourist resorts.

The Caribbean has long been a destination that offers tourist women opportunities for sexual experience, and large numbers of women from the United States, Canada, Britain, and Germany as well as smaller numbers of women from other European countries and from Japan (i.e., the same countries that send male sex tourists) engage in sexual relationships with local men while on holiday there (Karch and Dann 1981; Chevannes 1993; Pruitt and LaFont 1995). Preliminary analysis of data from Sanchez Taylor's survey of a sample of 104 single Western female tourists in Negril, Sosúa, and Boca Chica shows that almost 40 percent had entered into some form of sexual relationship with a local man.[3] The survey data further suggest that these were not chance encounters but rather that the sexually active female tourists visit the islands in order to pursue one or more sexual relationships. Only 9 percent of sexually active women were on their first trip; the rest had made numerous trips to the islands, and over 20 percent of female sex tourists reported having had two or more different local sexual partners in the course of a two- to three-week stay. Furthermore female sex tourists, as much as male sex tourists, view their sexual experiences as integral to their holiday—"When in Jamaica you have to experience everything that's on offer," one black American woman explained, while a white woman working as a tour representative for a U.S. package operator said: "I tell my single women: come down here to love them, fuck them, and leave them, and you'll have a great time here. Don't look to get married. Don't call them."

Like male sex tourists, these women differ in terms of their age, nationality, social class, and racialized identity, including among their ranks young "spice girl" teenagers and students as well as grandmothers in their sixties, working-class as well as middle-class professionals, or self-employed women. They also differ in terms of the type of sexual encounters they pursue and the way in which they interpret these encounters. Some are eager to find a man as soon as they get off the plane and enter into multiple, brief, and instrumental relationships; others want to be romanced and sweet-talked by one or perhaps two men during their holiday. Around 40 percent described their relationships with local men as "purely physical" and 40 percent described them as "holiday romances." Twenty percent said that they had found "true love." Almost all the sexually active women surveyed stated that they had "helped their partner(s) out financially" by buying them meals, drinks, gifts, or by giving cash, and yet none of them perceived these relationships as commercial sexual transactions. Asked

whether they had ever been approached by a gigolo/prostitute during their stay in Jamaica, 90 percent of them replied in the negative. The data collected in the Dominican Republic revealed similar patterns of denial.

The informal nature of the sexual transactions in these resorts blurs the boundaries of what constitutes prostitution for Western women just as it does for Western men, allowing them to believe that the meals, cash, and gifts they provide for their sexual partners do not represent a form of payment for services rendered but rather an expression of their own munificence. It is only when women repeatedly enter into a series of extremely brief sexual encounters that they begin to acknowledge that, as one put it, "It's all about money." Even this does not lead them to view themselves as prostitute users, however, and again it is notions of difference and Otherness that play a key role in protecting the sex tourist from the knowledge that they are paying for the sexual attentions they receive. As Others, local men are viewed as beings possessed of a powerful and indiscriminate sexuality that they cannot control, and this explains their eagerness for sex with tourist women, regardless of their age, size, or physical appearance. Again, the Other is not *selling* sex, just "doing what comes naturally."

As yet, the number of black female sex tourists in Sanchez Taylor's survey and interview sample is too small to base any generalizations upon,[4] but so far their attitudes are remarkably consistent with those voiced by the central character in Terry Macmillan's 1996 novel *How Stella Got Her Groove Back,* in which a black American woman finds "love and romance" with a Jamaican boy almost half her age and with certainly less than half her economic means.[5] Stella views her own behavior in a quite different light from that of white male sex tourists—she disparages an older white male tourist as "a dirty old man who probably has to pay for all the pussy he gets" (Macmillan 1996: 83). It is also interesting to note the ways in which Macmillan "Otherizes" local men: the Jamaican boy smells "primitive"; he is "exotic and goes with the island"; he is "Mr.

Expresso in shorts" (ibid: 142, 154). Like white female sex tourists interviewed in the course of research, Macmillan further explains the young Jamaican man's disinterest in Jamaican women and so his sexual interest in an older American woman by Otherizing local women through the use of derogatory stereotypes. Thus, Jamaican women are assumed to be rapacious, materialistic, and sexually instrumental—they only want a man who owns a big car and house and money— and so Jamaican men long for women who do not demand these things (i.e., American women who already possess them).

Like their male counterparts, Western female sex tourists employ fantasies of Otherness not just to legitimate obtaining sexual access to the kind of young, fit, handsome bodies that would otherwise be denied to them and to obtain affirmation of their own sexual desirability (because the fact is that some female sex tourists are themselves young and fit looking and would be easily able to secure sexual access to equally appealing male bodies at home), but also to obtain a sense of power and control over themselves and others as engendered, sexual beings and to affirm their own privilege as Westerners. Thus they continually stress their belief that people in the Caribbean "are different from Westerners." Sexual life is one of the primary arenas in which this supposed difference is manifest. More than half of the female sex tourists surveyed in Jamaica stated that Jamaicans are more relaxed about teenage sex, casual sex, and prostitution than Westerners. In response to open-ended questions, they observed that "Jamaican men are more up front about sex," that "Jamaicans are uninhibited about sex," that "Jamaicans are naturally promiscuous," and that "sex is more natural to Jamaicans." In interviews, female sex tourists also reproduced the notion of an opposition between the "civilized" West and the "primitive" Third World. One Scots grandmother in her early forties described the Dominican Republic as follows: "It's just like Britain before its industrial phase, it's just behind Britain, just exactly the same. Kids used to get beat up to go

up chimneys, here they get beaten up to go polish shoes. There's no difference."

Western female sex tourists' racisms, like those of male sex tourists, are also many-layered and nuanced by differences in terms of nationality, age, and racialized identity. There are older white American female sex tourists whose beliefs about "race" and attitudes toward interracial sex are based upon an ideology that is overtly white supremacist. The black male represents for them the essence of an animalistic sexuality that both fascinates and repels. While in their own country they would not want to openly enter a sexual relationship with a black man, in a holiday resort like Negril they can transgress the racialized and gendered codes that normally govern their sexual behavior, while maintaining their honor and reputation back home. As one Jamaican gigolo commented:

> While they are here they feel free. Free to do what they never do at home. No one looking at them. Get a Black guy who are unavailable at home. No one judge them. Get the man to make them feel good then they go home clean and pure.

This observation, and all the sexual hostility it implies, is born out by the following extract from an interview with a 45-year-old white American woman from Chicago, a regular sex tourist to Negril:

> [Jamaican men] are all liars and cheats. . . . [American women come up Negril because] they get what they don't get back home. A girl who no one looks twice at back home, she gets hit on all the time here, all these guys are paying her attention, telling her she's beautiful, and they really want her. . . . They're obsessed with their dicks. That's all they think of, just pussy and money and nothing else. . . . In Chicago, this could never happen. It's like a secret, like a fantasy and then you go home.

When asked whether she would ever take a black boyfriend home and introduce him to her friends and family, she was emphatic that she would not—"No, no, never. It's not like that. This is something else, you know, it's time out. Like a fantasy." This is more than simply a fantasy about having multiple anonymous sexual encounters without getting caught and disgraced. It is also a highly racialized fantasy about power and vengeance. Women like the sex tourist quoted above are looking for black men with good bodies, firm and muscle-clad sex machines that they can control, and this element of control should not be overlooked. It is also important to female sex tourists who reject white supremacist ideologies, and there are many of these, including white liberals and young white women who value Blackness as a "cool" commodity in the same way that many young white men do, and black American and black British female sex tourists.

These latter groups do not wish to indulge in the overtly hostile racialized sexual fantasy described by the woman quoted above, but they do want to live out other fantasies, whether they be "educating and helping the noble savage," or being the focus of "cool" black men's adoring gaze, or being the central character of a Terry Macmillan novel.[6] No matter what specific fantasy they pursue, female sex tourists use their economic power to initiate and terminate sexual relations with local men at whim, and within those relationships, they use their economic and racialized power to control these men in ways in which they could never command a Western man. These are unaccustomed powers, and even the female sex tourists who buy into exoticizing rather than hostile and denigrating racisms appear to enjoy them as such.

For white women, these powers are very clearly linked to their own whiteness as well as to their status and economic power as tourist women. Thus they contrast their own experience against that of local women (remarking on the fact that they are respected and protected and not treated like local women) *and* against their experience back home (commenting on how safe they feel in the Caribbean walking alone at night and entering bars and discos by themselves, observing that local men are far more attentive and chival-

rous than Western men). Take, for example, the comments of "Judy," a white American expatriate in the Dominican Republic, a woman in her late fifties and rather overweight:

> When you go to a disco, [white] men eye up a woman for her body, whatever. Dominicans don't care because they love women, they love women. It's not that they're indifferent or anything. They are very romantic, they will never be rude with you, while a white man will say something rude to you, while Dominican men are not like that at all. A white man will say to me, like, "slut" to me and I have been with a lot of Dominican men and they would never say anything like that to you. They are more respectful. Light cigarettes, open doors, they are more gentlemen. Where white men don't do that. So if you have been a neglected woman in civilization, when you come down here, of course, when you come down here they are going to wipe you off your feet.

The Dominican Republic presents women like Judy with a stage upon which to simultaneously affirm their femininity through their ability to command men and exact revenge on white men by engaging sexually with the competition, i.e., the black male. For the first time she is in a position to call the shots. Where back home white female sex tourists' racialized privilege is often obscured by their lack of gender power and economic disadvantage in relation to white men, in sex tourist resorts it is recognized as a source of personal power and power over others. Meanwhile, their beliefs about gender and sexuality prevent them from seeing themselves as sexually exploitative. Popular discourses about gender present women as naturally sexually passive and receptive, and men as naturally indiscriminate and sexually voracious. According to this essentialist model of gender and sexuality, women can never sexually exploit men in the same way that men exploit women because penetrative heterosexual intercourse requires the woman to submit to the male—she is "used" by him. No matter how great the asymmetry between female tourist and local male in terms of their age or economic, social, and racialized power, it is still assumed that the male derives benefits from sex above and beyond the purely pecuniary and so is not being exploited in the same way that a prostitute woman is exploited by a male client. This is especially the case when the man so used is socially constructed as a racialized, ethnic, or cultural Other and assumed to have an uncontrollable desire to have sex with as many women as he possibly can.

Conclusion

The demand for sex tourism is inextricably linked to discourses that naturalize and celebrate inequalities structured along lines of class, gender, and race/Otherness; in other words, discourses that reflect and help to reproduce a profoundly hierarchical model of human sociality. Although sex tourists are a heterogeneous group in terms of their background characteristics and specific sexual interests, they share a common willingness to embrace this hierarchical model and a common pleasure in the fact that their Third World tourism allows them either to affirm their dominant position within a hierarchy of gendered, racialized, and economic power or to adjust their own position upward in that hierarchy. In the Third World, neocolonial relations of power equip Western sex tourists with an extremely high level of control over themselves and others as sexual beings and, as a result, with the power to realize the fantasy of their choosing. They can experience sexual intimacy without risking rejection; they can evade the social meanings that attach to their own age and body type; they can transgress social rules governing sexual life without consequence for their own social standing; they can reduce other human beings to nothing more than the living embodiments of masturbatory fantasies.

In short, sex tourists can experience in real life a world very similar to that offered in fantasy to pornography users: "Sexuality and sexual activity are portrayed in pornography as profoundly distanced from the activities of daily life. The action in pornography takes place in what Griffin has termed 'pornotopia,' a world outside real time and space" (Harstock 1985: 175). To sex tourists, the resorts they visit are fantasy islands, variously peopled by Little Brown Fucking Machines, "cool" black women who love to party, "primitive smelling" black studs who only think of "pussy and money," respectful Latin gentlemen who love women. All the sex tourist has to do to attain access to this fantasy world is to reach into his or her pocket, for it is there that the sex tourist, like other individuals in capitalist societies, carries "his social power as also his connection with society" (Marx 1973: 94). That the Western sex tourist's pocket can contain sufficient power to transform others into Others, mere players on a pornographic stage, is a testament to the enormity of the imbalance of economic, social, and political power between rich and poor nations. That so many Westerners *wish* to use their power in this way is a measure of the bleakness of the prevailing model of human nature and the human sociality that their societies offer them.

Notes

1. In 1995 we were commissioned by ECPAT (End Child Prostitution in Asian Tourism) to undertake research on the identity, attitudes, and motivations of clients of child prostitutes. This involved ethnographic fieldwork in tourist areas in South Africa, India, Costa Rica, Venezuela, Cuba, and the Dominican Republic. We are currently working on an Economic and Social Research Council-funded project (Award no. R 000 23 7625), which builds on this research through a focus on prostitution and the informal tourist economy in Jamaica and the Dominican Republic. Taking these projects together, we have interviewed some 250 sex tourists and sexpatriates and over 150 people involved in tourist-related prostitution (women, children, and men working as prostitutes, pimps, procurers, brothel keepers, etc.).

2. The fact that not all men are prostitute users is something that is often forgotten in radical feminist analyses of prostitution which, as Hart has noted, encourage us to view "either all men as prostitutes' clients or prostitutes' clients as somehow standing

for/being symbolic of men in general" (Hart 1994: 53).

3. Because the survey aims to support exploration and theory development in a previously underresearched field, purposive (nonprobability) sampling methods were employed (Arber 1993: 72). Sanchez Taylor obtained a sample by approaching all single female tourists in selected locations (a particular stretch of beach, or a given bar or restaurant) and asking them to complete questionnaires.

4. Four out of eighteen single black British and American female tourists surveyed had entered into sexual relationships with local men. Sanchez Taylor also interviewed four more black female sex tourists.

5. In Negril, gigolos often refer to black American female sex tourists as "Stellas," after this fictional character.

6. Macmillan hints at the transgressive elements of a black Western female sex tourist's excitement—Stella's desire for the "primitive"-smelling younger man makes her feel "kind of slutty," but she likes the feeling.

References

Arber, Sarah. "Designing Samples." *Researching Social Life*, ed. Nigel Gilbert, 68–92. London: Sage, 1993.

Bishop, Ryan and Lillian S. Robinson. *Night Market: Sexual Cultures and the Thai Economic Miracle*. New York: Routledge, 1998.

Brace, Laura and Julia O'Connell Davidson. "Desperate Debtors and Counterfeit Love: The Hobbesian World of the Sex Tourist." *Contemporary Politics* 2.3 (1996): 55–78.

Chevannes, Barry. "Sexual Behaviour of Jamaicans: A Literature Review." *Social and Economic Studies* 42.1 (1993).

Graaf, Ron de, Ine Vanwesenbeck, Gertjan van Zessen, Straver Visser, and Jan Visser. "Prostitution and the Spread of HIV." *Safe Sex in Prostitution in The Netherlands*, 2–24, Amsterdam: Mr A. de Graaf Institute, 1992.

Grewal, Inderpal. *Home and Harem: Nation, Gender, Empire and the Cultures of Travel*. London, Leicester University Press 1996.

Hall, C. Michael. "Gender and Economic Interests in Tourism Prostitution: The Nature, Development and Implications of Sex Tourism in South-East Asia." *Tourism: A Gender Perspective*, ed. Vivien Kinnaird and D. Hall. London: Routledge, 1994.

Hart, Angie, "Missing Masculinity? Prostitutes' Clients in Alicante, Spain." *Dislocating Masculinity: Comparative Ethnographics*, ed. Andrea Cornwall and Nancy Lindisfarne, 48–65. London: Routledge, 1994.

Harstock, Nancy. *Money, Sex, and Power*. Boston: Northeastern University Press, 1985.

hooks, bell. *Black Looks: Race and Representation*. London: Turnaround; Boston: South End Press, 1992.

———. *Outlaw Culture: Resisting Representations*. London; Routledge, 1994.

Jeffreys, Sheila. *The Idea of Prostitution*. Melbourne: Spinifex, 1997.

Karch, Cecilia A. and G. H. S. Dann, "Close Encounters of the Third Kind." *Human Relations* 34 (1981): 249–68.

Kempadoo, Kamala. "Prostitution, Marginality, and Empowerment: Caribbean Women in the Sex Trade." *Beyond Law* 5.14 (1994): 69–84.

———. "Regulating Prostitution in the Dutch Caribbean." Paper presented at the 20th annual conference of the Caribbean Studies Association, Caraçao, Netherlands Antrilles, May 1995.

———. "Dominicanas en Curaçao: Miros y Realidades." *Genero y Sociedad* 4.1 (May–August 1996): 102– 30.

Kruhse-Mount Burton, Suzy. "Sex Tourism and Traditional Australian Male Identity." *International Tourism: Identity and Change*, ed. Marie-Françoise Lanfant, John Allcock, and Edward Bruner, 192–204. London: Sage, 1995.

Lee, Wendy. "Prostitution and Tourism in South-East Asia." *Working Women: International Perspectives on Labour and Gender Ideology*, ed. N. Redclift and M. Thea Sinclair, 79–103. London: Routledge, 1991.

Macmillan, Terry. *How Stella Got Her Groove Back*. New York: Penguin, 1996.

Marx, Karl. *Grundisse*. Harmondsworth, England: Penguin, 1973.

Morris-Jarra, Monica. "No Such Thing as a Cheap Holiday." *Tourism in Focus 26* (Autumn 1996): 6–7.

O'Connell Davidson, Julia. *Prostitution, Power and Freedom*. Cambridge: Polity Press, 1998.

Perio, Gaelle and Dominique Thierry. *Tourisme Sexuel au Bresil et en Colombie.* Rapport D'Enquete, TOURGOING, 1996.

Plumridge, Elizabeth and Jane Chetwynd. "Discourses of Emotionality in Commercial Sex." *Feminism & Psychology* 7.2 (1997): 165–81.

Pruitt, Deborah and Suzanne LaFont. "For Love and Money: Romance Tourism in Jamaica." *Annals of Tourism Research* 22.2 (1995): 422–40.

Sanchez Taylor, Jacqueline. "Marking the Margins: Research in the Informal Economy in Cuba and the Dominican Republic." Discussion Paper No. 597/1, Department of Sociology, University of Leicester, 1997.

Seabrook, Jeremy. *Travels in the Skin Trade: Tourism and the Sex Industry.* London: Pluto Press, 1997.

Shrage, Laurie, *Moral Dilemmas of Feminism.* London: Routledge, 1994.

Steller, Robert, *Perversion: The Erotic Form of Hatred,* London: Karnac, 1986.

Sturdevant, Saundra and Brenda Stolzfus. *Let the Good Times Roll: Prostitution and the U.S. Military in Asia.* New York: The New Press, 1992.

Truong, Than Dam. *Sex, Money and Morality: The Political Economy of Prostitution and Tourism in South East Asia.* London: Zed Books, 1990.

Young, Lola. *Fear of the Dark: "Race," Gender and Sexuality in the Cinema.* London: Routledge, 1996.

PART EIGHT

Men in Families

Are men still taking seriously their responsibilities as family breadwinners? Are today's men sharing more of the family housework and childcare than those in previous generations? The answers to these questions are complex, and often depend on which men we are talking about and what we mean when we say "family."

Many male workers long ago won a "family wage" and, with it, made an unwritten pact to share that wage with a wife and children. But today, as Barbara Ehrenreich argues in her influential book *The Hearts of Men*, increasing numbers of men are revolting against this traditional responsibility to share their wages, thus contributing to the rapidly growing impoverishment of women and children. Ehrenreich may be correct, at least with respect to the specific category of men who were labeled "yuppies" in the 1980s. But if we are looking at the growing impoverishment of women and children among poor, working-class,

and minority families, the causes have more to do with dramatic shifts in the structure of the economy—including skyrocketing unemployment among young black males—than they do with male irresponsibility. Increasing numbers of men have no wage to share with a family.

But how about the new dual-career family? Is this a model of egalitarianism, or do women still do what sociologist Arlie Hochschild calls "the second shift"—the housework and childcare that comes after they get home from work. In this section, Francine Deutsch examines dual-career families and observes how men get out of sharing housework and childcare. Deutsch makes clear that equality will come only when we have dual careers and dual-career families. Anne Shelton and Daphne John examine the different patterns among men of different ethnic groups.

Also in flux are notions of fatherhood and how this role may be changing. Are men becoming more nurturing and caring fathers, developing skills, like the men in Hollywood films such as *Knocked Up*, or simply loving their children more than life itself? The articles in this section cause us to expand the debate about fatherhood, recognizing the variety of fatherhoods that are evidenced by different groups of men, such as gay men (Judith Stacey). Scott Coltrane summarizes the research on the effects of involved fatherhood.

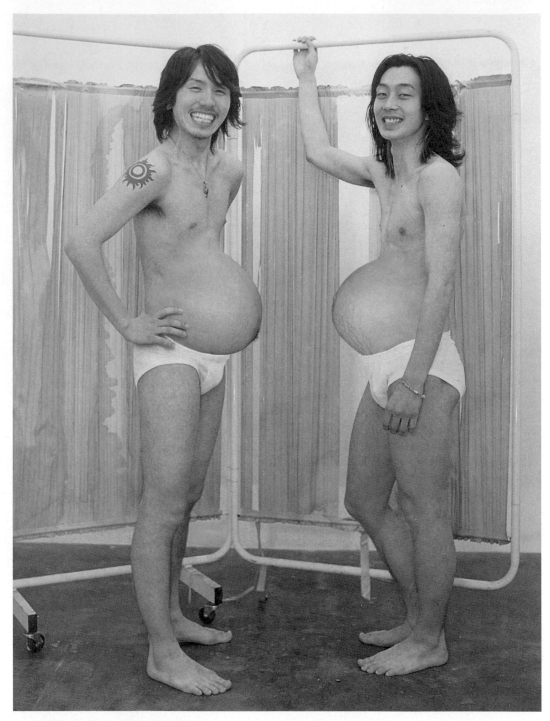

Hiroko Okada, Future Plan #2, 2003
© Hiroko OKADA. Courtesy Mizuma Art Gallery

Francine M. Deutsch

Strategies Men Use to Resist

Women's ambivalence alone certainly doesn't account for the unequal division of labor at home. The unequal men are hardly fighting to do an equal share of the work. In part, they feel entitled to their wives' domestic services, entitled to pursue unfettered careers, and entitled to relax after their day at the job. Yet they don't feel as entitled as their fathers did. They recognize that their wives are out doing paid labor as well. The men in my study virtually never justified their lack of involvement in household work by invoking some inherent right or privilege they held as men. Although even recent statistics show that women do much more of the household labor, the raw spoken claim of male privilege seems to have become taboo. Men do resist, but their strategies are largely indirect. They include: passive resistance, strategic incompetence, strategic use of praise, the adherence of inferior standards, and denial.

Passive Resistance

"Just say nothing!" seems to be the motto of some men who resist their wives' efforts to involve them in household work. The most obvious form of passive resistance is simply to ignore the request. When I asked one father how he responded to his wife's entreaties, he answered, "In one ear, and out the other."

From *Halving It All* by Francine Deutsch, Cambridge, MA: Harvard University Press, 1999.

Obliviousness can be another form of passive resistance. Ethan sits with his coffee oblivious to his children's requests for juice. Another mother reports a similar scene at her house:

> He plants himself on the couch. As soon as he's home from work sometimes . . . If there's something going on with kids, the kids could be screaming and yelling. He's totally oblivious to it. I'm listening to it (while preparing dinner) and I have to come out here and say something to them.

Sometimes men give in and perform a particular household duty, but their grouchiness while doing so becomes another form of passive resistance:

> He'll help do dishes once in a while . . . He might put up a stink, but he'll end up doing it. I think I . . . try to sleaze out of it (responsibility when at home) as much as I can . . . I try to dicker or make an excuse or something as my first response, but I usually end up, perhaps somewhat nastily, taking care of them (household chores).

Passive resistance is effective because it requires so much energy to overcome. Women, already tired from their double day, may give up the struggle if the cost of getting help looks higher than the benefits of that help. Having to ask a husband to pour the juice when a child asks may feel like more effort than it's worth. As one mother put it: "I have to direct him and it's easier for me to just do it." The sulking, unpleasant compliance of a husband who clearly resents doing a chore will probably cloud whatever satisfaction his wife feels in getting help. Small wonder that the next time she may very well shrink from trying to obtain his help.

Incompetence

Ruining the laundry, leaving grease on the dishes, ignoring children when one is supposed to be watching them, and forgetting to pick them up from activities are all examples of the strategy of incompetence. Incompetence has its rewards. It allows men to justify the gender-based distribution of domestic labor.

> Getting the kids dressed—these buttons are so tiny I can't do these tiny buttons . . . Poor kids, they're always getting dressed backwards.
>
> Dinnertime. Mom is the cook. When the kids hear that Daddy's going to be making dinner, they'd rather eat out. I'm not talented. I'm just not very good in the kitchen.
>
> I just don't possess the tools to deal with girls' clothing, whereas she can.

Women may think twice about trying to get their husbands to take more responsibility at home when the way they carry out those responsibilities creates more problems than it solves: "From time to time he's taken on laundry, but that always ends up really a disaster, something being stained or shrunk, so I don't want him to do laundry."

Ruined laundry or mismatched children's outfits may be annoying, but incompetent care for children can be downright frightening. One mother recounted an incident in which her husband forgot her specific instructions to pick up his eight-year-old son before the older one so that the younger child wouldn't be waiting alone. The eight-year-old did end up waiting on a corner for his father, not alone only because another mother discovered his predicament and waited with him. Not surprisingly, she concludes, "Sometimes I don't trust (my husband) . . . He just doesn't pay attention."

Likewise, another mother explained why she worries when her husband watches their two-year-old:

> The other day he was outside with her and he was sitting there reading the newspaper. I never do that, never sit there and read a newspaper, not because I have to see everything that she does. It was more of a safety thing . . . I would like to feel more confident that when he's alone with her he is watching out for her safety-wise. I sometimes think he's not as conscious of safety.

One might argue that men's "incompetence" in household chores is not a strategy, but simply reflects their lack of skill because of the way they were raised. Boys aren't taught how to take care of children and how to do laundry. According to this argument, even if their incompetence functions to relieve them of domestic responsibility, it doesn't mean that the incompetence is by design. There are two flaws in this argument.

First, although women may be socialized to feel the responsibility for childcare, many have not learned any of the necessary skills before they actually become parents. The difference between them and their husbands is that they know they have no choice. They have to learn how to button those tiny buttons, how to feed solid food, and how to soothe a crying infant. Although these women may have begun parenthood as incompetently as their husbands, the expectations that they and others hold for them as mothers mean that they simply learn what is necessary to learn.

Second, the skills in question can readily be learned. If one took the descriptions of men's incompetence at face value, one would wonder how these men held down jobs. Can it really be the case that a machinist or a man who holds a Ph.D. is incapable of running a washing machine? Women and men often say that women are the managers at home because the women are more organized, but how then do these "disorganized" men manage at work? If a man "forgot" important responsibilities at work the way the father just described "forgot" to pick up his eight-year-old son, he might soon be out of a job.

At heart the issue is not competence, but motivation. If someone wants to learn how to cook, do laundry, take care of children, and manage the household chores she or he can certainly do so. The equally sharing (and alternating-shift) fathers make eminently clear that competence in household skills is not the exclusive domain of women. Some women are not fooled by their husband's cries of incompetence. Listen to this mother's take on what happens when she asks for some help:

> He plays, you know, "How do you do this kind of thing?" and asks me fifteen questions so it would almost be easier for me to do it myself than to sit there and answer all his questions. That makes me angry because I feel like he's just playing stupid because he doesn't want to do it.

The strategy of incompetence often works. Like passive resistance, it is a way of making the cost of the struggle over the work at home too high. This mother sums it up succinctly: "If they act incompetent, then we have to act competent . . . I have this fear that if I didn't do it, then it wouldn't get done or it would be done incompetently." It is a fear that has basis in fact.

Praise

The flip side of men's self-portrayals of incompetence is their praise of their wives' skill in domestic labor. Although praise may be a sincere expression of appreciation, a benefit to its recipient, praise at home may also have the insidious effect of keeping the work within women's domain. The underlying message from men to their wives may sometimes be: "You're so good at it, you should do it." Sometimes the message is hardly subtle: "It would be a struggle for me to do the laundry. I don't think I do it as well as Roz. I think she is better with sort of the *peasant* stuff of life." And the father who said the kids wanted to

eat out when they heard Dad was the cook told me: "I only eat to survive, but Dale is just wonderful. She makes these fabulous dinners." In a few couples men used the praise they heaped on their wives to justify why childcare was divided traditionally in their households:

> I definitely wasn't as good as Roz. Roz's just good. She's good if they get a splinter. She's just good at all that stuff.

> She's wonderful (as a mother) . . . Some women, like I say, are geared to be businesswomen; Florence is geared to be a mother. She loves it. She's good at it. I feel real lucky to have her as a partner because it takes a lot of the burden off me.

Praise can be insidious precisely because women do derive satisfaction from a job well done at home and from receiving recognition for it. Ironically, praise may undermine women's struggle for more help because they don't want to lose the self-esteem they derive from husbands' admiring accolades.

Different Standards

Another strategy men use to resist work at home is to maintain different and lower standards. Their spoken or unspoken claim is that they don't care as much as their wives if the house is clean, if a nutritious dinner is served, or if children have after-school activities.

There are three ways that couples might respond to this difference. First, men could raise their standards to meet their wives'. This rarely happens among the unequal couples. Second, women could lower their standards, which occasionally does occur among this group. Most commonly, however, the difference in standards becomes a driving force behind an unequal division. The person who cares more takes the responsibility and does the work.

Women usually care more about keeping the house neat and clean because they, and not their husbands, are judged to be lacking if the house is a mess: "He wouldn't care if it wasn't dusted once every six months. I care because it's a reflection on me. Now that's another problem. Why should it be a reflection on me? He lives here too. But if anybody comes in here and the house is dirty, they're going to think that I'm a slob." Nonetheless, women are lowering their standards for household care, as sales of paper plates have increased and sales of floor wax have declined.

The problem of what children need is a more troubling one. When the welfare of children is involved, women often feel they can't compromise their standards. Denise gave up a camping trip because she thought one parent should be home with her kids. Other mothers changed their jobs so they could meet the school bus when their husbands wouldn't do it or take their children to the after-school activities that they cared about more than their husbands did.

Denial

Just as a magician tricks us by directing our gaze elsewhere while he makes his move, some fathers deny there is a problem by focusing attention elsewhere while their wives do the work at home. Denial takes a variety of forms. Men exaggerate their own contributions by comparing themselves to previous generations, attribute greater contributions of their wives to their wives' personalities or preferences, and obscure who's doing what by invoking rules and patterns that sound fair and equal.

Men often recall their own fathers' roles at home in order to understand their superior contributions. Ironically, some men who do far less than their wives even see themselves as progressive role models. One father in a dual-earner family said he did 35 percent of the childcare; his wife said 25 percent. Nevertheless, he sees himself as a model of equality. His exaggerated view of his contributions seems to stem from his implicit comparison to himself and his father. When I asked why mothers usually did more at home, he said, "Because of the roles of our parents." (His

analysis, of course, ignores that his wife leads a very different life from that of his mother, who was never employed outside the home.) He went on to describe his own contributions in glowing terms:

> We've joked and talked about many of the things that I try and do as far as helping and participating . . . I'm hoping that as our girls are selecting mates later in life, they remember how much I helped out and how caring and listening I was . . . One of the advantages for kids that I'm involved with parenting (is) that they will expect their spouses will be involved. I'm a strong advocate of equal rights of women.

No doubt he is a loving and caring father, but he is far from contributing an equal share at home. He does help out, but his enthusiasm for the benefits of their modern division of labor must be considered in light of the inequality between him and his wife and her response to their division: "Sometimes I get overwhelmed and tired, real tired." By focusing on what he is doing that his father didn't, this man seems to miss what his wife is doing that he is not.

Men sometimes obscure an unequal division of labor by talking about and perhaps thinking about themselves and their wives as interchangeable. When I asked men to describe a typical day, indicating who did what, they sometimes used the word "we." "We get the kids ready for school." "We unloaded the dishwasher." Invariably, on further investigation, "we" meant that their wives were doing it.

Men also suggested by a false interchangeability between themselves and their wives by invoking a rule for dividing household labor that ostensibly applied equally to each, but actually worked in their favor. For example, parents commonly reported that whoever was available did the task at hand. Although that might sound like an equitable procedure, it is not if the father arranges to be unavailable. Consider this family. The father describes the division of responsibility at night: "As far as helping with the homework it's fairly equal . . . We both tend to try to help out—whoever's free that night . . . It's not you're going to do the help in math or I'm going to help in math. It's who's free." That sounds equitable, but listen to his wife's description of what happens in the evening:

> That's been a bone of contention lately. Sawyer goes out a lot . . . He still runs a lot at night so that leaves me to deal with the homework . . . She (one of their children) needs a lot of help with math, so that any homework issues I've been dealing with, and getting the youngest ready for bed.

He goes out, so guess who is available?

Finally, fathers sometimes engage in denial when they acknowledge an inequity in the distribution of labor but attribute it to personality characteristics or personal preferences of their wives. Men exaggerated their wives' enjoyment of the family work. For example, this 75–25 father told me: "Cooking relaxes her. She likes to do it and she likes to keep busy for the most part." But when I talked to his wife, she *complained* that he didn't make dinner when he got home from work early.

By imagining their wives' desire and need to do the domestic labor, these men avoid acknowledging the inequity within the couple. This denial allows them to resist not only the work, but also the guilt they might feel if they viewed the situation accurately.

Clearly, men in the unequal families resist the work at home. But the unequal men are not villains. In fact, most are helpers, not slackers. They do relinquish some male privileges, even while they resist giving up others. However, they also ignore the need for their help, feign incompetence, manipulate their wives with praise, discourage them with very low household and parental standards, and avoid work by denying that there is any conflict at all. All of these strategies work to relieve men of household work without their having to admit directly that they simply

don't feel responsible for it. Despite the time their wives spend earning a paycheck, the unequal men often feel entitled to avoid picking up the slack at home. The myth implicitly promulgated by these men is that their wives do the work at home not simply because they are women, but because they notice it, they're better at it, and they enjoy it more.

Although these work-resisting strategies are used mostly by the unequal husbands, the equally sharing husbands are not perfect either. Some resist giving up at least a few traditional male privileges. Housework, in particular, seemed an area of contention. For example, in one of the most explicitly feminist equally sharing couples I interviewed, the father's "incompetence" in doing laundry sounded remarkably familiar. Even in the most equal of households, there may be vestiges of the old ways. Still, even if there are some pockets of resistance, for the most part the equally sharing fathers honor their wives' claims to equality.

Strong Women and Reasonable Men

Strong women and reasonable men resolve the conflict over domestic work by inventing equality. Equally sharing mothers are an assertive crew. They communicate in a clear and direct manner, and use whatever clout they have to elicit their husbands' cooperation. Their husbands acknowledge the strength of these women in establishing equality at home:

> Sally is very strong. There's no question about that. I think it's partly that Sally . . . makes it that we both share. She feels very strongly about that.
>
> I think the most important reason is that Bernice absolutely, completely insists on it.

However, part of the reason these women appear strong is their success, and although women's strength may be necessary in the fight for equality, it is not sufficient. The strength and assertiveness of the equally sharing mothers is matched by the sense of fairness evident in the behavior of the equally sharing fathers. Equally sharing men have relinquished male privileges to which at least some had initially felt entitled.

In fact, the equally sharing women may argue for principles of equality because they sense they have a shot at success with their husbands. The unequally sharing mothers, realizing the futility of trying for equality in their families, settle for trying to get their husbands to do a bit more. The equally sharing mothers may not have to resort to meltdowns because their husbands have already responded. The rage of the unequal women may express more than the frustration of trying to do the impossible. It may be the rage of impotence at their failure to get more help.

Compare the experience of the equally sharing mothers who won the battles for equality to that of Madeline, a legal services attorney with two children, who began parenthood with strong views about equal sharing. She and her husband agreed that when their first child was born each of them would take parental leave, and subsequently each of them would cut back on paid work to care for their new baby to avoid using too much daycare. Her husband, Aaron, was thrilled with his equally sharing role in the early years of parenting: "I was very excited about it. I had a paternity leave and . . . did sole care . . . and then worked a three- or four-day week for another year . . . There was a lot of time when I was just with my son and I considered that a privilege." Equal sharing was initially achieved in this family with little conflict. But perhaps signs of the dénouement were evident in the meaning Aaron ascribed to his sharing. The language he uses as he enthusiastically describes his role as a new parent is telling. It is the language of personal choice: "It was just great. It completely felt like my own choice and not something that I should do or that I had to do."

It is difficult to imagine a mother speaking these words. No matter how thrilled she is at spending time with a new infant, there is no denying that caring for a new baby is something she "should do." Aaron expresses the thrill of parenting at the same time that he asserts his entitlement not to do it. He immerses himself in parenthood the first time around because he wants to, not because he feels ultimately that it is his responsibility to do so. Thus, after their second child was born, when his career was getting off the ground and he had less passion and energy for parenting, he felt entitled to refuse to do it. He refused to take parental leave or cut back to part-time work. His wife told me:

> If you had come a year after William was born, then you would have found us struggling more about whose responsibility was what. I was feeling very much like Aaron was reneging on the commitment that we made about being with William . . . I had made my commitment and he wasn't keeping his part of the bargain.

Madeline was every bit as assertive as the equally sharing mothers. Yet, although she fought for her belief in equal responsibility for childcare clearly and directly, today she compromises her career while her husband takes a helper role at home. Aaron's analysis of what happens in "society" aptly describes what happened in his own family: "I think probably men feel they have the option to invest or not invest, whereas I think women feel they're the bottom line and they can't count on anyone else to do that."

Madeline may not appear as strong as other equally sharing mothers simply because she failed. Her husband did not honor her claims of equality. Aaron differed from the equally sharing men because those men accepted the justice of their wives' claims, even if they hadn't internalized as strong a feeling of responsibility for family life as their wives had. One extraordinarily honest equally sharing father acknowledged that although he "irrationally" wished his wife would create a more traditional family life, "rationally" he recognized that it wouldn't be fair: "I'm hardly a raging feminist, but I do have enough sense to see that that's a completely unfair distribution of labor."

Thus a sense of fairness motivates some of the equally sharing men to accept their wives' well-argued claims. Moreover, that sense of fairness drives some of the men to share even without a struggle. Let's not forget Paul, the father of five, who jumped in to help without prompting from his wife. His sense of fairness and love for his wife dictated that it wouldn't be right to shirk while she worked.

The sense of entitlement that men and women bring to marriage affects the content and conduct of their conflicts, but it also changes and develops over time. Feelings of entitlement lead women to fight for principles, make clear and rational demands, and back them up with power-assertive strategies. But the feelings of entitlement expressed by the equally sharing mothers can also be a product, rather than a precursor, of their success. When their husbands accept principles of equality, respond to their demands, or indicate that their relationships are more important than male privilege, they promote a feeling of entitlement in their wives.

For example, consider Paul's wife, Mary, the equally sharing mother of five who didn't demand equality or even fight for it. When I asked her whether she or Paul had more leisure time, she reflected for a few seconds (indicating there wasn't much difference between them) and then replied, "I don't know, maybe he has a little bit more," adding in a light-hearted tone, "I'll have to do something about that." Once achieved, equality feels like a right.

Conversely, when the unequal husbands resist, they undermine their wives' sense of entitlement to their help. Listen to this mother's story:

There's some things that aren't worth fighting over. I always know when (my husband) has been babysitting for a couple of hours because the living room looks like a demolition derby has come through. And the bathroom looks the same way . . . the dirty diapers are in there and

all the dirty clothes are all over the bathroom floor . . . So I just have learned that it's not worth wasting all kinds of extra energy. I just kind of do it, not necessarily that I like it. *He helps much more than a lot of fathers help.*

The futility of some struggles leads women to give up and to readjust their expectations. Instead of comparing their husbands' contributions to their own, they shift to comparing their husbands' contributions to those of other men. It is precisely that focus on within-gender comparison that maintains different senses of entitlement between men and women. If a husband does more than his peers, his wife may then conclude she is getting a good deal. But although she may be getting a good deal relative to other women, it's not so good when you compare it to what her husband is getting. The shift in comparisons, however, allows women to live with resistant husbands and not feel exploited.

Men's senses of entitlement are also, in part, products of the struggle with their wives. When you look at the equally sharing men now, they all seem eminently reasonable. For some, the reasonable stance was born out of serious strife with their wives. Interestingly, sometimes these men don't mention the conflicts that led up to their equally sharing role. For example, the husband who had expected his wife to "cook, clean, . . . and box his collars" made no mention of the strikes his wife used to get him to change. His transformation occurred so thoroughly that now his explanation for equal sharing refers only to his own sense of responsibility to do right by his children.

Discovering themselves acting like egalitarians, equally sharing fathers often pat themselves on the back for their enlightened stance. Meanwhile, their wives tout their own assertiveness and strength. Although they look like they have always been strong women and reasonable men, it is important not to forget that female strength and male reason are qualities that are sustained, lost, or developed in the creation of family life.

Anne Shelton
Daphne John

Ethnicity, Race, and Difference: A Comparison of White, Black, and Hispanic Men's Household Labor Time

Most of the recent research on household labor concerns the impact of women's labor force participation on the allocation of tasks or responsibilities. Researchers routinely recognize that women's household labor time is associated with their employment status, as well as with a variety of other sociodemographic characteristics, including age and education. A great deal has been written about the ways in which time commitments and sex role attitudes affect the division of household labor (Coverman 1985; Huber and Spitze 1983; Perrucci, Potter, and Rhoads 1978; Pleck 1985; Ross 1987). Men are by definition included in the analyses that focus on the division of household labor, but these studies typically ignore the relationship between men's work and family roles.

Some researchers have examined the relationship between men's work and family roles (Coverman 1985; Pleck 1977, 1985), but the relative scarcity of these studies means that although some questions about men's household roles have been examined, a number of issues remain unexamined. In particular, there has been little research on the impact of men's paid labor time on their household labor time and there has been only limited research on racial and ethnic variations in men's household labor time.

In this analysis we begin to examine some of the neglected issues in the study of men's house-

From *Men, Work, and Family*, Jane Hood (ed.), pp. 131–150. Sage Publications, 1993. Reprinted with permission.

hold labor time by focusing on how married men's paid labor time affects their family roles as defined by their household labor time and specific household tasks. Although there is less variation in men's paid labor time than in women's, there is some variation, and just as paid labor time affects women's household labor time, it may also affect men's. Moreover, the amount of time men have available to them may affect the specific household tasks they perform, with men with more time performing more nondiscretionary tasks than men who have less time available to them.

Recently, increased awareness of the need to examine links between gender and race have led many to argue that race and gender cannot, in fact, be discussed separately (Collins 1990; Reid and Comas-Diaz 1990; Zinn 1991). Moreover, "gender studies" should not be limited only to women. Therefore, we assess the impact of selected sociodemographic characteristics on men's household labor time with a special emphasis on race and ethnicity.

Literature Review

The changes in women's labor force participation have resulted in a large number of dual-earner couples. Kimmel (1987) notes that this shift has created not only new role demands for women, but also new demands for men. Just as women have expanded their roles in the paid labor force, men also have expanded their roles in the family. The transition in men's and women's roles may, however, vary by race and ethnicity because of the historically different patterns of black, white, and Hispanic women's labor force participation (Beckett and Smith 1981; McAdoo 1990).

Although researchers routinely examine the impact of women's paid labor time on the household division of labor, the impact of men's paid labor time on the household division of labor is generally ignored. The lack of attention to the impact of men's paid work time on their household labor time may reflect the fact that there is less variability in men's paid labor time than in women's. Those studies that have examined the impact of men's paid work time on their household labor time have yielded conflicting results (Barnett and Baruch 1987; Coverman and Sheley 1986; Pleck 1985; Thompson and Walker 1989). Some find that men's time spent in paid labor is negatively associated with their household labor time (Rexroat and Shehan 1987; Atkinson and Huston 1984), whereas others find no association (Kingston and Nock 1985). Because this research rarely focuses on racial/ethnic variation, we have little information about the ways that paid labor and household labor demands may be related differently for white, black, and Hispanic men.

Research on black and Hispanic households indicates that the images of the egalitarian black household and the gender-stratified Hispanic household may be inaccurate depictions of reality derived from superficial examinations. In the case of black households, egalitarianism is commonly attributed to black women's high rates of labor force participation (McAdoo 1990). If, however, black women's labor force participation reflects economic pressures rather than egalitarian sex role attitudes (Broman 1988, 1991), women's employment may be unrelated to the division of labor.

Research on the division of labor in black households does not consistently indicate how black and white households differ. Some research on the division of household labor finds that black families have a more egalitarian division of labor than white families (Beckett 1976; Beckett

and Smith 1981; Broman 1988, 1991). Other studies by J. A. Ericksen, Yancey, and E. P. Ericksen (1979) and Farkas (1976) also suggest that black men do more household labor than their white counterparts (see also Miller and Garrison 1982). However, Broman (1991, 1988) argues that although some egalitarian patterns do exist in black households, there is not gender equity. For example, in married couple households the proportions of men who state they do most of the household chores is much smaller than the proportion of women responding that they do all the household chores. Although unemployed men respond that they do more of the household chores more frequently than employed men, they do not make this claim nearly as often as women, regardless of women's employment status. Broman (1988) also notes that women are likely to report being primarily responsible for traditionally female tasks.

Other researchers argue that the image of the egalitarian black family is inaccurate (Cronkite 1977; Staples 1978; Wilson, Tolson, Hinton, and Kiernan 1990). For example, Wilson et al. (1990) point out that black women are likely to be responsible for child care and household labor. Cronkite (1977) says that black men prefer more internal differentiation in the household than do white men. That is, she argues that they prefer a more traditional division of household labor, with women responsible for housework and child care. Others claim that black families are similar to white families in egalitarianism and that the differences that do exist often are based on social class rather than on race per se (McAdoo 1990; Staples 1978). Staples (1978) also claims that class differences are consistent across race. McAdoo (1990) argues, in much the same vein, that black and white fathers are similarly nurturant to their children and that black and white middle- and upper-income fathers have similar parenting styles. In contrast to the view that black men are less traditional than white men, Ransford and Miller (1983) find that middle-class black men have more traditional sex role attitudes than white middle-class men.

The literature regarding the division of household labor within Hispanic households is more limited, and much of what is available deals only with Chicanos, excluding other Hispanics. The research on Hispanic households yields conflicting results. Golding (1990) finds that Mexican American men do less household labor than Anglo men, whereas Mexican American women do more household labor than Anglo women. Differences between Hispanic and Anglo men's housework and child care time, like the differences between black and white men, may be due to other differences between them (Golding 1990; McAdoo 1990; Staples 1978). Golding (1990) finds that education is correlated with ethnicity and household labor time such that after removing the effects of education, the impact of ethnicity on the division of labor in the household is not significant. Thus, although she finds a more traditional division of labor within Mexican American households than in Anglo households, this division of labor reflects educational differences rather than solely ethnicity effects. Similarly, Ybarra (1982) finds that although acculturation does not significantly affect who performs the household labor, wives' employment does. She finds that the division of labor in dual-worker households is more equal than in male provider households.

In other research, Mirandé (1979) discusses the patterns of shared responsibility for domestic work in Mexican American households. Although men's participation in household labor may give the appearance of egalitarianism, it does not necessarily indicate equality. For example, men may participate but spend less time than women. Vega and colleagues (1986) argue that Mexican American families are similar to Anglo families but that in terms of their adaptability to change in family roles they appear to be more flexible than Anglo families. Thus the male provider role may be less firmly entrenched in Mexican American than in Anglo households, resulting in a less rigid division of household labor. Similarly, Zinn (1980) asserts that Mexican American women's changing work roles may change their role identification.

There also is research indicating that decision making is not shared in Hispanic households (Williams 1990). Williams (1990) finds that Mexican American men continue to have more authority than wives, but that the patterns of decision making are not as traditional as in the past.

Some research suggests that the differences among white, black, and Hispanic men's family roles may reflect differences in the way that they internalize the provider role. Wilkie (1991) argues that black men's ability to fulfill the provider role may be associated with their rates of marriage (see also Tucker and Taylor 1989). Similarly, Stack (1974) found that when black men are unable to provide financially for their family, they also are less likely to participate in the household (e.g., housework and child care) (Cazenave 1979; Wilkie 1991). Although the findings of Wilkie (1991) and Tucker and Taylor (1989) do not directly indicate a relationship between the provider role and men's participation in the household, we can speculate that this association may exist. Thus, to the extent that there are differences among black, white, and Hispanic men's internalization of the provider role, we might also expect to find that the relationship between work and family roles varies by race/ethnicity.

We focus on the definition of egalitarianism based on the division of labor within the household. Hood (1983) notes that there are a number of ways in which an egalitarian marriage is defined. For our purposes, egalitarianism is defined in terms of household labor time. Some studies discuss decision making and role sharing, which are logically associated with the division of household labor, but which are not unproblematically related to it (Blumstein and Schwartz 1983).

A problem with much of the research on men's household labor time is the failure to incorporate wives' characteristics into the analyses. Just as men's paid labor time may act as a constraint on their household labor time, wives' paid labor time may create a demand for them to spend more time on household labor. The use of couples as the units of analysis in this chapter helps us understand the interaction between spouses' characteristics.

We further examine white, black, and Hispanic men's household labor time to determine the nature of the association between men's paid labor time and household labor time. In addition, we examine racial/ethnic differences in men's household labor time and assess the extent to which any observed differences may reflect differences in paid labor time, education, or other sociodemographic characteristics. We also incorporate wives' paid labor time and attitudes about family roles into our analysis to determine the ways in which husbands' and wives' characteristics interact to affect men's household labor time.

Data and Methods

The data for this study are from the 1987 National Survey of Families and Households (NSFH) (Sweet, Bumpass, and Call 1988), a national probability sample of 9,643 persons with an oversampling of 3,374 minority respondents, single parents, cohabiting persons, recently married persons, and respondents with stepchildren. One adult per household was selected randomly to be the primary respondent and his or her spouse/partner (if applicable) was also given a questionnaire designed for secondary respondents. Portions of the main interview with the primary respondent were self-administered, as was the entire spouse/partner questionnaire. In this analysis, we include only married respondents with a completed spouse questionnaire.

In the analyses to follow we begin by describing black, white, and Hispanic men's and women's household labor time. In addition to comparing household labor time across racial/ethnic groups, we also compare this time by work status.

In the second stage of the analysis, we examine the relationship between ethnicity and men's household labor time after controlling for a variety of other factors, including age, education, sex role attitudes, and both husbands' and wives' paid work. We use multiple regression analysis to determine if there are race/ethnic differences in

household labor time or in the impact of paid labor time on household labor time that are independent of sociodemographic differences between white, black, and Hispanic men.[1]

In addition to determining whether or not a race/ethnicity effect on household labor time exists once other characteristics have been taken into account, we look at the relationship between husbands' and wives' paid labor and household labor time. We expect to find that men who spend more time in paid work will spend less time on household labor once other characteristics have been held constant. Moreover, to the extent that wives' market work time may act as a demand on men, we expect to find that the more time wives spend in paid labor the more time husbands will spend on household labor, once other variables have been held constant.

Our analyses include separate estimates of white, black, and Hispanic men's and women's household labor time. Hispanics include Mexican Americans as well as other Hispanic respondents. Paid labor time is measured in hours usually spent per week at work for both respondents and spouses. Education and age are measured in years.

Respondents' and spouses' sex role attitudes are measured by their responses to two attitude items. Each item was scored from 1 to 5. Respondents were asked if they agreed with the following statements:

1. If a husband and a wife both work full-time, they should share household tasks equally.
2. Preschool children are likely to suffer if their mother is employed.

Responses to the two items were summed and divided by two so that the range of the summated measure is 1 to 5. A high score indicates more liberal sex role attitudes and a low score indicates more traditional sex role attitudes.

Presence of children was included as an independent variable in some of the analyses. A score of 0 indicates that the respondent has no children under the age of 18 in the household, whereas a score of 1 indicates that there are children under the age of 18 in the household.

Findings

Findings in Table 35.1 reveal that black and Hispanic men spend significantly more time on household labor than do white men. Women's household labor time also varies by race/ethnicity, but in a different pattern. Hispanic women spend significantly more time on household labor than white women. They also spend more time on household labor than black women, but a t-test of the difference is not significant. Nevertheless, the gap is of substantive interest because the lack of statistical significance is largely a function of inflated standard deviations due to the small number of black and Hispanic respondents. As the results in Table 35.1 indicate, the divergent patterns of variation in household labor time by race and gender combine in such a way that men's proportionate share of household labor also varies by ethnicity.

Black men spend an average of 25 hours per week on household labor compared to 19.6 hours for white men and 23.2 hours for Hispanic men. The absolute size of the gap between black and Hispanic men's household labor time is small, with both groups of men spending significantly more time on household labor than white men. Nevertheless, black men spend more time on household labor than Hispanic men, although the gap is not statistically significant. This pattern both partially confirms and contradicts earlier research. Black men's relatively high household labor time is consistent with the view that black households may have a more equal division of labor than other households. The data in Table 35.1 do not, however, allow us to determine the source of black men's household labor time investments. It is possible, for example, that on average, black men spend less time in paid labor and therefore more time on household labor. The pattern also could reflect a number of other possible differences in the sociodemographic characteristics of black and white men that we examine in a later section.

Hispanic men's relatively high time investment in household labor is consistent with previous research finding that Hispanic men participate at least as much as Anglo men in household labor, and contradicts those who argue that Hispanic men participate in household labor less than Anglo men. Of course, much of the research on Hispanic men's family roles examines decision making or the distribution of power, rather than household labor time. Most of the research on household labor assumes that it is onerous duty and that only someone without the power to

■ **TABLE 35.1**
Household Labor Time by Gender and Race/Ethnicity

	White	Black	Hispanic	T-Test Blk/Wht	T-Test Hsp/Wht	T-Test Blk/Hsp
Men	19.6	25.0	23.2	2.3**	2.2*	.6
	(19.3)	(28.7)	(19.2)			
Women	37.3	38.0	41.8	.3	1.9*	1.2
	(21.6)	(26.3)	(24.5)			
Men's % of Household Labor Time	34%	40%	36%			

Notes: *p ≤ .05; **p ≤ .01. Standard deviation in parentheses.

avoid it (or without any decision-making authority) will do it (Ferree 1987). Thus, researchers whose focus is on decision making often assume that egalitarian patterns of decision making are associated with an egalitarian division of household labor.

Women's household labor time also varies by race/ethnicity, with Hispanic women spending significantly more time on household labor than either black or white women. Hispanic women spend an average of 41.8 hours per week on household labor compared to 37.3 hours for white women and 38 hours per week for black women. Thus, Hispanic men and women spend significantly more time on household labor than white men and women, whereas black women's household labor time is not significantly different from white women's household labor time. Women's and men's different investments in household labor time affect men's proportionate share of household labor time. The data on black men and women indicate that black men do 40 percent of the household labor (done by men and women only) whereas Hispanic and Anglo men do 36 percent and 34 percent of the household labor, respectively. Thus, Table 35.1 confirms earlier research reporting that black households have a more equal division of household labor than white households and also confirms research indicating that Anglo and Hispanic households may have few differences in division of labor. In addition, the findings for Hispanic households suggest that there may be even more changes in the traditional patterns of Hispanic households than Williams's (1990) research on decision-making indicates.

We begin to examine the source of some of the gap in Table 35.2, where we present white, black, and Hispanic men's household labor time by employment status using multiple classification analysis. We do this in order to determine if black men's relatively high levels of household labor time reflect their lower paid labor time.

With respect to employment status, there are some interesting patterns. For both white and Hispanic men, those who are employed spend less time on household labor than those who are not employed, although the pattern is statistically significant only for white men. For blacks, however, the pattern is quite different. Black men who are not employed spend less time on household labor than black men who are employed, although the difference is not statistically significant. These findings indicate that the relationship between paid labor time and household labor time varies by race/ethnicity and that differences in black, white, and Hispanic men's household labor time are not simply a function of differences in their employment status.

The relationship between black men's employment status and their household labor time may indicate that black men who are not employed are different from nonemployed white and Hispanic men. To the extent that black men are not employed involuntarily, the results in Table 35.2 may reflect the age structure of those who are not employed. It also may indicate the presence of a distinct group of black men characterized by both low time investments in paid labor and low investments in household labor. The argument that the apparent egalitarianism of the black family may be a function of black men's

■ **TABLE 35.2**

Men's Household Labor Time by Race/Ethnicity and Employment Status

	White	Black	Hispanic
Employment Status			
Not employed	23.5	19.5	23.0
Employed PT (1-39 hrs.)	19.1	26.6	22.7
Employed FT	18.2	27.0	22.3
Eta	.12***	.13	.03
N	2798	183	164

Notes: We use 39 hours as our break between part-time and full-time in order to ensure an adequate n for the part-time category. Eta is a measure of association.

*** $p \leq .001$.

reduced hours in paid labor is not supported by these findings. If anything, these findings indicate that, among blacks, the division of household labor is likely to be more equal in households where the man is employed than in households where he is not. Although this is in some sense counterintuitive, it may indicate that the "breadwinner" role is internalized in such a way that even black men who are not employed may opt out of the family per se, rather than compensating for their reduced paid work with more household labor (Komarovsky 1940; Stack 1974). Among the men in this sample, the expression of their "opting out" may be to avoid household labor. (See Cazenave 1984; Hood 1986, for more discussion of the importance of subjective perceptions of work and family roles.)

Up to this point we have examined men's household labor time without taking into consideration a variety of sociodemographic characteristics, sex role attitudes, or wives' work status. Thus, some of the observed race/ethnic differences may reflect other differences among white, black, and Hispanic households. In Table 35.3 we examine the impact of race/ethnicity on men's household labor time by estimating the direct effect of race/ethnicity on household labor time as well as by estimating the ways that paid labor time may affect white, black, and Hispanic men's household labor time differently, after taking other factors into account. Thus, in Table 35.3 we can determine if the previously observed association between race/ethnicity and household labor time or the race/ethnic differences in the impact of paid labor time on household labor time are artifacts of other differences among white, black, and Hispanic men.

The results in Table 35.3 show that after controlling for respondents' education, age, children, men's sex role attitudes, wives' sex role attitudes and paid labor time, race/ethnicity is not significantly associated with men's household labor time. Thus, the differences among white, black, and Hispanic men's household labor time that we observed earlier appear to reflect other differences among them. For example, they may reflect dif-

■ **TABLE 35.3**

Regression of Men's Household Labor Time on Paid Labor Time, Race/Ethnicity, Presence of Children, Education, Age, Sex Role Attitudes, Wives' Paid Labor Time, and Wives' Sex Role Attitudes

	beta	standard error
Paid labor	−.10***	.02
Black	−3.4	2.4
Hispanic	−.67	3.2
Black/paid	.27***	.07
Hispanic/paid	.08	.08
Children	3.7***	.81
Education	−.15	.12
Age	.02	.03
Men's sex role attitudes	1.5***	.52
Wives' paid labor time	.07***	.02
Wives' sex role attitudes	.76	.51
Constant	13.4	3.4
R^2	.033	
N	2782	

Note: ***p ≤ .001.

ferences in social class or education as McAdoo (1990) and Golding (1990) have argued. They may also, however, reflect differences in the presence of children or in wives' paid labor time.

Although we find no direct effects of race/ethnicity on men's household labor time in our multivariate analysis, the differential effect of paid labor time on men's household labor time remains.[2] For white and Hispanic men, each additional hour spent in paid labor is associated with their spending slightly more than six fewer minutes per day on household labor. For black men, however, each additional hour in paid labor is associated with them spending more time on household labor, even after controlling for sociodemographic and household characteristics. Thus, the pattern we observed in the bivariate analyses is repeated in the multivariate analyses. The more time black men spend in paid labor the more time they spend on household labor, whereas the association between paid labor time and household labor time is negative for Anglo and Hispanic men.

There are a variety of possible explanations for the different association between paid labor time and household labor time for black men than for white or Hispanic men. Black men may define the breadwinner role more narrowly than white or Hispanic men, such that when they are not employed and unable to contribute to their family's financial well-being they may retreat from the family in other ways (Stack 1974). The race/ethnic variation in the association between men's paid labor time and household labor time may reflect differences in housing patterns. If households with nonemployed black men are more likely to live in apartments, and those with employed black men are more likely to live in single-family houses, the pattern we see may reflect the amount of household labor that must be done. The different association for white and Hispanic men may be the result of different housing patterns. That is, households with non-employed white or Hispanic men may not be as concentrated in apartments as is the case with black households. Thus there may be variation in the amount of household labor that must be done associated with men's employment status.

The pattern of the effects of some of the control variables is also interesting. For example, men with children spend more time on household labor than men without children, and men with more egalitarian sex role attitudes spend more time on household labor than men with more traditional attitudes. Wives' sex role attitudes are not associated with men's household labor time, but the more time wives spend in paid labor, the more time husbands spend on household labor. Interestingly, after controlling for other variables, men's age is not significantly associated with their household labor time.

In Table 35.4 we further examine the relationship between men's employment status and

■ **TABLE 35.4**

Men's Time Spent on Specific Household Tasks by Employment Status and Race/Ethnicity

	Not Employed	Employed Part-Time	Employed Full-Time
Preparing Meals			
White	3.3	2.9	2.3
Black	4.2	4.9	3.3
Hispanic	5.8	3.2	2.2
Beta	.09[+]	.09	.02
Washing Dishes			
White	2.7	2.2	1.9
Black	1.6	4.5	2.7
Hispanic	4.0	4.1	2.1
Beta	.06*	.22**	.05
Cleaning House			
White	2.3	1.8	1.7
Black	2.3	3.2	3.0
Hispanic	4.3	3.9	2.2
Beta	.08[+]	.20**	.11***
Outdoor Tasks			
White	7.5	5.0	5.6
Black	5.8	4.8	5.4
Hispanic	5.2	3.7	3.9
Beta	.06	.06	.06*
Shopping			
White	2.9	2.4	2.3
Black	2.7	2.6	4.0
Hispanic	2.5	3.5	3.1
Beta	.02	.08	.14***
Laundry			
White	.7	.8	1.2
Black	.9	1.5	.6
Hispanic	1.3	.4	.6
Beta	.06	.11	.08***
Paying Bills			
White	1.6	1.4	1.5
Black	2.5	2.2	2.4
Hispanic	2.1	4.1	2.5
Beta	.07	.26***	.09***
Auto Maintenance			
White	1.4	1.6	2.0
Black	1.4	2.5	3.4
Hispanic	2.1	3.2	2.9
Beta	.04	.21***	.08***
Driving			
White	1.2	1.3	1.5
Black	1.1	1.7	2.7
Hispanic	1.9	1.4	1.5
Beta	.04	.04	.08

Notes: Controlling for respondents' sex role attitudes, education, age, spouses' paid work time, spouses' sex role attitudes, and number of children. Beta is a partial measure of association. [+]$p \leq .10$; *$p \leq .05$; **$p \leq .01$; ***$p \leq .001$.

their household labor time by examining white, black, and Hispanic men's time spent on specific household tasks, after controlling for sociodemographic and household characteristics. Among those men employed full-time, black men spend more time than white and Hispanic men cleaning house, shopping, and repairing automobiles. Cleaning house and shopping are typically "female-typed" tasks indicating that employed black men's household labor time represents less gender stratification rather than simply more time spent on tasks typically done by men. Nevertheless, there are some "female-typed" tasks on which white men spend more time. White men employed full-time spend more time on laundry than black or Hispanic men. Not all of the differences in housework time result from variation in time spent on "female-typed" tasks. White and black men employed full-time spend more time than Hispanic men on outdoor tasks, and black and Hispanic men employed full-time spend more time paying bills than white men.

Among those who are employed part-time or not at all, Hispanic men are most likely to spend more time on specific household tasks than either white or black men, although in a number of cases black and Hispanic men's household task time is similar. Hispanic men employed part-time spend the most time cleaning house, but black men also spend more time cleaning house than white men. Similarly, black men spend significantly more time washing dishes than other men, although Hispanic men spend almost as much time as black men. Among those who are not employed, Hispanic men spend more time than black or white men preparing meals, washing dishes, and cleaning house; thus more time among "female-typed" tasks than other men.

The patterns observed in Table 35.4 indicate that there is more variation by race/ethnicity among men who are employed full-time than among those who are employed part-time or not at all. Although we should use care when comparing across employment statuses in Table 35.4 (because there may be sociodemographic differences among the groups), we can see that black

men's greater household labor time, with respect to white and Hispanic men, appears to be among those who are employed full-time, whereas there are fewer and less definite patterns among those employed fewer hours or not at all.

With respect to specific household tasks, Table 35.4 shows that black men who are employed full-time spend more time on a variety of household tasks, rather than on only a few or male-typed tasks. The pattern of greater involvement in traditionally female tasks among black men employed full-time indicates that among black households there are more egalitarian patterns of family work when the husband is employed than when he is not.

Conclusion

Our findings point to several important patterns. Just as women's paid labor time is associated with their household labor time, we find that men's paid labor time is associated with their household labor time. Thus, although there is less variation in men's paid labor time than in women's, there is enough that it warrants some research attention. Interestingly, the pattern of association between paid labor time and household labor time varies by race/ethnicity. Employed black men do more household labor than those who are not employed, whereas employed white and Hispanic men do less household labor than those who are not employed. These different patterns illustrate the dangers of analyses that fail to examine not only the direct effect of race/ethnicity on household labor time but also the way that race/ethnicity may affect the relationship among other variables. The relationship between men's work and family roles is not such that we can talk about a relationship: the relationship varies by race/ethnicity. This difference in the relationship between work and family suggests that we need to conduct more research on the nature of work and family trade-offs and how they vary by race and ethnicity.

Our analyses also indicate some differences in the family roles (as measured by household labor time) of white, black, and Hispanic men. Our findings from bivariate analyses show that Hispanic and black men spend more time on household labor than white men. Even with Hispanic women's relatively high levels of household labor time, Hispanic men's proportionate share of household labor time is higher than white men's. Black men's relatively high proportionate share of household labor time confirms earlier research indicating that black households may be more egalitarian than white households. Unlike some speculation, however, we find that this pattern is not the result of differences in black men's paid labor time, but that employed black men are the ones who are spending more time on household labor. This somewhat surprising finding indicates the need to examine the relationship between black men's work and family roles in more detail. Given previous findings about black men's attachment to family and work roles (Cazenave 1979), black men's attachments to the provider role as well as their perceptions of family obligations may be the most fruitful place to begin future studies. In addition, the different patterns observed indicate the complex nature of the work—family linkage for men more generally. Further analyses might also focus on the characteristics of nonemployed black men as compared to nonemployed white and Hispanic men to determine what may account for the different patterns of work and family role trade-offs.

Finally, we find that higher household labor time among black men employed full-time reflects their greater time investments in traditionally female tasks, rather than differences in time investments in "male-typed" tasks. In addition, the pattern of Hispanic men's time spent on specific household tasks indicates that they often spend more time on "female-typed" tasks than Anglo men. Thus, even though Anglo and Hispanic men's total household labor time is not significantly different once sociodemographic characteristics have been taken into account, Hispanic men may spend more time on typically "female-typed" tasks like meal preparation, washing dishes, and cleaning house than do Anglo men

(see also Mirandé 1985; Zinn 1980). In addition, our findings indicate that there may be more changes in the Hispanic household than some who have found changing patterns suggest (Mirandé 1985; Williams 1990).

In future research we must give more attention to racial/ethnic variation in men's family patterns as well as to the different trade-offs that men may make between work and family. We simply cannot assume that the trade-offs are the same for men as for women, just as we have often argued that we cannot assume that women's labor force experiences can be modeled in the same way that we model men's. At the same time, our findings argue for the systematic inclusion of ethnicity and race in studies of the work–family trade-off for both men and women. We need to examine differences among black, white, and Hispanic men's perceptions of their family responsibilities if we are to understand how they balance work and family responsibilities.

Notes

We appreciate the very helpful comments of Jane Hood, Norma Williams, Maxine Baca Zinn, and Marta Tienda.

1. The lack of statistical significance is a result of the relatively small number of black and Hispanic respondents in the survey.

2. To determine the differential effects of paid labor time for white, black, and Hispanic respondents we included interaction terms for race/ethnicity and paid labor time in our analysis. The nonsignificant effect for the interaction term between Hispanic and paid labor time indicates that the impact of paid labor time on Hispanic men's household labor time is not significantly different from the impact of paid labor time on white men's household labor time. The significant interaction term for black men indicates that there is a significant difference in the impact of paid labor time on black and white men's household labor time. By adding the coefficient for paid labor time to the coefficient for the black/paid labor time interaction term, we can see that even after controlling for sociodemographic and household characteristics, paid labor time is positively associated with black men's

household labor time. Thus, the more time black men spend in paid labor the more time they spend in household labor, whereas the association between paid labor time and household labor time is negative for Anglo and Hispanic men.

References

Atkinson, J., and Huston, T. L. 1984. "Sex Role Orientation and Division of Labor Early in Marriage." *Journal of Personality and Social Psychology* 46, no. 2: 330–345.

Barnett, R. C., and Baruch, G. K. 1987. "Determinants of Fathers' Participation in Family Work." *Journal of Marriage and the Family* 49: 29–40.

Beckett, J. O. 1976. "Working Wives: A Racial Comparison." *Social Work,* November, 463–471.

Beckett, J. O., and Smith, A. D. 1981. "Work and Family Roles: Egalitarian Marriage in Black and White Families." *Social Service Review* 55, no. 2: 314–326.

Blumstein, P., and Schwartz, P. 1983. *American Couples.* New York: Pocket Books.

Broman, C. 1988. "Household Work and Family Life Satisfaction of Blacks." *Journal of Marriage and the Family* 50: 743–748.

———. 1991. "Gender, Work-Family Roles, and Psychological Well-Being of Blacks." *Journal of Marriage and the Family* 53: 509–520.

Cazenave, N. 1979. "Middle-Income Black Fathers: An Analysis of the Provider Role." *Family Coordinator* 28: 583–593.

———. 1984. "Race, Socioeconomic Status, and Age: The Social Context of Masculinity." *Sex Roles* 11, no. 7–8: 639–656.

Collins, P. H. 1990. *Black Feminist Thought: Knowledge, Consciousness and the Politics of Empowerment.* Cambridge, Mass.: Unwin Hyman.

Coverman, S. 1985. "Explaining Husbands' Participation in Domestic Labor." *Sociological Quarterly* 26, no. 1: 81–98.

Coverman, S., and Sheley, J. F. 1986. "Change in Men's Housework and Child-Care Time, 1965–1975." *Journal of Marriage and the Family* 48: 413–422.

Cronkite, R. C. 1977. "The Determinants of Spouses' Normative Preferences for Family Roles." *Journal of Marriage and the Family* 39: 575–585.

Ericksen, J. A., Yancey, W. L., and Ericksen, E. P. 1979. "The Division of Family Roles." *Journal of Marriage and the Family* 41: 301–313.

Farkas, G. 1976. "Education, Wage Rates, and the Division of Labor Between Husband and Wife." *Journal of Marriage and the Family* 38: 473–483.

Ferree, M. M. 1987. "Family and Job for Working-Class Women: Gender and Class Systems Seen from Below." In N. Gerstel and H. E. Gross, eds., *Families and Work,* 289–301. Philadelphia: Temple University Press.

Golding, J. M. 1990. "Division of Household Labor, Strain and Depressive Symptoms Among Mexican Americans and Non-Hispanic Whites." *Psychology of Women Quarterly* 14: 103–117.

Hood, J. C. 1983. *Becoming a Two-Job Family.* New York: Praeger.

———. 1986. "The Provider Role: Its Meaning and Measurement." *Journal of Marriage and the Family* 48: 349–359.

Huber, J., and G. Spitze. 1983. *Sex Stratification: Children, Housework and Jobs.* New York: Academic Press.

Kimmel, M. S. 1987. "Rethinking 'Masculinity': New Directions in Research." In M. S. Kimmel, ed., *Changing Men: New Directions of Research on Men and Masculinity,* 9–24. Newbury Park, Calif.: Sage.

Kingston, P. W., and Nock, S. L. 1985. "Consequences of the Family Work Day." *Journal of Marriage and the Family* 47, no. 3: 619–630.

Komarovsky, M. 1940. *The Unemployed Man and His Family.* New York: Dryden.

McAdoo, H. P. 1990. "A Portrait of African American Families in the United States." In S. E. Rix, ed., *The American Woman 1990–1991: A Status Report,* 71–93. New York: Norton.

Miller, J., and Garrison, H. H. 1982. "Sex Roles: The Division of Labor at Home and in the Workplace." *Annual Review of Sociology* 8: 237–262.

Mirandé, A. 1979. "A Reinterpretation of Male Dominance in the Chicano Family." *Family Coordinator* 28, no. 4: 473–480.

———. 1985. *The Chicano Experience: An Alternative Perspective.* Notre Dame, Ind.: University of Notre Dame Press.

Perrucci, C. C., Potter, H. R., and Rhoads, D. L. 1978. "Determinants of Male Family-Role Performance." *Psychology of Women Quarterly* 3, no. 1: 53–66.

Pleck, J. H. 1977. "The Work-Family Role System." *Social Problems* 24: 417–427.

———. 1985. *Working Wives/Working Husbands.* Beverly Hills: Sage.

Ransford, E., and Miller, J. 1983. "Race, Sex, and Feminist Outlooks." *American Sociological Review* 48: 46–59.

Reid, P. T., and Comas-Diaz, L. 1990. "Gender and Ethnicity: Perspectives on Dual Status." *Sex Roles* 22, no. 7–8: 397–408.

Rexroat, C., and Shehan, C. 1987. "The Family Life Cycle and Spouses' Time in Housework." *Journal of Marriage and the Family* 49, no. 4: 737–750.

Ross, C. E. 1987. "The Division of Labor at Home." *Social Forces* 65, no. 3: 816–834.

Stack, C. B. 1974. *All Our Kin.* New York: Harper Colophon.

Staples, R. 1978. "Masculinity and Race: The Dual Dilemma of Black Men." *Journal of Social Issues* 34, no. 1: 169–183.

Sweet, J., Bumpass, L., and Call, V. 1988. *The Design and Content of the National Survey of Families and Households.* Working Paper NSFH-1. Madison: University of Wisconsin–Madison, Center for Demography and Ecology.

Thompson, L., and Walker, A. J. 1989. "Gender in Families: Women and Men in Marriage, Work and Parenthood." *Journal of Marriage and the Family* 51: 845–871.

Tucker, M. B., and Taylor, R. J. 1989. "Demographic Correlates of Relationship Status Among Black Americans." *Journal of Marriage and the Family* 51: 655–665.

Vega, W. A., Patterson, T., Sallis, J., Nader, P., Atkins, C., and Abramson, I. 1986. "Cohesion and Adaptability in Mexican American and Anglo Families." *Journal of Marriage and the Family* 48: 857–867.

Wilkie, J. R. 1991. "The Decline in Men's Labor Force Participation and Income and the Changing Structure of Family Economic Support." *Journal of Marriage and the Family* 53, no. 1: 111–122.

Williams, N. 1990. *The Mexican American Family: Tradition and Change.* Dix Hills, N.Y.: General Hall.

Wilson, M. N., Tolson, T. F. J., Hinton, I. D., and Kiernan, M. 1990. "Flexibility and Sharing of Childcare Duties in Black Families." *Sex Roles* 22, no. 7–8: 409–425.

Ybarra, L. 1982. "When Wives Work: The Impact on the Chicano Family." *Journal of Marriage and the Family* 44: 169–178.

Zinn, M. B. 1980. "Gender and Ethnic Identity Among Chicanos." *Frontiers* 2: 8–24.

———. 1991. "Family, Feminism, and Race in America." In J. Lorber and S. A. Farrell, eds., *The Social Construction of Gender,* 110–134. Newbury Park, Calif.: Sage.

Scott Coltrane

Fathering: Paradoxes, Contradictions, and Dilemmas

The beginning of the 21st century offers a paradox for American fathers: Media images, political rhetoric, and psychological studies affirm the importance of fathers to children at the same time that men are becoming less likely to live with their offspring. Although the average married father spends more time interacting with his children than in past decades, marriage rates have fallen, and half of all marriages are predicted to end in divorce. Additionally, the proportion of births to unmarried mothers has increased dramatically for all race and ethnic groups, and single-mother households have become commonplace. These contradictory tendencies—more father-child interaction in two-parent families but fewer two-parent families in the population—have encouraged new research on fathers and spawned debates about how essential fathers are to families and normal child development (Blankenhorn, 1995; Silverstein & Auerbach, 1999).

Scholars attribute the current paradox in fathering to various economic and social trends. Whereas most men in the 20th century were sole breadwinners, contemporary fathers' wages can rarely support a middle-class standard of living for an entire family. The weakening of the good-provider model, coupled with trends in fertility, marriage, divorce, and custody, has resulted in the average man spending fewer years living with children (Eggebeen, 2002). Simultaneously, how-

ever, men rank marriage and children among their most precious goals, single-father households have increased, and fathers in two-parent households are spending more time with co-resident children than at any time since data on fathers were collected (Pleck & Masciadrelli, 2003). Although married fathers report that they value their families over their jobs, they spend significantly more time in paid work and less time in family work than married mothers, with most men continuing to serve as helpers to their wives, especially for housework and child maintenance activities (Coltrane, 2000). Personal, political, religious, and popular discourses about fathers reveal similar ambivalence about men's family involvements, with ideals ranging from stern patriarchs to nurturing daddies, and public portrayals frequently at odds with the actual behavior of average American fathers (LaRossa, 1997). We can understand these contradictions by recognizing that fatherhood has gained symbolic importance just as men's family participation has become more voluntary, tenuous, and conflicted (Griswold, 1993; Kimmel, 1996).

In this chapter, I summarize how fathering practices have varied across cultures and through history; highlight how different social, economic, and political contexts have produced different types of father involvement; review how social scientists have measured father involvement; and examine findings about causes and consequences of father involvement. I end with a short analysis of debates over family policy and offer tentative predictions about the future of fathering in America.

From *Handbook of Contemporary Families: Considering the Past, Contemplating the Future*, Marilyn Coleman and Lawrence Ganong (Eds.), pp. 224–243. 2004. Thousand Oaks, CA: Sage.

Cross-Cultural Variation

Fatherhood defines a biological and social relationship between a male parent and his offspring. *To father* means to impregnate a woman and beget a child, thus describing a kinship connection that facilitates the intergenerational transfer of wealth and authority (at least in patrilineal descent systems such as ours). Fatherhood also reflects ideals about the rights, duties, and activities of men in families and in society and generalizes to other social and symbolic relationships, as when Christians refer to "God the Father," Catholics call priests "Father," and Americans label George Washington "the Father" of the country. Fatherhood thus reflects a normative set of social practices and expectations that are institutionalized within religion, politics, law, and culture. Social theories have employed the concept of *social fatherhood* to explain how the institution of fatherhood links a particular child to a particular man (whether father or uncle) in order to secure a place for that child in the social structure (Coltrane & Collins, 2001).

Fathering (in contrast to *fatherhood*) refers more directly to what men do with and for children. Although folk beliefs suggest that fathering entails behaviors fixed by reproductive biology, humans must learn how to parent. In every culture and historical period, men's parenting has been shaped by social and economic forces. Although women have been the primary caretakers of young children in all cultures, fathers' participation in child rearing has varied from virtually no direct involvement to active participation in all aspects of children's routine care. Except for breastfeeding and the earliest care of infants, there are no cross-cultural universals in the tasks that mothers and fathers perform (Johnson, 1988). In some societies, the social worlds of fathers and mothers were so separate that they rarely had contact and seldom performed the same tasks; in other societies, men participated in tasks like infant care and women participated in tasks like hunting (Coltrane, 1988; Sanday, 1981).

Drawing on worldwide cross-cultural comparisons, scholars have identified two general patterns of fathers' family involvement, one intimate and the other aloof. In the intimate pattern, men eat and sleep with their wives and children, talk with them during evening meals, attend births, and participate actively in infant care. In the aloof pattern, men often eat and sleep apart from women, spend their leisure time in the company of other men, stay away during births, and seldom help with child care (Whiting & Whiting, 1975). Societies with involved fathers are more likely than societies with aloof fathers to be peaceful, to afford women a role in community decision making, to have intimate husband–wife relationships, to feature more gender equality in the society, and to include nurturing deities of both sexes in their religions. Aloof-father societies are more likely to have religious systems with stern male gods, social institutions that exclude women from community decision making, marriage systems in which husbands demand deference from wives, and public rituals that focus on men's competitive displays of masculinity (Coltrane, 1988, 1996; Sanday, 1981).

Research on fathering among indigenous peoples such as the African Aka suggests why involved fathering and gender egalitarianism are associated (Hewlett, 1991). Anthropologists such as Hewlett have drawn on Chodorow's (1974) work to suggest that when fathers are active in infant care, boys develop an intimate knowledge of masculinity, which makes them less likely to devalue the feminine, whereas when fathers are rarely around, boys lack a clear sense of masculinity and construct their identities in opposition to things feminine by devaluing and criticizing women (Hewlett, 2000). In reviews of data on father involvement over the past 120,000 years, Hewlett concluded that fathers contribute to their children in many ways, with the relative importance of different contributions varying dramatically; that different ecologies and modes of production have a substantial impact on the contributions of fathers to their children; and that fathers' roles today are relatively unique in human history (Hewlett, 1991, 2000).

Historical Variation

Historical studies have focused on practices in Europe and North America, chronicling and emphasizing men's public lives: work, political exploits, literary accomplishments, scientific discoveries, and heroic battles. This emphasis shows how various economic, political, and legal practices have structured privileges and obligations within and beyond families. For example, the historical concept of family in the West is derived from the Latin *famulus,* meaning servant, and the Roman *familia,* meaning the man's domestic property. Linking institutional arrangements with linguistic forms tells us something important about men's relationships to families. Recent historical studies have focused more directly on men's ideal and actual behaviors in families, thereby documenting complexity and diversity in past fathering practices (e.g., Griswold, 1993; Kimmel, 1996; LaRossa, 1997; Mintz, 1998; Pleck & Pleck, 1997).

Before these studies, many scholars erroneously assumed that changes in fatherhood were linear and progressive (Coltrane & Parke, 1998). For example, early family history emphasized that peasant families were extended and governed by stern patriarchs, whereas market societies produced nuclear families, companionate marriages, and involved fathers. In fact, historical patterns of fathering have responded to a complex array of social and economic forces, varying considerably across regions, time periods, and ethnic or cultural groups. Although it is useful to identify how men's work and production have shaped their public and private statuses, actual family relations have been diverse, and fatherhood ideals have followed different trajectories in different regions of the same country (Griswold, 1993; Mintz, 1998; Pleck & Pleck, 1997).

The economy of the 17th and 18th centuries in Europe and America was based on agriculture and productive family households. For families that owned farms or small artisan shops, their place of work was also their home. Slaves, indentured servants, and others were expected to work on family estates in return for food, a place to live, and sometimes other rewards. In this pattern of household or family-based production, men, women, and children worked together. Regional variations could be large, and fathers and mothers often did different types of work, but many tasks required for subsistence and family survival were interchangeable, and both mothers and fathers took responsibility for child care and training (Coltrane & Galt, 2000).

Because most men's work as farmers, artisans, and tradesmen occurred in the family household, fathers were a visible presence in their children's lives. Child rearing was a more collective enterprise than it is today, with family behaviors and attitudes ruled primarily by duty and obligation. Men introduced sons to farming or craft work within the household economy, oversaw the work of others, and were responsible for maintaining harmonious household relations. The preindustrial home was a system of control as well as a center of production, and both functions reinforced the father's authority (Griswold, 1993). Though mothers provided most direct care for infants and young children, men tended to be active in the training and tutoring of children. Because they were moral teachers and family heads, fathers were thought to have greater responsibility for and influence on children than mothers and were also generally held responsible for how the children acted outside the home (Pleck & Pleck, 1997).

Because the sentimental individualism of the modern era had not yet blossomed, emotional involvement with children in the Western world during the 17th and early 18th centuries was more limited than today. Prevailing images of children also were different from modern ideas about their innocence and purity. Religious teachings stressed the corrupt nature and evil dispositions of children, and fathers were admonished to demand strict obedience and use swift physical punishment to cleanse children of their sinful ways.

Puritan fathers justified their extensive involvement in children's lives because women were seen as unfit to be disciplinarians, moral guides, or intellectual teachers. Griswold (1997) pointed out, however, that stern unaffectionate fathering, though not confined to Puritans, was not representative of all of the population. In fact, most American fathers attempted to shape and guide their children's characters, not break them or beat the devil out of them. As more privileged 18th-century fathers gained enough affluence to have some leisure time, many were affectionate with their children and delighted in playing with them (Griswold, 1997).

As market economies replaced home-based production in the 19th and 20th centuries, the middle-class father's position as household head and master and moral instructor of his children was slowly transformed. Men increasingly sought employment outside the home, and their direct contact with family members declined. As the wage labor economy developed, men's occupational achievement outside the household took on stronger moral overtones. Men came to be seen as fulfilling their family and civic duty, not by teaching and interacting with their children as before, but by supporting the family financially. The middle-class home, previously the site of production, consumption, and virtually everything else in life, became a nurturing, child centered haven set apart from the impersonal world of work, politics, and other public pursuits. The separate-spheres ideal became a defining feature of the late 19th and early 20th centuries (Bernard, 1981; Coltrane & Galt, 2000; Kimmel, 1996).

The ideal that paid work was only for men and that only women were suited to care for family members remained an unattainable myth rather than an everyday reality for most families. Many working-class fathers were not able to earn the family wage assumed by the separate-spheres ideal, and a majority of African American, Latino, Asian American, and other immigrant men could not fulfill the good-provider role that the cultural ideal implied. Women in these families either had to work for wages, participate in

production at home, or find other ways to make ends meet. Although the emerging romantic ideal held that women should be sensitive and pure keepers of the home on a full-time basis, the reality was that women in less advantaged households had no choice but to simultaneously be workers and mothers. In fact, many working-class and ethnic minority women had to leave their homes and children to take care of other people's children and houses (Dill, 1988). Even during the heyday of separate spheres in the early 20th century, minority women, young single women, widows, and married women whose husbands could not support them worked for wages.

As noted above, attempts to understand the history of fatherhood have often painted a simple before-and-after picture: *Before* the Industrial Revolution, families were rural and extended, and patriarchal fathers were stern moralists; *after* the Industrial Revolution, families were urban and nuclear, and wage-earning fathers became companionate husbands, distant breadwinners, and occasional playmates to their children. This before and after picture captures something important about general shifts in work and family life, but its simple assumption of unidirectional linear change and its binary conceptualization contrasting men's patriarchal roles in the past with egalitarian roles in the present is misleading (Coontz, 1992). Stage models of family history have ignored the substantial regional and race/ethnic differences that encouraged different family patterns (Pleck & Pleck, 1997). For example, as most of the United States was undergoing industrialization, large pockets remained relatively untouched by it. The experience of white planters in the antebellum South was both like and unlike that of men in the commercial and industrial North (Griswold, 1993). Another major drawback of early historical studies is the tendency to over-generalize for the entire society on the basis of the experience of the white middle class. Even during the heyday of separate spheres at the turn of the 20th century, minority and immigrant men were unlikely to be able to support a family. Race and class differences also intersect with regional differences: Not only did southern fathering practices differ from northern ones, but slave fathers and freedmen in the South had much different experiences than either group of white men (Griswold, 1993; McDaniel, 1994).

The Emergence of Modern Fathering

Throughout the 20th century, calls for greater paternal involvement coexisted with the physical presence, but relative emotional and functional absence, of fathers (LaRossa, 1997). Nevertheless, some fathers have always reported high levels of involvement with their children. By the 1930s, even though mothers bore most of the responsibility for care of homes and families, three out of four American fathers said they regularly read magazine articles about child care, and nearly as many men as women were members of the PTA (Kimmel, 1996). Increases in women's labor force participation during the 1940s briefly challenged the ideal of separate family and work roles, but in the postwar era, high rates of marriage and low rates of employment reinforced the ideology of separate spheres for men and women. The ideal father at mid-century was seen as a good provider who "set a good table, provided a decent home, paid the mortgage, bought the shoes, and kept his children warmly clothed" (Bernard, 1981, pp. 3–4). As they had during the earlier Victorian era, middle-class women were expected to be consumed and fulfilled by wifely and motherly duties. With Ozzie and Harriet–style families as the 1950s model, women married earlier and had more children than any group of American women before them. Rapid expansion of the U.S. economy fueled a phenomenal growth of suburbs, and the consumer culture from that era idolized domestic life on radio and television. Isolated in suburban houses, many mothers now had almost sole responsibility for raising children, aided by occasional reference to expert guides from pediatricians and child psychologists (Hays, 1996). Fathers of the 1950s were also told to get involved with child care—but not *too* involved (Kimmel,

1996). The separate spheres of white middle-class men and women were thus maintained, though experts deemed them permeable enough for men to participate regularly as a helper to the mother (Coltrane & Galt, 2000; Hays, 1996).

During the mid–20th century, separate-spheres ideology and the popularity of Freud's ideas about mother-infant bonding led to widespread acceptance of concepts like *maternal deprivation,* and few researchers asked who besides mothers took care of children, although some researchers began to focus on *father absence* during the baby boom era (roughly 1946–64). Empirical studies and social theories valued the symbolic significance of fathers' breadwinning, discipline, and masculine role modeling, even though few studies controlled for social class or measured what fathers actually did with children. Studies including fathers found that they were more likely than mothers to engage in rough and tumble play and to give more attention to sons than daughters (Parke, 1996; Pleck, 1997). In general, research showed that child care was an ongoing and taken-for-granted task for mothers but a novel and fun distraction for fathers (Thompson & Walker, 1989).

Compared to the wholesome but distant good-provider fathers pictured on television programs like *Ozzie and Harriet* and *Father Knows Best* in the 1950s, a new father ideal gained prominence in the 1980s (Griswold, 1993). According to Furstenberg (1988), "[T]elevision, magazines, and movies herald the coming of the modern father—the nurturant, caring, and emotionally attuned parent. . . . Today's father is at least as adept at changing diapers as changing tires" (p. 193). No longer limited to being protectors and providers, fathers were pictured on television and in magazines as intimately involved in family life. Fatherhood proponents focused on the potential of the new ideals and practices (Biller, 1976), but researchers in the 1980s reported that many fathers resisted assuming responsibility for daily housework or child care (Thompson & Walker, 1989). Some researchers claimed that popular images far exceeded men's actual behaviors

(LaRossa, 1988), and others suggested that men, on the whole, were less committed to families than they had been in the past (Ehrenreich, 1984). In the 1990s, researchers also began to examine how the modern ideal of the new father carried hidden messages about class and race, with some suggesting that the image of the sensitive and involved father was a new class/ethnic icon because it set middle-class fathers apart from working-class and ethnic minority fathers, who presented a more masculine image (Messner, 1993). Others suggested that the sensitive or androgynous parenting styles of new fathers might lead to gender identity confusion in sons (Blankenhorn, 1995).

Measuring Father Involvement

Before the 1980s, the rare researchers who included fathers focused on simple distinctions between father-present and father-absent families, finding that children from families with co-resident fathers generally fared better, on average, than those without co-resident fathers. Although the structural aspects of fatherhood (marriage, paternity, co-residence) sometimes correlate with various child and family outcomes, most researchers now agree that what fathers do with and for children is more important than co-residence or legal relationship to the mother and recommend that dichotomous measures (e.g., father presence/absence) be replaced by more nuanced ones.

The most influential refinement in fathering measurement was offered by Lamb, Pleck, Charnov, and Levine (1987), who suggested three components: (a) interaction, the father's direct contact with his child through caregiving and shared activities; (b) availability (or accessibility), a related concept concerning the father's potential availability for interaction, by virtue of being accessible to the child (whether or not direct interaction is occurring); and (c) responsibility, the role the father takes in ascertaining that the child is taken care of and in arranging for resources to be available for the child. Within each of these cate-

gories, two further distinctions should be made. First, it is critical to distinguish the amount from the quality of involvement: Both are important to child development and parental well-being (Parke, 1996). Second, absolute as well as relative (in relation to partner) indices of involvement are independent and may affect children and adults in different ways (Pleck, 1997).

A recent tabulation of father involvement assessment in 15 large social science family data sets showed that all but one measured father "presence/absence," with most also measuring some aspects of fathers' "availability," "teaching," "monitoring," or "affection." About half measured the fathers' "communication" or "emotional support," only a few measured "thought processes" (e.g., worrying, dreaming) or "planning" (e.g., birthdays, vacations, friend visits), and none measured "sharing interests" (e.g., providing for instruction, reading together) or "child maintenance" (e.g., cleaning or cooking for the child) (Federal Interagency Forum, 1998, pp. 144, 400; Palkovitz, 1997, pp. 209–210). Structural availability is thus the most common fathering indicator, with various routine parent-child interactions and support activities sometimes assessed, and with fathers' planning and responsibility rarely measured. In addition, many studies collect fathering data from just one reporter, even though self-reports of fathers' involvement tend to be higher than mothers' reports of fathers' involvement, especially for nonresident fathers (Coley & Morris, 2002; Smock & Manning, 1997).

Levels and Predictors of Fathers' Involvement

Research on fathering in two-parent households shows a noticeable and statistically significant increase in men's parenting involvement, both in absolute terms and in relation to mothers. Simultaneously, however, average levels of fathers' interaction with, availability to, and responsibility for children lag well behind those of mothers (Marsiglio, Amato, Day, & Lamb, 2000; Parke,

1996; Pleck & Masciadrelli, 2003). Measurement strategies vary, with time-use diaries generally producing the most accurate estimates of fathers' interaction and availability. On average, in the 1960s to early-1980s, fathers interacted with their children about a third as much as mothers and were available about half as much as mothers (Lamb et al., 1987). During the mid-1980s to early-1990s, the average co-resident father interacted about two fifths as much as mothers and was available to his children almost two thirds as much (Pleck, 1997). In the late 1990s, he was available to his children about three fourths as much as mothers, interacting on weekdays about two thirds as often, but over four fifths as much on weekends (Pleck & Masciadrelli, 2003; Yueng, Sandberg, Davis-Kean, & Hofferth, 2001). In an estimated 20% of two-parent families, men are now about as involved as mothers interacting with and being available to their children. At the same time, in most families, fathers share much less of the responsibility for the planning, scheduling, emotional management, housework, and other maintenance activities associated with raising children (Deutsch, 1999; Hochschild, 1989).

Researchers have begun to isolate the effects of income, race/ethnicity, education, family structure, marriage, employment, work schedules, and other factors on father involvement, though results are often incomplete or contradictory. For example, the relation between socioeconomic status and father involvement is complex. Income is often found to be positively correlated with father involvement among various ethnic groups (Fagan, 1998; Parke, 1996). Relative income contributions by wives are also associated with higher proportionate levels of father involvement in housework and child care (Coltrane, 2000; Yeung et al., 2001), though some studies still find that financially dependent husbands do less domestic work than others (Brines, 1994). Wealthier men do little routine family work, but the amount their wives do varies dramatically, with higher-earning wives more likely to purchase domestic services (e.g., child care, house cleaning, laundry) (Cohen, 1998; Oropesa, 1993).

Although most contemporary studies of fathering have been based on white, middle-class, two-parent families, we are beginning to get a more complete picture about similarities and differences across family types. When financial stability is hard to achieve, fathers only minimally involved with their children may nevertheless see themselves as "good fathers" because they work hard to provide financially. Because of inequities in the labor market, men of color are disproportionately likely to face difficulties being adequate providers (Bowman & Sanders, 1998; Hamer & Marchioro, 2002). Comparisons between white, African American, and Latino fathers suggest similar levels of involvement with infants and similar styles of engagement with young children (e.g., proportionately more play and less caretaking than mothers; Coltrane, Parke, & Adams, 2001; Toth & Xu, 1999). Contrary to cultural stereotypes, some research also shows that Latino fathers are more likely than their European American counterparts to spend time in shared activities with children, to perform housework and personal care, and to engage in monitoring and supervising children's activities (Coltrane et al., 2001; Toth & Xu, 1999; Yeung et al., 2001). Results for African American fathers in two-parent households are mixed, with most reporting levels of father-child interaction comparable to other race/ethnic groups, and several studies finding that black men do more housework than white men, net of other predictors (Ahmeduzzaman & Roopnarine, 1992; Broman, 1991; Hossain & Roopnarine, 1993; John & Shelton, 1997), and that nonresident black fathers contribute more to children than nonresident white fathers (Wilson, Tolson, Hinton, & Kiernan, 1990). Studies of African American and Latino fathers reveal a wide range of behaviors across families, depending on employment, income, education, gender and religious ideology, family structure, marital status, age of children, immigration status, neighborhood context, cultural traditions, and presence of extended or fictive kin, and a similar pattern of association between social contextual variables and levels and styles of paternal

ikening.
athers get
, infancy they
later in children's
, 1996).

& Steuve, 2001; Silverstein, 2002).

Fathers tend to spend more time with young children than they do with older children and adolescents, probably because younger children require more attention and care, even though many men feel more comfortable interacting with older children. Most research finds that a father's availability (as determined by work hours) is a strong predictor of his involvement in child care. When mothers of preschool children are employed, a father's time availability predicts whether he will serve as a primary caregiver (Brayfield, 1995; Casper & O'Connell, 1998). Fathers and mothers with nonoverlapping work shifts are the most likely to share child care (Presser, 1995). When mothers of school-aged children are employed more hours, their husbands tend to do a greater portion of the child care and housework, and fathers tend to be more involved to the extent that they view their wives' career prospects more positively (Pleck, 1997). For instance, Brewster (2000) found that fathers in the late 1980s and 1990s were likely to use nonworking discretionary hours for child care, whereas in the late 1970s and early 1980s they tended to use those hours for other activities.

As demonstrated in comprehensive reviews (Pleck, 1997; Pleck & Masciadrelli, 2003), father involvement is multiply determined, with no single factor responsible for the different types of involvement. In addition, studies often report contradictory effects of factors like income, education, age, family size, and birth timing. One of the most consistent findings is that men are more involved with sons than with daughters (Harris, Furstenberg, & Marmer, 1998; Harris & Morgan, 1991; Marsiglio, 1991; McBride, Schoppe, & Rane, 2002), especially with older children (Pleck, 1997). However, some recent studies have found no differences in father involvement by sex of child (Fagan, 1998; Hofferth, 2003), leading Pleck and Masciadrelli (2003) to suggest that

Lamb, Pleck, and colleagues suggested that for fathers to become actively involved, they required four facilitating factors: (a) motivation, (b) skills and self-confidence, (c) social approval, and (d) institutional support (Lamb et al., 1987; see also Pleck, 1997). Many studies find that fathers are more involved and show more warmth if they believe in gender equality (Cabrera et al., 2000; Hofferth, 1998), though others find no significant association (Marsiglio, 1991; Pleck, 1997). Others find that fathers get more involved when they have a strong fatherhood identity or actively embrace the father role (Beitel & Parke, 1998; Hawkins, Christiansen, Sargent, & Hill, 1993; Pasley, Ihinger-Tallman, & Buehler, 1993; Rane & McBride, 2000; Snarey, 1993). In general, fathers feel more competent as parents when they are more involved with their children, though it is difficult to say whether this competence is a precursor or a result of active fathering (Beitel & Parke, 1998; McHale & Huston, 1984). Evidence suggesting that competence leads to involvement comes from interventions designed to develop fathers' parenting skills (e.g., Cowan & Cowan, 2000; McBride, 1990). In terms of social support, fathers tend to be more involved when the children's mothers facilitate it, when the mothers had positive relationships with their own fathers when they were children (Allen & Hawkins, 1999; Cowan & Cowan, 2000; McBride & Mills, 1993; Parke, 1996), and when kin and other community members support father involvement (Pleck, 1997). Finally, institutional supports can include factors such as fewer work hours and more flexible work schedules (Pleck, 1993).

Another approach to identifying predictors of father involvement is based on a process model of parenting (Belsky, 1984; McBride et al., 2002). This framework suggests that fathering is shaped by three categories of influence: (a) characteristics of the father (e.g., personality, attitudes toward child rearing), (b) characteristics of the child (e.g., temperament, age, gender), and (c) contextual sources of stress and support (e.g., marital relationships, social support networks, occupational experiences). Many of these facilitating influences overlap with factors in the Lamb and Pleck model, but this approach also includes consideration of things like child temperament and parental stress. Emergent findings suggest that child temperament or other characteristics may have a larger influence on father–child involvement than mother–child involvement, probably because fathering is seen as more discretionary than mothering (Cabrera et al., 2000; McBride et al., 2002).

The nature of the marital relationship is also associated with paternal involvement, though causality is sometimes difficult to assess. Some find that greater marital satisfaction leads to greater father involvement (Parke, 1996), and others suggest that higher levels of men's relative contributions to child care lead to women's greater marital satisfaction (Brennan, Barnett, & Gareis, 2001; Ozer, Barnett, Brennan, & Sperling, 1998). In addition, satisfaction with men's levels of family involvement appears to be strongly related to mothers' and fathers' gender ideals and expectations. We cannot simply assume that more father involvement is better for all families. As the emerging gatekeeping literature (e.g., Allen & Hawkins, 1999; Beitel & Parke, 1998) attests, too much involvement by fathers can be interpreted as interference rather than helpfulness. In general, if family members want a father to be more involved, his participation has positive effects on family functioning. If family members feel that fathers should not change diapers or do laundry, then such practices can cause stress (Coltrane, 1996).

The Potential Influence of Fathers

As scholars pay more attention to fathers, they are beginning to understand what influence their involvement might have on child development. Most researchers find that father-child relationships are influential for children's future life chances (Federal Interagency Forum, 1998; Parke, 1996; Pleck & Masciadrelli, 2003). The focus of this research tends to be on the positive aspects of fathers' involvement, though it should be noted that because men are more likely than women to abuse children or to use inappropriate parenting techniques, increased male involvement can lead to increased risk and negative outcomes for children, particularly if the father figure does not have a long-term relationship with the mother (Finkelhor, Hotaling, Lewis, & Smith, 1990; Margolin, 1992; National Research Council, 1993; Radhakrishna, Bou-Saada, Hunter, Catellier, & Kotch, 2001).

Many researchers continue to focus on fathers' economic contributions to children and report that fathers' resources improve children's life chances. Longitudinal research shows that children from one-parent households (usually mother headed) are at greater risk for negative adult outcomes (e.g., lower educational and occupational achievement, earlier childbirth, school dropout, health problems, behavioral difficulties) than those from two-parent families (Marsiglio et al., 2000; McLanahan & Sandefur, 1994). Although comparisons between children of divorced parents and those from first-marriage families show more problems in the former group, differences between the two are generally small across various outcome measures and do not necessarily isolate the influence of divorce or of father involvement (Crockett, Eggebeen, & Hawkins, 1993; Furstenberg & Harris, 1993; Seltzer, 1994). For children with nonresident fathers, the amount of fathers' earnings (especially the amount that is actually transferred to children) is a significant predictor of children's well-being, including school grades and behavior problems (Amato & Gilbreth, 1999; McLanahan, Seltzer, Hanson, & Thomson, 1994; Marsiglio et al., 2000). Because the great majority of children from single-parent homes turn out to be happy, healthy, and productive adults, debates continue about how such large-group comparisons should be made and how we should interpret their results

in terms of fathers' economic or social contributions (Amato, 2000; Coltrane & Adams, 2003).

Earlier reviews suggested that the level of
father involvement has a smaller direct affect on
infant attachment ...

father interaction, though time spent parenting is
also related to competence (Lamb et al., 1987;
Marsiglio et al., 2000). Preschool children with
fathers who perform 40% or more of the within-
family child care show more cognitive competence, more internal locus of control, more
empathy, and less gender stereotyping than
preschool children with less involved fathers
(Lamb et al., 1987; Pleck, 1997). Adolescents
with involved fathers are more likely to have positive developmental outcomes such as self-control, self-esteem, life skills, and social competence,
provided that the father is not authoritarian or
overly controlling (Mosley & Thomson, 1994;
Pleck & Masciadrelli, 2003). Studies examining
differences between the presence of biological
fathers versus other father figures suggest that it is
the quality of the father–child relationship rather
than biological relationship that enhances the
cognitive and emotional development of children
(Dubowitz et al., 2001; Hofferth & Anderson,
2003; Silverstein & Auerbach, 1999). Reports of
greater father involvement when children were
growing up have also been associated with positive aspects of adult children's educational attainment, relationship quality, and career success
(Amato & Booth, 1997; Harris et al., 1998; Nock,
1998; Snarey, 1993). Because of methodological
inadequacies in previous studies such as not controlling for maternal involvement, most scholars
recommend more carefully controlled studies
using random samples and multirater longitudinal designs, as well as advocating caution in interpreting associations between fathering and
positive child outcomes (Amato & Rivera, 1999;
Parke, 1996; Pleck & Masciadrelli, 2003). It will
take some time to isolate the specific influence of
fathers as against the influence of mothers and
other social-contextual factors such as income,
education, schools, neighborhoods, communities,
kin networks, and cultural ideals.

We do know that when fathers share child
care and housework with their wives, employed
mothers assume total responsibility for family
work, evaluate the division of labor as more
... and enjoy higher lev-
ital satisfaction (Brennan ...,
2000; Deutsch, 1999). When men care for young
children on a regular basis, they emphasize verbal
interaction, notice and use more subtle cues, and
treat sons and daughters similarly, rather than
focusing on play, giving orders, and sex-typing
children (Coltrane, 1996, 1998; Parke, 1996).
These styles of father involvement have been
found to encourage less gender stereotyping
among young adults and to encourage independence in daughters and emotional sensitivity in
sons. Most researchers agree that these are worthy goals that could contribute to reducing sexism, promoting gender equity, and curbing
violence against women (but see Blankenhorn,
1995).

Demographic Contexts for Father Involvement

As Furstenberg, (1988) first noted, conflicting
images of fathers are common in popular culture,
with nurturing, involved "good dads" contrasted
with "bad dads" who do not marry the mother of
their children or who move out and fail to pay
child support. Recent research suggests that both
types of fathers are on the rise and that the demographic contexts for fatherhood have changed significantly over the past few decades. In many
industrialized countries, at the same time that
some fathers are taking a more active role in their
children's lives, growing numbers of men rarely
see their children and do not support them financially. In the United States, for example, single-
parent households are increasing, with only about
half of U.S. children eligible for child support
from nonresident parents via court order, and
only about half of those receive the full amount
(Scoon-Rogers, 1999). Both trends in fatherhood
—toward more direct involvement and toward
less contact and financial support—are responses

to the same underlying social developments, including women's rising labor force participation and the increasingly optional nature of marriage.

Marriage rates have fallen in the past few decades, with people waiting longer to get married and increasingly living together without marrying. Women are having fewer children than they did just a few decades ago, waiting longer to have them, and not necessarily marrying before they give birth (Eggebeen, 2002; Seltzer, 2000). One of three births in the United States is to an unmarried woman, a rate that is three times higher than it was in the 1960s, with rates for African American women highest, followed by Latinas, and then non-Hispanic whites (National Center for Health Statistics, 2000). It is often assumed that nonmarital births produce fatherless children, but recent studies show that most of the increase in nonmarital childbearing from the 1980s to the 1990s is accounted for by the increase in the number of cohabiting women getting pregnant and carrying the baby to term without getting married. Historically, if an unmarried woman became pregnant, she would marry to legitimate the birth. Today, only a minority of women do so.

In addition, an increasingly large number of American fathers live apart from their children because of separation or divorce. Because most divorcing men do not seek (or are not awarded) child custody following divorce, the number of divorced men who are uninvolved fathers has risen (Eggebeen, 2002; Furstenberg & Cherlin, 1991), although recent research shows that the actual involvement of fathers with children after divorce varies enormously, sometimes without regard to official postdivorce court orders (Braver, 1998; Hetherington & Stanley-Hagan, 1999; McLanahan & Sandefur, 1994; Seltzer, 1998). The number of men with joint physical (residential) custody has grown, though joint legal (decision-making) custody is still a more common postdivorce parenting arrangement (Maccoby & Mnookin, 1992; Seltzer, 1998). And although single-father households have increased in recent years, single-mother households continue to outpace them five to one. Demographers suggest that because of all these trends, younger cohorts will be less likely to experience sustained involved fathering than the generations that immediately preceded them (Eggebeen, 2002).

Marriage and the traditional assumption of fatherhood have become more fragile, in part because an increasing number of men face financial difficulties. Although men continue to earn about 30% higher wages than women, their real wages (adjusted for inflation) have declined since the early 1970s, whereas women's have increased (Bernstein & Mishel, 1997). As the U.S. economy has shifted from heavy reliance on domestic manufacturing to global interdependence within an information and service economy, working-class men's prospects of earning a family wage have declined. At the same time, women's labor force participation has risen steadily, with future growth in the economy predicted in the areas where women are traditionally concentrated (e.g., service, information, health care, part-time work). The historical significance of this shift cannot be overestimated. For most of the 19th and 20th centuries, American women's life chances were determined by their marriage decisions. Unable to own property, vote, or be legally independent in most states, daughters were dependent on fathers and wives were dependent on their husbands for economic survival. Such dependencies shaped family relations and produced fatherhood ideals and practices predicated on male family headship. As women and mothers have gained independence by entering the labor force in record numbers, it is not surprising that older ideals about marriage to a man legitimating childbearing have been challenged.

Gender and the Politics of Fatherhood

In the 1990s, popular books and articles revived a research and policy focus that had been popular in the 1960s: father absence. For example, Popenoe (1996) suggested that drug and alcohol abuse, juvenile delinquency, teenage pregnancy, violent crime, and child poverty were the result of father-lessness and that American society was in decline because it had abandoned traditional marriage and child-rearing patterns. Such claims about father absence often rely on evolutionary psychology and sociobiology and define fathers as categorically different from mothers (Blankenhorn, 1995; Popenoe, 1996). Even some proponents of nurturing fathers warn men against trying to act too much like mothers (Pruett, 1993). Following this reasoning, some argue for gender differentiated parenting measurement strategies: "[T]he roles of father and mother are different and complementary rather than inter-changeable and thus the standards for evaluating the role performance of fathers and mothers should be different" (Day & Mackey, 1989, p. 402). Some label the use of measures developed on mothers to study fathers and the practice of comparing fathers' and mothers' parenting as the *deficit model* (Doherty, 1991) or the *role inadequacy perspective* (Hawkins & Dollahite, 1997).

Because parenting is a learned behavior for both men and women, most social scientists focus on the societal conditions that create gender differences in parenting or find proximate social causes of paternal investment that outweigh assumed biological causes (e.g., Hofferth & Anderson, 2003). Nevertheless, questioning taken-for-granted cultural ideals about families can cause controversy. When Silverstein and Auerbach (1999) challenged assertions about essential differences between fathers and mothers in an *American Psychologist* article entitled "Deconstructing the Essential Father," they received widespread public and academic criticism. Their scholarly article (based on a review of research findings) was ridiculed as "silliness" and "junk science" by Wade Horn (1999; formerly of the National Fatherhood Initiative and now Assistant Secretary in the U.S. Department of Health and Human Services), and the U.S. House of Representatives debated whether to pass a resolution condemning the article (Silverstein, 2002). Clearly, debates about fathers, marriage, and family values carry symbolic meanings

that transcend scientific findings. The contentious political and scholarly debates about fathers that emerged in the 1990s appear to be framed by an older political dichotomy: Conservatives tend to focus on biological parenting differences and stress the importance of male headship and breadwinning, respect for authority, and moral leadership (Blankenhorn, 1995; Popenoe, 1996), whereas liberals tend to focus on similarities between mothers and fathers and stress the importance of employment, social services, and possibilities for more equal marital relations (Coontz, 1992; Silverstein & Auerbach, 1999; Stacey, 1996).

A full analysis of contemporary family values debates is beyond the scope of this chapter, but elsewhere I analyze marriage and fatherhood movements using data and theories about political opportunities, resource mobilization, and the moral framing of social issues (Coltrane, 2001; Coltrane & Adams, 2003; see also Gavanas, 2002). In general, cultural tensions in the larger society are mirrored in policy proposals and academic debates about the appropriate roles of fathers and the importance of marriage. One cannot adjudicate among various scholarly approaches to fathering without acknowledging gendered interests and understanding the political economy of expert knowledge production. Recent policies and programs promoting marriage and fatherhood using faith-based organizations are designed to advance a particular vision of fatherhood. Whether they will benefit the majority of American mothers and children is a question that cannot be resolved without more sophisticated research with controls for mothers' parenting and various other economic and social-contextual issues (Marsiglio et al., 2000; Marsiglio & Pleck, in press).

Prospects for the Future

The forces that are driving changes in fathers' involvement in families are likely to continue. In two-parent households (both married and cohabiting), men share more family work if their female partners are employed more hours, earn more money, and have more education. All three of these trends in women's attainment are likely to continue for the foreseeable future. Similarly, fathers share more family work when they are employed fewer hours and their wives earn a greater portion of the family income. Labor market and economic trends for these variables are also expected to continue for several decades. Couples also share more when they believe that family work should be shared and that men and women should have equal rights. According to national opinion polls, although the country has become slightly more conservative about marriage and divorce than it was in the 1970s and 1980s, the belief in gender equality continues to gain acceptance among both men and women. In addition, American women are waiting longer, on average, to marry and give birth, and they are having fewer children—additional factors sometimes associated with more sharing of housework and child care. Thus, I predict that increasing economic parity and more equal gender relations will allow women to buy out of some domestic obligations and/or recruit their partners to do more. Middle- and upper-class wives and mothers will rely on working-class and immigrant women to provide domestic services (nannies, housekeepers, child care workers, fast food employees, etc.), thereby reducing their own hours of family labor but simultaneously perpetuating race, class, and gender hierarchies in the labor market and in the society. Some fathers in dual-earner households will increase their contributions to family work, whereas others will perform a greater proportion of housework and child care by virtue of their wives' doing less. Other men will remain marginal to family life because they do not stay connected to the mothers of their children, do not hold jobs allowing them to support their children, or do not seek custody or make regular child support payments. These two ideal types—of involved and marginalized fathers—are likely to continue to coexist in the popular culture and in actual practice.

The context in which American couples negotiate fathering has definitely changed. The future is likely to bring more demands on fathers to be active parents if they want to stay involved with the mothers of their children. For fathers to assume more responsibility for active parenting, it may be necessary to change cultural assumptions that men are entitled to domestic services and that women are inherently predisposed to provide them. Further changes in fathering are likely to be driven by women's increasing independence and earning power. Ironically, women's enhanced economic position also makes them able to form families and raise children without the fathers being present. In the future, men will be even less able to rely on their superior earning power and the institution of fatherhood to maintain their connection to families and children. Increasingly, they will need to adopt different fathering styles to meet specific family circumstances and to commit to doing things men have not been accustomed to doing. Some men will be able to maintain their economic and emotional commitments to their children, whereas others will not. Some men will participate in all aspects of child rearing, whereas others will hardly see their children. Unless living wages and adequate social supports are developed for all fathers (as well as for mothers and children), we can expect that the paradoxes, contradictions, and dilemmas associated with fathering described in this chapter will continue for the foreseeable future.

Author's Note: This chapter incorporates some material from a November 21, 2002, National Council on Family Relations (NCFR) Annual Conference Special Session "Future Prospects for Increasing Father Involvement in Child Rearing and Household Activities," reprinted as "The Paradox of Fatherhood: Predicting the Future of Men's Family Involvement" in *Vision 2003* (Minneapolis, MN: NCFR/Allen Press). I thank Marilyn Coleman, Lawrence Ganong, Joseph Pleck, Carl Auerbach, and two anonymous reviewers for valuable feedback on an earlier draft of this chapter.

References

Ahmeduzzaman, M., & Roopnarine, J. L. (1992). Sociodemographic factors, functioning style, social support, and fathers' involvement with preschoolers in African American intact families. *Journal of Marriage and the Family, 54,* 699–707.

Allen, S. M., & Hawkins, A. J. (1999). Maternal gatekeeping. *Journal of Marriage and the Family, 61,* 199–212.

Amato, P. (2000). Diversity within single-parent families. In D. H. Demo, K. R. Allen, & M. A. Fine (Eds.), *Handbook of family diversity* (pp. 149–172). New York: Oxford University Press.

Amato, P., & Booth, A. (1997). *A generation at risk: Growing up in an era of family upheaval.* Cambridge, MA: Harvard University Press.

Amato, P., & Gilbreth, J. (1999). Nonresident fathers and children's well-being: A meta-analysis. *Journal of Marriage and the Family, 61,* 557–573.

Amato, P., & Rivera, F. (1999). Paternal involvement and children's behavior problems. *Journal of Marriage and the Family, 61,* 375–384.

Auerbach, C., Silverstein, L., & Zizi, M. (1997). The evolving structure of fatherhood. *Journal of African American Men, 2,* 59–85.

Beitel, A. H., & Parke, R. D. (1998). Paternal involvement in infancy: The role of maternal and paternal attitudes. *Journal of Family Psychology, 12,* 268–288.

Belsky, J. (1984). The determinants of parenting. *Child Development, 55,* 83–96.

Bernard, J. (1981). The good provider role: Its rise and fall. *American Psychologist, 36,* 1–12.

Bernstein, J., & Mishel, L. (1997). Has wage inequality stopped growing? *Monthly Labor Review, 120,* 3–17.

Biller, H. B. (1976). The father and personality development. In M. E. Lamb (Ed.), *The role of the father in child development.* New York: John Wiley.

Blankenhorn, D. (1995). *Fatherless America.* New York: Basic Books.

Bowman, P. J., & Sanders, R. (1998). Unmarried African American fathers. *Journal of Comparative Family Studies, 29,* 39–56.

Braver, S. L. (1998). *Divorced dads.* New York: Jeremy Tarcher/Putnam.

Brayfield, A. (1995). Juggling jobs and kids. *Journal of Marriage and the Family, 57,* 321–332.

Brennan, R. T., Barnett, R. C., & Gareis, K. C. (2001). When she earns more than he does: A longitudinal study of dual-earner couples. *Journal of Marriage and Family, 63,* 168–182.

Brewster, K. L. (2000, March). *Contextualizing change in fathers' participation in child care.* Paper presented at "Work and Family" Conference, San Francisco.

Brines, J. (1994). Economic dependency, gender, and the division of labor at home. *American Journal of Sociology, 100,* 652–688.

Broman, L. L. (1991). Gender, work, family roles, and psychological well-being of blacks. *Journal of Marriage and the Family, 53,* 509–520.

Cabrera, N., Tamis-LeMonda, C., Bradley, R., Hofferth, S., & Lamb, M. (2000). Fatherhood in the 21st century. *Child Development, 71,* 127–136.

Casper, L. M., & O'Connell, M. (1998). Work, income, the economy, and married fathers as child-care providers. *Demography, 35,* 243–250.

Chodorow, N. (1974). Family structure and feminine personality. In M. Z. Rosaldo & L. Lamphere (Eds.), *Woman, culture and society* (pp. 43–66). Palo Alto, CA: Stanford University Press.

Cohen, P. N. (1998). Replacing housework in the service economy: Gender, class, and race/ethnicity in service spending. *Gender and Society, 12,* 219–231.

Coley, R. L., & Morris, J. E. (2002). Comparing father and mother reports of father involvement among low-income minority families. *Journal of Marriage and the Family, 64,* 982–997.

Coltrane, S. (1988). Father-child relationships and the status of women. *American Journal of Sociology, 93,* 1060–1095.

Coltrane, S. (1996). *Family man.* New York: Oxford University Press.

Coltrane, S. (1998). *Gender and families.* Newbury Park, CA: Pine Forge/Alta Mira.

Coltrane, S. (2000). Research on household labor. *Journal of Marriage and the Family, 62,* 1209–1233.

Coltrane, S. (2001). Marketing the marriage "solution." *Sociological Perspectives, 44,* 387–422.

Coltrane, S., & Adams, M. (2003). The social construction of the divorce "problem": Morality, child victims, and the politics of gender. *Family Relations, 52,* 21–30.

Coltrane, S., & Collins, R. (2001). *Sociology of marriage and the family* (5th ed.). Belmont, CA: Wadsworth/Thomson Learning.

Coltrane, S., & Galt, J. (2000). The history of men's caring. In M. H. Meyer (Ed.), *Care work: Gender, labor, and welfare states* (pp. 15–36). New York: Routledge.

Coltrane, S., & Parke, R. D. (1998). *Reinventing fatherhood: Toward an historical understanding of continuity and change in men's family lives* (WP 98–12A). Philadelphia: National Center on Fathers and Families.

Coltrane, S., Parke, R. D., & Adams, M. (2001, April). *Shared parenting in Mexican-American and European-American families.* Paper presented at the biennial meeting of the Society for Research in Child Development, Minneapolis, MN.

Coontz, S. (1992). *The way we never were.* New York: Basic Books.

Cowan, C. P., & Cowan, P. A. (2000). *When partners become parents.* Mahwah, NJ: Lawrence Erlbaum.

Crockett, L. J., Eggebeen, D. J., & Hawkins, A. J. (1993). Fathers' presence and young children's behavioral and cognitive adjustment. *Journal of Family Issues, 14,* 355–377.

Day, R. D., & Mackey, W. C. (1989). An alternate standard for evaluating American fathers. *Journal of Family Issues, 10,* 401–408.

Deutsch, F. (1999). *Halving it all.* Cambridge, MA: Harvard University Press.

Dill, B. T. (1988). Our mother's grief: Racial ethnic women and the maintenance of families. *Journal of Family History, 13,* 415–431.

Doherty, W. J. (1991). Beyond reactivity and the deficit model of manhood. *Journal of Marital and Family Therapy, 17,* 29–32.

Dubowitz, H., Black, M. M., Cox, C. E., Kerr, M. A., Litrownik, A. J., Radhakrishna, A., English, D. J., Schneider, M. W., & Runyan, D. K. (2001). Father involvement and children's functioning at age 6 years: A multisite study. *Child Maltreatment, 6,* 300–309.

Eggebeen, D. (2002). The changing course of fatherhood. *Journal of Family Issues, 23,* 486–506.

Ehrenreich, B. (1984). *The hearts of men.* Garden City, NY: Anchor Press/Doubleday.

Fagan, J. A. (1998). Correlates of low-income African American and Puerto Rican fathers' involvement with their children. *Journal of Black Psychology, 3,* 351–367.

Federal Interagency Forum on Child and Family Statistics. (1998). Report of the Working Group on Conceptualizing Male Parenting (Marsiglio, Day, Evans, Lamb, Braver, & Peters). In *Nurturing fatherhood* (pp. 101–174). Washington, DC: Government Printing Office.

Finkelhor, D., Hotaling, G., Lewis, I., & Smith, C. (1990). Sexual abuse in a national survey of adult men and women. *Child Abuse and Neglect, 14,* 19–28.

Furstenberg, F. F. (1988). Good dads—bad dads. In A. Cherlin (Ed.), *The changing American family and public policy* (pp. 193–218). Washington, DC: Urban Institute Press.

Furstenberg, F. F., & Cherlin, A. (1991). *Divided families.* Cambridge, MA: Harvard University Press.

Furstenberg, F. F., & Harris, K. (1993). When and why fathers matter. In R. Lerman & T. Ooms (Eds.), *Young unwed fathers* (pp. 150–176). Philadelphia: Temple University Press.

Gavanas, A. (2002). The fatherhood responsibility movement. In B. Hobson (Ed.), *Making men into fathers* (pp. 213–242). New York: Cambridge University Press.

Griswold, R. L. (1993). *Fatherhood in America: A history.* New York: Basic Books.

Griswold, R. L. (1997). Generative fathering: A historical perspective. In A. J. Hawkins & D. Dollahite (Eds.), *Generative fathering* (pp. 71–86). Thousand Oaks, CA: Sage.

Hamer, J., & Marchioro, K. (2002). Becoming custodial dads: Exploring parenting among low-income and working-class African American fathers. *Journal of Marriage and the Family, 64,* 116–129.

Harris, K. H., Furstenberg, F. F., & Marmer, J. K. (1998). Paternal involvement with adolescents in intact families. *Demography, 35,* 201–216.

Harris, K. H., & Morgan, S. P. (1991). Fathers, sons and daughters: Differential paternal involvement in parenting. *Journal of Marriage and the Family, 53,* 531–544.

Hawkins, A. J., Christiansen, S. L., Sargent, K. P., & Hill, E. J. (1993). Rethinking fathers' involvement in child care. *Journal of Family Issues, 14,* 531–549.

Hawkins, A. J., & Dollahite, D. C. (1997). Beyond the role-inadequacy perspective of fathering. In A. J. Hawkins & D. C. Dollahite (Eds.), *Generative fathering: Beyond deficit perspectives* (pp. 3–16). Thousand Oaks, CA: Sage.

Hays, S. (1996). *The cultural contradictions of motherhood.* New Haven, CT: Yale University Press.

Hetherington, E. M., & Stanley-Hagan, M. M. (1999). Stepfamilies. In M. E. Lamb (Ed.), *Parenting and child development in "nontraditional" families* (pp. 137–159). Mahwah, NJ: Lawrence Erlbaum.

Hewlett, B. S. (1991). *The nature and context of Aka pygmy paternal infant care.* Ann Arbor: University of Michigan Press.

Hewlett, B. S. (2000). Culture, history, and sex: Anthropological contributions to conceptualizing father involvement. *Marriage and Family Review, 29,* 59–73.

Hochschild, A. R. (1989). *The second shift.* New York: Viking.

Hofferth, S. L. (1998). *Healthy environments, healthy children: Children in families.* Ann Arbor. Institute for Social Research, University of Michigan.

Hofferth, S. L. (2003). Race/ethnic differences in father involvement in two-parent families: Culture, context, or economy? *Journal of Family Issues, 24,* 185–216.

Hofferth, S. L., & Anderson, K. G. (2003). Are all dads equal? Biology versus marriage as a basis for paternal investment. *Journal of Marriage and the Family, 65,* 213–232.

Horn, W. (1999). Lunacy 101: Questioning the need for fathers. Retrieved April 29, 2003, from the Smart Marriages Web site: http://listarchives. his.com/smartmarriages/smartmarriages.9907/msg00011.html.

Hossain, Z., & Roopnarine, J. L. (1993). Division of household labor and child care in dual-earner African-American families with infants. *Sex Roles, 29,* 571–583.

Hunter, A. G., & Davis, J. E. (1994). Hidden voices of black men: The meaning, structure, and complexity of manhood. *Journal of Black Studies, 25,* 20–40.

John, D., & Shelton, B. A. (1997). The production of gender among black and white women and men: The case of household labor. *Sex Roles, 36,* 171–193.

Johnson, M. (1988). *Strong mothers, weak wives.* Berkeley: University of California Press.

Kimmel, M. (1996). *Manhood in America: A cultural history.* New York: Free Press.

Lamb, M. E., Pleck, J., Charnov, E., & Levine, J. (1987). A biosocial perspective on parental behavior and involvement. In J. B. Lancaster, J. Altman, & A. Rossi (Eds), *Parenting across the lifespan* (pp. 11–42). New York: Academic Press.

LaRossa, R. (1988). Fatherhood and social change. *Family Relations, 37,* 451–457.

LaRossa, R. (1997). *The modernization of fatherhood: A social and political history.* Chicago: University of Chicago Press.

Maccoby, E., & Mnookin, R. (1992). *Dividing the child.* Cambridge, MA: Harvard University Press.

Margolin, L. (1992). Child abuse by mother's boyfriends. *Child Abuse and Neglect, 16,* 541–551.

Marsiglio, W. (1991). Paternal engagement activities with minor children. *Journal of Marriage and the Family, 53,* 973–986.

Marsiglio, W., Amato, P., Day, R. D., & Lamb, M. E. (2000). Scholarship on fatherhood in the 1990s and beyond. *Journal of Marriage and the Family, 62,* 1173–1191.

Marsiglio, W., & Pleck, J. H. (in press). Fatherhood and masculinities. In R.W. Connell, J. Hearn, & M. Kimmel (Eds.), *The handbook of studies on men and masculinities.* Thousand Oaks, CA: Sage.

McBride, B. A. (1990). The effects of a parent education/play group program on father involvement on child rearing. *Family Relations, 39,* 250–256.

McBride, B. A., & Mills, G. (1993). A comparison of mother and father involvement with their preschool age children. *Early Childhood Research Quarterly, 8,* 457–477.

McBride, B. A., Schoppe, S., & Ranc, T. (2002). Child characteristics, parenting stress, and parental involvement: Fathers versus mothers. *Journal of Marriage and the Family, 64,* 998–1011.

McDaniel, A. (1994). Historical racial differences in living arrangements of children. *Journal of Family History, 19,* 57–77.

McHale, S. M., & Huston, T. L. (1984). Men and women as parents: Sex role orientations, employment, and parental roles with infants. *Child Development, 55,* 1349–1361.

McLanahan, S., & Sandefur, G. (1994). *Growing up with a single parent: What hurts, what helps.* Cambridge, MA: Harvard University Press.

McLanahan, S., Seltzer, J., Hanson, T., & Thomson, E. (1994). Child support enforcement and child well-being. In I. Garfinkel, S. S. McLanahan, & P. K. Robins (Eds.), *Child support and child well-being* (pp. 285–316). Washington, DC: Urban Institute.

Messner, M. (1993). "Changing men" and feminist politics in the U.S. *Theory and Society, 22,* 723–737.

Mintz, S. (1998). From patriarchy to androgyny and other myths. In A. Booth & A. C. Crouter (Eds.), *Men in families* (pp. 3–30). Mahweh, NJ: Lawrence Erlbaum.

Mosley, J., & Thomson, E. (1994). Fathering behavior and child outcomes. In W. Marsiglio (Ed.), *Fatherhood* (pp. 148–165). Thousand Oaks, CA: Sage.

National Center for Health Statistics. (2000, January). Nonmarital birth rates, 1940–1999. Retrieved on April 29, 2003, from the Centers for Disease Control and Prevention Web site: www.cdc.gov/nchs/data/nvsr/nvsr48.

National Research Council. (1993). *Understanding child abuse and neglect.* Washington, DC: National Academy Press.

Nock, S. (1998). *Marriage in men's lives.* New York: Oxford University Press.

Oropesa, R. S. (1993). Using the service economy to relieve the double burden: Female labor force participation and service purchases. *Journal of Family Issues, 14,* 438–473.

Ozer, E. M., Barnett, R. C., Brennan, R. T., & Sperling, J. (1998). Does childcare involvement increase or decrease distress among dual-earner couples? *Women's Health: Research on Gender, Behavior, and Policy, 4,* 285–311.

Padgett, D. L. (1997). The contribution of support networks to household labor in African American families. *Journal of Family Issues, 18,* 227–250.

Palkovitz, R. (1997). Reconstructing "involvement." In A. Hawkins & D. Dollahite (Eds.), *Generative fathering* (pp. 200–216). Thousand Oaks, CA: Sage.

Parke, R. D. (1996). *Fatherhood.* Cambridge, MA: Harvard University Press.

Pasley, K., Ihinger-Tallman, M, & Buehler, C. (1993). Developing a middle-range theory of father involvement postdivorce. *Journal of Family Issues, 14,* 550–576.

Pleck, E. H., & Pleck, J. H. (1997). Fatherhood ideals in the United States: Historical dimensions. In M. E. Lamb (Ed.), *The role of the father in child development* (3rd ed., pp. 33–48). New York: John Wiley.

Pleck, J. H. (1993). Are "family-supportive" employer policies relevant to men? In J. C. Hood (Ed.), *Men, work, and family* (pp. 217–237). Newbury Park, CA: Sage.

Pleck, J. H. (1997). Paternal involvement: Levels, sources, and consequences. In M. E. Lamb (Ed.), *The role of the father in child development* (3rd ed., pp. 66–103). New York: John Wiley.

Pleck, J. H., & Masciadrelli, B. P. (2003). Paternal involvement: Levels, sources, and consequences. In M. E. Lamb (Ed.), *The role of the father in child development* (4th ed.). New York: John Wiley

Pleck, J. H., & Steuve, J. L. (2001). Time and paternal involvement. In K. Daly (Ed.), *Minding the time in family experience* (pp. 205–226). Oxford, UK: Elsevier.

Popenoe, D. (1996). *Life without father: Compelling new evidence that fatherhood and marriage are indispensable for the good of children and society.* New York: Free Press.

Presser, H. B. (1995). Job, family, and gender. *Demography, 32,* 577–598.

Pruett, K. D. (1993). The paternal presence. *Families in Society, 74,* 46–50.

Radhakrishna, A., Bou-Saada, I. E., Hunter, W. M., Catellier, D. J., & Kotch, J. B. (2001). Are father surrogates a risk factor for child maltreatment? *Child Maltreatment, 6,* 281–289.

Rane, T. R., & McBride, B. A. (2000). Identity theory as a guide to understanding father's involvement with their children. *Journal of Family Issues, 21,* 347–366.

Sanday, P. R. (1981). *Female power and male dominance.* New York: Cambridge University Press.

Scoon-Rogers, L. (1999). Child support for custodial mothers and fathers. *Current Population Reports,* P60–196. Washington, DC: U.S. Bureau of the Census.

Seltzer, J. A. (1994). Consequences of marital dissolution for children. *Annual Review of Sociology, 20,* 235–266.

Seltzer, J. A. (1998). Father by law: Effects of joint legal custody on nonresident fathers' involvement with children. *Demography, 35,* 135–146.

Seltzer, J. A. (2000). Families formed outside of marriage. *Journal of Marriage and the Family, 62,* 1247–1268.

Silverstein, L. B. (2002). Fathers and families. In J. McHale & W. Grolnick (Eds.), *Retrospect and prospect in the psychological study of fathers* (pp. 35–64). Mahwah, NJ: Lawrence Erlbaum.

Silverstein, L. B., & Auerbach, C. F. (1999). Deconstructing the essential father. *American Psychologist, 54,* 397–407.

Smock, P., & Manning, W. (1997). Nonresident parents' characteristics and child support. *Journal of Marriage and the Family, 59,* 798–808.

Snarey, J. (1993). *How fathers care for the next generation.* Cambridge, MA: Harvard University Press.

Stacey, J. (1996). *In the name of the family.* Boston: Beacon.

Thompson, L., & Walker, A. J. (1989). Gender in families: Women and men in marriage, work, and parenthood. *Journal of Marriage and the Family, 51,* 845–871.

Toth, J. F., & Xu, X. (1999). Ethnic and cultural diversity in fathers' involvement: A racial/ethnic comparison of African American, Hispanic, and white fathers. *Youth and Society, 31,* 76–99.

Whiting, J., & Whiting, B. (1975). Aloofness and intimacy of husbands and wives. *Ethos, 3,* 183–207.

Wilson, M. N., Tolson, T. F. J., Hinton, I. D., & Kiernan, M. (1990). Flexibility and sharing of childcare duties in black families. *Sex Roles, 22,* 409–425.

Yueng, W. J., Sandberg, J. F., Davis-Kean, P. E., & Hofferth, S. L. (2001). Children's time with fathers in intact families. *Journal of Marriage and Family, 63,* 136–154.

Judith Stacey

Cruising to Familyland: Gay Hypergamy and Rainbow Kinship

*Promiscuity was rampant because in an all-male-subculture there was no one to say 'no'
—no moderating role like that a woman plays in the heterosexual milieu. (Shilts, 1987)*

*Because men are naturally promiscuous, two men will stick together as naturally as the
two north poles of a magnet. (Davis and Phillips, 1999)*

*There is room for both monogamous gay couples and sex pigs in the same big tent of gay
community. (Rofes, 1998: 221)*

Does masculine sexuality threaten bourgeois family and social order? Scholars, critics and activists who hold incommensurate ideological and theoretical views about gender, family and sexuality, nonetheless seem to share the belief that it does. To religious and social conservatives, gay male sexual culture signifies masculine libido incarnate, the dangerous antithesis of family and community. "In the Christian right imagination," as Arlene Stein points out, "homosexuals represent undisciplined male sexuality, freed of the 'civilizing' influence of women" (Stein, 2001: 107). "Untrammeled homosexuality can take over and destroy a social system," warns Paul Cameron, a leading anti-gay ideologue in the US. Indeed, Cameron unwittingly hints that sexual jealousy, marital frustration and not-so-latent homoerotic desire propel his hostility to homosexuality when he concedes that:

> Marital sex tends toward the boring end. Generally, it doesn't deliver the kind of sheer sexual pleasure that homosexual sex does. The evi-

dence is that men do a better job on men, and women on women, if all you are looking for is orgasm. (Quoted in Dreyfuss, 1999)

Quite a few mainstream gay male leaders, like the late journalist and AIDS victim Randy Shilts, agree that gay male sexual culture, which legitimates pursuit of recreational sex with an unlimited number of partners as an end in itself, represents the dangerous excesses of *masculine* sexuality. In *And the Band Played On,* Shilts charged unfettered masculine sexuality with escalating the epidemic spread of AIDS. In his view, gay baths, bars and cruising grounds serve masculine, rather than specifically homoerotic male desires: "Some heterosexual males confided that they were enthralled with the idea of the immediate, available, even anonymous sex a bathhouse offered, if they could only find women who would agree. Gay men, of course, agreed quite frequently" (Shilts, 1987: 89). Similarly, pessimistic assessments of undomesticated masculinity that undergird the views of reactionary antifeminists, like George Gilder (1986), echo in the discourse of mainstream gay men. For example, "the conservative case for gay marriage" that neoconservative gay journalist Andrew Sullivan puts forth maintains that:

From *Current Sociology,* March 2004, Vol. 52(2):
181–197 Sage Publications (London, Thousand Oaks,
CA, and New Delhi).

. . . the discipline of domesticity, of shared duties and lives, of the inevitable give-and-take of cohabitation and love with anyone, even of the same sex, tends to benefit men more than the option of constant, free-wheeling, etiolating bachelorhood. (Sullivan, 1997: 151)

Right-wing opponents of same-sex marriage endorse the diagnosis that masculine eros is antisocial, but reject the remedy Sullivan proposes as insufficient and naive. Thus, the scornful second extract at the start of this article by Britain's moralistic *Daily Mail* columnist Melanie Phillips concludes: "It is not marriage which domesticates men—it is women" (Davis and Phillips, 1999: 17).

Writing from an antithetical ideological perspective, the late gay sociologist Martin Levine likewise interpreted gay male cruising culture as an arena of hypermasculinity, where men operate free of the restraints that negotiating with women imposes on heterosexual men:

. . . without the "constraining" effects of feminine erotic standards, gay men were able to focus more overtly and obviously on the sexual activities in finding sexual partners. . . . Cruising, in this sense, is a most masculine of pastimes. Gay men were simply more honest—and certainly more obvious—about it. (Levine, 1998: 79–80)

Likewise, queer theorists, such as Michael Warner (1999), who also hold political and sexual values quite hostile to those of Andrew Sullivan as well as to the right-wing authors quoted above, nonetheless share Sullivan's view (or, in Warner's case, fear) that the contemporary gay rush to the altar and the nursery will erode the liberatory, transgressive character of queer sexual culture. Gays who have succumbed to what comedian Kate Clinton terms "mad vow disease," Warner charges, fail to recognize that "marriage has become the central legitimating institution by which the state penetrates the sexuality of its subjects; it is the 'zone of privacy' outside which sex is unprotected" (Warner, 1999: 128). Critics on all sides take gay male sexual culture to be a potent source of oppositional values and cultural resistance.

In short, sexual radicals and conservatives converge in viewing gay male sexual norms and practices as a realm of unadulterated masculine desire that is subversive to bourgeois domesticity and committed family ties. "If you isolate sexuality as something solely for one's own personal amusement," Paul Cameron warns, "and all you want is the most satisfying orgasm you can get—and that is what homosexuality seems to be—then homosexuality seems too powerful to resist" (quoted in Dreyfuss, 1999).

Yet, *is* orgasm, or even carnal pleasure, all that gay men are looking for when they cruise? And, more to the point, is that all they find? In this article, I draw from ethnographic research I conducted on gay male intimacy and kinship in Los Angeles to challenge these widely shared assumptions. Gay male cruising culture, I suggest, yields social and familial consequences far more complex and contradictory than most critics (or even a few fans) seem to imagine. The gay cruising arena of unencumbered, recreational sex certainly does disrupt conventional family norms and practices. At the same time, however, it also generates bonds of kinship and domesticity. Gay male sexual cruising serves, I suggest, as an underappreciated cultural resource for the creative construction of those "families of choice" (Weston, 1991; Weeks et al., 2001) and "invincible communities" (Nardi, 1999) that scholars have identified as the distinctive character of non-heterosexual family and kinship formations. In particular, the unfettered pursuit of masculine sexuality facilitates opportunities for individual social mobility and for forging rainbow kinship ties that have not yet attracted much attention from scholars or activists.

Gay "El Lay"

Los Angeles is home to the second largest, and likely the most socially diverse, yet comparatively understudied population of gay men on the planet. Arguably no city better symbolizes sexual excess, consumer culture and the antithesis of family values, and perhaps no population more so than the gay male denizens who crowd the bars, beats and boutiques of West Hollywood. To many observers, numerous gay men among them, "Weho" culture particularly signifies gay male decadence in situ, the epitome of the sexual culture that both Andrew Sullivan and Paul Cameron denounce. Cursory contact with gay culture in Los Angeles readily reinforces stereotypes about gay men's narcissistic preoccupation with erotic allure. Advertisements for corporeal beautification and modification flood the pages, airwaves and websites of the local gay male press: familiar and exotic cosmetic surgery and body sculpture procedures, including penile, buttock and pec implants; liposuction; laser resurfacing; hair removal or extensions; cosmetic dentistry; personal trainers and gym rat regimens; tattooing and tattoo removal; body piercing; hair coloring, growing and styling; tinted contact lenses; manicures, pedicures and body waxing; as well as color, style and fashion consultants and the commodified universe of couture, cosmetics and personal grooming implements that they service.

Nonetheless, conducting local field research on gay men's intimate affiliations from 1999 to 2003, I encountered tinker toys as often as tinsel. Los Angeles might well be the cosmetic surgery capital of "planet out," but much less predictably, the celluloid metropolis is also at the vanguard of gay fatherhood. Organized groups of "Gay Fathers" and of "Gay Parents" formed in the city as early as the mid-1970s and contributed to the genesis of Family Pride, Incorporated, currently among the leading national grassroots organizations of its kind anywhere (Miller, 2001: 226–9). Los Angeles also gave birth to Growing Generations, the world's first and only gay-owned, assisted reproduction agency founded to serve an international gay clientele.[1] Several of its first clients were among nine families who in 1998 organized the PopLuckClub (PLC), a pioneering local support group for gay fathers and their children.[2] The thriving PLC sponsors monthly gatherings, organizes special events and provides information, referrals, support and community to a membership that now includes nearly 200 fam-

ilies of varying shapes, sizes, colors and forms. A PLC subgroup of at-home dads and their children meet weekly for a play-date and lunch in a West Hollywood playground; single gay dads and "prospective SGDs" seeking "to meet others who understand how parenting affects our lives" hold monthly mixers that feature "friendly folks, scintillating snacks, and brilliant banter—about the best brand of diapers!" (PLC listserv, 2003); and additional PLC focus groups, for prospective gay dads or adoptive dads, for example, as well as satellite chapters in neighboring counties continually emerge.

Between June 1999 and June 2003, I conducted field research in the greater Los Angeles area that included lengthy multisession, family life history interviews with 50 self-identified gay men born between 1958 and 1973 and with members of their designated kin, as well as within their community groups, religious institutions and organizations, like the PLC. My primary subjects came of age and came out after the Stonewall era of gay liberation and after the AIDS crisis was widely recognized. Popular discourses about safe sex, the gayby boom, gay marriage, domestic partnerships and "families we choose" informed their sense of familial prospects. This is the first cohort of gay men young enough to be able to contemplate parenthood outside heterosexuality and mature enough to be in a position to choose or reject it. The men and their families include diverse racial, ethnic, geographic, religious and social class backgrounds.[3] They also practice varied relational and residential options. My research sample included 16 gay men who were single at the time of my study; 31 who were coupled, some in open relationships, others monogamous, most of whom cohabited, but several who did not; and a committed, sexually exclusive, trio. It included men who reside or parent alone, with friends, lovers, former lovers, biological, legal and adopted kin, and children of every "conceivable" origin.[4] More than a few of these men cruised their way to several genres of gay hypergamy and to unconventional forms of rainbow kinship.

Cruising to Kinship: Case Studies

In anthropological terminology, hypergamy designates a marriage system in which women, but not men, may "marry up" the social status ladder. In the classic situation, lower rank kin groups trade on the youth, beauty and fertility of their daughters in efforts to marry them (and thereby the fortunes of their natal families) to older, wealthier, often less attractive men from higher ranking families. Modern western residues of this preindustrial patriarchal pattern persist, of course, as the fact that there is a dictionary entry for "trophy wife" (but none for "trophy husband") underscores: "An attractive, young wife married to a usually older, affluent man" (*The American Heritage® Dictionary of the English Language*, 2000). The more pejorative and even more sexist definition for "gold-digger" ("a woman who seeks money and expensive gifts from men") reveals that heterosexual women still can barter youth, beauty and erotic appeal (and sometimes even fertility) for intimate affiliations with older men with greater economic, cultural and social resources (*The American Heritage® Dictionary of the English Language*, 2000).

Two Rainbow Families

And so can some gay men. Cruising culture, combined with the greater fluidity of gay male gender conventions, allows gay men to engage more frequently than is common in intimate encounters that cross conventional social borders. While the majority of these may be fleeting and anonymous, the sheer volume of gay erotic exchanges outside the customary bounds of public scrutiny and social segregation provides opportunities to form more enduring socially heterogeneous attachments. Brief sketches of two cases from my field research illustrate how gay men can cruise their way to creative, multicultural permutations of hypergamous kinship.

Ozzie and Harry—A Gay Pygmalion Fable[5]

Ozzie, Harry and their two young children, a picture-perfect, affluent, adoring nuclear family who own an elegant, spacious Spanish home, represent an utterly improbable, gay fairy-tale romance of love, marriage and the baby-carriage. A transracial, transnational, cross-class, interfaith couple who have been together eight years, Ozzie and Harry claim to have fallen in love at first sight on a Roman street in 1995. Harry, then 31 years old and a prosperous, white, Jewish, New England ivy-league educated, successful literary agent, was vacationing in Europe when he spotted and cruised 24-year-old Ozzie on a crowded street. Talented but undereducated, a Catholic Afro-Brazilian raised in an improverished single-mother family, Ozzie had migrated to Italy several years earlier as a guest worker.

Although the lovers met by cruising, they both claim to have fallen in love instantly. Ozzie says he told Harry that he loved him that very first night: "I just knew. I just told him what I felt." They report sharing all of their "hopes and dreams" from the moment they met, and preeminent among these was the desire to have children: "When we first met we talked about everything," Harry recalled:

> . . . and all of our dreams, and one of them was to have a family and what it meant to be gay, you know, if we were together, and what we would be giving up potentially, what the sacrifices might be; and so that was one of the things that was going to be a potential sacrifice was not being able to have children.

"Me too," Ozzie interjected. "I always knew I wanted to have children." "But we talked about how we didn't think it was possible to have them together," Harry continued. "We both talked about how it was a dream that we both had, and that it was kind of something that we thought we might have to forsake together."

The new lovers plunged headlong into a deeply romantic, intense, committed, monogamous love affair that seems only to have deepened after nearly a decade of bourgeois domesticity. After a year of transatlantic (and translinguistic) courtship, Harry sponsored his beloved's immigration to the US, financed

Ozzie's education in computer technology and vocal music, and assisted his rapid acquisition of fluency in English and bourgeois cultural habitus, all domains in which Ozzie proved gifted. After the couple celebrated their union with an interfaith commitment ceremony in 1998, they had dinner with a gay couple who had recently become fathers through surrogacy. "It was all kind of Kismet," Harry recalled. "They told us about their two sons, and we kind of admitted that it was something we fantasized about." Inspired by this example, Ozzie and Harry contacted Growing Generations and decided immediately to engage a "traditional" surrogate[6] in order to realize the dream of fatherhood that they had feared they would have to sacrifice on the altar of gay love. The agency successfully matched them with a white woman who has since borne them two babies—first a white daughter conceived with Harry's sperm, and three years later, a biracial, genetic half-sister, conceived with Ozzie's.

No gay union in my study encapsulates a more dramatic example of successful hypergamy, or one that transcends a wider array of social structural inequalities and cultural differences than the bond between Ozzie and Harry. Formally, the younger, buff and beautiful Ozzie occupies a disadvantaged position across a staggering number of social divisions and cultural resources—including income, wealth, education, occupation, race, nation, language, citizenship, not to mention access to the ongoing support of his natal world of kin, long-term friendship, community and culture. Moreover, because the co-parents share a strong prejudice against hired childcare, Ozzie has become a full-time, at-home parent and economically dependent on Harry, to boot. "We don't use babysitters at all," Harry boasted, as he burped their first infant daughter during my initial visit. "We don't want any nannies, babysitters, nothing," he emphasized, espousing a childrearing credo few contemporary mothers in the West could contemplate affording, even they were to desire it:

Nothing, NOTHING. We don't believe in it. No baby nurse, nothing. Just us; and one of us always will be with her. If you wait this long to do this. We're mature adults. I mean I'm 38. I have no dreams left, other than being a good dad and a good mate for my Ozzie.

"The same with me," Ozzie volunteered, draping both arms around his spouse with adoration. Initially, Harry had stayed home several months blissfully caring for their first newborn while Ozzie was employed. However, because Harry commands far greater earning power, he decided that it was in his family's interest that he resume the breadwinner role. He has supported Ozzie as full-time, at-home parent ever since.

Nonetheless, despite forms of structural inequity glaring enough to make Betty Friedan's (1963) critique of the feminine mystique seem tepid, this is no transvestite version of the male-dominant, female-dependent, breadwinner–homemaker patriarchal bargain of the 1950s' modern family. Defying all sociological odds, Ozzie seems to enjoy substantive and emotional parity with Harry both as partner and parent. In deference to Ozzie's jealous, possessive wishes, Harry relinquished friendships with his former lovers. Harry regards his breadwinner role to be a sacrificial burden rather than a creative outlet or source of status and power: "I hate work," Harry maintains. "It's a necessary evil." He conducts as much of his professional work from home as he can in order to participate as fully as possible in the hands-on burdens and blessings of early parenting—diapering, feeding, dressing, toilet-training, bathing, along with playing, reading, cuddling, educating, cajoling, consoling, disciplining and chauffeuring. Indeed, not only does Harry dread the unavoidable business trips that periodically separate him from his children and spouse, he seems genuinely to envy Ozzie's uninterrupted quotidian contact with the children. "I don't need to make my mark," Harry claims. "There's nothing else I need to accomplish. So that's the most important job [being a parent and mate] I have which is why it's a real conflict."

What's more, Harry has voluntarily relinquished the weighty patriarchal power of the purse by taking legal measures to fully share all property, as well as child custody of both daughters, with Ozzie. Few heterosexual marriages—whether hypergamous or homogamous—share resources, responsibilities, or romance so fully or harmoniously as these two seem to do.

Mother Randolph and his Foundling Boys

Dino, an 18-year-old, fresh "wetback," Salvadoran immigrant, was waiting at a bus stop in 1984 when a 45-year-old Anglo entertainment lawyer with a taste for young Latino men cruised by and picked him up. Discovering that his gregarious, sexy, young trick was homeless and unemployed, the lawyer brought Dino home to live and keep house for him for several weeks. There the eager youth began to acquire the mores and mentors, along with the mistakes, from which he has since built his life as an undocumented immigrant among chosen kin in gay L.A.

Among the mentors, Randolph eventually proved to be the most significant. Now in his mid-sixties, Randolph is a cultivated, but bawdy, financially secure and generous, former interior designer recently disabled by post-polio syndrome. Much earlier, Randolph had met his life partner of 17 years while cruising in a "stand-up sex club." Ten years into the committed, but sexually open, relationship that ensued, Randolph's lover shocked him by choosing to undergo male-to-female sex reassignment surgery. Randolph was traumatized, and the couple's relationship foundered. After a year-long separation and his lover's successful transition from male to female, however, Randolph recognized that his love for the person transcended his strong homoerotic sexual preference, and so the couple reunited. Paradoxically, this gender and sexual upheaval compelled Randolph to perform a semblance of the life of heterosexual masculinity that he had renounced as inauthentic, at considerable risk, but to his great relief, a full decade before the Stonewall rebellion.

Several years after her surgical transformation, however, Randolph's lover was diagnosed with AIDS, a cruel legacy of her prior life as a sexually active gay man. By then too, Randolph's post-polio syndrome symptoms had begun to emerge, and he lacked the physical ability to take care of his lover, or of himself. Blessed with ample financial, social and spiritual resources, Randolph gradually assembled a rainbow household staff of five gay men, who have come to regard him and each other as family.

Chance encounters through sexual cruising generated many of these relationships, as it had the union between Randolph and his lover. A former employee of Randolph's met Dino at a gay bar in 1993 and introduced him to his benefactor. By then Dino had been diagnosed as HIV-positive and was drinking heavily. Randolph has a long history and penchant for rescuing gay "lost boys," and so he hired Dino to serve as his household's primary live-in cook and manager. Now sober, grateful and devoted, Dino remains asymptomatic thanks to the health care that Randolph purchases for him. Dino resides at Randolph's Mondays through Fridays and spends weekends with his lover of five years, a 50-something, Anglo dental hygienist who cruised him at a Gay Pride parade. Dino's lover pays him weekly overnight conjugal visits in Randolph's household and also participates in the holiday feasts that Dino prepares for Randolph's expansive, extended, hired and chosen family.

Randolph employs three additional men who work staggered shifts as physical attendant, practical nurse and chauffeur, and a fourth as part-time gardener and general handyman. The day nurses are Mikey, a 23-year-old, white former street hustler and drug abuser, and Ricardo, the newest of Mikey's three roommates in another multicultural and intergenerational gay male household. The devoutly Catholic Ricardo, who is also 20-something, is a recent illegal Mexican immigrant still struggling with religious guilt over his homosexual desires. Randolph's night nurse, Bernard, is a married, closeted, bisexual African-American man in his fifties with whom Randolph used to enjoy casual sex. Finally, Randolph employs his friend Lawrence as his gardener, a white gay man now in his late forties and also HIV-positive, with whom Randolph has been close ever since they hooked up in a San Diego tea room more than three decades ago.

Randolph refers to Dino and his day nurses parentally as his "boys." "Well, I'm their father and their mother," he explains. Since Randolph's lover died in 1999, "these boys are certainly the most important family that I have these days. They mean more to me, and *for* me than anyone else." From his wheelchair-throne, "Mother Randolph," as he parodically identifies himself, presides with love, wit, wisdom and, it must be acknowledged, financial control, as well as responsibility, over a multicultural, mutually dependent, elastically extended, chosen family somewhat reminiscent of the black drag houses immortalized in the documentary *Paris Is Burning* (1990, directed by Jennie Livingston). Few of these intimate attachments remain erotic. However, a serendipitous series of hypergamous sexual encounters initiated most of the creative kin ties in this expansive rainbow "family of man."

The Gay Family Cruise

Most advocates and opponents of gay, recreational sexual cruising culture, whether straight or gay, believe it threatens mainstream "family values." To be sure, gay male cruising directly challenges norms of heteronormativity, monogamy and premarital chastity. Indeed, unless the pure pursuit of sexual pleasure is culturally sanctioned, in the face of "marital boredom," as Paul Cameron warns, "it seems too powerful to resist" and is often threatening to secure and stable intimate attachments. In fact, for reasons like these, a sizable constituency of gay men find sexual transgression to be as disturbing and threatening as does mainstream heterosexual culture. Although Ozzie and Harry met by cruising, they, along with many men "in the family," practice sexual exclusivity and strongly disapprove of polyamory and recreational sex. These more sex-

ually conservative family values appear to be particularly prevalent among gay men who are fathers, among the religiously observant, and the generation of gay men who came of age in the period immediately following discovery of the AIDS virus.

However, as my field research illustrates, the gay male arena of sexual sport also spawns less obvious, more productive effects on intimacy and kinship. Sexual cruising, as we have seen, initiates lasting familial ties more than is commonly recognized. Anonymous erotic encounters occasionally yield fairly conventional forms of love and "marriage." "Sexual encounters are often pursued as a route to more long-term, committed, emotional relationships," as Weeks et al. (2001: 144) observe. "Particularly for some men who are not in a couple relationship, casual sexual relationships can offer the potential for meeting the 'right' person." Or, as a gay friend of mine puts it more humorously, "Sex can be a great icebreaker." Randolph, as we have seen, cruised his deceased mate, Dino met his current lover, and even the implausibly idyllic, romantic, monogamous union and nuclear family formed by Harry and Ozzie commenced on a sexual cruise. Many other interviewees also reported histories of long-term relationships initiated through anonymous sexual encounters.[7]

Within what Giddens (1992) has termed the modern western "transformation of intimacy," the search for everlasting "confluent love" occupies a status akin to a religious quest. Just as Puritans who subscribed to the Protestant ethic took material success to signify their spiritual salvation, so do many believers in the "pure relationship" seek its earthly signs in the appearance of instantaneous erotic "chemistry." Syndicated gay sex advice columnist-provocateur Dan Savage endorses this comparatively mainstream family cruise route with uncharacteristic sentimentality:

> Desire brought my boyfriend and me together. And it's simple desire that brings most couples, gay or straight, together. Responsibly acted on, this desire is a good thing in and of itself, and it can often lead to other good things. Like strong, healthy families. (Savage, 2003)

Momentary sexual adventures also yield more innovative genres of "healthy" family life. Anonymous gay sexual encounters do not ordinarily lead to conjugal coupling, but not infrequently they commence enduring friendships that evolve into kin-like ties, whether or not sexual interest continues. Through such side-effects of casual sex, Randolph met his close friend and gardener; Dino acquired, at first temporary, and later his long-term lodging, employment and familial support; and Mikey repeatedly found refuge from Hollywood's mean streets. Thus, even when a gay man ostensibly *is* "only looking for the most satisfying orgasm" he can get, sexual cruising allows him to find a whole lot more. "Some people like the sport of chasing somebody and seeing if they can get them," Mother Randolph acknowledged. "For some people the game is worth more than the candle. My interest is specifically in the candle." When I asked Randolph, however, whether an orgasm constituted the candle, he quickly identified more enduring embers:

> Yes, and also the love-making, if it was that sort of situation. If I had a guy home in bed, I was big on foreplay and all of that. In fact, often I didn't want my partner to go home after fucking. I often liked them to stay over. And a lot of my sexual partners became eventual friends. Mr. Baldwin [the gardener] over there at the sink being one of them.

A venerable gay history of cruising to kinship and community long antedated the contemporary popularity of gay family discourse. Even in the first two decades of the 20th century, as George Chauncey's (1994) prize winning historical study, *Gay New York,* copiously documents, gay men frequented bars and bathhouses seeking not only quick sexual encounters, but also because they "formed more elaborate social relationships with the men they met there, and came to depend on them in a variety of ways." Chauncey draws on the extensive diaries of Charles Tomlinson Griffes, a successful early 20th-century composer who:

> . . . was drawn into the gay world by the baths not just because he had sex there, but because

he met men there who helped him find apartments and otherwise make his way through the city, who appreciated his music, who gave him new insights into his character, and who became his good friends. (Chauncey, 1994: 224)

Thus, socially heterogeneous intimate affiliations (whether long-term or more ephemeral) are among the underappreciated byproducts of gay cruising grounds. Thanks in part to this arena of sexual sport, interracial intimacy occurs far more frequently in the gay world, and particularly among gay men, than in heterosexual society. US census data indicate this contrast, even though, because they only tabulate co-residential couples who elected to self-identify as same-sex partners, they vastly understate the degree of both gay and interracial intimacy in the US. In 1990, the first time the US census form allowed co-residing, same-sex partners to declare their couple status, 14.6 percent of those who did so were interracial pairs, compared with only 5.1 percent of married heterosexual couples. In the 2000 Census, 15.3 percent of declared same-sex male couples and 12.6 percent of lesbians compared with 7.4 percent of married and 15 percent of unmarried heterosexual pairs bridged racial differences.[8] The percentage of interracial pairs in my nonrepresentative sample was substantially higher, a product, most likely, of my decision to stratify in order to encompass broad racial and social diversity. Of 31 men in my sample who identified themselves as coupled at the time of the interviews, 14 were paired with someone of a different race.[9]

One of the provocative byproducts of sexual cruising culture is the greater access to social mobility that it offers gay men from subordinate social classes, races and cultural milieux than their straight siblings and peers enjoy.[10] In the unvarnished prose of William J. Mann (1997), an established gay writer in the US, "the dick dock in Provincetown is a great equalizer. I've watched my share of condo owners suck off their share of houseboys." While it is likely that only a small percentage of those "houseboys" garner more than a quickly lit "candle" from these encounters, these nonetheless represent a social mobility opportunity very few of their non-gay peers enjoy. Marveling over his personal meteoric rise from working-class origins in a small factory town, Mann reflects:

> *"How the hell did you ever wind up here, kid?"* I've asked myself time and again . . . how did I end up sharing a house in the tony west end of Provincetown every summer for the entire summer, year after year? It's simple: I'm gay. Had I not been gay—had I been my brother, for example—I would never have discovered the access that led me to a different place. (Mann, 1997: 221)

Both Mann and his brother attended the same state university near their hometown. "But only *I* ventured into a world my parents had never known. Had I not been a gay kid," Mann recognizes, "I would never have been invited into that world." A visiting gay lecturer, for example, took the youthful Mann to dinner and later introduced him to prominent writers, and to a gay world: "I met people, I read books, I listened to speeches" (Mann, 1997: 221).

Ozzie, Dino, Mikey and Ricardo are among 10 of the 50 gay men in my study who have traversed even greater social, geographic, economic and cultural distances, all beneficiaries of what I am choosing to call gay hypergamy. But for its gender composition, the Cinderella fairy-tale character of Ozzie's marriage to Harry, represents hypergamy in nearly the classic anthropological sense of marrying up through an exchange of beauty and youth for cultural status and material resources. In no way do I mean to imply that Ozzie or Harry intentionally deployed strategic, let alone manipulative, bartering tactics in this exchange. By the same token, I do not believe that most contemporary, hypergamous, heterosexual marriages involve the cynical exploitation or motives connoted by terms like "gold-digger" or "trophy wife." Rather, I aim to highlight some unrecognized gender and social effects of the asymmetrical exchanges of sex appeal for status that represent the contemporary cultural residue of patriarchal hypergamy.

Expanding the concept somewhat, gay hypergamy can be used to designate even relatively brief and informal intimate affiliations between exotic, erotic youth and older men with greater material resources and cultural capital. Cruising on the "dick dock" in Provincetown, in the baths of old New York, at a bus stop in Los Angeles, and at beats, cottages, tea rooms and ports of call around the world (see, for example, Altman, 2001; Dowsett, 1996) allows for more democratic social mixing and matching and greater opportunities for upward mobility than heterosexual society generally offers. Whether or not the "candle" ignites a satisfying orgasm, it can melt social barriers—as icebreakers are meant to do—and thereby expand the bonds of kinship, as in the rainbow family ties between Mother Randolph and his adopted, and hired, "boys." In this respect, the world of sexual sport resembles athletic sport, which also provides some ghetto male youth opportunities for social mobility and cross-racial bonds, but because sexual sport is simultaneously more intimate and unregulated, it is also far more socially transgressive.[11]

It turns out that gay male "promiscuity" is not as inherently antithetical to healthy, committed, or even to comparatively conventional, family values, as its critics and some of its champions imagine. However, gay men who breach sexual norms often find themselves challenging social divides as well, cruising their way into hypergamous intimate attachments and a social rainbow of kinship bonds. The culture of unbridled masculine sexuality represents no utopian arena of egalitarian, liberated "sexual citizenship." Hypergamous, erotic exchanges among gay men that cross racial, generational and social class boundaries can yield the same sort of exploitative, abusive, humiliating and destructive effects on the more vulnerable party that women too often suffer in asymmetrical heterosexual exchanges. Gender does effect a crucial difference, however, in the social geometry of heterosexual and gay hypergamy. The exclusively masculine arena of gay hypergamy allows for greater reciprocity of sexual and cultural exchanges over the life-cycle than women can typically attain. The heterosexual double standard of beauty and aging inflicts severe erotic and romantic constraints on even very prosperous, high status, aging "gold-diggers" or "trophy" widows. Although aging gay men also suffer notable declines in their erotic options, they operate on a gender-free playing field. Unlike heterosexual women, formerly subordinate beneficiaries of gay hypergamy, like Ozzie and Dino, can come to enact the opposite side of the exchange over the life course. Gay men who cruise to higher status can anticipate ultimately enjoying the power to exchange whatever cultural and material capital they attained through gay hypergamy for intimacy with less socially privileged, younger, attractive men.

Gay men aboard the family cruise ship are reconfiguring eros, domesticity, parenthood and kinship in ways that simultaneously reinforce and challenge conventional gender and family practices and values.[12] Although by no means a utopian arena of race and class harmony, gay cruising does facilitate more democratic forms of intimate social (as well as sexual) intercourse across more social boundaries (including race, age, class, religion, nation, education, ideology and even sexual orientation) than occur almost anywhere else. Enduring bonds of chosen family and kinship are among the significant consequences of these transgressive assignations. Whether or not Melanie Phillips is correct in her view that men are "naturally promiscuous," she is clearly wrong that masculine erotic impulses preclude two men from forming enduring attachments. Whether for "monogamous gay couples" like Ozzie and Harry, or for unapologetic "sex pigs" like Mother Randolph and his foundlings, it turns out that sexual cruising can be a creative mode of family travel.

Notes

1. See www.growinggenerations.com

2. See www.popluckclub.org

3. My primary sample of 50 men included 10 Latinos, seven blacks, four Asians and 29 of white Anglo or Jewish origins. Nine men were also immigrants, both documented and undocumented, five of these from Latin America, two from the Caribbean and two from Europe. Religious upbringings and affiliations ranged from fundamentalist, Catholic, Jewish and Protestant, to Buddhist and atheist. Social class locations in the US are, of course, vastly more difficult to conceptualize or assign. The men's natal family backgrounds ranged from destitute to almost aristocratic, with the majority, unsurprisingly, from self-identified "middle-class" origins. Current income and occupational statuses encompassed the unemployed and indebted as well as extremely wealthy and successful members of the local professional, creative, managerial and community elite.

4. In order to study the broad array of paternal strategies and configurations, I intentionally oversampled gay fathers. Thus, 26 of the 50 men have some sort of paternal relationship to children, whether biological, social and/or legal, and whether or not their children reside with them.

5. I employ pseudonyms and have altered identifying details to protect privacy of informants.

6. In the terminology of assisted reproduction clinics in the US, a "traditional" surrogate is also the biological mother of a child conceived via alternative insemination with sperm, generally supplied by a contracting father. A "gestational" surrogate, in contrast, does not contribute genetic material to the child she bears under contract, but is hired to gestate an ovum supplied by an egg donor, fertilized in vitro and transplanted to her uterus.

7. Because I cannot reliably tally the aggregate number of couple relationships which all 50 interviewees have collectively experienced over their lifespans, I cannot provide meaningful data on the proportion of these that were initiated through sexual cruising. However, 10 of the 31 men who were in committed couple relationships when interviewed reported that they had met their mates in this way.

8. An analysis of these census data by the Williams Project at the UCLA School of Law examined 23 cities where most same-sex couples are concentrated. Project director William Rubenstein reports that 7 percent of married couples and 14.1 percent of unmarried heterosexual couples are interracial compared with 18.4 percent of same-sex couples in these urban areas. The project defines "interracial" as the mix of two racial groups and/or a Hispanic partner

and non-Hispanic partner. For more information, contact William Rubenstein, The Williams Project, UCLA School of Law.

9. Of these 14 interracial intimacies, eight were in black/white couples, four were Latino/white and two were an Asian/white couple. Additional men in the sample reported prior cross-racial unions.

10. Studies have found substantial differences in occupational ladders and career paths between heterosexual and non-heterosexual individuals. Nimmons (2002: 51) cites the as yet unpublished study by Dr. John Blandford at the University of Chicago, who analyzed a large sample from standard US census figures to find that gay men in same-sex partnered households were "greatly over-represented" compared with heterosexual counterparts in "Professional and Specialty" occupations, particularly in teaching, nursing and the arts. Gay men, however, were scarcely represented at all in traditionally masculine working-class jobs, such as heavy equipment operators, miners, explosive workers, brick layers, etc. Rothblum and Factor's (2001) study of lesbians and their straight sisters found that sisters who grew up in the same age cohort, of the same race/ethnicity and with parents of the same education, occupation and income displayed quite dissimilar outcomes on demographic variables. Lesbians were significantly more educated, more likely to live in urban areas and more geographically mobile than their heterosexual sisters.

11. See, for example, Messner (1992: 90): "several white and black men told me that through sport they had their first real contact with people from different racial groups, and for a few of them, good friendships began . . . competitive activities such as sport mediate men's relationships with each other in ways that allow them to develop a powerful bond while at the same time preventing the development of intimacy."

12. These contradictory practices have historical antecedents. Chauncey (1994: 290) describes the "idiom of kinship" popular in the early 20th century among gay men who used camp culture "to undermine the 'natural' categories of the family and to reconstitute themselves as members of fictive kinship systems." Men involved in relationships that enacted a gendered division of labor often defined themselves as "husbands" and "wives," thereby inverting and undermining the meaning of "natural" categories,

while repeated use simultaneously confirmed their significance.

Bibliography

Adam, Barry (2003) "The 'Defense of Marriage Act' and American Exceptionalism;" *Journal of the History of Sexuality* 12(2): 259–76.

Altman, Dennis (2001) *Global Sex*. Chicago, IL: University of Chicago Press.

Asher, Jon ben (2003) "Pope Declares Gay Families In authentic," *Integrity-L Digest* 28 January (#2003–29) from PlanetOut News Front; at: www.365Gay.com

Barbeau v. British Columbia (Attorney General) (2003) BCCA 251, Court of Appeal for British Columbia.

Bawer, Bruce (1993) *A Place at the Table: The Gay Individual in American Society*. New York: Simon and Schuster.

Browning, Frank (1994) *The Culture of Desire: Paradox and Perversity in Gay Lives Today*. New York: Vintage Books.

Budgeon, Shelley and Roseneil, Sasha (2002) "Cultures of Intimacy and Care Beyond 'The Family': Friendship and Sexual/Love Relationships in the Twenty-First Century," paper presented at the International Sociological Association, Brisbane, July.

Butler, Judith (1990) *Gender Trouble: Feminism and the Subversion of Identity*. New York: Routledge.

Chauncey, George (1994) *Gay New York: Gender, Urban Culture, and the Making of the Gay Male World 1890–1940*. New York: Basic Books.

Davis, Evan and Phillips, Melanie (1999) "Debate: Gay Marriage," *Prospect Magazine* 40 (April): 16–20.

Dowsett, Gary W. (1996) *Practicing Desire: Homosexual Sex in the Era of AIDS*. Stanford, CA: Stanford University Press.

Dreyfuss, Robert (1999) "The Holy War on Gays," *Village Voice* 18 March: 38–41.

Fagan, Craig (2002) "Buenos Aires Legalizes Same-Sex Unions"; at: www.salon.com/mwt/wire/2002/12/13/brazil_marriage/index.html

Friedan, Betty (1963) *The Feminine Mystique*. New York: Norton.

Giddens, Anthony (1992) *The Transformation of Intimacy: Sexuality, Love and Eroticism in Modern Societies*. Cambridge: Polity Press.

Gilder, George (1986) *Men and Marriage.* Gretna: Pelican.

Heath, Melanie and Stacey, Judith (2002) "Transatlantic Family Travail," *American Journal of Sociology* 108(3): 658–68.

Integrity Press Release (2003) "Integrity Uganda Begins Same Sex Blessings," 12 April; at: www.integrityusa.org/UgandaJournal/index.htm

Levine, Martin (1998) *Gay Macho: The Life and Death of the Homosexual Clone.* New York: New York University Press.

Lewin, Ellen (1998) *Recognizing Ourselves: Ceremonies of Lesbian and Gay Commitment.* New York: Columbia University Press.

Mann, William J. (1997) "A Boy's Own Class," in Susan Raffo (ed.) *Queerly Classed,* pp. 217–26. Boston, MA: South End Press.

Messner, Michael A. (1992) *Power at Play: Sports and the Problem of Masculinity.* Boston, MA: Beacon Press.

Miller, John C. (2001) "'My Daddy Loves Your Daddy': A Gay Father Encounters a Social Movement," in Mary Bernstein and Renate Reimann (eds) *Queer Families, Queer Politics: Challenging Culture and the State,* pp. 221–30. New York: Columbia University Press.

Nardi, Peter (1999) *Gay Men's Friendships: Invincible Communities* Chicago, IL: University of Chicago Press.

Nimmons, David (2002) *The Soul Beneath the Skin: The Unseen Hearts and Habits of Gay Men.* New York: St. Martin's Press.

"Oppose the Federal Marriage Amendment" (2003) at: www.petitiononline.com/0712t001/petition. html (accessed 30 May 2003).

PLC listserv (2003) "The Lusty Month of May Mixer," 5 May.

Rauch, Jonathan (1994) "A Pro-Gay, Pro-Family Policy," *Wall Street Journal* 29 November: A22.

Rofes, Eric (1998) *Dry Bones Breathe: Gay Men Creating Post-AIDS Identities and Cultures.* New York: Harrington Park Press.

Rothblum, Esther D. and Factor, Rhonda (2001) "Lesbians and Their Sisters as a Control Group: Demographic and Mental Health Factors," *Psychological Science* 12: 63–9.

Savage, Dan (2003) "G.O.P. Hypocrisy," *New York Times* 25 April: A31.

Shilts, Randy (1987) *And the Band Played On.* New York: St Martin's Press.

Stein, Arlene (2001) *The Stranger Next Door: The Story of a Small Community's Battle over Sex, Faith, and Civil Rights.* Boston, MA: Beacon Press.

Stuever, Hank (2001) "Is Gay Mainstream?," *Washington Post* 27 April: C1.

Sullivan, Andrew (1997) "The Conservative Case," in Andrew Sullivan (ed.) *Same-Sex Marriage: Pro and Con,* pp. 146–54. New York: Vintage Books.

The American Heritage® Dictionary of the English Language (2000) 4th edn. Boston, MA: Houghton Mifflin.

United States Congress (1996) *The Defense of Marriage Act: Committee on the Judiciary, United States Senate.* Washington, DC. US Government Printing Office.

Warner, Michael (1999) *The Trouble with Normal: Sex, Politics, and the Ethics of Queer Life.* New York: Free Press.

Weeks, Jeffrey, Heaphy, Brian and Donovan, Catherine (2001) *Same Sex Intimacies: Families of Choice and Other Life Experiments.* London: Routledge.

Weston, Kath (1991) *Families We Choose: Lesbians, Gays, Kinship.* New York: Columbia University Press.

Wetzstein, Cheryl (2003) "Bill to Define Marriage Tried Again in House as 2 States Mull Cases," *Washington Times;* at: www.washingtontimes. com/national/20030525-155459-1812r.htm

PART NINE

Masculinities in the Media and Popular Culture

Men are daily bombarded with images of masculinity—in magazines, television, movies, music, even the Internet. We see what men are supposed to look like, act like, be like. And social scientists are only now beginning to understand the enormous influence that the media have in shaping our ideas about what it means to be a man.

For one thing, it is clear that the media can create artificial standards against which boys as well as girls measure themselves. Just as idealized human female models can only approximate the exaggeratedly large breasts and exaggeratedly small waistline of Barbie, virtually no men can ap- proach the physiques of the cartoon version of Tarzan or even G.I. Joe. The original G.I. Joe had the equivalent of 12.2-inch biceps when he was introduced in 1964. Ten years later, his biceps measured the equivalent of 15.2 inches. By 1994, he had 16.4-inch biceps, and today his biceps measure a simulated 26.8 inches—nearly 7 inches larger than Mark McGwire's 20-inch mus- cles. "Many modern figures display the physiques of advanced bodybuilders and some display levels of muscularity far exceeding the outer limits of ac tual human attainment," notes Dr. Harrison Pope, a Harvard psychiatrist.

Media masculinities create standards against which men measure themselves. No wonder we often feel like we fail the test of physical manhood. At the same time, the media encourage us to eval uate and judge the manhood of others by those same standards. As the articles in this section suggest, we constantly "see" masculinity in the media—at the movies, in beer and liquor com- mercials (Mike Messner and Jeffrey Montez de Oca), on sports talk radio (David Nylund), in media coverage of wildlife management (Sine Anahita and Tamara Mix), and even in rock music (Sarah Williams).

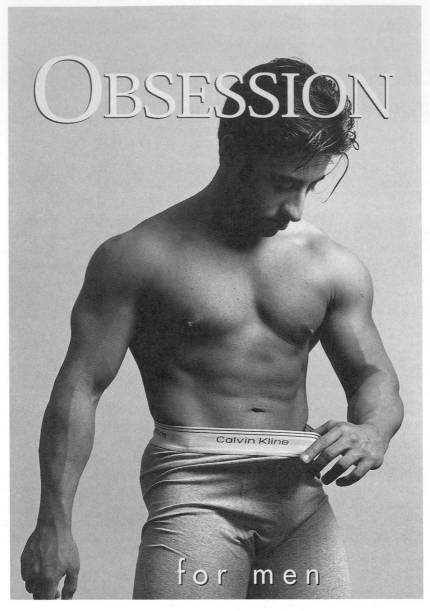

Image courtesy of www.adbusters.org.

Michael A. Messner

Jeffrey Montez de Oca

The Male Consumer as Loser: Beer and Liquor Ads in Mega Sports Media Events

The historical development of modern men's sport has been closely intertwined with the consumption of alcohol and with the financial promotion and sponsorship provided by beer and liquor producers and distributors, as well as pubs and bars (Collins and Vamplew 2002). The beer and liquor industry plays a key economic role in commercialized college and professional sports (Zimbalist 1999; Sperber 2000). Liquor industry advertisements heavily influence the images of masculinity promoted in sports broadcasts and magazines (Wenner 1991). Alcohol consumption is also often a key aspect of the more dangerous and violent dynamics at the heart of male sport cultures (Curry 2000; Sabo, Gray, and Moore 2000). By itself, alcohol does not "cause" men's violence against women or against other men; however, it is commonly one of a cluster of factors that facilitate violence (Koss and Gaines 1993; Leichliter et al. 1998). In short, beer and liquor are central players in "a high holy trinity of alcohol, sports, and hegemonic masculinity" (Wenner 1998).

Gender, Men's Sports, and Alcohol Ads

Although marketing beer and liquor to men is not new, the imagery that advertisers employ to pitch their product is not static either. Our analysis of

Adapted from *Signs: Journal of Women in Culture and Society* 2005, vol. 30, no. 3 © 2005 by The University of Chicago. All rights reserved.

past Super Bowls and *Sports Illustrated* beer and liquor ads suggests shifting patterns in the gender themes encoded in the ads.

Ads from the late 1950s through the late 1960s commonly depicted young or middle-aged white heterosexual couples happily sharing a cold beer in their suburban backyards, in their homes, or in an outdoor space like a park.

In these ads, the beer is commonly displayed in a clear glass, its clean, fresh appearance perhaps intended to counter the reputation of beer as a working-class male drink. Beer in these ads symbolically unites the prosperous and happy postwar middle-class couple. By the mid-1970s, women as wives and partners largely disappeared from beer ads. Instead of showing heterosexual couples drinking in their homes or backyards, these ads began primarily to depict images of men drinking with other men in public spaces. Three studies of beer commercials of the 1970s and 1980s found that most ads pitched beer to men as a pleasurable reward for a hard day's work. These ads told men that "For all you do, this Bud's for you." Women were rarely depicted in these ads, except as occasional background props in male-dominated bars (Postman et al. 1987; Wenner 1991; Strate 1992).

The 1950s and 1960s beer ads that depicted happy married suburban couples were part of a moment in gender relations tied to postwar culture and Fordist relations of production. White, middle-class, heterosexual masculinity was defined as synonymous with the male breadwinner, in symmetrical relation to a conception of femininity grounded in the image of the suburban housewife. In the 1970s and early 1980s, the focus on men's laboring bodies, tethered to their public leisure with other men, expressed an almost atavistic view of hegemonic masculinity at a time when women were moving into public life in huge numbers and blue-collar men's jobs were being eliminated by the tens of thousands.

Both the postwar and the postindustrial ads provide a gendered pedagogy for living a masculine lifestyle in a shifting context characterized by uncertainty. In contrast to the depiction of happy white families comfortably living lives of suburban bliss, the postwar era was characterized by anxieties over the possibility of a postwar depression, nuclear annihilation, suburban social dislocation, and disorder from racial and class movements for social justice (Lipsitz 1981; May 1988; Spigel 1992). Similarly, the 1970s and 1980s beer ads came in the wake of the defeat of the United States in the Vietnam War, the 1972 gas crisis, and the turbulence in gender relations brought on by the women's and gay/lesbian liberation movements.

The 2002 and 2003 ads that we examine here primarily construct a white male "loser" whose life is apparently separate from paid labor. He hangs out with his male buddies, is self-mocking and ironic about his loser status, and is always at the ready to engage in voyeurism with sexy fantasy women but holds committed relationships and emotional honesty with real women in disdain. To the extent that these themes find resonance with young men of today, it is likely because they speak to basic insecurities that are grounded in a combination of historic shifts: deindustrialization, the declining real value of wages and the male breadwinner role, significant cultural shifts brought about by more than three decades of struggle by feminists and sexual minorities, and challenges to white male supremacy by people of color and by immigrants. This cluster of social changes has destabilized hegemonic masculinity and defines the context of gender relations in which today's young men have grown toward adulthood.

Two Mega Sports Media Events

This article examines the gender and sexual imagery encoded in two mega sports media events: the 2002 and 2003 Super Bowls and the 2002 and 2003 *Sports Illustrated* swimsuit issues.

Mega sports media events are mediated cultural rituals (Dayan and Katz 1988) that differ from everyday sports media events in several key ways: sports media actively build audience anticipation and excitement throughout the year for these single events; the Super Bowl and the swimsuit issue are each preceded by major pre-event promotion and hype—from the television network that will broadcast the Super Bowl to *Sports Illustrated* and myriad other print and electronic media; the Super Bowl and the swimsuit issue are used as marketing tools for selling the more general products of National Football League (NFL) games and *Sports Illustrated* magazine subscriptions; the Super Bowl and the swimsuit issue each generate significant spin-off products (e.g., videos, books, "making of" TV shows, calendars, frequently visited Web pages); the Super Bowl and the swimsuit issue generate significantly larger audiences than does a weekly NFL game or a weekly edition of *Sports Illustrated;* and advertisements are usually created specifically for these mega sports media events and cost more to run than do ads in a weekly NFL game or a weekly edition of *Sports Illustrated.*

Super Bowl Ads

Since its relatively modest start in 1967, the NFL Super Bowl has mushroomed into one of the most expensive and most watched annual media events in the United States, with a growing world audience (Martin and Reeves 2001), the vast majority of whom are boys and men. Increasingly over the past decade, Super Bowl commercials have been specially created for the event. Newspapers, magazines, television news shows, and Web sites now routinely run pre–Super Bowl stories that focus specifically on the ads, and several media outlets run post–Super Bowl polls to determine which ads were the most and least favorite. Postgame lists of "winners" and "losers" focus as much on the corporate sponsors and their ads as on the two teams that—incidentally?—played a football game between the commercials.

Fifty-five commercials ran during the 2003 Super Bowl (not counting pregame and postgame shows), at an average cost of $2.1 million for each thirty-second ad. Fifteen of these commercials were beer or malt liquor ads. Twelve of these ads were run by Anheuser-Busch, whose ownership of this Super Bowl was underlined at least twenty times throughout the broadcast, when, after commercial breaks, the camera lingered on the stadium scoreboard, atop which was a huge Budweiser sign. This represented a slight increase in beer advertising since the 2002 Super Bowl, which featured thirteen beer or malt liquor commercials (eleven of them by Anheuser-Busch), at an average cost of $1.9 million per thirty-second ad. In addition to the approximately $31.5 million that the beer companies paid for the 2003 Super Bowl ad slots, they paid millions more creating and testing those commercials with focus groups. There were 137.7 million viewers watching all or part of the 2003 Super Bowl on ABC, and by far the largest demographic group watching was men, aged twenty-five to fifty-five.

Sports Illustrated Swimsuit Issue Ads

Sports Illustrated began in 1964 to publish an annual February issue that featured five or six pages of women modeling swimsuits, embedded in an otherwise normal sixty-four-page magazine (Davis 1997). This modest format continued until the late 1970s, when the portion of the magazine featuring swimsuit models began gradually to grow. In the 1980s, the swimsuit issue morphed into a special issue in which normal sports coverage gradually disappeared. During this decade, the issue's average length had grown to 173 pages, 20 percent of which were focused on swimsuit models. By the 1990s the swimsuit issue averaged

207 pages in length, 31 percent of which featured swimsuit models. The magazine has continued to grow in recent years. The 2003 issue was 218 pages in length, 59 percent of which featured swimsuit models. The dramatic growth in the size of the swimsuit issue in the 1990s, as well as the dropping of pretence that the swimsuit issue had anything to do with normal "sports journalism," were facilitated by advertising that began cleverly to echo and spoof the often highly sexualized swimsuit imagery in the magazine. By 2000, it was more the rule than the exception when an ad in some way utilized the swimsuit theme. The gender and sexual themes of the swimsuit issue became increasingly seamless, as ads and Sports Illustrated text symbiotically echoed and played off of each other. The 2002 swimsuit issue included seven pages of beer ads and seven pages of liquor ads, which cost approximately $230,000 per full page to run. The 2003 swimsuit issue ran the equivalent of sixteen pages of beer ads and thirteen pages of liquor ads. The ad space for the 2003 swimsuit issue sold for $266,000 per full-page color ad.

The millions of dollars that beer and liquor companies spent to develop and buy space for these ads were aimed at the central group that reads the magazine: young and middle-aged males. Sports Illustrated estimates the audience size of its weekly magazine at 21.3 million readers, roughly 76 percent of whom are males. Nearly half of the male audience is in the coveted eighteen- to thirty-four-year-old demographic group, and three quarters of the male Sports Illustrated audience is between the ages of eighteen and forty-nine. A much larger number of single-copy sales gives the swimsuit issue a much larger audience, conservatively estimated at more than 30 million readers.[1]

The Super Bowl and the Sports Illustrated swimsuit issue are arguably the biggest single electronic and print sports media events annually in the United States. Due to their centrality, size, and target audiences, we suggest that mega sports media events such as the Super Bowl and the swimsuit issue offer a magnified view of the dominant gender and sexual imagery emanating from the center of the sports-media-commercial complex.

Losers and Buddies, Hotties and Bitches

In the 2002 and 2003 beer and liquor ads that we examined, men's work worlds seem mostly to have disappeared. These ads are less about drinking and leisure as a reward for hard work and more about leisure as a lifestyle in and of itself. Men do not work in these ads; they recreate. And women are definitely back in the picture, but not as wives who are partners in building the good domestic life. It is these relations among men as well as relations between men and women that form the four dominant gender themes in the ads we examined. We will introduce these four themes by describing a 2003 Super Bowl commercial for Bud Lite beer.

Two young, somewhat nerdy-looking white guys are at a yoga class, sitting in the back of a room full of sexy young women. The two men have attached prosthetic legs to their bodies so that they can fake the yoga moves. With their bottles of Bud Lite close by, these voyeurs watch in delight as the female yoga teacher instructs the class to "relax and release that negative energy . . . inhale, arch, *thrust* your pelvis to the sky and exhale, *release* into the stretch." As the instructor uses her hands to push down on a woman's upright spread-eagled legs and says "focus, focus, focus," the camera (serving as prosthesis for male spectators at home) cuts back and forth between close-ups of the women's breasts and bottoms, while the two guys gleefully enjoy their beer and their sexual voyeurism. In the final scene the two guys are standing outside the front door of the yoga class, beer bottles in hand, and someone throws their fake legs out the door at them. As they duck to avoid being hit by the legs, one of them comments, "*She's* not very relaxed."

We begin with this ad because it contains, in various degrees, the four dominant gender themes

that we found in the mega sports media events ads:

1. Losers: Men are often portrayed as chumps, losers. Masculinity—especially for the lone man—is precarious. Individual men are always on the cusp of being publicly humiliated, either by their own stupidity, by other men, or, worse, by a beautiful woman.

2. Buddies: The precariousness of individual men's masculine status is offset by the safety of the male group. The solidity and primacy—and emotional safety—of male friendships are the emotional center of many of these ads.

3. Hotties: When women appear in these ads, it is usually as highly sexualized fantasy objects. These beautiful women serve as potential prizes for men's victories and proper consumption choices. They sometimes serve to validate men's masculinity, but their validating power also holds the potential to humiliate male losers.

4. Bitches: Wives, girlfriends, or other women to whom men are emotionally committed are mostly absent from these ads. However, when they do appear, it is primarily as emotional or sexual blackmailers who threaten to undermine individual men's freedom to enjoy the erotic pleasure at the center of the male group.

To a great extent, these four gender themes are intertwined in the Super Bowl "Yoga Voyeurs" ad. First, the two guys are clearly not good-looking, high-status, muscular icons of masculinity. More likely they are intended to represent the "everyman" with whom many boys and men can identify. Their masquerade as sensitive men allows them to transgress the female space of the yoga class, but they cannot pull the masquerade off and are eventually "outed" as losers and rejected by the sexy women. But even if they realize that they are losers, they do not have to care because they are so happy and secure in their bond with each other. Their friendship bond is cemented in frat-boy-style hijinks that allow them to share close-up voyeurism of sexy women who, we can safely assume, are way out of these men's league. In the end, the women reject the guys as pathetic losers. But the guys do not seem too upset. They have each other and, of course, they have their beers.

Rarely did a single ad in our study contain all four of these themes. But taken together, the ads show enough consistency that we can think of these themes as intertwined threads that together make up the ideological fabric at the center of mega sports media events. Next, we will illustrate how these themes are played out in the 2002 and 2003 ads, before discussing some of the strains and tensions in the ads.

Real Friends, Scary Women

Five twenty-something white guys are sitting around a kitchen table playing poker. They are laughing, seemingly having the time of their lives, drinking Jim Beam whiskey. The caption for this ad reflects the lighthearted, youthful mood of the group: "Good Bourbon, ice cubes, and whichever glasses are clean." This ad, which appeared in the 2002 *Sports Illustrated* swimsuit issue, is one in a series of Jim Beam ads that have run for the past few years in *Sports Illustrated* and in other magazines aimed at young men.[2] Running under the umbrella slogan of "Real Friends, Real Bourbon," these Jim Beam ads hail a white, college-age (or young college-educated) crowd of men with the appeal of playful male bonding through alcohol consumption in bars or pool halls. The main theme is the safety and primacy of the male group, but the accompanying written text sometimes suggests the presence of women. In one ad, four young white guys partying up a storm together and posing with arms intertwined are accompanied by the caption, "Unlike your girlfriend, they never ask where this relationship is going." These ads imply that women demand levels of emotional commitment and expression undesirable to men, while life with the boys (and the booze) is exciting, emotionally comfortable, and safe. The comfort that these ads suggest is that bonding and intimacy have clear (though mostly unspoken) boundaries that limit emotional expression in the male group. When drinking with the guys, a man can feel close to his friends, perhaps even drape an arm over a friend's shoulder, embrace him, or tell him that he loves him. But the context of alcohol consumption provides an escape hatch that contains and rationalizes the eruption of physical intimacy.

Although emotional closeness with and commitment to real women apparently are to be avoided, these ads also do suggest a role for women. The one ad in the Jim Beam series that includes an image of a woman depicts only a body part (*Sports Illustrated* ran this one in its 2000 swimsuit issue in 3-D). Four guys drinking together in a bar are foregrounded by a set of high-heeled legs that appear to be an exotic dancer's. The guys drink, laugh, and seem thoroughly amused with each other. "Our lives would make a great sitcom," the caption reads, and continues, "of course, it would have to run on cable." That the guys largely ignore the dancer affirms the strength and primacy of their bond with one another—they do not need her or any other women, the ad seems to say. On the other hand—and just as in the "Yoga Voyeurs" commercial—the female dancer's sexualizing of the chronotopic space affirms that the bond between the men is safely within the bounds of heterosexuality.

Although these ads advocate keeping one's emotional distance from women, a commitment to heterosexuality always carries the potential for developing actual relationships with women. The few ads that depict real women portray them consistently as signs of danger to individual men and to the male group. The ads imply that what men really want is sex (or at least titillation), a cold beer, and some laughs with the guys. Girlfriends and wives are undesirable because they push men to talk about feelings and demonstrate commitment to a relationship. In "Good Listener," a 2003 Super Bowl ad for Budweiser, a young white guy is sitting in a sports bar with his girlfriend while she complains about her best friend's "totally self-centered and insensitive boyfriend." As he appears to listen to this obviously boring "girl talk," the camera pulls to a tight close-up on her face. She is reasonably attractive, but the viewer is not supposed to mistake her for one of the model-perfect fantasy women in other beer ads. The close-up reveals that her teeth are a bit crooked, her hair a bit stringy, and her face contorts as she says of her girlfriend that "she has these *emotional* needs he can't meet." Repelled, the guy spaces out and begins to peer over her shoulder at the television. The camera takes the guy's point of view and focuses on the football game while the speaking woman is in the fuzzy margins of his view. The girlfriend's monologue gets transposed by a football announcer describing an exciting run. She stops talking, and just in time his gaze shifts back to her eyes. She lovingly says, "You're such a great listener." With an "aw-shucks" smile, he says "thanks," and the "Budweiser TRUE" logo appears on the screen. These ads suggest that a sincere face and a bottle of beer allow a guy to escape the emotional needs of his partner while retaining regular access to sex. But the apparent dangers of love, long-term commitment, and marriage remain. The most overtly misogynist ad in the 2003 Super Bowl broadcast was "Sarah's Mom." While talking on the phone to a friend, a young, somewhat nerdy-looking white guy prepares to meet his girlfriend's mother for the first time. His friend offers him this stern advice: "Well, get a good look at her. 'Cause in twenty years, that's what Sarah's gonna look like." The nerd expresses surprised concern, just as there is a knock on the door. Viewed through the door's peephole, the face of Sarah's mother appears as young and beautiful as Sarah's, but it turns out that Sarah's mother has grotesquely large hips, thighs, and buttocks. The commercial ends with the screen filled mostly with the hugeness of the mother's bottom, her leather pants audibly stretching as she bends to pet the dog, and Sarah shoveling chips and dip into her mouth, as

she says of her mother, "Isn't she incredible?" The guy replies, with obvious skepticism, "yeah."

The message to boys and men is disturbing. If you are nerdy enough to be thinking about getting married, then you should listen to your male friends' warnings about what to watch out for and what is important. If you have got to have a wife, make sure that she is, and always will be, conventionally thin and beautiful.

In beer ads, the male group defines men's need for women as sexual, not emotional, and in so doing it constructs women as either whores or bitches and then suggests ways for men to negotiate the tension between these two narrow and stereotypical categories of women. This, we think, is a key point of tension that beer and liquor companies are attempting to exploit to their advantage. They do so by creating a curious shift away from the familiar "madonna-whore" dichotomy of which Western feminists have been so critical, where wives/mothers/girlfriends are put on a pedestal and the women one has sex with are put in the gutter. The alcohol industry would apparently prefer that young men not think of women as madonnas. After all, wives and girlfriends to whom men are committed, whom they respect and love, often do place limits on men's time spent out with the boys, as well as limits on men's consumption of alcohol. The industry seems to know this: as long as men remain distrustful of women, seeing them either as bitches who are trying to ensnare them and take away their freedom or as whores with whom they can party and have sex with no emotional commitment attached, then men remain more open to the marketing strategies of the industry.

Winners and Losers

In the 2002 and 2003 Super Bowls, Budweiser's "How Ya Doin'?" ads featured the trope of a country bumpkin, or hick, in the big city to highlight the rejection of men who transgress the symbolic boundaries of the male peer group. These ads also illustrate the communication and emotional processes that police these boundaries. Men may ask each other "how's it goin'," but they do not want to hear how it's *really* goin'. It is these unspoken limits that make the group bond feel like an emotionally safe place: male buddies at the bar will not ask each other how the relationship is going or push each other to get in touch with their feminine sides. But men who transgress these boundaries, who do not understand the unwritten emotional rules of the male group, are suspect, are branded as losers, and are banished from the inner circle of the group.

Revenge of the Regular Guys

If losers are used in some of these ads to clarify the bounds of masculine normality, this is not to say that hypermasculine men are set up as the norm. To the contrary, overly masculine men, muscle men, and men with big cars who flash their money around are often portrayed as the real losers, against whom regular guys can sometimes turn the tables and win the beautiful women. In the ads we examined, however, this "regular guy wins beautiful fantasy woman" outcome was very rare. Instead, when the regular guy does manage to get the beautiful fantasy woman's attention, it is usually not in the way that he imagined or dreamed. A loser may want to win the attention of—and have sex with—beautiful women. But ultimately, these women are unavailable to a loser; worse, they will publicly humiliate him if he tries to win their attention. But losers can always manage to have another beer.

If white-guy losers risk punishment or humiliation from beautiful women in these ads, the level of punishment faced by black men can be even more severe. Although nearly all of the television commercials and print ads that we examined depict white people, a very small number do focus centrally on African Americans.[3] In "Pick-Up Lines," a Bud Lite ad that ran during the 2002 Super Bowl, two black males are sitting at a bar next to an attractive black female. Paul, the man in the middle, is obviously a loser; he's

wearing a garish shirt, and his hair looks like an Afro gone terribly wrong. He sounds a bit whiny as he confides in his male friend, "I'm just not good with the ladies like you, Cedric." Cedric, playing Cyrano de Bergerac, whispers opening pickup lines to him. The loser turns to the woman and passes on the lines. But just then, the bartender brings another bottle of beer to Cedric, who asks the bartender, "So, how much?" Paul, thinking that this is his next pickup line, says to the woman, "So, how much?" Her smile turns to an angry frown, and she delivers a vicious kick to Paul's face, knocking him to the floor. After we see the Budweiser logo and hear the voice-over telling us that Bud Lite's great taste "will never let you down," we see a stunned Paul rising to his knees and trying to pull himself up to his bar stool, but the woman knocks him down again with a powerful backhand fist to the face.

This Bud Lite "Pick-Up Lines" ad—one of the very few ads that depict relations between black men and black women—was the only ad in which we saw a man being physically beaten by a woman. Here, the African American woman as object turns to subject, inflicting direct physical punishment on the African American man. The existence of these very few "black ads" brings into relief something that might otherwise remain hidden: most of these ads construct a youthful white masculinity that is playfully self-mocking, always a bit tenuous, but ultimately lovable. The screwups that white-guy losers make are forgivable, and we nearly always see these men, in the end, with at least a cold beer in hand. By contrast, the intersection of race, gender, and class creates cultural and institutional contexts of suspicion and punishment for African American boys and men (Ferguson 2000). In the beer ads this translates into the message that a black man's transgressions are apparently deserving of a kick to the face.

Erotic Intertextuality

One of the dominant strategies in beer and liquor ads is to create an (often humorous) erotic tension among members of a "threesome": the male reader/viewer, a woman depicted as a sexy fantasy object, and a bottle of cold beer. This tension is accomplished through intertextual referencing between the advertising text and the sport text. For instance, on returning to live coverage of the Super Bowl from a commercial break, the camera regularly lingered on the stadium scoreboard, above which was a huge Budweiser sign.

One such occasion during the 2003 Super Bowl was particularly striking. Coors had just run its only commercial (an episode from its successful "Twins" series) during this mega sports media event that seemed otherwise practically owned by Anheuser-Busch. Immediately on return from the commercial break to live action, the handheld field-level camera focused one by one on dancing cheerleaders (once coming so close that it appears that the camera bumped into one of the women's breasts), all the while keeping the Budweiser sign in focus in the background. It was almost as though the producers of the Super Bowl were intent on not allowing the Coors "twins" to upstage Anheuser-Busch's ownership of the event.

Omnipresent advertising images in recent years have continued to obliterate the already blurry distinction between advertising texts and other media texts (Goldman and Papson 1996). This is surely true in the world of sport: players' uniforms, stadium walls, the corner of one's television screen, and even moments within telecasts are regularly branded with the Nike swoosh or some other corporate sign. When ads appropriate or make explicit reference to other media (e.g., other ads, celebrities, movies, television shows, or popular music), they engage in what Robert Goldman and Stephen Papson call "cultural cannibalism" (1998, 10). Audiences are then invited to make the connections between the advertised product and the cultural meanings implied by the cannibalized sign; in so doing, the audience becomes "the final author, whose participation is essential" (O'Donohoe 1997, 259). As with all textual analyses that do not include an audience study, we must be cautious in inferring how differently situated audiences might variously take

up, and draw meanings from, these ads. However, we suspect that experiences of "authorship" in the process of decoding and drawing intertextual connections are a major part of the pleasure of viewing mass media texts.

The 2002 and 2003 *Sports Illustrated* swimsuit issues offer vivid examples of texts that invite the reader to draw intertextual connections between erotically charged ads and other non-ad texts. Whereas in the past the *Sports Illustrated* swimsuit issue ran ads that were clearly distinct from the swimsuit text, it has recently become more common for the visual themes in the ads and the swimsuit text to be playfully intertwined, symbiotically referencing each other. A 2003 Heineken ad shows a close-up of two twenty-four-ounce "keg cans" of Heineken beer, side by side. The text above the two cans reads, "They're big. And yeah, they're real." As if the reference to swimsuit models' breast size (and questions about whether some of the models have breast implants) were perhaps too subtle, *Sports Illustrated* juxtaposed the ad with a photo of a swimsuit model, wearing a suit that liberally exposed her breasts.

For the advertisers and for *Sports Illustrated,* the payoff for this kind of intertextual coordination is probably large: for the reader, the text of the swimsuit issue becomes increasingly seamless, as ads and swimsuit text melt into each other, playfully, humorously, and erotically referencing each other. As with the Super Bowl ads, the *Sports Illustrated* swimsuit issue ads become something that viewers learn not to ignore or skip over; instead, the ads become another part of the pleasure of consuming and imagining.

In 2003, Miller Brewing Company and *Sports Illustrated* further developed the symbiotic marketing strategy that they had introduced in 2002. The 2003 swimsuit issue featured a huge Miller Lite ad that included the equivalent of fourteen full pages of ad text. Twelve of these pages were a large, pull-out poster, one side of which was a single photo of "Sophia," a young model wearing a bikini with the Miller Lite logo on the right breast cup. On the opposite side of the poster were four one-page photos and one two-page photo of Sophia posing in various biki-nis, with Miller Lite bottles and/or logos visible in each picture. As it did in the 2002 ad, Miller invites viewers to enter a contest to win a trip to the next *Sports Illustrated* swimsuit issue photo shoot. The site of the photo shoot fuses the text-based space of the magazine with the real space of the working models in exotic, erotic landscapes of desire that highlight the sexuality of late capi-talist colonialism (Davis 1997). The accompany-ing text invites the reader to "visit http://www.cnnsi.com" to "check out a 360 degree view of the *Sports Illustrated* swimsuit photo shoot." And the text accompanying most of the photos of Sophia and bottles of Miller Lite teasingly encourages the reader to exercise his consumer power: "So if you had to make a choice, which one would it be?"

This expansive ad evidences a multilevel symbiosis between *Sports Illustrated* and Miller Brewing Company. The playful tease to "choose your favorite" (model, swimsuit, and/or beer) invites the reader to enter another medium—the *Sports Illustrated* swimsuit Web site, which includes access to a *Sports Illustrated* swimsuit photo shoot video sponsored by Miller. The result is a multi-faceted media text that stands out as something other than mere advertisement and other than business-as-usual *Sports Illustrated* text. It has an erotic and commercial charge to it that simulta-neously teases the reader as a sexual voyeur and hails him as an empowered consumer who can freely choose his own beer and whichever sexy woman he decides is his "favorite."

"Life Is Harsh": Male Losers and Alcoholic Accommodation

In recent years, the tendency in the *Sports Illus-trated* swimsuit issue to position male readers as empowered individuals who can "win" or freely choose the sexy fantasy object of their dreams has begun to shift in other directions. To put it simply, many male readers of the swimsuit issue may find the text erotically charged, but most know that these are two-dimensional images of sexy

women who in real life are unavailable to them. In recent years, some swimsuit issue ads have delivered this message directly. In 1997, a two-page ad for Tequila Sauza depicted six women in short red skirts, posing flirtatiously, some of them lifting their blouses provocatively to reveal bare midriffs, or opening their blouses to reveal parts of their breasts. In small letters, across the six women's waists, stretching all the way across the two pages, the text reads, "We can say with 99.9% accuracy that there is no possible way whatsoever in this lifetime that you will ever get a date with one of these women." Then, to the side of the ad is written "LIFE IS HARSH. Your tequila shouldn't be." A similar message appears in other ads. For instance, in the 1999 swimsuit issue, a full-page photo of a Heineken bottle included the written text "The only heiny in this magazine you could actually get your hands on."

These ads play directly to the male reader as loser and invite him to accommodate to his loser status, to recognize that these sexy fantasy women, though "real," are unavailable to him, and to settle for what he can have: a good bottle of Tequila Sauza or a cold (rather than a hot) "Heiny." The Bud Lite Super Bowl commercials strike a similar chord. Many Bud Lite ads either titillate the viewer with sexy fantasy women, point to the ways that relationships with real women are to be avoided, or do both simultane-ously. The break that appears near the end of each Bud Lite ad contrasts sharply with the often negative depiction of men's relations with real women in the ad's story line. The viewer sees a close-up of a bottle of Bud Lite. The bottle's cap explodes off, and beer ejaculates out, as a male voice-over proclaims what a man truly can rely on in life: "For the great taste that won't fill you up, and never lets you down . . . make it a Bud Lite."

Revenge of the Losers

The accommodation theme in these ads may suc-ceed, momentarily, in encouraging a man to shift his feelings of being a sexual loser toward manly feelings of empowerment through the consumption of brand-name beers and liquor. If the women in the ads are responsible for heightening tensions that result in some men's sense of themselves as losers, one possible outcome beyond simply drinking a large amount of alcohol (or one that accompanies the consumption of alcohol) is to express anger toward women and even to take revenge against them. This is precisely a direction that some of the recent ads have taken.

A full-page ad in the 2002 swimsuit issue showed a large photo of a bottle of Maker's Mark Whiskey. The bottle's reflection on the shiny table on which it sits is distorted in a way that suggests an hourglass-shaped female torso. The text next to the bottle reads, "'Your bourbon has a great body and fine character. I WISH the same could be said for my girlfriend.' D. T., Birmingham, AL." This one-page ad is juxtaposed with a full-page photo of a *Sports Illustrated* model, provocatively using her thumb to begin to pull down the right side of her bikini bottom.

Together, the ad text and *Sports Illustrated* text angrily express the bitch-whore dichotomy that we discussed above. D. T.'s girlfriend is not pictured, but the description of her clearly indicates that not only does she lack a beautiful body; worse, she's a bitch. While D. T.'s girlfriend symbolizes the real woman whom each guy tolerates, and to whom he avoids committing, the juxtaposed *Sports Illustrated* model is the beautiful and sexy fantasy woman. She is unavailable to the male reader in real life; her presence as fantasy image highlights that the reader, like D. T., is stuck, apparently, with his bitchy girlfriend. But at least he can enjoy a moment of pseudo-empowerment by consuming a Maker's Mark whiskey and by insulting his girlfriend's body and character. Together, the Maker's Mark ad and the juxtaposed *Sports Illustrated* model provide a context for the reader to feel hostility toward the real women in his life.

This kind of symbolic male revenge toward women is expressed in a different way in a four-page Captain Morgan rum ad that appeared in the 2003 *Sports Illustrated* swimsuit issue. On the first page, we see only the hands of the cartoon character "Captain Morgan" holding a fire hose spraying water into the air over what appears to be a tropical beach. When one turns the page, a three-page foldout ad reveals that "the Captain" is spraying what appears to be a *Sports Illustrated* swimsuit issue photo shoot. Six young women in tiny bikinis are laughing, perhaps screaming, and running for cover (five of them are huddled under an umbrella with a grinning male character who looks suspiciously like Captain Morgan). The spray from the fire hose causes the women's bathing suits to melt right off their bodies. The readers do not know if the swimsuits are painted on or are made of meltable candy or if perhaps Captain Morgan's ejaculate is just that powerfully corrosive. One way or the other, the image suggests that Captain Morgan is doing a service to the millions of boys and men who read this magazine. Written across a fleeing woman's thigh, below her melting bikini bottom, the text reads "Can you say birthday suit issue?"

Two men—apparently photographers—stand to the right of the photo, arms raised to the heavens (with their clothing fully intact). The men in the picture seem ecstatic with religious fervor. The male reader is perhaps invited to identify with these regular guys: like them, he is always good enough to look at these beautiful women in their swimsuits but never good enough to get them to take it off for him. But here, "the Captain" was clever enough to strip the women naked so that he and all of his male buddies could enjoy a vengeful moment of voyeurism. The relational gender and sexual dynamics of this ad—presented here without overt anger and with cartoonish humor—allegorize the common dynamics of group sexual assaults (Beneke 1982). These sexy women have teased men enough, the ad suggests. First they arouse men, and then they inevitably make them feel like losers. They deserve to be stripped naked against their will. As in many male rape fantasies, the ad suggests that women ultimately find that they like it. And all of this action is facilitated by a bottle of rum, the Captain's magical essence.

Tension, Stabilization, and Masculine Consumption

We argued in our introduction that contemporary social changes have destabilized hegemonic masculinity. Examining beer and liquor ads in mega sports media events gives us a window into the ways that commercial forces have seized on these destabilizing tendencies, constructing fantasy narratives that aim to appeal to a very large group—eighteen- to thirty-four-year-old men. They do so by appealing to a broad zeitgeist among young (especially white, heterosexual) men that is grounded in widespread tensions in the contemporary gender order.[4] The sexual and gender themes of the beer and liquor ads that we examine in this article do not stand alone; rather they reflect, and in turn contribute to, broader trends in popular culture and marketing to young white males. Television shows like *The Man Show,* new soft-core porn magazines like *Maxim* and *FHM,* and radio talk shows like the syndicated *Tom Leykus Show* share similar themes and are targeted to similar audiences of young males. Indeed, radio talk show hosts like Leykus didactically instruct young men to avoid "girlie" things, to eschew emotional commitment, and to think of women primarily as sexual partners (Messner 2002, 107–8). These magazines and television and radio shows construct young male lifestyles saturated with sexy images of nearly naked, surgically enhanced women; unabashed and unapologetic sexual voyeurism shared by groups of laughing men; and explicit talk of sexual exploits with "hotties" or "juggies." A range of consumer products that includes—often centrally, as in *The Man Show*—consumption of beer as part of the young male lifestyle stitches together this erotic bonding among men. Meanwhile, real women are either absent from these media or they are disparaged as gold diggers (yes, this term has been resuscitated) who use sex to get men to spend money on them and trick them into marriage. The domesticated man is viewed as a wimpy victim who has subordinated his own pleasures (and surrendered his paychecks) to a

woman. Within this framework, a young man should have sex with as many women as he can while avoiding (or at least delaying) emotional commitments to any one woman. Freedom from emotional commitment grants 100 percent control over disposable income for monadic consumption and care of self. And that is ultimately what these shows are about: constructing a young male consumer characterized by personal and emotional freedom who can attain a hip lifestyle by purchasing an ever-expanding range of automobile related products, snack foods, clothes, toiletries, and, of course, beer and liquor.

At first glance, these new media aimed at young men seem to resuscitate a 1950s "*Playboy* philosophy" of men's consumption, sexuality, and gender relations (Ehrenreich 1983). Indeed, these new media strongly reiterate the dichotomous bitch-whore view of women that was such a linch-pin of Hugh Hefner's "philosophy." But today's tropes of masculinity do not simply reiterate the past; rather, they give a postfeminist twist to the *Playboy* philosophy. A half-century ago, Hefner's pitch to men to recapture the indoors by creating (purchasing) one's own erotic "bachelor pad" in which to have sex with women (and then send them home) read as a straightforwardly masculine project. By contrast, today's sexual and gender pitch to young men is delivered with an ironic, self-mocking wink that operates, we think, on two levels. First, it appears to acknowledge that most young men are neither the heroes of the indoors (as Hefner would have it) nor of the outdoors (as the 1970s and 1980s beer ads suggested). Instead, the ads seem to recognize that young white men's unstable status leaves them always on the verge of being revealed as losers. The ads plant seeds of insecurity on this fertile landscape, with the goal of creating a white guy who is a consistent and enthusiastic consumer of alcoholic beverages. The irony works on a second level as well: the throwback sexual and gender imagery—especially the bitch-whore dichotomization of women—is clearly a defensively misogynistic backlash against feminism and women's increasing autonomy and social power.

The wink and self-mocking irony allow men to have it both ways: they can engage in humorous misogynist banter and claim simultaneously that it is all in play. They do not take themselves seriously, so anyone who takes their misogyny as anything but boys having good fun just has no sense of humor. The humorous irony works, then, to deflect charges of sexism away from white males, allowing them to define themselves as victims, as members of an endangered species. We suspect, too, that this is a key part of the process that constructs the whiteness in current reconstructions of hegemonic masculinity. As we have suggested, humorous "boys-will-be-boys" misogyny is unlikely to be taken ironically and lightly when delivered by men of color.

Caught between the excesses of a hyper-masculinity that is often discredited and caricatured in popular culture and the increasing empowerment of women, people of color, and homosexuals, while simultaneously being undercut by the postindustrial economy, the "Average Joe" is positioned as the ironic, vulnerable but lovable hero of beer and liquor ads. It is striking that the loser is not, or is rarely, your "José Mediano," especially if we understand the construction as a way to unite diverse eighteen- to thirty-four-year-old men. This is to say that the loser motif constructs the universal subject as implicitly white, and as a reaction against challenges to hegemonic masculinity it represents an ongoing possessive investment in whiteness (Lipsitz 1998).

Our analysis suggests that the fact that male viewers today are being hailed as losers and are being asked to identify with—even revel in—their loser status has its limits. The beer and liquor industry dangles images of sexy women in front of men's noses. Indeed, the ads imply that men will go out of their way to put themselves in position to be voyeurs, be it with a TV remote control, at a yoga class, in a bar, or on the *Sports Illustrated*/Miller Beer swimsuit photo shoot Web site. But ultimately, men know (and are increasingly being told in the advertisements themselves) that these sexy women are not available to them.

Worse, if men get too close to these women, these women will most likely humiliate them. By contrast, real women—women who are not model-beautiful fantasy objects—are likely to attempt to ensnare men into a commitment, push them to have or express feelings that make them uncomfortable, and limit their freedom to have fun watching sports or playing cards or pool with their friends. So, in the end, men have only the safe haven of their male friends and the bottle.

This individual sense of victimization may feed young men's insecurities while giving them convenient scapegoats on which to project anger at their victim status. The cultural construction of white males as losers, then, is tethered to men's anger at and desire for revenge against women. Indeed, we have observed that revenge-against-women themes are evident in some of the most recent beer and liquor ads. And it is here that our analysis comes full circle. For, as we suggested in the introduction, the cultural imagery in ads aimed at young men does not simply come from images "out there." Instead, this imagery is linked to the ways that real people live their lives. It is the task of future research—including audience research—to investigate and flesh out the specific links between young men's consumption of commercial images, their consumption of beer and liquor, their attitudes toward and relationships with women, and their tendencies to drink and engage in violence against women.

Notes

1. In addition to *Sports Illustrated's* 3,137,523 average weekly subscribers, the company's rate card claims 1,467,228 single-copy sales of the swimsuit issue. According to the same multiplier of 6.55 readers per magazine that *Sports Illustrated* uses for estimating the total size of its weekly audience, the swimsuit issue audience is over 30 million. More than likely, the multiplier for the swimsuit issue is higher than that of the weekly magazine, so the swimsuit issue audience is probably much larger than 30 million.

2. Most of the Jim Beam "Real Friends" ads discussed here did not appear in the two *Sports Illustrated*

swimsuit issues on which we focus. However, it enhances our understanding of the gender themes in the Jim Beam ads to examine the thematic consistencies in the broader series of Jim Beam "Real Friends" ads.

3. Of the twenty-six beer and malt liquor ads in the two Super Bowls, twenty-four depicted people. Among the twenty-four ads that depicted people, eighteen depicted white people only, three depicted groups that appear to be of mixed race, and three focused on African American main characters. Thirteen of the twenty-four beer and liquor ads in the two *Sports Illustrated* swimsuit issues depicted people: twelve depicted white people only, and one depicted what appears to be the silhouette of an African American couple. No apparent Latino/as or Asian Americans appeared in any of the magazine or television ads.

4. These same beer companies target different ads to other groups of men. Suzanne Danuta Walters (2001) analyzes Budweiser ads, e.g., that are aimed overtly at gay men.

References

Beneke, Timothy. 1982. *Men on Rape*. New York: St. Martin's.

Collins, Tony, and Wray Vamplew. 2002. *Mud, Sweat, and Beers: A Cultural History of Sport and Alcohol*. New York: Berg.

Curry, Timothy. 2000. "Booze and Bar Fights: A Journey to the Dark side of College Athletics." In *Masculinities, Gender Relations, and Sport*, ed. Jim McKay, Donald F. Sabo, and Michael A. Messner, 162–75. Thousand Oaks, CA: Sage.

Davis, Laurel L. 1997. *The Swimsuit Issue and Sport: Hegemonic Masculinity in* Sports Illustrated. Albany, NY: SUNY Press.

Dayan, Daniel, and Elihu Katz. 1988. "Articulating Consensus: The Ritual and Rhetoric of Media Events." In *Durkheimian Sociology: Cultural Studies*, ed. Jeffrey C. Alexander, 161–86. Cambridge: Cambridge University Press.

Ehrenreich, Barbara. 1983. *The Hearts of Men: American Dreams and the Flight from Commitment*. New York: Anchor Doubleday.

Ferguson, Ann Arnett. 2000. *Bad Boys: Public Schools in the Making of Black Masculinity*. Ann Arbor: University of Michigan Press.

Goldman, Robert, and Stephen Papson. 1996. *Sign Wars: The Cluttered Landscape of Advertising*. New York: Guilford.

———. 1998. *Nike Culture: The Sign of the Swoosh*. Thousand Oaks, CA: Sage.

Koss, Mary, and John A. Gaines. 1993. "The Prediction of Sexual Aggression by Alcohol Use, Athletic Participation, and Fraternity Affiliation." *Journal of Interpersonal Violence* 8(1):94–108.

Leichliter, Jami S., Philip W. Meilman, Cheryl A. Presley, and Jeffrey R. Cashin. 1998. "Alcohol Use and Related Consequences among Students with Varying Levels of Involvement in College Athletics." *Journal of American College Health* 46(6):257–62.

Lipsitz, George. 1981. *Class and Culture in Cold War America: "A Rainbow at Midnight."* New York: Praeger.

———. 1998. *The Possessive Investment in Whiteness: How White People Profit from Identity Politics*. Philadelphia: Temple University Press.

Martin, Christopher R., and Jimmie L. Reeves. 2001. "The Whole World Isn't Watching (but We Thought They Were): The Super Bowl and U.S. Solipsism." *Culture, Sport, and Society* 4(2): 213–54.

May, Elaine Tyler. 1988. *Homeward Bound: American Families in the Cold War Era*. New York: Basic Books.

Messner, Michael A. 2002. *Taking the Field: Women, Men, and Sports*. Minneapolis: University of Minnesota Press.

O'Donohoe, Stephanie. 1997. "Leaky Boundaries: Intertextuality and Young Adult Experiences of Advertising." In *Buy This Book: Studies in Advertising and Consumption*, ed. Mica Nava, Andrew Blake, Ian McRury, and Barry Richards, 257–75. London: Routledge.

Postman, Neil, Christine Nystrom, Lance Strate, and Charlie Weingartner. 1987. *Myths, Men, and Beer: An Analysis of Beer Commercials on Broadcast Television, 1987*. Washington, DC: AAA Foundation for Traffic Safety.

Sabo, Don, Phil Gray, and Linda Moore. 2000. "Domestic Violence and Televised Athletic Events: 'It's a man thing.' " In *Masculinities, Gender Relations, and Sport*, ed. Jim McKay, Don Sabo, and Michael A. Messner, 127–46. Thousand Oaks, CA: Sage.

Sperber, Murray. 2000. *Beer and Circus: How Big-Time College Sports Is Crippling Undergraduate Education.* New York: Henry Holt.

Spigel, Lynn. 1992. *Make Room for TV: Television and the Family Ideal in Postwar America.* Chicago: University of Chicago Press.

Strate, Lance. 1992. "Beer Commercials: A Manual on Masculinity." In *Men, Masculinity, and the Media,* ed. Steve Craig, 78–92. Newbury Park, CA: Sage.

Walters, Suzanna Danuta. 2001. *All the Rage: The Story of Gay Visibility in America.* Chicago: University of Chicago Press.

Wenner, Lawrence A. 1991. "One Part Alcohol, One Part Sport, One Part Dirt, Stir Gently: Beer Commercials and Television Sports." In *Television Criticism: Approaches and Applications,* ed. Leah R. Vende Berg and Lawrence A. Wenner, 388–407. New York: Longman.

———. 1998. "In Search of the Sports Bar: Masculinity, Alcohol, Sports, and the Mediation of Public Space." In *Sport and Postmodern Times,* ed. Genevieve Rail, 303–32. Albany, NY: SUNY Press.

Zimbalist, Andrew. 1999. *Unpaid Professionals: Commercialism and Conflict in Big-Time College Sports.* Princeton, NJ: Princeton University Press.

David Nylund

When in Rome: Heterosexism, Homophobia, and Sports Talk Radio

I am negotiating the traffic in my car on a typical harried Monday morning. As an avid sports fan, I turn on my local sports radio station. A commercial plugging the local radio station is airing: "Your hair's getting thinner, your paunch is getting bigger. But you still think the young babes want you! That's because you listen to Sports 1140 AM—it's not just sports talk, it's culture." Next comes the loud, rhythmic guitar riffs from the Guns N' Roses song, "Welcome to the Jungle." As Axl Rose begins to sing the lyrics to the heavy metal song, an announcer bellows, "Live from Los Angeles. You're listening to the Jim Rome Show." Next, the distinct, brash voice of Jim Rome, the nation's most popular sports talk radio host, addresses his audience of 2 million sports fans:[1] "Welcome back to the Jungle. I am Van Smack. We have open phone lines. But clones, if you call, have a take and do not suck or you will get run."[2] Over the next 3 hours, the well-known host interviews famous sports figures, articulates his notoriously controversial opinions on various topics using urban slang, and takes phone calls from his loyal listeners/sports fans who speak in Rome-invented terms such as *Jungle Dweller, bang,* and *Bugeater.*[3] I listen to the program with mixed feelings. As a sports fan and long-time listener of sports talk radio, I find myself engrossed and amused; I want to know what each "in-group" term means. As a critical feminist scholar, I am uneasy with his confrontational and insulting style, not to mention the aggressive and

uncritical content of his speech. I wonder, "What will Rome say next?"[4]

The Jim Rome Show reflects a growing cultural trend in the United States—sports talk radio. According to sportswriter Ashley Jude Collie (2001), Jim Rome is the "hippest, most controversial, and brutally honest voice" (p. 53) in mediated sports. In addition to his nationally syndicated radio program that airs on more than 200 stations, the 40-year-old hosts ESPN's *Rome is Burning,* a weekly 1-hr television sports talk show (and his second show on ESPN). Rome began his radio career broadcasting University of California, Santa Barbara (UCSB), basketball games. After graduating from UCSB in 1986 and serving seven nonpaying radio internships, Rome earned a local weekend job at XTRA in San Diego, a powerful 77,000-watt station. The "clever fashioning of a streetwise persona" (Mariscal, 1999), his raspy voice, staccato delivery, and fiercely independent opinions separated him from the talk radio crowd, and he soon moved into hosting a primetime radio show. Eventually, his popularity earned him a television spot on ESPN2, *Talk2,* a cable show that Rome hosted in the early 90s. The Noble Sports Network syndicated Rome's radio show in 1995, and Premiere Radio Networks acquired the rights to the show 1 year later. Rome also hosted Fox Sports Net's *The Last Word,* a sports talk television program that ran from 1997 to 2002.

However, despite the variety of venues in which he plays, it is the radio show's format that contributes to Rome's controversiality and popularity. Loyal callers, whom he calls "clones," phone in with their opinion (referred to as a

From *Journal of Sport & Social Issues,* Volume 28, No. 2, May 2004, pp. 136–168.

"take") on what's happening in the world of sports. Rome listens intently and either "runs" the caller with a buzzer (meaning he disconnects the call) or he allows them to finish their take and says, "rack'em" (meaning he saves the call as an entry into the huge call-of-the-day contest). As opposed to other talk radio programs where there is some dialogical interaction between the caller and hosts, Rome and his callers do not engage in a back-and-forth interchange. The caller's comments are highly performative, full of insider language, and monological. Rome silently listens to the call and only comments when the caller is finished with his or her monologue or Rome disconnects the call. Rarely, if ever, does a caller disagree with Rome.[5] "Huge" calls are those that Rome considers good "smack" speech—his term for sports talk that is gloatful, uninhibited, and unbridled. According to Rome, only the strong survive in this 3-hr dose of smack and irreverence. Rome's in-group language and his unique interaction (or lack thereof) make his radio show distinctive. His "survival of the fittest" format is responsible for the show's reputation as sports version of hate-speech radio (Hodgson, 1999).

The Jim Rome Show epitomizes the growing trend of talk radio. Presented as a medium in which citizens/callers can freely "air their point of view," talk radio has become a very popular forum for large numbers of people to engage in debate about politics, religion, and sports. The media culture, with talk radio as a prominent discourse, plays a very powerful role in the constitution of everyday life, shaping our political values, gender ideologies, and supplying the material out of which people fashion their identities (Kellner, 1995). Hence, it is crucial for scholars to furnish critical commentary on talk radio; specifically, we should critique those radio texts that work to reinforce inequality.

Talk radio formats, particularly political talk radio, exploded in the 1980s as a result of deregulation, corporatization of radio, and niche marketing (Cook, 2001).[6] Deregulation, which loosened mass-media ownership and content restrictions,

renewed interest in radio as a capitalist investment and galvanized the eventual emergence of its two 1990s prominent showcase formats: hate radio talk shows and all-sports programming (Cook, 2001). By the late 1990s, there were more than 4,000 talk shows on 1,200 stations (Goldberg, 1998).[7] Sports talk radio formats have, according to cultural studies scholar Jorge Mariscal (1999), "spread like an unchecked virus" (p. 111). Currently, there are more than 250 all-sports stations in the United States (Ghosh, 1999).

As a result of deregulation and global capitalism, new media conglomerates emerged as the only qualified buyers of radio programming.[8] Infinity Broadcasting, the largest U.S. company devoted exclusively to owning and operating radio stations, owns WFAN[9] and Sacramento's local all-sports station, 1140 AM. Its competing company, Premiere Radio Network, owns the popular nationally syndicated programs hosted by Howard Stern, Rush Limbaugh, Dr. Laura, and Jim Rome. Schiller (1989) refers to this homogenizing, modulated trend as "corporate speech" (p. 40) that encourages censorship and contains public expression within corporate, capitalist ideologies that reinforce dominant social institutions.

With the corporatization of radio came niche marketing that caters to targeted demographic groups. Talk radio is aimed at a very desirable demographic: White middle-class men between the ages of 24 and 55 years. Research shows that talk-radio listeners are overwhelmingly men who tend to vote Republican (Armstrong & Rubin, 1989; Hutchby, 1996; Page & Tannenbaum, 1996). The most popular program, the *Rush Limbaugh Show,* has 20 million daily listeners who laugh along with the host as he rants and vents, opening a channel for the performance of the angry White male. Roedieger (1996) remarked, in a fascinating read of Limbaugh's cultural significance in the United States, that "banality can carry much more social power than genius where White consciousness is concerned" (p. 42). Douglas (2002) argued that although most of the research on talk radio is on the threat it poses to democracy, what is obvious, but far less discussed, is talk radio's central role in restoring masculine hegemony:

> Talk radio is as much—maybe even more—about gender politics at the end of the century than it is about party politics. There were different masculinities enacted on the radio, from Howard Stern to Rush Limbaugh, but they were all about challenging and overthrowing, if possible, the most revolutionary of social movements, feminism. The men's movement of the 1980s found its outlet—and that was talk radio. (Douglas, 2002, p. 485)

Similarly, sports talk radio, according to Goldberg (1998), enacts its White hegemony via hypermasculine posing, forceful opinions, and loudmouth shouting. Sports talk radio "pontificates, moralizes, politicizes, commercializes, and commodifies—as it entertains" (p. 213). Although Rome's masculine style is different from Limbaugh's and Stern's, all three controversial hosts have built reputations through their rambunctious, masculinist, and combative styles (Farred, 2000). With White male masculinity being challenged and decentered by feminism, affirmative action, gay and lesbian movements, and other groups' quest for social equality, sports talk shows, similar to talk radio in general, have become an attractive venue for embattled White men seeking recreational repose and a nostalgic return to a prefeminist ideal (Farred, 2000).

This article offers a critical analysis of the most prominent sports talk-radio program, *The Jim Rome Show*. My study does not critique and dissect *The Jim Rome Show* in isolation from other media texts or discourses about sports; rather, I aim to provide a historicized and contextualized study based in cultural studies methodology. I show how *The Jim Rome Show* is situated within a broader set of social, gender, racial, political, economic, and cultural forces. In particular, I examine the ways in which the show reinforces and (less obviously) calls into question heterosexism as well as what gender scholars call *hegemonic masculinity*. As a prelude to this analysis, I discuss

sports talk radio and its link to traditional masculinity, homophobia, and heterosexism.

Sports Talk Radio and Hegemonic Masculinity

Many cultural critics and feminists are interested in examining the media industry's participation in the construction and maintenance of oppressive gender and sexual ideologies. One such dominant ideology is hegemonic masculinity. Media critics and scholars of gender have described at least five distinctive features of hegemonic masculinity in U.S. culture: (a) physical force, (b) occupational achievement, (c) patriarchy, (d) frontiermanship, and (e) heterosexuality (Brod, 1987; Kimmel, 1994). Connell (1990) defined hegemonic masculinity as "the culturally idealized form of masculine character" (p. 83) that emphasizes "the connecting of masculinity to toughness and competitiveness," as well as "the subordination of women" and "marginalization of gay men" (p. 94). Connell also suggested that hegemonic masculinity is not a static phenomenon but is an always contested, historically situated, social practice.

Historically, sports have played a fundamental role in the construction and maintenance of traditional masculinity in the United States (Messner, 1992). Communications scholar Nick Trujillo (1996) stated, "No other institution in American culture has influenced our sense of masculinity more than sport" (p. 183). The mass media have benefited from institutionalized sports and have served to reaffirm certain features of hegemonic masculinity. As Trujillo (1994) wrote:

> Media coverage of sports reinforces traditional masculinity in at least three ways. It privileges the masculine over the feminine or homosexual image by linking it to a sense of positive cultural values. It depicts the masculine image as "natural" or conventional, while showing alternative images as unconventional or deviant. And it personalizes traditional masculinity by elevating its representatives to places of

heroism and denigrating strong females or homosexuals. (p. 97)

Mediated sports texts function largely to reproduce the idea that hegemonic masculinity and heterosexuality are natural and universal rather than socially constructed (Jhally, 1989). Because these dominant texts have detrimental effects on women, gays, lesbians, and some men, Trujillo argued that mediated sport should be analyzed and critiqued.

Many scholars have taken up Trujillo's call, and in the past decade we have seen an explosion of research on sports and mass media (Wenner, 2000). Most of these studies examine televised sports and its link to violent masculinity, sexism, and homophobia (Messner, Dunbar, & Hunt, 2000). However, scholars have also turned their attention to the impact and meaning of "sports talk."[10] Farred (2000) described sports talk as an "overwhelmingly masculinist (but not exclusively male), combative, passionate, and apparently open ended discourse" (p. 101). Farred described sports radio talk shows as "orchestrated and mediated by rambunctious hosts" providing a "robust, opinionated, and sometimes humorous forum for talking about sport" (p. 116). Likewise, Sabo and Jansen (2000) posited that sports talk serves as an important primer for gender socialization in current times. They wrote:

> Sports talk, which today usually means talk about mediated sports, is one of [the] only remaining discursive spaces where men of all social classes and ethnic groups directly discuss such values as discipline, skill, courage, competition, loyalty, fairness, teamwork, hierarchy, and achievement. Sports and sports fandom are also sites of male bonding. (p. 205)

Sports radio does appear to have a communal function and is a particularly interesting site to study how men perform relationships and community. Haag (1996) found something inherently democratizing about sports talk radio, for she thinks it promotes civic discourse and "teaches us how to make community of and for a lot of people who lead isolated, often lonely lives in Amer-

ica" (p. 460). Haag also suggested that sports talk radio serves a different function than political talk radio, despite serving a similar largely White middle-class audience, because the values that it emphasizes focus on community, loyalty, and decency. The appeal of sports talk radio, according to Haag, lies in the idiosyncrasies of its hosts and the regionalism of the issues covered, in direct opposition to the increased national corporate control of radio. Farred (2000), in speaking to the communal function of sports, suggested that sports talk on the radio can "temporarily break down barriers of race, ethnicity, and class." As he put it, "White suburbanites, inner-city Latino and African-American men can all support the New York Knicks or the Los Angeles Dodgers" (p. 103).

Why is sports talk radio so popular at this particular time in history? Examining the historical and social context of masculinity suggests some interesting answers. With post-Fordist industrialization came economic changes that challenged the ideology of hegemonic masculinity. Women's increased presence in the public sphere, along with the changes in men's work and increased visibility of sexual diversity, provoked a "crisis in masculinity" (Dworkin & Wachs, 2000).[11] This crisis made many men fearful of becoming "feminized." Consequently, organized sports, with its emphasis on strength and physicality, functions as a popular homosocial institution to counter men's fear of feminization in the new economy and to help men cope with changes in the gender and economic order (Messner, 1992; Pronger, 1990).

Thus, as Douglas argued about talk radio in general, the emergence of sports talk radio can be understood as another attempt to retain certain aspects of traditional male identity. Its popularity with men coincides with other current media trends, including men's magazines such as *Maxim* and *FHM,* or Comedy Central Cable Network's hypermasculine TV show, *The Man Show.* It can be argued that these forms represent a nostalgic (and perhaps an ironic) attempt to return to a prefeminist masculine ideal. In particular, White, middle-class, heterosexual men may feel threatened and uncertain with changes encouraged by feminism and gay rights. Sports talk radio may represent an attempt to symbolically reassert their superiority over women and homosexuals (Horrocks & Campling, 1994). In this vein, Goldberg (1998) suggested that sports talk radio, far from being a democratizing force (here disagreeing with Haag), reinscribes dominant discourses and is a leading forum for reproducing male domination. He contended that "Sports talk radio facilitates this masculine self-elevation, the ideological reproduction of hegemony—risk and cost free but for the price of the toll call" (p. 218).[12]

As a casual listener to *The Jim Rome Show* over the past 3 years, I have noticed themes of misogyny, violence, and heterosexual dominance appear to recur with considerable frequency. Rome's persona embodies an aggressive masculinity with unassailable expertise and authority. This aggressive persona climaxed in 1994 on the set of Rome's ESPN show *Talk 2* while interviewing NFL quarterback Jim Everett. During the interview, Everett knocked Rome off his chair after Rome taunted Everett by calling him "Chris" (i.e., female tennis star, Chris Evert), a veiled reference to the quarterback's reputed lack of toughness. Rome's reference to Everett as "Chris" on the show was not the first time he had done so. In fact, Rome has used this term on Everett throughout the 1993 NFL season on his local radio show on XTRA 690 AM. This hypermasculine event increased Rome's fame and reputation among some of his audience as a host who "tells it like it is" even if it means insulting someone. However, many in the media criticized Rome's lack of professionalism and predicted the end of his career (Sports Illustrated Editors, 1994). Although Rome left ESPN2 soon after the Everett incident, his radio career slowly continued to grow to the prominence it now holds. Rome's reputation as intolerant and abusive continues to this day because his rapid-fire, masculinist-laden opinion on sports provoked OutSports.com—a Web site that caters to gay and lesbian sports fans—to refer to him as "the commentator who makes a name for himself by saying stupid things with an obnoxious style, that for some reason, attracts many straight sports fans" (Buzinski, 2000, p. 5).[13]

As a cultural studies scholar and committed sports fan, I am compelled to study *The Jim Rome Show* to examine the sexism and homophobia present in the show. When in Rome do the clones do as the Romans do? This question led me to conduct a textual analysis that identifies those features that appear to reinforce or promote homophobia and sexism. I also researched audiences in various sports bars in the United States to achieve a better understanding of what *The Jim Rome Show* means to listeners. I was particularly curious whether certain audience members resist the dominant, hegemonic, textual themes.

Method

It is important to note that my research is influenced by my pleasure in listening to the show as a sports fan. Because I write as a scholar and as a fan, my study reflects these two levels of knowledge, which are not necessarily in conflict but are also not necessarily in perfect alliance. Being a fan allows me certain insights into sports talk radio that an academic who is not a fan might not have, particularly when his or her analysis of texts is isolated from actual audiences. I thus avoid Jenkins's (1992) critique of academic textual analysis that is distant from audiences and consequently "unable to link ideological criticism with an acknowledgment of the pleasures we find within popular texts"(p. 7).

To help work against the limitations of critiquing texts in isolation from context, I hung out in sports bars and interviewed listeners of *The Jim Rome Show* to better understand the complex relationship between audiences and texts. These interviews were conducted in sports bars in Sacramento, Tampa, Las Vegas, and Fresno (see the appendix for interview script). I conducted interviews with 18 people who described themselves as fans of *The Jim Rome Show*. The average age of participants was 32 years. Ten were White, three were African American, three were Latino, and two were Asian American. Sixteen of the participants were men, and two were women, all identified as heterosexual.[14] Given that my research was limited to a small number of participants and because the audience members I interviewed may not be representative of *The Jim Rome Show*'s North American audience, the results are not necessarily generalizable. Yet my hope is that my findings will promote future research on the ways that listeners decode sports talk radio texts.

As I reviewed each interview transcript, I made notes about its content, analyzing the responses to each question. I was particularly interested in looking for common themes, key phrases, ways of talking, and patterns of responses that occurred in my conversations with the participants. Instead of a positivist model of research, my audience research is provisional, partial, and situated in a particular social and historical location. As Ang (1996) stated, "Critical audience studies should not pretend to tell the 'truth' about 'the audience.' Its ambitions should be more modest" (p. 45).

Sports Bars

I chose to research sports bars because many of the patrons who frequent these spaces are avid listeners of *The Jim Rome Show*.[15] In addition, because it is a primary site for male bonding, the sports bar is an extension of the social practices and discourses evident in sports talk radio (Wenner, 1998). Nevertheless, conducting research as a sports fan in the highly masculinized space of a sports bar produced some interesting ethical dilemmas; specifically, the issue of power relations. I attempted to be self-reflexive of my privileged subject position (White, male, heterosexual, sports fan) as to not inadvertently reproduce male hegemony. This privilege was evident when I was discussing my research with a male friend who identifies as gay. As he said to me, "I could never do that research; a sports bar is a dangerous place for a gay man. I would feel very unsafe there." Taking his comments into account helps me to continually reflect on my privileged status as

researcher and straight, middle-class, White male fan. I also need to ask critical questions that invite my male participants to examine and interrogate masculinity.

Being a sports fan who has frequented many sports bars has advantages and disadvantages. The main risk is overidentifying with my research participants and not having enough critical distance. The main advantage of being a sports fan is that it helps to facilitate nuanced understandings and forms of access impossible from other subject positions. Conducting this study as a fan inspired me to a high degree of accountability— I have included verbatim materials, edited and selected from my taped interviews, as a way of privileging their voice (all the names of my research participants have been changed to preserve anonymity).

The sports bar is a fascinating site to conduct fieldwork. In his assessment of the cultural space of modern and postmodern sports bars, Wenner (1998) argued that alcohol, sports, and hegemonic masculinity operate as a "holy trinity." He distinguished the modern sports bar, a traditionally gendered place, from the postmodern sports bar, a place where gender relations are rearranged into a commodified hybrid. The modern sports bar, according to Wenner, is a place to talk to your male peers, have a drink, and watch and discuss sports—places I remember hanging out with my father and grandfather after Detroit Tigers' games. In contrast, the postmodern sports bar is "designed as an experience as opposed to a real place" (Wenner, 1998, p. 323). He wrote,

> The postmodern sports bar does not seek to stimulate the "authenticity" of a local place. Designed for out-of-towners to catch the game and for the realization that fewer and fewer people live in the places they were from, the postmodern sports bar offers "memorabilia in the generic." A wide net is cast so that there is some identity hook for everyone, no [matter] what their favorite team, level of fanship, or geographic past. (p. 325)

The bars I frequented were of the postmodern type that Wenner described. Distinct from the smell (I remember the local taverns in Detroit as smelling like men's locker rooms) and look of local sports bars (worn furniture, photos of local sports heroes, and virtually all men—no women—sitting at bar stools), the bars I conducted my research in were airy, bright, lively, loud, and smelled good. The bar areas looked very similar in each city—a large rectangular perimeter that resembled a large table with four corners and a "wet area" in the middle serviced by bartenders. In contrast to the local sports bar, the sexual geography of the postmodern bars I frequented was more egalitarian. Men and women worked as bartenders and waiters. During the time I spent observing, the majority of people sitting at the bar were men, but women also sat there without noticeable harassment. The space was a metaphor for postmodern culture in general—a constant tension between democratization and commodification. In this space, I found that male hegemony was still present as in the older bar context but in a more understated way. As Wenner (1998) wrote, "In the postmodern sports bar, male hegemony does not go away, it is merely transformed by its reframing" (p. 327).

In each bar I visited, I sat at the large bar area and began socializing with patrons, discussing sports and current events. After some small talk, I asked them if they listened to *The Jim Rome Show*. Virtually all the men I approached stated that they listened to the show. I then informed them of my research project and asked them to do an audiotaped interview about their experience of the show. All agreed enthusiastically after I assured them of confidentiality. The interviews, generally lasting 20 min, were enjoyable and surprisingly substantive and informative. Although the common initial explanation for listening to *The Jim Rome Show* was "it's entertaining," the conversations also focused on issues of homosexuality, masculinity, and other social topics. Often, people shared very personal stories and thanked me for an "enlightening" or "thought-provoking" experience. The interviews confirmed the notion that sports talk can provide an opportunity for men to discuss and even raise their awareness of gender and sexual issues that they might not otherwise have.

In addition to interviewing people at sports bars, I taped *The Jim Rome Show* from April 30 through September 7, 2001—roughly 390 hr of programming (130 shows). I listened to each taped show and classified the content of the program into two general categories: (a) discussion of sports that centers on statistics and player/team performance and (b) discussion of larger social and political issues including racism, sexism, and homophobia. In my estimation, roughly 80% of the content of *The Jim Rome Show* was devoted to the former whereas social issues were the main topic 20% of the time. I also grouped the sociopolitical content into two general categories: hegemonic and counterhegemonic and found that roughly 70% of the discussion on such issues was hegemonic in nature.[16] In addition to grouping the show's content into these categories, I transcribed portions of the program when sexuality was discussed to conduct a close "reading" of the text. During the period in which I transcribed and analyzed *The Jim Rome Show*, four instances stand out as particularly important moments, what journalists often call "pegs"—critical events that generate a flurry of coverage (Grindstaff, 1994). In this case, the pegs generated discussion of homosexuality, prompting further commentary on other sports media programs. In the pages that follow, I analyze four topics that were widely discussed on *The Jim Rome Show* and other sports media programs as well as among the fans I interviewed. My analysis is connected to the larger media and cultural context. The period in which I taped the show was/is representative of a post-Clinton/Lewinsky, post-Bush inauguration, and pre–September 11, 2001, period of U.S. history. I intend to show links between the topics discussed on *The Jim Rome Show* and larger mediated discourse in general. By examining these pegs and placing them in their historical context, I hope to provide a forum in which to think through some of the ways that capitalism, hegemonic masculinity, sexuality, race, class, and consumption operates in contemporary U.S. culture.

Hegemonic Themes

As stated earlier, my analysis of the text confirms that much of the discourse on the show contains themes of misogyny, violence, and heterosexual dominance including themes that reinforced sexism and lesbian baiting. The following examples highlight these instances. The first is from an infamous program date July 23. On this date, Rome was commenting on the breaking story that several professional male athletes (Patrick Ewing, Terrell Davis, and Dekembe Motumbo) had testified in an Atlanta court that they regularly attended a strip club (The Gold Club) and engaged in sex acts with the some of the club's dancers.[17] This tabloid-like story was a great opportunity for Rome to engage in his sardonic "smack" talk. Here are Rome's acerbic comments on Patrick Ewing's admission that he received "free oral sex" at the Gold Club:

> Want some free oral sex Patrick [Ewing]? Nah, I'm good. Maybe next time! Come on! He said he'd been there 10 times. He said he had free oral sex 2 times. And by the way, who's going to say 'no' to free oral sex? I mean, clones, would you like some free oral sex? Who's going to say no to that [laughing]? Most athletes go to a club or restaurant and get comped some free drinks, chicken wings. . . . not Patrick, he gets comped free oral sex.

> [later in his monologue] Meanwhile, a former stripper testified. And it's a good thing. We finally have some good testimony. She testified that she performed sex acts or witnessed other dancers perform sex acts on celebrities including Terrell Davis and Dekembe Motumbo. So in response to the proverbial question, "who wants to sex Motumbo?" The answer obviously is whichever skank's turn it is at the Gold Club.

In this section of the transcript, Rome employs a very common, taken-for-granted discourse—"the heterosexual male sexual drive discourse" (Hare-Mustin, 1994). This dominant ideology is predicated on the notion that women are objects (Rome misogynistically refers to the dancers as "skanks") who arouse men's heterosexual urges, which are assumed to be "natural and compelling" (Hare-Mustin, 1994, p. 24). Accordingly, men cannot control their primitive sexual yearnings, and women are blamed for inflaming them. This assumption, reproduced by Rome's rhetorical question, "who is going to turn down 'free' oral sex," reinforces women's subjugation as they become defined as existing solely for men's pleasure.

Rome's language takes on homophobic tones later in the same program. In this excerpt, Rome ridicules a former dancer's testimony:

> Finally we are getting somewhere. I thought Ewing's testifying of getting 'hummers' was going to be the best that the trial had to offer. Thankfully, it's not. In fact, not even close! After Patrick was done humiliating himself, one of the hookers got on the stand. That's when it really got good. A former dancer at the club starting naming names! This is just the beginning. This 'tramp' also testified that she went back to the hotel room of a former wrestling executive, to perform sex acts, not on him, but on his wife! Now, we are getting somewhere. Sex with athletes; lesbian sex acts with the wives of executives. That's what I was hoping for from the beginning! And this tramp also added that she and another dancer performed a lesbian sex show for Ewing and some friends before he was given free oral sex by other dancers. And perhaps the most amazing thing, this tramp that ratted everybody out, is now working at a day care center in Georgia. Wonderful. Who wouldn't want to leave their kids with a woman who used to be a hooker? There's no one I would trust my kids with more than a woman who used to perform lesbian sex shows for NBA centers and sex with wrestling executive's wives. What a perfect person to have around children! Man, I can't wait to see what happens today in the trial. I wonder who else's life will be ruined today?

Many of the callers on the September 9 program also reproduced male hegemony during their takes. Here is the call of the day:

> **Dan:** [Contemptuously] I feel sorry for those skanks. I mean Ewing, Motumbo![18] Hopefully, the dancers got time and a half! I guess

America has finally found a job worse than Assistant Crack Whore. About the only thing good to come out of this sordid mess is that Motumbo finally found a bar where his pickup line works.

Rome: [Laughing] Good job Dan!

Rome and his production staff chose this take as the call of the day, and in doing so, they support offensive, masculinist humor.[19] Dan's behavior reflects a common social practice for many men the desire to earn the homosocial approval of other, more powerful men such as Jim Rome. Rome has power over the discourse and decides that Dan's wit gives him the right to enter the homosocial space of male privilege. Yes, Dan attempts to hold the players accountable for their behavior. However, the underlying tone of Dan's comments—"crack whore" and "skanks"— are racialized and sexist.

Rome's comments on athletes receiving oral sex at a strip club references the Clinton/Lewinsky affair and the increasing media focus on sex scandals in the lives of public figures. Although the "tabloidization" of the media has many negative consequences, Lumby (2001) posited that it is not completely destructive. In fact, the increased media attention on private sexuality is because of, in part, the "feminist project of politicizing the private sphere and its attendant issues, such as sexual harassment, domestic violence, and child care" (p. 234). "Bad" tabloid style press may actually stem from some "good" political motives that have focused on issues that were once seen as merely personal. Yet the media focus on Clinton and Rome's focus on athletes at the Gold Club elides a feminist analysis of structures of power (Clinton with an intern or famous athletes with female sex workers). Hence, the entertainment value of sex scandals undermines the feminist goal of politicizing the private and reinforces "patriarchal sexuality morality: a proscription of sexual behavior outside the bounds of heterosexual monogamous marriage and the violation of that proscription by power and privileged males" (Jakobsen, 2001, p. 307).

Entertainment and Male Hegemony

How do fans themselves make sense of and respond to Rome's problematic masculinist commentary? Not surprising, many of the fans I spoke to found it humorous; "It's entertaining" was the most common response. In fact, 2 days after Rome's acerbic comments about the incidents at the Gold Club, the topic came up with George (all the names of my research participants have been changed to preserve anonymity), a 27-year-old White male, in a sports bar in Sacramento. While inquiring about what he finds appealing about Rome, he replied,

> I listen every day. He tells like it is. He lets it rip. He doesn't hold back. I like that! And he's entertaining! He pokes fun at people like the other day when Rome went off about the Ewing [Gold Club incident]. It's funny! It reminds me of locker room humor. Yes, I get a kick out of his smack talk. It's pure entertainment. Like when he trashes NASCAR and the WNBA.

His friend, John (a 26-year-old White male), echoed similar sentiments:

> Yeah, Rome is hilarious. I thought it was hilarious when he called Jim Everett, "Chris." That's what sticks in my head when someone says something about Rome. He's kind of like the Rush Limbaugh or Howard Stern of sports talk radio. Like he thinks he's God. But I don't mind it because he's entertaining. And it's a way for him to get the ratings and the market share. I admire that because I am a stockbroker. You need to market yourself to stand out. You need to be aggressive and controversial to be successful in today's society. The show makes men cocky—like the clones. I listen to it for the entertainment. And he does know his sports.

Such comments are fairly representative of the participants that I interviewed. Many men valorize Rome's "transnational business masculinity," a term coined by Connell (2000) to describe egocentrism, conditional loyalties, and a commitment to capital accumulation. In addition, as stated above, many participants found the program pleasurable because Rome is knowledgeable, authoritative, and comedic. Implied here is the notion that listening to Rome is a natural as well as an innocent pleasure. One person, when asked about the so-called harmlessness of the program, said, "If you don't like it, turn the radio dial. No one is forcing you to listen. Its just entertainment!" This is a common response to critiques of the negative effects of media culture and audience pleasure. Yet amusement is neither innate nor harmless. Pleasure is learned and closely connected to power and knowledge (Foucault, 1980b). As media scholar Douglas Kellner (1995) observed,

> We learn what to enjoy and what we should avoid. We learn when to laugh and when to cheer. A system of power and privilege thus conditions our pleasures so that we seek certain socially sanctioned pleasures and avoid others. Some people learn to laugh at racist jokes and others learn to feel pleasure at the brutal use of violence. (p. 39)

The media industry, therefore, often mobilizes pleasure around conservative ideologies that have oppressive effects on women, homosexuals, and people of color. The ideologies of hegemonic masculinity, assembled in the form of pleasure and humor, are what many of my participants found most enjoyable about *The Jim Rome Show,* including Rome's aggressive, masculinist, "expert" speech that ridicules others. Thus, many of the pleasurable aspects of the program may encourage certain male listeners to identify with the features of traditional masculinity.

Calling *The Rome Show:* Homosociality and Approval

I was also interested in what listeners of the program thought of callers' comments and if they had ever called the program themselves. Many enjoyed listening to callers such as Dan and found their commentary to constitute comical moments of the show. I was particularly interested in what calling in to the show might mean for men who subscribe to traditional masculinity.

One of the main aspects of traditional masculine homosociality involves men's striving and competing for prestige and approval within their peer groups (Wenner, 1998). This striving provides the basis for an affiliation. Many people I interviewed stated that the ultimate compliment would be for Jim Rome to approve of their take if they called. To have your call "racked" by the leading sports media personality would be a revered honor. What's more, from within the terms of hegemonic masculinity, having one's call rejected may signify a "failure" of masculinity. The following dialogue occurred between me and Fred (a 44-year-old Black male):

David: Have your called the program before?

Fred: No, I never have called. I thought about calling but I would hate to get run [Rome disconnecting the call]. Man, that would hurt! I sometimes think, "Man, I could give a good take . . . but if I call and 'suck' . . . you know . . . get run, start stuttering . . . man that would be embarrassing.

David: What would be embarrassing about getting run?

Fred: It's embarrassing 'cause it's Jim Rome. He's the man [laughing]! He's the pimp in the box![20] Man, if you get racked and are the caller of the day, you're the man!

As stated earlier in this article, some scholars believe that sports and the media expanded to create a homosocial institution that functions to assuage men's fear of feminization in current postmodern culture. Some of my interviews appear to confirm this view. When asked why *The Jim Rome Show* and other sports talk radio programs are so popular among heterosexual men, about one half of the men told me that they feel anxious and uncertain because of the changes in men's work and women's increasing presence in the public sphere. Moreover, several participants believed that sports talk provides a safe haven for men to bond and reaffirm their essential masculinity. Here's what a 27-year-old White male said in a bar in Tampa:

It's [*The Jim Rome Show*] a male bonding thing, a locker room for guys in the radio: You can't do it at work, everything's PC [politically correct] now! So the Rome Show is a last refuge for men to bond and be men. It's just in your car, Rome, and it's the audience that you can't see. I listen in the car and can let that maleness come out. I know its offensive sometimes to gays and women . . . you know . . . when men bond . . . but men need that! Romey's show gives me the opportunity to talk to other guy friends about something we share in common. And my dad listens to Romey also. So my dad and I bond also.

This comment is telling about the mixed effects of sports talk. On one hand, sports talk radio allows men to express a "covert intimacy"[21] (Messner, 1992) and shared meaning about a common subject matter. This bonding can bring forth genuine moments of closeness and should not necessarily be pathologized or seen as completely negative. However, much of the bonding is, as the interviewee stated, "offensive sometimes to gays and women." Many of the men I interviewed were speaking in a group context in the presence of other male peers. The gender displays (sexist and homophobic jokes, for example) by the men I interviewed in the homosocial space of a sports bar were interesting to observe as they confirmed Messner's (2002) point that men in groups define and solidify their boundaries through aggressive misogynistic and homophobic speech and actions. Underneath this bonding experience are homoerotic feelings that must be warded off and neutralized through joking, yelling, cursing, and demonizing anybody who does not conform to normative masculinity. Pronger (1990) argued the arena of sports is paradoxical: on one hand, sports is a primary for the expression of heterosexual masculinity, and on the other hand, there is a powerful homoerotic undercurrent subliminally present in sports. Sports radio operates similarly as an extension of this paradoxically homosocial and homoerotic space. Shields (1999), in his analysis of sports radio, stated, "It would be impossible to overstate

the degree to which sports talk radio is shadowed by the homosexual panic implicit in the fact that it consists almost entirely of a bunch of out-of-shape White men sitting around talking about Black men's buff bodies" (p. 50).

Lesbian Baiting

Sabo and Jansen (2000) suggested that radio talk shows are regular forums for men to lament and demonize lesbians or "dykes" in sport. A vivid example of lesbian baiting occurred on Jim Rome's September 7 show. Rome began the program with comments about a story in *Sports Illustrated* that claimed that ex-coach of the Detroit WNBA team, Nancy Lieberman, was rumored to have had an affair with one of her players. Consider Rome's bombastic and derisive comments about this rumor:

> Not surprisingly, Liebermen is divorced from her husband right now. I can't imagine why! I would think that your wife having a lesbian affair with one of your players would make your marriage that much stronger! Lieberman continues to deny the accusation, "I did nothing wrong. I was never in a relationship with her [the guard]. I mentored her to the best of my ability. If the media can write that Hilary Clinton's gay, write that Oprah Winfrey's gay, write that Rosie O'Donnell is gay, I guess that is the hand I am dealt with. Again, I did nothing wrong" end of quote. Wow! Look Nancy, stop the lies [Yelling]! . . . She has inferior ability. You are kicking it with her by the pool. You don't think your players are going to resent that? And leave Hilary, "Obese" Winfrey, and Rosie "O'Fat" out of this. I imagine they loved you tracking their name through this by pointing the finger at them as lesbians by the media.

This is another instance of Rome's loyalty to hegemonic masculinity. One way to interpret the above passage is that Rome is simply criticizing the unethical behavior of a coach supposedly having an affair with a player. Closer scrutiny, however, reveals that he is also marginalizing the presence of lesbians in sports.[22] Lesbians present a unique threat to the maintenance of male hegemony in sport as do women generally. The visibility of lesbians in sport contests the idea that sports are naturally a "manly" pursuit by rupturing cultural associations between masculinity and heterosexual potency. As Crosset (1995) posited, "The media industry has a stake in maintaining the image of sport as a resource for doing masculinity. It sells" (p. 126). For this reason, Rome's ridiculing of lesbians preserves male hegemony in sport.[23]

While talking to a heterosexual couple (both listened to the program and described themselves as committed sports fans), I asked the husband, Sam, what he made of Rome's sexist humor. Sam said that he thought it was ironic and should not be taken literally:

> **Sam:** I mean Rome's joking about lesbians and women is tongue in cheek. Neither he nor the clones mean it literally. I mean it's not like you are going to start gay bashing or treating your wife or daughter poorly! It's just playful satire!
>
> **Dave:** But why find that type of humor funny—humor at the expense of lesbians and women—even if it is tongue-in-cheek humor?
>
> **Sam:** I don't know, maybe men are feeling mixed . . . unsure about being all gender sensitive and politically correct.

Sam is suggesting that the humorous content of *The Jim Rome Show* provides men a space to playfully mediate the changing and tenuous nature of hegemonic masculinity; he describes Rome's misogyny as "ironic" not as sexist. However, as Jackson, Stevenson, and Brooks (2002) stated about satire and men's magazines (*Maxim* and *Loaded,* for example), "Irony allows you to have your cake and eat it. It allows you to express an unpalatable truth in a disguised form, while claiming it is not what you mean" (p. 103). Hence, irony, while making visible the ambivalence men feel toward traditional masculinity, ultimately works to mask oppressive, patriarchal aspects of this masculinity in the form of humor.

More interesting, Sam's wife Susan, a self-proclaimed feminist, fervently disagreed with her husband's views about the so-called innocence of the humor on the show:

> Okay, Jim Rome may know his sports. But he's a macho asshole like Rush or Stern. Sarcastic humor is not innocent [looking at Sam]! But I mostly hate the program because of the men I know that are fans of the show. I know some men at work who love the show, and call themselves, "clones." These guys have never grown up! It's like they are still in a fraternity! The Jim Rome Fraternity of men who never grow up! And they are all very sexist and make homophobic jokes all the time. I think Rome is dangerous and wrong.

Counterhegemonic Themes

As the above analysis illuminates, *The Jim Rome Show* reinforces male hegemony. However, a close reading of the show reveals some contradiction and fissures to hegemony. The following transcripts of the program exemplify times when the text and its voices (Jim Rome, audience members) partially subvert hegemonic masculinity and homophobia. The first example is from the show dated April 30 when the topic of bigotry was raised by Rome. Here, Rome, in his belligerent vocal style, is taking issue with the homophobic comments made by Chicago Cubs pitcher, Julian Tavares, about San Francisco Giants fans:

> Julian Tavarez, a pitcher for the Cubs said this about San Francisco Giants fans—his words not mine—"they are a bunch of a-holes and faggots." . . . You know, it would be nice to go a week without some racist or bigot comment . . . but no, Julian. Nice job Julian. . . . And here's a thought, Julian Rocker [reference to John Rocker, a pitcher who became famous for making racist and homophobic comments during an interview in *Sports Illustrated*], just because San Francisco has a significant gay population, I would be willing to bet that not everybody at a Giants game is a homosexual. Maybe. Can't document that. Just a thought . . . I feel pretty secure in saying that?

How do you come up with this garbage? I mean how do you get to the point where the proper response to heckling fans is to drop racist, anti-Semitic, or homophobic bombs on people? And even if you had those bigoted views, you would have the sense to keep it yourselves. They might realize that not everybody hates everybody else. I think there is only one solution to this problem of overcrowding in the racist frat house. We are going to have to have honorary members.

In this instance, the host clearly positions himself as antiracist and antihomophobic. This stance is noteworthy and a possible contradiction to dominant sports talk discourse. Rome uses his masculine authority to stand against the intolerance often engendered by homophobia.

Rome's comments on the subject appear to be progressive and reasonable.[24] On closer examination, however, Rome's location of the problem of homophobia in a few bigoted, intolerant individuals leaves unchallenged the larger societal structures that perpetuate heterosexism. The stance taken up by the host is rooted within liberal discourse, which reduces analysis to an individual, private endeavor (Kane & Lenskyj, 2000; Kitzinger, 1987) and forecloses any serious discussion of homophobia as structural and political issues related to power, gender, and sexuality. When Rome denounces a few athletes as "bigots," it prevents a wider analysis of the link between the institution of organized sports and its heterosexual, masculinist, and homophobic agenda. Addressing the thorny questions of sexuality, politics, power, and privilege would be a risky and bold move for *The Jim Rome Show*, as it would offer a more radical challenge to the institution of heterosexual privilege and sports.

The next seemingly subversive segment relates to an editorial letter in the May 2001 issue of *Out* magazine. In that issue, editor in chief, Lemon, stated that his boyfriend was a Major League baseball player. Lemon did not give names but hinted that the player was from an East Coast franchise. Rome and other mainstream media programs reacted quickly to the editorial. A media firestorm resulted in a rumor mill: Players, fans, owners, and sports talk radio hosts swapped guesses and anxieties over the athlete's identity.

On May 18, Rome's monologue pondered the questions, What would happen if that person's identity became public? What would it mean for baseball, gays, and lesbians in sports in general, and for the man himself? Given that Lemon's boyfriend would be the first athlete in one of the "big four" major league team sports (baseball, football, basketball, and hockey) to come out "during" his career, what effect would this have on the institution of sport? Rome decided to pose this question to one of his interview participants that day, well-respected baseball veteran Eric Davis.

> **Rome:** What would happen if a teammate of yours, or any baseball player, would come out of the closet and say, "I am gay"? What would the reaction be like? How badly would that go?
>
> **Eric:** I think it would go real bad. I think people would jump to form an opinion because everybody has an opinion about gays already. But I think it would be a very difficult situation because with us showering with each other . . . being around each other as men. Now, you're in the shower with a guy who's gay . . . looking at you . . . maybe making a pass. That's an uncomfortable situation. In society, they have never really accepted it. They want to come out. And if that's the cause fine but in sports, it would definitely raise some eyebrows. . . . I don't think it should be thrown at 25 guys saying, "yeah I am gay."
>
> [Rome changes the subject . . . no follow-up]

Rome asks a pointed question to Davis whose predictable homophobic response warrants more follow-up questions. Yet Rome shifts the subject to something less problematic, letting Davis off the hook. After Rome ends the interview, he addresses Davis's comments in another monologue:

That's [Eric Davis] a 17-year respected major league ballplayer. And I think that's a representative comment of a lot of these guys. . . . He is very highly regarded guy. This is why I asked him the question. And he answered it very honestly. He would be concerned about having a gay teammate. . . . For instance, when he's showering. Personally, I don't agree with the take. It's my personal opinion. However, I posed the question to see what the reaction would be. And this is what I have been saying since this story broke. This is why it would not be a good thing. This is why the editor of that magazine clearly was wrong and has never been in a locker-room or clubhouse. That's why it hasn't happened. Eric Davis' reaction is what you would expect. Not everybody would feel that way, but a large majority would. It would make it nearly impossible for a gay player to come out.

Here, Rome is aware of the difficulties that would occur for an openly gay ballplayer. However, he shares his opinion in the safety of his "expert" monologue, not in the presence of Eric Davis. He does not risk compromising his masculinity or his relationship with Davis by endorsing this unusually progressive stance in the presence of a famous ballplayer such as Davis. However, when a listener calls immediately after the Davis interview, Rome responds differently:

Joe: I never imagined my first take would be on gays but I had to call. Being gay, it matters to no one but gays themselves. Why don't you guys, girls or gays . . . whatever you guys are. Just do us a favor, do yourselves a favor and keep it to yourselves. I mean . . . [Rome runs the caller with the buzzer and disconnects the call]

Rome: I think that's a very convenient response—"It's an issue only because you make it an issue." I don't agree with that frankly. It's an issue because they are often persecuted against, harassed, assaulted, or killed in some cases. That's why it is an issue. They are fired from jobs, ostracized. It's not only an issue because they are making it an issue. What you are saying is keep your mouth shut, keep it in the closet; you are not accepting them for whom they are and what they are. It's not an issue because they are making it an issue. It's an issue because of people saying things like, "keep your mouth shut. . . . We don't want you around. . . . We don't want to know you people exist." That's why it's an issue because of that treatment.

Again, Rome takes a strong stance against homophobia and demonstrates a fairly nuanced appreciation of the injustices of homophobia and heterosexism. This position is worth mentioning, particularly in the context of a program referred to as "The Jungle" with an audience of mostly men steeped in traditional masculinity and for whom heterosexuality is the unquestioned norm. Rome's antihomophobic stance represents a fissure in hegemonic masculinity. It can potentially foster a new awareness in Rome's listeners and invite new voices into this important conversation about masculinity and sexuality, potentially spurring a rethinking of masculinity and sports. Cutting off the first-time caller because of his homophobic comment could be viewed as a productive accountable maneuver, which is notable because straight men do not have a rich history of holding other straight men responsible for homophobic slurs.[25]

The historic May 18 radio show generated further substantive discussion on the issue of sports and heterosexual dominance in various media sites. This included a two-part show on Jim Rome's Fox TV show, *The Last Word,* titled "The Gay Athlete." The show's guests included two out athletes: Diana Nyad and Billy Bean. The show's discussion was very rich with the host asking fairly nuanced and enlightened questions. Since this show, Rome has interviewed other athletes who have come out since they left professional sports including football players, Esera Tuaolo and David Kopay. In these interviews, Rome asked perceptive questions about the prevalence of homophobia in male sports and applauds their courage in coming out. ESPN also addressed the same topic and conducted a poll that showed that a substantial number of sports fans would have no problem with a gay athlete ("Outside the Lines," 2001). What's more, the *Advocate* magazine published an article by cultural critic Toby Miller (2001) where he argued that the media firestorm generated by Brendan Lemon's article could potentially create a moment "for unions and owners of the big four to issue a joint statement in support, to show that queers are a legitimate part of the big leagues" (p. 3).

Another significant moment occurred on the May 18 show when Rome read the "huge e-mail of the day," usually reserved for the nastiest comments. Rome chose an e-mail from "Mike from San Gabriel," who wrote the following:

Jim, Eric Davis is perhaps the quintessential baseball player/human being who has overcome tremendous odds in battling and overcoming cancer and physical challenges. He's faced and battled a disease that strikes fear into the heart, and understands that life must be taken a day at a time.

Yet, despite this brush with death and the clarity in some areas that it brings, Eric's reaction to your question regarding baseball players' reactions to knowing that a teammate is gay spoke volumes, and none of it particularly heartening. Eric's fear (speaking for the average baseball player, that is) that a gay player may be checking him out in the shower is representative of the stereotypes foisted upon homosexuals in our society, and in baseball in particular. I find it a little sad and ironic that an African-American player would espouse a viewpoint—fear, ignorance and intolerance—that for much of baseball's history had kept some of the best players in history—African-Americans—out of the Major Leagues.

Perhaps, though, baseball may play a progressive role in our society once again. Like it did in helping to erase the "color" barrier in the 1950s, so too it may be able to play a part in fostering tolerance and acceptance in society today. I think it's going to take someone the stature of a Jackie Robinson from the gay community to help allay the fears of baseball players, and in turn our society, before progress can be made. Until then, gay baseball players will be relegated to a shadowy world of fear and intolerance once reserved for African-Americans and other minorities.

Mike

Mike's comments caught the attention of the editor of Outsports.com, Mike Buzinski, who commented that Mike's e-mail of the day was "well-written" and "gay-positive." In the Web site article titled "Give the Media Good Marks: Coverage of Closeted Gay Baseball Player was Positive and Non-Judgmental," Buzinski (2001) went on to write:

Lesbian basketball fans and gay Major League Baseball players have been all the rage in the sports media the past two weeks. This alone is unprecedented. The mainstream media barely acknowledges the existence of gay athletes or fans. Having the issue raised in, among others, *The New York Times, The Los Angeles Times,* Internet discussion boards and sports talk radio is all to the good. Even better is that, overall, the coverage was balanced, informative and non-homophobic. (p. 1)

Later in the same article he refers to Jim Rome:

The tenor of talk radio (at least when I was listening) was not as Neanderthal as one might have expected. Jim Rome, the guy who called Jim Everett "Chris" a few years ago, has been very enlightened on the gay issue, saying it's nobody's business, while at the same time acknowledging the difficulties an "out" athlete might face. (p. 2)

Rome's stance against homophobia is groundbreaking and historic in sports talk radio.

Ultimately, however, the perspective articulated by "Mike" and supported by Rome once again confines the meaning of homophobia in sports to the intolerant or ignorant behavior of individuals and locates the responsibility for changing that behavior in gay players and/or Black athletes, who, after all, should "understand" about discrimination. Mike's letter and Rome's comments also innocently presume that African Americans have achieved equality in sports and in the larger society. This presumption, common in sports talk radio discourse, is informed by what Goldberg (1998) referred to as a "feel-good colorblindness of sports talk hosts" (p. 221).[26] Queer scholars have discussed how sexuality is often produced through the process of racialization (Gopinath, 1997; Munoz, 1999). By ignoring the intersection of race and sexuality, Rome saves sports from a more biting and transgressive critique, one that would expose the deep, institutional sexism and racism in sports. Instead, Rome refocuses the audience on the simple metaphors of sports—bad guy bigots and heroic gay athletes—rather than the larger discursive environment of sports and media that keep White, heterosexual masculinity at its center, thereby systematically excluding and oppressing all "others," including women, racial minorities, and gays.

Hence, there are contradictions in, and limitations to, Rome's "progressive" stance on sexuality. His comments espouse a liberal discourse that views homophobia as fearful behavior enacted by intolerant individuals.[27] Take, for example, Rome's careless dismissal of the caller who wants gays to stay in the closet. Although the caller's comments certainly reflect a homophobic viewpoint, Rome locates the blame in the caller as an individual, as if the caller is one of just a few, unenlightened bigots. A closer look at Rome's own discursive practices on the show, including homophobic references, jokes, and name calling, all point to the same homosocial fears that motivate the caller's concern. Perhaps the caller's comments are better understood as a reasonable (but repugnant) apprehension of gays and lesbians based on the widely shared perception that out gays and lesbians challenge heteronormativity and patriarchy. As Card (1995) pointed out, hatred and hostility toward homosexuals is not a pathological disorder of a few individuals. Rather, homophobia is a pervasive affliction that is not isolated in its effects.

Also embedded in this discourse is the assumption that the right, best way for gays and lesbians to live is out. Almost all parties in this dialogue refer to coming out, including Mike, Rome, Eric Davis, and the editor of *Out* magazine. As Gopinath (1997) observed, the "coming out narrative" assumes that people who have same-sex desire need to reveal their sexuality and become visible and also presupposes a universal gay subject. Coming out is viewed by Rome as a contested privilege, a "right," and the natural and logical next step in achieving "health" and an "authentic life." This identitarian narrative is supported by many people and institutions, including the mental health industry, straight allies, and in particular, by the dominant discourses of the urban gay community.

The Jim Rome Show suggests that coming out signifies freedom and egalitarianism. Although this stance can provide a very powerful option for persons who identify as gay or lesbian, coming out can also be another standard for sexual expression that people may feel obligated to meet. In addition, privileging the coming-out narrative can unwittingly work in the service of heteronormativity. Coming out requires that a person claim an identity as gay or lesbian. Foucault (1980a) suggested that claiming a fixed identity as homosexual may be personally liberating but unintentionally relocates heterosexuality in the privileged center. Because straights are not required to come out and claim a heterosexual identity, heterosexuality is assumed to be natural and normal. Although Rome and his callers discuss homosexuality, heterosexuality is never interrogated or discussed hence remaining an unmarked and naturalized category.

It is important to note that Rome's interviewing of out athletes such as Billy Bean and David Kopay is a unique outcome in the world of heteronormative sports. To allow visibility of the gay athletes cannot be taken lightly in terms of its potential ramifications. Yet it is equally important to ask which athletes are allowed to become visible? What is their social location? How is their sexuality represented? Virtually all the gay athletes who have been on *The Jim Rome Show* are White males (an exception is Esera Tuaolo who is Samoan) who define homosexuality as an essentialist identity. Foucault (1980b) contended that although visibility opens up some new political possibilities, it is also "a trap" because it creates new forms of surveillance, discipline, and limits. Sure, Bean and Kopay are given space to discuss their experience as a gay athlete, however it must be contained within a very limited, private discourse. Scholar Duggan (2001) claimed that much of the recent visibility of gays and lesbians are framed within a post-Stonewall, identitarian, private discourse. She referred to this discourse as homonormativity—"a politics that does not contest dominant heteronormative assumptions and institutions, but upholds and sustains them, while promising the possibility of a demobilized gay constituency and a privatized, depoliticized gay culture anchored in domesticity and consumption" (p. 179). According to Duggan, homonormativity is privatizing much as heteronormativity is, and each lends support to the other. As much as Rome's recognition of gays in the sporting world is noteworthy, it is very much contained with a homonormative frame that reproduces the sex and gender binary. Hence, Rome's show although it may be influenced by traditional gay and lesbian identity politics; it is not a queer space. Athletes, including women who perform a more transgressive, non-normative sexuality, are invisible in sports radio.

Don't Ask Don't Tell

Sexuality and sports was again the subject of discussion of Rome's show on August 29. On the program that day, Rome was interviewing heavyweight boxers Lennox Lewis and Hasim Rahman about their upcoming title fight. During the interview, a war of words broke out because Rahman questioned Lewis's heterosexuality. Lewis became quite perturbed stating, "I am not gay! I'm 100% a woman's man." This verbal conflict continued later that day on an ESPN interview program. During the ESPN taping, a physical scuffle broke out between the two boxers as they

pushed each other and rolled around on the ground. The following day, Rome discussed the incident, and the subsequent brawl on ESPN on his program focusing mainly on the question of whether the incident was staged to hype the fight. Rome argued that the harsh feelings between Rahman and Lewis were "genuine," that the incident was not staged. Yet in focusing on the theatrics or authenticity of the scuffle, Rome failed to address the inappropriateness of Rahman's homophobic slur.

The host did make an attempt, however, to address some of his callers' heterosexist/homophobic comments in the wake of the incident. On the August 30 radio show, many clones called pronouncing that Lewis' strong reaction to Rahman's assertion proves that Lewis is gay. Hence, homophobic gossip questioning Lewis' sexuality became the spotlight of the talk. In this next excerpt, Rome criticizes Rahman's allegations and the callers' fixations with Lewis' sexual orientation:

> Personally, I don't care. It's nobody's business what that guy [Lewis] does outside of the ring. It's nobody's business but Lennox's. I don't care. But apparently, he does. He says he is not. I don't care whether he is or isn't. I tell you what—HE'S NOT GOING TO STAND FOR ANYBODY SAYING HE IS. He made that pretty clear. I don't think Rahman should have said what he said. He should not have said quote, "That was gay of you to go to court to get me to fight." But, I tried to point out to Lennox that he's not calling you a homosexual, he's saying "it was gay to go to court." Lennox didn't want to hear it. He didn't make the distinction. And yes, it is a little peculiar that he got that hot that quickly, but I don't really care.

Here again, Rome takes up a "tolerant" position by asserting that sexual orientation should not matter and gossip about Lewis's sexuality is improper. Yet, by stating that sexual orientation makes no difference to him, Rome is once again invoking a liberal, privatized argument that contradicts his previous intolerance of the same "don't ask, don't tell position" held by a caller. In addition, his comments mirror the "don't ask, don't tell policy" on gays in the military. Queer theory scholar McWhorter (1999) critiqued this personalized approach to homophobia:

> When tolerant people insist that my homosexuality doesn't matter to them, they say in effect that my homosexuality is not a social or cultural phenomenon at all but rather some sort of brute quality inherent in me and totally disconnected from them; they say in effect that my homosexuality is a kind of object that is obviously there but has nothing to do with me as a person. Thus, this "tolerance" in the final analysis amounts basically to the same stance as that taken by reductivistic homophobes. (p. 3)

In summary, Rome's position of tolerance is praiseworthy. Yet his stance is less than revolutionary if one takes critiques such as McWhorter's into account. Rome's discourse replicates essentialism—the idea that sexuality can be reduced to some biological essence—an ideology that replicates heternormativity by failing to examine sexuality in a historical, social, and political context.

Many of the people I interviewed in sports bars appreciated that Rome and his show addressed larger, social issues. The overwhelming majority of interviewees respected and agreed with Rome's opinion or takes on the issues of gender and sexuality. For many, the show was the main forum for them to discuss and reflect on wider, political matters. The following is a conversation I had with Nick, a 26-year-old Latino male in Fresno that reflects the dominant discourse of don't ask, don't tell:

Nick: Romey is like a sports sociologist with humor. He's entertaining. He's really into the gay issue. He's an advocate for gay rights. I respect him for it but because he speaks his mind.

David: Why do you respect him for that?

Nick: Personally, I don't care what gays do. But it's not cool that gays have to stay in the closet. But I don't think gays in team sports won't work because so many athletes are macho and homophobic.

Nick's comments are fairly representative of the conversations I had with fellow fans. All 18 people I interviewed respected and agreed with Rome's tolerant position on the issue of homosexuality and sport—a position, although progressive in the context of sports talk radio, is limited because it ignores larger structures that promote heterosexism. Although all made it clear that they were heterosexual, my interviewees indicate that some men who listen to sports talk radio are somewhat open-minded on the issue of homosexuality and sports.

I don't know if this attitude is representative of the larger Rome audience. It may not be, because *The Jim Rome Show* Web site (www.jimrome.com) contained 16 pages in which self-described clones passionately opposed Rome's antihomophobic takes. Here's an example of the deep-seated homophobia expressed on the Web site message board. It reveals how those who subscribe to dominant masculinity feel threatened by Rome's position:

> My 13-year-old was working with me at my business today, and we were listening to Rome when he takes off in his "gay defender" mode. My son looks at me and says, "Dad, what's wrong with this guy? He thinks homosexuality is normal?" Well, clue-in Romey—it IS wrong: morally, and in every other way. Why you pander to this group is beyond comprehension.

There were other responses on the fan message board that questioned Rome's genuineness stating that his progressive stance on homophobia was primarily motivated as a marketing strategy to stir up controversy and recruit new listeners. Some on the message board found Rome's stance to be hypocritical as Rome himself has made homophobic references in the past. One of the men I interviewed also stated that Rome's position on homosexuality was hypocritical:

> A contradiction! He's totally a hypocrite. Here is a so-called gay advocate on one breath and in

the next breath, he refers to the LPGA as the "dyke" tours. And remember, he's the guy who got famous for calling Jim Everett, "Chrissie." Plus, he panders to athletes and celebrities such as Jay Mohr. I was listening to Romey in May when Mohr called Mike Hampton [a baseball pitcher] a "gay Curious George." Rome laughed at this and lauded Mohr's brilliant humor. He's not progressive. If he were progressive, he would confront homophobes. He's just another macho dude who's using social issues and controversy to gain market share, profits, and more radio affiliates.

Female Listeners

Because many of Rome's comments were sexist, I was also interested in finding out how women listeners experience the show. In addition to Susan, I interviewed Joan, a 31-year-old White woman hanging out in a bar in Las Vegas. Diverging from Susan's opinion, Joan believed Rome to be progressive on gender and sexual issues, In fact, she was the only person I interviewed who actually called the program. Here's part of our dialogue at a bar in Las Vegas:

Joan: I actually called. My voice was heard. He was cool. He didn't bag me. I didn't speak the clone language. I am me! I called to state that violence should stay in hockey—hockey is not hockey without violence—I feel very strong about that.

David: What was cool about Rome?

Joan: He's cool to women. He's not sexist or homophobic. He respected my call. I know sexist guys. I have lived with them. My ex-husband was one. He was very violent and mean. I lived in a bad environment. I left him and moved to Vegas. I no longer will be around men who are offensive or demeaning to women.

David: And you don't experience that from Rome, him saying sexist comments?

Joan: No, I don't feel that from him. I don't see him as demeaning to women. If he were a sexist, I wouldn't listen to his show.

Joan's comments could be seen as firmly grounded in postfeminist discourse that replicates hegemonic masculinity.[28] Her comments advocate continued violence in hockey, and she does not experience Rome as sexist despite Rome's repeated misogynistic references on the show. Joan presents herself as "one of the guys" and replicates a patriarchal view of the show and its contents. Her response is further indication the listeners of *The Jim Rome Show,* dependent on their social location, read the text in multiple ways.

Conclusion

At this historical moment when hegemonic masculinity has been partially destabilized by global economic changes and by gay liberation and feminist movements, the sports media industry seemingly provides a stable and specific view of masculinity grounded in heterosexuality, aggression, individuality, and the objectification of women. *The Jim Rome Show,* with its aggressive, male-talking host and masculinist themes, is located within this hypermasculine space.

However, my analysis indicates that *The Jim Rome Show* is not a simple, completely obnoxious site of monolithic masculine discourse. Rather, the show represents a complex, paradoxical, ambivalent, and polyvalent text. *The Jim Rome Show* fosters a mix of masculine styles, identities, and discourses, ranging from highly misogynistic to liberal humanist. My article notes some of the discontinuous and contradictory moments that disrupt hegemonic masculinity and heterosexual dominance; it considers Jim Rome's antihomophobic stance to be somewhat progressive given the context and hypermasculine discursive space of sports talk radio.

In my effort to recognize the complexity and contradictory elements of the text, I suggest that the antihomophobic tenor of the radio program, although laudable, is informed by a liberal-humanist approach that elides substantive interrogation and political discussion of the structures of heterosexual domination. Moreover, Rome's examination of homophobia focuses entirely on sexuality and sexual identity; issues of race fall by the wayside, making his analysis monothematic. Whiteness and hetero-normativity stay at the privileged center.

It is also important to note that *The Jim Rome Show* is a highly popular, commercialized radio program owned by a giant corporation (Premiere Radio Network) that privileges profits, niche marketing, and audience ratings over challenging oppressive practices and institutions. Consequently, Rome's show tends toward a more conservative "reproductive agency" (identification with corporate consumerism that stabilizes oppressive social institutions) than a more radical or transgressive "resistant agency" (Dworkin & Messner, 1999).

My audience analysis suggests that *The Jim Rome Show* may, in the end, stabilize the institution of heteronormativity. I showed how the textual content greatly influences the ways audience members understand the show's messages. The participants interviewed generally held conservative opinions about gender and sexuality that conform to the hegemonic masculine ideal. However, most of my interview participants did support Jim Rome's antihomophobic posture. Thus, further research should explore whether the text helps to transform the beliefs of men who have not yet acquired a sincere commitment to anti-homophobia.

In addition, future research needs to investigate how gays and lesbians may experience this discursive space. *The Jim Rome Show* has been specifically created for heterosexuals to publicly discuss sports. Even if Rome is sometimes anti-homophobic, how does this space feel for a gay or lesbian person? Even if Rome defends gays (and usually not lesbians), is his show a "safe haven" for queers? Does *The Jim Rome Show* simply re-create hierarchical power relations or is it a democratic site that opens up the potential for achieving real social justice? These questions are critical for future feminist inquiries into radio sports talk programs. Moreover, how has the discourse of the Rome show and other sports radio

programs changed since September 11, 2001? Has the discourse become more nationalistic?

It is also crucial to consider the role of pleasure in listening to sports talk radio while steering clear of the problems associated with uncritical, moralistic, and/or celebratory accounts of popular culture. I myself enjoy listening to the program even though I am aware of the sexist, homophobic themes. Pleasure is a double-edged sword: It provides opportunities for relaxation, bonding, but also makes the sexist and homophobic content seem more innocent and easier to dismiss or laugh off. Hence pleasure cannot be valorized per se but needs to be critically examined to determine whether the pleasure of a given moment in the text of the program is progressive, emancipatory, or destructive.

Regardless, it is important for critical media scholars and activists to leverage and build on those moments in the text that disrupt hegemonic masculinity and heterosexism. McKay, Messner, and Sabo (2000) suggested that there is a tendency for critical media studies and sports sociology to overemphasize negative outcomes for men in sports. They argued that this overemphasis on negative outcomes leads to a simplistic view of the incongruities in talk and commentary about sports.

Following this thesis, I think it is important for critical scholars and activists to be vigilant in noticing and promoting the possibilities for disruption and resistance within dominant media sport structures. The antihomophobic tenor of *The Jim Rome Show* is an opportunity to address heterosexual dominance in sports. Yes, Rome's radio program reveals the limits of liberal discourse, however, his progressive stance may be a starting point to influence men who are deeply embedded in hegemonic masculinity. Remember, Rome was not built in a day! Rome likely has more influence with many men who are recruited by the specifications of dominant masculinity than academic scholars and political activists. In other words, a radio community of men discussing sports may not be just simply reproducing hegemony—there is more complexity in this discursive space, including opportunities for men to engage in relationship building and to reinvent masculinity. Perhaps Haag's (1996) suggestion that sports talk discourse may serve as a blueprint for civic discourse has some merit here.

Although Rome's radio program is deeply embedded within corporate consumerism and tends more toward a more reproductive than resistant agency, it remains a potential channel for challenging hegemonic masculinity and homophobia. The contradictions, fissures, and ambivalences within the discursive space of *The Jim Rome Show* should not be trivialized. It is through those contradictory spaces that Rome's show may have potential for generating new conversations about masculinity and sexuality. Although *The Jim Rome Show* is situated within commercial culture, it does offer heterosexual men a rare public space for dialogue on homophobia and contemporary masculinity. Furthermore, I would assert that this discursive space is occupied in a multiplicity of ways, not all of which are immediately colonized by consumer capitalism. Hence, my study neither uncritically celebrates the show nor views the show in purely negative terms as a backlash against feminism and gay rights. Rather *The Jim Rome Show* offers a potential site to change gender relationships and identities, while concurrently reinscribing particular forms of traditional masculinity.

Appendix

In general, I asked the interviewed audience members the following questions:

1. How often do you listen to *The Jim Rome Show*?
2. What do you like most about the show?
3. What do you like least about the show?
4. What do you think the show means to most men who listen regularly to the program?
5. Why is the show popular with many men?
6. What is your view on Rome's position on various social issues?
7. Have you ever called the program?
8. What do you think of most of the takes of the callers?
9. What is your age? Race or ethnic group? Sex? Sexual orientation? Occupation if any? Sport participation?
10. What other television and radio programs do you consume?

Acknowledgments

Funding for this project was provided by a research grant from the Gay Lesbian Alliance Against Defamation (GLAAD), Center for Study of Media and Society. Permission granted by GLAAD to reprint/publish this article. Special thanks to Van Cagle, Kent Ono, Laura Grindstaff, Susan Kaiser, Gayatri Gopinath, Judith Newton, and Debora Nylund for their helpful suggestions as this article developed. I am also grateful to Van Cagle and GLAAD for their support of this project.

Notes

1. According to Arbitron ratings, *The Jim Rome Show* is ranked eighth in radio talk audience share. The most popular radio talk hosts, according to the ratings, are Rush Limbaugh and Dr. Laura. All three shows, Jim Rome, Rush Limbaugh, and Dr. Laura, are owned by Premiere Radio Network, a company worth U.S. $330 million dollars. These statistics are from Premiere Radio's Web site: www.premiereradio.com.

2. "Run" refers to the host hanging up on the caller.

3. Jim Rome's Web site (www.jimrome.com) has a 24-page glossary (known as "city jungle gloss") that lists his terms and the definitions. For instance," Jungle Dweller" refers to a frequent telephone contributor to Rome's show. "Bang" means to answer phone calls. "Bugeater" refers to a Nebraskan who is a fan of the Nebraska Cornhuskers' college football team.

4. The comment "What will Rome say next?" has been applied several times to listeners of the *Howard Stern Show,* for those who enjoy and despise it. This is (even) mentioned in the Howard Stern autobiographical movie, *Private Parts.*

5. Rome's relationship with his caller, similar to most talk-show power relations between caller and host, is quite asymmetrical. Hutchby (1996) in his study of the discourse in talk radio stated that although the host has an array of discursive and institutional strategies available to him or her to keep the upper hand, occasionally callers have some resources available to resist the host's powerful strategies. Hence, Hutchby argued that power is not a monolithic feature of talk radio. Hutchby's argument does not appear to work with *The Jim Rome Show* as callers hardly ever confront Rome's authority. Rather, Rome's callers want his approval.

6. Deregulation was championed by then FCC chairman Mark Fowler who sold it as a form of media populism and civic participation. However, this public marketing campaign masked increased economic consolidation and increased barriers to entry into this market for all but very powerful media conglomerates such as Infinity Broadcasting and Premiere Radio. Commenting about the success of conservative White male talk radio due to deregulation of the 1980s, Douglas (2002) claimed that Reaganism was successful by "selling the increased concentration of wealth as a move back toward democracy" (p. 491).

7. In 1960, there were just two radio stations in the United States that were dedicated to talk radio formats (Goldberg, 1998).

8. The other significant deregulatory move in the 1980s was the abandonment of the Fairness Doctrine, which the FCC announced it would no longer enforce. The doctrine required stations to offer access to air alternative opinions when controversial issues were discussed. The goal of the doctrine was to promote a balance of views. Opponents of the doctrine, including Fowler and Reagan, felt it inhibited freedom of speech. Stations, they argued, avoided giving airtime to opinionated individuals because of the requirement to broadcast competing points of view. Unrestricted by the Fairness Doctrine's mandate for balance, Limbaugh and a legion of ultraconservative imitators took off the gloves and revived the financial state of AM radio.

9. The largest sports station in the United States based in New York. WFAN is also the largest ad-billing radio station in the United States.

10. These popular hosts are known for being rude and abrupt to their callers. If the host disagrees with the callers' opinion, they are likely to be disconnected by being buzzed, flushed down the toilet, or run over by a bus.

11. The idea that contemporary masculinity is in crisis is an arguable point. Beynon (2002) suggested that it is misleading to assume that the current alleged crisis is new and unique to current times; that there are many historical periods when masculinity appeared to be in crisis. In fact, he argued that crisis is constitutive of masculinity itself.

12. Mariscal also disagreed with Haag's stating the national syndicated programs such as *The Jim Rome Show* undermines the regionalism of sports radio.

13. In a recent interview in *Sports Illustrated,* Rome stated he regrets the Everett interview and has matured into a well-reasoned interviewer. In the article, Rome stated that he was "wiser" because of being married and having a child (Deitsch, 2003).

14. I invited several women to be interviewed about *The Jim Rome Show.* However, only two stated that they listened to the show.

15. The local Sacramento sports talk affiliate runs a commercial that says, "Belly up to the bar and pour yourself a cold one! You are listening to your sports bar on the radio."

16. It is important to note that my coding scheme was based on my interpretation of what constitutes hegemony and counterhegemony; it is not an objective measure.

17. The court in Atlanta was prosecuting the owner of the Gold Club for mob connections and other illegalities. This event received a great deal of media attention.

18. Ewing and Motumbo are Black men. The caller of the day, Dan, is implying that they are unattractive men. Dan's disdainful "smack talk" could be understood to reproduce racist representations of Black athletes.

19. As a sidebar, Cook (2001) challenged the common notion that radio talk shows are a natural two-way dialogue between the caller and host that allow the caller to "freely air their point of view" (p. 62). The production process reveals that it is a complex, mediated process that constrains the dialogue through a range of in-studio control techniques. These hidden maneuvers include off-air talk decisions on what gets included on the program, what gets omitted, and time control cues. Cook argued that examining the complex relational politics in radio talk is important to ex-

amine to contest its negative power and influence.

20. The term *pimp in the box* refers to Rome's "pimping" of NHL hockey in Los Angeles during 1992–1993 when the Los Angeles Kings made it to the Stanley Cup Finals. Rome's show was the first in Los Angeles to actively talk about hockey on sports talk stations and book hockey players as guests. This made national news as Wayne Gretzky was to appear on the show following every playoff game the Kings played that season to the point where Gretzky thanked Rome during a televised interview after the Kings won Game 7 of the Western Conference Finals to advance to the Finals. After thanking Kings management and players he said, "To my friend Jim Rome, we've got the karma going."

21. Messner (1992) defined "covert intimacy" as doing things together rather than mutual talk about inner lives.

22. Rome has consistently "bashed" the LPGA and the WNBA, sports with lesbian visibility.

23. Rome has a history of marginalizing lesbian athletes including Martina Navratilova, referring to her as "Martin" because of embodying qualities that are usually associated with maleness, such as strength, authority, and independence. In her book, *Female Masculinity*, Halberstam (1998) made a compelling argument for a more flexible taxonomy of masculinity, including not only biological men, who have historically held the power in society, but also women who perform a traditionally masculine persona. Halberstam argued "a major step toward gender parity, and one that has been grossly overlooked, is the cultivation of female masculinity" (p.3). Utilizing Halberstam's framework, Heywood and Dworkin (2003) suggested that athletes who perform female masculinity, such as Navratilova, create fissures in the heterosexual male preserve of sport.

24. When I refer to Rome in this section, I am referring not to Rome, the individual person. Rather, I am referring to Rome's discourse.

25. However, it is important to note that Rome asserts his authority over a person with less power—a first-time caller. Rome doesn't take this strong a stance with Eric Davis, a high-status person who likely has more influence within the sports world. This textual example reveals the power relations of talk radio; hosts and famous athletes have more authority than callers.

26. Goldberg (1998) and Mariscal (1999) suggested that sports talk radio is more racialized than any other radio format.

27. Mariscal (1999), in his analysis of *The Jim Rome Show,* noted Rome's contradictory stance on race. At times, Rome is very progressive and antiracist, and other times Mariscal noted that Rome engaged in derogatory stereotypes toward Latinos. Mariscal stated that Rome's inconsistent stance on "racially charged topics reveal[s] the basic slippage in liberal discourse," (p. 116) a situation where citizens engage in post-civil rights speech that "slides easily from tepid antiracism to the reproduction of deeply ingrained racist clichés" (p. 116).

28. Postfeminism refers to the idea that women have already achieved full equality with men (Humm, 1995).

References

Ang, I. (1996). *Living room wars: Rethinking media audiences for a postmodern world.* New York: Routledge.

Armstrong, C. B., & Rubin, A. M. (1989). Talk radio as interpersonal communication. *Journal of Communication. 39*(2), 84–93.

Beynon, J. (2002). *Masculinities and culture.* Philadelphia: Open University Press.

Brod, H. (Ed.). (1987). *The making of masculinities.* Boston: Unwin Hyman.

Buzinski, J. (2000, July 13). *Week in review.* Available at www.outsports.com/

Buzinski, J. (2001, May 20). *Give the media good marks: Coverage of closeted gay baseball player was positive and non-judgmental.* Available at www.outsports.com/

Card, C. (1995). *Lesbian choices.* New York: Columbia University Press.

Collie, A. J. (2001, August 8). Rome rants. *American Way,* pp. 50–54, 56–57.

Connell, R. W. (1990). An iron man: The body and some contradictions of hegemonic masculinity. In M. A. Messner & D. F. Sabo (Eds.), *Sport, men, and the gender order* (pp. 83–95). Champaign, IL: Human Kinetics.

Connell, R. W. (2000). *The men and the boys.* Berkeley: University of California Press.

Cook, J. (2001). Dangerously radioactive: The plural vocalities of radio talk. In C. Lee & C. Poynton

(Eds.), *Culture and text: Discourse and methodology in social research and cultural studies* (pp. 59–80). New York: Rowman & Littlefield.

Crosset, T. W. (1995). *Outsiders in the clubhouse: The world of women's professional golf.* Albany: State University of New York Press.

Deitsch, R. (2003, May 12). Under review: Rome returning. *Sports Illustrated, 98,* 28.

Douglas, S. J. (2002). Letting the boys be boys: Talk radio, male hysteria, and political discourse in the 1980s. In M. Hilmes & J. Loviglio (Eds.), *Radio reader: Essays in the cultural history of radio* (pp. 485–504). New York: Routledge.

Duggan, L. (2001). The new homonormativity: The sexual politics of neoliberalism. In R. Castronovo & D. D. Nelson (Eds.), *Materalizing democracy: Toward a revitalized cultural politics* (pp. 175–194). Durham, NC: Duke University Press.

Dworkin, S. L., Messner, M.A. (1999). Just do what? Sports, bodies, gender. In J. Lorber, M. M. Ferree, & B. Hess (Eds.), *Revisioning gender* (pp. 341–364). Thousand Oaks, CA: Sage.

Dworkin, S. L. & Wachs, F. L. (2000). The morality/manhood paradox: Masculinity, sports, and the media. In M. A. McKay, M. A. Messner, & D. F. Sabo (Eds.), *Masculinities, gender relations, and sport* (pp. 47–66). Thousand Oaks, CA: Sage.

Farred, G. (2000). Cool as the other side of the pillow: How ESPN's Sportscenter has changed television sports talk. *Journal of Sport & Social Issues, 24*(2), 96–117.

Foucault, M. (1980a). *The history of sexuality: An introduction.* New York: Vintage.

Foucault, M. (1980b). *Power/knowledge: Selected interviews and other writings, 1972–1977.* (Colin Gordon, Ed. & Trans.). New York: Pantheon.

Ghosh, C. (1999, February 22). A guy thing: Radio sports talk shows. *Forbes,* p. 55.

Goldberg, D. T. (1998). Call and response: Sports, talk radio, and the death of democracy. *Journal of Sport & Social Issues, 22*(2), 212–223.

Gopinath, G. (1997). Nostalgia, desire, and diaspora: South Asian sexualities in motion. *Positions, 5*(2), 467–489.

Grindstaff, L. (1994). Abortion and the popular press: Mapping media discourse from *Roe* to *Webster.* In T. G. Jelen & M. A. Chandler (Eds.), *Abortion politics in the United States and Canada: Studies in public opinion* (pp. 58–88). Westport, CT: Praeger.

Haag, P. (1996). The 50,000 watt sports bar: Talk radio and the ethic of the fan. *South Atlantic Quarterly, 95*(2), 453–470.

Halberstam, J. (1998). *Female masculinity.* Durham, NC: Duke University Press.

Hare-Mustin, R. T. (1994). Discourses in the mirrored room: A postmodern analysis of therapy. *Family Process, 33,* 19–35.

Heywood, L., & Dworkin, S. L. (2003). *Built to win: The female athlete as cultural icon.* Minneapolis: University of Minnesota Press.

Hodgson, E. (1999, August 18). King of smack. *Fastbreak—The Magazine of the Phoenix Suns,* pp. 1–5.

Horrocks, R., & Campling, J. (1994). *Masculinity in crisis: Myths, fantasies and realities.* New York: Routledge.

Humm, M. (1995). *The dictionary of feminist theory* (2nd ed.). New York: Prentice Hall.

Hutchby, I. (1996). *Confrontation talk: Arguments, asymmetries, and power on talk radio.* Mahwah, NJ: Lawrence Erlbaum.

Jackson, P., Stevenson, N., & Brooks, K. (2002). *Making sense of men's magazines.* London: Polity.

Jakobsen, J. R. (2001). He has wronged America and women: Clinton's sexual conservatism. In L. Berlant & L. Duggan (Eds.), *Our Monica, ourselves: The Clinton affair and the national interest* (pp. 291–314). New York: New York University Press.

Jenkins, H. (1992). *Textual poachers: Television fans and participatory culture.* New York: Routledge.

Jhally, S. (1989). Cultural studies and the sports/media complex. In L. W. Wenner (Ed.), *Media, sports, and society* (pp. 70–93). Newbury Park, CA: Sage.

Kane, M. J., & Lenskyj, H. J. (2000). Media treatment of female athletes: Issues of gender and sexualities. In L. W. Wenner (Ed.), *Mediasport* (pp. 186–201). New York: Routledge.

Kellner, D. (1995). *Media culture: Cultural studies, identity, and politics between the modern and postmodern.* New York: Routledge.

Kimmel, M. (1994). Masculinity as homophobia. In H. Brod & M. Kaufman (Eds.), *Theorizing masculinities* (pp. 119–141). Thousand Oaks, CA: Sage.

Kitzinger, C. (1987). *The social construction of lesbianism.* Newbury Park, CA: Sage.

Lumby, C. (2001). The President's penis: Entertaining sex and power. In L. Berlant & L. Duggan (Eds.), *Our Monica, ourselves: The Clinton affair and the national interest* (pp. 225–236). New York: New York University Press.

Mariscal, J. (1999). Chicanos and Latinos in the jungle of sports talk radio. *Journal of Sport & Social Issues, 23*(1), 111–117.

McKay, M. A., Messner, M. A., & Sabo, D. F. (Eds.). (2000). *Masculinities, gender relations, and sport.* Thousand Oaks, CA: Sage.

McWhorter, L. (1999). *Bodies and pleasures: Foucault and the politics of sexual normalization.* Bloomington: Indiana University Press.

Messner, M. A. (1992). *Power at play: Sports and the problem of masculinity.* Boston: Beacon.

Messner, M. A. (2002). *Taking the field: Women, men, and sports.* Minneapolis: University of Minnesota Press.

Messner, M. A., Dunbar, M., & Hunt, D. (2000). The televised sports manhood formula. *Journal of Sport & Social Issues, 24*(4), 380–394.

Miller, T. (2001, June). Out at the ballgame. *Advocate,* pp. 1–3.

Munoz, J. E. (1999). *Disidentifications. Queers of color and the performance of politics.* Minneapolis: University of Minnesota Press.

Outside the lines: Homophobia and sports. (2001, May 31). ESPN.com. Available at http://espn.go.com/otl

Page, B. I., & Tannenbaum, J. (1996). Populistic deliberation and talk radio. *Journal of Communication, 46*(2), 33–53.

Pronger, B. (1990). *The arena of masculinity: Sports, homosexuality, and the meaning of sex.* New York: St. Martin's.

Roedieger, D. (1996). White looks: Hairy apes, true stories, and Limbaugh's laughs. *Minnesota Review, 47,* 41–52

Sabo, D. F., & Jansen, S. C. (2000). Prometheus unbound: Constructions of masculinity in the sports media. In L. W. Wenner (Ed.), *Mediasport* (pp. 202–217). New York: Routledge.

Schiller, H. (1989). *Culture, Inc.* New York: Oxford University Press.

Shields, D. (1999). *Black planet: Facing race during an NBA season.* New York: Crown.

Sports Illustrated Editors. (1994, April). The fall of Rome. *Sports Illustrated, 80,* 14.

Trujillo, N. (1994). *The meaning of Nolan Ryan.* College Station, TX: Texas A & M University Press.

Trujillo, N. (1996). Hegemonic masculinity on the mound: Media representations of Nolan Ryan and the American sports culture. In S. K. Foss (Ed.), *Rhetorical criticism: Exploration and practices* (pp. 181–203). Prospect Heights, IL: Waveland Press.

Wenner, L. W. (1998). The sports bar: Masculinity, alcohol, sports, and the mediation of public space. In G. Rail & J. Harvey (Eds.), *Sports and postmodern times: Gender, sexuality, the body, and sport* (pp. 301–322). Albany: State University of New York Press.

Wenner, L. W. (Ed.). (2000). *Mediasport.* New York: Routledge.

Sine Anahita

Tamara L. Mix

Retrofitting Frontier Masculinity for Alaska's War against Wolves

Masculinities shape relationships among people. They also shape people's relationships with nonhuman animals. In the long history of humanity's control of wolves, masculinity has determined the manner in which wolves are targeted, whether and how they are killed, and to what extent governments are involved. Alaska's recent reinstitution of aerial wolf control, in which wolves are shot from a low-flying airplane or helicopter, or from aircraft that land after tracking wolves from the air, dramatically illustrates these gender issues.

In this article, we analyze news articles about wolf control published during 14 years in the *Anchorage Daily News*. We apply Connell's (1993) ideas about frontier masculinity to create an understanding of Alaska's wolf politics. Frontier masculinity centers on cultural myths about real and imagined heroic frontiersmen and cowboys. We contend that in Alaska, frontier masculinity is constructed and sustained at the state level by influential policy makers and is promulgated by the major news media. As we document, there has been significant pressure against Alaska's wolf control policies, including major challenges to the frontier masculinity that shapes and supports these policies. But rather than letting go of frontier masculinity, we claim Alaska policy makers have retrofitted it to garner public support for dominion over Alaska's wolves. We call this retooled form "retro frontier masculinity." We claim that retro frontier masculinity has been developed as a response to systemic change.

From *Gender & Society* 20(3): 1–22. Copyright © 2006 Sociologists for Women in Society.

Frontier Masculinity in Alaska

In the U.S. national imagination, Alaska is mythologized as exceptional and unique in multiple ways (Kollin 2001). Many state policies support mythological aspects of the state, especially the myth of Alaska's being "the last frontier." Smelser (1998) describes how myths serve particular functions, including bonding disparate groups together in a collective denial of reality, and providing narratives that can be deployed for political ends. Alaska politicians exploit the myth of the state's exceptionalism as the last frontier for political advantage to mobilize their supporters and to attack their opposition. Kimmel (1996) documents that U.S. history has been shaped by chronic anxieties and insecurities about national masculinity and that the obsessive compulsion to constantly prove American masculinity spurred the quest to tame the western frontier. We claim that a particular form of masculinity plays a central role in the myth of Alaska as a modern-day frontier and is maintained and legitimized not only by the attitudes and actions of individual men and women but, more important for the purpose of this article, by state agencies and politicians working to maintain cultural hegemony through the regional media (Artz and Murphy 2000). Connell (1993) coined the term "frontier masculinity" to describe a form of masculinity built on the myths of the frontier, including the iconic Daniel Boone, cowboys, and Paul Bunyan. We find Connell's description of frontier masculinity to be an especially salient concept to use when exploring the gendered aspects of the wolf control issue in Alaska, so in this work we expand on his concept.

Like Connell's concept, Alaska's frontier masculinity is mythological and fantasy based. It is an idealized form of public masculinity, a state-level masculinity, more than it is a form of masculinity to which individual men are held accountable. Frontier masculinity as an ideal is built on romanticized understandings of wilderness (Bonnett 1996), rugged self-sufficiency, courage, masculine bodily strength (Little and Leyshon 2003), autonomous individualism (Miller 2004), and active subordination of nature (Kimmel 1987). From at least the mid-nineteenth century, U.S. men imagined frontiers as places to which they could escape stifling civilization and feminine domestication and where they could return to an authentic masculinity tested and honed by strenuous and virtuous labor (Kimmel 1996). Like the imagined Bunyan, who manhandled huge timber into submissive logs, or the fantasy cowboy who wrestled powerful steers to the ground for branding, men who defy death to overcome dangerous aspects of rurality and wilderness have long been hailed as masculine heroes (Emel 1995). For Kimmel (1987), the cowboy is the mythical icon of compulsive masculinity. Fierce, courageous, unemotional, unattached, and with the singular purpose of conquering nature, the cowboy embodies all of the mythical ideals of frontier masculinity.

Throughout its history, first as a territory, and then as a state, Alaska has been defined and understood as primarily male space, especially as a playground for white adventurers (Kollin 2001, 92), treasure seekers, and sport hunters. Frontier masculinity played a central role in 1890s–1920s gold rush Alaska and, before that, in the quest for riches through the fur trade. Indeed, the grizzled fur trapper and rugged gold prospector are celebrated cultural heroes of frontier masculinity, credited with battling a hostile and hazardous climate, vast wilderness, and dangerous animals to subordinate natural forces. The thousands of immigrants who flowed to Alaska in the wake of oil exploration in the 1970s–1980s carried with them their own visions of the myths of Alaska (Mitchell 2003). Today, the heavily masculinized oil industry is seen as the ultimate site for machismo and the romanticized cowboy hero, and the myth of frontier masculinity persists in the industry (Miller 2004).

Frontier masculinity has been constructed within the context of wilderness, an especially important element of the myth of Alaska as a frontier (Kollin 2001). Rural and wilderness areas are seen as sites where men can be real, masculine men, while men in cities are overly civilized, affected, and effeminate (Bell 2000). Wilderness areas are imagined as places where men can go wild and where they can experience masculine freedoms unavailable in stifling, feminized, domesticated cities (Bell 2000; Bonnett 1996; Kimmel 1996). Wilderness occupations are considered to be particularly manly, as men overpowering natural forces in their quest to make a living is highly valued (Strate 1992). Work has long functioned to help form masculine identities (Willott and Griffin 1996), with heavy, dirty, and dangerous work—the kinds of work traditionally available in Alaska and other frontiers—associated with especially manly men (Brandth 1995). Strength and power are central to constructions of rural masculinity (Little and Leyshon 2003) and are essential elements of frontier masculinity.

Hunting prowess may be the most significant aspect of Alaska's frontier masculinity. Hunting success is seen as necessary on an individual level, but more important for this article, masculine hunting success is a state issue and is a vital element of Alaska's myth of the frontier. Early-twentieth-century sportsmen writers helped create the myth that there is a moose behind every tree in Alaska (Kollin 2001) and that hunters barely need to aim accurately to bag a trophy bull. Hunting for sport or for food is a highly gendered activity (King 1991). Nationwide, less than 7 percent of women hunt (Luke 1998), and men are up to 20 times more likely to hunt regardless of any other demographic variable (Stedman and Heberlein 2001). In patriarchal cultures, violence is part of what it means to be a man (McBride 1995), including normative participation in blood sports such as trophy hunting (Adams 1991). Killing animals that are especially fierce, such as wolves or bears, has long been considered an indicator of manly virility (Emel 1995). Another way that hunting is gendered is revealed by the fact that hunters say that it makes them feel manly (Luke 1998). Within hunting cultures, hunting is valorized (Brightman 1996), and men who do not hunt, or who show sympathy for hunted animals (Emel 1995) are considered to not be "real men" (Murphy 2001, 68). In Alaska, hunting cannot be separated from the myth of frontier masculinity; indeed, hunting prowess is central to the concept.

Hunting communities justify hunting in multiple ways. They claim it as a God-given right (Keller et al. 1996; Woods 1997), as providing sustenance for families (Luke 1998), as a duty to protect crops against pests (Milbourne 2003a, 2003b; Woods 1997), as instinctual (King 1991; Luke 1998), as a cultural imperative (Fox 2002), as the most important way men obtain prestige and authority (Brightman 1996), and as sustaining traditional rural community life (Milbourne 2003a, 2003b). These key concepts reveal how hunting is intimately connected with issues of masculinity: the discourses surrounding natural rights, family provider, paternalist duty, instinct, traditional culture, route to authority, and sustaining traditional community life are all tightly woven with concepts of masculinity. Indeed, Emel (1995, 727) claims, "hunting and killing are definitive" of masculinity, and as we claim here, of the myth of frontier masculinity.

In Alaska, sport hunting is strongly supported by state policies. Many influential policy makers identify themselves as sport hunters, and state agencies and decision-making bodies have historically been controlled by the sport hunting lobby (Strohmeyer 2003). But here, as elsewhere, hunting is under siege, as an increasingly vocal anti-hunting movement exerts pressure on hunting communities and state government (Byrd 2002). We argue that because hunting and statewide hunter success are such integral parts of the myth of the frontier and of frontier masculinity, state agencies routinely intervene to sustain them.

Due to the dominance and pervasiveness of the myth of frontier masculinity in Alaska, its values are instituted into state policy on hunting and wildlife issues. In Alaska, wildlife policies, including those that address hunting, are largely set by the Alaska Board of Game. This agency has historically upheld policies of aggressive control and domination of wildlife, including targeting the entire wolf population in several areas of Alaska for eradication and burning vast amounts of forest to transform the areas into moose habitat to increase hunting opportunities. The key issue has traditionally been one of subordinating nature. Throughout most of Alaska's history, the board has comprised almost exclusively men, and like other states (Pacelle 1998), the board is dominated by individuals active in the hunting industry—sport hunters, fur trappers, and professional game guides (Luke 1998; Stedman and Heberlein 2001; Strohmeyer 2003). Ecofeminists note that values of aggressive control and domination of nature, wild places, and wild animals are strongly linked with patriarchal dominion (Donovan 1990; Seager 2003; Warren 1995). The policies instituted by Alaska's Board of Game have historically demonstrated the accuracy of this claim, as year after year, the board works to maintain frontier masculinity through the valorization of hunting (Brightman 1996) and aggressive subordination of wildlife, including Alaska's wolves.

The Wolf in Frontier Masculinity

Alaska has had a complicated historical relationship with its wild wolf packs. Wolves have long functioned as scapegoats all across the world (Keller et al. 1996; Kleese 2002; Lopez [1978] 1995; Moore 1994). As McBride (1995, 124) claims, whether the scapegoat is guilty of the accused crimes or not does not matter; it is "mythically guilty," and so it is considered unquestionably by community members to be, in fact, guilty. The problems of the community are foisted on the scapegoat, in this case wolves, and the scapegoat gets its just deserts: death. In Alaska, wolves have been placed in the time-honored role of scapegoat.

As early as the 1920s, the U.S. federal and Alaska territorial governments collaborated in predator control projects that targeted the territory's wolves for extermination, claiming wolves were competitors with sportsmen for trophy Dall sheep (Rawson 2001). Alaska's policies about wolves mirrored federal eradication policies throughout the United States. Especially in Western states, wolves were portrayed as not only useless to humans but also menacing, ferocious vermin that threatened stockmen's livelihoods (Jones 2002; Keller et al. 1996) and were undeserving of life, or even a merciful end to it (Emel 1995). In the late nineteenth and early twentieth centuries, it was considered unmanly for men to show emotion, including sympathy for the suffering of wolves as they were being killed (Emel 1995). In the 1930s, following publication of Murie's famous book, *The Wolves of Mt. McKinley*, wolf-killing projects in Alaska were cancelled, reinstituted, then cancelled again as public and scientific opinion favorable to wolves (Jones 2002) encountered stiff opposition from influential big game hunters (Rawson 2001). During the 1940s and much of the 1950s, wolf eradication programs continued throughout the territory, and untold numbers of wolves were killed by sportsmen on snowmobiles and through poisoning and trapping. The U.S. government aided the territory's efforts to eradicate wolves by financing a bounty system and by paying federal agents to shoot wolves from airplanes (Rawson 2001). Jay Hammond,[1] future governor of Alaska, boasted of killing 300 wolves from his plane in one month in the 1950s; his actions were hailed as heroic in the territory (Lopez [1978] 1995). But in the mid-1950s, new federal policy officially terminated some wolf control programs, and portending the nature of future conflicts, Alaska's residents bristled at what was termed outside interference with local wildlife issues. When Alaska became a state in 1959, one of the central tenets was that Alaska could set its own wildlife policies, free from federal interference (Rawson 2001).

Aerial wolf control programs and on-the-ground trapping and hunting of wolves continued to be unregulated in most of Alaska until the mid-1960s, when the state legislature for the first time classified wolves as big game animals and furbearers and required a hunting license to kill

wolves. The consequence of the reclassification from vermin to game meant that not only federal agents, but the general public, could shoot wolves from airplanes (Rawson 2001). In the 1970s, the burgeoning environmental movement helped pass the federal Airborne Hunting Act, claiming that killing wildlife from the air was unfair chase. The passage of the act put a stop to most of Alaska's wolf hunting by air. However, on-the-ground hunting of wolves for sport and fur continued, and wolves continued to be blamed for plummeting moose and caribou populations. In the 1980s and 1990s, public conflict about wolves escalated, both nationally and statewide, with sportsmen's groups pressuring Alaska's legislature and Board of Game to increase wolf eradication programs and with environmentalist groups working to protect the state's wolf packs. Meanwhile, elsewhere in the United States, wolves were protected under the 1966 federal Endangered Species Act (Kellert et al. 1996). Outside Alaska, in the mid-1990s, several wolf reintroduction projects and protection programs for the few wild wolf packs that survived widespread extermination earlier in the twentieth century were highly successful in reestablishing vibrant wolf populations in several states, although not without local conflict (Byrd 2002; Jones 2002). In Alaska, state policies fluctuated in the 1990s, sometimes authorizing wolf eradication programs and at other times restricting them, depending on who controlled the Alaska Board of Game, the state legislature, and the governorship.

In 2004, the state resumed its internationally controversial policy of exterminating wolves by air, and it continues to enact state policies that encourage land-based hunters and trappers to kill wolves. The result is that more than 15 percent of Alaska's wolves are killed legally each year, and influential policy makers are working to expand the state-sponsored aerial wolf extermination program. For example, in 2005, 89 percent of the wolves in one area were scheduled to be killed.

Throughout Alaska's historical relationship with its wolves, groups promoting a particular form of public, state-level masculinity—frontier masculinity (Connell 1993)—have controlled state policy through domination of the legislature and the state's wildlife management agencies. The fact that groups maintaining such ideologies have been the ones to control official policy-making institutions has meant that Alaska's wolf policies are designed to support sportsmen's and frontiersmen's values of subordination of wolves. This is in spite of marked resistance from most wildlife scientists, environmentalists, animal rights groups, and a majority of citizens in both the United States (Nie 2002; Pacelle 1998) and Alaska (Kellert 1985). Although many authors have noted the symbolic value of wolves (Byrd 2002; Jones 2002; Kellert et al. 1996; and Nie 2002), an area that is under-theorized is the gendered aspect of that symbolism.

Challenges and Changes to Frontier Masculinity

Economies and political systems may collapse, but hegemonic masculinities are collectively retooled to fit new realities (Brandth 1995; Campbell and Bell 2000; Ní Laoire 2001) so that control and subordination processes remain intact (Connell 2002). For Alaska men, frontier masculinity is no longer available as it was during the halcyon sport hunting, fur trading, gold rush, or oil pipeline days. We believe that because of multiple factors that have exerted significant pressure on traditional frontier masculinity, Alaska policy makers have retooled it so as to restore its hegemonic power.

One of the factors exerting pressure on frontier masculinity has been economic restructuring. Downsizing in extraction industries such as the oil industry (Miller 2004), timber industry (Sherman 2004), and gold mining, and the decline in the international market for fur, has eliminated many traditional Alaskan frontiersmen occupations. In addition, cultural imperialism has marginalized, and even obliterated, traditional forms of masculinity on which men have relied for generations (Connell 1993). Transnational capitalism has eroded the social acceptability of traditional Alaska frontier masculinity. The new internationally hegemonic form of masculinity is a trans-

national business masculinity (Connell 2002), a form of masculinity that is largely unavailable to Alaska men except, perhaps, in urban areas such as Anchorage. Still another factor that has exerted pressure on frontier masculinity is global climate change, which has caused shifts in migration patterns of birds, marine life, and land mammals; degraded wildlife habitat (Fox 2002); and is linked to plummeting moose populations (Alaska Regional Assessment Group 1999). For frontiersmen and sportsmen in Alaska, these changes are being experienced as declining hunter success. Fish and wildlife populations supported indigenous peoples in what was to become Alaska for thousands of years until significant white migration in the early part of the twentieth century taxed wildlife populations to near-extinction (Mitchell 2003). After federal and territorial governments instituted wolf-kill projects, caribou and moose populations exploded to unnaturally high numbers, resulting in huge, widespread populations easily exploited by hunters and giving rise to the mythical perception that there is a trophy moose behind every tree in the state (Kollin 2001). The phenomenal success of sport hunters during extensive wolf-eradication programs is part of the basis on which traditional frontier masculinity was built in the twentieth century. But after extensive wolf control was cut back, and after a series of population crashes among moose and caribou due to human manipulation of their population, habitat degradation, and overhunting by humans, sportsmen's hunting success was no longer guaranteed as it had been in the mythological halcyon days of frontier masculinity.

In Alaska discourse, shifts in transnational capitalism, economic restructuring, climate change, and overhunting are not typically blamed for the pressures on men and frontier masculinity. Wolves are the ones that have been blamed. As a Midwestern rancher explained, "while international markets and corporatization can be quite complex, wolves are relatively simple and can fit straight into the scope of a rifle" (Nie 2001, 8). In Alaska, blame is attributed to the lack of state policies that keep wolves under control and out of areas especially convenient for hunters. In fact, policy makers scapegoat wolves in spite of overwhelming scientific evidence that wolves are not primarily responsible for the decline of caribou and moose populations, for which they are blamed and targeted for eradication.

Structural changes, such as those described above, have gendered implications. For example, working-class men experience unemployment as emasculation (Fine et al. 1997). Men experiencing economic downsizing tighten their physical and financial control over wives and children as a way to shore up their power and sense of manliness (Sherman 2004). They may also increase their expression of misogyny and homophobia (Connell 1993) and project their anger toward women, ethnic minority communities, and other scapegoats (Fine et al. 1997) such as wolves (Moore 1994). Among men whose masculine identity is based on dominance over nature (Kruse 1999; Warren 1995), the inability to be successful at hunting, to dominate an animal by killing it, is a profound challenge to their masculinity (Emel 1995). Big game hunting is an ancient mode by which men gain authority and prestige (Brightman 1996), so when hunting is constrained in hunting communities, men lose a primary route by which they accrue power. Men who are near the bottom of a collapsing economy feel embattled (Fine et al. 1997; Moore 1994). Because they experience the situation as their traditional masculinity being under siege, they must find other ways to be men (Fine et al. 1997). This, we claim, is what is happening to Alaska men who have relied on frontier masculinity as their way to be manly.

As men come to feel embattled, and feel their masculine identity is under siege, they turn to their communities and to male-dominated institutions like the Alaska Game Board and the state legislature to help them craft new ways to be men. This underscores the fact that creating new ways for men to be manly is not an individual pursuit but is structured at the level of the state. Franzway, Court, and Connell (1989) analyze the state

as a gendered institution, claiming it is best viewed as a set of practices that institutionalize power relations, largely for the benefit of men. Connell (2001) further expands the idea that gendered practices are structural, and not just the property of individual men, when he describes the crisis tendency of dominant masculinities. According to Connell, when a dominant masculinity, such as frontier masculinity, is threatened, there are structural, often national attempts to reestablish and reaffirm the threatened masculinity. In U.S. history, one recurring strategy deployed to reaffirm masculinity is the reification of the cult of the outdoorsman. Originally emerging in the nineteenth century, it has been revived several times during masculinity's moments of national crisis (Connell 2001).

In Alaska, the newspaper resources we analyzed demonstrate that attempts to reestablish and reaffirm frontier masculinity occurred at the state level. We claim that Alaska policy makers retooled traditional frontier masculinity so as to restore its dominance but that they did so in ways that reflect new emphases. As we discuss, we call this retooled form retro frontier masculinity, in the sense that it is a revived form of an older masculinity.

Method

Our interest in this article is how a shifting, public, state-level masculinity has shaped the discourse and policy-making processes related to the wolf issue in Alaska. An analysis of newspaper accounts as the wolf issue unfolded during the course of 14 years provided us with rich longitudinal data. For this work, we conducted an interpretive content analysis of newspaper articles, editorials, and letters to the editor of the most influential and widely distributed paper in Alaska: the *Anchorage Daily News* (referred to hereafter as *ADN*; see Table 40.1). The *ADN* was selected for its frequent reporting of wolf control issues within a local and regional context. We examined articles during the period of 1 January 1990 to 31 May 2004. The first date was selected because it was a pivotal moment in wolf control,

■ **TABLE 40.1**

News Items Cited in the Text

Date	Author	Title
12 February 1990	Medred	Mechanized Predators Stalk Wolves from Sky; Officials Say Aerial Hunters Harassed Wolves to Near Exhaustion before Landing, Shooting
24 June 2001	Manning	Unexpected Results of Study Show Grizzlies Are Killing Moose Calves
27 October 1991	Hulen	Alaska's Wolves: Game Board Looks at Heated Proposals
1 November 1991	Hulen	Board Bans Some-Day Aerial Wolf Hunts
25 November 1992	Ahn	Collars Doom Wolves; Board Planned Ahead; Killers Will Track Packs
4 December 1992	Ahn	Proposal Could Foil Wolf Kills
7 December 1992	staff	Wolf Control: Hickel Backs Down, Heads for 'Summit'
20 December 1992	Bryson	Editor's Notes: We Alaskans
27 December 1992	Hickel	Wolf Hunt: Nation's Wildlife Leaders Invited to January Summit in Alaska
13 January 1993	Carey	Wolf: More Than an Animal, Bigger Than Alaska
22 November 1992	Doogan	God's Newspaper Doesn't Like the Killing of Wolves from Helicopters
2 December 1994	Rinehart	Wolf Kill Is Off
3 December 1994	Rinehart	Law Calls for Wolf, Bear Kills; Board Implements Predator Control
19 February 1995	staff	Park Service Needs Better Bean Counters
6 February 2000	Ruskin	'Flying through a Graveyard': Wolves Short of Prey, Hunters Say in McGrath
24 February 2000	Bellisle	Fish and Game Faces Cut Unless Policies Change
27 October 2002	Rosier	Murkowski Is What Alaska Deserves and What Our Fish, Wildlife Need
19 December 2002	Keller	How Will Governor Handle Wolves?
18 January 2003	Cockerham	Murkowski Game Board Heavy on Hunting Advocates
23 January 2003	Keppel	Finally, Game Board Will Serve Needs of Alaskans, Not Tourists
14 February 2003	Curtis, K. and J.	Come to Dinner and Let's Talk about Alaska's Divisive Subsistence Issues
6 March 2003	Manning	Predator Control Opinions Welcome
7 March 2003	Manning	Crowd Supports Predator Control
25 March 2003	Gay	Bill a 'Tool' to Manage Wolves
5 November 2003	Gay	Game Board OK's Aerial Wolf Hunts
11 December 2003	Gay	Governor Stands Firm on Aerial Wolf Control Plans: State Won't Be Cowed by Animal Rights Groups, Murkowski Says
15 March 2003	Manning	Predators Face Another Hard Hit: Board of Game Wants Wolves across Cook Inlet To Be Killed from Snowmachines or Aircraft
4 December 2003	Gay	No One Budges at Wolf Debate
21 August 2005	Hunter and Cockerham	State Has 'Lost a Giant' in Hammond (08/03/05)

as we discuss. We chose the second date because it was the final date of the aerial wolf control program for the year in which data collection was undertaken. In this article, we primarily focus our analysis on the news reports and indicate information from editorials and letters to the editor as they appear. Because we are particularly interested in how Alaska's state agencies and politicians control state wolf policies, we believe the *ADN* provides important insight and is a useful data source.

Articles were pulled from *ADN*'s online source, and key words were used to locate items: wolf control AND Alaska; predator control AND Alaska; aerial hunting AND Alaska; aerial trapping AND Alaska. We examined a total of 544 news reports, editorials, and letters to the editor and read them in chronological order. Through this examination, it became clear that a gendered framework provides an alternative way to analyze the shifting public discourse and policy-making discussions about wolves. Artz and Murphy (2000) document how mainstream newspapers such as the *ADN* work to uphold current hegemony, including hegemonic gender regimes, and our interpretive analysis of the newspaper articles confirms their claim.

A conventional content analysis typically codes manifest content, which is countable and supposedly objective (Berg 1995). However, for this article, we follow Berg's (1995) recommendation to code latent content because of its revelation of symbolic meanings attached to the manifest content. Because we are interested in how public masculinities shape public discourse, we utilize feminist narrative interpretive methods (DeVault 1999), allowing us to see that some of the latent content is gendered, even when "gender," "masculinity," or similar words do not actually appear in the text. Giving the newspaper materials a "gendered reading" (DeVault 1999), while conscious of our status as members of a particular group (sociologists interested in gender and environment), allows us to create alternative interpretations while a more casual reader might find gender and masculinity invisible.

Berg (1995) recommends that coding for latent content be accompanied by at least three independent examples to corroborate the researchers' interpretation as objective. DeVault (1999) critiques the pursuit of objectivity, noting that objective reality does not exist, that everything is socially constructed within a patriarchal social system. As mentioned previously, she recommends giving texts a gendered reading to render issues of gender visible and manifest. DeVault's argument notwithstanding, we believe we can meet Berg's recommendation of having three independent examples to corroborate our interpretation of latent content. Our claim about the newspaper resources we analyzed is that there is latent content about masculinities that can be utilized to interpret the wolf control issue. Our first independent example to corroborate our claim is that much of the discourse in the *ADN* is manifestly gendered. For example, *ADN* newspaper writers primarily use masculine pronouns to refer to hunters, making the assumption that they are men, and use masculine generics, such as "man" or "men" to refer to "people" and the term "flyboys" to describe the aerial hunters who kill wolves from the air. These examples corroborate our claim that there is latent gender content to be analyzed. Second, most of the actions described in the newspaper are performed by male actors, although the articles rarely point out this fact. This may make the gendered aspects of men's activities invisible to casual observers, but to gender scholars, this underscores how masculinity is generally not seen at all but is invisible (Connell 1993). Third, as Connell (1993) notes, masculinities are not just personal practices but are institutionalized and organized through the state, the family, and the media, such as newspapers. The media, of which the *ADN* is an example, are an institution recognized as instrumental in constructing and maintaining gender regimes (Connell 1996). Thus, we believe that these three independent examples—manifest gender content visible in the language used, the *ADN*'s assumption that primary actors in the wolf controversy are men, and the scholarly recognition that public media play a role in the maintenance of gender regimes—corroborate our gendered reading of the texts.

The Fading of Frontier Masculinity

By the 1990s, after a century of hegemony, frontier masculinity was enduring significant challenges. An iconographic moment occurred in 1990 when a group of prominent sportsmen was arrested and charged with illegally using airplanes to harass a pack of wolves before killing them (Medred, *ADN*, 12 February 1990). In the news article about the crime, the U.S. Fish and Wildlife investigator implied the men simply got carried away with the thrill of the hunt. In spite of the investigator's "boys will be boys" attitude, the men were charged with a series of crimes. The writer of the article was the outdoors editor for the *ADN*. Although ostensibly about the crime, most of the article lauded the mythological hunting reputation of Jack Frost, the ringleader arrested in the case. He noted that Frost had killed every species of large animal in the United States by bow and that he had received multiple awards from hunting organizations. The writer gave Frost esteemed status as an admired, untamed, rebellious sportsman, an "outlaw aerial wolf hunter." Throughout the article, frontier masculinity was valorized; however, evidence that this was a moment when frontier masculinity shifted from its previous hegemonic position is that Frost received a number of anonymous, threatening phone calls. This signaled a shift in the way the anonymous public felt about harassing and killing wolves from the air and in the violent performance of frontier masculinity for the purpose of subordinating nature.

Less than one year later, the influence of frontier masculinity on state wildlife policy after nearly one hundred years of control was waning. In 1991, the Alaska Board of Game instituted a series of new policies based on the recommendations of a 16-member alliance composed of both sports hunters and prowolf environmentalists. The new policies included limits on wolf hunting, including restricting same-day airborne hunt-

ing tactics, which allowed hunters to track wolves from the air, land, and shoot them. Sport hunters decried the limits, with one claiming killing wolves is "an essential freedom" and another saying, "I have as much a right and privilege to shoot a wolf as someone else has to watch a wolf" (Hulen, *ADN*, 27 October 1991). Doug Pope, chair of the Game Board, acknowledged the past role played by frontier masculinity, saying airborne hunting is "the last sort of remnant of the cowboy mentality that used to pervade here in Alaska, the sort of outlaw mentality" (Hulen, 1 November 1991). Pope decided the new policy would restrict airborne hunting to special cases, saying, "we're on the edge of a new era."

In successive years, frontier masculinity as embodied in the state's wolf control policies was increasingly challenged. One year after Pope's statement about new b board policies and the "new era," Governor Hickel appointed a staunch proponent of wolf control to replace him. The board once again talked about instituting widespread aerial wolf control, yielding to complaints by sportsmen that wolves competed with them for wild game. State biologists with the Division of Wildlife Conservation radio-collared 25 wolves with the intent of tracking them to their packs, then killing entire packs with shotguns from helicopters (Ahn, *ADN*, 25 November 1992). Five hundred wolves were targeted. The plan was presented to the public as rational and scientific, emphasizing the fact that it would be state biologists using the shotguns and helicopters. National outrage over Alaska's plan filled Governor Hickel's mailbox and jammed phone lines to the Division of Wildlife Conservation. A threatened national tourism boycott called by animal rights and environmental groups put the Game Board and state biologists on the defensive.

National criticism of the plan included proposed congressional legislation forbidding Alaska's plan and threats to investigate the state's use of radio-collars under Federal Communications Commission regulations (Ahn, *ADN*, 4 December 1992). In newspaper reports, frontier masculinity seemed to be vying with a form of masculinity that bristled with adolescent, schoolyard bullying language from national officials. For example, Representative DeFazio (D—Oregon) claimed the state would suffer "a black eye" if it went ahead with its plan. With national attention focused on Alaska's Board of Game and sport hunters, the threats to Alaska's frontier masculinity were obvious.

As a result of the international pressure, Governor Hickel, an *ADN* headline proclaimed, "backed down," canceled the proposed aerial wolf control plan, and called for a Wolf Summit (*ADN*, 7 December 1992), an event that became notorious. The governor, the report stated, used bad judgment in approving the plan, and now he had "a political disaster on his hands" (*ADN*, 7 December 1992). The article warned that sportsmen and the "hardliners in the Department of Fish and Game" who continued to press for aerial wolf control were promoting an issue that the rest of the United States would never allow, even though Alaska proponents "parade, posture, and pout." The article framed proponents of wolf control as stubborn, spoiled little boys.

Relying on the elements of frontier masculinity that had long shaped the wolf control issue, especially the taken-for-granted lethal subordination of wolves, no longer worked to justify why the state should carry on with its proposed wolf eradication plans. Governor Hickel, in response to a question from an NBC news journalist about why Alaska should institute wolf control, answered, "Well . . . you can't just let nature run wild" (Bryson, *ADN*, 20 December 1992). Nature must be dominated, according to Game Board policies shaped by frontier masculinity. A week later, Hickel, in a widely published letter (27 December 1992), said folks outside Alaska misunderstood the wolf issue. In a telling tactical shift, instead of claiming sportsmen's right to kill wolves, Hickel claimed wolves were preventing Alaska family men from meeting the nutritional needs of their families. Deploying strategic bewilderment, the governor said Alaska's family providers were confused about why animal rights advocates did not want their families to have food to eat. This change from the state's formerly steadfast maintenance

of sportsmen's right to dominate nature, to not allow it to "run wild," to an emphasis on men as embattled family providers unable to put food on their tables signals the shift of public policy to one shaped by what we call retro frontier masculinity.

The Emergence of Retro Frontier Masculinity

For many decades, the ideal of frontier masculinity, including the legacy of the mythological cowboy, framed the issue of wolf control. Emerging from the legacy of frontier masculinity are ideas about sportsmen's rights to unquestioned, total dominion over nature and wild animals. However, under the pressures of outrage over Alaska's aerial wolf control policies, the state's policy makers sought to reframe the issue. They did so by retooling and retrofitting frontier masculinity.

In the process of retrofitting frontier masculinity, policy makers continued to frame the wolf control issue as the right of sportsmen to subordinate nature but extended their frames (Snow et al. 1986) to include alternative, perhaps more compelling reasons for lethal wolf control. Frames are sets of interpretations of events made by a social movement to attract activists, to mobilize supporters, and to challenge the opposition (Snow et al. 1986). The new frames, or strategic emphases, included vilification of opponents as feminized, casting wolf hunters as paternalist protectors, reification of the masculine family provider role, and analysis of the issue as one fundamentally about competition. These emphases often overlap. A key part of the retrofit process is deploying values that have historical, even ancient, precedent, reframed for a new agenda.

Vilifying opponents as feminized is one of the reframed strategies undertaken as the state's policy makers sought to retrofit frontier masculinity. As Connell (2001) and Kimmel (1996) document, masculinity is constructed in opposition to anything feminine, and being associated with sissyhood is the ultimate insult. Previously, Alaska's policy makers had little need to vilify their opponents as feminized because the values of traditional frontier masculinity were hegemonic.

Early in 1993, policy makers realized that compromise on the wolf control issue might be necessary, but they had to reassure the public that compromise did not necessarily threaten the state's traditional form of masculinity. The tendency to compromise had not been part of frontier masculinity, in large part because any sign of sensitivity, compassion, or desire for nonhierarchical processes connoted wimpiness (Ducat 2004; Kimmel 1996). For example, Michael Carey, editor of the *ADN*, sought to assure readers that being against aerial wolf control did not necessarily make one less of a real Alaska man: "The legendary game warden, Sam White of Fairbanks, hardly a posy sniffer, had no use for aerial wolf hunting" because it gives hunters an unfair, nonsportsmanlike advantage over their prey (*ADN*, 13 January 1993). Embodying sportsmanlike values such as giving prey a "fair chance," he claimed, does not mean that a hunter is an effete, flower-loving environmentalist.

Another example of the tactic of vilification of opponents as feminized appeared in 1992 when an opinion writer wrote an article criticizing central players. He trivialized those opposed to state employees gunning down wolves from the air as "defenders of forest creatures" and characterized activists as "little old ladies with umbrellas" (*ADN*, 22 November 1992). The writer feminized those opposed to aerial wolf control as a way to delegitimate their stance.

In 1994, an event occurred that underscored the efficacy of accusations of sissyhood. Gordon Haber, an influential wolf biologist and activist, and an accompanying TV reporter, videotaped several wolves caught in state-set snares. The snares had been touted as humane because they supposedly instantly killed animals by strangulation. Haber's video, however, pictured wolves who were not only still alive but suffering dreadfully (Rinehart, *ADN*, 2 December 1994). The footage was graphic, grisly, horrifying, and widely published on TV newscasts, in national newspapers, and on the Internet. An Alaska Fish and Game employee was pictured on the videotape shooting a wolf point-blank five times before it succumbed. Immediately after the footage of the dying wolves was published, the newly elected Democratic governor, Tony Knowles, and the Fish and Game Commissioner, Carl Rosier, terminated the state's wolf control project. However, the next day, the Board of Game sought proposals on how to implement a new law passed by Republican state representatives requiring the state to manage wildlife populations for the sole benefit of human hunters (Rinehart, *ADN*, 3 December 1994). The law stated that if problems with game arose, the Department of Fish and Game was required to kill predators and burn timber before it could limit human hunting activities. Public criticism of killing wolves using "helicopters and machine guns" was discounted as mere "sissified squeamishness" (*ADN*, 19 February 1995). It has long been unmanly to show sympathy for wolves as they are being killed (Emel 1995). However, the tactic of publicly vilifying opponents as sissies emerged only when the values of frontier masculinity needed to be retooled.

Sportsmen's groups put pressure on the legislature during the eight years Knowles was governor, and prohunting legislators decimated budgets of agencies that did not comply with demands for aggressive wolf control projects. In 1996, and again in 2000, citizen's initiatives passed that forbade the state from instituting aerial wolf hunting, although the initiatives were circumvented on the inauguration of Knowles' Republican successor. But during his tenure, Knowles refused to allow lethal wolf control, called for an external scientific study, and allowed only nonlethal means of control such as relocation and sterilization programs. In addition, he sought to appoint members of the Alaska Board of Game who were moderate on wildlife issues and who represented ideological diversity. As a result, many letters to the editor contained derogatory remarks not only hinting at his lack of manliness but also questioning the masculinity of his appointees to the Game Board. Even after the new, pro-wolf control Governor Murkowski took office, letters continued to accuse Knowles of having run a sissified Game Board. In 2003, a letter writer expressed relief that Murkowski had appointed a Game Board with strong, pro-wolf control values.

"Eight years of gutless leadership concerning wolf control have come to an end. The powder-puff picks that former Gov. Tony Knowles had on the Game Board were there to serve the tourist industry, not to feed the people of remote Alaska" (Keppel, *ADN*, 23 January 2003). A couple of weeks later, a letter writer asked, "Why did they never attack Gov. Tony Knowles for instituting no effective predator control and turning our Game Board into a bunch of wolf huggers?" (Keith and Julie Curtis, *ADN*, 14 February 2003).

Another tactic that gained utility during the retrofitting of frontier masculinity was casting wolves as threatening and wolf hunters as protectors. Recalling that the hero of "Little Red Riding Hood" was the hunter who killed the wolf (Emel 1995), wolves were cast as a threat to children: "Participants talked of the danger the wolves pose for children walking to school in the dark," claimed one article (Ruskin, *ADN*, 6 February 2000). "Wolves often are spotted from classrooms, and parents fear for their children's safety," a woman claimed (Bellisle, 24 February 2000). This tactic, which played on ancient myths, raised the specter of innocent children being killed by bold, out-of-control wolves. The state's project to kill wolves was thus framed as a means to protect children. Skogen and Krange (2003) note that men in Norway who felt that their rural lifestyle was under siege utilized similar rhetorical strategies, claiming that the weakest members of their communities—elderly people, women, and children—were the most likely to be attacked by wolves and thus were in need of paternalist protection.

Related to the tactic of framing the wolf control issue as being necessary to protect children, women, and elderly people, with the emergence of retro frontier masculinity, the state's wolf policies began to emphasize the need for family men to have enough moose to hunt to provide meat for their families. Previously, this had been mostly a side issue, with sport hunters' rights to kill trophy bull moose or their right to kill wolves for sport taking discursive precedence. Part of the reframing of the wolf control issue, then, was a reification of the masculine family provider role.

In 2002, Republican Frank Murkowski was elected governor after running a campaign that promoted lethal wolf control to increase moose populations available to family providers. The National Rifle Association awarded Murkowski a grade of "A," while his opponent, Fran Ulmer, a woman who had been Knowles's lieutenant governor, received an "F" (Rosier, *ADN*, 27 October 2002). On inauguration, the new governor made it clear to opponents of wolf control that retro frontier masculinity would shape the state's wildlife policies. Murkowski was "now considering how radical a Board of Game he wants to nominate, and how fast to start wolf control," Leo Keller, a wildlife photographer, complained (*ADN*, 19 December 2002). "The cry to enslave Mother Nature and kill wolves with a false expectation of improving moose populations is growing throughout Alaska," he continued. "Will the new administration use the scientific data [which showed that bears accounted for most moose predation], or just approve the misguided, wanton killing of wolves?" Within a month, Keller had his answer. Murkowski replaced six out of seven members of the Board of Game, stacking it with professional game guides and sport hunters (Cockerham, *ADN*, 18 January 2003). The lone woman appointee was a professional game guide. The first sentence of the article describing the move portrayed Murkowski as a decisive, masculine warrior: Murkowski "waded into the predator control battlefield when he put his firm stamp on the Alaska Board of Game."

At the first Board of Game meeting after the 2002 gubernatorial election, 45 people complained about wolves. Many were hunters from an area where a study had documented not a general lack of moose but only a shortage of bull moose within a mile of town, indicating predation by humans, not wolves. However, families were said to be suffering for lack of meat, and a resident claimed, "we have so many wolves in our country that people are carrying handguns to the outhouse" (Manning, *ADN*, 7 March 2003). The board acted swiftly to demonstrate its newly restored muscle. Aerial wolf control plans were instituted, and the state attorney was directed to find a way to circumvent the anti–aerial wolf hunting amendment to the state's constitution that had earlier been passed by citizens. Meanwhile, polls showed 76 percent of Alaskans were opposed to state-sponsored lethal wolf control (Manning, *ADN*, 6 March 2003).

The legislature also whirled into action, passing bills allowing wolf control practices that had earlier been prohibited by voters. Ralph Seekins, a first-term senator, introduced a bill allowing the Board of Game to make a "preemptive strike against predators" (Gay, *ADN*, 25 March 2003). Passed by the legislature and signed by the new governor, the bill allowed preemptive strikes against predators even if moose or caribou populations were not threatened. Seekins claimed he wanted wolves killed "efficiently, effectively, and professionally" (Gay, *ADN*, 25 March 2003) by using state sharpshooters flying low in helicopters.

Another reframed strategic emphasis state policy makers utilized was to consider the wolf control issue in terms of fairness and competition. There are three elements to this: structuring aerial wolf hunts as a matter of fair competition between wolves and their pursuers, questioning whether wolves deserve fair competition, and framing wolf control as necessary to limit wolves' competition with family providers seeking to put meat on their family tables. An example of how the issue was framed in terms of making aerial wolf control a matter of fair competition between wolves and humans occurred in 2003. Murkowski, the new Republican governor, authorized aerial wolf control under strict limitations: volunteer pilots using their own resources, including planes, fuel, guns, and ammunition (Gay, *ADN*, 5 November 2003). Framing the wolf control issue as one fundamentally about fair competition, Murkowski said, "Humaneness is in the eye of the beholder. If you run 'em down in a helicopter and shoot 'em, that's pretty efficient. If you run 'em down in a Super Cub, that requires a little more skill and the wolf has probably got a better chance" (Gay, *ADN*, 11 December 2003). Alternately, some policy makers questioned whether

wolves even deserve to be treated with any fairness in competition. Said a member of an advisory committee to the Alaska Board of Game, "I don't believe in fair chase for vermin. If you're trying to get rid of them, why worry about it?" (Manning, *ADN*, 15 March 2003).

A third way that the idea of competition is utilized in retro frontier masculinity is describing wolf control projects as giving human hunters a competitive advantage against wolves in their mutual quest for meat. When, in 2003, the Board of Game announced plans to kill all wolves in a 1,700 square mile area, and to begin an equally aggressive wolf kill plan in another area, competition was a key part of the discussion. Paul Joslin of the Alaska Wildlife Alliance termed the hunt plans "a posse in the sky" (Gay, *ADN*, 4 December 2003). Priscilla Feral, head of Friends of Animals, told Representative Ralph Seekins, "That's barbaric and out of touch with Alaska and the rest of the world. . . . In 2003 it really is an ethical outrage to be blasting wolves with shotguns." Seekins's response was, "We have to eliminate the competition to feed Alaskans." More fundamentally, Seekins also revealed what is now obvious to all who have studied the wolf control issue: "This isn't about wolves. This is about who gets to control Alaska. . . . They want us to compromise and compromise and compromise until there's nothing left."

Reflections

In Alaska, wolves are reprising a role they have played for centuries: They are scapegoats at the state level, where they pay for the multiple pressures against masculinity with their lives. A legitimate question might be, Why wolves? Kellert et al. (1996) document that in the Yellowstone Park area, mountain lions are the major culprits in livestock predation and are responsible for many attacks on humans. Yet there is little mention of mountain lions as a problem in the local press. At the same time, mere discussion of a wolf reintroduction program elicited much negative publicity, including dire predictions of children's being killed in the park. Similarly, a scientist working in a particularly contentious area in Alaska documented that the majority of predation on moose was caused not by wolves but by bears (Manning, *ADN*, 24 June 2001). In fact, in his study, wolves accounted for only 16 percent of predation on moose, while black bears and grizzly bears together accounted for 81 percent. But even though bears have recently been blamed as culprits in predation on moose in Alaska, including being targeted for lethal and nonlethal methods of control, bears cannot be scapegoats the way wolves are. The scientist who did the study acknowledged that even suggesting bears be killed like wolves would be "unimaginable. . . . That's a place I don't think anyone wants to go. People have a lot of respect for them," he said. We claim there is more to the story of who plays the scapegoat role than respect for bears. First, because bears are among North America's most fierce animals, they are especially revered. In arctic and subarctic regions, the hunting of bears is viewed as "paradigmatically male" (Brightman 1996, 692) because of the status accorded to them. In contrast, wolves have long been attributed to the lowest status possible for animals, that of vermin, and killing vermin is considered socially acceptable, even desirable (Flynn 1999).

Second, Alaska inherited a culturally ingrained hatred of wolves handed down first from Europe, then from early American pioneers, then from Western expansionists (Kellert 1985). In fact, wolves were the target of the first wildlife laws passed by early American settlers, as a wolf bounty was established as early as 1630 (Kellert et al. 1996). Although it could be argued that bears have posed as many practical problems as wolves have, they are not subject to the kind of negative myths that have been foisted on wolves. Wolves have long been constructed in the popular imagination as symbolizing danger, while bears have escaped such symbolism. Evidence of this can be found in children's stories. Whereas the wolf is an evildoer blowing down houses of Little Pigs, or devouring Grandmother and attempting to eat Little Red Riding Hood, bears are benign, even if

they are annoyed at Goldilocks's trespassing on their private property without their permission. In addition, they are considered cuddly, as the popular teddy bear aptly illustrates.

Interestingly, Barclay (2002) claims that in colonial America, wolves were not as large a problem for colonists as they were for administrators who were responsible for the economic growth of the colonies and for attracting new settlers. Barclay argues that if wolves were indeed a problem, then settlers would not have needed the incentive of bounties to kill them; instead, settlers would have killed individual problem wolves, such as those caught killing livestock. He concludes that the newly emerged modern state abstracted the problem of a few wolves' being problems into a scary stereotype of wolves that threatened the safety of communities, then offered bounties for wolf heads as a way to attract new livestock producers and settlers. Barclay documents that the state has a history of strategically constructing myths about wolves, while there seems to be no evidence that the state has conducted similar myth making about bears.

There is also the mythological relationship bears share with masculinity. For example, the mythopoetic men's movement's celebration of the archetypal wild and hairy man (Bonnett 1996) seems bear-like. In contrast, labeling a man a "wolf" implies that he sexually harasses women, which is increasingly considered to be antisocial behavior. In addition, gay men have created a subculture of "bears," or masculinized men who celebrate hairy and large men (Hennen 2005). Bears seem to have a special link with masculinity that wolves do not.

This article argues that policy makers in Alaska retrofitted an earlier form of masculinity, frontier masculinity, as a way to garner public support for their controversial wolf control projects. While traditional frontier masculinity emphasized sportsmen's rights to kill wolves, the framing of the issue utilizing retro frontier masculinity employs new strategic emphases: vilifying opponents as feminized, casting wolf hunters as paternalist protectors, reifying the masculine family provider role, and framing the issue as fundamentally about competition. Retro frontier masculinity is deployed on a statewide basis, reflecting the fact that states are gendered.

We hope this work opens another area where sociologists may examine issues of gender. In particular, this work contributes to the analysis of how the state may construct and sustain a symbolic form of masculinity as a way to manage systemic threats to public manliness. Our ideas about retro frontier masculinity further strengthen sociological understandings about how masculinity not just is a property of individuals but also is deployed at the state level by policy makers seeking political advantage. In addition, our work highlights not only how masculinity is socially constructed but also how the social construction of masculinity is inherently interwoven with the social construction of frontiers, wilderness, scapegoats, and wolves and other wildlife. Finally, this work documents how the symbolic politics of masculinity have not only human victims but nonhuman ones as well. In Alaska, wolves are paying for the state's deployment of retro frontier masculinity with their lives.

Note

1. Hammond died in 2005 but continues to be seen as a mythical exemplar of Alaska masculinity: "'He was kind of a larger than life, quintessential Alaskan,' said Fred Dyson, a Republican state senator from Eagle River. 'He was a war hero, a man of great personal Christian faith, really a physical stud. He done it all. He fished, he hunted and lived in the Bush'" (Hunter and Cockerham, *ADN*, 21 August 2005).

References

Adams, Carol J. 1991. *The sexual politics of meat: A feminist-vegetarian critical theory*. New York: Continuum.

Alaska Regional Assessment Group. 1999. *The potential consequences of climate variability and change*. Fairbanks: Center for Global Change and Arctic System Research, University of Alaska Fairbanks.

Artz, Lee, and Bren Ortega Murphy. 2000. *Cultural hegemony in the United States*. Thousand Oaks, CA: Sage.

Barclay, Paul D. 2002. A "curious and grim testimony to a persistent human blindness": Wolf bounties in North America, 1630–1752. *Ethics, Place & Environment* 5 (1): 25–35.

Bell, David. 2000. Farm boys and wild men: Rurality, masculinity, and homosexuality. *Rural Sociology* 65 (4): 547–61.

Berg, Bruce L. 1995. *Qualitative research methods for the social sciences*. 2d ed. Boston: Allyn and Bacon.

Bonnett, Alastair. 1996. The new primitives: Identity, landscape and cultural appropriation in the mythopoetic men's movement. *Antipode* 28 (3): 273–91.

Brandth, Berit. 1995. Rural masculinity in transition: Gender images in tractor advertisements. *Journal of Rural Studies* 11 (2): 123–33.

Brightman, Robert. 1996. The sexual division of foraging labor: Biology, taboo, and gender politics. *Comparative Studies in Society and History* 38 (4): 687–729.

Byrd, Kimberly. 2002. Mirrors and metaphors: Contemporary narratives of the wolf in Minnesota. *Ethics, Place & Environment* 5 (1): 50–65.

Campbell, Hugh, and Michael Mayerfeld Bell. 2000. The question of rural masculinities. *Rural Sociology* 65 (4): 532–46.

Connell, R. W. 1993. The big picture: Masculinities in recent world history. *Theory and Society* 22: 597–623.

———. 1996. New directions in gender theory, masculinity research, and gender politics. *Ethnos* 61 (3/4): 157–76.

———. 2001. The social organization of masculinity. In *The masculinities reader*, edited by S. M. Whitehead and F. J. Barrett. Malden, MA: Polity.

———. 2002. Understanding men: Gender sociology and the new international research on masculinities. *Social Thought & Research* 24 (1/2): 13–31.

DeVault, Marjorie L. 1999. *Liberating method: Feminism and social research*. Philadelphia: Temple University Press.

Donovan, Josephine. 1990. Animal rights and feminist theory. *Signs: Journal of Women in Culture and Society* 15 (2): 350–75.

Ducat, Stephen J. 2004. *The wimp factor: Gender gaps, holy wars, and the politics of anxious masculinity.* Boston: Beacon.

Emel, Jody. 1995. Are you man enough, big and bad enough? An ecofeminist analysis of wolf eradication in the United States. *Society and Space: Environment and Planning D* 13:707–34.

Fine, M., L. Weis, J. Addelston, and J. Marusza. 1997. (In) secure times: Constructing white working-class masculinities in the late 20th century. *Gender & Society* 11 (1): 52–68.

Flynn, Clifton P. 1999. Animal abuse in childhood and later support for interpersonal violence in families. *Society and Animals* 7 (2): 161–72.

Fox, S. 2002. These are things that are really happening: Inuit perspectives on the evidence and impacts of climate change in Nunavut. In *The earth is faster now: Indigenous observations of Arctic environmental change*, edited by I. Krupnik and D. Jolly. Fairbanks, AK: Arctic Research Consortium.

Franzway, Suzanne, Dianne Court, and R. W. Connell. 1989. *Staking a claim: Feminism, bureaucracy and the state.* Boston: Allen & Unwin.

Hennen, Peter. 2005. Bear bodies, bear masculinity: Recuperation, resistance, or retreat? *Gender & Society* 19 (1): 25–43.

Jones, Karen. 2002. "A fierce green fire": Passionate pleas and wolf ecology. *Ethics, Place & Environment* 5 (1): 35–44.

Kellert, Stephen R. 1985. Public perceptions of predators, particularly the wolf and coyote. *Biological Conservation* 31:167–89.

Kellert, S. R., M. Black, C. R. Rush, and A. J. Bath. 1996. Human culture and large carnivore conservation in North America. *Conservation Biology* 10 (4): 977–90.

Kimmel, Michael S. 1987. The cult of masculinity: American social character and the legacy of the cowboy. In *Beyond patriarchy: Essays by men on pleasure, power, and change*, edited by Michael Kaufman. Toronto, Canada: Oxford University Press.

———. 1996. *Manhood in America: A cultural history.* New York: Free Press.

King, Roger J. H. 1991. Environmental ethics and the case for hunting. *Environmental Ethics* 13 (1): 59–85.

Kleese, Deborah. 2002. Contested natures: Wolves in late modernity. *Society and Natural Resources* 15:313–26.

Kollin, Susan. 2001. *Nature's state: Imagining Alaska as the last frontier.* Chapel Hill: University of North Carolina Press.

Kruse, Corwin R. 1999. Gender, views of nature, and support for animal rights. *Society and Animals* 7 (3): 179–98.

Little, Jo, and Michael Leyshon. 2003. Embodied rural geographies: Developing research agendas. *Progress in Human Geography* 27 (3): 257–72.

Lopez, Barry H. [1978] 1995. *Of wolves and men.* New York: Simon & Schuster.

Luke, Brian. 1998. Violent love: Hunting, heterosexuality, and the erotics of men's predation. *Feminist Studies* 24 (3): 627–55.

McBride, James. 1995. *War, battering, and other sports: The gulf between American men and women.* Atlantic Highlands, NJ: Humanities Press.

Milbourne, Paul. 2003a. The complexities of hunting in rural England and Wales. *Sociologia Ruralis* 43 (3): 289–308.

———. 2003b. Hunting ruralities: Nature, society and culture in "hunt countries" of England and Wales. *Journal of Rural Studies* 19:157–71.

Miller, Gloria E. 2004. Frontier masculinity in the oil industry: The experience of women engineers. *Gender, Work and Organization* 11 (1): 47–73.

Mitchell, Donald Craig. 2003. *Sold American: The story of Alaska Natives and their land, 1867–1959.* Fairbanks: University of Alaska Press.

Moore, Roland S. 1994. Metaphors of encroachment: Hunting for wolves on a central Greek mountain. *Anthropological Quarterly* 67 (2): 81–89.

Murphy, Peter F. 2001. *Studs, tools, and the family jewels: Metaphors men live by.* Madison: University of Wisconsin Press.

Ní Laoire, Caitrína. 2001. A matter of life and death? Men, masculinities, and staying "behind" in rural Ireland. *Sociologia Ruralis* 41 (2): 220–36.

Nie, Martin A. 2001. The sociopolitical dimensions of wolf management and restoration in the United States. *Human Ecology Review* 8 (1): 1–12.

———. 2002. Wolf recovery and management as value-based political conflict. *Ethics, Place, & Environment* 5 (1): 65–71.

Pacelle, Wayne. 1998. Forging a new wildlife management paradigm: Integrating animal protection values. *Human Dimensions of Wildlife* 3 (2): 42–50.

Rawson, Timothy. 2001. *Changing tracks: Predators and politics in Mt. McKinley National Park*. Fairbanks: University of Alaska Press.

Seager, Joni. 2003. Pepperoni or broccoli? On the cutting wedge of feminist environmentalism. *Gender, Place and Culture* 10 (2): 167–74.

Sherman, Jennifer. 2004. Remaking rural masculinity: Fatherhood and masculine identity in the spotted owl's shadow. Paper presented at the annual meeting of the Rural Sociological Society, Sacramento, CA, 14 August.

Skogen, Ketil, and Olve Krange. 2003. A wolf at the gate: The Anti-Carnivore Alliance and the symbolic construction of community. *Sociologia Ruralis* 43 (3): 309–25.

Smelser, Neil I. 1998. Collective myths and fantasies: The myth of the good life in California. In *The social edges of psychoanalysis*. Berkeley: University of California Press.

Snow, David A., E. Burke Rochford Jr., Steven K. Worden, and Robert D. Benford. 1986. Frame alignment processes, micromobilization, and movement participation. *American Sociological Review* 51:464–81.

Stedman, Richard C., and Thomas A. Heberlein. 2001. Hunting and rural socialization: Contingent effects of the rural setting on hunting participation. *Rural Sociology* 66 (4): 599–617.

Strate, L. 1992. Beer commercials: A manual on masculinity. In *Men, masculinity, and the media*, edited by S. Craig. Newbury Park, CA: Sage.

Strohmeyer, John. 2003. *Extreme conditions: Big oil and the transformation of Alaska*. Anchorage, AK: Cascade Press.

Warren, K. J. 1995. The power and the promise of ecological feminism. In *Earth ethics: Environmental ethics, animal rights, and practical applications*, edited by J. P. Sterba. Englewood Cliffs, NJ: Prentice Hall.

Willott, Sara, and Christine Griffin. 1996. Men, masculinity, and the challenge of long-term unemployment. In *Understanding masculinities*, edited by M. M. A. Ghaill. Philadelphia: Open University Press

Woods, Michael. 1997. Researching rural conflicts: Hunting, local politics and actor-networks. *Journal of Rural Studies* 14:321–40.

Sarah F. Williams

"A Walking Open Wound": Emo Rock and the "Crisis" of Masculinity in America[1]

How could we ever really know or love each other as long as we kept playing those roles that kept us from knowing or being ourselves? Weren't men as well as women still locked in lovely isolation, alienation, no matter how many sexual acrobatics they put their bodies through? Weren't men dying too young, suppressing fears and tears and their own tenderness? It seemed to me that men weren't really the enemy—they were fellow victims, suffering from an outmoded masculine mystique that made them feel unnecessarily inadequate when there were no bears to kill.[2]

In the late 1990s and early 2000s, amid synthpop- and boy band-saturated airwaves, a band from the suburban beach town of Boca Raton, Florida, began to make waves of their own—first through small crowds generated by Internet communities, and then reaching the masses splashed on the covers of major American music magazines and MTV. Although some would argue their musical style is a far cry from the bands originally saddled with this hardcore punk-derived moniker, Dashboard Confessional brought emo rock to the mainstream. As a musical style and genre, emo, or emotionally oriented rock, has gained credibility and wide acceptance in recent years due to the unparalleled popularity of bands such as Dashboard Confessional, The Get Up Kids, Saves the Day, Brand New, and Thursday as well as the publication of journalist Andy Greenwald's book *Nothing Feels Good: Punk Rock,*

Teenagers, and Emo.[3] Despite this recent publication and countless journalistic investigations into youth culture's attraction to these artists, there has yet to be an investigation into the actual musical characteristics of emo rock especially with respect to gender studies. Representations of gender stereotypes in popular music have dramatically come to the fore in academic scholarship during the last few years, which discusses everything from 80s New Wave to heavy metal and punk rock, yet little as current or curious as the emo phenomenon.[4] This study will examine the established codes of an extramusical idea such as masculinity as represented in emo rock.

In many ways, current emo rock embodies what journalists and sociologists have referred to as a so-called crisis of masculinity. Men, like women, have been imprisoned by cultural stereotypes not only in the way they reenact social gender codes but also in the subcultures, lyrics, images, and semiotics they choose to represent themselves as popular music artists. Definitions of manhood have shifted over the decades as our culture has moved from one of production, utility, and industry to one of consumption, ornament, and service.[5] This society of industry recognized the essence of masculinity to be stoicism, a backbreaking work ethic, a willingness to shoulder others' burdens, reliability, and unflinching resolve. Our current culture of consumption recognizes manhood, according to Susan Faludi, as "defined by appearance, by youth and attractiveness, by money and aggression, by posture and swagger and 'props,' by the curled lip and petulant sulk and flexed biceps."[6] Expressions of masculinity in popular music must work within these incredibly limited, culturally constructed

521

scenarios as well. As a more contemporary and mainstream expression of underground American punk and hardcore music, emo rock attempts, awkwardly at times, to reconcile the long-established codes of masculinity—musical representations of aggression, pomp, stoicism, misogyny, and determination—with more multifaceted human expressions of heartache, weakness, longing, and loss. For instance, how do emo artists today musically portray the gamut of masculine emotions in an underground genre that has heretofore been characterized by pounding, violent guitar distortion, extreme dynamics, and gritty, hostile vocal timbres? Emo rock, as I will elucidate, is one articulation of the adjustments and redefinitions that masculinity must experience in the face of numerous social shifts from consumer culture to feminist backlash.[7] Perhaps these "crises" and conflicts seemingly arise due to rigid social definitions of gender roles and their inability to adapt to the changing cultural landscape. Perhaps, also, the current state of the male identity is, as sociologist David Morgan notes, not so much in an actual "crisis," but rather "widely disseminated talk about crisis."[8]

"Manhood under Siege": Debate about the "Crisis"

Writers and academics—from sociologist Barbara Ehrenreich to journalist Susan Faludi—have examined the effects of social change on the American masculine identity for decades. They have noted, again, the shifts in cultural values and the rise and subsequent backlash of the feminist movement as contributing factors to what Susan Faludi refers to as "American manhood under siege."[9] Faludi, Michael Kimmel, E. Anthony Rotundo, and others have observed the effects of cultural and economic change on cultural perceptions of manhood in America. Before the Second World War, men's contribution to society, and therefore their worth, was bound up in endeavors that exhibited "social usefulness." The prevailing definition of manhood was those who "carried out their duties to family and community were men to admire."[10] Our culture shifted

toward one of celebrity, advertising, technology, consumption, and ornament, and saw the growth of the middle class, suburban sprawl, and service industries perceived as more "feminine" than industry. The movement of labor into office cubicles instead of the factory began to crush the putative individuality and initiative of the working-class male. The "hardness," as author David Riesman wrote about 1950s maleness, understood to be inherent in American masculinity was going "soft" as its spirit was dampened by the collective will of the corporation.[11] This whittling away at the masculine façade as economic provider continued through the 1990s and 2000s despite unemployment, corporate downsizing, and economic highs and lows. Faludi cautions against the viewing of the crisis of masculinity through the lens of these superficial social indicators and suggests, rather, that we consider the fact that:

> we have changed fundamentally from a society that produced a culture to a culture rooted in no real society at all. . . . Where we once lived in a society in which men in particular participated by being useful in public life, we now are surrounded by a culture that encourages people to play almost no functional public roles, only decorative or consumer ones.[12]

The social gender roles became murky—that is, men's roles in society as "breadwinners" and women's as "house makers" evolved beyond these caricature-like stereotypes. For generations of men whose identities were bound up in economy, labor, and wage, this represents a fairly major crisis of self and worth.[13] We can see, in many ways, the parallel between this realignment and renegotiation of the masculine identity in twenty-first-century American culture and the shift in musical aesthetics in hardcore punk and emo genres toward styles more multilayered and expressive.

Because concrete investigations into gender studies and culture began in earnest with the women's movement, feminism as a discipline has been the theoretical basis for the way in which studies of gender, and subsequently masculinities, have been developed. In that respect, theories of male identity and masculinity have been measured against and in relation to feminist methodologies. This influence is less about certain texts or scholarly publications as it is about, as David Morgan asserts, "the influence of a particular social and political movement which had certain consequences for the ways in which some men see their lives."[14] There have been several cultural responses to the feminist movement over the past few decades with direct respect to how men view their own sexuality and their identities within society. This should not be considered a unilateral direction of influence, however. Over time feminist critiques change and modify, as do masculinities, and the response of both men and women to feminism and vice versa evolve as our social environments change. Or, as Morgan again notes:

> "Wimp" can be a term of disapproval amongst feminists as well as amongst groups of men and it is not unknown for some feminists, certainly some women, to be heard saying that they prefer the old men to the new men on the grounds that at least one knew where one was with the old version. Men in their turn are responding to these responses from women and feminists.[15]

Sociologists have cited a "masculine mystique" as responsible for the stereotypes men were working against before, during, and after the feminist movement. The "mystique," or expectations of the male social role, dictated that men be iron-clad, impenetrable, stoic breadwinners—roles just as unattainable and unrealistic as the feminine social roles. One publication in the early 1980s in New York attempted to enlighten its readers on these problematic social constraints, especially the masculine façade:

> The American Male—brave, courageous, and bold. . . . He's the provider. He's the bedrock of the American family. He learns to repress emotions like fear, insecurity, compassion which leads to tears, and a certain kind of sensitivity allowed to be felt by women only.[16]

The author goes on to make note of this restrictive definition of masculinity. This unattainable ideal led to what Barbara Ehrenreich describes as "psychic alienation" and the beginnings of the men's liberation movement that, in the popular press, depicted men as "stepping out of [their] armor" and viewing the male role as a "disposable exoskeleton" one sheds to reveal the true man within.[17]

Yet this "softening" of the image of American masculinity came with a price as questions arose as to exactly how malleable the male role truly was:

> The qualities now claimed for the authentic male self—sensitivity, emotional ability, a capacity for self-indulgence, even unpredictability —were still, and despite the feminist campaign to the contrary, recognizably "feminine." How much could a man transform himself, in the name of androgynous progress, without ceasing to be . . . "all male," or visibly heterosexual?[18]

Although the men's liberation movement of the 1970s and 1980s attempted to widen definitions of American masculinity, it was in many ways responsible for the ghettoization and stigmatization of homosexuality and the sharp divide between gay and straight behaviors. This strong identification with one "camp" or the other allowed straight men to adopt or display various traits or behaviors usually reserved for stereotypically "effeminate" lifestyles while remaining firmly entrenched in heterosexuality. So we see again that masculinity has nothing to do, in the end, with the expressions of certain traits. Expressions of sexuality depend more on "the maintenance of certain kinds of relation ships, between men and women, and between men."[19] Thus the cultural segregation of the homosexual community and men's continued responses to feminism have contributed to the construction of American masculinity and men's perceptions of their own sexuality in relation to other social groups. The implications of the feminist movement and the general societal shifts in America can be represented, either consciously or unconsciously, in popular music art forms.

Since the inception of the Greek musical modes and their symbolic connections with coded expression, exactly how music communicates meaning has fascinated Western thinkers and composers. Scholars looked for new methodologies and vocabularies to approach popular music—a genre that relies more on aural compositions than written ones—when it became clear that popular and rock musics were eclipsing Western art music in social influence and popularity.[20] The lyrical content, instrumentation, fan base, history of the genre, and the very images of the performers are as important in the construction of meaning in music as are the sounds themselves. As a case in point, we have come to identify fast tempos, declamatory vocal styles, distorted guitars, and loud dynamics with an aggressive, oftentimes rage-filled sentiment in music—a sentiment usually upheld through secondary indicators such as the song lyrics and the constraints of the particular musical genres or subcultures of which the performance or musical ensemble is a part. Because most punk genres were historically male-dominated, as is the rock industry in general, and exhibited these particular musical codes, we consequently uphold these sonic tropes as symbolic of masculine pomp and prowess. Mediated by lyrics, images, performances, and marketing, the musical constructions of problematic concepts like sexuality can be subverted by various layers of representation.[21] Emo is a problematic genre of music in this respect—that is, it situates itself in the lineage of underground punk and hardcore genres, yet its artists strive to venture musically and lyrically beyond the aesthetic effects of nihilism, pessimism, and political frustration.

Emo's Beginnings

The musical representation of rage, anguish, and social defiance were heartily codified in the various punk movements that began in England in the late 1970s and spread west to the United States through New York to the opposite coast in Seattle. The musical roots of emo as a genre distinction lie in America's answer to the British punk invasion. Hardcore, as a genre categorization, has been in use since the mid-1980s when American youth began to rebel against what it

saw as the inauthenticity of New Wave and recapture the DIY spirit and raw aggression of punk. Started in Washington, D.C., by bands like Rites of Spring, Jawbreaker, and Minor Threat, with contributions by Southern California bands such as Black Flag and Social Distortion, hardcore retained the aggressive tempos, declamatory vocal styles, and shocking on-stage behavior characteristic of English punk in the late 1970s; however, the lyrical content of hardcore began to shift from outward rage against authority to inner feelings of emotional pain, depression, and loneliness.[22] Seventies punk was, in many ways, about a loss of control in a world of corrupt politics and class wars, whereas hardcore struggles with a loss of emotional grounding and a breakdown of the stoic masculine veneer. It is a movement that strives to retain the musical signifiers of aggressive masculinity while redirecting the focus of the lyrics to more personal and private topics that had heretofore gone unexplored in punk idioms. However, because of its musical and performative allegiance to antiestablishment, antimainstream punk genres, hardcore was destined to remain underground.

Hardcore was, among other things, about disaffected suburban youth raging against the affluence and yuppie greed of the "Gimme Decade" of the 1980s. Unlike the repressed, working-class punk bands in Britain, hardcore appeared in the vast cookie-cutter expanse of Southern California and the sprawling metropolis of Reagan-era Washington, D.C., led by middle-class, complacent youth. Historically, punk scenes emerge out of economic and cultural repression and recession. Not coincidentally, at the apex of the hardcore movement in 1982 the United States was experiencing price increases, record unemployment, and economic recession.[23] Hardcore as a vibrant scene was short-lived and, in many ways, was not transmittable to the mainstream because of its extreme aesthetic. Popular tastes in America seemed to favor the clean, electronic sounds of New Wave. In fact, in the years following the British punk movement and rise and fall of hardcore, American audiences saw the inception of MTV and the subsequent growth in the record industry due to the massive popularity of New Wave—a far cry from the raw and raucous sounds of punk upon which it was originally founded.[24]

Beyond the violent mosh pits and stage-diving crowd antics, hardcore also dealt with lyrical issues that did not find a ready audience in the 1980s in the midst of apparently superficial, "candy-coated" pop—that is, depression, identity crises, and other personal demons. For instance, the brawny, tattooed leader of the seminal hardcore band Black Flag, Henry Rollins, is featured on their 1981 record *Damaged* shattering a mirror with his bare fist. *Damaged* contains the requisite hardcore sound—breakneck tempos, rhythmic insistency, guitar distortion—and Rollins's signature growl. With songs about partying, beer, and women, at no point do we get a glimpse of an intimate timbre or the sensitive turn of a melodic phrase. Like all good hardcore, the musical emphasis is on speed and ferocity. However, one particularly revealing and vulnerable track, "Depression," begins with nebulous guitar feedback before launching into this typical hardcore punk sound. Rollins shouts the lyrics "Right here, all by myself / I ain't got no one else / the situation is bleeding me / there's no relief for a person like me." Yet the desperation in the lyrics is drowned out by the raw aggression of the music. Similarly, the catalogue of 1980s hardcore masters Minor Threat, in keeping with the hardcore aesthetic, does not contain one song over about two minutes and is monothematic in its overall soundscape. The band members throw themselves from the stage, destroy equipment, spit and scream static, monotone vocal lines, and write songs with tempos pushing 184 bpm. Yet the blatant self-consciousness of the lyrics begins to seep through in songs like "Little Friend." The lyrics describe a man on the edge: "No description / For what I feel / It's a non-emotion / It's something gray / Way down / Inside of me." After the third repetition of lead singer Ian McKaye's list of possible descriptors for his feelings—"anger," "fear," and "frustration," which is accompanied

by a primal scream—we experience an uncharacteristic decrease in energy and tempo in a wash of guitar feedback. McKaye and his band mates convey a sense of emotional authenticity in their lyrics despite musical characteristics that would incite the most fervent slam dancing and stage diving.

Like any punk genre, technical proficiency and musical display is not essential in the construction of style. As hardcore chronicler Steven Blush notes, hardcore focused on "speed and anger" without any reference to the experimental or avant-garde.[25] Lacking the self-indulgent guitar solos of heavy metal or classic rock, tempos were as fast as possible and vocals were aggressive and abrasive, bordering on speech-song monotonal growls. Hardcore was very much about a preservation of this musical style wherein the communication of aggression, anguish, frustration, and even emotional vulnerability were relegated representation through breakneck tempos, harsh, gritty vocal timbres, and very little deviation from simple formal structures. It was a step forward, however, from the unemotional, asexual working-class British punk whose image of authenticity and energy hardcore artists strove to recreate. Late 1990s emo rock was inspired by the musical ferocity of hardcore and its struggle to reconcile more complex human emotions with a wider palate of musical signifiers.

Punk's Softer Side

Emo rock, and even some of the more mainstream hardcore artists, creates musical paradoxes that mimic the "masculine mystique" that is widely discussed in current academic and popular discourse. Musical expressions of sex, gender, and sexuality are contingent on the perpetuation of gender stereotypes and social roles. As we experience shifts in our culture and those social roles come under increasing scrutiny, these conflicts and changes can manifest themselves in artistic representations like popular music and art.[26] Through the mix of punk styles and the occasional use of musical signifiers normally reserved for more "sensitive" or "feminine" styles of music—acoustic guitars, stringed instruments, intimate vocal styles—emo musically presents a conflicted, but evolving, portrait of modern manhood. This portrait has, for many years, brewed beneath the surface of the aggressive veneer of punk rock genres; the more mainstream musical sensibilities of emo bring this punk-related genre, and its program of honest vulnerability, to the forefront. To achieve this feat, emo captures the changes in cultural attitudes about masculinity and the musical signifiers of emotional weakness—that is, such "undesirable" qualities like vulnerability, femininity, weakness—while attempting to retain the musical signifiers of aggression that are the bedrock of the punk/hardcore musical style. The struggles and seemingly contradictory combinations that characterized the 1980s underground subgenre of hardcore paved the way for a new, more multifaceted representation of masculinity in modern emo rock that captures, and perhaps even encourages, the current metamorphoses of social sex roles.

Emo, as an underground genre, was created from a merging of hardcore and indie rock after the last gasp of the grunge movement and before the Britneys and boy bands of the late 1990s. Andy Greenwald describes the inception of this genre as a sort of "kinder and gentler" punk: "The songs were smoother, and the chords were chunkier and corralled into sloppy melodies. The voices weren't accusing, they were yearning."[27] Emo still displayed the fast tempos, double time drumbeats, and declamatory vocals, but the style was not as homogenous as hardcore. Emo has become a broader genre that now encompasses acoustic rock, thrash, metal, rap, and country. Exploring the addition of instruments like acoustic guitars, pianos, even violins and cellos, evocative sonorities like major seventh chords, and deceptive terrace dynamics, emo began to expand the musical possibilities for punk and hard rock genres. The lyrical content and program as well have shifted beyond the anguish of hardcore and the "general pain of being an outsider to the specific hurt of a bad relationship."[28]

It was the voice of disempowered, misunderstood teenagers across the country. In blunt, nonpoetic terms, the mission of the emo artists was to articulate the collective shortcomings, fears, and miseries of the masses through their music.

Emo is teen-centric. Regardless of the lead singer's age, the desired vocal timbre is a slightly prepubescent nasal quality with a diaphragmatic push that resembles the arrogant vocalizations of British punk. Emo music videos depict teen rites of passage such as proms, house parties gone wild, and anxiety over graduation. The album art for the band Saves the Day's *Through Being Cool* (1999) features the bored, disaffected, and slightly nervous artists as social outcasts, awkwardly lounging on a sagging futon while a high school house party rages in the background. Targeting music consumers in the midst of adolescence built emo a loyal, fanatic subcultural fan base.[29]

Jimmy Eat World, a certified platinum emo band from suburban Phoenix, is the perfect poster child for this burgeoning punk subgenre. The band members, regardless of their age, connect with the audience by casting themselves as equally awkward and gangly thirty-year-old men:

> Onstage [frontman Jim Adkins] is more craftsman than character, old and maybe gawkier than his fans but otherwise not that different from them. In "Pain," a lament delivered as if it were a call to arms, he sang as if he were trying to dissolve into the crowd of teenagers who were singing along.[30]

Musically, Jimmy Eat World displays a wider array of instrumentation, tempos, and structural forms than typical two-minute hardcore rants. In a song on their 1999 album *Clarity*, Adkins and fellow band members cater to their base with "Crush," a song about adolescent insecurity and regret. The lyrics read like a page from a high schooler's diary about a failed first goodnight kiss: "Hands around your waist / Take in restraint like a breath / It's your move / Settle for less again." Typical punk conventions such as repeated low guitar and bass eighth notes under short, detached vocal phrases accompany the verse sections, while the chorus and bridge sections are more melodic, eventually leading to a section in which the drums drop out and the vocals repeat "like a breath" amidst a distorted haze of feedback. This brief, but incredibly charged, pause occurs here leading to a more energized version of the chorus section, like the "restraint" of this transition section breaking free. This conceit—that is, the cathartic climax and release of this charged pause—is fairly common in modern emo songs. It could be considered indicative of signifiers of the climax-arousal song format that has historically signified masculine sexuality. However, given the lyrical content and other musical indicators such as instrumentation and complexity of form, it seems emo is beginning to challenge the rigid constraints of what it means to make music within a historically male-dominated subculture. Addressing the similar subject of unrequited love, The Get Up Kids' "Martyr Me" (2004) features the same type of subdued transition section, paring the instrumentation down to only vocals and acoustic guitar. A desperate "balcony scene-style" plea for what would presumably be a female savior from his life of ennui, the lead singer croons in almost affected youthful strains: "It's a good fight / Thrown in the towel / I'm just sinking water deep / But if all I have is defeat / [Chorus] Tonight if you're awake at all." After a build in momentum to a deceptive terrace dynamic—at the point we would expect the triumphant return of the chorus—we hear in fact a rather restrained section where we hear only the lead singer's voice accompanied by the earnest strum of an acoustic guitar. We are offered perhaps a window of vulnerability here—a point at which our troubadour would stand in a solitary spotlight and metamorphose the concert dynamic from one of raucous arena to intimate coffeehouse. Yet this window slams quickly after no more than a taste of this curious shift in aesthetic when the final restatement of the chorus returns at the original dynamic accompanied by the full electric instrumentation.

The darling of the emo movement, Dashboard Confessional lead singer Chris Carrabba, frequently strums an acoustic guitar with the same vehemence and aggression as any hard rocker plays an electric. A visual contraction, Carrabba's much-discussed good looks—with a perfectly coiffed 1950s-style James Dean, greaser haircut—are paired with intricate and elaborate tattoos up and down both arms, traditionally a social symbol for a punk or "deviant." Dashboard Confessional's fans are legendary in their fervent loyalty to the group and their almost cultlike behavior at live concerts. Obscuring Carrabba's own amplified vocals, scores of pathos-ridden teenagers scream the catalogue of lyrics, word for word, like a cathartic musical group therapy session. The band catapulted into the mainstream with their 2001 release, *The Places You Have Come to Fear the Most*, despite the fact that it was a stylistic departure for both the band and the genre itself. Although still containing songs that carried fairly active, punk-inspired drum beats and Carrabba's noticeably youthful tenor voice, the instrumentation was pared down to only, at times, Carrabba's voice and acoustic guitar. Historically the milieu of the sensitive, yet sexless, singer/songwriter, Carrabba appropriates this "feminine" instrument and refashions it for emo as a symbol of sincerity.[31] Relentless and rhythmic, Carrabba's guitar accompanies the lyrics to "Again I Go Unnoticed," the story of a stagnant relationship: "Another wasted night, / the television steals the conversation. / Exhale, another wasted breath, / again it goes unnoticed." Carrabba's voice still carries the punk/hardcore edgy grunt, but the symbolic sincerity of the acoustic guitar begs one to pay attention to the sentiments of vulnerability and pain in the lyrics. Appropriating the energy and rhythmic intensity of punk, Dashboard Confessional's subject matter and even the vocal timbre of its lead singer seems to betray its hardcore roots, a genre that has traditionally required *musical* aggression and machismo. Carrabba effortlessly shifts between a more guttural vocal style reserved for sexually aggressive and arrogant genres like punk and hard rock, and, with eyes closed and lips to microphone, a sweetly intimate falsetto croon.

On the more recent and amplified album *A Mark, A Mission, A Brand, A Scar*, Carrabba continues to vacillate between these aggressive, declamatory vocal styles and a more intimate falsetto on "Ghost of a Good Thing." Built on an accompaniment of acoustic guitar "power chords"—the root-fifth-octave voicing and preferred chord structure of heavy metal and hard rock—Carrabba warbles his way through the majority of the song in a delicate voice, so beautifully fragile one nervously waits for a prepubescent crack. In a brief return to the chorus, the "grain" of Carrabba's voice suddenly shifts, for the first and only time in the song, to a more nasal, declamatory vocal style accompanied by these assertive power chords. John Shepherd equates these nasal timbres to "reproducing physiologically the tension and experiential repression encountered as males engage with the public world," whereas the more thin, softer tones, produced in the head instead of the chest cavity, come to represent "male vulnerability" in hard rock genres.[32] Whether or not Carrabba or his fans are aware, these subtle vocal shifts project different characterizations and aid in the representation of not only this specific lead singer but also the set of characteristics that define emo as a genre. After this brief and jarring vocal episode, Carrabba returns to his softer style, later adding gentle acoustic guitar strums and arpeggios, tambourine, and even a Db major seventh chord—all signifiers of the more emotionally charged singer-songwriter style, *not* hardcore or hard rock.

Dashboard Confessional's title track to their 2001 acoustic album, "The Places You Have Come to Fear the Most," exhibits many of the aforementioned palate-broadening characteristics of the modern emo genre—including a charged pause for dramatic effect preceding the triumphant return of the chorus. However, this time, instead of reinforcing the musical conventions of punk and hard rock by launching back into a ragged vocal timbre after a softer transition section and charged, anxious pause, Chris

Carrabba jumps immediately into the final chorus material one octave higher, at the edge of his vocal range. In a voice that resembles sobbing rather than screaming, Carrabba cries: "This is one time that you can't fake it hard enough to please everyone, or anyone at all." In perhaps the most revealing moment in emo rock, audible gasping cries punctuate these lyrics and mimic the hysteria of weeping as Carrabba struggles for air while ferociously strumming his acoustic guitar. Although the lyrical content here does not deal with unrequited love or the pain of a breakup, Carrabba pens a sentiment similar to that of the hardcore bands that inspired his music-making—that is, the frustration with inauthenticity and the tribulations of living a "genuine" existence. Appropriating the acoustic guitar as a symbol of sincerity and honest poetics, Dashboard Confessional, and other emo bands, attempt to musically depict masculinity and the genre of emo as multifaceted. The semiotics of emotional pain, frustration, anger, love, arrogant masculinity, and aggression are sometimes seamlessly united and, at the same time, jarringly juxtaposed.

Conclusion

The so-called crisis of modern masculinity in America manifests itself in numerous ways. From changing attitudes toward male and female roles in the workplace and home to the types of instruments that are appropriate for use in certain popular music genres, these social and artistic shifts are always tenuous and self-conscious at the outset. Many emo bands and fans resent, subconsciously perhaps, the genre label itself because of the gender implications it implies. Riley Breckenridge of the emo band Thrice explains that "people run from the emo tag because being emotional entails being sensitive and crying and stuff like that. Most sixteen year olds or eighteen year olds don't want to admit that they ever cry or that they ever are sensitive."[33] Yet these artists seem to be caught between expressing a kind of populist sentiment—that is, most teenagers in America, including males, can relate to being dumped, feeling invisible, or dealing with bullies—and representing the firmly entrenched ideas of what it means to make male-centered rock music. Emo rock and hardcore first reinterpreted these signifiers of male sexual aggression—pounding, repetitive guitar chords, declamatory vocal styles—as representative of emotional pain, adolescent angst, and the frustration of a world bent on misunderstanding its nonconformist youth. The relentless strumming of the electric guitar coupled with driving drumbeats is straying from its original indicators of sexual frustration and aggressive, violent masculinity depicted by punk genres. Rather, the expansion of musical ideas, lyrics, and instrumentation are slowly becoming acceptable as an indicator of emotional turmoil, insecurities, vulnerability, and other emotions beyond one-dimensional stereotypes of men's experiences. By slowing down and addressing the changing emotional landscape of American men, emo has connected with its fan base in a way hardcore and punk artists were unable to accomplish. Fans of this more introspective version of hardcore still require the energy, authenticity, and volume that is expected of any subgenre of punk; however, now that the sonic landscape has grown to represent more faithfully the sentiments of the lyrics, emo bands are finding that their fans have stopped stage diving, and started listening.

Notes

1. Versions of this paper were presented at the International Association for the Study of Popular Music in Charlottesville, VA, in October 2004 and the Hawaii International Conference on Arts and Humanities in Honolulu, HI, in January 2006. I am grateful for many conversations on masculinity and rock music, emo in particular, with Dr. Jennifer Walshe, Dr. Jean Little-john, John Williams, Prof. Scott Lipscomb, and Joe Cannon whose insights and encouragement inspired this paper. I am also grateful for the comments and suggestions of those at IASPM, specifically Griffin Woodworth, Daniel Party, and Prof. Richard Peterson.

2. Betty Friedan, *The Feminine Mystique* (New York: W. W. Norton, 1963), 368.

3. Andy Greenwald, *Nothing Feels Good: Punk Rock, Teenagers, and Emo* (New York: St. Martin's Griffin, 2003).

4. See, for example, Simon Reynolds and Joy Press, *The Sex Revolts: Gender, Rebellion and Rock 'n' Roll* (Cambridge, MA: Harvard University Press, 1995); Lucy O'Brien, *Annie Lennox: Sweet Dreams are Made of This* (New York: St. Martin's Press, 1993), 77–79; Robert Walser, "Prince as Queer Post-structuralist," *Popular Music and Society* 18, no. 2 (1994): 79–90, and *Running With the Devil: Power, Gender and Madness in Heavy Metal Music* (Hanover, NH: University Press of New England, 1993); Robert Walser and Susan McClary, "Start Making Sense! Musicology Wrestles with Rock," in *On Record: Rock, Pop, and the Written Word*, ed. Simon Frith and Andrew Goodwin (London and New York: Routledge, 1990 [1988]), 277–300 (283). See also Simon Frith and Angela McRobbie, "Rock and Sexuality" in *On Record: Rock, Pop and the Written Word*, ed. Simon Frith and Andrew Goodwin (London and New York: Routledge, 1990 [1978]), 371–389 (374); Sheila Whiteley, *Women and Popular Music: Sexuality, Identity and Subjectivity* (London and New York: Routledge, 2000), "Little Red Rooster v. The Honky Tonk Woman: Mick Jagger, Sexuality, Style and Image," in *Sexing the Groove*, ed. Sheila Whiteley (London and New York: Routledge, 1997), 67–99, and *The Space Between the Notes: Rock and the Counter-Culture* (London and New York: Routledge, 1992); Lisa Lewis, *Gender Politics and MTV* (Philadelphia: Temple University Press, 1990), 43–54, 129–151; Susan McClary, *Feminine Endings* (Minneapolis: University of Minnesota Press, 1991), 148–168; Mark Simpson, "Dragging it Up and Down: The Glamorized Male Body," in *Male Impersonators: Men Performing Masculinity*, ed. Mark Simpson (London and New York: Routledge, 1994), 177–196; Gareth Palmer, "Bruce Springsteen and Masculinity," in *Sexing the Groove*, ed. Sheila Whiteley (London and New York: Routledge, 1997), 100–117.

5. See also Ian Biddle's chapter in this volume, Chapter 6.

6. Susan Faludi, *Stiffed: The Betrayal of the American Man* (New York: Harper-Collins, 1999), 38.

7. This idea of a "crisis" of masculinity and male identity is discussed by M. S. Kimmel in "The Contemporary 'Crisis' of Masculinity in Historical Perspective," in *The Making of Masculinities*, ed. H. Brod (Boston: Allen & Unwin, 1987), 121–154, and in "Re-

thinking 'Masculinity': New Directions in Research," in *Changing Men: New Directions in Research on Men and Masculinity*, ed. M. S. Kimmel (Newbury Park, CA: Sage, 1987). See also P. Hodson, *Men: An Investigation into the Emotional Male* (London: BBC/Ariel Books, 1984). These texts receive further commentary in David H. J. Morgan, *Discovering Men* (London and New York: Routledge, 1992), 6–23. For more popular psychology ruminations on the subject, see Robert Bly, *Iron John: A Book About Men* (New York: Vintage, 1992); Warren Farrell, *The Myth of Male Power* (New York: Berkley Publishing Group, 2001).

8. Morgan, *Discovering*, 7.

9. Faludi, *Stiffed*, 6.

10. E. Anthony Rotundo, *American Manhood* (New York: Basic Books, 1993), 13. See also Herb Gilmore, *The Hazards of Being Male* (New York: Signet, 1987), x.

11. See David Riesman, *The Lonely Crowd* (New Haven: Yale University Press, 1950), 18–41. Riesman's study focuses more on the effects of conformity in American society and the rise in white-collar labor. See also Barbara Ehrenreich, *The Hearts of Men: The American Dream and the Flight from Commitment* (Garden City, NY: Anchor Press, 1983), 34–35 for a detailed discussion of this work.

12. Faludi, *Stiffed*, 34–35.

13. See Ehrenreich, *Hearts*, 11–41, 169–182 for a discussion of what she refers to as the "breadwinner ethic."

14. Morgan, *Discovering*, 7.

15. Ibid., 18.

16. Philip Rice, "On Being Male in America," *Voice* (Spring 1981): 1.

17. Ehrenreich, *Hearts*, 127.

18. Ibid., 128. For more on the early men's liberation movement, see also Roger Horrocks, *Masculinity in Crisis: Myths, Fantasies and Realities* (London: St. Martin's Press, 1994), 89–91; Joseph H. Pleck, "The Male Sex Role: Definitions, Problems and Sources of Change," *Journal of Social Issues* 32 (1976): 155–164 (155); Jack Sawyer, "On Male Liberation," *Liberation* 15 (1970): 32–33 (32); Robert Brannon, "The Male Sex Role: Our Culture's Blueprint of Manhood, and What It's Done for Us Lately," in *The Forty-Nine Percent Majority*, ed. Deborah S. David and Robert Brannon (Reading, MA: Addison Wesley, 1976), 4–15.

19. Morgan, *Discovering*, 67.

20. See Walser and McClary, "Musicology," 277–292, for a discussion on musicology and its adaptations to include popular and rock music.

21. See Frith and McRobbie, "Rock," 371–373.

22. See Bernard Perusse, "Shouldn't All Music Be Emotional?," *The Gazette* (Montreal, Quebec), May 8, 2004, D1.

23. See Steven Blush, *American Hardcore: A Tribal History* (New York: Federal House, 2001), 29; Steven Taylor, *False Prophet: Field Notes from the Punk Underground* (Middletown, CT: Wesleyan University Press, 2003), 72. A similar situation occurred in England that spurred the British punk scene. See Jon Savage, *England's Dreaming: Anarchy, Sex Pistols, Punk Rock, and Beyond* (New York: St. Martin's Griffin, 1991), 108–110, for commentary on the social and economic conditions in England at the time punk surfaced in the late 1970s.

24. New Wave was, in many ways, an "art school" version of punk and hardcore youth sought a music that would reclaim the DIY authenticity and raw energy of punk without the cumbersome, intellectual baggage of New Wave. For more on the comparisons of New Wave to punk, see Dave Rimmer, *Like Punk Never Happened: Culture Club and the New Pop* (London: Faber & Faber, 1985), 7–23; David Szatmary, *A Time to Rock: A Social History of Rock and Roll* (New York: Schirmer Books, 1996), 236, 274–275; Legs McNeil and Gillian McCain, *Please Kill Me: The Uncensored Oral History of Punk* (New York: Grove Press, 1996), 405; Taylor, *False Prophet*, 71; Lawrence Grossberg, "Is There Rock after Punk?" in *On Record: Rock, Pop, and the Written Word*, ed. Simon Frith and Andrew Goodwin (London and New York: Routledge, 1990), 111–124; Simon Frith and Andrew Goodwin, "New Pop and its Aftermath," in *On Record: Rock, Pop and the Written Word*, ed. Simon Frith and Andrew Goodwin (London and New York: Routledge, 1990), 466–471; Blush, *American*, 12–14, 35–37.

25. Blush, *American*, 37.

26. See Blush, *American*, 35, for a commentary on hardcore as a male-dominated subgenre and its relationship to the beginnings of the Riot Grrrl feminist punk movement that began primarily in Olympia, Washington.

27. Greenwald, *Nothing*, 34.

28. Josh Tyrangiel, "Emotional Rescue," *Time* (May 27, 2002): 60. See also Alex Pappademas, "The Heart-

break Kid," *Spin* (October 2003): 66–69.

29. The particulars of emo's fan base are a topic beyond the scope of this current study. However, Andy Greenwald discusses the demographics and dynamics of emo fans at length in his book *Nothing Feels Good*. It is interesting to note that unlike punk and hardcore, there are nearly equal numbers of men and women at emo concerts and the participatory aspect of these live events—for example, singing the lyrics along with the band—are not specific to any one gender.

30. Kelefa Sanneh, "Are We Not Sensitive? We Are (Arena) Emo," *The New York Times*, April 16, 2005, 7. See also Aldin Vaziri, "Don't Say Emo to Jimmy Eat World," *The San Francisco Chronicle*, November 3, 2004, E2.

31. For commentary on the symbolic properties of rock instruments, specifically the guitar, see for example Steve Waksman, "Black Sound, Black Body: Jimi Hendrix, the Electric Guitar and the Meanings of Blackness," in *Instruments of Desire* (Cambridge, MA: Harvard University Press, 1999), 167–206; Mavis Bayton, "Women and the Electric Guitar," in *Sexing the Groove*, ed. Sheila Whiteley (London and New York: Routledge, 1997), 37–49.

32. John Shepherd, "Music and Male Hegemony," in *Music as Social Text* (Cambridge: Polity Press, 1991), 166.

33. Perusse, "Shouldn't," D1.

PART TEN

Violence and Masculinities

Nightly, we watch news reports of suicide bombings in the Middle East, terrorist attacks on the United States, racist hate crimes, gay-bashing murders, or Colombian drug lords and their legions of gun-toting thugs. Do these reports ever mention that virtually every single one of these terrorists, suicide bombers, or racist gang members is male?

This fact is so obvious that it barely needs to be mentioned. Virtually all the violence in the world today is committed by men. Imagine, for a moment, if all that violence were perpetrated entirely by women. Would that not be *the* story?

Take a look at the numbers: Men constitute 99 percent of all persons arrested for rape, 88 percent of those arrested for murder, 92 percent of those arrested for robbery, 87 percent for aggravated assault, 85 percent of other assaults, 83 percent of all family violence, and 82 percent of disorderly conduct. Nearly 90 percent of all murder victims are killed by men.

From early childhood to old age, violence is the most obdurate, intractable behavioral gender difference. The National Academy of Sciences puts the case starkly: "The most consistent pattern with respect to gender is the extent to which male criminal participation in serious crimes at any age greatly exceeds that of females, regardless of source of data, crime type, level of involvement, or measure of participation." "Men are always and everywhere more likely than women to commit criminal acts," write criminologists Michael Gottfredson and Travis Hirschi.[1]

What can we, as a culture, do to understand, let alone prevent the casual equation of masculinity and violence? The articles in this section approach that equation in a variety of arenas. James Gilligan describes how perceived humiliations are the pretext that legitimates the use of violence, and Jack Katz's ethnography of "badass" masculinity applies that model to street crime. Nick Pappas, Patrick McKenry, and Beth Catlett look at violence in sports, especially ice hockey. (Ice hockey is especially interesting because the rules of the game are so gendered: For men, aggression and fighting are prescribed, but female ice hockey strictly prohibits them.)

Tim Beneke describes how ordinary men might justify the use of violence and sexual aggression. Violence isn't only interpersonal; it is also institutional. Cynthia Enloe's chilling examination of the scandal at Abu Ghraib prison shows

THINK AGAIN (David John Attyah and S. A. Bachman) 1998–1999

how both individual and institutional ideals of masculinity lead to specifically gendered forms of humiliation and torture.

Note

1. National Academy of Sciences, cited in Michael Gottfredson and Travis Hirschi. *A General Theory of* *Crime* (Stanford: Stanford University Press, 1990), p. 145. See also Steven Barkan, "Why Do Men Commit Almost All Homicides and Assault?" in *Criminology: A Sociological Understanding* (Englewood: Prentice Hall, 1997); Lee Bowker, ed., *Masculinities and Violence* (Thousand Oaks, CA: Sage Publications, 1998).

Nick T. Pappas
Patrick C. McKenry
Beth Skilken Catlett

Athlete Aggression on the Rink and off the Ice: Athlete Violence and Aggression in Hockey and Interpersonal Relationships

Athletes recently have appeared on television and in news headlines because of their involvement in instances of aggression and violence. Although much of the documented violence takes place in the context of sports competition, not all athlete aggression is restricted to sports opponents. Indeed, the past decade has witnessed documentation of athlete aggression directed toward other males outside the sports arena, as well as aggression directed toward women in both intimate and nonintimate situations. What remains unclear, however, is whether athletic participation—in particular, the violent strategies learned in sport—contributes to the likelihood that athletes will be violent in interpersonal relationships (Coakley 1998; Crosset 1999).

Public concern about the links between sports participation and interpersonal violence has spawned work over the past decade that documents athlete violence, especially in the area of sexual aggression. Specifically, several studies have indicated that college athletes are overrepresented among those who are involved in aggressive and violent sexual behavior on college campuses. In a study of male undergraduates at a large southeastern university, Boeringer (1996) found that 60 percent of athletes reported at least one instance of using verbal coercion to obtain

sexual favors, 28 percent reported using alcohol and drugs to obtain sexual favors, and 15 percent reported using physical force. Moreover, Boeringer found that athletes reported higher percentages than nonathletes in all such categories of aggressive behavior. In a similar vein, Frintner and Rubinson (1993) found that although the population of male athletes at a large midwestern university was less than 2 percent of the male student population, 21 percent of the reported sexual assaults, 18 percent of the attempted sexual assaults, and 14 percent of the cases of sexual abuse were committed by members of sports teams or sports clubs on campus. Berkowitz (1992) similarly reported that in one review of alleged gang rapes by college students since 1980, twenty-two out of twenty-four documented cases were perpetuated by either members of fraternities or intercollegiate athletic teams. And Crosset, Benedict, and McDonald (1995) reviewed police records at twenty colleges and universities as well as the records of offices of judicial affairs and found that male athletes were overrepresented in reports of sexual assault; while athletes accounted for 3 percent of the male student population, they perpetrated 35 percent of the physical battering reports on the college campuses.

Young (1993) argues that the links between sport and interpersonal violence parallel the problems of violence elsewhere in society. In fact, this notion is consistent with research that indicates

Men and Masculinities, Vol. 6 No. 3, January 2004 291–312. © 2004 Sage Publications.

that violence in one social domain is highly correlated with violence in other domains (Fagan and Browne 1994; National Research Council 1996). Yet it should be noted that while much is known regarding athlete-athlete violence as a part of the sport, there is little empirical validation of athlete violence outside the sports arena (Benedict and Klein 1997; Coakley 1998; Young 2000). Moreover, while initial explorations have theorized a link between athletic participation and interpersonal violence, many studies have found only a weak association between sports violence and outside the sport violence (e.g., Koss and Gaines 1993) and some have found no association at all (Carson, Halteman, and Stacy 1997; Schwartz and Nogrady 1996).

The mixed results of early empirical research highlight the need to clarify the connections between athletic participation and violence. Indeed, researchers such as Boeringer (1996) and Crosset (1999, 2000) note the pressing need to explore the dynamics surrounding athlete violence beyond the sports context, including inquiries into how team members, coaches, and fans promote and defend violent behavior, variations in the experiences of athletes in different sports contexts, and the role of intervening variables that may be more predictive of male violence than athletic participation per se (Crosset 1999; Crowell and Burgess 1996). One intervening variable, alcohol consumption, is worth particular note. As Crosset (1999) argues, missing from current discussions of athletes and violence is any discussion of drinking. This omission is conspicuous in light of the strong association between drinking and sport. Furthermore, alcohol has been strongly implicated in much of the research on violence against women; although alcohol consumption is not necessarily considered a cause of such violence, many scholars theorize that it has a complex role in men's violence.

The need for such exploration is perhaps nowhere more pertinent than in the sport of hockey. In recent years, several incidents in professional hockey have resulted in an intensified concern regarding aggression and violence associated with the sport. For instance, Toronto Maple Leafs' Nick Kyupreos sustained a severe concussion that led to his early retirement from hockey. In another incident, Vancouver's Donald Brashhear was struck on the head by Boston's Marty McSorley; he missed 20 games because of the injury. Furthermore, several publicized incidents of athlete violence outside the sports context have caused substantial concern, in particular, about the links between male athletic participation and violence against women. One case, for example, involves AHL Wilkes-Barre rookie, Billy Tibbetts, who lost four seasons of hockey due to a jail sentence for raping a 15-year-old girl at a party.

Thus, the purpose of this study is to explore, through in-depth interviews with five former college/professional hockey players, the nature of aggression and violence in their sport and its relationship to violent interpersonal behaviors both inside and outside the sport. Violence is defined as male-to-male physical sport-related violence, male-to male physical out-of-sport interpersonal violence; and male-to-female physical, sexual, and emotional aggression and abuse.

Socialization for Violence

While an instinctive drive and a drive stimulated by frustration may partially explain sports aggression, Terry and Jackson (1985) contend that a powerful socialization process is the primary determinant of sport and sport-related violence. Hargreaves (1986) notes that sports offers an ideal means for males to develop and exhibit traditional masculine qualities including power, strength, and violence while rejecting traditionally ascribed feminine values. Terry and Jackson see sports aggression as behavior learned in a culture that reinforces and models violence. In sport, reinforcement for acts of violence emanate from a variety of sources, which may be grouped under three categories: (1) the immediate reference group of the athlete, especially coaches, teammates, and family; (2) the structure of the sport and the implementation of rules by governing bodies and referees; and (3) the attitude of the fans, media, courts of law, and society in general.

Reference Groups

Cultural ideals of sport and of masculinity combine to create a context within which violence in athletics is not only tolerated but encouraged (Messner 1995). Coaches and parents contribute to the legitimacy of sports violence as they argue that sport aggression prepares boys for success as a man in an adult world (Fine 1987). Messner and Sabo (1990) contend that male tolerance of risk and injury in sports is not a socially passive process but rather is one through which violence, injury, and disablement become reframed as masculinizing by society at all levels. Demonstration of these behaviors is thus linked to gender legitimacy.

In a review of biographies of athletes who come to understand the rewards of aggression and violence, Crosset (1999) suggests that these individuals learn from coaches and peers to be violent. Studies of hockey players, in particular, provide prototypic examples of such socializing influences. For instance, Smith (1979b) found that displays of toughness, courage, and willingness to fight are important means of establishing a positive identity among both peers and coaches in hockey. Moreover, Weinstein, Smith, and Wiesenthal (1995) found that players' aggression, demonstrated especially through fistfighting, often produced greater teammate and coach perceptions of player competence than playing or skating skills. In general, players who backed away from fights were often labeled as "chicken" and were viewed as exhibiting signs of personal failure and weak character. These authors suggest that players will often participate in hockey fights and violence to avoid demeaning labels, which are not easily removed.

Key concepts from West and Zimmerman's (1987) classic work on "doing gender" provide an apt interpretive framework for understanding the impact of hockey culture on athletes' displays of violence and aggression. Under this view, violent

behavior can be seen as a way of constructing oneself as masculine and demonstrating one's place in the masculinity hierarchy (Connell 1995). Violence and aggression may be displayed as a way to meet the gender expectations of the peer group as well as the hegemonic notions of masculinity more broadly (Coakley 1989; Levinson 1989).

Furthermore, Crosset (1999) argues that training for sport in the context of an already patriarchal society may also be training men to be violent toward women. For example, coaches employ images of antifemininity and castration to chastise players. The descriptive works of Curry (1991, 1998, 2000) found team dynamics that openly express support for violence against women and demonstrate how resistance to these norms is discouraged. Indeed, teammates in many contact sports clearly reinforce and model sexist behaviors, focusing on sex, aggression, and negative attitudes toward women (Curry 1991).

Structure of the Sport and Implementation of the Rules

Many athletes are presented with a conflict inherent to competitive sports—that is, they are presented with the apparent dilemma of having to win at all costs and yet, at the same time, to adhere to moral and ethical sport behavior. Young (1993) reflected this conflict when he compared professional sports to a hazardous and violent workplace with its own unique form of industrial disease. Male athletes are expected to be tough and to live up to cultural expectations of manliness, which often encourage the use of violence and performance-enhancing drugs such as steroids. Indeed, Messner (1990) contends that violent behaviors are occupational imperatives in contact sports with practical consequences if not performed. Athletes constantly are encouraged to ignore their own pain and at the same time are encouraged to inflict pain on others or they risk being belittled by their coaches and peers.

Smith (1979a) specifically describes the hockey subculture in terms of an occupational culture based on a theme of violence. By age 15, boys are identified by coaches for their ability to mete out and withstand illegal physical coercion—attributes desired by professional hockey teams. The structure of the system compels conformity to prevailing professional standards that include the necessity of employing violence. Weinstein, Smith, and Weisenthal (1995) found even among youth and preprofessional junior hockey teams that there was a strong imperative toward violence. These authors state that fighting and intimidation are essential elements in the tradition and culture of hockey.

From an early age, hockey players undergo a specialized socialization process in the production of a tough fighting unit; players are taught that competence is linked to aggressive play, including penalties (Vaz 1979, 1980; Weinstein, Smith, and Wiesenthal 1995). Toughness and willingness to fight are attributes that impress coaches and management (Smith 1983). Players understand the possibility of violence on the ice, and they know that fighting is advocated as a proactive means for not being easily intimidated and guarding against further aggression. Players also are required to create trouble for opponents and to employ tactics that create anxiety in adversaries (Faulkner 1974; Weinstein, Smith, and Wiesenthal 1995).

Attitudes of the Community and Society in General

In general, there appears to be widespread support, both institutional and community, for violence associated with sport, both within and outside the sports context. Institutional support for alleged perpetrators of violence outside the sport often blames the victims and fails to hold athletes responsible for their actions. The inability of institutions to hold athletes accountable also extends to the court system (Crosset 1999). In spite of higher rates of violence within sport communities, conviction rates present a striking difference that favors the accused athlete (Bene-

dict and Klein 1997). Benedict and Klein examined arrest and conviction rates for collegiate and professional athletes accused of felony sexual assaults against women and compared these with national crime data to determine differential patterns of treatment in the criminal justice system. In sum, these authors found that of 217 athletes who were initially reported to police for a felonious sex crime, only 24 percent were successfully prosecuted. The comparison national sample was 54 percent of arrests leading to conviction. In addition, Benedict (1997) found in their 150 case studies of reported violence that athletes were convicted in only 28 cases, mainly through plea-bargaining agreements. Only 10 cases went to trial, and 6 of these resulted in guilty verdicts.

Curry (2000), among others, has focused on the sports bar as a safe haven in the community arena for aggression outside the sport. Curry found that aggression and assault are encouraged by bars' privileging of male athletes—allowing them to drink for free, taking their sides during fights, and giving them an arena in which to operate. Curry describes the striving for status among peers in the bars through drinking, fighting, and public display of sexual activity. Indeed, Curry (1998) contends that these bars were permissive to the point of allowing the male athletes to take advantage of situations where they could prey on the physical inequalities of others.

Fans also play an important role in the reinforcement of violence, in particular within hockey culture. For example, in a national opinion poll, 39 percent of Canadians reported that they like to see fighting at hockey games (Macleans-Goldfarb 1970, cited in Smith 1979a). In a similar vein, Smith (1979b) found that 61 percent of the players he surveyed perceived spectators at these games as approving of fighting.

Based on this overview of the literature and the socialization into a culture of violence theoretical perspective, the following research questions were developed and addressed: (1) In what ways does participation in hockey promote a culture of aggression and violence? and (2) To what extent does hockey aggression and violence affect off-ice behavior, and what factors seem influential?

Method

Participants in this study were five former hockey players whose ages ranged between twenty-five and thirty years old with a mean age of twenty-six years. Four of the five athletes consisted of former players that the researcher formerly coached at the collegiate level. Each of the athletes had competed at either the collegiate level, the professional minor league level, or both. Four of the athletes played collegiate hockey, two of the athletes played professionally in the minor leagues, and one player played both college and professional hockey. Three of the five players were Canadian and played Canadian junior hockey before playing collegiate or professional hockey. It is important to note that the style of Canadian junior hockey is fundamentally different from collegiate hockey in that it allows and encourages fighting to a much greater extent than American collegiate hockey. The two American players had competed at either the high school and/or prep school level before playing collegiate hockey.

The first author has a history of extensive involvement in the culture of ice hockey, with a keen understanding of the perspectives of the players, as well as the phenomenon of violence inside and outside the sports arena. This experience has occurred through participation in American and Canadian junior hockey, over five years of professional playing experience in both the minor leagues and in Europe, and coaching at numerous levels, including three years at the men's collegiate level. It is through being deeply involved in the culture of ice hockey as both a player and a coach over the span of twenty years that the first author has a unique, insider knowledge of ice hockey and its associated violence.

In fact, the first author's unique position as a participant observer within the culture of hockey allowed him ready access for recruitment of players to participate in this study. Four of the five informants were players that the first author coached in college, and the fifth was a referral from one of the four former players. Each of these athletes has at least ten years of professional competition and is thought to be fully immersed into the culture of ice hockey. In addition, the researcher has a long personal and professional relationship with the four players he coached.

The primary source of data for this study was in-depth interviews. The interviews can be considered as semistructured because they were guided by a set of predetermined questions with a number of branching questions that were used to facilitate more detail and more focused attention to the study's domains of interest. Probing questions were also used in a spontaneous manner to prompt elaboration and specificity. The questions were derived from previous inquiries into sport violence as well as previous focused discussions with participants in ice hockey regarding the use of violence. Five major questions were asked during the interviews: (1) Describe your overall experience as a player in organized hockey; (2) How do you think contact sports such as hockey promote violence/aggression within the sport itself; (3) Describe any situations of violence/aggression perpetrated by athletes that you have either seen, heard of, or participated in that occurred outside of sports competition; (4) What are some of the ways that you think participation in hockey encourages off-ice aggression; and (5) What are some ways to prevent athlete violence and aggression off-ice. The participants determined the settings for the interviews, which, in four of the five cases were their homes; this helped to ensure privacy and confidentiality.

It is important to note that these participants were asked to (1) discuss their own personal involvement in hockey, both on and off the ice and (2) to comment on their observations of others in the sport and their overall view of violence and aggression associated with the culture of hockey. Because the principal investigator had a strong personal connection to and history with the respondents, and because he wanted to ensure honest and open exploration of sensitive topics such as violence, sexual aggression, and alcohol and drug use, he did not insist that participants specify whether their narrative responses pertained to their own personal experiences or experiences observed of other athletes. Thus, these participants are best considered key informants who inform this in-depth exploration of the culture of violence and aggression among hockey players.

The data analysis began with a verbatim transcription of the audio-recorded interviews. Once this was completed, a qualitative content analysis was conducted by two independent coders. Specifically, coders first identified and subsequently organized themes that emerged from the transcribed text. The interview responses were examined for salient topics covered, patterns, regularities, and differences within and across the cases. Then, initially coded categories were generated from the topics and patterns, and these coding schemes were developed, continuously modified, and redefined through the data collection process and afterwards (Miles and Huberman 1994). Finally, the topics and patterns were placed into conceptually focused analytical themes related to the study's theoretical foundation (Berg 1998; Bogdan and Biklen 1992).

Results

All of the participants' narratives contained detailed accounts of both their own and other athletes' involvement in violence and aggression within the context of sports competition, as well as outside of the competitive arena. These narratives described varied experiences with and observations of aggression perpetrated against teammates, opponents, bystanders, and women. Moreover, each of the participants provided their own subjective insights about the interconnections between hockey and aggression/violence. In this analysis, we first discuss, in an introductory fashion, the participants' accounts of the extent of violence in ice hockey. Next, we review the ways in which hockey socialization and athletes' notions of masculinity combine to create a culture of aggression and violence. We then turn to an examination of two central factors—consumption of alcohol and the objectification of

women—that contribute to exporting violence outside the athletic arena.

Frequency of Violence

All of the research participants were easily able to identify a number of situations in which they had either participated in violence or they had observed such violence among their friends and teammates. Moreover, these narratives illustrate the way in which such violence and aggression is considered routine in this population. For example, one athlete described his social life in this way:

> It seemed like every time we would go out . . . at someone's house or a bar . . . at least once a weekend, there would probably be a fight . . . if you took a random sample of 20 guys that did-n't play sports and went out on a Friday or Saturday, I don't think you would find the frequency in them getting into fights compared to the 20 guys that I hung out with that I played hockey with.

The narrative accounts of two other participants reflected parallel sentiments with respect to the conventions of aggression and violence in this community:

> More things I've seen has been guys hitting other guys—in a bar—get a couple of drinks in some of these guys, and they want to fight everyone as if they're invincible—the worst I've seen is that guys will get a bunch of teeth knocked out or their face beat in—black eyes and brown eyes and all of that . . .

> I mean, I had quite a lot of brawls in the summer—one time, a guy had sold drugs to my younger sister and I confronted the guy, and he brought back a bunch of his friends, and I went after the whole gang of them and . . . I beat them up quite badly . . . they beat me over the head with a fishing bat and they cut me open, but I'd also cut a bunch of them open pretty bad too—and I went to the hospital and they had come after me at the hospital. I was out of town very shortly after that, so that was good.

These players' perspectives align well with extant research that asserts that conformity to a violent sport ethic is common and that this conformity can lead male athletes to see aggression as a natural part of their sport and a natural part of who they are as athletes and men (Young 1993). The question that remains, however, is, Are people who choose to play heavy contact sports more likely than others to see aggression as an appropriate way to deal with life stressors? An answer to this question is embedded within the research participants' reflections on the potential causes of aggressive behavior among hockey players. In particular, several respondents speculated that men with aggressive tendencies may be attracted to the sport of hockey:

> It's the old what-came-first-the-chicken-or-the-egg syndrome—were these guys violent before they played hockey or did they become violent because they played hockey . . . I think that guys I played with . . . had some antisocial behavior and had it before they ever got into hockey, and then you mix the two and you can get yourself into a lot of trouble. . . . I played junior C in Canada, and guys were getting out of jail on weekends to play hockey—you know, get in trouble with the law and all sorts of crazy stuff before they were really ever really involved with the game, and I think the game for them was almost a chance to vent their anger or whatever it was they were dealing with in a way that wouldn't get them thrown [back] into jail . . .

> I played against guys that do a lot of fighting in hockey that were just plain whacked—you know, that would sit there across from you before the game, hyperventilating and stuff, some of them I knew that were actually crazy—but . . . with one guy in particular, I knew that he had a chemical imbalance and he just happens to also be a really good hockey player that snaps . . .

> I think, from my experiences, with some of these guys who are getting into trouble on the ice have a lot more going on off the ice than you think. The rink becomes the hunting grounds for a lot of these guys, and I don't know all their stories in and out, but troubled guys getting in trouble on the ice as well whether it's family, school, or what. . . . I think it's a place for violence to come out—because it's allowed.

These narratives are somewhat inconsistent with a sports socialization perspective. That is, these informants' speculations that men with preexisting aggressive tendencies actualize such proclivities within the acceptable context of hockey play is somewhat contrary to an explanation that emphasizes the socialization of the athlete in which violence learning takes place within sport culture. However, the multifaceted interpretations offered by the informants in this study are compatible with Coakley's (1989) assertion that the origins of this phenomenon are heterogeneous, and that there is no single cause of violence in sport.

Hockey Socialization and the Culture of Masculinity

The socialization of hockey differs from socialization for other contact sports because fighting plays a central role in hockey competition. Indeed, according to Gruneau and Whitson (1993), high rates of violence in hockey are to be expected because physical contact affords opportunities for hockey sticks to be defined and used as weapons, and norms within the community celebrate toughness and a willingness to fight, seek retribution, and intimidate opponents. According to the participants in this study, this context promotes a unique set of dynamics that is unlike most other contact sports. Players enhance their value to their team by demonstrating toughness through display of fighting skills; indeed, the ability to fight effectively becomes a coveted trait, operating even as a means to indirectly win games through intimidation of the opposition and targeting of key opposing players. Fighting is seen to be far more important than skating skills to player success (Weinstein, Smith, and Wiesenthal 1995). These concepts can be seen in the following observations of three study participants:

> Hockey definitely promotes violence. . . . I mean, they have a penalty for fighting . . . and just the reasoning behind that is that they say hey, we don't want fighting in the game, but if they didn't want fighting in the game, they wouldn't have a penalty for it—they would just

basically kick the person out of the sport . . . and just the nature of the sport . . . how you win a game—you're physically dominant over another person—being bigger, stronger, faster than the person . . . it's just inherent in the nature of the sport . . . that promotes violence . . .

Hockey players or others in a contact sport could be prone to instigate a fight . . . hockey players instigating fights is part of the game . . . instigating a fight can work to your advantage . . . you can get them [opposition] off their game . . . you know . . . make them push themselves, push their manhood . . . I'm not sure if it [hockey] makes you more prone to violence, but it almost does . . .

Actually, it [fighting] was the thing that was paying my meal ticket so to speak, you know— and you get good at it and you have to do it— or you weren't going to play or they would find somebody else that would do it. I mean, if I was going to make it to the NHL, I was going to have to fight my way there, and it wasn't going to be through some other role on the team, and you have your role on the team.

The narrative data in this study also reflect the pressure that hockey players feel from coaches who are perceived to promote aggression in their players. These athletes' accounts are replete with references to coaches' win-at-all-cost mentality, as well as descriptions of the ethically questionable methods that a number of their former coaches used against their players to motivate them toward aggressive behavior. For example, one player described the way in which a coach used aggression himself as a sort of modeling strategy:

There's pressure from all around. The coaches will use name calling or in some situations use physical—not to hurt, but wrestle you around a bit—if they don't think you are doing your job and being aggressive and taking guys out of the play, that kind of thing. I've been in situations where coaches have used their hand or their stick in certain ways to get you fired up—hand in the back of the head, stick in the balls, you know.

Other coaches may not have engaged in aggressive behavior themselves, but players certainly believed that their coaches had a role in encouraging aggression, perhaps by active promotion or simply tacit acceptance of violent and aggressive behavior. The following narratives serve as prototypic examples:

Your teammates may expect you to watch their back . . . but, generally, it's the coach that will tell you to start with the violence . . . to agitate—sometimes those are elements that the team is lacking . . . it really is . . . coaches like guys . . . who take a hit . . . most coaches I've played with have not had a problem with sending someone out . . . a heavy person [enforcer] out . . . if they believe that a rival would possibly injure one of his good players . . . it makes sense . . . you've got to keep your scorers to win the game . . .

I've been involved in situations before where people are asked to go and fight [by the coach]. Someone is being dirty on the ice—takes a cheap shot at a smaller guy and basically they [coach] will . . . say, hey, I want you to go fight that guy just because they don't want them to take liberties and try to intimidate . . . so that's a definite influence, and, of course, you are rewarded by the coaches . . .

I smacked a guy in the dressing room one time and the coach asked me why I did it at the next practice. I said he shot his mouth off in front of the whole team and I told him to shut it or I was going to smack him—if I back down in front of the whole team and let him shoot his mouth off, how do you expect these guys to rely on me the next game out there—he [coach] said that's fine.

These quotes are consistent with Crosset's (1999) findings that athletes fully understand that their knowledge of the rewards for being mean are linked to coaching behaviors.

Fan pressures and influences also promote aggression and violence because the reinforcement through cheering and positive comments is extremely appealing to the athletes. Although winning was usually viewed as being most important, the use of aggression and violence could at times be considered an extremely significant secondary aspect in terms of what hockey fans wanted to see. The pressure players felt as a result of spectator comments is described through the following accounts:

> The first thing that comes into my head is the cheering every time somebody gets hit into the boards and a fight breaks out everyone stands up and cheers—that kind of thing, and when they see blood. A lot of fans came to see that and they got bored if there wasn't some kind of violence going on. In my personal conversations with them and how they react to the game, it was enough for me to see that they wanted to see that violence thing, and it does promote it— I mean, when the crowd is behind you and cheer when you knock people into the boards— I'm not going to lie, it gets you fired up and wants to make you do more banging of guys into the boards, and lots of times, if it takes that to get the team fired up, then that's what you're going to do. It always helps to get the fans behind you—they definitely have a role in promoting violence in the sport.

> Like even at universities or . . . back in the days of juniors . . . basically, if you go out in a fight and beat someone up . . . after the game . . . you'd get recognition for that—fans would come up to you and say, that's a great fight you were in, you really beat the crap out of that guy . . . and, basically, you're getting rewarded for . . . fighting with someone, and people remember that . . . if you're constantly getting rewarded for something you do . . . you're going to do that again and again.

Such findings are consistent with Smith's (1979b) findings that 61 percent of the players perceived spectators at hockey games approved of fighting.

The reinforcement of violent behaviors can be usefully framed with the observations offered by Vaz (1980). He found that violence is virtually non-existent among young boys just starting to play hockey. But as they are influenced by older players and professionals within the hockey community, rough play is encouraged and "under cer-

tain conditions, failure to fight is variously sanctioned by coaches and players" (145). This hockey subculture plays itself out against a larger backdrop of conventions of masculinity in contemporary society. For instance, several players discussed the ways in which hockey players are likely to equate manliness with a willingness to engage in violent behavior. Three narratives, in particular, illustrate this inclination:

> I think of people that you know and hang out with . . . expect you to be strong, kind of macho, and stick up or you know stick up for yourself . . . someone would never walk up to you and say, hey that was a great move you made walking away from fighting that guy, I mean I probably never heard that in my life but I definitely heard a person being put down because he backed away from a physical confrontation both on the ice and off the ice . . . you were generally perceived as weak if you didn't go fight . . . it would lower their opinion of you whereas if you went out and fought . . . you were generally seen . . . in higher standards . . . you're a team guy, you're a guy that would stick up for the other players . . . you were tough . . . you're a lot of things that people respected back then . . .

> I think it's more trying to prove yourself . . . trying to prove your physical dominance . . . to yourself, your coach, your teammates, the fans that you know . . . hey, I might of lost the last fight, but hey, I'm strong enough to win this fight against this guy . . . and trying to make yourself look better in front of . . . especially your teammates . . . your teammates tend to remember a lot of things that I think most of the fans that come will forget . . .

> If someone were to try to fight you on the ice and you backed away . . . it would be more perceived as he's weak, he's backed away from a physical confrontation and generally most people don't want to be seen like that . . . so I think there was a lot of pressure to stick up for yourself and I think the same goes over into your social behavior often . . . you're kind of expected to stick up for yourself and people think you should and kind of have the perception that if you are not, you're not as manly.

As this last narrative reflects, embedded within many of these players' narratives is the implicit recognition that the tendency to draw parallels between manliness and violence extends beyond the competitive arena into broader social relations (cf. Coakley 1989). For example, one player described the similarities between problem solving in hockey competition and problem solving in social relationships in this way:

> You might have something like guys having problems in school and with their girlfriend or . . . away from home and pressure from not being around his family . . . maybe at an older level, like in juniors, maybe leaving home for the first time, a combination of all those things contributing to maybe a little bit more of a downer attitude—not feeling good about themself—and maybe having to beat someone up to feel better about themself—you get a lot of that with athletes.

As this thematic analysis indicates, hockey socialization and players' ideals of masculinity combine to create a culture of aggression and violence within the sport. Specifically, the socializing influences on which the research participants focused their attention included hockey competition per se, teammates, coaches, and fans. Cultural imagery surrounding masculinity—in particular, ideals of physical dominance, strength, and toughness—joins with these primary hockey influences to create a culture within which violence and aggression are not only tolerated but even encouraged. Moreover, the narrative data in this study demonstrate that the conventions of aggression and violence that typify sports competition apply as well in the nonsports environment. In fact, one player's narrative powerfully illustrates his belief that this link is indeed inevitable:

> They make demands on athletes to be tough because they want to see it, it [aggression] automatically carries over when you see some guy who's huge and charged with beating his wife. It's like, what—so they think this is some sort of surprise, because if you're paying a guy three million dollars a year to knock somebody's block off, do you expect them to turn it off? No way, and you're praising him to be this animal, you know, you want him to be a destructive force on the field but then you want him to be some sort of pussy cat off the field?

In addition to discussing this inherent connection between violence within and outside of sports competition, the athletes discussed two factors that promoted the exportation of violence outside the athletic context: (1) consumption of alcohol and (2) objectification of women.

Alcohol Consumption

Previous research—for example, Gallmeier (1988)— has found that alcohol use is nearly universal among professional hockey players. Its use is apparently related to the extreme pressures of the game, as well as to the desire to suppress or deaden feelings. Likewise, all of the participants in this study discussed the common role of alcohol in the lives of hockey players. Moreover, these athletes associated violence with consumption of alcohol and other substances. For some, alcohol consumption was mentioned merely as a contextual feature in their descriptions of violent episodes. Some of the participants, however, perceived alcohol as a causal agent, explaining that it facilitated the transition of violence from the competitive venue into everyday social interaction. One player explained it in this way:

> It is the major factor of talk and off-ice violence—alcohol and testosterone and after-sport smack talking—you know, I was doing this and I did that and I played great, and when they start drinking, they think that they can do anything . . . it's the major factor in off-ice violence. Alcohol is the thing that leads to fights—in my experience in college, there wasn't one sober, off-ice violence [incident] that I ever witnessed or heard of or anything—never.

Other players may not have identified alcohol as "the major factor" but they certainly described, with great clarity, the role alcohol and drugs often play in creating a context within which athletes can act out their machismo. Two narratives illustrate this phenomenon:

> Alcohol after a game adds a strange element— I think it makes a person more conducive to violence off the ice—definitely—just because beer and muscles . . . you feel a little bit more invincible once you have a six-pack in you . . . that much more macho . . . alcohol is good for socializing, helps you relax, but it can also get people on edge . . . especially more high-strung people . . .

> I think it just adds fuel to the fire—if you've already got a kid who's aggressive by nature and you throw a catalyst in there [alcohol], it just makes everything worse—especially with hockey as there's a lot of drinking that goes on with it—you mix that with guys who are maybe lonely or depressed and you got trouble off the ice—if things are going on on the ice that they may not be happy with and then you're drinking and doing drugs, it makes everything worse—so it's just adding fuel to the fire.

In essence, all these players describe some way that alcohol and drugs act to promote aggression and violence. Indeed, these findings are consistent with previous work in this area. For instance, although alcohol has not been identified as the cause of abuse, it has been associated with violence and is thought to play a complex role in its occurrence; it may impair reasoning and communication, be part of premeditated strategy (Crowell & Burgess 1996), and/or be used to excuse violent behavior (Benedict 1997). Furthermore, the complex relationship between alcohol, violence, and constructions of masculinity that is implicated in the narrative data in this study is mirrored by Messerschmidt (1993), who theorizes that alcohol cannot be separated from demonstrating masculinity as it is often used to decrease communication and increase men's capacity to be violent.

Although the athletes in this study talked about the connection between alcohol and violence rather generally, there is research to indicate that excessive alcohol use within male peer groups contributes to sexual violence against women (Koss and Dinero 1988). In addition, Koss and Gaines (1993) linked alcohol consumption, athletic participation, and violence against women; they found that while athletic participation per se was associated with sexual aggression, alcohol consumption was even more highly correlated with sexual aggression. Thus, this analysis now turns to an examination of the role of hockey players' sexual relationships with women.

Objectification of Women

Commentaries, theoretical analyses, and empirical studies have begun to focus on whether participation in certain sports is related to misogyny, high rates of physical and sexual assault, and the occurrence of rape and gang rape (Coakley 1998). For instance, Sanday (1990) argues that when men become emotionally bound together in all-male groups that emphasize physical dominance, they often express their sense of togetherness by demeaning women. The narrative data in this study provide support for these assertions. For example, two participants talk extensively about the way in which their peers objectify women:

> I think that date rape is prevalent among the jock culture. There are things that are not violent but they just seem kind of wrong that guys do in terms of how they relate to women—off ice. They treat women like objects—sexual objects. They talk about them as if they aren't there, as if they [the athletes] were in the locker room talking . . . and don't care what they say at all because they think they're still going to have sex or whatever. Things like that machismo group mentality, that locker room mentality, comes out in off-ice behavior . . . treating women really bad . . . like one-nighters or short-term girlfriends or someone they didn't care very much, just as objects or sex partners.

> Locker room talk [is] definitely machismo without doubt, and that carries over when the team is all out . . . you're talking to a girl and all the team's around and they say, what are you going to do to her—and all that stuff. That kind of

talk breeds, does breed that kind of certain be-havior in the group when men have the group thing going with a not-caring attitude towards women—that kind of carries over when a guy's with a girl—he doesn't care what happens to the girl as long as he is getting what he wants—or getting what the group wants—like, sometimes, I've heard where two guys will have sex with one woman, group sex, or, if she's drunk or passed out or whatever—sometimes, the girl's into it—and that's a rarity—and then you hear about that stuff in the locker room—I mean, it happens, and sometimes they're willing and sometimes they're not—I'm not sure . . . if they're kind a coaxed, you know, 'cause there are more than one male in the room—stuff like that.

From the first author's knowledge of athlete behavior, these players are describing situations that are very common to the male sport culture, and they reflect only a small extent of the actual sexual behaviors that occur. It has been this researcher's experience that objectification of women occurs as a natural outgrowth and con-tinuation of traditional male socialization that begins in early childhood. Such socialization encourages boys and men to see women as infe-rior and as sexual objects who are supposed to meet the needs of men. The culture of hockey reinforces this objectification because of the focus on traditional male behaviors conducive to sports success and the large amount of time men spend exclusively with other males. These conversa-tions occur frequently as part of the bonding experience.

Moreover, according to the athlete infor-mants in this study, such demeaning attitudes and talk often carry over into actual violent behaviors. One player's account provides an apt illustration:

A guy back in juniors I played with when he was 16—a tough kid off the farm—cucumber farm—he got his girlfriend pregnant—knocked her up—she was about 15—and while I never saw it—he was actually taken away right out of the rink one night because she went to the cops and told them he had been beating her when she was even pregnant with the kid—so that

was probably one of the worst stories I had heard because there was a baby involved.

Two other players also commented on their knowledge of violence against women. Although these athletes do not concede to engaging in vio-lence against women themselves, they discuss it as if it is a somewhat routine occurrence within male hockey cultures:

Yeah, I remember certain things that had hap-pened. . . . My friends would get abusive with their girlfriends and stuff like that. I definitely know people that have gotten like that—not necessarily hit, but they'd be abusive and kind of push them and things like that, and we'd al-ways stop them.

I'd heard stories of guys roughing up a girl a bit. Most of it was guys talking about other guys they knew that were in situations like that.

Summary and Conclusions

The findings of this study indicate that interper-sonal aggression is common in the lives of these hockey players, both on and off the ice. For these hockey professionals, aggressive behaviors were seen as manifestations of existent tendencies as well as products of sport socialization. Future studies should examine personality characteris-tics and psychological symptoms of particularly aggressive athletes to determine the role of indi-vidual factors as opposed to the culture of sport in producing violent behaviors. Increasingly, studies of interpersonal violence are employing biopsy-chosocial perspectives, noting the relevance of all three domains in predicting violence (e.g., McK-enry, Julian, and Gavazzi 1995).

The participants in this study readily explored the ways in which hockey socialization created a context within which violence and aggression are not only tolerated but also encouraged. Much was said about the culture of hockey itself as an insti-gating mechanism of male violence. Clearly, hockey was viewed as a violent sport and a sports culture that encouraged violent behaviors on the ice; the players, management, and indeed the fans expected and desired it. It was not mindless violence but functional despite some prohibition. Consistent with Weinstein, Smith, and Wiesenthal's (1995) survey of youth and preprofessional junior hockey players, violent behaviors were seen as only mildly penalized and generally viewed as essential for team and individual player success. For example, referees do not intervene in professional hockey fights as long as only two players are involved, and teammates and coaches judge players' competence more on their willingness to engage in violence (especially fist fighting) than playing and skating skills. Messner (1995) notes that men are raised to view the world as competitive and hierarchal, taught to get the job done regardless of the consequences to others—what Balkan (1966) termed "unmitigated agency." Thus, when tasks become more important than people, violence is sometimes a problem-solving mechanism, for example, intentionally hurting an opposing player. Aggression and violence were important components to competitive success, and they were not limited to the ice rink; a united front perpetuating violent behaviors carried over to social situations. In addition, coaches often were negligent, if not somewhat encouraging, of players remaining tough and aggressive off the ice.

A culture of masculinity can be seen to characterize the teams the players described. The athletes tended to share a set of ideological beliefs related to traditional forms of masculine expression, for example, preoccupation with achievement and maintaining status through fighting or risk taking, acquiring an identity of toughness (Weisfeld et al. 1987). Research has found that hockey players with the strongest levels of endorsement of traditional masculine ideologies are more likely to fight than are other players (Weinstein, Smith, and Wiesenthal 1995). Kilmartin (2000) contends that violent behaviors by athletes are motivated by one athlete's perception that another is trying to hurt him. This too was represented in the players' comments regarding the need to be on guard, the necessity to protect oneself from the violence inherent in the game, and the dominance perspective wherein the athlete is

constantly battling against teammates and opposition who are motivated toward domination. The culture of masculinity was also seen in the pack mentality that emerged among the players and carried over to off-ice activities. The strong bonds that emerged reinforced aggressive behaviors but also resulted in strong bonds of allegiance and loyalty.

In his examination of sport and violence, Young (2000) asserts that while knowledge of player violence within sport is substantial, little is actually known about other forms of sport-related violence. This in-depth exploration of hockey culture begins to fill this knowledge gap; its unique contribution is a more nuanced understanding of athletes' expressions of aggression and violence outside the sports context. As noted previously, the players in this study viewed aggression in broader social relationships as a logical extension of on-ice violent behavior. This relationship between participation in violence in sport and in other social contexts is consistent with the well-established relationship between and among various types of violent displays consistently found in the literature (Fagan and Browne 1994, Levinson 1989). Moreover, when asked specifically to provide explanations for off-ice violence based on their experiences, many mentioned the role of alcohol specifically, but also in combination with other factors. The players typically drew a causal relationship between alcohol use and violent behaviors. Alcohol was used to a great extent to self-medicate as a means of handling the stresses associated with the game. Gustafson (1986) contends that alcohol is a societally sanctioned aggressive solution for men to use when frustrated. Also, hockey seems to be a culture that is defined, in part, by the use of alcohol in leisure. Others have noted that drinking is a cultural symbol of masculinity (Lemle and Mishkind 1989). The complex role that alcohol plays in aggression should be explored in greater depth, especially as it interacts with social situations, psychological factors, and other drugs.

The informants in this study also identified athletes' tendency to objectify women as a factor that contributes to the exportation of violence off the ice. Interestingly, the men defined sexual abuse of women broadly to include verbal aggression and general disrespectful behaviors, that is, treatment of women as sexual objects. Some connected sexual aggression or violence to what they termed a locker-room-talk mentality wherein certain male sexual bravado in the peer culture was carried off the ice to their relationships with women. The respondents tended to differentiate between general physical violence and sexual aggression or violence, seeing the latter as less serious and more understandable than general physical violence. In general, the athletes seemed to speak of a culture that had a lesser regard for women.

In general, the findings of this study have illuminated men's subjective experiences as participants in the sport of hockey. As such, they have brought personal insights to bear on our understanding of aggression and violence in sports. Because this was a small-scale intensive study, the voices of a variety of other participants who could have provided more insights into couple violence were excluded, for example, actual male aggressors of women and women victims. The researchers rely on the perspectives of respondents who had a particularly close relationship with the first author; perhaps a larger number of informants who were not acquainted with the researcher would have yielded additional information. Many questions remain to be addressed. Because violent behaviors first emerge in high school and continue into college play, these would be useful arenas for generating a fuller understanding of the development of violent behaviors in this sport. Other sports have also been associated with violence outside the sport itself, for example, football and basketball; a question emerges as to whether the development of violence is similar for other sports. In addition, as more women enter contact sports, it would be interesting to see if they create a similar sport culture and become more aggressive both in and outside the sport. Factors that have been implicated in domestic vi-

olence research in general, for example, masculine identity, family-of-origin issues, male peer group influences, and stress need to be explored in future work on this topic.

References

Balkan, D. 1966. *The duality of human existence.* Chicago: Rand McNally.

Benedict, J. R. 1997. *Public heroes, private felons.* Boston: Northeastern University Press.

Benedict, J., and A. Klein. 1997. Arrest and conviction rates for athletes accused of sexual assault. *Sociology of Sport Journal* 14:86–94.

Berg, B. L. 1998. *Qualitative research methods in the social sciences.* Needham Heights, MA: Allyn & Bacon.

Berkowitz, A. 1992. College men as perpetrators of acquaintance rape and sexual assault: A review of recent literature. *Journal of American College Health* 40:157–65.

Boeringer, S. 1996. Influences of fraternity membership, athletics, and male living arrangements on sexual aggression. *Violence Against Women* 2:135–47.

Bogdan, R. C., and S. K. Biklen. 1992. *Qualitative research for education: An introduction to theory and methods.* 2d ed. Boston: Allyn & Bacon.

Carson, S. K., W. A. Halteman, and G. Stacy. 1997. Athletes and rape: is there a connection? *Perceptual and Motor Skills* 85:1379–83.

Coakley, J. J. 1998. *Sport in society: issues and controversies.* Boston: Irwin McGraw-Hill.

Connell, R. W. 1995. *Masculinities.* Los Angeles: University of California Press.

Crosset, T. W. 1999. Male athletes' violence against women: A critical assessment of the athletic affiliation, violence against women debate. *Quest* 51:244–57.

———. 2000. Athletic affiliation and violence against women: toward a structural prevention project. In *Masculinities, gender relations, and sport,* edited by J. McKay, M. A. Messner, and D. Sabo, 147–61. Thousand Oaks, CA: Sage.

Crosset, T. W., J. R. Benedict, and M. M. McDonald. 1995. Male student-athletes reported for sexual assault: A survey of campus. *Journal of Sport and Social Issues* 19:126–40.

Crowell, N., and A. Burgress, eds. 1996. *Understanding violence against women.* Washington, DC: National Academy Press.

Curry, T. J. 1991. Fraternal bonding in the locker room: A profeminist analysis of talk about competition and women. *Sociology of Sport Journal* 8:119–35.

———. 1998. Beyond the locker room: Campus bars and college athletes. *Sociology of Sport Journal* 15:205–15.

———. 2000. Booze and bar fights: A journey to the dark side of college athletics. In *Masculinities, gender relations, and sport,* edited by J. McKay, M. A. Messner, and D. Sabo, 162–75. Thousand Oaks, CA: Sage.

Fagan, J., and A. Browne. 1994. Violence between spouses and intimates: Physical aggression between women and men in intimate relationships. In *Understanding and preventing violence: social influences,* edited by A. J. Reiss, Jr., and J. A. Roth, 115–292. Washington, DC: National Academy Press.

Faulkner, R. 1974. Making violence by doing work, selves, situations and the world of professional hockey. *Sociology of Work and Occupations* 1:288–312.

Fine, G. A. 1987. *With the boys: Little league baseball and preadolescent culture.* Chicago: University of Chicago Press.

Frintner, M. P., and L. Rubinson. 1993. Acquaintance rape: The influence of alcohol, fraternity, and sports team membership. *Journal of Sex Education and Therapy* 19:272–84.

Gallmeier, C. P. 1988. Juicing, burning, and tooting: Observing drug use among professional hockey players. *Arena Review* 12:1–12.

Gruneau, R., and D. Whitson. 1993. *Hockey night in Canada: Sport, identities, and cultural politics.* Toronto, Canada: Garamond.

Gustafson, R. 1986. Threat as a determinant of alcohol-related aggression. *Psychological Reports* 58:287–97.

Hargreaves, J. 1986. Where's the virtue? Where's the grace? A discussion of the social production of gender relations in and through sport. *Theory, Culture, and Society* 3:109–21.

Kilmartin, C. T. 2000. *The masculine self.* Boston: McGraw-Hill.

Koss, M. P., and T. E. Dinero. 1988. Predictors of sexual aggression among a national sample of male

college students. *Annals of the New York Academy of Sciences* 528:133–46.

Koss, M. P., and J. A. Gaines. 1993. The prediction of sexual aggression by alcohol use, athletic participation, and fraternity affiliation. *Journal of Interpersonal Violence* 8:94–108.

Lemle, R., and M. E. Mishkind. 1989. Alcohol and masculinity. *Journal of Substance Abuse Treatment* 6:213–22.

Levinson, D. 1989. *Family violence in cross cultural perspective.* Newbury Park, CA: Sage.

McKenry, P. C., T. W. Julien, and N. Gavazzi. 1995. Toward a biopsychosocial model of domestic violence. *Journal of Marriage and the Family* 57:307–20.

Messerschmidt, J. W. 1993. *Masculinities and crime: Critique and reconceptualization of theory.* Lanham, MD: Rowman & Littlefield.

Messner, M. 1990. When bodies are weapons: Masculine violence in sport. *International Review for the Sociology of Sport* 25:203–21.

———. 1995. Boyhood, organized sports, and the construction of masculinity. In *Men's lives,* edited by M. A. Kimmel and M. S. Messner, 102–14. Boston: Allyn & Bacon.

Messner, M., and D. Sabo. 1990. *Sports, men, and the gender order: Critical feminist perspectives.* Champaign, IL: Human Kinetics.

Miller, M. B., and A. M. Haberman. 1994. *Qualitative data analyses: A new sourcebook of methods.* Newbury Park, CA: Sage.

National Research Council. 1996. *Understanding violence against women.* Washington, DC: National Academy Press.

Sanday, P. 1990. *Fraternity gang rapes: Sex, brotherhood, and privilege on campus.* New York: New York University Press.

Schwartz, M., and C. Nogrady. 1996. Frat membership, rape myths, and sexual aggression on a college campus. *Violence Against Women* 2:158–62.

Smith, M. D. 1979a. Hockey violence: A new test of the violent subculture hypothesis. *Social Problems* 27:235–47.

———. 1979b. Towards an explanation of hockey violence: A reference other approach. *Canadian Journal of Sociology* 4:105–24.

———. 1983. *Violence and sport.* Toronto, Canada: Butterworths.

Terry, P. C., and J. J. Jackson. 1985. The determinants and control of violence in sport. *Quest* 37:27–37.

Vaz, E. W. 1979. Institutionalized rule violation and control in organized minor league hockey. *Canadian Journal of Sports Sciences* 4:83–90.

———. 1980. The culture of young hockey players: Some initial observations. In *Jock: Sports and male identity,* edited by D. F. Sabo and R. Runfola, 142–57. Englewood Cliffs, NJ: Prentice Hall.

Weinstein, M. D., D. S. Smith, and D. L. Wiesenthal. 1995. Masculinity and hockey violence. *Sex Roles* 33:831–47.

Weisfeld, G. E., D. M. Muczenski, C. C. Weisfeld, and D. R. Omark. 1987. Stability of boys' social success among peers over an eleven-year period. In *Interpersonal relations: family, peers, and friends,* edited by J. A. Meacham, 58–80. Basel, UK: Karger.

West, C., and D. H. Zimmerman. 1987. Doing gender. *Gender & Society* 1:125–51.

Young, K. 1993. Violence, risk, and liability in male sports culture. *Sociology of Sport Journal* 10: 373–96.

———. 2000. Sport and violence. In *Handbook of sports studies,* edited by J. Coakley and E. Dunning, 23–59. London: Sage.

James Gilligan

Culture, Gender, and Violence: "We Are Not Women"

Even those biological factors that do correlate with increased rates of murder, such as age and sex, are not primary determinants or independent causes of violent behavior. They do not spontaneously, in and of themselves, create violent impulses; they act only to increase the predisposition to engage in violence, when the individual is exposed to the social and psychological stimuli that do stimulate violent impulses. In the absence of those stimuli, these biological factors acting alone do not seem to stimulate or cause violence spontaneously or independently.

That is good news; for while we cannot alter or eliminate the biological realities of age and sex, which are made by God, we can bring about fundamental changes in the social and cultural conditions that expose people to increased rates and intensities of shame and humiliation, since culture and society are made by us. In this chapter I will analyze some of the cultural patterns, values, and practices that stimulate violence, and how they might be altered to prevent violence.

When these conditions are altered the exposure of human populations to shame is dramatically reduced—and so is violence. Those economically developed democracies all over the world that have evolved into "welfare states" since the end of the Second World War, including all of Western Europe, Japan, Canada, Australia, and New Zealand, offer universal and free health care, generous public housing, unemployment and family leave policies, and so on. Every one of those countries has a more equitable (and hence less shame-inducing) socioeconomic system than the United States does. There is a much greater sharing of the collective wealth of the society as measured, for example, by the smaller gap between the income and wealth of the most and least affluent segments of their populations. Our rate of violent crime (murder, rape) is from two to twenty times as high as it is in any of the other economically developed democracies. This is precisely what the theory presented in this book would predict.

Other cultures have also altered their social conditions so as to protect their members from exposure to overwhelming degrees of shame and humiliation, and have experienced the dramatic diminution in rates of violence that the theory espoused in this book would lead us to expect. They demonstrate the degree to which rates of violence are determined by social, cultural, and economic conditions. One example would be those societies that practice what has been called "primitive Christian communism," and are truly classless societies whose economic systems are based on communal sharing—Anabaptist sects such as the Hutterites, Mennonites, and Amish. One remarkable feature of these societies is that the incidence of violence in them is virtually zero. The Hutterites, for example, do not appear to have had a single confirmed case of murder, rape, aggravated assault, or armed robbery since they arrived in America more than a hundred years ago. They also practice a strict and absolute pacifism, which is why they had to emigrate to

America from Europe in the last century—to escape becoming victims of genocide at the hands of governments there, which were persecuting them. While that aspect of their experience is one reason why I do not propose them as a model for our own society to emulate in any concrete, literal way, they do demonstrate that violence does not have to be universal; and that altering social, cultural, and economic conditions can dramatically reduce, and for all practical purposes eliminate, human violence from the face of the earth.

One apparent exception to the generalizations I am making here is Japan, which has often been cited as a "shame culture." If frequent exposure and intense sensitivity to shame (in the absence of a correspondingly powerful exposure to guilt) stimulates violence toward others, then why does Japan have a relatively low homicide and high suicide rate—the same pattern that characterizes those societies that have sometimes been called "guilt cultures," namely, the European and other economically developed "welfare state" democracies? There are two answers to that question, one that refers to the period before World War II, and the other, the time since then.

During both periods, Japan has been described by those who know it best as an intensely homogeneous and conformist society, with strong pressures against individual deviations from group norms and behaviors. That social pattern had, and still has, a powerful influence on the patterns of Japanese violence. Until the end of the Second World War, Japan was an extremely violent society—indeed, one of the most violent in the history of the world; they have been described, both by themselves and by their neighbors, as "a nation of warriors" since they first emerged as an independent nation two to three thousand years ago. However, that violence was directed almost entirely toward non-Japanese. Some cultures, such as Japan's, have been more successful than others in channeling the homicidal behavior of their members toward members of other cultures, so that it is labeled warfare or genocide, rather than toward members of their own culture, which is called murder.

Thus, the Japanese engaged in a degree of violence toward their Asian neighbors from 1930 to 1945 that was just as genocidal as what the Germans perpetrated in Europe. When compared to the number of suicides that Japanese citizens committed during the first half of this century, the number of homicides that they committed (in the form of warfare) during that same period was astronomical—exactly as the theory proposed in this book would predict.

However, since 1945 the social and economic conditions in Japan have changed remarkably. Japan today has the lowest degree of economic inequity among its citizens in the world (as judged by the World Bank's measures of relative income and wealth). So it is not surprising that Japan also has a remarkably low frequency both of violent crime and of structural violence. For if socioeconomic inequities expose those at the bottom of the ladder to intense feelings of inferiority; if relative equality protects people from those feelings; and if inferiority feelings stimulate violent impulses, then it is not surprising that Japan's current socioeconomic structure would be marked by a low level of violence toward others, as indeed it is—even if the Japanese are unusually sensitive to feelings and experiences of shame, and even if (as some observers have claimed) they are not especially sensitive to or likely to experience guilt feelings. For their socioeconomic system, even if it does revolve primarily around sensitivity to shame rather than guilt, actively protects most individuals from being exposed to overwhelming degrees of shame, and also provides them with nonviolent (e.g., economic) means by which to prevent or undo any "loss of face" that is experienced.

If the main causes of violence are these social and psychological variables (shame versus honor), an apparent anomaly lies in the fact that men are and always have been more violent than women, throughout history and throughout the world. If shame stimulates violence; if being treated as inferior stimulates shame; and if women have been treated throughout history as inferior to men, then why are women less violent than men? (And they are indeed vastly less likely than men are to commit homicide, suicide, warfare, and assault, in every culture and every period of history.)

The Making of "Manhood" and the Violence of Men

To understand this apparent anomaly, we must examine the cultural construction of masculinity and femininity, and the contrasting conditions under which the two sexes, once they have been cast into patriarchally defined "gender roles," are exposed to feelings of private shame or public dishonor. To understand physical violence we must understand male violence, since most violence is committed by males, and on other males. And we can only understand male violence if we understand the sex roles, or gender roles, into which males are socialized by the gender codes of their particular cultures. Moreover, we can only understand male gender roles if we understand how those are reciprocally related to the contrasting but complementary sex or gender roles into which females are socialized in that same culture, so that the male and female roles require and reinforce each other.

Gender codes reinforce the socialization of girls and women, socializing them to acquiesce in, support, defend, and cling to the traditional set of social roles, and to enforce conformity on other females as well. Restrictions on their freedom to engage in sexual as well as aggressive behavior is the price women pay for their relative freedom from the risk of lethal and life-threatening violence to which men and boys are much more frequently exposed (a dubious bribe, at best, and one which shortchanges women, as more and more women realize).

The outpouring of scholarship across disciplines on the asymmetrical social roles assigned to males and females by the various cultures and civilizations of the world, including our own, has included works in history, economics, literary theory, philosophy, sociology, anthropology, psychology, science, law, religious studies, ethnic studies, and women's studies. One thing all this work has made clear to me (and to many others) is that listening to women (for the first time), and opening up a dialogue between men and women, rather than merely continuing what has throughout most of the history of civilization been primarily a male monologue, is a necessary prerequisite for learning how to transform our civilization into a culture that is compatible with life. And to do that requires that men and women both learn to interact in ways that have simply not been permitted by the gender codes of the past.

My work has focused on the ways in which male gender codes reinforce the socialization of boys and men, teaching them to acquiesce in (and support, defend, and cling to) their own set of social roles, and a code of honor that defines and obligates these roles. Boys and men are exposed thereby to substantially greater frequencies of physical injury, pain, mutilation, disability, and premature death. This code of honor requires men to inflict these same violent injuries on others of both sexes, but most frequently and severely on themselves and other males, whether or not they want to be violent toward anyone of either sex.

Among the most interesting findings reported by social scientists is the fact that men and women stand in a markedly different relationship to the whole system of allotting honor in "cultures of honor." For example, one observation that has been made recurrently is that men are the only possible sources, or active generators (agents), of honor. The only active effect that women can have on honor, in those cultures in which this is a central value, is to destroy it. But women do have that power: They can destroy the honor of the males in their household. The culturally defined symbol system through which women in patriarchies bring honor or dishonor to men is the world of sex—that is, female sexual behavior. In this value system, which is both absurd from any rational standpoint and highly dangerous to the continued survival of our species given its effect of stimulating male violence, men delegate to women the power to bring dishonor on men. That is, men put their honor in the hands of "their" women. The most emotionally powerful means by which women can dishonor men (in this male construction) is by engaging in nonmarital sex, i.e., by being too sexually active or aggressive ("unchaste" or "unfaithful") before, during, or even after marriage.

These themes are prominent in one well-known "culture of honor," for example, the American South. Bertram Wyatt-Brown illustrated this by quoting from a letter Lucius Quintus Cincinnatus Lamar wrote to Mary Chesnut in 1861, in which he compares the men of the South to Homer's heroes, who "fought like brave men, long and well," and then went on to say "We are men, not women." The real tragedy for Lamar, as Wyatt-Brown saw, was that "for him, as for many, the Civil War was reduced to a simple test of manhood."

And women can adopt those same views of manhood, as Mary Chesnut recounts in her diary: " 'Are you like Aunt Mary? Would you be happier if all the men in the family were killed?' To our amazement, quiet Miss C. took up the cudgels—nobly: 'Yes, if their life disgraced them. There are worse things than death.'" These attitudes are exactly the same as those of the men I have known in maximum-security prisons.

That the same relative differences between the two gender roles can be found in many civilizations throughout history and throughout the world emphasizes the importance of understanding that it is men who are expected to be violent, and who are honored for doing so and dishonored for being unwilling to be violent. A woman's worthiness to be honored or shamed is judged by how well she fills her roles in sexually related activities, especially the roles of actual or potential wife and mother. Men are honored for activity (ultimately, violent activity); and they are dishonored for passivity (or pacifism), which renders them vulnerable to the charge of being a non-man ("a wimp, a punk, and a pussy," to quote the phrase that was so central to the identity of the murderer I analyzed in Chapter Three). Women are honored for inactivity or passivity, for

not engaging in forbidden activities. They are shamed or dishonored if they are active where they should not be—sexually or in realms that are forbidden (professional ambition, aggressiveness, competitiveness and success; or violent activity, such as warfare or other forms of murder). Lady Macbeth, for example, realized that to commit murder she would have to be "unsex'd," i.e., freed from the restraints on violence that were imposed on her by virtue of her belonging to the female sex; and even then, she was unable to commit murder herself, but had to shame her husband into committing murder for her, so that she could only participate in violent behavior vicariously (just as she could only gain honor vicariously, through the honor she would obtain through being his queen when he became king).

Further evidence that men are violence objects and women, sex objects, can be found by examining the kinds of crimes that are committed against each sex. Men constitute, on the average, 75 percent or more of the victims of lethal physical violence in the United States—homicide, suicide, so-called unintentional injuries (from working in hazardous occupations, engaging in violent athletic contests, and participating in other high-risk activities), deaths in military combat, and so on. And throughout the world, men die from all these same forms of violence from two to five times as often as women do, as the World Health Organization documents each year. Women, on the other hand, according to the best available evidence, seem to be the victims of sex crimes (such as rape and incest) more often than men are. Both men and women seem to feel that men are more acceptable as objects of physical violence than women are, for both sexes kill men several times more often than they kill women. Even in experimental studies conducted by psychologists, both men and women exhibit greater readiness and willingness to inflict pain on men than on women, under otherwise identical conditions. Studies of child abuse in those countries in which reasonably accurate statistics are available find that boys are more often victims of lethal or life-threatening violent child abuse (being treated as violence objects), whereas girls are more often victims of sexual abuse (being treated as sex objects)—with few exceptions. Virtually every nation that has had a military draft has decided either that only men should be drafted, or that only men should be sent into combat. Again, none of this should surprise us, given the competition between men for status, valor, bravery, heroism—and honor—in patriarchal societies.

We cannot think about preventing violence without a radical change in the gender roles to which men and women are subjected. The male gender role generates violence by exposing men to shame if they are not violent, and rewarding them with honor when they are. The female gender role also stimulates male violence at the same time that it inhibits female violence. It does this by restricting women to the role of highly unfree sex objects, and honoring them to the degree that they submit to those roles or shaming them when they rebel. This encourages men to treat women as sex objects, and encourages women to conform to that sex role; but it also encourages women (and men) to treat men as violence objects. It also encourages a man to become violent if the woman to whom he is related or married "dishonors" him by acting in ways that transgress her prescribed sexual role.

Since culture is itself constructed, by all of us, if we want to take steps to diminish the amount of violence in our society, both physical and sexual, we can take those steps. To speak of eliminating the sexual asymmetry that casts men and women into opposing sex roles is to speak of liberating both men and women from arbitrary and destructive stereotypes, and to begin treating both women and men as individuals, responding to their individual goals and abilities, rather than to the group (male or female) to which they belong.

There is a deep and tragic paradox about civilization. On the one hand, it has been, up to now, the most life-enhancing innovation the human species has created. The sciences have made it possible for more people to live, and to live longer lives, and to live better lives, freer of pain and illness, cold and hunger, than was ever possible before civilization was invented; and the many forms of art that could not and did not exist except under conditions of civilization are among the main things that make life worth living. But the paradox is that civilization has also increased both the level of human violence, and the scale of the human potential for violence, far beyond anything that any precivilized human culture had done. In the past, the primary threat to human survival was nature, now it is culture. Human suffering before civilization was mainly pathos; since the creation of civilization, it has become, increasingly, tragedy. In fact, it would not be going too far to say that violence is the tragic flaw of civilization. The task confronting us now is to see whether we can end the tragic (violent) element of civilization while maintaining its life-enhancing aspects.

Why has civilization resulted in the most enormous augmentation of human violence since the human species first evolved from its primate forebears? I believe that that question can only be answered by taking into account the psychology of shame. Shame not only motivates destructive behavior, it also motivates constructive behavior. It is the emotion that motivates the ambition and the need for achievement that in turn motivates the invention of civilization.

But—and this is the crux of the matter—this same emotion, shame, that motivates the ambition, activity, and need for achievement that is necessary for the creation of civilization also motivates violence. And when the enormous increase in technological power that civilization brings with it is joined to the enormous increase in violent impulses that shame brings with it, the stage is set for exactly the drama that the history (that is, the civilization) of the world shows us—namely, human social life as an almost uninterrupted, and almost uninterruptedly escalating, series of mass slaughters, "total" and increasingly genocidal wars, and an unprecedented threat to the very continuation not only of civilization itself (which brought this situation about, it cannot be emphasized too strongly) but much more importantly, of the human species for the sake of whose survival civilization was invented in the first place.

Through my clinical work with violent men and my analysis of the psychodynamics of shame and guilt, I have come to view the relationship between civilization and violence in a way that is the diametrical opposite of Freud's. Freud saw violence as an inevitable, spontaneously occurring, natural, innate, instinctual impulse, and civilization and morality as attempts at "taming," neutralizing, inhibiting, or controlling that violent impulse. I see violence, in contrast, as defensive, caused, interpretable, and therefore preventable; and I see civilization, as it has existed up to now (because of class, caste and age stratification, and sexual asymmetry), as among the most potent causes of violence.

One of the puzzles of this century is the phenomenon of Nazism: how could one of the most civilized nations on earth have been capable of such uncivilized, barbaric behavior? (One could ask the same question about Japan's record in World War II.) But from the perspective being elaborated here, genocide is not a regression or an aberration from civilization, or a repudiation of it. It is the inner destiny of civilization, its core tendency—its tragic flaw. Genocide has characterized the behavior of most of the great world civilizations, from ancient Mesopotamia to Rome, to medieval Europe, to the African slave trade and the conquest of the Americas, to the Holocaust and atomic weapons.

How to deal with violence, then? The moral value system (which I will call "shame-ethics") that underlies the code of honor of those patriarchal cultures and subcultures in which behavioral norms are enforced primarily by the sanctions of shame versus honor, such as the Mafia, urban street gangs, and much of the rest of American culture, rationalizes, legitimates, encourages, and even commands violence: it does not prohibit or inhibit it.

The kind of morality that I am calling guilt-ethics (that says "Thou shalt not kill") is an attempt at a kind of therapy, an attempt to cure the human propensity to engage in violence, which is stimulated by shame-ethics. And that was a noble attempt, which one can only wish had been successful. Why has it not worked? I think that the analysis of violence presented in this book can enable us to see the answer to that question. The reason that guilt-ethics has not solved and cannot solve the problem of violence is because it does not dismantle the motivational structure that causes violence in the first place (namely, shame, and the shame-ethics that it motivates). Guilt, and guilt-ethics, merely changes the direction of the violence that shame has generated, it does not prevent the violence in the first place. It primarily redirects, onto the self, the violent impulses that shame generates toward other people. But it does not prevent violence, or even inhibit it. Suicide is no solution to the problem of homicide; both forms of violence are equally lethal. Masochism is no solution to the problem of sadism; both forms of pathology are equally destructive and painful.

Neither shame nor guilt, then, can solve the problem of violence; shame causes hate, which becomes violence (usually toward other people), and guilt merely redirects it (usually onto the self). But to say simply that we need more love, and less shame and guilt, is vacuous. What we really need is to be able to specify the conditions that can enable love to grow without being inhibited by either shame or guilt. And it is clear that shame and guilt do inhibit love. Shame inhibits people from loving others, because shame consists of a deficiency of self-love, and thus it motivates people to withdraw love from others and ration it for the self. Guilt, on the other hand, inhibits self-love, or pride, which the Christian guilt-ethic calls the deadliest of the seven deadly sins. Guilt motivates people to hate themselves, not love themselves, because the feeling of guilt is the feeling that one is guilty and therefore deserves punishment (pain, hate), not reward (pleasure, love).

If we approach violence as a problem in public health and preventive medicine then we need to ask: What are the conditions that stimulate shame and guilt on a socially and epidemiologically significant scale? The conditions that are most important are relative poverty, race and age discrimination, and sexual asymmetry. If we wish to prevent violence, then, our agenda is political and economic reform.

The social policies that would be most effective in preventing violence are those that would reduce the amount of shame. To reduce the amount of shame, we need to reduce the intensity of the passive, dependent regressive wishes that stimulate shame. And to reduce the intensity of those wishes, we must gratify those wishes; by taking better care of each other, especially the neediest among us—particularly beginning in childhood, when the needs for love and care are most intense and peremptory. To quote again the phrase that Dostoevsky put in the mouth of Father Zossima, we then would recognize that "all are responsible for all."

We have a horror of dependency in this country—particularly dependency on the part of men. No wonder we have so much violence—especially male violence. For the horror of dependency is what causes violence. The emotion that causes the horror of dependency is shame. Men, much more than women, are taught that to want love or care from others is to be passive, dependent, unaggressive and unambitious or, in short, unmanly; and that they will be subjected to shaming, ridicule, and disrespect if they appear unmanly in the eyes of others. Women, by contrast, have traditionally been taught that they will be honored if, and only if, they accept a role that restricts them to the relatively passive aim of arranging to be loved by men and to depend on men for their social and economic status, foregoing or severely limiting or disguising activity, ambition, independence, and initiative of their own. This set of injunctions decreases women's vulnerability to behaving violently, but it also inhibits women from participating actively or directly in the building of civilization, in part by reducing them to the role of men's sex objects.

We Americans, as a society, appear to be horrified by the thought that a man could be dependent on anyone (other than himself), and that a woman could be dependent on anyone (other than "her man," that is, her father or husband). The extent of our horror of dependency can be seen in our horror of what is somewhat misleadingly called "welfare dependency"—whether it is the "dependency" on society of an unemployed or disabled man, of an unmarried mother, or of a child without a father. This conceals, or rather reveals, that we as a nation do less for our own citizens than does any other democracy on earth; less health care, child care, housing, support to families, and so on. So that we end up shaming and blaming those whose needs are exposed. Therefore it is not surprising that we also have more violence than does any other democracy on earth, as well as more imprisonment—since we shame some people for having needs that all people have.

For needs that are repressed do not get met, nor do they just disappear. The return of repressed needs, in unconscious, disguised form, is what the various symptoms of psychopathology consist of. One form in which repressed needs for care return is chronic institutionalization—that is, long-term imprisonment or mental hospitalization—which allows us as a society to punish massively, while we gratify grudgingly, those needs of which we are so intolerant.

In fact, the violence of our society reveals our shame at being less "independent" than we "declared" ourselves to be two centuries ago. In contemporary America, to want love, to depend on others, to be less than completely self-sufficient, is to be shamed by all the institutions of our society, from welfare offices to mental hospitals to prisons. One can pretend that one is in an institution only because one is so tough and dangerous and scary, so active and aggressive, and so independent of the community's standards, that the courts insisted on locking one up against one's own wishes. But nevertheless, it is true that for many men in our society it is only in prison that one is given three meals a day, a warm bed to sleep in at night, a roof over one's head, and people who care enough about one to make sure that one is there every night.

Those are among the reasons why the most effective way to increase the amount of violence and crime is to do exactly what we have been doing increasingly over the past decades, namely, to permit—or rather, to force—more and more of our children and adults to be poor, neglected, hungry, homeless, uneducated, and sick. What is particularly effective in increasing the amount of violence in the world is to widen the gap between the rich and the poor. We have not restricted that strategy to this country, but are practicing it on a worldwide scale, among the increasingly impoverished nations of the third world; and we can well expect it to culminate in increasing levels of violence, all over the world.

Relative poverty—poverty for some groups coexisting with wealth for others—is much more effective in stimulating shame, and hence violence, than is a level of poverty that is higher in absolute terms but is universally shared. Shame exists in the eye of the beholder—though it is more likely to exist there if the beheld is perceived as richer and more powerful than oneself. In that archaic, prescientific language called morality, this gap is called injustice; but most people throughout the world still think in moral terms, and the perception that one is a victim of injustice is what causes shame, which in turn causes violence.

From the standpoint of public health, then, the social psychology of shame, discrimination, and violence becomes central to any preventive psychiatry. The causes and consequences of the feelings of shame as well as their psychodynamic parameters have become more urgently compelling as a focus of investigation, given the potential ultimacy of violence in a nuclear age, as well as the continuing high rate of violence in American society. In my analysis of the psychological consequences of the feelings of shame, I have set out to show how such seemingly trivial events as personal experiences of chagrin or embarrassment can explode into epidemics of violence, just as the physical consequences of organisms as insignificant as microbes can have the gravest implications for public health. As Rudolph Virchow, who helped to lay the foundations of preventive medicine and public health more than a century ago, put it, "Medicine is a social science, and politics is simply medicine on a larger scale."

If cleaning up sewer systems could prevent more deaths than all the physicians in the world, then perhaps reforming the social, economic, and legal institutions that systematically humiliate people can do more to prevent violence than all the preaching and punishing in the world. The task before us now is to integrate the psychodynamic understanding of shame and guilt with the broader social and economic factors that intensify those feelings to murderous and suicidal extremes on a mass scale.

ARTICLE 44

Tim Beneke

Men on Rape

Rape may be America's fastest growing violent crime; no one can be certain because it is not clear whether more rapes are being committed or reported. It *is* clear that violence against women is widespread and fundamentally alters the meaning of life for women; that sexual violence is encouraged in a variety of ways in American culture; and that women are often blamed for rape.

Consider some statistics:

- In a random sample of 930 women, sociologist Diana Russell found that 44 percent had survived either rape or attempted rape. Rape was defined as sexual intercourse physically forced upon the woman, or coerced by threat of bodily harm, or forced upon the woman when she was helpless (asleep, for example). The survey included rape and attempted rape in marriage in its calculations. (Personal communication)
- In a September 1980 survey conducted by *Cosmopolitan* magazine to which over 106,000 women anonymously responded, 24 percent had been raped at least once. Of these, 51 percent had been raped by friends, 37 percent by strangers, 18 percent by relatives, and 3 percent by husbands. 10 percent of the women in the survey had been victims of incest. 75 percent of the women had been "bullied into making love." Writer Linda Wolfe, who reported on the survey, wrote in reference to such bullying: "Though such harassment stops short of rape, readers reported that it was nearly as distressing."

- An estimated 2–3 percent of all men who rape outside of marriage go to prison for their crimes.[1]
- The F.B.I. estimates that if current trends continue, one woman in four will be sexually assaulted in her lifetime.[2]
- An estimated 1.8 million women are battered by their spouses each year.[3] In extensive interviews with 430 battered women, clinical psychologist Lenore Walker, author of *The Battered Woman*, found that 59.9 percent had also been raped (defined as above) by their spouses. Given the difficulties many women had in admitting they had been raped, Walker estimates the figure may well be as high as 80 or 85 percent (personal communication). If 59.9 percent of the 1.8 million women battered each year are also raped, then a million women may be raped in marriage each year. And a significant number are raped in marriage without being battered.
- Between one in two and one in ten of all rapes are reported to the police.[4]
- Between 300,000 and 500,000 women are raped each year outside of marriage.[5]

What is often missed when people contemplate statistics on rape is the effect of the *threat* of sexual violence on women. I have asked women repeatedly, "How would your life be different if rape were suddenly to end?" (Men may learn a lot by asking this question of women to whom they are close.) The threat of rape is an assault upon the meaning of the world; it alters the feel of the human condition. Surely any attempt to comprehend the lives of women that fails to take issues of violence against women into account is misguided.

Through talking to women, I learned: *The threat of rape alters the meaning and feel of the night.* Observe how your body feels, how the night feels, when you're in fear. The constriction in your chest, the vigilance in your eyes, the rubber in your legs. What do the stars look like? How does the moon present itself? What is the difference between walking late at night in the dangerous part of a city and walking late at night in the country, or safe suburbs? When I try to imagine what the threat of rape must do to the night, I think of the stalked, adrenalated feeling I get walking late at night in parts of certain American cities. Only, I remind myself, it is a fear different from any I have known, a fear of being raped.

It is night half the time. If the threat of rape alters the meaning of the night, it must alter the meaning and pace of the day, one's relation to the passing and organization of time itself. For some women, the threat of rape at night turns their cars into armored tanks, their solitude into isolation. And what must the space inside a car or an apartment feel like if the space outside is menacing?

I was running late one night with a close woman friend through a path in the woods on the outskirts of a small university town. We had run several miles and were feeling a warm, energized serenity.

"How would you feel if you were alone?" I asked.

"Terrified!" she said instantly.

"Terrified that there might be a man out there?" I asked, pointing to the surrounding moonlit forest, which had suddenly been transformed into a source of terror.

"Yes."

Another woman said, "I know what I can't do and I've completely internalized what I can't do. I've built a viable life that basically involves never leaving my apartment at night unless I'm directly going some place to meet somebody. It's unconsciously built into what it occurs to women to do." When one is raised without freedom, one may not recognize its absence.

The threat of rape alters the meaning and feel of nature. Everyone has felt the psychic nurturance of nature. Many women are being deprived of that nurturance, especially in wooded areas near cities. They are deprived either because they cannot experience nature in solitude because of threat, or because, when they do choose solitude in nature, they must cope with a certain subtle but nettlesome fear.

Women need more money because of rape and the threat of rape makes it harder for women to earn money. It's simple: if you don't feel safe walking at night, or riding public transportation, you need a car. And it is less practicable to live in cheaper, less secure, and thus more dangerous neighborhoods if the ordinary threat of violence that men experience, being mugged, say, is compounded by the threat of rape. By limiting mobility at night, the threat of rape limits where and when one is able to work, thus making it more difficult to earn money. An obvious bind: women need more money because of rape, and have fewer job opportunities because of it.

The threat of rape makes women more dependent on men (or other women). One woman said: "If there were no rape I wouldn't have to play games with men for their protection." The threat of rape falsifies, mystifies, and confuses relations between men and women. If there were no rape, women would simply not need men as much, wouldn't need them to go places with at night, to feel safe in their homes, for protection in nature.

The threat of rape makes solitude less possible for women. Solitude, drawing strength from being alone, is difficult if being alone means being afraid. To be afraid is to be in need, to experience a lack; the threat of rape creates a lack. Solitude requires relaxation; if you're afraid, you can't relax.

The threat of rape inhibits a woman's expressiveness. "If there were no rape," said one woman, "I could dress the way I wanted and walk the way I wanted and not feel self-conscious about the responses of men. I could be friendly to people. I wouldn't have to wish I was ugly. I wouldn't have to make myself small when I got on the bus. I wouldn't have to respond to verbal abuse from men by remaining silent. I could respond in kind."

If a woman's basic expressiveness is inhibited, her sexuality, creativity, and delight in life must surely be diminished.

The threat of rape inhibits the freedom of the eye. I know a married couple who live in Manhattan. They are both artists, both acutely sensitive and responsive to the visual world. When they walk separately in the city, he has more freedom to look than she does. She must control her eye movements lest they inadvertently meet the glare of some importunate man. What, who, and how she sees are restricted by the threat of rape.

The following exercise is recommended for men.

Walk down a city street. Pay a lot of attention to your clothing; make sure your pants are zipped, shirt tucked in, buttons done. Look straight ahead. Every time a man walks past you, avert your eyes and make your face expressionless. Most women learn to go through this act each time we leave our houses. It's a way to avoid at least some of the encounters we've all had with strange men who decided we looked available.[6]

To relate aesthetically to the visual world involves a certain playfulness, spirit of spontaneous exploration. The tense vigilance that accompanies fear inhibits that spontaneity. The world is no longer yours to look at when you're afraid.

I am aware that all culture is, in part, restriction, that there are places in America where hardly anyone is safe (though men are safer than women virtually everywhere), that there are many ways to enjoy life, that some women may not be so restricted, that there exist havens, whether psychic, geographical, economic, or class. But they are *havens*, and as such, defined by threat.

Above all, I trust my experience: no woman could have lived the life I've lived the last few years. If suddenly I were restricted by the threat of rape, I would feel a deep, inexorable depression. And it's not just rape; it's harassment, battery, Peeping Toms, anonymous phone calls, exhibitionism, intrusive stares, fondlings—all con-

tributing to an atmosphere of intimidation in women's lives. And I have only scratched the surface; it would take many carefully crafted short stories to begin to express what I have only hinted at in the last few pages. I have not even touched upon what it might mean for a woman to be sexually assaulted. Only women can speak to that. Nor have I suggested how the threat of rape affects marriage.

Rape and the threat of rape pervade the lives of women, as reflected in some popular images of our culture.

"She Asked for It"—Blaming the Victim[7]

Many things may be happening when a man blames a woman for rape.

First, in all cases where a woman is said to have asked for it, her appearance and behavior are taken as a form of speech. "Actions speak louder than words" is a widely held belief; the woman's actions—her appearance may be taken as action—are given greater emphasis than her words; an interpretation alien to the woman's intentions is given to her actions. A logical extension of "she asked for it" is the idea that she wanted what happened to happen; if she wanted it to happen, she *deserved* for it to happen. Therefore, the man is not to be blamed. "She asked for it" can mean either that she was consenting to have sex and was not really raped, or that she was in fact raped but somehow she really deserved it. "If you ask for it, you deserve it," is a widely held notion. If I ask you to beat me up and you beat me up, I still don't deserve to be beaten up. So even if the notion that women asked to be raped had some basis in reality, which it doesn't, on its own terms it makes no sense.

Second, a mentality exists that says: a woman who assumes freedoms normally restricted to a man (like going out alone at night) and is raped is doing the same thing as a woman who goes out in the rain without an umbrella and catches a cold. Both are considered responsible for what happens to them. That men will rape is taken to be a legitimized given, part of nature, like rain or snow. The view reflects a massive abdication of responsibility for rape on the part of men. It is so much easier to think of rape as natural than to acknowledge one's part in it. So long as rape is regarded as natural, women will be blamed for rape.

A third point. The view that it is natural for men to rape is closely connected to the view of women as commodities. If a woman's body is regarded as a valued commodity by men, then of course, if you leave a valued commodity where it can be taken, it's just human nature for men to take it. If you left your stereo out on the sidewalk, you'd be asking for it to get stolen. Someone will just take it. (And how often men speak of rape as "going out and *taking* it.") If a woman walks the streets at night, she's leaving a valued commodity, her body, where it can be taken. So long as women are regarded as commodities, they will be blamed for rape.

Which brings us to a fourth point. "She asked for it" is inseparable from a more general "psychology of the dupe." If I use bad judgment and fail to read the small print in a contract and later get taken advantage of, "screwed" (or "fucked over"), then I deserve what I get; bad judgment makes me liable. Analogously, if a woman trusts a man and goes to his apartment, or accepts a ride hitchhiking, or goes out on a date and is raped, she's a dupe and deserves what she gets. "He didn't *really* rape her" goes the mentality—"he merely took advantage of her." And in America it's okay for people to take advantage of each other, even expected and praised. In fact, you're considered dumb and foolish if you don't take advantage of other people's bad judgment. And so, again, by treating them as dupes, rape will be blamed on women.

Fifth, if a woman who is raped is judged attractive by men, and particularly if she dresses to look attractive, then the mentality exists that she attacked him with her weapon so, of course, he counter-attacked with his. The preview to a popular movies states: "She was the victim of her own *provocative beauty*." Provocation: "There is a line which, if crossed, will *set me off* and I will lose control and no longer be responsible for my behavior. If you punch me in the nose then, of course, I will not be responsible for what happens: you will have provoked a fight. If you dress, talk, move, or act a certain way, you will have provoked me to rape. If your appearance *stuns* me, *strikes* me, *ravishes* me, *knocks me out*, etc., then I will not be held responsible for what happens; you will have asked for it." The notion that sexual feeling makes one helpless is part of a cultural abdication of responsibility for sexuality. So long as a woman's appearance is viewed as a weapon and sexual feeling is believed to make one helpless, women will be blamed for rape.

Sixth, I have suggested that men sometimes become obsessed with images of women, that images become a substitute for sexual feeling, that sexual feeling becomes externalized and out of control and is given an undifferentiated identity in the appearance of women's bodies. It is a process of projection in which one blurs one's own desire with her imagined, projected desire. If a woman's attractiveness is taken to signify one's own lust and a woman's lust, then when an "attractive" woman is raped, some men may think she wanted sex. Since they perceive their own lust in part projected onto the woman, they disbelieve women who've been raped. So long as men project their own sexual desires onto women, they will blame women for rape.

And seventh, what are we to make of the contention that women in dating situations say "no" initially to sexual overtures from men as a kind of pose, only to give in later, thus revealing their true intentions? And that men are thus confused and incredulous when women are raped because in their sexual experience women can't be believed? I doubt that this has much to do with men's perceptions of rape. I don't know to what extent women actually "say no and mean yes"; certainly it is a common theme in male folklore. I have spoken to a couple of women who went through periods when they wanted to be sexual but were afraid to be, and often rebuffed initial sexual advances only to give in later. One point is clear: the ambivalence women may feel about having sex is closely tied to the inability of men to fully accept them as sexual beings. Women have been traditionally punished for being openly and freely sexual; men are praised for it. And if many men think of sex as achievement of possession of a valued commodity, or aggressive degradation, then women have every reason to feel and act ambivalent.

These themes are illustrated in an interview I conducted with a 23-year-old man who grew up in Pittsburgh and works as a file clerk in the financial district of San Francisco. Here's what he said:

"Where I work it's probably no different from any other major city in the U.S. The women dress up in high heels, and they wear a lot of makeup, and they just look really *hot* and really sexy, and how can somebody who has a healthy sex drive not feel lust for them when you see them? I feel lust for them, but I don't think I could find it in me to overpower someone and rape them. But I definitely get the feeling that I'd like to rape a girl. I don't know if the actual act of rape would be satisfying, but the *feeling* is satisfying.

"These women look so good, and they kiss ass of the men in the three-piece suits who are *big* in the corporation, and most of them relate to me like 'Who are *you*? Who are *you* to even *look* at?' They're snobby and they condescend to me, and I resent it. It would take me a lot longer to get to first base than it would somebody with a three-piece suit who had money. And to me a lot of the men they go out with are superficial assholes who have no real feelings or substance, and are just trying to get ahead and make a lot of money. Another thing that makes me resent these women is thinking, 'How could she want to hang out with somebody like that? What does that make her?'

"I'm a file clerk, which makes me feel like a nebbish, a nerd, like I'm not making it, I'm a failure. But I don't really believe I'm a failure because I know it's just a phase, and I'm just doing it for the money, just to make it through this phase. I catch myself feeling like a failure, but I realize that's ridiculous."

What exactly do you go through when you see these sexy, unavailable women? "Let's say I see a woman and she looks really pretty and really clean and sexy, and she's giving off very feminine, sexy vibes. I think, 'Wow, I would love to make love to her,' but I know she's not really interested. It's a tease. A lot of times a woman knows that she's looking really good and she'll use that and flaunt it, and it makes me feel like she's laughing at me and I feel *degraded*.

"I also feel dehumanized, because when I'm being teased I just turn off, I cease to be human. Because if I go with my human emotions I'm going to want to put my arms around her and kiss her, and to do that would be unacceptable. I don't like the feeling that I'm supposed to stand there and take it, and not be able to hug her or kiss her; so I just turn off my emotions. It's a feeling of humiliation, because the woman has forced me to turn off my feelings and react in a way that I really don't want to.

"If I were actually desperate enough to rape somebody, it would be from wanting the person, but it would be a very spiteful thing, just being able to say, 'I have power over you and I can do anything I want with you,' because really I feel that *they* have power over *me* just by their presence. Just the fact that they can come up to me and just melt me and make me feel like a dummy makes me want revenge. They have power over me so I want power over them. . . .

"Society says that you have to have a lot of sex with a lot of different women to be a real man. Well, what happens if you don't? Then what are you? Are you half a man? Are you still a boy? It's ridiculous. You see a whiskey ad with a guy and two women on his arm. The implication is that real men don't have any trouble getting women."

How does it make you feel toward women to see all these sexy women in media and advertising using their looks to try to get you to buy something? "It makes me hate them. As a man you're taught that men are more powerful than women, and that men always have the upper hand, and that it's a man's society; but then you see all these women and it makes you think, 'Jesus Christ, if we have all the power how come all the beautiful women are telling us what to buy?' And to be honest, it just makes me hate beautiful women because they're using their power over me. I realize they're being used themselves, and they're doing it for money. In *Playboy* you see all these beautiful women who look so sexy and they'll be giving you all these looks like they want to have sex so bad; but then in reality you know that except for a few nympho-maniacs, they're doing it for the money; so I hate them for being used and for using their bodies in that way.

"In this society, if you ever sit down and real-ize how manipulated you really are it makes you pissed off—it makes you want to take control. And you've been manipulated by women, and they're a very easy target because they're out walking along the streets, so you can just grab one and say, 'Listen, you're going to do what I want you to do,' and it's an act of revenge against the way you've been manipulated.

"I know a girl who was walking down the street by her house, when this guy jumped her and beat her up and raped her, and she was black and blue and had to go to the hospital. That's beyond me. I can't understand how somebody could do that. If I were going to rape a girl, I wouldn't hurt her. I might *restrain* her, but I wouldn't *hurt* her. . . .

"The whole dating game between men and women also makes me feel degraded. I hate being put in the position of having to initiate a rela-tionship. I've been taught that if you're not aggressive with a woman, then you've blown it.

She's not going to jump on *you*, so *you've* got to jump on *her*. I've heard all kinds of stories where the woman says, 'No! No! No!' and they end up making great love. I get confused as hell if a woman pushes me away. Does it mean she's try-ing to be a nice girl and wants to put up a good appearance, or does it mean she doesn't want any-thing to do with you? You don't know. Probably a lot of men think that women don't feel like real women unless a man tries to force himself on her, unless she brings out the 'real man,' so to speak, and probably too much of it goes on. It goes on in my head that you're complimenting a woman by actually staring at her or by trying to get into her pants. Lately, I'm realizing that when I stare at women lustfully, they often feel more threatened than flattered."

Notes

1. Such estimates recur in the rape literature. See *Sexual Assault* by Nancy Gager and Cathleen Schurr, Grosset & Dunlap, 1976, or *The Price of Coercive Sexu-ality* by Clark and Lewis, The Women's Press, 1977.

2. *Uniform Crime Reports*, 1980.

3. See *Behind Closed Doors* by Murray J. Strauss and Richard Gelles, Doubleday, 1979.

4. See Gager and Schurr (above) or virtually any book on the subject.

5. Again, see Gager and Schurr, or Carol V. Horos, *Rape*, Banbury Books, 1981.

6. From "Willamette Bridge" in *Body Politics* by Nancy Henley, Prentice-Hall, 1977, p. 144.

7. I would like to thank George Lakoff for this in-sight.

ARTICLE 45

Cynthia Enloe

Wielding Masculinity inside Abu Ghraib: Making Feminist Sense of an American Military Scandal

Since the mid-1970s, feminists have been crafting skills to explain when and why organizations become arenas for sexist abuse. One of the great contributions of the work done by the "Second Wave" of the international women's movement has been to throw light on what breeds sex discrimination and sexual harassment inside organizations otherwise as dissimilar as a factory, a stock brokerage, a legislature, a university, a student movement, and a military (Bowers, 2004; Kwon, 1999; Ogasawara, 1998; Stockford, 2004, Whitworth, 2004). All of the Abu Ghraib reports' authors talked about a "climate," an "environment," or a "culture," having been created inside Abu Ghraib that fostered abusive acts. The conditions inside Abu Ghraib were portrayed as a climate of "confusion," of "chaos." It was feminists who gave us this innovative concept of organizational climate.

In April, 2004, a year after the US government launched its massive military invasion of Iraq, a series of shocking photographs of American soldiers abusing Iraqi prisoners began appearing on television news programs and the front pages of newspapers around the world. American male and female soldiers serving as prison guards in a prison called Abu Ghraib were shown deliberately humiliating and torturing scores of Iraqi men held in detention and under interroga-

tion. The American soldiers were smiling broadly. They appeared to be taking enormous pleasure in humiliating their Iraqi charges.

Most people who saw these photographs—people in Seattle and Seoul, Miami and Madrid, Bangkok and Boston—can still describe the scenes. An American male soldier standing self-satisfied with his arms crossed and wearing surgical blue rubber gloves, while in front of him, an American woman soldier, smiling at the camera, is leaning on top of a pile of naked Iraqi men forced to contort themselves into a human pyramid. An American woman soldier, again smiling, holding a male Iraqi prisoner on a leash. An American woman soldier pointing to a naked Iraqi man's genitals, apparently treating them as a joke. American male soldiers intimidating naked Iraqi male prisoners with snarling guard dogs. An Iraqi male prisoner standing alone on a box, his head hooded, electrical wires attached to different parts of his body. An Iraqi male prisoner forced to wear women's underwear. Not pictured, but substantiated, were Iraqi men forced to masturbate and to simulate oral sex with each other, as well as an Iraqi woman prisoner coerced by several American male soldiers into kissing them (Hersh, 2004a).

What does a feminist curiosity reveal about the causes and the implications of the American abuses of Iraqi prisoners at Abu Ghraib? Few of the US government's official investigators or the mainstream news commentators used feminist insights to make sense of what went on in the prison. The result, I think, is that we have not

From "Wielding Masculinity Inside Abu Ghraib: Making Feminist Sense of an American Military Scandal," by Cynthia Enloe. *Asian Journal of Women's Studies* 10(3): 89–102. © 2004. Used by permission of the author.

really gotten to the bottom of the Abu Ghraib story. One place to start employing a feminist set of tools is to explain why one American woman military guard in particular captured the attention of so many media editors and ordinary viewers and readers: the twenty-one-year-old enlisted army reservist Lynndie England.

What proved shocking to the millions of viewers of the prison clandestine photos were several things. First, the Abu Ghraib scenes suggested there existed a gaping chasm between, on the one hand, the US Bush administration's claim that its military invasion and overthrow of the brutal Saddam Hussein regime would bring a civilizing sort of "freedom" to the Iraqi people and, on the other hand, the seemingly barbaric treatment that American soldiers were willfully meting out to Iraqis held in captivity without trial. Second, it was shocking to witness such blatant abuse of imprisoned detainees by soldiers representing a government that had signed both the international Geneva Conventions against mistreatment of wartime combatants and the UN Convention Against Torture, as well as having passed its own anti-torture laws.

Yet there was a third source of shock that prompted scores of early media commentaries and intense conversations among ordinary viewers: seeing women engage in torture. Of the seven American soldiers, all low-ranking Army Reserve military police guards, whom the Pentagon charged and initially court-martialed, three were women. Somehow, the American male soldier, the man in the blue surgical gloves (his name was Charles Graner), was not shocking to most viewers and so did not inspire much private consternation and/or a stream of op-ed columns. Women, by conventional contrast, were expected to appear in wartime as mothers and wives of soldiers, occasionally as military nurses and truck mechanics, or most often as the victims of the wartime violence. Women were not—according to the conventional presumption—supposed to be the wielders of violence, certainly not the perpetrators of torture. When those deeply gendered presumptions were turned upside down, many

people felt a sense of shock. "This is awful; how could this have happened?"

Private First Class Lynndie England, the young woman military guard photographed holding the man on a leash, thus became the source of intense public curiosity. The news photographers could not restrain themselves two months later, in early August, 2004, from showing England in her army camouflaged maternity uniform when she appeared at Fort Bragg for her pre-trial hearing. She had become pregnant as a result of her sexual liaison with another enlisted reservist while on duty in Abu Ghraib. Her sexual partner was Charles Graner. Yet Charles Graner's name was scarcely mentioned. He apparently was doing what men are expected to do in wartime: have sex and wield violence. The public's curiosity and its lack of curiosity thus matched its pattern of shock. All three were conventionally gendered. Using a feminist investigatory approach, one should find this lack of public and media curiosity about Charles Graner just as revealing as the public's and media's absorbing fascination with Lynndie England.

Responding to the torrent of Abu Ghraib stories coming out of Iraq during the spring and summer of 2004, President George W. Bush and his Secretary of Defense, Donald Rumsfeld, tried to reassure the public that the graphically abusive behavior inside the prison was not representative of America, nor did it reflect the Bush administration's own foreign policies. Rather, the Abu Ghraib abuses were the work of "rogue" soldiers, a "few bad apples." The "bad apple" explanation always goes like this: the institution is working fine, its values are appropriate, its internal dynamics are of a sort that sustain positive values and respectful, productive behavior. Thus, according to the "bad apple" explanation, nothing needs to be reassessed or reformed in the way the organization works; all that needs to happen to stop the abuse is to prosecute and remove those few individuals who refused to play by the established rules. Sometimes this may be true. Some listeners to the Bush administration's "bad apple" explanation, however, weren't reassured. They wondered if the Abu Ghraib abuses were not produced by just a few bad apples found in a solid, reliable barrel, but, instead, were produced by an essentially "bad barrel." They also wondered whether this "barrel" embraced not only the Abu Ghraib prison, but the larger US military, intelligence and civilian command structures (Hersh, 2004b; Hersh, 2004c; Human Rights Watch, 2004).

What makes a "barrel" go bad? That is, what turns an organization, an institution, or a whole system into one that at least ignores, perhaps even fosters abusive behavior by the individuals operating inside it? This question is relevant for every workplace, every political system, every international alliance. Here too, feminists have been working hard over the past three decades to develop a curiosity and a set of analytical tools with which we can all answer this important question. So many of us today live much of our lives within complex organizations, large and small—work places, local and national governments, health care systems, criminal justice systems, international organizations. Feminist researchers have revealed that virtually all organizations are gendered: that is, all organizations are shaped by the ideas about, and daily practices of, masculinities and femininities (Bunster-Burotto, 1985; Ehrenreich, 2004; Enloe, 2000; Whitworth, 2004). Ignoring the workings of gender, feminist investigators have found, makes it impossible for us to explain accurately what makes any organization "tick." That failure makes it impossible for us to hold an organization accountable. Yet most of the hundred-page long official reports into the Abu Ghraib abuse scandal were written by people who ignored these feminist lessons. They acted as if the dynamics of masculinity and femininity among low-level police and high level policy-makers made no difference. That assumption is very risky.

A series of US Senate hearings, along with a string of Defense Department investigations tried to explain what went wrong in Abu Ghraib and why. The most authoritative of the Defense Department reports were the "Taguba Report,"

the "Fay/Jones Report" (both named after generals who headed these investigations) and the "Schlesinger Report" (named after a civilian former Secretary of Defense who chaired this investigatory team) (Human Rights Watch, 2004; Jehl, 2004; Lewis and Schmitt, 2004; Schmitt, 2004; Taguba, 2004). In addition, the CIA was conducting its own investigation, since its officials were deeply involved in interrogating—and often hiding in secret prisons—captured Afghans and Iraqis. Moreover, there were several human rights groups and journalists publishing their own findings during 2004. Together, they offered a host of valuable clues as to why this institutional "barrel" had gone bad. First was the discovery that lawyers inside the Defense and Justice Departments, as well as the White House, acting on instructions from their civilian superiors, produced interpretations of the Geneva Conventions and US law that deliberately shrank the definitions of "torture" down so far that American military and CIA personnel could order and conduct interrogations of Iraqis and Afghans in detention using techniques that otherwise would have been deemed violations of US and international law.

Second, investigators found that an American general, Geoffrey Miller, commander of the US prison at Guantanamo Bay, Cuba, was sent by Secretary Rumsfeld to Iraq in September, 2003, where he recommended that American commanders overseeing military prison operations in Iraq start employing the aggressive interrogation practices that were being used on Afghan and Arab male prisoners at Guantanamo. Somewhat surprisingly, General Miller later was named by the Pentagon to head the Abu Ghraib prison in the wake of the scandal. Third, investigators discovered that the intense, persistent pressure imposed on the military intelligence personnel by the Defense Department to generate information about who was launching insurgent assaults on the US occupying forces encouraged those military intelligence officers to put their own pressures on the military police guarding prisoners to "soften up" the men in their cell blocks, thus undercutting the military police men's and women's own chain of command (which led up to a female army general, Janice Karpinski, who claimed that her authority over her military police personnel had been undermined by intrusive military intelligence officers). This policy change, investigators concluded, dangerously blurred the valuable line between military policing and military interrogating. A fourth finding was that non-military personnel, including CIA operatives and outside contractors hired by the CIA and the Pentagon, were involved in the Abu Ghraib military interrogations in ways that may have fostered an assumption that the legal limitations on employing excessive force could be treated cavalierly: We're under threat, this is urgent, who can be bothered with the Geneva Conventions or legal niceties?

Did it matter where the women were inside the prison and up and down the larger American military and intelligence hierarchies—as low level police reservists, as a captain in the military intelligence unit, as a general advising the chief US commander in Iraq? Investigators apparently didn't ask. Did it matter what exactly Charles Graner's and the other male military policemen's daily relationships were to their female colleagues, who were in a numerical minority in the military police unit, in the military interrogation unit and in the CIA unit all stationed together at Abu Ghraib? The official investigators seemed not to think that asking this question would yield any insights. Was it significant that so many of the abuses perpetrated on the Iraqi prisoners were deliberately sexualized? Was hooding a male prisoner the same (in motivation and in result) as forcing him to simulate oral sex? No one seemed to judge these questions to be pertinent. Was it at all relevant that Charles Graner, the older and apparently most influential of the low-ranking guards charged, had been accused of physical intimidation by his former wife? No questions asked, no answers forthcoming. Among all the lawyers in the Defense and Justice Departments and in the White House who were ordered to draft guidelines to permit the US government's officials to sidestep the Geneva Conventions outlawing torture, were there any subtle pressures imposed on them to appear "manly" in a time of war? This question too seems to have been left on the investigative teams' shelves to gather dust.

Since the mid-1970s, feminists have been crafting skills to explain when and why organizations become arenas for sexist abuse. One of the great contributions of the work done by the "Second Wave" of the international women's movement has been to throw light on what breeds sex discrimination and sexual harassment inside organizations otherwise as dissimilar as a factory, a stock brokerage, a legislature, a university, a student movement, and a military (Bowers, 2004; Kwon, 1999; Ogasawara, 1998; Stockford, 2004; Whitworth, 2004). All of the Abu Ghraib reports' authors talked about a "climate," an "environment," or a "culture," having been created inside Abu Ghraib that fostered abusive acts. The conditions inside Abu Ghraib were portrayed as a climate of "confusion," of "chaos." It was feminists who gave us this innovative concept of organizational climate.

When trying to figure out why in some organizations women employees were subjected to sexist jokes, unwanted advances, and retribution for not going along with the jokes or not accepting those advances, feminist lawyers, advocates and scholars began to look beyond the formal policies and the written work rules. They explored something more amorphous but just as, maybe even more, potent: that set of unofficial presumptions that shapes workplace interactions between men and men, and men and women. They followed the breadcrumbs to the casual, informal interactions between people up and down the organization's ladder. They investigated who drinks with whom after work, who sends sexist jokes to whom over office email, who pins up which sorts of pictures of women in their lockers or next to the coffee machine. And they looked into what those people in authority did not do. They discovered that inaction is a form of action: "turning a blind eye" is itself a form of action. Inaction sends out signals to everyone in the organization about what is condoned. Feminists labeled these webs of presumptions, informal interactions, and deliberate inaction an organization's "climate." As feminists argued successfully in court, it is not sufficient for a stock brokerage or a college to include anti-sexual harassment guidelines in their official handbooks; employers have to take explicit steps to create a workplace climate in which women would be treated with fairness and respect.

By 2004, this feminist explanatory concept—organizational "climate"—had become so accepted by so many analysts that their debt to feminists had been forgotten. Generals Taguba, Jones and Fay, as well as former Defense Secretary Schlesinger, may never have taken a Women's Studies course, but when they were assigned the job of investigating Abu Ghraib they were drawing on the ideas and investigatory skills crafted for them by feminists.

However, more worrisome than their failure to acknowledge their intellectual and political debts was those journalists' and government investigators' ignoring the feminist lessons that went hand in hand with the concept of "climate." The first lesson: to make sense of any organization, we always must dig deep into the group's dominant presumptions about femininity and masculinity. The second lesson: we need to take seriously the experiences of women as they try to adapt to, or sometimes resist those dominant gendered presumptions—not because all women are angels, but because paying close attention to women's ideas and actions will shed light on why men with power act the way they do.

It is not as if the potency of ideas about masculinity and femininity had been totally absent from the US military's thinking. Between 1991 and 2004, there had been a string of military scandals that had compelled even those American senior officials who preferred to look the other way to face sexism straight on. The first stemmed from the September, 1991, gathering of American navy aircraft carrier pilots at a Hilton hotel in Las Vegas. Male pilots (all officers), fresh from their victory in the first Gulf War, lined a hotel corridor and physically assaulted every

woman who stepped off the elevator. They made the "mistake" of assaulting a woman navy helicopter pilot who was serving as an aide to an admiral. Within months members of Congress and the media were telling the public about "Tailhook"—why it happened, who tried to cover it up (Office of the Inspector General, 2003). Close on the heels of the Navy's "Tailhook" scandal came the Army's Aberdeen training base sexual harassment scandal, followed by other revelations of military gay bashing, sexual harassment and rapes by American male military personnel of their American female colleagues (Enloe, 1993; 2000).

Then in September, 1995, the rape of a local school girl by two American male marines and a sailor in Okinawa sparked public demonstrations, new Okinawan women's organizing and more US Congressional investigations. At the start of the twenty-first century American media began to notice the patterns of international trafficking in Eastern European and Filipina women around American bases in South Korea, prompting official embarrassment in Washington (an embarrassment which had not been demonstrated earlier when American base commanders turned a classic "blind eye" toward a prostitution industry financed by their own male soldiers because it employed "just" local South Korean women). And in 2003, three new American military sexism scandals caught Washington policy-makers' attention: four American male soldiers returning from combat missions in Afghanistan murdered their female partners at Fort Bragg, North Carolina; a pattern of sexual harassment and rape by male cadets of female cadets—and superiors' refusal to treat these acts seriously—as revealed at the US Air Force Academy; and testimonies by at least sixty American women soldiers returning from tours of duty in Kuwait and Iraq described how they had been sexually assaulted by their male colleagues there—with, once again, senior officers choosing inaction, advising the American women soldiers to "get over it" (Jargon, 2003; Lutz and Elliston, 2004; The Miles Foundation, 2004; Moffeit and Herder, 2004).

So it should have come as no surprise to American senior uniformed and civilian policy makers seeking to make sense of the abuses perpetrated in Abu Ghraib that a culture of sexism had come to permeate many sectors of US military life. If they had thought about what they had all learned in the last thirteen years—from Tailhook, Aberdeen, Fort Bragg, Okinawa, South Korea and the US Air Force Academy—they should have put the workings of masculinity and femininity at the top of their investigatory agendas. They should have made feminist curiosity one of their own principal tools. Perhaps Tillie Fowler did suggest to her colleagues that they think about these military sexual scandals when they began to delve into Abu Ghraib. A former Republican Congresswoman from Florida, Tillie Fowler, had been a principal investigator on the team that looked into the rapes (and their cover-ups) at the US Air Force Academy. Because of her leadership in that role, Fowler was appointed to the commission headed by James Schlesinger investigating Abu Ghraib. Did she raise this comparison between the Air Force Academy case and Abu Ghraib? Did her male colleagues take her suggestion seriously?

Perhaps eventually the investigators did not make use of the feminist lessons and tools because they imagined that the lessons of Tailhook, the Air Force Academy and Okinawa were relevant only when all the perpetrators of sexualized abuse are men and all the victims are women. The presence of Lynndie England and the other women in Abu Ghraib's military police unit, they might have assumed, made the feminist tools sharpened in these earlier gendered military scandals inappropriate for their explorations. But the lesson of Tailhook, Okinawa and the most recent military scandals was not that the politics of masculinity and femininity matter only when men are the perpetrators and women are the victims. Instead, the deeper lesson of all these other military scandals is that we must always ask: Has this organization (or this system of interlocking organizations) become masculinized in ways that privilege certain forms of masculinity, feminize its oppositiion and trivialize most forms of femininity?

With this core gender question in mind, we might uncover significant dynamics operating in Abu Ghraib and in the American military and civilian organizations that were supposed to be supervising the prison's personnel. First, American military police and their military and CIA intelligence colleagues might have been guided by their own masculinized fears of humiliation when they forced Iraqi men to go naked for days, to wear women's underwear and to masturbate in front of each other and American women guards. That is, belief in an allegedly "exotic," frail Iraqi masculinity, fraught with fears of nakedness and homosexuality, might not have been the chief motivator for the American police and intelligence personnel; it may have been their own home-grown American sense of masculinity's fragility—how easily manliness can be feminized—that prompted them to craft these prison humiliations. In this distorted masculinized scenario, the presence of women serving as military police might have proved especially useful. Choreographing the women guards' feminized roles so that they could act as ridiculing feminized spectators of male prisoners might have been imagined to intensify the masculinized demoralization. Dominant men trying to utilize at least some women to act in ways that undermine the masculinzed self-esteem of rival men is not new.

What about the American women soldiers themselves? In the US military of 2004 women comprised 15 percent of active duty personnel, 17 percent of all Reserves and National Guard (and a surprising 24 percent of the Army Reserves alone). From the very time these particular young women joined this military police unit, they, like their fellow male recruits, probably sought to fit into the group. If the reserve military police unit's evolving culture—perhaps fostered by their superiors for the sake of "morale" and "unit cohesion"—was one that privileged a certain form of masculinized humor, racism and bravado, each woman would have had to decide how to deal with that. At least some of the women reservist recruits might have decided to join in, play the roles assigned to them in order to gain the hoped-for reward of male acceptance. The facts that the Abu Ghraib prison was grossly understaffed during the fall or 2003 (too few guards for spiraling numbers of Iraqi detainees), that it was isolated from other military operations, and that its residents endured daily and nightly mortar attacks, would only serve to intensify the pressures on each soldier to gain acceptance from those unit members who seemed to represent the group's dominant masculinized culture. And Lynndie England's entering into a sexual liaison with Charles Graner? We need to treat this as more than merely a "lack of discipline." We need to ask what were the cause and effect dynamics between their sexual behaviors and the abuses of prisoners and staging of the photographs. Feminists have taught us never to brush off sexual relations as if they have nothing to do with organizational and political practices.

Then there is the masculinization of the military interrogators' organizational cultures, the masculinization of the CIA's field operatives and the workings of ideas about "manliness" shaping the entire US political system. Many men and women—as lawyers, as generals, as Cabinet officers, as elected officials—knew full well that aggressive interrogation techniques violated both the spirit and the language of the Geneva Conventions, the UN Convention Against Torture and the US federal law against torture. Yet during the months of waging wars in Afghanistan and Iraq most of these men and women kept silent. Feminists have taught us always to be curious about silence. Thus we need to ask: Did any of the American men involved in interrogations keep silent because they were afraid of being labeled "soft," or "weak," thereby jeopardizing their status as "manly" men. We need also to discover if any of the women who knew better kept silent because they were afraid that they would be labeled "feminine," thus risking being deemed by their colleagues untrustworthy, political outsiders.

We are not going to get to the bottom of the tortures perpetrated by Americans at Abu Ghraib unless we make use of a feminist curiosity and unless we revisit the feminist lessons derived from the scandals of Tailhook, Fort Bragg, Annapolis, Okinawa and the Air Force Academy. Those tools and lessons might shed a harsh light on an entire American military institutional culture and maybe even the climate of contemporary American political life. That institutional culture and that political climate together have profound implications not only for Americans. They are being held up as models to emulate in Korea, Japan, the Philippines, Afghanistan and Iraq. That, in turn, means that the insights offered by feminist analysts from those societies who have such intimate experiences with this US institutional culture and this political climate are likely to teach Americans a lot about themselves.

References

Bowers, Simon (2004), "Merrill Lynch Accused of 'Institutional Sexism,' " *The Guardian*, (London), June 12.

Bunster-Burotto, Ximena (1985), "Surviving beyond Fear: Women and Torture in Latin America," *Women and Change in Latin America*, eds. June Nash and Helen Safa, South Hadley, MA: Bergin and Garvey Publishers: 297–325.

Enloe, Cynthia (1993), *The Morning After: Sexual Politics at the End of the Cold War*, Berkeley: University of California Press.

——— (2000), *Maneuvers: The International Politics of Militarizing Women's Lives*, Berkeley and London: University of California Press.

Ehrenreich, Barbara (2004), "All Together Now," Op. Ed., *New York Times*, July 15.

Hersh, Seymour (2004a), "Annals of National Security: Torture at Abu Ghraib," *The New Yorker*, May 10: 42–47.

——— (2004b), "Annals of National Security: Chain of Command," *The New Yorker*, May 17: 38–43.

——— (2004c), "Annals of National Security: The Gray Zone," *The New Yorker*, May 24: 38–44.

Human Rights Watch (2004), *The Road to Abu Ghraib*, New York: Author.

Jargon, Julie (2003), "The War Within," Westword, January.

Jehl, Douglas (2004), "Some Abu Ghraib Abuses are Traced to Afghanistan," *The New York Times*, August 26.

Kwon, Insook (1999), "Militarization in My Heart," unpublished PhD Dissertation, Women's Studies Program, Clark University, Worcester, MA, USA.

Lewis, Neil A. and Eric Schmitt (2004), "Lawyers Decided Bans on Torture Didn't Bind Bush," *New York Times*, June 8.

Lutz, Catherine and Jori Elliston (2004), "Domestic Terror," *Interventions: Activists and Academics Respond to Violence*, eds. Elizabeth Castelli and Janet Jackson, New York: Palgrave.

The Miles Foundation (2004), "Brownback/Fitz Amendment to S. 2400," email correspondence, June 14, from Milesfdn@aol.com.

Moffeit, Miles and Amy Herder (2004), "Betrayal in the Ranks," *The Denver Post*, May, Available on the Web at: http://www.denverpost.com.

Office of the Inspector General (2003), *The Tailhook Report, US Department of Defense*, New York: St. Martin's Press.

Ogasawara, Yuko (1998), *Office Ladies and Salaried Men: Power, Gender and Work in Japanese Companies*, Berkeley and London: University of California Press.

Schmitt, Eric (2004), "Abuse Panel Says Rules on Inmates Need Overhaul," *The New York Times*, August 25.

Stockford, Marjorie A. (2004), *The Bellwomen: The Story of the Landmark AT&T Sex Discrimination Case*, New Brunswick, NJ: Rutgers University Press.

Taguba, Antonio (2004), "Investigation of the 800th Military Police Brigade," Washington, D.C.: US Department of Defense, April.

Whitworth, Sandra (2004), *Men, Militarism and UN Peacekeeping: A Gendered Analysis*, Boulder, CO: Lynne Rienner Publishers.

PART ELEVEN

Men, Movements, and the Future

Q: Why did you decide to record again?

A: Because *this* housewife would like to have a career for a bit! On October 9, I'll be 40, and Sean will be 5 and I can afford to say, "Daddy does something else as well." He's not accustomed to it—in five years I hardly picked up a guitar. Last Christmas our neighbors showed him "Yellow Submarine" and he came running in, saying, "Daddy, you were singing . . . Were you a Beatle?" I said, "Well—yes, right."

—John Lennon, interview for *Newsweek*, 1980

Are men changing? If so, in what directions? Can men change even more? In what ways should men be different? We posed many of these questions at the beginning of our exploration of men's lives, and we return to them here, in the book's last section, to examine the directions men have taken to enlarge their roles, to expand the meaning of masculinity, to change the rules.

The articles in this section address the possibility and the direction of change for men: How shall we, as a society, understand masculinity in the modern world? The Statement of the United Nations Commission on the Status of Women outlines the importance of involving men in the global struggles for gender equality.

On the more personal side of the ledger, Jackson Katz and Mark Anthony Neal examine the ways in which individual men, of different races, are stepping up for equality and, in the process, redefining masculinity. Eric Anderson shows how putting men in gender-integrated contexts can foster the development of egalitarian views of women. And finally, Allan Johnson links the personal and the political as he unravels the gender "knot."

Commission on the Status of Women
Forty-Eighth Session, March 1–12, 2004

The Role of Men and Boys in Achieving Gender Equality

Agreed conclusions March 12, 2004, as adopted

1. The Commission on the Status of Women recalls and reiterates that the Beijing Declaration and Platform for Action[1] encouraged men to participate fully in all actions towards gender equality and urged the establishment of the principle of shared power and responsibility between women and men at home, in the community, in the workplace and in the wider national and international communities. The Commission also recalls and reiterates the outcome document adopted at the twenty-third special session of the General Assembly entitled "Gender equality, development and peace in the twenty-first century"[2] which emphasized that men must take joint responsibility with women for the promotion of gender equality.

2. The Commission recognizes that men and boys, while some themselves face discriminatory barriers and practices, can and do make contributions to gender equality in their many capacities, including as individuals, members of families, social groups and communities, and in all spheres of society.

3. The Commission recognizes that gender inequalities still exist and are reflected in imbalances of power between women and men in all spheres of society. The Commission further recognizes that everyone benefits from gender equality and that the negative impacts of gender inequality are borne by society as a whole and emphasizes, therefore, that men and boys, through taking responsibility themselves and working jointly in partnership with women and girls, are essential to achieving the goals of gender equality, development and peace. The Commission recognizes the capacity of men and boys in bringing about change in attitudes, relationships and access to resources and decision making which are critical for the promotion of gender equality and the full enjoyment of all human rights by women.

4. The Commission acknowledges and encourages men and boys to continue to take positive initiatives to eliminate gender stereotypes and promote gender equality, including combating violence against women, through networks, peer programmes, information campaigns, and training programmes. The Commission acknowledges the critical role of gender-sensitive education and training in achieving gender equality.

5. The Commission also recognizes that the participation of men and boys in achieving gender equality must be consistent with the empowerment of women and girls and acknowledges that efforts must be made to address the undervaluation of many types of work, abilities and roles associated with women. In this regard, it is important that resources for gender equality initiatives for men and boys do not compromise equal

opportunities and resources for women and girls.

6. The Commission urges Governments and, as appropriate, the relevant funds and programmes, organizations and specialized agencies of the United Nations system, the international financial institutions, civil society, including the private sector and non-governmental organizations, and other stakeholders, to take the following actions:

a) Encourage and support the capacity of men and boys in fostering gender equality, including acting in partnership with women and girls as agents for change and in providing positive leadership, in particular where men are still key decision makers responsible for policies, programmes and legislation, as well as holders of economic and organizational power and public resources;

b) Promote understanding of the importance of fathers, mothers, legal guardians and other caregivers, to the well being of children and the promotion of gender equality and of the need to develop policies, programmes and school curricula that encourage and maximize their positive involvement in achieving gender equality and positive results for children, families and communities;

c) Create and improve training and education programmes to enhance awareness and knowledge among men and women on their roles as parents, legal guardians and caregivers and the importance of sharing family responsibilities, and include fathers as well as mothers in programmes that teach infant child care development;

d) Develop and include in education programmes for parents, legal guardians and other caregivers information on ways and means to increase the capacity of men to raise children in a manner oriented towards gender equality;

e) Encourage men and boys to work with women and girls in the design of policies and programmes for men and boys aimed at gender equality and foster the involvement of men and boys in gender mainstreaming efforts in order to ensure improved design of all policies and programmes;

f) Encourage the design and implementation of programmes at all levels to accelerate a socio-cultural change towards gender equality, especially through the upbringing and educational process, in terms of changing harmful traditional perceptions and attitudes of male and female roles in order to achieve the full and equal participation of women and men in the society;

g) Develop and implement programmes for pre-schools, schools, community centers, youth organizations, sport clubs and centres, and other groups dealing with children and youth, including training for teachers, social workers and other professionals who deal with children to foster positive attitudes and behaviours on gender equality;

h) Promote critical reviews of school curricula, textbooks and other information education and communication materials at all levels in order to recommend ways to strengthen the promotion of gender equality that involves the engagement of boys as well as girls;

i) Develop and implement strategies to educate boys and girls and men and women about tolerance, mutual respect for all individuals and the promotion of all human rights;

j) Develop and utilize a variety of methods in public information campaigns on the role of men and boys in promoting gender equality, including through approaches specifically targeting boys and young men;

k) Engage media, advertising and other related professionals, through the development of training and other programmes, on the importance of promoting gender equality, non-stereotypical portrayal of women and girls and men and boys and on the harms caused by portraying women and girls in a demeaning or exploitative manner, as well as on the enhanced participation of women and girls in the media;

l) Take effective measures, to the extent consistent with freedom of expression, to combat the growing sexualization and use of pornography in media content, in terms of the rapid development of ICT, encourage men in the media to refrain from presenting women as inferior beings and exploiting them as sexual objects and commodities, combat ICT- and media-based violence against women including criminal misuse of ICT for sexual harassment, sexual exploitation and trafficking in women and girls, and support the development and use of ICT as a resource for the empowerment of women and girls, including those affected by violence, abuse and other forms of sexual exploitation;

m) Adopt and implement legislation and/or policies to close the gap between women's and men's pay and promote reconciliation of occupational and family responsibilities, including through reduction of occupational segregation, introduction or expansion of parental leave, flexible working arrangements, such as voluntary part-time work, teleworking, and other home-based work;

n) Encourage men, through training and education, to fully participate in the care and support of others, including older persons, persons with disabilities and sick persons, in particular children and other dependants;

o) Encourage active involvement of men and boys through education projects and peer-based programmes in eliminating gender stereotypes as well as gender inequality in particular in relation to sexually transmitted infections, including HIV/AIDS, as well as their full participation in prevention, advocacy, care, treatment, support and impact evaluation programmes;

p) Ensure men's access to and utilization of reproductive and sexual health services and programmes, including HIV/AIDS-related programmes and services, and encourage men to participate with women in programmes designed to prevent and treat all forms of HIV/AIDS transmission and other sexually transmitted infections;

q) Design and implement programmes to encourage and enable men to adopt safe and responsible sexual and reproductive behaviour, and to use effectively methods to prevent unwanted pregnancies and sexually transmitted infections, including HIV/AIDS;

r) Encourage and support men and boys to take an active part in the prevention and elimination of all forms of violence, and especially gender-based violence, including in the context of HIV/AIDS, and increase awareness of men's and boys' responsibility in ending the cycle of violence, inter alia, through the promotion of attitudinal and behavioural change, integrated education and training which prioritize the safety of women and children, prosecution and rehabilitation of perpetrators, and support for survivors, and recognizing that men and boys also experience violence;

s) Encourage an increased understanding among men how violence, including trafficking for the purposes of commercialized sexual exploitation, forced marriages and forced labour, harms women, men and children and undermines gender equality, and consider measures aimed at eliminating the demand for trafficked women and children;

t) Encourage and support both women and men in leadership positions, including political leaders, traditional leaders, business leaders, community and religious leaders, musicians, artists and athletes to provide positive role models on gender equality;

u) Encourage men in leadership positions to ensure equal access for women to education, property rights and inheritance rights and to promote equal access to information technology and business and economic opportunities, including in international trade, in order to provide women with the tools that enable them to take part fully and equally in economic and political decision-making processes at all levels;

v) Identify and fully utilize all contexts in which a large number of men can be reached, particularly in male-dominated institutions, industries and associations, to sensitize men on their roles and responsibilities in the promotion of gender equality and the full enjoyment of all human rights by women, including in relation to HIV/AIDS and violence against women;

w) Develop and use statistics to support and/or carry out research, inter alia, on the cultural, social and economic conditions, which influence the attitudes and behaviours of men and boys towards women and girls, their awareness of gender inequalities and their involvement in promoting gender equality;

x) Carry out research on men's and boys' views of gender equality and their perceptions of their roles through which further programmes and policies can be developed and identify and widely disseminate good practices. Assess the impact of efforts undertaken to engage men and boys in achieving gender equality;

y) Promote and encourage the representation of men in institutional mechanisms for the advancement of women;

z) Encourage men and boys to support women's equal participation in conflict prevention, management and conflict resolution and in post-conflict peace-building;

7. The Commission urges all entities within the UN system to take into account the recommendations contained in these agreed conclusions and to disseminate these agreed conclusions widely.

Notes

1. Report of the Fourth World Conference on Women, Beijing 4–15 September 1995 (United Nations publications, Sales No. E.96.IV.13).

2. A/RES/S-23/3, annex.

Jackson Katz

More Than a Few Good Men

"As long as we take the view that these are problems for women alone to solve, we cannot expect to reverse the high incidence of rape and child abuse . . . and domestic violence. We do know that many men do not abuse women and children; and that they strive always to live with respect and dignity. But until today the collective voice of these men has never been heard, because the issue has not been regarded as one for the whole nation. From today those who inflict violence on others will know they are being isolated and cannot count on other men to protect them. From now on all men will hear the call to assume their responsibility for solving this problem."—President Nelson Mandela, 1997, National Men's March, Pretoria, South Africa

Since the very beginning of the women-led movements against domestic and sexual violence in the 1970s, there have been men who personally, professionally, and politically supported the work of those women. In addition, over the past several decades there have been repeated attempts by men to create organizations and targeted initiatives to address men's roles in ending men's violence against women. Some of the early efforts were undertaken by groups of concerned men who responded to the challenge from women's organizations to educate, politicize, and organize other men. Some of these men chose to volunteer in supportive roles with local rape crisis cen-

Reproduced by permission of Jackson Katz, "More than a Few Good Men" (2006) pp. 253–270 in *The Macho Paradox* by Jackson Katz.

ters or battered women's programs. Others contributed to the development of the fledgling batterer intervention movement in the late 1970s and 1980s. Some of the better known programs for batterers were Emerge in Cambridge, Massachusetts; RAVEN (Rape and Violence End Now) in St. Louis, Missouri; and Men Stopping Violence in Atlanta, Georgia. Still other men created political and activist educational organizations, like the National Organization for Men Against Sexism (NOMAS), which has held "Men and Masculinity" conferences annually since 1975; the Oakland Men's Project in the San Francisco Bay Area; Men Stopping Rape in Madison, Wisconsin; DC Men Against Rape; and Real Men, an anti-sexist men's organization I co-founded in Boston in 1988.

The rapidly growing field of "men's work" also produced community centers that combine batterer-intervention and counseling services for men with educational outreach and social activism. One of the groundbreaking programs in this field is the Men's Resource Center of Western Massachusetts, founded in Amherst in 1982. In the 1990s anti-sexist men's initiatives in the U.S. and around the world increased dramatically. One of the most visible has been the White Ribbon Campaign, an activist educational campaign founded by a group of men in Canada in 1991. They started the WRC in response to a horrific incident on December 6, 1989, at the University of Montreal, where an armed twenty-five-year-old man walked into a classroom, separated the women from the men and proceeded to shoot the women. Before he finished his rampage, he had murdered fourteen women in cold blood—and shaken up an entire country. The significance of the white ribbon—which has been adopted on hundreds of college campuses and communities in the U.S. as well as a number of other countries—is that men wear it to make a visible and public pledge "never to commit, condone, nor remain silent about violence against women."

Despite these notable efforts over the past thirty years, the movement of men committed to ending men's violence against women has only recently picked up significant momentum. There are more men doing this work in the United States and around the world than ever before. Halfway through the first decade of the twenty-first century there is reason for optimism, especially about the emergence of a new generation of anti-sexist men. But there are nowhere near enough men yet involved to make a serious dent in this enormous problem. Several key challenges lie ahead:

- How to increase dramatically the number of men who make these issues a priority in their personal and professional lives
- How to expand the existing infrastructure of men's anti-rape and domestic violence prevention groups, and other campus and community-based initiatives
- How to institutionalize gender violence prevention education at every level of the educational system
- How to build multiracial and multiethnic coalitions that unite men across differences around their shared concerns about sexist violence and the sexual exploitation of children
- How to insure that federal, state, and local funding for efforts to reduce gender violence are maintained and expanded in the coming years
- And finally, how to make it socially acceptable—even cool—for men to become vocal and public allies of women in the struggle against all forms of men's violence against women and children

A "Big Tent" Approach

As I have made clear in this book, there is much that we can do to prevent men's violence against women—if we find the collective will in male culture to make it a priority. I am convinced that millions of men in our society are deeply concerned about the abuse, harassment, and violence we see—and fear—in the lives of our daughters, mothers, sisters, and lovers. In fact, a recent poll conducted for Lifetime Television found that 57 percent of men aged sixteen to twenty-four believe gender violence is an "extremely serious" problem. A 2000 poll conducted by the Family Violence Prevention Fund found that one-quarter of men would do more about the issue if they were asked. And some compelling social norms research on college campuses suggests that one of the most significant factors in a man's decision to intervene in an incident is his perception of how other men would act in a similar situation. Clearly, a lot of men are uncomfortable with other men's abusive behaviors, but they have not figured out what to do about it—or have not yet mustered the courage to act on their own. So there is great potential to increase dramatically the number of men who commit personal time, money, and institutional clout to the effort to reduce men's violence against women. But in order to achieve this we need to think outside the box about how to reach into the mainstream of male culture and social power.

One promising approach employs elements of what might be called "big tent" movement building. The big tent concept comes from politics, where it has been used most famously to describe efforts to unite various constituencies and single-issue special-interest groups under the Republican Party label. A number of questions arise when this concept is applied to gender violence prevention: How do we attract individuals and organizations not known for their advocacy of the issues of men's violence? What are some of the necessary compromises required in order to broaden the coalition of participating individuals and groups? What are some of the costs and benefits of engaging new partners, who might not have the depth of experience or the ideological affinities of the majority of women and men currently in the movement?

Growing pains always accompany growth. A bigger movement will inevitably create new conflicts. One way to think about the question of broadening the base of the movement is to consider the concept embodied in the geometric model of the Venn diagram. The Venn diagram captures the idea that coalition building involves identifying shared objectives between groups with different interests, not creating a perfect union between fully compatible partners. The diagram consists of two overlapping circles. In this case we might say that one circle represents the needs and interests of the battered women's and rape crisis movements. The other circle represents any men's organization that has not historically been part of these movements. Clearly, there are large areas where the circles do not overlap. But the big tent approach does not dwell on the areas of disconnection. It focuses on the center area, where there are points of agreement and shared objectives. If individuals and groups of men and women can agree that reducing men's violence against women is an urgent objective, then perhaps they can agree for the moment to table their other differences.

Challenges

There are obvious downsides to incautiously expanding the big tent. Take, for example, the costs and benefits of working with men in the sports culture. Many women in domestic and sexual violence advocacy have long seen the benefit to partnering with athletic teams or utilizing high-profile male athletes in public service campaigns. But some of these same women worry about the potential risks inherent in such collaboration. They fear that a male athlete who speaks out publicly against men's violence could undermine the integrity of the movement if his private behavior does not match his public rhetoric. Happily, in recent years this fear has begun to dissipate as more male athletes speak out, in part because with increased men's participation there is less pressure on any one man to be the "perfect" poster child for anti-violence efforts. We can also never lose sight of the fact that professional sports teams are not social justice organizations. They are businesses that sometimes have huge investments in players. Say a team takes a public stand against men's violence, and then at some point one of its star players is arrested for domestic violence or sexual assault. Is the team likely to respond based on what they think is best for the community, or for their own bottom line?

The participation of faith-based organizations in the big tent presents significant opportunities, but comes with its own unique set of challenges. As the Rev. Dr. Marie Fortune, a pioneer in the movements against domestic and sexual violence and founder of the FaithTrust Institute in Seattle, Washington, points out, "Millions of men participate in faith-based communities whose leaders, often male, typically enjoy significant moral authority and shape in important ways the values and behaviors of men in their congregations." There are male clergy in every denomination who are strong allies of women in the domestic and sexual violence prevention movements. But many clergy and religious leaders have received no training on the issue of men's violence against women. To this day many male

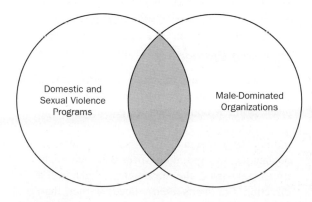

Domestic and
Sexual Violence
Programs

Male-Dominated
Organizations

clergy are reluctant to take strong public stands on issues of sexual and domestic violence. What further complicates matters is that many religious traditions have "reflected and reinforced," in the words of Rev. Fortune, "patriarchal values that have been at the core of violence against women." But perhaps even more troubling are the clergy sex abuse scandals that have become routine in recent years. It is plain to see that even men with impeccable religious credentials can be private hypocrites.

The participation of faith-based organizations in gender violence prevention also raises the question of how much ideological incompatibility is tolerable in the quest for big tent inclusiveness. Can feminist religious and secular leaders work in coalition with religious leaders who have resisted the advancement of women in the family and the pulpit? Can progressive religious and secular leaders who support full sexual equality work side by side with religious leaders who oppose gay civil rights?

Similar questions arise about an organization like the Boy Scouts. Scouting plays an important role in the lives of millions of boys and adolescent males. Many local Boy Scout chapters have participated in events of domestic violence and sexual assault awareness month. But if the Scouts went a step further and made participation in gender violence prevention a major nationwide organizational goal, they could have a tremendous impact, especially since the Scouts have a presence in many communities where there is currently little male participation in domestic and sexual violence programs. But many progressive organizations refuse to work with the Boy Scouts because their official policy discriminates against openly gay scouts and scoutmasters. Does their anti-gay stance make the Boy Scouts an unacceptable coalition partner in the struggle against teen-relationship abuse and sexual assault?

Until now most men in the movement to end men's violence against women have been pro-feminist and politically liberal or progressive. But this does not preclude them from framing one aspect of the gender-violence issue in language

about crime and punishment that resonates with conservatives. In fact, many politically conservative men have played an important role in this fight—particularly men in law enforcement, the military, and government. After all, domestic and sexual violence are more than social problems; they are crimes. Nonetheless, millions of abusive men continue to receive suspended sentences, probation, and other light penalties, which signals that their crimes are not taken seriously. In order to be effective, decisive action is required by police, prosecutors, and judges. The goal of punishment is to send the message to would-be perps that the price for transgression is steep. Conservative as well as progressive men who take the idea of personal responsibility seriously should support policies that hold law-breakers accountable, and advocacy that strengthens the community's desire to do so. But a criminal justice approach is also fraught with potential problems. For one thing, there are not enough jail cells to house all the men who could be prosecuted for domestic and sexual violence. As I have discussed, class bias and racism are factors in any discussion about the criminal justice system. Efforts to attract conservative men's support by emphasizing a law enforcement approach might exact too high a cost—and jeopardize the increased participation of people of color who are concerned about both gender violence *and* the over-representation of men in color in the "prison industrial complex." In addition, since most gender violence—including the vast majority of rape—is currently not reported, it is questionable how effective a criminal justice approach can be.

Men and Women

The special challenge of gender violence prevention politics is that women's trust of men is not a given. Some women are understandably wary of men's motivations and skeptical about their commitment to gender justice. As increasing numbers of men get involved, they worry that men might try to "take over" the movement, or take it in a direction that suits men's needs rather than women's. Women are always eager to see whether men "walk their talk." For example, an administrator in a domestic-violence agency recently told me about a talented young man who had applied for a youth outreach position. He seemed to know the issues really well, she explained, and he grasped some of the subtle racial and ethnic issues involved in this work. He also had an engaging personal style. But he had not yet mastered the "micro-politics" of how to interact with women in positions of leadership. He often cut off women co-presenters, or talked over them in an effort to prove his knowledge. Was it worth the risk of hiring him?

For their part, some men are well-meaning but oblivious to the sensitivities required for effective inter-gender collaboration on an issue where women have historically been the leaders. For example, I have heard stories too many times about earnest young men on college campuses who were inspired to start anti-rape groups, but neglected first to check in with women who were already engaged in rape prevention work, like the director of the campus women's center. These sorts of political missteps can cause unnecessary tension and discord at the earliest stages and can undermine successful coalition-building.

Even so, there are numerous examples across the country of men and women working together to create and sustain sexual and domestic violence prevention initiatives. In fact, many successful college men's anti-violence programs have actually been started by women. Among the more well-known are Men Against Violence at Louisiana State University, begun by Dr. Luoluo Hong, and the Fraternity Anti-Violence Education Project at West Chester University in Pennsylvania, led by Dr. Deborah Mahlstedt.

What Can Men Do?

At a small state college in the Northeast, a controversy erupted in early 2005 when the editors of the student newspaper distributed a sex survey across campus that included a question about which professor on campus they would most like to "get it on with." The person chosen was the coordinator of the women's studies program,

who responded with a lengthy letter to the editor in which she wrote that it was "offensive and hurtful" to be disrespected by students in this way, and as a professional it undermined her ability to do her job. In her letter she posed a number of questions for an alternative survey, including one to men which asked, "What are you willing to do to help reduce rape and sexual assault among college students?" In response, a male columnist for the student newspaper wrote dismissively: "I will not rape anyone. Is there anything more I should add to this?" The student's response might have been glib and a bit obnoxious, but he spoke for a lot of men. Many of them have never even considered the wide range of choices men have to reduce rape and sexual assault, and every other type of gender violence. What follows is a brief discussion about how men can be effective anti-sexist agents, both as individuals and in their various public and private leadership roles within institutions.

Have the Courage to Look Inward

One of the most important steps any man can take if he wants to be an ally to women in the struggle against gender violence is to be honest with himself. A key requirement for men to become effective anti-sexist agents is their willingness to examine their own attitudes and behaviors about women, sex, and manhood. This is similar to the sort of introspection required of anti-racist whites. It is not an easy process, especially when men start to see that they have inadvertently perpetuated sexism and violence through their personal actions, or their participation in sexist practices in male culture. Because defensiveness is the enemy of introspection, it is vital that men develop ways to transcend their initial defensive reactions about men's mistreatment of women and move toward a place where they are grounded enough to do something about it.

Support Survivors

In a social climate where women who report sexual and domestic violence are often disbelieved and called "accusers," it is crucial that men personally and publicly support survivors—girls and boys, women and men. This can mean the offer of a supportive ear in a conversation, or a shoulder for a friend to cry on. It can also mean challenging others—men and women—who seek to discredit victims' accounts of their victimization. For example, when a girl or woman reports a sexual assault and her alleged attacker is a popular guy with a network of supporters, people often rally around him—even when they have nothing more than his word to go on that she is lying. Sadly, some of them try to smear her character and reputation. It is not fair to assume the man's guilt; he is entitled to a presumption of innocence until proven guilty. But alleged victims are entitled to a presumption as well—the presumption that they are telling the truth about what was done to them. They also have the right to be treated with respect, and to expect the people around them to defend their integrity if it is ever questioned.

Seek Help

Men who are emotionally, physically, or sexually abusive to women and girls need to seek help now. But first they have to acknowledge to themselves that they have a problem. I once gave a speech about men's violence against women at a big state university in the West. After the event was over, a blond-haired college student in jeans and a T-shirt approached me in the main lobby of the student center. His voice quivered as he said, "I just realized that I have done bad things to women." He did not elaborate, nor did I ask him to. But I could tell he had a troubled conscience by the look in his eyes, and because he waited nearly half an hour to talk to me. The question of what to do about men who have been abusive will take on ever greater urgency as more men become involved in the movement against gender violence. Many men who were formerly abusive to women have become effective professionals in batterer intervention programs. They share their personal stories and serve as models for how men can grow and change. This is crucial because millions of men have committed mild or severe acts of cruelty toward women and children, and whether they were charged with and convicted of

a crime or not, we have to figure out ways to integrate most of them back into our families and communities. Of course, sometimes this is easier said than done. For example, in recent years families in communities across the U.S. have faced the challenge of living in neighborhoods alongside convicted child molesters. This raises another set of questions: When do the rights of children and their parents to be free from the threat of sexual abuse and violence out-weigh the rights of men (or women) who have served their sentences and are seeking to rebuild their lives? If a man has committed acts of sexual or domestic violence, should those acts define him for the rest of his life?

Refuse to Condone Sexist and Abusive Behavior by Friends, Peers, and Coworkers

As I have argued in this book, if we want to dramatically increase the number of men who make men's violence against women a priority, it is not useful to engage them as perpetrators or potential perpetrators. Instead, it makes sense to enlist them as empowered bystanders who can do something to confront abusive peers, or who can help to create a climate in male peer culture that discourages some men's sexist attitudes and behaviors. This is often easier said than done, because it can be quite awkward for men to confront each other about how they talk about and treat women. Consider an experience I had when I was in my early thirties at a wedding of an old friend of mine. A few minutes after I was introduced to the best man at a cocktail reception the day before the wedding, he confidently told me and a group of other guys a tasteless joke about battered women. I was not sure how to react. If I said something, I feared that it could create a chill between us, and this was the first day of a long weekend. But if I did not say something, I feared my silence might imply approval of the joke. I felt similar to how I would have felt if a white friend had told a racist joke. There was an added concern: How could I—or anyone else—know the full context of his joke-telling? The guy may have been personally harmless, but at the very least his gender politics were suspect, and at the worst he also may have been a closeted batterer who was subtly seeking public approval for his private behavior. I managed to mutter a feeble objection, something like, "Surely you have other topics to joke about." But I never told the guy how I really felt.

Sometimes men who take a strong stand against gender violence can face serious interpersonal consequences for their efforts. Mike LaRiviere, a police officer who is deeply committed to domestic and sexual violence prevention, trains police across the country in domestic violence policies and procedures. He recounts an incident many years ago when he was relatively new to his small-city New England police force. He and his more senior partner answered a domestic violence call, and when they arrived at the apartment it was obvious that the man had assaulted the woman. Mike thought it was clear they should make an arrest, both for the victim's safety and to hold the man accountable for what he had done. But the senior partner had another idea.

He just wanted to tell the guy to cool down. Mike and he had a hushed but heated conversation in another room about what to do. They finally arrested the man, but for the next five or six months, Mike's partner barely spoke with him. The atmosphere in the squad car was tense and chilly, which in police work can be dangerous as well as unpleasant, because you can never be certain that someone who seethes with resentment will always have your back.

In spite of how difficult it can be for men to challenge each other about sexism, it does happen. In fact, it might happen more often than many people realize. In any case, it is important for men to hear each other's stories about this type of intervention, so they can see that other men feel as they do and so they can get potentially useful ideas. I heard one such story about a bachelor party road trip that Al Emerick, a leader of Men Against Violence Against Women in Jacksonville, Florida, took a couple of years ago with some friends. They were a group of well-off white guys in their thirties who had been playing poker together for nine years. There were four married men in the car along with the groom, and

the discussion came up about strip clubs. The best man was ready to drop a pile of one-dollar bills on some "fine ladies' asses." Al said he would not be joining them, and the guys immediately got on him. "Whattya gay?" "What's the big deal, the wife's not here." "Cut loose." Because the guys had known Al for quite some time, they knew he was no prude, nor were his objections based on his religious beliefs. But they did know he had been working with a men's group that was affiliated with the local domestic violence shelter. He told them he did not want to take part because he had a problem with the objectification of women—even when it is voluntary. As he tells it, this group of friends spent two hours in an "intense but wonderful" conversation about sexism, domestic violence, male privilege, power, and control. In the course of the conversation Al fielded a range of predictable challenges like: "I'm not an abuser because I look at chicks." He countered with questions like, "What about men in the audience who might be abusers or rapists? By us being there and supporting the action, aren't we reinforcing their behaviors?" In the end, they never went to the strip clubs. Since that event, they have had further conversations about these issues, and according to Al, one of the guys has even offered to help produce a public service announcement for the anti-sexist men's group.

Make Connections between Men's Violence against Women and Other Issues

Gender violence contributes to a wide range of social problems that include youth violence, homelessness, divorce, alcoholism, and the transmission of HIV/AIDS. Men who care about these problems need to educate themselves about the relationship between gender violence and these issues, and then integrate this understanding in their work and daily life.

Perhaps nowhere are the effects of gender violence more pronounced than with HIV/AIDS, the global pandemic that has already killed twenty million people and infected forty-five million. Across the world, there is an inextricable linkage between men's violence against women and transmission of the virus. Forms of gender violence that are fueling transmission include sexual coercion and rape, men's refusal to wear condoms, and married or monogamous men's solicitation of prostitutes followed by unprotected sex with their wives or partners. Gender violence also takes the form of civil and customary laws that perpetuate male privilege and prerogative and deny women's human rights. This might include civil and customary laws that do not recognize marital rape or the dangers of early marriage, as well as systematic prohibitions against females inheriting wealth and property—a reality that ultimately forces millions of widows and daughters to lives of abject poverty and economic dependence on men. But according to M.I.T. research fellow and United Nations consultant Miriam Zoll, while heterosexual transmission may be the primary route of HIV/AIDS infection today, few HIV-prevention programs actually address the underlying gender, power, and sexual dynamics between men and women that contribute to infection, including violence. In a 2004 report entitled "Closing the HIV/AIDS Prevention Gender Gap?" Zoll surveyed men's and women's attitudes about gender and sexuality on several continents. She found that men and women's cultural definitions and perceptions of masculinity and femininity often reinforced men's power over women in ways that make sexually transmitted infections more likely. In the report, Zoll featured the work of men and women who are implementing promising gender-based prevention strategies. For example, Dean Peacock is a white South African who lived for many years in the U.S., where he worked in San Francisco as a facilitator in a batterer intervention program. Peacock returned to South Africa a couple of years ago to lead HIV prevention work with men in a program called Men As Partners, sponsored by Engender Health and Planned Parenthood of South Africa. As Zoll reports, from his unique vantage point Peacock observed with groups of men in prevention trainings in South Africa many of the same ideas about masculinity that he encountered with batterers in the U.S.: "A real man doesn't negotiate with a woman." "A real

man doesn't use condoms." "A real man doesn't worry about his health status." "A real man doesn't get tested." "A real man has sex with multiple partners." Even so, Peacock says that men in South Africa with whom he has worked are very open to gender equitable work. "The paradox of the HIV/AIDS epidemic is that it has opened the door to gender equality. We say to these men, 'If you work with us, your life will become richer.' We appeal to them as moral agents. We ask them, 'What is your responsibility to take this to the community, to challenge other men's behaviors, to confront men who are violent, to confront other men who are placing their partners at risk?' "

Contribute Financial Resources

Men with significant financial resources need to think creatively about what they can do to help support the growing number of domestic and sexual-assault prevention initiatives that target boys and men. This is the cutting edge of prevention work, and the field is new enough that a small number of wealthy men could make an enormous impact. Ted Waitt, founder of the Gateway Computer Company, has been one of the early leaders in this area. Philanthropic individuals and organizations can and should continue to fund services for women and girls who are victims and survivors of men's violence, especially when state and federal funds are being cut; funds that target work with men and boys should never compete with funds for direct services for women and girls. But they should not have to, because the pool of available resources should increase as more influential men get involved and bring new ideas and energy to the task of preventing men's violence against women.

Be Creative and Entrepreneurial

A number of enterprising men have used their imagination and creativity to raise other men's awareness of sexism, and to challenge the sexist attitudes and behaviors of men around them. Any list of these individuals is necessarily subjective and abbreviated, but I would nonetheless like to spotlight a handful of exemplary anti-sexist activist men. Chris Kilmartin, a professor of psychology at Mary Washington University, performs a one-man show around the country where he uses his skills as a stand-up comedian to satirize traditional masculinity. His first solo theatre performance was called *Crimes against Nature*, and his most recent show is entitled *Guy Fi: The Fictions That Rule Men's Lives*. Through these dramatic presentations and scholarship, Kilmartin has helped to expand the focus of sexual assault prevention to include discussions about the pressures on young men to conform to gender norms that limit their humanity as well as set them up to hurt women.

Another man who has made a unique contribution to this work is Hank Shaw, who in 2000 produced a glossy brochure about men and gender violence that is called, "It's Time for Guys to Put an End to This." Shaw, whose day job is in marketing and corporate communications, wanted to reach average guys with a piece written in "guy language" for men who would likely never read a book about gender violence. The brochure, tens of thousands of which have been distributed across the U.S., Canada, and elsewhere, is cleverly written and beautifully illustrated, and contains such features as the "Mancipation Proclamation": "Henceforth guys are no longer under any gender-oriented, testosterone-derived, penis-related or penis-associated obligation to hurt, harass, or otherwise mess up (or mess with) the lives of female employees, coworkers, students, family members, friends, neighbors, or other female personages who may or may not be personally known to the party of the first part. When all people of the male persuasion get this message, it will spare everyone a whole lot of grief. Plus it will save the country about a gazillion dollars per year."

Another man who has become influential in the gender violence prevention field is Don McPherson, the former professional football player and star quarterback for Syracuse University in the late 1980s. One of the first highly successful black quarterbacks, McPherson runs the Sports Leadership Institute at Adelphi University in New York, and travels widely and gives speeches about violence toward women and what it means to be a man to a variety of high school, college, and professional audiences. What makes McPherson an effective gender violence prevention educator is that while he has the credentials as "The Man" due to his success in sports, he openly admits that he was never comfortable in the role that so many men fantasize about: "I had to carry myself in a different way," he told Oprah Winfrey, "sometimes not showing emotion, not showing weakness or any kind of vulnerability. It meant being in control all of the time. Most people expected me to be shallow . . . I struggled with who I really was on the inside versus my need to be a part of the guys who were cool." In his popular lecture, entitled, "You Throw Like a Girl," McPherson makes the connection between what the culture expects of "real men," and men's widespread mistreatment of women.

New technologies are changing the nature of social activism, and this is as true for anti-sexist men's work as it is for any social movement. In particular, the Internet and the Web have become indispensable tools in anti-sexist men's organizing. The ability to instantaneously transmit information and facilitate connection between people across the country and the world continues to amaze some of us who have vivid memories from the 1980s and 1990s of standing on street corners handing out leaflets. One man who has made a significant contribution to harnessing the power of the Internet is Marc Dubin, founder and executive director of CAVNET, Communities Against Violence Network, at www.cavnet.org. CAVNET is a diverse network of professionals and advocates who work on issues related to violence against women and children, human rights, genocide, and crime victims with disabilities. People in the network regularly share a wealth of information and resources—including points of contact for anti-sexist men's organizations nationally and internationally. Dubin, who works tirelessly—and virtually without pay—to maintain and expand CAVNET's database and connect people to each other, is a former federal prosecutor with extensive experience prosecuting domestic violence, sexual assault, rape, child abuse, and hate crimes. He formerly served as special counsel to the Violence Against Women Office at the United States Department of Justice and is an expert in the federal civil rights of people with disabilities.

Start Anti-Sexist Men's Groups

The power of individuals to catalyze change increases exponentially when they work together to create new institutions and organizations. A growing number of organizations have made significant contributions in recent years to gender violence prevention efforts with men and boys. Some of these groups have paid staff and operate along the lines of traditional non-profit educational organizations; others are more grass roots and volunteer-oriented. It is not possible to provide anything close to a comprehensive list of these various initiatives, but consider a handful of examples from around the country: The Washington, D.C.-based group Men Can Stop Rape regularly conducts anti-rape trainings with high school, college, and community organizations. Their "strength campaign" posters and other materials have been widely circulated. The Institute on Domestic Violence in the African American Community, headed by Dr. Oliver Williams, regularly brings together scholars and activists to discuss issues of particular interest to men (and women) of color, such as the potential role of the hip-hop generation in preventing men's violence against women. The anti-rape men's group One in Four has chapters on dozens of college campuses. In 1999, a group of men in the famous fishing town of Gloucester, Massachusetts—carpenters and clergy, bartenders and bankers—started Gloucester Men Against Domestic Abuse. They march annually in the town's popular Fourth of July parade and sponsor a billboard that says "Strong Men Don't Bully," a public testimonial of sorts that features the names of five hundred Gloucester men. The Men's Leadership Forum in San Diego, California, is a high-profile annual conference held on Valentine's Day. Since

2001, MLF has brought together a diverse group of men and boys (and women) from across the city to learn how men in business, labor unions, the sports culture, education, the faith community, and the human services can contribute to ending men's violence against women. Some men are politicized about sexism out of concern for their daughters, or as a result of things that have happened to them. One of the most effective organizations that addresses these concerns is Dads and Daughters, a Duluth, Minnesota-based advocacy group led by Joe Kelly. Part of the mission of DADS is to mobilize concerned fathers to challenge companies whose marketing is sexist and exploitative—especially when it involves the sexualization of young girls or adolescents, or treats men's violence against women as a joke.

In addition to some of these now well-established organizations, anti-sexist men on college campuses and in local communities have worked—often in collaboration with women's centers or domestic and sexual violence programs—to educate men and boys about the role men can play in confronting and interrupting other men's abusive behaviors. One venue for this collaboration has been the proliferating number of V-Day events held on college campuses. While V-Day is woman-centered, male students have played all sorts of supportive roles, such as organizing outreach efforts to men and coproducing and promoting performances of the Eve Ensler play *The Vagina Monologues*.

Some anti-sexist men's efforts have been ad hoc and customized to fit the needs and experiences of various communities. For example, in 2003 a group of Asian American men in Seattle organized to support the local chapter of the National Asian Pacific American Women's Forum in their opposition to a restaurant that was promoting "naked sushi" nights, where patrons took sushi off the bodies of semi-nude models wrapped in cellophane. And in the summer of 2004, a group of men (and women) in the "punk, indie, alternative" music scene organized a Different Kind of Dude Fest in Washington, D.C. Along the lines of the Riot Girrls and Girlfest,

Hawaii, they sought to use art as an organizing tool. Their goal was to call attention to the ways in which progressive political punk culture, while promising liberation from other forms of social conformity and oppression, nonetheless helped to perpetuate sexism and patriarchal domination. The organizers of the music festival also explicitly affirmed the need for men to be allies of feminists in the fight for gender justice and social equality.

Champion Institutional Reform

Men who hold positions of power in government, non-profit organizations, business, and labor unions can do much to prevent men's violence against women if they take two critical steps: 1.) Recognize domestic and sexual violence prevention as a leadership issue for men, and 2.) Start to think creatively about how they can push their institutions to address it. The problem is that many men in positions of institutional authority do not yet see gender violence prevention in this way. That is why I strongly suggest that public or private institutions who want to begin serious primary prevention initiatives first arrange trainings for men in positions of senior leadership—and the more senior, the better. If done well, gender violence prevention training for men can be transformative. Men often come out of such trainings with an entirely new sensibility about their professional and personal responsibilities to women and children, as well as to other men. This is important because in the long term, dramatic reductions in the incidence of men's violence against women in the U.S. and around the world will only come about when people with power—which often means *men* in power—make gender violence issues a priority. Among other things, this means that male leaders must set and maintain a tone—in educational institutions, corporations, the military—where sexist and abusive behavior is considered unacceptable and unwelcome, not only because women don't like it but because other men will not stand for it. This sounds good, but people often ask me how to get powerful men to take these issues seriously. For example, how do you convince male legislators,

educational administrators, business leaders, or military commanders to attend gender violence prevention training? There are a variety of strategies, but the bottom line is that they do not necessarily have to be motivated—at least initially—by altruism or concerns about social justice. They need instead to be persuaded that prevention is a widely shared institutional goal, and that it is their responsibility to be as knowledgeable and proactive about these issues as possible.

Think and Act Locally and Globally

The focus of this book has been mostly on the U.S., but obviously men's violence against women is an issue everywhere in the world. Since 9/11, many Americans have learned what many people around the world have long known—in the modern era, what happens in foreign cultures thousands of miles away can affect people right here at home, sometimes in ways that are impossible to predict. That is the irrevocable reality of the global environment in which we now live. As I have maintained throughout, gender violence is best seen not as aberrational behavior perpetrated by a few bad men but as an expression of much more deeply seated structures of male dominance and gender inequality. This is much easier to see when you are looking at someone else's culture. For example, in radical fundamentalist Islamic countries, women have few rights, and in many instances men's violence against them is legal and even expected—especially when they defy male authority. In other words, men's violence against women functions in some cultures to maintain a highly authoritarian, even fascistic male power structure. In that sense, gender violence is clearly a political crime with potentially far-reaching consequences. As a result, the way that men in distant lands treat women—individually and as a group—cannot be dismissed as a private family or cultural matter. It has too much bearing on political developments that could affect all of us—like the possibility of nuclear war, or the constant threat of terrorist attacks.

At the same time, it is tempting for some Americans to hear and read about the way men mistreat women in foreign cultures and attribute that mistreatment to cultural deficiencies and even barbarism. But it is important to remember that by world standards, the incidence of men's violence against women here in the U.S. is embarrassingly high. No doubt many American men would be offended to hear people in other countries speculating about the shortcomings of American men—and the inferiority of the culture that produced them.

Fortunately, the growing movement of men who are speaking out about men's violence against women is international in scope. There are anti-sexist men's initiatives in scores of countries across the world. In addition, one of the most promising developments in the history of international human rights law is the growing international movement to identify men's violence against women as a human rights issue. A pivotal moment in that movement came in 2001, when the United Nations war crimes tribunal named rape and sexual slavery as war crimes. And today, a number of international organizations—most prominently Amnesty International—have begun to focus on gender violence and link the physical and sexual exploitation of women to a host of other social and political problems. One of the major challenges for American anti-sexist men in the coming years will be to make connections between men's violence against women in the U.S. with violence around the world, and to support efforts everywhere to reduce men's violence and advance gender equality—not only because it is the right thing to do, but also because it is arguably in our national interest.

What's in It for Men?

Men who occupy positions of influence in boys' lives—fathers, grandfathers, older brothers, teach-ers, coaches, religious leaders—need to teach them that men of integrity value women and do not tolerate other men's sexism or abusive behavior. Obviously they have to lead by example. But that is not enough. In a cultural climate where the objectification of women and girls has accelerated, and boys are exposed to ever more graphic displays of brutality toward women disguised as "entertainment," men need to preemptively provide clear guidelines for boys' behavior. This does not always have to be defined in negative terms, e.g., "Don't hit women." It can be framed as a positive challenge to young men, especially if they aspire to something more special than being "one of the guys" at all costs.

In fact, when I give talks about men's violence against women to groups of parents, I am often asked by parents of sons if there is something positive we can offer young men as a substitute for what we are taking away from them. "We constantly say to our kids, 'Don't do this, don't do that, I wish you wouldn't listen to this music.' We tell them they shouldn't treat girls a certain way, they shouldn't act tough. We spend a lot of time telling our sons what they shouldn't be. It's so negative. Why shouldn't they just tune us out? What's in it for them?"

My answer is really quite simple, and it is as true for the fathers as it is for the sons. When we ask men to reject sexism and the abuse of women, we are not taking something away from them. In fact, we are giving them something very valuable—a vision of manhood that does not depend on putting down others in order to lift itself up. When a man stands up for social justice, non-violence, and basic human rights—for women as much as for men—he is acting in the best traditions of our civilization. That makes him not only a better man, but a better human being.

Mark Anthony Neal

New Black Man

Why write a book like *New Black Man*? What's to be gained by calling forth a generation of pro-feminist, anti-homophobic, nurturing black men? Scholars all have an intellectual project, a basic issue that they seek to address during the course of their careers. My goal has always been to address the concept of black community. Although many have interpreted the fissures and crevices within the so-called black community (particularly in the post-civil-rights era) as evidence of weakness, I believe that a diversity of ideas and identities actually strengthens our communities. I've been committed to doing work that highlights the value of those who have been marginalized in our communities, including but not limited to black youth, black women (and black feminists in particular), and black gays and lesbians.

I've been equally committed to using my work and my civic voice to challenge the real violence—physical, rhetorical, and emotional—that we inflict on those marginalized bodies in our communities. It's not enough to close ranks around those who we marginalize; we need to take aim at the very forms of privilege that allow folks to continue to be marginalized. As a heterosexual black man in my late thirties, I have access to modes of privilege within black communities and the larger society, namely patriarchy and social status. These are privileges that many of those marginalized within our communities simply don't possess. *New Black Man* is my attempt to talk openly and honestly about those

privileges, especially black male privilege, and to think out loud about the ways that black men can develop relationships with their mothers, daughters, sisters, friends, and colleagues that are pro-feminist and anti-sexist. There's no doubt in my mind that Black America must address sexism, misogyny, and homophobia at this point in our history. Below are just a few things for us to think about when pursuing the life of a *New Black Man*.

Understanding Black Male Privilege

Too often when I discuss black male privilege with black men, they fall back on defense mechanisms that highlight the effects of racism and unemployment in the lives of black men. There's no question that these issues are real challenges to black men, but just because black men are under siege in White America, it doesn't mean that they don't exhibit behaviors that do real damage to others, particularly within black communities. What many of these young men want to do is excuse the behavior of black men because of the extenuating circumstances under which black manhood is lived in our society. What they are suggesting is that black male behaviors that oppress women, children, and gays and lesbians in our community are understandable given the amount of oppression that some black men face from White America. This is unacceptable because one form of oppression cannot be used to justify another. Furthermore, it neglects the fact that others, some black women, for example, are also oppressed by White America because of their race and gender.

Countless conferences, books, pamphlets, articles, and online discussions are devoted to the crises that black men face, and the violence that is manifested against them, but there is comparatively little discussion of the very violence that black men often wield against black women. In fact, conversations about black male violence against black women and children are often interpreted as being part of the very racism that black men face. Those who speak out about black male violence are seen as traitors. We must get to a point where black male violence against black women, children, gays, and lesbians is openly challenged for what it is—behavior that is deeply harmful to the entire black community—and not just in the cases where the culprit is some young black male of the hip-hop generation. It has been too easy to blame the indiscretions and crimes of hip-hop generation figures like R. Kelly, Mystikal, or Tupac on the moral failings of the hip-hop generation, when we should be owning up to the fact that their behavior might have been influenced by their perceptions of how black male privilege operates in our communities.

Black Feminism Is Not the Enemy

One of the main attributes of black male privilege is the unwillingness or incapability to fully understand the plight of black women in our communities. Yes, there are acknowledgments of incidents where black women are affected by blatant racism, but fewer when black women are affected because they are *black women* as opposed to being simply black people. Black feminism has sought to address this issue, creating a body of writings and activist events that highlight the conditions of black women globally. For example, it was not surprising that during the vice-presidential debate in October 2004 neither Vice-President Dick Cheney nor Democratic nominee John Edwards were aware that for black women between the ages of twenty-five and thirty-four, HIV disease was the largest cause of death. Tellingly, the debate was hosted by television journalist Gwen Ifill, an African-American woman. Black feminism has sought to make such information available and a topic of conversation,

especially among the black political leadership.

Much of the violence against black women happens close to home, so it shouldn't be surprising that black men come under close scrutiny and criticism by black feminism. Yes, some of the criticism is very angry, and admittedly not all of it is constructive (as with criticisms of white racism), but it is absolutely necessary in a society where black women's critical voices are so often silenced. For those black men who don't understand the anger that many black women feel toward them, it might be helpful to think about the amount of anger that many blacks still harbor toward whites, given the history of racism in this country. Indeed, some black men have oppressed black women in ways that closely resemble the historical oppression of blacks by whites in American society.

Very often those black men who are critical of feminism simply have not done their homework. They are responding to hearsay they've heard on call-in talk shows or read online, rather than actually reading any black feminist writings themselves. These men should check themselves, and check out a book by Audre Lorde, June Jordan, Barbara Christian, Pat Parker, Cheryl Clarke, Barbara Smith, Patricia Hill-Collins, Jewelle Gomez, Beverly Guy-Sheftall, Johnetta Cole, Cathy Cohen, Sharon Patricia Holland, Gwendolyn Pough, Joy James, and Alice Walker, Sonia Sanchez, Nikki Giovanni, and Masani Alexis DeVeaux—just a few of the women who have contributed to the body of literature known as Black Feminist Thought. Black feminism is wide ranging, and is concerned not only with dealing with violence against black women and girls, but also pressing issues of patriarchy, black women's healthcare, sex, and sexuality, black women's education, and racism. We do no justice to the legitimate issues that these women and others have raised if we don't seriously engage their work.

Black men also need to be serious about finding out the issues that affect the black women in their lives. For example, some studies have shown that eighty percent of black women in the United States will suffer from some form of fibroid disease and yet most black men are unaware of the fact, largely because they view it, like menstrual cycles, as simply a "woman's issue." Could we ever imagine a malady that affected eighty percent of all black men in the United States that the majority of black women would be unaware of? Of course not.

Real Black Men Are Not Homophobes

The prevailing notion on the ground is that real black men ain't "fags." This concept not only goes against any notion of community, it also simply isn't true. Black gay men have been valuable contributors to all aspects of black life in the United States. The same faulty logic that suggests real black men ain't "fags" also suggests that black women are lesbians because black men have failed to live up to some "Strong Black Man" ideal, as if black lesbians were solely motivated by their displeasure with black men as opposed to their own social, cultural, and sexual desires. In either case, the presence of black gays and lesbians is often interpreted as a sign of failed black masculinity.

It's time that we start championing a movement where "real black men are not homophobes," given the damage that homophobia does in our community. Such a movement would encourage black men to forcefully challenge homophobia wherever they encounter it, whether it's expressed as heterosexist jokes on the *Tom Joyner in the Morning Show*, BET's *Comic View*, or in the kinds of homophobic violence, rhetorical and literal, that circulate regularly in our churches, on college campuses, in barbershops, within hip-hop, and other institutions within black communities. It's not enough for us to simply eradicate homophobia in our own lives, we need to make the message loud and clear that homophobia is not welcome in our communities. We also need to think differently about black masculinity and understand that black men exhibit a range of attitudes and behaviors that don't always fit neatly into some mythical notion of a "Strong

Black Man." We do incredible damage to ourselves and to those around us by submitting to an idea that there is some little box that all black men must fit into. We are bigger than that.

Real Black Fathers Are Loving Fathers

It has long been believed that the only responsibilities black men have in relation to their families are to provide financially and to dispense discipline. Although these are important aspects of parenting, this model of fatherhood does not allow black men to be emotionally available to their children and wives as nurturers. The idea that black men can be nurturers is often viewed skeptically, as evidence of some kind of weakness. Therefore, many black men who are unable to find work often think that they aren't good fathers because the only model of fatherhood they know is one where black men are, above all else, providers. I suspect this thinking can be directly correlated to the number of black men who have chosen to be involved in the illicit underground drug economy.

This narrow view of fatherhood can take men away from their sons and daughters by means of incarceration or worse, death, and it can prompt men to leave their families because they feel unfit as fathers if they fall upon hard times. We need black men to be there for their children, not just financially, but physically and emotionally. So it is crucial that we establish new rules of fatherhood that allow black men to be good fathers regardless of their temporary economic status.

Rethinking black fatherhood goes hand-in-hand with rethinking black masculinity. We need to applaud black fathers who see themselves as partners in the full range of parenting activities, and who take seriously their roles as nurturers. We need to build a model of black feminist fatherhood, one in which black men aren't just the protectors of their daughters, but also seriously consider how black girls and black women live in the world and the challenges and dangers that they are liable to face. In a world where young black girls are so often silenced and invisible, black fathers have a responsibility, along with black mothers, to create the spaces where the plight of black girls is taken seriously. This also requires sensitizing young black boys, both our sons and those that we come in contact with on a regular basis, to the importance of black girls and black women.

Hip-Hop Is Not the Enemy, but It Is a Problem

Like it or not, hip-hop is the soundtrack of black youth. It's been so easy to point to the moral failings of the hip-hop generation, particularly in relation to the sexism, misogyny, and homophobia that circulates in some of the music and videos, but those moral failings are often just a reflection of how the larger society and black communities think about black women, children, gays, and lesbians. Many criticisms of hip-hop simply deflect attention from equally disturbing practices within more traditional and acceptable black institutions. Too often, the crticisms of hip-hop are done without a real understanding of how ideas, knowledge, language, emotions, and relationships are cultivated by the hip-hop generation. It's not as if the hip-hop generation is beyond scrutiny, but if our elders are going to hold us accountable, they should at least make an effort to understand our worldview and the reasons why we make the choices we make. The world that the post–civil-rights generation(s) inhabits is fundamentally different from the one that produced the freedom movement of the 1950s and 1960s, and our elders need to acknowledge that fact. Our demons are not their demons, and our elders do us no good pretending that our current dilemma is somehow the product of our moral failings and our inability to pay homage to the freedom fighters who came before us. That said, the hip-hop generation also needs to appreciate the sacrifices made by our elders and accept

that there are worthwhile lessons to be learned from their examples.

Just as hip-hop has been used to help politicize the hip-hop generation, it must also be used to create better gender relationships within the hip-hop generation. We need to make language available to young men in hip-hop that will help them rethink their gender politics. Young men often see hip-hop as a haven to articulate their frustrations with women—girlfriends, mothers, baby-mamas, groupies—but they are rarely capable of turning the critique upon themselves in order to interrogate their own roles in creating and maintaining dysfunctional relationships with women. The dialogue with young men is beginning in the work of black feminists of the hip-hop generation—Gwendolyn Pough and Joan Morgan come immediately to mind—and it is valuable work that I hope will continue to engage hip-hop music and those who listen and produce it, so that an honest conversation takes place, not just scolding and finger-wagging.

Young black women, of course, are also learning about and expressing their gender and sexuality through hip-hop. Talk about women and hip-hop, or hip-hop and gender, is often reduced to issues of misogyny and homophobia. Although these critiques *must* be made, the conversation typically remains focused on how men portray women in their lyrics and music videos. Rarely do we discuss how women use hip-hop to articulate their view of the world, a view that may or may not be predicated on what the men in hip-hop (or their lives) might be doing. For example, many black women hip-hop artists, scholars, and journalists speak about "desire" (sexual and otherwise) and the ways that women artists articulate desire in their art. Unfortunately, these issues are rarely discussed in mainstream discussions about hip-hop. Perhaps some of the critical energy focused so much on what black men in hip-hop are saying about women would be better spent by learning to listen to the voices of black women themselves.

Becoming a New Black Man

> I am a man of my times, but the times don't know it yet!
>
> —Erik Todd Dellums as Bayard Rustin in *Boycott*

Finally, it is important the readers remember that I am not *the* New Black Man, but rather that the New Black Man is a metaphor for an imagined life—a way to be "strong" as a black man in new ways: strong commitment to diversity in our communities, strong support for women and feminism, and strong faith in love and the value of listening. I struggle, and often falter, to live up to these ideals every day of my life. It's a challenge, but one I know is well worth facing for myself, for my wife, and for my beautiful daughters. After reading these words, I hope you will join me, men and women, in making the New Black Man the man of our times.

Eric Anderson[1]

"I Used to Think Women Were Weak": Orthodox Masculinity, Gender Segregation, and Sport

Introduction

There have been numerous investigations into the socialization of males into the institutional and organizational norms of masculinity in organized, competitive male team sports (henceforth, simply "team sports"). These findings mostly agree that team sports promote an orthodox form of masculinity that promotes socionegative (sexist, misogynistic, and antifeminine) attitudes toward women (Anderson, 2005b; Bryson, 1987; Burstyn, 1999; Burton-Nelson, 1995; Crosset, 1990; Curry, 1991; Hughes and Coakley, 1991; Messner, 1992, 2002; Muir and Seitz, 2004; Nixon, 1994; Pronger, 1990; Robidoux, 2001; Sabo and Panepinto, 1990; Schacht, 1996). Yet few have formally questioned the influence that segregating males from females has on producing these attitudes (Boeringer, 1996, 1999; Caudwell, 2003; Messner, 2002). Based on qualitative research, I first theorize a model of the cultural *and* structural influences that help reproduce orthodox masculinity among men in team sports. I then explain how competitive male team sport athletes might maintain socionegative attitudes toward women even in a time when institutional sexism has been shown to be decreasing (Bryant, 2003; Burton-Nelson, 1995; Johnson, 1998; Reskin and Roos, 1990).

Findings suggest that the complex reproduction of orthodox masculinity in men's team sports, the kind of sports Messner (2002) describes as the institutional center of sports—such as football, basketball, and hockey—are largely influenced by segregating males into a homophobic, sexist, antifeminine, and misogynistic gender regime that only promotes those who aptly conform to the orthodox sporting ethos (Anderson, 2005a; Connell, 1987; Ewald and Jiobu, 1985; Hughes and Coakley, 1991; Nixon, 1994; Robidoux, 2001). It is suggested that in this top-down socialization system, acquiescence to masculine norms grows greater as one matriculates through the sporting hierarchy, potentially withering away at an individual's agency to contest the bifurcated gender system (Anderson, 2005a; Foucault, 1977; Goffman, 1961; Robidoux, 2001).

Then, utilizing data from heterosexual men who were first socialized into the masculinized sport of high school football but later joined the feminized sport of collegiate cheerleading, I show that despite years of socialization into orthodox masculinity, informants largely reconstruct their views regarding women. Virtually all informants who had not previously respected women's athleticism reported changing their attitudes; and all informants said that they had learned to better respect women's leadership abilities and to value their friendship.

The results are not conclusive, and this research does not examine the effect that gender integration has on *women's* experiences and out-

From *Sociological Forum* 23 (2) 2008, pp. 257–280. Copyright © 2008. Reproduced with permission of Blackwell Publishing Ltd.

comes in sport; however, it does suggest that there may be important socionegative implications for gender-segregating competitive sporting programs. Perhaps of most concern, it questions whether the hegemonic view of segregating the sexes in order to protect women from men's violence does not, instead, engender such violence.

Theory and Methods

To understand how men's team sports reproduce orthodox notions of masculinity, particularly sexism and misogyny, I tie together several theoretical concepts, linking them to a set of grounded observations and in-person semi-structured interviews, upon which a theoretical model is built. To understand the relationship between men's team sports and these socionegative attitudes, I rely on a sociofeminist theory of masculinity that maintains gender is produced through a complex interaction of institutional power, organizational culture, and individual agency (Acker, 1990; Anderson, 2005a; Dilorio, 1989; Martin and Collinson, 1999; Messner, 1997, 2002; Thorne, 1993; West and Zimmerman, 1987).

The study consists of a nationally representative sample of 68 self-identified heterosexual male university cheerleaders who formerly played high school football, but later, when they were unable to make their university football teams, became collegiate cheerleaders.[2] Because these men had never played institutionalized team sports on a gender-integrated team (I use gender integration as synonymous with sex integration), the design allows for the influence of gender segregation and gender integration to be analyzed. In this manner it is more reliable than simply comparing the attitudes of current football players to cheerleaders. However, because most failed high school football players do not try to become university cheerleaders, a self-selection process cannot be ruled out; it is possible that those most influenced by the masculinization process of football may not join cheerleading. Still, almost all the informants report that upon entering cheerleading they held sexist views regarding women's

athleticism and almost half reported maintaining misogynistic views (largely seeing women as sex objects), so conclusions about the affect of gender integration are likely relevant to other groups of men in conservative gender environments too.

My orientation into the culture of collegiate cheerleading began with informal discussions among friends who were collegiate male cheerleaders and through the analysis of cheerleading web sites. Twelve collegiate male cheerleaders were then contacted on America Online by using the member profile search, which provides a search engine for accessing AOL's 33 million subscribers. After conversing with these cheerleaders through instant messaging, they were asked for in-depth, taped telephone interviews. From these initial informants, I used snowball and theoretical sampling techniques to obtain an additional 12 interviews.

The 44 other informants were acquired over 2 years of attending local, regional, and several national collegiate cheerleading competitions, each drawing thousands of athletes from throughout the United States. Here, informants were strategically selected and asked if they were willing to participate in my academic research. In total, 68 interviews with self-identified heterosexual male cheerleaders were transcribed and coded (Gubrium and Holstein, 1997). The men, between 18 and 23 years of age, represent diverse regions and city sizes from throughout the United States, and consequently reflect the racial and class composite of men who cheer in the United States. Eighty percent are white, middle-class men, so generalizations are limited accordingly.

The semi-structured interviews began by asking informants to discuss their life history in sport and the process by which they came into cheerleading. I asked them to retrospectively reflect about their perceptions of women's athleticism and leadership qualities throughout their socialization and matriculation in sport, as well as how they view women today. Although it is recognized that retrospective attitudinal accounts can be problematic (Gubrium and Holstein, 1997), their recollections are supported by the large body of literature regarding men in team sports. Then, in order to see if these responses varied in the presence of others, 12 informal group interviews (60–120 minutes) were conducted on gender-integrated cheerleading teams, in which both men and women were asked about their social networks.

In addition to these interviews, I conducted 300 hours of participant observation on four strategically selected gender-integrated cheerleading teams. These teams were solicited in advance of a major competition and each agreed to be observed and interviewed over a 4-day competition period. Observations also took place at practices in their home states and while socializing away from the athletic arena. Field notes (with either a micro recorder or pocket-sized memo pad) were recorded outside their direct presence, as not to interrupt the socializing process. My experience as a coach, and knowledge of kinesiology and sport psychology, enabled me to both speak their language and help with their athletic endeavors, thus influencing their willingness to be observed.

Orthodox Masculinity in Sport

Gendered institutions are always dynamic arenas of tension and struggle, but perhaps there is no other institution in which gender is more naturalized than sport (Caudwell, 2003; Davis, 1990; McKay, 1997; Messner, 2000). As a highly segregated, homophobic, sexist, and misogynistic gender regime, sport not only contributes to the gender order, but it also reproduces a conservative and stabilizing form of masculinity that renders considerable costs for both sexes (Anderson, 2005a; Burstyn, 1999; Connell, 1987, 2002; Demetriou, 2001; Messner, 1992, 2002). Of concern to this research is not so much what these outcomes are, but to examine how team sports manage to reproduce themselves as organizations that value orthodox masculinity. I then explore how this process might be disrupted through gender-integrating sport.

The tenets used to define orthodox masculinity include, but are not limited to, a number of achieved variables: including risk taking, homophobia, self-sacrifice, the marginalizing of others, a willingness to inflict bodily damage, and the acceptance of pain and injury. Of specific concern for this research, however, is that orthodox masculinity looks disparagingly at femininity and thus helps reproduce patriarchy (Anderson, 2005a,b; Eveslage and Delaney, 1998; Hughes and Coakley, 1991; Kimmel, 1994; Messner, 1992; Pronger, 1990; Muir and Seitz, 2004; Schacht, 1996). This is something Connell and Messerschmidt (2005:844) reconfirmed: "To sustain a given pattern of hegemony requires the policing of men as well as the exclusion or discrediting of women."

Because of the sexist and (often) misogynistic ethos associated with the presence of orthodox masculinity among men in team sports, the performance of femininity by men, or transgression of masculinized boundaries, is deemed highly contentious and is severely penalized (Adler and Adler, 1998; Anderson, 2005a; Davis, 1990; Hughes and Coakley, 1991; McGuffey and Rich, 1999). Those who do not make athletics their top priority or those who refuse to make sacrifices for the sake of victory are deemed *loose cannons* and are stigmatized as not being *team players*. Men who play within feminized terrains, like cheerleading, gymnastics, or ice skating, are generally subordinated by those who play within masculinized terrains, like football and basketball, a status that makes them the targets of homophobic and misogynistic discourse (Adams, 1993; Anderson, 2000, 2002, 2005a; Davis, 1990; Eveslage and Delaney, 1998; Muir and Seitz, 2004). The collective policing of these masculine borders is so severe that I have previously described competitive team sport athletes as members of a cult of athleticism (Anderson, 2005a). These are men who tithe their agency and vow complacency to rigid team norms. As members of this cult, these men express near uniformity in thought and action—reverent to the ideology of orthodox masculinity.

These identity management techniques are considered a reflection of the social process of hegemonic masculinity (Connell, 1987); however, it is important to clarify that I use orthodox masculinity and *not* hegemonic masculinity as a category of dominance. Although Connell (1995) describes the contemporary form of hegemonic masculinity as including sexist and antifeminine attitudes, she does not give a categorical label to this group. This makes it easy to erroneously conflate the process of hegemonic masculinity with an archetype of masculinity, something Connell and Messerschmidt (2005:854) firmly reject: "While we welcome most modifications of hegemonic masculinity . . . we reject those usages that imply a fixed character type, or an assemblage of toxic traits."

It would also be inappropriate to use hegemonic masculinity as an archetype because the hegemonic position of men requires them to possess both the *achieved* and *ascribed* variables that align with social masculine dominance. Orthodox masculinity, as I define it (Anderson, 2005b), only refers to the conformity of the achieved variables that currently align with social dominance, something that *all* men can attempt to approximate. Connell offers no archetype for this group of men. Accordingly, the social process of dominance in this article is understood by men *acting* in accord with orthodox masculinity, despite their ascribed traits. These men are then said to perform in opposition to traditionally subordinated and marginalized masculinities (Anderson, 2005b; Connell, 1987, 1995; Messner, 1992, 2002).

Costs Associated with Orthodox Masculinity in Sport

There are *many* costs associated with orthodox masculinity for men and women. Researchers have examined how males construct hierarchies around athleticism in school culture, and how those who are marginalized by this stratification suffer emotionally (Anderson, 2005a; Pollack, 1998), socially (Anderson, 2005a; Plummer,

1999), and sometimes physically (Anderson, 2000; Messner, 1992, 2002). This is particularly true for gay males, who are almost altogether marginalized by athletic culture (Anderson, 2000, 2002, 2005a; Hekma, 1998; Pronger, 1990; Wolf Wendel *et al.*, 2001). Few males are immune from social victimization under this system—and none escape the physical. This is made salient when watching the violence men afflict on each other in team sports, violence that is naturalized as "just part of the game" (Messner, 1992, 2000; Papas *et al.*, 2004; Smith, 1983).

However, men are not the only ones who suffer from such masculine stratification. Although the use of sport in reproducing men's social, political, and financial dominance over women (Bourdieu, 2001; Burton-Nelson, 1995; Connell, 1987) is somewhat outside the scope of this analysis—as is the positioning of men over women within the institution of sport itself. Rather, of concern to this analysis is that the socializing of men into this violent ethos may have serious implications for the symbolic and physical violence that men commit against women.

Team sports are *at least* partially responsible for the promotion of antifeminine, sexist, and misogynistic attitudes among male athletes (Anderson, 2005a; Messner, 2002; Muir and Seitz, 2004; Plummer, 1999; Pollack, 1998; Schacht, 1996). Male athletes (in general) and team sport athletes (in particular) have been shown to objectify women—often viewing them as sexual objects to be conquered (Burstyn, 1999; Burton-Nelson, 1995; Curry, 1991; Messner, 1992, 2002; Schacht, 1996). Others suggest that, in the same manner that team sport participation has been shown to influence violence against other men (Kreager, 2004), the socialization of men into team sports might also influence symbolic, domestic, and public violence against women (Boeringer, 1996, 1999; Crosset, 2000; Crosset *et al.*, 1995; Koss and Gaines, 1993; Loy, 1995; Papas *et al.*, 2004). Crosset *et al.* (1995) have shown that while student-athletes make up only 3.7% of the men at Division 1 universities, they are responsible for 19% of sexual assault reports to campus judicial affairs offices.

More recently, Crosset (2000) has shown that football, basketball, and hockey players—notably team sport athletes—are responsible for 67% of the sexual assaults reported by student athletes, although they only comprise 30% of the student athlete populace.

Despite these findings, hegemonic views continue to attribute sport as a sociopositive institution in U.S. culture, concealing a great number of social problems that sport, or at least the way we do sport, generates (Carlson *et al.*, 2005; Jeziorski, 1994; Gerdy, 2002). Accordingly, this research critically examines not the outcomes of sport, but the influence that gender segregation has on those outcomes.

Reproducing Orthodox Masculinity in Sport

No form of masculinity is self-reproducing. The reproductive process is laden with social tension and ultimately *can* fail (Anderson, 2005b). But in the arena of sport, the process of reproducing orthodox masculinity has proven resilient (Pronger, 1990). Men's team sports have consistently resisted the cultural and institutional challenges of both women and gay men (Anderson, 2002, 2005a; Messner, 2002). It is this reproduction process, the specific mechanisms that explain the resiliency of orthodox masculinity in the sport setting, which I now address.

To do this I employ a theoretical model, in four steps, that explains the synergy of the dominant cultural and structural variables that produce and influence the reproduction of orthodox masculinity in men's team sports. The research component of this article then examines the influence gender-integrating sport might have on disrupting this masculinist system.

Step 1: Socialize Them Young

Americans attribute to team sports a *large number* of sociopositive characteristics. Parents believe that sport will teach their sons' moral character, self-restraint, and a sense of fair play. One of the more resilient myths is that team sports teach boys how to work together and to get along well with each other (Miracle and Rees, 1994). But researchers find that the most salient benefits of athletic participation are found in elevated self-esteem, better school attendance, educational aspirations, higher rates of university attendance, and perhaps even postschooling employment (Eccles and Barber, 1999; Carlson *et al.*, 2005; Jeziorski, 1994; Marsh, 1992, 1993; Sabo *et al.*, 1989). I maintain that these quantitative investigations are somewhat misleading because they fail to examine whether the benefits associated with sporting participation are the result of something intrinsic to team sports, or whether they simply reflect the physical, symbolic, and emotional dominance that a socially elite group of males exhibit over marginalized men and women in most jockocratic school cultures (Anderson, 2005a). In other words, do male athletes have higher self-esteem because they score goals, or is this a statistical reflection of the lowering of nonathletes' self-esteem in response to being subordinated by athletes who are culturally and institutionally glorified in the U.S. school system? When these studies do examine the socionegative attributes of team sport participation (Miller *et al.*, 2005), they often examine variables that lend themselves to quantifiable analysis, like disciplinary referrals. Thus, they fail to examine the more important socionegative variables (those that do not lend themselves to quantification), like the volitional and unintentional damage inflicted on those who do not fit this masculine mold.

However, what is important to this analysis is not whether sports deliver these sociopositive outcomes; rather, what is important is that Americans *believe* they do, something reflected in team sport participation rates. Compared to the 6% of U.S. parents who discourage athletic participation, 75% encourage it (Miracle and Rees, 1994). Largely a fact that the United States remains one of the few Western countries to intertwine public education with athletic programs (Gerdy, 2002), some U.S. high schools report participation rates as high as 72% (Carlson *et al.*, 2005). Thus, there exists great cultural and institutional pressure for boys to participate in these types of sports (Anderson, 2005a; Messner, 2002; Miracle and Rees,

1994; Plummer, 1999; Pollack, 1998). Their participation is pressured by peers, made compulsory by parents, or is mandated through public education. As a result, if there is any institution described as being *all-important* in the lives of boys and young men—it most certainly is sport.

Step 2: Separate the Sexes

Largely a product of men's desires, men and women occupy separate spaces in the sporting world (Anderson, 2005a; Crosset, 1990; Frye, 1999; Hargreaves, 1993; Kidd, 1990; Pronger, 1990; Whitson, 1990). Few other institutions naturalize the segregation of men and women so near perfectly as do team sports (Davis, 1990; Messner, 2000, 2002). Although occupational sex segregation is declining in other institutions (Cotter *et al.*, 1995; Johnson, 1998; Reskin and Roos, 1990; Rotolo and Wharton, 2004), formal and traditional reasoning has left team sports a largely unexamined arena of gender segregation (Caudwell, 2003; Messner, 2000, 2002). Although this segregation has *many* male-driven purposes, it is important to note that feminist separation also occurs in sport.

One can certainly understand the feminist desire to play sports away from men, particularly where women are protected from the violence of male athleticism (Kreager, 2004; Smith, 1983). Gender segregation in team sports is therefore confirmed by both men and women. It is then naturalized through notions of "opposite" phenotypes (Davis, 1990; Messner, 2000) and myths about boys' elevated levels of innate aggression and athletic advantage over girls (Butterfield and Loovis, 1994; Messner, 2002). Collectively, sex segregation in sport, as Messner (2002:12) describes, is "grounded in a mutually agreed-upon notion of boys' and girls' 'separate worlds.'"

Step 3: Control the Environment

Athletes who emulate the institutional creed of orthodox masculinity are usually selected over players who break from its tenets, influencing them to adopt the gendered norms associated with orthodox masculinity. Ewald and Jiobu

(1985) show that some athletes so overly adhere to the norms of sporting culture that they disrupt family relationships, work responsibilities, and even their physical health—all guided by a masculine creed of *giving it all*. I have previously shown that gay athletes largely remain closeted for these same reasons, fearing that coming out will thwart their athletic progress (Anderson, 2002, 2005a).

Hughes and Coakley (1991:311) describe this social deviance as *over-conformity* to the sport ethic, saying: "The likelihood of being chosen or sponsored for continued participation is increased if athletes overconform to the norms of sport." Of course, athletes do not see overconformity as problematic, rather "they see it as confirming and reconfirming their identity as athletes. . . ." Building on Hughes and Coakley's (1991) over-conformity theory, I examine the structural mechanisms that help reproduce sport as a site of orthodox masculinity by highlighting the near-total institutional aspects of team sports.

Goffman (1961) describes a total institution as an enclosed social system in which the primary purpose is to control all aspects of a person's life. Foucault's (1977) description of the military serves as a useful example. Foucault maintained that, through intense regimentation and implementation of a standard ideal of behavior, the military has the ability to transform peasants into soldiers. He posited that men become more docile to the system because their growing identity as a soldier is one of a withering of agency—that the longer a soldier remains in the institution of soldiering, the less agency he has to contest it. Though I do not maintain that competitive, institutionalized team sports *are* a total institution (athletes do have the freedom to quit sport), I do argue that team sports approximate a "near-total" institution. This is because, much like the military, sport uses myths of glory, patriotism, and masculine idolatry, along with corporeal discipline and structures of rank, division, uniform, rules, and punishment, to subordinate individual agency and construct a fortified ethos of orthodox masculinity (Britton and Williams, 1995; Woodward, 2000).

When athletes think in alignment with their teammates, they are given social prestige and are publicly lauded; they are honored by their institutions and celebrated by fans and community (Bissinger, 1990; Messner, 1992, 2002). Hughes and Coakley (1991:311) say: "Athletes find the action and their experiences in sport so exhilarating and thrilling that they want to continue participating as long as possible." Coakley (1998: 155) later adds, "they love their sports and will do most anything to stay involved." Thus, it is understandable that from *their perspective* sport is a socially positive vessel. And while I think the reasons athletes will do almost anything to remain in team sports are more complicated than just the thrill one receives from playing them, the point remains that athletes who withstand the selection process do so because of their outstanding athletic ability *and* their willingness to conform to orthodox masculinity. In doing so, they limit who they befriend, shut out other cultural influences, and are therefore less exposed to those who do not fit orthodox masculine requisites (Anderson, 2005a; Robidoux, 2001).

Conversely, athletes who do not adhere to the tenets of orthodox masculinity are sanctioned by verbal insults and are less likely to be given valued playing positions (Anderson, 2002; Bean, 2003; Hughes and Coakley, 1991; Hekma, 1998). Coming out of the closet, "acting feminine," or being told that one is not a team player are marks of shame that are likely to drive nonconformists from the sporting terrain (Hekma, 1998). Thus, desiring peer recognition and social promotion, athletes normally put team expectations before individual concerns, sacrificing individual agency and contributing to the reproduction of a rigid, masculine sporting culture. Of particular concern to this research, this virtually necessitates that those who aspire to the next level must publicly disengage with any stigmatized notion of sexual or gender ideology that is inconsistent with orthodox masculinity (Anderson, 2005a; Messner, 2002).

From an early age, then, athletes befriend each other on and off the field. Their social lives are routinely dictated by a rigid athletic schedule of practices, competitions, and other team functions. Team sport athletes, from this and other research, report that the further they matriculate through the ranks, the less freedom exists to inhabit any social space outside this network and the more their identity narrows in order to be competitive with other men (Anderson, 2005a; Messner, 1992; Nixon, 1994; Robidoux, 2001).

I suggest that this might make gender construction in team sports different from the type of agency-laden gender construction that West and Zimmerman (1987) or Thorne (1993) suggest occurs more broadly. This is because, from youth to adulthood, males socialized into competitive team sports follow a subtle but increasingly institutionalized gender ideology: an incipient notion of gender that slowly erodes individual agency and restructures athletes as highly masculinized conformists in thought and action. The subordination required for retaining one's sporting status, or being selected for advancement, wears away at their agency to construct oppositional masculinities. This is then justified by the prevalent belief that homogeneity is required in sports to produce desirable results (Sabo and Panepinto, 1990), even though there is only a small and dubious relationship between a group's social cohesion and athletic success (Granovetter, 1983; Mullen and Cooper, 1994).

Step 4: Selectively Recruit Coaches

Not every boy who dreams of making it to the National Football League will. Certainly, the thousands of male collegiate cheerleaders who used to play football did not. Instead of making it to the top, most athletes self-segregate out, are selected out, graduate out, drop out, or are forced out of organized sporting participation through injury. Those who remain are endowed with social capital and this influences longstanding members to define their master identity as that of *an athlete*—making it all the more difficult for them to break from the gendered ideology embedded in athletic identities and esteemed in athletic cultures (Anderson, 2005a; Messner, 1987).

However, centering one's identity on athleticism carries measurable risks. Sport is a volatile field where careers end on poor plays or missteps, and athletes can, at a moment's notice, be cut from a team (Bean, 2003). In fact, as an athlete, the only thing that he can be assured of is that his career will end; and relative to other occupations, it will do so early. Thus, whether an athlete suddenly loses his association with his athletic identity, or his body ages out of competitive form, all are forced to disengage with competitive sport. And when this happens, they are generally no longer valued in the sport setting (Messner, 1987).

Men who drop out, are forced out, or otherwise do not make the next level of sport often find themselves detached from the masculine prestige they once enjoyed—something sport psychologists call the disengagement effect (Greendorfer, 1992). Athletes who rode atop the masculine hierarchy feel the greatest loss upon disengaging from that elite status. So, for those with no further opportunity to play competitive sports, coaching becomes one of the few alternative venues for getting back into the game. Sport almost always draws leaders from those who overconformed to the previous cohort's ideals, something perceived to give them expertise as coaches (Anderson, forthcoming). As coaches, these ex-athletes rely on hero-athlete narratives to promote their individual experience and to inspire a new generation of boys into a similar ethos of orthodox masculinity (Anderson, 2005a, 2007; Hughes and Coakley, 1991). But for every athlete who has been highly merited by sport, there are many more that did not make the cut, often those who had horrifying experiences in sport.

Those who were marginalized or publicly humiliated in sports are rarely represented in coaching positions. Their stories are seldom told in popular culture. Books are not published, sponsorships are not given, and movies are not made about those who *did not* achieve success in sport. Even when stories of gay (or otherwise marginalized athletes) are told, they normally depict a heroic underdog (Anderson, 2000). In this manner, only highly selective stories are being told about sport; stories that glamorize the struggle and romance of the sporting-hero genre (Stangle, 2001). These stories, fictional or real, make for great entertainment but they falsely bestow on sport qualities that only exist for a few. Conversely, when marginalized athletes drop out, are pushed out, or otherwise leave the sporting arena, their perceptions of how sport ought to operate go with them. Those who were marginalized by sports and those who were too intimidated to play them in the first place, do not go on to coach; and their ideas about how sports ought to function go unheard. Sport is essentially closed to voices of dissent.

Within competitive team sports, then—and from a very early age—athletes are normally removed from the presence of women. They are selected to the next level of play only if they adhere to the tenets of orthodox masculinity, where they are influenced by the top-down modeling of the near-total institution. Finally, the institution itself excludes input from those not within its dominant framework. Thus, this system is more than just culturally hegemonic, it is also structural. Not just structural in the sense of a social, historical, and institutionalized pattern, but literally structured by codified rules of segregation, reminiscent of the same rules that once formally segregated blacks from whites. It is a resilient system that reproduces a more conservative form of gender expression among men, helping make sport a powerful gender regime despite the gains of second-wave feminism that characterizes the broader culture (Bryant, 2003; Johnson, 1998; Reskin and Roos, 1990).

Disrupting Orthodox Masculinity in Sport

The fact that thousands of former high school football players yearly enter the culturally feminized world of collegiate cheerleading (Anderson, 2005b; Davis, 1990; Hanson, 1995) might seem antithetical to the effectiveness of my reproduction model. After all, if the sanctions are so great for breaking this masculine mold, why would so many ex-team-sport athletes choose to transgress into cheerleading, where they are likely to be ridiculed?

The answer is that, for most men, the system *is* sufficiently seamless—preventing most ex-team-sport athletes from breaking its mandates. However, for those who do (my informants), it seems that their transgression is not viewed so much a violation of orthodox masculinity, but as an ironic attempt to remain within it. Most of the 68 heterosexual football players in this study maintained that they entered the sport of cheerleading precisely *because* they failed to make the next level of sport. Cut from their masculinized identities as football players, they reeled in the dissonance between their personal and public personas and desired to get back in the game—any game. But because most of the men who devoted their youth to football were not trained in the rigors of other competitive team sports, they were unable to make, or assumed they would not be able to make, other collegiate athletic teams. Thus, cheerleading became the most likely entry for these informants to be part of a team again. "Everybody knew me in high school," John said. "I was 'John, the football player.' Here [in college] nobody knew me. Cheerleading was a way to get back on the field." "I had been a football player all my life," Tim said. "Everything revolved around it. I thought I'd play in college, but I didn't make it. I couldn't believe it. So I'm not on the field now, but it's better than being in the bleachers."

To be clear, most athletes' transition from football to cheerleading is not without tension. Entering a feminized terrain is especially difficult for men who previously ostracized male cheerleaders (Anderson, 2005b). But the transition is aided by existing male cheerleaders who vigorously recruit ex-football players: assuring them access to socially elite women. It was common to hear: "In cheerleading, you get to be around all these beautiful women."

Sentiment regarding men who participate in cheerleading has also been strategically crafted to maintain that male cheerleaders are anything but "girly men." On the contrary, they are promoted as "real" men: heterosexual, brave, and strong enough to hold a woman (or two) above their heads, yet agile enough to perform the complex gymnastic routines also required of them (Anderson, 2005b; Davis, 1990). One university's cheerleading recruitment poster illustrated both these heterosexualizing and masculinizing tactics: "Want strong muscles? Want to toss girls? Our Cheer Team needs stunt men!! No experience needed."

It is also important to know that the type of cheerleading examined in this research is not simply that of cheering for men's team sports. Cheerleading squads today compete against one another in complex performances, where men and women dance, cheer, stunt, and tumble to rhythmically synchronized, high-energy music. Higher, faster, and more dangerous are the hallmarks of successful squads, and these qualities demand cheerleaders (of both sexes) to be more than peppy supporters; they must also be courageous acrobats and spirited showmen. Thus, men's roles in the sport have changed significantly over the years (Davis, 1990; Hanson, 1995). Whereas men in cheerleading never used to "fly" into the air or unlock their arms from rigid straight-armed positions when dancing, today half the men's squads were shown to do precisely this. Men dance, stunt, and even allow themselves to be thrown into the air, landing safely in the arms of other men (Anderson, 2005b).

Finally, the transition from the masculinized world of high school football to the feminized world of collegiate cheerleading is made easier because of the geographical relocation that often occurs when attending college, removing informants from their previous social network and placing them more safely out of reach of peer devaluation. This helped many of the informants explore cheerleading with *less* social risk than would have occurred had they decided to explore cheerleading in high school.

I Used to Think Women Were Weak

Jeff and Tony practiced putting a female athlete into the air by holding her above their heads, but after growing bored with the combination, Jeff said, "My turn" and the athletes switched positions so that Jeff was standing atop the outstretched arms of one man and one woman. After practice he said, "I never would have guessed women could do that before I joined cheer. It's not like I'm a hundred pounds you know." Like Jeff, virtually all the informants viewed men as maintaining an athletic advantage in sport (before and after joining cheerleading) but about 70% of the informants said they had no idea that women could be *this* athletic. This struck me as strange, considering most had seen women cheering on their football sidelines in high school. "Yeah, you see them doing some of this stuff on the sidelines," Jeff said, "but you don't really get an idea of just how physically tough it is until you try it." Tony agreed, "I never really thought about how hard it must be to do what they do. Not until I tried it."

Accordingly, most of the informants maintain that they never really had their preconceptions about the inferiority of female athleticism challenged. Like Jeff, Jim recalled that he used to believe that women were physically incapable of competing with men. He said, "I used to think women were weak, but now I know that's not true." David added, "I never thought women were so athletic before. I hated women's sports. But these women are *athletes*. They do stuff I'd never do and I bet there are a lot of sports women can do better in." Brad summed up much of the sentiment.

> I didn't appreciate women as athletes before. [In high school] I heard that another school had a girl on their [football] team and I thought that was wrong. My teammates and I were talking about it, and we all agreed that a woman just couldn't handle what we could. Now I see that women can handle a lot and they aren't as fragile as I thought they were.

Participant observations show why these men have upgraded their views on women's athletic abilities. In cheerleading, men see women performing highly dangerous feats that require the same strength, balance, and fearlessness that they claim masculinizes them (Davis, 1990). And even though men do most of the heavy lifting in the co-ed division of cheerleading, they need only watch the all-women's division to see the same stunts performed by women (Adams and Bettis, 2003; Anderson, 2005b; Hanson, 1995).

Furthermore, virtually all the men expressed a new-found appreciation for the leadership qualities and coaching abilities that women exhibit in cheerleading. Perhaps this is because virtually all the collegiate female cheerleaders competed in high school, and this gives them considerable knowledge of the sport. Watching David, a wide-eyed new male recruit trying to learn a complicated and dangerous stunt illustrated this.

David listened to Emily's directions, asked for clarification, and relaxed at her encouragement. Immediately after landing the stunt, he turned to hug her, beaming with self-pride. He then awaited her congratulations and smiled again upon receiving it. It makes sense that men listen to women in cheerleading: when one is contemplating flying through the air, performing a back flip, or holding a person above one's head, listening to the experts prevents injuries.

Finally, data from interviews and participant observations also indicate that many of these men rethought their misogynistic attitudes, particularly regarding women as sex objects. Relying on retrospective reports, about half the men said they maintained misogynistic attitudes before joining cheerleading; mostly in that they hyper-sexualized women and desired to socially exclude them from male preserves of power (Muir and Seitz, 2004; Schacht, 1996). Yet most (not all) of these men maintain that cheerleading helped them undo this thinking. Dan enthusiastically said: "Oh, we totally learn to respect women, I mean they [teammates] are like our sisters." Ronnie confirmed: "Yeah, I never really understood women too much before, but my teammates are a family to me. I have grown real close to them, and now I can often see things from their perspective." Ryan said:

> In high school it was all about the cheerleaders making signs for our games or baking us cookies. I mean, we hung out with them at parties, but it was nothing like what occurs here [in cheerleading]. We didn't travel with them or have team dinners and stuff. I never really had female friends in high school . . . I never really got to know them like I do now.

These results suggest that the sex segregation existent in Ryan's high school effectively denied him the opportunity to befriend women as equal members, not only in social networks but as equal members in sport sharing responsibility for the outcome of a game. I asked Ryan if his high school social network of friends was also comprised of mostly men. "Yeah, my teammates. That's really all I socialized with," he said. Conversely, in collegiate cheerleading, Ryan was able to make friends with women in ways he was not able to in high school. Will concurred, "I've never before had best-friends that weren't men. But now, some of my best friends are women."

This theme was also explored in the 12 group interviews. Here, all the cheerleaders and several coaches were asked about the social interaction between men and women. Collectively, both men and women, coaches and athletes, near-unanimously maintained that cohesion occurs between the sexes. Jill (a player) said: "The men in cheerleading learn a new respect for women in this sport. They learn that not only are we good athletes, but we are smart athletes and competent leaders, too." Highlighting how gender integration might also change women's views of men, Lindsay (a coach) said: "These guys have given me a new understanding of men, and they aren't all that bad." Another female coach added:

> Oh yeah, they become like family. I mean they spend so much time together, they change in the same locker rooms sometimes, and they just get real comfortable, even with bodily issues. I

can't imagine a more cohesive group of athletes than you find in cheerleading.

Data from this research clearly indicate that there exists a significant sociopositive attitudinal shift regarding women. Informants near-unanimously maintained that they enhanced their beliefs about the athleticism of women; all but a handful reported that they had learned to see women as more than sex objects. Finally, *all* the athletes report having learned to respect and value women as friends, teammates, and competent leaders in the sport of cheerleading. Thus, in the sex-integrated sport of collegiate cheerleading, even once sexist and misogynistic men were able to witness the athleticism of women, befriend them in ways that they were previously unable to, and to learn of their sexual and gendered narratives—humanizing them in the process. And while not all men were equally affected by their experience in cheerleading, the considerable results observed highlight the question of how much of men's antifeminine, sexist, and misogynistic attitudes might be prevented if team sports were structurally gender integrated across all sports and among all age cohorts.

Discussion

Research has shown that male team sports influence an orthodox form of masculinity that devalues femininity and promotes sexism and misogyny (Anderson, 2005a; Griffin, 1998; Messner, 1992, 2002). Burstyn (1999), Crosset (1990), Kimmel (1990) Messner (1992, 2002), and others (Muir and Seitz, 2004) have suggested that this is mostly the result of organizational culture and/or historical processes. Within these cultural models, sport is ironically viewed as a sociopositive institution that socializes males through a top-down process of peer-influenced collective culture. Boys and men are thought to adopt socionegative views about women in order to become part of the in-group and to establish their masculine worth among peers (Plummer, 1999). Building on these cultural theories, I utilize qualitative methods to also examine the influence of the *structure* of team sports; theorizing a model to help elicit the mechanisms of the production and reproduction of orthodox masculinity in team sport settings.

Findings lead me to suggest that, in the gender-segregated arena of sport, the extreme regimentation and inordinate amount of time required to excel often deprives men of experiences outside the athletic arena, where they might otherwise be introduced to the athletic abilities and sexual/gendered narratives of women. Instead, in the homosocial world of men's team sports, males are socialized into an ethos in which women are valued as sexual objects and devalued as athletes (Anderson, 2005a; Curry, 1991; Schacht, 1996). This is made more possible because there are no women to contest these narrow understandings, and also because coaches are recruited from a pool of ex-athletes who matriculated through the same system. Essentially, I suggest that because team sports are nearly compulsory for U.S. youth, young boys are indoctrinated into a masculinized, homophobic, and sexist gender regime from early childhood—an institution they cannot easily escape. Even if boys are fortunate enough to enter a gender-integrated sports team when young, by the time they reach high school, gender segregation is the norm. Additionally, the demands of competitive sport often consume such quantities of time that it also structures men into off-the-field social networks of teammates—positioning them into a near-total masculine institution. Bereft of alternative gender narratives, and desiring social promotion among their peers, boys and men are more willing to subject their agency to orthodox masculinity, which remains predicated in antifeminine, sexist, and (frequently) misogynistic thinking. In this aspect, segregation on the field is complicated by the effect of a near-total institution off the field.

In addition to providing a model for how orthodox masculinity is reproduced among team sport athletes, my research also suggests how this process might be interrupted. Data clearly shows that when these same men become familiar with the experiences of women (in the gender-integrated sport of cheerleading), almost all adopt a new gender strategy that looks more favorably on women (none downgraded their position). Although some of this change may occur because of the liberalizing attitudes of university life in general (Ohlander *et al.*, 2005), I attribute much of their reconstruction to the gender-integrated sport of cheerleading. Here, the time constraints of training and travel structures athletes into mixed-sex social networks, at least part of the time. Here, men are likely to have conversations with women about sex, gender, sport, and life—the kind of conversations they were often unable to have in a homosocial culture such as football. In partaking in these conversations, informants not only prevailed themselves to hearing the multiple narratives of women, but they also saw them as worthy and competent athletes, teammates, coaches, and leaders. In cheerleading, even men who were once highly sexist were able to socialize and develop cohesion with women as participants of equal agency and responsibility for team performance and outcomes—something that works against gender stereotyping. Coupled with a more inclusive institutional and organizational setting (Anderson, 2005b), these men were influenced to undo much of their separatist and sexist thinking.

The findings of this research may stand out as odd compared to research showing that the integration of men and women does not always deter gender stereotyping (Jackson and Warren, 2000; Harvey and Stables, 1984). I suggest that team sports may be uniquely effective in reducing gender stereotypes because they necessitate that men and women work together for the accomplishment of victory. It makes sense that men relying on women to obtain their athletic goals look more favorably on women compared to when they compete directly against them. Conversely, it is also possible that part of these results are influenced by the feminized nature of cheerleading and the process these men go through to rectify their masculinity with this feminized terrain (Anderson, 2005b). Either way, these findings indicate that the gender-integrated nature of cheerleading may help *disrupt* the reproduction of orthodox masculinity among men in gender-segregated team sports. This research therefore carries serious implications for the structure on which U.S. team sports operate, calling for further investigation into the effects of gender integrating men's and women's team sports.

I do not claim gender integration to be a panacea for the sexual, social, ethical, and gender-related problems associated with sports; men's team sports are far too entwined with other masculinist systems and institutions for that. Furthermore, this research does not address what effect gender desegregating team sports might have on female athletes, particularly considering that women have been shown to be subordinated by men within other integrated terrains (Britton and Williams, 1995; Connell, 1987; Reskin and Roos, 1990; Williams, 1995). Nor does this research address how gender-integrated team sports might impact on the number of sociopositive attributes that Sabo *et al.* (2004) correlate with women's sporting participation.[3] But whereas dominant ideology maintains that gender segregation is valuable because it shelters women from men's violence, I question whether violence against women might instead be promoted through sporting segregation. If gender segregation in sport is even *partially* responsible for men's violence against women, then this research should serve as a call for further academic inquiry into the effects of gender integrating sports.

Still, it is recognized that gender desegregating sport is a politically charged proposition, and I am aware that among traditionalists of sport the potential implications of these findings may not be received favorably. But only by examining both sides of this question will we come to a better understanding of the impact gender segregation has on athletic culture. Hegemonic perspectives that value gender segregation in sport—whether they be masculinist or feminist in origin—should not stop us from academically examining a counterproposition. As Frye (1999:361) says: "If you are doing something that is so strictly forbidden by the patriarchs, you must be doing something right."

Notes

1. Department of Education, University of Bath, BA2 7AY, United Kingdom; e-mail: E.Anderson@bath.ac.uk or EricAndersonD@aol.com.

2. Informants were included only if they had played football throughout their 4 years of high school and had not previously played competitive, institutionalized team sports with women. The sample consisted of athletes in equal parts from the U.S. West, South, East, and Midwest.

3. Sabo *et al.* (2004) show that correlated with women's athletic participation is an improvement in physical health, elevated self-esteem, improved academic standing, greater career mobility, reduced rates of pregnancy, and even reduced sexual victimization. What is not clear however is whether these findings are the result of athletic participation alone or whether they are predicated on gender-segregated athletic participation.

References

Acker, Joan. 1990. "Hierarchies, Jobs, Bodies: A Theory of Gendered Organizations.," *Gender & Society* 4: 139–158.

Adams, Marie Louise 1993. "To be an Ordinary Hero: Male Figure Skaters and the Ideology of Gender," In T. Haddad (ed.), *Men and Masculinities*. Toronto: Canadian School Press.

Adams, Natalie, and Pamela Bettis. 2003. "Commanding the Room in Short Skirts: Cheering as the Embodiment of Ideal Girlhood," *Gender & Society* 17: 1: 73–91.

Adler, Patricia, and Peter Adler. 1998. *Peer Power: Preadolescent Culture and Identity*. New Brunswick, NJ: Rutgers University Press.

Anderson, Eric. 2000. *Trailblazing: The True Story of America's First Openly Gay Track Coach*. Hollywood, CA: Alyson Publications.

Anderson, Eric. 2002. "Openly Gay Athletes: Contesting Hegemonic Masculinity in a Homophobic Environment," *Gender & Society* 16: 6: 860–877.

Anderson, Eric. 2005a. *In the Game: Gay Athletes and the Cult of Masculinity*. New York: State University of New York Press.

Anderson, Eric. 2005b. "Orthodox and Inclusive Masculinity: Competing Masculinities Among Heterosexual Men in a Feminized Terrain," *Sociological Perspectives* 48: 3: 337–355.

Anderson, Eric. 2007. "Coaching Identity and Social Exclusion," In Jim Denison (ed), *Coaching Knowledges: Understanding the Dynamics of Sport Performance*: pp. 24–50. London: A & C Black Publishers.

Bean, Billy, with Chris Bull. 2003. *Going the Other Way: Lessons from a Life In and Out of Major-Leaguer Baseball*. New York: Marlowe and Company.

Bissinger, H. G. 1990. *Friday Night Lights: A Town, a Team, and a Dream*. Boston: Addison-Wesley.

Boeringer, S. B. 1996. "Influence of Fraternity Membership, Athletics and Male Living Arrangements on Sexual Aggression," *Violence Against Women* 2: 134–147.

Boeringer, S. B. 1999. "Associations of Rape-Supportive Attitudes with Fraternal and Athletic Participation," *Violence Against Women* 5: 81–90.

Bourdieu, Pierre. 2001. *Masculine Domination*. Stanford, CA: Stanford University Press.

Britton, Dana M., and Christine Williams. 1995. " 'Don't Ask, Don't Tell, Don't Pursue:' Military Policy and the Construction of Heterosexual Masculinity," *Journal of Homosexuality* 30: 1: 1–21.

Bryant, Alyssa. 2003. "Changes in Attitudes Toward Women's Roles: Predicting Gender-Role Traditionalism Among College Students," *Sex Roles* 48: 3/4: 131–142.

Bryson, Lois. 1987. "Sport and the Maintenance of Masculine Hegemony," *Women's Studies International Forum* 10: 349–360.

Burstyn, Varda. 1999. *The Rites of Men: Manhood, Politics, and the Culture of Sport*. Toronto: University of Toronto Press.

Burton-Nelson, Mariah. 1995. *The Stronger Women Get the More Men Love Football: Sexism and the American Culture of Sports*. New York: Avon Books.

Butterfield, S. A., and E. M. Loovis. 1994. "Influence of Age, Sex, Balance, and Sport Participation in Development of Kicking by Children in Grades K–8," *Perceptual and Motor Skills* 79: 121–138.

Carlson, Deven, Leslie Scott, Michael Planty, and Jennifer Thompson. 2005. *What is the Status of High School Athletes 8 Years After Graduation?* Report released by the National Center for Educational Statistics. Washington, DC: U.S. Department of Education.

Caudwell, Jane. 2003. "Sporting Gender: Women's Footballing Bodies as Sites/Sights for the (Re)Articulation of Sex, Gender, and Desire," *Sociology of Sport Journal* 20: 4: 371–386.

Coakley, Jay. 1998. *Sport in Society: Issues and Controversies*. Boston: McGraw-Hill.

Connell, R. W. 1987. *Gender and Power*. Stanford, CA: Stanford University Press.

Connell, R. W. 1995. *Masculinities*. Berkeley, CA: University of California Press.

Connell, R. W. 2002. *Gender*. London: Polity.

Connell, R. W., and James Messerschmidt. 2005. "Hegemonic Masculinity: Rethinking the Concept," *Gender & Society* 19: 6: 829–859.

Cotter, David A., Joann M. DeFiore, Joan D. Hermsen, Brenda Marsteller Kowaleski, and Reeve Vanneman. 1995. "Occupational Gender Desegregation in the 1980s," *Work and Occupations* 22: 3–21.

Crosset, Todd 1990. "Masculinity, Sexuality, and the Development of Early Modern Sport," In Michael Messner and Donald Sabo (eds.), *Sport, Men and the Gender Order: Critical Feminist Perspectives*: pp. 55–66. Champaign, IL: Human Kinetics.

Crosset, Todd 2000. "Athletic Affiliation and Violence Against Women: Toward a Structural Prevention Project," In Jim McKay, Michael Messner and Donald Sabo (eds.), *Masculinities, Gender Relations, and Sport*: pp. 147–161. Thousand Oaks, CA: Sage.

Crosset, Todd, Jeffrey Benedict, and Mark MacDonald. 1995. "Male Student Athletes Reported for Sexual Assault: A Survey of Campus Police Departments and Judicial Affairs Offices," *Journal of Sport and Social Issues* 19: 126–140.

Curry, Tim. 1991. "Fraternal Bonding in the Locker Room: A Profeminist Analysis of Talk About Competition and Women," *Sociology of Sport Journal* 8: 2: 119–135.

Davis, Laurel. 1990. "Male Cheerleaders and the Naturalization of Gender," In Michael Messner and Donald Sabo (eds.), *Sport, Men and the Gender Order*: pp. 153–161. Champaign, IL: Human Kinetics.

Demetriou, D. Z. 2001. "Connell's Concept of Hegemonic Masculinity: A Critique," *Theory and Society* 30: 3: 337–361.

Dilorio, Judith. 1989. "Feminism, Gender, and the Ethnographic Study of Sport," *Arena Review* 13: 1: 49–59.

Eveslage, Scott, and Kevin Delaney. 1998. " 'Trash Talking' at Hardwick High: A Case Study of Insult Talk on a Boy's Basketball Team," *International Review for the Sociology of Sport* 33: 239–253.

Ewald, K., and R. M. Jiobu. 1985. "Explaining Positive Deviance: Becker's Model and the Case of Runners and Bodybuilders," *Sociology of Sport Journal* 2: 144–156.

Foucault, Michel. 1977. *Discipline and Punish: The Birth of the Prison.* New York: Vintage.

Frye, Marilyn 1999. "Some Reflections on Separatism and Power," In Janet Kourany, James Sterba and Rosemarie Tong (eds.), *Feminist Philosophies*, 2nd edn.: pp. 359–366. Upper Saddle River, NJ: Prentice Hall.

Gerdy, John. 2002. *Sports: The All American Addiction.* Jackson, MS: University Press of Mississippi.

Goffman, Erving. 1961. *Asylums: Essays on the Social Situation of Mental Patients and Other Inmates.* New York: Double Day.

Granovetter, Mark. 1983. "The Strength of Weak Ties: A Network Theory Revisited," *Sociological Theory* 1: 201–233.

Greendorfer, Susan. 1992. "A Critical Analysis of Knowledge Construction in Sport Psychology," In Thelma Horn (ed.), *Advances in Sport Psychology*: pp. 201–215. Champaign, IL: Human Kinetics.

Griffin, Pat. 1998. *Strong Women, Deep Closets: Lesbians and Homophobia in Sport.* Champaign, IL: Human Kinetics.

Gubrium, Jaber, and James Holstein. 1997. *The New Language of Qualitative Method.* New York: Oxford University Press.

Hanson, Mary Ellen. 1995. *Go! Fight! Win! Cheerleading in American Culture.* Bowling Green, OH: Bowling Green State University Popular Press.

Hargreaves, Jennifer 1993. "The Victorian Cult of the Family and the Early Years of Female Sport," In Eric Dunning, Joseph Maguire and Robert E. Pearson (eds.), *The Sports Process: A Comparative and Developmental Approach.* Champaign, IL: Human Kinetics.

Harvey, T. J., and A. Stables. 1984. "Gender Differences in Subject Preference and Perception of Subject Importance Among Third Year Secondary School Pupils in Single-Sex and Mixed Comprehensive Schools," *Educational Studies* 10: 3: 243–253.

Hekma, Gert. 1998. " 'As Long as They Don't Make an Issue of it . . .' ": Gay Men and Lesbians in Organized Sports in the Netherlands," *Journal of Homosexuality* 35: 1: 1–23.

Hughes, Robert, and Jay Coakley. 1991. "Positive Deviance Among Athletes: The Implications of Overconformity to the Sport Ethic," *Sociology of Sport Journal* 8: 4: 307–325.

Jackson, C., and J. Warren. 2000. "The Importance of Gender as an Aspect of Identity at Key Transition Points in Compulsory Education," *British Educational Research Journal* 26: 3: 375–388.

Jeziorski, Ronald. 1994. *The Importance of School Sports in American Education and Socialization.* New York: University Press of America.

Johnson, Robert. 1998. *Destined for Equality: The Inevitable Rise of Women's Status.* Cambridge, MA: Harvard University Press.

Kidd, Bruce 1990. "The Men's Cultural Center: Sports and the Dynamic of Women's Oppression/Men's Repression," In Michael Messner and Donald Sabo (eds.), *Sport, Men and the Gender Order*: pp. 31–45. Champaign IL: Human Kinetics.

Kimmel, Michael 1990. "Baseball and the Reconstitution of American Masculinity, 1880–1920," In Michael Messner and Donald Sabo (eds.), *Sport, Men and the Gender Order: Critical Feminist Perspectives*: pp. 55. Champaign, IL: Human Kinetics.

Kimmel, Michael. 1994. "Homophobia as Masculinity: Fear, Shame, and Silence in the Construction of Gender Identity," In H. Brod and M. Kaufman (eds.), *Theorizing Masculinities*: pp. 119–141. Thousand Oaks, CA: Sage.

Koss, Mary, and J. Gaines. 1993. "The Prediction of Sexual Aggression by Alcohol Use, Athletic Participation and Fraternity Affiliation," *Journal of Interpersonal Violence* 8: 94–108.

Kreager, Derek 2004. "Unnecessary Roughness? School Sports, Peer Networks, and Male Adolescent Violence," Presented at the Annual Meetings of the American Criminological Society, Nashville, TN.

Loy, John. 1995. "The Dark Side of Agon: Fratriarchies, Performative Masculinities, Sport Involvement, and the Phenomenon of Gang

Rape," In Karl Heinrich, Bette Rutten and Alfred Rutten (eds), *International Sociology of Sport: Contemporary Issues*: pp. 263–281. Stuttgart, Germany: Verlag SN.

Marsh, Herbert. 1992. "Extracurricular Activities: Beneficial Extension of the Traditional Curriculum of Subversion of Academic Goals," *Journal of Educational Psychology* 84: 553–562.

Marsh, Herbert. 1993. "The Effects of Participation in Sport During the Last Two Years of High School," *Sociology of Sport Journal* 10: 18–43.

Martin, Patricia Yancey, and David Collinson. 1999. "Gender and Sexuality in Organizations," In Myra Mars Ferree, Judith Lorber and Beth Hess (eds.), *Revisioning Gender*: pp. 285–310. Thousand Oaks, CA: Sage.

McKay, Jim. 1997. *Managing Gender: Affirmative Action and Organizational Power in Australian, Canadian, and New Zealand Sport*. Albany, NY: State University of New York Press.

McGuffey, C. Shawn, and Lindsay B. Rich. 1999. "Playing in the Gender Transgression Zone: Race, Class, and Hegemonic Masculinity in Middle Childhood," *Gender and Society* 13: 5: 608–610.

Messner, Michael. 1987. "The Meaning of Success: The Athletic Experience and the Development of Identity," In Harry Brod (ed.), *The Making of Masculinities: The New Men's Studies*: pp. 193–209. Boston: Allen and Unwin.

Messner, Michael. 1992. *Power at Play: Sports and the Problem of Masculinity*. Boston: Beacon Press.

Messner, Michael. 1997. *Politics of Masculinities: Men in Movements*. Alta Mira, CA: Alta Mira Press.

Messner, Michael. 2000. "Barbie Girls vs. Sea Monsters: Children Constructing Gender," *Gender & Society* 14: 765–784.

Messner, Michael. 2002. *Taking the Field: Women, Men and Sports*. Minneapolis, MN: University of Minnesota Press.

Miller, Kathleen, Merrill Melnick, Grace Barnes, Michael Farrell, and Don Sabo. 2005. "Untangling the Links Among Athletic Involvement, Gender, Race, and Adolescent Academic Outcomes," *Sociology of Sport Journal* 22: 2: 178–193.

Miracle, Andrew W., and C. Roger Rees. 1994. *Lessons of the Locker Room: The Myth of School Sports*. Amherst, NY: Prometheus Books.

Muir, Kenneth, and Trina Seitz. 2004. "Machismo, Misogyny, and Homophobia in a Male Athletic

Subculture: A Participant-Observation Study of Deviant Rituals in Collegiate Rugby," *Deviant Behavior* 25: 303–327.

Mullen, B., and C. Cooper. 1994. "The Relation Between Group Cohesiveness and Performance: An Integration," *Psychological Bulletin* 115: 210–227.

Nixon, Howard. 1994. "The Relationship of Friendship Networks, Sports Experiences, and Gender to Expressed Pain Thresholds," *Sociology of Sport Journal* 13: 1: 78–86.

Ohlander, Julie, Jeanne Batalova, and Judith Treas. 2005. "Explaining Educational Influences on Attitudes Toward Homosexuality," *Social Science Research* 38: 4: 781–799.

Papas, Nick, Patrick McHenry, and Beth Catlett. 2004. "Athlete Aggression on the Rink and Off the Ice," *Men and Masculinities* 6: 3: 291–312.

Plummer, David. 1999. *One of the Boys: Masculinity, Homophobia and Modern Manhood*. New York: Huntington Park Press.

Pollack, William. 1998. *Real Boys: Rescuing Our Sons From the Myths of Boyhood*. New York: Owl Books.

Pronger, Brian. 1990. *The Arena of Masculinity: Sport, Homosexuality, and the Meaning of Sex*. New York: St. Martin's Press.

Reskin, Barbara, and Patricia Roos. 1990. *Job Queues, Gender Queues. Explaining Women's Inroads into Male Occupations*. Philadelphia, PA: Temple University Press.

Robidoux, Michael. 2001. *Men at Play: A Working Understanding of Professional Hockey*. Quebec: McGill-Queen's University Press.

Rotolo, Thomas, and Amy Wharton. 2004. "Living Across Institutions: Exploring Sex-Based Homophily in Occupations and Voluntary Groups," *Sociological Perspectives* 46: 1: 59–82.

Sabo, Donald, Merrill Melnick, and B. Vanfossen. 1989. *The Women's Sports Foundation Report: Minorities in Sport*. New York: Women's Sports Foundation.

Sabo, Donald, Michael Miller, Merrill Melnick, and Leslie Heywood. 2004. *Their Lives Depend on It: Sport, Physical Activity, and the Health and Well-Being of American Girls*. East Meadow, NY: Women's Sports Foundation.

Sabo, Donald, and Joe Panepinto. 1990. "*Football Ritual and the Social Reproduction of Masculinity*," In Michael Messner and Donald Sabo (eds.), *Sport,*

Men and the Gender Order: Critical Feminist Perspectives: pp. 115–126. Champaign, IL: Human Kinetics.

Schacht, Steven P. 1996. "Misogyny On and Off the 'Pitch': The Gendered World of Male Rugby Players," *Gender & Society* 10: 550–565.

Smith, Michael. 1983. *Violence in Sport*. Toronto: Butterworths.

Stangle, Jane. 2001. "Comment's on Eric Anderson's *Trailblazing,*" *Sociology of Sport Journal* 18: 4: 471–475.

Thorne, Barrie. 1993. *Gender Play: Girls and Boys in School*. London: Rutgers University Press.

West, Candice, and Don Zimmerman. 1987. "Doing Gender," *Gender & Society* 1: 125–151.

Whitson, Dave. 1990. "Sport in the Social Construction of Masculinity," In Michael Messner and Donald Sabo (eds.), *Sport, Men and the Gender Order: Critical Feminist Perspectives*: pp. 55. Champaign, IL: Human Kinetics.

Williams, Christine 1995. *Still a Man's World: Men Who Do "Women's Work."* Berkeley, CA: University of California Press.

Wolf Wendel, Lisa, Douglas Toma, and Christopher Morphew. 2001. "How Much Difference is Too Much Difference? Perceptions of Gay Men and Lesbians in Intercollegiate Athletics," *Journal of College Student Development* 42: 5: 465–479.

Woodward, Rachel. 2000. "Warrior Heroes and Little Green Men: Soldiers, Military Training, and the Construction of Rural Masculinities," *Rural Sociology* 65: 4: 6–40.

Allan Johnson

Unraveling the Gender Knot

What is the knot we want to unravel? In one sense, it is the complexity of patriarchy as a system—the tree, from its roots to the smallest outlying twig. It is misogyny and sexist ideology that keep women in their place. It is the organization of social life around core patriarchal principles of control and domination. It is the powerful dynamic of fear and control that keeps the patriarchal engine going. But the knot is also about our individual and collective paralysis around gender issues. It is everything that prevents us from seeing patriarchy and our participation in it clearly, from the denial that patriarchy even exists to false gender parallels, individualistic thinking, and cycles of blame and guilt. Stuck in this paralysis, we can't think or act to help undo the legacy of oppression.

To undo the patriarchal knot we have to undo the knot of our paralysis in the face of it. A good place to begin is with two powerful myths about how change happens and how we can contribute to it.

Myth #1: "It's Always Been This Way, and It Always Will Be" Given thousands of years of patriarchal history, it's easy to slide into the belief that things have always been this way. Even thousands of years, however, are a far cry from what "always" implies unless we ignore the more than 90 percent of humanity's time on Earth that pre-

ceded it. Given all the archaeological evidence pointing to the existence of goddess-based civilizations and the lack of evidence for perpetual patriarchy, there are plenty of reasons to doubt that life has always been organized around male dominance or any other form of oppression. . . . So, when it comes to human social life, the smart money should be on the idea that nothing has always been this way or any other.

This should suggest that nothing *will* be this way or any other, contrary to the notion that patriarchy is here to stay. If the only thing we can count on is change, then it's hard to see why we should believe for a minute that patriarchy or any other kind of social system is permanent. Reality is always in motion. Things may appear to stand still, but that's only because we have short attention spans, limited especially by the length of a human life. If we take the long view—the *really* long view—we can see that everything is in process all the time. Some would argue that everything *is* process, the space between one point and another, the movement from one thing toward another. What we may see as permanent end points—world capitalism, Western civilization, advanced technology, and so on—are actually temporary states on the way to other temporary states. Even ecologists, who used to talk about ecological balance, now speak of ecosystems as inherently unstable. Instead of always returning to some steady state after a period of disruption, ecosystems are, by nature, a continuing process of change from one arrangement to another and never go back to just where they were.

Social systems are also fluid. A society isn't some hulking *thing* that sits there forever as it is. Because a system only happens as people participate in it, it can't help but *be* a dynamic process of creation and recreation from one moment to the next. In something as simple as a man following the path of least resistance toward controlling conversations (and a woman letting him do it), the reality of patriarchy in that moment comes into being. This is how we *do* patriarchy, bit by bit, moment by moment. It is also how individuals can contribute to change—by choosing paths of *greater* resistance, as when men resist the urge toward control and women resist their own subordination. Since we can always choose paths of greater resistance or create new ones entirely, systems can only be as stable as the flow of human choice and creativity, which certainly isn't a recipe for permanence. In the short run, patriarchy may look stable and unchangeable. But the relentless process of social life never produces the exact same result twice in a row, because it's impossible for everyone to participate in any system in an unvarying and uniform way. Added to this are the dynamic interactions that go on among systems—between capitalism and the state, for example, or between families and the economy—that also produce powerful and unavoidable tensions, contradictions, and other currents of change. Ultimately, systems can't help but change, whether we see it or not.

Oppressive systems often *seem* stable because they limit our lives and imaginations so much that we can't see beyond them. But this masks a fundamental long-term instability caused by the dynamics of oppression itself. Any system organized around control is a losing proposition because it contradicts the essentially uncontrollable nature of reality and does such violence to basic human needs and values. As the last two centuries of feminist thought and action have begun to challenge the violence and break down the denial, patriarchy has become increasingly vulnerable. This is one reason why male resistance, backlash, and defensiveness are now so intense. . . .

Patriarchy is also destabilized as the illusion of masculine control breaks down. Corporate leaders alternate between arrogant optimism and panic, while governments lurch from one crisis to another, barely managing to stay in office, much less solving major social problems such as poverty, violence, health care, middle-class angst, and the excesses of global capitalism. Computer technology supposedly makes life and work more efficient, but it does so by chaining people to an escalating pace of work and giving them less rather than more control over their lives. The loss of control in pursuit of control is happening on a larger level, as well. As the patriarchal obsession with control deepens its grip on everything from governments and corporations to schools and religion, the overall degree of control actually becomes less, not more. The scale on which systems are out of control simply increases. The stakes are higher and the capacity for harm is greater, and together they fuel an upward spiral of worry, anxiety, and fear.

As the illusion of control becomes more apparent, men start doubting their ability to measure up to patriarchal standards of manhood. We have been here before. At the turn of the twentieth century, there was widespread white male panic in the United States about the "feminization" of society and the need to preserve masculine toughness. From the creation of the Boy Scouts to Teddy Roosevelt's Rough Riders, a public campaign tried to revitalize masculinity as a cultural basis for revitalizing a male-identified society and, with it, male privilege. A century later, the masculine backlash is again in full bloom. The warrior image has re-emerged as a dominant masculine ideal, from *Rambo, Diehard*, and *Under Siege* to right-wing militia groups to corporate takeovers to regional militarism to New Age Jungian archetypes in the new men's movement.[1]

Neither patriarchy nor any other system will last forever. Patriarchy is riddled with internal contradiction and strain. It is based on the false and self-defeating assumption that control is the answer to everything and that the pursuit of more control is always better than contenting ourselves with less. The transformation of patriarchy has been unfolding ever since it emerged seven thousand years ago, and it is going on still. We can't know what will replace it, but we can be confident that patriarchy will go, that it *is* going at every moment. It's only a matter of how quickly, by what means, and toward what alternatives, and whether each of us will do our part to make it happen sooner rather than later and with less rather than more human suffering in the process.

Myth #2: The Myth of No Effect and Gandhi's Paradox   Whether we help change patriarchy depends on how we handle the belief that nothing we do can make a difference, that the system is too big and powerful for us to affect it. In one sense the complaint is valid: if we look at patriarchy as a whole, it's true that we aren't going to make it go away in our lifetime. But if changing the entire system through our own efforts is the standard against which we measure the ability to do something, then we've set ourselves up to feel powerless. It's not unreasonable to want to make a difference, but if we have to see the final result of what we do, then we can't be part of change that's too gradual and long term to allow that. We also can't be part of change that's so complex that we can't sort out our contribution from countless others that combine in ways we can never grasp. Problems like patriarchy are of just that sort, requiring complex and long-term change coupled with short-term work to soften some of its worst consequences. This means that if we're going to be part of the solution to such problems, we have to let go of the idea that change doesn't happen unless we're around to see it happen and that what we do matters only if we make it happen. In other words, if we free ourselves of the expectation of being in control of things, we free ourselves to act and participate in the kind of fundamental change that transforms social life.

To get free of the paralyzing myth that we cannot, individually, be effective, we have to change how we see ourselves in relation to a long-term, complex process of change. This begins by changing how we relate to time. Many changes can come about quickly enough for us to see them happen. When I was in college, for example, there was little talk about gender inequality as a social problem, whereas now there are women's studies programs all over the country. But a goal like ending gender oppression takes more than this and far more time than our short lives can encompass. If we're going to see ourselves as part of that kind of change, we can't use the human life span as a significant standard against which to measure progress. . . .

[W]e need to get clear about how our choices matter and how they don't. Gandhi once said that nothing we do as individuals matters, but that it's vitally important that we do it anyway. This touches on a powerful paradox in the relationship between society and individuals. In terms of the patriarchy-as-tree metaphor, no individual leaf on the tree matters; whether it lives or dies has no effect on much of anything. But collectively, the leaves are essential to the whole tree because they photosynthesize the sugar that feeds it. Without leaves, the tree dies. So, leaves both matter and they don't, just as we matter and we don't. What each of us does may not seem like much, because in important ways, it *isn't* much. But when many people do this work together, they can form a critical mass that is anything but insignificant, especially in the long run. If we're going to be part of a larger change process, we have to learn to live with this sometimes uncomfortable paradox rather than going back and forth between momentary illusions of potency and control and feelings of helpless despair and insignificance.

A related paradox is that we have to be willing to travel without knowing where we're going. We need faith to do what seems right without necessarily knowing the effect that will have. We have to think like pioneers who may know the *direction* they want to move in or what they would like to find, without knowing where they will wind up. Because they are going where they've never been before, they can't know whether they will ever arrive at anything they might consider a destination, much less what they had in mind when they first set out. If pioneers had to know their destination from the beginning, they would never go anywhere or discover anything. In similar ways, to seek out alternatives to patriarchy, it has to be enough to move *away* from social life organized around dominance and control and to move *toward* the certainty that alternatives are possible, even though we may not have a clear idea of what those are or ever experience them ourselves. It has to be enough to question how we think about and experience different forms of power, for example, how we see ourselves as gendered people, how oppression works and how we participate in it, and then open ourselves to experience what happens next. When we dare ask core questions about who we are and how the world works, things happen that we can't foresee; but they don't happen unless we *move*, if only in our minds. As pioneers, we discover what's possible only by first putting ourselves in motion, because we have to move in order to change our position—and hence our perspective—on where we are, where we've been and where we *might* go. This is how alternatives begin to appear: to imagine how things might be, we first have to get past the idea that things will always be the way they are.

In relation to Gandhi's paradox, the myth of no effect obscures the role we can play in the long-term transformation of patriarchy. But the myth also blinds us to our own power in relation to other people. We may cling to the belief that there is nothing we can do precisely because we know how much power we do have and are afraid to use it because people may not like it. If we deny our power to affect people, then we don't have to worry about taking responsibility for how we use it or, more significant, how we don't. This reluctance to acknowledge and use power comes up in the simplest everyday situations, as when a group of friends starts laughing at a sexist joke and we have to decide whether to go along. It's a moment in a sea of countless such moments that constitutes the fabric of all kinds of oppressive systems. It is a crucial moment, because the group's seamless response to the joke reaffirms

the normalcy and unproblematic nature of it and the sexism behind it. It takes only one person to tear the fabric of collusion and apparent consensus. . . .

Our power to affect other people isn't simply about making them feel uncomfortable. Systems shape the choices that people make primarily by providing paths of least resistance. We typically follow those paths because alternatives offer greater resistance or because we aren't even aware that alternatives exist. Whenever we openly choose a different path, however, we make it possible for people to see both the path of least resistance they're following and the possibility of choosing something else. This is both radical and simple. When most people get on an elevator, for example, they turn and face front without ever thinking why. We might think it's for purely practical reasons—the floor indicators and the door we'll exit through are at the front. But there's more going on than that, as we'd discover if we simply walked to the rear wall and stood facing it while everyone else faced front. The oddness of what we were doing would immediately be apparent to everyone, and would draw their attention and perhaps make them uncomfortable as they tried to figure out why we were doing that. Part of the discomfort is simply calling attention to the fact that we make choices when we enter social situations and that there are alternatives, something that paths of least resistance discourage us from considering. If the possibility of alternatives in situations as simple as where to stand in elevator cars can make people feel uncomfortable, imagine the potential for discomfort when the stakes are higher, as they certainly are when it comes to how people participate in oppressive systems like patriarchy.

If we choose different paths, we usually won't know if we affect other people, but it's safe to assume that we do. When people know that alternatives exist and witness other people choosing them, things become possible that weren't before. When we openly pass up a path of least resistance, we *increase* resistance for other people around that path because now they must reconcile their choice with what they've seen us do, something they didn't have to deal with before. There's no way to predict how this will play out in the long run, and certainly no good reason to think it won't make a difference.

The simple fact is that we affect one another all the time without knowing it. . . . This suggests that the simplest way to help others make different choices is to make them myself, and to do it openly so they can see what I'm doing. As I shift the patterns of my own participation in patriarchy, I make it easier for others to do so as well, *and harder for them not to.* Simply by setting an example—rather than trying to change them—I create the possibility of their participating in change in their own time and in their own way. In this way I can widen the circle of change without provoking the kind of defensiveness that perpetuates paths of least resistance and the oppressive systems they serve.

It's important to see that in doing this kind of work we don't have to go after people to change their minds. In fact, changing people's minds may play a relatively small part in changing systems like patriarchy. We won't succeed in turning diehard misogynists into practicing feminists. At most, we can shift the odds in favor of new paths that contradict core patriarchal values. We can introduce so many exceptions to patriarchal rules that the children or grandchildren of diehard misogynists will start to change their perception of which paths offer the least resistance. Research on men's changing attitudes toward the male provider role, for example, shows that most of the shift occurs *between* generations, not within them.[2] This suggests that rather than trying to change people, the most important thing we can do is contribute to the slow sea change of entire cultures so that patriarchal forms and values begin to lose their "obvious" legitimacy and normalcy and new forms emerge to challenge their privileged place in social life.

In science, this is how one paradigm replaces another.[3] For hundreds of years, for example, Europeans believed that the stars, planets, and sun revolved around Earth. But scientists such as Copernicus and Galileo found that too many of their astronomical observations were anomalies that didn't fit the prevailing paradigm: if the sun and planets revolved around Earth, then they wouldn't move as they did. As such observations accumulated, they made it increasingly difficult to hang on to an Earth-centered paradigm. Eventually the anomalies became so numerous that Copernicus offered a new paradigm, for which he, and later Galileo, were persecuted as heretics. Eventually, however, the evidence was so overwhelming that a new paradigm replaced the old one.

In similar ways, we can think of patriarchy as a system based on a paradigm that shapes how we think about gender and how we organize social life in relation to it. The patriarchal paradigm has been under attack for several centuries and the defense has been vigorous, with feminists widely regarded as heretics who practice the blasphemy of "male bashing." The patriarchal paradigm weakens in the face of mounting evidence that it doesn't work, and that it produces unacceptable consequences not only for women but, increasingly, for men as well. We help to weaken it by openly choosing alternative paths in our everyday lives and thereby providing living anomalies that don't fit the prevailing paradigm. By our example, we contradict patriarchal assumptions and their legitimacy over and over again. We add our choices and our lives to tip the scales toward new paradigms that don't revolve around control and oppression. We can't tip the scales overnight or by ourselves, and in that sense we don't amount to much. But on the other side of Gandhi's paradox, it is crucial where we "choose to place the stubborn ounces of [our] weight."[4] It is in such small and humble choices that patriarchy and the movement toward something better actually happen.

Stubborn Ounces: What Can We Do?

What can we do about patriarchy that will make a difference? I don't have the answers, but I do have some suggestions.

Acknowledge That Patriarchy Exists

A key to the continued existence of every oppressive system is people being unaware of what's going on, because oppression contradicts so many basic human values that it invariably arouses opposition when people know about it. The Soviet Union and its East European satellites, for example, were riddled with contradictions that were so widely known among their people that the oppressive regimes fell apart with barely a whimper when given half a chance. An awareness of oppression compels people to speak out, breaking the silence on which continued oppression depends. This is why most oppressive cultures mask the reality of oppression by denying its existence, trivializing it, calling it something else, blaming it on those most victimized by it, or drawing attention away from it to other things. . . .

It's one thing to become aware and quite another to stay that way. The greatest challenge when we first become aware of a critical perspective on the world is simply to hang on to it. Every system's paths of least resistance invariably lead *away* from critical awareness of how the system works. Therefore, the easiest thing to do after reading a book like this is to forget about it. Maintaining a critical consciousness takes commitment and work; awareness is something we either maintain in the moment or we don't. And the only way to hang on to an awareness of patriarchy is to make paying attention to it an ongoing part of our lives.

Pay Attention

Understanding how patriarchy works and how we participate in it is essential for change. It's easy to have opinions; it takes work to know what we're talking about. The easiest place to begin is by reading, and making reading about patriarchy part of our lives. Unless we have the luxury of a personal teacher, we can't understand patriarchy without reading, just as we need to read about a foreign country before we travel there for the first time, or about a car before we try to work under the hood. Many people assume they already know what they need to know about gender since everyone has a gender, but they're usually wrong. Just as the last thing a fish would discover is water, the last thing we'll discover is society itself and something as pervasive as gender dynamics. We have to be open to the idea that what we think we know about gender is, if not wrong, so deeply shaped by patriarchy that it misses most of the truth. This is why feminists talk with one another and spend time reading one another's work—seeing things clearly is tricky business and hard work. This is also why people who are critical of the status quo are so often self-critical as well: they know how complex and elusive the truth really is and what a challenge it is to work toward it. People working for change are often accused of being orthodox and rigid, but in practice they are typically among the most self-critical people around. . . .

Reading, though, is only a beginning. At some point we have to look at ourselves and the world to see if we can identify what we're reading about. Once the phrase "paths of least resistance" entered my active vocabulary, for example, I started seeing them all over the place. Among other things, I started to see how easily I'm drawn to asserting control as a path of least resistance in all kinds of situations. Ask me a question, for example, and the easiest thing for me to do is offer an answer whether or not I know what I'm talking about. "Answering" is a more comfortable mode, an easier path, than admitting I don't know or have nothing to say.[5] The more aware I am of how powerful this path is, the more I can decide whether to go down it each time it presents itself. As a result, I listen more, think more, and talk less than I used to. . . .

Little Risks: Do Something

The more we pay attention to what's going on, the more we will see opportunities to do something about it. We don't have to mount an expedition to find those opportunities; they're all over the place, beginning in ourselves. As I became aware of how I gravitated toward controlling conversations, for example, I also realized how easily men dominate group meetings by controlling the agenda and interrupting, without women objecting to it. This pattern is especially striking in groups that are mostly female but in which most of the talking nonetheless comes from a few men. I would find myself sitting in meetings and suddenly the preponderance of male voices would jump out at me, an unmistakable hallmark of male privilege in full bloom. As I've seen what's going on, I've had to decide what to do about this little path of least resistance and my relation to it that leads me to follow it so readily. With some effort, I've tried out new ways of listening more and talking less. At times it's felt contrived and artificial, like telling myself to shut up for a while or even counting slowly to ten (or more) to give others a chance to step into the space afforded by silence. With time and practice, new paths have become easier to follow and I spend less time monitoring myself. But awareness is never automatic or permanent, for patriarchal paths of least resistance will be there to choose or not as long as patriarchy exists.

As we see more of what's going on, questions come up about what goes on at work, in the media, in families, in communities, in religion, in government, on the street, and at school—in short, just about everywhere. The questions don't come all at once (for which we can be grateful), although they sometimes come in a rush that can feel overwhelming. If we remind ourselves that it isn't up to us to do it all, however, we can see plenty of situations in which we can make a difference, sometimes in surprisingly simple ways. Consider the following possibilities:

• *Make noise, be seen.* Stand up, volunteer, speak out, write letters, sign petitions, show up. Like every oppressive system, patriarchy feeds on silence. Don't collude in silence. . . .

• *Find little ways to withdraw support from paths of least resistance and people's choices to follow them, starting with ourselves.* It can be as simple as not laughing at a sexist joke or saying we don't think it's funny; or writing a letter to the editor objecting to sexism in the media. . . .

• *Dare to make people feel uncomfortable, beginning with ourselves.* At the next local school board

meeting, for example, we can ask why principals and other administrators are almost always men (unless your system is an exception that proves the rule), while the teachers they control are mostly women. Consider asking the same thing about church, workplaces, or local government. . . .

It may seem that such actions don't amount to much until we stop for a moment and feel our resistance to doing them—our worry, for example, about how easily we could make people feel uncomfortable, including ourselves. If we take that resistance to action as a measure of power, then our potential to make a difference is plain to see. The potential for people to feel uncomfortable is a measure of the power for change inherent in such simple acts of not going along with the status quo.

Some will say that it isn't "nice" to make people uncomfortable, but oppressive systems like patriarchy do a lot more than make people feel uncomfortable, and it certainly isn't "nice" to allow them to continue unchallenged. Besides, discomfort is an unavoidable part of any meaningful process of education. We can't grow without being willing to challenge our assumptions and take ourselves to the edge of our competencies, where we're bound to feel uncomfortable. If we can't tolerate ambiguity, uncertainty, and discomfort, then we'll never go beneath the superficial appearance of things or learn or change anything of much value, including ourselves.

• *Openly choose and model alternative paths.* As we identify paths of least resistance—such as women being held responsible for child care and other domestic work—we can identify alternatives and then follow them openly so that other people can see what we're doing. Patriarchal paths become more visible when people choose alternatives, just as rules become more visible when someone breaks them. Modeling new paths creates tension in a system which moves toward resolution. . . .

• *Actively promote change in how systems are organized around patriarchal values and male privilege.* There are almost endless possibilities here because social life is complicated and patriarchy is everywhere. We can, for example,

—Speak out for equality in the workplace.

—Promote diversity awareness and training.

—Support equal pay and promotion for women.

—Oppose the devaluing of women and the work they do, from the dead-end jobs most women are stuck in to the glass ceilings that keep women out of top positions.

—Support the well-being of mothers and children and defend women's right to control their bodies and their lives.

—Object to the punitive dismantling of welfare and attempts to limit women's access to reproductive health services.

—Speak out against violence and harassment against women wherever they occur, whether at home, at work, or on the street.

—Support government and private support services for women who are victimized by male violence.

—Volunteer at the local rape crisis center or battered women's shelter.

—Call for and support clear and effective sexual harassment policies in workplaces, unions, schools, professional associations, churches, and political parties, as well as public spaces such as parks, sidewalks, and malls.

—Join and support groups that intervene with and counsel violent men.

—Object to theaters and video stores that carry violent pornography. . . .

—Ask questions about how work, education, religion, family, and other areas of family life are shaped by core patriarchal values and principles. . . .

• *Because the persecution of gays and lesbians is a linchpin of patriarchy, support the right of women and men to love whomever they choose*. Raise awareness of homophobia and heterosexism. . . .

• *Because patriarchy is rooted in principles of domination and control, pay attention to racism and other forms of oppression that draw from those same roots*. . . .

[P]atriarchy isn't problematic just because it emphasizes *male* dominance, but because it promotes dominance and control as ends in themselves. In that sense, all forms of oppression draw support from common roots, and whatever we do that draws attention to those roots undermines *all* forms of oppression. If working against patriarchy is seen simply as enabling some women to get a bigger piece of the pie, then some women probably will "succeed" at the expense of others who are disadvantaged by race, class, ethnicity, and other characteristics. . . . [I]f we identify the core problem as *any* society organized around principles of control and domination, then changing *that* requires us to pay attention to all of the forms of oppression those principles promote. Whether we begin with race or gender or ethnicity or class, if we name the problem correctly, we'll wind up going in the same general direction.

• *Work with other people.* This is one of the most important principles of participating in social change. From expanding consciousness to taking risks, it makes all the difference in the world to be in the company of people who support what we are trying to do. We can read and talk about books and issues and just plain hang out with other people who want to understand and do something about patriarchy. Remember that the modern women's movement's roots were in consciousness-raising groups in which women did little more than sit around and talk about themselves and their lives and try to figure out what that had to do with living in patriarchy. It may not have looked like much at the time, but it laid the foundation for huge social movements. One way down this path is to share a book like this one with someone and then talk about it. Or ask around about local groups and organizations that focus on gender issues, and go find out what they're about and meet other people. . . . Make contact; connect to other people engaged in the same work; do whatever reminds us that we aren't alone in this.

• *Don't keep it to ourselves.* A corollary of looking for company is not to restrict our focus to the tight little circle of our own lives. It isn't enough to work out private solutions to social problems like patriarchy and other forms of oppression and keep them to ourselves. It isn't enough to clean up our own acts and then walk away, to find ways to avoid the worst consequences of patriarchy at home and inside ourselves and think that's taking responsibility. Patriarchy and oppression aren't personal problems and they can't be solved through personal solutions. At some point, taking responsibility means acting in a larger context, even if that means just letting one other person know what we're doing. It makes sense to start with ourselves; but it's equally important not to *end* with ourselves.

If all of this sounds overwhelming, remember again that we don't have to deal with everything. We don't have to set ourselves the impossible task of letting go of everything or transforming patriarchy or even ourselves. All we can do is what *we* can *manage* to do, secure in the knowledge that we're making it easier for other people—now and in the future—to see and do what *they* can do. So, rather than defeat ourselves before we start:

- *Think small, humble, and doable rather than large, heroic, and impossible.* Don't paralyze yourself with impossible expectations. It takes very little to make a difference. . . .
- *Don't let other people set the standard for us. Start where we are and work from there. . . . set reasonable goals* ("What small risk for change

will I take *today?*"). As we get more experienced at taking risks, we can move up our lists. . . .

In the end, taking responsibility doesn't have to be about guilt and blame, about letting someone off the hook or being on the hook ourselves. It is simply to acknowledge our obligation to make a contribution to finding a way out of patriarchy, and to find constructive ways to act on that obligation. We don't have to do anything dramatic or Earth-shaking to help change happen. As powerful as patriarchy is, like all oppressive systems, it cannot stand the strain of lots of people doing something about it, beginning with the simplest act of speaking its name out loud.

Notes

1. See James William Gibson, *Warrior Dreams: Violence and Manhood in Post-Vietnam America* (New York: Hill and Wang, 1994).

2. J. R. Wilkie, "Changes in U.S. Men's Attitudes Towards the Family Provider Role, 1972–1989." *Gender & Society* 7, no. 2 (1993): 261–279.

3. The classic statement of how this happens is by Thomas S. Kuhn, *The Structure of Scientific Revolutions* (Chicago: University of Chicago Press, 1970).

4. This is a line from a poem by Bonaro Overstreet that was given to me by a student many years ago. I have not been able to locate the source.

5. Or, as someone once said to me about a major corporation that valued creative thinking, "It's not OK to say you don't know the answer to a question here."

CONTRIBUTORS

SINE ANAHITA is an assistant professor of sociology and women's studies at the University of Alaska Fairbanks. She is particularly interested in issues of gender, sexuality, and rurality, especially as these are shaped in Alaska and the circumpolar North. Other current work focuses on structural water inequalities in Alaska.

ERIC ANDERSON is an American sociologist at the University of Bath, in England. He is well known for his research on sport, masculinities, sexualities, and homophobia. Dr. Anderson is the foremost researcher on the relationship between gay male athletes and sport. He has authored several books and peer-reviewed articles, including the award-winning *In the Game: Gay Athletes and the Cult of Masculinity*. His forthcoming book, *Inclusive Masculinities*, examines the changing nature of men's gendered behaviors. His autobiography, *Trailblazing: America's First Openly Gay High School Coach*, has been widely acclaimed.

TIM BENEKE is a freelance writer and editor living in the San Francisco Bay Area. He is the author of *Men on Rape* and *Proving Manhood*.

GREG BORTNICHAK will soon graduate from college and put his barista days behind him. He plays guitar and cello in his band, "The Sparta Philharmonic." This article originally appeared in *Men Speak Out: Views on Gender, Sex, and Power*, ed. Shira Tarrant (Routledge, 2008).

ROCCO L. (CHIP) CAPRARO, Senior Associate Dean and Assistant Professor of History, is the founding coordinator of the men's studies program and founding director of the rape prevention education program for men at Hobart and William Smith Colleges, Geneva, New York. He received his B.A. from Colgate University and his Ph.D. from Washington University, and is a consultant and public speaker in the areas of gender and diversity, with an emphasis on masculinity, and is currently writing a brief history of rock and roll from a men's studies perspective.

MONICA J. CASPER is Professor of Social and Behavioral Sciences and Director of Humanities, Arts, and Cultural Studies at Arizona State University's New

College of Interdisciplinary Arts and Sciences. She is co-author of *Missing Bodies: The Politics of Visibility*, author of *The Making of the Unborn Patient: A Social Anatomy of Fetal Surgery*, and editor of *Synthetic Planet: Chemical Politics and the Hazards of Modern Life*. With Lisa Jean Moore, she co-edits the NYU Press series *Biopolitics*.

BETH SKILKEN CATLETT is Assistant Professor of Women's Studies at DePaul University. She received her doctorate from the Ohio State University, where her studies focused on feminist approaches to studying families. She has been particularly interested in applying a feminist paradigm to understanding male aggression.

SCOTT COLTRANE is Dean of the College of Arts and Sciences, University of Oregon. His research focuses on families, gender, and social inequality.

ANGELA COWAN is a postgraduate student in the Department of Sociology at the University of Newcastle. Her thesis topic is an investigation of the discursive world of young children. She is a trained primary school teacher and has worked as an observer on a number of psychiatric research projects.

JULIA O'CONNELL DAVIDSON is Professor of Sociology at the University of Nottingham in the United Kingdom with a focus on gender, race, class and global inequalities, and contract, employment relations, selfhood, and human rights. She has conducted studies of entrepreneurial prostitution, sex tourism, and children's involvement in the global sex trade.

BARRY DEUTSCH lives in Portland, Oregon, in a bright blue house with pink trim, which is kept filled with housemates, children, and cats. Barry is a graduate of Portland State University, where he studied women's studies and economics. At PSU, Barry created a political comic strip for the student newspaper, which went on to win two Oregon Newspaper Publisher's Association awards, as well as the national Charles M. Schulz award, given once each year to the nation's best college cartoonist. Barry's political cartoons appear in the economics magazine

Dollars and Sense. Barry's graphic novel *Hereville*, about the adventures of a kick-ass 11-year-old Orthodox Jewish girl who wants to fight dragons, will be published by Abrams in 2010. *The Washington Post* described "Hereville" as what happens when "Buffy the Vampire Slayer" is crossed with Isaac Bashevis Singer. Barry's blog and links to Barry's comics can be found at www.amptoons.com.

FRANCINE M. DEUTSCH is Professor of Psychology at Mount Holyoke College, and the author of *Halving It All: How Equality Shared Parenting Works* (1999, Harvard University Press), a study of the division of domestic labor among dual-earner couples. Her articles on gender and the family have been published in *Journal of Personality* and *Social Psychology, Psychology of Women Quarterly, Sex Roles, Journal of Family Issues,* and *Current Directions in Psychology.* Her most recent research examines the gendered life plans of Chinese college seniors in the People's Republic of China, and plans for egalitarian marriage among graduating college seniors in the United States.

CYNTHIA ENLOE is Research Professor at Clark University. Among her recent books are *Maneuvers: The International Politics of Militarizing Women's Lives; Curious Feminist: Searching for Women in a New Age of Empire;* and *Globalization and Militarism: Feminists Make the Link.*

YEN LE ESPIRITU is Professor of Ethnic Studies at the University of California, San Diego. She is the author of *Asian American Panethnicity: Bridging Institutions and Identities, Filipino American Lives,* and *Asian American Women and Men: Labor, Laws, and Love.* She is also serving as the President of the Association of Asian American Studies.

JULES FEIFFER is a syndicated cartoonist and was a regular contributor to *The Village Voice.*

ANN FERGUSON is Assistant Professor of Women's Studies and African American Studies at Smith College. She received her Ph.D. in Sociology from the University of California at Berkeley.

JAMES GILLIGAN has been on the faculty of the Department of Psychiatry at the Harvard Medical School since 1966, for whom he directed mental health services for the Massachusetts prison system for many years; and is Director of the Center for the Study of Violence, Immediate Past President of the International Association for Forensic Psychother-

apy, author of *Violence: Reflections on a National Epidemic* and *Preventing Violence,* and a member of the Academic Advisory Council of the National Campaign Against Youth Violence.

PEGGY C. GIORDANO is a distinguished research professor of sociology at Bowling Green State University. Her research centers on basic social network processes, including friendships and dating relationships, and the ways in which these influence a variety of developmental outcomes, especially adolescent sexual behavior and delinquency involvement.

DAVID GRAZIAN is Associate Professor of Sociology at the University of Pennsylvania, and the author of *Blue Chicago: The Search for Authenticity in Urban Blues Clubs* (University of Chicago Press, 2003) and *On the Make: The Hustle of Urban Nightlife* (University of Chicago Press, 2008). His research interests broadly include the sociology of culture, urban sociology, social interaction, ethnographic methods, and social theory. He is currently writing a textbook on the sociology of popular culture.

CHONG-SUK HAN is an Assistant Professor of Sociology (Teaching/Instructional) at Temple University. His research focuses on the intersection of race, gender, and sexuality, particularly among gay Asian American men. His publications have appeared in a number of journals including *Sexuality and Culture, Social Identities, AIDS Education and Prevention,* and *Contemporary Justice Review,* among others. In 2006, he was the recipient of the Martin Levine Dissertation Award from the Sexualities Section of the American Sociological Association.

SHAUN R. HARPER is an Assistant Professor and Research Associate in the Center for the Study of Higher Education at The Pennsylvania State University.

KEVIN D. HENSON is Associate Professor of Sociology at Loyola University Chicago. He is the author of *Just a Temp* (1996) and co-editor of *Unusual Occupations* (2000). His research focuses on gender and nonstandard employment. He has written about the role of clerical temporary employment in recreating racial and gender inequalities, and is currently working on a project on traveling nurses.

ROBERT JENSEN is a journalism professor at the University of Texas at Austin and board member of the Third Coast Activist Resource Center. His latest book, *All My Bones Shakee,* will be published in 2009 by Soft Skull Press. He also is the author of *Getting Off: Pornography and the End of Masculinity* (South End Press, 2007); *The Heart of Whiteness: Confronting Race, Racism and White Privilege* (City Lights, 2005); *Citizens of the Empire: The Struggle to Claim Our Humanity* (City Lights, 2004); and *Writing Dissent: Taking Radical Ideas from the Margins to the Mainstream* (Peter Lang, 2002). Jensen can be reached at rjensen@uts.cc.utexas.edu and his articles can be found online at http://uts.cc.utexas.edu/~rjensen/index.html.

DAPHNE JOHN is associate professor and chair of the department of sociology at Oberlin College. Her teaching and research focuses on issues related to work and family, and gender stratification.

ALLAN G. JOHNSON is a writer, teacher, and public speaker who has worked on issues of privilege, oppression, and social inequality since receiving his Ph.D. in sociology from the University of Michigan in 1972. After almost 30 years of college teaching, he now devotes himself entirely to writing and public speaking. His books include *The Forest and the Trees,* 2nd ed. (2008), *The Blackwell Dictionary of Sociology,* 2nd ed. (2000), *The Gender Knot,* rev. ed. (2005), and *Privilege, Power, and Difference,* 2nd ed. (2005). His work has been translated into several languages and excerpted in numerous anthologies. For more information or to contact him, go to www.agjohnson.us

ELLEN JORDAN is Senior Lecturer in the Department of Sociology at the University of Newcastle. She was for many years a teacher in primary schools. Her major research interests are women's work in nineteenth-century Britain and gender construction in early childhood.

EMILY W. KANE is the Whitehouse Professor of Sociology, and a member of the Program in Women and Gender Studies, at Bates College in Lewiston, Maine. Much of her research focuses on beliefs about gender inequality, including quantitative analysis of such beliefs in the United States and cross-nationally, and on gender and parenting. She is currently working on a book based on the qualitative interview data included in her article within this collection. She is also interested in community engagement, teaching courses and working on research that addresses the intersections of social inequality, public sociology, and community-based research.

JACKSON KATZ is co-founder of the mixed-gender, racially diverse Mentors in Violence Prevention (MVP) program, the leading gender violence prevention initiative in college and professional athletics. He is the creator and co-creator of educational videos including "Tough Guise" (2000), "Wrestling With Manhood" (2002), and "Spin the Bottle" (2004). His book *The Macho Paradox: Why Some Men Hurt Women and How All Men Can Help* was published by Sourcebooks in 2006. He lectures widely in the United States and internationally about masculinities, media, and violence.

MICHAEL S. KIMMEL is Professor of Sociology at SUNY at Stony Brook. His books include *Changing Men* (1987), *Men Confront Pornography* (1990), *Men in the United States* (1992), *Manhood in America* (1996), *The Politics of Manhood* (1996), *The Gendered Society* (2000), and *Guyland* (2008). He is the editor of *Men and Masculinities,* a scholarly journal, and national spokesperson for the National Organization for Men Against Sexism (NOMAS).

PAUL KIVEL is a trainer, activist, writer, and a violence prevention educator. He is the author of several books including *Men's Work, Uprooting Racism,* and *Boys Will Be Men.* He is also co-author of several widely used curricula including Making the Peace, Young Men's Work, and Young Women's Lives. His newest book is *You Call This a Democracy? Who Benefits, Who Pays, and Who Really Decides.* He can be reached at pkivel@mindspring.com, or at www.paulkivel.com.

BARBARA KRUGER is an artist in New York City.

THOMAS J. LINNEMAN is Associate Professor and Chair of Sociology at The College of William and Mary. His research interests include sexualities, masculinities, the media, religion, and social change. He is the author of *Weathering Change: Gays and Lesbians, Christian Conservatives, and Everyday Hostilities* (New York University Press, 2003), as well as "How Do You Solve a Problem Like Will Truman? The Feminization of Gay Masculinities on Will & Grace" (*Men and Masculinities,* 2008).

MEIKA LOE is Assistant Professor of Sociology and Women's Studies at Colgate University in New York. She is the author of *The Rise of Viagra: How the Little Blue Pill Changed Sex in America,* NYU Press, 2004.

MONICA A. LONGMORE is a professor of sociology at Bowling Green State University. Her interests include social psychological processes, including the nature and consequences of dimensions of the self-concept, especially the impact of self-conceptions on adolescent dating and sexual behavior.

PETER LYMAN was University Dean of Libraries at the University of California, Berkeley.

WENDY D. MANNING is a professor of sociology at Bowling Green State University and director of the Center for Family and Demographic Research. Her research focuses on relationships that exist outside the boundaries of marriage, including cohabitation, adolescent dating, and nonresident parenting.

MARTHA MCCAUGHEY is Professor of Women's Studies and Sociology at Appalachian State University. Her work examines the body, gender, science, technology, and popular culture. She is most recently the author of *The Caveman Mystique: Pop-Darwinism and the Debates Over Sex, Violence, and Science* (Routledge, 2008).

PATRICK MCKENRY is a professor of Human Development and Family Science at the Ohio State University. He received his doctorate from the University of Tennessee in Child and Family Studies. His research has focused on family conflict, including domestic violence. He has published over 100 journal articles and book chapters.

MICHAEL A. MESSNER is Professor of Sociology and Gender Studies at the University of Southern California. He is co-editor of *Through the Prism of Difference: Readings on Sex and Gender* (1997). His books include *Power at Play: Sports and the Problem of Masculinity* (1992), and *Politics of Masculinities: Men in Movements* (1997).

ALFREDO MIRANDE is Professor of Sociology and Ethnic Studies at the University of California, Riverside. He is the author of *The Age of Crisis, la Chicana, The Chicano Experience,* and *Gringo Justice.*

TAMARA L. MIX is an assistant professor of sociology at Oklahoma State University. Her interests include environmental sociology, inequality, and social movements. Current projects focus on issues of environmental and social justice and involve an analysis of stakeholders in Alaska's predator control program and studies of communities affected by environmental hazards.

JEFFREY MONTEZ DE OCA is a doctoral candidate in sociology at the University of Southern California. He teaches classical and contemporary theory as well as media analysis. His dissertation examines postwar physical education and American football's relation to cold war masculinities.

LISA JEAN MOORE, Professor of Sociology and Women's Studies at Purchase College SUNY, is the co-author of "Missing Bodies: The Politics of Visibility." She has also written *Sperm Counts: Overcome by Man's Most Precious Fluid* (NYU Press 2007) and *Gendered Bodies* co-written with Judith Lorber (Oxford University Press 2007). Other work appears in journals such as *Hypatia, Feminist Studies, Body and Society, Social Text,* and *Men and Masculinities.*

PETER M. NARDI is Professor of Sociology at Pitzer College. He has published articles on AIDS, anti-gay crimes and violence, magic and magicians, and alcoholism and families. His books include *Men's Friendships* (1993) and *Growing Up Before Stonewall* (1994), with David Sanders and Judd Marmor. He has served as co-president of the Los Angeles chapter of the Gay and Lesbian Alliance Against Defamation.

MARK ANTHONY NEAL is the author of four books, *What the Music Said: Black Popular Music and Black Public Culture* (1998), *Soul Babies: Black Popular Culture and the Post-Soul Aesthetic* (2002), *Songs in the Keys of Black Life: A Rhythm and Blues Nation* (2003), and *New Black Man: Rethinking Black Masculinity* (2005). Neal is also the co-editor (with Murray Forman) of *That's the Joint!: The Hip-Hop Studies Reader* (2004). Neal is Professor of Black Popular Culture in the Department of African and African American Studies at Duke University.

DAVID NYLUND is a doctoral student in cultural studies at the University of California, Davis, and an assistant professor of social work at California State University, Sacramento. He is the author of *Treating Huckleberry Finn: A New Narrative Approach with Kids Diagnosed ADHD/ADD* (Jossey-Bass, 2000).

NICK T. PAPPAS is a graduate of the Ohio State University in Human Development and Family Science. He is a former professional hockey player and coach and former adjunct professor at Indiana University of Pennsylvania. Dr. Pappas is the founder of Personal & Athletic Solutions, working as a motivational speaker and personal life coach (www.drnickpappas.com).

C. J. PASCOE is completing a dissertation entitled, "'Dude, You're a Fag': Masculinity in High School," about the social construction of masculinity in adolescence among both boys and girls.

BETH A. QUINN is an Associate Professor in the Department of Sociology at Montana State University-Bozeman. She received her Ph.D. in Criminology, Law, and Society from the University of California-Irvine. Drawing primarily on feminist and masculinity theories and neo-institutional organizational theory, her research focuses on legal complaint-making and discrimination law. This research has been published in journals such as *Law and Social Inquiry* and *Gender & Society*. She is currently exploring how human resources understand and deal with sexual harassment law.

M. ROCHLIN is the creator of "The Heterosexual Questionnaire."

JACKIE KRASAS ROGERS'S research interests include gender and racial inequality in work and employment. She explores issues of inequality and employment in her book entitled, *Temps: The Many Faces of the Changing Workplace*. The book documents and analyzes the experiences both of temporary clerical workers and temporary lawyers. Presently, Professor Rogers is working as part of an interdisciplinary research team funded by the National Science Foundation to investigate the underrepresentation of women in the information technology field. Her work has appeared in *Gender & Society* and *Work & Occupations*.

DON SABO is a Professor of Social Sciences at D'Youville College in Buffalo, New York. He has co-authored *Humanism in Sociology, Jock: Sports & Male Identity*, and *Sport, Men and the Gender Order: Critical Feminist Perspectives*. His most recent books include, *Sex, Violence and Power in Sports: Rethinking Masculinity*, and *Men's Health & Illness: Gender, power & the Body*. He has conducted many national surveys on gender issues in sport, is a trustee of the Women's Sports Foundation, and co-authored the 1997 Presidents' Council on Physical Fitness and Sports report "Physical Activity & Sport in the Lives of Girls."

RITCH C. SAVIN-WILLIAMS is Professor of Human Development at Cornell University. He is co-editor, with Kenneth M. Cohen, of *The Lives of Lesbians, Gays, and Bisexuals* (Harcourt Brace 1996).

KRISTEN SCHILT is an Assistant Professor of Sociology at the University of Chicago. Her research examines gender inequality in the workplace through the lens of transgender workplace experiences.

ANNE SHELTON is professor in the department of sociology and anthropology at the University of Texas at Arlington. She is author of *Women, Men and Time: Gender Differences in Paid Work, Housework and Leisure*, Westport, CT: Greenwood, 1992.

KATHLEEN F. SLEVIN is Chancellor Professor of Sociology at The College of William and Mary. Her research interests include aging, gender, and work. With Toni Calasanti she is the co-editor of *Age Matters: Realigning Feminist Thinking* (Routledge, 2006) and a Gender Lens Series book: *Gender, Social Inequalities, and Aging* (AltaMira Press, 2001).

JUDITH STACEY is Professor of Sociology and Professor of Gender and Sexuality at New York University. She is author of many articles and books on gender, sexualities and families, including *In the Name of the Family: Rethinking Family Values in a Postmodern Age* (Boston: Beacon Press, 1996).

GLORIA STEINEM is a founding editor of *Ms.*, and the author of *Outrageous Acts and Everyday Rebellions* and *Revolution from Within*.

JACQUELINE SANCHEZ TAYLOR is a researcher on adult sex tourism and child sexual exploitation in Latin America, India, South Africa, and the Caribbean. Her Ph.D. focuses on sexual economic exchanges between female tourists and local men in Jamaica and the Dominican Republic. She is currently a sociology lecturer at the University of Leeds.

KAREN WALKER has completed her doctorate in the Department of Sociology at the University of Pennsylvania. She is Vice President of Research at Public/Private Ventures in Philadelphia.

CHRISTINE L. WILLIAMS is Professor of Sociology at the University of Texas at Austin. She is author of *Gender Differences at Work* (1989), *Still a Man's World* (1997), and editor of *Doing "Women's Work": Men in Nontraditional Occupations* (1993).

SARAH F. WILLIAMS received a PhD from the Northwestern University School of Music, with a dissertation entitled "Now Rise Internal Tones: Representations of Early Modern English Witchcraft in Sound and Music." She has taught courses at

Northwestern on gender and popular music, and rock music and media culture, and on women in music at DePaul University in Chicago. Dr. Williams has presented her research internationally on the acoustic properties of witchcraft, authenticity in American cowboy music, and technology and androgyny in 1980s New Wave music. She is also a freelance journalist and makes regular contributions to *Play Music* magazine, and currently resides in San Diego, California.